# THE BOOK OF THE STATES

### 2000-01 EDITION
### VOLUME 33

The Council of State Governments
Lexington, Kentucky

Headquarters: (859) 244-8000
Fax: (859) 244-8001
E-mail: info@csg.org
Internet: www.csg.org

ISBN 0-87292-877-2

# The Council of State Governments

## Council Offices

**Headquarters:**
Daniel M. Sprague, Executive Director
2760 Research Park Drive, P.O. Box 11910
Lexington, KY 40578-1910
Phone: (859) 244-8000
Fax: (859) 244-8001
E-mail: info@csg.org
Internet: www.csg.org

**Eastern:**
Alan V. Sokolow, Director
5 World Trade Center, Suite 9241
New York, NY 10048
Phone: (212) 912-0128
Internet: www.csgeast.org

**Midwestern:**
Michael H. McCabe, Director
641 E. Butterfield Road, Suite 401
Lombard, IL 60148
Phone: (630) 810-0210
Internet: www.csgmidwest.org

**Southern:**
Colleen Cousineau, Director
3355 Lenox Road, Suite 1050
Atlanta, GA 30326
Phone: (404) 266-1271
Internet: www.slcatlanta.org

**Western:**
Kent Briggs, Director
121 Second Street, 4th Floor
San Francisco, CA 94105
Phone: (415) 974-6422
Internet: www.csgwest.org
Denver, CO: (303) 572-5454

**Washington, D.C.:**
Jim Brown, General Counsel & Director
Hall of the States
444 N. Capitol Street, NW, Suite 401
Washington, DC 20001
Phone: (202) 624-5460
Internet: www.csg-dc.org

Copyright 2000
The Council of State Governments
2760 Research Park Drive • P.O. Box 11910
Lexington, Kentucky 40578-1910

Manufactured in the United States of America

Publication Sales Department
1-800-800-1910

Paperback Price: $79.00
Order # BOS0001P
ISBN # 0-87292-878-0

Hard Cover Price: $99.00
Order # BOS0001HC
ISBN # 0-87292-877-2

# The Book of the States' Staff Acknowledgements

*Publishing House Staff*

Audrey Curry, Publishing House Coordinator
Fred J. Vickers, Senior Editor
Bill Voit, Senior Project Director
Nancy Vickers, Publications Assistant

*Production Staff*

Matthew Brown, Electronic Publishing Specialist
Lisa Eads, Production/Print Liaison
Connie LaVake, Production Systems Administrator
Skip Olson, Graphic Design Coordinator
Darren Shannon, Electronic Publishing Assistant

*Additional CSG Staff*

James Carroll, Information Specialist
Keon S. Chi, Senior Fellow
Chester Hicks, Regional Coordinator
Don Hunter, Manager, Information and Membership Services
Ed Janairo, Help Desk and Training Coordinator
Cindy Lackey, Policy Analyst
Trudi Matthews, Policy Analyst
Malissa McAlister, Policy Analyst
David Moss, Research Assistant
John Mountjoy, Regional Coordinator
Elaine Stuart, Managing Editor
Matt Tewksbary, Technology Assistant

# Contents

# CONTENTS

## Chapter Three
## THE LEGISLATURES .................................................................................................. 63

*From citizen-lawmakers to full-time legislators, the legislatures run the gamut —
includes information on legislative organization, operation and action, session length,
legislative procedure, compensation, bill introductions and enactments , committee
appointments, and a review of administrative regulations.*

**Chapter Four**
**THE JUDICIARY** .................................................................................................................. 129
*The fundamentals of state justice systems includes information on state courts of last resort,*
*intermediate information on state courts of last resort, intermediate appellate courts and*
*general trial courts, selection/retention and removal of judges, and compensation of judges*
*and judicial administrators.*

**JUDICIARY**

**Chapter Five**
**ELECTIONS, CAMPAIGN FINANCE AND INITIATIVES** ................................................... 153
*Democracy in action — includes information on offices up for election 2000-2009, methods of*
*nominating candidates, formulas for election dates, polling hours, voting statistics, campaign*
*finance laws, and procedures for initiative, referenda and recalls.*

**Elections**

# CONTENTS

## Chapter Six
## STATE FINANCES ................................................................................................ 253

*With significant changes in fiscal federalism anticipated and new responsibilities devolving from Washington to the states, the importance of state finances has rarely been so critical — includes information on state budgetary procedures and fund management, revenues and expenditures, state debt, taxes, federal government grants and payments to states, and federal program spending by state.*

## Chapter Seven
## MANAGEMENT, REGULATION AND PERSONNEL ............................................ 335

*Staffing the states — includes information on personnel systems, information resource
management, and regulatory activities. Also: statistics on employment, payrolls and retirement
systems, and tables on licensing and regulation of selected non-health occupations and professions.*

### PERSONNEL

### INFORMATION/RECORDS MANAGEMENT

### STATE PURCHASING

### PUBLIC EMPLOYMENT

# CONTENTS

*Includes information on public school attendance, higher education institutions and their full-time
faculty salaries, fees and room rates at higher education institutions, prison populations,
child labor laws, and health care and highway spending.*

# CONTENTS

## Chapter Ten
## STATE PAGES ....................................................................................................... 459

*Everything you always wanted to know about the states — includes capitals, population, land areas, historical data, executive branch officials, legislative leaders, judges of high courts, state mottoes, flowers, songs, birds and other items unique to the states and other U.S. jurisdictions.*

## Chapter Eleven
## STATE GOVERNMENT IN REVIEW ............................................................................ 495

*Selected CSG resources about the governors' priorities for 2000, controlling air pollution, incentives to create, attract or retain businesses, gaming, Medicaid managed care, and state efforts to retain and recruit information technology employees.*

### AIR QUALITY

# Foreword

The 2000-01 edition of *The Book of the States* represents the 33rd volume of this premier reference work on state government. As noted in the Foreword to the first volume produced in 1935, "your interest in this book will vary with your interest in state government." We can assure you that if you have any interest in state government, you will have a keen interest in the essays and tables included here.

The Council of State Governments has served state government across the country for over 66 years, and we are proud that *The Book of the States* has been our flagship publication since the beginning. We trust that this volume reflects the challenges and opportunities facing states today. As states confront a greater diversity and complexity of issues presented by new global linkages and rapidly changing technologies, CSG's mission is more important than ever. We pledge that through all of our products and services, CSG will be a partner to state governments and state leaders, a champion of excellence in their institutions, and an active participant in putting the best and newest ideas and solutions into practice.

May 2000

Daniel M. Sprague
*Executive Director*
The Council of State Governments

## ACKNOWLEDGMENTS

The project staff wish to thank the hundreds of individuals in the states who provided data and information, the authors who graciously shared their expertise, and the thousands of state officials who, through their daily work, contributed to the story of state government presented in this volume.

# STATE GOVERNANCE, MANAGEMENT AND POLICIES: TRENDS AND ISSUES

*State governments across the nation have been on the upswing, constantly reforming their governance structures, improving administration and management and innovating policies and programs. This article highlights efforts to improve the capacity of state government, raises pertinent issues and questions, and suggests options for state policy-makers to consider.*

**by Keon S. Chi**
**Senior Fellow, CSG**

## Governance

### Legislative Branch

*Legislative Reform*

The legislative reform movement began in the wake of reapportionment in the 1960s. Since then, state legislatures have undergone a steady transformation to face new challenges. The organizational structures and institutional procedures of state legislatures as a whole remain as diverse and complex as ever. Some are highly professional legislative bodies with full-time legislators and year-round sessions, others are citizen legislatures made up of part-time lawmakers, and still others are hybrid legislatures with characteristics of both.

Compared to situations 30 to 40 years ago, lawmakers in most states now have more professional staff services. Most have several agencies to support both houses, and individual legislators employ staff members for constituent relations or committee work. Other improvements include higher legislative salaries, improved facilities, and furnished and equipped individual offices. Moreover, nearly every state now enforces ethics laws for legislators and lobbyists. All but seven states hold annual sessions, instead of biennial sessions. Special sessions frequently are held at the request of governors and legislators. The most obvious change in recent decades is that most legislatures now meet annually. Only four states held annual legislative sessions 50 years ago: that number increased to 34 in 1975 and 43 in 2000. Biennial sessions still are held in Arkansas, Kentucky, Montana, Nevada, North Dakota, Oregon and Texas. State legislatures now are more active during the interim periods between regular sessions, when standing committees often meet. As a result, the legislative workload has expanded. Legislators introduced more bills and enacted more laws in recent session than in earlier decades.

States also have increased the number of standing and joint committees. At the same time that the number of legislative leadership positions has increased, there has been a perceived decline in the authority of legislative leaders. This has been attributed to leadership selection methods, campaign finance reforms and, more recently, legislative term limits. In most states, the size of the legislature in most states is unchanged from 40 years ago. In the past four decades, Connecticut, Illinois, Massachusetts, Ohio and Vermont are among the few that have reduced the size of their legislative chambers. In 2000, the Minnesota Legislature at the request of the governor considered a constitutional amendment to switch to a unicameral legislature, patterned after Nebraska, but failed to pass it.

### Lobbying Laws

An unprecedented movement has taken place in many states in the past several years to deal with government accountability and public integrity. Many states now have comprehensive ethics laws. Yet more needs to be done to meet public expectations. As national polls indicate, the widespread perception is that some state legislators are obligated to moneyed private interests. To many people, the power of special interest groups seems to drown out the voice of the average person. Lobbyists also have noted the negative perceptions of their trade.

Discussions on legislator-lobbyist interactions focus on: How can we change public misperceptions of legislative lobbying? How should legislators regulate their conduct and that of lobbyists? And, how can legislators and lobbyists improve the legislative environment without jeopardizing the flow of information and communication?

There are several actions state legislators might consider. To help the public better understand the complexity of legislative lobbying, legislators might want to initiate and/or participate in civic education programs. Legislators should disclose to the public their interactions

with lobbyists. States should examine legislative standards of conduct to promote public integrity and to gain public trust. Further, states should revise legislative codes of ethics and revamp their lobbying enforcement agencies to address individual and institutional responsibility. Public integrity is ensured only when legislators realize a strong sense of accountability. Only by demonstrating and practicing accountability can legislators earn public trust.

### Legislative Term Limits

In 1990, voters in California, Colorado and Oklahoma approved the first term-limit ballot initiatives. Term limits won voter approval in 11 states in 1992, one in 1993, four in 1994 and one in 1995. Only the Utah Legislature imposed term limits on itself by law in 1994. In 1998, a total of 217 legislators in seven states were ineligible for re-election due to term limits. In 2000, legislators in nine chambers in five states (Arizona, Florida, Montana, Ohio and South Dakota) were scheduled to be termed out.

Supporters of legislative term limits argue that such measures will prohibit career politicians from continuously enjoying the advantages of incumbency and will bring in new members to represent voter interests. Critics of term limits decry the loss of institutional memory and argue that term limits deprive voters of the right to re-elect veteran legislators. The irony is that in most states these reasons for or against term limits have not been seriously debated in legislative chambers. Instead, such pro and con arguments have taken place mostly in the media. Legislative term limits have faced court tests in more than a dozen states in recent years. In 1998, courts struck down term-limit laws in three states and upheld them in several others. As of mid-2000, legislative term limits remained intact in 18 states.

There are many questions to ask about the term-limits movement in states. Major concerns for state legislators center around the effects of term limits, especially in three areas: demographic characteristics of state legislators, institutionalized changes and legislative behavior. What effects will legislative term limits have on the workings of state legislatures? What do legislators, staff members and lobbyists say about the effects of term limits? Is it constitutional to limit the number of terms state legislators can serve? Why have some courts ruled term-limit laws unconstitutional? Who has jurisdiction over state legislative term limits, state or federal courts? What are the implications of previous court rulings for other states, with or without legislative term limits? Finally, what options do state legislators have in dealing with term limits? And what procedural recommendations should lawmakers consider in improving legislative procedures under term limits?

There are several policy options for consideration. For example, states may want to allow lawmakers an equal number of years of consecutive service in both chambers with no lifetime ban. They may want to limit the number of consecutive years of service in the legislature as an institution, not for each chamber. States may consider staggered term-limits dates for newly elected legislators so they can attain leadership positions. States also may consider sharing positions of influence by eliminating the seniority system as the criterion for electing leaders. In addition, states may consider new leadership roles and styles and a new way to set the legislative agenda. They may want to readdress legislators' roles, their learning curve, and their communications with fellow legislators and constituents.

## Campaign Finance Reform

There exists a widespread perception among the public that money makes a significant difference in most, if not all, election outcomes. Unless the influence of big or improper money is reduced public confidence may continue to wane in government. In recent years, with a variety of innovative ideas, many states have tried to regulate the way candidates raise and spend money. Yet there is room for further reform. State policy-makers might want to consider several alternatives to campaign-finance practices. By requiring candidates and state agencies to report and disclose information on campaign finance in a more timely and comprehensive manner, for example, the public can be better informed of the candidates' financial status. Although the trend of limiting campaign contributions is likely to continue, state leaders are expected to be more mindful of constitutional issues, particularly in view of recent court decisions regarding contributors' First Amendment rights.

State leaders are likely to find room for improvement in the area of the independence, authority and capability of state agencies enforcing campaign finance laws. Reporting and disclosure is meaningless unless the state deals with campaign-finance law violations. Half the states have experimented with public financing with limited success. States are likely to try to find alternatives to the check-off and add-on systems and additional resources for campaign finance. Strengthening state political parties so they can play a larger role in campaign finance may help candidates wean themselves from wealthy individual and special-interest contributions.

## Legislative Information Technology

The Internet has drastically changed state legislative operations and information systems. Every state legislature now has a colorful Web site with information about the workings of the lawmaking body. In most states, legislative information is available to legislators and staff, state officials in the other branches, lobbyists and the public. Moreover, legislators in many states use computers on the floor of the chamber, thus creating new dimensions in the legislative process. The scope of information available has expanded steadily over the years. In most states, digitized legislative information includes: administrative rules, bill status, bill text, resolution status, legislative analysis, committee meeting schedules and notices, committee reports, and legislative calendars, journals, rules and procedures, reports and voting records. In addition, many legislative Web sites now provide links to other states' Web sites, policy organizations, interest groups and federal agencies.

These developments open the door to questions about the effect of legislative information technology. Key questions include: Does information technology help or hinder legislative effectiveness and efficiency? What new politics or measures might be needed to strengthen the legislative branch in an era of rapidly changing information technology? These are some of the issues relevant to the use of technology in the state legislative process. The main question, however, is not whether more technology should or should not be used in the legislative process, but how best to use it, keeping in mind that we live in a new era of electronic government and electronic democracy. Therefore, state legislators might want to adopt new policies and regulations on the appropriate use of technology.

## Executive Branch

### Restructuring

Every year, government restructuring, ranging from comprehensive statewide organizational change to partial, targeted agency reorganization occurs in one-third of the states. In most cases, governors initiate restructuring efforts. For fiscal 2000, for example, more than 15 governors proposed major government restructuring. These restructuring proposals included creating new departments, changing the department-level status of agencies, reorganizing workforce development efforts and eliminating boards and commissions. Recent comprehensive restructuring has followed the traditional principles of executive reorganization, such as: grouping agencies into broad functional areas; establishing departments to enhance the span of control and make accountable the chief executive and legislature; delineating single lines of authority; administering departments by single heads; curtailing independent boards or commissions; reducing confusion in service delivery for the public, and producing cost savings and efficiency.

States routinely partially reorganize. Some states dealt with the proliferation and fragmentation of state agencies by creating an "umbrella agency" for functional areas such as human services, transportation, general services and administration. Proponents contend that comprehensive agencies would give top-level agency heads better administrative control without disturbing the authority of other cabinet-level agencies. Other advantages include more effective planning, better resource allocation and improved efficiency and accountability. On the other hand, critics contend problems of umbrella agencies include program complexity, inefficiency, poor coordination and uncoordinated services.

The two basic approaches used in executive reorganization are centralization and decentralization, whether called restructuring, reinventing or reengineering. There seems to be no single direction for state reorganization efforts. One trend in executive restructuring has been toward creating more cabinet systems. The number of states using a cabinet model grew from 14 in 1965 to 40 in 2000. Authorization mechanisms for adopting a cabinet system include constitutional and statutory provisions, gubernatorial executive orders and tradition. Cabinets perform varied roles, and the nature and number of cabinet members also differ from state to state. Cabinets can help identify priority issues, serve as a policy-making body, allow the chief executive to maintain closer contract with the executive departments and give visibility to decisions.

In the area of elective executive officers, two trends are notable. The number of popularly elected executive offices in state government has remained the same over the past two decades, except for a slight decrease in the numbers of comptrollers, chief state education officers and public utility commissioners. Terms of office, however, have changed. Currently, governors in 48 states serve four-year terms, while governors in New Hampshire and Vermont serve two-year terms. While 18 states had no term limits on governors in 1980, only nine did in 2000. Twenty-two of the 42 states with lieutenant governors place restrictions on the number of terms they can serve. Term limits apply to other constitutional officers in many states.

### Civil Service Reform

As of 2000, states employed more than 5 million workers and most of those were covered by civil-service systems. A wide range of problems exists in many civil-service systems, however. Common complaints about the half-century old systems include time-consuming hiring processes, job classifications, lengthy dismissal processes, rigid reduction-in-force policies, job performance unrelated to rewards, and restrictions on agency managers. In response, many states have initiated reforms in recent years. A 1996 survey by the National Association of State Personnel Executives found revisions underway in 45 states in classification systems, in compensation in 27 states, and in merit testing in 26 states. Classification and compensation are frequently mentioned as ripe for reform. In 1993, the National Commission on the State and Local Public Service (Winter Commission) recommended reducing job classifications from thousands to no more than a dozen. The commission's report also advocated a simple pay structure to allow agency managers to use greater discretion in rewarding productive employees. Many governors also have called for radical reform of classification systems. Yet, the numbers of job classifications in many states have remained unchanged since 1993.

One recent development in the classification area is the use of broadbanding. Under broadbanding, a state pares away many salary grades and ranges, collapsing them into fewer job classes. The most common reason for adopting this practice is to complement the move to a flatter organization. Other reasons are to encourage a broadly skilled work force, support a new work culture or climate, support career-development opportunities and minimize job analysis and evaluation costs.

Another significant management development in state human resources is Georgia's unique approach to reforming its classification system. In that state, workers hired after July 1996 have been placed in an unclassified service not covered by the merit system and are employed at will. Although the state has reported positive outcomes of the reform, it is premature to evaluate the effectiveness of such a change. One challenge faced by state personnel executives, including those in Georgia, is the need to refine their strategic visions for human-resource management. States have

many opportunities to revamp their civil service systems, and need innovative ideas from personnel executives, strong gubernatorial leadership and continued legislative commitment.

## Judiciary Branch

### Court Systems

State court systems are evolving constantly. Like the other two branches of state government, the judicial branch also has been targeted by reformers over the years. Early critics pointed to the fragmentation and duplication of courts, overlapping jurisdictions, the absence of a central administrative organization and unqualified judges who were chosen more for party service than judicial merit. Since the 1970s, many states have responded to reformers' recommendations. Despite years of reforms, organizational patterns of state court systems remain diverse in their structures, jurisdictions, names, and methods of selecting and retaining judges.

### Judges

The number of justices in the state courts of last resort has remained about the same, ranging from five to nine in most states, even though caseloads have increased in recent decades. In contrast, the number of the second tier of state courts — intermediate appellate courts — has increased sharply. Similarly, the number of intermediate appellate judges more than doubled in recent years to nearly 900. The number of such judges ranges from three in Alaska, Idaho and North Dakota to 63 in New York, 88 in California and 89 in Texas.

The organization of state trial courts is more diverse than that of appellate courts. As of 1995, 44 states had trial-court systems on two levels: general and limited jurisdictions. General jurisdiction courts tend to be partly state funded, while limited jurisdiction courts typically are supported by municipal or county funds. Perhaps reflecting growing caseloads, the total number of trial court judges was 8,791 in 1995, compared with 5,612 two decades earlier. In some states, including Arkansas, Illinois and Iowa, however, the number of trial court judges decreased in the past 20 years. But across the states, the average number of judges in trial courts increased.

State courts are faced with mounting pressures from increased workloads and complexity. At the same time, limited financial resources restrict their ability to respond to changing demands. More than a dozen states recently established futures commissions and others produced strategic planning documents to suggest ways to make court systems more effective and efficient.

# Management and Administration

## Federalism

The most remarkable federalism issue for the states in recent years was the enactment of the Unfunded Mandate Reform Act of 1995. This act gives state and local elected officials the chance to seek a roll call vote on the floor of the House or Senate on any proposed unfunded mandate. Another major victory for the states was the new Executive Order No. 13132 signed by President Clinton on Aug. 4, 1999 after more than a year of negotiations between state and federal officials. The executive order, which became effective on Nov. 2, 1999, emphasizes consultation with state and local elected officials and sets forth fundamental principles of federalism, federalism policy-making criteria, and special requirements for pre-emption, legislative proposals, and intergovernmental consultation, and grants increased flexibility for state and local waivers.

The 106th Congress also considered bills designed to strengthen the standing of states in the federal system: the Federalism Accountability Act and the Federalism Act. The State Flexibility Clarification Act, a refinement of the Unfunded Mandate Reform Act, instructs the Congressional Budget Office to score a reduction in federal matching funds as a mandate. The other, the Financial Assistance Accountability Act, simplifies the grant application process for states. Perhaps the most noticeable victory for the states in 1999 was the tobacco settlement case. The Clinton Administration had claimed that states owed the federal government more than half of the money due them as part of the master settlement agreement with the tobacco industry. State legislators and governors mobilized behind anti-recoupment language inserted in the emergency appropriations bill that made its way through Congress.

Recently, governors made strong arguments in favor of a new federalism by calling for clarifying the roles and responsibilities of the levels of government. They said, "It is important to decide which level of government should create regulations and which level should enforce them and that it is critical to coordinate and rationalize federal, state and local tax systems."

Regarding the federal budget proposal for fiscal 2001, the nation's governors said that the federal government must first uphold its current funding commitments to states, including health and human services programs, transportation trust funds and senior prescription drugs. The governors also responded to the Congressional moratorium on Internet taxes. The governors said, "States will continue to work towards simplifying and streamlining their own state sales tax systems. The governors oppose efforts by the federal government to restrict or interfere with states' ability to collect existing tax liabilities."

State legislators also have urged the administration to protect state sovereignty by including in the fiscal 2001 federal budget measures such as maintaining the shared commitment to welfare reform and children's health through full funding of TANF (Temporary Assistance to Needy Families) and SCHIP (State Children's Health Insurance Program); maintaining state-federal entitlement and mandatory programs, such as Medicaid and child welfare; restoring full funding of $2.38 billion to the Social Services Block Grant; increasing funding for the Child Care and Development Block Grant; providing a comprehensive proposal for funding school construction; protecting the guaranteed funding levels set for highways; providing full funding for aviation programs; providing full funding for state revolving funds; and maintaining funding for child support programs.

## Quality Management

Over the years, governors and other state

policy-makers have experimented with improvements in public management and service delivery. In the 1960s and 1970s, for example, many states adopted the planning-programming-budgeting system. In the 1980s, states promoted management by objective and zero-based budgeting. Today, however, quality initiatives have replaced these management approaches in most states. Total quality management is a management approach that emphasizes meeting or exceeding public expectations for products or services. TQM emphasizes excellence in customer service and empowers workers to pursue a never-ending search for quality improvement. Quality management focuses on customers, teamwork and continuous improvement.to

It is not easy to implement quality practices, however. The critical factors for successful quality initiatives in state government are leadership commitment, employee participation, flexible operational systems, result orientation and customer satisfaction.

For successful quality initiatives, governors and agency directors must "walk the talk" with organizational commitment and resources. Successful quality initiatives require a greater emphasis on employee participation in decision-making. Such initiatives should create a process that lets employees identify ways to continually improve the quality and productivity of their workplace.

State policy-makers need to streamline their work procedures by instituting a shorter chain of command. The overall management and service delivery system should be focused on results. The most important factor for a successful quality initiative is customer satisfaction. Finally, state managers and employees must be convinced that quality government is not a fad. They must overcome resistance from others who tend to favor the status quo.

*Privatization and Outsourcing*

In recent years, states have used the privatization approach to save money and provide better services. With support from governors, agency heads and legislative leaders, state agencies have privatized more functions and services — a trend state officials expect will continue in the next few years. Six out of 10 state officials who responded to a 1997 survey conducted by The Council of State Governments said privatization activity had expanded in their state or agency, while the rest said such activity had remained about the same in the past five years. State transportation agencies led executive departments in the number of privatized programs and services. Other departments with high numbers of privatized programs were general services and administration, corrections and social services. The CSG survey also showed that outsourcing is the most widely used method of privatizing functions and services, with eight out of 10 activities using this method. Some agencies use a carefully crafted decision-making process. Overall, however, most state agencies have initiated privatization projects on an ad hoc basis without a standard decision-making, monitoring or evaluating process.

State officials consider cost the most important factor in determining whether to privatize a service, function or program. Before initiating major privatization projects, however, policy-makers should determine if constitutional, statutory, federal or internal regulatory barriers exist. Recently, many states have enacted privatization laws to revise civil service systems, which protect state workers and prohibit outsourcing functions or services. In most cases, the strongest resistance to privatization comes from employee organizations. Some states have addressed employee concerns by reassigning personnel within government, allowing employees to compete with private vendors and consulting with private organizations. The success or failure of privatized services depends on how the option is used. Agency managers have to plan, manage and monitor privatization activities carefully. They also should be aware that privatization does not mean the delegation of government authority or responsibility. Policy-makers are ultimately accountable to clients and taxpayers for privatized services.

# Policies

A recent survey of governors and legislative leaders by The Council of State Governments indicated that education, economic development, health care and tax relief topped the policy issues states were considering in 2000.

## Education Policy

Today, education remains the No. 1 public policy issue in most states as expressed in governors' state-of-state addresses. Governors mentioned early education, teacher quality, professional development, teacher salaries, school construction, school safety, standards-based reforms, literacy, technology, school choice, class size, postsecondary, access and technology. Governors mentioned less frequently math and science promotion, a longer school year, full-day kindergarten, exit exams and equity.

What can and should the states do to improve public education? Among reform proposals, state policy-makers might consider redefining educational goals, school finance, facilities, teacher training, data collection, alternatives to public school and accountability. State policy-makers might want to examine the education clause in their state constitution to ensure it is up-to-date and sets meaningful educational goals. Over the past two decades, many states have revised their constitutional provisions on educational goals. Educational goals should be realistic and measurable. In the past 10 years, more than 30 states have been sued for unequal educational spending. About half these states, under court orders, have implemented radical changes in funding public schools. Heavy reliance on local property taxes for education presents a major problem in achieving equal funding. In some states, courts declared educational systems unconstitutional because some districts had such poor school facilities. State policy-makers might consider alternative ways of raising revenues for education. States need to invest more in school facilities to boost student performance. More money is needed to reduce class sizes and to make educational technology available to every school, especially in poor districts.

States need to improve teacher recruiting and training programs. Today, four out of five teachers in public schools are ill prepared to teach the subject matter of their classes. Some states are setting new standards for classroom teachers to ensure they are experts in the subjects they teach. States need to devise new ways to compare student performance in their states with that of students in other states.

States might also consider alternative ways of providing public education, at least on an experimental basis. In the past decades, more states have implemented school choice, vouchers and charter schools. While it is premature to judge the effectiveness of such alternatives, state policy-makers might consider introducing competition to public education.

States also need to consider new systems to hold schools accountable to parents and taxpayers. Many states are considering school report cards, takeovers of low performance schools, and education and financial accountability for principals, administrators and teachers.

Educational reform is complicated by politics. As long as Congress and the president disagree, little change can be expected at the national level. Moreover, reform in public education is not likely without support from powerful teachers' unions. Yet several states, despite these obstacles, have successfully implemented educational reform.

## Economic Development and Growth Management

*Business Incentives*

During the past few decades, states have offered tax and financial incentives to qualified companies to create, retain or expand jobs. The number of states offering employee-wage rebates almost tripled in the past 10 years. Many states also have customized company-specific incentives to lure large businesses. As a result, interstate competition has intensified. In response to a 1999 CSG survey, respondents from 32 states said their states increased the number of incentive programs in the past five years, while the number of such incentive programs remained unchanged in 14 states. Two states decreased the number. These figures can be compared with the 1994 CSG survey data: 38

states had an increase in business incentives; 10 states' activities remained the same and two states experienced a decrease during the previous five years. Over the next five years, a majority of the states expect to maintain incentive activities at current levels.

Recently, some state and local government officials and observers have questioned the effectiveness of incentives. State policy-makers might consider issues, such as business location, cost-benefit studies, legislative guidelines, interstate competition and emerging trends. Tax and financial incentives, albeit relevant, are not the primary factor in determining businesses' location. State policy-makers should rely on a formal cost-benefit model, not anecdotal examples, to gauge the effectiveness of tax and financial incentives. State legislators need to clearly define guidelines when debating business incentive packages and evaluating job-creation proposals. State policy-makers should refrain from engaging in bidding wars in which they offer large, customized incentive packages to large companies at the expense of existing companies, small or large.

The number of states creating tax and financial incentives is likely to stay the same or decline in the next few years according to the CSG survey. More states appear to be concerned about the return on their business-incentives investment. Regarding interstate competition, some policy consultants argue that when a state lures an existing company from another state, the "winning" state should pay the other state. An increasing number of states are reforming business regulations, including permits, environmental protection rules and workers' compensation laws. States also need to consider fairer competition in the global market, in line with international trade agreements.

*Growth Management*

Recently, various governors have expressed concern about the impact of economic growth. The chief executives in more than half the states addressed some aspects of the growth issue in their state-of-the-state addresses. Some used the phrase "smart growth" to describe their initia-

tives; others focused on specific policies, such as anti-sprawl efforts, open-space and farmland preservation, land-use planning, brownfields redevelopment, urban revitalization and transportation planning. Some governors also are trying to make their states more attractive to high tech companies. Many people are concerned about the negative impacts of urban sprawl.

## Health and Human Services

*Managed Care*

The debate over health-care problems continues, and cost and access for children and senior citizens tend to dominate reform activities. In particular, state policy-makers and administrators debate how to control spending for public health-care programs while expanding coverage of uninsured persons. Based on recent trends and forecasts, state policy-makers have options for health-care cost-control initiatives, ranging from managed care and purchasing alliances to preventive and primary health-care programs.

In implementing managed care, the challenges are how to cover the disabled and elderly, monitor cost shifting and obtain federal waivers. The emerging patterns in purchasing alliances include consolidating health-benefit plans of state employees with those of small businesses, Medicaid recipients and uninsured individuals. Key issues include utilization and payment levels, risk pools and anti-trust laws. The absence of reliable data makes it difficult to determine the quality of health services. Major issues are standardization, electronic transfer and barriers to data collection efforts. States need to reform health-insurance policies, especially those affecting purchasing alliances and small businesses, to control costs and expand coverage. Issues include guaranteed insurance, pre-existing conditions, portability and community rating.

Current trends in incremental Medicaid reform efforts are expansion of eligibility, emphasis on managed care and negotiated rates with providers. Major issues include federal waivers, block grants and the Employee Retirement

Income Security Act. States need to emphasize preventive and primary health care and increase health. awareness. States might take advantage of prevention programs such as early periodic screening. Key issues include lack of public awareness of preventive programs, preventable hospitalization and barriers to expanded primary care.

Health cost-control efforts should not be confined to programmatic reforms. Other issues include restructuring administrative agencies, changing organizational dynamics and defining new roles for the states in the health care field. Traditionally, states protected public health and safety, purchased health care, developed and trained health care resources and established rules governing health care providers and health marketplace activities. Now, states are expected to perform several new roles, including directing overall policy development, controlling health care expenditures, and explaining health-insurance coverage to the public.

*Replacing Welfare*

In 1996, Congress replaced the 60-year old Aid to Families with Dependent Children program with the new Temporary Assistance to Needy Families program. Under the TANF program, states were required to prepare and certify welfare-to-work plans by July 1, 1997, indicating how they intend to move welfare recipients to work. The total block grant was estimated to be $16.4 billion for each year from fiscal 1996 to 2003. Each state receives a fixed amount — based on historical expenditures for AFDC benefits and administration, EA (Emergency Assistance) and JOBS (Job Opportunities and Basic Skills). The law has affected most of the 12.8 million people on welfare and almost all of the 25.6 million people receiving food stamps. It has changed benefits for more than one-fifth of the families with children.

To implement the TANF program, each state was encouraged to have clear goals and objectives for its welfare-to-work system to improve the process for determining eligibility and offer incentives and sanctions. States were to provide support services, such as child care, transporta-tion and health services, to help families leave welfare within the federal time limits. In addition, states were encouraged to address preventive measures to enhance child support collections, reduce teen-pregnancy rates and promote recipients' responsibility. State policy-makers should mobilize community-based organizations and offer new incentives to businesses to create jobs for welfare recipients. To meet federal work requirements and implement effective welfare-to-work programs, state policy-makers should consider restructuring human service agencies and changing the culture of welfare administration for welfare workers and recipients.

It is encouraging that both the number of welfare recipients and welfare expenditures have declined in recent years. In some states, the number of welfare recipients dropped by more than half. As of March 1999, the nation's welfare rolls had dropped 47 percent from its 1994 peak, and in six states welfare rolls fell by more than 70 percent. Most states predict that the number of welfare recipients will decrease even more in the next few years. The reduced number of welfare recipients is attributed to several factors: a strong economy that created more jobs; tougher child-support enforcement measures that kept more children off the rolls; stringent work requirements in many demonstration projects that encouraged work instead of welfare; and improved administration and management using more sophisticated information systems.

Many critics of the 1996 law had forecast potential problems with states' welfare systems. Virtually no one predicted that states would receive more federal money under TANF. In 1999, for example, federal payments to the states were $6 billion higher than they would have been under the old law. The fact is that states' welfare rolls have dropped significantly while federal financing, by law, remains fixed at historic highs. On average, the federal government now awards states 64 percent more per family than it did before the welfare reform law took effect. In 12 states, the federal payment per welfare case more than doubled.

## Fiscal Policy

*Tobacco Settlement*

The 1999 tobacco settlement may be regarded as one of the biggest plums states received in recent history. Under a lawsuit settled between 46 states and the major tobacco companies, states are expected to receive $206 billion over the next 25 years. The suit sought to recover public-health costs of tobacco-related illnesses. However, the Clinton Administration had claimed that states owed the federal government more than half of the money due them as part of the master settlement agreement with the tobacco industry. State legislators and governors mobilized behind anti-recoupment language inserted in the emergency appropriations bill that Congress enacted.

According to "The Fiscal Survey of States," (June 1999), by the National Governors' Association and the National Association of State Budget Officers, most states planned to use of tobacco settlement funds for health and smoking-cessation programs. In 1999, governors in 25 states proposed to use funds for health programs; 23 states, for children's health programs; 21 states, for smoking-cessation programs; and governors in 12 states proposed to use funds for education programs. Other proposals include creating budget stabilization funds and initiating capital spending. Most of the proposals for construction spending are health-related, such as constructing rural health centers and converting hospitals to other health users. The NASBO report also said that in more than one-half of the states, governors were recommending that tobacco settlement funds be segregated in separate funds. Examples of separate funds include trust funds, nonprofit corporations, and funds earmarked for medical research. In about one fifth of the states, the governor's budget does not include any proposed use of the tobacco settlement funds because of the uncertainty of the timing of the actual receipt of these funds.

*Lotteries and Casinos*

Recently, lotteries and casinos have become a major revenue source for many states. In 1999, lotteries operated in 37 states, the District of Columbia and Puerto Rico. According to a 1998 survey of lottery states by The Council of State Governments, about two-thirds of the states anticipated an increase in lottery players in the next few years. Survey respondents from more than 20 lottery states predicted their state will introduce additional types of games in the next few years. No states limit the number of lottery retailers by law. Several states have increased prize money to attract more players and reduced state revenues or administrative costs. Percentages of prize money awarded ranged from a low of 50 percent of revenues in Arizona to a high of 70 percent of revenues in Massachusetts. On average, states award 55 percent of gross revenues for prizes. The percent of revenues that goes to the state ranges from a low of 22 percent in Massachusetts to a high of 40 percent in Pennsylvania. The average is about 32 percent. More states now earmark lottery proceeds for specific programs rather than using them for general funds. Only 10 states currently transfer lottery profits to their general fund, compared with 22 states that did in 1994. Since 1994, the number of states using some or all lottery revenues for education has increased from 12 to 17. With these and other trends in mind, state officials are raising questions about their lottery's future: How should the state improve the way it regulates lottery games, retailers, procurement, conducts oversight, watches for fraud and abuse, and advertises? How should the state deal with compulsive gamblers and underage players? Perhaps, more importantly, how should the state measure true costs and benefits of lotteries?

Casino gambling was legal only in Nevada and Atlantic City 10 years ago. Today, however, more than 20 states allow casinos. Casinos are found in small towns and urban areas, riverboats, Indian reservations and racetracks. Casinos promote job creation, residential development, tourism and tax revenues. The most important contributing factor might be public and policy-makers' attitudes toward casinos. Ten years ago, less than half the U.S. public said casino gambling was acceptable. Today, a vast majority of adult Americans say that casinos are acceptable for themselves and others. Casinos largely attract players from the state where they are located. Most states expect more casino players in the next few years, and casino revenues are expected to grow as a result. Yet, most states have not conducted comprehensive studies on casino players' demographic backgrounds, whether casinos benefit the local economy or contribute to their revenue base. Most states have not assessed costs and benefits. State policy-makers are considering options for the number of licenses, regulations, tax rates, credit controls, underage players, treatment for problem gamblers, Indian gambling and Internet gambling. There are other issues relevant to interstate competition and federal-state-tribal relations. States need more facts so that they can determine whether casino operations are meeting the state's desired purposes and objectives.

*E-commerce Taxation*

In the past few years, the number of businesses and consumers shopping online has increased at an astonishing rate. Online retail sales of $20 billion in 1999 are expected to increase to $184 billion by 2004. Today's typical electronic customers are male, better educated and have higher incomes than Main Street shoppers, but the gap in buyers based on gender, age and Internet access — the so-called "digital divide" — is narrowing. More women, teenagers and people without household Internet access are expected to join the rising tide of e-commerce. To develop rational tax policies on e-commerce at all levels of government, Congress passed and President Clinton signed the Internet Tax Freedom Act of 1998. The act created the Advisory Commission on Electronic Commerce, and charged it to report to Congress on April 3, 2000. In the meantime, the federal government placed a three-year moratorium on state and local taxation on e-commerce.

Representatives of state and local government organizations argued before Congress that the moratorium unfairly pre-empted their authority. At the Commission meetings, state and local governments called for levying state sales and use taxes on e-commerce on several grounds. Internet remote sellers should not be given a tax advantage over local merchants. Imposition of sales and use taxes on e-commerce is necessary for a level playing field for all customers. If left untaxed, e-commerce as it grows would further erode the sales-tax base of many state and local governments. Although dealing with numerous taxing jurisdictions is challenging for multistate, remote sellers, software is available to do the job. If states and local governments cannot collect sales and use taxes on e-commerce, substantial revenue losses would affect public services. Opponents contend that sales and use taxes on e-commerce would reduce the volume of online retail sales, negatively affecting the economy. The strongest arguments against taxing e-commerce relate to the administrative burdens imposed on sellers by differing tax rates and tax collections for more than 7,000 state and local taxing jurisdictions.

Most states rely heavily on sales and use taxes, which provide more than one-third of all state revenues. The 45 states with such taxes collected more than $150 billion in 1998. Currently, 34 of the 45 states with state sales/user taxes allow local governments to levy additional sales taxes to provide public services such as education, police and fire protection, transportation and health services. So, the issue is: How can state and local governments reform their sales tax systems to deal more effectively with e-commerce?

Many reformers propose that states adopt uniform policies on tax rates, vendor registration, tax remittance and audit requirements, exemptions for business purchases and definitions of products and services. State and local sales and use tax systems could be simplified by eliminating tax compliance burdens for remote sellers, especially in tax returns, payments, tax audits, tax-rate monitoring and record-keeping requirements. They propose to shift e-commerce sales tax administration to third-party entities, such as software and credit card companies. They are asking states to adopt uniform legislation on e-commerce taxation either on a regional or national basis by states themselves before Congress makes the current moratorium on e-commerce taxation permanent.

In April 2000, the Advisory Commission on Electronic Commerce submitted its final report to Congress, recommending in part that the current moratorium of sales and use taxes be extended for a period of five years barring e-commerce taxation on sales of digitized goods and products, and that state and local governments work with the National Conference of Commissioners on Uniform State Laws in drafting a uniform sales and use tax act that would simplify state and local sales and use taxation policies. The U.S. House on May 10, 2000 approved a bill to extend the tax moratorium for five more years.

## Prospects for States

State leaders and others at the start of the new millennium are asking, "What are the major forces that are likely to shape the future of state government?" While this is a loaded and difficult question, trends in the past two decades point to five such forces: federalism, public-private interactions, technology, public participation and state leaders.

First, federalism is a formidable force in shaping the role and responsibility of state governments. How the states will deal with public policy issues depends upon the changing nature of federal-state-local relations. To shape federalism, state leaders will need to continue their campaigns for more federal actions designed to strengthen the standing of the states in the federal system such as the Federalism Accountability Act and the Federalism Act of 1999. It is also important to continue the work of the "federalism summits" held in 1995 and 1997 by representatives of The Council of State Governments and other major state leadership organizations. These meetings were designed to improve the "partnership equilibrium" of federal and state governments. The principles adopted by the summits include requiring Congress to justify its constitutional authority to act on each given bill, limit and clarify federal pre-emption of state laws and federal regulations on states, streamline block-grant funding and simplify financial reporting requirements.

Second, relations with the private sector will have a considerable impact on the future of the states, especially in administration and management. Public-private interactions at the state level during the past 20 years have grown in three areas: government restructuring and cost control studies, planning and management, and alternative service delivery. Many states have included private-sector representatives on government reorganization task forces to identify cost-reduction measures patterned after private-sector practices, Most states also have established public-private partnership projects aimed at strategic planning and benchmarking, economic development and management improvement. The most prominent and controversial area of public-private sector alliances in recent years has been and will remain to be privatization. The extent of outsourcing government services to private vendors is likely to shape the future of state government operations.

Third, technology already is shaping state government operations. State governments need information technology to operate effectively. Electronic democracy and electronic government are creating new dimensions in government and raising new questions and problems. The technology applications most widely available to state agencies are cellular phones, e-mail, the Internet, paging and voice mail. States have launched major initiatives in automation, emergency management, fleet management, procurement reform and telecommunications. Many states now use computers in their legislative chambers and courtrooms. Technology is a formidable force in all branches of state government.

Fourth, the future of the states depends on the extent and form of public participation in the workings of state government. In light of relatively lower levels of public confidence in state policy-makers, the public could either shun participation or seek to shape policy through statewide campaigns for voter initiatives where allowed. Recent campaigns have targeted taxation, education, lobbying, campaign finance and legislative term limits. The public also could help shape state legislative processes by directly accessing activity in legislative chambers through the Internet and other technology applications, bypassing traditional media coverage. The extent of citizen participation can be a determining factor in improving state government management.

Finally, elected and appointed state leaders have not only the authority and resources to shape the future of the states in many, if not all, policy and program areas. They are and should be the key movers and shakers of state government. While the national government has an impact on states, state leaders have a considerable amount of flexibility and discretion under the U.S. Constitution. States have a vast amount of reserved powers to exercise, ranging from the power to streamline government structures to reform state educational systems. Leadership and management styles can make a difference in the way states are run. State leaders and managers need to initiate or replicate innovations on a continuing basis to meet the challenges of the future.

## Selected References

Keon S. Chi. *Lobbying Reform*, Lexington, Ky.: The Council of State Governments, September 1996.

Keon S. Chi. *Replacing Welfare*, Lexington, Ky.: The Council of State Governments, April 1997.

Keon S. Chi. *State Health Care Cost Control*, Lexington, Ky.: The Council of State Governments, August 1995.

Keon S. Chi. *Total Quality Management*, Lexington, Ky.: The Council of State Governments, October 1994.

Keon S. Chi and Daniel J. Hofmann. *State Business Incentives: Trends and Options for the Future*, Second Edition, Lexington, Ky.: The Council of State Governments, 2000.

Keon S. Chi and Cindy Jasper. *Private Practices: A Review of Privatization in State Government*, Lexington, Ky.: The Council of State Governments, 1998.

Keon S. Chi and Cindy Jasper. *Reforming School Finance*, Lexington, Ky.: The Council of State Governments, October 1997.

Keon S. Chi and Drew Leatherby. *State Legislative Term Limits*, Lexington, Ky.: The Council of State Governments, February 1998.

Keon S. Chi and Drew Leatherby. *States Ante Up: Regulating Lotteries and Casinos*, Lexington, Ky.: The Council of State Governments, October 1998.

*Managing for Success: A Profile of State Government for the 21st Century*, Lexington, Ky.: The Council of State Governments, 1997.

*Restoring Balance to the American Federal System: A Report of the Proceedings of the 1995 States' Federalism Summit*, Lexington, Ky.: The Council of State Governments, 1996.

*State Government Organization Charts*, Lexington, Ky.: The Council of State Governments, 1995.

*The Book of the States: 1998-99*, Lexington, Ky.: The Council of State Governments, 1998.

*The Fiscal Survey of States*. Washington, D.C.: National Governors' Association and National Association of State Budget Officers, June 1999.

# Chapter One

# STATE CONSTITUTIONS

*The framework for state governments — includes
information on the constitutions, amendment
procedures, and constitutional commissions.*

For additional information on Chapter One contact
The States Information Center, at The Council of State Governments,
(859) 244-8253 or E-mail: sic@csg.org.

# Table 1.1
## GENERAL INFORMATION ON STATE CONSTITUTIONS
### (As of January 1, 2000)

| State or other jurisdiction | Number of constitutions* | Dates of adoption | Effective date of present constitution | Estimated length (number of words) | Number of amendments Submitted to voters | Number of amendments Adopted |
|---|---|---|---|---|---|---|
| Alabama | 6 | 1819, 1861, 1865, 1868, 1875, 1901 | Nov. 28, 1901 | 310,296 (a,b) | 913 | 664(c ) |
| Alaska | 1 | 1956 | Jan. 3, 1959 | 15,988 (b) | 37 | 28 |
| Arizona | 1 | 1911 | Feb. 14, 1912 | 28,876 | 227 | 125 |
| Arkansas | 5 | 1836, 1861, 1864, 1868, 1874 | Oct. 30, 1874 | 40,720 | 179 | 85 (d) |
| California | 2 | 1849, 1879 | July 4, 1879 | 54,645 | 834 | 500 |
| Colorado | 1 | 1876 | Aug. 1, 1876 | 45,679 | 282 | 135 |
| Connecticut | 4 | 1818 (f), 1965 | Dec. 30, 1965 | 16,608 (b) | 30 | 29 |
| Delaware | 4 | 1776, 1792, 1831, 1897 | June 10, 1897 | 19,000 | (e) | 132 |
| Florida | 6 | 1839, 1861, 1865, 1868, 1886, 1968 | Jan. 7, 1969 | 38,000 | 116 | 86 |
| Georgia | 10 | 1777, 1789, 1798, 1861, 1865, 1868, 1877, 1945, 1976, 1982 | July 1,1983 | 37,849 (b) | 68 (g) | 51 (g) |
| Hawaii | 1(h) | 1950 | Aug. 21, 1959 | 20,774 (b) | 113 | 95 |
| Idaho | 1 | 1889 | July 3, 1890 | 23,442 (b) | 202 | 115 |
| Illinois | 4 | 1818, 1848, 1870, 1970 | July 1,1971 | 13,700 | 17 | 11 |
| Indiana | 2 | 1816, 1851 | Nov. 1, 1851 | 10,315 (b) | 74 | 42 |
| Iowa | 2 | 1846, 1857 | Sept. 3, 1857 | 12,616 (b) | 57 | 52 (i) |
| Kansas | 1 | 1859 | Jan. 29, 1861 | 12,616 (b) | 120 | 91 (i) |
| Kentucky | 4 | 1792, 1799, 1850, 1891 | Sept. 28, 1891 | 23,911 (b) | 70 | 36 |
| Louisiana | 11 | 1812, 1845, 1852, 1861, 1864, 1868, 1879, 1898, 1913, 1921, 1974 | Jan. 1, 1975 | 54,112 (b) | 153 | 107 |
| Maine | 1 | 1819 | March 15, 1820 | 13,500 | 198 | 168 (j) |
| Maryland | 4 | 1776, 1851, 1864, 1867 | Oct. 5, 1867 | 41,349 | 249 | 214 (k) |
| Massachusetts | 1 | 1780 | Oct. 25, 1780 | 36,700 (l) | 146 | 118 |
| Michigan | 4 | 1835, 1850, 1908, 1963 | Jan. 1, 1964 | 25,530 (b) | 57 | 23 |
| Minnesota | 1 | 1857 | May 11, 1858 | 11,547 (b) | 213 | 118 |
| Mississippi | 4 | 1817, 1832, 1869, 1890 | Nov. 1, 1890 | 24,323 (b) | 155 | 121 |
| Missouri | 4 | 1820, 1865, 1875, 1945 | March 30, 1945 | 42,000 | 156 | 99 |
| Montana | 2 | 1889, 1972 | July 1, 1973 | 13,726 (b) | 43 | 23 |
| Nebraska | 2 | 1866, 1875 | Oct. 12, 1875 | 20,048 | 319 (m) | 213 (m) |
| Nevada | 1 | 1864 | Oct. 31, 1864 | 20,700 | 206 | 128 |
| New Hampshire | 2 | 1776, 1784 | June 2, 1784 | 9,200 | 282 (n) | 143 (n) |
| New Jersey | 3 | 1776, 1844, 1947 | Jan. 1, 1948 | 17,800 | 65 | 52 |
| New Mexico | 1 | 1911 | Jan. 6, 1912 | 27,200 | 264 | 139 |
| New York | 4 | 1777, 1822, 1846, 1894 | Jan. 1, 1895 | 51,700 | 287 | 217 |
| North Carolina | 3 | 1776, 1868, 1970 | July 1, 1971 | 11,000 | 38 | 30 |
| North Dakota | 1 | 1889 | Nov. 2, 1889 | 20,564 | 249 (o) | 137 (o) |
| Ohio | 2 | 1802, 1851 | Sept. 1, 1851 | 36,900 | 263 | 159 |
| Oklahoma | 1 | 1907 | Nov. 16, 1907 | 79,153 (b) | 314 (p) | 161 (p) |
| Oregon | 1 | 1857 | Feb. 14, 1859 | 49,326 (b) | 434 | 220 |
| Pennsylvania | 5 | 1776, 1790, 1838, 1873, 1968 (q) | 1968 (q) | 27,503 (b) | 32 (q) | 26 (q) |
| Rhode Island | 2 | 1842 (f) | May 2, 1843 | 10,233 (b) | 105 | 59 |
| South Carolina | 7 | 1776, 1778, 1790, 1861, 1865, 1868, 1895 | Jan. 1, 1896 | 22,500 | 665 (r) | 480 (r) |
| South Dakota | 1 | 1889 | Nov. 2, 1889 | 25,315 (b) | 206 | 105 |
| Tennessee | 3 | 1796, 1835, 1870 | Feb. 23, 1870 | 15,300 | 57 | 34 |
| Texas | 5 (s) | 1845, 1861, 1866, 1869, 1876 | Feb. 15, 1876 | 80,806 (b) | 564 (t) | 390 |
| Utah | 1 | 1895 | Jan. 4, 1896 | 11,000 | 146 | 96 |
| Vermont | 3 | 1777, 1786, 1793 | July 9, 1793 | 8,295 (b) | 210 | 52 |
| Virginia | 6 | 1776, 1830, 1851, 1869, 1902, 1970 | July 1, 1971 | 21,092 (b) | 42 | 34 |
| Washington | 1 | 1889 | Nov. 11, 1889 | 50,237 (b) | 163 | 92 |
| West Virginia | 2 | 1863, 1872 | April 9, 1872 | 26,000 | 116 | 67 |
| Wisconsin | 1 | 1848 | May 29, 1848 | 14,392 (b) | 181 | 133 (i) |
| Wyoming | 1 | 1889 | July 10, 1890 | 31,800 | 111 | 68 |
| American Samoa | 2 | 1960, 1967 | July 1, 1967 | 6,000 | 14 | 7 |
| No. Mariana Islands | 1 | 1977 | Jan. 9, 1978 | 11,000 | 55 | 51 (u, v) |
| Puerto Rico | 1 | 1952 | July, 25, 1952 | 9,281 | 6 | 6 |

See footnotes at end of table.

# GENERAL INFORMATION ON STATE CONSTITUTIONS — Continued

*Source*: Dr. Janice May, The University of Texas at Austin

*The constitutions referred to in this table include those Civil War documents customarily listed by the individual states.

(a) The Alabama constitution includes numerous local amendments that apply to only one county. An estimated 70 percent of all amendments are local. A 1982 amendment provides that after proposal by the legislature to which special procedures apply, only a local vote (with exceptions) is necessary to add them to the constitution.

(b) Computer word count.

(c ) One Alabama amendment on the 1998 ballot was excluded because a dispute over the election result had not been resolved.

(d) Eight of the approved amendments have been superseded and are not printed in the current edition of the constitution. The total adopted does not include five amendments proposed and adopted since statehood.

(e) Proposed amendments are not submitted to the voters in Delaware.

(f) Colonial charters with some alterations served as the first constitutions in Connecticut (1638, 1662) and in Rhode Island (1663).

(g) The Georgia constitution requires amendments to be of "general and uniform application throughout the state," thus eliminating local amendments that accounted for most of the amendments before 1982.

(h) As a kingdom and republic, Hawaii had five constitutions.

(i) The figure includes amendments approved by the voters and later nullified by the state supreme court in Iowa (three), Kansas (one), Nevada (six) and Wisconsin (two).

(j) The figure does not include one amendment approved by the voters in 1967 that is inoperative until implemented by legislation.

(k) Two sets of identical amendments were on the ballot and adopted in the 1992 Maryland election. The four amendments are counted as two in the table.

(l) The printed constitution includes many provisions that have been annulled. The length of effective provisions is an estimated 24, 122 words (12,400 annulled in Massachusetts, and in Rhode Island before the "rewrite" of the constitution in 1986, it was 11,399 words (7,627 annulled).

(m) The 1998 Nebraska ballot contained 18 separate popositions in the form of 10 amendments with subparts. The voters approved 14 of the 18 proposals.

(n) The constitution of 1784 was extensively revised in 1792. Figure show proposals and adoptions since the constitution was adopted in 1784.

(o) The figures do not include submission and approval of the constitution of 1889 itself and of Article XX; these are constitutional questions included in some counts of constitutional amendments and would add two to the figure in each column.

(p) The figures include five amendments submitted to and approved by the voters which were, by decisions of the Oklahoma or U.S. Supreme Courts, rendered inoperative or ruled invalid, unconstitutional, or illegally submitted.

(q) Certain sections of the constitution were revised by the limited convention of 1967-68. Amendments proposed and adopted are since 1968.

(r ) In 1981 approximately two-thirds of 626 proposed and four-fifths of the adopted amendments were local. Since then the amendments have been statewide propositions.

(s) The Constitution of the Republic of Texas preceded five state constitutions.

(t) The number of proposed amendments to the Texas Constitution excludes three proposed by the legislature but not placed on the ballot.

(u) By 1992 49 amendments had been proposed and 47 adopted. Since then, one was proposed but rejected in 1994, all three proposals were ratified in 1996 and in 1998, of two proposals one was adopted.

(v) The total excludes one amendment ruled void by a federal district court.

## Table 1.2
## CONSTITUTIONAL AMENDMENT PROCEDURE: BY THE LEGISLATURE
### Constitutional Provisions

| State or other jurisdiction | Legislative vote required for proposal (a) | Consideration by two sessions required | Vote required for ratification | Limitation on the number of amendments submitted at one election |
|---|---|---|---|---|
| Alabama | 3/5 | No | Majority vote on amendment | None |
| Alaska | 2/3 | No | Majority vote on amendment | None |
| Arizona | Majority | No | Majority vote on amendment | None |
| Arkansas | Majority | No | Majority vote on amendment | 3 |
| California | 2/3 | No | Majority vote on amendment | None |
| Colorado | 2/3 | No | Majority vote on amendment | None (b) |
| Connecticut | (c) | (c) | Majority vote on amendment | None |
| Delaware | 2/3 | Yes | Not required | No referendum |
| Florida | 3/5 | No | Majority vote on amendment (d) | None |
| Georgia | 2/3 | No | Majority vote on amendment | None |
| Hawaii | (e) | (e) | Majority vote on amendment (f) | None |
| Idaho | 2/3 | No | Majority vote on amendment | None |
| Illinois | 3/5 | No | (g) | 3 articles |
| Indiana | Majority | Yes | Majority vote on amendment | None |
| Iowa | Majority | Yes | Majority vote on amendment | None |
| Kansas | 2/3 | No | Majority vote on amendment | 5 |
| Kentucky | 3/5 | No | Majority vote on amendment | 4 |
| Louisiana | 2/3 | No | Majority vote on amendment (h) | None |
| Maine | 2/3 (i) | No | Majority vote on amendment | None |
| Maryland | 3/5 | No | Majority vote on amendment | None |
| Massachusetts | Majority (j) | Yes | Majority vote on amendment | None |
| Michigan | 2/3 | No | Majority vote on amendment | None |
| Minnesota | Majority | No | Majority vote in election | None |
| Mississippi | 2/3 (k) | No | Majority vote on amendment | None |
| Missouri | Majority | No | Majority vote on amendment | None |
| Montana | 2/3 (i) | No | Majority vote on amendment | None |
| Nebraska | 3/5 | No | Majority vote on amendment (f) | None |
| Nevada | Majority | Yes | Majority vote on amendment | None |
| New Hampshire | 3/5 | No | 2/3 vote on amendment | None |
| New Jersey | (l) | (l) | Majority vote on amendment | None (m) |
| New Mexico | Majority (n) | No | Majority vote on amendment (n) | None |
| New York | Majority | Yes | Majority vote on amendment | None |
| North Carolina | 3/5 | No | Majority vote on amendment | None |
| North Dakota | Majority | No | Majority vote on amendment | None |
| Ohio | 3/5 | No | Majority vote on amendment | None |
| Oklahoma | Majority | No | Majority vote on amendment | None |
| Oregon | (o) | No | Majority vote on amendment (p) | None |
| Pennsylvania | Majority (p) | Yes (p) | Majority vote on amendment | None |
| Rhode Island | Majority | No | Majority vote on amendment | None |
| South Carolina | 2/3 (q) | Yes (q) | Majority vote on amendment | None |
| South Dakota | Majority | No | Majority vote on amendment | None |
| Tennessee | (r) | Yes (r) | Majority vote in election (s) | None |
| Texas | 2/3 | No | Majority vote on amendment | None |
| Utah | 2/3 | No | Majority vote on amendment | None |
| Vermont | (t) | Yes | Majority vote on amendment | None |
| Virginia | Majority | Yes | Majority vote on amendment | None |
| Washington | 2/3 | No | Majority vote on amendment | None |
| West Virginia | 2/3 | No | Majority vote on amendment | None |
| Wisconsin | Majority | Yes | Majority vote on amendment | None |
| Wyoming | 2/3 | No | Majority vote in election | None |
| American Samoa | 2/3 | No | Majority vote on amendment (u) | None |
| No. Mariana Islands | 3/4 | No | Majority vote on amendment | None |
| Puerto Rico | 2/3 (v) | No | Majority vote on amendment | 3 |

See footnotes at end of table.

## CONSTITUTIONAL AMENDMENT PROCEDURE: BY THE LEGISLATURE — Continued

*Source*: Dr. Janice May, University of Texas at Austin

(a) In all states not otherwise noted, the figure shown in the column refers to the proportion of elected members in each house required for approval of proposed constitutional amendments.

(b) Legislature may not propose amendments to more than six articles of the constitution in the same legislative session.

(c) Three-fourths vote in each house at one session, or majority vote in each house in two sessions between which an election has intervened.

(d) Majority vote on amendment except amendment for "new state tax or fee" not in effect on Nov. 7, 1994 requires two-thirds of voters in the election.

(e) Two-thirds vote in each house at one session, or majority vote in each house in two sessions.

(f) Majority vote on amendment must be at least 50 percent of the total votes cast at the election (at least 35 percent in Nebraska); or, at a special election, a majority of the votes tallied which must be at least 30 percent of the total number of registered voters.

(g) Majority voting in election or three-fifths voting on amendment.

(h) If five or fewer political subdivisions of the state are affected, majority in state as a whole and also in affected subdivision(s) is required.

(i) Two-thirds of both houses.

(j) Majority of members elected sitting in joint session.

(k) The two-thirds must include not less than a majority elected to each house.

(l) Three-fifths of all members of each house at one session, or majority of all members of each house for two successive sessions.

(m) If a proposed amendment is not approved at the election when submitted, neither the same amendment nor one which would make substantially the same change for the constitution may be again submitted to the people before the third general election thereafter.

(n) Amendments concerning certain elective franchise and education matters require three-fourths vote of members elected and approval by three-fourths of electors voting in state on the amendment.

(o) Majority vote to amend constitution, two-thirds to revise ("revise" includes all or a part of the constitution).

(p) Emergency amendments may be passed by two-thirds vote of each house, followed by ratification by majority vote of electors in election held at least one month after legislative approval. There is an exception for an amendment containing a supermajority voting requirement, which must be ratified by an equal supermajority.

(q) Two-thirds of members of each house, first passage; majority of members of each house after popular ratification.

(r) Majority of members elected to both houses, first passage; two-thirds of members elected to both houses, second passage.

(s) Majority of all citizens voting on amendment.

(t) Two-thirds vote senate, majority vote house, first passage; majority both houses, second passage. As of 1974, amendments may be submitted only every four years.

(u) Within 30 days after voter approval, governor must submit amendment(s) to U.S. Secretary of the Interior for approval.

(v) If approved by two-thirds of members of each house, amendment(s) submitted to voters at special referendum; if approved by not less than three-fourths of total members of each house, referendum may be held at next general election.

## Table 1.3
## CONSTITUTIONAL AMENDMENT PROCEDURE: BY INITIATIVE
## Constitutional Provisions

| State or other jurisdiction | Number of signatures required on initiative petition | Distribution of signatures | Referendum vote |
|---|---|---|---|
| Arizona | 15% of total votes cast for all candidates for governor at last election. | None specified. | Majority vote on amendment. |
| Arkansas | 10% of voters for governor at last election. | Must include 5% of voters for governor in each of 15 counties. | Majority vote on amendment. |
| California | 8% of total voters for all candidates for governor at last election. | None specified. | Majority vote on amendment. |
| Colorado | 5% of total legal votes for all candidates for secretary of state at last general election. | None specified. | Majority vote on amendment. |
| Florida | 8% of total votes cast in the state in the last election for presidential electors. | 8% of total votes cast in each of 1/2 of the congressional districts. | Majority vote on amendment except amendment for "new state tax or fee" not in effect Nov. 7, 1994 requires 2/3 of voters voting in election. |
| Illinois (a) | 8% of total votes cast for candidates for governor at last election. | None specified. | Majority voting in election or 3/5 voting on amendment. |
| Massachusetts (b) | 3% of total votes cast for governor at preceding biennial state election (not less than 25,000 qualified voters). | No more than 1/4 from any one county. | Majority vote on amendment which must be 30% of total ballots cast at election. |
| Michigan | 10% of total voters for all candidates at last gubernatorial election. | None specified. | Majority vote on amendment. |
| Mississippi | 12% of total votes for all candidates for governor in last election. | No more than 20% from any one congressional district. vote cast at election. | Majority vote on amendment and not less than 40% of total. |
| Missouri | 8% of legal voters for all candidates for governor at last election. | The 8% must be in each of 2/3 of the congressional districts in the state. | Majority vote on amendment. |
| Montana | 10% of qualified electors, the number of qualified electors to be determined by number of votes cast for governor in preceding general election. | The 10% to include at least 10% of qualified electors in each of 2/5 of the legislative districts. | Majority vote on amendment. |
| Nebraska | 10% of total votes for governor at last election. | The 10% must include 5% in each of 2/5 of the counties. of total vote at the election. | Majority vote on amendment which must be at least 35%. |
| Nevada | 10% of voters who voted in entire state in last general election. | 10% of total voters who voted in each of 75% of the counties. | Majority vote on amendment in two consecutive general elections. |
| North Dakota | 4% of population of the state. | None specified. | Majority vote on amendment. |
| Ohio | 10% of total number of electors who voted for governor in last election. | At least 5% of qualified electors in each of 1/2 of counties in the state. | Majority vote on amendment. |
| Oklahoma | 15% of legal voters for state office receiving highest number of voters at last general state election. | None specified. | Majority vote on amendment. |
| Oregon | 8% of total votes for all candidates for governor at last election at which governor was elected for four-year term. | None specified. | Majority vote on amendment except for supermajority equal to supermajority voting requirement contained in proposed amendment. |
| South Dakota | 10% of total votes for governor in last election. | None specified. | Majority vote on amendment. |
| No. Mariana Islands | 50% of qualified voters of commonwealth. | In addition, 25% of qualified voters in each senatorial district. | Majority vote on amendment if legislature approved it by majority vote; if not, at least 2/3 vote in each of two senatorial districts in addition to a majority vote. |

*Source*: Dr. Janice May, University of Texas at Austin
(a) Only Article IV, the Legislature, may be amended by initiative petition.
(b) Before being submitted to the electorate for ratification, initiative measures must be approved at two sessions of a successively elected legislature by not less than one-fourth of all members elected, sitting in joint session.

## Table 1.4
## PROCEDURES FOR CALLING CONSTITUTIONAL CONVENTIONS
### Constitutional Provisions

| State or other jurisdiction | Provision for convention | Legislative vote for submission of convention question (a) | Popular vote to authorize convention | Periodic submission of convention question required (b) | Popular vote required for ratification of convention proposals |
|---|---|---|---|---|---|
| Alabama | Yes | Majority | ME | No | Not specified |
| Alaska | Yes | No provision (c,d) | (c) | 10 years (c) | Not specified (c) |
| Arizona | Yes | Majority | (e) | No | MP |
| Arkansas | No | No | | | |
| California | Yes | 2/3 | MP | No | MP |
| Colorado | Yes | 2/3 | MP | No | ME |
| Connecticut | Yes | 2/3 | MP | 20 years (f) | MP |
| Delaware | Yes | 2/3 | MP | No | No provision |
| Florida | Yes | (g) | MP | No | Not specified |
| Georgia | Yes | (d) | No | No | MP |
| Hawaii | Yes | Not specified | MP | 9 years | MP (h) |
| Idaho | Yes | 2/3 | MP | No | Not specified |
| Illinois | Yes | 3/4 | (i) | 20 years; 1988 | MP |
| Indiana | No | No | | | |
| Iowa | Yes | Majority | MP | 10 years; 1970 | MP |
| Kansas | Yes | 2/3 | MP | No | MP |
| Kentucky | Yes | Majority (j) | MP (k) | No | No provision |
| Louisiana | Yes | (d) | No | No | MP |
| Maine | Yes | (d) | No | No | No provision |
| Maryland | Yes | Majority | ME | 20 years; 1970 | MP |
| Massachusetts | No | | No | Not specified | |
| Michigan | Yes | Majority | MP | 16 years; 1978 | MP |
| Minnesota | Yes | 2/3 | ME | No | 3/5 voting on proposal |
| Mississippi | No | No | | | |
| Missouri | Yes | Majority | MP | 20 years; 1962 | Not specified (l) |
| Montana | Yes (m) | 2/3 | MP | 20 years | MP |
| Nebraska | Yes | 3/4 | MP (o) | No | MP |
| Nevada | Yes | 2/3 | ME | No | No provision |
| New Hampshire | Yes | Majority | MP | 10 years | 2/3 voting on proposal |
| New Jersey | No | No | | | |
| New Mexico | Yes | 2/3 | MP | No | Not specified |
| New York | Yes | Majority | MP | 20 years; 1957 | MP |
| North Carolina | Yes | 2/3 | MP | No | MP |
| North Dakota | No | No | | | |
| Ohio | Yes | 2/3 | MP | 20 years; 1932 | MP |
| Oklahoma | Yes | Majority | (e) | 20 years | MP |
| Oregon | Yes | Majority | (e) | No | No provision |
| Pennsylvania | No | No | | | |
| Rhode Island | Yes | Majority | MP | 10 years | MP |
| South Carolina | Yes | (d) | ME | No | No provision |
| South Dakota | Yes | (d) | (d) | No | (p) |
| Tennessee | Yes (q) | Majority | MP | No | MP |
| Texas | No | No | | | |
| Utah | Yes | 2/3 | ME | No | MP |
| Vermont | No | No | | | |
| Virginia | Yes | (d) | No | No | MP |
| Washington | Yes | 2/3 | ME | No | Not specified |
| West Virginia | Yes | Majority | MP | No | Not specified |
| Wisconsin | Yes | Majority | MP | No | No provision |
| Wyoming | Yes | 2/3 | ME | No | Not specified |
| American Samoa | Yes | (r) | No | No | ME (s) |
| No. Mariana Islands | Yes | Majority (t) | 3-Feb | No (u) in each of 2 senatorial districts | MP and at least 2/3 in |
| Puerto Rico | Yes | 2/3 | MP | No | MP |

See footnotes at end of table.

# PROCEDURES FOR CALLING CONSTITUTIONAL CONVENTIONS — Continued

*Source*: Dr. Janice May, University of Texas at Austin

*Key:*

MP — Majority voting on the proposal.

ME — Majority voting in the election.

(a) In all states not otherwise noted, the entries in this column refer to the proportion of members elected to each house required to submit to the electorate the question of calling a constitutional convention.

(b) The number listed is the interval between required submissions on the question of calling a constitutional convention; where given, the date is that of the first required submission of the convention question.

(c) Unless provided otherwise by law, convention calls are to conform as nearly as possible to the act calling the 1955 convention, which provided for a legislative vote of a majority of members elected to each house and ratification by a majority vote on the proposals. The legislature may call a constitutional convention at any time.

(d) In these states, the legislature may call a convention without submitting the question to the people. The legislative vote required is two-thirds of the members elected to each house in Georgia, Louisiana, South Carolina and Virginia; two-thirds concurrent vote of both branches in Maine; three-fourths of all members of each house in South Dakota; and not specified in Alaska, but bills require majority vote of membership of each house. In South Dakota, the question of calling a convention may be initiated by the people in the same manner as an amendment to the constitution (see Table 1.3) and requires a majority vote on the question for approval.

(e) The law calling a convention must be approved by the people.

(f) The legislature shall submit the question 20 years after the last convention, or 20 years after the last vote on the question of calling a convention, whichever date is last.

(g) The power to call a convention is reserved to the people by petition.

(h) The majority must be 50 percent of the total votes cast at a general election or at a special election, a majority of the votes tallied which must be at least 30 percent of the total number of registered voters.

(i) Majority voting in the election, or three-fifths voting on the question.

(j) Must be approved during two legislative sessions.

(k) Majority must equal one-fourth of qualified voters at last general election.

(l) Majority of those voting on the proposal is assumed.

(m) The question of calling a constitutional convention may be submitted either by the legislature or by initiative petition to the secretary of state in the same manner as provided for initiated amendments (see Table 1.3).

(n) Two-thirds of all members of the legislature.

(o) Majority must be 35 percent of total votes cast at the election.

(p) Convention proposals are submitted to the electorate at a special election in a manner to be determined by the convention. Ratification by a majority of votes cast.

(q) Conventions may not be held more often than once in six years.

(r) Five years after effective date of constitutions, governor shall call a constitutional convention to consider changes proposed by a constitutional committee appointed by the governor. Delegates to the convention are to be elected by their county councils. A convention was held in 1972.

(s) If proposed amendments are approved by the voters, they must be submitted to the U.S. Secretary of the Interior for approval.

(t) The initiative may also be used to place a referendum convention call on the ballot. The petition must be signed by 25 percent of the qualified voters or at least 75 percent in a senatorial district.

(u) The legislature was required to submit the referendum no later than seven years after the effective date of the constitution. The convention was held in 1985; 45 amendments were submitted to the voters.

**Table 1.5**
**STATE CONSTITUTIONAL COMMISSIONS**
**(Operative during January 1, 1998 to January 1, 2000)**

| State | Name of commission | Method and date of creation and period of operation | Membership: number and type | Funding | Purpose of commission | Proposals and action |
|---|---|---|---|---|---|---|
| Florida | Florida Constitution Revision Commission | Constitution: Florida Constitution Art. XI, secs. 2 (a) and 2 (c), as amended in 1988 and 1996. Established every 20 years within 30 days after legislature adjournment and must present constitutional proposals 180 days before general election. 1997-98 commission: June 1997-May 1998 | 37: attorney general ex officio. 36 appointed: by governor (15), by speaker of House (9), by president of Senate (9), by chief justice of Supreme Court with advice of justices (3). 3 alternates. Governor designates chair. | $1.8 million appropriation | To review constitution and propose necessary revision directly to voters. | June 1997- March 1998 meetings. 10 substantive commission committees. 15 public hearings scheduled at various locations. Internet home page, monthly news letters, journal, manual, TV call-in. Hundreds of citizen and member proposals. Commission approved 33 in form of constitutional amendments for Nov. 1998 ballot. Voters adopted 8 for substantial revision covering all articles and schedule. Subjects included: equal and basic rights, education as fundamental right and state duty, gun control, public campaign financing, environmental protection, cabinet reform, appointment option for trial judges. |
| Utah | Utah Constitutional Revision Commission | Statutory: Ch. 89, *Laws of Utah,* 1969; amended by Ch. 107, *Laws* 1977, which made the commission permanent as of July 1 1977. (Codified as Ch. 54, Title 63, *Utah Code Annotated,* 1953.) | 16: 1 ex officio, 9 appointed - by the speaker of the House (3), president of the Senate (3), and governor (3) - no more than 2 of each group to be from same party; and 6 additional members appointed by the 9 previously appointed members. | Appropriations through 1995 totaled $1,023,000. In recent years, annual appropriations have been $55,000. | Study constitution and recommend desirable changes including proposed drafts. | Mandated to report recommendations at least 60 days before legislature convenes. Voter action on commission recommendations through 1997 include: approval of revised articles on legislature, executive, judiciary, elections and rights of suffrage, revenue and taxation, education, and corporations. In 1998: voters approved 4 commission recommended amendments; commission report to legislature on election cycle and on local government provisions (1997 draft revised). In 1999: study of judicial retention elections. |

*Source:* Dr. Janice May, University of Texas at Austin
*Note:* No constitutional conventions were held from January 1, 1998 through January 1, 2000.

# Table 1.6
## STATE CONSTITUTIONAL CHANGES BY METHOD OF INITIATION: 1992-93, 1994-95, 1996-97 and 1998-1999

| Method of installation | Number of states involved | | | | Total proposals | | | | Total adopted | | | | Percentage adopted | | | |
|---|---|---|---|---|---|---|---|---|---|---|---|---|---|---|---|---|
| | 1992-93 | 1994-95 | 1996-97 | 1998-99 | 1992-93 | 1994-95 | 1996-97 | 1998-99 | 1992-93 | 1994-95 | 1996-97 | 1998-99 | 1992-93 | 1994-95 | 1996-97 | 1998-99 |
| All methods | 43 | 43 | 42 | 46 | 239 | 233 | 233 | 296 | 160 | 168 | 178 | 229‡ | 66.1* | 70.3* | 76.3* | 77.2*‡ |
| Legislative proposal | 42 | 41 | 42 | 46 | 201 | 202 | 193 | 266 | 137 | 158 | 159 | 210‡ | 67.1* | 76.2* | 82.4* | 78.8*‡ |
| Constitutional initiative | 13 | 13 | 12 | 12 | 34 | 31 | 40 | 21 | 21 | 10 | 19 | 11 | 61.7 | 32.2 | 47.5 | 52.4 |
| Constitutional convention | 1 | ... | ... | 1 | 1 | ... | ... | ... | 0.0 | ... | ... | ... | 0.0 | ... | ... | ... |
| Constitutional commission | 1 | ... | ... | ... | 3 | ... | ... | 9 | 2 | ... | ... | 8 | 66.6 | ... | ... | 88.9 |

*Source:* Dr. Janice May, University of Texas at Austin
*Key:*
* — In calculating these percentages, the amendments adopted in Delaware (where proposals are not submitted to the voters) are excluded.
‡ — One Alabama amendment is excluded from adoptions because the election results are in dispute.
... — Not applicable

# Table 1.7
## SUBSTANTIVE CHANGES IN STATE CONSTITUTIONS: PROPOSED AND ADOPTED 1992-93, 1994-95, 1996-97 and 1998-1999

| Subject matter | Total proposed | | | | Total adopted | | | | Percentage adopted | | | |
|---|---|---|---|---|---|---|---|---|---|---|---|---|
| | 1992-93 | 1994-95 | 1996-97 | 1998-99 | 1992-93 | 1994-95 | 1996-97 | 1998-99 | 1992-93 | 1994-95 | 1996-97 | 1998-99 |
| Proposals of statewide applicability | 211* | 199* | 194* | 250* | 139† | 141† | 146† | 188† | 64.9* | 68.8* | 75.2* | 74.8* |
| Bill of Rights | 18 | 26 | 22 | 34 | 15 | 19 | 17 | 31 | 83.3 | 73.0 | 77.2 | 91.1 |
| Suffrage & elections | 8† | 9 | 13 | 7 | 8 | 6 | 12 | 7 | 100.0 | 66.6 | 92.3 | 100.0 |
| Legislative branch | 42 | 30 | 27 | 40 | 31 | 23 | 12 | 29 | 73.8 | 76.6 | 44.4 | 72.5 |
| Executive branch | 15 | 16 | 15 | 17 | 13 | 12 | 10 | 10 | 86.6 | 75.0 | 66.6 | 58.8 |
| Judicial branch | 12† | 22 | 15* | 19 | 9 | 19 | 17 | 16 | 75.0 | 77.2 | 93.3 | 84.2 |
| Local government | 10 | 9 | 7 | 15 | 6 | 7 | 5 | 10 | 60.0 | 77.7 | 71.4 | 66.6 |
| Finance & taxation | 54 | 49 | 41 | 61 | 29 | 30 | 31 | 46 | 53.7 | 61.2 | 75.6 | 75.4 |
| State & local debt | 4 | 5 | 9 | 6 | 2 | 2 | 8 | 4 | 50.0 | 40.0 | 88.8 | 66.6 |
| State functions | 25 | 17 | 21 | 24 | 9 | 11 | 17 | 14 | 36.0 | 52.9 | 80.9 | 58.3 |
| Amendment & revision | 2 | 6 | 4 | 3 | 1 | 4 | 3 | 3 | 50.0 | 66.6 | 75.0 | 100.0 |
| General revision proposals | 0 | 0 | 0 | 1 | 0 | 0 | 0 | 1 | 0.0 | 0.0 | 0.0 | 100.0 |
| Miscellaneous proposals | 23 | 10 | 20 | 23‡ | 16 | 8 | 14 | 17‡ | 69.5 | 80.0 | 70.0 | 77.2 |
| Local amendments | 28 | 34 | 39 | 46 | 21 | 27 | 32 | 41†† | 75.7 | 79.4 | 82.0 | 91.1†† |

*Source:* Dr. Janice May, University of Texas at Austin
*Key:*
* — Excludes Delaware where proposals are not submitted to voters.
† — Includes Delaware.
‡ — Includes two amendments that provided for substantial editing: Delaware (gender-neutral changes) and Texas (removal of obsolete and duplicative provisions)
†† — Excludes one Alabama amendment pending resolution of dispute over election results.

## Table 1.8
## STATE CONSTITUTIONAL CHANGES BY CONSTITUTIONAL INITIATIVE (1998-99)

| State | Number of proposals | Number of adoptions | Percentage adopted |
|---|---|---|---|
| Arizona | 1 | 1 | 100.0 |
| Arkansas | 0 | 0 | 0.0 |
| California | 2 | 1 | 50.0 |
| Colorado | 4 | 1 | 25.0 |
| Florida | 0 | 0 | 0.0 |
| Illinois | 0 | 0 | 0.0 |
| Massachusetts | 0 | 0 | 0.0 |
| Michigan | 0 | 0 | 0.0 |
| Mississippi | 1 | 0 | 0.0 |
| Missouri | 1 | 1 | 100.0 |
| Montana | 1 | 1 | 100.0 |
| Nebraska | 1 | 0 | 0.0 |
| Nevada | 1* | 1* | 100.0* |
| North Dakota | 1 | 1 | 100.0 |
| Ohio | 0 | 0 | 0.0 |
| Oklahoma | 1 | 0 | 0.0 |
| Oregon | 5 | 3 | 60.0 |
| South Dakota | 2 | 1 | 50.0 |
| Total | 21 | 11 | 52.4 |

*Source*: Dr. Janice May, University of Texas at Austin

*Nevada voters approved for the second time one initiative and for the first time one initiative. To become effective, constitutional initiatives require voter approval in two elections. The new initiative was not counted in the table.

# Chapter Two

# EXECUTIVE BRANCH

*Who's who and what's what for the offices of governor, lieutenant governor, secretary of state, attorney general, treasurer and many others — includes information on terms of office, methods of selection, qualifications, salaries, and powers and duties.*

For additional information on Chapter Two contact
The States Information Center, at The Council of State Governments,
(859) 244-8253 or E-mail: sic@csg.org.

## Table 2.1
## THE GOVERNORS, 2000

| State or other jurisdiction | Name and party | Length of regular term in years | Date of first service | Present term ends | Number of previous terms | Maximum consecutive terms allowed by constitution | Joint election of governor and lieutenant governor (a) | Official who succeeds governor | Birthdate | Birthplace |
|---|---|---|---|---|---|---|---|---|---|---|
| Alabama | Don Siegelman (D) | 4 | 1/99 | 1/03 | ... | 2 | No | LG | 2/24/46 | AL |
| Alaska | Tony Knowles (D) | 4 | 12/94 | 12/02 | 1 | 2 | Yes | LG | 1/1/43 | OK |
| Arizona | Jane Dee Hull (R) | 4 | 9/97 (b) | 1/03 | 1 (b) | 2 (c) | (q) | SS | 8/8/35 | MO |
| Arkansas | Mike Huckabee (R) | 4 | 7/96 (c) | 1/03 | 1 (c) | 2 (c) | No | LG | 8/24/55 | AR |
| California | Gray Davis (D) | 4 | 1/99 | 1/03 | ... | 2 | No | LG | 12/26/42 | NY |
| Colorado | Bill Owens (R) | 4 | 1/99 | 1/03 | ... | 2 | Yes | LG | 10/22/50 | TX |
| Connecticut | John G. Rowland (R) | 4 | 1/95 | 1/03 | 1 | ... | Yes | LG | 5/24/57 | CT |
| Delaware | Thomas R. Carper (D) | 4 | 1/93 | 1/01 | 1 | 2 (j) | No | LG | 1/23/47 | WV |
| Florida | Jeb Bush (R) | 4 | 1/99 | 1/03 | ... | 2 | Yes | LG | 2/11/53 | TX |
| Georgia | Roy Barnes (D) | 4 | 1/99 | 1/03 | ... | 2 | No | LG | 3/11/48 | GA |
| Hawaii | Benjamin J. Cayetano (D) | 4 | 12/94 | 12/02 | 1 | 2 | Yes | LG | 11/14/39 | HI |
| Idaho | Dirk Kempthorne (R) | 4 | 1/99 | 1/03 | ... | 2 | No | LG | 10/29/51 | CA |
| Illinois | George H. Ryan (R) | 4 | 1/99 | 1/03 | ... | ... | Yes | LG | 2/24/34 | IL |
| Indiana | Frank O'Bannon (D) | 4 | 1/97 | 1/01 | 1 | 2 | Yes | LG | 1/30/30 | KY |
| Iowa | Tom Vilsack (D) | 4 | 1/99 | 1/03 | ... | ... | Yes | LG | 12/13/50 | PA |
| Kansas | Bill Graves (R) | 4 | 1/95 | 1/03 | 1 | 2 | Yes | LG | 1/9/53 | KS |
| Kentucky | Paul E. Patton (D) | 4 | 12/95 | 12/03 | 1 | 2 | Yes | LG | 5/26/37 | KY |
| Louisiana | Mike Foster (R) | 4 | 1/96 | 1/04 | 1 | 2 | No | LG | 7/11/30 | LA |
| Maine | Angus S. King Jr. (I) | 4 | 1/95 | 1/03 | 1 | 2 | (q) | PS | 3/31/44 | VA |
| Maryland | Parris N. Glendening (D) | 4 | 1/95 | 1/03 | 1 | 2 | Yes | LG | 6/11/42 | NY |
| Massachusetts | Argeo Paul Cellucci (R) | 4 | 7/97 (d) | 1/03 | 1 (d) | ... | Yes | LG | 4/24/48 | MA |
| Michigan | John Engler (R) | 4 | 1/91 | 1/03 | 2 | 2 (k) | Yes | LG | 10/12/48 | MI |
| Minnesota | Jesse Ventura (Reform) (t) | 4 | 1/99 | 1/03 | ... | ... | No | LG | 7/15/51 | MN |
| Mississippi | David Ronald Musgrove (D) | 4 | 1/00 | 1/04 | ... | 2 | No | LG | 7/29/56 | MS |
| Missouri | Mel Carnahan (D) | 4 | 1/93 | 1/01 | 1 | 2 (j) | No | LG | 2/11/34 | MO |
| Montana | Marc Racicot (R) | 4 | 1/93 | 1/01 | 1 | 2 (l) | Yes | LG | 7/24/48 | MT |
| Nebraska | Mike Johanns (R) | 4 | 1/99 | 1/03 | ... | 2 (m) | Yes | LG | 6/18/50 | NE |
| Nevada | Kenny C. Guinn (R) | 4 | 1/99 | 1/03 | ... | 2 | No | LG | 8/24/36 | AR |
| New Hampshire | Jeanne Shaheen (D) | 2 | 1/97 | 1/01 | 1 | ... | (q) | PS | 1/28/47 | MO |
| New Jersey | Christine T. Whitman (R) | 4 | 1/94 | 1/02 | 1 | 2 | (q) | PS | 9/26/46 | NY |
| New Mexico | Gary E. Johnson (R) | 4 | 1/95 | 1/03 | 1 | 2 | Yes | LG | 1/1/53 | ND |
| New York | George E. Pataki (R) | 4 | 1/95 | 1/03 | 1 | ... | Yes | LG | 6/24/45 | NY |
| North Carolina | James B. Hunt Jr. (D) | 4 | 1/77 | 1/01 | 3 (e) | 2 | No | LG | 5/16/37 | NC |
| North Dakota | Edward T. Schafer (R) | 4 | 12/92 | 12/00 | 1 | ... | Yes | LG | 8/8/46 | ND |
| Ohio | Bob Taft (R) | 4 | 1/99 | 1/03 | ... | 2 | Yes | LG | 1/8/42 | OH |
| Oklahoma | Frank Keating (R) | 4 | 1/95 | 1/03 | 1 | 2 | No | LG | 2/10/44 | MO |
| Oregon | John A. Kitzhaber (D) | 4 | 1/95 | 1/03 | 1 | 2 | (p) | SS | 3/5/47 | WA |
| Pennsylvania | Tom Ridge (R) | 4 | 1/95 | 1/03 | 1 | 2 | Yes | LG | 8/26/45 | PA |
| Rhode Island | Lincoln Almond (R) | 4 | 1/95 | 1/03 | 1 | 2 | No | LG | 6/16/36 | RI |
| South Carolina | Jim Hodges (D) | 4 | 1/99 | 1/03 | ... | 2 | No | LG | 11/19/56 | SC |

See footnotes at end of table.

# THE GOVERNORS, 2000 — Continued

| State or other jurisdiction | Name and party | Length of regular term in years | Date of first service | Present term ends | Number of previous terms | Maximum consecutive terms allowed by constitution | Joint election of governor and lieutenant governor (a) | Official who succeeds governor | Birthdate | Birthplace |
|---|---|---|---|---|---|---|---|---|---|---|
| South Dakota | William J. Janklow (R) | 4 | 1/79 | 1/03 | 3 (f) | 2 | Yes | LG | 9/13/39 | IL |
| Tennessee | Don Sundquist (R) | 4 | 1/95 | 1/03 | 1 | 2 | No | SpS (s) | 3/15/36 | IL |
| Texas | George W. Bush (R) | 4 | 1/95 | 1/03 | 1 | ... | No | LG | 7/6/46 | CT |
| Utah | Micheal O. Leavitt (R) | 4 | 1/93 | 1/01 | 1 | 3 (n) | Yes | LG | 2/11/51 | UT |
| Vermont | Howard Dean (D) | 2 | 8/91 (g) | 1/01 | 3 (g) | ... | No | LG | 11/17/48 | NY |
| Virginia | James S. Gilmore III (R) | 4 | 1/98 | 1/02 | ... | (o) | No | LG | 10/6/49 | VA |
| Washington | Gary Locke (D) | 4 | 1/97 | 1/01 | ... | (p) | No | LG | 1/21/50 | WA |
| West Virginia | Cecil H. Underwood (R) | 4 | 1/56 | 1/01 | 1 (h) | 2 | (f) | PS | 11/5/22 | WV |
| Wisconsin | Tommy G. Thompson (R) | 4 | 1/87 | 1/03 | 3 | ... | Yes | LG | 11/19/41 | WI |
| Wyoming | Jim Geringer (R) | 4 | 1/95 | 1/03 | 1 | 2 | (f) | SS | 4/24/44 | WY |
| American Samoa | Tauese P. F. Sunia (D) | 4 | 1/97 | 1/01 | ... | 2 | Yes | LG | 8/29/41 | AS |
| Guam | Carl T.C. Gutierrez (D) | 4 | 1/95 | 1/03 | ... | 2 | Yes | LG | 10/15/41 | GU |
| No. Mariana Islands | Pedro P. Tenorio (R) | 4 | 1/94 | 1/02 | 2 (i) | 2 | Yes | LG | 4/18/34 | CNMI |
| Puerto Rico | Pedro J. Rossello (D) (r) | 4 | 1/93 | 1/01 | 1 | ... | (f) | SS | 4/5/44 | PR |
| U.S. Virgin Islands | Charles W. Turnbull (D) | 4 | 1/99 | 1/03 | ... | (o) | Yes | LG | 2/5/35 | VI |

*Sources*: National Governors' Association and The Council of State Governments.

Key:
D — Democrat
I — Independent
R — Republican
LG — Lieutenant Governor
SS — Secretary of the Senate
PS — President of the Senate
SpS — Speaker of the Senate
... — Not applicable

(a) The following also choose candidates for governor and lieutenant governor through a joint nomination process: Florida, Kansas, Maryland, Minnesota, Montana, North Dakota, Ohio, Utah, American Samoa, Guam, No. Mariana Islands and U.S. Virgin Islands.

(b) Governor Hull, as secretary of state, became Governor in September 1997 after Governor Fife Symington resigned. She was elected in November 1997 to a full four-year term. She is not eligible to serve another term.

(c) Governor Huckabee, as lieutenant governor, became Governor in July 1996 after Governor Jim Guy Tucker resigned. He was elected to a full four-year term in November 1998. He is eligible to serve one more term.

(d) Governor Cellucci, as lieutenant governor, became Governor in July 1997 after Governor William F. Weld resigned. He was elected to a full four-year term in November 1998.

(e) Served 1977-1981, 1981-1985 and 1993-1997.

(f) Served 1979-83 and 1983-87.

(g) Governor Dean, as lieutenant governor, became Governor in August 1991 after the death of Governor Richard A. Snelling. He was elected to full two-year terms in November 1992, November 1994, November 1996 and November 1998.

(h) Served from 1957-1961.

(i) Governor Tenorio served previous terms from 1981 to 1985 and from 1985 to 1989.

(j) Absolute two-term limitation, but terms need not be consecutive.

(k) The term of office is limited to two four-year terms; however, the law became effective after Governor Engler was first elected in 1990, so he is grandfathered.

(l) Absolute limit of eight years of service out of every sixteen years.

(m) After two consecutive terms as Governor, the candidate must wait four years before becoming eligible to run again.

(n) The term of office is limited to three consecutive four-year terms; however, because this provision was passed during Governor Leavitt's administration, he has been grandfathered from the provision and is eligible to serve one additional term.

(o) Governor cannot serve immediate successive terms.

(p) Absolute limit of eight years of service out of every fourteen years.

(q) No lieutenant governor.

(r) Governor Rossello also is a member of the New Progressive Party.

(s) Official bears the additional title of "lieutenant governor."

(t) Governor Ventura was elected on the Reform ticket. He switched to the Independance Party of Minnesota after his election.

# Table 2.2
# THE GOVERNORS: QUALIFICATIONS FOR OFFICE

| State or other jurisdiction | Minimum age | State citizen (years) | U.S. citizen (years) | State resident (years) | Qualified voter (years) |
|---|---|---|---|---|---|
| Alabama* | 30 | 7 | 10 | 7 | ... |
| Alaska | 30 | ... | 7 | 7 | ★ |
| Arizona | 25 | 5 | 10 | ... | ... |
| Arkansas | 30 | ... | ★ | 7 | ... |
| California* | 18 | ... | 5 | 5 | ★ |
| Colorado* | 30 | ... | ★ | 2 | ... |
| Connecticut | 30 | ... | ... | ... | ★ |
| Delaware* | 30 | ... | 12 | 6 | ... |
| Florida | 30 | ... | ... | 7 | ★ |
| Georgia* | 30 | ... | 15 | 6 | ... |
| Hawaii | 30 | ★ | ... | 5 | ★ |
| Idaho | 30 | ... | ★ | 2 | ... |
| Illinois | 25 | ... | ★ | 3 | ... |
| Indiana | 30 | ... | 5 | 5 | ... |
| Iowa | 30 | ... | ★ | 2 | ... |
| Kansas | ... | ... | ... | ... | ... |
| Kentucky | 30 | 6 | ★ | 6 | ... |
| Louisiana | 25 | 5 | 5 | ... | ★ |
| Maine | 30 | ... | 15 | 5 | ... |
| Maryland | 30 | ... | (a) | 5 | 5 |
| Massachusetts | ... | ... | ... | 7 | ... |
| Michigan | 30 | ... | ... | ... | 4 |
| Minnesota | 25 | ... | ★ | 1 | ... |
| Mississippi | 30 | ... | 20 | 5 | ... |
| Missouri | 30 | ... | 15 | 10 | ... |
| Montana | 25 | ★ | ★ | 2 | ... |
| Nebraska | 30 | 5 | 5 | 5 | ... |
| Nevada* | 25 | 2 | ... | 2 | ★ |
| New Hampshire | 30 | ... | ... | 7 | ... |
| New Jersey | 30 | ... | 20 | 7 | ... |
| New Mexico | 30 | ... | ★ | 5 | ★ |
| New York | 30 | ... | ★ | 5 | ★ |
| North Carolina* | 30 | ... | 5 | 2 | ... |
| North Dakota | 30 | ... | ★ | 5 | ★ |
| Ohio | 18 | ... | ★ | ★ | ★ |
| Oklahoma* | 31 | ... | ★ | ... | 10 |
| Oregon | 30 | ... | ★ | 3 | ... |
| Pennsylvania | 30 | ... | ★ | 7 | ... |
| Rhode Island | ... | ... | ... | ... | ★ |
| South Carolina | 30 | 5 | ★ | 5 | ★ |
| South Dakota | 18 | ... | 2 | 2 | ... |
| Tennessee | 30 | 7 | ★ | ... | ... |
| Texas | 30 | ... | ★ | 5 | ... |
| Utah* | 30 | 5 | ... | 5 | ★ |
| Vermont* | ... | ... | ... | 4 | ... |
| Virginia | 30 | ... | ★ | 5 | 5 |
| Washington | 18 | ... | ★ | ... | ★ |
| West Virginia | 30 | 5 | ... | 1 | ★ |
| Wisconsin | 18 | ... | ★ | ... | ★ |
| Wyoming | 30 | ... | ★ | 5 | ★ |
| American Samoa* | 35 | ... | ★ | 5 | ... |
| Guam | 30 | ... | 5 | 5 | ★ |
| No. Mariana Islands* | 35 | ... | ... | 10 | ★ |
| Puerto Rico | 35 | 5 | 5 | 5 | ... |
| U.S. Virgin Islands* | 30 | ... | 5 | 5 | ★ |

*Source*: The Council of State Governments' survey, January 2000; except as noted by * where information is from *The Book of the States 1998-99*.

*Key*:
★— Formal provision; number of years not specified.
... — No formal provision.
(a) *Crosse v. Board of Supervisors of Elections* 243 Md. 555, 221A.2d431 (1966) — opinion rendered indicated that U.S. citizenship was, by necessity, a requirement for office.

(b) No person convicted of a felony is eligible to hold office until final discharge from state supervision.

(c) No person in default as a collector and custodian of public money or property shall be eligible to public office; no person convicted of a felony shall be eligible unless restored to civil rights.

## Table 2.3
## THE GOVERNORS: COMPENSATION

| State or other jurisdiction | Salary | Governor's office staff (a) | Access to state transportation | | | Travel allowance | Official residence |
|---|---|---|---|---|---|---|---|
| | | | Automobile | Airplane | Helicopter | | |
| Alabama* | $94,655 | 22 | ★ | ★ | ★ | (b) | ★ |
| Alaska | 81,648 | 67 | ★ | ... | ... | (b) | ★ |
| Arizona | 95,000 | 150 (a) | ★ | ★ | ... | (b) | ... |
| Arkansas | 68,448 | 55 | ★ | ... | ... | (c) | ★ |
| California* | 165,000 (d) | 86 | ★ | ... | ... | (c) | (e) |
| Colorado* | 90,000 | 39 | ★ | ★ | ... | (f) | ★ |
| Connecticut | 78,000 | 38 | ★ | ... | ... | (f) | ★ |
| Delaware* | 107,000 | 25 | ★ | ★ | ★ | (b) | ★ |
| Florida | 117,240 | 310 | ★ | ★ | ... | (b) | ★ |
| Georgia* | 111,480 | 43 | ★ | ★ | ★ | (f) | ★ |
| Hawaii | 94,780 | 69.5 (g) | ★ | ... | ... | (f) | ★ |
| Idaho | 95,500 | 21 | ★ | ★ | ... | (f) | ★ |
| Illinois | 140,200 | 125 | ★ | ★ | ★ | (b) | ★ |
| Indiana | 77,200 | 35 | ★ | ★ | ★ | (b) | ★ |
| Iowa | 104,352 | 19 | ★ | ★ | ... | (b) | ★ |
| Kansas | 91,742 | 29 | ★ | ★ | ... | (f) | ★ |
| Kentucky | 97,608 | 40 | ★ | ★ | ★ | (b) | ★ |
| Louisiana | 95,000 | 100 | ★ | ★ | ★ | (b) | ★ |
| Maine | 70,000 | 21 | ★ | ... | ★ | (b) | ★ |
| Maryland | 120,000 | 82 | ★ | ★ | ★ | (f) | ★ |
| Massachusetts | 135,000 | 86 | ★ | ... | ★ | (f) | ... |
| Michigan | 151,245 | 93 | ★ | ★ | ★ | (b) | ★ |
| Minnesota | 120,303 | 45 | ★ | ★ | ★ | (f) | ★ |
| Mississippi | 101,800 | 33 | ★ | ★ | ★ | (f) | ★ |
| Missouri | 112,755 | 38 | ★ | ★ | ... | (c) | ★ |
| Montana | 83,672 | 18 | ★ | ★ | ★ | (b) | ★ |
| Nebraska | 65,000 | 15 | ★ | ★ | ★ | (b) | ★ |
| Nevada* | 117,000 | 23 | ★ | ★ | ... | (c) | ★ |
| New Hampshire | 93,263 | 23 | ★ | ★ | ... | (f) | ★(j) |
| New Jersey | 130,000 (n) | 156 | ★ | ... | ★ | $61,000 | ★ |
| New Mexico | 90,000 | 27 | ★ | ★ | ★ | $79,200 (c) | ★ |
| New York | 179,000 | 203 | ★ | ★ | ★ | (b) | ★ |
| North Carolina | 107,132 | 81 | ★ | ★ | ★ | $11,500 | ★ |
| North Dakota | 76,884 | 17 | ★ | ★ | ... | (f) | ★ |
| Ohio | 119,225 | 66 | ★ | ★ | ★ | (f) | ★ |
| Oklahoma* | 101,040 | 34 | ★ | ★ | ... | (f) | ★ |
| Oregon | 88,300 | 29 | ★ | ... | ... | (f) | ★ |
| Pennsylvania | 135,559 | 90 | ★ | ... | ... | (b) | ★ |
| Rhode Island | 95,000 | 49 | ★ | ★ | ... | N.A. | ... |
| South Carolina | 106,078 | 34 | ★ | ★ | ★ | (f) | ★ |
| South Dakota | 89,898 | 24 | ★ | ★ | ... | (f) | ★ |
| Tennessee | 85,000 | 40 | ★ | ★ | ... | (f) | ★ |
| Texas | 115,345 | 198 | ★ | ★ | ★ | (b) | ★ |
| Utah* | 93,000 | 17 | ★ | ★ | ... | $57,100 | ★ |
| Vermont* | 88,026 | 18 | ★ | ... | ... | (f) | ... |
| Virginia | 110,000 (k) | 36 | ★ | ★ | ★ | (b) | ★ |
| Washington | 132,000 | 36 | ★ | ★ | ... | (f) | ★ |
| West Virginia | 99,000 | 42 | ★ | ★ | ★ | (l) | ★ |
| Wisconsin | 115,699 | 47 | ★ | ★ | ... | (f) | ★ |
| Wyoming | 95,000 | 16 | ★ | ★ | ... | (c) | ★ |
| American Samoa* | 50,000 | 23 | ★ | ... | ... | $105,000 (c) | ★ |
| Guam | 90,000 | 42 | ★ | ... | ... | $218/day | ★ |
| No. Mariana Islands* | 70,000 | 16 | ★ | ... | ... | (f, m) | ★ |
| Puerto Rico | 70,000 | 22 | ★ | ★ | ★ | (f) | ★ |
| U.S. Virgin Islands* | 80,000 | 17 | ★ | ... | ... | (f) | ★ |

See footnotes at end of table.

# THE GOVERNORS: COMPENSATION — Continued

*Source*: The Council of State Governments' legislative survey January 2000, except where noted by * where data are from *The Book of the States, 1998-99.*

*Note*: In some states, the leadership positions in the house are not empowered by the law or by the rules of the chamber, but rather by the party members themselves. Entry following slash indicates number of individuals holding specified position.

*Key:*
EH — Elected or confirmed by all members of the house.
EC — Elected by party caucus.
AS — Appointed by speaker.
AL — Appointed by party leader.
. . . — Position does not exist or is not selected on a regular basis.

(a) Appointed by minority floor leader.

(b) Official title is deputy speaker. In Hawaii, American Samoa and Puerto Rico, vice speaker.

(c) Four deputy majority leaders are appointed by majority leader and 16 assistant majority leaders are appointed by the speaker in consultation with the majority leader; three majority whips are appointed by speaker in consultation with the majority lead

(d) Minority leader pro tempore, three deputy minority leaders, six assistant minority leaders and one minority whip appointed by minority leader.

(e) Approved by house members.

(f) Official titles: assistant majority leader is deputy majority leader, majority floor leader is majority floor whip, assistant majority floor leader is freshman majority whip, assistant minority leader is Republican leader pro tem. Other titles of minority floor leaders are designated by party affiliation (Republican).

(g) Official titles: majority floor leader is deputy majority leader, majority caucus chairman is majority conference chairperson, minority floor leader is deputy minority leader, and minority caucus chairman is minority conference chairperson.

(h) Appointed by minority floor leader.

(i) Additional positions include minority agenda chair (EC) and minority policy chair (EC).

(j) Appointed only in the speaker's absence.

(k) Majority leader also serves as majority floor leader; assistant majority leader also serves as assistant majority floor leader; minority leader also serves as minority floor leader; assistant minority leader also serves as assistant minority floor lea

(l) Additional positions include deputy speaker pro tem, parliamentarian, deputy majority leader, 13 deputy majority whips and 3 deputy minority whips.

(m) Majority leader also serves as majority floor leader.

(n) Official title is assistant majority leader.

(o) Official title is assistant minority whip.

(p) Speaker and minority leader are also caucus chairmen.

(q) Majority leader also serves as majority floor leader; minority leader also serves as minority floor leader.

(r) Unicameral legislature; see entries in Table 3.6, "Senate Leadership Positions — Methods of Selection."

(s) Official titles: minority leader is Democratic leader and assistant minority leader is deputy Democratic leader.

(t) Additional positions include four deputy speakers (EC), three assistant majority whips (EC), majority budget officer (EC), minority leader pro tem (EC), and three deputy minority leaders (EC).

(u) Official titles: majority caucus chairman is majority conference leader and minority caucus chairman is conference chairman.

(v) Additional positions: deputy speaker (AS), assistant speaker (AS), assistant speaker pro tem (AS), minority leader pro tem (AL), assistant minority leader pro tem (AL), deputy majority leader (AS), deputy minority leader (AL), deputy majority whip (AS deputy minority whip (AL), assistant majority whip (AS), assistant minority whip (AL), majority conference vice-chairman (AS), minority conference vice-chairman (AL), majority conference secretary (AS), minority conference secretary (AL), majority steering committee chairman (AS), majority steering committee vice-chairman (AS), minority steering committee chairman (AL), minority steering committee vice-chairman (AL), majority program committee chairman (and minority program committee chairman (AL).

(w) Official titles: majority caucus chairman is majority conference chairman; minority caucus chairman is minority conference chairman.

(x) Additional positions include assistant majority whip (EH) and assistant minority whip (EH).

(y) Additional positions include assistant majority whip and minority caucus secretary.

(z) Majority leader also serves as majority caucus chairman; minority leader also serves as minority caucus chairman.

(aa) Official titles: minority leader is Republican leader and minority whip is Republican whip.

(bb) Additional positions include first deputy speaker (AS).

(cc) Official title is senior speaker pro tem.

(dd) Official title is deputy minority leader.

(ee) Additional positions include two deputy majority whips, three assistant majority whips, and two freshman whips.

(ff) Official title is chief deputy majority whip.

(gg) Additional positions include three assistant majority whips (EC).

(hh) Additional positions include assistant majority whip and assistant minority whip (EC).

(ii) Speaker is elected in caucus but the formal nomination and election by acclamation take place the first day of the session by the entire body of house.

(jj) Assistant majority leader also serves as majority whip; assistant minority leader also serves as minority whip.

(kk) Additional positions include three assistant minority whips, all positions are established by caucus rule and can change each biennium.

(ll) Additional position is caucus vice chair (EC).

(mm) Speaker also serves as majority leader.

(nn) Official title is floor leader.

(oo) Official title is alternate floor leader.

# Table 2.4
## THE GOVERNORS: POWERS

| State or other jurisdiction | Budget-making power | | Veto power (a) | | | | | Authorization for reorganization through executive order (b) | Other statewide elected officials (c) | |
|---|---|---|---|---|---|---|---|---|---|---|
| | Full responsibility | Shares responsibility | No item veto | Item veto-2/3 legislators present to override | Item veto-majority legislators elected to override | Item veto-3/5 legislators elected to override | Item veto-at least 2/3 legislators elected to override | | Number of officials | Number of agencies |
| Alabama* | ★ | … | … | … | ★ | … | … | … | 9 | 7 |
| Alaska | C,S | … | … | … | … | … | … | C | 1 | 0 (d) |
| Arizona | ★(f) | … | … | … | … | … | ★ | … | 9 | 7 |
| Arkansas | ★ | … | … | … | ★ | … | … | … | 6 | 0 |
| California* | ★ | … | … | … | ★ | … | ★ | S | 7 | 7 |
| Colorado* | … | ★ | … | … | … | … | ★★ | … | 4 | 4 |
| Connecticut | ★ | … | … | … | … | … | ★★ | … | 5 | 5 |
| Delaware* | ★ | … | ★ | (m) | … | … | … | C | 1 | 1 |
| Florida | … | ★ | … | … | … | ★ | ★ | S | 7 | 7 |
| Georgia | ★ | … | … | … | … | … | ★ | S | 12 | 8 |
| Hawaii | ★ | … | … | … | … | … | … | … | 1 | 1 |
| Idaho | ★ | … | ★ | ★ | … | … | … | … | 6 | 6 |
| Illinois | ★ | … | … | … | ★ | ★ | … | C | 5 | 5 |
| Indiana | ★ | … | ★ | … | … | … | … | … | 7 | 7 |
| Iowa | ★ | … | … | ★ | ★ | … | ★ | … | 7 | 6 |
| Kansas | ★ | … | … | ★ | … | … | … | C | 5 | 4 |
| Kentucky | … | (n) | ★(e) | … | … | … | ★(e) | S | 6 | 6 |
| Louisiana | … | ★ | … | … | … | … | … | … | 8 | 8 |
| Maine | ★ | … | ★ | … | … | … | … | … | 0 | 0 |
| Maryland | ★ | … | … | ★ | … | … | … | C | 3 | 3 |
| Massachusetts | ★(f) | … | … | ★ | … | … | ★ | C | 5 | 10 |
| Michigan | ★ | … | … | … | … | … | ★★ | C | 35 | 20 |
| Minnesota | … | … | … | … | … | … | ★★ | S | 5 | 5 |
| Mississippi | … | ★ | … | … | … | … | ★ | S | 7 | 7 |
| Missouri | ★(f) | … | … | … | … | … | ★ | C,S, Common Law | 5 | 5 |
| Montana | ★ | … | … | ★ | … | … | ★ | S | 5 | 5 |
| Nebraska | C (f) | … | ★ | … | … | C | … | … | 5 | 5 |
| Nevada | ★ | … | ★ | … | … | … | … | … | 5 | 5 |
| New Hampshire | ★(f) | … | … | … | … | … | … | … | 5 | 5 |
| New Jersey | ★ | … | … | … | … | … | … | … | 0 | 0 |
| New Mexico | ★ | … | … | ★ | … | … | ★ | … | 0 | 0 |
| New York | ★ | … | … | ★★ | … | … | … | … | 9 | 7 |
| North Carolina* | … | ★ | … | … | … | … | ★(e) | … | 3 | 20 |
| North Dakota | ★(f) | … | C | … | ★ | ★ | ★ | C | 9 | 9 |
| Ohio | ★(f) | … | … | … | … | ★ | … | … | 12 | 17 |
| | | | | | | | | | 5 | 5 |

# THE GOVERNORS: POWERS — Continued

| State or other jurisdiction | Budget-making power | | Veto power (a) | | | | | Authorization for reorganization through executive order (b) | Other statewide elected officials (c) | |
|---|---|---|---|---|---|---|---|---|---|---|
| | Full responsibility | Shares responsibility | No item veto | Item veto-2/3 legislators present to override | Item veto-majority legislators elected to override | Item veto-3/5 legislators elected to override | Item veto-at least 2/3 legislators elected to override | | Number of officials | Number of agencies |
| Oklahoma* | ★(f) | ... | ... | ... | ... | ... | ★ | S | 10 | 8 |
| Oregon | ★(f) | ... | ... | ★ | ... | ... | ... | ... | 5 | 5 |
| Pennsylvania | ... | ★ | ... | ... | ... | ... | ★ | ... | 4 | 4 |
| Rhode Island | ★(f) | ... | ★ | ... | ... | ... | ... | ... | 4 | 4 |
| South Carolina | ... | ★ | ... | ★ | ... | ... | ... | ... | 8 | 4 (h) |
| South Dakota | ★ | ... | (i) | ... | ... | ... | ★ | C | 9 | 7 |
| Tennessee | ★ | ... | (j) | ... | ★ | ... | ... | S | 0 | 0 |
| Texas | ... | ★ | (j) | ★★ | ... | ... | ... | ... | 9 | 6 |
| Utah* | ... | ★ | ... | ★★ | ... | ... | ... | S | 5 | 17 |
| Vermont* | ★ | ... | ★ | ... | ... | ... | ... | S | 5 | 5 |
| Virginia | ★ | ... | ... | ★★ | ... | ... | ... | S (k) | 2 | 2 |
| Washington | ★ | ... | ... | ★★ | ... | ... | ... | ... | 8 | 8 |
| West Virginia | ★ | ... | ... | ★★ | ... | ... | ★ | S: Common Law | 10 | 6 |
| Wisconsin | ★ | ... | ... | ★(l) | ... | ... | ★ | ... | 5 | 5 |
| Wyoming | ★ | ... | ... | ... | ... | ... | ★ | ... | 4 | 4 |
| American Samoa* | ... | ★ | ... | ... | ... | ... | ★ | S | 1 | 1 |
| Guam | ★ | ... | (j) | ... | ... | ... | ★ | ★ | 0 | 0 |
| No. Mariana Islands* | ... | ★ | (j) | ... | ... | ... | ★ | ★ | 1 | 1 |
| Puerto Rico | ★(f) | ... | ... | ... | ... | ... | ... | ... | 0 | 0 |
| U.S. Virgin Islands* | ★ | ... | ... | ... | ... | ... | ... | ★ | 1 | 1 |

*Source:* The Council of State Governments' survey, January 2000; except as noted by * where information is from *The Book of the States* 1998-99.

*Key:*

★ — Yes; provision for.

... — No; not applicable.

C — Constitutional

S — Statutory

(a) In all states, except North Carolina , governor has the power to veto bills passed by the state legislature. The information presented here refers to the governor's power to item veto within a bill and the votes needed in the state legislature to override the item veto. For additional information on vetoes and veto overrides, as well as the number of days the governor is allowed to consider bills, see Table 3.16, "Enacting Legislation: Veto, Veto Overrides and Effective Date."

(b) For additional information on executive orders, see Table 2.5, "Gubernatorial Executive Orders: Authorization, Provisions, Procedures."

(c) Includes only executive branch officials who are popularly elected either on a constitutional or statutory basis (elected members of state boards of education, public utilities commissions, university regents, or other state boards or commissions are also included; the number of agencies involving theses officials is also listed.

(d) Lieutenant governor's office is part of governor's office.

(e) In New York, governor has item veto over appropriations. In Louisiana, governor has item veto over appropriations bill only.

(f) Full responsibility to propose; legislature adopts or revises and governor signs or vetoes.

(g) Governor has no veto power.

(h) Divisions within governor's office.

(i) Line item veto authority over the budget bill. Simple majority override. Veto authority over legislation. Simple majority override.

(j) The governor has an item veto over appropriations only.

(k) For shifting agencies between secretarial offices; all other reorganizations require legislative approval.

(l) In Wisconsin, governor has "partial" veto over appropriation bills. The partial veto is broader than item veto.

(m) Governor may only veto a specific appropriation within a general appropriation bill or an entire bill. 2/3 of both houses can override.

(n) The Governor has full responsibility to propos budget. Legislature may make changes; governor can veto.

(o) North Dakota has a governor's veto and a line item veto on appropriations bills.

## Table 2.5
## GUBERNATORIAL EXECUTIVE ORDERS: AUTHORIZATION, PROVISIONS, PROCEDURES

| State or other jurisdiction | Authorization for executive orders | Civil defense disasters, public emergencies | Energy emergencies and conservation | Other emergencies | Executive branch reorganization plans and agency creation | Create advisory, study or investigative committees/commissions | Respond to federal programs and requirements | State personnel administration | Other administration | Filing and publication procedures | Subject to administrative procedure act | Subject to legislative review |
|---|---|---|---|---|---|---|---|---|---|---|---|---|
| Alabama* | S,I (a) | ★(a) | ★(a) | ★(b) | | | | | | ★(c,d) | | |
| Alaska | I | ★ | ★(a) | ★(a) | C | ★ | ★ | ★ | | S | | C |
| Arizona | S,I(e) | ★ | ★(a) | ★(a) | | ★ | ★ | ★ | ★ | ★(c) | | |
| Arkansas | S | ★ | ★ | ★ | ★ | ★ | ★ | ★ | ★ | ★ | | |
| California* | S | ★ | ★ | ★(f) | ★ | ★ | ★ | ★ | | ★ | | |
| Colorado* | S,I | ★ | ★ | ★ | ★ | ★ | ★ | ★ | | ★ | | |
| Connecticut | S | ★ | ★ | ★ | ★ | ★ | ★ | ★ | | ★ | | |
| Delaware* | C | ★ | ★ | ★(h) | ★ | ★ | ★ | ★(qq) | ★(a,g) | ★(c) | | |
| Florida* | C,S | ★(pp) | ★(aa) | ★ | ★ | ★ | ★ | ★ | ★(i,j,oo) | ★(c) | | |
| Georgia* | S,I | ★ | ★ | ★ | ★ | ★ | ★ | ★ | ★ | ★ | | |
| Hawaii | C | ★ | | | | | | | ★(k) | | | |
| Idaho | S | S | I | I | | I | I | | | ★(c) | | |
| Illinois | C | S | I | I | | I | I | I | | ★(c) | | ★(l) |
| Indiana | S,I | ★ | ★ | | ★ | ★ | ★ | | | ★ | | |
| Iowa | S | | ★ | | | | | | | | | |
| Kansas | C,S | ★ | ★ | ★(o) | ★ | ★ | ★ | ★ | ★(p,q,r) | ★(c,d,n) | ★ | ★(t,u) |
| Kentucky | C,S | ★ | ★ | ★ | ★ | ★ | ★ | ★ | ★ | ★(c) | | ★ |
| Louisiana | S (g) | S | S | | ★ | I | I | I | ★ | ★(n) | ★ | |
| Maine | S | ★ | ★ | ★(v,w) | ★ | C,S | ★ | | ★ | ★(d) | ★ | |
| Maryland | C,S | ★ | ★ | ★(f,v) | ★ | C,S | ★ | ★ | ★(x) | ★ | | ★(y) |
| Massachusetts | C,I | ★ | ★ | ★(f,v) | ★ | ★ | ★ | ★ | | ★(n) | | |
| Michigan | C,S | ★ | ★(aa) | ★ | ★ | ★ | ★ | ★ | ★(r) | ★(c) | ★ | ★(z) |
| Minnesota | S | ★ | S | ★ | ★ | ★ | S | S | ★(bb) | ★(c,n) | | ★(y) |
| Mississippi | S | ★ | S | ★ | ★ | ★ | ★ | S | ★(cc,dd) | ★(c) | | ★(y) |
| Missouri | C,S,Common Law | ★ | I | ★ | ★ | ★ | ★ | ★ | ★(y) | ★(y) | | ★(y,ee) |
| Montana | S,I | S | S | ★ | ★ | ★ | S | ★ | S,C | ★(c) | | |
| Nebraska | I | S | S | S | | S | S | ★ | I | | | |
| Nevada | S,I | ★ | I | I | | ★ | ★ | ★ | ★(q) | ★ | | |
| New Hampshire | S | ★ | ★(a) | ★(ff) | | ★ | ★ | ★ | ★(dd) | ★ | | |
| New Jersey | C,S,I | ★ | ★ | ★ | (gg) | ★ | ★ | ★ | | | | |
| New Mexico | C | ★ | ★ | ★ | H | ★ | ★ | ★ | S,C | | | |
| New York | I | S | S | S | S,C | S | S | S | I | ★ | | |
| North Carolina | S,I | ★ | S | S | I | I | I | S | ★(q) | S | | |
| North Dakota | S,I | ★ | S | ★ | | I | I | S | S,C | S | | ★(y) |
| Ohio | I | ★ | ★ | ★ | ★ | ★ | ★ | ★ | ★ | ★(c) | | (j,r,s,t,bb,dd) |

# GUBERNATORIAL EXECUTIVE ORDERS: AUTHORIZATION, PROVISIONS, PROCEDURES — Continued

| State or other jurisdiction | Authorization for executive orders | Provisions | | | | | | | | Procedures | | |
|---|---|---|---|---|---|---|---|---|---|---|---|---|
| | | Civil defense, disasters, public emergencies | Energy emergencies and conservation | Other emergencies | Executive branch reorganization plans and agency creation | Create advisory, coordinating, study or investigative committees/commissions | Respond to federal programs and requirements | State personnel administration | Other administration | Filing and publication procedures | Subject to administrative procedure act | Subject to legislative review |
| Oklahoma* | S,I | ★ | ★ | ★(v) | ★ | … | … | ★ | ★(gg) | ★(c) | ★ | ★(y) |
| Oregon | S | ★ | … | ★(n,v,x,hh) | … | ★ | ★ | … | …(ii) | ★(c) | … | … |
| Pennsylvania | C,S | ★ | … | … | … | ★ | ★ | … | ★(ii) | ★(c,n) | … | … |
| Rhode Island | S (a) | ★(dd) | ★ | ★(j,hh) | … | (a) | … | … | ★(m) | ★(c,d,jj) | … | … |
| South Carolina | I (e) | … | … | … | … | ★ | ★ | ★ | … | … | ★ | ★ |
| South Dakota | C | … | ★ | ★ | (kk) | … | ★ | … | ★(t) | ★(c) | … | ★ |
| Tennessee | S,I | ★ | ★ | ★ | ★ | ★ | ★ | ★ | ★ | ★(c) | ★ | ★ |
| Texas | S,I | ★ | ★ | ★ | (kk) | ★ | ★ | … | … | ★(c) | … | … |
| Utah* | S | ★ | ★ | … | ★ | ★ | ★ | … | … | ★(ll) | ★ | … |
| Vermont* | S,I | ★ | ★ | ★(g) | ★ | ★ | ★ | ★ | … | … | … | ★(mm) |
| Virginia | S,I | ★ | ★ | ★(g) | ★(nn) | ★ | ★ | ★ | ★ | ★(c) | … | … |
| Washington | S | ★ | … | … | S,I | S,I | ★ | S,I | ★ | ★(c,n) | … | … |
| West Virginia | S,I (e) | ★ | ★ | ★ | S,I | S,I | ★ | ★ | S,I (e,i) | ★(c,n) | ★ | … |
| Wisconsin | S | ★ | … | ★ | ★ | ★ | ★ | ★ | ★(q,dd,gg) | ★(c) | ★ | … |
| Wyoming | S | I | ★ | ★ | ★ | I | ★ | … | … | … | … | ★ |
| American Samoa* | C,S | ★ | ★ | ★ | (kk) | ★ | ★ | ★ | ★ | ★(rr) | ★(rr) | … |
| Guam | C | ★ | I | ★ | C | S,I | S | ★ | ★ | S | I | … |
| No. Mariana Islands* | C | ★ | I | ★ | … | ★ | S | ★ | ★ | S | I | … |
| Puerto Rico | I | ★ | … | ★ | … | S,I | S | ★ | ★ | … | … | ★ |
| U.S. Virgin Islands* | C | ★ | ★ | ★ | ★ | ★ | ★ | ★ | ★ | ★ | … | ★ |

See footnotes at end of table.

# GUBERNATORIAL EXECUTIVE ORDERS: AUTHORIZATION, PROVISIONS, PROCEDURES — Continued

*Source:* The Council of State Governments' survey, January 2000; except as noted by * where data are from *The Book of the States 1998-99.*

*Key:*

C — Constitutional
S — Statutory
I — Implied
★ — Formal provision.
. . . — No formal provision.

(a) Broad interpretation of gubernatorial authority.
(b) To activate or veto environmental improvement authorities.
(c) Executive orders must be filed with secretary of state or other designated officer. In Idaho, must also be published in state general circulation newspaper.
(d) Governor required to keep record in office. In Maine, also sends copy to Legislative Counsel, State Law Library, and all county law libraries in state.
(e) Some or all provisions implied from constitution.
(f) To regulate distribution of necessities during shortages.
(g) Broad grant of authority.
(h) Local financial emergency, shore erosion, polluted discharge and energy shortage.
(i) To reassign state attorneys and public defenders.
(j) To suspend certain officials and/or other civil actions.
(k) Delegation of authority over real property (e.g., to counties for park purposes).
(l) Only if involves a change in statute.
(m) To transfer allocated funds.
(n) Included in state register or code.
(o) To give immediate effect to state regulation in emergencies.
(p) To control administration of state contracts and procedures.
(q) To impound or freeze certain state matching funds.
(r) To reduce state expenditures in revenue shortfall.
(s) To designate game and wildlife areas or other public areas.
(t) Appointive powers.
(u) To suspend rules and regulations of the bureaucracy.
(v) For fire emergencies.
(w) For financial institution emergencies.
(x) To control procedures for dealing with public.
(y) Reorganization plans and agency creation.
(z) Legislative appropriations committees must approve orders issued to handle a revenue shortfall.

(aa) If an energy emergency is declared by the state's Executive Council or legislature.
(bb) To assign duties to lieutenant governor, issue writ of special election.
(cc) To control prison and pardon administration.
(dd) To administer and govern the armed forces of the state.
(ee) For meeting federal program requirements.
(ff) To declare air pollution emergencies.
(gg) Relating to local governments.
(hh) To declare water, crop and refugee emergencies.
(ii) To transfer funds in an emergency.
(jj) Must be published in register if they have general applicability and legal effect.
(kk) Can reorganize, but not create.
(ll) Filed with legislature.
(mm) Only executive branch reorganization.
(nn) To shift agencies between secretarial offices; all other reorganizations require legislative approval.
(oo) By executive order, governor may also suspend collection of fines and forfeitures, grant reprieves not exceeding 60 days and with approval of 3 cabinet members, grant full or conditional pardons, restore civil rights, commute punishment and remit fines and forfeiture for offenses.
(pp) Governor may also delineate an interjurisdictional area to prepare , plan, mitigate or respond to emergency.
(qq) Governor may also declare an office vacant.
(rr) If executive order fits definition of rule.

## Table 2.6
## STATE CABINET SYSTEMS

| State or other jurisdiction | State statute | State constitution | Governor created | Tradition in state | Appointed to specified office (a) | Elected to specified office (a) | Gubernatorial appointment regardless of office | Number of members in cabinet (including governor) | Frequency of cabinet meetings | Open cabinet meetings |
|---|---|---|---|---|---|---|---|---|---|---|
| | *Authorization for cabinet system* | | | | *Criteria for membership* | | | | | |
| Alabama* | ... | ... | ... | ★ | ... | ... | ★ | 28 | Gov.'s discretion (a) | ... |
| Alaska | ... | ... | ★ | ... | ★ | ... | ... | 18 | Regularly | ★(b) |
| Arizona | ... | ... | ★ | ... | ★ | ... | ★ | 38 | Monthly | ... |
| Arkansas | ★ | ... | ... | ... | ★ | ... | ... | 18 | Regularly | ... |
| California* | ★ | ... | ★ | ... | ★ | ... | ★ | 13 | Every two weeks | ... |
| Colorado* | ... | ★ | ... | ... | ★ | ... | ... | 21 | Gov.'s discretion | ★ |
| Connecticut | ★ | ... | ... | ... | ★ | ... | ... | 24 | Gov.'s discretion | ... |
| Delaware* | ★ | ... | ... | ... | ★ | ... | ★ (c) | 17· | Gov.'s discretion | ... |
| Florida | ... | ★ | ... | ... | ... | ★ | ... | 7 | Every two weeks | ★ |
| Georgia* | | | | ---------- (d) ---------- | | | | | | |
| Hawaii | ... | ... | ... | ★ | ★ | ★ | ... | 17 | Gov.'s discretion | ... |
| Idaho | | | | ---------- (d) ---------- | | | | | | |
| Illinois | ... | ... | ... | ... | ★(e) | ★ | ... | 28 | Gov.'s discretion | ... |
| Indiana | | | | ---------- (d) ---------- | | | | | | |
| Iowa | | | | ---------- (e) ---------- | | | | | | |
| Kansas | ... | ... | ★ | ... | ... | ... | ★ | 16 | Gov.'s discretion | ... |
| Kentucky | ★ | ... | ... | ... | ★ | ... | ... | 20 | Gov.'s discretion | ... |
| Louisiana | ★ | ★ | ... | ... | ★ | ★ | ... | 13 | Gov.'s discretion | ... |
| Maine | ... | ... | ... | ★ | ... | ... | ★(c) | 17 | Weekly | ... |
| Maryland | ★ | ... | ... | ... | ★(c) | ... | ... | 23 | Gov.'s discretion | ... |
| Massachusetts | ★ | ... | ... | ... | ★ | ... | ... | 12 | Weekly | ... |
| Michigan | ... | ★ | ... | ... | ★ | ★ | ★ | 21 | Gov.'s discretion | ... |
| Minnesota | ... | ... | ★ | ... | ★ | ... | ... | 26 | Regularly | ... |
| Mississippi | | | | ---------- (d) ---------- | | | | | | |
| Missouri | ... | ★ | ... | ★ | ★ | ... | ... | 17 | Gov.'s discretion | ... |
| Montana | ... | ... | ★ | ... | ★ | ... | ... | 17 | Bi-weekly | ★ |
| Nebraska | ★ | ... | ... | ... | ★ | ... | ... | 27 | Gov.'s discretion | ... |
| Nevada* | | | | ---------- (d) ---------- | | | | | | |
| New Hampshire | | | | ---------- (d) ---------- | | | | | | |
| New Jersey | ★ | ★ | ... | ... | ★ | ... | ... | 18 | Gov.'s discretion | ... |
| New Mexico | ★ | ... | ... | ... | ★ | ... | ... | 17 | Weekly | ... |
| New York | ... | ... | ... | ★ | ★ | ... | ... | 25 | Gov.'s discretion | ... |
| North Carolina* (f) | ★ | ★ | ★ | ... | ... | ... | ★ | 10 | Monthly | ... |
| North Dakota (g) | | | | ---------- (d) ---------- | | | | | | |
| Ohio | ★ | ... | ... | ... | ★ | ... | ★ | 25 | Gov.'s discretion | ... |
| Oklahoma* | ★ | ... | ★ | ... | ... | ... | ★ | 16 (h) | Gov.'s discretion | ... |
| Oregon | | | | ---------- (d) ---------- | | | | | | |
| Pennsylvania | ★ | ... | ... | ... | ★(c) | ... | ... | 19 | Weekly | ★ |
| Rhode Island | | | | ---------- (i) ---------- | | | | | | |
| South Carolina | ★ | ... | ... | ... | ... | ... | ★(c ) | 13 | Gov.'s discretion | ... |
| South Dakota | ... | ... | ★ | ... | ★ | ... | ★ | 22 | Gov.'s discretion | ... |
| Tennessee | ★ | ... | ... | ★ | ★ | ... | ... | 22 | Gov.'s discretion | ★ |
| Texas | | | | ---------- (d) ---------- | | | | | | |
| Utah* | ... | ... | ★ | (i) | ★ | ... | ... | 19 | Monthly | ... |
| Vermont* | ★ | ... | ... | ... | ★ | ... | ... | 6 | Gov.'s discretion | ... |
| Virginia | ★ | ... | ... | ... | ★ | ... | ... | 9 | Gov.'s discretion | ... |
| Washington | ... | ... | ★ | ... | ★ | ... | ... | 28 | Bi-weekly, weekly during legislative session | ... |
| West Virginia | ★ | ... | ... | ... | ★ | ... | ... | 9 | Bi-monthly | ... |
| Wisconsin | ★ | ... | ... | ... | ★ | ... | ... | 16 | Gov.'s discretion | ★ |
| Wyoming | ★ | ... | ... | ... | ★ | ... | ... | 15 | Gov.'s discretion | ★ |
| American Samoa* | ★ | ★ | ... | ... | ★ | ... | ★ | 16 | Gov.'s discretion | ★ |
| Guam | ... | ... | ★ | ... | ★ | ... | ... | 55 | Bi-monthly | ... |
| No. Mariana Islands* | ... | ★ | ... | ... | ★ | ... | ... | 16 | Gov.'s discretion | ★ |
| Puerto Rico | ★ | ★ | ... | ... | ★ | ... | ... | 18 | Gov.'s discretion | ... |
| U.S. Virgin Islands* | ★ | ... | ... | ... | ... | ... | ★ | 16 | Monthly or as needed | ... |

See footnotes at end of table.

## STATE CABINET SYSTEMS — Continued

*Source*: The Council of State Governments' survey January 2000, except as noted by * where data are from *The Book of the States*, 1998-99.

*Key*:

★ — Yes

... — No

(a) Individual is a member by virtue of election or appointment to a cabinet-level position.

(b) Except when in executive session.

(c) With the consent of the senate.

(d) No formal cabinet system. In Idaho, however, sub-cabinets have been formed, by executive order; the chairmen report to the governor when requested.

(e) Sub-cabinets meet quarterly.

(f) Constitution provides for a Council of State made up of elective state administrative officials, which makes policy decisions for the state while the cabinet acts more in an advisory capacity.

(g) Cabinet consists of agencies, created by legislation; directors of agencies appointed by the governor.

(h) Includes secretary of state; most other cabinet members are heads of state agencies.

(i) In Rhode Island, department heads require advice and consent of the Senate. In Utah, department heads serve as cabinet; meets at discretion of governor, but when first appointed, department heads also require advice and consent of Senate.

## Table 2.7
## THE GOVERNORS: PROVISIONS AND PROCEDURES FOR TRANSITION

| State or other jurisdiction | Legislation pertaining to gubernatorial transition | Appropriation available to gov-elect | Provision for: Gov-elect's participation in state budget for coming fiscal year | Gov-elect to hire staff to assist during transition | State personnel to be made available to assist gov-elect | Office space in buildings to be made available to gov-elect | Acquainting gov-elect staff with office procedures and routing office functions | Transfer of information (files records, etc.) |
|---|---|---|---|---|---|---|---|---|
| Alabama* | ... | ... | ● | (a) | ● | ● | ● | ... |
| Alaska | ... | ... | ... | ... | ● | ● | ● | ★ |
| Arizona | ... | ... | ★ | ... | ● | ● | ● | ● |
| Arkansas | ★ | $ 60,000 (b) | ● | ● | ● | ● | ● | ● |
| California* | ★ | 450,000 | ★ | ★ | ★ | ★ | ● | ● |
| Colorado* | ★ | 10,000 | ... | ★ | ★ | ★ | ★ | ★ |
| Connecticut | ★ | 25,000 | ● | ★ | ● | ★ | ... | ★ |
| Delaware* | ★ | (c) | (d) | (e) | ● | ★ | ● | ● |
| Florida | ... | 300,000 | ★ | ★ | ● | ★ | ● | ● |
| Georgia* | ★ | ★ | ● | ★ | ★ | ★ | ● | ★ |
| Hawaii | ★ | 100,000 | ★ | ★ | ★ | ★ | ● | ★ |
| Idaho | ★ | 15,000 | ★ | ★ | ★ | ★ | ★ | ★ |
| Illinois | ★ | (f) | ★ | ★(g) | ★ | ★ | ★ | ★ |
| Indiana | ★ | 40,000 | ★ | ★ | ★ | ★ | ★ | ★ |
| Iowa | ★(h) | 10,000 | ★ | ★ | ●(i) | ● | ● | ★(j) |
| Kansas | ★ | 100,000 | ★ | ★ | ★ | ★ | ★ | ★ |
| Kentucky | ★ | Unspecified | ★ | ★ | ★ | ★ | ★ | ★ |
| Louisiana | ★ | 10,000 | ★ | ★ | ★ | ● | ● | ● |
| Maine | ★ | 5,000 | ★ | ★ | ★(k) | ● | ★ | ● |
| Maryland | ★ | (l) | ... | ★ | ★ | ★ | ★ | ★ |
| Massachusetts | ... | ★ | ★ | ● | ● | ● | ● | ★ |
| Michigan | ★ | 1,000,000 (m) | ● | ★ | ★ | ● | ★ | ● |
| Minnesota | ★ | 50,000 | ★ | ★ | ★ | ★ | ● | ★ |
| Mississippi | ★ | 60,000 | ★ | ★ | ★ | ★ | ★ | ★ |
| Missouri | ★ | 100,000 | ★ | ★ | ● | ★ | ● | ●(n) |
| Montana | ★ | 50,000 | ★ | ★ | ★ | ★ | ★ | ★ |
| Nebraska | ... | ● | ★ | ● | ● | ● | ● | ● |
| Nevada* | ★ | 5,000 | ★ | ... | ● | ● | ● | ★(h) |
| New Hampshire | ★ | 75,000 | ★ | ★ | ★ | ★ | ★ | ... |
| New Jersey | ★ | Unspecified | ★ | ★ | ★ | ★ | ● | ★ |
| New Mexico | ★ | (f) | ★ | ★ | ● | ★ | ● | ● |
| New York | ... | ● | ● | ● | ● | ● | ● | ● |
| North Carolina | ★ | 50,000 (o) | ●(p) | ★ | ★ | ★ | ● | ● |
| North Dakota | ● | 10,000 | (r) | (a) | ● | ... | ● | ★ |
| Ohio | ★ | 250,000 (z) | ... | ★ | ★ | ★ | ... | (y) |
| Oklahoma* | ★ | 40,000 | ★ | ★ | ... | ● | ... | ● |
| Oregon | ★ | 20,000 | ★ | ★ | ★ | ★ | ★ | ★ |
| Pennsylvania | ★ | 100,000 | ... | ★ | ● | ● | ● | ... |
| Rhode Island | ... | ● | ★ | ●(a) | ● | ● | ● | ● |
| South Carolina | ★ | 50,000 (s) | ... | ★ | ★ | ★ | ★ | ★ |
| South Dakota | ● | 10,000 (t) | ● | ● | ● | ● | ● | ● |
| Tennessee | ★ | ★ | ★ | ★ | ★ | ★ | ★ | ★ |
| Texas | ... | ..... | ★ | ★ | ● | ● | ● | ● |
| Utah* | ... | Unspecified | ... | ... | ... | ... | ... | ... |
| Vermont* | ... | (c) | ★(u) | ● | ● | ● | ... | (v) |
| Virginia | ... | (c) | ... | ★(n) | ★(n) | ★(n) | ★(n) | ★(n) |
| Washington | ★ | ★ | ● | ★ | ● | ★ | ● | ● |
| West Virginia | ... | ..... | ... | ... | ... | ● | ● | ... |
| Wisconsin | ★ | Unspecified | ★ | ★ | ★ | ★ | ★ | ★ |
| Wyoming | ... | (f) | ... | ... | ● | ● | ● | ● |
| American Samoa* | ... | Unspecified | ★(w) | ★ | ● | ● | ★ | ● |
| Guam | ★ | (x) | ... | ... | ★ | ★ | ★ | ... |
| No. Mariana Islands* | ★ | Unspecified | ... | ★ | ★ | ★ | ★ | ★ |
| Puerto Rico | ... | 250,000 (o) | ● | ● | ● | ● | ● | ● |
| U.S. Virgin Islands* | ... | (x) | ... | (e) | ... | ... | ... | ... |

See footnotes at end of table.

# THE GOVERNORS: PROVISIONS AND PROCEDURES FOR TRANSITION — Continued

*Source*: The Council of State Governments' survey, January 2000; except as noted by * where data are from *The Book of the States, 1998-99.*
*Key*:

. . . — No provisions or procedures.
★ — Formal provisions or procedures.
● — No formal provisions, occurs informally.
(a) Governor usually hires several incoming key staff during transition.
(b) Made available in 1983.
(c) Determined prior to each election by legislature.
(d) Can participate in budget office hearings before taking office.
(e) Subject to appropriations.
(f) Legislature required to make appropriation; no dollar amount stated in legislation. In New Mexico, $50,000 was made available in 1990. In Wyoming, $12,500 for transition following 1994 election. In Illinois, $200,000 for transition following 1990 election.
(g) On a contractual basis.
(h) Pertains only to funds.
(i) Provided on irregular basis.
(j) Arrangement for transfer of criminal files.
(k) Budget personnel.

(l) Provided in annual budget in transition year.
(m) Made available in 1990.
(n) Activity is traditional and routine, although there is no specific statutory provision.
(o) Inaugural expenses are paid from this amount.
(p) New governor can submit supplemental budget.
(q) If necessary, submit request to State Emergency Commission.
(r) Responsible for submitting budget for coming biennium.
(s) Governor's executive budget recommendation for FY 94-95 is to increase this appropriation to $150,000 for transition purposes. This will require legislative approval in the 94-95 Appropriations Bill.
(t) Made available for 1996.
(u) Responsible for the preparation of the budget; staff made available.
(v) Not transferred, but use may be authorized.
(w) Can submit reprogramming or supplemental appropriation measure for current fiscal year.
(x) Appropriations given upon the request of governor-elect.
(y) By discetion of director of budget and management.
(z) Made available in 1998.

# Table 2.8
# IMPEACHMENT PROVISIONS IN THE STATES

| State or other jurisdiction | Governor and other state executive and judicial officers subject to impeachment | Legislative body which holds power of impeachment | Vote required for impeachment | Legislative body which conducts impeachment trial | Chief justice presides at impeachment trial (a) | Vote required for conviction | Official who serves as acting governor if governor impeached (b) | Legislature may call special session for impeachment |
|---|---|---|---|---|---|---|---|---|
| Alabama | ★ (c) | H | ... | S | ★ | 2/3 mbrs. | LG | ★ |
| Alaska | ★ | S | 2/3 mbrs. | H | (d) | 2/3 mbrs. | LG | ★ |
| Arizona | ★ (e) | H | maj. mbrs. | S | ★ (f) | 2/3 mbrs. | SS | ★ |
| Arkansas | ★ | H | ... | S | ★ | 2/3 mbrs. | PS | ... |
| California | ★ | H | ... | S | ... | 2/3 mbrs. | LG | ... |
| Colorado | ★ | H | maj. mbrs. | S | ★ | 2/3 mbrs. | LG | ... |
| Connecticut | ★ | H | ... | S | ★ | 2/3 mbrs. present | LG | ... |
| Delaware | ★ | H | 2/3 mbrs. | S | ★ | 2/3 mbrs. | LG | ... |
| Florida | ★ | H | 2/3 mbrs. | S | ★ | 2/3 mbrs. present | LG | ★ |
| Georgia | ★ | H | ... | S | ★ | 2/3 mbrs. | LG | ... |
| Hawaii | ★ (g) | H | ... | S | ★ | 2/3 mbrs. | LG | ★ |
| Idaho | ★ | H | ... | S | ★ | 2/3 mbrs. | LG | ... |
| Illinois | ★ | H | maj. mbrs. | S | ... | 2/3 mbrs. | LG | ★ |
| Indiana | ★ | H | ... | S | ... | 2/3 mbrs. | LG | ★ |
| Iowa | ★ | H | ... | S | ... | 2/3 mbrs. present | LG | ★ |
| Kansas | ★ | H | ... | S | ★ | 2/3 mbrs. | LG | ... |
| Kentucky | ★ | H | ... | S | ... | 2/3 mbrs. present | LG | ★ |
| Louisiana | ★ | H | ... | S | ... | 2/3 mbrs. | LG | ★ |
| Maine | ★ | H | ... | S | ... | 2/3 mbrs. present | PS | ... |
| Maryland | ★ | H | maj. mbrs. | S | ... | 2/3 mbrs. | LG | ... |
| Massachusetts | ★ | H | maj. mbrs. | S (h) | ★ | 2/3 mbrs. | LG | ★ |
| Michigan | ★ | H | maj. mbrs. | S | ... | 2/3 mbrs. present | LG | ... |
| Minnesota | ★ | H | 2/3 mbrs. present | S | ... | 2/3 mbrs. present | LG | ... |
| Mississippi | ★ | H | ... | S | (i) | (i) | LG | ... |
| Missouri | ★ | H | ... | (j) | (k) | (k) | LG | ... |
| Montana | ★ | H | 2/3 mbrs. | S | ... | 2/3 mbrs. | LG | ★ |
| Nebraska | ★ (e) | S (j) | maj. mbrs. | S (k) | (k) | (k) | LG | ★ |
| Nevada | ★ | H | maj. mbrs. | S | ★ | 2/3 mbrs. | LG | ... |
| New Hampshire | ★ (l) | H | maj. mbrs. | S | ★ | ... | PS | ... |
| New Jersey | ★ | H | maj. mbrs. | S | ★ | 2/3 mbrs. | PS | ★ |
| New Mexico | ★ | H | maj. mbrs. | S (m) | ★ | 2/3 mbrs. | LG | ★ |
| New York | ★ | H | maj. mbrs. | S | ... | 2/3 mbrs. present | LG | ★ |
| North Carolina | ★ | H | ... | S | ★ | 2/3 mbrs. present | LG | ★ |
| North Dakota | ★ (e) | H | maj. mbrs. | S | ★ | 2/3 mbrs. | LG | ... |
| Ohio | ★ (l) | H | maj. mbrs. | S | ★ | 2/3 mbrs. | LG | ... |
| Oklahoma | ★ (c) | H | ... | S | ★ | 2/3 mbrs. present | LG | ★ |
| Oregon | ★ | H | ... | S | (n) | ... | LG | ★ |
| Pennsylvania | ★ | H | 1/4 mbrs. (o) | S | ... | 2/3 mbrs. present | LG | ... |
| Rhode Island | ★ | H | 2/3 mbrs. | S | ★ | 2/3 mbrs. | LG | ... |
| South Carolina | ★ | H | ... | S | ... | 2/3 mbrs. | LG | ... |

See footnotes at end of table.

# IMPEACHMENT PROVISIONS IN THE STATES — Continued

| State or other jurisdiction | Governor and other state executive and judicial officers subject to impeachment | Legislative body which holds power of impeachment | Vote required for impeachment | Legislative body which conducts impeachment trial | Chief justice presides at impeachment trial (a) | Vote required for conviction | Official who serves as acting governor if governor impeached (b) | Legislature may call special session for impeachment |
|---|---|---|---|---|---|---|---|---|
| South Dakota | ★ (e) | H | maj. mbrs. | S | ★ | 2/3 mbrs. | LG | ... |
| Tennessee | ★ | H | ... | S | ★ | 2/3 mbrs. (p) | PS | ★ |
| Texas | ★ | H | ... | S | ... | 2/3 mbrs. present | LG | ... |
| Utah | ★ (e) | H | 2/3 mbrs. | S | ★ | 2/3 mbrs. | LG | ... |
| Vermont | ★ | H | 2/3 mbrs. | S | ... | 2/3 mbrs. present | LG | ... |
| Virginia | ★ | H | maj. mbrs. | S | ... | 2/3 mbrs. present | LG | ★ |
| Washington | ★ (e) | H | ... | S | ★ | 2/3 mbrs. | LG | ★★ |
| West Virginia | ★ | H | maj. mbrs. | S | ★ | 2/3 mbrs. | PS | ★ |
| Wisconsin | ★ | H | maj. mbrs. | S | ... | 2/3 mbrs. present | LG | ... |
| Wyoming | ★ (e) | H | maj. mbrs. | S | ★ | 2/3 mbrs. | SS | ... |
| Dist. of Columbia | ... | | | | | | | |
| American Samoa | (r) | H | 2/3 mbrs. | S | ★ | 2/3 mbrs. | ... | ... |
| Guam | (q) | | | | | | | |
| No. Mariana Islands | ★ (s) | H | 2/3 mbrs. | S | ... | 2/3 mbrs. | LG | ... |
| Puerto Rico | ★ (s) | H | 2/3 mbrs. | S | ★ | 3/4 mbrs. | SS | ★ |
| U.S. Virgin Islands | (q) | | | | | | | |

*Source:* State constitutions and statutes.

*Note:* The information in this table is based on a literal reading of the state constitutions and statutes. For information on other methods for removing state officials, see Table 4.5, "Methods for Removal of Judges and Filling of Vacancies," and Table 5.23, "State Recall Provisions: Applicability to State Officials and Petition Circulation."

*Key:*

★ — Yes; provision for.

. . . — Not specified, or no provision for.

H — House or Assembly (lower chamber).

S — Senate.

LG — Lieutenant governor.

PS — President or speaker of the Senate.

SS — Secretary of state.

(a) Presiding justice of state court of last resort. In many states, provision indicates that chief justice presides only on occasion of impeachment of governor.

(b) For provisions on official next in line in succession if governor is convicted and removed from office, refer to Table 2.1, "The Governors."

(c) Includes justices of Supreme Court. Other judicial officers not subject to impeachment.

(d) A Supreme Court justice designated by the court.

(e) With exception of certain judicial officers. In Arizona and Washington–justices of courts not of record. In Nevada, Utah and Wyoming–justices of the peace. In North Dakota and South Dakota–county judges, justices of the peace, and police magistrates.

(f) Should the Chief Justice be on trial, or otherwise disqualified, the Senate shall elect a judge of the Supreme Court to preside.

(g) Governor, lieutenant governor, and any appointive officer for whose removal the consent of the Senate is required.

(h) House elects three members to prosecute impeachment.

(i) All impeachments are tried before the state Supreme Court, except that the governor or a member of the Supreme Court is tried by a special commission of seven eminent jurists to be elected by the Senate. A vote of 5/7 of the court of special commission is necessary to convict.

(j) Unicameral legislature; members use the title "senator."

(k) Court of impeachment is composed of chief justice and all district court judges in the state. A vote of 2/3 of the court is necessary to convict.

(l) All state officers while in office and for two years thereafter.

(m) Court for trial of impeachment composed of president of the Senate, senators (or major part of them), and judges of Court of Appeals (or major part of them).

(n) No provision for impeachment. Public officers may be tried for incompetency, corruption, malfeasance, or delinquency in office in same manner as criminal offenses.

(o) Vote of 2/3 members required for an impeachment of the governor.

(p) Vote of 2/3 of members sworn to try the officer impeached.

(q) Removal of elected officials by recall procedure only.

(r) Governor, lieutenant governor.

(s) Governor and Supreme Court justices.

## Table 2.9
## CONSTITUTIONAL AND STATUTORY PROVISIONS FOR LENGTH AND NUMBER OF TERMS OF ELECTED STATE OFFICIALS

| State or other jurisdiction | Governor | Lt. governor | Secretary of state | Attorney general | Treasurer | Auditor | Comptroller | Education | Agriculture | Labor | Insurance | Other |
|---|---|---|---|---|---|---|---|---|---|---|---|---|
| Alabama | 4/2 | 4/2 | 4/2 | 4/2 | 4/2 | 4/2 | ... | ... | 4/2 (a) | ... | ... | |
| Alaska | 4/2 (b) | 4/- | (c) | ... | (d) | ... | ... | ... | ... | ... | ... | |
| Arizona | 4/2 (b) | (e) | 4/2 (b) | 4/2 (b) | 4/2 (b) | ... | ... | 4/2 (b) | ... | ... | ... | Corporation Comm.–6/0; Mine inspector–2/(f) |
| Arkansas | 4/2 | 4/2 | 4/2 | 4/2 | 4/2 | 4/2 | (g) | ... | ... | ... | ... | Land Cmsr.–4/2 |
| California | 4/2 | 4/2 | 4/2 | 4/2 | 4/2 | ... | 4/2 | 4/2 | ... | ... | ... | |
| Colorado | 4/2 | 4/2 | 4/2 | 4/2 | 4/2 | ... | ... | ... | ... | ... | ... | Regents of Univ. of Colo.–6/-; Bd. of Education–6/- |
| Connecticut | 4/- | 4/- | 4/- | ... | 4/- | ... | 4/- | ... | ... | ... | ... | |
| Delaware | 4/2 (h) | 4/- | ... | 4/- | 4/- | 4/- | ... | ... | ... | ... | 4/- | |
| Florida | 4/(i) | 4/- | 4/- | 4/- | 4/- | ... | 4/- | 4/- | 4/- | ... | (j) | |
| Georgia | 4/2 (b) | 4/- | 4/- | 4/- | ... | ... | ... | 4/- | 4/- | 4/- | 4/- | |
| Hawaii | 4/2 | 4/2 | (c) | ... | (g) | ... | ... | ... | ... | ... | ... | |
| Idaho | 4/(b) | 4/- | 4/- | 4/- | 4/- | 4/- | ... | 4/- | ... | ... | ... | |
| Illinois | 4/- | 4/- | 4/- | 4/- | 4/- | ... | 4/- | ... | ... | ... | ... | |
| Indiana | 4/(b) | 4/- | 4/(b) | ... | 4/(l) | 4/(l) | (k) | ... | (c) | ... | ... | |
| Iowa | 4/- | 4/- | 4/- | ... | 4/- | 4/- | ... | ... | ... | ... | ... | |
| Kansas | 4/2 | 4/2 | 4/- | 4/2 | ... | ... | ... | ... | ... | ... | ... | Bd. of Education–4/- |
| Kentucky | 4/2 | 4/2 | 4/2 | 4/2 | 4/2 | 4/2 | (g) | ... | 4/2 | 4/2 | ... | Railroad Comm.–4/- |
| Louisiana | 4/(b) | 4/- | 4/- | 4/- | 4/- | ... | (m) | 4/- | 4/- | ... | 4/- | Bd. of Education–4/-; Elections Cmsr.–4/- |
| Maine | 4/2(b) | (n) | ... | ... | ... | ... | ... | ... | ... | ... | ... | |
| Maryland | 4/2 (b) | 4/- | ... | 4/- | ... | ... | 4/- | ... | ... | ... | ... | |
| Massachusetts | 4/- | 4/- | 4/- | 4/- | 4/- | 4/- | ... | ... | ... | ... | ... | |
| Michigan | 4/2 | 4/2 | 4/2 | 4/2 | ... | ... | (g) | ... | ... | ... | ... | Bd. of Education–8/- |
| Minnesota | 4/- | 4/- | 4/- | 4/- | 4/(aa) | 4/- | (g) | ... | ... | ... | (o) | |
| Mississippi | 4/2(h) | 4/2 (b) | 4/- | 4/- | 4/- | 4/- | (g) | ... | ... | ... | ... | |
| Missouri | 4/2 (h) | 4/- | 4/- | 4/- | 4/2 (h) | 4/- | ... | ... | ... | ... | ... | |
| Montana | 4/(p) | 4/(p) | 4/(p) | 4/(p) | ... | 4/(p) | ... | 4/(p) | ... | ... | ... | |
| Nebraska | 4/2 (b) | 4/2 (b) | 4/2 (b) | 4/2 (b) | 4/2 (b) | 4/2 (b) | ... | ... | ... | ... | ... | Regents of Univ. of Neb.–6/-; Bd. of Education–4/-; Public Service Comm.–6/- |
| Nevada | 4/2 | 4/2 | 4/2 | 4/2 | 4/2 | ... | 4/2 | ... | ... | ... | ... | |
| New Hampshire | 2/- | (n) | ... | ... | ... | ... | ... | ... | ... | ... | ... | Exec. Council–2/- |
| New Jersey | 4/2 (b) | (n) | ... | ... | ... | ... | ... | ... | ... | ... | ... | |
| New Mexico | 4/2 (b) | 4/2 (b) | 4/2 (b) | 4/2 (b) | 4/2 (b) | 4/2 (b) | (q) | ... | ... | ... | ... | Cmsr. of Public Lands–4/2 (b); Bd. of Education–4/-; Corporation Comm.–6/- |
| New York | 4/- | 4/- | ... | 4/- | ... | (d) | 4/- | ... | ... | ... | ... | |
| North Carolina | 4/(b) | 4/(b) | 4/- | 4/- | 4/- | 4/- | ... | 4/- | 4/- | 4/- | 4/- | |
| North Dakota | 4/- | 4/- | 4/- | 4/- | 4/- | 4/- | ... | 4/- | 4/- (r) | 4/- (r) | 4/- | Public Service Comm.–6/-; Tax Cmsr.–4/- |
| Ohio | 4/(b) | 4/(i) | 4/(i) | 4/(i) | 4/(i) | 4/(i) | (q) | ... | ... | ... | ... | |
| Oklahoma | 4/2(b) | 4/(b) | ... | 4/(b) | 4/(b) | 4/(b) | ... | 4/(b) | ... | 4/- | 4/- | |
| Oregon | 4/(l) | (e) | 4/(l) | ... | 4/(l) | ... | (q) | ... | ... | ... | ... | |
| Pennsylvania | 4/2 | 2 | ... | 4/- | 4/2 (b) | 4/2 (s) | (4/2) | ... | ... | ... | ... | |
| Rhode Island | 4/2 | 4/2 (b) | 4/2 (b) | 4/2 (b) | 4/2 (b) | ... | ... | ... | ... | ... | ... | |
| South Carolina | 4/2 (b) | (4/2) | 4/- | 4/- | 4/- | ... | 4/- | 4/- | 4/- | ... | ... | Adjutant General–4/- |
| South Dakota | 4/2 (b) | 4/2 (b) | 4/(b) | 4/(b) | 4/(b) | 4/(b) | (k) | ... | ... | ... | ... | Cmsr. of School & Public Lands–4/- (b) |
| Tennessee | 4/2 (b) | (n) | ... | ... | ... | (d) | ... | ... | ... | ... | ... | |
| Texas | 4/- | 4/- | ... | 4/- | (d) | ... | 4/- | ... | ... | ... | ... | Bd. of Education–6/-; Cmsr. of General Land Off.–4/-; Railroad Comm.–6/- |
| Utah | 4/- | 4/- | (c) | 4/- | 4/- | 4/- | ... | ... | ... | ... | ... | |
| Vermont | 2/- | 2/- | 2/- | ... | 2/- | 2/- | (g) | ... | ... | ... | ... | |

See footnotes at end of table.

## LENGTH AND NUMBER OF TERMS — Continued

| State or other jurisdiction | Governor | Lt. governor | Secretary of state | Attorney general | Treasurer | Auditor | Comptroller | Education | Agriculture | Labor | Insurance | Other |
|---|---|---|---|---|---|---|---|---|---|---|---|---|
| Virginia | 4/ (z) | 4/U | ... | 4/U | ... | ... | ... | ... | ... | ... | ... | |
| Washington | 4/- | 4/- | 4/- | 4/- | 4/- | 4/- | (q) | 4/- | ... | ... | ... | Cmsr. of Public Lands–4/- |
| West Virginia | 4/2 (t) | (n) | 4/- | 4/- | 4/- | 4/- | (k) | ... | 4/- | ... | ... | |
| Wisconsin | 4/- | 4/- | 4/- | 4/- | 4/- | ... | ... | 4/- | ... | ... | ... | |
| Wyoming | 4/- (p) | (e) | 4/- | ... | 4/- | 4/- | (k) | 4/- | ... | ... | ... | |
| Dist. of Columbia | 4/- (u) | (4/2) | ... | ... | ... | ... | ... | ... | ... | ... | ... | Chmn. of Council of Dist. of Col.–4/U |
| American Samoa | 4/2 (v) | (4/2) | (c) | ... | ... | ... | (q) | ... | ... | ... | ... | |
| Guam | 4/2 (b) | (4/2) | (c) | ... | ... | ... | (w) | ... | ... | ... | (x) | |
| No. Mariana Islands | 4/ (l) | 4/- | ... | ... | ... | ... | (q) | ... | (y) | ... | (o) | |
| Puerto Rico | 4/- | (e) | ... | ... | ... | ... | ... | ... | ... | ... | ... | |
| U.S. Virgin Islands | 4/2 (b) | 4/- | (c) | ... | (g) | ... | (g) | ... | ... | ... | (c) | |

*Note*: First entry in a column refers to number of years per term. Entry following the slash refers to the maximum number of consecutive terms allowed. Blank cells indicate no specific administrative official performs function. Footnotes specify if a position's functions are performed by an appointed official under a different title. This table reflects a literal reading of the state constitutions and statutes.

*Key*:

- — No provision specifying number of terms allowed.

0 — Provision specifying officeholder may not succeed self.

U — Provision specifying individual may hold office for an unlimited number of terms.

. . . . — Position is appointed or elected by governmental entity (not chosen by electorate).

(a) Commissioner of agriculture and industries.

(b) After two consecutive terms, must wait four years and/or one full term before being eligible again.

(c) Lieutenant governor performs function.

(d) Comptroller performs function.

(e) Secretary of state is next in line of succession to the governorship.

(f) No Mine Inspector shall serve more than four consecutive terms in that office.

(g) Finance administrator performs function.

(h) Absolute two-term limitation, but not necessarily consecutive.

(i) Eligible for eight consecutive years.

(j) State treasurer also serves as insurance commissioner.

(k) State auditor performs function.

(l) Eligible for eight out of any period of 12 years.

(m) Head of administration performs function.

(n) President or speaker of the Senate is next in line of succession to the governorship. In Tennessee, speaker of the Senate has the statutory title "lieutenant governor."

(o) Commerce administrator performs function.

(p) Eligible for eight out of 16 years.

(q) State treasurer performs function.

(r) Constitution provides for a secretary of agriculture and labor. However, the legislature was given constitutional authority to provide for (and has provided for) a department of agriculture, and a commissioner of labor distinct from the commissioner of agriculture.

(s) Treasurer must wait four years before being eligible to the office of auditor general.

(t) A person who has been elected or who has served as governor during all or any part of two consecutive terms shall be ineligible for the office of governor during any part of the term immediately following the second of the two consecutive terms.

(u) Mayor.

(v) Limit is statutory.

(w) General services administrator performs function.

(x) Taxation administrator performs function.

(y) Natural resources administrator performs function.

(z) Cannot serve consecutive terms, but after 4 year respite can seek reelection.

(aa) Office of the state treasurer will be abolished on the first Monday in January 2003.

## Table 2.10
## SELECTED STATE ADMINISTRATIVE OFFICIALS: METHODS OF SELECTION

| State or other jurisdiction | Governor | Lieutenant governor | Secretary of state | Attorney general | Treasurer | Adjutant general | Administration | Agriculture | Banking | Budget |
|---|---|---|---|---|---|---|---|---|---|---|
| Alabama | CE | CE | CE | CE | CE | GS | G | CE | GS | G |
| Alabama | CE | CE | CE | CE | CE | GS | G | CE | B | G |
| Alaska | CE | CE | (a-1) | GS | AG | GS | GS | AG | AG | GOC |
| Arizona | CE | CE (a-2) | CE | CE | CE | G | G | G | G | G |
| Arkansas | CE | CE | CE | CE | CE | G | G | B | G | AG |
| California | CE | CE | CE | CE | CE | GS | GS(c) | GS | GS | GS |
| Colorado | CE | CE | CE | CE | CE | GS | GS | GS | CS | G |
| Connecticut* | CE | CE | CE | CE | CE | GE | GE | GE | GE | CS |
| Delaware | CE | CE | GS | CE | CE | GS | GS | GS | G | GS |
| Florida | CE | CE | CE | CE | CE | GS | GS | CE | CE | G |
| Georgia* | CE | CE | CE | CE | G | N.A. | N.A. | CE | N.A. | G |
| Hawaii | CE | CE | (a-1) | GS | (a-6) | GS | (a-9) | GS | AG | GS |
| Idaho | CE | CE | CE | CE | CE | G | G | G | G | G(a-15) |
| Illinois | CE | CE | CE | CE | CE | GE | GS | GS | GS | G |
| Indiana | CE | CE | CE | SE | CE | AG | AG | LG | AG | AG |
| Iowa | CE | CE | CE | CE | CE | GS | (a-16) | CE | GS | GS |
| Kansas | CE | CE | CE | CE | CE | GS | GS | GS | GS | G |
| Kentucky | CE | CE | CE | CE | CE | CE | G | CE | G | G |
| Louisiana | CE | CE | CE | CE | CE | GS | GS | CE | GLS | A |
| Maine | CE | (t) | CL | CL | CL | GLS | GLS | GLS | A | A |
| Maryland | CE | CE | GS | CE | CL | G | CL(a-16) | CL | A | CL |
| Massachusetts | CE | CE | CE | CE | CE | G | G | CG | G | CG |
| Michigan | CE | CE | CE | CE | GS | GS | GS | B | GS | GS |
| Minnesota | CE | CE | CE | CE | CE | G | GS | GS | A | (a-15) |
| Mississippi | CE | CE | CE | CE | CE | GS | GS | SE | GS | A |
| Missouri | CE | CE | CE | CE | CE | G | GS | GS | AGS | AGS |
| Montana* | CE | CE | CE | CE | CE | GS | GS | GS | A | G |
| Nebraska | CE | CE | CE | CE | CE | GS | GS | GS | GS | A |
| Nevada | CE | CE | CE | CE | CE | G | G | BA | A | (a-5) |
| New Hampshire | CE | (t) | CL | GC | CL | GC | GC | GC | GC | (hh) |
| New Jersey* | CE | (t) | GS | GS | GS | GS | (a-16) | BG | GS | A |
| New Mexico | CE | CE | CE | CE | CE | G | (a-16) | B | G | G |
| New York | CE | CE | GS | CE | A | G | (a-16) | GS | GS | G |
| North Carolina* | CE | CE | SE | SE | SE | G | G | SE | G | G |
| North Dakota | CE | CE | CE | CE | CE | G | ... | CE | GS | G |
| Ohio* | CE | CE | CE | C | CE | G | G | G | A | G |
| Oklahoma | CE | CE | GS | CE | CE | GS | GS | B | GS | (a-15) |
| Oregon | CE | (a-2) | CE | SE | CE | G | GS | GS | A | A |
| Pennsylvania | CE | CE | GS | CE | CE | GS | G | GS | GS | G |
| Rhode Island | CE | CE | CE | CE | CE | G | G | AGS | AGS | AGS |
| South Carolina* | CE | CE | CE | CE | CE. | CE | B | CE | (a-4) | AB |
| South Dakota | CE | G | CE | CE | CE | G | G | G | A | (a-15) |
| Tennessee | CE | (t,vv) | CL | CT | CL | G | (a-16) | G | G | A |
| Texas | CE | CE | G | CE | CE | G | (a-16) | SE | B | G |
| Utah | CE | CE | (a-1) | CE | CE | G | GS | G | G | G |
| Vermont | CE | CE | CE | SE | CE | SL | GS | GS | GS | (a-15) |
| Virginia* | CE | CE | GB | CE | GB | GB | GB | GB | B | GB |
| Washington | CE | CE | CE | CE | CE | G | G | G | G | G |
| West Virginia | CE | (t) | CE | CE | CE | GS | G | CE | GS | A, CS |
| Wisconsin | CE | CE | CE | CE | CE | G | GS | GS | A | A |
| Wyoming | CE | (a-2) | CE | G | CE | G | GS | GS | A | A |
| American Samoa* | CE | CE | (a-1) | GB | GB | N.A. | GB | GB | N.A. | GB |
| No. Mariana Islands | CE | CE | ... | GS | G | ... | G | G | G | G |
| U.S. Virgin Islands* | CE | CE | (a-1) | G | G | G | G | G | (a-1) | G |

*Source*: The Council of State Governments' survey of state personnel agencies, January 2000, except where noted by * where data are from The Book of the States, 1998-99.

*Note*: The chief administrative officials responsible for each function were determined from information given by the states for the same function as listed in State Administrative Officials Classified by Function, 1999, published by The Council of State Governments.

*Key:*
N.A. — Not available.
. . . — No specific chief administrative official or agency in charge of function.
CE — Constitutional, elected by public.
CL — Constitutional, elected by legislature.
SE — Statutory, elected by public.
SL — Statutory, elected by legislature.
L — Selected by legislature or one of its organs
CT — Constitutional, elected by state court of last resort.

*Appointed by:*
G — Governor
GS — Governor
GB — Governor
GE — Governor
GC — Governor
GD — Governor
GLS — Governor
GOC — Governor & Council
LG — Lieutenant Governor
LGS — Lieutenant Governor
AT — Attorney General
SS — Secretary of State
C- Cabinet Secretary
CG— Cabinet Secretary

*Approved by:*
Senate (in Nebraska, unicameral legislature)
Both houses
Either house
Council
Departmental board
Appropriate legislative committee & Senate

Senate

Governor

## SELECTED OFFICIALS: METHODS OF SELECTION — Continued

| State or other jurisdiction | Civil rights | Commerce | Community affairs | Comptroller | Consumer affairs | Corrections | Economic development | Education | Election administration | Emergency management |
|---|---|---|---|---|---|---|---|---|---|---|
| Alabama | CE | G | G | CS | CS | G | G | B | CE | G |
| Alaska | BG | GS | . . . | AG | AG | GS | AG | GS | LG | AG |
| Arizona | AT | G | G(a-7) | AG | A | G | G(a-7) | G | CE(a-2) | G |
| Arkansas | . . . | G | G | G | CE | B | G | BG | (b) | G |
| California | GS | GS | G | CE | GS | GS | GS(a-7) | CE | CS | GS |
| Colorado | CS | G | CS | CS | AT | GS | G | B | SS | CS |
| Connecticut* | B | B | A | CE | GE | GE | GE | B | CS | A |
| Delaware | G | GS | . . . | AG | AT | GS | GS | GS | GS | AG |
| Florida | A | G | GS | CE | A | GS | N.A. | CE | SS | A |
| Georgia* | G | B | B | CE | G | N.A. | N.A. | CE | (j) | A |
| Hawaii | B | GS | G | GS | A | GS | GS | B | B | G |
| Idaho | G | G | A | (a-23) | (a-3) | B | A | CE | SS | A |
| Illinois | GS | GS | GS | CE | CE | GS | GS | B | B | GS |
| Indiana | AG | LG | N.A. | CE | AT | AG | LT | CE | (l) | AG |
| Iowa | GS | GS | A | GS | AT | GS | GS | GS | (n) | GS |
| Kansas | B | CE/GS | A | A | AT | GS | (q) | B | (r) | CS |
| Kentucky | G | (a-11) | G | (a-15) | (a-3) | G | G | B | B | AG |
| Louisiana | A | GS | A | GS | AG | GS | GS | BG | CE | A |
| Maine | B | GLS(a-11) | . . . | A | A | GLS | GLS | GLS | A | A |
| Maryland | N.A.* | AG* | N.A.* | CE* | A* | AGS* | GS* | B* | G* | AG* |
| Massachusetts | G | (a-11) | GLS* | G | G | CG | G | B | GE* | B* |
| Michigan | B | GS | N.A. | CS | CS | GS | N.A. | B | (y) | CS |
| Minnesota | GS | N.A | A | (a-15) | AT | GS | A | GS | (aa) | A |
| Mississippi | . . . | GS | A | GS | A | GS | GS | B | A | G |
| Missouri | AGS | (a-11) | N.A. | A | (a-3) | GS | GS | BG | SS | A |
| Montana* | A | GS | A | GS | A | GS | CS | CE | SS | CS |
| Nebraska | B | GS | A | A | A | GS | GS | B | A | A |
| Nevada | G | G | N.A. | CE | A | G | GD | B | (nn) | A |
| New Hampshire | CS | GC | G | AGC | AT | GC | AGC | B | (a-2) | G |
| New Jersey* | A | GS | GS | (a-6) | A | GS | A | GS | A | A |
| New Mexico | G | (a-11) | G | (a-4) | G | GS | GS | B | G | G |
| New York | GS | GS | (a-2) | CE | GS | GS | GS | B | G | A |
| North Carolina* | AG | G | AG | GC | (a-3) | G | AG | SE | G | AG |
| North Dakota | G | G | CE | A | CS | G | G | CE | CS | A |
| Ohio* | B | G | A | (a-4) | B | G | G | B | A | A |
| Oklahoma | B | GS | (a-7) | A | B | B | (a-7) | CE | L | GS |
| Oregon | A | . . . | G | A | (pp) | GS | GS | SE | A | AG |
| Pennsylvania | B | GS | A | G | AT | GS | GS | GS | A | G |
| Rhode Island | B | (a-11) | G | AGS | AT | G | G | B | G | G |
| South Carolina* | BG | GS | N.A. | CE | B | GS | (a-7) | CE | B | A |
| South Dakota | A | G | (a-11) | (a-23) | A | G | G | G | SS | G |
| Tennessee | BA | (a-11) | (a-11) | A | A | G | G | G | SS | A |
| Texas | B | G | G | CE | (a-3) | B | (a-7) | B | (xx) | A |
| Utah | A | GS | GS | A | A | GS | A | B | G | A |
| Vermont | (aaa) | GS | GS | (a-15) | AT | AG | AGS | BG | (bbb) | AG |
| Virginia* | GB | GB | GB | GB | N.A. | GB | (ccc) | GB | GB | GB |
| Washington | G | G | G | (a-4) | A | G | G | CE | A | A |
| West Virginia | GS | GS | GS | CE | AT | GS | (a-8) | (ddd) | (a-2) | GS |
| Wisconsin | A | GS | A | CS | (fff) | GS | CS | CE | B | GS |
| Wyoming | CS | BG | BG | CE | AT | GS | BG | CE | CS | N.A. |
| American Samoa* | N.A. | GB | (a-7) | (a-4) | (a-3) | A | (a-7) | GB | G | G |
| No. Mariana Islands | GS | GS | GS | GS | A | G | G | B | G | G |
| U.S. Virgin Islands* | G | G | G | (a-15) | G | G | N.A. | G | B | G |

Appointed by:
A — Agency head
AB — Agency head
AG — Agency head
AGC — Agency head
AGS Agency head
ALS — Agency head
ASH — Agency head
B — Board or commission
BG — Board
BGS — Board
BS — Board or commission
BA — Board or commission
CS — Civil Service
LS — Legislative Committee

Approved by:

Board

Governor
Governor & Council

Appropriate legislative committee
Senate president & House speaker

Governor
Governor & Senate
Senate
Agency head

Senate

(a) Chief administrative official or agency in charge of function:
(a-1) Lieutenant Governor
(a-2) Secretary of state
(a-3) Attorney general
(a-4) Treasurer
(a-5) Administration
(a-6) Budget
(a-7) Commerce
(a-8) Community affairs
(a-9) Comptroller
(a-10) Consumer affairs
(a-11) Economic development
(a-12) Education (chief state school officer)
(a-13) Energy
(a-14) Environmental protection

## SELECTED OFFICIALS: METHODS OF SELECTION — Continued

| State or other jurisdiction | Employment services | Energy | Environment protection | Finance | Fish & wildlife | General services | Health | Higher education | Highways | Historic preservation |
|---|---|---|---|---|---|---|---|---|---|---|
| Alabama | CS | CS | B | G | CS | CS | B | B | G | B |
| Alaska* | AG | AG | GS | AG | GS | AG | AG | AG | AG | A |
| Arizona | AG | A | G | G | G | AG | G | G | AG | A |
| Arkansas | G | G | BG | G | B | AG | BG | BG | B | A |
| California | GS | B | GS | GS | GS | GS | GS | B | GS | G |
| Colorado | GS | G | CS | CS | CS | CS | GS | GS | (a-29) | B |
| Connecticut* | A | A | GE | GE | (e) | GE | GE | B | A | B |
| Delaware | GS | A | GS | GS | AG | GS | AG | B | GS | AG |
| Florida | A | A | GS | A | B | GS | GS | B | GS | SS |
| Georgia* | A | N.A. | A | (a-4) | A | A | A | B | (a-29) | A |
| Hawaii | CS | CS | G | (a-6) | CS | (a-25) | GS | B | CS | (a-19) |
| Idaho | G | A | A | G | B | A | G | B | (a-29) | B |
| Illinois | GS | GS | GS | G | GS | GS | GS | B | G | GS |
| Indiana | AG | LG | AG | (a-6) | A | (a-5) | AG | AG | (a-29) | N.A. |
| Iowa* | GS | A | A | (o) | A | GS | GS | (p) | A | A |
| Kansas | GS | A | A | . . . | CS | GS | GS | B | GS | G |
| Kentucky | AG | AG | G | G | B | (a-5) | G | B | AG | AG |
| Louisiana | A | GS | GS | GS | GS | GS | GS | B | GS | A |
| Maine | A | G | GLS | GLS(a-5) | GLS | A | GLS | B | GLS(a-29) | B/BG |
| Maryland | N.A.* | A* | N.A.* | GS | A | GS | GS | G | A | A |
| Massachusetts | CG | CG | CG | (a-5) | CG | (a-5) | CG | B | G | B* |
| Michigan | N.A. | . . . | GS | (a-6) | CS | CS | GS | CS | (a-29) | CS |
| Minnesota | A | A | A | GS | A | (a-5) | GS | B | A | N.A. |
| Mississippi | B | A | GS | GS | BGC | A | B | B | B | B |
| Missouri | A | A | A | (a-5) | (dd) | A | GS | B | B | N.A. |
| Montana* | CS | CS | G | G | CS | CS | G | B | G | CS |
| Nebraska | A | A | GS | (ee) | (ff) | A | GS | B | GS | B |
| Nevada | A | CS | A | (a-9) | GB | N.A. | AG | B | (a-29) | G |
| New Hampshire | GC | G | GC | (a-5) | BGC | CS | AGC | B | (a-29) | GC |
| New Jersey* | A | GS | GS | (a-6) | B | A | GS | B | (a-29) | A |
| New Mexico | (a-18) | GS | GS | GS | G | GS | GS | B | GS | G |
| New York | (a-18) | (hhh) | GS | (a-9) | A | GS | GS | (a-12) | (a-29) | (a-20) |
| North Carolina* | G | AG | AG | (a-6) | BG | (a-5) | AG | B | AG | AG |
| North Dakota | G | CS | CS | A | G | G | G | B | G | CS |
| Ohio* | G | A | G | (a-6) | A | G | G | B | (a-29) | B |
| Oklahoma | (mm) | GS | B | G | B | (a-5) | B | B | B | B |
| Oregon | GS | GS | B | A | B | (a-5) | AG | B | (a-29) | B |
| Pennsylvania | G | A | G | G | (rr) | GS | GS | G | G | A |
| Rhode Island | G | (a-24) | G | (a-6) | AGS | AGS | AG | B | B | B |
| South Carolina* | B | A | A | B | B | AB | BGS | B | (a-29) | A |
| South Dakota | A | A | G | G | A | (a-5) | G | B | A | A |
| Tennessee | A | A | N.A. | G | B | G | (ww) | B | (a-29) | AG |
| Texas | B | A | B | (a-9) | B | B | B | B | (a-29) | B |
| Utah | GS | A | GS | A | A | A | (yy) | B | GS | A |
| Vermont | GS | GS | . . . | AGS | AGS | AGS | AG | N.A. | (a-29) | (qq) |
| Virginia* | GB | GB | GB | GB | B | GB | GB | B | GB | GB |
| Washington | A | . . . | G | G | B | (a-5) | G | B | (a-29) | A |
| West Virginia | GS | GS | GS | GS | A, CS | G | GS | (eee) | GS | A |
| Wisconsin | A | A | A | A | (ggg) | (a-5) | A | N.A. | A | CS |
| Wyoming | A | A | GS | CE | GS | (a-5) | GS | B | GS | GS |
| American Samoa* | A | GB | GB | (a-4) | GB | G | GB | (a-12) | (a-29) | A |
| No. Mariana Islands | G | G | G | GS | G | B | GS | B | GS | G |
| U.S. Virgin Islands* | (a-18) | G | G | G | N.A. | N.A. | G | CE | G | G |

(a-15) Finance
(a-16) General services
(a-17) Highways
(a-18) Labor
(a-19) Natural Resources
(a-20) Parks and recreation
(a-21) Personnel
(a-22) Post-audit
(a-23) Pre-audit
(a-24) Public utility regulation
(a-25) Purchasing
(a-26) Revenue
(a-27) Social services
(a-28) Tourism
(a-29) Transportation
(a-30) Welfare

(b) Responsibilities shared between Secretary of State (CE); and Supervisor of Elections (CE).

(c) Responsibilities shared between Director, Department of General Services (GS); and Chief Deputy Director, same department (A).

(d) Method not specified.

(e) Responsibilities shared between Director, Fisheries Division (CS); and Director, Wildlife Division (CS).

(f) Responsibilities shared between Commissioner, Department of Mental Retardation (GE); and Commissioner, Department of Mental Health & Addiction Services (GE).

(g) Responsibilities shared between Director, Division of Alcoholism, Drug Abuse and Mental Health (AG); and Director, Division of Mental Retardation (GS).

(h) Responsibilities shared between Secretary, Department of Services for

## SELECTED OFFICIALS: METHODS OF SELECTION — Continued

| State or other jurisdiction | Information systems | Insurance | Labor | Licensing | Mental health & retardation | Natural resources | Parks & recreation | Personnel | Planning | Post audit |
|---|---|---|---|---|---|---|---|---|---|---|
| Alabama | CS | G | G | ... | G | G | CS | B | G | L |
| Alaska | AG | AG | GS | AG | AG | GS | AG | AG | ... | L |
| Arizona | A | G | G | ... | A | G | G | A | G(a-6) | G |
| Arkansas | G | G | G | ... | BA | A | G | AG | ... | L |
| California | GS | CE | GS | GS(a-10) | GS | GS | GS | G | G | G |
| Colorado | G | G | GS | GS | CS | GS | CS | CS | (a-6) | L |
| Connecticut* | GE | GE | GE | GB | (f) | CS | CS | A | (a-13) | L |
| Delaware | GS | CE | GS | AG | AG | GS | AG | GS | G | CE |
| Florida | A | CE | GS | SS | A | GS | A | A | G | L |
| Georgia* | A | CE | CE | A | A | B | A | G | G | G |
| Hawaii | CS | AG | GS | (a-7) | CS | GS | CS | GS | ... | (k) |
| Idaho | (a-5) | G | G | G | N.A. | ... | B | G | (a-7) | A |
| Illinois | GS | GS | GS | GS | GS | GS | GS | AG | ... | L |
| Indiana | AG | AG | AG | (m) | AG | AG | AG | AG | ... | AG |
| Iowa* | GS | GS | GS | GS | A | GS | A | GS | (a-11) | CE |
| Kansas | A | SE | A | B | A | GS | GS | A | B | L |
| Kentucky | (s) | G | G | AG | G | G | G | G | (a-6) | CE |
| Louisiana | A | CE | GS | A | GS | GS | LGS | B | A | CL |
| Maine | A | GLS | GLS | A | GLS | GLS | A | A | G | SL |
| Maryland | A | GS | GS | A | A(v) | GS | A | A | GS | A |
| Massachusetts | C | G | G | G | CG(w) | CG | (x)* | CG | (a-11) | CE |
| Michigan | CS | GS | CS | GS | GS | B | CS | B | ... | CL |
| Minnesota | A | N.A. | GS | A | A | GS | A | GS | GS | (bb) |
| Mississippi | B | SE | ... | ... | (cc) | GS | BGS | BS | A | CE |
| Missouri | A | GS | GS | A | A | GS | A | G | (a-6) | CE |
| Montana* | CS | A | G | CS | CS | G | CS | CS | (a-6) | L |
| Nebraska | A | GS | GS | A | A | GS | B | A | GS | CE |
| Nevada | G | A | A | ... | GD | G | ... | A | (a-5) | L |
| New Hampshire | AGC | GC | GC | ... | AGC | GC | AGC | AGC | G | CS |
| New Jersey* | G | GS | GS | A | A | GS | A | GS | A | A |
| New Mexico | G | G | GS | G | (ii) | GS | G | G | ... | CE |
| New York | (a-16) | GS | GS | (jj) | GS | (a-14) | GS | GS | (a-11) | (a-9) |
| North Carolina* | AG | SE | SE | ... | AG | G | AG | G | AG | SE |
| North Dakota | G | CE | G | CE | CS | CS | G | A | ... | (kk) |
| Ohio* | A | G | A | G | (ll) | G | A | A | (a-6) | CE |
| Oklahoma | (oo) | CE | CE | ... | B | (a-28) | (a-28) | GS | ... | CE |
| Oregon | A | GS | SE | ... | AG | GOC | B | A | B | A |
| Pennsylvania | G | GS | GS | GS | (ss) | GS | A | G | G | CE |
| Rhode Island | A | A | AGS | A | G | (a-14) | A | A | A | (tt) |
| South Carolina* | AB | GS | GS | (a-18) | B | B | GS | AB | AB | B |
| South Dakota | G | A | G | A | (uu) | G | A | G | (a-15) | L |
| Tennessee | A | G | G | A | A | G | A | G | N.A. | CL |
| Texas | B | G | B | B | B | B | B | A | (a-6) | L |
| Utah | A | GS | A | A | AG | GS | AG | GS | G | CE |
| Vermont | A | GS | GS | A | AG | GS | AGS | AGS | ... | CE |
| Virginia* | GB | SL | GB | GB | GB | GB | GB | GB | (a-6) | SL |
| Washington | G | CE | G | G | A | CE | G | G | (a-15) | CE |
| West Virginia | G | GS | GS | ... | GS | GS | GS | A | GS | L |
| Wisconsin | A | GS | GS | GS | CS | GS | CS | GS | (a-6) | L |
| Wyoming | A | GS | G | AG | A | G | GS | A | G | CE |
| American Samoa* | (a-29) | G | N.A. | N.A. | (a-27) | AG | GB | A | (a-7) | G |
| No. Mariana Islands | G | G | G | B | GS | GS | G | GS | G | GS |
| U.S. Virgin Islands* | (a-6) | (a-1) | G | N.A. | G | (a-19) | G | G | G | G |

Children, Youth and Their Families (GS); and Secretary, Department of Health and Social Services (GS).

(i) Responsibilities shared between Director, Division of Licensing, Department of State (SS); and Secretary, Department of Professional Regulation (N.A.).

(j) Responsibilities shared between the Secretary of State (CE); and Director, Election Division (A).

(k) Responsibilities shared between State Auditor (L); and Division Head, Division of Audit (CS).

(l) Responsibilities shared between Co-Directors in Election Commission (AG); appointed by the Governor, subject to approval by the Chairs of the State Republican/Democratic parties.

(m) Responsibilities shared between Executive Director, Health Professions Bureau; and Executive Director, Professional Licensing Agency (G).

(n) Responsibilities shared between Secretary of State (CE); and Director of Elections (CS).

(o) Responsibilities shared between Director, Department of Revenue; and Director, Department of Management (GS).

(p) Responsibilities shared between Director, Department of Education (GS); and Executive Secretary, Board of Regents (B).

(q) Responsibilities shared between Secretary, Department of Commerce and Housing (GS); Director, Division of Existing Industry, same department (A); Director,

Business Development Division, same department (A); and President Kansas Inc. (B).

(r) Responsibilities shared between Secretary of the State (CE); and Deputy Assistant for Elections (SS).

(s) Responsibilities shared between Chief Information Office, Governor's Office for Technology (G); and Executive Director, Information Resources Management, Finance & Administration (AG).

## SELECTED OFFICIALS: METHODS OF SELECTION — Continued

| State or other jurisdiction | Pre-audit | Public library development | Public utility regulation | Purchasing | Revenue | Social services | Solid waste management | State police | Tourism | Transportation | Welfare |
|---|---|---|---|---|---|---|---|---|---|---|---|
| Alabama | CS | B | SE | CS | G | B | CS | G | G | G | G |
| Alaska | (a-15) | AG | AG | (a-16) | GB | GS | CS | AG | AG | GS | AG |
| Arizona | A(a-9) | G | G | A | G | G | G | G | G | GS | A |
| Arkansas | AG | G | BG | AG | AG | G | AG | G | AG | B | G |
| California | CE(a-9) | GS | G | GS | B | GS | B | GS | N.A. | GS | GS(a-27) |
| Colorado | CS | A | GS | CS, AB | GS | GS | CS | CS | . . . | GS | GS |
| Connecticut* | (a-9) | A | GE | A | GE | GE | CS | GE | A | GE | CS |
| Delaware | CE | AG | AG | AG | AG | GS | B | AG | A | GS | AG |
| Florida | GOC | SS | B | A | GOC | GS | A | A | N.A. | A | A |
| Georgia* | G | AB | N.A. | A | N.A. | A | A | B | A | BG | A |
| Hawaii | CS | B | G | GS | GS | GS | CS | . . . | (a-11) | GS | CS |
| Idaho | CE | A | GS | A | GS | A | . . . | G | A | B | A |
| Illinois | CE | SS | CE | A | GS | GS | A | GS | A | GS | GS |
| Indiana* | CE | AG | AG | AG | AG | A | A | AG | LG | AG | AG |
| Iowa* | (a-26) | BA | GS | A | GS | A | A | A | A | GS | A |
| Kansas | CS | GS | GS | A | GS | GS | A | GS | A | GS | A |
| Kentucky | G | G | G | (a-15) | G | G | AG | G | G | G | G |
| Louisiana | A | BGS | BS | A | GS | GS | GS | GS | LGS | GS | GS |
| Maine | A | B | G | CS | A | GLS | CS | AGS | A | GLS | A |
| Maryland | A | A | GS | A | A | A | A | GS | A | GS | GS |
| Massachusetts | (a-9)* | B | G | CG | CG | CG | A* | G | CG | G | CG |
| Michigan | CL | CL | GS | CS | GS | GS | CS | GS | N.A. | GS | GS |
| Minnesota | A | A | A | A | GS | A | A | A | G | GS | A |
| Mississippi | . . . | BS | B | A | GS | . . . | A | GS | A | B | GS |
| Missouri | (a-9) | B | GS | A | GS | GS | A | GS | A | (a-17) | A |
| Montana* | . . . | B | SE | CS | G | G | CS | AT | CS | CS | G |
| Nebraska | A | B | B | A | GS | GS | A | GS | A | GS | GS |
| Nevada | (a-5) | G | G | CS | G | G | (a-14) | CS | GB | BG | AG |
| New Hampshire | CS | AGC | GC | CS | GC | AGC | AGC | GC | AGC | GC | AGC |
| New Jersey* | (a-6) | N.A. | GS | A | A | GS | A | GS | A | GS | A |
| New Mexico | G | G | CE | G | GS | GS | CS | GS | GS | (a-17) | GS |
| New York | (a-9) | (a-12) | GS | (a-16) | GS | GS | (a-14) | GS | (a-11) | GS | (a-27) |
| North Carolina* | (a-22) | AG | AG | AG | G | AG | AG | N.A. | AG | G | N.A. |
| North Dakota | A | CS | CE | CS | CE | G | CS | A | G | G | G |
| Ohio* | (a-22) | B | B | A | B | G | A | A | A | G | G |
| Oklahoma | (a-9) | B | (lll) | A | G | B | A | GS | B | B | (a-30) |
| Oregon | . . . | B | GS | A | GS | GS | A | GS | A | GS | AG |
| Pennsylvania | CE | A | GS | A | GS | G | A | GS | A | GS | GS |
| Rhode Island* | . . . | G | G | A | A | G | A | G· | A | G | A |
| South Carolina* | (a-9) | B | B | A | GS | GS | A | A | GS | B | (a-27) |
| South Dakota | CE | A | CE | A | G | G | A | G | G | G | (a-27) |
| Tennessee | (a-9) | SS | SE | A | G | A | A | G | G | G | G |
| Texas | (a-9) | A | B | A | (a-9) | G | A | B | A | B | L |
| Utah | A | A | A | A | GS | (zz) | A | A | A | GS | GS |
| Vermont | (a-15) | AGS | GS | A | AGS | AG | A | A | A | GS | GS |
| Virginia* | (a-9) | GB | SL | CS | GB | GB | (a-14) | GB | CS | GB | (a-27) |
| Washington | (a-4) | G | G | A | G | G | A | G | A | B | (a-27) |
| West Virginia | GS | B | G | A | GS | GS | B | GS | GS | GS | GS |
| Wisconsin | CS | CS | GS | CS | GS | GS | CS | GS | GS | GS | A |
| Wyoming | CE | A | G | CS | GS | GS | A | GS | BG | GS | GS |
| American Samoa* | (a-4) | (a-12) | N.A. | A | (a-4) | GB | GB | GB | (a-7) | GB | N.A. |
| No. Mariana Islands | GS | B | B | G | G | GS | GS | GS | B | GS | GS |
| U.S. Virgin Islands* | N.A. | G | N.A. | N.A. | G | G | G | G | G | N.A. | G |

(t) In Maine, New Hampshire, New Jersey, Tennessee and West Virginia, the Presidents (or Speakers) of the Senate are next in line of succession to the Governorship. In Tennessee, the Speaker of the Senate bears the statutory title of Lieutenant Governor.

(u) Responsibilities shared between Commissioner, Environmental Protection Department (GLS); and Commissioner, Department of Conservation (GLS).

(v) Responsibilities shared between Director, Mental Hygiene Administration (A); and Director, Developmental Disabilities Administration, Department of Health and Mental Hygiene (GS).

(w) Responsibilities shared between Commissioner, Department of Mental Retardation (BA); and Commissioner, Department of Mental Health, Executive Office of Human Services (BA).

(x) Responsibilities shared between Director, Division of Forests and Parks, Department of Environmental Management (BA); and Director, Recreational Facilities, Metropolitan District Commission (BA).

(y) Responsibilities shared between Secretary of State (CE); and Director, Bureau of Elections (CS).

(z) Responsibilities shared between Chief, Wildlife Division, Department of Natural Resources; and Chief, Fisheries Division, same department (CS).

(aa) Responsibilities shared between Secretary of State (CE); and Director, Election Division, Office of the Secretary of State (A).

(bb) Responsibilities shared between State Auditor (CE); and Legislative Auditor (L).

(cc) Responsibilities shared between Bureau Chief, Alcohol and Drug Abuse Division, Department of Mental Health; and Director, Department of Mental Health (BS).

(dd) Responsibilities shared between Acting Chief, Division of Fisheries, Department of Conservation; Chief, Division of Wildlife, same department (B).

(ee) Responsibilities shared between State Tax Commissioner, Department of Revenue (GS); Administrator, Budget Division, Department of Administrative Services (A); and Auditor of Public Accounts (CE).

(ff) Responsibilities shared between Division Administrator, Wildlife Division, Game & Parks Commission (A); and Division Administrator, Fisheries Division, same commission (A).

(gg) Responsibilities shared between Director Mental Health & Human Services, Department of Health & Human Services; and Director; same department (GS).

(hh) Responsibilities shared between Commissioner, Department of Administration Services (GC); and Assistant Commissioner & Budget Office, Budget Office same department (AGC).

(ii) Responsibilities shared between Division Director II, Long Term Services Division, Department of Health (G); and Division II Director, Behavioral Health Services Division, same department (G).

(jj) Responsibilities shared between Executive Coordinator, Office of Professional Responsibility (AG); Commissioner, State Education Department (B); and Secretary of State (GS).

(kk) Responsibilities shared between Legislative Budget Analyst/Auditor, Legislative Council (A); and State Auditor (CE).

(ll) Responsibilities shared between Director, Department of Mental Health; and Director, Department of Mental Retardation and Developmental Disabilities (G).

(mm) Responsibilities shared between Administator and Secretary of Human Resources, Office of Personnel Management (G); and Executive Director, Employment Security Commission (B).

(nn) Responsibilities shared between Secretary of State (CE); Deputy Secretary of State for Elections, Office of Secretary of State (SS); and Chief Deputy Secretary of State, same office (SS).

(oo) Responsibilities shared between Director, Data Processing & Planning Division, Department of Transportation (A); and Director, Information Services Division Management, Office of State Finance (A).

(pp) Responsibilities shared between Manager, Insurance Division, Con

(qq) Responsibilities shared between Director, Division for Historic Preservation, Agency of Commerce and Community Affairs (A); and Historic Preservation Officer (GS).

(rr) Responsibilities shared between Executive Director, Fish Commission (B); and Executive Director, Game Commission (B).

(ss) Responsibilities shared between Deputy Secretary, Mental Health, Department of Public Welfare (G); and Deputy Secretary, Mental Retardation, same department (G).

(tt) Responsibilities shared between Chief General Audit Section, Office of Accounts and Control, Department of Administration, (A); and Auditor General (L).

(uu) Responsibilities shared between Director, Division of Mental Health, Department of Human Services (A); and Secretary same department (G).

(vv) Elected to the Senate by the public and elected Lieutenant Governor by the Senate.

(ww) Responsibilities shared between Chief Health Officer, Department of Health (A); and Commissioner, same department (G).

(xx) Responsibilities shared between Secretary of State (G); and Deputy Assistant Secretary of State (A).

(yy) Responsibilities shared between Executive Director, Department of Health (GS); and Director, Division of Health Care Financing, same department (A).

(zz) Department of Human Services.

(aaa) Responsibilities shared between Chief, Public Protection Division, Office of the Attorney General (AT); and Executive Director, Human Rights Commission (B).

(bbb) Responsibilities shared between Secretary of State (CE); and Director of Elections, Office of Secretary of State (A).

(ccc) Responsibilities shared between Secretary, Commerce and Trade (GB); and Director, Department of Economic Development (GB).

(ddd) Responsibilities shared between Cabinet Secretary, Department of Education and the Arts (G); and Superintendent, Department of Education (B).

(eee) Responsibilities shared between University System Chancellor, Board of Trustees for Higher Education, Department of Education and the Arts (B); Chancellor, State College System (B); and Chancellor, State College System, Department of Education (B); and Cabinet Secretary, Department of Education and the Arts (G).

(fff) Responsibilities shared between Administrator, Trade and Consumer Protection Division, Agriculture, Trade and Consumer Protection (A); and Director, Office of Consumer Protection, Department of Justice (CS).

(ggg) Responsibilities shared between Director, Bureau of Fisheries Management & Habitat Protection, Department of Natural Resources (CS); and Director, Bureau of Wildlife Management, Division of Resource Management (CS).

(hhh) Ex officio by virtue of other office.

(iii) Responsibilities shared between Director, Parks & Recreation, Department of Wildlife, Fisheries & Parks (BGC); and Department Director, same department (A).

(kkk) However, HR functions are decentralized in Texas.

(lll) Responsibilities shared between Director, Public Utility Division, Corporation Commission (A); and 3 Commissioners, Corporation Commission (CE).

## Table 2.11
## SELECTED STATE ADMINISTRATIVE OFFICIALS: ANNUAL SALARIES

| State or other jurisdiction | Governor | Lieutenant governor | Secretary of state | Attorney general | Treasurer | Adjutant general | Administration | Agriculture | Banking | Budget |
|---|---|---|---|---|---|---|---|---|---|---|
| Alabama | $94,655 | $48,870 | $66,722 | $124,951 | $66,722 | $71,235 | $88,819 | $66,258 | $84,000 | $71,235 |
| Alaska | 81,648 | $76,176 | (a-1) | 83,292 | (a-9) | 86,292 | $86,292 | N.A. | 92,844 | 86,292 |
| Arizona | 95,000 | (a-2) | 70,000 | 90,000 | 70,000 | 89,980 | 118,100 | 89,739 | 89,610 | 104,998 |
| Arkansas | 68,448 | 33,083 | 42,780 | 57,040 | 42,780 | 82,250 | 109,945 | 74,011 | 97,981 | 83,044 |
| California | 165,000 | 123,750 | 123,750 | 140,250 | 132,000 | 126,503 | (e) | 126,358 | 126,358 | 126,358 |
| Colorado | 90,000 | 68,500 | 68,500 | 80,000 | 68,500 | 108,000 | 108,000 | 108,000 | 86,628 | 108,156 |
| Connecticut* | 78,000 | 55,000 | 50,000 | 60,000 | 50,000 | 64,000 (c) | 84,000 (c) | 64,000 (c) | 64,000 (c) | 94,763 (c) |
| Delaware | 107,000 | 47,900 | 95,500 | 105,200 | 84,800 | 83,100 | 89,100 | 89,100 | 102,200 | 58,900 |
| Florida | 117,240 | 112,304 | 116,056 | 116,056 | 116,056 | 103,604 | 107,940 | 116,056 | 116,056 | 109,272 |
| Georgia* | 111,480 | 72,812 | 89,538 | 102,211 | 96,804 | 97,279 | 86,814 | 89,545 | 86,835 | 109,020 |
| Hawaii | 94,780 | 90,041 | (a-1) | 85,302 | (a-6) | 131,600 | (a-9) | 85,302 | 74,655 | 85,302 |
| Idaho | 95,500 | 25,250 | 77,500 | 85,500 | 77,500 | 91,000 | 74,485 | 77,875 | 77,459 | (a-15) |
| Illinois | 140,200 | 107,200 | 123,700 | 123,700 | 107,200 | 79,960 | 103,100 | 99,000 | 102,600 | 95,000 |
| Indiana | 77,200 (t) | 64,000 | 66,000 | 79,400 | 66,000 | 94,259 | 86,615 | 71,561 | 83,759 | 86,528 |
| Iowa | 104,352 | 73,047 | 82,940 | 99,379 | 82,940 | 101,878 | 96,800 | 82,940 | 66,333 | 102,993 |
| Kansas | 91,742 | Waived | 71,270 | 81,958 | 71,270 | 85,119 | 90,240 | 85,200 | 68,406 | 80,730 |
| Kentucky | 97,068 | 82,521 | 82,521 | 82,521 | 82,521 | 86,822 | 76,532 | 82,521 | 83,316 | 97,067 |
| Louisiana | 95,000 | 85,008 | 85,000 | 85,000 | 85,000 | 119,088 | 129,361 | 85,000 | 82,152 | 93,984 |
| Maine | 70,000 | (z) | 48298 (c) | 62,670 (c) | 48298 (c) | 56,784 (c) | 56,784 (c) | 56784 (c) | 53,498 (c) | 50,294 (c) |
| Maryland | 120,000 | 100,000 | 70,000 | 100,000 | 100,000 | 79,135 (c) | 91,880 (c) | 91,880 (c) | 68,210 (c) | 106,745 (c) |
| Massachusetts | 135,000 | 120,000 | 120,000 | 122,500 | 120,000 | 103,604 | 104,699 | 84,468 | 96,891 | 85,879 |
| Michigan | 151,245 | 100,671 | 124,900 | 124,900 | 108,000 | 107,983 | 113,984 | 104,003 | 105,987 | 107,991 |
| Minnesota | 120,303 ** | 66,168 | 66,168 | 93,981 | 66,168 | 108,576 | 97,300 | 97,300 | 92,812 | (a-15) |
| Mississippi | 101,800 | 60,000 | 75,000 | 90,800 | 75,000 | 80,000 | 85,000 | 75,000 | 85,000 | 55,993 (c) |
| Missouri | 112,755 | 68,188 | 90,471 | 97,899 | 90,471 | 77,880 | 99,013 | 92,952 | 74,063 | 88,032 |
| Montana* | 83,672 ** | 53,407 | 62,848 | 66,756 | 70,420 | 70,420 | 70,420 | 40,420 | 70,420 | 70,420 |
| Nebraska | 65,000 | 47,000 | 52,000 | 64,500 | 49,500 | 60,968 | 71,400 | 69,870 | 71,400 | 81,422 |
| Nevada | 117,000 | 50,000 | 80,000 | 110,000 | 80,000 | 78,964 | 92,914 | 74,160 | 69,620 | (a-5) |
| New Hampshire | 93,263 | (z) | 74,372 | 83,256 | 74,372 | 78,827 | 83,256 | 62,171 | 78,827 | 57,725 (c) |
| New Jersey* | 130,000**(qqq) | (z) | 100,225 | 100,225 | 100,225 | 100,225 | (a-16) | 100,225 | 100,225 | 95,000 |
| New Mexico | 90,000 | 65,000 | 65,000 | 72,500 | 65,000 | 83,454 | 83,502 | 104,080 | 70,000 | 74,256 |
| New York | 179,000 | 151,500 | 120,800 | 151,500 | 86,860 | 120,800 | (a-16) | 120,800 | 127,000 | 147,490 |
| North Carolina* | 107,132 | 94,552 | 94,552 | 94,552 | 94,552 | 79,554 | 92,378 | 94,552 | 94,552 | 113,875 |
| North Dakota | 76,884 | 63,180 | 58,260 | 65,753 | 58,260 | 101,952 | N.A. | 58,260 | 61,440 | (oo) |
| Ohio* | 119,225 ** | 57,637 | 82,347 | 85,509 | 82,347 | 90,355 | 95,326 | 90,376 | 62,005 | 106,683 |
| Oklahoma | 101,140 | 75,530 | 65,000 | 94,349 | 82,004 | 103,604 | 75,000 | 74,000 | 90,000 | (a-15) |
| Oregon | 88,300 | (a-2) | 67,900 | 72,800 | 67,900 | 92,832 | 112,812 | 92,932 | 84,264 | (a-5) |
| Pennsylvania | 135,559 | 113,870 | 97,603 | 112,785 | 112,785 | 97,603 | 112,500 | 97,603 | 97,603 | 112,500 |
| Rhode Island | 95,000 | 80,000 | 80,000 | 85,000 | 80,000 | 75,993 | 95,220 | 57,812 | 69,561 | 98,515 |
| South Carolina* | 106,078 | 46,545 | 92,007 | 92,007 | 92,007 | 92,007 | 111,296 (c) | 92,007 | (a-4) | 72,154 (c) |
| South Dakota | 89,898 | 65,270 (ww) | 61,090 | 76,357 | 61,090 | 77,251 | 75,046 | 75,046 | 79,456 | (a-15) |
| Tennessee | 87,276 ** | 49,500 | 120,000 | 112,068 | 120,000 | 84,540 | (a-15) | 84,540 | 84,540 | 78,864 |
| Texas | 115,345 | (t) | 112,352 | 92,217 | 92,217 | 89,500 | (a-16) | 92,217 | 105,000 | 118,200 |
| Utah | 93,000 | 72,300 | (a-1) | 78,200 | 72,300 | 80,576 | 90,890 | 80,575 | 80,575 | 94,525 |
| Vermont | 88,026 | 46,030 | 69,493 | 83,491 | 69,493 | 65,603 | 83,428 | 69,076 | 72,820 | (a-15) |
| Virginia* | 110,000 | 32,000 | 76,346 | 97,500 | 93,573 | 71,666 | 82,417 | 73,185 | 103,136 | 94,778 |
| Washington | 132,000 (aaa) | 69,000 | 75,900 | 120,000 | 92,500 | 103,604 | 99,362 | 99,362 | 99,362 | (a-15) |
| West Virginia | 99,000 | (z) | 65,000 | 75,000 | 70,000 | 70,000 | 70,000 | 70,000 | 55,000 | 67,500 |
| Wisconsin | 115,699 | 60,182 | 54,610 | 112,274 | 54,610 | 84,500 | 105,001 | 95,269 | 80,582 | 91,417 |
| Wyoming | 95,000 | (a-2) | 77,000 | 78,500 | 77,000 | 79,244 | 75,000 | 69,000 | 58,500 | 64,583 |
| No. Mariana Islands | 70,000 | 70,000 | . . . | 70,000 | 45,000 | . . . | 54,000 | 40,800 (c) | 40,800 | 54,000 |
| U.S. Virgin Islands* | 80,000 | 75,000 | (a-1) | 65,000 | 48,459 | 65,000 | 65,000 | 65,000 | (a-1) | 65,000 |

*Source*: The Council of State Governments' survey of state personnel agencies, January 2000, except where noted by * where data are from *The Book of the States, 1998-99*.

** Data are from *The Book of the States, 2000-2001*, Table 2.3.

*Note*: The chief administrative officials responsible for each function were determined from information given by the states for the same function as listed in *State Administrative Officials Classified by Function*, 2000, published by The Council of State Governments.

*Key*:

N.A. — Not available.

. . . . — No specific chief administrative official or agency in charge of function.

(a) Chief administrative official or agency in charge of function:
(a-1) Lieutenant governor.
(a-2) Secretary of state.

(a-3) Attorney general.
(a-4) Treasurer.
(a-5) Administration.
(a-6) Budget.
(a-7) Commerce.
(a-8) Community affairs.
(a-9) Comptroller.
(a-10) Consumer affairs.
(a-11) Economic development.
(a-12) Education (chief state school officer).
(a-13) Energy.
(a-14) Environmental protection.
(a-15) Finance.
(a-16) General services.
(a-17) Highways.

## SELECTED OFFICIALS: ANNUAL SALARIES — Continued

| State or other jurisdiction | Civil rights | Commerce | Community affairs | Comptroller | Consumer affairs | Corrections | Economic development | Education | Election administration | Emergency management |
|---|---|---|---|---|---|---|---|---|---|---|
| Alabama | (a-3) | $104,319 | $71,235 | $72,784 (c) | $54,083 (c) | $80,449 | $71,235 | $153,502 | $66,722 | $71,235 |
| Alaska | $86,244 | N.A. | 86,292 | 74,592 | 62,784 | 86,292 | N.A. | 86,292 | 83,124 | 74,592 |
| Arizona | 97,789 | 107,133 | (a-7) | 83,200 | 91,499 | 120,822 | (a-7) | 84,988 | (a-2) | 69,325 |
| Arkansas | ... | (a-11) | (a-27) | (a-15) | $74,637 | 105,143 | 98,378 | 108,375 | (a-2) | 58,514 |
| California | 118,514 | 126,358 | 97,572 | 132,000 | 118,514 | 126,358 | (a-7) | 140,250 | (f) | 104,570 |
| Colorado | 88,536 | 90,000 | 108,000 | 98,004 | 86,148 | 108,000 | 90,000 | 127,200 | 61,392 | 72,840 |
| Connecticut* | 64,000 (c) | ... | 72,000 (c) | 50,000 | 64,000 (c) | 89,000 (c) | 72,000 (c) | 84,000 (c) | 61,642 (c) | 69,340 (c) |
| Delaware | 58,900 | (a-2) | ... | 85,700 | 84,263 | 95,500 | 95,500 | 120,500 | 61,400 | 61,900 |
| Florida | 50,933 | ... | 101,143 | 106,870 | 66,837 | 108,004 | ... | 106,870 | 70,448 | 87,763 |
| Georgia* | 73,183 | 103,764 | 103,764 | (a-4) | 87,768 | 86,832 | (a-7) | 91,578 | 75,204 | 95,178 |
| Hawaii | 75,000 | 85,302 | 74,800 | 85,302 | 65,700 | 85,302 | 85,302 | 90,041 | 77,966 | 76,404 |
| Idaho | 59,010 | 82,181 | 52,416 | 67,500 | (a-3) | 95,014 | 58,351 | 77,500 | 77,500 | 62,650 |
| Illinois | 77,444 | 89,357 | (a-7) | 96,804 | (a-3) | 104,369 | (a-7) | 149,203 | 86,760 | 72,233 |
| Indiana | 59,094 | (a-1) | 46,752 | (a-23) | 69,545 | 82,212 | 70,199 | 63,099 | (u) | 82,328 |
| Iowa | 70,000 | 96,800 | 76,939 | (a-6) | 82,700 | 92,700 | 109,166 | 110,919 | (a-2) | 58,899 |
| Kansas | 58,879 | 96,661 | 59,704 | 65,037 | 61,036 | 86,069 | (x) | 112,000 | 66,206 | 49,025 |
| Kentucky | 75,870 | (a-11) | 77,343 | (a-15) | (a-3) | 82,273 | 140,000 | 151,938 | 71,691 | 78,324 |
| Louisiana | 27,040 | (a-11) | ... | (a-5) | 75,000 | 78,000 | 83,200 | 119,616 | 85,000 | 64,152 |
| Maine | 40,414 (c) | (a-11) | N.A. | 50,294 (c) | 46,904 (c) | 56,784 (c) | 56,784 (c) | 56,784 (c) | 55,744 (c) | 40,414 (c) |
| Maryland | 73,462 (c) | 104,195 (c)* | 65,660 (c)* | 100,000* | 65,660 (c)* | 76,585 (c)* | 104,195 (c)* | 119,000* | 65,660 (c)* | 56,293 (c)* |
| Massachusetts | 71,351 | (a-11) | 69,015* | 103,502 | 102,500 | 110,750 | 93,454 | 149,450 | 69,015* | 70,295 |
| Michigan | 103,982 | 103,982 | N.A. | 92,123 | 99,577 | 107,991 | N.A. | 108,409 | (a-2) | 84,543 |
| Minnesota | 97,300 | N.A. | 88,928 | (a-15) | 62,995 | 97,300 | 97,300 | 185,000 | (ff) | 64,519 |
| Mississippi | ... | 76,822 | 54,571 | 85,000 | 52,800 | 85,000 | 76,822 | 144,000 | 48,062 | 65,000 |
| Missouri | 64,740 | (a-11) | 73,146 | 82,488 | (a-3) | 92,952 | 92,952 | - 115,284 | 63,600 | 70,236 |
| Montana* | 51,230 | 70,420 | 48,197 | 70,420 | 51,904 | 70,420 | 58,477 | 62,848 | 35,256 | 43,848 |
| Nebraska | 72,610 | (a-11) | 52,217 | 78,250 | 75,381 | 83,812 | 76,500 | 112,062 | 48,126 | 64,748 |
| Nevada | 61,167 | 92,914 | N.A. | (Call) | 55,575 | 92,914 | 82,068 | 92,914 | 46,350 | 59,670 |
| New Hampshire | 53,333 | 83,256 | 67,303 | 65,508 | 65,508 | 64,394 (c) | 62,171 | 83,256 | (a-2) | 64,890 |
| New Jersey* | 83,483 | 100,225 | 100,225 | (a-6) | 91,639 | N.A. | 78,928 | 100,225 | 63,000 | 81,285 |
| New Mexico | 52,333 | (a-11) | 62,400 | (a-4) | 71,577 | 83,502 | 83,502 | 93,147 | 55,120 | 66,323 |
| New York | 109,800 | 120,800 | (a-2) | 151,500 | 101,600 | 136,000 | 120,800 | 136,000 | 109,800 | 100,253 |
| North Carolina* | 52,354 | 92,378 | 72,632 | 117,669 | (a-3) | 92,378 | 86,164 | 94,552 | 76,089 | 71,760 |
| North Dakota | (a-18) | (a-11) | 58,260 | (pp) | 47,532 | 66,696 | 92,772 | 59,436 | 28,584 | 51,312 |
| Ohio* | 82,950 | 92,132 | 91,270 | (a-4) | 103,376 | 101,650 | 97,781 | 135,845 | 74,547 | 57,554 |
| Oklahoma | 58,200 | 103,600 | 73,000 | 72,000 | 55,316 | 81,000 | N.A. | 88,511 | 71,957 | 44,553 |
| Oregon | 76,356 | ... | 90,912 | 84,264 | (fff) | 107,508 | 102,384 | 67,900 | 92,832 | 76,356 |
| Pennsylvania | 97,467 | 103,025 | 73,213 | 105,300 | 78,005 | 108,448 | 103,025 | 108,448 | 62,729 | 74,817 (c) |
| Rhode Island | 52,955 | ... | ... | 85,647 | ... | 85,647 | ... | 130,933 | 69,561 | 69,502 |
| South Carolina* | 65,755 (c) | 100,661 | N.A. | 92,007 | 74,378 (c) | 104,328 (c) | (a-7) | 92,007 | 54,820 (c) | 40,823 (c) |
| South Dakota | N.A. | 75,046 | (a-11) | (a-23) | 44,643 | 76,939 | 81,952 | 77,251 | 46,300 | 53,830 |
| Tennessee | 67,740 | (a-11) | (a-11) | 78,600 | 40,488* | 84,540 | 89,976 | 89,976 | 76,020 | 70,476 |
| Texas | 56,958 | (a-7) | 110,000 | 92,217 | (a-3) | 150,000 | 89,500 | 164,748 | (ggg) | 72,600 |
| Utah | 62,452 | 78,885 | 86,860 | (a-15) | 62,450 | 94,525 | 79,575 | 128,412 | 34,410 | 77,500 |
| Vermont | (zz) | 75,462 | 75,462 | (a-15) | 62,629 | 80,142 | 61,214 | 90,000 | (hhh) | 57,532 |
| Virginia* | 62,318 | 104,097 | 104,097 | 94,241 | ... | 100,369 | 116,113 | 116,113 | 62,318 | 70,984 |
| Washington | 77,250 | 99,362 | 92,136 | (a-4) | 107,400 | 99,362 | 99,362 | 94,394 | 70,332 | 65,316 |
| West Virginia | 40,000 | 65,000 | 105,000 | 70,000 | 72,000 | 70,000 | (a-8) | (bbb) | (a-2) | 40,000 |
| Wisconsin | 79,870 | 89,751 | 69,501 | 87,805 | 82,339 | 100,754 | 73,441 | 88,089 | 91,935 | 75,001 |
| Wyoming | 46,560 | 135,000 | (a-7) | 77,000 | 38,000 | 72,000 | (a-7) | 77,000 | 34,037 | 48,118 |
| No. Mariana Islands | N.A. | 57,000 | 48,000 | 54,000 | 50,000 (c) | 40,800 | 40,800 | 80,000 | 48,000 | 40,800 |
| U.S. Virgin Islands * | 37,000 | 65,000 | 65,000 | (a-15) | 65,000 | 65,000 | 65,000 | 65,000 | 55,000 | 45,000 |

(a-18) Labor.
(a-19) Natural resources.
(a-20) Parks and recreation.
(a-21) Personnel.
(a-22) Post audit.
(a-23) Pre-audit.
(a-24) Public utility regulation.
(a-25) Purchasing.
(a-26) Revenue.
(a-27) Social services.
(a-28) Tourism.
(a-29) Transportation.
(a-30) Welfare.

(b) $50/session day, $3,780/month for office expense and mileage.
(c) Minimum figure in range: top of range follows:
 Alabama: Comptroller, $110,973; Consumer affairs, $82,498; Employment services, $88,819; Energy, $76,518; Fish & Wildlife, $88,819; General services, $88,819; Information systems, $110,973; Parks & recreation, $88,819; Pre-Audit, $110,973; Purchasing, $88,819; Solid waste management, $82,498.
 Connecticut: Adjutant general, $87,000; Administration, $106,000; Agriculture, $87,000; Banking, $87,000; Budget, $121,728; Civil rights, $87,000; Community affairs, $95,000; Consumer affairs, $87,000; Corrections, $106,000; Economic development, $95,000; Education, $106,000; Elections administration, $79,069; Emergency management, $88,943; Employment services, $87,000; Energy, $87,000; Environmental protection, $95,000; Finance, $106,000.
 Florida: Energy, $96,499.
 Hawaii: Employment services, $85,512; Energy, $90,732; Fish & wildlife, $81,444; Highways, $85,512; Information systems, $85,512; Mental health

## SELECTED OFFICIALS: ANNUAL SALARIES — Continued

| State or other jurisdiction | Employment services | Energy | Environmental protection | Finance | Fish & wildlife | General services | Health | Higher education | Highway | Historic preservation |
|---|---|---|---|---|---|---|---|---|---|---|
| Alabama | $58,295 (c) | $50,151 (c) | $104,500 | $71,235 | $58,295 (c) | $58,295 (c) | $173,604 | $148,408 | $95,670 (d) | $75,000 |
| Alaska | 80,244 | 74,592 | 86,292 | N.A. | 86,292 | 89,484 | 92,448 | N.A. | 83,124 | 67,488 |
| Arizona | 62,483 | 60,964 | 115,000 | 92,664 | 101,345 | 89,232 | 117,500 | 72,342 | 100,984 | 54,392 |
| Arkansas | 103,813 | 83,943 | 91,506 | 109,945 | 93,309 | 90,285 | 156,712 | 111,417 | 118,742 | 70,783 |
| California | 118,514 | 113,287 | 126,358 | 126,358 | 118,514 | 118,514 | 118,514 | 141,672 | 118,514 | 80,628 |
| Colorado | (a-18) | 85,000 | 98,088 | (a-9) | 100,704 | 89,328 | 108,000 | 108,000 | 108,000 | 80,148 |
| Connecticut* | 64,000 (c) | 64,000 (c) | 72,000 (c) | 84,000 (c) | (h) | 95,000 | 95,000 | 114,000 | 83,500 | 63,087 |
| Delaware | (a-18) | 44,511 | (a-19) | 102,200 | 75,300 | (a-5) | 132,100 | 65,800 | 95,500 | 74,100 |
| Florida | 92,520 (m) | 47,452 (c) | 107,940 | 89,815 | 110,754 | 107,940 | 149,060 | 255,000 | 113,482 | 82,241 |
| Georgia* | 77,850 | N.A. | 99,234 | (a-4) | 85,524 | (a-5) | 135,570 | 215,384 | (a-29) | 79,404 |
| Hawaii | 62,520 (c) | 66,336 (c) | 72,886 | (a-6) | 59,544 (c) | (a-25) | 85,302 | 167,184 | 62,520 (c) | (a-19) |
| Idaho | 76,440 | 66,040 | 80,018 | 9,880 | 94,162 | 53,560 | 88,005 | 109,741 | 111,426 | 62,005 |
| Illinois | 107,200 | 99,000 | 99,000 | (s) | (a-19) | (a-5) | 107,200 | 175,100 | 101,256 | 84,100 |
| Indiana | 81,489 | 54,274 | 86,615 | (a-6) | 74,918 | (a-5) | 111,270 | 129,000 | (a-29) | 47,151 |
| Iowa | 96,054 | 81,536 | 81,536 | (a-6) | 81,536 | (a-5) | 96,800 | (w) | 89,544 | 79,100 |
| Kansas | 87,204 | 44,587 | 80,725 | (y) | 43,451 | (a-5) | 87,189 | 125,000 | (a-29) | 71,821 |
| Kentucky | 76,927 | 70,811 | 85,271 | 91,163 | 90,000 | (a-5) | 150,091 | 233,000 | 94,756 | 89,250 |
| Louisiana | N.A. | 73,800 | 80,808 | (a-5) | 75,000 | (a-5) | 99,432 | 160,425 | (a-29) | 49,788 |
| Maine | N.A. | 50,294 (c ) | 56,784 (c ) | (a-5) | 56,784 (c) | 50,294 (c) | 56,784 (c) | N.A. | (a-29) | 51,792 (c) |
| Maryland | 60,798 (c)* | 65,660 (c) * | 89,330 (c) *| 106,745 (c) | 63,384 | (a-5) | 106,745 (c) | 99,025 (c) | (a-29) | 65,660 (c) |
| Massachusetts | 87,000 | 83,897 | 89,876 | (a-5) | 89,001 | (a-5) | 110,750 | 80,067* | 87,683 | 68,210* |
| Michigan | N.A. | . . . | 108,054 | (a-6) | 83,729 | 100,767 | 107,991 | 84,982 | (a-29) | 93,438 |
| Minnesota | 85,712 | 87,675 | 74,312 | 97,300 | N.A. | 97,300 | 97,300 | 92,143 | 97,300 | N.A. |
| Mississippi | 70,000 | 54,572 (c) | 85,000 | 85,000 | 80,000 | 65,260 (c) | 130,314 (c) | 160,000 | 85,000 | 70,000 |
| Missouri | 86,136 | 73,176 | 81,024 | 93,211 | (hh) | 74,604 | 119,028 | 143,196 | 110,004 | 49,152 |
| Montana* | 52,732 | 58,477 | 70,420 | 70,420 | 70,420 | 42,999 | 70,420 | 113,368 | 70,420 | 46,702 |
| Nebraska | 47,900 | 55,977 | 81,600 | (ii) | (jj) | 70,048 | 83,640 | 110,118 | 83,641 | 82,131 |
| Nevada | 76,501 | 53,453 | 86,084 | (a-9) | 73,290 | N.A. | 76,500 | 177,833 | (a-29) | 67,108 |
| New Hampshire | 74,372 | 56,780 | 81,046 | (a-5) | 62,171 | 53,333 | 62,175 (c) | 53,288 | (a-29) | 65,508 |
| New Jersey* | 79,507 | 100,225 | 100,225 | (a-6) | 75,894 | 85,000 | 100,225 | 95,000 | 100,225 | 84,349 |
| New Mexico | 83,502 | 83,502 | 83,502 | 83,502 | 81,501 | 83,502 | 83,502 | 83,502 | 83,502 | N.A. |
| New York | (a-18) | 120,800 | 136,000 | (a-9) | 107,054 | 136,000 | 136,000 | (a-12) | (a-29) | (a-20) |
| North Carolina* | 117,520 | 59,293 | 72,056 | (a-6) | 72,569 | (a-5) | 115,632 | 240,000 | 110,676 | 61,917 |
| North Dakota | 67,104 | N.A. | 75,384 | (oo) | 67,092 | (a-5) | 101,916 | 145,860 | (a-29) | 46,740 |
| Ohio* | 95,202 | 72,571 | 96,408 | (a-6) | 77,064 | 95,326 | 94,120 | 157,394 | (a-29) | N.A. |
| Oklahoma | (ss) | 5,600 | 82,000 | 90,000 | 81,576 | (a-5) | 110,000 | 215,000 | 133,203 | 62,000 |
| Oregon | 92,832 | 84,264 | 92,832 | 102,384 | 92,832 | (a-5) | 92,832 | 141,828 | (a-29) | 95,000 |
| Pennsylvania | 95,000 | 85,379 | 97,300 | (a-6) | (iii) | 103,025 | 108,448 | 85,100 | 105,800 | 87,316 |
| Rhode Island | 96,890 | (a-24) | 93,614 | (a-6) | 61,024 | 88,861 | 110,059 | 125,687 | (a-29) | 63,129 |
| South Carolina* | 107,014 | 44,157 (c) | 74,097 (c) | 111,296 (c) | 79,268 (c) | 74,097 (c) | 104,328 (c) | 86,603 (c) | (a-29) | 33,552 (c) |
| South Dakota | 63,668 | 38,396 | (a-19) | 76,481 | 64,459 | (a-5) | 75,046 | 140,370 | 72,841 | 49,796 |
| Tennessee | 89,976 | 51,264 | N.A. | 120,000 | 84,540 | 84,540 | 128,848 | 142,536 | (a-29) | 49,968 |
| Texas | 120,000 | N.A. | 112,500 | (a-9) | 115,000 | N.A. | 148,680 | 150,000 | (a-29) | 77,500 |
| Utah | 103,000 | 53,077 | 94,525 | 93,815 | 86,485 | 79,720 | (jjj) | N.A. | (a-29) | 64,185 |
| Vermont | 72,072 | 78,852 | N.A. | 74,568 | 61,006 | 75,462 | 91,728 | 112,732 | (a-29) | 61,755 |
| Virginia* | 82,417 | 95,036 | 96,911 | 104,097 | 85,335 | 82,417 | 113,558 | 113,800 | 96,187 | 71,666 |
| Washington | 75,732 | N.A. | 99,362 | 122,877 | 99,362 | 99,326 | 99,362 | 116,400 | (a-29) | 56,340 |
| West Virginia | 65,000 | (a-14) | 65,000 | (a-5) | 68,292 | 70,000 | (ccc) | (ddd) | (a-29) | 41,484 |
| Wisconsin | 93,365 | 73,441 | 102,350 | 78,699 | (eee) | (a-5) | 99,573 | N.A. | (a-29) | 107,904 |
| Wyoming | 56,953 | 46,000 | 71,000 | 77,000 | 77,973 | (a-5) | 72,000 | 85,000 | (a-29) | 62,000 |
| No. Mariana Islands | 40,800 | 40,800 | 48,000 | 54,000 | 40,800 | 54,000 | 60,000 | 70,000 (c) | 54,000 | 40,800 |
| U.S. Virgin Islands* | (a-18) | 54,500 | 65,000 | 65,000 | 55,000 | N.A. | 65,000 | 61,600 | 46,000 | 48,627 |

& retardation, $73,872; Parks & recreation, $85,512; Post audit, $85,512; Pre-Audit, $85,512; Solid waste management, $81,444; Welfare, $85,512.

Maine: Secretary of State, $70,886; Attorney general, $91,208; Treasurer, $70,886; Adjutant General, $83,470; Administration, $83,470; Agriculture, $83,470; Banking, $78,499; Budget, $73,466; Civil Rights, $56,451; Commerce, $83,470; Comptroller, $73,466; Consumer Affairs, $68,806; Corrections, $83,470; Economic Development, $ 83,470; Education, $83,470; Emergency Management, $ 59,176; Energy, $73,466; Environmental Protection, $83,470; Finance, $83,470; Fish & Wildlife, $83,470; General Services, $73,466; Health, $83,470; Highways, $83,470; Historic Preservation, $75,650; Information Systems, $83,470; Insurance, $83,470; Labor, $83,470; Licensing, $68,806; Mental Health, $ 83,470; Natural Resources, $83,470; Parks & Recreation, $73,466; Personnel, $73,466; Planning, $83,470; Post Audit, $75,650; Pre-Audit, $73,466; Public Library,$ 70,886; Purchasing, $63,461; Revenue, $78,499; Social Services, $83,470; Solid Waste Management,

$53,602; State Police, $ 73,466; Tourism, $63,461; Transportation, $83,470; Welfare, $67,350

Maryland: Adjutant general, $96,741; Administration, $112,415; Agriculture, $112,415; Banking, $83,304; Budget, $130,696; Civil rights, $89,764; Commerce, $128,146*; Community affairs, $80,754*; Consumer affairs, $80,754*; Corrections, $84,191*; Economic development, $128,196*; Election administration, $80,754*; Emergency management, $69,234*; Employment services, $74,774*; Energy, $80,754*; Environmental protection, $109,865*; Finance, $130,696; Health, $130,696; Higher education, $121,203; Historic preservation, $83,304; Information systems, $104,277; Labor, $112,245; Natural resources, $121,203; Parks and recreation, $83,304; Personnel, $96,741; Planning, $104,277; Post-audit, $120,000; Pre-audit, $89,764; Public library development, $83,304; Purchasing, $83,304; Revenue, $89,764; Social services, $89,764; Solid waste management, $83,304; Police, $121,203; Tourism, $89,764; Transportation, $130,696.

## SELECTED OFFICIALS: ANNUAL SALARIES — Continued

| State or other jurisdiction | Information systems | Insurance | Labor | Licensing | Mental health & retardation | Natural resources | Parks & recreation | Personnel | Planning | Post audit |
|---|---|---|---|---|---|---|---|---|---|---|
| Alabama | $72,784 (c) | $71,014 (d) | $71,235 | ... | $106,750 | $71,235 | $58,295 (c) | $116,589 | $71,235 | $121,888 |
| Alaska | 83,124 | 83,124 | 86,292 | $74,592 | 69,780 | 86,292 | 74,592 | 80,244 | N.A. | N.A. |
| Arizona | 87,672 | 99,000 | 101,337 | ... | 89,232 | 62,803* | 105,705 | 88,271 | 104,998 | 98,987 |
| Arkansas | 99,456 | 91,923 | 90,491 | ... | 90,464 | 49,016 | 85,647 | 83,044 | ... | 111,976 |
| California | 118,524 | 132,000 | 126,358 | (a-10) | 118,514 | 126,358 | 118,514 | 118,514 | 96,000* | 126,358 |
| Colorado | 84,516 | 95,000 | 108,000 | 108,000 | 89,556 | 108,000 | 98,256 | 89,556 | (a-6) | 99,745 |
| Connecticut* | 70,000 | 87,000 | 83,500 | 75,500 | (i) | 96,317 | 96,853 | 90,420 | 75,000 | N.A. |
| Delaware | 102,200 | 81,100 | 89,100 | 66,000 | (j) | 95,500 | 79,300 | 95,500 | 79,260 | 81,000 |
| Florida | 92,705 | (a-4) | 107,940 | 85,324 | (n) | (a-14) | 96,142 | 84,810 | 109,272 | 111,024 |
| Georgia* | 83,478 | 89,508 | 89,537 | 81,798 | 115,014 | 98,256 | 79,014 | 100,242 | (a-6) | 88,872 |
| Hawaii | 65,520 (c) | 74,655 | 85,302 | (a-7) | 54,012 (c,p) | 85,302 | 62,520 (c) | 85,302 | ... | (c, q) |
| Idaho | (a-5) | 72,342 | 76,440 | 53,997 | 59,030 | ... | 85,966 | 74,485 | (a-7) | 77,500 |
| Illinois | (a-5) | 90,700 | 90,700 | 90,700 | 115,600 | 99,000 | (a-19) | 76,140 | ... | 104,700 |
| Indiana | 78,819 | 73,814 | 82,000 | (v) | 79,984 | 86,615 | 72,364 | 79,794 | ... | 76,794 |
| Iowa | 96,803 | 92,062 | 79,926 | 55,100 | 78,749 | 94,000 | 81,536 | 95,000 | (a-11) | 82,940 |
| Kansas | 89,010 | 71,270 | 78,042 | 58,869 | 82,004 | (a-20) | 88,646 | 79,335 | 93,001 | 91,676 |
| Kentucky | (kkk) | 79,008 | 91,163 | 60,115 | 77,943 | 80,406 | 81,034 | 91,163 | (a-6) | 82,521 |
| Louisiana | 89,928 | 85,000 | 95,000 | 67,236 | 145,596 | 88,812 | 66,204 | 96,192 | 65,268 | 114,000 |
| Maine | 50,294 (c) | 56,784 (c) | 56,784 (c) | 46,904 (c) | 56,784 (c) | (aa) | 50,294 (c) | 50,294 (c) | 50,294 (c) | 51,792 (c) |
| Maryland | 85,262 (c) | 97,550 | 91,880 (c) | 88,000 | (bb) | 99,025 (c) | 68,210 (c) | 79,135 (c) | 85,262 (c) | 95,000 (c) |
| Massachusetts | 97,285 | 91,404 | 85,000 | 86,265 | (cc) | 93,181 | (dd) * | 104,699 | (a-11)* | 120,000 |
| Michigan | 93,438 | 105,987 | 99,451 | 103,982 | 107,991 | 104,003 | 93,250 | 109,182 | ... | 117,548 |
| Minnesota | 95,338 | N.A. | 97,300 | 92,812 | 96,904 | 97,300 | 85,712 | 97,301 | 97,301 | (gg) |
| Mississippi | 85,000 | 75,000 | ... | ... | (c, lll) | (a-14) | (c, mmm) | 75,000 | 55,992 (c) | 75,000 |
| Missouri | 105,011 | 88,585 | 92,952 | 71,784 | 173,820 | 92,926 | 77,892 | 82,056 | (a-6) | 90,471 |
| Montana* | 64,540 | 58,658 | 70,420 | 48,197 | 61,911 | 70,420 | 48,197 | 50,425 | (a-6) | 74,690 |
| Nebraska | 91,537 | 69,360 | 66,510 | 71,348 | 83,130 (kk) | 67,485 | 82,000 | 67,000 | 71,400 | 49,500 |
| Nevada | 92,914 | 80,343 | 92,914 | ... | 90,640 | 92,914 | ... | 78,050 | (a-5) | 88,919 |
| New Hampshire | 74,372 | 78,827 | 62,171 | ... | 78,827 | 83,256 | 62,171 | 74,372 | 67,303 | 53,332 |
| New Jersey* | 84,500 | 100,225 | 100,225 | 91,639 | 87,026 | 100,225 | 76,688 | 100,225 | 85,000 | 95,000 |
| New Mexico | 83,502 | 71,999 | 83,502 | 83,502 | (ll) | 83,502 | 72,783 | 81,501 | ... | 65,000 |
| New York | (a-16) | 120,800 | 127,000 | (mm) | 136,000 (nn) | (a-14) | 120,800 | 120,800 | (a-11) | (a-9) |
| North Carolina* | 104,245 | 94,552 | 94,552 | ... | 94,871 | 92,378 | 69,742 | 92,378 | 75,474 | 94,552 |
| North Dakota | 95,000 | 58,262 | 55,000 | (a-2) | 51,936 | 56,448 | 59,014 | 61,812 | ... | (qq) |
| Ohio* | 83,096 | 90,376 | 75,130 | 92,123 | (rr) | 96,616 | 75,154 | 82,888 | (a-6) | 82,347 |
| Oklahoma | (tt) | 82,004 | 69,056 | ... | 94,910 | (a-28) | (a-28) | 65,000 | ... | 82,004 |
| Oregon | 124,428 | N.A. | 67,900 | ... | 102,384 | 84,264 | 92,832 | 92,832 | 84,264 | 102,384 |
| Pennsylvania | 105,300 | 97,603 | 108,448 | 77,550 | (uu) | 108,448 | 91,627 | 106,400 | 105,000 | 112,785 |
| Rhode Island | 98,515 | 69,561 | 96,980 | 69,561 | 105,053 | 75,993 | 61,024 | 85,647 | 98,515 | (vv) |
| South Carolina* | 74,097 (c) | 74,378 (c) | 72,850 (c) | (a-18) | 94,549 (c) | 79,268 (c) | 72,850 (c) | 72,154 (c) | 85,214 | 77,190 (c) |
| South Dakota | 91,790 | 64,459 | 75,046 | 31,033 | (xx) | 75,046 | 72,867 | 72,867 | (a-15) | 76,889 |
| Tennessee | 98,472 | 84,540 | 89,976 | 66,300 (yy) | 89,976 | 84,540 | 65,004 | 84,540 | N.A. | (a-9) |
| Texas | 97,200 | 157,500 | 120,000 | 70,000 | 135,000 | 97,000 | 115,000 | 81,920 | (a-6) | 96,200 |
| Utah | 86,485 | 80,576 | 80,576 | 57,587 | 133,485 | 90,055 | 86,485 | 94,525 | (a-6) | 74,600 |
| Vermont | 75,962 | 72,820 | 69,472 | 55,890 | 83,928 | 75,462 | 71,385 | 67,392 | ... | 69,493 |
| Virginia* | 94,778 | 103,136 | ... | 48,290 (c) | 94,778 | 104,097 | 71,666 | 82,417 | ... | 108,944 |
| Washington | 99,362 | 86,000 | 103,000 | 99,362 | 92,268 | 94,394 | 97,850 | 99,362 | (a-15) | 92,500 |
| West Virginia | 74,500 | 55,000 | 55,000 | ... | 70,000 | 65,000 | 65,000 | 50,000 | (a-5) | 56,937 |
| Wisconsin | 91,206 | 86,702 | 95,136 | 87,619 | 62,724 | 102,350 | 71,176 | 86,702 | (a-6) | 92,901 |
| Wyoming | 64,910 | 62,000 | 62,400 | N.A. | 104,916 | 63,000 | 62,000 | 61,483 | 63,000 | 77,000 |
| No. Mariana Islands | 40,800 (c) | 40,800 (c) | 40,800 | 45,360 | 60,000 | 80,000 | 40,800 | 54,000 | 50,000 | 80,000 |
| U.S. Virgin Islands* | 65,000 | (a-1) | 65,000 | (a-10) | 62,000 | 65,000 | 65,000 | 60,000 | 55,000 | 60,000 |

Michigan: Emergency management, $89,209; General services, $95,118; Historic preservation, $95,118; Information systems, $95,118; Parks & recreation, $95,118; Purchasing, $95,118; Revenue, $105,152; Solid waste management, $95,118.

Mississippi: Budget, $83,585; Commerce, $97,443; Community affairs $85,837; Consumer affairs, $68,400; Economic development, $97,443; Elections administration, $71,688; Energy, $85,837; General services, $97,143; Health, $160,000; Mental health & retardation, $83,585; Parks & recreation, $92,288; Planning, $83,585; Purchasing, $70,290; Solid waste management, $67,575; Tourism, $85,837.

New Hampshire: Budget, $74,372; Corrections, $81,046; Health, $78,827. Licensing, $90,608.

Ohio: Commerce, $86,965.

Pennsylvania: Emergency Management, $100,382.

South Carolina: Administration, $155,282; Budget, $108,232; Civil rights, $91,749; Commerce, $140,443; Consumer affairs, $103,774; Corrections, $145,560; Elections administration, $76,486; Energy, $69,249; Environmental protection, $111,145; Finance, $155,282; Fish & wildlife, $110,596; General services, $111,145; Health, $145,560; Higher education, $120,829; Historic preservation, $52,617; Information systems, $111,145; Insurance, $103,774; Labor, $101,642; Mental health & retardation, $131,915; Natural resources, $110,596; Parks & recreation, $101,642; Personnel, $108,232; Post-audit, $107,696; Public library development, $79,162; Public utility regulation, $85,987; Purchasing, $69,249; Revenue, $131,915; Social services, $145,560; Solid waste management, $72,016; State police, $96,746; Tourism, $101,642; Transportation, $131,915.

Virginia: Licensing, $76,346.

Northern Mariana Islands: Agriculture, $45,000; Consumer affairs, $70,000; Higher education, $80,000; Information systems, $45,000; Insurance, $45,000.

## SELECTED OFFICIALS: ANNUAL SALARIES — Continued

| State or other jurisdiction | Pre-audit | Public library development | Public utility regulation | Purchasing | Revenue | Social services | Solid waste management | State police | Tourism | Transportation | Welfare |
|---|---|---|---|---|---|---|---|---|---|---|---|
| Alabama | (a-9) | $96,000 | $81,000 | $58,295 (c) | $110,973 (d) | $102,600 | $54,083 (c) | $52,733 | $71,235 | $95,670 (d) | $102,600 |
| Alaska | N.A. | 89,484 | 83,124 | 89,484 | N.A. | 86,292 | 67,488 | 89,484 | 74,592 | 86,292 | 74,592 |
| Arizona | (a-9) | 106,267 | 73,000 | 75,712 | 110,872 | 115,000 | 74,801 | 110,988 | 92,242 | 110,301* | 89,232 |
| Arkansas | 56,504 | 76,656 | 85,261 | 77,475 | 83,044 | 113,877 | 47,270 | 79,520 | 62,433 | 118,742 | 113,877 |
| California | (a-9) | 99,576 | 113,287 | 118,514 | 118,514 | 118,514 | 113,287 | 126,358 | . . . | 118,514 | 118,514 |
| Colorado | (a-9) | 90,485 | 96,794 | 98,004 | 108,000 | 108,000 | 89,556 | 98,304 | . . . | 108,000 | 108,000 |
| Connecticut* | (a-9) | 68,123 | 103,360 | 60,000 | 83,500 | 95,000 | 95,954 | 91,128 | 92,505 | 107,586 | 95,000 |
| Delaware | 81,000 | 70,200 | 72,700 | 67,200 | 99,700 | 102,200 (k) | 75,700 | 102,500 | 63,428 | 95,500 | 91,700 |
| Florida | (a-26) | 88,334 | 116,823 | 92,520 | 117,687 | 107,940 (o) | 80,625 | 100,102 | N.A. | 110,052 | 89,863 |
| Georgia* | (a-22) | 89,424 | 86,184 | 67,782 | 88,104 | 89,424 | 74,832 | 101,220 | 95,376 | 150,000 | (a-27) |
| Hawaii | 52,520 (c) | 85,302 | 77,964 | 77,964 | 85,302 | 85,302 | 59,544 (c) | . . . | (a-11) | 85,302 | 62,520 (c) |
| Idaho | (a-9) | 52,062 | 74,984 | 60,840 | 65,000 | 788,208 | 54,413* | 75,005 | 57,970 | 111,426 | 74,693 |
| Illinois | (a-9) | 85,386 | 102,800 | 71,520 | 107,200 | 104,700 | 80,952 | 99,000 | 80,952 | 107,200 | 107,200 |
| Indiana | 66,000 | 74,802 | 84,713 | 53,121 | 84,713 | 94,224 | 71,837 | 94,260 | 73,927 | 86,320 | 75,428 |
| Iowa | 96,516 | 89,544 | 96,800 | 81,536 | (a-23) | 81,536 | 70,803 | 85,446 | 74,984 | 103,508 | 74,568 |
| Kansas | (ooo) | 72,360 | 106,101 | 69,963 | 87,975 | 94,345 | 68,994 | 76,590 | 59,000 | 93,828 | 82,004 |
| Kentucky | (a-15) | 83,087 | 92,531 | (a-15) | 91,163 | 95,598 | 66,101 | N.A. | 91,163 | 91,163 | 95,598 |
| Louisiana | 73,404 | 85,800 | 75,000 | 66,636 | 80,000 | 88,000 | 76,752 | 78,000 | 66,204 | 108,000 | 78,000 |
| Maine | (a-9) | 48,298 (c) | 95,314 | 45,302 (c) | 53,498 (c) | 56,784 (c) | 38,418 (c) | 50,294 (c) | 45,302 (c) | 56,784 (c) | 48,152 (c) |
| Maryland | 73,462 (c) | 68,210 (c) | 91,880 | 68,210 (c) | 73,462 (c) | 73,462 (c) | 668,210 (c) | 99,025 (c) | 73,462 (c) | 106,745 (c) | (a-27) |
| Massachusetts | (a-9) | 78,372 | 94,049 | 95,952 | 104,699 | 104,485 | 68,048* | 109,937 | 71,914 | 95,845 | 108,580 |
| Michigan | N.A. | 83,095 | 85,900 | 89,617 | N.A. | 107,991 | 93,292 | 103,982 | N.A. | 103,982 | 107,991 |
| Minnesota | 91,997 | 78,321 | 85,879 | 94,044 | 97,300 | 88,469 | 84,000 | 89,951 | 91,225 | 97,300 | 75,586 |
| Mississippi | . . . | 70,000 | 65,000 | 47,122 (c) | 91,000 | . . . | 45,639 (c) | 80,000 | 54,572 (c) | 85,000 | 85,000 |
| Missouri | (a-9) | 73,200 | 91,185 | 76,128 | 99,013 | 95,086 | 56,580 | 79,692 | 74,964 | (a-17) | 82,620 |
| Montana* | . . . | 49,506 | 57,819 | 43,095 | 70,420 | 70,420 | 48,478 | 54,400 | 57,162 | 70,420 | (a-27) |
| Nebraska | 78,250 | 66,838 | 58,999 | (a-16) | 76,498 | 85,680 | 58,691 | 65,280 | 46,201 | (a-17) | 85,607 |
| Nevada | (a-5) | 78,050 | 86,084 | 70,261 | 92,914 | 93,310 | (a-14) | 84,606 | 82,068 | 92,914 | 87,550 |
| New Hampshire | 62,166 | 62,171 | 83,256 | 48,828 | 83,256 | 81,045 | 74,372 | 74,372 | 53,332 | 83,256 | 81,045 |
| New Jersey* | (a-22) | N.A. | 100,225 | 86,100 | 92,247 | 100,225 | 71,802 | 94,461 | 84,500 | 100,225 | 87,000 |
| New Mexico | 75,691 | 61,000 | 72,500 | 66,872 | 83,502 | 83,502 | 49,922 | 83,502 | 83,502 | (a-17) | 83,502 |
| New York | (a-9) | (a-12) | 127,000 | (a-16) | 127,000 | 136,000 | (a-14) | 127,000 | (a-11) | 136,000 | (a-27) |
| North Carolina* | (a-22) | 71,418 | 95,592 | 81,120 | 92,378 | 89,411 | 50,921 | 90,394 | 78,352 | 92,378 | 96,629 |
| North Dakota | 70,920 | 56,244 | 58,260 | 43,200 | 58,260 | 98,472 | 50,160 | 63,240 | 54,631 | 76,236 | 98,472 |
| Ohio* | (a-22) | 75,816 | 99,557 | 82,867 | 90,376 | 106,683 | 70,699 | 86,278 | 65,811 | 105,560 | 106,683 |
| Oklahoma | (a-9) | 64,730 | (ppp) | 69,201 | 74,371 | 123,000 | 68,696 | 85,000 | 72,000 | 133,203 | N.A. |
| Oregon | . . . | 84,264 | 97,476 | 76,356 | 102,384 | 112,812 | 69,300 | N.A. | 79,464 | 112,632 | 102,384 |
| Pennsylvania | (a-4) | 70,025 | 105,525 | 60,010 | 103,025 | 97,800 | 87,316 | 103,025 | 54,924 | 108,848 | 108,448 |
| Rhode Island | 85,647 | 98,515 | 79,211 | 88,861 | 98,515 | 113,901 | . . . | 100,478 | | 104,820 | 113,901 |
| South Carolina* | (a-9) | 56,738 (c) | 61,631 (c) | 44,157 (c) | 94,549 (c) | 104,328 (c) | 45,922 (c) | 64,498 (c) | 72,850 (c) | 94,549 (c) | (a-27) |
| South Dakota | 61,090 | 50,440 | 71,240 | 44,531 | 75,046 | 89,585 | 49,940 | 76,481 | 75,046 | 81,952 | (a-27) |
| Tennessee | 78,600 | 98,800 | 84,540 | 70,764 | 84,540 | 69,948 | 66,780 | 84,540 | 84,540 | 84,540 | 85,540 |
| Texas | (a-9) | 78,000 | 77,233 | N.A. | (a-9) | 157,500 | 91,100 | 102,000 | 89,500 | 145,000 | 105,000 |
| Utah | (a-15) | 69,614 | 73,498 | 79,720 | 86,861 | 99,556 | 86,485 | 79,720 | 71,765 | 103,001 | 103,001 |
| Vermont | (a-15) | 66,997 | 90,168 | 63,211 | 71,552 | 84,760 | 67,371 | 95,614 | 62,878 | 79,934 | 85,051 |
| Virginia* | (a-9) | 76,024 | 103,136 | 82,417 | 94,778 | 94,778 | (a-14) | 99,323 | 116,113 | 96,187 | 94,778 |
| Washington | (a-4) | 89,583 | 99,362 | 72,096 | 105,060 | 122,877 | 73,836 | 103,000 | 68,230 | 111,464 | (a-27) |
| West Virginia | (a-5) | 62,500 | 70,000 | 74,500 | 70,000 | 70,000 | 58,980 | 70,000 | 65,000 | 70,000 | (a-27) |
| Wisconsin | 55,899 | 89,475 | 89,500 | 77,521 | 93,851 | 99,573 | 93,845 | 85,002 | 89,997 | 104,043 | 99,573 |
| Wyoming | 77,000 | 61,893 | 69,195 | 49,707 | 71,000 | 72,000 | 62,113 | 75,000 | 135,000 | 75,000 | (a-27) |
| No. Mariana Islands | 54,000 | 39,900 | 70,000 | 40,800 | 42,559 | 48,000 | 54,000 | 54,000 | 70,000 | 54,000 | 48,000 |
| U.S. Virgin Islands* | (a-15) | 43,000 | 49,500 | 65,000 | 65,000 | 65,000 | 65,000 | 65,000 | 65,000 | 43,000 | 53,000 |

(d) By merit system employee at higher rate of pay.

(e) Responsibilities shared between Director, Department of General Services, $118,514; and Chief Deputy Director, same department, $108,324.

(f) Responsibilities shared between Chief, Political Reform, $80,244; and Chief, Elections, $91,512.

(g) Responsibilities shared between Chief, Financial and Performance Audits, Department of Finance, $88,608; and Auditor General, $88,608.

(h) Responsibilities shared between Director, Fisheries Division, $72,115 - $92,505; and Director, Wildlife Division, $55,689 - $75,501.

(i) Responsibilities shared between Commissioner, Department of Mental Retardation, $84,000 - $106,000; and Commissioner, Department of Mental Health, $84,000 - $106,000.

(j) Responsibilities shared between Acting Director, Division of Alcoholism, Drug Abuse and Mental Health, Department of Health and Social Services, $113,700; and Director, Division of Mental Retardation, same department, $91,700.

(k) Responsibilities no longer shared.

(l) Combined with Planning.

(m) Combined with Labor.

(n) Responsibilities shared between Director of Mental Health, Department of Children and Family Services, $83,890; and Director, Substance Abuse, same department, $77,738.

# SELECTED OFFICIALS: ANNUAL SALARIES — Continued

(o) Combined with Welfare.

(p) Responsibilities no longer shared.

(q) Responsibilities shared between State Auditor, Office of the Auditor, $85,302; and Division Head, Division of Audit, Department of Accounting & General Services, $62,520.

(r) Responsibilities shared between Director, Department of Commerce, $79,019; and Administrator, Division of Community Development, $41,766.

(s) Responsibilities shared between Director, Bureau of the Budget, $95,000; and Director, Department of Revenue, $107,200.

(t) In Texas, the salary of the Lieutenant Governor is the same as a Senator when serving as President of the Senate ($7200/year) and the same as Governor when serving as Governor.

(u) Responsibilities shared between Co-Directors, Election Commission, $50,500.

(v) Responsibilities shared between Executive Director, Health Professions Bureau, $54,274; and Executive Director, Professional Licensing Agency, $61,915.

(w) Responsibilities shared between Acting Director, Department of Education, $82,347; and Executive Director, Board of Regents, $105,986.

(x) Responsibilities shared between Secretary, Department of Commerce and Housing, $96,661; Director, Division of Existing Industry, same department, $69,404; Director, Business Development Division, same department, $60,708; and President, Kansas Inc., $87,984.

(y) Responsibilities shared between Director, Division of the Budget, $80,730; and Secretary, Department of Administration, $90,240.

(z) In Maine, New Hampshire, New Jersey, Tennessee and West Virginia, the presidents (or speakers) of the Senate are next in line of succession to the governorship. In Tennessee, the speaker of the Senate bears the statutory title of lieutenant governor.

(aa) Responsibilities shared between Commissioner, Environmental Protection Department, $77,896; and Commissioner, Department of Conservation, $77,896.

(bb) Responsibilities shared between Director, Mental Hygiene Administration, $79,135 - $96,741; and Director, Developmental Disabilities Administration, Department of Health and Mental Hygiene, $$79,135 - $96,741.

(cc) Responsibilities shared between Commissioner, Department of Mental Retardation, $103,413; and Commissioner, Department of Mental Health, Executive Office of Human Services, $103,413.

(dd) Responsibilities shared between Director, Division of Forests and Parks, Department of Environmental Management, $70,666; and Director, Recreational Facilities, Metropolitan District Commission, $70,666.

(ee) Responsibilities shared between Chief, Wildlife Division, Department of Natural Resources, $66,190 - $95,118; and Chief, Fisheries Division, same department, $66,190 - $95,118.

(ff) Responsibilities shared between Secretary of State, $66,168; and Director, Election Division, Office of the Secretary of State, $53,286.

(gg) Responsibilities shared between State Auditor, $72,182; and Legislative Auditor, $90,744.

(hh) Responsibilities shared between Chief, Division of Fisheries, Department of Conservation, $61,656; Chief, Division of Protection, same department, $51,960; and Chief, Division of Wildlife, same department, $61,656.

(ii) Responsibilities shared between State Tax Commissioner, Department of Revenue, $76,498; Administrator, Budget Division, Department of Administrative Services, $81,422; and Auditor of Public Accounts, $49,500.

(jj) Responsibilities shared between Administrator, Wildlife Division, Game & Parks Commission, $55,773; and Administrator, Fisheries Division, same commission; $55,832.

(kk) Responsibilities no longer shared.

(ll) Responsibilities shared between Division Director II, Long Term Services Division, Department of Health, $69,048; and Division Director II, Behavioral Health Services Division, same department, $66,013.

(mm) Responsibilities shared between Commissioner, State Education Department, $136,000; Secretary of State, Department of State, $120,800; and Executive Director, Office of Professional Responsibility, $107,054.

(nn) Responsibilities no longer shared.

(oo) Responsibilities shared between same department, Director, Office of Management and Budget, $79,692; and Director, Fiscal Management Division,$70,920.

(pp) Responsibilities shared between Director, Office of Management & Budget, $79,692; and Director of Fiscal Management, same department, $70,920.

(qq) Responsibilities shared between Legislative Budget Analyst/Auditor, Legislative Council, $89,916; and State Auditor, State Auditor's Office, $58,262.

(rr) Responsibilities shared between Director, Department of Mental Health, $102,419; and Director, Department of Mental Retardation and Developmental Disabilities, $96,387.

(ss) Responsibilities shared between Secretary of Human Resources, Office of Personnel Management, $65,000; and Executive Director, Employment Security Commission, $81,000.

(tt) Responsibilities shared between Director, Data Processing & Planning Division, Department of Transportation, $58,446; and Manager, Information Services Division Management, Office of State Finance, $99,000.

(uu) Responsibilities shared between Deputy Secretary, Mental Health, Department of Public Welfare, $102,400; and Deputy Secretary, Mental Retardation, same department, $97,600.

(vv) Responsibilities shared between Chief, General Audit Section, Office of Accounts and Control, Department of Administration; and Auditor General, salaries not available.

(ww) Annual salary for duties as presiding officer of the Senate.

(xx) Responsibilities shared between Director, Division of Mental Health, Department of Human Services, $59,186; and Secretary, same department, $76,377.

(yy) Responsibilities shared between Director, Regulatory Boards, Department of Commerce & Insurance, $58,596; and Director, Health Related Boards, $44,208.

(zz) Responsibilities shared between Chief, Public Protection Division, Office of the Attorney General, $62,629; and Executive Director, Human Rights Commission, $51,293.

(aaa) Annually returns $31,000 of salary to general fund.

(bbb) Responsibilities shared between Secretary, Department of Education and the Arts, $70,000; and Superintendent, Department of Education, $146,000.

(ccc) Responsibilities shared between Secretary, Department of Health & Human Resources, $70,000; and Commissioner, Bureau of Public Health, salary not available.

(ddd) Responsibilities shared between Secretary, Department of Education and the Arts, $70,000; Chancellor, State College System, Department of Education, $160,000; and Chancellor, Board of Trustees for Higher Education, Department of Education and the Arts, $160,000.

(eee) Responsibilities shared between Director, Bureau of Fisheries Management and Habitat Protection, Division of Resource Management, $60,539; and Director, Bureau of Wildlife Management, same division, $65,219.

(fff) Responsibilities shared between Manager, Insurance Division, Consumer Protection, $69,300; and Consumer Information Officer, Civil Enforcement Division, Department of Justice, $44,568.

(ggg) Responsibilities shared between Secretary of State, $112,352; and Deputy Assistant, Office of Secretary of State, $80,136.

(hhh) Responsibilities shared between Secretary of State, $69,493; and Director of Elections, Office of the Secretary of State, $52,395.

(iii) Responsibilities shared between Executive Director, Fish Commission, $89,252; and Executive Director, Game Commission, $87,316.

(jjj) Responsibilities shared between Executive Director, Department of Health, $103,000; and Director, Division of of Health Care Financing, Department of Health, $79,720.

(kkk) Responsibilities shared between Chief Information Office, Governor's Office of Technology, $131,250; and Executive Director, Information Resources Management, Finance & Administration, $83,757.

(lll) Responsibilities shared between Director, Department of Mental Health, $85,000; and Bureau Chief, Division of Alcohol & Drug Abuse, same department, $55,993.

(mmm) Responsibilities shared between Director, Parks & Recreation, Department of Wildlife, Fisheries & Parks, $80,000; and Department Director, same department, $61,816.

(ooo) Responsibilities shared between Central Account Service Manager, Division of Accounts & Reports, Department of Administration, $64,147; and Team Leader, Audit Services, same division and department, $54,080.

(ppp) Responsibilities shared between Commissioners, Corporations Commission, varying salary levels for four commissioners, $68,000; $72,000; $76,000; and $82,004.

(qqq) Governor voluntarily accepts a reduced salary of $85,000.

## Table 2.12
## LIEUTENANT GOVERNORS: QUALIFICATIONS AND TERMS

| State or other jurisdiction | Minimum age | State citizen (years) (a) | U.S. citizen (years) | State resident (years) | Qualified voter (years) | Length of term (years) | Maximum consecutive terms allowed |
|---|---|---|---|---|---|---|---|
| Alabama | 30 | 7 | 10 | 7 | . . . | 4 | 2 |
| Alaska* | 30 | 7 | 7 | 7 | ★ | 4 | . . . |
| Arizona | | | | (b) | | | |
| Arkansas | 30 | 7 | ★ | 7 | ★ | 4 | 2 |
| California | 18 | . . . | 5 | 5 | ★ | 4 | (c) |
| Colorado* | 30 | . . . | ★ | 2 | . . . | 4 | 2 |
| Connecticut | 30 | . . . | . . . | . . . | ★ | 4 | . . . |
| Delaware | 30 | . . . | 12 | 6 | . . . | 4 | 2 |
| Florida | 30 | . . . | . . . | 7 | ★ | 4 | (c) |
| Georgia | 30 | 6 | 15 | 6 | ★ | 4 | . . . |
| Hawaii | 30 | . . . | ★ | 5 | ★ | 4 | 2 |
| Idaho | 30 | . . . | ★ | 2 | . . . | 4 | 2 |
| Illinois | 25 | . . . | ★ | ★ | . . . | 4 | . . . |
| Indiana | 30 | . . . | 5 | 5 | . . . | 4 | . . . |
| Iowa | 30 | . . . | 2 | 2 | . . . | 4 | . . . |
| Kansas | . . . | . . . | . . . | . . . | . . . | 4 | 2 |
| Kentucky | 30 | 6 | ★ | 6 | . . . | 4 | 2 |
| Louisiana | 25 | 5 | 5 | . . . | ★ | 4 | . . . |
| Maine | | | | (b) | | | |
| Maryland* | 30 | . . . | (d) | 5 | 5 | 4 | 2 |
| Massachusetts | 18 | . . . | . . . | 7 | . . . | 4 | 2 |
| Michigan | 30 | . . . | . . . | . . . | 4 | 4 | 2 |
| Minnesota | 25 | ★ | ★ | 1 | . . . | 4 | 2 |
| Mississippi | 30 | . . . | 20 | 5 | . . . | 4 | 2 |
| Missouri | 30 | . . . | 15 | 10 | . . . | 4 | . . . |
| Montana | 25 | . . . | ★ | 2 | . . . | 4 | (e) |
| Nebraska | 30 | 5 | 5 | 5 | . . . | 4 | 2 |
| Nevada | 25 | 2 | . . . | 2 | ★ | 4 | 2 |
| New Hampshire | | | | (b) | | | |
| New Jersey | | | | (b) | | | |
| New Mexico | 30 | 5 | ★ | 5 | ★ | 4 | 2 |
| New York | 30 | 5 | ★ | 5 | . . . | 4 | . . . |
| North Carolina | 30 | . . . | 5 | 2 | . . . | 4 | 2 |
| North Dakota | 30 | . . . | ★ | 5 | ★ | 4 | . . . |
| Ohio | . . . | . . . | ★ | . . . | ★ | 4 | 2 |
| Oklahoma | 31 | . . . | ★ | . . . | 10 | 4 | . . . |
| Oregon | | | | (b) | | | |
| Pennsylvania* | 30 | . . . | ★ | 7 | . . . | 4 | 2 |
| Rhode Island | 18 | . . . | ★ | ★ | ★ | 4 | 2 |
| South Carolina | 30 | 5 | 5 | 5 | . . . | 4 | 2 |
| South Dakota | . . . | . . . | 2 | 2 | . . . | 4 | 2 |
| Tennessee | | | | (b) | | | |
| Texas | 30 | . . . | ★ | 5 | . . . | 4 | . . . |
| Utah | 30 | 5 | . . . | 5 | ★ | 4 | 3 (f) |
| Vermont | . . . | . . . | . . . | 4 | . . . | 2 | . . . |
| Virginia | 30 | . . . | ★ | 5 | 5 | 4 | . . . |
| Washington | 18 | ★ | ★ | ★ | ★ | 4 | (c) |
| West Virginia | | | | (b) | | | |
| Wisconsin | 18 | . . . | ★ | . . . | ★ | 4 | . . . |
| Wyoming | | | | (b) | | | |
| American Samoa* | 35 | . . . | ★ | 5 | . . . | 4 | . . . |
| Guam* | 30 | . . . | 5 | 5 | ★ | 4 | 2 |
| No. Mariana Islands | 35 | . . . | . . . | 10 | ★ | 4 | . . . |
| Puerto Rico | | | | (b) | | | |
| U.S. Virgin Islands | 30 | . . . | 5 | 5 | 5 | 4 | 2 |

*Source*: The Council of State Governments' Survey, January 2000, except as noted by * where information is from *The Book of the States* 1998-99.

*Note*: This table includes constitutional and statutory qualifications.

*Key*:

★ — Formal provision; number of years not specified.

. . . — No formal provision.

(a) Some state constitutions have requirements for "state citizenship." This may be different from state residency.

(b) No lieutenant governor. In Tennessee, the speaker of the Senate, elected from Senate membership, has statutory title of "lieutenant governor."

(c) Eligible for eight consecutive years.

(d) Crosse v. Board of Supervisors of Elections 243 Md. 555, 221 A.2d431 (1966)–opinion rendered indicated that U.S. citizenship was, by necessity, a requirement for office.

(e) Eligible for eight out of 16 years.

(f) Eligible for 12 consecutive years.

## Table 2.13
## LIEUTENANT GOVERNORS: POWERS AND DUTIES

| State or other jurisdiction | Presides over Senate | Appoints committees | Breaks roll-call ties | Assigns bills | Authority for governor to assign duties | Member of governor's cabinet or advisory body | Serves as acting governor when governor out of state |
|---|---|---|---|---|---|---|---|
| Alabama | ★ | ★(a) | ★ | ★ | ... | ... | ★(b) |
| Alaska* | ... | ... | ... | ... | ★ | ★ | ★(c) |
| Arizona | ------------------------------- (d) ------------------------------- |
| Arkansas | ★ | ... | ★ | ★ | ... | ... | ★ |
| California | ★ | ... | ★ | ... | ★ | ... | ★ |
| Colorado* | ... | ... | ... | ... | ★ | ★ | ★ |
| Connecticut | ★ | ... | ★ | ... | ... | ★ | ★ |
| Delaware (e) | ★ | ... | ★ | ★ | ★ | ★ | ★ |
| Florida | ... | ... | ... | ... | ★ | ... | ... |
| Georgia | ★ | ★(a) | ... | ★ | ★ | ... | ... |
| Hawaii | ... | ... | ... | ... | ★ | ... | ★ |
| Idaho | ★ | ... | ★ | ... | ★ | ... | ★ |
| Illinois | ... | ... | ... | ... | ★ | ★ | (j) |
| Indiana (f) | ★ | ... | ★ | ... | ★ | ★ | ... |
| Iowa | ... | (a) | ... | ... | ★ | (l) | (j) |
| Kansas | ... | ... | ... | ... | ★ | ★ | ★ |
| Kentucky | ... | ... | ... | ... | ★ | ★ | ... |
| Louisiana | ... | ... | ... | ... | ★ | ... | ★ |
| Maine* | ------------------------------- (g) ------------------------------- |
| Maryland* | ... | ... | ... | ... | ★ | ★ | ★ |
| Massachusetts | ... | ... | ★ | ★ | ★ | ★ | ★ |
| Michigan | ★ | ... | ★ | ... | ★ | ★ | ★ |
| Minnesota | ... | ... | ... | ... | ★ | ★ | ★ |
| Mississippi | ★ | ★(a) | ★ | ★ | ... | ... | ★ |
| Missouri | ★ | ... | ★ | ... | ★ | ... | ★ |
| Montana | ... | ... | ... | ... | ★ | ★ | ★(b) |
| Nebraska | ★(h) | ... | ★(i) | ... | ★ | ... | ★ |
| Nevada | ★ | ... | ★ | ... | ... | ★ | ★(j) |
| New Hampshire | ------------------------------- (g) ------------------------------- |
| New Jersey | ------------------------------- (g) ------------------------------- |
| New Mexico | ★ | ... | ★ | ... | ★ | ★ | ★ |
| New York | ★ | ... | ★ | ... | ★ | ★ | ★ |
| North Carolina | ★ | ... | ★ | ... | ★ | ★(k) | ★ |
| North Dakota | ★ | ... | ★ | ★ | ★ | ★ | ★ |
| Ohio | ... | ... | ... | ... | (l) | ★ | (m) |
| Oklahoma | ★ | ... | ★ | ... | ★ | ★ | ★ |
| Oregon | ------------------------------- (d) ------------------------------- |
| Pennsylvania* | ★ | ... | ★(i) | ★ | ★ | ★ | ... |
| Rhode Island | ★ | ... | ★ | ... | ... | ... | ... |
| South Carolina | ★ | ★ | ★ | ★ | ... | ... | ★(j) |
| South Dakota | ★ | (n) | ★ | ★ | ★ | ★ | (o) |
| Tennessee | ------------------------------- (g) ------------------------------- |
| Texas | ★ | ★(a) | (a) | ★ | ... | ... | ★ |
| Utah | ... | ... | ... | ... | ★ | ★ | ... |
| Vermont | ★ | ★(a) | ★ | ★ | ... | ... | ★ |
| Virginia | ★ | ... | H | ... | ★ | ★ | ... |
| Washington | ★ | ... | ... | ... | ★ | ... | ★ |
| West Virginia | ------------------------------- (g) ------------------------------- |
| Wisconsin | ... | ... | ... | ... | ★ | ★ | (p) |
| Wyoming | ------------------------------- (d) ------------------------------- |
| American Samoa* | ... | ... | ... | ... | ★ | ★ | ★ |
| Guam* | (h) | ... | ... | ... | ★ | ★ | ★ |
| No. Mariana Islands | ... | ... | ... | ... | ★ | (q) | ★ |
| Puerto Rico | ------------------------------- (d) ------------------------------- |
| U.S. Virgin Islands | ... | ... | ... | ... | ★(l) | ★ | ★ |

See footnotes at end of table.

## LIEUTENANT GOVERNORS: POWERS AND DUTIES — Continued

*Source*: The Council of State Governments' survey, January 2000, except as noted by * where information is from *The Book of the States 1998-99*.

Key:

★— Provision for responsibility.

. . . — No provision for responsibility.

(a) Appoints all standing committees. Alabama–appoints some special committees; Georgia–appoints all senate members of conference committees and all senators who serve on interim study committees; Iowa– appoints some special committees; Mississippi–appoints members of conference, joint and special committees; Texas– Has the authority to appoint all committees and assign all bills, but that authority is pursuant to provisions in the Senate's rules; Vermont–appoints all committees as a member of the Committee on Committees.

(b) After 20 days absence. In Montana, after 45 days.

(c) Alaska constitution identifies two types of absence from state; (1) temporary absence during which the lieutenant serves as acting governor; and (2) continuous absence for a period of six months, after which the governor's office is declared vacant and lieutenant governor succeeds to the office.

(d) No lieutenant governor; secretary of state is next in line of succession to governorship.

(e) Constitutional duty includes President of the Board of Pardons.

(f) By statute, lieutenant governor serves as Director of Department of Commerce and Commissioner of Agriculture.

(g) No lieutenant governor; senate president or speaker is next in line of succession to governorship. In Tennessee, speaker of the senate bears the additional statutory title of "lieutenant governor."

(h) Unicameral legislative body. In Guam, that body elects own presiding officer.

(i) Except on final enactments.

(j) Only in emergency situations.

(k) Member of Council of State per state constitution. Also sits on Governor's Cabinet, by invitation.

(l) Presides over cabinet meetings in absence of governor.

(m) Only if governor asks the lieutenant to serve in that capacity, in the former's absence.

(n) Conference committees.

(o) Only in event of governor's continuous absence from state.

(p) Only in situations of an absence which prevents governor from discharging duties which need to be undertaken prior to his return.

(q) The lieutenant governor is an automatic member of the Governor's cabinet.

## Table 2.14
## SECRETARIES OF STATE: QUALIFICATIONS FOR OFFICE

| State or other jurisdiction | Minimum age | U.S. citizen (years) | State resident (years) | Qualified voter (years) | Method of selection to office |
|---|---|---|---|---|---|
| Alabama | 25 | 7 | 5 | ★ | E |
| Alaska | --------------------------------------- (a) --------------------------------------- | | | | |
| Arizona | 25 | 10 | 5 | . . . | E |
| Arkansas | 18 | . . . | . . . | . . . | E |
| California | 18 | ★ | ★ | ★ | E |
| Colorado | 25 | ★ | 2 | ★ | E |
| Connecticut | 18 | . . . | . . . | ★ | E |
| Delaware | . . . | . . . | ★ | . . . | A |
| Florida | 30 | ★ | 7 | ★ | E |
| Georgia | 25 | 10 | 4 | ★ | E |
| Hawaii | --------------------------------------- (a) --------------------------------------- | | | | |
| Idaho | 25 | ★ | 2 | . . . | E |
| Illinois | 25 | ★ | 3 | . . . | E |
| Indiana* | . . . | . . . | . . . | . . . | E |
| Iowa | . . . | . . . | . . . | . . . | E |
| Kansas | . . . | . . . | . . . | . . . | E |
| Kentucky | 30 | ★ | 2 (b) | ★ | E |
| Louisiana | 25 | 5 | 5 (b) | ★ | E |
| Maine* | . . . | . . . | . . . | . . . | (c) |
| Maryland | . . . | (d) | (d) | . . . | A |
| Massachusetts* | 18 | ★ | 5 | ★ | E |
| Michigan | 18 | ★ | ★ | ★ | E |
| Minnesota | 21 | ★ | ★ | ★ | E |
| Mississippi | 25 | 5 | 5 (b) | 5 | E |
| Missouri | . . . | ★ | 1 | . . . | E |
| Montana (e) | 25 | ★ | 2 | ★ | E |
| Nebraska (f) | 19 | ★ | . . . | . . . | E |
| Nevada | 25 | ★ | 2 | ★ | E |
| New Hampshire | . . . | ★ | ★ | ★ | (c) |
| New Jersey | . . . | ★ | ★ | ★ | A |
| New Mexico | 30 | ★ | 5 | ★ | E |
| New York | . . . | . . . | . . . | . . . | A |
| North Carolina | 21 | ★ | ★ | ★ | E |
| North Dakota | 25 | ★ | 5 | ★ | E |
| Ohio | 18 | . . . | ★ | ★ | E |
| Oklahoma | 31 | ★ | . . . | 10 | A |
| Oregon | 18 | ★ | ★ | ★ | E |
| Pennsylvania | . . . | . . . | . . . | . . . | A |
| Rhode Island | 18 | ★ | 30 days | ★ | E |
| South Carolina | . . . | ★ | ★ | ★ | E |
| South Dakota | . . . | . . . | ★ | . . . | E |
| Tennessee | . . . | . . . | . . . | . . . | (c) |
| Texas | . . . | . . . | . . . | . . . | A |
| Utah | --------------------------------------- (a) --------------------------------------- | | | | |
| Vermont | . . . | . . . | . . . | . . . | B |
| Virginia | . . . | . . . | . . . | . . . | A |
| Washington | 18 | ★ | ★ | ★ | E |
| West Virginia | 18 | ★ | 30 days | 30 days | E |
| Wisconsin | 18 | ★ | ★ | ★ | E |
| Wyoming* | 25 | ★ | ★ | ★ | E |
| American Samoa | --------------------------------------- (a) --------------------------------------- | | | | |
| Guam | --------------------------------------- (a) --------------------------------------- | | | | |
| No. Mariana Islands | --------------------------------------- (a) --------------------------------------- | | | | |
| Puerto Rico | . . . | 5 | 5 | . . . | A |
| U.S. Virgin Islands | --------------------------------------- (a) --------------------------------------- | | | | |

*Source*: The Council of State Governments' survey, January 2000, except as noted by * where data are from *The Book of the States*, 1998-1999.

*Note*: This table contains constitutional and statutory provisions. "Qualified voter" provision may infer additional residency and citizenship requirements.

*Key*:

★ — Formal provision; number of years not specified.

. . . . — No formal provision.

A — Appointed by governor.

E — Elected by voters.

(a) No secretary of state.

(b) State citizenship requirement.

(c) Chosen by joint ballot of state senators and representatives. In Maine and New Hampshire, every two years. In Tennessee, every four years.

(d) No formal provision but customary and political tradition.

(e) No person convicted of a felony is eligible to hold public office until final discharge from state supervision.

(f) No person in default as a collector and custodian of public money or property shall be eligible to public office; no person convicted of a felony shall be eligible unless restored to civil rights.

Table 2.15
# SECRETARIES OF STATE: ELECTION AND REGISTRATION DUTIES

| State or other jurisdiction | Chief election officer | Determines ballot eligibility of political parties | Receives initiative and/or referendum petition | Files certificate of nomination or election | Supplies election ballots or materials to local officials | Files candidates' expense papers | Files other campaign reports | Conducts voter education programs | Registers charitable organizations | Registers corporations (a) | Processes and/or commissions notaries public | Registers securities | Registers trade names/marks |
|---|---|---|---|---|---|---|---|---|---|---|---|---|---|
| | Election | | | | | | | | Registration | | | | |
| Alabama | ★ | ★ | ... | ★ | ★ | ★ | ★ | ★ | ... | ★ | ... | ... | ★ |
| Alaska (b) | ★ | ★ | ★ | ★ | ★ | ... | ... | ★ | ... | ... | ★ | ... | ... |
| Arizona | ★ | ★ | ★ | ★ | ... | ★ | ★ | ... | ★ | ... | ★ | ... | ★ |
| Arkansas | ★ | ★ | ★ | ★ | ★ | ★ | ★ | ★ | ★ | ★ | ★ | ... | ★ |
| California | ★ | ★ | ★ | ★ | ★ | ★ | ★ | ★ | ... | ★ | ★ | ... | ★ |
| Colorado | ★ | ★ | ★ | ★ | ... | ★ | ★ | ... | ★ | ★ | ★ | ... | ★ |
| Connecticut | ★ | ★ | ... | ★ | ★ | ★ | ★ | ★ | ★ | ★ | ★ | ... | ★ |
| Delaware | ... | ... | ... | (c) | ... | ... | (d) | ... | ★(e) | ★ | ★ | ... | ★ |
| Florida | ★ | ★ | ... | ★ | ★ | ★ | ★ | ★ | ... | ★ | ★ | ... | ★ |
| Georgia | ★ | ★ | ... | ★ | ★ | ★ | ★ | ★ | ★ | ★ | ... | ★ | ★ |
| Hawaii (b) | ... | ... | ... | ... | ... | ... | ... | ... | ... | ... | ... | ... | ... |
| Idaho | ★ | ★ | ★ | ★ | ★ | ★ | ★ | ★ | ... | ★ | ★ | ... | ★ |
| Illinois | ... | ... | ★ | ★ | ... | ... | ... | ... | ... | ★ | ★ | ★ | ★ |
| Indiana* | ★ | ... | ... | ★ | ... | ★ | ★ | ★ | ... | ★ | ★ | ★ | ★ |
| Iowa | ★ | ★ | ... | ★ | ★ | ... | ... | ... | ... | ★ | ★ | ... | ★ |
| Kansas | ★ | ★ | ... | ★ | ★ | ★ | ★ | ★ | ★ | ★ | ★ | ... | ★ |
| Kentucky | ★ | ★ | ... | ★ | ... | ... | ... | ★ | ... | ★ | ★ | ... | ★ |
| Louisiana | ★ | ★ | ... | ★ | ★ | ★(f) | ★(f) | ★ | ... | ★ | ★ | ★ | ★ |
| Maine* | ★ | ★ | ★ | ★ | ★ | ... | ... | ★ | ... | ★ | ★ | ... | ★ |
| Maryland | (p) | ... | ★ | ★ | ... | ... | ★(g) | ... | ★ | ... | ★ | ... | ★(h) |
| Massachusetts* | ★ | ★ | ★ | ★ | ... | (d) | (d) | ★ | ... | ★ | ★ | ... | ★ |
| Michigan | ★ | ... | ★ | ★ | ★ | ★ | ★ | ★ | ... | ★ | ★ | ... | ★ |
| Minnesota | ★ | ★ | ... | ★ | ★ | ... | ... | ★ | ... | ★ | ... | ... | ★ |
| Mississippi | (i) | ★ | ★ | ★ | ★ | ★ | ★ | ★ | ★ | ★ | ★ | ★ | ★ |
| Missouri | ★ | ★ | ★ | ★ | ... | ... | ... | ★ | (e) | ★ | ★ | ★ | ★ |
| Montana | ★ | ★ | ★ | ★ | ★ | ... | ... | ★ | ... | ★ | ★ | ... | ★ |
| Nebraska | ★ | ★ | ★ | ★ | ★ | ... | ... | ★ | ... | ★ | ★ | ... | ★ |
| Nevada | ★ | ★ | ★ | ★ | ★ | ★ | ★ | ★ | ★ | ★ | ★ | ★ | ★ |
| New Hampshire | ★ | ★ | ★ | ★ | ★ | ★ | ★ | ★ | ★ | ★ | ★ | ★ | ★ |
| New Jersey (j) | ... | ... | ... | ... | ★ | ... | ... | ... | ... | ... | ... | ... | ... |
| New Mexico | ★ | ★ | ★ | ★ | ★ | ★ | ★ | ★ | ... | ... | ★ | ... | ★ |
| New York | ... | ... | ... | ... | ... | ... | ... | ... | ... | ★ | ... | ... | ★ |
| North Carolina | ... | ... | ... | ... | ... | ... | ... | ... | ★ | ★ | ★ | ★ | ★ |
| North Dakota | ★ | ★ | ★ | ★ | ★ | ★ | ★ | ★ | ★ | ★ | ★ | ... | ★ |
| Ohio | ★ | ★ | ★ | ★ | ★ | ★ | ★ | ★ | ... | ★ | ... | ... | ★ |
| Oklahoma | ... | ... | ★ | ★(k) | ... | ... | ... | ... | ★ | ★ | ★ | ... | ★ |
| Oregon | ★ | ★ | ★ | ★ | ★ | ★ | ★ | ★ | (e) | ★ | ★ | ... | ... |
| Pennsylvania | ★ | ★ | ... | ★(l) | ★ | ★ | ★ | ★ | ★ | ★ | ★ | ... | ★ |
| Rhode Island | ... | ... | N.A. | ★ | ★ | (d) | (d) | ★ | ★ | ★ | ★ | ... | ★ |
| South Carolina | ... | ... | ... | ... | ... | ... | ... | ... | ★ | ★ | ★ | ... | ★ |
| South Dakota | ★ | ★ | ★ | ★ | ★ | ★ | ★ | ★ | ... | ★ | ★ | ... | ★ |
| Tennessee | (m) | ★ | ... | ★ | ... | ... | ... | ... | ★ | ★ | ★ | ... | ★ |
| Texas | ★ | ★ | ... | ★ | ★ | ... | ... | ★ | ... | ★ | ★ | ... | ★ |
| Utah (b) | ★ | ★ | ★ | ★ | ★ | ★ | ★ | ★ | N.A. | N.A. | N.A. | N.A. | N.A. |
| Vermont | ★ | ★ | N.A. | ★(n) | ★ | ★ | ★ | ★ | ... | ★ | ... | ... | ★ |
| Virginia | ... | ... | ★ | ... | ... | ... | ... | ... | ... | ... | ★ | ... | (p) |
| Washington | ★ | ★ | ★ | ★ | ... | ... | ... | ★ | ★ | ★ | ... | ... | ★ |
| West Virginia | ★ | ★ | N.A. | ★ | ★ | ★ | ★ | ★ | ★ | ★ | ★ | ... | ★ |
| Wisconsin | ... | ... | N.A. | N.A. | ... | ... | ... | ... | ... | ... | ★ | ... | ★ |
| Wyoming* | ★ | ★ | ★ | ★ | ... | ★ | ★ | ★ | ★ | ★ | ★ | ★ | ★ |
| American Samoa (b) | ... | ... | ... | ... | ... | ... | ... | ... | ... | ... | ... | ... | ... |
| Guam (b) | ... | ... | ... | ... | ... | ... | ... | ... | ... | ... | ... | ... | ... |
| Puerto Rico | ... | ... | ... | ... | ... | ... | ... | ... | ★ | ★ | ★ | ... | ★ |
| U.S. Virgin Islands (b) | ... | ... | ... | ... | ... | ... | ... | ... | ★ | ★(o) | ★ | ... | ★ |

See footnotes at end of table.

# SECRETARIES OF STATE: ELECTION AND REGISTRATION DUTIES — Continued

*Source*: The Council of State Governments' survey, January 2000, except as noted by * where data are from *The Book of the States*, 1998-99.

*Key*:

★ — Responsible for activity.

. . . — Not responsible for activity.

N.A. — Not applicable.

(a) Unless otherwise indicated, office registers domestic, foreign and non-profit corporations.

(b) No secretary of state. Duties indicated are performed by lieutenant governor. In Hawaii, election related responsibilities have been transferred to an independent Chief Election Officer.

(c) Files certificates of election for publication purposes only; does not file certificates of nomination.

(d) Federal candidates only.

(e) Incorporated organizations only.

(f) Candidates for Congress only.

(g) Accepts disclosures of persons doing business with the state who also make political contributions.

(h) Registers trade/service marks, but trade names are registered at a different agency. In Maryland, the trade name would be registered with the Secretary of State if it were also the trade/service mark of the entity.

(i) State Election Commission composed of governor, secretary of state and attorney general.

(j) Functions have moved.

(k) Files certificates of national elections only; does not file certificates of nomination.

(l) Certificates of nomination are filed only for special elections or when vacancies in nominations occur.

(m) Secretary appoints state coordinator of elections.

(n) Files certificates of election for House of Representatives only.

(o) Both domestic and foreign profit; but only domestic non-profit.

(p) The Secretary of State is not the chief election officer, but a member of the Board of State Canvassers.

## Table 2.16
## SECRETARIES OF STATE: CUSTODIAL, PUBLICATION AND LEGISLATIVE DUTIES

| State or other jurisdiction | Custodial | | | | Publication | | | | | Legislative | | | |
|---|---|---|---|---|---|---|---|---|---|---|---|---|---|
| | Archives state records and regulations | Files state agency rules and regulations | Administers uniform commercial code provisions | Files other corporate documents | State manual or directory | Session laws | State constitution | Statutes | Administrative rules and regulations | Opens legislative sessions (a) | Enrolls or engrosses bills | Retains copies of bills | Registers lobbyists |
| Alabama | ... | ... | ★ | ★ | ... | ★ | ★ | ★ | ... | ... | ... | ★ | ... |
| Alaska (b) | ... | ★ | ... | ... | ... | ★ | ... | ★ | ★ | ★ | ... | ★ | ... |
| Arizona | ... | ★ | ★ | ... | ★ | ... | ★ | ★ | ★ | ... | ... | ★ | ★ |
| Arkansas | ... | ★ | ★ | ★ | ★ | ★ | ★ | ★ | ★ | ... | ... | ★ | ★ |
| California | ★ | ★ | ★ | ★ | ★ | ★ | ★ | ★ | ... | ... | ... | ★ | ★ |
| Colorado | ... | ★ | ★ | ★ | ... | ... | ★ | ... | ... | ... | ... | ★ | ★ |
| Connecticut | ★(c) | ★ | ★ | ★ | ★ | ... | ★ | ... | ... | S | ... | ★ | ... |
| Delaware | ★ | ★ | ★ | ★ | ... | ... | ... | ... | ★ | ... | ... | ... | ... |
| Florida | ★ | ★ | ★ | ★ | ... | ★ | ★ | ... | ★ | ... | ... | ... | ... |
| Georgia | ★ | ★ | ... | ★ | ★ | ★ | ★ | ★ | ★ | ... | ... | ★ | ... |
| Hawaii (b) | ... | ★ | ... | ... | ... | ... | ... | ... | ... | ... | ... | ... | ... |
| Idaho | ... | ... | ★ | ★ | ★ | ★ | ★ | ... | ... | ... | ... | ★ | ★ |
| Illinois | ★ | ★ | ★ | ★ | ★ | ★ | ★ | ... | ★ | H | ... | ★ | ★ |
| Indiana* | ... | ★ | ★ | ★ | ... | ... | ★ | ... | ... | H | ... | ★ | ... |
| Iowa | ... | ... | ★ | ★ | ★ | ... | ★ | ... | ... | ... | ... | ★ | ... |
| Kansas | ... | ★ | ★ | ★ | ... | ★ | ... | ... | ★ | ★ | ★ | ★ | ★ |
| Kentucky | ★ | ... | ★ | ★ | ... | ★ | ... | ... | ... | ... | ★ | ... | ... |
| Louisiana | ★ | ... | ★ | ★ | ★ | ★ | ... | ... | ... | ... | ... | ★ | ... |
| Maine* | ★ | ★ | ★ | ★ | ... | ... | ★ | ... | ★ | ... | ... | ★ | ... |
| Maryland | ... | ★ | ... | ... | ... | ... | ... | ... | ★ | ... | ... | ★(g) | ... |
| Massachusetts* | ★ | ★ | ★ | ★ | ★ | ★ | ★ | ★ | ★ | ... | ... | ★ | ★ |
| Michigan | ★ | ★ | ★ | ★ | ... | ... | ... | ... | ... | ... | ... | ★ | ★ |
| Minnesota | ... | ★ | ★ | ★ | ★ | ... | ★ | ... | ... | H | ... | ★ | ... |
| Mississippi | ★ | ★ | ★ | ★ | ★ | ★ | ★ | ... | ★ | ★ | ★ | ★ | ★ |
| Missouri | ★ | ★ | ★ | ★ | ★ | ... | ★ | ... | ★ | H | ... | ★ | ... |
| Montana | ★ | ★ | ★ | ★ | ... | ... | ★ | ... | ★ | H | ... | ★ | ... |
| Nebraska | ★ | ★ | ★ | ★ | ... | ★ | ... | ★ | ... | ... | ★ | ... | ... |
| Nevada | ... | ★ | ★ | ... | ... | ... | ... | ... | ★ | ... | ★ | ... | ... |
| New Hampshire | ★ | ... | ★ | ★ | ★ | ... | ★ | ... | ... | ... | ★ | ★ | ★ |
| New Jersey | ★ | ... | ... | ... | ★ | ... | ★ | ... | ... | ... | ... | ... | ... |
| New Mexico | ... | ★ | ★ | ★ | ★ | ★ | ★ | ★ | ... | H | ... | ★ | ★ |
| New York | ★ | ★ | ★ | ★ | ... | ... | ★ | ... | ★ | ... | ... | ★ | ★ |
| North Carolina | ... | ... | ★ | ★ | ★ | ★ | ★ | ... | ... | ... | ... | ★ | ★ |
| North Dakota | ... | ★ | ★ | ★ | ★ | ... | ... | ... | ... | ... | ... | ★ | ★ |
| Ohio | ... | ★ | ★ | ★ | ... | ★ | ★ | ... | ... | ... | ... | ★ | ... |
| Oklahoma | ... | ★ | ... | ★ | ... | ★ | ★ | ... | ★ | ... | ... | ★ | ... |
| Oregon | ★ | ★ | ★ | ★ | ★ | ... | ... | ... | ★ | ... | ... | ★ | ... |
| Pennsylvania | ... | ... | ★ | ★ | ... | ... | ... | ... | ... | ... | ... | ★ | ... |
| Rhode Island | ★ | ★ | ★ | ★ | ★ | ... | ★ | ... | ★ | ... | ... | ★ | ★ |
| South Carolina | ... | ... | ★ | ★ | ... | ... | ... | ... | ... | ... | ... | ★ | ... |
| South Dakota | ... | ★ | ★ | ★ | ★ | ... | ★ | ... | ... | H | ... | ... | ★ |
| Tennessee | ★ | ★ | ★ | ★ | ★ | ★ | ★ | ★ | ★ | ... | ... | ★ | ... |
| Texas | ... | ★ | ★ | ★ | ... | ★ | ... | ... | ★ | H(e) | ... | ★ | ... |
| Utah (b) | ... | ... | ... | ... | ... | ... | ... | ... | ... | ... | ... | ★ | ★ |
| Vermont | ★ | ★ | ★ | ★ | ★ | ★ | ★ | ... | ... | H(e) | ... | ★ | ★ |
| Virginia | ... | ... | ... | ... | ★ | ... | ... | ... | ... | ... | ... | ... | ★ |
| Washington | ★ | ... | ... | ★ | ... | ... | ... | ... | ... | ... | ... | ... | ... |
| West Virginia | ★(c) | ★ | ★ | ★ | ... | ... | ... | ... | ★ | ... | ... | ★ | ... |
| Wisconsin | ★ | ★ | ... | ... | ... | ... | ... | ... | ★ | ... | ... | ★ | ... |
| Wyoming* | ... | ★ | ★ | ★ | ★ | ... | ★ | ... | ... | H | ... | ★ | ★ (f) |
| American Samoa (b) | ... | ... | ... | ... | ... | ... | ... | ... | ... | ... | ... | ... | ... |
| Guam (b) | ... | ... | ★ | ... | ... | ... | ... | ... | ... | ... | ... | ... | ... |
| Puerto Rico | ... | ★ | ★ | ★ | ... | ★ | ★ | ★ | ★ | ... | ... | ... | ... |
| U.S. Virgin Islands (b) | ... | ★ | ★ | ★ | ... | ... | ... | ★ | ... | ... | ★ | ★ | ... |

*Source*: The Council of State Governments' survey, January 2000, except as noted by * where data are from *The Book of the States, 1998-99*.

Key:

★ — Responsible for activity.

. . . — Not responsible for activity.

(a) In this column only: H–Both houses; H–House; S–Senate.

(b) No secretary of state. Duties indicated are performed by lieutenant governor.

(c) The secretary of state is keeper of public records, but the state archives is a department of the state library.

(d) Functions regarding corporations, UCC and state directory have moved.

(e) Until speaker is elected.

(f) Only groups supporting or opposing legislation which was subject to a statewide initiative or referendum within the past four years.

(g) Responsible for custody of bills passed by the General Assembly until Governor signs the bills, chapterizes and transmits the bills to the Court of Appeals and returns vetoed bills to General Assembly before session.

# Table 2.17
## ATTORNEYS GENERAL: QUALIFICATIONS FOR OFFICE

| State or other jurisdiction | Minimum age | U.S. citizen (years) | State resident (years) | Qualified voter (years) | Licensed attorney (years) | Membership in the state bar (years) | Method of selection to office |
|---|---|---|---|---|---|---|---|
| Alabama | 25 | 7 | 5 | ... | ... | ... | E |
| Alaska | ... | ★ | ... | ... | ... | ... | A |
| Arizona | 25 | 10 | 5 | ... | ... | ... | E |
| Arkansas | 18 | ★ | ★ | ★ | ... | ... | E |
| California | 18 | ... | ... | ... | (a) | (a) | E |
| Colorado | 25 | ★ | 2 | ... | ★ | (b) | E |
| Connecticut | 18 | ★ | ★ | ★ | 10 | 10 | E |
| Delaware | ... | ... | ... | ... | ... | ... | E |
| Florida* | 30 | ... | 7 | ★ | 5 | 5 | E |
| Georgia | 25 | 10 | 4 | ... | 7 | 7 | E |
| Hawaii | ... | ★ | 1 | ... | (c) | ... | A |
| Idaho* | 30 | ★ | 2 | ... | ★ | ★ | E |
| Illinois | 25 | ★ | 3 | ... | ... | ... | E |
| Indiana* | ... | ... | (d) | ... | ★ | ... | E |
| Iowa | ... | ... | ... | ... | ... | ... | E |
| Kansas | ... | ... | ... | ... | ... | ... | E |
| Kentucky | 30 | 2 | 2 (d) | ... | 8 | 2 | E |
| Louisiana | 25 | 5 | 5 (d) | ★ | 5 | 5 | E |
| Maine* | ... | ... | ... | ... | ... | ... | (e) |
| Maryland | ... | ★(f) | 10 (d) | ★ | 10 | 10 (c) | E |
| Massachusetts | ... | ... | 5 | ... | ... | ★ | E |
| Michigan | 18 | ★ | 30 days | ★ | (a) | (a) | E |
| Minnesota | 21 | ★ | 30 days | ★ | ... | ... | E |
| Mississippi | 26 | ... | 5 (d) | ... | 5 | 5 | E |
| Missouri | ... | ★ | 1 | ... | ... | ... | E |
| Montana (g) | 25 | ★ | 2 | ... | 5 | ★ | E |
| Nebraska (h) | ... | ... | ... | ... | ... | ... | E |
| Nevada | 25 | ★ | 2 (d) | ★ | ... | ... | E |
| New Hampshire | ... | ... | ... | ... | ★ | ★ | A |
| New Jersey | 18 (c) | ... | ★ | ... | ... | ... | A |
| New Mexico | 30 | ... | 5 | ... | ★ | ... | E |
| New York | 30 | ★ | 5 | ... | (c) | ... | E |
| North Carolina | 21 | ... | ... | ★ | ★ | (c) | E |
| North Dakota | 25 | ★ | 5 | ★ | ★ | ★ | E |
| Ohio | 18 | ★ | ★ | ★ | (a) | ... | E |
| Oklahoma | 31 | ★ | 10 | 10 | ... | ... | E |
| Oregon* | 18 | ★ | 6 mos. | ★ | ... | ... | E |
| Pennsylvania* | 30 | ★ | 7 | ... | ★ | ★ | E |
| Rhode Island | 18 | ★ | ★ | ★ | ... | ... | E |
| South Carolina | 18 | ★ | 30 days | ★ | ... | ... | E |
| South Dakota | ... | ★ | ★ | ... | (c) | (c) | E |
| Tennessee | ... | ... | ... | ... | ... | ... | (i) |
| Texas | ... | ... | ... | ... | (c) | (c) | E |
| Utah | 25 | ... | 5 (d) | ★ | ★ | ★ | E |
| Vermont | ... | ... | ... | ... | ... | ... | E |
| Virginia | 30 | ★ | 5 (j) | ... | ... | 5 (j) | E |
| Washington | ... | ★ | ★ | ★ | ★ | ★ | E |
| West Virginia | 25 | ★ | 5 (d) | ★ | ... | ... | E |
| Wisconsin | ... | ★ | ★ | ... | ... | ... | E |
| Wyoming | ... | ... | ★ | ★ | 4 | 4 | A |
| American Samoa* | ... | ... | (a) | ... | (c) | (c) | A |
| Guam | ... | ... | ... | ... | ... | ... | A |
| No. Mariana Islands | ... | ... | 3 | ... | 5 | ... | A |
| Puerto Rico | 21 (c) | ★ | ... | ... | (c) | (c) | A |
| U.S. Virgin Islands | 21 | ★ | ... | ... | (k) | ... | A |

## ATTORNEYS GENERAL: QUALIFICATIONS FOR OFFICE - continued

*Source*: The Council of State Governments' survey, January 2000, except as noted by * where information is from *The Book of the States, 1998-99*.

*Note*: This table contains constitutional and statutory provisions. "Qualified voter" provision may infer additional residency and citizenship requirements.

*Key*:

★ — Formal provision; number of years not specified.

. . . — No formal provision.

A — Appointed by governor.

E — Elected by voters.

(a) No statute specifically requires this, but the State Bar act can be interpreted as making this a qualification.

(b) Licensed attorneys are not required to belong to the bar association.

(c) Implied.

(d) State citizenship requirement.

(e) Chosen biennially by joint ballot of state senators and representatives.

(f) Crosse v. Board of Supervisors of Elections 243 Md. 555, 2221A.2d431 (1966)–opinion rendered indicated that U.S. citizenship was, by necessity, a requirement for office.

(g) No person convicted of a felony is eligible to hold public office until final discharge from state supervision.

(h) No person in default as a collector and custodian of public money or property shall be eligible to public office; no person convicted of a felony shall be eligible unless restored to civil rights.

(i) Appointed by judges of state Supreme Court.

(j) Same as qualifications of a judge of a court of record.

(k) Must be admitted to practice before highest court.

## Table 2.18
## ATTORNEYS GENERAL: PROSECUTORIAL AND ADVISORY DUTIES

| State or other jurisdiction | Authority in local prosecutions: | | | | Issues advisory opinions: | | | | | Reviews legislation: | |
|---|---|---|---|---|---|---|---|---|---|---|---|
| | Authority to initiate local prosecutions | May intervene in local prosecutions | May assist local prosecutor | May supersede local prosecutor | To state executive officials | To legislators | To local prosecutors | On the interpretation of statutes | On the constitutionality of bills or ordinances | Prior to passage | Before signing |
| Alabama | A | A,D | A,D | A | ★ | ★ | ★ | ★ | ... | ★ | ... |
| Alaska | (a) | (a) | (a) | (a) | ★ | ★ | ... | ★ | ★ | ★ | ★ |
| Arizona | A,B,C,D,F | B,D | B,D | B | ★ | ★ | ★ | ★ | ★ | ★ | ... |
| Arkansas | ... | D | D | ... | ★ | ★ | ★ | ★ | ★ | ... | ... |
| California | A,B,D,E,F | A,B,D,E | A,B,D,E | A,B,D,E | ★ | ★ | ★ | ★ | ★ | ★ | ★ |
| Colorado | B,F | B | D,F (b) | B | ★ | ★ | ★ | ★ | ★ | ★ | ★ |
| Connecticut | ... | ... | ... | ... | ★ | (c) | ★ | ★ | ★ | ★ | ★ |
| Delaware | A,B,C,E,F,G | A,B C,E,F,G | A,B,C,E,F,G | A,B,C,E,F,G | ★ | ★ | ★ | ★ | ★ | ★ | ★ |
| Florida* | F (b,d) | D (b,d) | D | ... | ★ | ★ | ★ | ★ | ... | ★ | ★ |
| Georgia | A,B,F | A,B,D,G | A,B,D,F | B | ★ | ★ | ★ | ★ | ... | ★ | ★ |
| Hawaii | E | A,D,G | A,D | A,G | ★ | ★ | ★ | ★ | ★ | ★ | ★ |
| Idaho* | B,D,F | ... | D | ... | ★ | ★ | ★ | ★ | ★ | ★ | ★ |
| Illinois | A,D,E,F,G (b) | A,D,E,G | D,E,F,G | A,D,E,F,G | ★ | ★ (f) | ★ | ★ | ★ | (g) | (g) |
| Indiana* | F (b) | ... | A,D,E | G | ★ | ★ | ★ | ★ | ★ | B | ★ |
| Iowa | D,F | D | D | ... | ★ | ★ | ★ | ★ | ★ | ★ | ★ |
| Kansas | A,B,C,D,F | A,D | D | A,F | ★ | ★ | ★ | ★ | ★ | (g) | (g) |
| Kentucky | A,B,D,E,F,G | B,D,G | B,D,F | G | ★ | ★ | ★ | ★ | ★ | ★ | ... |
| Louisiana | G | G | D | G | ★ | ★ | ★ | ★ | ★ | (g) | (g) |
| Maine* | A | A | A | A | ★ | ★ | ... | ★ | ★ | ★ | ★ |
| Maryland | B,C,F | B,C,D | B,C,D | B,C | ★ | ★ | ★ | ★ | ★ | ★ | ★ |
| Massachusetts | A | A | A,D | A | ★ | ★ (h) | ★ | ★ | ★ | (g) | (g) |
| Michigan | A | A | D | A | ★ | ★ | ★ | ★ | ★ | ★ | ★ |
| Minnesota | B,F | B,D,G | A,B,D,G | B | ★ | ★ (h) | ★ | ★ | ... | ... | (g) |
| Mississippi | B,D,E,F | D | B,D,F | E | ★ | ★ | ★ | ★ | ★ | (g) | (g) |
| Missouri | F | G | B | ... | ★ | ★ | ★ | ★ | ... | ★ | ★ |
| Montana | B,D,E,F | A,B,D,E | A,B,D,E,F | A,B,E | ★ | ★ (i) | ★ | ★ | ... | (e) | (g) |
| Nebraska | A | A | A,D | A | ★ | ★ | ★ | ★ | ★ | ... | ... |
| Nevada | D,F,G (d) | D (d) | (d,j) | ★ | ★ | ... | ★ | ★ | ★ (k) | ... | ... |
| New Hampshire | A | A | A | A | ★ | ... (i) | ... | ★ | ★ | ★ | ★ |
| New Jersey | A | A,B,D,G | A,D | A,B,D,G | ★ | ★ | ★ | ★ | ★ | ★ | ★ |
| New Mexico | A,B,C,D,E,F(b)(j) | G | D | G | ★ | ★ | ★ | ★ | ★ | ★ | ★ |
| New York | B,F | B,D,F | D | B | ★ | ★ (h) | ★ | ★ | ★ | ★ | ★ |
| North Carolina | ... | D | D | ... | ★ | ★ | ★ | ★ | ★ | ★ | ... |
| North Dakota | A,D,E,F,G | A,D,G | A,B,D,E,F,G | A,G | ★ | ★ | ★ | ★ | ... | (f) | (g) |
| Ohio | B,C,F | B,F | F | B,C | ★ | ★ (i) | ★ | ★ | ... | ... | ... |
| Oklahoma | B,C,F | B,C | B,C | ... | ★ | ★ | ★ | ★ | ★ (l) | ... | ★ (g) |
| Oregon* | B,F | B,D | B,D | B | ★ | ★ | ★ | ★ | ★ | (g) | (g) |
| Pennsylvania* | A,D,F,G | D,G | D | G | ★ | ... | ... | ★ | ... | ★ | ★ |
| Rhode Island | A | A | A | ... | ★ | ★ | ... | ★ | ★ | ... | ... |
| South Carolina | A,D,E,F (b) | A,B,C,D,E,F | A,D | A,E | ★ | (m) | A,D | B,C (c) | B,C | ★ C (n) | ★ C,B (g) |
| South Dakota | A,B,C (n) | A,D | A,D | A,E | ★ | ★ | ★ | ★ | ★ | ... | ... |
| Tennessee | D,F,G (b) | D,G (b) | D | ... | ★ | ★ | ★ | ★ | ★ | (g) | (g) |
| Texas | F | ... | D | ... | ★ | ★ | ★ | ★ | ★ | ★ | ★ |
| Utah | A,B,D,E,F,G | E,G | D,E | E | ★ | ★ (m) | ★ | ★ | ★ | (g) | (g) |
| Vermont | A | A | A | ... | ★ | ★ | ★ | ★ | ★ | ★ | ★ |
| Virginia | B,F | B,D,F | B,D,F | B | ★ | ★ | ★ | ★ | ★ | ★ | ★ |
| Washington | B,D,G | B,D,G | D | B | ★ | ★ | ★ | ★ | ★ | ★ | ★ |
| West Virginia | ... | ... | D | ... | ★ | (c) | ★ | ★ | ★ | (e) | (e) |
| Wisconsin | B,C,D,F | B,C,D | D | B | ★ | ★ | ★ | ★ | ★ | ★ | ★ |
| Wyoming | B,D (d),F | B,D | B,D | ... | ★ | ★ | ★ | ★ | ... | ★ | ★ |
| American Samoa* | A (o) | (o) | (o) | (o) | ★ | ... | (o) | (e) | (e) | (g) | (g) |
| Guam | A | A | A | A | ★ | ★ | ★ | ★ | ★ | (g) | B |
| No. Mariana Islands | A | ... | ... | ... | ★ | ... | ... | ★ | ★ | ★ | ★ |
| Puerto Rico | A,B,E | A,B,E | A,E | A,B,E | ★ | ★ | ... | ★ | ★ | ★ | ★ |
| U.S. Virgin Islands* | A (o) | (o) | (o) | (o) | ★ | ★ | ... | ★ | ★ | ... | ★ |

See footnotes at end of table.

## ATTORNEYS GENERAL: PROSECUTORIAL AND ADVISORY DUTIES — Continued

*Source:* The Council of State Governments' survey, January 2000, except as noted by * where information is from *The Book of the States 1998-99.*

*Key:*

A — On own initiative.

B — On request of governor.

C — On request of legislature.

D — On request of local prosecutor.

E — When in state's interest.

F — Under certain statutes for specific crimes.

G — On authorization of court or other body.

★ — Has authority in area.

. . . — Does not have authority in area.

(a) Local prosecutors serve at pleasure of attorney general.

(b) Certain statutes provide for concurrent jurisdiction with local prosecutors.

(c) To legislative leadership.

(d) In connection with grand jury cases.

(e) No legal authority, but sometimes informally reviews laws at request of legislature.

(f) Opinion may be issued to officers of either branch of General Assembly or to chairman or minority spokesman of committees or commissions thereof.

(g) Only when requested by governor or legislature.

(h) To legislature as a whole not individual legislators.

(i) To either house of legislature, not individual legislators.

(j) Will prosecute as a matter of practice when requested.

(k) On the constitutionality of legislation.

(l) Bills, not ordinances.

(m) Only when requested by legislature.

(n) Has concurrent jurisdiction with states' attorneys.

(o) The attorney general functions as the local prosecutor.

## Table 2.19
## ATTORNEYS GENERAL: CONSUMER PROTECTION ACTIVITIES, SUBPOENA POWERS AND ANTITRUST DUTIES

| State or other jurisdiction | May commence civil proceedings | May commence criminal proceedings | Represents the state before regulatory agencies (a) | Administers consumer protection programs | Handles consumer complaints | Subpoena powers (b) | Antitrust duties |
|---|---|---|---|---|---|---|---|
| Alabama | ★ | ★ | ★ | ★ | ★ | ● | A,B |
| Alaska | ★ | ★ | ★ | ★ | ★ | ★ | B,C |
| Arizona | ★ | . . . | . . . | ★ | ★ | ★ | A,B,C |
| Arkansas | ★ | . . . | ★ | ★ | ★ | ★ | B |
| California | ★ | ★ | ★ | ★ | ★ | ★ | A,B,C,D (c) |
| Colorado | ★ | ★ | ★ | ★ | ★ | ★ | A,B,C,D (d) |
| Connecticut | ★ | (e) | ★ | ★ | ★ | ● | A,B,D |
| Delaware | ★ | ★ | ★ | ★ | ★ | ★ | A,B,D |
| Florida* | ★ | ★ (f) | ★ | ★ (e) | ★ | ★ | A,B,C,D |
| Georgia | ★ | ★ | ★ | . . . | . . . | ● | B,C |
| Hawaii | ★ | ★ | ★ | ★ (e,g) | (g) | ★ | A,B,C,D |
| Idaho* | ★ | . . . | ★ | ★ | ★ | ★ | D |
| Illinois | ★ | . . . | . . . | ★ | ★ | ★ | A,B,C,D |
| Indiana* | ★ | . . . | ★ | ★ | ★ | (e) | B,D |
| Iowa | ★ | ★ | ★ | ★ | ★ | ● | A,B,C,D |
| Kansas | ★ | ★ | ★ | ★ | ★ | ★ | B,C,D |
| Kentucky | ★ | ★ | ★ | ★ | ★ | ★ | A,B,D |
| Louisiana | ★ | (f) | ★ | ★ | ★ | ★ | A,B,C,D |
| Maine* | ★ | ★ | ★ | ★ | ★ | ★ | A,B,C |
| Maryland | ★ | ★ | ★ | ★ | ★ | ★ | B,C,D |
| Massachusetts | ★ | ★ | ★ | ★ | ★ | ★ | A,B,C,D |
| Michigan | ★ | . . . | . . . | ★ | ★ | ● | B,C,D |
| Minnesota | ★ | . . . | ★ | ★ | ★ | ● | A,B,C,D |
| Mississippi | ★ | ★ | ★ | ★ | ★ | ● | A,B,C,D |
| Missouri | ★ | ★ | ★ | ★ | ★ | ● | A,B,C,D |
| Montana | ★ (h) | ★ (h) | (e) | . . . | . . . | ● | A,B,C,D |
| Nebraska | ★ | ★ | ★ | ★ | ★ | ● | A,B,C,(d),D |
| Nevada | ★ | ★ | . . . | ★ | ★ | ● | A,B,C,D |
| New Hampshire | ★ | ★ | ★ | . . . | ★ | ● | A,B,C,D |
| New Jersey | ★ | ★ | ★ | ★ | ★ | ★ | A,B,C,D |
| New Mexico | ★ | ★ | ★ | ★ | ★ | ● | A,B,C,D |
| New York | ★ | ★ | . . . | ★ | ★ | ★ | A,B,C,D |
| North Carolina | ★ | (e) | ★ | ★ | ★ | ★ | A,B,D |
| North Dakota | ★ | . . . | ★ | ★ | ★ | ★ | A,B,C,D |
| Ohio | ★ | ★ | ★ | ★ | ★ | ★ | A,B,C,D |
| Oklahoma | ★ | (e) | (e) | ★ | ★ | ● | B,D |
| Oregon* | ★ | ★ | ★ | ★ | ★ | ● | A,B,C,D |
| Pennsylvania* | ★ | ★ | ★ | ★ | ★ | ● | A (i),B (j),C (j),D |
| Rhode Island | ★ | ★ | ★ | ★ | ★ | ★ | A,B,C,D |
| South Carolina | ★ (a) | ★ (c) | ★ | . . . | ★ | ● | A,B,C,D |
| South Dakota | ★ | ★ | ★ | ★ | ★ | ● | A,B,C,D |
| Tennessee | ★ | (e, f) | (e) | . . . | . . . | ★ | B,C,D |
| Texas | ★ | . . . | ★ | ★ | ★ | ● | A,B,D |
| Utah | ★ (d) | ★ | ★ | . . . | ★ (g) | ● | A (k),B,C,D (k) |
| Vermont | ★ | ★ | ★ | ★ | ★ | ★ | A,B |
| Virginia | ★ | (e) | ★ | ★ (g) | ★ (g) | ● | A,B,C,D |
| Washington | ★ | (e) | ★ | ★ | ★ | ● | A,B,D |
| West Virginia | ★ | . . . | ★ | ★ | ★ | ★ | A,B,D |
| Wisconsin | ★ | (e) | ★ | . . . | . . . | ★ | A,B,C,D |
| Wyoming | ★ | . . . | ★ | ★ | ★ | ● | . . . |
| American Samoa* | ★ | ★ | ★ | ★ | ★ | . . . | . . . |
| Guam | ★ | ★ | ★ | ★ | ★ | ● | A,B,C,D |
| No. Mariana Islands | ★ | ★ | ★ | ★ | ★ | ★ | B,C,D |
| Puerto Rico | ★ | ★ | ★ | ★ (e) | ★ (e) | ★ | A,B,C,D |
| U.S. Virgin Islands* | ★ | ★ (l) | ★ | . . . | . . . | ● | B (m),C |

*Source:* The Council of State Governments' survey, January 2000, except as noted by * where information is from *The Book of the States 1998-99.*

*Key:*

A — Has parens patriae authority to commence suits on behalf of consumers in state antitrust damage actions in state courts.

B — May initiate damage actions on behalf of state in state courts.

C — May commence criminal proceedings.

D — May represent cities, counties and other governmental entities in recovering civil damages under federal or state law.

★ — Has authority in area.

. . . — Does not have authority in area.

(a) May represent state on behalf of: the "people" of the state; an agency of the state; or the state before a federal regulatory agency.

(b) In this column only: ★ broad powers and ● limited powers.

(c) When permitted to intervene.

(d) Attorney general has exclusive authority.

(e) To a limited extent.

(f) May commence criminal proceedings with local district attorney.

(g) Attorney general handles legal matters only with no administrative handling of complaints.

(h) Only when requested by the state department of commerce or by a county attorney.

(i) In federal courts only.

(j) For bid rigging violations only.

(k) Opinion only, since there are no controlling precedents.

(l) May prosecute in inferior courts. May prosecute in district court only by request or consent of U.S. Attorney General.

(m) May initiate damage actions on behalf of jurisdiction in district court.

## Table 2.20
## ATTORNEYS GENERAL: DUTIES TO ADMINISTRATIVE AGENCIES AND OTHER RESPONSIBILITIES

| State or other jurisdiction | Serves as counsel for state | Appears for state in criminal appeals | Issues official advice | Interprets statutes or regulations | Conducts litigation: On behalf of agency | Conducts litigation: Against agency | Prepares or reviews legal documents | Represents the public before the agency | Involved in rule-making | Reviews rules for legality |
|---|---|---|---|---|---|---|---|---|---|---|
| Alabama | A,B,C | ★ (a) | ★ | ★ | ★ | ★ | ★ | (b) | (b) | ★ |
| Alaska | A,B,C | ★ | ★ | ★ | ★ | ★ | ★ | . . . | ★ | ★ |
| Arizona | A,B,C | (a) | ★ | ★ | ★ | ★ | ★ | . . . | ★ | ★ |
| Arkansas | A,B,C | ★ (a) | ★ | ★ | ★ | (b) | ★ | ★ | ★ | ★ |
| California | A,B,C | ★ (a) | ★ | ★ | ★ | ★ | ★ | . . . | . . . | . . . |
| Colorado | A,B,C | (b) | ★ | ★ | ★ | ★ | ★ | (e) | ★ | ★ |
| Connecticut | A,B,C | (b) | ★ | ★ | ★ | (b) | ★ | (b) | ★ | ★ |
| Delaware | A,B,C | ★ (a) | ★ | ★ | ★ | ★ | ★ | ★ | ★ | ★ |
| Florida* | A,B,C | ★ (a) | ★ | ★ | ★ | (b) | ★ | (b) | ★ | . . . |
| Georgia | A,B,C | (b,c) | ★ | ★ | ★ | ★ | ★ | . . . | ★ | ★ |
| Hawaii | A,B,C | (b,c) | ★ | ★ | ★ | ★ | ★ | ★ | ★ | ★ |
| Idaho* | A,B,C | ★ (a) | ★ | ★ | ★ | . . . | ★ | . . . | ★ | ★ |
| Illinois | A,B,C | (b,c) | ★ | ★ | ★ | ★ | ★ | ★ | . . . | . . . |
| Indiana* | A,B,C | ★ (a) | ★ | ★ | ★ | . . . | ★ | . . . | ★ | ★ |
| Iowa | A,B,C | ★ (a) | ★ | ★ | ★ | ★ | ★ | (f) | (f) | ★ |
| Kansas | A,B,C | ★ (a) | ★ | ★ | ★ | ★ | ★ | . . . | . . . | ★ (a) |
| Kentucky | A,B,C | ★ | ★ | ★ | ★ | ★ | ★ | (e) | (b) | (b) |
| Louisiana | A,B,C | (c) | ★ | ★ | ★ | . . . | ★ | . . . | . . . | ★ |
| Maine* | A,B,C | (d) | ★ | ★ | ★ | (b) | ★ | (b) | ★ | ★ |
| Maryland | A,B,C | ★ | ★ | ★ | ★ | (b) | ★ | ★ | ★ | ★ |
| Massachusetts | A,B,C | (b,c,d) | ★ | ★ | ★ | ★ | ★ | ★ | ★ | ★ |
| Michigan | A,B,C | (b,c,d) | ★ | ★ | ★ | ★ | ★ | ★ | . . . | . . . |
| Minnesota | A,B,C | (c,d) | ★ | ★ | (a) | ★ | ★ | ★ | ★ | ★ |
| Mississippi | A,B,C | ★ | ★ | ★ | ★ | ★ | ★ | ★ | ★ | ★ |
| Missouri | A,B,C | ★ | ★ | ★ | ★ | . . . | ★ | . . . | ★ | ★ |
| Montana | A,B,C (b) | ★ | ★ | ★ | (b) | ★ | (b) | . . . | (b) | (b) |
| Nebraska | A,B,C | ★ | ★ | ★ | ★ | ★ | ★ | . . . | . . . | ★ |
| Nevada | A,B,C | ★ (d) | ★ | ★ | ★ | . . . | ★ | (b) | ★ | ★ |
| New Hampshire | A,B,C | ★ (a) | ★ | ★ | ★ | ★ | ★ | ★ | ★ | ★ |
| New Jersey | A,B,C | ★ (d) | ★ | ★ | ★ | ★ | ★ | . . . | ★ | ★ |
| New Mexico | A,B,C | ★ (a) | ★ | ★ | ★ | ★ | ★ | ★ | ★ | ★ |
| New York | A,B,C | (b) | . . . | ★ | ★ | (b) | ★ | (b) | . . . | . . . |
| North Carolina | A,B,C | ★ | ★ | ★ | ★ | ★ | ★ | (b) | ★ | ★ |
| North Dakota | A,B,C | (b) | ★ | ★ | ★ | ★ | ★ | . . . | ★ | ★ |
| Ohio | A,B,C | (b) | ★ | ★ | ★ | ★ | ★ | ★ | ★ | . . . |
| Oklahoma | A,B,C | ★ (a) | ★ | ★ | ★ | (b) | ★ | (b) | ★ | ★ |
| Oregon* | A,B,C | ★ | (a) | ★ | ★ | (b) | ★ | . . . | ★ | ★ |
| Pennsylvania* | A,B,C | ★ | ★ | ★ | ★ | ★ | ★ | . . . | ★ | ★ |
| Rhode Island | A,B,C | ★ (a) | ★ | ★ | ★ | ★ | ★ | ★ | ★ | ★ |
| South Carolina | A,B,C | ★ (d) | (a) | ★ | ★ | (b) | ★ | . . . | ★ | ★ |
| South Dakota | A,B,C | ★ (a) | ★ | ★ | ★ | . . . | ★ | . . . | . . . | . . . |
| Tennessee | A,B,C | ★ (a) | ★ | ★ | ★ | . . . | ★ | (f) | (f) | . . . |
| Texas | A,B,C | (c) | ★ | ★ | ★ | ★ | ★ | . . . | ★ | ★ |
| Utah | A,B,C | ★ (a) | ★ | ★ | ★ | ★ | ★ | (b) | ★ | ★ |
| Vermont | A,B,C | ★ | ★ | ★ | ★ | ★ | ★ | ★ | ★ | ★ |
| Virginia | A,B,C | ★ (a) | ★ | ★ | ★ | ★ | ★ | ★ (g) | ★ | ★ |
| Washington | A,B,C | (c,g) | ★ | ★ | ★ | ★ | ★ | ★ (b) | ★ | ★ |
| West Virginia | A,B,C | ★ (a) | ★ | ★ | ★ | (g) | ★ | ★ | ★ | . . . |
| Wisconsin | A,B,C | ★ | ★ | ★ | ★ | (b) | ★ | ★ | (b) | (b) |
| Wyoming | A,B,C | ★ (a) | ★ | ★ | ★ | ★ | ★ | . . . | ★ | ★ |
| American Samoa* | A,B,C | ★ (a) | ★ | ★ | ★ | . . . | ★ | . . . | ★ | ★ |
| Guam | A,B,C | ★ | ★ | ★ | (d) | ★ | ★ | (b) | ★ | ★ |
| No. Mariana Islands | A,B,C | ★ | ★ | ★ | ★ | . . . | ★ | . . . | ★ | ★ |
| Puerto Rico | A,B,C | ★ | ★ | ★ | ★ | . . . | ★ | . . . | ★ | ★ |
| U.S. Virgin Islands* | A,B,C (h) | ★ | ★ | ★ | ★ | ★ | ★ | . . . | ★ | ★ |

*Source:* The Council of State Governments' survey, January 2000, except as noted by * where information is from *The Book of the States 1998-99*.

*Key:*
A — Defend state law when challenged on federal constitutional grounds.
B — Conduct litigation on behalf of state in federal and other states' courts.
C — Prosecute actions against another state in U.S. Supreme Court.
★ — Has authority in area.
. . . — Does not have authority in area.
(a) Attorney general has exclusive jurisdiction.

(b) In certain cases only.
(c) When assisting local prosecutor in the appeal.
(d) Can appear on own discretion.
(e) Public Service Commission only.
(f) Consumer Advocate Division represents the public in utility rate making hearings and rule making proceedings.
(g) If authorized by the governor.
(h) Except in cases in which the U.S. Attorney is representing the Government of the U.S. Virgin Islands.

## Table 2.21
## TREASURERS: QUALIFICATIONS FOR OFFICE

| State or other jurisdiction | Minimum age | U.S. citizen (years) | State citizen (years) | Qualified voter (years) | Method of selection to office |
|---|---|---|---|---|---|
| Alabama | 25 | 7 | 5 | ... | E |
| Alaska | ... | ... | ... | ... | A |
| Arizona | 25 | 10 | 5 | ... | E |
| Arkansas* | 18 | ★ | ... | ★ | E |
| California | 18 | ★ | ★ | ... | E |
| Colorado | 25 | ★ | 2 | ... | E |
| Connecticut* | 21 | ★ | ... | ★ | E |
| Delaware | ... | ... | ... | ... | E |
| Florida | 30 | ... | 7 | ★ | E |
| Georgia | ... | ... | ... | ... | (a) |
| Hawaii | ... | ★ | 1 | ... | A |
| Idaho | 25 | ★ | 2 | ... | E |
| Illinois | 25 | ★ | 3 | ... | E |
| Indiana* | ... | ... | (b) | ★ | E |
| Iowa | 18 | ... | ... | ... | E |
| Kansas | ... | ... | ... | ... | E |
| Kentucky | 30 | ... | 2 (c) | ... | E |
| Louisiana* | 25 | 5 | 5 | ★ | E |
| Maine | ... | ... | ★ | ... | L |
| Maryland | ... | ... | ... | ... | L |
| Massachusetts | ... | ... | 5 | ... | E |
| Michigan | ... | ... | ... | ... | A |
| Minnesota | 21 | ★ | 20 days | 20 days | E |
| Mississippi | 25 | ★ | 5 | ★ | E |
| Missouri | ... | ★ | 1 | ... | E |
| Montana | ... | ... | ... | ... | A |
| Nebraska* | ... | ★ | ★ | ★ | E |
| Nevada | 25 | ★ | 2 | ★ | E |
| New Hampshire | ... | ... | ... | ... | L |
| New Jersey | ... | ... | ... | ... | A |
| New Mexico | 30 | ★ | 5 | ★ | E |
| New York | ... | ... | ... | ... | A |
| North Carolina | 21 | ★ | ★ | ★ | E |
| North Dakota | 25 | ★ | ★ | ★ | E |
| Ohio* | 18 | ★ | 30 days | 30 days | E |
| Oklahoma | 31 | 10 | 10 | 10 | E |
| Oregon | 18 | ★ | ★ | ... | E |
| Pennsylvania | ... | ... | ... | ... | E |
| Rhode Island | 18 | ★ | ★ | 30 days | E |
| South Carolina | ... | ★ | ★ | ★ | E |
| South Dakota | ... | ... | ... | ... | E |
| Tennessee | ... | ... | ... | ... | L |
| Texas | ------------------------------------------------(d)------------------------------------------------ | | | | |
| Utah | 25 | ★ | 5 | ★ | E |
| Vermont | ... | ... | 2 | ... | E |
| Virginia | ... | ... | ... | ... | A (e) |
| Washington | ... | ★ | ★ | 30 days | E |
| West Virginia | 18 | ★ | ★ | ★ | E |
| Wisconsin | ... | ... | ... | ... | E |
| Wyoming* | 25 | ★ | ★ | ★ | E |
| Dist. of Columbia | ... | ... | ... | ... | (f) |
| Guam | 18 | 5 | 5 | ★ | ★ |
| Puerto Rico | ... | ... | ... | ... | A |
| U.S. Virgin Islands* | ... | ... | ... | ... | A |

*Source:* The Council of State Governments' survey, January 2000, except as noted by * where information is from *The Book of the States, 1998-99.*

*Note:* "Qualified Voter" provision may infer additional residency and citizenship requirements.

*Key:*

★ — Formal provision; number of years not specified.
. . . — No formal provision.
A — Appointed by the governor.
E — Elected by the voters.
L — Elected by the legislature.

(a) Appointed by State Depository Board.
(b) Residency requirements while in office.
(c) State resident and citizen requirement.
(d) No longer has a state treasurer, effective September 1, 1996. Duties transferred to the Comptroller of Public Accounts.
(e) Subject to confirmation by the General Assembly.
(f) Appointed by the chief financial officer.

## Table 2.22
## TREASURERS: DUTIES OF OFFICE

| State or other jurisdiction | Investment of excess funds | Investment of retirement and/or trust funds | Management of bonded debt | Bond issue | Debt service | Arbitrage rebate | Unclaimed property | Deferred compensation | Linked deposits | College savers program |
|---|---|---|---|---|---|---|---|---|---|---|
| Alabama | ★ | ★ | ... | ★ | ★ | ★ | ★ | ... | ★ | ★ |
| Alaska (n) | ★ | ★ (a) | ★ | ★ | ★ | ★ | ★ | ★ | ... | ★ |
| Arizona | ★ | ★ (a) | ... | ... | ... | ★ | ★ | ... | ... | ... |
| Arkansas* | ★ | ★ | ... | ... | ★ | ... | ... | ... | ... | ... |
| California | ★ | ★ | ★ | ★ | ★ | ★ | ... | ... | ... | ★ |
| Colorado | ★ | (d) | ... | ★(b) | ... | ... | ★ | (d) | ... | ★(I) |
| Connecticut* | ★ | ★ | ★ | ★ | ★ | ★ | ★ | ... | ... | ★ |
| Delaware | ★ | ... | ★ | ★ | ★ | ★ | ... | ★ | ... | ★(o) |
| Florida | ★ | ★ (p) | (d) | (d) | (d) | ... | ... | ★ | ... | (d) |
| Georgia | ★ | ... | ... | ... | ... | ... | ... | ... | ... | ... |
| Hawaii | ★ | ★ (a) | ★ | ★ | ★ | ★ | ★ | ... | ... | ★ |
| Idaho | ★ | ... | ★ | ★ | ★ | ... | ... | ... | ... | ... |
| Illinois | ★ | ★ (a) | ★(c) | ... | ★ | ★ | ★ | ... | ★ | ★ |
| Indiana* | ★ | ★ | ... | ... | ... | ... | ... | ... | ... | ★ |
| Iowa | ★ | ... | ★ | ★ | ... | ... | ★ | ... | ★ | ★ |
| Kansas | ★ | ... | ... | ★ | ★ | ... | ★ | ... | ... | ... |
| Kentucky | ★ | (d) | ... | ... | ... | ... | ★(b) | ... | N.A. | ... |
| Louisiana* | ★ | ... | ★ | ★ | ★ | ★ | ... | ... | ★ | ★ |
| Maine | ★ | ★ | ★ | ★ | ★ | ★ | ★ | ... | ★ | ★ |
| Maryland | ★ | ... | ★(c) | ★(c) | ★ | ★ | ... | ... | ★ | ... |
| Massachusetts | ★ | ★ | ★ | ★ | ★ | ★ | ★ | ★ | ★ | ★ |
| Michigan | ★ | ★ | ★ | ★ | ★ | ... | ★ | ★ | ★ | ★ |
| Minnesota | (d) | (d) | ★ | ... | ★ | ... | ★ | (d) | ... | (d) |
| Mississippi | ★ | (d) | ★ | ★ | ★ | ★ | ★ | (d) | ... | ★ |
| Missouri | ★ | (d) | (d) | (d) | ★ | ★ | ★ | ... | ★ | (d) |
| Montana | ... | ... | ★(b) | ★(b) | ★(b) | ★(b) | ... | ... | ... | ... |
| Nebraska* | ★ | ★ | ... | ... | ... | ... | ★ | ... | ... | ... |
| Nevada | ★ | ★ (e) | ★ | ★ | ★ | ... | ... | ... | ... | ★ |
| New Hampshire | ★ | ★ | ★ | ★ | ★ | ★ | ★ | ★ | ... | ★ |
| New Jersey | ... | ... | ★ | ★ | ★ | ★ | ★ | ... | ... | ★ |
| New Mexico | ★ | ★ (f) | ★ | (d) | ★ | ★ | ... | ... | ... | ... |
| New York | ★(g) | ... | ... | ... | ... | ... | ... | ... | ★(q) | ★(h) |
| North Carolina | ★ | ★ | ★ | ★ | ★ | ★ | ★ | ... | ... | ... |
| North Dakota | ★ | ... | ... | ... | ... | ... | ... | ... | .. | ... |
| Ohio* | ★ | ... | ... | ★ | ... | ... | ... | ... | ★ | ★ |
| Oklahoma | ★ | ... | ... | ... | ... | ... | ★ | ... | ★ | ★ |
| Oregon | ★ | ★ | ★ | ★ | ★ | ★(i) | (r) | ★(j) | ... | ★ |
| Pennsylvania | ★ | ★ | ... | ★ | ... | ... | ★ | ★(a) | ★ | ★ |
| Rhode Island | ★ | ★ | ★ | ★ | ★ | ★ | ★ | ★ | ★ | ★ |
| South Carolina | ★ | ★ (s) | ★ | ★ | ★ | ★ | ★ | ★ | ★ | ... |
| South Dakota | ★ | (d) | ... | ... | ★ | ... | ★ | ... | ... | ★ |
| Tennessee | ★ | ★ | ... | ... | ... | ... | ★ | ... | ★ | ★ |
| Texas | ------------------------------(k)------------------------------ | | | | | | | | | |
| Utah | ★ | ★ (e) | ★ | ★ | ★ | ★ | ★ | ... | ... | ★(j) |
| Vermont | ★ | ★ | ★ | ★ | ★ | ★ | ★ | ★ | ... | ... |
| Virginia | ★ | ★ (a) | ★ | ★ | ★ | ★ | ★ | ... | ... | (d) |
| Washington | ★ | (d) | ★ | ★ | ★ | ★ (i) | ... | (d) | ... | (d) |
| West Virginia | ... | (d) | ... | (t) | (c ) | ... | ★ | ... | N.A. | ★ |
| Wisconsin | ... | ... | ... | ... | ... | ... | ★ | ... | ... | ★ |
| Wyoming* | ★ | ★ (d) | ★ | ★ (m) | ★ | ★ | ★ | ★ | N.A. | ★(d) |
| Dist. of Columbia | ★ | ★ | ★ | ★ | ★ | ★ | ... | ★ | ... | ... |
| Guam | ★ (a) | ... | ... | ... | ★ (b) | ★(b) | ★(b) | ... | ★(b) | N.A. |
| Puerto Rico | ★ | ★ | ★ | ★ | ★ | ★ | ... | ... | ... | ... |

*Source*: The Council of State Governments' survey, January 2000, except as noted by * where information is from *The Book of the States, 1998-99.*

*Note*: For additional information on functions of the treasurers' offices, see Tables 6.5 - 6.7.

*Key*:
★ — Responsible for activity.
. . . — Not responsible for activity.
N.A. — Not available.

(a) State treasurer does invest certain trust funds, however, retirement funds are invested by the state retirement system. In Alaska, the commissioner of Revenue is sole fiduciary for certain trust funds; however, retirement funds are invested by State Pension Investment Board.
(b) Portions.
(c) General Obligation.
(d) As board member only.
(e) Except for Public Employees Retirement System.

# TREASURERS: DUTIES OF OFFICE - continued

(f) Short term.

(g) Commissioner of Taxation and Finance invests funds of a number of state entities, but does not invest the state's general fund monies. Commissioner serves as joint custodian of the general fund, but the state comptroller invests general fund monies.

(h) Not administered by Treasury.

(i) Contract out for actual services.

(j) Investment only.

(k) No longer has a state treasurer, effective September 1, 1996. Duties transferred to the Comptroller of Accounts.

(l) Short term portfolio only.

(m) State Board of Investments.

(n) The state of Alaska does not have a state treasurer. The Commissioner of Revenue, who is appointed by the Governor, is the person with these duties of office.

(o) Chair, Delaware College Investment Plan Board

(p) Treasurer's duties include investment of trust funds. As a member of 3 member State Board of Administration, shares responsibility for investing retirment funds.

(q) Both Treasurer and State Comptroller have programs.

(r ) State Land Board

(s) Treasurer's office invests fixed income securities. The Budget & Control Board invests in equities.

(t) Financial Advisor on certain issues.

# Chapter Three

# THE
# LEGISLATURES

*From citizen-lawmakers to full-time legislators, the legislatures run the gamut — includes information on legislative organization, operation and action, session lengths, legislative procedure, compensation, bill introductions and enactments, committee appointments, and a review of administrative regulations.*

For additional information on Chapter Three contact
The States Information Center, at The Council of State Governments,
(859) 244-8253 or E-mail: sic@csg.org.

## Table 3.1
## NAMES OF STATE LEGISLATIVE BODIES AND CONVENING PLACES

| State or other jurisdiction | Both bodies | Upper house | Lower house | Convening place |
|---|---|---|---|---|
| Alabama | Legislature | Senate | House of Representatives | State House |
| Alaska | Legislature | Senate | House of Representatives | State Capitol |
| Arizona | Legislature | Senate | House of Representatives | State Capitol |
| Arkansas | General Assembly | Senate | House of Representatives | State Capitol |
| California | Legislature | Senate | Assembly | State Capitol |
| Colorado | General Assembly | Senate | House of Representatives | State Capitol |
| Connecticut | General Assembly | Senate | House of Representatives | State Capitol |
| Delaware | General Assembly | Senate | House of Representatives | Legislative Hall |
| Florida | Legislature | Senate | House of Representatives | The Capitol |
| Georgia | General Assembly | Senate | House of Representatives | State Capitol |
| Hawaii | Legislature | Senate | House of Representatives | State Capitol |
| Idaho | Legislature | Senate | House of Representatives | State Capitol |
| Illinois | General Assembly | Senate | House of Representatives | State House |
| Indiana | General Assembly | Senate | House of Representatives | State House |
| Iowa | General Assembly | Senate | House of Representatives | State Capitol |
| Kansas | Legislature | Senate | House of Representatives | State Capitol |
| Kentucky | General Assembly | Senate | House of Representatives | State Capitol |
| Louisiana | Legislature | Senate | House of Representatives | State Capitol |
| Maine | Legislature | Senate | House of Representatives | State House |
| Maryland | General Assembly | Senate | House of Delegates | State House |
| Massachusetts | General Court | Senate | House of Representatives | State House |
| Michigan | Legislature | Senate | House of Representatives | State Capitol |
| Minnesota | Legislature | Senate | House of Representatives | State Capitol |
| Mississippi | Legislature | Senate | House of Representatives | New Capitol |
| Missouri | General Assembly | Senate | House of Representatives | State Capitol |
| Montana | Legislature | Senate | House of Representatives | State Capitol |
| Nebraska | Legislature | (a) | | State Capitol |
| Nevada | Legislature | Senate | Assembly | Legislative Building |
| New Hampshire | General Court | Senate | House of Representatives | State House |
| New Jersey | Legislature | Senate | General Assembly | State House |
| New Mexico | Legislature | Senate | House of Representatives | State Capitol |
| New York | Legislature | Senate | Assembly | State Capitol |
| North Carolina | General Assembly | Senate | House of Representatives | State Legislative Building |
| North Dakota | Legislative Assembly | Senate | House of Representatives | State Capitol |
| Ohio | General Assembly | Senate | House of Representatives | State House |
| Oklahoma | Legislature | Senate | House of Representatives | State Capitol |
| Oregon | Legislative Assembly | Senate | House of Representatives | State Capitol |
| Pennsylvania | General Assembly | Senate | House of Representatives | Main Capitol Building |
| Rhode Island | General Assembly | Senate | House of Representatives | State House |
| South Carolina | General Assembly | Senate | House of Representatives | State House |
| South Dakota | Legislature | Senate | House of Representatives | State Capitol |
| Tennessee | General Assembly | Senate | House of Representatives | State Capitol |
| Texas | Legislature | Senate | House of Representatives | State Capitol |
| Utah | Legislature | Senate | House of Representatives | State Capitol |
| Vermont | General Assembly | Senate | House of Representatives | State House |
| Virginia | General Assembly | Senate | House of Delegates | State Capitol |
| Washington | Legislature | Senate | House of Representatives | Legislative Building |
| West Virginia | Legislature | Senate | House of Delegates | State Capitol |
| Wisconsin | Legislature | Senate | Assembly (b) | State Capitol |
| Wyoming | Legislature | Senate | House of Representatives | State Capitol |
| Dist. of Columbia | Council of the District of Columbia | (a) | | District Building |
| American Samoa | Legislature | Senate | House of Representatives | Maota Fono |
| Guam | Legislature | (a) | | Congress Building |
| No. Mariana Islands | Legislature | Senate | House of Representatives | Civic Center Building |
| Puerto Rico | Legislative Assembly | Senate | House of Representatives | The Capitol |
| U.S. Virgin Islands | Legislature | (a) | | Capitol Building |

*Source:* The Council of State Governments, *Directory I - Elective Officials* 2000

(a) Unicameral legislature. Except in Dist. of Columbia, members go by the title Senator.
(b) Members of the lower house go by the title Representative.

# Table 3.2
## LEGISLATIVE SESSIONS: LEGAL PROVISIONS

| State or other jurisdiction | Regular sessions | | | | Special sessions | | |
|---|---|---|---|---|---|---|---|
| | Legislature convenes | | | Limitation on length of session (a) | Legislature may call | Legislature may determine subject | Limitation on length of session |
| | Year | Month | Day | | | | |
| Alabama | Annual | Jan. Apr. Feb. | 2nd Tues. (b) 3rd Tues. (c, d) 1st Tues. (e) | 30 L in 105 C | No | Yes (f) | 12 L in 30 C |
| Alaska | Annual | Jan. Jan. | 2nd Mon. 3rd Mon. (g) | 120 C (h) | By 2/3 vote of members | Yes (i) | 30 C |
| Arizona | Annual | Jan. | 2nd Mon. | (j) | By petition, 2/3 members, each house | Yes (i) | None |
| Arkansas | Biennial-odd year | Jan. | 2nd Mon. | 60 C (h) | No | Yes (f,k) | (k) |
| California | (l) | Jan. | 1st Mon. (d) | None | No | No | None |
| Colorado | Annual | Jan. | 2nd Wed. | 120 C | By request, 2/3 members, each house | Yes (i) | None |
| Connecticut | Annual (m) | Jan. Feb. | Wed. after 1st Mon. (n) Wed. after 1st Mon. (o) | (p) | Yes (q) | (q) | None (r) |
| Delaware | Annual | Jan. | 2nd Tues. | June 30 | Joint call, presiding officers, both houses | Yes | None |
| Florida | Annual | Mar. | Tues. after 1st Mon. (d) | 60 C (h) | Joint call, presiding officers, both houses | Yes (f) | 20 C (h) |
| Georgia | Annual | Jan. | 2nd Mon. | 40 L | By petition, 3/5 members, each house | Yes (i) | (s) |
| Hawaii | Annual | Jan. | 3rd Wed. | 60 L (h) | By petition, 2/3 members, each house | Yes | 30 L (h) |
| Idaho | Annual | Jan. | Mon. on or nearest 9th day | None | No | No | 20 C |
| Illinois | Annual | Jan. | 2nd Wed. | None | Joint call, presiding officers, both houses | Yes (i) | None |
| Indiana | Annual | Jan. | 2nd Mon. (d, t) | odd-61 L or Apr. 30; even-30 L or Mar. 15 | No | No | 30 L or 40 C |
| Iowa | Annual | Jan. | 2nd Mon. | (u) | No | No | None |
| Kansas | Annual | Jan. | 2nd Mon. | odd-None; even-90 C (h) | Petition to governor of 2/3 members, each house | Yes | None |
| Kentucky | Biennial-even year | Jan. | Tues after 1st Mon. (d) | 60 L (v) | No | No | None |
| Louisiana | Annual | Mar. Apr. | last Mon. (d, n) last Mon. (m, o) | odd-60 L in 85 C; even-30 L in 45 C | By petition, majority, each house | Yes (i) | 30 C |
| Maine | (l,m) | Dec. Jan. | 1st Wed. (b) Wed. after 1st Tues. (o) | 3rd Wed. of June (h) 3rd Wed. of April (h) | Joint call, presiding officers, with consent of majority of members of each political party, each house | Yes (i) | None |
| Maryland | Annual | Jan. | 2nd Wed. | 90 C (g) | By petition, majority, each house | Yes | 30 C |
| Massachusetts | Annual | Jan. | 1st Wed. | (w) | By petition (x) | Yes | None |
| Michigan | Annual | Jan. | 2nd Wed. (d) | None | No | No | None |
| Minnesota | (y) | Jan. | Tues. after 1st Mon. (n) | 120 L or 1st Mon. after 3rd Sat. in May (y) | No | Yes | None |

# LEGISLATIVE SESSIONS: LEGAL PROVISIONS — Continued

| State or other jurisdiction | Regular sessions | | | | Special sessions | | |
|---|---|---|---|---|---|---|---|
| | Legislature convenes | | | Limitation on length of session (a) | Legislature may call | Legislature may determine subject | Limitation on length of session |
| | Year | Month | Day | | | | |
| Mississippi | Annual | Jan. | Tues. after 1st Mon. | 125 C (h, z); 90 C (h, z) | No | No | None |
| Missouri | Annual | Jan. | Wed. after 1st Mon. | May 30 | By petition, 3/4 members, each house | Yes | 30 C (aa) |
| Montana | Biennial-odd year | Jan. | 1st Mon. | 90 L | By petition, majority, each house | Yes | None |
| Nebraska | Annual | Jan. | Wed. after 1st Mon. | odd-90 L (h); even-60 L (h) | By petition, 2/3 members | Yes | None |
| Nevada | Biennial-odd year | Jan. | 3rd Mon. | 60 C (u) | No | No | 20 C (u) |
| New Hampshire | Annual | Jan. | Wed. after 1st Tues. (d) | 45 L | By 2/3 vote of members, each house | Yes | 15 L (u) |
| New Jersey | Annual | Jan. | 2nd Tues. | None | By petition, majority, each house | Yes | None |
| New Mexico | Annual (m) | Jan. | 3rd Tues. | odd-60 C; even-30 C | By petition, 3/5 members, each house | Yes (i) | 30 C |
| New York | Annual | Jan. | Wed. after 1st Mon. | None | By petition, 2/3 members, each house | Yes (i) | None |
| North Carolina | (y) | Jan. | 3rd Wed. after 2nd Mon. (n) | None | By petition, 3/5 members, each house | Yes | None |
| North Dakota | Biennial-odd year | Jan. | Tues. after Jan. 3, but not later than Jan. 11 (d) | 80 L (bb) | No | Yes | None |
| Ohio | Annual | Jan. | 1st Mon. | None | Joint call, presiding officers, both houses | Yes | None |
| Oklahoma | Annual | Feb. | 1st Mon. (cc) | 160 C | By vote, 2/3 members, each house | Yes (i) | None |
| Oregon | Biennial-odd year | Jan. | 2nd Mon. after 1st Tues. | None | By petition, majority, each house | Yes | None |
| Pennsylvania | Annual | Jan. | 1st Tues. | None | By petition, majority each house | No | None |
| Rhode Island | Annual | Jan. | 1st. Tues. | 60 L (u) | No | No | None |
| South Carolina | Annual | Jan. | 2nd Tues. (d) | 1st Thurs. in June (h) | No | Yes | None |
| South Dakota | Annual | Jan. | 2nd Tues. | odd-40 L; even-35 L | No | No | None |
| Tennessee | Annual | Jan. | (dd) | 90 L (u) | By petition, 2/3 members, each house | Yes | 30 L (u) |
| Texas | Biennial-odd year | Jan. | 2nd Tues. | 140 C | No | No | 30 C |
| Utah | Annual | Jan. | 3rd. Mon. | 45 C | No | No | 30 C (ee) |
| Vermont | (y) | Jan. | Wed. after 1st Mon. (n) | None | No | Yes | None |
| Virginia | Annual | Jan. | 2nd Wed. | odd-30 C (h); even-60 C (h) | By petition, 2/3 members, each house | Yes | None |
| Washington | Annual | Jan. | 2nd Mon. | odd-105 C; even-60 C | By vote, 2/3 members, each house | Yes | 30 C |
| West Virginia | Annual | Feb. Jan. | 2nd Wed. (c, d) 2nd Wed. (e) | 60 C (h) | By petition, 3/5 members, each house | Yes (ff) | None |
| Wisconsin | Annual (gg) | Jan. | 1st Mon. (n) | None | No | No | None |

See footnotes at end of table.

# LEGISLATIVE SESSIONS: LEGAL PROVISIONS — Continued

| State or other jurisdiction | Regular sessions | | | | Special sessions | | |
|---|---|---|---|---|---|---|---|
| | Legislature convenes | | | Limitation on length of session (a) | Legislature may call | Legislature may determine subject | Limitation on length of session |
| | Year | Month | Day | | | | |
| Wyoming .................. | Annual (m) | Jan. Feb. | 2nd Tues. (n) 3rd Mon. (o) | odd-40 L; even-20 L | No | Yes | None |
| Dist. of Columbia .......... | (hh) | Jan. | 2nd day | None | | | |
| American Samoa ........... | Annual | Jan. July | 2nd Mon. 2nd Mon. | 45 L 45 L | No | No | None |
| Guam .................. | Annual | Jan. | 2nd Mon. (ii) | None | No | No | None |
| No. Mariana Islands ...... | Annual | (jj) | (d, jj) | 90 L (jj) | Upon request of presiding officers, both houses | Yes (i) | 10 C |
| Puerto Rico ...... | Annual | Jan. | 2nd Mon. | None | No | No | 20 C |
| U.S. Virgin Islands ........ | Annual | Jan. | 2nd Mon. | None | No | No | None |

*Sources:* State constitutions and statutes. The information in this table was compiled in 1998.

*Note:* Some legislatures will also reconvene after normal session to consider bills vetoed by governor. Connecticut—if governor vetoes any bill, secretary of state must reconvene General Assembly on second Monday after the last day on which governor is either authorized to transmit or has transmitted every bill with his objections, whichever occurs first: General Assembly must adjourn *sine die* not later than three days after its reconvening. Hawaii—legislature may reconvene on 45th day after adjournment *sine die*, in special session, without call. Louisiana—legislature meets in a maximum five-day veto session on the 40th day after final adjournment. Missouri—if governor returns any bill on or after the fifth day before the last day on which legislature may consider bills (in even-numbered years), legislature automatically reconvenes on first Wednesday following the second Monday in September for a maximum 10 C sessions. New Jersey—legislature meets in special session (without call or petition) to act on bills returned by governor on 45th day after *sine die* adjournment of the regular session; if the second year expires before the 45th day, the day preceding the end of the legislative year. Utah—if 2/3 of the members of each house favor reconvening to consider vetoed bills, a maximum five-day session is set by the presiding officers. Virginia—legislature reconvenes on sixth Wednesday after adjournment for a maximum three-day session (may be extended to seven days upon vote of majority of members elected to each house). Washington—upon petition of 2/3 of the members of each house, legislature meets 45 days after adjournment for a maximum five-day session.

Key:
C — Calendar day
L — Legislative day (in some states called a session day or workday; definition may vary slightly, however, generally refers to any day on which either house of legislature is in session).
(a) Applies to each year unless otherwise indicated.
(b) General election year (quadrennial election year).
(c) Year after quadrennial election.
(d) Legal provision for organizational session prior to stated convening date. Alabama—in the year after quadrennial election, second Tuesday in January for 10 C. California—in the even-numbered general election year, first Monday in December for an organizational session, recess until the first Monday in January of the odd-numbered year. Florida—in general election year, 14th day after election. Indiana—third Tuesday after first Monday in November. Kentucky—in odd-numbered year, Tuesday after first Monday in January for 10 L. Louisiana—in year after general election, second Monday in January, not to exceed 3 L. Michigan—held in odd-numbered year. New Hampshire—in even-numbered year, first Wednesday in December. North Dakota—in December. South Carolina—in even-numbered year, Tuesday after certification of election of its members for a maximum three-day session. West Virginia—in year after general election, on second Wednesday in January. No. Mariana Islands—in year after general election, second Monday in January.

(e) Other years.
(f) By 2/3 vote each house.
(g) Following a gubernatorial election year.
(h) Session may be extended by vote of members in both houses. Alaska—2/3 vote for 10-day extension. Arkansas—2/3 vote. Florida—3/5 vote. Hawaii—petition of 2/3 membership for maximum 15-day extension. Kansas—2/3 vote. Maine—2/3 vote for maximum 10 L. Maryland—3/5 vote for maximum 30 C. Mississippi—2/3 vote for 30 C extension, no limit on number of extensions. Nebraska—4/5 vote. South Carolina—2/3 vote. Virginia—2/3 vote for 30 C extension. West Virginia—2/3 vote (or if budget bill has not been acted upon three days before session ends, governor issues proclamation extending session). Puerto Rico—joint resolution.
(i) Only if legislature convenes itself. Special sessions called by the legislature are unlimited in scope in Arizona, Georgia, Maine, and New Mexico.
(j) No constitutional or statutory provision; however, legislative rules require that regular sessions adjourn no later than Saturday of the week during which the 100th day of the session falls.
(k) After governor's business has been disposed of, members may remain in session up to 15 C by a 2/3 vote of both houses.
(l) Regular sessions begin after general election, in December of even-numbered year. In California, legislature meets in December for an organizational session, recesses until the first Monday in January of the odd-numbered year and continues in session until Nov. 30 of next even-numbered year. In Maine, session which begins in December of general election year runs into the following year (odd-numbered); second session begins in next even-numbered year.
(m) Second session limited to consideration of specific types of legislation. Connecticut—individual legislators may only introduce bills of a fiscal nature, emergency legislation and bills raised by committees. Louisiana—fiscal matters. Maine—budgetary matters; legislation in the governor's call; emergency legislation; legislation referred to committees for study. New Mexico—budgets, appropriations and revenue bills; bills drawn pursuant to governor's message; vetoed bills. Wyoming—budget bills.
(n) Odd-numbered years.
(o) Even-numbered years.
(p) Odd-numbered years—not later than Wednesday after first Monday in June; even-numbered-years not later than Wednesday after first Monday in May.
(q) Constitution provides for regular session convening dates and allows that sessions may also be held "... at such other times as the General Assembly shall judge necessary." Call by majority of legislators is implied.
(r) Upon completion of business.
(s) Limited to 40 L unless extended by 3/5 vote and approved by the governor, except in cases of impeachment proceedings.

# LEGISLATIVE SESSIONS: LEGAL PROVISIONS — Continued

(t) Legislators may reconvene at any time after organizational meeting; however, second Monday in January is the final date by which regular session must be in process.

(u) Indirect limitation; usually restrictions on legislator's pay, per diem, or daily allowance.

(v) May not extend beyond April 15.

(w) Legislative rules say formal business must be concluded by Nov. 15th of the 1st session in the biennium, or by July 31st of the 2nd session for the biennium.

(x) Joint rules provide for the submission of a written statement requesting special session by a specified number of members of each chamber.

(y) Legal provision for session in odd-numbered year; however, legislature may divide, and in practice has divided, to meet in even-numbered years as well.

(z) 90 C sessions every year, except the first year of a gubernatorial administration during which the legislative session runs for 125 C.

(aa) 30 C if called by legislature; 60 C if called by governor.

(bb) No legislative day is shorter than a natural day.

(cc) Odd number years will include a regular session commencing on the first Tuesday after the first Monday in January and recessing not later than the first Monday in February of that year. Limited constitutional duties can be performed.

(dd) Commencement of regular session depends on concluding date of organizational session. Legislature meets, in odd-numbered year, on second Tuesday in January for a maximum 15 C organizational session, then returns on the Tuesday following the conclusion of the organizational session.

(ee) Except in cases of impeachment.

(ff) According to a 1955 attorney general's opinion, when the legislature has petitioned to the governor to be called into session, it may then act on any matter.

(gg) The legislature, by joint resolution, establishes the session schedule of activity for the remainder of the biennium at the beginning of the odd-numbered year.

(hh) Each Council period begins on January 2 of each odd-numbered year and ends on January 1 of the following odd-numbered year.

(ii) Legislature meets on the first Monday of each month following its initial session in January.

(jj) 60 L before April 1 and 30 L after July 31.

## Table 3.3
## THE LEGISLATORS: NUMBERS, TERMS, AND PARTY AFFILIATIONS
### (As of April 2000)

| State or other jurisdiction | Senate | | | | | | House | | | | | | Senate and House totals |
|---|---|---|---|---|---|---|---|---|---|---|---|---|---|
| | Democrats | Republicans | Other | Vacancies | Total | Term | Democrats | Republicans | Other | Vacancies | Total | Term | |
| All states ..................... | 1,048 | 950 | 11 | 6 | 2,079 | ... | 2,897 | 2,582 | 19 | 14 | 5,532 | ... | 7,611 |
| Alabama ......................... | 23 | 12 | ... | ... | 35 | 4 | 69 | 36 | ... | ... | 105 | 4 | 140 |
| Alaska ............................ | 5 | 15 | ... | ... | 20 | 4 | 14 | 26 | ... | ... | 40 | 2 | 60 |
| Arizona .......................... | 14 | 16 | ... | ... | 30 | 2 | 22 | 38 | ... | ... | 60 | 2 | 90 |
| Arkansas ........................ | 29 | 6 | ... | ... | 35 | 4 | 74 | 23 | ... | 3 | 100 | 2 | 135 |
| California ....................... | 24 | 15 | ... | 1 | 40 | 4 | 47 | 32 | 1 (a) | ... | 80 | 2 | 120 |
| Colorado ........................ | 15 | 20 | ... | ... | 35 | 4 | 25 | 40 | ... | ... | 65 | 2 | 100 |
| Connecticut .................... | 19 | 17 | ... | ... | 36 | 2 | 96 | 55 | ... | ... | 151 | 2 | 187 |
| Delaware ........................ | 13 | 8 | ... | ... | 21 | 4 | 15 | 26 | ... | ... | 41 | 2 | 62 |
| Florida ........................... | 15 | 24 | ... | 1 | 40 | 4 | 47 | 73 | ... | ... | 120 | 2 | 160 |
| Georgia .......................... | 33 | 22 | ... | 1 | 56 | 2 | 102 | 78 | ... | ... | 180 | 2 | 236 |
| Hawaii ........................... | 23 | 2 | ... | ... | 25 | 4 | 38 | 12 | ... | 1 | 51 | 2 | 76 |
| Idaho ............................. | 4 | 31 | ... | ... | 35 | 2 | 12 | 58 | ... | ... | 70 | 2 | 105 |
| Illinois ........................... | 27 | 32 | ... | ... | 59 | (b) | 62 | 56 | ... | ... | 118 | 2 | 177 |
| Indiana .......................... | 19 | 31 | ... | ... | 50 | 4 | 53 | 47 | ... | ... | 100 | 2 | 150 |
| Iowa .............................. | 20 | 30 | ... | ... | 50 | 4 | 44 | 56 | ... | ... | 100 | 2 | 150 |
| Kansas ........................... | 13 | 27 | ... | ... | 40 | 4 | 48 | 77 | ... | ... | 125 | 2 | 165 |
| Kentucky ........................ | 18 | 20 | ... | ... | 38 | 4 | 64 | 35 | ... | 1 | 100 | 2 | 138 |
| Louisiana ....................... | 28 | 11 | ... | ... | 39 | 4 | 75 | 30 | ... | ... | 105 | 4 | 144 |
| Maine ............................ | 19 | 15 | 1 (a) | ... | 35 | 2 | 81 | 69 | 1 (a) | ... | 151 | 2 | 186 |
| Maryland ....................... | 32 | 15 | ... | ... | 47 | 4 | 106 | 35 | ... | ... | 141 | 4 | 188 |
| Massachusetts ................ | 32 | 8 | ... | ... | 40 | 2 | 128 | 29 | 1 (a) | 2 | 160 | 2 | 200 |
| Michigan ........................ | 15 | 23 | ... | ... | 38 | 4 | 52 | 58 | ... | ... | 110 | 2 | 148 |
| Minnesota ...................... | 40 (c) | 26 (d) | 1(a) | ... | 67 | 4 | 63(c) | 70 (d) | 1 (a) | ... | 134 | 2 | 201 |
| Mississippi ..................... | 34 | 18 | ... | ... | 52 | 4 | 86 | 33 | 3 (a) | ... | 122 | 4 | 174 |
| Missouri ......................... | 18 | 16 | ... | ... | 34 | 4 | 86 | 76 | 1 (a) | ... | 163 | 2 | 197 |
| Montana ......................... | 18 | 32 | ... | ... | 50 | 4 | 41 | 59 | ... | ... | 100 | 2 | 150 |
| Nebraska ........................ | ----------Nonpartisan election---------- | | | | 49 | 4 | ------------------------------Unicameral------------------------ | | | | | | 49 |
| Nevada ........................... | 9 | 12 | ... | ... | 21 | 4 | 28 | 14 | ... | ... | 42 | 2 | 63 |
| New Hampshire .............. | 12 | 12 | ... | ... | 24 | 2 | 153 | 244 | 1 (a) | 2 | 400 | 2 | 424 |
| New Jersey ..................... | 16 | 24 | ... | ... | 40 | 4 (e) | 32 | 48 | ... | ... | 80 | 2 | 120 |
| New Mexico .................... | 25 | 17 | ... | ... | 42 | 4 | 40 | 30 | ... | ... | 70 | 2 | 112 |
| New York ....................... | 23 | 36 | ... | 2 | 61 | 2 | 98 | 52 | ... | 0 | 150 | 2 | 211 |
| North Carolina ............... | 35 | 15 | ... | ... | 50 | 2 | 66 | 54 | ... | ... | 120 | 2 | 170 |
| North Dakota ................. | 18 | 31 | ... | ... | 49 | 4 | 34 | 63 | ... | 1 | 98 | 4 | 147 |
| Ohio .............................. | 12 | 21 | ... | ... | 33 | 4 | 39 | 59 | ... | 1 | 99 | 2 | 132 |
| Oklahoma ...................... | 33 | 15 | ... | ... | 48 | 4 | 61 | 40 | ... | ... | 101 | 2 | 149 |
| Oregon ........................... | 13 | 17 | ... | ... | 30 | 4 | 25 | 35 | ... | ... | 60 | 2 | 90 |
| Pennsylvania .................. | 20 | 30 | ... | ... | 50 | 4 | 100 | 103 | ... | ... | 203 | 2 | 253 |
| Rhode Island .................. | 42 | 8 | ... | ... | 50 | 2 | 85 | 12 | 1 (a) | 2 | 100 | 2 | 150 |
| South Carolina ............... | 24 | 22 | ... | ... | 46 | 4 | 57 | 67 | ... | ... | 124 | 2 | 170 |
| South Dakota .................. | 13 | 22 | ... | ... | 35 | 2 | 19 | 51 | ... | ... | 70 | 2 | 105 |
| Tennessee ....................... | 18 | 15 | ... | ... | 33 | 4 | 61 | 38 | ... | ... | 99 | 2 | 132 |
| Texas ............................. | 15 | 16 | ... | ... | 31 | 4 | 78 | 71 | ... | 1 | 150 | 2 | 181 |
| Utah .............................. | 11 | 18 | ... | ... | 29 | 4 | 21 | 54 | ... | ... | 75 | 2 | 104 |
| Vermont ......................... | 17 | 13 | ... | ... | 30 | 2 | 77 | 67 | 6 (f) | ... | 150 | 2 | 180 |
| Virginia ......................... | 20 | 20 | ... | ... | 40 | 4 | 47 | 52 | 1 (a) | ... | 100 | 2 | 140 |
| Washington ..................... | 27 | 22 | ... | ... | 49 | 4 | 49 | 49 | ... | ... | 98 | 2 | 147 |
| West Virginia .................. | 29 | 5 | ... | ... | 34 | 4 | 75 | 25 | ... | ... | 100 | 2 | 134 |
| Wisconsin ....................... | 17 | 16 | ... | ... | 33 | 4 | 44 | 55 | ... | ... | 99 | 2 | 132 |
| Wyoming ........................ | 10 | 20 | ... | ... | 30 | 4 | 17 | 43 | ... | ... | 60 | 2 | 90 |
| Dist. of Columbia (g) ..... | 11 | 2 | ... | ... | 13 | 4 | ------------------------------Unicameral------------------------ | | | | | | 13 |
| American Samoa ............. | ----------Nonpartisan election---------- | | | | 18 | 4 | ----------Nonpartisan election---------- | | | | 20 | 2 | 38 |
| Guam ............................. | 3 | 12 | ... | ... | 15 | 2 | ------------------------------Unicameral------------------------ | | | | | | 15 |
| No. Mariana Islands ...... | 0 | 7 | 1(m) | 1 | 9 | 4 | 6 | 11 | 1(a) | ... | 18 | 2 | 27 |
| Puerto Rico .................... | 19 (i) | 8 (j) | 1 (k) | ... | 28 | 4 | 37 (i) | 16 (j) | 1 (k) | ... | 54 | 4 | 82 |
| U.S. Virgin Islands ......... | 6 | 2 | 7 (l) | ... | 15 | 2 | ------------------------------Unicameral------------------------ | | | | | | 15 |

# THE LEGISLATORS: NUMBERS, TERMS, AND PARTY AFFILIATIONS — Continued

*Source*: The Council of State Governments, *Directory I - Elective Officials 2000*.

(a) Independent.

(b) The entire Senate is up for election every 10 years, beginning in 1972. Senate districts are divided into three groups. One group elects senators for terms of four years, four years and two years; the second group for terms of four years, two years and four years; the third group for terms of two years, four years, and four years.

(c) Democrat-Farmer-Labor.

(d) Independent-Republican.

(e) The first senatorial term at the beginning of each decade is 2 years.

(f) Independent (2); Progressive (4).

(g) Council of the District of Columbia.

(h) Statehood

(i) New Progressive Party.

(j) Popular Democratic Party.

(k) Puerto Rico Independent Party.

(l) Independent (5); Independent Citizens Movement (2).

(m) Reform.

## Table 3.4
## MEMBERSHIP TURNOVER IN THE LEGISLATURES: 2000

| State or other jurisdiction | Senate | | | House | | |
|---|---|---|---|---|---|---|
| | Total number of members | Number of membership changes | Percentage change of total | Total number of members | Number of membership changes | Percentage change of total |
| Alabama | 35 | 0 | 0 | 105 | 0 | 0 |
| Alaska | 20 | 0 | 0 | 40 | 2 | 5 |
| Arizona | 30 | 0 | 0 | 60 | 0 | 0 |
| Arkansas | 35 | 0 | 0 | 100 | 3 | 3 |
| California | 40 | 0 | 0 | 80 | 1 | 1 |
| Colorado | 35 | 0 | 0 | 65 | 4 | 6 |
| Connecticut | 36 | 0 | 0 | 151 | 3 | 2 |
| Delaware | 21 | 0 | 0 | 41 | 0 | 0 |
| Florida | 40 | 1 | 3 | 120 | 4 | 3 |
| Georgia | 56 | 0 | 0 | 180 | 1 | 5 |
| Hawaii | 25 | 0 | 0 | 51 | 0 | 0 |
| Idaho | 35 | 0 | 0 | 70 | 4 | 6 |
| Illinois | 59 | 2 | 3 | 118 | 1 | 1 |
| Indiana | 50 | 1 | 2 | 100 | 1 | 1 |
| Iowa | 50 | 0 | 0 | 100 | 2 | 2 |
| Kansas | 40 | 0 | 0 | 125 | 1 | 1 |
| Kentucky | 38 | 0 | 0 | 100 | 1 | 1 |
| Louisiana | 39 | 10 | 25 | 105 | 21 | 20 |
| Maine | 35 | 0 | 0 | 151 | 1 | 5 |
| Maryland | 47 | 0 | 0 | 141 | 2 | 1 |
| Massachusetts | 40 | 2 | 5 | 160 | 8 | 5 |
| Michigan | 38 | 1 | 3 | 110 | 0 | 0 |
| Minnesota | 67 | 4 | 6 | 134 | 1 | 1 |
| Mississippi | 52 | 8 | 15 | 122 | 25 | 20 |
| Missouri | 34 | 0 | 0 | 163 | 4 | 2 |
| Montana | 50 | 0 | 0 | 100 | 0 | 0 |
| Nebraska | 49 | 3 | 6 | Unicameral | | |
| Nevada | 21 | 0 | 0 | 42 | 0 | 0 |
| New Hampshire | 24 | 1 | 4 | 400 | 4 | 1 |
| New Jersey | 40 | 1 | 3 | 80 | 0 | 0 |
| New Mexico | 42 | 0 | 0 | 70 | 0 | 0 |
| New York | 61 | 2 | 3 | 150 | 1 | 5 |
| North Carolina | 50 | 0 | 0 | 120 | 2 | 2 |
| North Dakota | 49 | 0 | 0 | 98 | 0 | 0 |
| Ohio | 33 | 0 | 0 | 99 | 9 | 9 |
| Oklahoma | 48 | 0 | 0 | 101 | 0 | 0 |
| Oregon | 30 | 0 | 0 | 60 | 0 | 0 |
| Pennsylvania | 50 | 0 | 0 | 203 | 0 | 0 |
| Rhode Island | 50 | 0 | 0 | 100 | 0 | 0 |
| South Carolina | 46 | 1 | 2 | 124 | 5 | 4 |
| South Dakota | 35 | 0 | 0 | 70 | 1 | 1 |
| Tennessee | 33 | 0 | 0 | 99 | 0 | 0 |
| Texas | 31 | 1 | 3 | 150 | 0 | 0 |
| Utah | 29 | 0 | 0 | 75 | 1 | 1 |
| Vermont | 30 | 0 | 0 | 150 | 3 | 2 |
| Virginia | 40 | 4 | 10 | 100 | 8 | 8 |
| Washington | 49 | 1 | 2 | 98 | 1 | 1 |
| West Virginia | 34 | 1 | 3 | 100 | 3 | 3 |
| Wisconsin | 33 | 0 | 0 | 99 | 0 | 0 |
| Wyoming | 30 | 0 | 0 | 60 | 5 | 8 |
| Dist. of Columbia | 13 | 0 | 0 | Unicameral | | |
| American Samoa | 18 | 1 | 6 | 20 | 0 | 0 |
| Guam | 15 | 0 | 0 | Unicameral | | |
| No. Mariana Islands | 9 | 1 | 10 | 18 | 9 | 50 |
| Puerto Rico | 28 | 1 | 4 | 54 | 3 | 6 |
| U.S. Virgin Islands | 15 | 0 | 0 | Unicameral | | |

*Source:* The Council of State Governments, *Directory I Elective Officials 2000*

*Note:* Turnover calculated after 1999 legislative elections.

## Table 3.5
## THE LEGISLATORS: QUALIFICATIONS FOR ELECTION

| State or other jurisdiction | House Minimum age | House U.S. citizen (years) | House State resident (years) | House District resident (years) | House Qualified voter (years) | Senate Minimum age | Senate U.S. citizen (years) | Senate State resident (years) | Senate District resident (years) | Senate Qualified voter (years) |
|---|---|---|---|---|---|---|---|---|---|---|
| Alabama | 21 | … | 3 (a) | 1 | … | 25 | … | 3 (a) | 1 | ★ |
| Alaska | 21 | … | 3 | 1 | ★ | 25 | … | 3 | 1 | … |
| Arizona | 25 | ★ | 3 | 1 | … | 25 | ★ | 3 | 1 | … |
| Arkansas | 21 | ★ | 2 | 1 | … | 25 | ★ | 2 | 1 | … |
| California | 18 | 3 | 3 | 1 | ★ | 18 | 3 | 3 | 1 | ★ |
| Colorado | 25 | ★ | … | 1 | ★ | 25 | ★ | … | 1 | ★ |
| Connecticut | 18 | … | 3 (a) | ★ | ★ | 18 | … | 3 (a) | ★ | … |
| Delaware | 24 | … | 3 (a) | ★ | … | 27 | … | 3 (a) | ★ | ★ |
| Florida | 21 | … | 2 | 1 | ★ | 21 | … | 2 | 1 | … |
| Georgia | 21 | ★ | 2 (a) | 1 | … | 25 | ★ | 2 (a) | 1 | ★ |
| Hawaii | 18 | … | 3 | (b) | ★ | 18 | … | 3 | (b) | ★ |
| Idaho | 18 | … | … | 1 | ★ | 18 | … | … | 1 | … |
| Illinois | 21 | ★ | … | 2 (c) | … | 21 | ★ | … | 2 (c) | ★ |
| Indiana | 21 | ★ | 2 | 1 | … | 25 | ★ | 2 | 1 | … |
| Iowa | 21 | ★ | 1 | 60 days | … | 25 | ★ | 1 | 60 days | … |
| Kansas | 18 | … | 2 (a) | 1 | ★ | 18 | … | 6 (a) | H | ★ |
| Kentucky | 24 | … | 2 | 1 | … | 30 | … | 2 | 1 | … |
| Louisiana | 18 | 5 | 1 | 3 mo. | … | 18 | 5 | 1 | 3 mo. | … |
| Maine | 21 | … | 1 (a) | 6 mo. (d) | ★ | 25 | … | 1 (a) | 6 mo. (d) | ★ |
| Maryland | 21 | … | … | … | ★ | 25 | … | 5 | ★ | ★ |
| Massachusetts | 18 | ★ | … | 1 | ★ | 18 | ★ | 5 | ★ | ★ |
| Michigan | 21 | … | 1 | (b) | ★ | 21 | … | 1 | (b) | … |
| Minnesota | 18 | … | 1 | 6 mo. | ★ | 18 | … | 1 | 6 mo. | ★ |
| Mississippi | 21 | … | 4 (a) | 2 | 2 | 25 | … | … | 2 | 4 |
| Missouri | 24 | … | 1 | 1 (e) | 2 | 30 | … | 1 | 1 (e) | 3 |
| Montana | 18 | … | 1 | 6 mo. (f) | ★ | 18 | … | 1 | 6 mo. (f) | ★ |
| Nebraska | | | | | | 21 | … | 1 (a) | 1 | ★ |
| Nevada | 21 | … | 1 (a) | 1 | ★ | 21 | … | 1 (a) | 1 | … |
| New Hampshire | 18 | … | 2 | ★ | … | 30 | … | 7 | ★ | … |
| New Jersey | 21 | … | 2 (a) | 1 | ★ | 30 | … | 4 (a) | 1 | … |
| New Mexico | 21 | … | … | ★ | … | 25 | … | … | ★ | … |
| New York | 18 | ★ | 5 | 1 (g) | ★ | 18 | ★ | 5 | 1 (g) | ★ |
| North Carolina | (h) | … | 1 | 1 | ★ | 25 | … | 2 (a) | 1 | ★ |
| North Dakota | 18 | … | 1 | (b) | ★ | 18 | … | 1 | (b) | … |
| Ohio | 18 | … | … | 1 | ★ | 18 | … | … | 1 | … |
| Oklahoma | 21 | … | … | (b) | ★ | 25 | … | … | (b) | ★ |
| Oregon | 21 | ★ | … | 1 | … | 21 | ★ | 1 | 1 | … |
| Pennsylvania | 21 | … | … | 1 | … | 25 | … | … | 1 | … |
| Rhode Island | 18 | … | … | 1 | ★ | 18 | … | … | … | ★ |
| South Carolina | 21 | … | … | (b) | ★ | 25 | … | … | (b) | ★ |

See footnotes at end of table.

# THE LEGISLATORS: QUALIFICATIONS FOR ELECTION — Continued

| State or other jurisdiction | House | | | | | Senate | | | | |
|---|---|---|---|---|---|---|---|---|---|---|
| | Minimum age | U.S. citizen (years) | State resident (years) | District resident (years) | Qualified voter (years) | Minimum age | U.S. citizen (years) | State resident (years) | District resident (years) | Qualified voter (years) |
| South Dakota | 21 | ★ | 2 | (b) | ★ | 21 | ★ | 2 | (b) | ★ |
| Tennessee | 21 | ★ | 3 (a) | 1 (b) | ★ | 30 | ★ | 3 | 1 (b) | ★ |
| Texas | 21 | ★ | 2 | 1 | ★ | 26 | ★ | 5 | 1 | ★ |
| Utah | 25 | ★ | 3 | 6 mo. (b) | ★ | 25 | ★ | 3 | 6 mo. (b) | ★ |
| Vermont | 18 | ... | 2 | 1 | ★ | 18 | ... | 2 | 1 | ... |
| Virginia | 21 | ... | ... | ★ | ★ | 21 | ★ | ... | ★ | ★ |
| Washington | 18 | ★ | ... | (b) | ★ | 18 | ... | ... | (b) | ★ |
| West Virginia | 18 | ... | 5 (a) | 1 | ★ | 25 | ... | 5 (a) | 1 | ★ |
| Wisconsin | 18 | ... | 1 | (b) | ★ | 18 | ... | 1 | (b) | ★ |
| Wyoming | 21 | ★ | (a) | 1 | ... | 25 | ★ | (a) | 1 | ... |
| Dist. of Columbia | U | U | ★ | U | U | 18 | ... | 1 | ★ | ... |
| American Samoa | 25 | ★(i) | 5 | 1 | U | 30 (j) | ★(i) | 5 | 1 | ★ |
| Guam | U | U | ★ | U | U | 25 | ★ | 5 | 1 | ... |
| No. Mariana Islands | 21 | ... | 3 | ... | ★ | 25 | ... | 5 | ... | ★ |
| Puerto Rico (k) | 25 | ... | 2 | 1 (l) | ... | 30 | ... | 2 | 1 (l) | ... |
| U.S. Virgin Islands | 21 | ★ | ... | 3 | ... | 21 | ... | 3 | 3 | ★ |

Sources: State constitutions and statutes.

Note: Many state constitutions have additional provisions disqualifying persons from holding office if they are convicted of a felony, bribery, perjury or other infamous crimes.

Key:

U — Unicameral legislature; members are called senators, except in District of Columbia.

★ — Formal provision; number of years not specified.

... — No formal provision.

(a) State citizenship requirement.

(b) Must be a qualified voter of the district; number of years not specified.

(c) Following redistricting, a candidate may be elected from any district that contains a part of the district in which he resided at the time of redistricting, and reelected if a resident of the new district he represents for 18 months prior to reelection.

(d) If the district was established for less than six months, residency is length of establishment of district.

(e) Only if the district has been in existence for one year; if not, then legislator must have been a one year resident of the district(s) from which the new district was created.

(f) Shall be a resident of the county if it contains one or more districts or of the district if it contains all or parts of more than one county.

(g) After redistricting, must have been a resident of the county in which the district is contained for one year immediately preceding election.

(h) A conflict exists between two articles of the constitution, one specifying age for House members (i.e., "qualified voter of the state") and the other related to general eligibility for elective office (i.e., "every qualified voter . . . who is 21 years of age . . . shall be eligible for election").

(i) Or U.S. national.

(j) Must be registered matai.

(k) Read and write the Spanish or English language.

(l) When there is more than one representative district in a municipality, residence in the municipality shall satisfy this requirement.

# Table 3.6
## SENATE LEADERSHIP POSITIONS — METHODS OF SELECTION

| State or other jurisdiction | President | President pro tem | Majority leader | Assistant majority leader | Majority floor leader | Assistant majority floor leader | Majority whip | Majority caucus chairman | Minority leader | Assistant minority leader | Minority floor leader | Assistant minority floor leader | Minority whip | Minority caucus chairman |
|---|---|---|---|---|---|---|---|---|---|---|---|---|---|---|
| Alabama | (a) | ES | AT | ... | ... | ... | ... | ... | AP | ... | ... | ... | ... | ... |
| Alaska | ES | EC | EC | ... | ... | ... | EC | ... | EC | ... | ... | ... | EC | ... |
| Arizona* | ES | AP | EC | ... | ... | ... | EC | ... | EC | EC | ... | ... | EC | ... |
| Arkansas | (a) | ES | EC | ... | EC | ... | EC | EC | EC | ... | ... | ... | EC | EC |
| California | (a) | ES | ... | ... | EC | ... | EC | EC | EC | ... | EC | ... | ... | EC |
| Colorado | ES | ES | EC | EC | ... | ... | AT | ... | EC | EC | ... | ... | AL | ... |
| Connecticut (b) | (a) | ES | AT | AT | ... | ... | ... | ... | EC | AL/8 | ... | ... | EC | ... |
| Delaware | (a) | EC (c) | EC | EC (mm) | ... | ... | EC | ... | EC (d) | EC (e) | EC/2 | ... | EC | ... |
| Florida | ES | ES | EC | ... | ... | ... | EC | ... | EC | ... | ... | ... | EC | ... |
| Georgia | (a) | ES | EC | ... | ... | ... | EC | EC | EC | ... | ... | ... | EC | EC |
| Hawaii | ES | ES (f) | EC | EC | EC | ... | EC (j) | EC | EC | EC | EC | ... | EC | EC |
| Idaho | (a) | ES | EC | ... | ... | ... | EC | AP | EC | EC | EC | ... | EC | AL |
| Illinois | ES | ... | AP (g) | AP/6 | AT | ... | AT | EC | EC | AL/5 | EC | ... | EC | EC |
| Indiana | (a) | ES | EC | EC | AT | AT | AT | EC | EC | EC | EC | AT | EC | EC |
| Iowa | ES | ES | EC | EC | ... | ... | ... | ... | EC | EC | EC | ... | EC | EC |
| Kansas (h) | ES | ES (f) | EC | EC (i) | EC (i) | ... | EC (j) | (j) | EC | EC | EC | (l) | EC | EC |
| Kentucky | ES | ES | EC | EC | ... | ... | EC | EC | EC | EC | EC | ... | EC | EC |
| Louisiana | ES | ES | EC (l) | EC (l) | (l) | (l) | ... | ... | EC (l) | EC (l) | (l) | (l) | ... | ... |
| Maine* | ES | AP (k) | AP (n) | AP,AL (o) | (m) | (o) | AP,AL | ... | EC | EC (l) | (l) | ... | EC | ... |
| Maryland (m) | ES | ES | AP (n) | AP,AL (o) | ... | ... | AP,AL | EC | EC | ... | ... | ... | EC | ... |
| Massachusetts* | EC (p) | ... | AP | AP/2 | ... | ... | ... | (p) | EC (p) | AL/3 | ... | ... | EC (p) | (p) |
| Michigan | (a) | ES | EC | EC | EC | EC | EC | EC | EC | EC | EC | EC | EC | EC |
| Minnesota | ES | ES | EC | EC | EC | EC | AL/4 | ... | EC | EC/6 | EC | EC | EC/6 (q) | ... |
| Mississippi | (a) | ES | EC | ... | ... | ... | EC | EC | EC | EC | ... | ... | EC | ... |
| Missouri | (a) | ES | EC | EC | EC | EC | EC | EC | EC | EC | EC | EC | EC | EC |
| Montana | ES | ES | EC | ES | ES | ... | ES | ... | ES | ES | ES | ... | ES | ... |
| Nebraska (U) | ES (r) | ES (r) | ... | ... | ... | ... | ... | ... | ... | ... | ... | ... | ... | ... |
| Nevada | (a) | ES | EC | EC | EC | EC | EC | EC | EC | EC | EC | EC | EC | EC |
| New Hampshire (s) | ES | ES | EC | EC/3 | ... | ... | EC | EC | EC | EC/3 | EC | EC | EC | EC |
| New Jersey (t) | ES | ES | EC | EC/3 | ... | ... | EC | EC | EC | EC/3 | EC | EC | EC | EC |
| New Mexico | (a) | ES | EC (u) | ... | EC (u) | ... | EC | EC | EC | AL/3 | EC | EC | EC | EC |
| New York* (v) | (a) ES | ES (w) | (w) | AT/2 | ... | ... | AT | AT (x) | EC | AL/3 | ... | ... | AL | AL (x) |
| North Carolina (y) | (a) | ES | EC | EC | ... | ... | EC | EC | EC | EC | ... | EC | AL | EC |
| North Dakota | (a) | ES | EC | EC | ... | ... | ES | EC | ES (p) | ES | ES | EC | ES | (p) |
| Ohio (z) | ES (p) | ES | EC | EC | ... | ... | ES | (p) | EC (p) | EC | EC | ES | EC (aa) | (p) |
| Oklahoma | (a) | ES | EC | EC | ... | ... | EC | EC | EC | EC | EC | EC | EC | EC |
| Oregon | ES | ES | EC | AL/7 | ... | ... | EC | (p) | EC (p) | EC/3 | EC/3 | ... | EC/1 | (p) |
| Pennsylvania* | (a) | ES | EC | EC | ... | ... | EC | EC | EC (aa) | EC/3 | ... | ... | EC (aa) | EC |
| Rhode Island* (y) | (a) | ES | EC | AL/6 (bb) | ... | ... | AL | ... | EC | AL/2 (bb) | ... | ... | AL | ... |
| South Carolina* | (a) | ES | ... | ... | ... | ... | ... | ... | ... | ... | ... | ... | ... | ... |

See footnotes at end of table.

## SENATE LEADERSHIP POSITIONS — METHODS OF SELECTION — Continued

| State or other jurisdiction | President | President pro tem | Majority leader | Assistant majority leader | Majority floor leader | Assistant majority floor leader | Majority whip | Majority caucus chairman | Minority leader | Assistant minority leader | Minority floor leader | Assistant minority floor leader | Minority whip | Minority caucus chairman |
|---|---|---|---|---|---|---|---|---|---|---|---|---|---|---|
| South Dakota | (a) | ES | EC/2 | EC | ... | ... | EC/2 | ... | EC | EC | ... | ... | EC/2 | ... |
| Tennessee | ES (s) | AP (cc) | EC (cc) | ... | ... | ... | ... | EC (cc) | EC (cc) | ... | ... | ... | ... | EC (cc) |
| Texas | (a) | ES | EC | EC | ... | ... | ... | ... | EC | EC | ... | ... | ... | ... |
| Utah (dd) | ES (ee) | ... | EC | ... | ... | ... | EC | ... | EC | ... | ... | ... | EC | ... |
| Vermont | (a) | ES | EC | EC (ff) | EC (ff) | ... | (ff) | ... | EC | EC (ff) | EC (ff) | ... | (ff) | EC (cc) |
| Virginia | (a) | ES | EC | ... | EC | ... | EC | EC | EC (nn) | ... | EC | ... | EC | EC |
| Washington (gg) | (a) | ES | EC | ... | EC | ... | AP | EC | EC (hh) | EC (hh) | EC (hh) | EC (hh) | EC (hh) | EC (hh) |
| West Virginia* | ES | AP | AP | ... | ... | ... | AP | EC | EC | ... | EC | ... | AL | EC |
| Wisconsin | ES | ES | EC | EC | EC | ... | EC | EC | EC | EC | EC | ... | EC | EC |
| Wyoming | ES | ES (f) | ... | ... | ... | ... | ... | EC | EC | ... | ... | ... | ... | EC |
| Dist. of Columbia* (U) | (ii) | (jj) | ... | ... | ... | ... | ... | ... | ... | ... | ... | ... | ... | ... |
| American Samoa* (U) | ES | ES (f) | ... | ... | ... | ... | ... | ... | ... | ... | ... | ... | ... | ... |
| Guam* (U) | ES (r) | ES (f) | EC | EC | ... | ... | EC | ... | EC | EC | ... | ... | EC | ... |
| No. Mariana Islands* | ES (h) | ... | (h) | ... | ES (kk) | ... | ... | ... | EC | ... | EC (ll) | ... | ... | ... |
| Puerto Rico* | ES (p) | ES (f) | EC | ... | EC (ll) | ... | ... | (p) | EC/2 (p) | ... | EC (ll) | ... | ... | (p) |
| U.S. Virgin Islands* (U) | ES | ES (f) | ES | ... | (n) | ... | ... | (n) | ... | ... | ... | ... | ... | ... |

Source: The Council of State Governments' survey, January 2000, except where noted by * where data are from The Book of the States, 1998-99.

Note: In some states, the leadership positions in the Senate are not empowered by the law or by the rules of the chamber, but rather by the party members themselves. Entry following slash indicates number of individuals holding specified position.

Key:
ES — Elected or confirmed by all members of the Senate.
EC — Elected by party caucus.
AP — Appointed by president.
AT — Appointed by president pro tempore.
AL — Appointed by party leader.
(U) — Unicameral legislative body.
. . . — Position does not exist or is not selected on a regular basis.
(a) Lieutenant governor is president of the Senate by virtue of the office.
(b) Additional positions include deputy president pro tem, two deputy majority leaders (EC), minority leader pro tem, and two deputy minority leaders (appointed by minority leader and approved by party caucus).
(c) Approved by Senate members.
(d) Preferred title is Democratic leader.
(e) Official title is minority leader pro tempore.
(f) Official title is vice president. In Guam, vice speaker.
(g) The president can, at his or her discretion, serve as majority leader and usually does.
(h) Additional positions include minority agenda chair (EC).
(i) Assistant majority leader also serves as majority party caucus chairperson.
(j) Official title is assistant majority leader/whip.
(k) Appointed only in the president's absence.

(l) Majority leader also serves as majority floor leader; assistant majority leader also serves as assistant majority floor leader; minority leader; minority leader also serves as minority floor leader; assistant minority leader also serves as assistant minority floor leader.
(m) Other positions include deputy majority leader, deputy majority whip and assistant deputy majority whip; these positions are appointed by president and majority leader.
(n) Majority leader also serves as majority floor leader.
(o) Official title is deputy majority leader. Also serves as assistant majority floor leader.
(p) President and minority floor leader are also caucus chairmen. In Ohio and Puerto Rico, president and minority leader. In Oregon, majority leader and minority leader.
(q) Official title is assistant minority leader/minority whip.
(r) Official title is speaker. In Tennessee, official also has the statutory title of "lieutenant governor."
(s) Additional positions include a Republican leader and a Democratic leader.
(t) Additional positions include deputy majority leader (EC), two deputy assistant minority leaders (EC), and minority leader pro tem (EC).
(u) Majority leader also serves as majority floor leader. Minority leader also serves as minority floor leader.
(v) Additional positions include vice-president pro tem (AT), deputy majority leader (AT), majority program development chairman (AT), deputy minority leader (AL), senior assistant majority leader (AT), majority conference vice-chairman (AT), minority conference vice-chairman (AL), majority conference secretary (AL), deputy majority whip (AT), majority steering committee chairman (AT), minority conference secretary (AL), assistant majority whip (AT), and assistant minority whip (AL).
(w) President pro tempore is also majority leader.
(x) Majority caucus chairman: official title is majority conference chairman. Minority caucus chairman: official title is minority conference chairman.
(y) Additional positions include deputy president pro tempore.
(z) Additional positions include assistant president pro tempore (ES) and assistant minority whip (ES).

# SENATE LEADERSHIP POSITIONS — METHODS OF SELECTION — Continued

(aa) Customary title of minority party leaders is the party designation (Democratic).

(bb) Assistant majority leader: official title is deputy majority leader. Assistant minority leader: official title is deputy minority leader.

(cc) President pro tem: official title is speaker pro tem. Official titles of majority party leaders: Democratic; official titles of minority party leaders: Republican.

(dd) Additional positions include assistant majority whip (EC) and assistant minority whip (EC).

(ee) The president is elected in caucus but is formally and officially nominated and elected by acclamation on the 1st day of session by the entire body of senate.

(ff) Assistant majority leader also serves as majority whip. Assistant minority whip also serves as minority whip.

(gg) Additional positions include vice president pro tem (ES), majority assistant whip (EC), and Republican assistant whip (EC).

(hh) Customary title of minority party leaders is the party designation (Republican).

(ii) Chairman of the Council, which is an elected position.

(jj) Appointed by the chairman; official title is chairman pro tem.

(kk) Official title is floor leader.

(ll) Office title is alternate floor leader.

(mm) Official title is majority leader pro tempore.

(nn) Serves as minority floor leader.

## Table 3.7
## HOUSE LEADERSHIP POSITIONS — METHODS OF SELECTION

| State or other jurisdiction | Speaker | Speaker pro tem | Majority leader | Assistant majority leader | Majority floor leader | Assistant majority floor leader | Majority whip | Majority caucus chairman | Minority leader | Assistant minority leader | Minority floor leader | Assistant minority floor leader | Minority whip | Minority caucus chairman |
|---|---|---|---|---|---|---|---|---|---|---|---|---|---|---|
| Alabama | EH | EH | EC | … | … | … | … | … | EC | … | … | … | … | … |
| Alaska* | EH | EC | EC | … | … | … | EC | … | EC | EC | … | EC | EC | EC |
| Arizona* | EH | AS | EC | … | … | … | EC | … | EC | EC | … | EC | EC | EC |
| Arkansas | EH | AS | EC | EC | … | … | EC | … | EC | EC | … | EC | EC | EC |
| California | EH | AS | … | EC | AS | … | EC | … | EC | EC | EC | … | AL (a) | EC |
| Colorado | EH | AS | EC | EC | … | … | EC (c) | EC | EC | EC | … | EC | EC | EC |
| Connecticut | EH | AS/3 (b) | EC | (c) | … | … | AS (c) | AS (z) | EC | AL/8 (d) | AL/8 (d) | … | AL | EC |
| Delaware | EC (e) | EH | EC | AS | AS (z) | … | EC | AS (z) | EC | … | AL | AL | AL | EC |
| Florida | EH | EH | AS | AS | AS (z) | … | AS | AS (g) | EC | AL/6 | AL/2 (g) | (h) | AL | AL (g) |
| Georgia | EH | EH | EC | EC | EC | … | EC | EC | EC | AL/6 | EC | (h) | EC | (h) |
| Hawaii | EH (b) | EH (b) | EC | EC | EC | EC | EC | EC | EC | EC | EC | … | EC | EC |
| Idaho | EH | EH | EC | EC | EC | EC | EC | EC | EC | EC | EC | … | EC | EC |
| Illinois | EH | AS | AS | AS/6 | AS/2 (g) | … | AS | AS (g) | EC | AL/6 | EC | … | EC | AL (g) |
| Indiana | EH | … | EC | EC | EC | … | EC | EC | EC | AL/6 | EC | (h) | (h) | (h) |
| Iowa | EH | AS | EC | EC | EC | … | EC | EC | EC | EC | EC | … | EC | EC |
| Kansas (i) | EH | EH | EC | EC | EC | … | EC | EC | EC | EC | EC | … | EC | EC |
| Kentucky | EH | EH | EC | EC | EC | … | EC | EC | EC | EC | EC | … | EC | EC |
| Louisiana | EH | AS | AS | AS/6 | … | … | AS | AS | EC | AL | … | … | AL | … |
| Maine* | EC (k) | AS (j) | EC (k) | EC (k) | (k) | (k) | EC | EC (k) | EC (k) | EC (k) | (k) | (k) | EC | EC |
| Maryland (l) | EH | EH | AS (m) | EC | (m) | AS | AS | (p) | EC | AL/8 | AL | … | … | … |
| Massachusetts* | EC (p) | … | AS | AS/2 | … | … | EC | (p) | EC (p) | AL | EC | … | EC | (p) |
| Michigan | EH | EH | EC (q) | EC/8 | EC | … | EC | (p) | EC (p) | EC | EC | … | EC | (p) |
| Minnesota | EH | AS | … | … | (q) | … | AS | AS | EC | AL/8 | (q) | … | EC | EC |
| Mississippi | EH | EH | EC | EC | EC | … | EC | EC | EC | … | … | … | … | … |
| Missouri* | EH | EH | EC | EC | EC | EC | EC | EC | EC | EC | EC | … | EC | EC |
| Montana | EH | EH | EH | … | EH | … | EH | EH | EH (p) | EH | EH | EH | EH | EH |
| Nebraska | (r) | … | … | … | … | … | … | … | … | … | … | … | … | … |
| Nevada | EH | AS (b) | AS | … | … | EC | EC | EC | EC | AL (s) | EC | … | EC | EC (u) |
| New Hampshire (t) | EH | AS (b) | AS | AS | EC | EC | AS | AS | AS (s) | EC/4 | EC | … | AL | EC |
| New Jersey (t) | EH | EH | EC | EC/3 | EC | … | EC | EC | EC | … | … | … | EC | EC |
| New Mexico | EH | EH | EC (m) | … | EC (m) | EC | EC | EC | EH (p) | AL | EC | … | EC | EC (u) |
| New York*(v) | EH | AS | AS (m) | AS | … | … | AS | AS (w) | EC | AL/2 | … | EC | AL | EC |
| North Carolina | EH | EH | EC | EC | … | … | EC | EC | EC | AL/2 | EC | … | AL | AL (w) |
| North Dakota | EH | EH | EC | EC | … | … | EC | EC | EC | EC | EC | … | EC | EC |
| Ohio (x) | EH (p) | EH | EC | EC | EH | … | EH | EC | EH (p) | EH | EC/3 (dd) | … | EH | (p) |
| Oklahoma (y) | EH | EH | EC (z) | AS/2 | AS | AS/7 | AS/2 | EC | EC (z) | AL/2 | EC/3 | … | EC/2 | EC |
| Oregon | EH | EH | EC | … | EC | … | EC | (z) | EC (z) | AL/2 | … | … | EC/3 | (z) |
| Pennsylvania | EH | AS (cc) | EC | AL/6 | EC | … | EC | (z) | EC (aa) | AL/2 | EC/3 | … | EC (aa) | (z) |
| Rhode Island* (bb) | EH | AS (cc) | EC | EC/11 (n) | EC | … | EC | EC | EC | EC | … | … | EC | EC |
| South Carolina* (ee)* | EH | EH | EC | EC | EC | … | EC (ff) | … | EC | EC | … | … | EC | EC |

See footnotes at end of table.

# HOUSE LEADERSHIP POSITIONS — METHODS OF SELECTION — Continued

| State or other jurisdiction | Speaker | Speaker pro tem | Majority leader | Assistant majority leader | Majority floor leader | Assistant majority floor leader | Majority whip | Majority caucus chairman | Minority leader | Assistant minority leader | Minority floor leader | Assistant minority floor leader | Minority whip | Minority caucus chairman |
|---|---|---|---|---|---|---|---|---|---|---|---|---|---|---|
| South Dakota (gg) | EH | EH | EC | EC | . . . | . . . | EC/4 | . . . | EC | EC | . . . | . . . | EC/2 | . . . |
| Tennessee | EH | EH | EC | EC | EC | EC | EC | . . . | EC | EC | EC | EC | EC | EC |
| Texas | EH | AS | EC | . . . | . . . | . . . | EC | . . . | EC | . . . | EC | . . . | EC | EC |
| Utah (hh) | EH (ii) | . . . | EC | EC (i) | . . . | . . . | EC | . . . | EC (jj) | EC (jj) | . . . | . . . | EC | . . . |
| Vermont | EH | . . . | EC | . . . | . . . | . . . | (jj) | . . . | EC | . . . | EC | . . . | (jj) | . . . |
| Virginia | EH | EH | EC (q) | . . . | (q) | EC/2 | EC | EC (q) | EC (q) | . . . | (q) | EC | (EC) | EC |
| Washington (kk) | EH | EH | EC | . . . | . . . | . . . | EC | EC (ll) | EC | . . . | EC | . . . | (EC) | EC |
| West Virginia | EH | AS | AS | EC | . . . | . . . | AS | EC | EC | AL | AL | . . . | . . . | AL |
| Wisconsin | EH | EH | EC | . . . | . . . | . . . | EC | EC | . . . | EC | . . . | EC | EC | EC |
| Wyoming | . . . | EH | . . . | . . . | EC | . . . | . . . | . . . | . . . | . . . | EC | EC | EC | EC |
| Dist. of Columbia* | (r) | EH (b) | . . . | | | | | | | | | | | |
| American Samoa* | (r) | EH | . . . | | | | | | | | | | | |
| Guam* | EH (mm) | . . . | (mm) | . . . | EH (nn) | . . . | . . . | . . . | EC | . . . | EC (oo) | . . . | . . . | . . . |
| No. Mariana Islands* | . . . | EH (b) | EC | EC (oo) | . . . | . . . | . . . | (o) | (p) | . . . | . . . | EC (oo) | . . . | (p) |
| Puerto Rico* | EH (p) | . . . | EC | | | | | | | | | | | |
| U.S. Virgin Islands* | (r) | | | | | | | | | | | | | |

*Source:* The Council of State Governments' legislative survey January 2000, except where noted by * where data are from *The Book of the States, 1998-99.*

*Note:* In some states, the leadership positions in the house are not empowered by the law or by the rules of the chamber, but rather by the party members themselves. Entry following slash indicates number of individuals holding specified position.

Key:
EH — Elected or confirmed by all members of the house.
EC — Elected by party caucus.
AS — Appointed by speaker.
AL — Appointed by party leader.
. . . — Position does not exist or is not selected on a regular basis.

(a) Appointed by minority floor leader.
(b) Official title is deputy speaker. In Hawaii, American Samoa and Puerto Rico, vice speaker.
(c) Four deputy majority leaders are appointed by majority leader and 16 assistant majority leaders are appointed by the speaker in consultation with the majority leader; three majority whips are appointed by speaker in consultation with the majority lead
(d) Minority leader pro tempore, three deputy minority leaders, six assistant minority leaders and one minority whip appointed by minority leader.
(e) Approved by house members.
(f) Official titles: assistant majority leader is deputy majority leader, majority floor leader is majority floor whip, assistant majority floor leader is freshman majority whip, assistant minority leader is Republican leader pro tem. Other titles of minority floor leaders are designated by party affiliation (Republican).
(g) Official titles: majority floor leader is deputy majority leader, majority caucus chairman is majority conference chairperson, minority floor leader is deputy minority leader, and minority caucus chairman is minority conference chairperson.

(h) Appointed by minority floor leader.
(i) Additional positions include minority agenda chair (EC) and minority policy chair (EC).
(j) Appointed only in the speaker's absence.
(k) Majority leader also serves as majority floor leader; assistant majority leader also serves as assistant majority floor leader; minority leader also serves as minority floor leader; assistant minority leader also serves as assistant minority floor lea
(l) Additional positions include deputy speaker pro tem, parliamentarian, deputy majority leader, 13 deputy majority whips and 3 deputy minority whips.
(m) Majority leader also serves as majority floor leader.
(n) Official title is assistant majority leader.
(o) Official title is assistant minority whip.
(p) Speaker and minority leader are also caucus chairmen.
(q) Majority leader also serves as majority floor leader; minority leader also serves as minority floor leader(r)
Unicameral legislature; see entries in Table 3.6, "Senate Leadership Positions — Methods of Selection."
(s) Official titles: minority leader is Democratic leader and assistant minority leader is deputy Democratic leader.
(t) Additional positions include four deputy speakers (EC), three assistant majority whips (EC), majority budget officer (EC), minority leader pro tem (EC), and three deputy minority leaders (EC).
(u) Official titles: majority caucus chairman is majority conference leader and minority caucus chairman is conference chairman.

# HOUSE LEADERSHIP POSITIONS — METHODS OF SELECTION — Continued

(v) Additional positions: deputy speaker (AS), assistant speaker (AS), assistant speaker pro tem (AS), minority leader pro tem (AL), assistant minority leader pro tem (AL), deputy majority leader (AS), deputy minority leader (AL), deputy majority whip (AS) deputy minority whip (AL), assistant majority whip (AS), assistant minority whip (AL), majority conference vice-chairman (AS), minority conference vice-chairman (AL), majority conference secretary (AS), minority conference secretary (AL), majority steering committee chairman (AS), majority steering committee vice-chairman (AS), minority steering committee chairman (AL), minority steering committee vice-chairman (AL), majority program committee chairman (and minority program committee chairman (AL).

(w) Official titles: majority caucus chairman is majority conference chairman; minority caucus chairman is minority conference chairman.

(x) Additional positions include assistant majority whip (EH) and assistant minority whip (EH).

(y) Additional positions include assistant majority whip and minority caucus secretary.

(z) Majority leader also serves as majority caucus chairman; minority leader also serves as minority caucus chairman.

(aa) Official titles: minority leader is Republican leader and minority whip is Republican whip.

(bb) Additional positions include first deputy speaker (AS).

(cc) Official title is senior speaker pro tem.

(dd) Official title is deputy minority leader.

(ee) Additional positions include two deputy majority whips, three assistant majority whips, and two freshman whips.

(ff) Official title is chief deputy majority whip.

(gg) Additional positions include three assistant majority whips (EC).

(hh) Additional positions include assistant majority whip and assistant minority whip (EC).

(ii) Speaker is elected in caucus but the formal nomination and election by acclamation take place the first day of the session by the entire body of house.

(jj) Assistant majority leader also serves as majority whip; assistant minority leader also serves as minority whip.

(kk) Additional positions include three assistant minority whips, all positions are established by caucus rule and can change each biennium.

(ll) Additional position is caucus vice chair (EC).

(mm) Speaker also serves as majority leader.

(nn) Official title is floor leader.

(oo) Official title is alternate floor leader.

## Table 3.8
## METHOD OF SETTING LEGISLATIVE COMPENSATION
## (As of March 24, 1999)

| State or other jurisdiction | Constitution | Legislature | Compensation commission | Legislators' salaries tied or related to state employees' salaries |
|---|---|---|---|---|
| Alabama | ★ | . . . | ★ | . . . |
| Alaska | . . . | ★ | ★ | . . . |
| Arizona | . . . | . . . | ★ (a) | . . . |
| Arkansas | ★ | ★ | . . . | . . . |
| California | ★ | . . . | ★ | . . . |
| Colorado | . . . | ★ | . . . | . . . |
| Connecticut | . . . | . . . | ★ (b) | . . . |
| Delaware | . . . | ★ | ★ | . . . |
| Florida | . . . | ★ | . . . | Statute provides members same percentage increase as state employees. |
| Georgia | . . . | ★ | . . . | . . . |
| Hawaii | . . . | . . . | ★ (c) | . . . |
| Idaho | . . . | . . . | ★ | . . . |
| Illinois | . . . | ★ | ★ | Employment cost index, wages and salaries for state and local government workers. |
| Indiana | . . . | ★ | . . . | . . . |
| Iowa | . . . | ★ | ★ | . . . |
| Kansas | . . . | ★ | . . . | . . . |
| Kentucky | . . . | . . . | ★ | . . . |
| Louisiana | . . . | ★ | . . . | . . . |
| Maine | ★ | ★ | ★ | . . . |
| Maryland | . . . | . . . | ★ (d) | . . . |
| Massachusetts | . . . | ★ | . . . | . . . |
| Michigan | . . . | . . . | ★ (e) | . . . |
| Minnesota | . . . | ★ | ★ | . . . |
| Mississippi | . . . | ★ | . . . | . . . |
| Missouri | ★ | ★ | . . . | |
| Montana | . . . | ★ | . . . | Tied to executive branch pay matrix. |
| Nebraska | ★ | ★ | . . . | . . . |
| Nevada | . . . | ★ | . . . | . . . |
| New Hampshire | ★ | . . . | . . . | . . . |
| New Jersey | ★ | ★ | ★ | . . . |
| New Mexico | ★ | ★ | . . . | . . . |
| New York | ★ | ★ | . . . | . . . |
| North Carolina | . . . | ★ | . . . | . . . |
| North Dakota | . . . | ★ | ★ | . . . |
| Ohio | ★ | ★ | . . . | . . . |
| Oklahoma | . . . | ★ | ★ | . . . |
| Oregon | . . . | ★ | . . . | . . . |
| Pennsylvania | . . . | ★ | . . . | . . . |
| Rhode Island | ★ | . . . | . . . | . . . |
| South Carolina | . . . | ★ | . . . | . . . |
| South Dakota | ★ | ★ | . . . | . . . |
| Tennessee | ★ | ★ | . . . | . . . |
| Texas | ★ | . . . | . . . | . . . |
| Utah | . . . | . . . | ★ | . . . |
| Vermont | . . . | ★ | . . . | . . . |
| Virginia | ★ | ★ | . . . | . . . |
| Washington | ★ | ★ | ★ | . . . |
| West Virginia | . . . | . . . | ★ (f) | . . . |
| Wisconsin | . . . | ★ (g) | . . . | . . . |
| Wyoming | . . . | ★ | . . . | . . . |
| Dist. of Columbia | . . . | ★ | . . . | . . . |

See footnotes at end of table.

# METHOD OF SETTING LEGISLATIVE COMPENSATION — Continued

*Source:* National Conference of State Legislatures.
*Key:*
★ — Method used to set compensation.
. . . — Method not used to set compensation.
(a) Arizona commission recommendations are put on ballot for a vote of the people.
(b) The Connecticut General Assembly takes independent action pursuant to recommendations of a Compensation Committee.
(c) Hawaii commission recommendations effective unless legislature or governor disapproves by official action. Any change in salary that becomes effective does not apply to the legislature to which the recommendation was submitted.

(d) Maryland commission meets before each four-year term of office and presents recommendations to General Assembly for its action. Recommendations may be reduced or rejected, not increased.
(e) If resolution is offered, it is put to legislative vote; if legislature does not vote recommendations down, the new salaries take effect 1/1 of the new year.
(f) Submits, by resolution and must be concurred by at least four members of the commission. The Legislature must enact the resolution into law and may reduce, but shall not increase, any item established in such resolution.
(g) Approved by Joint Committee on Employment Relations and governor.

## Table 3.9
## LEGISLATIVE COMPENSATION: REGULAR SESSIONS
### (As of March 24, 1999)

| State or other jurisdiction | Salaries Regular sessions Per diem salary (a) | Limit on days | Annual salary | Travel allowance (as of March 24, 1999) Cents per mile | Round trips home to capital during session | Per diem living expenses |
|---|---|---|---|---|---|---|
| Alabama | $10/C | ... | ... | (b) | One | $2,280/m plus $50 three times/w for committee meetings attended (U). Out-of-state travel, actual expenses. |
| Alaska | ... | ... | $24,012 | (f) | ... | $173 (U). |
| Arizona | ... | ... | $24,000 | 30 | ... | $35/d for the 1st 120 days of regular session and for special session and $10/d thereafter; members residing outside Maricopa County receive an additional $25/d for the 1st 120 days of regular session and for special session and an additional $10/d thereafter (U). Set by statute. |
| Arkansas* | ... | ... | $12,500 | 31/House 32.5/Senate 31/Sen. Int. | Weekly | $89/d (V) tied to federal rate. |
| California | ... | ... | $99,000 | 24 | ... | $121/d Sunday through Saturday (U). Tied to federal rate. |
| Colorado | ... | ... | $30,000 | 20 24/4wd | ... | $45 ($99 for members outside Denver metro area) (V). Per diem is determined by the legislature. |
| Connecticut | ... | ... | $21,788 | 31 | ... | None. |
| Delaware | ... | ... | $29,574 | 25 (c) | ... | None. |
| Florida | ... | ... | $26,388 | 29 | ... | $102/d; not to exceed $3,640 for the house; not to exceed $4093.26 for the senate for the regular session (V). |
| Georgia (e) | ... | ... | $11,347.80 | 25 | ... | $75 (U) set by the legislature; $2,200 per diem differential account with max of 50 days. |
| Hawaii | ... | ... | $32,000 | ... | ... | $80 for members living outside Oahu; $10/d for members living on Oahu (V) set by the legislature. |
| Idaho | ... | ... | $14,760 | 26 | ... | $75 ($40 for legislators who do not establish a second residence in Boise) (U) set by commission. |
| Illinois | ... | ... | $50,803 | 32.5 | ... | $85 (U) tied to federal rate. |
| Indiana | ... | ... | $11,600 | 28 | ... | $112 (U) tied to federal rate. |
| Iowa | ... | ... | $20,758 | 24 | ... | $86 ($65 for Polk Cty. members) (U) set by the legislature. |
| Kansas | $72.06/C | ... | ... | 31 | ... | $80 (U) tied to federal rate. |
| Kentucky* | $151.00/C (i) ... $107.48/C (i) | ... | ... | (V) | ... | $88/d (U) tied to federal rate. |
| Louisiana | ... | ... | $16,800 | 32.5 | ... | $97 (U) tied to federal rate. Additional $6,000/yr (U) expense allowance. |
| Maine (j) | ... | ... | $10,500 - 1st $7,500 - 2nd | 24 | Weekly | For legislative session days and authorized committee meetings (V): $38 housing, $32 meals set by commission and the legislature. |
| Maryland | ... | ... | $30,591 | 29 | ... | Lodging $96; meals tied to federal rate and compensation commision (V). |
| Massachusetts | ... | ... | $46,410 | (g) | ... | $9-50 depending on distance from State House |
| Michigan | ... | ... | $55,054 | 31 | ... | $10,000 yearly expense allowances for session and interim (V) set by compensation commission. |
| Minnesota | ... | ... | $31,140 | (k) | ... | $56/legislative day (U) set by legislature. |
| Mississippi | ... | ... | $10,000 | 31 | ... | $99/d (U). |
| Missouri | ... | ... | $26,802.96 | 29.5 | ... | $68.80/d when present (U) tied to federal rate. |
| Montana* | $59.672/L | ... | ... | ... | Four | $75 (U) tied to rates in adjoining states. |
| Nebraska | ... | ... | $12,000 | 30 | Weekly | $84 ($34 if member resides within 50 miles of capitol) (V) tied to federal rate. |
| Nevada* | $130 | 60 | ... | (f) | ... | Federal rate for capitol area (V). |
| New Hampshire | ... | 2 yr. term | $200 | 38 for first 45 miles, 19 thereafter | ... | None. |
| New Jersey | ... | ... | $35,000 | ... | ... | None. |

See footnotes at end of table.

## LEGISLATIVE COMPENSATION:
## REGULAR SESSIONS — Continued

| State or other jurisdiction | Salaries — Regular sessions | | | Travel allowance (as of March 24, 1999) | | Per diem living expenses |
|---|---|---|---|---|---|---|
| | Per diem salary (a) | Limit on days | Annual salary | Cents per mile | Round trips home to capital during session | |
| New Mexico | ... | ... | ... | 32.5 (f) | ... | $124 (V) tied to federal rate. |
| New York | ... | ... | $79,500 | 29 | ... | $89; $130 in New York City metro area(V) set by legislature. |
| North Carolina | ... | ... | $13,951 | 29 | Weekly | $104 (U) set by statute. |
| North Dakota | $111/C | ... | ... | 25 | Weekly | $650/m housing (V). $250/m additional compensation |
| Ohio | ... | | $42,426.90 | 27 | Weekly | None. |
| Oklahoma | ... | ... | $38,400 | 32.5 (f) | ... | $97 (U) tied to federal rate. |
| Oregon* | ... | ... | $14,496 | 30 | ... | $87 (U) tied to federal rate. |
| Pennsylvania | ... | ... | $59,245.74 | 32.5 (f) | ... | $115 (V) tied to high/low substantiation method of revenue procedure 98-64. |
| Rhode Island | ... | ... | $10,768 | 32.5 | ... | None. |
| South Carolina | ... | ... | $10,400 | 31 | ... | $88/L (U); (V) for non statewide session days; for non session days $35/d; plus $1,000/m treated as income, not an approved expense plan. |
| South Dakota | ... | ... | $12,000/2 yr | 24 (l) | ... | $95/L (U) set by the legislature. |
| Tennessee | ... | ... | $16,500 | 26 (m) | ... | $114 (U). Request for per diem form must be submitted to Legislative Administration. |
| Texas* | ... | ... | $7,200 | 28(h) | ... | $118 (U) set by Ethics Commission. |
| Utah | $100/C | ... | ... | 31 | ... | $46/d and $76 for housing regardless of location (U) tied to federal rate. |
| Vermont | ... | ... | $536/w | 32.5 | ... | $50 for lodging and $37 for meals; commuters: $32 for meals (U) set by the legislature. |
| Virginia | ... | ... | Senate- $18,000 House- $17,640 | 27 | ... | $114 (U) tied to federal rate. |
| Washington | ... | ... | $28,300 | 31 | One | $82 (U) tied to federal rate. |
| West Virginia | ... | ... | $15,000 | 32 | Weekly | $85 (U); noncommuters $45 (U). |
| Wisconsin | ... | ... | $41,809 | 29 | Weekly | $75 maximum (U) set by the legislature. |
| Wyoming | $125/C | ... | ... | 35 | ... | $80 (U) set by the legislature. |
| Dist. of Columbia | ... | ... | $80,605 | ... | ... | None. |
| Guam | ... | ... | $55,307.20 | (n) | ... | None. |
| Puerto Rico | ... | ... | $40,000 | ... | ... | $93 within 50 km of capitol; $103 if outside 50 km (U). |
| U.S. Virgin Islands | ... | ... | $65,000 | ... | ... | $30/d in winter; $20/d in summer (V) set by the legislature. |

*Source:* National Conference of State Legislatures.

*Note:* In many states, legislators who receive an annual salary or per diem salary also receive an additional per diem amount for living expenses. Consult appropriate columns for a more complete picture of legislative compensation during sessions. For information on interim compensation and other direct payments and services to legislators, see Table 3.10, *"Legislative Compensation: Interim Payments and Other Direct Payments."*

\* — Biennial session. In Arkansas, Oregon and Texas, legislators receive an annual salary.

Key:
C — Calendar day
L — Legislative day
(U) — Unvouchered
(V) — Vouchered
d — day
w — week
m — month
y — year
. . . — Not applicable
(a) Legislators paid on a per diem basis receive the same rate during a special session.
(b) $50-75/day for in-state travel.
(c) Official business only.
(d) Varies - funds come from office expense allowance.

(e) $2,200 per diem differential rate. Georgia law states the maximum per diem plus per diem differential is $119/d. The per diem differential account is made up of the difference between the maximum allowance less the actual per diem paid x 50 days.
(f) Tied to federal mileage rate.
(g) Between $5-50 determined by distance from State House.
(h) An allowance in Texas for single, twin and turbo engines from .40 - $1/mile is also given.
(i) In Kentucky, per diem salary of $151.00/C is for members elected in 1998. The rate of $107.48/C applies to members up for re-election in 2000.
(j) In Maine, legislators who "commute" daily are eligible to be reimbursed for their mileage at the standard rate of .24/mile up to $38/day. This is termed "mileage in lieu of lodging."
(k) House: range of $60-550 for in-district mileage. Senate: a reasonable allowance.
(l) .24/mile for one round trip from Pierre to home each weekend. One trip is paid at .05/mile. During the interim, .24/mile for scheduled committee meetings.
(m) Members residing 100 miles from the capitol may be reimbursed a coach class airline ticket, limited to 1 per week of session or a committee meeting upon approval.
(n) Reimbursed for fuel purchase receipts.

# Table 3.10
## LEGISLATIVE COMPENSATION: INTERIM PAYMENTS AND OTHER DIRECT PAYMENTS

| State or other jurisdiction | Per diem compensation and living expenses for committee or official business during interim (as of March 1999) | Other direct payments or services to legislators (as of March 1999) |
|---|---|---|
| Alabama | $2280/m plus $50/d per diem. | None. |
| Alaska | $65/d (V); must work at least 4 hrs. or attend public meeting | $6,000/y for postage, stationary and other legislative expenses. Staffing allowance determined by rules and presiding officers, depending on time of year. |
| Arizona | $35/d with prior approval of presiding officer (V) set by statute. | None. |
| Arkansas | Legislators must sign in with budget officers. $89/d (V) tied to federal rate. Members are required to sign a "Per Diem Sheet" at each interim meeting/function. | Legislators are entitled to receive a maximum reimbursement of $9,600/y for legislative expenses. |
| California | $121/d; expenses over $121/d with receipt. | $240,000/y covers non-specified salary expenses, travel costs, publications, printing, postage, etc. |
| Colorado | Members are reimbursed for actual expenses. | $2,000/y |
| Connecticut | None. | Senato's receive $5,500/y and Representatives receive $4,500/y for staffing allowance. |
| Delaware | None. | None. |
| Florida | $50/d per diem or actual hotel plus $3 breakfast; $6 lunch; $12 dinner for authorized travel during committee weeks (V) set by Florida statutes. | $1,566 41/m for office expenses. |
| Georgia (a) | $75/d and .25/mile for committee service (V) set by the legislature. A committee roster is submitted with the members who attended the meeting. Those that did not attend do not get paid. | $4,800,y reimbursable expense account. If the member requests and provides receipts, the member is reimbursed for personal services, office equipment, rent, supplies, transportation, telecommunications, etc. |
| Hawaii | $10/d for official business on island of legal residence; $80/d for business on another island (V) set by the legislature. | House $4,500/m for Jan.-April staffing. Senate varies between $350-500/d for staffing allowance. |
| Idaho | None. | $500/y for unvouchered constituent expense. No staffing allowance. |
| Illinois | None. | Senators receive $67,000/y and Representatives $57,000/y for office expenses, including district offices and staffing. |
| Indiana | $112/d (V) tied to federal rate. | $25/d, 7 days a week during interim only. No staffing allowance. |
| Iowa | $86/d (U) set by the legislature. | $200/m to cover district constituency postage, travel, telephone and other expenses. No staffing allowance. |
| Kansas | $80/d. expenses for members attending interim committee as a member of that committee (V) tied to federal rate. Also, $270 for 20 pay periods ($5,400) considered taxable income. | $5,400/y which is taxable income to the legislators. Staffing allowances vary for leadership who have their own budget. Legislators provided with secretaries during the session only. |
| Kentucky | $1,435/m interim monthly expenses (U). Actual expenses up to a maximum for meals. | None. |
| Louisiana | Actual state government rate for lodging (V). $97/d (U) tied to federal rate. | $500/m pluse a $1,500 supplemental allowance for vouchered office expenses, rent, travel mileage in district, telephone and supplies. $2,000/m starting salary up to $3,000/m with annual increases paid directly to staff person. |
| Maine | Up to $32/d for meals. Actual for lodging if required with receipt; $38 without receipt (V) set by legislature and compensation commission. | None. |
| Maryland | $96/d lodging; $30/d meals related to official business (V) tied to federal rate and compensation commission. | Members, $18.265/y for normal expenses of an office with limits on postage, telephone and publications. Members must document expenses. Legislators must use $5,800 for clerical services. Senators receive one administrative assistant & session assistance. Delegates receive $10,000 from house staff accounting for clerical employee with benefits. |
| Massachusetts | $9-50 for expenses depending on distance from capitol (V). | $3,600/y for office expenses. |
| Michigan | None. | $61,904/y for printing, mailings, travel, furniture and district offices. Senate Majority party receives $207,044; Senate Minority party receives $126,247 for staffing. |

See footnotes at end of table.

# LEGISLATIVE COMPENSATION: INTERIM PAYMENTS AND OTHER DIRECT PAYMENTS — Continued

| State or other jurisdiction | Per diem compensation and living expenses for committee or official business during interim (as of March 1999) | Other direct payments or services to legislators (as of March 1999) |
|---|---|---|
| Minnesota | $56/d per approval of committee chair or leadership (U) set by the legislature. | None. |
| Mississippi | $1,500/during interim (U). | None. |
| Missouri | None. | $1,000/m to cover all reasonable and necessary business expenses. |
| Montana | In state rates $23/d for meals, receipt not required (U). $36.40 lodging, receipt not required (V). Claim form required. | None. |
| Nebraska | None. Actual expense reimbursed. | No allowance; however, each member is provided with two full-time capitol staff year-round. |
| Nevada | $69/d for meeting attendance in-state (V) set by the legislature. | None. |
| New Hampshire | None. | None. |
| New Jersey | None. | $750/y for equipment and supplies. $100,000/y for district office personnel, furnishings and benefits. |
| New Mexico | $124/d Nov. 1-April 30; $131/d May 1-Oct. 31 (V) tied to federal rate. | None. |
| New York | $89/d; $130/d for New York City metro area and out-of-state travel (V) set by the legislature. Paid for official duties performed outside their elected district. | Staff allowance set by majority leader for majority members and by minority leader for minority members. Staff allowance covers both district and capitol; geographic location; seniority and leadership responsibilities will cause variations; only one district office is permitted. |
| North Carolina | $104/d (V) set by statute. | Non-leaders receive $6,708/y for any legislative expenses not otherwise provided. Full-time secretarial assistance is provided during session. |
| North Dakota | During interim committee meetings, members receive $62.50/d, $20/d meals (U); $39 plus tax/d lodging (V) plus round trip mileage reimbursement at state employee mileage rate. All members receive a $250/m allowance for expenses. | None. |
| Ohio | None. | None. |
| Oklahoma | $25/d (U) set by the legislature. | $350/y for unvouchered office supplies plus seven rolls of stamps. |
| Oregon | $87/d committee and task force meetings (U) tied to federal rate. | $2,635/session; interim allowance is $400-550/m depending on geographic size of district. Staffing allowance of $3,756/m during session; $1,144/m during interim. |
| Pennsylvania | $115 (V) tied to high/low substantiation method of revenue procedure 98-64. | $27,500/y for operation of district offices. Staffing is determined by the Senate Floor Leader. |
| Rhode Island | None. | None. |
| South Carolina | Member attending official meetings in- or out-of-state is eligible for $88/d subsistence and $35/d per diem (V). | Senate $3,400/y for postage, stationery and telephone.  House $1,800/y for telephone and $600/y for postage. |
| South Dakota | $95 for each day of a committee meeting (U). Travel expenses are paid at state rates. | None. |
| Tennessee | $114/d (U) tied to federal rate. A request for per diem must be submitted to Legislative Administration. | $525/m for expenses in district and staff intrastate travel (U). |
| Texas | Senators receive $118/d for legislative business in Travis County, not to exceed 10 d/m (U). Representatives receive $118/d in Travis County, not to exceed 12 d/m (V). Per diem amount is determined by the Ethics Commission, number of days determined by Senate Caucus and the Committee on House Administration. | Senate: $25,000/m for staff salaries. House $9,750/m for staff salaries, supplies stationery, postage, district office rental, telephone expense, etc. |
| Utah | $42/d (U); $76/d for lodging (V). | None. |
| Vermont | $105/d for meeting day for actual meals and housing (U) set by the legislature. | None. |
| Virginia | $100/d for committee meetings. | $750/m; leadership receives $1,000/m for office expenses incurred through their district offices, stationery and business cards.  Legislators receive a staffing allowance of $29,028/y,: leadership receives $43,541/y. |
| Washington | $82/d (V) tied to federal rate; if traveling in a "high cost" region, receipts are required. | No staffing allowance. $450 for legislative expenses, for which the legislator has not been otherwise entitled to reimbursement. |
| West Virginia | $85/d, except $45/d for commuters (U). | None. |

See footnotes at end of table.

# LEGISLATIVE COMPENSATION: INTERIM PAYMENTS AND OTHER DIRECT PAYMENTS — Continued

| State or other jurisdiction | Per diem compensation and living expenses for committee or official business during interim (as of March 1999) | Other direct payments or services to legislators (as of March 1999) |
|---|---|---|
| Wisconsin | Per diem is paid year round up to $75/m (U). | Senate receives $66,000/two-year session plus a mailing for the district each year. Covers district mileage, copying and special documents; capitol expenses include printing, postage, subscriptions, phone etc. Senators receive $155,465/two year session for staffing. Assembly members receive $12,500 plus an allowance for district size-min. $870, max. $2,900 that covers printing and postage. Staff salary paid by state. |
| Wyoming | $80/d (V) set by the legislature. | None. |
| Dist. of Columbia | None. | None. |
| Guam | None. | None. |
| Puerto Rico | $93/d within 50 km of the capitol; $103/d beyond the 50 km limit (U). | Senate receives $7,500/m for staffing. House members receive $10,000/m for staffing. Senators receive an allowance that covers day-to-day operations. Staffing allowances vary with staffing requests. |
| U.S. Virgin Islands | None. | |

*Source:* National Conference of State Legislatures.

*Note:* For more information on legislative compensation, see Table 3.9, "Legislative Compensation: Regular Sessions." Although the definition of "per diem" is daily expence allowance, it is also used in some states to refer to an interim salary that is taxed and reported as income seperate from the annual salary.

*Key:*
(U) — Unvouchered.
(V) — Vouchered.
d — day.
m — month.
w — week.
y — year.

(a) In Georgia, $2,200 per diem differential account. A maximum of fifty (50) days can be claimed. Georgia state law states the maximum per diem plus per diem differential is $119/d. The per diem differential account is made up of the difference between the maximum allowance less the actual per diem paid x 50 days.

## Table 3.11
## ADDITIONAL COMPENSATION FOR SENATE LEADERS
### (As of March 24, 1999)

| State | Presiding Officer | Majority Leader | Minority Leader | Other Leaders |
|---|---|---|---|---|
| Alabama | None | None | None | None |
| Alaska | $500 | None | None | None |
| Arizona | $500 | None | None | None |
| Arkansas | None | None | None | President pro tem, $14,000 |
| California | None | None | None | None |
| Colorado | All leaders receive $99/day salary during interim when in attendance at committee or leadership meetings and committee meetings. | | | |
| Connecticut | $8,320 | $6,877 | $6,877 | Deputy min. and maj. ldrs., $5,018/year; asst. maj. and min. ldrs. and maj. and min. whips $3,302/year |
| Delaware | $11,940 | $9,299 | $9,299 | Maj. and min. whips $5,856 |
| Florida | $10,236 | None | None | None |
| Georgia | $75,724.56* | $2,400 | $2,400 | President pro tem, $4,800; admin. flr. ldr., $2,400; asst. admin. flr. ldr., $1,200 |
| Hawaii | $37,000 | None | None | None |
| Idaho | $3,000 | None | None | None |
| Illinois | $20,621 | None | $20,621 | Asst. maj. and min. ldr., $15,465; maj. and min. caucus chair, $15,465 |
| Indiana | $6,500 | $5,000 | $5,500 | Asst. pres. pro tem $2,500; asst. maj. flr. ldr. and maj. caucus chair, $1,000; maj. caucus chair, $5,000; min. asst. flr. ldr. and min. caucus chair, $4,500; maj. and min. whips, $1,500; asst. min. caucus chair, $500 |
| Iowa | $11,256 | $11,256 | $11,256 | Pres. Pro Tem $1,198 |
| Kansas | $11,409.32/yr | $10,293.14/yr | $10,293.14/yr | Asst. maj., min. ldrs., vice pres., $5,823.22/yr |
| Kentucky | $38/day for members elected in 1998; $26.87 for members not up for re-election | $30/day for members elected in 1998; $21.49 for members not up for re-election | $30/day for members elected in 1998; $21.49 for members not up for re-election | Maj., min. caucus chairs and whips, $23/day for members elected in 1998; $16.13/day for members not up for re-election |
| Louisiana | $32,000 | None | None | None |
| Maine | 150% of base salary | 125% of base salary | 125% of base salary | Asst. maj. and min. ldrs., 112.5% of base salary |
| Maryland | $10,000 | None | None | None |
| Massachusetts | $35,000 | $22,500 | $22,500 | Asst. maj. and min. ldr., $15,000 |
| Michigan | $5,250 | $22,050 | $17,850 | Maj. flr. ldr., $10,500; min. flr. ldr., $8,400 |
| Minnesota | None | $43,596* | $43,596 | Asst. maj. ldr., $32,697* |
| Mississippi | None | None | None | Pro tem resolution, $5,000/yr |
| Missouri | $2,500 | $1,500 | $1,500 | Pro tem, $1,500 |
| Montana | $5/day during session | None | None | None |
| Nebraska | None | None | None | None |
| Nevada | $900 | $900 | $900 | Pres. Pro tem, $900 |
| New Hampshire | $50/two-yr term | None | None | None |
| New Jersey | 1/3 above annual salary | None | None | None |
| New Mexico | None | None | None | None |
| New York | $41,500 | None | $34,500 | 22 other leaders with compensation ranging from $13,000 to $34,000 |
| North Carolina | $38,151* and $16,956 expense allowance | $17,048* and $7,992 expense allowance | $17,048* and $7,992 expense allowance | Dep. pro tem: $21,739* and $10,032 expense allowance |
| North Dakota | None | $10/day | $10/day | Asst. ldrs., $5/day |
| Ohio | $66,133 base salary | President pro tem $60,340 | $60,340 salary | Asst. pres. pro tem, $56,838; maj. whip, $53,340; asst. min. ldr., $55,090; min. whip, $49,842; asst. min. whip, $44,385 |

See footnotes at end of table.

## ADDITIONAL COMPENSATION FOR SENATE LEADERS — Continued

| State | Presiding Officer | Majority Leader | Minority Leader | Other Leaders |
|---|---|---|---|---|
| Oklahoma | $17,932 | $12,364 | $12,364 | None |
| Oregon | $1,208/month | None | None | None |
| Pennsylvania | $33,240.64 | $26,593.78 | $26,593.78 | Maj. and min. whip, $20,182; maj. and min. caucus chair, $12,584; maj. and min. policy chairs, maj.and min. caucus admin., $8,310 |
| Rhode Island | None | None | None | None |
| South Carolina | Lt. gov. holds this position | None | None | President pro tem, $11,000 |
| South Dakota | None | None | None | None |
| Tennessee | $49,500* plus $750/yr of ex officio duties | None | None | None |
| Texas | None | None | None | None |
| Utah | $1,000 | $500 | $500 | Maj. whip, asst. maj. whip, min. whip and asst. min. whip, $500 |
| Vermont | $593/week during session. No add'l salary | None | None | None |
| Virginia | None | None | None | None |
| Washington | Lt. gov. holds this position | $32,300 | $32,300 | None |
| West Virginia | $50/day during session; $100/day interim for a maximum of 80 days | $25/day during session | $25/day during session | None |
| Wisconsin | None | None | None | None |
| Wyoming | $3/day | None | None | None |
| District of Columbia | $10,000 (council chair) | Not applicable | Not applicable | Not applicable |
| Puerto Rico | $68,000/yr | $46,000/yr | $46,000/yr | None |
| Guam | None | None | None | None |
| U.S. Virgin Islands | $10,000 | None | None | None |

Source: National Conference of State Legislatures.
*Total annual salary for this leadership position.

## Table 3.12
## ADDITIONAL COMPENSATION FOR HOUSE LEADERS
### (As of March 24, 1999)

| State | Speaker | Majority leader | Minority leader | Other |
|---|---|---|---|---|
| Alabama | $2/day (limit 60 days) | None | None | None |
| Alaska | $500 | None | None | None |
| Arizona | None | None | None | None |
| Arkansas | $14,000/yr | None | None | $2,400 Spkr. designate |
| California | None | None | None | None |
| Colorado | All leaders receive $99/day salary during interim when in attendance at committee or leadership matters. | | | |
| Connecticut | $8,320 | $6,877 | $6,877 | Dep. spkr., dep. maj. and min. ldrs., $5,018/yr; asst. maj. and min. ldrs.; maj. and min whips, $3,302/yr |
| Delaware | $11,940 | $9,299 | $9,299 | Maj. and min. whips, $5,856 |
| Florida | $10,236 | None | None | None |
| Georgia | $62,811.48 | $2,400 | $2,400 | Admin. flr. ldr., $2,400; Asst. admin. flr. ldr., $1,200; spkr. pro tem, $4,800 |
| Hawaii | $37,000 | None | None | None |
| Idaho | $3,000 | None | None | None |
| Illinois | $20,621 | $17,398 | $20,621 | Dpty. maj. and min., $14,821; asst. maj. and asst. min., $13,531; maj. and min. conference chair, $13,531 |
| Indiana | $6,500 | $5,000 | $5,500 | Maj. caucus chair: $5,000; min. caucus chair, $4,500; Asst. min. flr. ldr., $4,500; maj. flr. ldr., $1,000; maj. whip, $1,500; min. whip, $1,500 |
| Iowa | $11,256 | $11,256 | $11,256 | Speaker pro tem, $1,198 |
| Kansas | $11,409.32/yr | $10,293.14/yr | $10,293.14/yr | Asst. maj. and min. ldrs., spkr. pro tem, $5,823.22/yr |
| Kentucky | $38/day | $30/day | $30/day | Maj. and min. caucus chairs & whips, $23/day |
| Louisiana | $32,000* | None | None | Speaker pro tem, $24,500* |
| Maine (e) | 150% of base salary | 125% of base salary | 125% of base salary | Asst. maj. and min. ldrs., 112.5% of base salary |
| Maryland | $10,000 | None | None | None |
| Massachusetts | $35,000 | $22,500 | $22,500 | Asst. maj. and min. ldr., $15,000 |
| Michigan | $23,000 | None | $17,000 | Spkr. pro tem, $5,000; min. flr. ldr., $8,000; maj. flr. ldr., $10,000 |
| Minnesota | $43,596* | $43,596* | $43,596* | None |
| Mississippi | None | None | None | None |
| Missouri | $2,500 | $1,500 | $1,500 | None |
| Montana | $5/day during session | None | None | None |
| Nebraska | None | None | None | None |
| Nevada | $900 | $900 | $900 | Speaker pro tem, $900 |
| New Hampshire | $50/two-year term | None | None | None |
| New Jersey | 1/3 above annual salary | None | None | None |
| New Mexico | None | None | None | None |
| New York | $41,500 | $34,500 | $34,500 | 31 leaders with compensation ranging from $9,000 to $25,000 |
| North Carolina | $38,151 and $16,956 expense allowance | $17,048 and $7,992 expense allowance | $17,048 and $7,992 expense allowance | Speaker pro tem, $21,739 and $10,032 expense allowance |
| North Dakota | $10/day | $10/day | $10/day | Asst. ldrs., $5/day |
| Ohio | $66,133 base salary | $56,838 base salary | | $60,340 base salary Spkr. pro tem, $60,340; asst. maj. ldr., $53,340; asst. min. ldr., $55,090; maj. whip, $49,842; min. whip, $49,842; asst. maj. whip, $46,342; asst. min. whip, $44,385 |
| Oklahoma | $17,932 | $12,364 | $12,364 | Speaker pro tem, $12,364 |
| Oregon | $1,208/month | None | None | None |
| Pennsylvania | $32,186.62 | $25,750.52 | $25,750.52 | Maj. and min. whips, $19,542; maj. and min. caucus chairs, $12,185; maj. and min. policy chairs, $8,047; maj. and min. caucus admin., $8,047 |
| Rhode Island | None | None | None | None |
| South Carolina | $11,000/yr | None | None | Speaker pro tem, $3,600/yr |

See footnotes at end of table.

## ADDITIONAL COMPENSATION FOR HOUSE LEADERS — Continued

| State | Speaker | Majority leader | Minority leader | Other |
|---|---|---|---|---|
| South Dakota | None | None | None | None |
| Tennessee | $45,000* plus $750/yr for ex-officio duties | None | None | None |
| Texas | None | None | None | None |
| Utah | $1,000 | $500 | $500 | Whips and asst. whips, $500 |
| Vermont | $593/week during session plus an additional $9,172 in salary | None | None | None |
| Virginia | $18,681 | None | None | None |
| Washington | $36,300* | None | $32,300* | None |
| West Virginia | $50/day during session; $100/day during interim for a maximum of 80 days | $25/day during session | $25/day during session | Up to four add'l people named by presiding officer receive $100 for a maximum of 30 days |
| Wisconsin | $25/month | None | None | None |
| Wyoming | $3/day | None | None | None |
| District of Columbia | $10,000 (chair of council) | Not applicable | Not applicable | Not applicable |
| Puerto Rico | $68,000/yr | $46,000/yr | $46,000/yr | None |
| Guam | None | None | None | None |
| U.S. Virgin Islands | None | None | None | None |

*Source*: National Conference of State Legislatures.
*Total annual salary for this leadership position.
*Key:*
(a) Only additional compensation for leaders is a per diem for everyday of work during interim; other members get one day of per diem per week during interim.
(b) Base salary.
(c) All leaders receive $99/d salary during interim when in attendance at cmte. or leadership matters.
(d) Official title is deputy speaker; in Hawaii, vice speaker; in Rhode Island, senior speaker pro tem.
(e) Total annual salary.

## Table 3.13
## STATE LEGISLATIVE RETIREMENT BENEFITS
### (As of March 24, 1999)

| State or other jurisdiction | Participation | Requirements for regular retirement | Contribution rate | Monthly benefit estimates | | | Benefit formula | Same as state employee |
|---|---|---|---|---|---|---|---|---|
| | | | | 4 yrs. | 12 yrs. | 20 yrs. | | |
| Alaska | Optional | Age 60 | Employee 6.75%; employer 14.92% | Not yet vested | $500 | $900 | 2% (first 10 yrs.); 2.25% (second 10 yrs.); or 2.5% (third 10 yrs.) x monthly salary avg. over highest consecutive yrs. x yrs. of service | Yes |
| Arizona | Optional | Age 65, 5+ yrs. service; age 62, 10+ yrs. service; age 60, 25+ yrs. service | 7% | $333.33 | $1,000 | $1,667 | 4%/yr. of credited service x 3 yr. avg; maximum 80% of member's avg. yearly salary | No |
| Arkansas | Optional | Age 65, 10 yrs. service; age 55, 12 yrs. service; or 30 yrs. service | Non-contributory | Not eligible | $420(a) | $700(b) | $35/mo. x yrs. service (c) | No |
| California | N.A. | | | | | | | |
| Colorado | Mandatory | Age 60, 5 yrs. service | 8% of gross salary | Not yet vested | $350 | $729 | 2.5% x HAS x creditable service through 20 yrs. plus 1.5% x HAS for 21 through 40 yrs. Maximum benefit = 80% of employees HAS (e) | No |
| Connecticut | Mandatory | Age 55 with 10 yrs. service | Members prior to 7/1/97-0 after 1/1/97 -2% | Not yet vested | $276 | $460 | (.0133 x avg. annual salary) + (.005 x avg. annual salary in excess of breakpoint [specified dollar amount for each yr.]) x yrs. credited service | Yes |
| Delaware | Mandatory | Age 62, 5 yrs. service | 3% of total monthly compensation in excess of $500 | N.A. | N.A. | N.A. | Years of service x highest rate of payment being paid to any retired member of the General Assembly | No |
| Florida | Optional | Age 62, 30 yrs. service; or vested with 8 yrs. and age 62 | 23.27% | (e) | (e) | (e) | Yrs. creditable service x percent value x average final compensation = annual option 1 benefit | No |
| Georgia | Optional | Age 60, 8 yrs. service | Employee pays 4% + $7; employer 5% + $7 | 0 | $336 (f) | $336 (f) | $28 x yrs. service x yrs. of service = monthly benefit; employee is penalized 5% for each yr. below age 62 | No |
| Hawaii | Optional 10 yrs. of service | 55 yrs. if less than | 7.80% | 0 | Varies | Varies | 3.5 x years of service as legislator x highest average salary plus annuity based on contributions as an elected offical | No |
| Idaho | Mandatory | 5 yrs. service minimum; age 65 unreduced; age 55 reduced | 6.97% | $77 | $236 | $383 | Avg. monthly salary for highest 42 consecutive months x .01917 x months of service divided by 12 | Yes |
| Illinois | Optional | Age 55, 8 yrs. service; age 62, 4 yrs. service | 8.5% for retirement; 2% for survivors; 1% for automatic increases for 11.5% total | 12% of final salary | 45% of final salary | 85% of final salary | 3% of each of 1st 4 yrs.; 3.5% for each of next 2 yrs.; 4% for each of next 2 yrs.; 4.5% for each of the next 4 yrs.; 5% for each yr. above 12 | No |
| Indiana | Mandatory | None | Employee 5% of taxable income; employer 20% | Varies | Varies | Varies | Years of service x 1.1% x highest one-year salary | No |

See footnotes at end of table.

# STATE LEGISLATIVE RETIREMENT BENEFITS — Continued

| State or other jurisdiction | Participation | Requirements for regular retirement | Contribution rate | Monthly benefit estimates | | | Benefit formula | Same as state employee |
|---|---|---|---|---|---|---|---|---|
| | | | | 4 yrs. | 12 yrs. | 20 yrs. | | |
| Iowa | Optional | Age 55; 4 yrs. service | 3.7% | $140 | $337.50 | $700 | 60% x avg of highest 3 yrs. x yrs. of service divided by 30 (maximum no. of yrs.) | Yes |
| Kansas | Optional | Age 65, age 62; 10 yrs. of service or age plus yrs.of service equals 85 pts. | 4% | N.A. | N.A. | N.A. | 3 highest yrs. x 1.75% x yrs. service divided by 12 | No |
| Kentucky | Mandatory | N.A. | $114.58/month | N.A. | N.A. | N.A. | N.A. | Yes |
| Louisiana | N.A. | | | | | | | |
| Maine | Mandatory (g) | Age 60 (if 10 yrs of service on 7/1/93) and age 62 (if less than 10 yrs of service on 7/1/93) | Employee 7.65%; legislative retirement system 14.08% ME State Retirement system 22.03% | Varies | Varies | Varies | 1/50 average final compensation x number of years of creditable service | No |
| Maryland | Optional | Age 60, with 8 yrs; Age 50, 8+yrs creditable services (early reduced retirement) | 5% of annual salary | 0 | $891 | $1,485 | 3% of legislative salary for each yr of creditable service up to a max of 22 yrs. 3 months | No |
| Massachusetts | Mandatory | Age 65, 32 yrs. Service | Depending on yr. entered 5%, 7% or 9% | N.A. | N.A. | N.A. | N.A. | Yes (i) |
| Michigan | Optional | Age 55 with 5 yrs. or age plus service equals 70 | 7%-13% | Varies | Varies | Varies | Depends on when service started | No |
| Minnesota | Mandatory | Age 62 (reduced amount available at age 60), 6 yrs. service | 9% | 0 | $759 | $1,645 | 2.5% x 5 yr. avg. salary/yr. service, except yrs. served before 1979 earn 5% up to 8 yrs. | No |
| Mississippi | Mandatory | 55 yrs. or 25 yrs. of service | Regular: 7.25%: Legislator: 9.75%: State: supplemental 3%/6.33% | Varies | Varies | Varies | N.A. | Yes |
| Missouri | Mandatory | Age 55, & 3 full biennial assemblies | Non-contributory (i) | $300 | $900 | $1,500 | $150/mo. per biennial assembly served plus average monthly compensation | No |
| Montana | Optional | Age 60, 5 yrs. service; age 65 regardless of yrs of service; or 30 yrs of service regardless of age | 6.8% | $87 | $263 | $439 | 1/56 x yrs. service x final avg. salary | Yes |
| Nevada | Mandatory | 10 yrs. service | 15% of session salary | 0 | $300 | $500 | Minimum service = 10 years; number of years x $24 = monthly allowance | No |
| New Jersey | Mandatory | Age 60, 8 yrs. service; age 55 (early retirement with 25 yrs.) | 5%/yr. | N.A. | N.A. | N.A. | Effective 1/74 all legislators received 3% per yr pension allowance; before 1974, members received 1/60th | No |

See footnotes at end of table.

The Council of State Governments 93

# STATE LEGISLATIVE RETIREMENT BENEFITS — Continued

| State or other jurisdiction | Participation | Requirements for regular retirement | Contribution rate | Monthly benefit estimates | | | Benefit formula | Same as state employee |
|---|---|---|---|---|---|---|---|---|
| | | | | 4 yrs. | 12 yrs. | 20 yrs. | | |
| New Mexico | Optional | Age 65, 5+ yrs.; 64, 8+ yrs., 63, 11+ yrs., 60, 12+ yrs. or any age with 14+ yrs. of credited service | $100 per year | $83.33 | $250 | $416.66 | $250 x yrs. of service (after 1959) | No |
| New York | Mandatory | Depends on tier set by date Minimum 10 yrs. service | Varies (0-3%); | 0 | Varies | Varies | Depends on tier set by date of initial membership | Yes |
| North Carolina | Mandatory | Age 65, 5 yrs. service | 24.58% | 0 | 48.2% of annual compensation | 75% of annual compensation | Final compensation x 4.02% x yrs. service | No |
| Ohio | Optional | Age 60, 5 yrs. service; age 55, 25 yrs. service; any age, 30 yrs. service | Legislator 8.5%; state 13.31% | No benefits | Varies | Varies | 2.1% of final avg. salary x years of service | Yes |
| Oklahoma | Optional | Age 60, 6 yrs. service | 4.5%-10% | $426.68 at 10% | $1,280.04 at 10% | $2,133.40 at 10% | Avg. participating salary x yrs. service x computation factor depending on optional contributions ranging from .019 x .040 | No |
| Oregon | Optional | Age 55, 30 yrs. service | 14.97% of subject wages | N.A. | N.A. | N.A. | 1.67% x yrs. service and final avg. monthly salary | Yes |
| Pennsylvania | Optional | Age 50, 3 yrs. service 8 continuous years as a member of the senate | 5% of gross salary | N.A. | N.A. | N.A. | 2% x final avg. salary x credited yrs. service x withdrawal factor if under regular retirement age (50 for legislators) | Yes |
| Rhode Island (j) | No | | | | | | | |
| South Carolina | Mandatory | Age 60, 8 yrs. service; 30 yrs of service regardless of age | 10% | 0 | $1,079 | $1,800 | 4.82% of annual compensation x yrs. Service | No |
| Tennessee | Optional | Age 55, 4 yrs. service | 5.43% | $280 | $840 | $1,375 | $70 x yrs. service with a $1,375 monthly | No |
| Texas | Optional | Age 60, 8 yrs. service; age 50, 12 yrs. service | 8% | Not eligible | $2,288.25 | $3,813.75 | 2.25% x district judges salary x length of service | No |
| Utah | Mandatory | Age 65, 4 yrs. service | Non-contributory | Varies | Varies | Varies | $10/mo. x yrs. service: adjusted semi annually according to consumer price index, ltd. to max of 4% | No |
| Virginia | Mandatory | Age 50 with 30 yrs. of service | 10.78% of monthly salary | Varies | Varies | Varies | 1.7% of average final compensation x yrs. of service | Yes |
| Washington | Optional | Several plans are offered; requirements vary depending on plan chosen | N.A. | N.A. | N.A. | N.A. | N.A. | No |
| West Virginia | Optional | Age 60, with 5 plus yrs. service. | 4.5% | Not eligible | $300 | $500 | 2% of final avg. salary x yrs. service | Yes |
| Wisconsin | Mandatory | Age 55, 5 yrs. service | 0.463% | $3,200 | $12,800 | $16,400 | 2% for each yr. of service x last salary | Yes |

See footnotes at end of table.

# STATE LEGISLATIVE RETIREMENT BENEFITS — Continued

| State or other jurisdiction | Participation | Requirements for regular retirement | Contribution rate | Monthly benefit estimates | | | Benefit formula | Same as state employee |
|---|---|---|---|---|---|---|---|---|
| | | | | 4 yrs. | 12 yrs. | 20 yrs. | | |
| Dist. of Columbia ......... | Mandatory | Age 62, 5 yrs. service; age 55, 30 yrs service; age 60, 20 yrs service | Before 10/1/87, 7%; after 10/1/87, 5% | 0 | Varies | Varies | Multiply high 3 yrs. average pay by indicator under applicable yrs. and mon months of service. | Yes |
| Puerto Rico ......... | Optional | Age 55 with 30 yrs. service | Approximately 9% | 0 | 18% of average 3 salaries | 30% of average 3 salaries | Less than 10 yrs. 0%; 1.5% per yr. | Yes |
| Guam ......... | Optional | Age 60 with 30 yrs.; age 55 with 15 yrs. service | 5% or 8.5% | Varies | Varies | Varies | An amount equal to 2% of avg. annual salary for each of first 10 yrs. of service and 2.5% of avg. annual salary for each yr. of service over 10 yrs. | Yes |
| U.S. Virgin Islands ......... | Optional | Age 60 with 10 yrs. Service | 8% | N.A. | Varies | Varies | At age 60 with at least 10 yrs. of service, at 2.5% for each year of service or at any time with at least 30 yrs. service | Yes |

*Source*: National Conference of State Legislatures.
*Note*: The following states do not have legislative retirement benefits: Alabama, Nebraska, New Hampshire, North Dakota, South Dakota, Vermont and Wyoming.
*Key*:
N.A. — Not available
(a) $480 for leadership.
(b) $800 for leadership.
(c) House Speaker or Senate President Pro Tem is $40/mo. x yrs. service.
(d) HAS = 1/12 x avg. 3 highest annual salaries earned during calendar yr. periods on which PERA contributions were paid; 15% limit applies to annual salary increases during 3 yrs. prior to retirement. Partial yr. salaries can be combined.

(e) Based on highest 5 yrs of salary.
(f) Member is 62 with maximum benefit option.
(g) Members may request a waiver if they can document that participation would increase their total tax liability
(h) Emp.oyee vested after 10 yrs.
(i) If evaluated separately from general employee plan, contribution rate is 27.94%. The current contribution rate, which includes employees is 10.3%.
(j) Constitution has been amended effective 1/95. Any legislator elected after this date is not eligible to join the State Retirement System, but will be compensated for $10,000/yr. with cost of living increases to be adjusted annually.

## Table 3.14
## BILL PRE-FILING, REFERENCE, AND CARRYOVER

| State | Pre-filing of bills allowed (b) | Bills referred to committee by: | | Bill referral restricted by rule (a) | | Bill carryover allowed (c) |
|---|---|---|---|---|---|---|
| | | Senate | House | Senate | House | |
| Alabama | ★ (d) | President (e) | Speaker | L | . . . | ★ (f) |
| Alaska | ★ (g) | President | Speaker | L | L | ★ |
| Arizona | ★ | President | Speaker | . . . | L | . . . |
| Arkansas | ★ | President | Speaker | L | L | . . . |
| California | ★ | Rules Cmte. | Rules Cmte. | L | . . . | ★ (h) |
| Colorado | ★ | President | Speaker | . . . | . . . | . . . |
| Connecticut | ★ | Pres. Pro Tempore | Speaker | L | L | . . . |
| Delaware | ★ | Pres. Pro Tempore | Speaker | . . . | L | ★ |
| Florida | ★ | President | Speaker | L | M | . . . |
| Georgia | ★ (i) | President (e) | Speaker | . . . | L | ★ |
| Hawaii | (j) | President | Speaker | . . . | . . . | ★ |
| Idaho | (k) | President (e) | Speaker | . . . | . . . | . . . |
| Illinois | ★ | Rules Cmte. | Rules Cmte. | . . . | . . . | ★ |
| Indiana | ★ | Pres. Pro Tempore | Speaker | M | . . . | . . . |
| Iowa | ★ | President | Speaker | M | M | ★ |
| Kansas | ★ | President | Speaker | L | L | ★ |
| Kentucky | ★ | Cmte. on Cmtes. | Cmte. on Cmtes. | L | L | . . . |
| Louisiana | ★ | President (l) | Speaker (l) | L | L | . . . |
| Maine | ★ (m) | ------Secy. of Senate and Clerk of House (n)------ | | . . . | . . . | ★ |
| Maryland | ★ | President | Speaker | L | L | . . . |
| Massachusetts | ★ | Clerk (l) | Clerk (l) | M | M | ★ |
| Michigan | . . . | Majority Ldr. | Speaker | . . . | . . . | ★ |
| Minnesota | ★ (o) | President | Speaker | M | M | ★ |
| Mississippi | ★ | President (e) | Speaker | . . . | . . . | . . . |
| Missouri | ★ | Pres. Pro Tempore | Speaker | . . . | . . . | . . . |
| Montana | ★ | President | Speaker | . . . | . . . | . . . |
| Nebraska | ★ | Reference Cmte. | U | L | U | ★ (p) |
| Nevada | ★ | (q) | | L | . . . | ★ |
| New Hampshire | ★ | President | Speaker | . . . | L | ★ |
| New Jersey | ★ (m) | President | Speaker | . . . | . . . | ★ |
| New Mexico | ★ | (r) | Speaker | M | M | . . . |
| New York | ★ | Pres. Pro Tempore (s) | Speaker | M | M | ★ |
| North Carolina | . . . | Clerk (t) | Speaker | M | L | ★ |
| North Dakota | ★ | President (e) | Speaker | M | M | . . . |
| Ohio | ★ | Reference Cmte. | Reference Cmte. | . . . | M | ★ |
| Oklahoma | ★ | Pres. Pro Tempore | Speaker | M | . . . | ★ |
| Oregon | ★ | President | Speaker | L | ★ | . . . |
| Pennsylvania | ★ | President (e) | Speaker | M | M | . . . |
| Rhode Island | ★ | President (e) | Speaker | L | M | ★ |
| South Carolina | ★ | President | Speaker | . . . | M | ★ |
| South Dakota | ★ | President (e) | Speaker | . . . | . . . | . . . |
| Tennessee | ★ | Speaker | Speaker | . . . | . . . | ★ |
| Texas | ★ | President (e) | Speaker | . . . | L | . . . |
| Utah | ★ | President | Speaker | . . . | . . . | . . . |
| Vermont | ★ | President (e) | Speaker | L | L | . . . |
| Virginia | ★ | Clerk | Clerk (u) | L | L | ★ |
| Washington | ★ | (v) | (v) | . . . | . . . | ★ |
| West Virginia | ★ | President | Speaker | . . . | . . . | ★ |
| Wisconsin | . . . | President | Speaker | . . . | . . . | ★ (p) |
| Wyoming | ★ (m) | President | Speaker | M | M | . . . |

See footnotes at end of table.

# BILL PRE-FILING, REFERENCE, AND CARRYOVER — Continued

*Source:* State legislative rule books and manuals. The information in this table was compiled in 1998.

*Key:*

★ — Yes

. . . — No

L — Rules generally require all bills be referred to the appropriate committee of jurisdiction.

M — Rules require specific types of bills be referred to specific committees (e.g., appropriations, local bills).

U — Unicameral legislature.

(a) Legislative rules specify all or certain bills go to committees of jurisdiction.

(b) Unless otherwise indicated by footnote, bills may be introduced prior to convening each session of the legislature. In this column only: ★ —pre-filing is allowed in both chambers (or in the case of Nebraska, in the unicameral legislature); . . . — pre-filing is not allowed in either chamber.

(c) Bills carry over from the first year of the legislature to the second (does not apply in Arkansas, Kentucky, Montana, Nevada, North Dakota, Oregon and Texas, where legislatures meet biennially). Bills generally do not carry over after an intervening legislative election.

(d) Except between the end of the last regular session of the legislature in any quadrennium and the organizational session following the general election.

(e) Lieutenant governor is the president of the Senate.

(f) No motion to carry over all bills on the calendar to reach a certain bill shall be in order.

(g) Maximum 10 bills per member.

(h) Bills introduced in the first year of the regular session and passed by the house of origin on or before the January 31st constitutional deadline are carryover bills.

(i) Pre-filing of bills allowed; however, must formally file again when the sessions starts.

(j) House only in even-numbered years.

(k) House members may prefile bills during the first 10 days in December before the next regular legislative session.

(l) Subject to approval or disapproval. Louisiana–majority members present. Massachusetts–by presiding officer and Committee on Steering and Policy.

(m) Prior to convening of first regular session only.

(n) For the joint standing committee system. Secretary of the Senate and Clerk of House, after conferring, suggest an appropriate committee reference for every bill, resolve and petition offered in either house. If they are unable to agree, the question of reference is referred to a conference of the President of the Senate and Speaker of the House. If the presiding officers cannot agree, the question is resolved by the Legislative Council.

(o) Prior to convening of second regular session only.

(p) Any bill or joint resolution on which final action has not been taken at the conclusion of the last general-business floor period in the odd-numbered year shall be carried forward to the even-numbered year.

(q) Motion for referral can be made by any member.

(r) Senator introducing the bill endorses the name of the committee to which the bill is referred. If an objection is made, the Senate determines the committee to which the bill is referred.

(s) Also serves as majority leader.

(t) Under the supervision of the chairman of the Senate Committee on Rules and Operation.

(u) Under the direction of the speaker.

(v) By the membership of the chamber.

## Table 3.15
## TIME LIMITS ON BILL INTRODUCTION

| State | Time limit on introduction of bills | Procedures for granting exception to time limits |
|---|---|---|
| Alabama | Senate: 24th day of regular session (a). House: no limit | Majority vote after consideration by Rules Committee. |
| Alaska | 35th C day of 2nd regular session (b). | 2/3 vote of membership (concurrent resolution). |
| Arizona | House: 29th day of regular session; 10th day of special session. Senate: 22nd day of regular session; 10th day of special session. | Permission of Rules Committee. |
| Arkansas | 55th day of regular session (50th day for appropriations bills). | 2/3 vote of membership of each house. |
| California | Deadlines may set during session. | Approval of Committee on Rules and 2/3 vote of membership. |
| Colorado | House: 22nd L day of regular session. Senate: 17th L day of regular session (c). | House, Senate Committees on Delayed Bills may extend deadline. |
| Connecticut | Depends on schedule set out by joint rules adopted for biennium (d). | 2/3 vote of members present. |
| Delaware | House: no limit. Senate: no limit. | |
| Florida | House: noon 1st day of regular session; committee bills noon 14th day of regular session (c,e). Senate: noon 4th L day of regular session (c,f). | Committee on Rules and Calendar determines whether existence of emergency compels bill's consideration. |
| Georgia | House: 30th L day of regular session because of Senate ruling. Senate: 33rd L day of regular session. | House: unanimous vote. Senate: 2/3 vote of membership. |
| Hawaii | Actual dates established during session. | Majority vote of membership. |
| Idaho | House: 20th day of session (e); 36th day of session (g). Senate: 12th day of session (e); 36th day of session (g). | |
| Illinois | House: determined by speaker (c,e). Senate: determined by president. | House: rules governing limitations may not be suspended except for bills determined by a majority of members of the Rules Comm. to be an emergency bill, & appropriations bills implementing the budget. |
| Indiana | House: Jan. 24 1st regular session; Jan. 10 of 2nd regular session. Senate: Jan. 21 of 1st regular session; Jan. 13 of 2nd regular session. | Senate: rules may be suspended by affirmative vote of majority of members; suspensions approved by Rules Committee, adopted by majority of members present. House: 2/3 vote of membership. Senate: consent of Rules and Legislative Procedures Committee. |
| Iowa | House: Friday of 6th week of 1st regular session (e, h, i); Friday of 2nd week of 2nd regular session (e, h, i). Senate: Friday of 7th week of 1st regular session (e, h); Friday of 2nd week of 2nd regular session (e, h). | Constitutional majority. |
| Kansas | 36th day of regular session for committees (j). | Resolution adopted by majority of members of either house may make specific exceptions to deadlines. |
| Kentucky | House: 38th L day of regular session. Senate: no introductions during last 20 L days of session. | Majority vote of membership of each house. |
| Louisiana | 30th C day of odd-year session; 10th C day of even-year session. | 2/3 vote of elected members of each house. |
| Maine | 1st Wednesday in December of 1st regular session; deadlines for 2nd regular session established by Legislative Council. | Approval of majority of members of Legislative Council. |
| Maryland | No introductions during last 35 C days of regular session. | 2/3 vote of elected members of each house. |
| Massachusetts | 1st Wednesday in December even-numbered years, preceding regular session (k). 1st Wednesday in November odd-numbered years, preceding regular session (k). | 2/3 vote of members present and voting. |
| Michigan | No limit. | |
| Minnesota | House: Actual date established during session (e, l). Senate: no limit. | 2/3 vote of members. |
| Mississippi | No introductions after 21st day of session (c, m). | 2/3 vote of members present and voting. |
| Missouri | 60th L day of regular session (c). | Majority vote of elected members each house; governor's request for consideration of bill by special message. |
| Montana | General bills & resolutions: 10th L day; revenue bills: 17th L day; committee bills and resolutions: 36th L day; committee bills implementing provisions of a general appropriation act: 75th L day; committee revenue bills: 62nd L day; interim study resolutions: 75th L day (c, n). | 2/3 vote of members. |
| Nebraska | 10th L day of any session (c, o). | 3/5 vote of elected membership for standing or special committees to introduce bills after 10th L day. |
| Nevada | 15th C day of regular session (p). | Affirmative vote of majority of members elected. |
| New Hampshire | Actual dates established during session. | 2/3 vote of members present. |

See footnotes at end of table.

# TIME LIMITS ON BILL INTRODUCTION — Continued

| State | Time limit on introduction of bills | Procedures for granting exception to time limits |
|---|---|---|
| New Jersey | Assembly: No printing of bills after September 1 during 2nd session. Senate: no limit. | Majority vote of members. |
| New Mexico | 28th C day of odd-year session (c, q); 13th C day of even-year session (c, q). | 2/3 vote of membership of each house. |
| New York | Assembly: for unlimited introduction of bills, 1st Tuesday in March; for introduction of 10 or fewer bills, last Tuesday in March (r, s). Senate: 1st Tuesday in March (s, t). | Unanimous vote. |
| North Carolina | House: 1st Thursday in February of 1st biennial session (u). Senate: March 27 for local bills. May 1 for budget bills. | House: 2/3 of members present and voting. Senate: 2/3 vote of membership. |
| North Dakota | House: 10th L day (v). Senate: 15th L day (v); resolutions: 18th L day (w); bills requested by executive agency or Supreme Court: Dec. 10 prior to regular session. | 2/3 vote or approval of majority of Committee on Delayed Bills. |
| Ohio | No limit. | |
| Oklahoma | January 30 for house of origin in 1st session (x); | 2/3 vote of membership. |
| Oregon | House: 36th C day of session (y). Senate: 36th C day following election of Senate president (z). | 2/3 vote of membership. |
| Pennsylvania | No limit (aa). | |
| Rhode Island | House: First Tuesday in February. Senate: February 5 for 1998. | House: 2/3 vote of members present. Senate: majority present and voting. |
| South Carolina | House: April 15 of regular session; May 1 for bills first introduced in Senate (c). Senate: May 1 of regular session for bills originating in House (c). | House: 2/3 vote of members present and voting. Senate: 2/3 vote of membership. |
| South Dakota | 40-day session: 15th L day; committee bills and joint resolutions, 16th L day. 35-day session: 10th L day; committee bills and joint resolutions, 11th L day; bills introduced at request of department, board, commission or state agency: 1st L day (c, bb). | 2/3 vote of membership. |
| Tennessee | House: general bills, 10th L day of regular session (cc). Senate: general bills, 10th L day or regular session; resolutions, 40th L day (cc). | Unanimous consent of Committee on Delayed Bills, or upon motion approved by 2/3 vote of members present. |
| Texas | 60th C day of regular session (dd). | 4/5 vote of members present and voting. |
| Utah | 42nd day of regular session (c). | 2/3 vote of members. |
| Vermont | House, individual introductions: 1st session, March 1; 2nd session, Feb. 1. Committees: 10 days after 1st Tue. in March (ee). Senate, individual and comm: 1st session, 53rd C day; 2nd session, sponsor requests bill drafting 25th C day before session (ff). | Approval by Rules Committee. |
| Virginia | Deadlines may be set during session. | |
| Washington | (Constitutional limit) No introductions during final 10 days of regular session (c, gg). | 2/3 vote of elected members of each house. |
| West Virginia | House: 50th day of regular session (c). Senate: 41st day of regular session (c, f). | 2/3 vote of members present. |
| Wisconsin | No limit. | |
| Wyoming | House: 15th L day of session. Senate: 12th L day of session (c). | 2/3 vote of elected members of either house. |

See footnotes at end of table.

# TIME LIMITS ON BILL INTRODUCTION — Continued

*Source:* State legislative rule books and manuals. The infomation in this table was compiled in 1998.

*Key:*

C — Calendar

L — Legislative

(a) Not applicable to local bills, advertised or otherwise.

(b) Not applicable to bills sponsored by any joint committees.

(c) Not applicable to appropriations bills. In West Virginia, supplementary appropriations bills or budget bills.

(d) Not applicable to (1) bills providing for current government expenditures; (2) bills the presiding officers certify are of an emergency nature; (3) bills the governor requests because of emergency or necessity; and (4) the legislative commissioners' revisor's bills and omnibus validating act.

(e) Not applicable to standing committee bills.

(f) Not applicable to local bills and joint resolutions.

(g) Not applicable to House State Affairs, Appropriations, Education, Revenue and Taxation, or Ways and Means committees, nor to Senate State Affairs, Finance, or Judiciary and Rules committees.

(h) Unless written request for drafting bill has been filed before deadline.

(i) Not applicable to bills co-sponsored by majority and minority floor leaders.

(j) Not applicable to Senate Ways and Means; Federal and State Affairs and the select committees of either house; or House committees on Calendar and Printing, Appropriations and Taxation.

(k) Not applicable to messages from governor, reports required or authorized to be made to legislature, petitions filed or approved by voters of cities or towns (or by mayors and city councils) for enactment of special legislation and which do not affect the powers and duties of state departments, boards, or commissions.

(l) Not applicable to bills recommended by conference committee reports, Rules and Legislative Administration Committee, the Senate, or the governor.

(m) Not applicable to revenue, local and private bills.

(n) Not applicable to joint resolutions concerning administration.

(o) Not applicable to "A" bills and those introduced at the request of the governor.

(p) Requests submitted to legislative counsel for bill drafting. Does not apply to standing committees or to member who has requested bill drafting before 16th C day of session.

(q) Not applicable to bills to provide for current government expenses; bills referred to legislature by governor by special message setting forth emergency necessitating legislation.

(r) Does not apply to bills introduced by Rules Committee, by message from the Senate, with consent of the speaker or by members elected at special election who take office on or after the first Tuesday of March.

(s) In no case may a bill be introduced on Fridays, unless submitted by governor or introduced by Rules Committee or by message from Senate.

(t) Bills recommended by state department or agency must be submitted to office of temporary president not later than March 1. Bills proposed by governor, attorney general, comptroller, Department of Education or office of court administration must be submitted to office of temporary president no later than first Tuesday in April.

(u) Not applicable to local and public bills or bills establishing districts for Congress or state or local entities.

(v) No member other than majority and minority leaders may introduce more than five bills in House after the 5th L day; three bills in Senate after 10th L day.

(w) Not applicable to resolutions proposing amendments to U.S. Constitution or directing legislative counsel to carry out a study (deadline, 34th L day).

(x) Final date for consideration on floor in house of origin during first session. Bills introduced after date are not placed on calendar for consideration until second session.

(y) Not applicable to measures approved by Committee on Legislative Rules and Reorganization or by speaker; appropriation or fiscal measures sponsored by Committees on Appropriations; true substitute measures sponsored by standing, special or joint committees; or measures drafted by legislative counsel.

(z) Not applicable to measures approved by Rules Committee, appropriation or fiscal measures sponsored by Committee on Ways and Means or measures requested for drafting by legislative counsel.

(aa) Resolutions fixing the last day for introduction of bills in the House are referred to the Rules Committee before consideration by the full House.

(bb) Not applicable to governor's bills.

(cc) Not applicable to certain local bills.

(dd) Not applicable to local bills, resolutions, emergency appropriations or all emergency matters submitted by governor in special messages to the legislature.

(ee) Not applicable to Appropriations or Ways and Means committees.

(ff) Not applicable to Appropriations or Finance committees.

(gg) Not applicable to substitute bills reported by standing committees for bills pending before such committees.

# Table 3.16
## ENACTING LEGISLATION: VETO, VETO OVERRIDE AND EFFECTIVE DATE

| State or other jurisdiction | Governor may item veto appropriation bills — Amount | Governor may item veto appropriation bills — Other (b) | Days allowed governor to consider bill (a) — During session: Bill becomes law unless vetoed | Days allowed governor to consider bill (a) — After session: Bill becomes law unless vetoed | Days allowed governor to consider bill (a) — After session: Bill dies unless signed | Votes required in each house to pass bills or items over veto (c) | Effective date of enacted legislation (d) |
|---|---|---|---|---|---|---|---|
| Alabama | ★ | ★ | 6 | 20P | 10A | Majority elected | Immediately (e) |
| Alaska | ★ (f) | ... | 15 | 10A | | 2/3 elected (g) | 90 days after enactment |
| Arizona | ★ | ★ | 5 | 10A | | 2/3 elected | 90 days after adjournment |
| Arkansas | ★ | ★ | 5 | 20A (h) | | Majority elected | 90 days after adjournment |
| California | ★ (f) | ... | 12 (i) | (i) | | 2/3 elected | (j) |
| Colorado | ★ | ★ | 10 (h) | 30A (h) | | 2/3 elected | Immediately (k) |
| Connecticut | ★ | ★ | 5 | 15P (h) | | 2/3 elected | Oct. 1 |
| Delaware | ★ | ★ | 10 | 15P (h) | 30A (h) | 3/5 elected | Immediately |
| Florida | ★ | ★ | 7 (h) | 15P (h) | | 2/3 elected | 60 days after adjournment |
| Georgia (l) | ★ | ★ | 6 (h) | 40A (h,m) | | 2/3 elected | July 1 (n) |
| Hawaii (l) | ★ (f) | ... | 10 (o,p) | 45A (o,p) | (p) | 2/3 elected | Immediately |
| Idaho | ★ | ★ | 5 | 10A | | 2/3 elected | 60 days after adjournment |
| Illinois | ★ (f) | ... | 60 (h) | 60P (h) | | 3/5 elected (g) | (n) |
| Indiana | ... | ★ | 7 | 7P (h) | | Majority elected | (q) |
| Iowa | ★ | ... | 3 | (r) | (r) | 2/3 elected | July 1 (n) |
| Kansas | ★ | ... | 10 (h) | 10P | | 2/3 elected | Upon publication |
| Kentucky | ★ | ★ | 10 | 10A | | Majority elected | 90 days after adjournment |
| Louisiana (l) | ★ | ★ | 10 (h) | 20P (h) | | 2/3 elected | Aug. 15 |
| Maine | ... | ★ | 10 | (m) | | 2/3 present | 90 days after adjournment |
| Maryland (l) | ... | ★ | 6 | 30P (m) | | 3/5 elected | June 1 (s) |
| Massachusetts | ★ (f) | ★ | 10 | 25A (h) | 10P | 2/3 present | 90 days after enactment |
| Michigan | ★ (f) | ★ | 14 (h) | 5A | 14P (h) | 2/3 elected and serving | 90 days after adjournment |
| Minnesota | ★ | ... | 3 | 10A | 14A | 2/3 elected (t) | Aug. 1 (t) |
| Mississippi | ★ | ★ | 5 | 15P (m) | | 2/3 elected | 60 days after enactment |
| Missouri | ★ | ... | 15 (h) | 45P (h,m) | | 2/3 elected | 90 days after adjournment (t,u) |
| Montana (l) | ★ (v) | ★ | 10 (h) | 25A (h) | | 2/3 present | Oct. 1 (t) |
| Nebraska | ★ | ... | 5 | 5A | | 3/5 elected | 3 months after adjournment |
| Nevada | ★ | ... | 5 | 10A | | 2/3 elected | Oct. 1 |
| New Hampshire | ... | ★ | 5 | | 5P | 2/3 elected | 60 days after enactment |
| New Jersey | ★ (f) | ... | 45 (h,w) | (w) | (w) | 2/3 elected | July 4; other dates usually specified |
| New Mexico | ★ | ... | 3 | | 20A | 2/3 present | 90 days after adjournment (t) |
| New York | ★ | ... | 10 | | 30A | 2/3 elected | 20 days after enactment |
| North Carolina (l) | ... | ★ | 10 | 30A | 10A | 3/5 elected | 30 days after adjournment |
| North Dakota | ★ | ★ | 3 | 15A | | 2/3 elected | (x) |
| Ohio | ★ | ★ | 10 | 10A | | 3/5 elected | 90 days after filed with secretary of state |
| Oklahoma | ★ | ... | 5 | 30A (o) | 15A | 2/3 elected (g) | 90 days after adjournment |
| Oregon | ★ | ★ | 5 (o) | 30A (o) | | 2/3 present | 90 days after adjournment |
| Pennsylvania | ★ | ★ | 10 (h) | 30A (h) | | 2/3 elected | 60 days after enactment |
| Rhode Island | ... | ★ | 6 | 10A (h) | | 3/5 present | Immediately |
| South Carolina | ★ | ... | 5 | (m) | | 2/3 present | 20 days after enactment |

See footnotes at end of table.

# ENACTING LEGISLATION: VETO, VETO OVERRIDE AND EFFECTIVE DATE — Continued

| State or other jurisdiction | Governor may item veto appropriation bills | | Days allowed governor to consider bill (a) | | | Votes required in each house to pass bills or items over veto (c) | Effective date of enacted legislation (d) |
|---|---|---|---|---|---|---|---|
| | Amount | Other (b) | During session | After session | | | |
| | | | Bill becomes law unless vetoed | Bill becomes law unless vetoed | Bill dies unless signed | | |
| South Dakota | ★ | ★ | 5 (h) | 15A (h) | | 2/3 elected | 90 days after adjournment (n) |
| Tennessee | ★ (f) | ... | 10 | 10A | | Majority elected | 40 days after enactment |
| Texas | ★ | ... | 10 | 20A | | 2/3 present | 90 days after adjournment |
| Utah | ★ | ... | 10 | 20A (h) | | 2/3 elected | 60 days after adjournment |
| Vermont | ... | ... | 5 | | 3A | 2/3 present | July 1 |
| Virginia | ★ | ★ | 7 (h) | | 30A (h) | 2/3 present (y) | July 1 (z) |
| Washington | ★ | ★ | 5 | 20A | | 2/3 present | 90 days after adjournment |
| West Virginia | ★ (f) | ★ | 5 | 15A (aa) | | Majority elected (g) | 90 days after enactment |
| Wisconsin | ★ | ... | 6 | | 6P | 2/3 present | Day after publication date |
| Wyoming | ★ | ★ | 3 | 15A (h) | | 2/3 elected | Immediately |
| American Samoa | ★ | ... | 10 | | 30A | 2/3 elected | 60 days after adjournment (bb) |
| Guam | ★ | ★ | 10 | | 30P | 2/3 elected | Immediately (cc) |
| No. Mariana Islands | ... | ... | 40 (h,dd) | | | 2/3 elected | Immediately |
| Puerto Rico | (f) | ★ | 10 | | 30P (h) | 2/3 elected | Specified in act |
| U.S. Virgin Islands | ★ | ★ | 10 | | 30P (h) | 2/3 elected | Immediately |

See footnotes at end of table.

# ENACTING LEGISLATION: VETO, VETO OVERRIDE AND EFFECTIVE DATE — Continued

*Sources:* State constitutions and statutes.

*Note:* Some legislatures reconvene after normal session to consider bills vetoed by governor. Connecticut–if governor vetoes any bill, secretary of state must reconvene General Assembly on second Monday after the last day on which governor is either authorized to transmit or has transmitted every bill with his objections, whichever occurs first; General Assembly must adjourn *sine die* not later than three days after its reconvening. Hawaii–legislature may reconvene on 45th day after adjournment *sine die*, in special session, without call. Louisiana–legislature meets in a maximum five-day veto session on the 40th day after final adjournment. Missouri–if governor returns any bill on or after the fifth day before the last day on which legislature may consider bills (in even-numbered years), legislature automatically reconvenes on first Wednesday following the second Monday in September for a maximum 10-calendar day session. New Jersey–legislature meets in special session (without call or petition) to act on bills returned by governor on 45th day after *sine die* adjournment of the regular session; if the second year expires before the 45th day, the day preceding the end of the legislative year. Utah–if two-third of the members of each house favor reconvening to consider vetoed bills, a maximum five-day session is set by the presiding officers. Virginia–legislature reconvenes on sixth Wednesday after adjournment for a maximum three-day session (may be extended to seven days upon vote of majority of members elected to each house). Washington–upon petition of two-third of the members of each house, legislature meets 45 days after adjournment for a maximum five-day session.

Key:
★ — Yes
. . . — No
A — Days after adjournment of legislature.
P — Days after presentation to governor.
(a) Sundays excluded, unless otherwise indicated.
(b) Includes language in appropriations bill.
(c) Bill returned to house of origin with governor's objections.
(d) Effective date may be established by the law itself or may be otherwise changed by vote of the legislature. Special or emergency acts are usually effective immediately.
(e) Penal acts, 60 days.
(f) Governor can also reduce amounts in appropriations bills. In Hawaii, governor can reduce items in executive appropriations measures, but cannot reduce nor item veto amounts appropriated for the judicial or legislative branches.
(g) Different number of votes required for revenue and appropriations bills. Alaska–three-fourth elected. Illinois–appropriations reductions, majority elected. Oklahoma–emergency bills, three-fourth elected. Virginia–budget and supplemental appropriations, two-third elected.
(h) Sundays included.
(i) A bill presented to the governor that is not returned within 12 days (excluding Saturdays, Sundays and holidays) becomes a law; provided that any bill passed before Sept. 1 of the second calendar year of the biennium of the legislative session and in the possession of the governor on or after Sept. 1 that is not returned by the governor on or before Sept. 30 of that year becomes law. The legislature may not present to the governor any bill after Nov. 15 of the second calendar year of the biennium of the session. If the legislature, by adjournment of a special session prevents the return of a bill with the veto message, the bill becomes law unless the governor vetoes within 12 days by depositing it and the veto message in the office of the secretary of state.
(j) For legislation enacted in regular sessions: Jan. 1 next following 90-day period from date of enactment. For legislation enacted in special sessions: 91 days after adjournment. Does not apply to statutes calling elections, statutes providing for tax levies or appropriations for the usual current state expenses or urgency statutes, all of which take effect immediately.
(k) An act takes effect on the date stated in the act, or if no date is stated in the act, then on its passage.
(l) Constitution withholds right to veto constitutional amendments.

(m) Bills vetoed after adjournment are returned to the legislature for reconsideration. Georgia–bills vetoed during last three days of session and not considered for overriding, and all bills vetoed after *sine die* adjournment may be considered at next session. Maine–returned within three days after the next meeting of the same legislature which enacted the bill or resolution. Maryland–reconsidered at the next meeting of the same General Assembly. Mississippi–returned within three days after the beginning of the next session. Missouri–bills returned on or after the 5th day before the last day to consider bills legislature automatically reconvenes on the first Wednesday following the second Wednesday in September not to exceed 10 calendar days. South Carolina–within two days after the next meeting.

(n) Effective date for bills which become law on or after July 1. Georgia–Jan. 1, unless a specific date has been provided for in legislation. Illinois–a bill passed after June 30 does not become effective prior to July 1 of the next calendar year unless legislature by a three-fifth vote provides for an earlier effective date. Iowa–if governor signs bill after July 1, bill becomes law on Aug. 15; for special sessions, 90 days after adjournment. South Dakota–91 days after adjournment.

(o) Except Sundays and legal holidays. In Hawaii, except Saturdays, Sundays, holidays and any days in which the legislature is in recess prior to its adjournment. In Oregon, except Saturdays and Sundays.

(p) The governor must notify the legislature 10 days before the 45th day of his intent to veto a measure on that day. The legislature may convene on the 45th day after adjournment to consider the vetoed measures. If the legislature fails to reconvene, the bill does not become law. If the legislature reconvenes, it may pass the measure over the governor's veto or it may amend the law to meet the governor's objections. If the law is amended, the governor must sign the bill within 10 days after it is presented to him in order for it to become law.

(q) No act takes effect until it has been published and circulated in the counties, by authority, except in cases of emergency.

(r) Governor must sign or veto all bills presented to him. Any bill submitted to the governor for his approval during the last three days of a session must be deposited by him in the secretary of state's office within 30 days after adjournment with his approval or objections.

(s) Bills passed over governor's veto are effective in 30 days or on date specified in bill, whichever is later.

(t) Different date for fiscal legislation. Minnesota, Montana–July 1. Missouri, New Mexico–immediately.

(u) In event of a recess of 30 days or more, legislature may prescribe, by joint resolution, that laws previously passed and not effective shall take effect 90 days from beginning of recess.

(v) No appropriation can be made in excess of the recommendations contained in the governor's budget except by a three-fifth vote. The excess is subject to veto by the governor.

(w) On the 45th day after the date of presentation, a bill becomes law unless the governor returns it with his objections, except that (1) if the legislature is in adjournment *sine die* on the 45th day, a special session is convened (without petition or call) for the sole purpose of acting upon bills returned by the governor; (2) any bill passed between the 45th day and the 10th day preceding the end of the second legislative year must be returned by the governor by the day preceding the end of the second legislative year; (3) any bill passed or reenacted within 10 days preceding the expiration of the second legislative year becomes law if signed prior to the seventh day following such expiration, or the governor returns it to the house of origin and two-third elected members agree to pass the bill prior to such expiration.

(x) August 1 bill filed with secretary of state; if enacted between August 1 and January 1 of following year, 90 days after its filing. Appropriations and tax bills: July 1.

(y) Must include majority of elected members.

(z) Special sessions–first day of fourth month after adjournment.

(aa) Five days for appropriations bills.

(bb) Laws required to be approved only by the governor. An act required to be approved by the U.S. Secretary of the Interior only after it is vetoed by the governor and so approved takes effect 40 days after it is returned to the governor by the secretary.

(cc) U.S. Congress may annul.

(dd) Twenty days for appropriations bills.

## Table 3.17
## LEGISLATIVE APPROPRIATIONS PROCESS: BUDGET DOCUMENTS AND BILLS

| State or other jurisdiction | Legal source of deadline | | Budget document submission — Submission date relative to convening | | | | | Budget bill introduction | | |
|---|---|---|---|---|---|---|---|---|---|---|
| | Constitutional | Statutory | Prior to session | Within one week | Within two weeks | Within one month | Over one month | Same time as budget document | Another time | Not until committee review of budget document |
| Alabama | ★ | ... | ... | 2nd day | ... | ... | ... | ★ | ... | ... |
| Alaska | ... | ★ | Dec. 15 | ★ | ... | ... | ... | ... | ★ (a) | ... |
| Arizona* | ... | ★ | ★ | ... | ... | ... | ... | ... | ... | ★ |
| Arkansas | ... | ★ | ... | ... | ... | ... | ★ | ... | ... | ★ |
| California | ★ | ... | ... | ... | ... | ★ | ... | ★ | ... | ... |
| Colorado | ... | ★ | ★ (b) | ... | ... | ... | ... | ... | ... | ★ |
| Connecticut | ... | ★ | ... | (a) | ... | ... | ... | ★ | ... | ... |
| Delaware | ... | ★ | ... | ... | ... | by Feb. 1 | ... | ★ (c) | ... | ... |
| Florida | ★ | ★ | 45 days | ... | ... | ... | ... | ... | ... | ★ (c) |
| Georgia | ★ | ... | ... | ★ | ... | ... | ... | ★ | ... | ... |
| Hawaii | ... | ★ | 30 days | ... | ... | ... | ... | ... | ★ | ... |
| Idaho | ... | ★ | ... | ★ | ... | ... | ... | ... | ... | ★ |
| Illinois | ... | ★ | ... | ... | ... | ... | ★ | ... | ★ | ... |
| Indiana | ... | ★ | ... | ... | ... | ... | ... | ★ | ... | ... |
| Iowa | ... | ★ | ... | ... | ... | ★ (a) | ... | ... | ... | ★ (c) |
| Kansas | ... | ★ | ... | ... | ★ (e) | ... | ... | ... | ★ | ... |
| Kentucky | ... | ★ | ... | ... | ★ (a,e) | ... | ... | ★ | ... | ... |
| Louisiana | ... | ★ | (f) | (f) | ... | ... | ... | (g) | ... | ... |
| Maine* | ... | ★ | ... | ★ (a,e) | ... | ... | ... | ★ | ... | ... |
| Maryland | ★ | ... | ... | ★ (e) | ... | ... | ... | ★ (h) | ... | ... |
| Massachusetts* | ... | ★ | ... | ... | ... | ★ | ... | ★ (i) | ... | ... |
| Michigan* | ... | ★ | ... | ... | ... | ★ (e) | ... | ★ | ... | ... |
| Minnesota | ... | ★ | ... | ... | ... | ★ (a) | ... | ... | ... | ★ (j) |
| Mississippi* | ... | ★ | ... | 1st day | ... | ... | ... | ... | ... | ★ |
| Missouri* | ★ | ... | ... | ... | ... | ★ | ... | ... | ★ | ... |
| Montana | ... | ★ | ★ | ... | ... | ... | ... | ... | ★ | ... |
| Nebraska | ... | ★ | ... | ... | ... | ★ (a,e) | ... | ★ (c) | ... | ... |
| Nevada | ... | ★ | ... | ... | ★ | ... | ... | ... | ... | ★ |
| New Hampshire | ... | ★ | ... | ... | ... | ... | ★ (a) | ★ | ... | ... |
| New Jersey | ... | ★ | ... | ... | ... | ★ (e) | ... | ... | ... | ★ (k) |
| New Mexico | ... | ★ | ... | ... | ... | (l) | ... | (d) | ... | ... |
| New York* | ★ | ... | ... | ... | ★ (e) | ... | ... | ★ (m) | ... | ... |
| North Carolina | ... | ... | ... | ... | ... | ... | (k) | ★ | ... | ... |
| North Dakota | ... | ★ | (n) | ... | ... | ... | ... | ... | ... | ★ |
| Ohio | ... | ★ | ... | ... | ... | ★ (e) | ... | ★ | ... | ... |
| Oklahoma | ... | ★ | Oct. 1 | ★ | ... | ... | ... | ★ | ... | ... |
| Oregon | ... | ★ | Dec. 1 (e) | ... | ... | ... | ... | ... | ★ (a) | ... |
| Pennsylvania | ... | ★ | ... | ... | ... | ★ (e,o) | ... | ... | ... | ★ |
| Rhode Island* | ... | ★ | ... | ... | ... | ... | ★ | ★ | ... | ... |
| South Carolina | ... | ★ | (a,b) | ... | ... | ... | ... | ... | ... | ★ |
| South Dakota | ... | ★ | ★ (a) | ... | ... | ... | ... | ... | ★ (p) | ... |
| Tennessee | ... | ★ | ... | ... | ★ (a,e) | ★ (a,e) | ... | ★ | ... | ... |
| Texas | ... | ★ | ... | 6th day | ... | ... | ... | ... | ★ | ... |
| Utah | ... | ★ | (q) | ★ (r) | ... | ... | ... | ... | ★ (s) | ... |
| Vermont | ... | ★ | ... | ... | ... | ★ | ... | ... | ... | ★ |
| Virginia | ... | ★ | Dec. 20 | ... | ... | ... | ... | ★ | (a) | ... |
| Washington | ... | ★ | Dec. 2 (u) | ... | ... | ... | ... | ... | (v) | ... |
| West Virginia | ★ | ... | ... | 1st day (e) | ... | ... | ... | ★ | ... | ... |
| Wisconsin | ... | ★ | ... | ... | ... | ★ (w) | ... | ★ | ... | ... |
| Wyoming | ... | ★ | Dec. 1 | ... | ... | ... | ... | ... | ... | ★ |
| No. Mariana Islands | ... | ★ | (a) | ... | ... | ... | ... | ... | (x) | ★ |
| Puerto Rico | ... | ★ | ... | ... | ... | ★ | ... | ... | ... | ★ |
| U.S. Virgin Islands | ... | ★ | May 30 | ... | ... | ★ (y) | ... | ★ | ... | (z) |

See footnotes at end of table.

# LEGISLATIVE APPROPRIATIONS PROCESS: BUDGET DOCUMENTS AND BILLS — Continued

*Source*: The Council of State Governments' legislative survey January 2000, except where noted by * where data are from *The Book of the States, 1998-99*.

Key:
★ - Yes
. . . - No

(a) Specific time limitations: Alaska-4th legislative day; Connecticut-odd numbered years no later than the first session day following the third day in February, in even numbered years on the day the General Assembly convenes; Iowa-no later than February 1; Kentucky-10th legislative day; Maine-by Friday following the first Monday in January; Minnesota-fourth Tuesday in January during biennial session; Nebraska-by January 15; New Hampshire-by February 15; Oregon-Dec. 15 in even-numbered years; South Carolina-first Tuesday in January; South Dakota-first Tuesday after the first Monday in December; Tennessee-on or before February 1; No. Mariana Islands-no later than 6 months before the beginning of the fiscal year.

(b) Copies of agency budgets to be presented to the legislature by November 1. Governor's budget usually is presented in January.

(c) Executive budget bill is introduced and used as a working tool for committee. Delaware-after hearings on executive bill, a new bill is then introduced; the committee bill is considered by the legislature.

(d) New Mexico repealed a statutory deadline in 1999. The deadline for budget bill introduction now relies on joint rules regarding third reading and final passage in house of origin.

(e) Later for first session of a new governor; Kansas-21 days; Kentucky-15th legislative day; Maine-by Friday following first Monday in February; Maryland-10 days after convening; Michigan-within 60 days; Nebraska-February 1; New Jersey-March 15; New York-February 1; Ohio-by March 15; Oregon-February 1; Pennsylvania-first full week in March; Tennessee- March 1; West Virginia-10 days, in odd-numbered years.

(f) The governor shall submit his executive budget to the Joint legislative Committee on the budget no later than 45 days prior to each regular session; except that in the first year of each term, the executive budget shall be submitted no later than 30 days prior to the regular session. Copies shall be made available to the entire legislature on the first day of each regular session.

(g) Bills appropriating monies for the general operating budget and ancillary appropriations, bills appropriating funds for the expenses of the legislature and the judiciary must be submitted to the legislature for introduction no later than 45 days prior to each regular session, except that in the first year of each term, such appropriation bills shall be submitted no later than 30 days prior to the regular session.

(h) Appropriations bill other than the budget bill (supplementary) may be introduced at any time. They must provide their own tax source and may not be enacted until the budget bill is enacted.

(i) General appropriations bills only.

(j) The Executive Branch usually submits budget bills shortly after the budget is submitted. There is no statutory requirement that this occur.

(k) By custom only. No statutory or constitutional provisions.

(l) Statutes provide for submission by the 25th legislative day; however, the executive budget is usually presented by the first day of the session.

(m) Governor has 30 days to amend or supplement the budget; he may submit any amendments to any bills or submit supplemental bills.

(n) For whole legislature. Legislative Council's Budget Section receives budget during legislature's December organizational session.

(o) Submitted by governor as soon as possible after General Assembly organizes, but not later than the first full week in February.

(p) No later than the 16th legislative day by rule.

(q) Governor must submit budget to Legislative Fiscal Analyst 30 days prior to session.

(r) Must submit to the legislature no later than 3 days after session begins.

(s) Joint legislative rules require budget bill to be introduced 3 days prior to the constitutionally mandated end of the session.

(t) Must submit to fiscal analyst 30 days prior to session.

(u) For fiscal period other than biennium, 20 days prior to first day of session.

(v) Even-numbered years.

(w) No set time.

(x) Last Tuesday in January. A later submission date may be requested by the governor.

(y) By enacting annual appropriations legislation.

(z) Prior to September 30.

## Table 3.18
## FISCAL NOTES: CONTENT AND DISTRIBUTION

| State or other jurisdiction | Content | | | | | | Distribution — Legislators | | | Appropriations committee | | | |
|---|---|---|---|---|---|---|---|---|---|---|---|---|---|
| | Intent or purpose of bill | Cost involved | Projected future cost | Proposed source of revenue | Fiscal impact on local government | Other | All | Available on request | Bill sponsor | Members | Chairman only | Fiscal staff | Executive budget staff |
| Alabama | ... | ★ | ... | ★ | ★ | ★ (a) | ... | ★ | ★ | ... | ... | ... | ... |
| Alaska | ... | ★ | ★ | ★ (b) | ★ (c) | ★ (d) | ★ | ... | ... | ... | ... | ... | ... |
| Arizona* | ★ | ★ | ★ | ★ | ★ | ★ (e) | ★ | ★ | ... | ... | ... | ★ | ★ |
| Arkansas (f) | ... | ★ | ★ | ... | ★ | ★ | ★ | ... | ... | ... | ... | ... | ... |
| California | ★ | ★ | ★ | ★ | ★ | ★ | ... | ★ | ★ | ★ | ... | ★ | ★ |
| Colorado | ★ | ★ | ★ | ★ | ★ | ★ | ... | ... | ★(gg) | ... | ... | ... | ... |
| Connecticut | ★ (g) | ★ | ★ | ★ (b) | ★ | ★ (h) | ★ | ... | ... | ★ (i) | ... | ★ | ★ |
| Delaware | ... | ★ | ★ | ... | ... | ★ (j) | ... | ★ | ... | ★ | ... | ★ | ★ |
| Florida* | ... | ★ | ★ | ★ | ★ | ★ (k) | ★ | ... | ... | ... | ... | ... | ... |
| Georgia | ... | ★ | ★ | ★ | ★ | ★ (k) | ★ | ★ | ... | ... | ... | ... | ... |
| Hawaii | ... | ... | ... | ... | ... | ★ | ... | ... | ... | ... | ★ | ★ | ★ |
| Idaho | ★ | ★ | ★ | ... | ★ | ★ | ★ | ... | ... | ... | ... | ... | ... |
| Illinois | ... | ★ | ★ | ★ | ★ | ... | ★ (l) | ★ (l) | ... | ... | ... | ... | ... |
| Indiana* | ★ | ★ | ★ | ★ | ★ | ★ | ... | ... | ... | ... | ★ | ★ | ★ |
| Iowa | ... | ★ | ★ | ★ | ★ | ★ | ... | ... | ... | ... | ... | ... | ... |
| Kansas | ★ | ★ | ★ | ★ | ★ | ... | ... | ★ | ★ | ... | ★ (m) | ★ | ★ |
| Kentucky | ★ | ★ | ★ | ★ | ★ | ★ (n) | ... | ★ | ★ | ★ (m) | ... | ★ | ... |
| Louisiana | ... | ★ | ★ | ... | ★ | ... | ★ | ★ | ... | ... | ★(o) | ... | ... |
| Maine* | ... | ★ | ★ | ★ | ★ | (p) | ★ | ... | ... | ... | ... | ... | ... |
| Maryland | ... | ★ | ★ | ★ | ★ | ★ | ... | ★ | ★ | ... | ... | ... | ... |
| Massachusetts* | ... | ★(q) | ★ | ... | ... | ★ | ★ | ... | ... | ★ | ... | ... | ... |
| Michigan* | ★ | ★ | ★ | ★ | ★ | ★ (r) | ★ (s) | ★ | ... | ... | ... | ★ | ... |
| Minnesota | ★ | ★ | ★ | ... | ★ | ★ (k) | ★ | ★ | ★ | ... | ★ | ★ | ★ |
| Mississippi* | ★ | ★ | ★ | ... | ★ | ... | ★ | ... | ... | ★ | ... | ★ | ★ |
| Missouri* | ... | ★ | ★ | ★ | ★ | ★ | ... | ... | ... | ... | ... | ... | ... |
| Montana | ... | ★ | ★ | ... | ★ | ★ (k) | ★ | ... | ... | ... | ... | ★ | ★ |
| Nebraska | ... | ★ | ★ | ... | ... | ★ (k) | ★ | ... | ... | ... | ... | ★ | ... |
| Nevada | ... | ★ | ★ | ★ | ★ | ★ | ★ | ... | ... | ... | ... | ... | ... |
| New Hampshire | ★ | ★ | ★ | ★ | ★ | ★ | ... | ... | ... | ... | ... | ★ | ★ |
| New Jersey | ★ | ★ | ★ | ★ | ★ | ★ (r) | ★ | ... | ... | ... | ... | ... | ... |
| New Mexico | ★ | ★ | ★ | ... | (t) | ★ (u) | ... | (v) | ... | ... | ★ (v) | ... | ... |
| New York* | ... | ★ | ★ | ... | ★ | ★ (n) | ... | ★ | ★ | ★ | ... | ★ | ... |
| North Carolina | ... | ★ | ★ | ... | ★ | ★ (k) | ★ | ... | ... | ... | ... | ... | ... |
| North Dakota (w) | ... | ★ | ★ (x) | ★ | ★ | ★ (n) | ... | ★ | ... | ... | ... | ★ (z) | ★ |
| Ohio | ★ | ★ | ★ | ★ | ★ | ★ | ★ | ★(hh) | ★ | (aa) | (aa) | ... | ... |
| Oklahoma (bb) | ★ | ★ | ... | ★ | ... | ★ (j) | ... | ★ | ★ | ... | ★ | ★ | ... |
| Oregon | ★ | ★ | ★ | ★ | ★ | ★ (e) | ★ | ... | ... | ... | ... | ... | ★ |
| Pennsylvania | ... | ★ | ★ | ★ | ★ | ★ (n) | ★ | ... | ... | ... | ... | ★ | ★ |
| Rhode Island* | ... | ★ | ★ | ... | ★ | ★ (cc) | ... | ★ | ... | ... | ★ | ★ | ★ |
| South Carolina | ... | ★ | ★ | ★ | ★ | ... | ★ | ★ | ... | ★ | ... | ★ | ★ |
| South Dakota | ... | ★ | ★ | ★ | ★ | ★ (n) | ★ | ★ | ... | ... | ... | ... | ... |
| Tennessee | ★ | ★ | ★ | ★ | ★ | ★ | ★ | ★ | ★ | ★ | ... | ★ | ★ |
| Texas | ... | ★ | ★ | ★ | ★ | ★ (n) | ★ | ★ | ★ | ★ (m) | ... | ... | ★ |
| Utah | ... | ★ | ★ | ★ | ★ | ★(ii) | ★ | ... | ... | ... | ... | ... | ★ |
| Vermont | ★ | ★ | ★ | ★ | ... | ... | ... | ★ | ... | ★ | ... | ... | ... |
| Virginia | ★ | ★ | ★ | ★ (dd) | ★ | ★ | ... | ★ | ★ | ★ | ... | ... | ... |
| Washington | ★ | ★ | ★ | ★ | ★ | ... | ... | ★ | ★ (m) | ... | ★ | ★ (ee) | ... |
| West Virginia | ★ | ★ | ★ | ★ | ★ | ... | ... | ... | ★ (m) | ... | ... | ... | ... |
| Wisconsin | ★ | ★ | ★ | ★ | ★ | ★ | ★ | ★ | ★ | ★ | ... | ★ | ★ |
| Wyoming | ... | ★ | ★ | ★ | ... | ★ | (ff) | ... | ... | ... | ... | ... | ... |
| No. Mariana Islands | ★ | ★ | ★ | ★ | ★ | ★ | ... | ... | ... | ... | ★ | ★ | ★ |
| U.S. Virgin Islands | ★ | ★ | ... | ★ | ★ | ... | ★ | ... | ★ | ★ | ... | ★ | ... |

See footnotes at end of table.

# FISCAL NOTES: CONTENT AND DISTRIBUTION — Continued

*Source*: The Council of State Governments' legislative survey January 2000, except where noted by * where data are from *The Book of the States, 1998-99*.

*Note*: A fiscal note is a summary of the fiscal effects of a bill on government revenues, expenditures and liabilities.

*Key*:

★ - Yes

. . . - No

(a) Fiscal notes are included in bills for final passage calendar.

(b) Contained in the bill and in the fiscal note.

(c) Information on fiscal impact is requested by the last committee to which the bill is referred on the day it is introduced. This provision will be repealed July 1, 1998.

(d) Fiscal notes are attached to the bill before it is reported from the first committee of referral. Governor's bills must have fiscal note before introduction. Once fiscal notes are submitted, they are copied and available to all.

(e) Assumptions (methodology/explanation of fiscal figures).

(f) Only retirement, corrections, and local government bills require fiscal notes.

(g) May be included but not required.

(h) Fiscal notes may also reflect: savings, positions and estimated impact on revenues; assumptions (methodology/explanation of fiscal figures); bill proposing changes in retirement system of state or local government must have an actuarial note; other relevant data; technical or mechanical defects may be noted.

(i) For both the Appropriations and the Finance, Revenue and Bonding Committees, preliminary notes are prepared for committee meetings.

(j) Relevant data and prior fiscal year cost information.

(k) Mechanical defects in bill.

(l) A summary of the fiscal note is attached to the summary of the relevant bill in the Legislative Synopsis and Digest. Fiscal notes are prepared for the sponsor of the bill and are attached to the bill on file in either the office of the clerk of the House or the Secretary of the Senate.

(m) Or to the committee to which referred.

(n) In North Dakota a bill that impacts workers' compensation benefits or premiums must have an actuarial impact statement. A bill proposing changes in the retirement system of state or local government must have an actuarial note. In Kentucky, a bill which fiscally affects state or local corection services must have a fiscal impact statement.

(o) Prepared by the Legislative Fiscal Office when a state agency is involved and prepared by Legislative Auditor's office when a local board or commission is involved; copies sent to House and Senate staff offices respectively.

(p) Distributed to chairs of committee to which bill was referred; the sponsor; the presiding officers of the Senate and the House; the non-partisan staff of the committee to which the bill was referred; and the State Budget officer (Executive).

(q) Fiscal notes are prepared only if cost exceeds $100,000 or matter has not been acted upon by the Joint Committee on Ways and Means.

(r) Other relevant data.

(s) Analyses prepared by the Senate Fiscal Agency are distributed to Senate members only; Fiscal notes prepared by the House Fiscal Agency are prepared for bills being voted on in any standing committee and are distributed to the chairperson and all committee members.

(t) Occasionally.

(u) The impact of revenue bills is reviewed by the Legislative Finance Committee and executive agencies.

(v) Legislative Finance Committee staff prepare fiscal notes for Appropriations Committee chairman; other fiscal impact statements prepared by Legislative Finance Committee and executive agencies are available to anyone upon request.

(w) Notes required only if impact is $5,000 or more.

(x) A four-year projection.

(y) All members of appropriations receive.

(z) Only select fiscal staff.

(aa) Fiscal notes are prepared for bills before being voted on in any standing committee and are given to the chairman and all committee members.

(bb) Fiscal notes are prepared only in the House.

(cc) Technical or mechanical defects may be noted.

(dd) The Dept. of Planning and Budget and other relevant state agencies, including the Dept. of Taxation , prepare impact statements, The Joint Legislative Audit And Review Commission (JLARC) prepares review statements as requested by committee chairpersons.

(ee) Distributed to appropriate fiscal and policy staff.

(ff) Fiscal notes are included with the bill upon introduction

(gg) A copy of the fiscal note is initially provided to the bill sponsor and to the chairman of the committee of reference to which the bill is assigned. A copy is then provided to every legislator.

(hh) After distribution to committee members, fiscal notes are made available to the public, inlcuding posting the notes on the Internet.

(ii) Fiscal notes are to include cost estimates on all proposed bills that anticipate direct expenditures by any Utah resident and the cost to the overall Utah resident population.

## Table 3.19
## BILL AND RESOLUTION INTRODUCTIONS AND ENACTMENTS:
## 1998 AND 1999 REGULAR SESSIONS

| State or other jurisdiction | Duration of session** | Introductions | | Enactments | | Measures vetoed by governor | Length of session |
|---|---|---|---|---|---|---|---|
| | | Bills | Resolutions | Bills | Resolutions | | |
| Alabama | Jan. 1-April 27, 1998 | 1,698 | 551 | 577 | 426 | 0 | 30L |
| | Mar. 2-June 9, 1999 | 1,352 | 590 | 377 | 314 | 0 | 30L |
| Alaska | Jan. 12-May 13 ,1998 | 356 | 68 | 142 | 43 | 8 (a) | 122C |
| | Jan. 19-May 19, 1999 | 438 | 105 | 94 | 39 | 4 (a) | 121C |
| Arizona* | Jan. 10-April 17, 1994 | 1,160 | 60 | 380 | 17 | 0 | 98C |
| | Jan. 9-April 13, 1995 | 957 | 70 | 300 | 23 | 8 | 95C |
| Arkansas | No regular session in 1998 | | | | | | |
| | Jan. 11-April 30, 1999 | 2,258 | 163 | 1,598 | 118 | 3 | 89C |
| California | Jan. 5-Sept. 1, 1998 | 2,118 | 231 | 1,083 | 180 | 351 | 132L |
| | Dec. 7,1998 - Sept. 10,1999 | 3,053 | 227 | 1027 | 144 | 246 | 124L |
| Colorado | Jan. 7-May 6, 1998 | 620 | 132 | 353 | 95 | 16 | 120C |
| | Jan. 6-May 5, 1999 | 624 | 144 | 369 | 116 | 5 | 120C |
| Connecticut | Feb. 4-May 6, 1998 | 1,383 | 226 | 273 | 226 | 1 | 68L |
| | Jan. 6-June 9, 1999 | 3,799 | 286 | 307 | 286 | 1 | 110L |
| Delaware | Jan. 13-June 30, 1998 | 553 | 113 | 270 | 10 | 13 | 52L |
| | Jan. 12-June 30, 1999 | 682 | 82 | 259 | 11 | 1 | 54L |
| Florida | Mar. 3-May 1, 1998 | 2,565 | 200 | 536 | 187 | 17 | 60C |
| | Mar. 2-April 30, 1999 | 2,409 | 167 | 489 | 164 | 10 | 60C |
| Georgia | Jan. 12-Mar. 19, 1998 | 2,117 | 1,338 | 524 | 989 | 13 | 40L |
| | Jan. 12-Mar. 24, 1999 | 1,386 | 1,125 | 461 | 968 | 6 | 40L |
| Hawaii | Jan. 21-May 14, 1998 | 2,554 | 672 | 334 | 188 | 23 | 65L |
| | Jan. 20-May 4, 1999 | 3,397 | 851 | 349 | 225 | 45 | 60L |
| Idaho | Adjourned Mar. 20, 1998 | 710 | 74 | 438 | 41 | 10 | 71C |
| | Jan. 11-Mar. 19, 1999 | 666 | 88 | 401 | 52 | 4 | 68C |
| Illinois | Jan. 6-May 22, 1998 | 906 | 20 | 131 | 1 | 2 | (c) |
| | Jan. 12-May 27, 1999 | 1,786 | 26 | 274 | 1 | 1 | (c) |
| Indiana | Nov. 11, 1997-Feb. 27, 1998 | 888 | 24 | 179 | 2 | 0 | (c) |
| | Nov. 11, 1998-April 29, 1999 | 1,504 | 50 | 34 | 6 | 11 (a) | (c) |
| Iowa | Jan. 12-April 22, 1998 | 980 | 9 | 225 | 2 | 16 (d) | 101C |
| | Jan. 11-April 29, 1999 | 1,264 | 27 | 208 | 1 | 14 (d) | 109C |
| Kansas | Jan.12-May 26, 1998 | 760 | 40 | 203 | 14 | 1(d) | (c) |
| | Jan. 11-May 25, 1999 | 942 | 65 | 173 | 19 | 0(d) | 68L |
| Kentucky | Jan. 6-April 15, 1998 | 1,369 | 364 | 552 | 312 | 4(d) | 60L |
| | No regular session in 1999 | | | | | | |
| Louisiana | April 27-June 10, 1998 | 440 | 329 | 76 | 254 | 0 | 60L |
| | Mar. 29-June 21, 1999 | 3,397 | 756 | 1,425 | 647 | 0 | 59L |
| Maine* | Jan. 5-April 14, 1994 | 615 | 11 | 340 | 0 | 12 (a) | 39L |
| | Dec. 7-June 30, 1995 | 1,586 | 33 | 607 | 2 | 1 | 70L |
| Maryland | Jan. 14-April 13, 1998 | 2,227 | 39 | 784 | 12 | 102 | 90C |
| | Jan. 13-April 12, 1999 | 2,049 | 35 | 705 | 13 | 125 | 90C |
| Massachusetts* | Jan. 8, 1992-Jan. 5, 1993 | 7,353 | 0 | 414 | 0 | 39 (a) | (c) |
| | Jan. 6, 1993-Jan. 4, 1994 | 7,667 | 0 | 498 | 0 | 53 (a) | (c) |
| Michigan | Jan. 14-Dec. 22, 1998 | 1,417 | 12 | 551 | 1 | 20 | (e) |
| | Jan. 13-Dec. 10, 1999 | 2,133 | 27 | 276 | 0 | 4 | 87L |
| Minnesota | Jan. 20, 1998-April 9, 1998 | 3,051 | 4 | 157 | 4 | 15(d) | 46L |
| | Jan. 5, 1999-May 17, 1998 | 4,760 | 70 | 250 | 3 | 18(d) | 67L |
| Mississippi | Jan. 6-April 5, 1998 | 3,212 | 345 | 598 | 164 | 11 | 90C |
| | Jan. 5-April 7, 1999 | 3,011 | 342 | 596 | 212 | 12 | 93C |
| Missouri* | Jan. 5-May 13, 1994 | 1,256 | 45 | 180 | 3 | 6 | 129C |
| | Jan. 4-May 12, 1995 | 1,242 | 63 | 170 | 4 | 5 | 129C |
| Montana | No regular session in 1998 | | | | | | |
| | Jan. 4-April 21, 1999 | 1,212 | 69 | 589 | 59 | 4(a) | 87L |
| Nebraska | Jan. 7-April 14, 1998 | 472 | 182 | 119 | 170 | 14(a) | 60L |
| | Jan. 6-May 27, 1999 | 883 | 282 | 327 | 260 | 9(a) | 89L |
| Nevada | No regular session in 1998 | | | | | | |
| | Feb. 1-May 31,1999 | 1,263 | 195 | 646 | 147 | 4(a) | 120C |
| New Hampshire | Jan. 7-Sept. 24, 1998 | 991 | 49 | 388 | 24 | 5 | 21L |
| | Jan. 6, 1999-Jan. 5, 2000 | 855 | 64 | 347 | 30 | 2 | 27L |
| New Jersey | Jan. 13, 1998-Jan. 7, 1999 | 5,866 | 776 | 155 | 8 | 60 | (c) |
| | Jan. 12, 1999-Jan.10, 2000 | N.A. | N.A. | 441 | 18 | N.A. | (c) |
| New Mexico | Jan. 20-Feb. 19, 1998 | 883 | 39 | 145 | 7 | 27 | 30C |
| | Jan. 19-Mar. 20, 1999 | 1,655 | 54 | 449 | 6 | 150 | 60C |
| New York* | Jan. 8-July 30, 1992 | 17,667 | 3,731 | 846 | 3,731 | 51 (d) | 151L |
| | Jan. 6-July 7, 1993 | 14,596 | 3,607 | 720 | 3,607 | 93 (d) | 152L |
| North Carolina | May 11-Oct. 29, 1998 | 1,036 | 43 | 230 | 14 | 0 | 101L |
| | Jan. 27-July 21, 1999 | 2,664 | 63 | 462 | 22 | 0 | 103L |

See footnotes at end of table.

## INTRODUCTIONS AND ENACTMENTS: REGULAR SESSIONS — Continued

| State or other jurisdiction | Duration of session* | Introductions | | Enactments | | Measures vetoed by governor | Length of session |
|---|---|---|---|---|---|---|---|
| | | Bills | Resolutions | Bills | Resolutions | | |
| North Dakota | No regular session in 1998 | | | | | | |
| | Jan. 5-April 17, 1999 | 937 | 140 | 562 | 108 | 7(a) | 71L |
| Ohio (f) | (g) | 273 | 49 | 127 | 24 | 0 | (c) |
| | Jan. 4-Dec. 30, 1999 | 757 | 97 | 128 | 45 | 0(d) | (c) |
| Oklahoma | Feb. 2-May 29, 1998 | 673 | 17 | 185 | 6 | 16 | 69L |
| | Jan. 5-May 28, 1997 | 807 | 26 | 223 | 5 | 9 | 70L |
| Oregon | No regular session in 1998 | | | | | | |
| | Jan. 10-July 24, 1999 | 3,103 | 205 | 1,170 | 86 | 69 | 195C |
| Pennsylvania* (i) | Jan. 3, 1995-Nov. 26, 1996 | 4,764 | 640 | 377 | 464 | 1 | (c) |
| Rhode Island* | Jan. 4-July 17, 1994 | 3,565 | (j) | 959 | 490 | 38 | 85L |
| | Jan. 3-Nov. 17, 1995 | 3,708 | (j) | 445 | 522 | 24 | 77L |
| South Carolina* | Jan. 9-June 27, 1996 | 1,342 | N.A. | 314 | N.A. | 21 (a) | (c) |
| | Jan. 14-June 17, 1997 | 1,389 | 775 | 257 | 553 | 19 (a) | 64L |
| South Dakota | Jan. 13-Mar. 16, 1998 | 572 | 12 | 297 | 3 | 7 | 34L |
| | Jan. 12-Mar. 23, 1999 | 556 | 14 | 260 | 2 | 7(a) | 39L |
| Tennessee | Jan. 13-May 30, 1998 | N.A. | N.A. | N.A. | N.A. | 3 | (c) |
| | Jan. 12-May 28, 1999 | 3996(l) | 1,033 | 1,078(l) | N.A. | 2 | (c) |
| Texas | No regular session in 1998 | | | | | | |
| | Jan. 12-May 31, 1999 | 5,766 | 142 | 1,622 | 17 | 0 | 140C |
| Utah | Jan. 19-Mar. 4, 1998 | 691 | 63 | 425 | 38 | 7 | 45C |
| | Jan. 18-Mar. 3, 1999 | 640 | 44 | 384 | 27 | 5 | 45C |
| Vermont | Jan. 8-June 13, 1998 | 334 | N.A. | 105 | 130 | 0 | (c) |
| | Jan. 6-May 15, 1999 | 776 | N.A. | 72 | 166 | 0 | (c) |
| Virginia | Jan. 14-Mar. 17, 1998 | 2,150 | 795 | 902 | 634 | 37 | 63L |
| | Jan. 13-Feb. 27, 1999 | 1,954 | 782 | 1039 | 682 | 23 | 46L |
| Washington | Jan. 12-Mar. 12, 1998 | 1,500 | 58 | 348 | 6 | 69(d) | 60C |
| | Jan. 11-April 25, 1999 | 2,402 | 70 | 400 | 14 | 26(d) | 105C |
| West Virginia | Jan. 14-Mar. 21, 1998 | 1,881 | 160 | 343 | 46 | 16 | 69C |
| | Jan. 13-Mar. 22, 1999 | 1,756 | 124 | 306 | 115 | 11(a) | 69C |
| Wisconsin | Jan. 6, 1997-Jan.4, 1999 | 1,521 | 213 | 338 | 78 | 9(d) | 727C |
| | Jan. 4, 1999-Jan. 1, 2001 | 929 | 124(k) | 25(k) | 5(k) | 3(k)(d) | 726C |
| Wyoming | Feb. 19-Mar. 12, 1998 | N.A. | N.A. | N.A. | N.A. | N.A. | 24L |
| | Jan. 12-Mar. 3, 1999 | N.A. | N.A. | N.A. | N.A. | N.A. | 36L |
| Puerto Rico* | Jan. 8-June 30, 1996 | 524 | 1,468 | 238 | 602 | 4 | 65L |
| | Jan. 13-June 30, 1997 | 2,205 | 1,651 | 212 | 678 | 4 | 101C |
| | Aug. 18-Nov. 18, 1997 | | | | | | |
| U.S. Virgin Islands* | Jan. 9-Dec. 19, 1996 | 169 | 30 | 67 | 23 | 26 | 20L |
| | Jan. 13 -Nov. 18,1997 | 178 | 9 | 60 | 6 | 7 (a) | 14C |

*Source*: The Council of State Governments legislative survey, January 2000 except where noted by * where data are from *The Book of the States, 1998-99.*

** Actual adjournment dates are listed regardless of constitutional or statutory limitations. For more information on provisions, see Table 3.2, "Legislative Sessions: Legal Provisions."

*Key*:

C - Calendar day.

L - Legislative day (in some states, called a session or workday; definition may vary slightly; however, it general refers to any day on which either chamber of the legislature is in session.)

N.A. - Not available.

(a) Number of vetoes overridden: Alaska:1998-4, 1999-2; Florida: 1998-2; Illinois: 1998-17, 1999-6; Kentucky: 1; Maine: 1994-1; Massachusetts: 1992-7, 1993- 6; Minnesota: 1999 1; Montana: 1; Nebraska: 1998-8, 1999-9; Nevada: 1; North Dakota: 1999-1; South Carolina: 1996-11, 1997-8; South Dakota: 1999-1, 1997-1; Washington: 1996-1; West Virginia 1999-7; U.S. Virgin Islands: 1997-3.

(b) Recessed for two weeks.

(c) Length of session: Illinois: 1998 Senate 43L and House 50L, 1999 Senate 54L and House 60L; Indiana: 1998 Senate 26L and House 29L, 1999 Senate 53L and House 55L;Kansas: 1998 Senate 67L and House 68L; Massachusetts: 1992 Senate 37L and House 144L, 1993 Senate 49L and House 150L; New Jersey: 1998 Senate 35L and Assembly 39L, 1999 Senate 29L and Assembly 33L; Ohio: 1998 Senate 255L and House 215L, 1999 Senate 129L and House 114L; Pennsylvania: Senate 136L and House 152L; South Carolina: 1996 Senate 67L and House 66L. Tennessee: 1998 Senate 37L and 38L, 1999 Senate 37L and House 38L. Vermont 1998: Senate 87L and House 83L, 1999 Senate 74L and House 75L.

(d) Line item or partial vetoes. Iowa - includes line item vetoes; Kansas 1998: 7 appropriations - line items, 1999: 1 appropriations line item. Kentucky - includes 2 line item vetoes in budget bill. Minnesota - includes 4 line -item veto items in 1998, 12 line-item veto items in 1999. New York - includes line item vetoes in appropriation bills. North Dakota 1999: 1 line item veto; 2 line item vetoes. Ohio: 1999 - some line items in budget bills were vetoed. Oklahoma 1998: 2 line item vetoes, 1999: 1 line item veto. Washington 1998: includes 28 vetos and 41 partial vetos, 1999: includes 6 vetoes and 20 partial vetos. Wisconsin 1997-1999 session: includes 1 veto and 8 partial vetoes, 1999-2001 session: includes 1 veto and 2 partial vetoes.

(e)1998 Senate 77L and House 87L.

(f) Preliminary information.

(g) Senate: Jan. 6-Dec. 30, 1998, House: Jan. 6-Dec. 29, 1998.

(j) Bills and resolutions are not counted separately.

(k) Data as of December 1999.

(l) Tennessee 1999: bill introductions is the combined total of the Senate and House introductions, including companion bills and carry-overs from previous session. Tennessee enacted 539 public chapters in 1999. Each chapter has 1 House and 1 Senate bill.

## Table 3.20
## BILL AND RESOLUTION INTRODUCTIONS AND ENACTMENTS:
## 1998 AND 1999 SPECIAL SESSIONS

| State or other jurisdiciton | Duration of session** | Introductions | | Enactments | | Measures vetoed by governor | Length of session |
|---|---|---|---|---|---|---|---|
| | | Bills | Resolutions | Bills | Resolutions | | |
| Alabama | No special session in 1998 | | | | | | |
| | Mar. 26-April 5, 1999 (g) | 0 | 0 | 0 | 0 | 0 | 11L |
| | Nov. 15-Nov. 29, 1999 | 141 | 92 | 65 | 51 | 0 | 7 |
| Alaska | May 26- June 1, 1998 | 3 | 3 | 1 | 0 | 0 | 7C |
| | July 20- July 21, 1998 | 2 | 2 | 0 | 0 | 0 | 2C |
| | May 20- May 25, 1999 | 2 | 2 | 2 | 1 | 0 | 6C |
| | Sept. 22-Sept.30, 1999 | 0 | 3 | 2 | 0 | (h) | 9C |
| Arizona* | March 28-30, 1994 | 16 | 0 | 8 | 0 | 0 | 3C |
| | June 15-17, 1994 | 12 | 2 | 5 | 2 | 0 | 3C |
| | March 14-16, 1995 | 18 | 0 | 9 | 0 | 0 | 3C |
| | March 23-28, 1995 | 4 | 0 | 1 | 0 | 0 | 6C |
| | Oct. 17, 1995 | 2 | 0 | 1 | 0 | 0 | 1C |
| Arkansas | No special session in 1998 | | | | | | |
| | Jan. 11-April 30, 1999 | 2,258 | 163 | 1,598 | 118 | 3 | 89L |
| California | Jan. 5-Sept.1, 1998 | 2 | 2 | 1 | 2 | 1 | 44L |
| | Jan. 19-Mar. 26, 1999 | 49 | 2 | 5 | 1 | 0 | 26L |
| Colorado | Sept. 14-Sept. 16, 1998 | 18 | 11 | 1 | 7 | 0 | 3C |
| Connecticut | June 22, 1998 | 1 | 5 | 1 | 5 | 0 | 1L |
| | Dec. 15, 1998 | 1 | 5 | 1 | 5 | 0 | 1L |
| | June 14, 1999 | 2 | 5 | 2 | 5 | 0 | 1L |
| Delaware | Oct. 7, 1998 | 1 | 0 | 1 | 0 | 0 | 1C |
| | Oct. 28, 1999 | 1 | 0 | 0 | 0 | 0 | 1C |
| Florida | No special sessions in 1998/1999 | | | | | | |
| Georgia | No special sessions in 1998/1999 | | | | | | |
| Hawaii | No special sessions in 1998/1999 | | | | | | |
| Idaho | No special session in 1998 | | | | | | |
| Illinois | No special sessions in 1998 | | | | | | |
| | Dec. 13, 1999 | N.A. | N.A. | N.A. | N.A. | N.A. | N.A. |
| Indiana | No special sessions in 1998/1999 | | | | | | |
| Iowa | No special sessions in 1998/1999 | | | | | | |
| Kansas | No special sessions in 1998/1999 | | | | | | |
| Kentucky | No special sessions in 1998/1999 | | | | | | |
| Louisiana | Mar. 23-April 17, 1998 | 379 | 182 | 173 | 159 | 3 | 18L |
| | No special session in 1999 | | | | | | |
| Maine* | No special session in 1994 | | | | | | |
| | Nov. 28-Nov. 30, 1995 | 13 | 0 | 8 | 0 | 0 | 3L |
| Maryland | No special sessions in 1998/1999 | | | | | | |
| Massachusetts* | No special sessions in 1994/1995 | | | | | | |
| Michigan* | No special sessions in 1994/1995 | | | | | | |
| Minnesota | April 20-22, 1998 | 16 | 0 | 3 | 0 | 0 | 3L |
| | No special session in 1999 | | | | | | |
| Mississippi | No special session in 1998 | | | | | | |
| | (f) | | | | | | |
| Missouri* | Sept. 22-Nov. 17, 1994 (b) | 0 | 0 | 0 | 0 | 0 | 9L |
| | No special session in 1995 | | | | | | |
| Montana | No special session in 1998 | | | | | | |
| | June 15-16,1999 | 4 | N.A. | 4 | N.A. | N.A. | 2L |
| Nebraska | May 13-15, 1998 | 3 | 0 | 3 | 0 | 0 | 7L |
| | No special session in 1999 | | | | | | |
| Nevada | No special sessions in 1998/1999 | | | | | | |
| New Hampshire | No special sessions in 1998/1999 | | | | | | |
| New Jersey* | No special session in 1996 (c) | | | | | | |
| New Mexico | April 29-May 4, 1998 | 127 | 0 | 18 | 0 | 2(a) | 6C |
| | May 4-May 13, 1999 | 86 | 1 | 23 | 1 | 12 | 10C |
| New York* | No special sessions in 1992/1993 | | | | | | |
| North Carolina | Mar. 24-April 30, 1998 | 8 | 2 | 1 | 1 | 0 | 23L |
| | Dec. 15-16, 1999 | 6 | 2 | 1 | 1 | 0 | 2L |
| North Dakota | No special sessions in 1998/1999 | | | | | | |
| Ohio | No special sessions in 1998/1999 | | | | | | |
| Oklahoma | June 15-19, 1998 | 4 | 0 | 0 | 0 | 0 | 5L |
| | Jan. 20-June 6, 1999 | 11 | 0 | 1 | 0 | 0 | 13L |
| Oregon | No special sessions in 1998/1999 | | | | | | |
| | No special session in 1997 | | | | | | |

See footnotes at end of table.

## INTRODUCTIONS AND ENACTMENTS: SPECIAL SESSIONS — Continued

| State or other jurisdiciton | Duration of session** | Introductions | | Enactments | | Measures vetoed by governor | Length of session |
|---|---|---|---|---|---|---|---|
| | | Bills | Resolutions | Bills | Resolutions | | |
| Pennsylvania* | March 11-June 28, 1996 | 60 | 5 | 11 | 3 | 0 | (d) |
| | No special session in 1997 | | | | | | |
| Rhode Island* | No special sessions in 1994/1995 | | | | | | |
| South Carolina* | 27-Jun-96 | N.A. | N.A. | N.A. | N.A. | N.A. | 1L |
| | No special session in 1997 | | | | | | |
| South Dakota | No special sessions in 1998/1999 | | | | | | |
| Tennessee | No special session in 1998 | | | | | | |
| | Mar. 29-April 22, 1999 | 110 | 167 | 0 | N.A. | 0 | 0 |
| | Nov. 11-Nov. 18, 1999 | 79 | 77 | N.A. | N.A. | N.A. | (d) |
| Texas | No special sessions in 1998/1999 | | | | | | |
| Utah | No special sessions in 1998/1999 | | | | | | |
| Vermont | No special sessions in 1998/1999 | | | | | | |
| Virginia | Apr. 23- Apr. 24, 1999 | 12 | 23 | 2 | 23 | 0 | 2L |
| | No special session in 1999 | | | | | | |
| Washington | No special session in 1998 | | | | | | |
| | May 17-May 19, 1999 | 22 | 0 | 12 | 0 | (e) | 3C |
| West Virginia | Mar. 21, 1998 | 9 | 4 | 9 | 4 | 0 | 1L |
| | July 14, 1998 | 4 | 3 | 4 | 3 | 0 | 1L |
| | Mar. 22, 1999 | 9 | 9 | 5 | 5 | 0 | 1L |
| | May 18-June 19, 1999 | 11 | 0 | 11 | 0 | 0 | N.A. |
| | Aug. 17, 1999 | 1 | 0 | 1 | 0 | 0 | 1L |
| Wisconsin | April 21-May 13, 1998 | 13 | 4 | 0 | 0 | 0 | 23C |
| | Oct. 29-Nov. 17, 1999 | 3 | 1 | 1 | 0 | 0 | 20C |
| Wyoming* | No special sessions in 1996 | | | | | | |
| Puerto Rico | May 31-June 6, 1997 | 15 | 0 | 3 | 0 | (e) | 7L |
| | 9-Jul-96 | 2 | 1 | 4 | 1 | 0 | 1C |
| | 11-Jul-96 | 2 | 1 | 4 | 1 | 0 | 1C |
| | July 14-22, 1997 | 16 | 12 | 2 | 0 | 0 | 4C |
| U.S. Virgin Islands | Dec. 19, 1996 | 5 | 0 | 1 | 0 | 0 | 1L |
| | 1-Apr-97 | 1 | 0 | 0 | 0 | 0 | 1L |

*Source:* The Council of State Governments' legislative survey January 2000, except where noted by * where data are from *The Book of the States, 1998-99.*

** Actual adjournment dates are listed regardless of constitutional or statutory limitations. For more information on provisions, see Table 3.2, "Legislative Sessions: Legal Provisions."

*Key:*
N.A. — Not Available
C — Calendar day.
L — Legislative day (in some states, called a session or workday; definition may vary slightly; however, it generally refers to any day on which either chamber of the legislature is in session).
(a) Number of vetoes overridden: New Mexico: 1998-1

(b) Special session held on Impeachment proceedings.
(c) Special session will convene to consider bills from the 1996-1997 session which have been returned by the governor.
(d) Length of session: Pennsylvania: 1996-Senate 34L and House 37L.
(e) One line item veto. Washington: 1999-3 partial vetoes.
(f) Mississippi's Legislature convened for 1 day to vote on a gubernatorial appointee. The actual convening date was not provided in time for this publication.
(g) Alabama convened this special session to resolve a dispute over control of the Senate, hence no bills or resolutions were introduced or enacted.
(h) From the regular session.

## Table 3.21
## STAFF FOR INDIVIDUAL LEGISLATORS

| State or other jurisdiction | Senate Capitol Personal | Shared | District | House Capitol Personal | Shared | District |
|---|---|---|---|---|---|---|
| Alabama | YR | YR/2 | ... | ... | YR/10 | ... |
| Alaska | N.A. | N.A. | N.A. | N.A. | N.A. | N.A. |
| Arizona* | ... | YR/2 (b) | ... | ... | YR/2 (b) | ... |
| Arkansas | ... | YR | ... | ... | YR | ... |
| California | YR | ... | YR | YR | ... | YR |
| Colorado | (c,d) | YR (e) | ... | (c) | YR (e) | ... |
| Connecticut | YR | YR (f) | ... | ... | YR/4 (f) | ... |
| Delaware | SO | YR/2 | ... | SO | YR/2 | ... |
| Florida | YR (g)* | ...* | (g)* | YR (g) | ... | YR (g) |
| Georgia | ... | YR/3 (e) | ... | ... | YR/5 (e) | ... |
| Hawaii | YR | ... | ... | YR | ... | ... |
| Idaho | ... | SO/.75 | ... | ... | SO/1.5 | ... |
| Illinois | YR | YR/2 (h) | YR (i) | YR | YR/1 (h) | YR (i) |
| Indiana | ... | YR/3 | ... | ... | YR/3 | ... |
| Iowa | SO | ... | ... | SO | ... | ... |
| Kansas | SO (e) | ... | ... | ... | SO/3 (e) | ... |
| Kentucky | ... | YR (j) | ... | ... | YR (j) | ... |
| Louisiana | (k) | YR (l) | YR (k) | (k) | YR (l) | YR (k) |
| Maine* | ... | SO/15 (m) | ... | ... | SO/45 (n) | ... |
| Maryland (z) | YR (a) (c) | SO | (w) | YR (a) (c) | SO (z) | (w) |
| Massachusetts* | YR | ... | ... | YR | ... | ... |
| Michigan | YR | ... | ... | YR | ... | ... |
| Minnesota | YR (o) | IO/2 (o) | ... | ... | YR/3 | ... |
| Mississippi | ... | YR | ... | ... | YR | ... |
| Missouri* | YR | ... | YR | YR | IO/1 | ... |
| Montana | ... | SO | ... | ... | SO | ... |
| Nebraska | YR | ... | ... | ----------Unicameral---------- | | |
| Nevada | SO (e) | YR | ... | SO (e) | YR | ... |
| New Hampshire | ... | SO | ... | ... | YR | (g) |
| New Jersey | YR (g) | ... | (g) | YR (g) | ... | ... |
| New Mexico | SO | SO | ... | SO | SO | YR |
| New York* | YR | ... | YR | YR | YR | ... |
| North Carolina | SO (e) | YR | ... | SO (e) | YR | ... |
| North Dakota | ... | SO/(e) | ... | ... | SO/(e) | (r) |
| Ohio | YR (p) | YR (q) | (r) | YR (s) | YR (q) | ... |
| Oklahoma | YR | ... | ... | SO (c,e) | IO/7 | ... |
| Oregon | YR | ... | ... | YR | ... | YR |
| Pennsylvania* | YR | ... | YR | YR | YR | ... |
| Rhode Island* | ... | YR/8 | ... | ... | YR/7 | ... |
| South Carolina* | YR | YR/(t) | ... | SO | SO/1 | ... |
| South Dakota | ... | ... | ... | ... | ... | ... |
| Tennessee | YR | ... | ... | YR | ... | YR |
| Texas | YR | ... | YR | YR | ... | ... |
| Utah | (u) | SO (c) | ... | (u) | SO(c) | ... |
| Vermont | ... | YR | ... | ... | YR | (s) |
| Virginia | SO (g) | ... | (g) | SO (g) | SO/2 | (w) |
| Washington | YR (v) | ... | (w) | YR | ... | ... |
| West Virginia | SO | ... | ... | ... | SO/17 | ... |
| Wisconsin | YR (x) | YR (x) | (x) | YR | YR (x) | (w) |
| Wyoming | ... | ... | ... | ... | ... | ... |
| No. Mariana Islands* | YR (y) | (y) | ... | YR (y) | (y) | ... |
| Puerto Rico* | YR (y) | ... | (x) | YR (y) | ... | (x) |
| U.S. Virgin Islands* | YR (y) | ... | ... | ----------Unicameral---------- | | |

See footnotes at end of table.

# STAFF FOR INDIVIDUAL LEGISLATORS — Continued

*Source*: The Council of State Governments' legislative survey January 2000, except where noted by * where data are from *The Book of the States, 1998-99*.

*Note*: For entries under column heading "Shared," figures after slash indicated approximate number of legislators per staff person, where available.

*Key*:

. . . — Staff not provided for individual legislators.

YR — Year-round.

SO — Session only.

IO — Interim only.

(a) Varies from year-to-year; it is up to legislator whether to have staff in capitol, district office, or elsewhere. Staff can move around as well as work part-year.

(b) Includes only majority and minority policy and research staff, not secretarial staff.

(c) Majority and minority leadership have a year-round secretarial staff.

(d) Legislators are allocated $1,000 during the session for personal staff assistance.

(e) Secretarial staff; in North Dakota contracted with a professional secretarial service to provide a joint steno pool of 8 people.

(f) Each senator is provided with one constituent case worker; all Senate and House members receive support from a centralized caucus staff.

(g) Personal and district staff are the same.

(h) Majority and minority offices provide staff year-round.

(i) District office expenses allocated per year from which staff may be hired.

(j) Leadership offices provide staff support year-round. Individual legislators have access to clerical support year-round, augmented during a session.

(k) Each legislator may hire as many assistants as desired, but pay from public funds ranges from $2,000 to $3,000 per month per legislator. Assistant(s) generally work in the district office but may also work at the capitol during the session.

(l) The six caucuses are assigned one full-time position each (potentially 24 legislators per one staff person).

(m) Majority and minority offices provide staff support year-round. Legislators have access to limited secretarial support during the session through the office of the Secretary of the Senate.

(n) Majority and minority offices provide staff support year-round and additional secretarial support during the session.

(o) Each majority party senator has one year-round secretary; some minority party senators share secretarial staff (YR/2).

(p) One secretary and one legislative aide per senator. Senate president and other leaders have one or more additional staff members.

(q) Majority and Minority Caucus staff positions provide services to respective members.

(r) Some legislators have established district offices at their own expense.

(s) One secretary per house member. Members in the minority caucus share constituent aides and legislative research assistants. Speaker has Executive Assistant, Administrative Aide, and a Legislative Aide. Minority Leader has an Executive Assistant and an Administrative Aide. Other leadership positions, both Majority and Minority, have Administrative Assistants and Legislative Aides as do Committee Chairs and Vice Chairs. Some members have chosen fewer staff; other members have an Administrative Aide.

(t) One secretary per two senators for 32 of the members; one secretary for each of the committee chairs.

(u) Legislators are provided student interns during session.

(v) Leadership, caucus chair, and Ways and Means Committee chair have two full-time staff each. All other legislators have one full-time staff year round and one additional staff session only.

(w) Full-time staff may move to the district office during interim period.

(x) Some of personal staff may work in the district office. Total of all staff salaries for each senator must be within limits established by the Senate.

(y) Individual staffing and staff pool arrangements are at the discretion of the individual legislator

(z) Maryland Senators can hire an administrative aide on a year round basis. This is a regular employee with benefits. The Senators may also hire a session secretary for the annual legislative session. This is a temporary non-benefited employee. Salaries are limited to amounts listed in the annual budget. Delegates may hire an administrative aid on a year round basis. This is regular employee with benefits. Since each legislative district includes one senator and three delegates, the amount included in the House budge for a delegate's aide is limited to 1/3 of the amount provided for a senator. The budget provides funding so that three delegates may share one session secretary of the annual legislative session. This is a temporary non-benefitted employee.

## Table 3.22
## STAFF FOR LEGISLATIVE STANDING COMMITTEES

| State or other jurisdiction | Committee staff assistance — Senate Prof. | Senate Cler. | House Prof. | House Cler. | Source of staff services** — Joint central agency (a) Prof. | Joint Cler. | Chamber agency (b) Prof. | Chamber Cler. | Caucus or leadership Prof. | Caucus Cler. | Committee or committee chairman Prof. | Committee Cler. |
|---|---|---|---|---|---|---|---|---|---|---|---|---|
| Alabama | ... | ★ | ★ | ★ | B | ... | ... | B | ★ | ... | ★ | ★ |
| Alaska | ★ | ★ | ★ | ★ | ★ | ★ | ... | B | ★ | ★ | ★ | ★ |
| Arizona* | ★ | ★ | ★ | ★ | B | ... | ... | B | B | ... | B | B |
| Arkansas | ★ | ★ | ★ | ★ | B | B | ... | ... | ... | ... | ... | ... |
| Califorina | ★ | ★ | ★ | ★ | ... | ... | ... | ... | ... | ... | B | B |
| Colorado | ★ | ... | ★ | ... | B | ... | ... | ... | ... | ... | ... | ... |
| Connecticut | ★ (c) | ★ (c) | ★ (c) | ★ (c) | B (c) | ... | ... | ... | ... | B (c) | ... | ... |
| Delaware | ● | ★ | ● | ★ | B | ... | B | ... | ... | B | ... | ... |
| Florida* | ★ | ★ | ★ | ★ | ... | ... | ... | ... | ... | B | B | B |
| Georgia | ... | ★ (d) | ... | ★ (d) | B | ... | B | ... | ... | ... | ... | ... |
| Hawaii | ● | ★ | ★ | ★ | B | B | B | B | B | B | B | B |
| Idaho | ★ | ★ | ★ | ★ | B | B | ... | ... | ... | ... | B | B |
| Illinois | ★ | ★ | ★ | ★ | ... | ... | B | B | B | B | ... | ... |
| Indiana* | ★ | ● | ★ | (e) | B | ... | ... | S | ... | S | ... | ... |
| Iowa | ★ | ... | ★ | ... | B | ... | ... | B (f) | B | ... | ... | B (f) |
| Kansas | ★ | ★ | ★ | ★ | B | B (g) | ... | ... | ... | ... | ... | ... |
| Kentucky | ★ | ★ | ★ | ★ | B | B | ... | ... | ... | ... | ... | ... |
| Louisiana | ★ (h) | ★ | ★ (h) | ★ | B | B | B | B | B | B | B (i) | B (i) |
| Maine* | ★ (c) | ★ (c,j) | ★ (c) | (c,j) | B | ... | ... | ... | ... | ... | ... | ... |
| Maryland | ★ (k) | ★ (k) | ★ (k) | ★ (k) | B | ... | ... | ... | ... | ... | ... | ... |
| Massachusetts* | ★ | ★ | ★ | ★ | ... | ... | ... | ... | ... | ... | ... | ... |
| Michigan* | ★ | ★ | ★ | ★ | B | ... | ... | H | B | ... | B | S |
| Minnesota | ★ | ★ | ★ | ★ | ... | ... | B | ... | H | H | B | B |
| Mississippi* | ● | ★ | ● | ★ | ... | ... | B | B | ... | ... | B | B |
| Missouri* | ★ | ★ | ★ | ... | B | ... | B | B | ... | ... | ... | B |
| Montana | ★ | ★ | ★ | ★ | B | ... | ... | B | ... | ... | ... | ... |
| Nebraska | ★ | ★ | U | U | ... | ... | ... | ... | ... | ... | U | U |
| Nevada | ★ | ★ (j) | ★ | ★ (j) | B | ... | ... | B | ... | ... | ... | ... |
| New Hampshire | ● | ★ | ★ | ★ | B | ... | ... | ... | B | ... | ... | ... |
| New Jersey | ★ | ★ | ★ | ★ | B | B | ... | ... | ... | ... | ... | ... |
| New Mexico | ★ | ★ | ★ | ★ | ... | ... | ... | ... | B | B | B | ... |
| New York* | ★ | ★ | ★ | ★ | B | B | B | B | B | B | B | B |
| North Carolina | ★ | ★ (l) | ★ | ★ (l) | B | ... | ... | ... | ... | ... | ... | ★ (l) |
| North Dakota | (h) | ★ | (h) | ★ | B | ... | ... | B | ... | ... | ... | ... |
| Ohio | ★ | ★ | ★ | ★ | B | ... | ... | ... | ... | ... | B (m) | B (m) |
| Oklahoma | ★ | ★ | ★ | ★ (l) | ... | ... | B | B | B | B | ... | H |
| Oregon | ★ | ★ | ★ | ★ | B | B | ... | ... | ... | ... | B | B |
| Pennsylvania | ★ | ★ | ★ | ★ | B | B | ... | ... | B | B | B | B |
| Rhode Island* | ★ | ★ | ★ | ★ | B | B | B | B | B | B | B | B |
| South Carolina | ★ | ★ | ★ | ★ | ... | ... | B | B | H | H | B | B |
| South Dakota | ★ | ★ | ★ | ★ | B | ... | ... | ... | ... | B | ... | ... |
| Tennessee | ★ | ★ | ★ | ★ | B | ... | ... | B (n) | ... | ... | S | B |
| Texas | ★ | ★ | ★ | ★ | B | ... | ... | B | ... | ... | B | B |
| Utah | ★ | ★ | ★ | ★ | B | B | ... | B | ... | ... | B | B |
| Vermont | ★ | ★ | ★ | ★ | B | B | ... | ... | ... | ... | ... | ... |
| Virginia | ★ | ★ | ★ | ★ | B | ... | B | B | ... | ... | (i) | (i) |
| Washington | ★ | ★ | ★ | ★ | ... | ... | ... | ... | B | B | B (o) | B (o) |
| West Virginia | ★ | ★ | ★ | ★ | B | B | B | B | B | B | B | B |
| Wisconsin | ★ | ★ | ★ | ★ | B | ... | B | ... | ... | ... | B | B |
| Wyoming | ★ | ★ | ★ | ★ | B | ... | ... | B | ... | B | ... | B |
| No. Mariana Islands | ★ | ★ | ★ | ★ | B (p) | B (p) | ... | ... | ... | ... | B (p) | B (p) |
| Puerto Rico | ★ | ★ | ★ | ★ | B (p) | B (p) | B (p) | B (p) | B (p) | B (p) | B (p) | B (p) |
| U.S. Virgin Islands | ★ | ★ | U | U | S (p) | S (p) | S (p) | S (p) | S (p) | S (p) | S (p) | S (p) |

See footnotes at end of table.

# STAFF FOR LEGISLATIVE STANDING COMMITTEES — Continued

*Source:* The Council of State Governments' legislative survey January 2000, except where noted by * where data are from *The Book of the States, 1998-99.*

** — Multiple entries reflect a combination of organizations location of services.

*Key:*

★ — All committees
● — Some committees
. . . — Services not provided
B — Both chambers
H — House
S — Senate
U — Unicameral

(a) Includes legislative council or service agency or central management agency.

(b) Includes chamber management agency, office of clerk or secretary and House or Senate research office.

(c) Standing committees are joint House and Senate committees.

(d) Provided on a pool basis.

(e) Provided on an ad hoc basis.

(f) The Senate secretary and House clerk maintain supervision of committee clerks. During the session each committee selects its own clerk.

(g) Senators select their secretaries and notify the central administrative services agency; all administrative employee matters handled by the agency.

(h) House and Senate Appropriations Committees have Legislative Council fiscal staff at their hearings.

(i) Staff is assigned to each committee but work under the direction of the chairman.

(j) Clerical staff hired during session only.

(k) Committees hire additional staff on a contractual basis during session only under direction of chairman.

(l) Member's personal secretary serves as a clerk to the committee or subcommittee that the member chairs.

(m) Member's personal legislative aide and secretary or administrative assistant serve as staff to the committee that the member chairs. The Majority Caucus Director of Finance also works with the House Finance and Appropriations Committee, but not exclusively. The chair of the Senate Finance Committee has one additional aide to assist with committee work.

(n) Bill clerks during session only.

(o) Each chamber has a non-partisan research staff which provides support services to committees (including chairmen).

(p) In general, the legislative service agency provides legal and staff assistance for legislative meetings and provides associated materials. Individual legislators hire personal or committee staff as their budgets provide and at their own discretion.

## Table 3.23
## STANDING COMMITTEES: APPOINTMENT AND NUMBER

| State or other jurisdiction | Committee members appointed by: | | Committee chairpersons appointed by: | | Number of standing committees during regular 1999 session (a) | |
|---|---|---|---|---|---|---|
| | Senate | House | Senate | House | Senate | House |
| Alabama | P (b),PT | S | P (b),PT | S | 24 | 23 |
| Alaska | CC (c) | CC (c) | CC (c) | CC (c) | 17 (d) | 17 (d) |
| Arizona | P | S | P | S | 11 (d) | 25 (d) |
| Arkansas | CC | (e) | CC | S | 16 | 15 |
| California | CR | S (f) | CR | S | 25 | 30 |
| Colorado | MjL, MnL | S | MjL | S | 11 | 11(d) |
| Connecticut | PT | S | PT | S | (f) | (f) |
| Delaware | PT | S (g) | PT | S | 25 | 24 |
| Florida | P | S | P | S | 19 (d) | 44 (d) |
| Georgia | P (b) | S | P (b) | S | 23 | 33 |
| Hawaii | P (h) | (i) | P (h) | (i) | 12 | 18 |
| Idaho | PT (j) | S | PT | S | 10 | 14 |
| Illinois | P, MnL | S, MnL | P | S | 17 | 34 |
| Indiana | PT | S | PT | S | 19 | 18 |
| Iowa | MJL, MnL (k) | S | MjL (k) | S | 15 | 16 |
| Kansas | (l) | S | (l) | S | 16 (d) | 20 (d) |
| Kentucky | CC | CC | CC | CC | 13 | 19 |
| Louisiana | P | S (m) | P | S | 17 | 17 |
| Maine | P | S | P | S | 4 (f) | 6 (f) |
| Maryland | P | S | P | S | 6 (d) | 8 (d) |
| Massachusetts | P | S, MnL | P | S | 8 (f) | 11 (f) |
| Michigan | MjL | S | MjL | S | 19 (d) | 23 (d) |
| Minnesota | (n) | S | (n) | S | 27 | 27 |
| Mississippi | P (b,o) | S (o) | P (b, o) | S (o) | 35 | 35 |
| Missouri | PT (p) | S, MnL | PT | S | 21 (d) | 46 (d) |
| Montana | CC | S | CC | S | 13 | 13 |
| Nebraska | CC | U | CC | U | 14 | U |
| Nevada | (q) | S | (q) | S | 9 | 12 |
| New Hampshire | P (r) | S (s) | P (r) | S | 18 (d) | 24 (d) |
| New Jersey | P | S | P | S | 14 (d) | 20 (d) |
| New Mexico | CC | S | CC | S | 9 | 17 |
| New York | PT (t) | S | PT (t) | S | 32 | 37 |
| North Carolina | PT | S | PT | S | 24 | 40 |
| North Dakota | CC | S | CC | S | 11 | 11 |
| Ohio | (u) | S | (u) | S | 13 (d) | 22 (d) |
| Oklahoma | PT, MnL | S | PT | S | 22 (d) | 28 (d) |
| Oregon | P | S | P | S | 13(d) | 9(d) |
| Pennsylvania | PT | CC (v) | PT | S | 22 | 25 |
| Rhode Island | MjL | S | MjL | S | 6 (d) | 9 (d) |
| South Carolina | E (w) | S | E | E | 14 | 7 |
| South Dakota | (x) | S | (x) | S | 13 | 13 |
| Tennessee | S | S | S | S | 9 | 14 |
| Texas | P (b) | S (y) | P (b) | S | 13 | 38 |
| Utah | P | S | P | S | 11 | 15 |
| Vermont | CC | S | CC | S | 12 | 15 |
| Virginia | E | S | (z) | S | 11 | 20 |
| Washington | P (b,aa) | S (bb) | P (b,aa) | S (cc) | 15 | 19 |
| West Virginia | P | S | P | S | 18 (d) | 15 (d) |
| Wisconsin | (dd) | S | (dd) | S | 14 (d) | 40 (d) |
| Wyoming | P (ee) | S (ee) | P (ee) | S (ee) | 12 | 12 |
| Dist. of Columbia | (ff) | U | (ff) | U | 9 | U |
| No. Mariana Islands | P | S | P | S | 8 | 7 |
| U.S. Virgin Islands | P | U | P | U | 9 | U |

See footnotes at end of table.

# STANDING COMMITTEES: APPOINTMENT AND NUMBER — Continued

*Sources:* State legislative rule books and manuals.

*Key:*
CC — Committee on Committees
CR — Committee on Rules
E — Election
MjL — Majority Leader
MnL — Minority Leader
P — President
PT — President pro tempore
S — Speaker
U — Unicameral Legislature

(a) According to state Internet sites and Senate and House clerk offices, May 2000.

(b) Lieutenant governor is president of the senate.

(c) Report of Committee on Committees is subject to approval by majority vote of chamber's membership.

(d) Also, joint standing committees. Alaska, 4; Arizona, 1; Colorado, 12; Florida, 6; Kansas, 16; Maryland, 12, (joint statutory); Michigan, 1; Mississippi, 1; Missouri 11; New Hampshire, 5; New Jersey, 3; Ohio, 5; Oklahoma, 3; Oregon, 2; Rhode Island, 7; West Virginia, 8; Wisconsin, 8.

(e) Members of the standing committees shall be selected by House District Caucuses with each caucus selecting five members for each "A" standing committee and five members for each "B" standing committee.

(f) Substantive standing committees are joint committees. Connecticut, 22; Maine, 17; Massachusetts, 23.

(g) Shall include members of both political parties.

(h) President appoints committee members and chairs; minority members on committees are nominated by minority party caucus.

(i) By resolution, with members of majority party designating the chair, vice-chairs and majority party members of committees, and members of minority party designating minority party members.

(j) Committee members appointed by the senate leadership under the direction of the president pro tempore, by and with the senate's advice.

(k) Appointments made after consultation with the president.

(l) Committee on Organization, Calendar and Rules.

(m) Speaker appoints only 12 of the 19 members of the Committee on Appropriations.

(n) Subcommittee on Committees of the Committee on Rules and Administration.

(o) Senate: except Rules Committee; House: except Rules and Management Committees.

(p) Membership shall be composed of majority and minority party members in the same proportion as in the total membership of the senate.

(q) Committee composition and leadership usually determined by party caucus.

(r) Appointments made after consultation with the minority leader.

(s) Speaker appoints minority members with advice of the minority floor leader.

(t) President pro tempore is also majority leader.

(u) Appointed by senate.

(v) Makes recommendation to the house.

(w) Seniority system is retained in process.

(x) Presiding officer announces committee membership after selection by president pro tempore, majority and minority leaders.

(y) A maximum of one-half of the membership on each standing committee, exclusive of the chair and vice chair, is determined by seniority; the remaining membership is appointed by the speaker.

(z) Senior members of the majority part on the committee is the chair.

(aa) Confirmed by the senate.

(bb) By each party caucus.

(cc) By majority caucus.

(dd) Committee on Senate Organization.

(ee) With the advice and consent of the Rules and Procedures Committee.

(ff) Chair of the Council.

## Table 3.24
## RULES ADOPTION AND STANDING COMMITTEES: PROCEDURE

| State | Constitution permits each legislative body to determine its own rules | Committee meetings open to public* | | Specific, advance notice provisions for committee meetings or hearings | Voting/roll call provisions to report a bill to floor |
|---|---|---|---|---|---|
| | | Senate | House | | |
| Alabama | ★ | ★ | ★ | Senate: none<br>House: 24 hours. | Senate: final vote on a bill is recorded.<br>House: recorded vote taken upon request by a member. |
| Alaska | Sec. 12, Art. II "The houses of each legislature shall adopt uniform rules of procedure." | ★ (a) | ★ (a) | For meetings, by 4:00 p.m. on the preceding Thurs.; for hearings, 5 days. | Roll call vote on any measure taken upon request by any member of either house. |
| Arizona | ★ | ★ | ★ | Senate: agenda submitted to secretary 5 days prior to meeting.<br>House: agenda available on previous day prior to meeting. | Senate: roll call vote taken upon request.<br>House: roll call vote required for final action on any bill. |
| Arkansas | ★ | ★ | ★ | Senate: 2 days<br>House: 24 hours | Senate: roll call votes are recorded.<br>House: each member's vote is recorded upon request by a member. |
| California | ★ | ★ (a) | ★ | Senate: none<br>House: none | Senate: disposition of bills by roll call vote only.<br>House: committee action on bills recorded by roll call vote. |
| Colorado | ★ | ★ | ★ | Senate: final action on a measure is prohibited unless notice is posted 1 calendar day prior to its consideration.<br>House: none | Senate: final action by recorded roll call vote.<br>House: final action by recorded roll call vote. |
| Connecticut | ★ | ★ | ★ | ** 1 day | ** Votes on favorable or unfavorable report recorded to show the names of members voting. |
| Delaware | ★ | ★ | ★ (a) | Senate: agenda released the day before meetings.<br>House: agenda for meetings released on last legislative day of preceding week. | Senate: results of any committee vote are recorded.<br>House: results of any committee vote are recorded. |
| Florida | ★ | ★ | ★ | Senate: during session–4 hours notice for first 50 days, 2 hours thereafter.<br>House: during session–4 days notice for first 45 calendar days, 24 hours thereafter. | Senate: vote on final passage is recorded.<br>House: vote on final passage is recorded. |
| Georgia | ★ | ★ | ★ | Senate: a list of committee meetings shall be posted by 10:00 a.m. the preceding Friday.<br>House: none | Senate: recorded roll call taken if one-third members sustain the call for yeas and nays.<br>House: recorded roll call taken if one-fifth members sustain the call for yeas and nays. |
| Hawaii | ★ | ★ (a) | ★ (a) | Senate: 72 hours before 1st referral committee meetings, 48 hours before subsequent referral committee meetings.<br>House: 48 hours. | Senate: final vote is recorded.<br>House: a record is made of a committee quorum and votes to report a bill out. |
| Idaho | ★ | ★ (a) | ★ (a) | Senate: none<br>House: none | Senate: bills can be voted out by voice vote or roll call.<br>House: bills can be voted out by voice vote or roll call. |
| Illinois | ★ | ★ (a) | ★ (a) | Senate: 6 days<br>House: 6 days | Senate: votes on all legislative measures acted upon are recorded.<br>House: votes on all legislative matters acted upon are recorded. |
| Indiana | ★ | ★ | ★ | Senate: 48 hours<br>House: prior to adjournment or the meeting day next preceeding the meeting | Senate: all final votes are recorded.<br>House: all final votes are recorded. |
| Iowa | ★ | ★ | ★ | Senate: none<br>House: none | Senate: final action on any bill or resolution is by roll call.<br>House: committee reports include the roll call vote on final disposition. |
| Kansas | ★ | ★ | ★ | Senate: none<br>House: none | Senate: vote recorded for any action on a bill upon request by a member.<br>House: the total for and against actions are recorded. |

See footnotes at end of table.

# RULES ADOPTION AND STANDING COMMITTEES: PROCEDURE — Continued

| State | Constitution permits each legislative body to determine its own rules | Committee meetings open to public* | | Specific, advance notice provisions for committee meetings or hearings | Voting/roll call provisions to report a bill to floor |
|---|---|---|---|---|---|
| | | Senate | House | | |
| Kentucky | ★ | ★ | ★ | Senate: none<br>House: none | Senate: each member's vote recorded on the disposition of each bill.<br>House: each member's vote recorded on the disposition of each bill. |
| Louisiana | ★ | ★ (a) | ★ (a) | Senate: no later than 1:00 p.m. the preceding day.<br>House: no later than 4:00 p.m. the preceding day. | Senate: any motion to report an instrument is decided by a roll call vote.<br>House: any motion to report an instrument is decided by a roll call vote. |
| Maine | **Implied as part of organizational session. | ★ | ★ | **public hearings must be advertised 2 weekends in advance. | **Recorded vote is required to report a bill out of committee. |
| Maryland | ★ | ★ | ★ | Senate: none<br>House: none | Senate: the final vote on any bill is recorded.<br>House: the final vote on any bill is recorded. |
| Massachusetts | ★ | ★ | ★ (a) | Senate: 48 hours for public hearings.<br>House: 48 hours for public hearings. | Senate: voice vote or recorded roll call vote at the request of 2 committee members.<br>House: recorded vote upon request by a member. |
| Michigan | ★ | ★ | ★ | Senate: none<br>House: none | Senate: committee reports include the vote of each member on any bill.<br>House: the daily journal reports the roll call on all motions to report bills. |
| Minnesota | ★ | ★ | ★ (a) | Senate: 3 days<br>House: 3 days | Senate: recorded vote upon request of one member. Upon the request of 3 members, the record of a roll call vote and committee report are printed in the journal.<br>House: recorded roll call vote upon request by a member. |
| Mississippi | ★ | ★ | ★ (a) | Senate: none<br>House: none | Senate: bills are reported out by voice vote or recorded roll call vote.<br>House: bills are reported out by voice vote or recorded roll call vote. |
| Missouri | ★ | ★ | ★ | Senate: none<br>House: 1 day | Senate: yeas and nays are reported in journal.<br>House: bills are reported out by a recorded roll call vote. |
| Montana | ★ | ★ | ★ | Senate: 3 legislative days<br>House: none | Senate: every vote of each member is recorded and made public.<br>House: every vote of each member is recorded and made public. |
| Nebraska | U | ★ (a) | ★ | public hearings, 7 calendar days. | Roll call votes are taken on final action. |
| Nevada | ★ | ★ | ★ | Senate: none<br>House: none | Senate: recorded vote is taken upon final committee action on bills.<br>House: recorded vote is taken on any matter pertaining to bill at chair's request. |
| New Hampshire | ★ | ★ | ★ | Senate: 5 days<br>House: 4 days | Senate: committees may report a bill out by voice or recorded roll call vote.<br>House: committees may report a bill out by voice or recorded roll call vote. |
| New Jersey | ★ | ★ | ★ (a) | Senate: 5 days<br>House: 5 days | Senate: the chair reports the vote of each member present on a motion to report a bill.<br>House: the chair reports the vote of each member present on motions with respect to bills. |
| New Mexico | ★ | ★ | ★ | Senate: none<br>House: none | Senate: the vote on the final report of the committee taken by yeas and nays. Reported roll call upon request when voice vote is uncertain.<br>House: the vote on the final reort of the committee taken by yeas and nays. Reported roll call upon request when voice vote is uncertain. |
| New York | (b) | ★ (a) | ★ (a) | Senate: 1 week<br>House: 1 week | Senate: each report records the vote of each Senator.<br>House: at the conclusion of a committee meeting a roll call vote is taken on each of the bills considered. |
| North Carolina | (c) | ★ (a) | ★ | Senate: none<br>House: public hearings, 5 calendar days | Senate: no roll call vote may be taken in any committee.<br>House: roll call vote taken on any question when requested by member & sustained by one-fifth of members present. |
| North Dakota | ★ | ★ | ★ | Senate: notice posted the preceding Wed. or Thurs., depending on the committee.<br>House: notice posted the preceding Wed. or Thurs., depending on the committee. | Senate: minutes include recorded roll call vote on each bill referred out.<br>House: minutes include recorded roll call vote on each bill referred out. |
| Ohio | ★ | ★ | ★ | Senate: 2 days<br>House: 5 days | Senate: bills are reported out by recorded roll call vote.<br>House: every member present must vote and all votes are recorded. |

## RULES ADOPTION AND STANDING COMMITTEES: PROCEDURE — Continued

| State | Constitution permits each legislative body to determine its own rules | Committee meetings open to public* | | Specific, advance notice provisions for committee meetings or hearings | Voting/roll call provisions to report a bill to floor |
|---|---|---|---|---|---|
| | | Senate | House | | |
| Oklahoma | ★ | ★ | ★ | Senate: none<br>House: 3 legislative days for public hearings that are requested by members. | Senate: recommendations to the Senate of legislative measures are by recorded roll call vote.<br>House: bills may be reported out by voice vote or by signing a written report. |
| Oregon | ★ | ★ | ★ | Senate: 24 hours<br>House: 24 hours | Senate: the vote on all official actions is recorded.<br>House: motions on measures before a committee are by recorded roll call vote. |
| Pennsylvania | ★ | ★ (a) | ★ (a) | Senate: none<br>House: none | Senate: every member, unless excused, must attend and vote on each question; absentee members may vote in writing. Votes and results are open to the public.<br>House: all votes are recorded. |
| Rhode Island | ★ | ★ (a) | ★ (a) | Senate: 2 days<br>House: 3 days | Senate: "public bills" are decided by a recorded roll call vote other bills by yeas and nays.<br>House: bills are reported out by recorded roll call vote. |
| South Carolina | ★ | ★ (b) | ★ (b) | Senate: 24 hours<br>House: 24 hours | Senate: no bill may be polled out unless at least 2/3 of the members are polled. Poll results are certified and published in journal.<br>House: generally, bills can be reported out by voice vote or roll call vote. |
| South Dakota | ★ | ★ | ★ | **1 legislative day | **Final disposition of a bill requires a majority vote of the members by roll call. |
| Tennessee | ★ | ★ | ★ | Senate: 6 days<br>House: 72 hours when House is recessed or adjourned. | Senate: aye and no votes cast by name on each question are recorded.<br>House: bills are reported out by recorded roll call vote. |
| Texas | ★ | ★ (a) | ★ (a) | Senate: 24 hours<br>House: 24 hours | Senate: bills are typically reported by recorded roll call vote.<br>House: committee reports include the record vote by which the report was adopted, including the vote of each member. |
| Utah | ★ | ★ | ★ | Senate: 24 hours<br>House: 24 hours | Senate: each member present votes on every question and all votes are recorded.<br>House: each member present votes on every question and all votes are recorded. |
| Vermont | (d) | ★ | ★ | Senate: none<br>House: none | Senate: vote is recorded for each committee member for every bill considered.<br>House: vote is recorded for each committee member for every bill considered. |
| Virginia | ★ | ★ (a) | ★ | Senate: none<br>House: none | Senate: generally, a recorded vote is taken for each measure.<br>House: vote of each member is taken and recorded for each measure. |
| Washington | ★ | ★ | ★ | Senate: 5 days<br>House: 5 days | Senate: bills reported from a committee carry a majority report which must be signed by a majority of the committee.<br>House: every vote to report a bill out of committee is by yeas and nays; the names of the members voting are recorded in the report. |
| West Virginia | ★ | ★ (a) | ★ (a) | Senate: none<br>House: none | Senate: each member of the committee when a yea or nay vote is taken.<br>House: recorded vote taken on motions to report a bill. |
| Wisconsin | ★ | ★ | ★ | Senate: a list of public hearings is filed Monday of the preceding week.<br>House: a list of public hearings is filed Monday of the preceding week. | Senate: number of ayes and noes, and members absent or not voting are reported. House: number of yeas and nays recorded. |
| Wyoming | ★ | ★ | ★ | Senate: by 3:00 p.m. of previous day.<br>House: by 3:00 p.m. of previous day. | Senate: bills are reported out by recorded roll call vote.<br>House: bills are reported out by recorded roll call vote. |

*Sources:* State constitutions, rule books and manuals.
*Key:*
★ — Yes
* — Notice of committee meetings may also be subject to state open meetings laws; in some cases, listed times may be subject to suspension or enforceable only to the extent "feasible" or "whenever possible."
** — Joint rules/committees.
U — Unicameral.

(a) Certain matters may be discussed in executive session. (Other states permit meetings to be closed for various reasons, but their rules do not specifically mention "executive session.")
(b) Not referenced specifically, but each body publishes rules and there are joint rules.
(c) Not referenced specifically, but each body publishes rules.
(d) The Senate is referenced specifically as empowered to "make its own rules."

## Table 3.25
# LEGISLATIVE REVIEW OF ADMINISTRATIVE REGULATIONS: STRUCTURES AND PROCEDURES

| State | Type of reviewing committee | Rules reviewed | Time limits in review process |
|---|---|---|---|
| Alabama | Mbrs. Legislative Council | P | 35 days for action by committee. |
| Alaska* | Joint bipartisan | P,E | . . . |
| Arizona | Joint bipartisan | P,E | . . . |
| Arkansas | Joint bipartisan | P,E | . . . |
| California | | P,E | Regulation review conducted by independent executive branch agency |
| Colorado (b) | Joint bipartisan | E | Every newly adopted or amended rule expires on May 15 of the following year. Each year the committee sponsors a bill before the General Assembly which extends the adopted or amended rules due to expire. |
| Connecticut* | Joint bipartisan | P,E | 65 days for action by committee. |
| Delaware | | P | The Attorney General shall review any rule or regulation promulgated by any state agency and inform the issuing agency in writing as to the potential of the rule or regulation to result in a taking of private property before the rule or regulation may become effective. |
| Florida | Joint bipartisan | P,E | . . . |
| Georgia | Standing committee | P | The agency notifies the Legislative Counsel 30 days prior to the effective dates of proposed rules. |
| Hawaii | Legislative agency (c) | P,E | . . . |
| Idaho | Germane joint subcommittees | P | All rules expire one year after adoption and must be reauthorized through legislative action. All pending rules reviewed by standing committees of the legislature. Rules imposing fees must be approved or are deemed rejected. Other pending rules are deemed approved unless rejected. |
| Illinois | Joint bipartisan | P,E | If the committee objects to a proposed rulemaking, the agency can modify, adopt or withdraw the rulemaking within 90 days. If the agency does not act within 90 days, the rulemaking is automatically withdrawn. If the committee determines a proposed rulemaking is objectionable and constitutes a threat to public interest, safety or welfare, it may prohibit adoption of the rulemaking for 180 days. |
| Indiana | Joint bipartisan | E | The Administrative Rules Oversight Committee conducts hearings on complaints about the rules. It issues nonbinding advisory recommendations. |
| Iowa | Joint bipartisan | P,E | The committee meets monthly and can delay the effective date of a proposed rule until the adjournment of the next legislative session, giving the legislature an opportunity to review the rule. The legislature can rescind any rule by joint action of the two houses. |
| Kansas | Joint bipartisan | P,E | Agencies must give a 60-day notice to the public and the Joint Committee of their intent to adopt or amend specific rules and regulation, a copy of which must be provided to the committee. Within the 60-day comment period, the Joint Committee must review and comment, if it feels necessary, on the proposals. Final rules and regulations are resubmitted to the committee to determine whether further expression of concern is necessary. |
| Kentucky | Joint bipartisan subcommittee | P,E | Within 45 days after publication of an administrative regulation in "The Administrative Register," or within 45 days of the receipt of a statement of consideration by the subcommittee. |
| Louisiana* (b) | Standing committee | P,E | All proposed rules and fees are submitted to designated standing committees of the legislature. If a rule or fee is unacceptable, the committee sends a written report to the governor. The governor has 10 days to disapprove the committee report. If both Senate and House committees fail to find the rule unacceptable, or if the governor disapproves the action of a committee within 10 days, the agency may adopt the rule change. (d) |
| Maine | Jt. standing policy cmtes. | P,E | Proposed rules identified as major substantive must be reviewed by the legislature before they are finally adopted. The legislature may approve, approve with changes or disapprove final adoption of major substantive rules. Failure of the legislature to act permits the agency to finally adopt the rule. Any group of 100 or more registered voters, or any person directly, substantially, or adversely affected by an existing rule may file an application for review with the executive director of the Legislative Council. One-third or more of the appropriate standing committee must request a review within 15 days of receipt of the application. |
| Maryland (b) | Joint bipartisan | P,E | The committee has 45 days from the date the regulation is published to comment or object to the regulation. |
| Massachusetts* (b) | Public hearing by agency | P | In Massachusetts, the General Court (Legislature) may by statute authorize an administrative agency to promulgate regulations. The promulgation of such regulations are then governed by Chapter 30A of the Massachusetts General Laws. Chapter 30A requires 21 day notice to the public of a public hearing on a proposed regulation. After public hearing the proposed regulation is filed with the State Secretary who approves it if it is in conformity with Chapter 30A. The State Secretary maintains a register entitled "Massachusetts Register" and the regulation does not become effective until published in the register. The agency may promulgate amendments to the regulations following the same process. |

See footnotes at end of table.

## LEGISLATIVE REVIEW OF ADMINISTRATIVE REGULATIONS: STRUCTURES AND PROCEDURES — Continued

| State | Type of reviewing committee | Rules reviewed | Time limits in review process |
|---|---|---|---|
| Michigan | Joint bipartisan | P | Joint Committee on Administrative Rules (JCAR) has 21 days to approve a formal notice of objection. If no objection is made, the rules may be filed and go into effect. If JCAR does formally object, bills to block the rules are automatically introduced and placed directly on the Senate and House calendars for action. If the bills are not enacted within 21 days, the rules may be filed and go into effect. Also, as specified in the Michigan Constitution, the committee can meet and suspend rules during the interim between legislative session for any rules during the interim. |
| Minnesota | ---------------------------------------------------------- (e) ---------------------------------------------------------- | | |
| Mississippi* | ---------------------------------------------------------- (a) ---------------------------------------------------------- | | |
| Missouri | Joint bipartisan | P,E | The committee must disapprove a final order of rulemaking within 30 days upon receipt or the order of rulemaking is deemed approved. |
| Montana | Germane joint bipartisan committees | P,E | . . . |
| Nebraska | ---------------------------------------------------------- (a) ---------------------------------------------------------- | | |
| Nevada | Joint bipartisan | P | If the committee objects to a rule, it is returned to the agency for revision in accordance with legislative intent and statuory authority. |
| New Hampshire | Joint bipartisan | P | Preliminary objections must be filed within 45 days of agency filing of final proposal. A vote to sponsor joint resolutions must be filed within 45 days of the objection response deadline. |
| New Jersey | The legislature | P,E | . . . |
| New Mexico | ---------------------------------------------------------- (g) ---------------------------------------------------------- | | |
| New York | Joint bipartisan commission | P,E | Agencies must give at least 45 days notice of proposed rule making to the public and the joint commission. While there is no statutory time limit for the commission's review, any commission comments or objections are typically submitted prior to agency adoption. Agency adoption may occur until expiration of the notice of proposed rule making, which is 180 days after its publication in the "State Register," unless extended for an additional 185 days by the agency upon public notice. Whenever a proposed rule is substantially revised, the agency must give at least 30 days notice of revised rule making to the public and the joint commission. |
| North Carolina* | Public membership appointed by legislature | P,E | The Rules Review Commission must review a permanent rule submitted to it on or before the 20th of the month by the last day of the next month. The commission must review a permanent rule submitted to it after the 20th of the month by the last day of the second subsequent month. |
| North Dakota | Interim committee | P | The committee has 90 days from the time a rule is published to initially consider a rule and may carry over for one additional meeting its decision on whether to declare the rule void. |
| Ohio | Joint bipartisan | P,E | Proposed rules are submitted to the committee 65 days prior to adoption. The committee has 30 days to review refiled rules. The committee has 90 days to review rules submitted without change. |
| Oklahoma (b) | Standing cmte. or cmte. appointed by leadership of both houses | P,E | The legislature has 30 legislative days to disapprove a permanent rule. The legislature may disapprove any rule at any time by joint resolution. |
| Oregon (h) | Joint bipartisan | E | . . . |
| Pennsylvania | Standing committees and an independent commission | P,E | Standing committees have 20 days to review the final form regulation. The independent commission has 30 days to review the final form regulation. (f) |
| Rhode Island* | ---------------------------------------------------------- (a) ---------------------------------------------------------- | | |
| South Carolina | Standing committees | P | 120 days for action by committee or legislature. |
| South Dakota | Joint bipartisan | P | A proposed or provisional rule can be suspended until July 1 following the next legislative session if five of the committee's six members agree. |
| Tennessee | Joint standing committee | P | All permanent rules take effect 75 days after filing with the secretary of state. Rules filed in a calendar year expire on June 30 of the following year unless extended by the General Assembly. |
| Texas | ---------------------------------------------------------- (a) ---------------------------------------------------------- | | |
| Utah | Joint bipartisan | P,E | Each rule in effect on February 28 of each year expires May 1 of that year unless reauthorized by the legislature in annual legislation. |
| Vermont* | Joint bipartisan | P,E | All final proposed rules must be submitted to the committee, which has 30 days to review them. Within 14 days of receiving an objection the agency must respond in writing. If the committee still objects it may file its objections with the secretary of state. |

See footnotes at end of table.

## LEGISLATIVE REVIEW OF ADMINISTRATIVE REGULATIONS: STRUCTURES AND PROCEDURES — Continued

| State | Type of reviewing committee | Rules reviewed | Time limits in review process |
|---|---|---|---|
| Virginia (b) | Standing committee | P,E | Legislative review is optional. Within 21 days after the receipt of an objection, the agency shall file a response with the registrar, the objecting legislative committee and the governor. After an objection is filed, the regulation unless withdrawn by the agency shall become effective on a date specified by the agency which shall be after the 21-day extension period. |
| Washington * (b) | Joint bipartisan | P,E | If the committee determines that a proposed rule does not comply with legislative intent, it notifies the agency, which must schedule a public hearing within 30 days of notification. The agency notifies the committee of its action within seven days after the hearing. If a hearing is not held or the agency does not amend the rule, the objection may be filed in the state register and referenced in the state code. The committee's powers, other than publication of its objections, are advisory. |
| West Virginia | Joint bipartisan | P | Committee reports and bills authorizing reviewed rules must be filed with the full legislature no later than 40 days before the 60th day of each regular legislative session. |
| Wisconsin | Joint bipartisan | P,E | The standing committee has 30 days to conduct its review for a proposed rule. The time limit can be extended in various ways. If a standing committee objects to a proposal rule, the joint committee also must object before legislation is introduced to sustain the objection. The joint committee may suspend an existing rule at any time. The suspension is followed by legislation to sustain that action. |
| Wyoming | Joint bipartisan | P,E | . . . |

*Source*: The Council of State Governments survey, January 2000, except where noted by * where data are from *The Book of the States, 1998-1999*.

*Key*:
P — Proposed rules
E — Existing rules
. . . — No formal time limits
(a) No formal rule review is performed by both legislative and executive branches.
(b) Review of rules is performed by both legislative and executive branches.
(c) In Hawaii, the legislative reference bureau assists agencies to comply with uniform format of style. This does not affect the status of rules.
(d) If a committee of either house fails to find a fee unacceptable or if the governor disapproves a committee's finding that a fee was unacceptable, it can be adopted. Committee action on proposed rules must be taken within 6 to 31 days after the agency reports to the committee on its public hearing (if any) and whether it is making changes on proposed rules.
(e) As of December, 1995 The Legislative Commission to Review Administrative Rules (LCRAR) is scheduled to cease operating, effective July 1, 1996. The Legislative Coordinating Commission (LCC) may perform the statutory functions of the LCRAR as it deems necessary. Contact the LCC for more information.

(f) Proposed regulations-standing committee may submit comments to the agency within 20 days of the close of the public comment period. Independent Regulatory Review Commission (IRRC) may submit comments to the agency within 10 days after the expiration of the standing committees' review period. Final regulations - standing committees have 20 days to approve or disapprove a final rule. The IRRC has within 10 days after the expiration of the standing committees' review period or at its next regular scheduled meeting, whichever is later, to approve or disapprove a final regulation. The independent commission may review existing regulations and make recommendations to the agency.

(g) No formal review is performed by legislature. Periodic review and report to legislative finance committee is required of certain agencies.

(h) Oregon created a second kind of review. An executive department agency must submit a proposed rule to a member or committee of the legislative assembly (the recipient differs depending upon the rule) and then, if requested, a standing or interim committee must review the rule and return its comments to the adopting agency.

## Table 3.26
## LEGISLATIVE REVIEW OF ADMINISTRATIVE REGULATIONS: POWERS

| State | Reviewing committee's powers: | | | Legislative powers: |
|---|---|---|---|---|
| | Advisory powers only (a) | No objection constitutes approval of proposed rule | Committee may suspend rule | Method of legislative veto of rules |
| Alabama | ... | ★ | ★ | Joint resolution (b) |
| Alaska* | (c) | (c) | ... | Statute (c) |
| Arizona | ★ | N.A. | N.A. | Statute |
| Arkansas | (d) | N.A. | N.A. | Statute (d) |
| California | ----- (e) ----- | | | |
| Colorado | ... | ★ | ... | Statute (f) |
| Connecticut* | ... | ★ | ... | Statute (g) |
| Delaware | (h) | N.A. | N.A. | N.A. |
| Florida | ★ | ... | (i) | Statute |
| Georgia | ... | ★ | ... | Resolution (j) |
| Hawaii | ★ | ... | (e) | No formal mechanism for legislature's review of administrative rules except as may be required by specific statute. |
| Idaho | ... | ★ | ... | Concurrent resolution (k) |
| Illinois | ... | ... | ★ | Joint resolution |
| Indiana | ★(l) | ... | N.A. | (m) |
| Iowa | ... | ★ | ★ proposed rules | Joint resolution |
| Kansas | ... | N.A. | ... | Statute |
| Kentucky | ... | ★ | ... | Statute |
| Louisiana* | ... | ★ | (n) | Concurrent resolution to suspend, amend or repeal adopted rules or fees. For proposed rules and emergency rules, see footnote (n). |
| Maine | ... | ★ | N.A. | (o) |
| Maryland | (p) | ... | ... | Majority vote of committee. Governor can override. |
| Massachusetts* | ... | ... | ... | The legislature may pass a bill which would supersede a regulation if signed into law by the governor. |
| Michigan | ... | ... | (q) | Concurrent resolution (r) |
| Minnesota | ----- (s) ----- | | | |
| Mississippi* | ----- (e) ----- | | | |
| Missouri | ... | ★ | ★ | Statute, concurrent resolutions (t) |
| Montana | ... | ... | ★(b) | Statute |
| Nebraska | ----- (e) ----- | | | |
| Nevada | ... | ★ | ★ | Vote of committee suspends regulation until the final day of next regular legislative session. Concurrent resolution of legislature required to extend suspension indefinitely. |
| New Hampshire | ★ | (u) | N.A. | Statute (v) |
| New Jersey | ----- (w) ----- | | | |
| New Mexico | ----- (e) ----- | | | |
| New York | ★ | N.A. | N.A. | The legislature may pass a bill which would supercede a regulation if signed into law by the governor. |
| North Carolina* | ★ | ... | ... | Any member of the General Assembly may introduce a bill to disapprove a rule that has been approved by the commission and that has not become effective or has become affective by executive order. (x) |
| North Dakota | ... | ★(y) | ★ | (z) |
| Ohio | ... | (aa) | ★ | Concurrent resolution. Adopt within jurisdiction of committee or extended until House and Senate have held five voting sessions. |
| Oklahoma | ★ | ★ | ... | Joint resolution or concurrent resolution if within review period. |
| Oregon | ★ | N.A. | N.A. | (cc) |
| Pennsylvania | Standing committees Independent commission | ★ | N.A. | Concurrent resolution (dd) |
| Rhode Island* | ----- (e) ----- | | | |
| South Carolina | ... | ★ | ... | Joint resolution (ee) |
| South Dakota | ... | ★ | ★ | Statute |
| Tennessee | ... | ★ | ★ | Statute (ff) |
| Texas | ----- (e) ----- | | | Statute |
| Utah | ... | ... | ... | Statute (ff) |
| Vermont* | ★(gg) | ★ | N.A. | Statute |

**Table 3.26**
# LEGISLATIVE REVIEW OF ADMINISTRATIVE REGULATIONS: POWERS - continued

| | Reviewing committee's powers: | | | Legislative powers: |
|---|---|---|---|---|
| State | Advisory powers only (a) | No objection constitutes approval of proposed rule | Committee may suspend rule | Method of legislative veto of rules |
| Virginia (e) ........................... | ★(hh) | N.A. | (ii) | N.A. |
| Washington* ......................... | ★(jj) | N.A. | (kk) | N.A. |
| West Virginia ....................... | ★ | . . . | . . . | (ll) |
| Wisconsin ............................. | . . . | ★ | ★ | Statute (mm) |
| Wyoming .............................. | (nn) | N.A. | . . . | Statute (oo) |

*Source*: The Council of State Governments survey, January 2000, except where noted by * where data are from *The Book of the States, 1998-1999*.

*Key*:
★ — Yes
. . . — No
N.A. — Not applicable

(a) This column is defined by those legislatures or legislative committees that can only recommend changes to rules but have no power to enforce a change.

(b) A rule disapproved by the reviewing committee is reinstated at the end of the next session if a joint resolution in the legislature fails to sustain committee action.

(c) Committee powers are advisory. Veto authority of the committee was ruled unconstitutional. However, the legislature can pass legislation for presentment to the executive to annul a rule.

(d) A legislative council subcommittee reviews the rules and regulations, makes recommendations to the full Legislative Council (a committee of the General Assembly). Members of the General Assembly may submit legislation that addresses agency authority to enact or modify rules or regulations.

(e) No formal mechanism for legislative review of administrative rules. In Virginia, legislative review is optional. In Hawaii, the legislative reference bureau assists agencies in complying to a uniform format of style. This does not affect the status of rules.

(f) All newly adopted or amended rules expire on May 15 of the year following adoption or amendment. The legislature exercises sunset control over rules. Each year a bill is filed that extends all rules promulgated the previous year, except for those rules specifically designated by the committee.

(g) By February 15 of each regular session, the committee submits for study to the General Assembly a copy of all disapproved regulations. The General Assembly may by resolution sustain or reverse a vote of disapproval.

(h) During the legislative interim, July 1 and the second Tuesday in January, the chairperson of a standing committee of either house, may, by majority vote, draft a committee report setting forth its suggestions and recommendations and to request the President Pro Tempore of the Senate or the Speaker of the House to call a special session to consider the committee's recommendations. Each committee report shall be forwarded to the Sunset Committee.

(i) Committee may submit recommendation for suspension to full legislature, which may enact a statute suspending a rule.

(j) The reviewing committee must introduce a resolution to override a rule within the first 30 days of the next regular session of the General Assembly. If the resolution passes by less than a two-thirds majority of either house, the governor has final authority to affirm or veto the resolution.

(k) All rules are terminated one year after adoption unless the legislature reauthorizes the rule.

(l) Governor can veto rules with or without cause.

(m) Legislature has authority to intervene only after a rule is adopted. The committee meets during the interim but can affect a rule only through recommending a change in statute.

(n) If the committee determines that a proposed rule is unacceptable, it submits a report to the governor who then has 10 days to accept or reject the report. If the governor rejects the report, the rule change may be adopted by the agency. If the governor accepts the report, the agency may not adopt the rule. Emergency rules become effective upon adoption or up to 60 days after adoption as provided in the rule, but a standing committee or governor may void the rule by finding it unacceptable within 2-61 days after adoption and reporting such finding to agency within four days.

(o) Certain proposed rules must be reviewed by the legislature before they may be adopted. The legislature must enact legislation to approve, approve with changes or disapprove final adoption. If the legislature determines an existing rule is inappropriate or unnecessary, it may direct the Office of Policy and Legal Analysis to draft legislation to amend the statutory authority of the agency to amend the rule.

(p) The committee can delay regulations for a limited time before the regulations are adopted.

(q) Committee can suspend rules during interim.

(r) JCAR has 21 days to approve a formal notice of objection.

(s) As of December, 1995 The Legislative Commission to Review Administrative Rules (LCRAR) is scheduled to cease operating, effective July 1, 1996. The Legislative Coordinating Commission (LCC) may perform the Statutory functions of the LCRAR as it deems necessary. Contact the LCC for more information.

(t) The General Assembly may revoke or suspend rules or portions thereof. Missouri uses a concurrent resolution which must be presented to the governor, but the legislature has 30 days in which to act on a resolution regardless of when it is heard by JCAR.

(u) Failure to object or approve within 45 days of agency filing of final proposal constitutes approval.

(v) The committee can temporarily suspend adoption of a rule via voting to sponsor a joint resolution. The legislature may permanently block regulation via legislation.

(w) Article V, Section IV of the Constitution, as amended in 1992, says the legislature may review any rule or regulation to determine whether the rule or regulation is consistent with legislative intent. The legislature transmits its objections to existing or proposed rules or regulations to the governor and relevant agency via concurrent resolutions. The legislature may invalidate or prohibit an existing or proposed rule from taking effect by a majority vote of the authorized membership of each house.

(x) If an agency does not amend a rule to address an objection of the commission, the commission may send written notice to leadership in both houses. The General Assembly may enact legislation disapproving the rule.

(y) Unless formal objections are made or the rule is declared void, rules are considered approved.

(z) The committee can void a rule.

(aa) Committee does not approve rules. Committee can recommend invalidation of all or part of a rule. Inaction on a rule is not considered approval or consent of legality of a rule.

(bb) Neither the governor nor the legislature has veto authority over rules.

(cc) The committee reports to the legislature during each regular session on the review of rules by the committee.

(dd) The committee has 14 days to introduce a concurrent resolution, which then must be passed by both chambers within 10 legislative days or 30 calendar days, followed by presentment to the governor.

(ee) Must be passed within 120-day review period and presented to the governor for signature.

(ff) The legislature exercises sunset control over rules. Each year a bill is filed that extends all rules promulgated the previous year, except for those rules specifically designated by the committee. In Tennessee, standing committees may suspend effectiveness of proposed rules.

(gg) LCAR cannot veto on delay adoption of rule, but can object. Objection has the effect of removing the presumption of validity that normally attached to rules.

(hh) Rules objected to become effective 21 days after receipt of objection by the Registrar of Regulations. .

(ii) Standing committee of both houses in concurrence with governor may suspend effective date until the end of the next General Assembly session.

(jj) Objections are published in the Washington State Register.

(kk) By a majority vote of the committee members, the committee may request the governor to approve suspension of a rule. If the governor approves, the suspension is effective until 90 days after the end of the next regular session.

(ll) State agencies have no power to promulgate rules without first submitting proposed rules to the legislature which must enact a statute authorizing the agency to promulgate the rule. If the legislature, during a regular session disapproves all or part of any legislative rule, the agency may not issue the rule nor take action to implement all or part of the rule unless authorized to do so. However, the agency may resubmit the same or a similar proposed rule to the committee.

(mm) Bills are introduced simultaneously in both houses.

(nn) Legislative Management Council can recommend action be taken by the full legislature.

(oo) Action must be taken before the end of the next succeeding legislative session to nullify a rule.

# Table 3.27
## SUMMARY OF SUNSET LEGISLATION

| State | Scope | Preliminary evaluation conducted by | Other legislative review | Other oversight mechanisms in bill | Phase-out period | Life of each agency (in years) | Other provisions |
|---|---|---|---|---|---|---|---|
| Alabama | C | Legis. Auditor Other Agency is Dept. of Examiners of Public Accounts | Standing Cmte. | Perf. audit | No later than Oct. 1 of the year following the regular session or a time as may be specified in the Sunset bill. | (usually 4) | Schedules of licensing boards and other enumerated agencies are repealed according to specified time tables. |
| Alaska | C | Legis. Auditor | Standing Cmte. | Perf. audit | 1/y | Varies (usually 4) | ... |
| Arizona* | S | Off. of the Auditor General | Legis. Cmtes. of reference | Perf. audit | 6/m | 10 | Jt. Legis. Audit Cmte. selects agencies for review and assigns responsibilities for hearings to the legis. cmtes. of reference. |
| Arkansas | (b) | ... | ... | ... | ... | ... | Automatic repeal of professional and vocational licensing boards if legislature does not extend the operation of the board by a specified date. |
| California | S | St. Legis. Sunset Review Cmte. (c) | ... | ... | ... | Varies | |
| Colorado | R | Dept. of Regulatory Agencies | Legis. Cmtes. of reference | (d) | 1/y | up to 10 | Advisory cmtes. are reviewed at least once after establishment, all regulatory functions of the state are reviewed. |
| Connecticut | (e) | ... | ... | ... | ... | ... | |
| Delaware | C | Agencies under review submit reports to Del. Sunset Comm. based on criteria for review and set forth in statute. Comm. staff conducts separate review. | ... | Per. audit | Dec. 31 of next succeeding calendar year | 4 | Yearly sunset review schedules must include at least nine agencies. If the number automatically scheduled for review or added by the General Assembly is less than a full schedule, additional agencies shall be added in order of their appearance in the Del Code to comlete the review schedule. |
| Florida* | R | ... | Subject area committees handle some sunset review. | Perf. audit, progress revie | ... | 10 | Automatic repeal if legislature fails to reenact legislation by a specific date. |
| Georgia | R | Dept. of Audits | Standing Cmtes. | Perf. audit | 1/y | 6-Jan | A performance audit of each regulatory agency must be conducted upon the request of the Senate or House standing committee to which an agency has been assigned for oversight and review. (f) |
| Hawaii | R | Legis. Auditor | Consumer Protection Cmte. of each house | Perf. eval. | None | 10-Jun | Schedules the various professional and vocational licensing programs for repeal according to a specified timetable. Proposed new regulatory measures must be referred to the Auditor for sunrise analysis. |
| Idaho | (g) | | | | | | |
| Illinois | R | Bur. of the Budget | Standing Cmte. | ... | ... | 10 (max.) | Automatic repeal if legislature fails to reenact legislation by a specific date. |
| Indiana | S | Off. of Fiscal and Management Analysis | ... | Perf. audit, Perf. eval. | ... | 10 | ... |
| Iowa | (h) | --- No program --- | | | | | |
| Kansas | | Administrative Regulation Review Subcommittee | Joint committee with subject matter jurisdiction. | ... | ... | ... | ... |
| Kentucky | R | | ... | ... | ... | ... | Executive reorganization orders which are not enacted into law at next regular session expire and previous organization is reinstated. |

See footnotes at end of table.

Key:
C — Comprehensive    R — Regulatory    S — Selective    D — Discretionary    d — day    m — month    y — year    ... — Not applicable

# SUMMARY OF SUNSET LEGISLATION — Continued

| State | Scope | Preliminary evaluation conducted by | Other legislative review | Other oversight mechanisms in bill | Phase-out period | Life of each agency (in years) | Other provisions |
|---|---|---|---|---|---|---|---|
| Louisiana | C | Standing cmtes. of the two houses with subject matter jurisdiction. | ... | Perf. eval. | 1/y | Up to 6 | Act provides for termination of a department and all and offices in a department. Also permits committees to select particular agencies or offices for more extensive evaluation. Provides for review by Jt. Legis. Cmte. on Budget of programs that were not funded during the prior fiscal year for possible repeal. |
| Maine* | C | Legislative Committee having jurisdiction over relevant policy area. | Selective review of major substantive rules of agencies. | ... | ... | Subject to review at least every 10/yrs. with provisions for selected earlier reviews. | ... |
| Maryland | R | Dept. of Legislative Services | Standing Cmtes. | Perf. eval. | 2/y | 10 | Sunset cycle reviews completed in 1993 and will resume again in 1998 |
| Massachusetts* | | ------------------------------------- No program ------------------------------------- | | | | | |
| Michigan | (g) | ... | ... | ... | ... | ... | ... |
| Minnesota | (g) | ... | ... | ... | ... | ... | ... |
| Mississippi | (i) | ... | ... | ... | ... | ... | ... |
| Missouri | | ------------------------------------- No program ------------------------------------- | | | | | |
| Montana | (g) | ... | ... | ... | ... | ... | ... |
| Nebraska | (g) | ... | ... | ... | ... | ... | ... |
| Nevada | (g) | ... | ... | ... | ... | ... | ... |
| New Hampshire | (j) | ... | ... | ... | ... | ... | ... |
| New Jersey | (g) | ... | ... | ... | ... | ... | ... |
| New Mexico | R | Legis. Finance Cmte. | ... | Perf. eval., Progress | (k) | 7-May | Legis. Finance Cmte. is responsible for introducing legislation to continue any agency reviewed. |
| New York* | (g) | ... | ... | ... | ... | ... | ... |
| North Carolina | (l) | ... | ... | ... | ... | ... | ... |
| North Dakota | | ------------------------------------- No program ------------------------------------- | | | | | |
| Ohio | S | Standing Cmtes. | ... | ... | (m) | Up to 4 | ... |
| Oklahoma | R,C | Jt. Cmte. on Sunset Review | Appropriations and Budget Cmte. | Prog. review | 1/y | 6 | ... |
| Oregon | (n) | ... | (n) | ... | ... | ... | ... |
| Pennsylvania* | (g) | ... | ... | ... | ... | ... | ... |
| Rhode Island* | (o) | ... | ... | ... | ... | ... | ... |
| South Carolina* | R | Legis. Audit Council | Reorganization Comm., Standing Cmtes. | Perf. audit | 1/y | 6 | ... |
| South Dakota | (p) | ... | ... | ... | ... | ... | ... |
| Tennessee | C | Jt. Govt. Operations Cmte. | ... | Perf. audit | 1/y | 8-Jan | Sunrise review provision 2/y after creation of entity. |
| Texas | S | Sunset Advisory Comm. | ... | Perf. eval. | 1/y | 12 | The Sunset Advisory Comm. chair and vice-chair rotate reappointment. |
| Utah | D | Interim Study Cmte. | ... | ... | ... | Up to maximum of 10/y | Legis. Audit Cmte. may at its discretion coordinate the audit of state agencies with the Interim Cmte. |

See footnotes at end of table.

Key:
C — Comprehensive   R — Regulatory   S — Selective   D — Discretionary   d — day   m — month   y — year   ... — Not applicable

# SUMMARY OF SUNSET LEGISLATION — Continued

| State | Scope | Preliminary evaluation conducted by | Other legislative review | Other oversight mechanisms in bill | Phase-out period | Life of each agency (in years) | Other provisions |
|---|---|---|---|---|---|---|---|
| Vermont | S | Legis. Council staff | Senate and House Government Operations Cmtes. | ... | None | ... | Reviews only focus on the need for regulation of professions and occupations. Statutory preference is for the least restrictive form of regulation necessary to protect the public. |
| Virginia | S(g) | ... | Standing Cmtes. | ... | ... | ... | General assembly places sunset on selective programs and acts. The duration varies as does the subject of the legislation. |
| Washington | C | Jt. Legis. Audit and Review Cmte. | Standing Cmtes. | ... | 1/y | Varies | ... |
| West Virginia | S | Jt. Cmte. on Govt. Operations | Performance Evaluation and Research Division | Perf. audit | 1/y | 6 | Jt. Cmte. on Govt. Operations composed of five House members, five Senate members and five citizens appointed by governor. Agencies may be reviewed more frequently. |
| Wisconsin | (g) | ... | ... | ... | ... | ... | ... |
| Wyoming | (q) | ... | ... | ... | ... | ... | ... |

*Source:* The Council of State Governments' survey, January 2000 except where noted by * where data are from *The Book of the States, 1998-99.*

Key:
C - Comprehensive
R - Regulatory
S - Selective
D - Discretionary
d — day
m — month
y — year
. . . — Not applicable
* — Sunset activity terminated.
(a) A onetime review of selected programs ended in 1983.
(b) Review by the Jt. Legislative Sunset Review Cmte. of professional and vocational licensing boards terminates on January 1, 2004. Sunset clauses are included in other selected programs and legislation.
(d) Bills need adoption by the legislature.
(e) Sunset legislation suspended in 1983. Next review cycle is scheduled for 2003.
(f) The automatic sunsetting of an agency every six years was eliminated in 1992. The legislature must pass a bill in order to sunset a specific agency.

(g) While they have not enacted sunset legislation in the same sense as the other states with detailed information in this table, the legislatures in Idaho, Michigan, Minnesota, Montana, Nebraska, Nevada, New Jersey, New York, Pennsylvania, Virginia and Wisconsin have included sunset clauses in selected programs or legislation.
(h) Sunset legislation terminated July 1992. Legislative oversight of designated state agencies, consisting of audit, review and evaluation, continues.
(i) Sunset Act terminated December 31, 1984.
(j) New Hampshire's Sunset Committee was repealed July 1, 1986.
(k) Agency termination is scheduled on July 1 of the year prior to the scheduled termination of statutory authority for that agency.
(l) North Carolina's sunset law terminated on July 30, 1981. Successor vehicle, the Legislative Committee on Agency Review, operated until June 30, 1983.
(m) Agencies subject to 101.84 of the Ohio Revised Code must be renewed or duties transferred by the General Assembly as they expire.
(n) Sunset legislation was repealed in 1993. Joint Legislative Audit Committee still serves as legislative review body.

# Chapter Four

# THE JUDICIARY

*The fundamentals of state justice systems — includes information on state courts of last resort, intermediate appellate courts and general trial courts, selection/retention and removal of judges, and compensation of judges and judicial administrators.*

For additional information on Chapter Four contact
The States Information Center, at The Council of State Governments,
(859) 244-8253 or E-mail: sic@csg.org.

# Table 4.1
## STATE COURTS OF LAST RESORT

| State or other jurisdiction | Name of court | Justices chosen (a) | | No. of judges (b) | Term (in years) (c) | Chief justice | |
|---|---|---|---|---|---|---|---|
| | | At large | By district | | | Method of selection | Term of service as chief justice |
| Alabama | S.C. | ★ | | 9 (d) | 6 | Popular election | 6 years |
| Alaska | S.C. | ★ | | 5 | 10 | By court | 3 years (e) |
| Arizona | S.C. | ★ | | 5 | 6 | By court | 5 years |
| Arkansas | S.C. | ★ | | 7 | 8 | Popular election | 8 years |
| California | S.C. | ★ | | 7 | 12 | Appointed by governor | 12 years |
| Colorado | S.C. | ★ | | 7 | 10 | By court | Indefinite |
| Connecticut | S.C. | ★ | | 7 (f) | 8 | Legislative appointment (g) | 8 years |
| Delaware | S.C. | ★ | | 5 | 12 | Appointed by governor | 12 years |
| Florida | S.C. | (h) | | 7 | 6 | By court | 2 years |
| Georgia | S.C. | ★ | | 7 | 6 | By court | 4 years |
| Hawaii | S.C. | ★ | | 5 | 10 | Appointed by governor, with consent of Senate (i) | 10 years |
| Idaho | S.C. | ★ | | 5 | 6 | By court | 4 years |
| Illinois | S.C. | | ★ | 7 | 10 | By court | 3 years |
| Indiana | S.C. | ★ | | 5 | 10 (j) | Judicial nominating commission appointment | 5 years |
| Iowa | S.C. | ★ | | 9 | 8 | By court | 8 years or duration of term |
| Kansas | S.C. | ★ | | 7 | 6 | Rotation by seniority | Indefinite |
| Kentucky | S.C. | | ★ | 7 | 8 | By court | 4 years |
| Louisiana | S.C. | ★ | ★ | 7 (k) | 10 | By seniority of service | Duration of service |
| Maine | S.J.C. | ★ | | 7 | 7 | Appointed by governor | 7 years |
| Maryland | C.A. | | ★ | 7 | 10 | Appointed by governor | Indefinite |
| Massachusetts | S.J.C. | ★ | | 7 (l) | To age 70 | Appointed by governor (m) | To age 70 |
| Michigan | S.C. | ★ | | 7 | 8 | By court | 2 years |
| Minnesota | S.C. | ★ | | 7 | 6 | Popular election | 6 years |
| Mississippi | S.C. | | ★ | 9 (n) | 8 | By seniority of service | Duration of service |
| Missouri | S.C. | ★ | | 7 | 12 | By court (o) | 2 years |
| Montana | S.C. | ★ | | 7 | 8 | Popular election | 8 years |
| Nebraska | S.C. | | ★(p) | 7 | 6 (q) | Appointed by governor from Judicial Nominating Commission | Duration of service |
| Nevada | S.C. | ★ | | 5 | 6 | Rotation | 2 years |
| New Hampshire | S.C. | ★ | | 5 | To age 70 | Appointed by governor with approval of elected executive council | To age 70 |
| New Jersey | S.C. | ★ | | 7 | 7 (r) | Appointed by governor, with consent of Senate | Duration of service |
| New Mexico | S.C. | ★ | | 5 (s) | 8 | By court | 2 years |
| New York | C.A. | ★ | | 7 | 14 | Appointed by governor from Judicial Nomination Commission | 14 years |
| North Carolina | S.C. | ★ | | 7 | 8 | Popular election | 8 years |
| North Dakota | S.C. | ★ | | 5 | 10 | By Supreme and district court judges | 5 years (t) |
| Ohio | S.C. | ★ | | 7 | 6 | Popular election | 6 years |
| Oklahoma | S.C. | | ★ | 9 | 6 | By court | 2 years |
| | C.C.A. | | ★ | 5 | 6 | By court | 2 years |
| Oregon | S.C. | ★ | | 7 | 6 | By court | 6 years |
| Pennsylvania | S.C. | ★ | | 7 | 10 | Rotation by seniority | Duration of term |
| Rhode Island | S.C. | ★ | | 5 | Life | Appointed by governor from Judicial Nominating Commission | Life |
| South Carolina | S.C. | ★ | | 5 | 10 | Legislative election | 10 years |

See footnotes at end of table.

# STATE COURTS OF LAST RESORT — Continued

| State or other jurisdiction | Justices chosen (a) At large | By district | Name of court | No. of judges (b) | Term (in years) (c) | Chief justice Method of selection | Term of service as chief justice |
|---|---|---|---|---|---|---|---|
| South Dakota | | ★ (u) | S.C. | 5 | 8 | By court | 4 years |
| Tennessee | ★ | | S.C. | 5 | 8 | By court | 4 years |
| Texas | ★ | | S.C. | 9 | 6 | Partisan election | 6 years |
| Texas | ★ | | C.C.A. | 9 | 6 | Partisan election | 6 years (v) |
| Utah | ★ | | S.C. | 5 | 10 (w) | By court | 4 years |
| Vermont | ★ | | S.C. | 5 | 6 | Appointed by governor from Judicial Nomination Commission, with consent of Senate | 6 years |
| Virginia | ★ | | S.C. | 7 | 12 | Seniority | Indefinite |
| Washington | ★ | | S.C. | 9 | 6 | By court | 4 years |
| West Virginia | | ★ | S.C.A. | 5 | 12 | Rotation by seniority | 1 year |
| Wisconsin | ★ | | S.C. | 7 | 10 | Seniority | Until declined |
| Wyoming | ★ | | S.C. | 5 | 8 | By court | At the pleasure of the court |
| Dist. of Columbia | ★ | | C.A. | 9 | 15 | Judicial Nominating Commission appointment | 4 years |
| American Samoa | ★ | | H.C. | 8 (x) | (y) | Appointed by Secretary of the Interior | (w) |
| Puerto Rico | ★ | | S.C. | 7 | To age 70 | Appointed by Governor, with consent of Senate | To age 70 |

*Sources:* Court Statistics Project, *State Court Caseload Statistics*, 1998 (National Center for State Courts 1999) and State Court Organization 1998; state constitutions, statutes and court administration offices.

Key:
S.C. — Supreme Court
S.C.A. — Supreme Court of Appeals
S.J.C. — Supreme Judicial Court
C.A. — Court of Appeals
C.C.A. — Court of Criminal Appeals
H.C. — High Court

(a) See Table 4.4, "Selection and Retention of Judges," for details.
(b) Number includes chief justice.
(c) The initial term may be shorter. See Table 4.4, "Selection and Retention of Judges," for details.
(d) 9 justices sit in panels of 5 or en banc.
(e) A justice may serve more than one term as chief justice, but may not serve consecutive terms in that position.
(f) 7 justices sit in panels of 5 (membership rotates daily); upon order of chief justice, 6 or 7 may sit on panel.
(g) Governor nominates from candidates submitted by Judicial Selection Commission.
(h) Regional (5), Statewide(2), Regional based on District of Appeal.
(i) Judicial Selection Commission nominates.

(j) Initial two years; retention 10 years.
(k) Includes one assigned from courts of appeal.
(l) 7 justices sit on the court, and 5 justices sit en banc.
(m) Chief Justices are appointed, until age 70, by the Governor with the advice and consent of the Executive (Governor's) Council.
(n) 9 justices sit in panels of 3 and en banc.
(o) Selection is typically rotated among the judges.
(p) Chief justice chosen statewide; associate judges chosen by district.
(q) More than three years for first election and every six years thereafter.
(r) Followed by tenure.
(s) 5 justices sit in panels of 3.
(t) Or expiration of term, whichever is first.
(u) Initially chosen by district; retention determined statewide.
(v) Presiding judge of Court of Criminal Appeals.
(w) Initial three years; retention 10 years.
(x) Chief judges and associate judges sit on appellate and trial divisions.
(y) For good behavior.

# Table 4.2
## STATE INTERMEDIATE APPELLATE COURTS AND GENERAL TRIAL COURTS: NUMBER OF JUDGES AND TERMS

| State or other jurisdiction | Intermediate appellate court | | | General trial court | | |
|---|---|---|---|---|---|---|
| | Name of court | No. of judges | Term (years) | Name of court | No. of judges | Term (years) |
| Alabama | Court of Criminal Appeals | 5 | 6 | Circuit Court | 131 | 131 |
| | Court of Civil Appeals | 5 | 6 | | | |
| Alaska | Court of Appeals | 3 | 8 | Superior Court | 40 (a) | 40 (a) |
| Arizona | Court of Appeals | 22 | 8 | Superior Court | 136 (ii) | 136 (ii) |
| Arkansas | Court of Appeals | 12 | 8 | Chancery/Probate Court and Circuit Court | 106 (b) | 106 (b) |
| California | Court of Appeals | 93 | 12 | Superior Court | 1,012 (c) | 1,012 (c) |
| Colorado | Court of Appeals | 16 | 8 | District Court | 154 (d) | 154 (d) |
| Connecticut | Appellate Court | 9 | 8 | Superior Court | 167 | 167 |
| Delaware | ... | ... | ... | Superior Court | 17 | 17 |
| | | | | Court of Chancery | (e) | (e) |
| Florida | District Courts of Appeals | 61 | 6 | Circuit Court | 468 | 468 |
| Georgia | Court of Appeals | 10 | 6 | Superior Court | 175 | 175 |
| Hawaii | Intermediate Court of Appeals | 4 | 10 | Circuit Court | 27 (f) | 27 (f) |
| Idaho | Court of Appeals | 3 | 6 | District Court | 37 (g) | 37 (g) |
| Illinois | Appellate Court | 42 (h) | 10 | Circuit Court | 497 (i) | 497 (i) |
| Indiana | Court of Appeals | 15 (k) | 10 (l) | Superior Court, Probate Court and Circuit Court | 279 | 279 |
| Iowa | Court of Appeals | 6 | 6 | District Court | 328 (m) | 328 (m) |
| Kansas | Court of Appeals | 10 | 4 | District Court | 156 (n) | 156 (n) |
| Kentucky | Court of Appeals | 14 | 8 | Circuit Court | 108 | 108 |
| Louisiana | Court of Appeals | 54 | 10 | District Court | 222 (o) | 222 (o) |
| Maine | ... | ... | ... | Superior Court | 16 | 16 |
| Maryland | Court of Special Appeals | 13 | 10 | Circuit Court | 140 | 140 |
| Massachusetts | Appeals Court | 14 | ... | Superior Court | 80 | 80 |
| Michigan | Court of Appeals | 28 | 6 | Circuit Court | 210 | 210 |
| Minnesota | Court of Appeals | 16 | 6 | District Court | 254 | 254 |
| Mississippi | Court of Appeals | 10 | 4 | Circuit Court | 49 | 49 |
| Missouri | Court of Appeals | 32 | 12 | Circuit Court | 135 (q) | 135 (q) |
| Montana | ... | ... | ... | District Court | 37 (r) | 37 (r) |
| Nebraska | Court of Appeals | 6 | 6 (s) | District Court | 53 | 53 |
| Nevada | ... | ... | ... | District Court | 51 | 51 |
| New Hampshire | ... | ... | ... | Superior Court | 28 (u) | 28 (u) |
| New Jersey | Appellate Division of Superior Court | 32 | 7 (v) | Superior Court | 384 (w) | 384 (w) |
| New Mexico | Court of Appeals | 10 | 8 | District Court | 72 | 72 |
| New York | Appellate Division of Supreme Court | 56 | 5 (y) | Supreme Court and County Court | 496 | 496 |
| | Appellate Terms of Supreme Court | 15 | 5 (y) | | | |
| North Carolina | Court of Appeals | 12 | 8 | Superior Court | 99 (aa) | 99 (aa) |
| North Dakota | ... | ... | ... | District Court | 43 | 43 |
| Ohio | Court of Appeals | 66 | 6 | Court of Common Pleas | 372 | 372 |

See footnotes at end of table.

# STATE INTERMEDIATE APPELLATE COURTS AND GENERAL TRIAL COURTS - Continued

| State or other jurisdiction | Intermediate appellate court | | | General trial court | | |
| --- | --- | --- | --- | --- | --- | --- |
| | Name of court | No. of judges | Term (years) | Name of court | No. of judges | Term (years) |
| Oklahoma | Court of Appeals | 12 | 6 | District Court | 131 | 4 |
| Oregon | Court of Appeals | 10 | 6 | Circuit Court | 40 (a) | 6 |
| | | | | Tax Court | | 6 |
| Pennsylvania | Superior Court | 15 | 10 | Court of Common Pleas | 136 (ii) | 10 |
| | Commonwealth Court | 9 | 10 | | 106 (b) | 10 |
| Rhode Island | ... | ... | ... | Superior Court | 1,012 (c) | Life |
| South Carolina | Court of Appeals | 9 | 6 | Circuit Court | 154 (d) | 6 |
| South Dakota | ... | ... | ... | Circuit Court | 167 | 8 |
| Tennessee | Court of Appeals | 12 | 8 | Chancery Court | 17 | 8 |
| | Court of Criminal Appeals | 12 | 8 | Circuit Court | (e) | 8 |
| | | | | Criminal Court | 468 | 8 |
| | | | | Probate Court | 175 | (ee) |
| Texas | Court of Appeals | 80 | 6 | District Court | 27 (f) | 4 |
| Utah | Court of Appeals | 7 | 10 (ff) | District Court | 37 (g) | 6 |
| Vermont | ... | ... | ... | Superior Court and District Court | 497 (i) | 6 |
| Virginia | Court of Appeals | 10 | 8 | Circuit Court | 279 | 8 |
| Washington | Court of Appeals | 21 | 6 | Superior Court | 328 (m) | 4 |
| West Virginia | ... | ... | ... | Circuit Court | 156 (n) | 8 |
| Wisconsin | Court of Appeals | 16 | 6 | Circuit Court | 108 | 6 |
| Wyoming | ... | ... | ... | District Court | 222 (o) | 6 |
| Dist. of Columbia | ... | ... | ... | Superior Court | 16 | 15 |
| Puerto Rico | Circuit Court of Appeals | 33 | 16 | Court of First Instance | 140 | 12 |

*Sources:* Court Statistics Project, *State Court Caseload Statistics, 1998* (National Center for State Courts 1999) and *State Court Organization 1998*.

Key:
... — Court does not exist in jurisdiction or not applicable.
(a) Plus eight masters.
(b) There are 30 circuit court judges who serve four-year terms. Chancery probate court consists of 33 judges who serve six-year terms. (43 additional judges serve both circuit and chancery courts)
(c) Plus 205 commissioners.
(d) Plus 32 magistrates.
(e) One chancellor and four vice-chancellors.
(f) Plus 15 family judges.
(g) Plus 81 full-time magistrate/judges.
(h) Plus 10 supplemental judges.
(i) Plus 318 associate judges, and 50 permissive associate judges.
(j) Associate judges 4 years.
(k) Plus one tax court judge.
(l) Two years initial; 10 years retention.
(m) Includes 112 district judges, 54 district associate judges, 7 senior judges, 12 associate juvenile judges, 135 part-time magistrates, one associate probate judge, and 7 alternate district associate judges.
(n) Plus 69 district magistrates.
(o) Plus eleven commissioners.
(p) To age 70.
(q) Plus 175 associate circuit judges.
(r) Plus six judges for water court and one for workers' compensation court.
(s) More than three years for first election and every six years thereafter.
(t) The initial term is for 3 years but not more than 5 yrs.
(u) Plus 11 full-time marital masters.
(v) Followed by tenure.
(w) Plus 21 surrogates.
(x) On reapportionment till age 70.
(y) Or duration.
(z) Fourteen years for Supreme Court; 10 years for county court.
(aa) Plus 100 clerks with estate jurisdiction.
(bb) Plus 77 associate judges and 73 special judges.
(cc) Plus 21 masters-in-equity.
(dd) Plus 8 law magistrates, 7 part-time law magistrates, 92 full-time clerk magistrates, and 58 part-time clerk magistrates.
(ee) Locally determined.
(ff) Three years initial; 10 years retention.
(gg) Plus 7 domestic court commissioners.
(hh) District and superior court judges also serve as family court judges.
(ii) Plus two part time judges.

## Table 4.3
## QUALIFICATIONS OF JUDGES OF STATE APPELLATE COURTS AND GENERAL TRIAL COURTS

| State or other jurisdiction | Years of minimum residence | | | | Minimum age | | Legal Credentials | |
|---|---|---|---|---|---|---|---|---|
| | In state | | In district | | | | | |
| | A | T | A | T | A | T | A | T |
| Alabama | 1 | 1 | ... | 1 | ... | ... | Licensed attorney | Licensed attorney |
| Alaska | 5 | 5 | ... | ... | ... | ... | 8 years practice | 5 years practice |
| Arizona | 10 (a) | 5 | (b) | 1 | ... | 30 | (c) | (d) |
| Arkansas | 2 | 2 | (b) | ... | 30 | 28 | 8 years practice | 6 years practice/bench |
| California | ... | ... | ... | ... | ... | ... | 10 years state bar | 10 years state bar |
| Colorado | ★ | ★ (e) | ... | ★ | ... | ... | 5 years state bar | 5 years state bar |
| Connecticut | ★ | ★ | (f) | (f) | ... | ... | 10 years state bar | Member of the bar |
| Delaware | ★ | ★ | (f) | (g) | ... | ... | "Learned in law" | "Learned in law" |
| Florida | ★(h) | ★ | (i) | ★(j) | ... | ... | 10 years state bar | 5 years state bar |
| Georgia | ★ | 3 | ... | ... | ... | 30 | 7 years state bar | 7 years state bar |
| Hawaii | ★ | ★ | ... | ... | ... | ... | 10 years state bar | 10 years state bar |
| Idaho | 2 | 1 | ... | ... | 30 | ... | 10 years state bar | 10 years state bar |
| Illinois | ★ | ★ | ★ | ★ | ... | ... | Licensed attorney | ... |
| Indiana | ... | 1 | (b) | ★ | ... | ... | 10 years state bar (k) | ... |
| Iowa | ... | ... | ... | ★ | ... | ... | Licensed attorney | |
| Kansas | ... | ... | ... | ★ | 30 | ... | 10 years active and continuous practice (l) | 5 years state bar |
| Kentucky | 2 | 2 | 2 | 2 | ... | ... | 8 years state bar and licensed attorney | 8 years state bar |
| Louisiana | 2 | 2 | 2 | 2 | ... | ... | 5 years state bar | 5 years state bar |
| Maine | ... | ... | ... | ... | ... | ... | " Learned in law" | "Learned in law" |
| Maryland | 5 | 5 | 6 mos. | 6 mos. | 30 | 30 | State bar member | State bar member |
| Massachusetts | ... | ... | ... | ... | ... | ... | ... | No law degree required |
| Michigan | ... | ... | (b) | ... | ... | ... | State bar member (m) | State bar member |
| Minnesota | ... | ... | (n) | ... | ... | ... | State bar member | State bar member |
| Mississippi | 5 | 5 | ... | ... | 30 | 26 | 5 years state bar | 5 years practice |
| Missouri | (o) | (o) | (b) | ★ | 30 | 30 | State bar member | State bar member |
| Montana | 2 | 2 | ... | ... | ... | ... | 5 years state bar | 5 years state bar |
| Nebraska | 3 (p) | ... | ★ | ★ | 30 | 30 | 5 years practice | 5 years practice |
| Nevada | 2 | 2 | ... | ... | 25 | 25 | State bar member | ... |
| New Hampshire | ... | ... | ... | ... | ... | ... | ... | ... |
| New Jersey | ... | (q) | ... | (q) | ... | ... | Admitted to practice in state for at least 10 years | 10 years practice of law |
| New Mexico | 3 | 3 | ... | ★ | 35 | 35 | 10 years active practice(r) | 6 years active practice |
| New York | ★ | ★ | (s) | (s) | ... | 18 | 10 years state bar | 10 years state bar |
| North Carolina | ... | N.A. | ... | ★ | ... | ... | State bar member | State bar member |
| North Dakota | ★(p) | ★ | ... | ★ | ... | ... | License to practice law | State bar member |
| Ohio | ★(p) | ★ | (t) | ★ | ... | ... | 6 years practice | 6 years practice |
| Oklahoma | ... | (u) | 1 | ★ | 30 | ... | 5 years state bar | (v) |
| Oregon | 3 | 3 | ... | (w) | ... | ... | State bar member | State bar member |
| Pennsylvania | 1 | 1 | (f) | ★ | ... | ... | State bar member | State bar member |
| Rhode Island | ... | ... | ... | ... | 21 | ... | License to practice law | State bar member |
| South Carolina | 5 | 5 | ... | ... | 32 | 32 | 8 years state bar | 8 years state bar |
| South Dakota | ★ | ★ | ★ | ★ | ... | ... | State bar member | State bar member |
| Tennessee | 5 | 5 | ★(x) | 1 | 35 | 30 | Qualified to practice law | Qualified to practice law |
| Texas | ★ | ... | ... | 2 | 35 | 25 | (y) | (z) |
| Utah | 5 (aa) | 3 | ... | ★ | 30 | 25 | State bar member | State bar member |
| Vermont | 5 | 5 | ... | (bb) | ... | ... | 5 years state bar | 5 years state bar |
| Virginia | ... | ★ | ... | ★ | ... | ... | 5 years state bar | 5 years state bar |
| Washington | 1 | 1 | 1 | 1 | ... | ... | (cc) | State bar member |
| West Virginia | 5 | ★ | ... | ★ | 30 | 30 | 10 years state bar | 5 years state bar |
| Wisconsin | 10 days | 10 days | 10 days | 10 days | ... | ... | 5 years state bar | 5 years state bar |
| Wyoming | 3 | 2 | ... | ... | 30 | 28 | 9 years state bar | ... |
| Dist. of Columbia | ★ | ★ | 90 days | 90 days | ... | ... | 5 years state bar | 5 years state bar (dd) |
| No. Mariana Islands | ... | ... | ... | ... | ... | 30 | N.A. | N.A. |
| Puerto Rico | 5 | ... | ... | ... | ... | ... | 10 years state bar | 7 years state bar |

See footnotes at end of table.

# QUALIFICATIONS OF JUDGES — Continued

*Sources*: National Center for State Courts, *State Court Organization* 1998

Key:

A — Judges of courts of last resort and intermediate appellate courts.

T — Judges of general trial courts.

★ — Provision; length of time not specified.

. . . — No specific provision.

(a) For court of appeals, five years.

(b) No local residency requirement stated for Supreme Court. Local residency required for Court of Appeals.

(c) Supreme Court- ten years state bar, Court of Appeals - five years state bar.

(d) Admitted to the practice of law in Arizona for five years.

(e) State residency requirement for District Court, no residency requirement stated for Denver Probate Court, Denver Juvenile Court or Water Court.

(f) Local residency not required.

(g) Court of Chancery does not have residency requirement, Superior Court requires residency.

(h) For District Courts of Appeal must reside within the territorial jurisdiction of the court.

(i) Initial appointment, must be resident of district at the time of original appointment.

(j) Circuit court judge must reside within the territorial jurisdiction of the court.

(k) In the Supreme Court and the Court of Appeals, five years service as a general jurisdiction judge may be substituted.

(l) Relevant legal experience, such as being a member of a law faculty or sitting as a judge, may qualify under the 10 year requirement.

(m) Supreme Court: state bar member and practice at least five years.

(n) No residency requirement stated for Supreme Court, Court of Appeals varies.

(o) At the appellate level must have been a state voter for nine years. At the general trial court level must have been a state voter for three years.

(p) No state residency requirement specified for Court of Appeals.

(q) For Superior court: out of a total of 416 authorized judgeships (includ-ing thirty-three in the appellate division), there are restricted superior court judgeships that require residence within the particular county of assignment at time of appointment and reappointment; there are 142 unrestricted judgeships for which assignment of county is made by the chief justice.

(r) Supreme Court and Court of Appeals : and/or judgeship in any court of the state.

(s) No local residency requirement stated for Court of Appeals, local residency requirement for presiding judge of Supreme Court, Appellate Divisions.

(t) No local residency requirement for Supreme Court, Court of Appeals requires district residency.

(u) Six months if elected.

(v) District Court: judges must be a state bar member for four years or a judge of court record. Associate judges must be a state bar member for two years or a judge of a court of record.

(w) Local residency requirement for Circuit Court, no residency requirement stated for Tax Court.

(x) Supreme Court: One justice from each of three divisions and two seats at large. Court of Appeals and Court of Criminal Appeals: Must reside in the grand division served.

(y) Ten years practicing law or a lawyer and judge of a court of record at least 10 years.

(z) District Court: judges must have been a practicing lawyer or a judge of a court in this state, or both combined, for four years.

(aa) Supreme Court is five; Court of Appeals is three.

(bb) No local residency requirement stated for Superior Court, District Court must reside in geographic unit.

(cc) Supreme Court: State bar member; Courts of Appeals: five years state bar.

(dd) Superior Court: Judge must also be an active member of the unified District of Columbia bar and have been engaged, during the five years immediately preceding the judicial nomination, in the active practice of law as an attorney by the United States, of District of Columbia government.

## Table 4.4
# SELECTION AND RETENTION OF JUDGES

| State or other jurisdiction | How selected and retained |
|---|---|
| **Alabama** | Appellate, circuit, district and probate judges elected on partisan ballots. Municipal court judges appointed by the governing body of the municipality (majority vote of its members). |
| **Alaska** | Supreme Court, court of appeals, superior court and district court judges appointed by governor from nominations submitted by Judicial Council. Supreme Court, court of appeals and superior court judges approved or rejected on nonpartisan retention ballot at first general election held more than three years after appointment. Reconfirmation every 10, eight and six years, respectively. District court judges approved or rejected at first general election held more than two years after appointment. Reconfirmation every four years. District court magistrates appointed by and serve at pleasure of presiding judge of superior court in each judicial district. |
| **Arizona** | Supreme Court justices and court of appeals judges appointed by governor from a list of not less than three nominees submitted by a nine-member Commission on Appellate Court Appointments. Superior court judges (in counties with population greater than 250,000) appointed by governor from a list of not less than three nominees submitted by a nine-member commission on trial court appointments. Judges initially hold office for term ending 60 days following next regular general election after expiration of two-year term. Judges who file declaration of intention to be retained in office run at next regular general election on nonpartisan retention ballot. Superior court judges in counties having population less than 250,000 elected on nonpartisan ballot; justices of the peace elected on partisan ballot; police judges and magistrates selected as provided by charter or ordinance; Tucson city magistrates appointed and reappointed by mayor and council from nominees submitted by nonpartisan Merit Selection Commission on magistrate appointments. |
| **Arkansas** | All elected on partisan ballot. |
| **California** | Supreme Court and courts of appeal judges appointed by governor, confirmed by Commission on Judicial Appointments. Judges run unopposed on nonpartisan retention ballot at next general election after appointment. Superior court judges elected on nonpartisan ballot with counties having the option to use selection method described above; judges elected to full term at next general election on nonpartisan ballot. Municipal court and justice court judges initially appointed by governor and county board of supervisors, respectively, retain office by election on non-partisan ballot. |
| **Colorado** | Supreme Court and court of appeals judges appointed by governor from nominees submitted by Supreme Court Nominating Commission. District judges appointed by governor from nominees submitted by Judicial District Nominating Commission. After initial appointive term of two years, judges run on nonpartisan retention ballot. Municipal judges appointed by municipal governing body. Denver County judges appointed by mayor from list submitted by nominating commission; judges run on nonpartisan retention ballot. |
| **Connecticut** | Judges of the Supreme Court, appellate court, and district court appointed by Legislature from nominations submitted by governor exclusively from candidates submitted by the Judicial Selection Commission. Judicial Review Council makes recommendations on nominations for reappointment. Probate judges elected on partisan ballots. |
| **Delaware** | All appointed by governor from list submitted by a judicial nominating commission (which is established by executive order) with consent of majority of Senate. |
| **Florida** | Supreme Court and district courts of appeal judges appointed by governor from nominees submitted by appropriate judicial nominating commission. Judges run for retention at next general election preceding expiration of term. Circuit and county court judges elected on nonpartisan ballots. |
| **Georgia** | Supreme Court, court of appeals, superior court, and state court judges elected on nonpartisan ballots. For the magistrate courts, the chief magistrate is selected in a partisan election; additional magistrates are appointed by the chief magistrate with the consent of the judges of the superior court. Probate judges and justices of peace elected on partisan ballots. Juvenile and municipal court judges appointed. |
| **Hawaii** | Supreme Court and intermediate court of appeals justices and circuit court judges nominated by Judicial Selection Commission (on list of four to six names) and appointed by governor with consent of Senate. Judges reappointed to subsequent terms by the Judicial Selection Commission. District court judges nominated by Commission (on list of at least six names) and appointed by chief justice. |
| **Idaho** | Supreme Court and court of appeals justices and district court judges elected on nonpartisan ballot. Magistrates appointed on nonpartisan merit basis by District Magistrates Commission and run for retention in first general election next succeeding the 18-month period following initial appointment; thereafter, run every four years. |
| **Illinois** | Supreme Court, appellate court and circuit court judges nominated at primary elections or by petition and elected at general or judicial elections on partisan ballot. Judges run in uncontested retention elections for subsequent terms. Circuit court associate judges are appointed by circuit judges for four-year terms. |
| **Indiana** | Supreme Court justices and court of appeals judges are appointed by governor from list of three nominees submitted by seven-member Judicial Nominating Commission. Judges serve until next general election after two years from appointment date; thereafter, run for retention on record. Circuit, superior and county judges in most counties run on partisan ballot. Circuit court judges in Vanderburgh County run on a nonpartisan ballot. Superior court judges in Allen County run on a nonpartisan ballot. The majority of superior court judges in Lake County, and all superior court judges in St. Joseph and Vanderburgh counties, are appointed by the governor upon recommendation of the Judicial Nominating Commission. Probate court and city court judges are selected by partisan elections. |
| **Iowa** | Supreme Court, court of appeals and district court judges appointed by governor from lists submitted by nominating commissions. Judges serve an initial one-year term until January 1 following next general election, then run on records for retention. Judicial magistrates appointed by county judicial magistrate appointing commission. District associate judges are appointed by the district judges of the judicial election district from persons nominated by the County Magistrate Appointing Commission, and stand for retention every four years thereafter. |

See footnotes at end of table.

## SELECTION AND RETENTION OF JUDGES — Continued

| State or other jurisdiction | How selected and retained |
|---|---|
| Kansas | Supreme Court and court of appeals judges appointed by governor from nominations submitted by Supreme Court Nominating Commission. Judges serve until second Monday in January following first general election after one year in office; thereafter run on record for retention every six (Supreme Court) and four (court of appeals) years. District judges in 17 judicial districts are appointed by governor through nonpartisan commission plan. District judges in 14 judicial districts are elected on partisan ballot. |
| Kentucky | All judges elected on nonpartisan ballot. |
| Louisiana | All justices and judges elected on partisan basis, but state has open primary which requires all candidates to appear on a single ballot. |
| Maine | All appointed by governor with confirmation of the Senate, except probate judges who are elected on partisan ballot. Governor reappoints and Senate reconfirms for seven-year terms. |
| Maryland | Court of Appeals and court of special appeals judges nominated by judicial nominating commission, and appointed by governor with advice and consent of Senate. Judges run on record for retention at next general election after one year of service. Judges of circuit courts and Supreme Bench of Baltimore City nominated by commission and appointed by governor. Judges of circuit court run on nonpartisan ballot in first general election after year of service (may be challenged by other candidates). District court judges nominated by commission and appointed by governor, subject to Senate confirmation. Judges of the district court appointed by governor, with Senate confirmation. Judges of the orphans' court are selected in nonpartisan elections. |
| Massachusetts | All nominated and appointed by governor with advice and consent of Governor's Council. Judicial Nominating Commission, established by executive order, submits names on nonpartisan basis to governor. |
| Michigan | Nominated in party conventions, all except district court magistrates are elected on nonpartisan ballot at general election. District court magistrates appointed by district court judges, with approval of county board of commissioners. |
| Minnesota | All elected on nonpartisan ballot. |
| Mississippi | All elected on nonpartisan ballot, except municipal court judges who are appointed by governing authority of each municipality. |
| Missouri | Judges of Supreme Court, court of appeals and the circuit courts of Jackson, Clay, Platte, and St. Louis counties appointed initially by governor from nominations submitted by judicial selection commissions. Judges run for retention after one year in office. All other judges elected on partisan ballot. |
| Montana | All elected on nonpartisan ballot. Judges unopposed in reelection effort, run for retention. Water court judges are appointed by chief justice; Workers' Compensation judges are appointed by the governor. |
| Nebraska | All judges appointed initially by governor from nominees submitted by judicial nominating commissions. Judges run for retention on non-partisan ballot in general election following initial three-year term; subsequent terms are six years. |
| Nevada | All elected on nonpartisan ballot. |
| New Hampshire | All appointed by governor and confirmed by majority vote of elected five-member executive council. |
| New Jersey | Judges of Supreme Court, superior court, tax court and municipal court appointed by governor with advice and consent of Senate, except judges of municipal courts serving a single municipality who are appointed by the governing body. Judges are reappointed for seven-year terms by the governor (to age 70) with the advice and consent of Senate. Surrogates selected in partisan elections. |
| New Mexico | Supreme Court, court of appeals, district and metropolitan judges appointed by governor from list submitted by a judicial nominating commission. At next general election, after appointment, judges run for full terms in partisan, contested election. The elected judge runs for subsequent terms in uncontested retention elections. Judges of probate court and municipal and magistrate courts are selected in partisan elections. |
| New York | All elected on partisan ballot, except judges of Court of Appeals, who are appointed by governor from list submitted by commission on judicial nomination with advice and consent of Senate. Governor also appoints judges of court of claims and designates members of appellate division of supreme court. Mayor of New York City appoints judges of criminal and family courts in the city from list submitted by a judicial nominating commission, established by mayor's executive order. |
| North Carolina | All elected on partisan ballot, except special judges of superior court who are appointed by governor, and magistrates, who are appointed by senior resident superior court judge. |
| North Dakota | All elected on nonpartisan ballot. |
| Ohio | All nominated in partisan primary elections, but in general elections, party affiliations not listed on ballot. Court of claims judges may be appointed by chief justice of Supreme Court from ranks of Supreme Court, court of appeals, court of common pleas or retired judges. |
| Oklahoma | Supreme Court, Court of Criminal Appeals, court of appeals and Workers' Compensation Court judges appointed by governor from list of three names submitted by judicial nominating commission. Judges run for retention on nonpartisan ballot at first general election following completion of one year's service; Workers' Compensation Court judges reappointed by governor. District and associate district judges elected on nonpartisan ballot. Special judges appointed by district judges within judicial administrative districts. Municipal judges appointed by governing body of municipality. |
| Oregon | All judges elected on nonpartisan ballot for six-year terms, except municipal judges who are generally appointed and serve as prescribed by city council. |
| Pennsylvania | All initially elected on partisan ballot and thereafter on nonpartisan retention ballot, except magistrates (Pittsburgh) who are appointed by mayor with advice and consent of city council. |
| Rhode Island | All judges appointed by governor from list submitted by Judicial Nominating Commission, with the separate advice and consent of the Senate and House of Representatives. All judges hold office during good behavior. |

## SELECTION AND RETENTION OF JUDGES — Continued

| State or other jurisdiction | How selected and retained |
|---|---|
| **South Carolina** | Supreme Court, court of appeals, circuit court and family court judges elected by legislature from names submitted on a nonpartisan basis by Judicial Merit Selection Commission. Probate judges elected on partisan ballot. Magistrates appointed by governor with advice and consent of Senate. Municipal judges appointed by mayor and aldermen of city. |
| **South Dakota** | Supreme Court justices appointed by governor from nominees submitted by Judicial Qualifications Commission. Justices run for retention at first general election after three years in office. Circuit court judges elected on nonpartisan ballot. Magistrates appointed by presiding judge of judicial court with approval of Supreme Court. |
| **Tennessee** | Judges of the Supreme Court and intermediate appellate courts appointed initially by governor from list of three nominees submitted by Appellate Court Nominating Commission. Judges run on nonpartisan retention ballot at biennial general election held more than 30 days after occurrence of vacancy. All other judges elected on partisan ballot, except some municipal and city court judges, who are appointed by governing body of city. |
| **Texas** | All elected on partisan ballot (method of selection for municipal judges determined by city charter or local ordinance). |
| **Utah** | Supreme Court, district court, circuit court and juvenile court judges appointed by governor from list of at least three nominees submitted by Judicial Nominating Commission. Judges run unopposed for retention in general election following initial three-year term; thereafter run on record for retention every 10 (Supreme Court) and six (other courts of record) years. |
| **Vermont** | Supreme Court justices, superior court and district and family court judges nominated by Judicial Nominating Board and appointed by governor with advice and consent of Senate. Judges retained by vote of general assembly for six-year terms. |
| **Virginia** | All full-time judges elected by majority vote of legislature. |
| **Washington** | Supreme Court, court of appeals, superior court and district court judges elected on nonpartisan ballot. Municipal judges in cities having a population greater than 400,000 are elected on nonpartisan ballot; municipal judges in cities of less than 400,000 appointed in manner determined by city legislative body. |
| **West Virginia** | Supreme Court of Appeals judges, circuit court judges and magistrates elected on partisan ballot. Municipal judges selected according to city charter. |
| **Wisconsin** | Supreme Court, court of appeals and circuit court judges elected on nonpartisan ballot. Municipal court judges selected according to bylaw or ordinance adopted by city council, town board or village board. |
| **Wyoming** | Supreme Court justices, district and county court judges appointed by governor from list of three nominees submitted by Judicial Nominating Commission. Judges run for retention on nonpartisan ballot at first general election occurring more than one year after appointment. Justices of the peace elected on nonpartisan ballot. Municipal (police) judges appointed by mayor with consent of council. |
| **Dist. of Columbia** | Court of Appeals and superior court judges nominated by president of the United States from a list of persons recommended by District of Columbia Judicial Nominating Commission; appointed upon advice and consent of U.S. Senate. |
| **American Samoa** | Chief justice and associate justice(s) appointed by the U.S. Secretary of the Interior pursuant to presidential delegation of authority. Associate judges appointed by governor of American Samoa on recommendation of the chief justice, and subsequently confirmed by the Senate of American Samoa. |
| **Guam** | All appointed by governor with consent of legislature from list of nominees submitted by Judicial Council; thereafter, run on record for retention every seven years. |
| **No. Mariana Islands** | All appointed by governor with advice and consent of Senate. |
| **Puerto Rico** | All appointed by governor with advice and consent of Senate. |
| **U.S. Virgin Islands** | All appointed by governor with advice and consent of legislature. |

*Sources: Judicial Selection in the United States: A Compendium of Provisions,* 3rd Edition (Chicago: American Judicature Society), Forthcoming 2000; "Judicial Selection in the States: Appellate and General Jurisdiction Courts," American Judicature Society.

*Note:* Unless otherwise specified, judges included in this table are in the state courts of last resort and intermediate appellate and general trial courts.

## Table 4.5
# METHODS FOR REMOVAL OF JUDGES AND FILLING OF VACANCIES

| State or other jurisdiction | How removed | Vacancies: how filled |
|---|---|---|
| Alabama | Judicial Inquiry Commission investigates, receives or initiates complaints concerning any judge. Complaints are filed with the Court of the Judiciary, which is empowered to remove, suspend, censure or otherwise discipline judges in the state.<br>Judges are subject to impeachment. | By gubernatorial appointment.. At next general election held after appointee has been in office one year, office is filled for a full term. In some counties, vacancies in circuit and district courts are filled by gubernatorial appointment on nominations made by judicial commission. |
| Alaska | Justices and judges subject to impeachment for malfeasance or misfeasance in performance of official duties.<br>On recommendation of Judicial Qualifications Commission or on its own motion, Supreme Court may suspend judge without salary when judge pleads guilty or no contest or is found guilty of a crime punishable as felony under state or federal law or of any other crime involving moral turpitude under that law. If conviction is reversed, suspension terminates and judge is paid salary for period of suspension. If conviction becomes final, judge is removed from office by Supreme Court.<br>On recommendation of Judicial Qualifications Commission, Supreme Court may censure or remove a judge for action (occurring not more than six years before commencement of current term) which constitutes willful misconduct in office, willful and persistent failure to perform duties, habitual intemperance or conduct prejudicial to the administration of justice that brings the judicial office into disrepute. The court may also retire a judge for disability that seriously interferes with the performance of duties and is (or is likely to become) permanent. | By gubernatorial appointment, from nominations submitted by Judicial Council. |
| Arizona | Judges subject to recall election. Electors, equal in number to 25 percent of votes cast in last election for judge, may petition for judge's recall.<br>All Supreme Court, court of appeals, and superior court judges (judges of courts of record) are subject to impeachment.<br>On recommendation of Commission on Judicial Qualifications or on its own motion, Supreme Court may suspend without salary, a judge who pleads guilty or no contest or is found guilty of a crime punishable as felony or involving moral turpitude under state or federal law. If conviction is reversed, suspension terminates and judge is paid salary for period of suspension. If conviction becomes final, judge is removed from office by Supreme Court.<br>Upon recommendation of Commission on Judicial Qualifications, Supreme Court may remove a judge for willful misconduct in office, willful and persistent failure to perform duties, habitual intemperance or conduct prejudicial to the administration of justice that brings the office into disrepute. The Court may also retire a judge for a disability that seriously interferes with performance of duties and is (or is likely to become) permanent. | Vacancies on Supreme Court, court of appeals, and superior courts (in counties with population over 250,000) are filled by the governor from judicial appointment commission lists. Vacancies on superior courts in counties of less than 250,000 may be filled by by gubernatorial appointment until next general election when judge is elected to fill remainder of unexpired term. Vacancies on justice courts are filled by appointment by county board of supervisors. |
| Arkansas | Supreme, appellate, circuit and chancery court judges are subject to removal by impeachment or by the governor upon the joint address of two-thirds of the members elected to each house of the General Assembly.<br>On recommendation of Judicial Discipline & Disability Commission, the Supreme Court may suspend, with or without pay, or remove a judge for conviction of any offense punishable as a felony under the laws of Arkansas or the United States; for conviction of a criminal act that reflects adversely on the judge's honesty, trustworthiness or fitness as a judge in other respects; for conduct involving dishonesty, fraud, deceit or misrepresentation; for conduct that is prejudicial to the administration of justice; for a willful violation of the Code of Judicial Conduct or the Rules of Professional Responsibility; for willful and persistent failure to perform the duties of office; or for habitual intemperance in the use of alcohol or other drugs. | By gubernatorial appointment. Appointee serves remainder of unexpired term if it expires at next general election. |
| California | All judges subject to impeachment for misconduct.<br>All judges subject to recall election.<br>On recommendation of the Commission on Judicial Performance or on its own motion, the Supreme Court may suspend a judge without salary when the judge pleads guilty or no contest or is found guilty of a crime punishable as a felony or any other crime that involves moral turpitude under that law. If conviction is reversed, suspension terminates and judge is paid salary for period of suspension. If conviction becomes final, judge is removed from office by Supreme Court.<br>Commission on Judicial Performance, may remove judge for willful misconduct in office, persistent failure or inability to perform duties, habitual intemperence or conduct prejudicial to the administration of justice that brings the office into disrepute, subject to petition to Supreme Court. The commission may also retire a judge for disability that seriously interferes with performance of duties and is (or is likely to become) permanent. | Vacancies on appellate courts are filled by gubernatorial appointment with approval of Commission on Judicial Appointments until next general election at which time appointee has the right to become a candidate. Vacancies on superior courts are filled by gubernatorial appointment for remainder of unexpired term; on justice courts by appointment of county board of supervisors or by nonpartisan special election. |

# METHODS FOR REMOVAL OF JUDGES AND FILLING OF VACANCIES — Continued

| State or other jurisdiction | How removed | Vacancies: how filled |
|---|---|---|
| Colorado | Supreme, appeals and district court judges are subject to impeachment for high crimes and misdemeanors or malfeasance in office by two-thirds vote of Senate.<br>Supreme Court, on its own motion or upon petition, may remove a judge from office upon final conviction for a crime punishable as a felony under state or federal law or of any other crime involving moral turpitude under that law.<br>Upon recommendation of Commission on Judicial Discipline, Supreme Court may remove or discipline a judge for willful misconduct in office, willful or persistent failure to perform the duties of office, intemperance or violation of judicial conduct, or for disability that seriously interferes with performance and is (or is likely to become) permanent.<br>Denver county judges are removed in accordance with charter and ordinance provisions. | By gubernatorial appointment (or mayoral appointment in case of Denver county court) from names submitted by appropriate judicial nominating commission. |
| Connecticut | Supreme and superior court judges are subject to removal by impeachment or by the governor on the address of two-thirds of each house of the General Assembly.<br>On recommendation of Judicial Review Council or on its own motion, the Supreme Court may remove or suspend a judge of the Supreme or superior court after an investigation and hearing. If the investigation involves a Supreme Court justice, such judge is disqualified from participating in the proceedings. If a judge becomes permanently incapacitated and cannot adequately fulfill the duties of office, the judge may be retired for disability by the Judicial Review Council on its own motion or on application of the judge. | If General Assembly is in session, vacancies are filled by governor exclusively from candidates submitted by the Judicial Selection Commission and appointed by the General Assembly. Otherwise vacancies are filled temporarily by gubernatorial appointment. |
| Delaware | Judges are subject to impeachment for treason, bribery or any high crime or misdemeanor.<br>The Court on the Judiciary may (after investigation and hearing) censure or remove a judge for willful misconduct in office, willful and persistent failure to perform the duties of office or an offense involving moral turpitude or other persistent misconduct in violation of judicial ethics. The Court may also retire a judge for permanent mental or physical disability interfering with the performance of duties. | Vacancies are filled by governor, with consent of majority of all members of senate, from nominees whose names are submitted by judicial nominating commission. |
| Florida | Supreme Court, district courts of appeal and circuit court judges are subject to impeachment for misdemeanors in office.<br>On recommendation of Judicial Qualifications Commission, Supreme Court may discipline or remove a judge for willful or persistent failure to perform duties or for conduct unbecoming to a member of the judiciary, or retire a judge for a disability that seriously interferes with the performance of duties and is (or is likely to become) permanent. | By gubernatorial appointment, from nominees recommended by appropriate judicial nominating commission. |
| Georgia | Judges are subject to impeachment for cause.<br>Upon recommendation of the Judicial Qualifications Commission (after investigation of alleged misconduct), the Supreme Court may retire, remove or censure any judge. | By gubernatorial appointment (by executive order) on nonpartisan basis from names submitted by Judicial Nominating Commission. |
| Hawaii | Upon recommendation of the Commission on Judicial Discipline (after investigation and hearings), the Supreme Court may reprimand, discipline, suspend (with or without salary), retire or remove any judge as a result of misconduct or disability. | Vacancies on Supreme, intermediate court of appeals and circuit courts are filled by gubernatorial appointment (subject to consent of Senate) from names submitted by Judicial Selection Committee. Vacancies on district courts are filled by appointment by chief justice from names submitted by Committee. |
| Idaho | Judges are subject to impeachment for cause.<br>Upon recommendation by Judicial Council, Supreme Court (after investigation) may remove judges of Supreme Court, court of appeals and district court judges.<br>District court judges (or judicial district sitting *en banc*), by majority vote in accordance with Supreme Court rules, may remove magistrates for cause. District Magistrate's Commission may remove magistrates without cause during first 18 months of service. | Vacancies on Supreme Court, court of appeals and district courts are filled by gubernatorial appointment from names submitted by Judicial Council for unexpired term. Vacancies in magistrates' division of district court are filled by District Magistrate's Commission for remainder of unexpired term. |
| Illinois | Judges are subject to impeachment for cause.<br>The Judicial Inquiry Board files complaints with the Courts Commission which may remove, suspend without pay, censure or reprimand a judge for willful misconduct in office, persistent failure to perform duties or other conduct prejudicial to the administration of justice or that brings the judicial office into disrepute. The Commission may also suspend (with or without pay) or retire a judge for mental or physical disability. | Vacancies on Supreme, appellate and circuit courts are filled by appointment by supreme court until general election. |
| Indiana | Upon recommendation of the Judicial Qualifications Commission or on its own motion, the Supreme Court may suspend or remove an appellate judge for pleading guilty or no contest to a felony crime involving moral turpitude. The Supreme Court may also retire, censure or remove a judge for other matters.<br>The Supreme Court may also discipline or suspend without pay a non-appellate judge. | Vacancies on Supreme Court and court of appeals are filled by governor from list of three nominees presented by judicial nominating commission. Vacancies on circuit courts are filled by gubernatorial appointment until general election. Vacancies on most superior courts are filled by gubernatorial appointment. |

## METHODS FOR REMOVAL OF JUDGES AND FILLING OF VACANCIES — Continued

| State or other jurisdiction | How removed | Vacancies: how filled |
|---|---|---|
| **Iowa** | Supreme and district court judges are subject to impeachment for misdemeanor or malfeasance in office.<br>Upon recommendation of Commission on Judicial Qualifications, the Supreme Court may retire a Supreme, district or associate district judge for permanent disability, or remove such judge for failure to perform duties, habitual intemperance, willful misconduct, conduct which brings the office into disrepute or substantial violations of the canons of judicial ethics.<br>Judicial magistrates may be removed by a tribunal in the judicial election district of the magistrate's residence. | Governor fills vacancies from lists submitted by judicial nominating commission. |
| **Kansas** | All judges are subject to impeachment for treason, bribery or other high crimes and misdemeanors.<br>Supreme Court justices are subject to retirement upon certification to the governor (after a hearing by the Supreme Court Nominating Commission) that such justice is so incapacitated as to be unable to perform adequately the duties of office.<br>Upon recommendation of the Judicial Qualifications Commission, the Supreme Court may retire for incapacity, discipline, suspend or remove for cause any judge below the Supreme Court level. | Vacancies on Supreme Court and court of appeals are filled on nonpartisan basis by governor from nominations submitted by Supreme Court nominating commission. Vacancies on district courts (in areas where commission plan has not been adopted) are filled by gubernatorial appointment until next general election, when vacancy is filled for remainder of unexpired term; in areas where commission plan has been adopted, vacancies are filled by gubernatorial appointment from names submitted by judicial nominating commission. |
| **Kentucky** | Judges are subject to impeachment for misdemeanors in office.<br>Retirement and Removal Commission, subject to rules of procedure established by Supreme Court, may retire for disability, suspend without pay or remove for good cause any judge. The Commission's actions are subject to review by Supreme Court. | By gubernatorial appointment (from names submitted by appropriate judicial nominating commission) or by chief justice if governor fails to act within 60 days. Appointees serve until next general election after their appointment at which time vacancy is filled. |
| **Louisiana** | Judges are subject to impeachment for commission or conviction of felony or malfeasance or gross misconduct.<br>Upon investigation and recommendation by Judiciary Commission, Supreme Court may censure, suspend (with or without salary), remove from office or retire involuntarily a judge for misconduct relating to official duties, willful and persistent failure to perform duties, persistent and public conduct prejudicial to the administration of justice that brings the office into disrepute, or conduct while in office which would constitute a felony or conviction of felony. The Court may also retire a judge for disability which is (or is likely to become) permanent. | Vacancies are filled by Supreme Court appointment if remainder of unexpired term is six months or less; if longer than six months, vacancies are filled in special election. |
| **Maine** | Judges are subject to removal by impeachment or by governor upon the joint address of the legislature.<br>Upon recommendation of the Committee on Judicial Responsibility and Disability, the Supreme Judicial Court may remove, retire or discipline any judge. | Vacancies are filled by governor, subject to review by joint standing committee on the judiciary and to Senate confirmation. |
| **Maryland** | Judges are subject to impeachment.<br>Judges of Court of Appeals, court of special appeals, trial courts of general jurisdiction and district courts are subject to removal by governor on judge's conviction in court of law, impeachment, or physical or mental disability. Judges are also subject to removal upon joint address of the legislature.<br>Upon recommendation of the Commission on Judicial Disabilities (after hearing), the Court of Appeals may remove or retire a judge for misconduct in office, persistent failure to perform duties, conduct prejudicial to the proper administration of justice, or disability that seriously interferes with the performance of duties and is (or is likely to become) permanent.<br>Elected judges convicted of felony or misdemeanor relating to public duties and involving moral turpitude may be removed from office by operation of law when conviction becomes final. | Vacancies are filled by governor with advice and consent of senate, from names submitted by judicial nominating commission. |
| **Massachusetts** | Judges are subject to impeachment.<br>The governor, with the consent of the Executive Council, may remove judges upon joint address of the legislature, and may also (after a hearing and with consent of the Council) retire a judge because of advanced age or mental or physical disability.<br>The Commission on Judicial Conduct, using rules of procedure approved by the Supreme Judicial Court, may investigate the action of any judge that may, by consequence of willful misconduct in office, willful or persistent failure to perform his duties, habitual intemperance or other conduct prejudicial to the administration of justice, bring the office into disrepute. | Vacancies are filled by governor, with advice and consent of Executive Council, from names submitted by judicial nominating commission. |

# METHODS FOR REMOVAL OF JUDGES AND FILLING OF VACANCIES — Continued

| State or other jurisdiction | How removed | Vacancies: how filled |
|---|---|---|
| Michigan | Judges are subject to impeachment.<br>With the concurrence of two-thirds of the members of the legislature, the governor may remove a judge for reasonable cause insufficient for impeachment.<br>Upon recommendation of Judicial Tenure Commission, Supreme Court may censure, suspend (with or without salary), retire or remove a judge for conviction of a felony, a physical or mental disability or a persistent failure to perform duties, misconduct in office, habitual intemperance or conduct clearly prejudicial to the administration of justice. | Vacancies in all courts of record are filled by gubernatorial appointment from nominees recommended by a bar committee. Appointee serves until next general election at which successor is selected for remainder of unexpired term. Vacancies on municipal courts are filled by appointment by city councils. |
| Minnesota | Supreme and district court judges are subject to impeachment.<br>Upon recommendation of Board of Judicial Standards, Supreme Court may censure, suspend (with or without salary), retire or remove a judge for conviction of a felony, physical or mental disability or persistent failure to perform duties, misconduct in office, habitual intemperance or conduct prejudicial to the administration of justice. | Statutory plan to fill vacancies on district courts requires governor to appoint from nominees recommended by a judicial nominating commission. Vacancies on other levels of court filled by gubernatorial appointment (no nominating commission). Appointee serves until general election occurring more than one year after appointment at which time a successor is elected to serve a full term. |
| Mississippi | Judges are subject to impeachment.<br>For reasonable cause which is not sufficient for impeachment, the governor may, on joint address of legislature, remove judges of Supreme and inferior courts.<br>Upon recommendation of Commission on Judicial Performance, Supreme Court may remove, suspend, fine, publicly censure or reprimand a judge for conviction of a felony (in a court outside the state), willful misconduct, willful and persistent failure to perform duties, habitual intemperance or conduct prejudicial to the administration of justice which brings the office into disrepute. The Commission may also retire any judge for physical or mental disability that seriously interferes with performance of duties and is (or is likely to become) permanent. | By gubernatorial appointment, from names submitted by a nominating commission. The office is filled for remainder of unexpected term at next state or congressional election held more than seven months after vacancy. |
| Missouri | Upon recommendation of Commission on Retirement, Removal and Discipline, Supreme Court may retire, remove or discipline any judge.<br>Judges subject to impeachment for crime, misconduct, habitual drunkenness, willful neglect of duty, corruption in office, incompetency, or any offense involving moral turpitude or oppression in office. | Vacancies on Supreme Court, court of appeals, and circuit courts that have adopted commission plan are filled by governor from list of nominees submitted by judicial nominating commission. Vacancies on other circuit courts and municipal court are filled, respectively, by special election and mayoral appointment. |
| Montana | All judges are subject to impeachment.<br>Upon recommendation of Judicial Standards Commission, Supreme Court may suspend a judge and remove same upon conviction of a felony or other crime involving moral turpitude. The Supreme Court may retire any judge for a disability that seriously interferes with the performance of duties, and that is (or may become) permanent. The Court may also censure, suspend or remove any judge for willful misconduct in office, willful and persistent failure to perform duties, violation of canons of judicial ethics adopted by the Supreme Court or habitual intemperance. | Vacancies on Supreme and district courts are filled by gubernatorial appointment (with confirmation by Senate) from names submitted by judicial nominating commission. Vacancies on municipal and city courts are filled by appointment by city council for remainder of unexpired term. |
| Nebraska | Judges are subject to impeachment. In case of impeachment of Supreme Court justice, judges of district court sit as court of impeachment with two-thirds concurrence required for conviction. In case of other judicial impeachments, Supreme Court sits as court of impeachment.<br>Upon recommendation of the Commission on Judicial Qualifications, the Supreme Court may reprimand, discipline, censure, suspend or remove a judge for willful misconduct in office, willful failure to perform duties, habitual intemperance, conviction of crime involving moral turpitude, disbarment or conduct prejudicial to the administration of justice that brings the office into disrepute. The Supreme Court also may retire a judge for physical or mental disability that seriously interferes with performance of duties and is (or is likely to become) permanent. | Vacancies are filled by governor from list of at least two nominees submitted by judicial nominating commission. |

# METHODS FOR REMOVAL OF JUDGES AND FILLING OF VACANCIES — Continued

| State or other jurisdiction | How removed | Vacancies: how filled |
|---|---|---|
| Nevada | All judges, except justices of peace, are subject to impeachment.<br>Judges are also subject to removal by legislative resolution and by recall election.<br>The Commission on Judicial Discipline may censure, retire or remove a Supreme Court justice or district judge for willful misconduct, willful or persistent failure to perform duties or habitual intemperance, or retire a judge for advanced age which interferes with performance of duties for mental or physical disability that is (or is likely to become) permanent, subject to appeal to the Supreme Court. | Vacancies on Supreme or district courts are filled by gubernatorial appointment from among three nominees submitted by Commission on Judicial Selection. Vacancies on justice courts are filled by appointment by board of county commissioners or by special election. |
| New Hampshire | Judges are subject to impeachment.<br>Governor, with consent of Executive Council, may remove judges upon address of both houses of legislature. | Vacancies are filled by governor and approved by majority vote of five-member Executive Council. |
| New Jersey | Supreme and superior court judges are subject to impeachment by the legislature.<br>Except for Supreme Court justices, judges are subject to a statutory removal proceeding that is initiated by the filing of a complaint by the Supreme Court on its own motion or the governor or either house of the legislature acting by a majority of its total membership. Prior to institution of the formal proceedings, complaints are usually referred to the Supreme Court's Advisory Committee on Judicial Conduct, which conducts a preliminary investigation, makes findings of fact and either dismisses the charges or recommends that formal proceedings be instituted. The Supreme Court's determination is based on a plenary hearing procedure, although the Court is supplied with a record created by the Committee. The formal statutory removal hearing may be either before the Supreme Court sitting *en banc* or before three justices or judges (or combination thereof) specifically designated by chief justice.<br>If Supreme Court certifies to governor that it appears a Supreme Court or superior court judge is so incapacitated as to substantially prevent the judge from performing the duties of office, the governor appoints a commission of three persons to inquire into the circumstances. On their recommendation, the governor may retire the justice or judge from office, on pension, as may be provided by law. | Vacancies on Supreme Court and superior court, county, district, tax, and municipal courts are filled by governor with advice and consent of Senate. |
| New Mexico | Judges are subject to impeachment.<br>Upon recommendation of the Judicial Standards Commission, the Supreme Court may discipline or remove a judge for willful misconduct in office, willful and persistent failure or inability to perform duties or habitual intemperance, or retire a judge for disability that seriously interferes with performance of duties and is (or is likely to become) permanent. | Vacancies on Supreme Court, Court of Appeals and district courts are filled by gubernatorial appointment from names submitted by judicial nominating commission. |
| New York | All judges are subject to impeachment.<br>Court of Appeals and Supreme Court judges may be removed by two-thirds concurrence of both houses of legislature.<br>Court of claims, county court, surrogate's court, family court, civil and criminal court (NYC) and district court judges may be removed by two-thirds vote of the Senate on recommendation of governor.<br>Commission on Judicial Conduct may determine that a judge be admonished, censured or removed from office for cause, or retired for disability, subject to appeal to the Court of Appeals. | Vacancies on Court of Appeals and appellate division of Supreme Court are filled by governor with advice and consent of Senate, from among nominees recommended by judicial nominating commission. Vacancies in elective judgeships (outside NYC) are filled at next general election for full term; until election, governor makes appointment (with consent of Senate if in session). |
| North Carolina | Upon recommendation of Judicial Standards Commission, Supreme Court may censure or remove a court of appeals or trial court judge for willful misconduct in office, willful and persistent failure to perform duties, habitual intemperance, conviction of a crime involving moral turpitude, conduct prejudicial to the administration of justice that brings the office into disrepute, or mental or physical incapacity that interferes with the performance of duties and is (or is likely to become) permanent.<br>Upon recommendation of Judicial Standards Commission, a seven-member panel of the court of appeals may censure or remove (for the above reasons) any Supreme Court judge. | Vacancies on Supreme, appeals and superior courts are filled by gubernatorial appointment until next general election. |
| North Dakota | Supreme and district court judges are subject to impeachment for habitual intemperance, crimes, corrupt conduct, malfeasance or misdemeanor in office. Governor may remove county judges after hearing.<br>All judges are subject to recall election.<br>On recommendation of Commission on Judicial Qualifications or on its own motion, Supreme Court may suspend a judge without salary when judge pleads guilty or no contest or is found guilty of a crime punishable as a felony under state or federal law or any other crime involving moral turpitude under that law. If conviction is reversed, suspension terminates and judge is paid salary for period of suspension. If conviction becomes final, judge is removed by Supreme Court.<br>Upon recommendation of Commission on Judicial Qualifications, Supreme Court may censure or remove a judge for willful misconduct, willful failure to perform duties, willful violation of the code of judicial conduct or habitual intemperance. The Court may also retire a judge for disability that seriously interferes with the performance of duties and is (or is likely to become) permanent. | Vacancies on Supreme and district courts are filled by gubernatorial appointment from nominees submitted by Judicial Nominating Committee until next general election, unless governor calls for a special election to fill vacancy for remainder of term.<br>Vacancies on county courts are filled by appointment by board of county commissioners from names submitted by nominating commission. |

# METHODS FOR REMOVAL OF JUDGES AND FILLING OF VACANCIES — Continued

| State or other jurisdiction | How removed | Vacancies: how filled |
|---|---|---|
| **Ohio** | Judges are subject to impeachment.<br>Judges may be removed by concurrent resolution of two-thirds members of both houses of legislature or removed for cause upon filing of a petition signed by 15 percent of electors in preceding gubernatorial election.<br>The Board of Commissioners on Grievances and Discipline of the Judiciary may disqualify a judge from office when judge has been indicted for a crime punishable as a felony under state or federal law. Board may also remove or suspend a judge for willful and persistent failure to perform duties, habitual intemperance, conduct prejudicial to the administration of justice or which would bring the office into disrepute, or suspension from practice of law, or retire a judge for physical or mental disability that prevents discharge of duties. Judge may appeal action to Supreme Court. | Vacancies are filled by gubernatorial appointment until next general election when successor is elected to fill unexpired term. If unexpired term ends within one year following such election, appointment is made for unexpired term. |
| **Oklahoma** | Judges are subject to impeachment for willful neglect of duty, corruption in office, habitual intemperence, incompetency or any offense involving moral turpitude.<br>Upon recommendation of Council on Judicial Complaints, chief justice of Supreme Court may bring charges against any judge in the Court on the Judiciary. Court on the Judiciary may order removal of judge for gross neglect of duty, corruption in office, habitual drunkenness, an offense involving moral turpitude, gross partiality in office, or oppression in office. Judge may also be retired (with or without salary) for mental or physical disability that prevents performance of duties, or for incompetence to perform duties. | Vacancies on Supreme Court, Court of Appeals, and Court of Criminal Appeals are filled by governor form list of candidates submitted by judicial nominating commission. For Court of Appeals vacancies, judge is elected to fill unexpired term at next general election. |
| **Oregon** | On recommendation of Commission on Judicial Fitness, Supreme Court may remove a judge for conviction of a felony or crime involving moral turpitude, willful misconduct in office, willful or persistent failure to perform judicial duties, habitual intemperance, illegal use of narcotic drugs or willful violation of rules of conduct prescribed by Supreme Court of general incompetence. A judge may also be retired for mental or physical disability after certification by Commission. Judge may appeal to Supreme Court. | Vacancies on Supreme Court, court of appeals and circuit courts are filled by gubernatorial appointment, until next general election when judge is selected to fill unexpired term. |
| **Pennsylvania** | All judges are subject to impeachment for misdemeanor in office.<br>Upon complaint by Judicial Conduct Board, Court of Judiciary Discipline may remove a judge subject to appeal to Supreme Court. | By gubernatorial appointment (with advice and consent of Senate), from names submitted by appropriate nominating commission. Appointee serves until next election if the election is more than 10 months after vacancy occurred. |
| **Rhode Island** | All judges are subject to impeachment.<br>The Supreme Court on its own motion may suspend a judge who pleaded guilty or no contest or was found guilty of a crime punishable as a felony under state or federal law or any other crime involving moral turpitude.<br>Upon recommendation of the Commission on Judicial Tenure and Discipline, the Supreme Court may censure, suspend, reprimand or remove from office a judge guilty of a serious violation of the canons of judicial ethics or for willful or persistent failure to perform duties, a disabling addiction to alcohol, drugs or narcotics, or conduct that brings the office into disrepute. The Supreme Court may also retire a judge for physical or mental disability that seriously interferes with the performance of duties and is (or is likely to become) permanent.<br>Whenever the Commission recommends removal of a Supreme Court justice, the Supreme Court transmits the findings to the Speaker of the House of Representatives, recommending the initiation of proceedings for the removal of the justice by resolution of the legislature. | Vacancies on Supreme Court are filled by the two houses of the legislature in grand committee until the next election. In case of a judge's temporary inability, governor may appoint a person to fill vacancy. Vacancies on superior, family and district courts are filled by gubernatorial appointment (with advice and consent of Senate). |
| **South Carolina** | Judges are subject to removal by impeachment or by governor on address of two-thirds of each house of the legislature.<br>Upon review of findings of fact, conclusions of law, and recommendation of the Board of Commissioners on Judicial Standards, the Supreme Court can discipline, suspend, remove, retire or hold in contempt a judge who has been convicted of a crime of moral turpitude, has violated the Code of Judicial Conduct or the Rules of Professional Conduct, persistently failed to perform his judicial duties, or is persistently incompetent or neglectful in the performance of his judicial duties or is habitually intemperate, consistently fails to timely issue his official orders, decrees, or opinions or otherwise perform his official duties without just cause or excuse, or for disability. | Vacancies on the Supreme Court, court of appeals, and circuit court are filled by joint public vote of general assembly, from list of nominees supplied by judicial screening committee. |
| **South Dakota** | Supreme Court justices and circuit court judges are subject to removal by impeachment.<br>Upon recommendation of Judicial Qualifications Commission, Supreme Court may remove a judge from office. | Vacancies on Supreme and circuit courts are filled by gubernatorial appointment from names submitted by Judicial Qualifications Commission for balance of unexpired term. |
| **Tennessee** | Judges are subject to impeachment for misfeasance or malfeasance in office.<br>Upon recommendation of the Court on the Judiciary, the legislature (by concurrent resolution) may remove a judge for willful misconduct in office or physical or mental disability. | Vacancies on Supreme, circuit, criminal, and chancery courts are filled by gubernatorial appointment until next biennial election. |

# METHODS FOR REMOVAL OF JUDGES AND FILLING OF VACANCIES — Continued

| State or other jurisdiction | How removed | Vacancies: how filled |
|---|---|---|
| Texas | Supreme Court, court of appeals and district court judges are subject to removal by impeachment or by joint address of both houses.<br>Supreme Court may remove district judges from office. District judges may remove county judges and justices of the peace.<br>Upon recommendation of removal by State Commission on Judicial Conduct, Supreme Court selects review tribunal. Decision of review tribunal may be appealed to the Supreme Court. | Vacancies on appellate and district courts are filled by gubernatorial appointment until next general election, at which time a successor is chosen. Vacancies on county courts are filled by appointment by county commissioner's court until next election when successor is chosen. Vacancies on municipal courts are filled by governing body of municipality for remainder of unexpired term. |
| Utah | All judges, except justices of the peace, are subject to impeachment.<br>Following investigations and hearings, the Judicial Conduct Commission may order the reprimand, censure, suspension, removal or involuntary retirement of any judge for willful misconduct, final conviction of a crime punishable as a felony under state or federal law, willful or persistent failure to perform judicial duties, disability that seriously interferes with performance, or conduct prejudicial to the administration of justice that brings the judicial office into disrepute. Prior to implementation, the Supreme Court reviews the order.<br>Lay justices of the peace may be removed for willful failure to participate in judicial education program. | Vacancies on Supreme, district and circuit courts are filled by gubernatorial appointment from candidates submitted by appropriate nominating commission. |
| Vermont | Upon review of the findings of the Judicial Conduct Board, all judges are subject to impeachment.<br>Supreme Court may discipline, impose sanctions on, or suspend from duties any judge in the state. | If Senate is in session, vacancies on Supreme, superior, and district courts are filled by governor, with advice and consent of Senate, from list of nominees submitted by judicial nominating board. Otherwise, by governor's appointment from nominees list. |
| Virginia | All judges are subject to impeachment.<br>Upon certification of charges against judge by Judicial Inquiry and Review Commission, Supreme Court may remove a judge. | If General Assembly is in session, vacancies are filled by majority vote of both houses. Otherwise by gubernatorial appointment, with appointee serving until 30 days after commencement of next legislative session. |
| Washington | A judge of any court of record is subject to impeachment.<br>After notice, hearing and recommendation by Judicial Qualifications Commission, Supreme Court may censure, suspend or remove a judge for violating a rule of judicial conduct. The Supreme Court may also retire a judge for disability that seriously interferes with the performance of duties and is (or is likely to become) permanent. | Vacancies on appellate and general trial courts are filled by gubernatorial appointment until next general election when successor is elected to fill remainder of term. |
| West Virginia | Judges are subject to impeachment for maladministration, corruption, incompetency, gross immorality, neglect of duty or any crime or misdemeanor.<br>Upon review of recommendations of the Judicial Hearing Board, the Supreme Court of Appeals may censure or suspend a judge for any violation of the judicial code of ethics or retire a judge who is incapable of performing duties because of advancing age, disease or physical or mental infirmity. | Vacancies on appellate and general trial courts are filled by gubernatorial appointment. If unexpired term is less than two years (or such additional period not exceeding three years), appointee serves for remainder of term. If unexpired term is more than three years, appointee serves until next general election, at which time successor is chosen to fill remainder of term. |
| Wisconsin | All judges are subject to impeachment.<br>Supreme Court, court of appeals and circuit court judges are subject to removal by address of both houses of legislature with two-thirds of members concurring, and by recall election.<br>As judges of courts of record must be licensed to practice law in state, removal of judge may also be by disbarment.<br>Upon review of the findings of fact, conclusions of law and recommendation of the Judicial Commission, the Supreme Court may reprimand, censure, suspend or remove for cause or disability any judge or justice for a willful violation of a rule of the Code of Judicial Ethics, willful or persistent failure to perform official duties, habitual intemperance, due to consumption of intoxicating beverages or use of dangerous drugs, which interferes with the proper performance of judicial duties, or conviction of a felony. | Vacancies on Supreme Court, court of appeals and circuit courts are filled by gubernatorial appointment from nominees submitted by nominating commission. |

# METHODS FOR REMOVAL OF JUDGES AND FILLING OF VACANCIES — Continued

| State or other jurisdiction | How removed | Vacancies: how filled |
|---|---|---|
| **Wyoming** | All judges, except justices of peace, are subject to impeachment. Upon recommendation of Judicial Supervisory Commission, the Supreme Court may retire or remove a judge. After a hearing before the panel of three district judges, the Supreme Court may remove justices of the peace. | Vacancies are filled by governor from list of three nominees submitted by judicial nominating commission. Vacancies on justice of peace courts are filled by appointment by county commissioners until next general election. |
| **Dist. of Columbia** | Commission on Judicial Disabilities and Tenure may remove a judge upon conviction of felony (including a federal crime), for willful misconduct in office, willful and persistent failure to perform judicial duties or for other conduct prejudicial to the administration of justice which brings the office into disrepute. | Vacancies are filled by president of United States, with consent of U.S. Senate, from list of persons recommended by Judicial Nominating Commission. |
| **Puerto Rico** | Supreme Court justices are subject to impeachment for treason, bribery or other felonies and misdemeanors involving moral turpitude. Supreme Court may remove other judges for cause (as provided by judiciary act) after a hearing on charges brought by order of chief justice, who disqualifies self from final proceedings. | Vacancies are filled as in initial selection. |

*Source:* American Judicature Society (Summer 1997). Used with permission.

## Table 4.6
# COMPENSATION OF JUDGES OF APPELLATE COURTS AND GENERAL TRIAL COURTS

| State or other jurisdiction | Appellate courts | | | | General trial courts | Salary |
|---|---|---|---|---|---|---|
| | Court of last resort | Salary | Intermediate appellate court | Salary | | |
| Alabama | Supreme Court | $124,950 | Court of Criminal Appeals | $123,784 (b) | Circuit courts | $84,564 |
| | | | Court of Civil Appeals | 123,784 | | |
| Alaska | Supreme Court | 112,224 | Court of Appeals | 106,020 | Superior courts | 103,776 |
| Arizona | Supreme Court | 118,000 | Court of Appeals | 115,500 | Superior courts | 113,000 |
| Arkansas | Supreme Court | 114,101 | Court of Appeals | 110,493 | Chancery courts | 106,878 |
| | | | | | Circuit courts | 106,878 |
| California | Supreme Court | 135,018 | Court of Appeals | 126,580 | Superior court | 110,612 |
| Colorado | Supreme Court | 95,090 | Court of Appeals | 90,590 | District courts | 86,090 |
| Connecticut | Supreme Court | 119,962 (a) | Appellate Court | 111,546 (a) | Superior courts | 106,558 (a) |
| Delaware | Supreme Court | 125,200 | . . . | . . . | Superior courts | 119,200 |
| Florida | Supreme Court | 145,083 | District Court of Appeals | 130,576 | Circuit courts | 117,020 |
| Georgia | Supreme Court | 129,283 | Court of Appeals | 128,463 | Superior courts | 110,772 (b) |
| Hawaii | Supreme Court | 93,780 | Intermediate Court | 89,780 | Circuit courts | 86,780 |
| Idaho | Supreme Court | 94,423 | Court of Appeals | 93,423 | District courts | 88,499 |
| Illinois | Supreme Court | 147,024 | Appellate Court | 138,376 | Circuit courts | 126,978 |
| Indiana | Supreme Court | 115,000 (c) | Court of Appeals | 110,000 (c) | Circuit courts | 90,000 |
| | | | | | Superior courts | 90,000 |
| Iowa | Supreme Court | 109,900 | Court of Appeals | 105,700 | District courts | 100,500 |
| Kansas | Supreme Court | 107,079 | Court of Appeals | 103,371 | District courts | 93,509 |
| Kentucky | Supreme Court | 108,927 | Court of Appeals | 104,480 | Circuit courts | 100,034 |
| Louisiana | Supreme Court | 103,336 | Court of Appeals | 97,928 | District courts | 92,520 |
| Maine | Supreme Judicial Court | 97,536 | . . . | . . . | Superior courts | 91,440 |
| Maryland | Court of Appeals | 119,850 | Court of Special Appeals | 112,850 | Circuit courts | 109,050 |
| Massachusetts | Supreme Judicial Court | 123,243 | Appeals Court | 114,045 | Trial court | 109,492 |
| Michigan | Supreme Court | 134,752 | Court of Appeals | 123,972 | Circuit courts | 114,539 |
| Minnesota | Supreme Court | 107,765 | Court of Appeals | 101,543 | District courts | 95,320 |
| Mississippi | Supreme Court | 102,300 | Court of Appeals | 95,500 | Chancery courts | 94,700 |
| | | | | | Circuit courts | 94,700 |
| Missouri | Supreme Court | 114,348 | Court of Appeals | 106,797 | Circuit courts | 98,947 |
| | | | | | Municipal division of circuit courts up to 87,235 | |
| Montana | Supreme Court | 83,550 | . . . | . . . | District courts | 77,439 |
| Nebraska | Supreme Court | 106,223 | Court of Appeals | 100,912 | District courts | 98,256 |
| Nevada | Supreme Court | 116,127 | . . . | . . . | District courts | 106,500 (a) |
| New Hampshire | Supreme Court | 100,404 | . . . | . . . | Superior courts | 94,128 |
| New Jersey | Supreme Court | 132,250 | Appellate division of Superior Court | 124,200 | Superior courts | 115,000 |
| New Mexico | Supreme Court | 87,773 | Court of Appeals | 83,384 | District courts | 79,215 |
| New York | Court of Appeals | 151,200 | Appellate divisions of Supreme Court | 144,000 | Supreme courts | 136,700 |
| North Carolina | Supreme Court | 110,687 (a) | Court of Appeals | 106,075 (a) | Superior courts | 100,310 (a) |
| North Dakota | Supreme Court | 83,807 | . . . | . . . | District courts | 77,340 |
| Ohio | Supreme Court | 113,850 | Court of Appeals | 106,050 | Courts of common pleas | 97,550 |
| Oklahoma | Supreme Court | 97,807 | Court of Appeals | 93,530 | District courts | 88,511 |
| Oregon | Supreme Court | 93,600 | Court of Appeals | 91,500 | Circuit courts | 85,300 |
| | | | | | Tax court | 88,000 |
| Pennsylvania | Supreme Court | 127,951 | Superior Court | 123,944 | Courts of common pleas | 111,122 |
| | | | Commonwealth Court | 123,944 | | |
| Rhode Island | Supreme Court | 118,650 (a) | . . . | . . . | Superior courts | 106,825 (a) |
| South Carolina | Supreme Court | 109,380 | Court of Appeals | 106,645 | Circuit courts | 103,911 |
| South Dakota | Supreme Court | 92,118 | . . . | . . . | Circuit courts | 86,044 |
| Tennessee | Supreme Court | 112,068 | Court of Criminal Appeals | 106,848 | Chancery courts | 102,240 |
| | | | | | Circuit courts | 102,240 |
| | | | | | Criminal courts | 102,240 |
| Texas | Supreme Court | 113,000 | Court of Appeals | 107,350 | District courts | 101,700 (b) |
| Utah | Supreme Court | 105,492 | Court of Appeals | 100,692 | District courts | 95,900 |
| Vermont | Supreme Court | 94,932 | . . . | . . . | Superior courts | 90,176 |

See footnotes at end of table.

## COMPENSATION OF JUDGES OF APPELLATE COURTS AND GENERAL TRIAL COURTS — Continued

| State or other jurisdiction | Appellate courts | | | | | General trial courts | Salary |
|---|---|---|---|---|---|---|---|
| | Court of last resort | Salary | Intermediate appellate court | Salary | | | |
| Virginia | Supreme Court | 128,352 | Court of Appeals | 121,936 | | Circuit courts | 119,154 |
| Washington | Supreme Court | 120,000 | Court of Appeals | 114,000 | | Superior courts | 108,300 |
| West Virginia | Supreme Court | 95,000 | ... | ... | | Circuit courts | 90,000 |
| Wisconsin | Supreme Court | 112,318 | Court of Appeals | 105,960 | | Circuit courts | 99,961 |
| Wyoming | Supreme Court | 93,000 | ... | ... | | District courts | 83,700 |
| Dist. of Columbia | Court of Appeals | 145,500 | ... | ... | | Superior courts | 136,700 |
| American Samoa | High Court | 74,303 | ... | ... | | ... | ... |
| Guam | ... | 126,000 | ... | ... | | Superior courts | 100,000 |
| No. Mariana Islands | Commonwealth Supreme Court | 126,000 | ... | ... | | ... | 120,000 |
| Puerto Rico | Supreme Court | 100,000 | Appellate Court | 90,000 | | Superior courts | 80,000 |
| | | | | | | District courts | 65,000 |
| U.S. Virgin Islands | Territorial courts | 100,000 | ... | ... | | ... | ... |

Source: National Center for State Courts, *Survey of Judicial Salaries* (Fall 1999).

Note: Compensation is shown according to most recent legislation, even though laws may not yet have taken effect.

(a) The base pay is supplemented by increments for length of service.

(b) Median salary. If more than half the salaries are the same as the minimum or the maximum salary, then the median (the midpoint above which half the salaries fall) is either the minimum or maximum salary.

(c) In Indiana, subsistence allowance is $3,000.

## Table 4.7
## SELECTED DATA ON COURT ADMINISTRATIVE OFFICES

| State or other jurisdiction | Title | Established | Appointed by (a) | Salary |
|---|---|---|---|---|
| Alabama | Administrative Director of Courts (b) | 1971 | CJ | $100,230 |
| Alaska | Administrative Director | 1959 | CJ(b) | 110,220 |
| Arizona | Administrative Director of Courts | 1960 | SC | 95,207 to 138,049 |
| Arkansas | Director, Administrative Office of the Courts | 1965 | CJ (c) | 79,919 |
| California | Administrative Director of the Courts | 1960 | JC | 126,580 to 135,000 |
| Colorado | State Court Administrator | 1959 | SC | (d) |
| Connecticut | Chief Court Administrator (e) | 1965 | CJ | 125,296 (f) |
| Delaware | Director, Administrative Office of the Courts | 1971 | CJ | 97,700 |
| Florida | State Courts Administrator | 1972 | SC | 106,710 |
| Georgia | Director, Administrative Office of the Courts | 1973 | JC | 93,299 |
| Hawaii | Administrative Director of the Courts | 1959 | CJ (b) | 85,302 |
| Idaho | Administrative Director of the Courts | 1967 | SC | 89,193 |
| Illinois | Administrative Director of the Courts | 1959 | SC | 138,376 |
| Indiana | Executive Director, Division of State Court Administration | 1975 | CJ | 87,400 |
| Iowa | Court Administrator | 1971 | SC | 76,700 to 115,400 |
| Kansas | Judicial Administrator | 1965 | CJ | 93,509 |
| Kentucky | Administrative Director of the Courts | 1976 | CJ | 100,032 |
| Louisiana | Judicial Administrator | 1954 | SC | 97,928 |
| Maine | Court Administrator | 1975 | CJ | 84,000 |
| Maryland | State Court Administrator (b) | 1955 | CJ | 107,775 |
| Massachusetts | Chief Justice for Administration & Management | 1978 | SC | 118,496 |
| Michigan | State Court Administrator | 1952 | SC | 113,984 |
| Minnesota | State Court Administrator | 1963 | SC | 95,320 |
| Mississippi | Court Administrator | 1974 | SC | 82,567 |
| Missouri | State Courts Administrator | 1970 | SC | 84,312 |
| Montana | State Court Administrator | 1975 | SC | 62,722 |
| Nebraska | State Court Administrator | 1972 | CJ | 86,859 |
| Nevada | Director, Office of Court Administration | 1971 | SC | 78,019 |
| New Hampshire | Director of the Administrative Office of the Court | 1980 | SC | 80,999 |
| New Jersey | Administrative Director of the Courts | 1948 | CJ | 124,200 |
| New Mexico | Director, Administrative Office of the Courts | 1959 | SC | 83,593 |
| New York | Chief Administrator of the Courts (g) | 1978 | CJ (h) | 147,600 |
| North Carolina | Director, Administrative Office of the Courts | 1965 | CJ | 103,193 |
| North Dakota | Court Administrator (i) | 1971 | CJ | 74,444 |
| Ohio | Administrative Director of the Courts | 1955 | SC | 100,006 |
| Oklahoma | Administrative Director of the Courts | 1967 | SC | 93,530 |
| Oregon | Court Administrator | 1971 | SC | 91,500 |
| Pennsylvania | Court Administrator | 1968 | SC | 120,299 |
| Rhode Island | State Court Administrator | 1969 | CJ | 95,300 |
| South Carolina | Director of Court Administration | 1973 | CJ | 88,000 |
| South Dakota | State Court Administrator | 1974 | SC | 76,376 |
| Tennessee | Director | 1963 | SC | 98,364 |
| Texas | Administrative Director of the Courts (j) | 1977 | SC | 92,217 |
| Utah | Court Administrator | 1973 | SC | 95,900 |
| Vermont | Court Administrator (k) | 1967 | SC | 90,168 |
| Virginia | Executive Secretary to the Supreme Court | 1952 | SC | 112,145 |
| Washington | Administrator for the Courts | 1957 | SC (l) | 95,945 |
| West Virginia | Administrative Director of the Supreme Court of Appeals | 1975 | SC | 65,000 |
| Wisconsin | Director of State Courts | 1978 | SC | 105,960 |
| Wyoming | Court Coordinator | 1974 | SC | 70,000 to 85,000 |
| Dist. of Columbia | Executive Officer, Courts of D.C. | 1971 | (m) | 136,700 |
| American Samoa | Court Administrator | 1977 | CJ | 27,092 |
| Guam | Administrative Director of Superior Court | N.A. | CJ (n) | 73,000 |
| Puerto Rico | Administrative Director of the Courts | 1952 | CJ | 96,000 |
| U.S. Virgin Islands | Court/Administrative Clerk | N.A. | N.A. | 75,000 |

See footnotes at end of table.

# Table 4.7
## SELECTED DATA ON COURT ADMINISTRATIVE OFFICES - Continued

*Source*: Salary information was taken from National Center for State Courts, *Survey of Judicial Salaries* (Fall 1999).

Key:

SC — State court of last resort.

CJ — Chief justice or chief judge of court of last resort.

JC — Judicial council.

N.A. — Not available.

(a) Term of office for all court administrators is at pleasure of appointing authority.

(b) With approval of Supreme Court.

(c) With approval of Judicial Council.

(d) Set by Supreme Court.

(e) Administrator is an associate judge of the Supreme Court.

(f) Base pay supplemented by increments for length of service.

(g) If incumbent is a judge, the title is Chief Administrative Judge of the Courts.

(h) With advice and consent of Administrative Board of the Courts.

(i) Serves as executive secretary to Judicial Council.

(j) Serves as executive director of Judicial Council.

(k) Also clerk of the Supreme Court.

(l) Appointed from list of five submitted by governor.

(m) Joint Committee on Judicial Administration.

(n) Presiding judge of Superior Court (general trial court).

# Chapter Five

# ELECTIONS, CAMPAIGN FINANCE AND INITIATIVES

*Democracy in action — includes information on offices up for election 2000-2009, methods of nominating candidates, formulas for election dates, polling hours, voting statistics, campaign finance laws, and procedures for initiative, referenda and recalls.*

For additional information on Chapter Five contact
The States Information Center, at The Council of State Governments,
(859) 244-8253 or E-mail: sic@csg.org.

# Table 5.1
## STATE EXECUTIVE BRANCH OFFICIALS TO BE ELECTED: 2000-2009

| State or other jurisdiction | 2000 | 2001 | 2002 | 2003 | 2004 |
|---|---|---|---|---|---|
| Alabama | ... | ... | G,LG,AG,AR,A,SS,T | ... | ... |
| Alaska (a) | ... | ... | G | ... | ... |
| Arizona | ... | ... | G,AG,SS,SP,T (b) | ... | ... |
| Arkansas | ... | ... | G,LG,AG,A,SS,T | ... | ... |
| California | ... | ... | G,LG,AG,C,SS,SP,T (c,h) | ... | ... |
| Colorado (d) | ... | ... | G,LG,SS,T | ... | ... |
| Connecticut* | ... | ... | G,LG,AG,C,SS,T | ... | ... |
| Delaware* | G,LG (c) | ... | AG,C,T | ... | G,LG |
| Florida | (e) | ... | G,LG,AG,AR,CFO (dd) | ... | ... |
| Georgia | (e) | ... | G,LG,AG,AR,SS,SP (e,f) | ... | ... |
| Hawaii | (g) | ... | G,LG | ... | ... |
| Idaho | ... | ... | G,LG,AG,SS,SP,T (h) | ... | ... |
| Illinois | ... | ... | G,LG,AG,C,SS,T | ... | ... |
| Indiana* | G,LG,AG,SP | ... | A,SS,T | ... | G,LG,AG,SP |
| Iowa* | ... | ... | G,LG,AG,AR,SS,T | ... | ... |
| Kansas | (i) | ... | G,LG,AG,SS,T (i) | ... | ... |
| Kentucky* | ... | ... | ... | G,LG,AG,AR,A,SS,T | ... |
| Louisiana (j) | ... | ... | ... | G,LG,AG,AR,SS,T | ... |
| Maine (k) | ... | ... | G | ... | ... |
| Maryland | ... | ... | G,LG,AG,C | ... | ... |
| Massachusetts* | ... | ... | G,LG,AG,SS,T | ... | ... |
| Michigan (l) | ... | ... | G,LG,AG,SS | ... | ... |
| Minnesota | ... | ... | G,LG,AG,A,SS (z) | ... | ... |
| Mississippi | ... | ... | ... | G,LG,AG,AR,A,SS,T (m) | ... |
| Missouri | G,LG,AG,SS,T | ... | A | ... | G,LG,AG,SS,T |
| Montana | G,LG,AG,A,SS,SP | ... | ... | ... | G,LG,AG,A,SS,SP |
| Nebraska (n) | ... | ... | G,LG,AG,A,SS,T | ... | ... |
| Nevada* | (o) | ... | G,LG,AG,C,SS,T | ... | ... |
| New Hampshire | G | ... | G | ... | G |
| New Jersey | ... | G | ... | ... | ... |
| New Mexico | ... | ... | G,LG,AG,A,SS,T | ... | ... |
| New York | ... | ... | G,LG,AG,C | ... | ... |
| North Carolina* | G,LG,AG,AR,A,SS,SP,T (p) | ... | ... | ... | G,LG,AG,AR,A,SS,SP,T (q) |
| North Dakota (r) | G,LG,AG,AR,A,SS,SP,T(cc) | ... | ... | ... | G,LG,AG,AR,A,SS,SP,T(cc) |
| Ohio | (s) | ... | G,LG,AG,A,SS,T (s) | ... | (s) |
| Oklahoma | (u) | ... | G,LG,AG,A,SP,T(q,u) | ... | (u) |
| Oregon | AG,SS,T | ... | G,SP (v) | ... | AG,SS,T |
| Pennsylvania | AG,A,T (w) | ... | G,LG | ... | AG,A,T (w) |
| Rhode Island | ... | G,LG,AG,SS,T | ... | ... | ... |
| South Carolina | ... | G,LG,AG,AR,C,SS,SP,T(x) | ... | ... | ... |

See footnotes at end of table.

Key:
.:: — No regularly scheduled elections
G — Governor
LG — Lieutenant Governor
AG — Attorney General
AR — Agriculture

A — Auditor
C — Comptroller
SS — Secretary of State
SP — Superintendent of public instruction (bb)
T — Treasurer
CFO—Chief Financial Officer

# STATE EXECUTIVE BRANCH OFFICIALS TO BE ELECTED — Continued

| State or other jurisdiction | 2000 | 2001 | 2002 | 2003 | 2004 |
|---|---|---|---|---|---|
| South Dakota (y) | ... | ... | G,LG,AG,A,SS,T | ... | ... |
| Tennessee (aa) | | | G | ... | ... |
| Texas (aa) | | | G,LG,AG,AR,C | ... | ... |
| Utah | G,LG,AG,A,T (aa) | ... | (aa) | ... | G,LG,AG,A,T(aa) |
| Vermont | G,LG,AG,A,SS,T | ... | G,LG,AG,A,SS,T | ... | G,LG,AG,A,SS,T |
| Virginia | ... | G,LG,AG | ... | ... | ... |
| Washington | G,LG,AG,A,SS,SP,T (f) | | ... | ... | G,LG,AG,A,SS,SP,T (f) |
| West Virginia* | G,AG,AR,A,SS,T | | ... | ... | G,AG,AR,A,SS,T |
| Wisconsin | ... | SP | G,LG,AG,SS,T | ... | ... |
| Wyoming | ... | ... | G,A,SS,SP,T | ... | ... |
| U.S. Virgin Islands | ... | ... | G,LG | ... | ... |
| **Totals for year** | | | | | |
| Governor | 11 | 2 | 37 | 3 | 11 |
| Lieutenant Governor | 9 | 1 | 31 | 3 | 9 |
| Attorney General | 11 | 1 | 28 | 3 | 11 |
| Agriculture | 3 | 0 | 6 | 3 | 3 |
| Auditor | 8 | 0 | 8 | 2 | 8 |
| Chief Financial Officer | 0 | 0 | 1 | 0 | 0 |
| Comptroller | 0 | 0 | 9 | 0 | 0 |
| Secretary of State | 8 | 0 | 25 | 3 | 8 |
| Supt. of Public Inst. (bb) | 5 | 1 | 7 | 0 | 5 |
| Treasurer | 9 | 0 | 24 | 3 | 9 |

*Key:*
... — No regularly scheduled elections
G — Governor
LG — Lieutenant Governor
AG — Attorney General
AR — Agriculture

A — Auditor.
C — Comptroller
SS — Secretary of State
SP — Superintendent of public instruction (dd)
T — Treasurer

# STATE EXECUTIVE BRANCH OFFICIALS TO BE ELECTED — Continued

| State or other jurisdiction | 2005 | 2006 | 2007 | 2008 | 2009 |
|---|---|---|---|---|---|
| Alabama | ... | G,LG,AG,AR,A,SS,T | ... | ... | ... |
| Alaska (a) | ... | G,LG | ... | ... | ... |
| Arizona | ... | G,AG,SS,SP,T (b) | ... | ... | ... |
| Arkansas | ... | G,LG,AG,A,SS,T | ... | ... | ... |
| California | ... | G,LG,AG,SS,SP,T(c,h) | ... | ... | ... |
| Colorado (d) | ... | G,LG,AG,SS,T | ... | ... | ... |
| Connecticut* | ... | G,LG,AG,C,SS,T | ... | ... | ... |
| Delaware* | ... | AG,C,T | ... | G,LG | ... |
| Florida | ... | G,LG,AG,AR,CFO (dd) | ... | ... | ... |
| Georgia | ... | G,LG,AG,AR,SS,SP (e,f) | ... | ... | ... |
| Hawaii | ... | G,LG | ... | ... | ... |
| Idaho | ... | G,LG,AG,SS,SP,T (h) | ... | ... | ... |
| Illinois | ... | G,LG,AG,C,SS,T | ... | ... | ... |
| Indiana* | ... | A,SS,T | ... | G,LG,AG,SP | ... |
| Iowa | ... | G,LG,AG,AR,A,SS,T | ... | ... | ... |
| Kansas | ... | G,LG,AG,SS,T (i) | ... | ... | ... |
| Kentucky* | ... | ... | G,LG,AG,AR,A,SS,T | ... | ... |
| Louisiana (j) | ... | G | G,LG,AG,AR,SS,T | ... | ... |
| Maine(k) | ... | ... | ... | ... | ... |
| Maryland | ... | G,LG,AG,C | ... | ... | ... |
| Massachusetts* | ... | G,LG,AG,A,SS,T | ... | ... | ... |
| Michigan (l) | ... | G,LG,AG,SS | ... | ... | ... |
| Minnesota | ... | G,LG,AG,A,SS (z) | ... | ... | ... |
| Mississippi | ... | ... | G,LG,AG,AR,A,SS,T(m) | ... | ... |
| Missouri | ... | A | ... | G,LG,AG,SS,T | ... |
| Montana | ... | G,LG,AG,A,SS,T | ... | G,LG,AG,A,SS,SP | ... |
| Nebraska (n) | ... | G,LG,AG,C,SS,T | ... | ... | ... |
| Nevada* | ... | G | ... | ... | ... |
| New Hampshire | ... | G | ... | G | ... |
| New Jersey | G | ... | ... | ... | G |
| New Mexico (p) | ... | G,LG,AG,A,SS,T | ... | ... | ... |
| New York | ... | G,LG,AG,C | ... | ... | ... |
| North Carolina* | ... | ... | ... | G,LG,AG,AR,A,SS,SP,T (p) | ... |
| North Dakota (t) | ... | ... | ... | G,LG,AG,AR,A,SS,SP,T(ff) | ... |
| Ohio | ... | G,LG,AG,A,SS,T (s) | ... | (s) | ... |
| Oklahoma (t) | ... | G,LG,AG,A,SP,T(q,u) | ... | (u) | ... |
| Oregon | ... | G,SP (v) | ... | AG,SS,T | ... |
| Pennsylvania | ... | G,LG | ... | AG,A,T (w) | ... |
| Rhode Island | ... | G,LG,AG,SS,T | ... | ... | ... |
| South Carolina | ... | G,LG,AG,AR,C,SS,SP,T (x) | ... | ... | ... |

See footnotes at end of table.

Key:
... — No regularly scheduled elections
G — Governor
LG — Lieutenant Governor
AG — Attorney General
AR — Agriculture

A — Auditor
C — Comptroller
SS — Secretary of State
SP — Superintendent of public instruction (dd)
T — Treasurer

# STATE EXECUTIVE BRANCH OFFICIALS TO BE ELECTED — Continued

| State or other jurisdiction | 2005 | 2006 | 2007 | 2008 | 2009 |
|---|---|---|---|---|---|
| South Dakota (y) | ... | G,LG,AG,A,SS,T | ... | ... | ... |
| Tennessee | ... | G | ... | ... | ... |
| Texas | ... | G,LG,AG,AR,C | ... | ... | ... |
| Utah | ... | ... | ... | G,LG,AG,A,T | ... |
| Vermont | ... | G,LG,AG,A,SS,T | ... | G,LG,AG,SS,T | ... |
| Virginia | G,LG,AG | ... | ... | ... | G,LG,AG |
| Washington | ... | ... | ... | G,LG,AG,A,SS,SP,T (f) | ... |
| West Virginia * | SP | ... | ... | G,AG,AR,A,SS,T | SP |
| Wisconsin | ... | G,LG,AG,SS,T | ... | ... | ... |
| Wyoming | ... | G,A,SS,SP,T | ... | ... | ... |
| U.S. Virgin Islands | ... | G,LG | ... | ... | ... |
| **Totals for year** | | | | | |
| Governor | 2 | 37 | 3 | 11 | 2 |
| Lieutenant Governor .. | 1 | 31 | 3 | 9 | 2 |
| Attorney General | 1 | 28 | 3 | 11 | 2 |
| Agriculture | 0 | 6 | 3 | 3 | 1 |
| Auditor | 0 | 8 | 2 | 8 | 2 |
| Chief Financial Officer . | 0 | 1 | 0 | 0 | 0 |
| Comptroller | 0 | 9 | 0 | 0 | 0 |
| Secretary of State | 0 | 25 | 3 | 8 | 1 |
| Supt. of Public Inst. (ee) | 1 | 7 | 0 | 5 | 1 |
| Treasurer | 0 | 24 | 3 | 9 | 1 |

*Sources:* State election administration offices, except where noted by * where data are from *The Book of the States, 1998-99.*

*Note:* This table shows the executive branch officials up for election in given year. Footnotes indicate other offices (e.g., commissioners of labor, insurance, public service, etc.) also up for election in a given year. The data contained in this table reflect information available at press time.

*Key:*

... — No regularly scheduled elections
G — Governor
CFO — Chief Financial Officer
LG — Lieutenant Governor
AG — Attorney General
SP — Superintendent of public instruction(bb)
AR — Agriculture
T — Treasurer

A — Auditor
C — Comptroller
CFO —Chief Financial Officer
SS — Secretary of State
SP — Superintendent of public instruction (bb)
T — Treasurer

(a) Election of school boards established to maintain system of state dependent public school systems established in areas of the unorganized borough and military reservations not served by other public school systems.
(b) Mine inspector—4 year term; corporation commissioners (e)—6 year terms.
(c) Insurance commissioner and Board of Equalization.
(d) State board of education (7)—6 year terms; University of Colorado regents (9)—6 year terms.
(e) Public service commissioners (5)—6 year terms; 1996—2, 1998—1, 2000—2. Commissioner of labor—4 year term. Special election to fill secretary of state vacancy in 1996.
(f) Insurance commissioner, commissioner of public lands.
(g) State board of education (13)—4 year terms; 1996—7, 1998—6, 2000—7.

(h) Controller.
(i) Commissioner of insurance 1998; 2002. Board of education members (10)—4 year terms, 1996—5, 1998—5, 2000—5, 2002—5.
(j) Commissioner of elections—4 year term; commissioner of insurance—4 year term; board of elementary and secondary education (8)—4 year terms; public service commissioners (5)—6 year terms.
(k) In Maine the legislature elects constitutional officers (AG,A,SS,T) in even-numbered years.
(l) Michigan State University trustees (8)—8 year terms; University of Michigan regents (8)—8 year terms; Wayne State University governors (8)—8 year terms; board of education (8)—8 year terms, 1996—2, 1998—2, 2000—2.
(m) Commissioner of insurance, transportation commissioners (3), public service commissioners (3).
(n) Public service commissioners (5)—6 year terms; state board of education (8)—4 year terms; state university regents (8)—6 year terms.
(o) State board of education (11)—4 year terms, 1996—5, 1998-6, 2000—5.
(p) Commissioner of public lands—4 year terms, 1998; board of education (10)—6 year terms; corporation commissioners (3)—6 year terms.
(q) Commissioner of labor; commissioner of insurance.
(r) Commissioner of labor—4 year term, 1998; commissioner of insurance—4 year term, 1998; tax commissioner—4 year term, 1998; public service commissioner (3)—6 year terms.
(s) State board of education (19)—6 year terms, 1996—6; 1998—7; 2000—6.
(t) Corporation commissioner (3)—6 year terms, 1996, 1998, 2000; commissioner of insurance—4 year term, 1998; commissioner of labor—4 year term, 1998.
(u) In Oklahoma, 1 of 3 corporation commissioners elected for 6 year term.
(v) Commissioner of labor and industries—4 year term.

# STATE EXECUTIVE BRANCH OFFICIALS TO BE ELECTED — Continued

(w) In Pennsylvania, auditor general.

(x) Adjutant general—4 year term.

(y) Commissioner of school and public lands; public utility commissioners (3) 6 year terms; board of education (15)—6 year terms, 1996, 1998, 2000.

(z) In Minnesota the office of Treasurer is abolished effective 2003.

(aa) Commissioner of general land office—4 year term; railroad commissioners (3) 6 year terms; board of education (15)—6 year terms; members of State Board of Education serve staggered 4 year term (9–4 year terms, 1996–8, 1998–7, 2000–8.).

(bb) Superintendent of public instruction or commissioner of education.

(cc) In North Dakota, depending on the outcome of a constitutional measure appearing on the June 13, 2000 primary election ballot, the office of Treasurer may be abolished.

(dd) An amendment adopted by voters in 1998 merges the cabinet offices of treasurer and comptroller into one chief financial office; reduces cabinet membership to chief financial officer, attorney general, agriculture commissioner; secretary of state and education commissioner are eliminated from the elected cabinet. This takes effect in 2002.

## Table 5.2
## STATE LEGISLATURES: MEMBERS TO BE ELECTED, 2000–2009

| State or other jurisdiction | Total legislators Senate | Total legislators House | 2000 Senate | 2000 House | 2001 Senate | 2001 House | 2002 Senate | 2002 House | 2003 Senate | 2003 House | 2004 Senate | 2004 House |
|---|---|---|---|---|---|---|---|---|---|---|---|---|
| Alabama | 35 | 105 | ... | ... | ... | ... | 35 | 105 | ... | ... | ... | ... |
| Alaska | 20 | 40 | 10 | 40 | ... | ... | 10 | 40 | ... | ... | 10 | 40 |
| Arizona | 30 | 60 | 30 | 60 | ... | ... | 30 | 60 | ... | ... | 30 | 60 |
| Arkansas | 35 | 100 | 17 | 100 | ... | ... | 18 | 100 | ... | ... | 17 | 100 |
| California | 40 | 80 | 20 | 80 | ... | ... | 20 | 80 | ... | ... | 20 | 80 |
| Colorado | 35 | 65 | 18 | 65 | ... | ... | 17(g) | 65 | ... | ... | 18(g) | 65 |
| Connecticut | 36 | 151 | 36 | 151 | ... | ... | 36 | 151 | ... | ... | 36 | 151 |
| Delaware* | 21 | 41 | 11 | 41 | ... | ... | 21 | 41 | ... | ... | 10 | 41 |
| Florida | 40 | 120 | 20 | 120 | ... | ... | (a) | 120 | ... | ... | 20 | 120 |
| Georgia | 56 | 180 | 56 | 180 | ... | ... | 56 | 180 | ... | ... | 56 | 180 |
| Hawaii | 25 | 51 | 13 | 51 | ... | ... | 25 | 51 | ... | ... | 12 | 51 |
| Idaho | 35 | 70 | 35 | 70 | ... | ... | 35 | 70 | ... | ... | 35 | 70 |
| Illinois | 59 (b) | 118 | 19 | 118 | ... | ... | 59 | 118 | ... | ... | (c) | 118 |
| Indiana* | 50 | 100 | 25 | 100 | ... | ... | 25 | 99 | ... | ... | 25 | 99 |
| Iowa | 50 | 100 | 25 (e) | 100 | ... | ... | 25 (e) | 100 | ... | ... | 25(d) | 100 |
| Kansas | 40 | 125 | 40 | 125 | ... | ... | ... | 125 | ... | ... | 40 | 125 |
| Kentucky* | 38 | 100 | 19 | 100 | ... | ... | 19 | 100 | ... | ... | 19 | 100 |
| Louisiana | 39 | 105 | ... | ... | ... | ... | ... | ... | 39 | 105 | ... | ... |
| Maine | 35 | 151 | 35 | 151 | ... | ... | 35 | 151 | ... | ... | 35 | 151 |
| Maryland | 47 | 141 | ... | ... | ... | ... | 47 | 141 | ... | ... | ... | ... |
| Massachusetts* | 40 | 160 | 40 | 160 | ... | ... | 40 | 160 | ... | ... | 40 | 160 |
| Michigan | 38 | 110 | ... | 110 | ... | ... | 38 | 110 | ... | ... | ... | 110 |
| Minnesota | 67 | 134 | 67 | 134 | ... | ... | 67 | 134 | ... | ... | 67 | 134 |
| Mississippi | 52 | 122 | ... | ... | ... | ... | ... | ... | 52 | 122 | ... | ... |
| Missouri | 34 | 163 | 17 | 163 | ... | ... | 17 | 163 | ... | ... | 17 | 163 |
| Montana | 50 | 100 | 25 | 100 | ... | ... | 25 | 100 | ... | ... | 25 | 100 |
| Nebraska | 49 | U | 25 | U | ... | ... | 24 | U | ... | ... | 25 | U |
| Nevada* | 21 | 42 | 10 | 42 | ... | ... | 11 (f) | 42 | ... | ... | 10 | 42 |
| New Hampshire | 24 | 400 | 24 | 400 | ... | ... | 24 | 400 | ... | ... | 24 | 400 |
| New Jersey | 40 | 80 | ... | ... | 40 | 80 | ... | ... | 40 | 80 | ... | ... |
| New Mexico | 42 | 70 | 42 | 70 | ... | ... | ... | 70 | ... | ... | 42 | 70 |
| New York | 61 | 150 | 61 | 150 | ... | ... | 61 | 150 | ... | ... | 61 | 150 |
| North Carolina* | 50 | 120 | 50 | 120 | ... | ... | 50 | 120 | ... | ... | 50 | 120 |
| North Dakota | 49 | 98 | 24 (d) | 48 (d) | ... | ... | 25 (e) | 50 | ... | ... | 24 | 48 |
| Ohio | 33 | 99 | 16 (d) | 99 | ... | ... | 17 | 99 | ... | ... | 16 | 99 |
| Oklahoma | 48 | 101 | 24 | 101 | ... | ... | 24 | 101 | ... | ... | 24 | 101 |
| Oregon | 30 | 60 | 15 | 60 | ... | ... | 15 | 60 | ... | ... | 15 | 60 |
| Pennsylvania | 50 | 203 | 25 | 203 | ... | ... | 25 | 203 | ... | ... | 25 | 203 |
| Rhode Island | 50 | 100 | 50 | 100 | ... | ... | 38 | 75 | ... | ... | 38 | 75 |
| South Carolina | 46 | 124 | 46 | 124 | ... | ... | ... | 124 | ... | ... | 46 | 124 |

See footnotes at end of table.

# STATE LEGISLATURES: MEMBERS TO BE ELECTED, 2000-2009

| State or other jurisdiction | Total legislators | | 2000 | | 2001 | | 2002 | | 2003 | | 2004 | |
|---|---|---|---|---|---|---|---|---|---|---|---|---|
| | Senate | House | Senate | House | Senate | House | Senate | House | Senate | House | Senate | House |
| South Dakota ............. | 35 | 70 | 35 | 70 | ... | ... | 35 | 70 | ... | ... | 35 | 70 |
| Tennessee ................. | 33 | 99 | 16 | 99 | ... | ... | 17 | 99 | ... | ... | 16 | 99 |
| Texas ........................ | 31 | 150 | 15 | 150 | ... | ... | 31 | 150 | ... | ... | 15 | 150 |
| Utah ......................... | 29 | 75 | 14 | 75 | ... | ... | 15 | 75 | ... | ... | 14 | 75 |
| Vermont .................... | 30 | 150 | 30 | 150 | ... | ... | 30 | 150 | ... | ... | 30 | 150 |
| Virginia .................... | 40 | 100 | ... | ... | 40 | 100 | ... | ... | 40 | 100 | ... | ... |
| Washington ............... | 49 | 98 | 25 | 98 | ... | ... | 24 | 98 | ... | ... | 25 | 98 |
| West Virginia* ........... | 34 | 100 | 17 | 100 | ... | ... | 17 | 100 | ... | ... | 17 | 100 |
| Wisconsin ................. | 33 | 99 | 16 | 99 | ... | ... | 17 | 99 | ... | ... | 16 | 99 |
| Wyoming ................... | 30 | 60 | 15 | 60 | ... | ... | 15 | 60 | ... | ... | 16 | 60 |
| U.S. Virgin Islands ...... | 15 | U | 15 | U | ... | ... | 15 | U | ... | ... | 15 | U |
| **Totals** ................... | 1,999 | 5,440 | 1,188 | 4,737 | 40 | 180 | 1,272 | 4,982 | 171 | 407 | 1,089 | 4,711 |

See footnotes at end of table.

# STATE LEGISLATURES: MEMBERS TO BE ELECTED, 2000-2009 — Continued

| State or other jurisdiction | 2005 Senate | 2005 House | 2006 Senate | 2006 House | 2007 Senate | 2007 House | 2008 Senate | 2008 House | 2009 Senate | 2009 House |
|---|---|---|---|---|---|---|---|---|---|---|
| Alabama | ... | ... | 35 | 105 | ... | ... | 35 | 105 | ... | ... |
| Alaska | ... | ... | 10 | 40 | ... | ... | 10 | 40 | ... | ... |
| Arizona | ... | ... | 30 | 60 | ... | ... | 30 | 60 | ... | ... |
| Arkansas | ... | ... | 18 | 100 | ... | ... | 17 | 100 | ... | ... |
| California | ... | ... | 20 | 80 | ... | ... | 20 | 80 | ... | ... |
| Colorado | ... | ... | 17 (g) | 65 | ... | ... | 18 (g) | 65 | ... | ... |
| Connecticut | ... | ... | 36 | 151 | ... | ... | 36 | 151 | ... | ... |
| Delaware* | ... | ... | 11 | 41 | ... | ... | 10 | 41 | ... | ... |
| Florida* | ... | ... | 20 | 120 | ... | ... | 20 | 120 | ... | ... |
| Georgia | ... | ... | 56 | 180 | ... | ... | 56 | 180 | ... | ... |
| Hawaii | ... | ... | 13 | 51 | ... | ... | 12 | 51 | ... | ... |
| Idaho | ... | ... | 35 | 70 | ... | ... | 35 | 70 | ... | ... |
| Illinois | ... | ... | (c) | 118 | ... | ... | (c) | 118 | ... | ... |
| Indiana* | ... | ... | 25 | 99 | ... | ... | 25 | 100 | ... | ... |
| Iowa | ... | ... | 25 (e) | 100 | ... | ... | 25 (d) | 100 | ... | ... |
| Kansas | ... | ... | | 125 | ... | ... | 40 | 125 | ... | ... |
| Kentucky* | ... | ... | 19 | 100 | ... | ... | 19 | 100 | ... | ... |
| Louisiana | ... | ... | | | 39 | 105 | | 151 | ... | ... |
| Maine | ... | ... | 35 | 151 | ... | ... | 35 | 151 | ... | ... |
| Maryland | ... | ... | 47 | 141 | ... | ... | | | ... | ... |
| Massachusetts* | ... | ... | 40 | 160 | ... | ... | 40 | 160 | ... | ... |
| Michigan | ... | ... | 38 | 110 | ... | ... | | 110 | ... | ... |
| Minnesota | ... | ... | | 134 | ... | ... | 67 | 134 | ... | ... |
| Mississippi | ... | ... | | | 52 | 122 | | | 52 | 122 |
| Missouri | ... | ... | 17 | 163 | ... | ... | 17 | 163 | ... | ... |
| Montana | ... | ... | 25 | 100 | ... | ... | 25 | 100 | ... | ... |
| Nebraska | ... | ... | 24 | U | ... | ... | 24 | U | ... | ... |
| Nevada* | ... | ... | 11 | 42 | ... | ... | 11 | 42 | ... | 25 |
| New Hampshire | ... | ... | 24 | 400 | ... | ... | 24 | 400 | ... | ... |
| New Jersey | ... | 80 | | | 40 | 80 | | | ... | 80 |
| New Mexico | ... | ... | | 70 | ... | ... | 42 | 70 | ... | ... |
| New York | ... | ... | 61 | 150 | ... | ... | 61 | 150 | ... | ... |
| North Carolina* | ... | ... | 50 | 120 | ... | ... | 50 | 120 | ... | ... |
| North Dakota | ... | ... | 25 | 50 | ... | ... | 24 | 48 | ... | ... |
| Ohio | ... | ... | 17 | 99 | ... | ... | 16 | 99 | ... | ... |
| Oklahoma | ... | ... | 24 | 101 | ... | ... | 24 | 101 | ... | ... |
| Oregon | ... | ... | 15 | 60 | ... | ... | 15 | 60 | ... | ... |
| Pennsylvania | ... | ... | 25 | 203 | ... | ... | 25 | 203 | ... | ... |
| Rhode Island | ... | ... | 38 | 75 | 38 | 75 | 50 | 100 | ... | ... |
| South Carolina | ... | ... | | 124 | ... | ... | 46 | 124 | ... | ... |

See footnotes at end of table.

# STATE LEGISLATURES: MEMBERS TO BE ELECTED, 2000-2009 — Continued

| State or other jurisdiction | 2005 | | 2006 | | 2007 | | 2008 | | 2009 | |
|---|---|---|---|---|---|---|---|---|---|---|
| | Senate | House | Senate | House | Senate | House | Senate | House | Senate | House |
| South Dakota | ... | ... | 35 | 70 | ... | ... | 35 | 70 | ... | ... |
| Tennessee | ... | ... | 17 | 99 | ... | ... | 16 | 99 | ... | ... |
| Texas | ... | ... | 16 | 150 | ... | ... | 16 | 150 | ... | ... |
| Utah | ... | ... | 15 | 75 | ... | ... | 14 | 75 | ... | ... |
| Vermont | ... | ... | 30 | 150 | ... | ... | 30 | 150 | ... | ... |
| Virginia | ... | 100 | ... | ... | 40 | 100 | ... | ... | ... | 100 |
| Washington | ... | ... | 24 | 98 | ... | ... | 25 | 98 | ... | ... |
| West Virginia* | ... | ... | 17 | 100 | ... | ... | 17 | 100 | ... | ... |
| Wisconsin | ... | ... | 17 | 99 | ... | ... | 16 | 99 | ... | ... |
| Wyoming | ... | ... | 15 | 60 | ... | ... | 15 | 60 | ... | ... |
| U.S. Virgin Islands | ... | ... | 15 | U | ... | ... | 15 | U | ... | ... |
| Totals | 0 | 180 | 1,153 | 4,841 | 169 | 482 | 1,139 | 5,033 | 131 | 407 |

*Sources:* State elections administration offices, except where noted by * where data are from *The Book of the States, 1998-99.*

*Note:* This table shows the number of legislative seats up for election in a given year. As a result of redistricting, states may adjust some elections. The data contained in this table reflect information available at press time. See Table 3.3, "The Legislators: Numbers, Terms, and Party Affiliations," for specific information on legislative terms.

*Key:*

. . . — No regularly scheduled elections

U — Unicameral legislature

(a) Senators shall be elected for terms of four years, those from odd-numbered districts in the years the numbers of which are multiples of four and those from even-numbered years the numbers of which are not multiples of four;except, at the election next numbers of which are not multiples of four;except, at the election next following a reapportionment, some senators shall be elected for terms of two years when necessary to maintain staggered terms.

(b) The entire Senate is up for election every 10 years, beginning in 1972. Senate districts are divided into three groups. One group of senators is elected for terms of four years, four years and two years; two years, four years and four years; four years, two years and four years.

(c) After redistricting there will be a lottery for which districts in the Senate will receive the set of terms.

(d) Even-numbered Senate districts.

(e) Odd-numbered Senate districts. 1998 election will fill district 44 vacancy. Also, house members from odd-numbered districts will be elected to four-year terms in 1998. While House Members from even-numbered districts will be elected to two-year terms in 1998 and for four-year terms beginning in 2000.

(f) In Nevada, reapportionment after the census of 2000 will likely add senate and assembly districts for the 2002 elections.

(g) In Colorado, the number of senate seats will depend upon the 2002 reapportionment plan.

## Table 5.3
## METHODS OF NOMINATING CANDIDATES FOR STATE OFFICES

| State or other jurisdiction | Method(s) of nominating candidates |
|---|---|
| Alabama .......................... | Primary election; however, the state executive committee or other governing body of any political party may choose instead to hold a state convention for the purpose of nominating candidates. |
| Alaska ............................... | Primary election. |
| Arizona ........................... | Primary election. |
| Arkansas ......................... | Primary election. |
| California ........................ | Primary election or independent nomination procedure. |
| Colorado ......................... | Assembly/primary; however, a political party may hold a pre-primary assembly (no later than 65 days before the primary) for the designation of candidates. Each candidate who receives at least 30 percent of the delegates' vote of those present and voting is certified as a candidate for the office by the assembly with the candidate receiving the most votes listed first. If no candidate receives at least 30 percent of the vote, a second ballot shall be taken on all candidates, and the two candidates with the highest number of votes will be certified for the office by the assembly. If any candidate receives less than 10 percent of the votes from the assembly, they are precluded from petitioning further. Minor parties may nominate one candidate per office directly to the general election ballot. |
| Connecticut ..................... | Convention/primary election. Major political parties hold state conventions (convening not earlier than the 68th day and closing not later than the 50th day before the date of the primary) for the purpose of endorsing candidates. If no one challenges the endorsed candidate, no primary election is held. However, if anyone (who received at least 15 percent of the delegate vote on any roll call at the convention) challenges the endorsed candidate, a primary election is held to determine the party nominee for the general election. |
| Delaware* ........................ | Primary election. |
| Florida ............................ | Primary election. |
| Georgia ........................... | Primary election. |
| Hawaii ............................. | Primary election. |
| Idaho ............................... | Primary election. New parties nominate candidates for general election after qualifying for ballot status. |
| Illinois ............................ | Primary election. |
| Indiana* .......................... | Primary election held for the nomination of candidates for governor and U.S. senator; state party conventions held for the nomination of candidates for other state offices. |
| Iowa ................................ | Primary election; however, if there are more than two candidates for any nomination and none receives at least 35 percent of the primary vote, the primary is deemed inconclusive and the nomination is made by the party convention. (Applicable only for recognized political parties. |
| Kansas ............................. | Primary election; however, candidates of any political party that receive less than 5 percent but more than 1 percent of the total votes cast for statewide offices in the general election must nominate candidates by either caucus or convention. |
| Kentucky* ....................... | Primary election. A slate of candidates for governor and lieutenant governor that receives the highest number of its party's votes but which number is less than 40 percent of the votes cast for all slates of candidates of that party, shall be required to participate in a runoff primary with the slate of candidates of the same party receiving the second highest number of votes. |
| Louisiana* ....................... | Primary election. Open primary system requires all candidates, regardless of party affiliation, to appear on a single ballot. Candidate who receives over 50 percent of the vote in the primary is elected to office; if no candidate receives a majority vote, a runoff election is held between the two candidates who received the most votes. |
| Maine ............................... | Primary election. |
| Maryland ........................ | Primary election. |
| Massachusetts* .............. | Primary election. |
| Michigan ......................... | Primary election held for nomination of candidates for governor, U.S. congressional seats, state senators and representatives; court of appeals, circuit and district courts; state conventions held for nomination of candidates for lieutenant governor, secretary of state and attorney general. State convention also held to nominate candidates for Justice of Supreme Court, State Board of Education, Regents of University of Michigan, Trustees of Michigan State University, Governors of Wayne State University. |
| Minnesota ....................... | Primary election. |
| Mississippi ...................... | Primary election. |
| Missouri ......................... | Primary election. |
| Montana .......................... | Primary election. |
| Nebraska ......................... | Primary election. |
| Nevada* ........................... | Primary election. |
| New Hampshire .............. | Primary election. Non-party candidates may petition for general election ballot. |
| New Jersey ...................... | Primary election. Independent candidates are nominated by petition for the general election. |
| New Mexico .................... | Convention/primary election. |
| New York* ....................... | Committee meeting/primary election. The person who receives the majority vote at the state party committee meeting becomes the designated candidate for nomination; however, all other persons who received at least 25 percent of the convention vote may demand that their names appear on the primary ballot as candidates for nomination. |
| North Carolina* ............. | Primary election, or ballot access by petition. |
| North Dakota ................. | Convention/primary election. Political parties hold state conventions for the purpose of endorsing candidates. Endorsed candidates are automatically placed on the primary election ballot, but other candidates may also petition their name on the ballot. |
| Ohio ................................ | Primary election. |

See footnotes at end of table.

# METHODS OF NOMINATING CANDIDATES FOR STATE OFFICES — Continued

| State or other jurisdiction | Method(s) of nominating candidates |
|---|---|
| Oklahoma | Primary election. |
| Oregon | Primary election, assembly of electors, minor party conventions and independent nomination procedure. |
| Pennsylvania | Primary election, and nomination papers for minor political parties and political bodies. |
| Rhode Island | Primary election. |
| South Carolina | Primary election for Republicans and Democrats; party conventions held for five minor parties. All must file proper forms with their political party between March 16 and March 30. |
| South Dakota | Primary election. Any candidate who receives a plurality of the primary vote becomes the nominee; however, if no individual receives at least 35 percent of the vote for the candidacy for the offices of governor, U.S. senator, or U.S. congressman, a runoff election is held two weeks later. Attorney general, secretary of state, auditor, treasurer, school and public lands commissioner, and public utilities commissioner are nominated by party convention. |
| Tennessee | Primary election. |
| Texas | Primary election. New parties nominate candidates for general election after qualifying for ballot access. |
| Utah | Convention/primary election. Delegates are elected at neighborhood caucus meetings to attend county and state conventions and select party members to run at the regular primary election. |
| Vermont | Primary election, for major parties. Independent candidates may file by petition, minor parties organized in at least 10 towns may nonimate candidates at state committee meetings. |
| Virginia | Primary election; however, the state executive committee or other governing body of any political party may choose instead to hold a state convention for the purpose of nominating candidates (party opting for convention can only make nomination 32 days prior to date on which primary elections are normally held). |
| Washington | Primary election. |
| West Virginia* | Primary election; however, executive committees may make nomination in case of certain vacancies on ballot. |
| Wisconsin | Primary election. |
| Wyoming | Primary election. |
| Dist. of Columbia | Primary election. |
| U.S. Virgin Islands | Primary election. |

*Sources*: State election administration offices, except where noted by *
where data are from *The Book of The States, 1998-99.*

*Note*: The nominating methods described here are for state offices; procedures may vary for local candidates. Also, independent candidates may have to petition for nomination.

## Table 5.4
## ELECTION DATES FOR NATIONAL, STATE AND LOCAL ELECTIONS (Formulas)

| State or other jurisdiction | National Primary | National Runoff | National General | State Primary | State Runoff | State General | Local Primary | Local Runoff | Local General |
|---|---|---|---|---|---|---|---|---|---|
| Alabama | June, 1st T | ... | Nov., ★ | June, 1st T | June, Last T | Nat. | V | V | V |
| Alaska | Aug., 4th T | ... | Nov., ★ | Nat. | ... | Nat. | Nat. | ... | V |
| Arizona | 8 T Prior | ... | Nov., ★ | 8th T Prior | ... | Nat. | March 2nd T | May 3rd T | 8 T prior to Nat. or Nat. |
| Arkansas | 3 wks. Prior | June, 2nd T (a) | Nov., ★ | Nat. | Nat. | Nat. | Nat. | Nat. | Nat. |
| California | March, ★ | ... | Nov., ★ | V | ... | Nat. | V | ... | Nat. |
| Colorado | Aug., 2nd T | ... | Nov., ★ (b) | Nat. | ... | Nat. (b) | ... | ... | Nat. or May, 1st M (c) |
| Connecticut | 56th day Prior (N)(d) 1st T in March (P) | ... | Nov., ★ | 56th day Prior | ... | Nat. | State | ... | Nat. |
| Delaware* | Sept., 1st S After 1st M | ... | Nov., ★ (b) | ... | Nat. | Nat. | ... | ... | (d) |
| Florida | 9th T Prior | 5th T Prior | Nov., ★ (b) | Nat. | Nat. | Nat. (b) | ... | Nat. | Nat. (b) |
| Georgia | July, 3rd T | 21 days AP | Nov., ★ (b) | July, 3rd T | 21 days AP | Nat. (b) | July, 3rd T | 21 days AP | Nat.( b) |
| Hawaii | Sept., 2nd Last S | ... | Nov., ★ | Nat. | ... | Nat. | Nat. | ... | Nat. |
| Idaho | May, 4th T | ... | Nov., ★ | Nat. | ... | Nat. | Nat. | ... | Nat. |
| Illinois | March, 3rd T | ... | Nov., ★ | Feb., Last T | ... | Nat. | Nat. | ... | April, 1st T (c) |
| Indiana* | May, ★ | ... | Nov., ★ (b) | Nat. | ... | Nat. | Nat. | ... | Nat. |
| Iowa | June, ★ | ... | Nov., ★ | Nat. | ... | Nat. (b) | Nat. | ... | Nat. |
| Kansas | Aug., 1st T | ... | Nov., ★ (b) | Nat. (d) | ... | Nat. (d) | 5 wks. Prior (f) | ... | April 1st T (f) |
| Kentucky* | May, 1st T after 4th M | ... | Nov., ★ | Nat. | (g) | Nat. | Nat. | ... | Nat. |
| Louisiana (h) | Oct., 1st S | ... | Nov., ★ | Oct., 2nd to last S | ... | 4th S AP | V | ... | V |
| Maine | June, 2nd T | ... | Nov., ★ | June, 2nd | ... | Nov. (p) | ... | ... | V |
| Maryland | Sept., 2nd T After 1st M | ... | Nov., ★ | Nat. | ... | Nat. | Nat. | ... | Nat. |
| Massachusetts* | 7th T Prior | ... | Nov., ★ | V | ... | Nat. | V | ... | V |
| Michigan | Aug., ★ (b,i) | ... | Nov., ★ (b) | Nat.(b) | ... | Nat. (b) | V | ... | V |
| Minnesota | Sept., 1st T after 2nd M | ... | Nov., ★ | Nat. | ... | Nat. | Nat. (d) | ... | Nat. (d) |
| Mississippi | June, 1st T (j) | 3rd T AP | Nov., ★ | May, 1st T (d) | 3rd T AP | Nat. (d) | May, 1st T (d) | 2nd T AP | June, ★ (d) |
| Missouri | Aug., ★ | ... | Nov., ★ | Nat. | ... | Nat. | Nat. | ... | Nat. |
| Montana | June, ★ | ... | Nov., ★ | Nat. | ... | Nat. | Sept., 1st T after 2nd M (d) | ... | Nat. (f) |
| Nebraska | May, 1st T After 2nd M | ... | Nov., ★ | Nat. | ... | Nat. | Nat. | ... | Nat. |
| Nevada* | Sept., 1st T | ... | Nov., ★ | Nat. | ... | Nat. | Nat. | ... | Nat. |
| New Hampshire | Sept., 2nd T (b) | ... | Nov., ★ (b) | ... | ... | Nat. | ... | ... | Mar., 2nd T or May, 2nd T |
| New Jersey | June, ★ | ... | Nov., ★ | June, ★ | ... | Nat. | June, ★ | ... | Nat. |
| New Mexico | June, 1st T | ... | Nov., ★ | Nat. | ... | Nat. | Nat. | Sept., 2 wks AP (d) | Nat. |
| New York | March, 1st T (P) | ... | Nov., ★ | Sept., ★ | ... | Nat. | State | ... | Nat. |
| North Carolina* | May, ★ | ... | Nov., ★ | V | 4 wks. AP | Nat. | V | V | V |
| North Dakota | June, 2nd T | ... | Nov., ★ | June, 2nd T | ... | Nat. | June, 2nd T | ... | June, 2nd T (e) |
| Ohio | March, ★ T (P) | ... | Nov., ★ | Nat. (d) | ... | Nat. | Nat. (d) | ... | Nat. (d) |

See footnotes at end of table.

Key:
★ — First Tuesday after first Monday.
M — Monday.
T — Tuesday.
TH — Thursday.
S — Saturday.
Nat. — Same date as national elections.

State — Same date as state elections.
Prior — Prior to general election.
(P) — Presidential election years.
(N) — Non-presidential election years.
AP — After primary.
V — Varies.

# ELECTION DATES FOR NATIONAL, STATE AND LOCAL ELECTIONS — Continued

| State or other jurisdiction | National Primary | National Runoff | National General | State Primary | State Runoff | State General | Local Primary | Local Runoff | Local General |
|---|---|---|---|---|---|---|---|---|---|
| Oklahoma | Aug., 4th T (k) / Mar., 2nd T (P) | Sept., 3rd T | Nov., ★ (b) | Nat. | Nat. | Nat. (b) | Nat. | Nat. | Nat. (b) |
| Oregon | May, 3rd T (b) | ... | Nov., ★ (b) | May, 3rd T (b) | ... | Nat. | May, 3rd T (b) | ... | Nat. |
| Pennsylvania | April, 4th T (P)(l) | ... | Nov., ★ | Nat. | ... | Nat. | Nat. | ... | Nat. |
| Rhode Island | Sept., 2nd T After 1st M | ... | Nov., ★ | Nat. | ... | Nat. | Nat. | ... | Nat. |
| South Carolina | June, 2nd T | 2nd T AP | Nov., ★ | Nat. (d) | Nat. | Nat. | Nat. (d) | Nat. | Nat. (d) |
| South Dakota | June, 1st T | 2nd T AP | Nov., ★ | June, 1st T | 2nd T AP | Nat. | State (m) | ... | Nat. (m) |
| Tennessee | Aug., 1st TH (b) / March, 2nd T (P) | ... | Nov., ★ (b) | Nat. | ... | Nat. | May, 1st T (n) / March, 2nd T (P) | ... | Aug., 1st TH (b) |
| Texas | March, 2nd T | Apr., 2nd T | Nov., ★ (b) | Nat. | Nat. | Nat. | Nat. | Nat. | Nat. |
| Utah | June, 4th T | ... | Nov., ★ (b) | Nat. | ... | Nat. | Nat. | ... | Nat. |
| Vermont (o) | Sept., 2nd T | ... | Nov., ★ | ... | ... | Nat. | ... | ... | March, 1st T |
| Virginia (r) | June, 2nd T | ... | Nov., ★ | Nat. (f) | ... | Nat. (f) | Nat. or March, 1st T | ... | Nat. or May, 1st T |
| Washington | Sept., 3rd T (p) | ... | Nov., ★ | Nat. | ... | Nat. | Nat. | ... | Nat. |
| West Virginia* | May, 2nd T | ... | Nov., ★ | Nat. | ... | Nat. | Nat. | ... | Nat. |
| Wisconsin | Sept., 2nd T | ... | Nov., ★ | Nat. | ... | Nat. (q) | Feb., 3rd T | ... | April 1st T |
| Wyoming | Aug., 1st T After 3rd M | ... | Nov., ★ | Nat. | ... | Nat. | Nat. | ... | Nat. |
| U.S. Virgin Islands | ... | ... | ... | Sept., 2nd S | 14 day AP | Nov., 1st T | Sept., 2nd S | 14 days AP | Nov., 1st T |

Source: State election administration offices, except where noted by * where data are from *The Book of the States, 1998-99.*

Note: This table describes the basic formulas for determining when national, state and local elections will be held. For specific information on a particular state, the reader is advised to contact the specific state election administration office. National elections are defined as elections for president, U.S. Senate and U.S. House of Representatives. In some cases, states have elected to provide specific data on variations between national elections in presidential and non-presidential years. Where provided, these variations have been noted.

Key:
★ — First Tuesday after first Monday.
M — Monday.
T — Tuesday.
TH — Thursday.
S — Saturday.
Nat. — Same date as national elections.

State — Same date as state elections.
Prior — Prior to general election.
(P) — Presidential election years.
(N) — Non-presidential election years.
AP — After primary.
V — Varies.

(a) In Arkansas, a general primary is scheduled for the second Tuesday in June. A preferential primary is held three weeks before the general primary; should no candidate receive a majority vote, the general (runoff) primary is held.

(b) Even years.

(c) Unless that date conflicts with Passover, then 1st Tuesday following last day of Passover.

(d) In Delaware, elections are determined by city charter. In Iowa, partisan election only. In Kansas, state and county elections. In Minnesota, county elections only. In Mississippi, state and county elections are held together; municipal elections are held in separate years. In Montana, municipalities only. In New York, runoff in New York City only. In Ohio, municipalities and towns in odd years and counties in even years. In South Carolina, school boards vary.

(e) Cities only.

(f) Odd years.

(g) Held 35 days after the date of the May primary if necessary for governor and lieutenant governor race.

(h) Louisiana has an open primary which requires all candidates, regardless of party affiliation, to appear on a single ballot. If a candidate receives over 50 percent of the vote in the primary, that candidate is elected to the office. If no candidate receives a majority vote, then a single election is held between the two candidates receiving the most votes. For national elections, the first vote is held on the first Saturday in October of even-numbered years with the general election held on the first Tuesday after the first Monday in November. For state elections, the election is held on the second to last Saturday in October with the runoff being held on the fourth Saturday after first election. Local elections vary depending on the location and the year.

(i) Applies to federal, state, county, and township offices. County and township officers elected every four years in conjunction with presidential elections. Cities may hold their primaries and elections at different times depending on charter or governing statutes. Villages generally hold primary in February and elections in March on an annual basis. Schools for the most part hold annual elections in June.

(j) Except in presidential election year when congressional races correspond to Super Tuesday.

(k) The primary election is held on the 4th Tuesday in August in each even-numbered year, including presidential election years. The presidential preferential primary is held on the 2nd Tuesday in March during presidential election years.

(l) Except the 1994 election which would have landed on a Jewish holiday. It was held on May 10, 1994.

(m) County officials.

(n) County party has the option of having a county primary in conjunction with the presidential primary in March or the regular May date.

(o) In Vermont, if there is a tie in a primary or general election (and a recount does not resolve the tie) the appropriate superior could order a recessed election, among the tied candidates only, within three weeks of the recount. In state primary runoffs, the runoff election must be proclaimed within 7 days after primary; after proclamation, election is held 15-22 days later. Local elections are held by annual town meetings which may vary depending on town charter.

(p) Other election dates for special elections include: Feb. *, March 2T, April *, May, 4T or date of presidential primary.

(q) Superintendent of public instruction, Supreme Court, court of appeals and circuit court justices are elected with local officials.

(r) Beginning in 2000, presidential primaries will be held in presidential election years ( at the option of each party's governing committee) and other primaries normally held in March, will be the last Tuesday of February.

## Table 5.5
## POLLING HOURS: GENERAL ELECTIONS

| State or other jurisdiction | Polls open | Polls close | Notes on hours (a) |
|---|---|---|---|
| Alabama | No later than 8 a.m. | Between 6 and 8 p.m. | Polls must be open at least 10 consecutive hours; hours set by county commissioner. |
| Alaska | 7 a.m. | 8 p.m. | |
| Arizona | 6 a.m. | 7 p.m. | |
| Arkansas | 7:30 a.m. | 7:30 p.m. | |
| California | 7 a.m. | 8 p.m. | |
| Colorado | 7 a.m. | 7 p.m. | |
| Connecticut | 6 a.m. | 8 p.m. | |
| Delaware* | 7 a.m. | 8 p.m. | |
| Florida | 7 a.m. | 7 p.m. | |
| Georgia | 7 a.m. | 7 p.m. | |
| Hawaii | 7 a.m. | 6 p.m. | |
| Idaho | 8 a.m. | 8 p.m. | Polls may open earlier at option of county clerk, but not earlier than 7 a.m. Polls may close earlier if all registered electors in a precinct have voted. |
| Illinois | 6 a.m. | 7 p.m. | |
| Indiana* | 6 a.m. | 6 p.m. local time | |
| Iowa | 7 a.m. | 9 p.m. | |
| Kansas | Between 6 and 7 a.m. | Between 7 and 8 p.m. | Hours may be changed by county election officer, but polls must be open at least 12 consecutive hours between 6 a.m. and 8 p.m. |
| Kentucky* | 6 a.m. | 6 p.m. (prevailing time) | Only persons still in line at 6 p.m. may vote until 7 p.m. |
| Louisiana | 6 a.m. | 8 p.m. | |
| Maine | Between 6 and 10 a.m. | 8 p.m. | Towns with population less than 100 may close after all registered voters have voted. |
| Maryland | 7 a.m. | 8 p.m. | |
| Massachusetts* | 7 a.m. | 8 p.m. | |
| Michigan | 7 a.m. | 8 p.m. | |
| Minnesota | 7 a.m. | 8 p.m. | Municipalities of less than 500 may establish hours of no later than 10 a.m. to 8 p.m. |
| Mississippi | 7 a.m. | 7 p.m. | |
| Missouri | 6 a.m. | 7 p.m. | |
| Montana | 7 a.m. | 8 p.m. | In precincts of over 200 registered voters. |
| | noon | 8 p.m. | In precincts of less than 200 registered voters, polls may close when all registered electors have voted. |
| Nebraska | 7 a.m. | 7 p.m. (MST) | |
| | 8 a.m. | 8 p.m. (CST) | |
| Nevada* | 7 a.m. | 7 p.m. | |
| New Hampshire | Varies | Varies (cities) | All polls open not later than 11 a.m. and close not earlier than 7 p.m. In cities, city council shall determine polling hours at least 30 days prior to state elections. |
| | 11 a.m. | 7 p.m. (towns) | |
| New Jersey | 7 a.m. | 8 p.m. | |
| New Mexico | 7 a.m. | 7 p.m. | |
| New York | 6 a.m. | 9 p.m. | |
| North Carolina* | 6:30 a.m. | 7:30 p.m. | All voters standing in line at 7:30 p.m. will be allowed to vote. |
| North Dakota | Between 7 and 9 a.m. | Between 7 and 9 p.m. | In precincts where less than 75 votes were cast in previous elections, polls may open at noon. |
| Ohio | 6:30 a.m. | 7:30 p.m. | |
| Oklahoma | 7 a.m. | 7 p.m. | |
| Oregon | 7 a.m. | 8 p.m. | |
| Pennsylvania | 7 a.m. | 8 p.m. | |
| Rhode Island | Between 6 and 9 a.m. | 9 p.m. | Opening hours vary across cities and towns. |
| South Carolina | 7 a.m. | 7 p.m. | |
| South Dakota | 7 a.m. | 7 p.m. (MST) | |
| | 8 a.m. | 8 p.m. (CST) | |
| Tennessee | No standard opening time | 7 p.m. (CST) | Must be open at least 10 hours and no more than 13 hours. |
| | | 8 p.m. (EST) | |
| Texas | 7 a.m. | 7 p.m. | |
| Utah | 7 a.m. | 8 p.m. | |
| Vermont | Between 6 and 10 a.m. | 7 p.m. | |
| Virginia | 6 a.m. | 7 p.m. | |
| Washington | 7 a.m. | 8 p.m. | |
| West Virginia* | 6:30 a.m. | 7:30 p.m. | |
| Wisconsin | 7 a.m. | 8 p.m. | 1st, 2nd, 3rd class cities. |
| | Between 7 and 9 a.m. | 8 p.m. | 4th class cities, towns and villages. |
| Wyoming | 7 a.m. | 7 p.m. | |
| Dist. of Columbia | 7 a.m. | 8 p.m. | |
| U.S. Virgin Islands | 7 a.m. | 7 p.m. | |

Sources: State election administration offices, except where noted by * where data are from *The Book of the States, 1998-99.*

Note: Hours for primary, municipal and special elections may differ from those noted.

(a) In all states, voters standing in line when the polls close are allowed to vote; however, provisions for handling those voters vary across jurisdictions.

# Table 5.6
## VOTER REGISTRATION INFORMATION

| State or other jurisdiction | Mail registration allowed for all voters | Closing date for registration before general election (days) | Persons eligible for absentee registration (a) |
|---|---|---|---|
| Alabama | ★ | 10 | M/O |
| Alaska | ★ | 30 | (b) |
| Arizona | ★ | 29 | (b) |
| Arkansas | ★ | 30 | (b) |
| California | ★ | 29 | (b) |
| Colorado | ★ | 29 | (b) |
| Connecticut | ★ | 14 (c) | (b) |
| Delaware* | ★ | 20 | (b) |
| Florida | ★ | 29 | (b) |
| Georgia | ★ | (d) | (b) |
| Hawaii | ★ | 30 | (b) |
| Idaho | ★ | (e) | (b) |
| Illinois | ★ | 29 | M/O |
| Indiana* | ★ | 29 (f) | C,D,E,M/O,O,P,T |
| Iowa | ★ | 10 | (b) |
| Kansas | ★ | 14 | (b) |
| Kentucky* | ★ | 28 | (b) |
| Louisiana | ★ | 30 | (b) |
| Maine | ★ | Election day | (b) |
| Maryland | ★ | 25 | (b) |
| Massachusetts* | ★ | 20 | (b) |
| Michigan | ★ | 30 | (b) |
| Minnesota | ★ | Election day (g) | (b) |
| Mississippi | ★ | 30 | (b) |
| Missouri | ★ | 28 | (b) |
| Montana | ★ | 30 | (b) |
| Nebraska | ★ | (h) | (b) |
| Nevada* | ★ | 30 | M/O |
| New Hampshire | . . . | 10 (i) | B,D,E,R,S,T |
| New Jersey | ★ | 29 | (b) |
| New Mexico | ★ | 28 | T |
| New York | ★ | 25 | (b) |
| North Carolina* | ★ | 25 | (b) |
| North Dakota | | (j) | |
| Ohio | ★ | 30 | (b) |
| Oklahoma | ★ | 24 | (b) |
| Oregon | ★ | 20 | (b) |
| Pennsylvania | ★ | 30 | B,D,M/O,O,P,R,S,T |
| Rhode Island | ★ | 30 | D |
| South Carolina | ★ | 30 | B,C,D,S(n) |
| South Dakota | ★ | 15 | (b) |
| Tennessee | ★ | 30 | (b) |
| Texas | ★ | 30 | (b) |
| Utah | ★ | 8 (k) | (l) |
| Vermont | ★ | 17 | (m) |
| Virginia | ★ | 28 | T(o) |
| Washington | ★ | 30 | M/O |
| West Virginia* | ★ | 30 | (b) |
| Wisconsin | ★ | Election day (k) | (b) |
| Wyoming | ★ | (g) | (b) |
| Dist. of Columbia | ★ | 30 | (b) |
| American Samoa | ★ | 30 | M/O |
| Guam | ★ | 10 | (b) |
| Puerto Rico | . . . | 50 | (b) |
| U.S. Virgin Islands | . . . | 30 | M/O |

See footnotes at end of table.

# VOTER REGISTRATION INFORMATION — Continued

*Sources*: State election administration offices, except where noted by *
where data are from *The Book of the States 1998-99.*

*Key*:

★ — Mail registration allowed.

. . . — Mail registration not allowed.

*Note*: Previous editions of this chart contained a column for "Automatic cancellation of registration for failure to vote for ___ years". However, the National Voter Registration Act requires a confirmation notice prior to any cancellation and thus effectively bans any automatic cancellation of voter registration.

(a) In this column: B–Absent on business; C–Senior citizen; D–Disabled persons; E–Not absent, but prevented by employment from registering; M/O–No absentee registration except military and oversees citizens as required by federal law; O–Out of state; P–Out of precinct( or municipality in PA); R–Absent for religious reasons; S–Students; T–Temporarily out of jurisdiction.

(b) All voters. See column on mail registration.

(c) Closing date differs for primary election. In Connecticut, 1 day; Delaware, 21 days.

(d) Fifth Monday prior to election.

(e) With county clerk, within 24 days before an election; eligible voters may also register on election day at polling place.

(f) Absent uniformed services voters and overseas voters may be registered until the final poll list is prepared up to 10 days before election day.

(g) Minnesota–21 days or election day; Wyoming–30 days or primary election day, or general election day.

(h) 2nd Friday before election day.

(i) Also, at polls on election day.

(j) No voter registration.

(k) By mail: Utah, 20 days; Wisconsin, 13 days.

(l) There are several criteria including religious reasons, disabled, etc., or if the voter otherwise expects to be absent from the precinct on election day.

(m) Anyone unable to register in person.

(n) In South Carolina, all the following are eligible for absentee registration in addition to those categories already listed: electors with a death in the family within 3 days before the election; overseas military, Red Cross, U.S.O. government employees, and their dependents and spouses residing with them; persons on vacation; persons admitted to the hospital as emergency patients 4 days prior to election; persons confined to jail or pre-trial facility pending disposition of arrest/trial; and persons attending sick/disabled persons.

(o) In Virginia, the following temporarily out of jurisdiction persons are eligible for absentee registration: (1)uniformed services voters on active duty, merchant marine, and persons temporarily residing overseas by virtue of employment (and spouse/dependents of these persons residing with them), who are not normally absent from their locality, or have been absent and returned to reside within 28 days prior to an election, may register in person up to and including the day of the election; (2) members of uniformed services discharged from active duty during 60 days preceding election (and spouse/dependents) may register, if otherwise qualified, in person up to and including the day of the election.

## Table 5.7
## VOTING STATISTICS FOR GUBERNATORIAL ELECTIONS

| State or other jurisdiction | Date of last election | Primary election | | | | | General election | | | | | | | | |
|---|---|---|---|---|---|---|---|---|---|---|---|---|---|---|---|
| | | Republican | Democrat | Reform | Other | Total votes | Republican | Percent | Democrat | Percent | Reform | Percent | Other | Percent | Total votes |
| Alabama | 1998 | 359,014 | 358,179 | 0 | 0 | 717,193 | 554,746 | 42 | 760,155 | 57.8 | 0 | 0 | 2,941 | 0.2 | 1,314,901 |
| Alaska (a) | 1998 | 60,194 | 43,669 | 136 | 5,194 | 109,057 | 39,331 | 17.86 | 112,879 | 51.27 | 0 | 0 | 67,967 | 30.87 | 220,177 |
| Arizona | 1998 | 239,703 | 136,282 | 136 | 1,734 | 377,855 | 620,188 | 61 | 361,552 | 35.5 | 0 | 0 | 35,876 | 3.5 | 1,017,616 |
| Arkansas | 1998 | 57,208 | unopposed | 0 | 0 | 57,208 | 421,989 | 59.77 | 272,923 | 38.66 | 11,099 | 1.57 | 0 | 0 | 706,011 |
| California | 1998 | 2,167,133 | 3,600,264 | 0 | 229,867 | 5,997,264 | 3,218,030 | 38.38 | 4,860,702 | 57.97 | 0 | 0 | 306,464 | 3.65 | 8,385,196 |
| Colorado | 1998 | 214,210 | 144,191 | 0 | 0 | 358,401 | 645,806 | 49.3 | 631,655 | 48.2 | 0 | 0 | 33,478 | 2.5 | 1,310,939 |
| Connecticut | 1998 | (c) | N.A. | 0 | 0 | N.A. | 628,707 | 64 | 354,187 | 36 | 0 | 0 | 16,641 | 0.2 | 999,535 |
| Delaware | 1996 | N.A. | N.A. | N.A. | N.A. | N.A. | N.A. | N.A. | N.A. | N.A. | N.A. | N.A. | N.A. | N.A. | N.A. |
| Florida | 1998 | N.A. | N.A. | 0 | 0 | N.A. | 2,191,105 | 55.3 | 1,773,054 | 44.7 | 0 | 0 | 282 | 0 | 4,206,659 |
| Georgia | 1998 | 418,542 | 420,987 | 0 | 0 | 1,170,433 | 790,201 | 44.1 | 941,076 | 52.5 | 0 | 0 | 61,531 | 3.4 | 1,792,808 |
| Hawaii | 1998 | 157,549 | 110,880 | 0 | 725 | 269,154 | 198,952 | 48.2 | 204,206 | 49.5 | 0 | 0 | 4,398 | 1.1 | 407,556 |
| Idaho | 1998 | 127,990 | 26,973 | 0 | 0 | 154,963 | 258,095 | 67.7 | 110,815 | 29.1 | 0 | 0 | 12,338 | 3.2 | 381,248 |
| Illinois | 1998 | 707,406 | 950,307 | 0 | 0 | 1,824,806 | 1,714,094 | 51 | 1,594,191 | 47.5 | 0 | 0 | 50,420 | 1.5 | 3,358,705 |
| Indiana | 1996 | N.A. | N.A. | N.A. | N.A. | N.A. | N.A. | N.A. | N.A. | N.A. | N.A. | N.A. | N.A. | N.A. | N.A. |
| Iowa | 1998 | 162,393 | 115,490 | 368 | 0 | 278,251 | 444,787 | 46.5 | 500,231 | 52.3 | 0 | 0 | 11,400 | 1.2 | 956,418 |
| Kansas | 1998 | 310,150 | 103,481 | 0 | 0 | 413,631 | 544,882 | 73.4 | 168,243 | 22.6 | 7,830 | 1.1 | 21,710 | 2.9 | 742,665 |
| Kentucky | 1999 | 41,537 | unopposed | | 0 | 41,537 | 128,788 | 22 | 352,099 | 61 | 88,930 | 15 | 6,934 | 1 | 576,751 |
| Louisiana | 1999 | (b) | (b) | | 0 | (b) | N.A. | N.A. | N.A. | N.A. | N.A. | N.A. | N.A. | N.A. | N.A. |
| Maine | 1998 | 57,832 | 45,218 | 0 | 0 | 103,050 | 79,716 | 18.9 | 50,506 | 12 | 0 | 0 | 290,787 | 69.1 | 421,009 |
| Maryland | 1998 | 224,772 | 455,807 | 0 | 0 | 680,579 | 486,937 | 31.3 | 935,144 | 60.1 | 365 | 0 | 134,548 | 8.6 | 1,556,994 |
| Massachusetts | 1998 | N.A. | N.A. | N.A. | N.A. | N.A. | 967,160 | 50.8 | 901,843 | 47.4 | 0 | 0 | 34,333 | 1.8 | 1,903,336 |
| Michigan | 1998 | 533,081 | 729,665 | 0 | 0 | 1,262,746 | 1,883,005 | 62.2 | 1,143,574 | 37.8 | 0 | 0 | 525 | 0 | 3,027,104 |
| Minnesota | 1998 | 140,124 | 494,069 | 0 | 0 | 651,362 | 716,880 | 34.3 | 587,060 | 28.1 | 773,713 | 37 | 12,865 | 0.6 | 2,090,518 |
| Mississippi | 1999 | 153,149 | 545,555 | 0 | 0 | 698,704 | 370,691 | 48.52 | 379,034 | 49.2 | 8,208 | 1.07 | 6,005 | 0.79 | 763,938 |
| Missouri | 1996 | 282,313 | 425,770 | 0 | 0 | 710,636 | 866,268 | 40.4 | 1,224,801 | 57.2 | 0 | 0 | 51,449 | 2.4 | 2,142,518 |
| Montana | 1996 | 121,316 | 73,881 | 0 | 0 | 195,197 | 320,768 | 80.7 | 76,471 | 19.3 | 0 | 0 | 0 | 0 | 397,239 |
| Nebraska | 1998 | 190,941 | 167,109 | 0 | 0 | 358,050 | 288,741 | 49.2 | 292,771 | 49.9 | 0 | 0 | 5,030 | 0.9 | 586,542 |
| Nevada | 1998 | 126,570 | 91,966 | 0 | 0 | 218,536 | 223,892 | 53 | 182,281 | 43 | 0 | 0 | 14,816 | 4 | 420,989 |
| New Hampshire | 1998 | 73,078 | 30,351 | 0 | 0 | 103,609 | 98,473 | 30.9 | 210,769 | 66.1 | 0 | 0 | 9,698 | 3 | 318,940 |
| New Jersey | 1997 | 147,731 | 372 | 0 | 0 | 519,405 | 1,133,394 | 46.9 | 1,107,968 | 45.8 | 0 | 0 | 176,982 | 7.3 | 2,418,344 |
| New Mexico | 1998 | N.A. | N.A. | 0 | 0 | N.A. | 271,948 (d) | 55 | 226,755 | 45 | 0 | 0 | 0 | 0 | 498,703 |
| New York | 1998 | unopposed | 738,083 | 0 | 0 | 738,083 | 2,571,991 (d) | 52 | 1,518,992 | 30 | 0 | 0 | 894,949 | 18 | 2,414,041 |
| North Carolina | 1996 | 279,610 | 588,926 | 0 | 0 | 868,356 | 1,097,053 | 42.8 | 1,436,638 | 55.9 | 0 | 0 | 32,494 | 1.4 | 2,618,326 |
| North Dakota | 1996 | 48,412 | 46,049 | 0 | 0 | 94,754 | 174,937 | 66.2 | 89,349 | 33.8 | 0 | 0 | 12 | 0 | 264,298 |
| Ohio | 1998 | 657,915 | 915,626 | 2,009 | 0 | 1,575,550 | 1,678,721 | 50.05 | 1,498,956 | 44.69 | 111,468 | 3.32 | 65,068 | 1.194 | 3,354,213 |
| Oklahoma | 1998 | unopposed | 284,062 | 0 | 0 | 284,062 | 139,347 | 45.62 | 160,008 | 52.38 | 6,098 | 2 | 0 | 0 | 305,453 |
| Oregon | 1998 | 214,565 | 309,745 | 0 | 0 | 524,310 | 334,001 | 30 | 717,061 | 64 | 10,144 | 1 | 51,892 | 5 | 1,113,198 |
| Pennsylvania | 1998 | N.A. | N.A. | N.A. | N.A. | N.A. | 1,736,844 | 57 | 938,745 | 31 | 0 | 0 | 349,352 | 12 | 3,025,041 |
| Rhode Island | 1998 | N.A. | N.A. | N.A. | N.A. | N.A. | 156,180 | 51 | 129,105 | 42 | 1848 | 0 | 19,250 | 7 | 306,483 |
| South Carolina | 1998 | 158,049 | unopposed | 0 | 0 | 158,049 | 484,088 | 45.8 | 570,070 | 54 | 0 | 0 | 2,276 | 0.2 | 1,056,434 |

See footnotes at end of table.

# VOTING STATISTICS FOR GUBERNATORIAL ELECTIONS — Continued

| State or other jurisdiction | Date of last election | Primary election | | | | | General election | | | | | | | | |
|---|---|---|---|---|---|---|---|---|---|---|---|---|---|---|---|
| | | Republican | Democrat | Reform | Other | Total votes | Republican | Percent | Democrat | Percent | Reform | Percent | Other | Percent | Total votes |
| South Dakota | 1998 | unopposed | unopposed | 0 | 0 | 0 | 166,621 | 64 | 85,443 | 32.9 | 0 | 0 | 8,093 | 3.1 | 260,187 |
| Tennessee | 1998 | 387,860 | 298,466 | 0 | 0 | 686,326 | 669,973 | 69 | 278,750 | 29 | 0 | 0 | 18,513 | 2 | 967,336 |
| Texas | 1998 | 596,839 | 492,419 | 0 | 0 | 1,089,258 | 2,550,821 | 68.23 | 1,165,592 | 31.18 | 0 | 0 | 21,665 | 0.57 | 3,738,078 |
| Utah | 1996 | (c) | (c) | 0 | 0 | (c) | 503,693 | 75 | 98,178 | 23.3 | 0 | 0 | 11,570 | 1.7 | 671,879 |
| Vermont | 1998 | 52,531 | 17,948 | 0 | 0 | 70,479 | 89,726 | 41.1 | 121,425 | 55.6 | 0 | 0 | 6,969 (e) | 2 | 218,120 |
| Virginia | 1997 | (c) | (c) | 0 | 0 | (c) | 969,062 | 55.8 | 738,971 | 42.6 | 25,955 | 1.5 | 2,326 | 0.1 | 1,736,314 |
| Washington | 1996 | 396,038 | 631,217 | 0 | 3,742 | 1,030,997 | 940,538 | 42 | 1,296,492 | 58 | 0 | 0 | 0 | 0 | 2,237,030 |
| West Virginia | 1996 | 133,972 | 329,057 | 0 | 0 | 463,029 | 324,518 | 51.6 | 287,870 | 45.8 | 0 | 0 | 16,171 | 2.6 | 628,559 |
| Wisconsin | 1998 | 275,519 | 219,273 | 0 | 0 | 497,476 | 1,047,716 | 59.7 | 679,553 | 38.7 | 0 | 0 | 28,745 | 1.6 | 1,756,014 |
| Wyoming | 1998 | 84,179 | 33,502 | 0 | 0 | 117,681 | 97,235 | 56 | 70,754 | 40 | 0 | 0 | 6899 | 4 | 174,988 |

*Source:* State election administration offices.

N.A.— not available.

(a) The state recognizes two other political parties and the one limited party.

(b) Louisiana has an open primary which requires all candidates, regardless of party affiliation, to appear on a single ballot. If a candidate receives over 50 percent of the vote in the primary, he is elected to the office. If no candidate receives a majority vote, then a single election is held between the two candidates receiving the most votes.

(c) Candidate nominated by convention.

(d) Total includes the Conservative Party. Governor Pataki was the candidate for both parties.

(e) Includes Liberty Union Party (major party) and minor party candidates for governor.

## Table 5.8
## VOTER TURNOUT FOR PRESIDENTIAL ELECTIONS: 1988, 1992 AND 1996
## (In thousands)

| State | 1996 Voting age population (a) | Number registered | Number voting (b) | 1992 Voting age population (a) | Number registered | Number voting (b) | 1988 Voting age population (a) | Number registered | Number voting (b) |
|---|---|---|---|---|---|---|---|---|---|
| Alabama | 3,220 | 2,471 | 1,534 | 3,056 | 2,367 | 1,688 | 3,010 | 2,451 | 1,378 |
| Alaska | 410 | 415 | 245 | 404 | 315 | 261 | 370 | 293 | 203 |
| Arizona | 3,233 | 2,245 | 1,404 | 2,749 | 1,965 | 1,516 | 2,605 | 1,798 | 1,204 |
| Arkansas | 1,873 | 1,369 | 884 | 1,774 | 1,318 | 951 | 1,614 | 1,203 | 828 |
| California | 19,527 | 15,662 | 10,263 | 20,863 | 15,101 | 11,374 | 19,052 | 14,004 | 10,195 |
| Colorado | 2,843 | 2,285 | 1,551 | 2,501 | 2,003 | 1,597 | 2,489 | 2,037 | 1,432 |
| Connecticut | 2,300 | 1,900 | 750 | 2,535 | 1,962 | 1,616 | 2,492 | 1,795 | 1,443 |
| Delaware | 547 | (c) | 271 | 525 | 340 | 290 | 490 | 318 | 250 |
| Florida | 11,043 | 8,078 | 5,444 | 10,586 | 6,542 | 5,439 | 9,614 | 6,047 | 4,413 |
| Georgia | 5,396 | 3,811 | 2,299 | 4,750 | 3,177 | 2,321 | 4,665 | 2,941 | 1,810 |
| Hawaii | 882 | 545 | 370 | 856 | 464 | 383 | 824 | 444 | 369 |
| Idaho | 858 | 700 | 492 | 740 | 611 | 482 | 701 | 572 | 409 |
| Illinois | 11,431 | 6,663 | 4,418 | 8,568 | 6,600 | 5,164 | 8,550 | 6,357 | 4,697 |
| Indiana | 4,146 | 3,500 | 2,135 | 4,108 | 3,180 | 2,347 | 4,068 | 2,866 | 2,169 |
| Iowa | 2,138 | 1,776 | 1,252 | 2,075 | 1,704 | 1,355 | 2,068 | 1,690 | 1,226 |
| Kansas | 1,823 | 1,257 | 1,129 | 1,881 | 1,366 | 1,162 | 1,829 | 1,266 | 993 |
| Kentucky | 2,928 | 2,391 | 1,388 | 2,779 | 2,076 | 1,493 | 2,746 | 2,026 | 1,323 |
| Louisiana | 3,137 | (c) | 1,784 | 2,992 | 2,247 | 1,790 | 3,010 | 2,232 | 1,628 |
| Maine | 934 | 1,001 | 606 | 930 | 975 | 679 | 893 | 855 | 555 |
| Maryland | 3,811 | 2,577 | 1,794 | 3,719 | 2,463 | 1,999 | 3,491 | 2,310 | 1,747 |
| Massachusetts | 4,623 | (c) | 2,556 | 4,607 | 3,346 | 2,774 | 4,535 | 3,275 | 2,633 |
| Michigan | 7,072 | 6,677 | 3,849 | 6,947 | 6,147 | 4,275 | 6,791 | 5,953 | 3,669 |
| Minnesota | 3,412 | 2,730 | 2,211 | 3,278 | 2,711 | 2,356 | 3,161 | 2,917 | 2,125 |
| Mississippi | 1,961 | 1,826 | 894 | 1,826 | 1,640 | 1,008 | 1,867 | 1,596 | 932 |
| Missouri | 3,902 | 3,343 | 2,158 | 3,858 | 3,067 | 2,391 | 3,281 | 2,943 | 2,094 |
| Montana | 647 | 590 | 417 | 570 | 530 | 418 | 586 | 506 | 379 |
| Nebraska | 1,208 | 1,015 | 677 | 1,167 | 951 | 744 | 1,167 | 899 | 661 |
| Nevada | 1,180 | 778 | 464 | 1,013 | 650 | 506 | 780 | 445 | 350 |
| New Hampshire | 860 | 755 | 514 | 830 | 661 | 545 | 823 | 650 | 451 |
| New Jersey | 6,124 | (c) | 3,076 | 5,948 | 4,060 | 3,344 | 5,905 | 4,011 | 3,100 |
| New Mexico | 1,224 | 838 | 580 | 1,104 | 707 | 591 | 1,101 | 675 | 535 |
| New York | 13,564 | 9,161 | 6,439 | 13,609 | 9,196 | 7,069 | 13,480 | 8,612 | 6,486 |
| North Carolina | 5,800 | 4,300 | 2,515 | 5,217 | 3,817 | 2,612 | 4,913 | 3,432 | 2,134 |
| North Dakota | 437 | (c) | 272 | 463 | (c) | 315 | 483 | (c) | 309 |
| Ohio | 8,300 | 6,638 | 4,534 | 8,146 | 6,538 | 4,940 | 7,970 | 6,275 | 4,394 |
| Oklahoma | 2,419 | 1,823 | 1,206 | 2,328 | 2,302 | 1,390 | 2,404 | 2,199 | 1,171 |
| Oregon | 2,344 | 1,962 | 1,399 | 2,210 | 1,775 | 1,499 | 2,044 | 1,528 | 1,235 |
| Pennsylvania | 9,197 | 6,806 | 4,506 | 9,129 | 5,993 | 4,961 | 9,060 | 5,876 | 4,536 |
| Rhode Island | 751 | 603 | 390 | 776 | 554 | 425 | 764 | 549 | 385 |
| South Carolina | 2,872 | 1,814 | 1,203 | 2,646 | 1,537 | 1,237 | 2,479 | 1,435 | 1,041 |
| South Dakota | 530 | 456 | 324 | 500 | 448 | 336 | 507 | 440 | 313 |
| Tennessee | 3,660 | 3,056 | 1,894 | 3,861 | 2,726 | 1,982 | 3,598 | 2,417 | 1,636 |
| Texas | 13,698 | 10,541 | 5,612 | 12,524 | 8,440 | 6,154 | 12,270 | 8,202 | 5,427 |
| Utah | 1,322 | 1,050 | 691 | 1,159 | 965 | 780 | 1,078 | 807 | 662 |
| Vermont | 430 | 385 | 261 | 420 | 383 | 293 | 407 | 348 | 247 |
| Virginia | 5,089 | 3,323 | 2,417 | 4,842 | 3,055 | 2,559 | 4,544 | 2,877 | 2,192 |
| Washington | 4,122 | 3,078 | 2,294 | 3,818 | 2,814 | 2,287 | 3,417 | 2,499 | 1,865 |
| West Virginia | 1,414 | (c) | 636 | 1,350 | 956 | 684 | 1,398 | 969 | 653 |
| Wisconsin | 3,786 | (d) | 2,196 | 3,677 | (d) | 2,531 | 3,536 | (d) | 2,192 |
| Wyoming | 343 | 241 | 216 | 322 | 235 | 203 | 328 | 226 | 186 |

*Sources*: 1988, 1992 and 1996 data provided by Committee for the Study of the American Electorate, with update by the state election administration offices. 1992 base data provided by state election offices, as available; remaining data provided by Committee for the Study of the American Electorate. U.S. Congress, Clerk of the House, Statistics of the Presidential and Congressional Election. The Council of State Governments survey of election officials, January 2000.

(a) Estimated population, 18 years old and over. Includes armed forces in each state, aliens, and institutional population.
(b) Number voting is number of ballots cast in presidential race.
(c) Information not available.
(d) No statewide registration required. Excluded from totals for persons registered.

**Table 5.9**
**CAMPAIGN FINANCE LAWS: GENERAL FILING REQUIREMENTS**
**(As of December 31, 1999)**

| State or other Jurisdiction | Statements required from | Statements filed with | Time for filing |
|---|---|---|---|
| Alabama | Political committees. | Secretary of state: for statewide and judicial offices, state senate, house of representatives, and district attorney. Judge of probate in county of candidate's residence: for county and local offices. State Ethics Comm'n. Statement of economic interests. | 45 days before and between 10 and 5 days before an election; annually on January 31. |
| Alaska | State candidates, municipal candidates, and political groups in municipalities of more than 1,000 residents; an individual, group, or person making an independent expenditure; individuals contributing $500 to any group or candidate. | Alaska Public Offices Commission The state has a voluntary electronic filing system. | 30 days and one week before election; 10 days after election; and annually on February 15 for contributions/expenditures not reported the prior year. Contributions exceeding $250 made within nine days before election must be reported within 24 hours. |
| Arizona | Candidates and political committees. | Secretary of state: for state offices and state measures (including state legislature). Clerk of board of supervisors: for local judges seeking retention and county offices. City or town clerk: for city or town offices or measures. | In regular election year, June 30 report for period from January 1 through May 31; pre-election report not less than 12 days before the election, complete through 20 days before election; post-election report due 30 days after the election, complete through 20 days after the election. In other years, a report is filed by January 31 covering activity from 21 days after last general election to December 31 of next (non-election) year. |
| Arkansas | Candidates whose cumulative contributions exceed $500; exploratory committees; approved political action committees; independent expenditure committees. | Secretary of state and county clerk of county where candidate resides. | Generally, a monthly report due within 15 days after the end of each month; pre-election report due 7 days before any election; final monthly report 30 days after the end of the month in which the election is held; other reporting dates for non-candidate committees. |
| California | Candidates, committees, and elected officeholders. (a) Certain non-committee contributors of $5,000 are required to file reports. | Secy. of state, registrar-recorder of Los Angeles and San Francisco and clerk of county of residence; legislative candidates, board of equalization, court of appeals and superior court judges file with secy. of state, clerk of county with largest number of registered voters in the district affected and clerk of county of domicile. (b) Filings will be available electronically beginning with the 2000 primary. | Semi-annual: July 31 and January 31 for all candidates and committees, whether or not they received contributions or made expenditures, and all elected officers, except judges, whose salary is $100 or more per month. Judges and elected officers whose salary is less than $100 per month file only if they received contributions or made expenditures. Periodic: For elections in June or November of even-numbered years: March 22, 12 days before June election, October 5, and 12 days before the November election. (c) |
| Colorado | Candidates, political committees, issue committees, political parties; persons making independent expenditures of $1,000 or more. | Non-municipal elections: either secretary of state (statewide, legislative, district, or multi-county candidates) or the appropriate county clerk and recorder (other officers). Municipal elections: municipal clerk Non-statewide multi-county issues: county clerk and recorder of each involved county | First day of each month beginning the sixth full month before the major election, 14 days before, and 14 days after the major election in election years. Reports are required quarterly in off-election years. Independent expenditure reports due within 24 hours after obligating funds for the expenditure. |
| Connecticut | Candidates, political committees, and party committees spending or receiving more than $1,000 in any election; certain persons making independent expenditures. | Generally with secretary of state, with local candidates and referendum committees filing with town clerks. State-wide candidates raising or spending $250,000 or more must file electronically; other committees may also file electronically. Reports to be available on the Internet and through secretary of state's office. | Generally: 2nd Thursday of January, April, July, October; 7th day before regular state election; 45 days after election and 30 days after primary. State central committees: January 30, April 10, July 10; 12 days before any election. Supplemental reports: 7 days after distribution of surplus, or, if deficit, 90 days after primary or election, then 30 days after increase in deficit. |

See footnotes at end of table.

## CAMPAIGN FINANCE LAWS: GENERAL FILING REQUIREMENTS — Continued

| State or other jurisdiction | Statements required from | Statements filed with | Time for filing |
|---|---|---|---|
| Delaware | Candidates and committees. | State election commissioner. | 30 days and eight days before election; December 31 of year of election; December 31 of year after election, and annually on December 31 until contributions and expenditures are balanced and the fund is closed. |
| Florida | Candidates, political committees, committees of continuous existence, political party executive committees, and persons making independent expenditures of $100 or more unless no funds have been received or reportable expenditures made during reporting period. | Candidates file with officer before whom candidate qualifies, with copy to supervisor of elections in candidate's county of residence for other than statewide candidates. Statewide committees file with Division of Elections, while other committees file with county supervisor of elections. Filing is generally to be made on diskette, with reports available electronically. | Generally by the 10th day of each calendar quarter after treasurer is appointed through last day of qualifying for office and on the 4th, 18th, and 32nd days preceding first and second primaries; and on the 4th and 18th days immediately preceding the general election for an opposed candidate, political committee, or committee of continuous existence.

Candidates receiving public funds file on the 4th, 11th, 18th, 25th, and 32nd days prior to first primary and general election, and on the 4th, 11th, 18th, and 25th days prior to the second primary. Any candidate who becomes unopposed files within 90 days of that date. |
| Georgia | Candidates, political committees, persons (individual, partnership, committee, association, corporation, labor organization, or any other organization or group of persons) who accept contributions for, make contributions to, or make expenditures on behalf of, candidates, or to bring about the approval or rejection by voters of a proposed constitutional amendment or statewide referendum, and receives or spends $500 or more to bring about (or oppose) recall of a public officer. | Secretary of state for statewide candidates and statewide referenda. Superintendent of elections in county of candidate's residence for general assembly candidates (and ballot questions and recalls) with copy to secretary of state. County superintendent of elections or city clerks for other offices and elections. | 45 days and 15 days before and 10 days after primary; 15 days before general election (6 days before general election runoff); and December 31 of election year; supplemental report due December 31 of each year in office for winning candidates. |
| Hawaii | Candidates, parties, and committees which contribute in the aggregate $1,000 or more in an election period; committees that form within 10 days before an election and spend $1,000 or more. | Original and a copy with Campaign Spending Commission. In counties of less than 200,000 voters, file original and two copies with either Commission or clerk in county where candidate resides. | For candidates, on July 30 before the primary election and 10 working days before each election; 20 days after primary, and 30 days after a general or special election. Supplemental reports in the event of surplus or deficit over $250 are filed on the 5th day after the last day of election year, and every six months thereafter. |
| Idaho | Candidates, political committees, and any person who makes an expenditure of more than $100 other than by a contribution to a candidate or political committee. | Secretary of state. | By October 10 before general election, and 7 days before and 30 days after election. Measure committees file April 30 and July 30 reports. Supplemental reports in the event of an unexpended balance or expenditure deficit are filed annually on January 31. |
| Illinois | Treasurers of state and local political committees. | State Board of Elections for state political committees; State Board of Elections and county clerk for political committees acting as both state and local political committee. Electronic filing is required of candidates and committees that cross certain contribution, expenditure, or loan thresholds. All political committee reports are available via a searchable database on the Internet. | Reports of campaign contributions: 15 days before each election. Semi-annual reports of contributions and expenditures: January 31 and July 31. |

# CAMPAIGN FINANCE LAWS: GENERAL FILING REQUIREMENTS — Continued

| State or other jurisdiction | Statements required from | Statements filed with | Time for filing |
|---|---|---|---|
| Indiana | Political committees, candidate committees, regular party committees, and political action committees. (d) | Election Division for most. (e) | 18 days before election or convention; 20 days after convention if no pre-convention report was filed; annually by third Wednesday in January (by March 1 for political party committee). Public utilities file special report annually. Those with gaming interests file quarterly reports of ownership. |
| Iowa | Candidates and committees receiving contributions or making expenditures in excess of $500 or incurring debt greater than $500 in a calendar year. | Statewide office and state offices elected on less than statewide basis: Ethics and Campaign Disclosure Board. County, city, or school office: county election commissioner. State statutory political committee and other state-level political committees: Board. Other statutory political committee: county election commissioner and copy to Board. Committees may file electronically at their option. | May 19, July 19, October 19, and January 19 annually, except for committees for city and school office candidates who file five days before the election and the first of the month thereafter. In years in which no primary or general election is held, a state or city committee is not required to file the May and July reports. A candidate's committee is not required to file the May, July, and October reports in a a year the candidate does not stand for election. |
| Kansas | Candidates, political committees, party committees, constitutional amendment committees, and persons making independent expenditures of more than $100. | State offices elected statewide and political committees supporting same: with secretary of state. Constitutional amendments: Kansas Gov't'l Ethics Comm'n. State offices elected on less than statewide basis: with secretary of state and county election officer of residence. Local offices and political committees supporting same: county election officer. Disclosure information is available online. | Generally, eight days before election, and January 10 each year. Constitutional amendment committees file each February 15, 15 days before, and 15 days after elections. |
| Kentucky | Candidates, campaign committees, permanent committees, political issues committees, inaugural committees, political party executive committees, exploratory committees, fundraisers, contributing organizations (when in excess of $100), and those making independent expenditures of $500 or more in any one election. | Kentucky Registry of Election Finance. Duplicate reports filed with clerk in county where candidate resides. The Registry is currently working on an electronic filing and reporting system. | Candidates and campaign committees: 32nd and 15th day before an election, and 30 days after an election. If account is not closed at that time, a supplemental report is due, and filing will continue on an annual basis until a zero balance is shown. Candidates have five days from filing deadline to file with Registry. State committees: 30 days after registration, and not less than three days after the 56th, 42nd, 28th, and 14th days before an election, and each 30 days after an election until zero balance in account. Party executive committees: 30 days after an election. Permanent committees: last day of each calendar quarter. |
| Louisiana | Candidates for major or district office; candidates for other offices who receive contributions of greater than $200 from any one source or make expenditures of greater than $5,000; political committees; persons not a candidate who make independent expenditures or accept contributions other than to or from a candidate or committee in excess of $500; persons who accept contributions or make expenditures in excess of $200 to support or oppose recalls or propositions. | Supervisory Committee on Campaign Finance Disclosure. Electronic filing is required for statewide office candidates with more than $50,000 in loans or receipts. | Candidates and committees: 180th, 90th, 30th, & 10th day before primary; 10th day before and 40th day after general election. Election day reports due 10 days after each election. Annual reports by February 15 for most surpluses/deficits. Special report required within 48 hrs. after receipt of a contribution of certain amounts, or expenditures to certain persons from 20 days before election through election day. |
| Maine | Candidates, political committees, political action committees, party committees, and person making independent expenditures in excess of $50. | Commission on Governmental Ethics and Election Practices. | Six days before and 42 days after each election; gubernatorial candidates also file January 15 and July 15 in non-election years if they received or spent more than $1,000 in that year, and 42 days before an election. Party committees file semiannually and before general election. Special reports may be required of candidates receiving public financing. |

See footnotes at end of table.

# CAMPAIGN FINANCE LAWS: GENERAL FILING REQUIREMENTS — Continued

| State or other jurisdiction | Statements required from | Statements filed with | Time for filing |
|---|---|---|---|
| **Maryland** | Candidates receiving contributions of $300 or more; political committees; party central committees; slates. | Candidates and their noncontinuing committees and slates filed with the board with which candidate filed statement of candidacy. Party central committees, all continuing committees and government contractors file with the State Board of Elections. Statewide candidates must file electronically; reports available online November 1999. | Fourth Tuesday before primary, second Friday before any election, and earlier of the third Tuesday after general election or before taking office. Central and continuing committees also file annually on the date of the last general election. If there is a surplus or deficit, six months after general election, one year after general election, and annually on the election anniversary until the surplus or deficit is eliminated. |
| **Massachusetts** | Candidates and political committees. | City or town candidates (except for citywide candidates in cities of 100,000 or more): with city or town clerk or election commission. Other candidates: with director of campaign and political finance. Certain candidates will begin filing electronically in 2002, while certain committees must do so by 2004. Some information from reports is available online from Office of Campaign and Political Finance. | Candidates for General Court, PACs, People's Committees, local party committees: eight days before primary, 8 days before general election, and January 20 of each year. Candidates for statewide, Governor's Council, county and city office in cities of 100,000 or more, and state political party committees: third business day after designating depository, fifth day of each month (and 20th day in last six months of election year), and January 20 of each year. |
| **Michigan** | Candidates, political and independent committees, party committees and ballot question committees; certain persons making independent expenditures. | Secretary of state: candidates for state elective office, judicial office, and all political party committees and political action committees. County clerk: candidates for local office. State court administrator: special report for judicial office candidates. Electronic filing is voluntary, and certain reports are available online. | Candidate committees, party committees, ballot question committees: 11 days before and 30 days after election; committees other than political and independent committees: not later than January 31 of each year; political or independent committees (PACs) filing on state level: January 31, July 25, October 25 in odd years; April 25, July 25, and October, 25 in even years. |
| **Minnesota** | Candidates, party committees, political committees, political committees and persons making independent expenditures of more than $100. | Campaign Finance and Public Disclosure Board for most candidates. Electronic reporting is voluntary. | Candidates for statewide, legislative, and high court offices file 15 days before a primary and ten days before a general election and January 31 annually. (f) |
| **Mississippi** | Candidates and political committees. | Secy. of state if candidate for statewide, state district or legislative office; circuit clerk of appropriate county; municipal clerk for municipal office. Scanned reports are available; candidates may file via e-mail or disk. | For years other than 1999 and every fourth year thereafter: seven days before any election; January 31 to cover the entire prior calendar year. For 1999 and every fourth year thereafter, detailed reporting dates are specified. |
| **Missouri** | Committees, candidates who spend or receive more than $500 or receive a single contribution of more than $250, and persons making independent expenditures of $500 or more. | Missouri Ethics Commission for statewide office candidates and committees, and candidates for the supreme or appellate courts. Candidates for legislative office, circuit court, and county clerk file with the Commission and election authority of the candidate's place of residence. Requirements vary for other candidates. Continuing committee reports and reports from candidates filing electronically are available on-line. | Eight days before election day for period closing 12th day before election; 30 days after election day for period closing 25th day after election; and quarterly on 15th day of the month to include activity for period ending on last day of quarter. (g) |

# CAMPAIGN FINANCE LAWS: GENERAL FILING REQUIREMENTS — Continued

| State or other jurisdiction | Statements required from | Statements filed with | Time for filing |
|---|---|---|---|
| Montana | Candidates and political committees (except in certain school districts and special district elections). | Commissioner of political practices and election administrator of county where candidate is resident or political committee has headquarters. District court judicial candidates file with commissioner and election administrator in county where election held or in county seat with greatest population if election is in more than one county. | Statewide office candidates and related political committees: pre-election year quarterly reports on the fifth day after each quarter; March 10th and September 10th in an election year; 15 and five days before an election; not more than 20 days after an election; March 10th and September 10th of each year following an election until closing report is filed. State district office candidates and related political committees: 12th day before election, not more than 20 days after election, and whenever closing report is filed. Local office candidates and related political committees: same as for state district office if contributions or expenditures to campaign exceed $500. Statewide ballot issue committee: pre-election year reports on the fifth day following each quarter; March 10th, and tenth day of subsequent month through September; 15 and 25 days before election; within 20 days after election. Independent committees: 12th day before election, not more than 20 days after election, and when closing report is due at the end of the calendar year is due. (h) |
| Nebraska | Candidate committees, political party committees, independent committees, and ballot question committees upon raising, receiving, or spending more than $5,000 in a calendar year. (i) | Nebraska Accountability and Disclosure Commission. Copies to be filed with election commissioner or county clerk, as appropriate, depending on the type of committee. | By 30th day and tenth day before a primary or general election, and 40th day after primary election and 70th day after general election. Annual statement due by January 31 for preceding year if statements not required to be filed during previous years. (j) |
| Nevada | State, district, county, township, and city office candidates; persons that make candidate-related independent expenditures; ballot question advocacy persons and groups; and committees for the recall of a public officer. Persons include individuals, business and social organizations, non-governmental legal entities, PACs, political parties, and party-sponsored committees. | Secy. of state: candidate for statewide office, state senator, or assemblyman in multi-county district, or any other office with multi-county district; person making independent expenditures for a candidate elected from other than a single city or county; committee for the recall of a public officer; and ballot question advocacy group for a question voted on in other than a single county or city. County clerk: candidate for state senator or assemblyman voted on in a single county; county or township office; person making independent expenditures for a candidate elected only from the county; and ballot question advocacy group for a question voted on only in the county. City clerk: candidate for city office; person making independent expenditures for a candidate elected only from the city; and ballot question advocacy group for a question voted on only in the city. | Candidate at primary or general election: seven days before primary, seven days before general election, and 15th day of 2nd month after general election. City office candidate: seven days before city primary, seven days before city general election, and 15th day of 2nd month after city general election. Candidate at recall election: contributions report 30 days after election and expenses report 60 days after election. Candidate at special district office election: seven days before election, contributions report 30 days after election, and expenses report 60 days after election. Recall candidate: contribution report 30 days after special election and expenses report 60 days after special election. If no special election, 30 days after a district court determines a recall petition is legally insufficient. Recall committee: if petition for recall not filed, 30 days after notice of intent to circulate petition expired; if court does not order special recall election, 30 days after court decision; and if court orders special recall election, seven days before and 30 days after election. Person making candidate-related independent expenditures and ballot question advocacy group: seven days before primary election or city primary election, as appropriate; seven days before general election or city general election, as appropriate; and 15th day of second month after election. |
| New Hampshire | Candidates for governor, councilor, state senator, representative to General Court, and county office whose expenditures exceed $500, and political committees (including political party committees) whose receipts or expenditures exceed $500. | Secretary of state. | Wednesday 12 weeks before election (except political committee of candidate or political party), Wednesday three weeks before election, and second Wednesday after election. Every six months after election until obligations satisfied or surplus depleted. (k) |

See footnotes at end of table.

# CAMPAIGN FINANCE LAWS: GENERAL FILING REQUIREMENTS — Continued

| State or other jurisdiction | Statements required from | Statements filed with | Time for filing |
|---|---|---|---|
| **New Jersey** | Candidate committees and joint candidates committees (except periodic election fund reports not required if total amount to be expended for candidacy by all sources does not exceed $2,400 for candidate committee, $4,700 for joint candidates committee with two candidates, or $7,000 for joint candidates committee with three or more candidates, although aggregate contributions over $300 from single source must be reported); political committees that raise or expend $1,200 or more in an election; continuing political committees; political party committees; and legislative leadership committees. | New Jersey Election Law Enforcement Commission. In case of candidates for non-statewide office, a copy is filed with the county clerk of county where candidate seeks office, except candidates for state legislative office file in county where candidate resides. State candidate reports only accessible electronically at ELEC offices. | Candidates, joint candidates committees, and political committees: 29th day and 11th day before election and 20th day after election. If exempted from periodic reporting, file contributions report on scheduled date if aggregate contribution of more than $300 received. Candidate committees and joint candidates committees: quarterly reports by April 15th, July 15th, October 15th, and January 15th of calendar quarters in year candidate not running for election. Continuing political committees, political party committees, and legislative leadership committee: by April 15th, July 15th, October 15th, and January 15th of each calendar year. (I) |
| **New Mexico** | Public officials, candidates or treasurers of candidates' campaign committees (except candidates filing statements that they anticipate receiving or spending less than $1,000 for non-statewide office or $2,500 for statewide office in primary or general election), and treasurers of political committees. | Secretary of state: statewide elective offices, multi-county state legislative offices (but may file with county clerk of resident county), judicial offices for judicial districts (except magistrates), multi-county district offices, and political committees. County clerk: county elective offices, magistrates, and single-county state legislative offices. Voluntary electronic filing program in operation, with reports filed via disk, modem, or e-mail. Reports available electronically only at secretary of state's office. | All public officials and candidates: annually by second Monday in May. In election year, public officials who are candidates and candidates who have not filed statements of exceptions: by second Monday in October, by Thursday before election, and by 30th day after election. Undeclared candidates below reporting threshold of $1,000 for non-statewide office or $2,500 for statewide office for contributions or expenditures: second Monday in May for primary or second Monday in October for general election. Supplemental report of contribution or pledge to contribute for $500 or more in non-statewide election or for $2,500 or more in statewide election received after 5:00 p.m. on Tuesday before election due within 24 hours of receipt, except if received after 5:00 p.m. on Friday before election, then due by noon of Monday before election. |
| **New York** | Candidates and political committees, however, filing is not required for candidates or their authorized political committees (1) that do not expend more than $50 in a calendar year or $1,000 in an election cycle, (2) before an uncontested primary election, or (3) for an election in a city, town, or village or less than 10,000 unless total receipts or expenditures exceed $1,000. | Candidates: presidential electors, state executive or legislative offices, supreme court justices, constitutional convention delegates, and multi-county party positions (if not wholly within New York City), with State Board of Elections; other public offices (except village offices and party positions in a single county or New York City), with city or county board of elections, as appropriate; and village offices if election not on general election day, with county board of elections. Political committees: with State Board of Elections, except committees taking part solely in an election for a candidate required to file with a local board of elections, are also required to file with the county board of elections. Committees file with the county board of elections. Committees are required to file with other boards in certain instances. Electronic filing to be available effective January 1, 1999, applicable to all contributions greater than $1,000. | Primary election: 32nd and 11th day before and 10th day after contested primary election. Runoff primary: 4th day before and 10th day after primary. General election: 32nd day and 11th day before and 27th day after the election. Periodic statements are also required by January 15 and July 15 in each subsequent year until activities terminated. Contributions or loans of more than $1,000 received after close of second pre-election filing period must be reported within 24 hours of receipt. Political committees are to file by January 15th and July 15th of each year after statement of treasurer and depository filed. |

# CAMPAIGN FINANCE LAWS: GENERAL FILING REQUIREMENTS — Continued

| State or other jurisdiction | Statements required from | Statements filed with | Time for filing |
|---|---|---|---|
| **North Carolina** | Candidates, political committees (including political party committees), and referendum committees; individuals making independent expenditures over $100. Candidates and political party committees whose contributions, loans, and expenditures will not exceed $3,000 can be exempted from reporting. | State Board of Elections: with respect to candidates for state-wide or multi-county offices and statewide referenda. County board of elections: with respect to candidates for single-county district and county offices and county referenda, and, except where municipality conducts the election, candidates for municipal office and municipal referenda. Otherwise, file with municipal board of elections with respect to candidates for municipal office and municipal referenda, where municipality conducts election (note: county boards conduct most municipal elections). Voluntary state candidate electronic filing is expected to be effective with the 1998 elections. Certain report data is already available online. | All candidates and committees: organizational report due within 10 days of filing of candidacy or organization of committee. (m) |
| **North Dakota** | Candidates for statewide or legislative office who receive any contributions during a calendar year; political parties that receive contributions; political committees administering PACs; persons who receive contributions concerning statewide referenda and initiatives; and corporations, cooperative corporations, limited liability companies, or associations that spend money to promote passage or defeat of a measure. | Secretary of state: state and legislative office candidates; political parties; political committees; statewide initiative/ referendum group or person; and corporations, cooperative corporations, limited liability companies, and associations. | Pre-election statement: 12th day before election. Year-end statement: January 31 of following year. Supplemental statement for contribution of $500 or more received in 20-day period before an election must be filed within 48 hours by statewide or legislative office candidate and by referendum/initiative group or person. |
| **Ohio** | Candidate campaign committees, political action committees, political contributing entities, legislative campaign funds, and political parties (excluding campaign committees for candidates for municipal office paying $5,000 or less, member of a local board of education, or township trustee or clerk certifying that in one election period aggregate contributions and expenditures will not exceed $2,000 and no individual contribution will exceed $100). | Secy. of state: statewide and state board of education offices, state political committees, and state and national political parties. County board of elections: offices within county and multi-county district (file in county with greatest population), county political committees, and county political parties. | Twelfth day before and 38th day after an election: annual statement on the last business day of January except in year post-general election statement is filed. Monthly statements of contributions for July, August, September of general election year required by campaign committee of statewide office candidate. From 19th day before general election through general election day, a two-business-day statement required if campaign committee receives contribution causing aggregate contributions from contributor to exceed $2,500 in case of designated state executive office candidate or $500 in case of supreme court candidate. From 19th day before primary to primary a two-business-day report each time personal-funds candidate and no-limits opponent receive aggregate contributions from contributor exceeding $2,000. |
| **Oklahoma** | State elections: State office candidate or candidate committee accepting more than $500 in aggregate; PAC in state election that contributes or expends $500 in calendar year; and committee of political party with state office candidates. State offices and state officer elected by statewide vote, state senator, state representative, district judge, associate district judge, and district attorney. Local elections: county and other local office candidates or candidate committees and PACs and political party committees in local election receiving or expending more than $200 in campaign. | State Ethics Commission: state and county candidates/ candidate committees and other non-local committees. Municipal clerk: municipal candidates/committees and supporting/opposing committees. Clerk of board of education: school board candidates/committees and supporting/ opposing committees. Electronic filing is optional. Campaign finance information is available online. | State office elections: quarterly reports: January 15, April 15, July 15, and October 15 (ballot-measure PACs file by 10th of each month). Pre-election report eight days before primary, runoff primary, and general election (report between primary and runoff primary replaces October 15 report). Candidate committee which doesn't accept contributions or make expenditures exceeding $500 in aggregate may be exempted. Aggregate contribution or independent expenditure of $500 or more after closing date for pre-election reporting period must be reported within 24 hours of receipt. County and local elections: 10th day before primary, runoff primary, and general election, and 40th day after general election. If necessary, supplemental reports within six months and 10 days after general election and by January 15 of subsequent years. PAC in local proposition/measure election: 10th day before election, 40th day after election, and supplemental reports if necessary. |

See footnotes at end of table.

# CAMPAIGN FINANCE LAWS: GENERAL FILING REQUIREMENTS — Continued

| State or other jurisdiction | Statements required from | Statements filed with | Time for filing |
|---|---|---|---|
| Oregon | Candidates (or their principal campaign committees) and political committees; chief petitioners for initiative, referendum, and recall petitions. A non-federal office candidate who serves as own treasurer and does not expect aggregate contributions to exceed $300 in the primary or general election is exempt. | Secretary of state: statewide, state, and congressional district office. County clerk: non-city office within a county. County clerk in county where the chief administrative officer is located: multi-county district office. Chief city election officer: city office. | Candidates and committees: 21-30 days and five-eight days before election and 30 days after election. If $500 in contributions received after the ninth day and before the day preceding the election, a pre-election supplemental statement is due on the day before the election. If the post-election statement shows an unexpended balance of contributions or expenditure deficit, a post-election annual supplemental statement is required by September 10th until there is no balance or deficit. Chief petitioners: 15th day after petition filing deadline; annually by September 10th if did not qualify for ballot and have surplus or deficit. |
| Pennsylvania | Candidates and political committees if amount received or expended or liabilities incurred exceed $250 during a reporting period. | Report concerning candidate: office with which a candidate files nomination documents, either the Secy. of the commonwealth or appropriate county board of elections. If report concerns both candidates who file nomination documents with the secy. and those who file with county boards, then with the secy. of the commonwealth. Electronic filing is voluntary for all candidates. Reports are available online. | Statewide office candidates and political committees influencing statewide election: by sixth Tuesday and second Friday before primary and general election. All other committees: second Friday before primary and general election. All candidates and political committees: 30 days after election and annual report on January 31 of each year until no balance or debt; then termination report may be filed. Contribution of $500 or more received or independent expenditure of $500 or more made after final pre-election report must be reported within 24 hours. |
| Rhode Island | Candidates, political action committees, and state and municipal party committees that receive contributions of over $100 from one source in a calendar year, or spend more than $1,000 in the aggregate on behalf of a candidate or question. | State Board of Elections. | Pre-election reports at 90-day intervals on 3/31, 6/30, 9/30, and 12/31 after date person becomes candidate or campaign treasurer appointed. Twenty-eighth and seventh day before a primary, general, or special election (in a contested primary), and 28th day after an election (final report). Political party committee must file annual report by March 1. Ongoing reports due 120 days after election and at 90-day intervals thereafter on 3/31, 6/30, 9/30, and 12/31 until dissolution of campaign fund or completion of a committee's business regarding the past election. |
| South Carolina | Candidates and committees. | State Ethics Commission: non-legislative candidates and non-legislative committees. State Senate or House of Representatives' ethics committee, as appropriate: legislative candidates and caucus committees. | Initial report: if receipt or expenditures of contributions exceeds $500. 10 days after threshold amount met; if $500 threshold not met, 15 days before an election. Subsequent reports: 10 days after each calendar quarter, whether before or after an election, and 15 days before an election; however, if a pre-election report is due within 30 days of the end of a quarter, a combined report is due no later than 15 days before the election. Independent expenditure by committee within 20 days before an election to be reported immediately if more than $10,000 for statewide office candidate or $2,000 for any other candidate. Final report may be filed at any time when contributions no longer received or expenditures made or incurred. |
| South Dakota | State executive, state legislative, and county office candidates or candidate's committees; school board candidates in districts of more than 2,000 students or candidate's committees; PACs that participate in an election; political party committees; persons or ballot question committees involved with a question or constitutional amendment at a statewide election; and persons and political committees involved with a question at a non-statewide election. | Secy. of state: state office and legislative office candidates and candidate's committees, political party committees, political action committees, and persons involved with a statewide question. County auditor: county office candidates and candidate's committees. School business manager: school board candidates and candidates committees. Person in charge of an election: persons and committees involved with a non-statewide question. | State office candidates, candidates' committees, political action committees, and political party committees: last Tuesday prior to primary and general election, and by February 1 for preceding calendar year or remainder not covered by previous report. No pre-primary report for unopposed candidate or county party committee. If a contribution of $500 or more is received within nine days prior to an election, statement must be filed within 48 hours. Legislative and county office candidates: by July 1 and December 31 of election year. No pre-primary report for an unopposed candidate. School board candidates: Seven days before election. If a contribution of $500 or more is received within Nine days prior to an election, statement must be filed within 48 hours. Person or committee involved with a statewide question: by July 1 of election year and last Tuesday before election; annually thereafter by February 1. Person or committee involved with non-statewide question: 10 days before and 30 days after election. |

# CAMPAIGN FINANCE LAWS: GENERAL FILING REQUIREMENTS — Continued

| State or other jurisdiction | Statements required from | Statements filed with | Time for filing |
|---|---|---|---|
| Tennessee | Candidates and political campaign committees (except candidates for part-time public office paid less than $500 per month unless it is a chief administrative officer office or candidate expenditures exceed $1,000). | Registry of Election Finance: state office candidates and political campaign committees in state elections. Appropriate county election commission: local office candidates and committees for local elections. General Assembly candidates and their political committees file a copy with county election commission where the candidate resides. | Candidates, single-candidate political campaign committees, and single-measure political campaign committees: if political treasurer appointed more than one year before election, by February 1 each year through year of election; in election year, seven days before and 48 days after each election. If unexpended balance, continuing obligations or expenditure deficit exists after the post-election statement is filed, a supplemental annual statement must be filed. Multi-candidate political campaign committees: within 10 days after each quarter. (n) |
| Texas | Candidates, officeholders, specific-purpose political committees and general-purpose political committees (except political party county executive committees with aggregate contributions and expenditures of $5,000 or less in a calendar year). | Texas Ethics Commission or county clerk. (o) | Report due dates: semiannual reports (by July 15 and January 31) and pre-election reports (by 30th and eighth day before each election, and if run-off election, by eighth day before election). (p) |
| Utah | Candidates for governor, lt. governor, state auditor, state treasurer, or attorney general or candidate's personal campaign committee; legislative candidates (state senator, state representative, and leadership positions), state and local school board office candidates; political party committees; PAC that receives contributions or makes expenditures of $750 or more in calendar year; political issues committee that receives political issues contributions of $750 or more or makes political issues expenditures of $50 or more in calendar year; corporation that makes political purpose or political issues expenditures of $750 or more in calendar year. (q) | Lieutenant Governor: state executive, legislative, and state school board candidates; PACs; political issues committees; and corporations. County clerk: local school board and county office candidates. City recorder: city office candidates. | State executive/legislative office candidates: interim reports due seven days before party convention if contest. State executive/legislative office candidates and state/local school board candidates: interim reports due seven days before primary, September 15th, and seven days before general election. Summary report due January 5th after general election year, and annually until statement of dissolution filed. Candidates in county, first class city, second class city, and third class city with population of 10,000 or more: If local ordinance, at least once within two weeks before election (counties) or seven days before general election (cities). If no ordinance, 30 days after primary if lost, seven days before general election, and 30 days after general election. Political party committees: interim reports due September 15th and seven days before general election in regular general election year, summary report due on January 5th after general election year. PACs, political issues committees, and corporations: annually by January 5th, September 15th, and 7 days before general election. |
| Vermont | State executive office candidates, state legislative, county and local office candidates who have accepted contributions or made expenditures of $500 or more; political parties; and political committees that have accepted contributions or made expenditures of $500 or more in a calendar year. | Secy. of state: state executive office candidates, political committees, and political parties. Officer with whom candidate files nomination papers: state legislative, county, and local office candidates. State legislative candidates file with secretary of state and the clerk of the candidate's senate or house district. | State executive office and state legislative candidates, political committees, and political parties: 40 days before primary; 25th day of each month after primary and continuing to general election; not later than 40 days after general election and July 15th in odd-numbered years. Post-general election report is a final report for candidates; political committees and political parties may file a final report at any time. Political committees and political parties in local election: 10 days before and 10 days after each election. County office candidates: 10 days before primary; 10 days before general election; within 40 days after general election (final report); and July 15th and annually thereafter until all contributions and expenditures have been accounted for and indebtedness and surplus have been eliminated. Local office candidates: 10 days before and 10 days after the election. |

See footnotes at end of table.

# CAMPAIGN FINANCE LAWS: GENERAL FILING REQUIREMENTS — Continued

| State or other jurisdiction | Statements required from | Statements filed with | Time for filing |
|---|---|---|---|
| Virginia | Candidates or their campaign committees, political committees (including PACs, unexempted political party committees, and organized party groups of election officials) anticipating contributions or expenditures over $200, and inaugural fund committees. Exempted political party committees (committees other than state party committees, district party committees, county or city party committees for counties or cities with a population of more than 100,000, or organized political party groups of elected officials) report when contributions accepted or contributions or expenditures made exceed $10,000 (or higher amount set by state board of elections) in aggregate in calendar year. Persons to report independent expenditures exceeding $500 in a statewide election of $200 in any other election. Earmarked contributions received by political party committee or organized party group of elected officials to be reported. | State Board of Elections: all statewide and General Assembly candidates, persons, political committees, and inaugural fund committees. Electoral board where candidate resides: all candidates for general assembly and local office. Also, reports of single large pre-election contributions to statewide candidates. County, city, or local district party committee also filed with. Electronic filing and online reporting to be available in 1999. | Candidates for office filled at November general election: For non-election year—July 15 of election year and January 15 of following year. For election year—April 15, eighth day before June primary, July 15, September 15, October 15, eighth day before November election, 30th day after November election, January 15 of following year. Schedule followed until final report filed. Candidates for local offices filled at May general election: eighth day before primary (municipal primary candidates only), eighth day before election, June 15 of election year, July 15 following election, January 15 of next year, and January 15 of each following year until final report filed. Candidates for offices at a special election not held on regular election date: eighth day before election, 30th day after election and prior to taking office, January 15 and July 15 of following years until final report filed. Political committees: File in accordance with applicable schedule for (1) candidates for office filled at November general election, except political party committee not required to file report due on 30th day after November general election, or (2) candidates for local office filled at May general election, or (3) candidates for nomination or election to office filled at special election held on a date other than regularly scheduled general election. Must comply with election-year filing schedule for each year it seeks to influence the outcome of an election. Inaugural fund committees: March 15 immediately following inauguration, July 15 of inauguration year. Contributions of more than $1,000 for statewide office or $500 for any other office received after threshold must be reported within 72 hours. Such contributions received within the 72 hours preceding election day must be reported no later than the day before the election. |
| Washington | Candidates and political committees except in election campaigns for federal elective office and precinct committee officer. Candidates and political committees concerning an office whose constituency covers less than an entire county and contains less than 5,000 voters and in jurisdictions with less than 1,000 voters are exempted unless the exemption is voided by local ordinance or by petition filed by voters in the jurisdiction. | Public Disclosure Commission and auditor or elections officer of county in which the candidate resides. Continuing political committees file reports with the Public Disclosure Commission and auditor or elections officer of county in which the committee maintains its office or headquarters or in which treasurer resides (if there is no office or headquarters). Electronic filing is authorized; mandatory in 2001 for continuing political committees that expended $10,000 in contributions or expenditures since last report exceed $200. Certain contribution information is currently available online. | At time campaign treasurer is designated; 21st and seventh day before and by the 10th day of the month following an election; 10th day of each month in which no other reports are required if a contribution is received or expenditure made total $200 since last report; and at time campaign fund is closed and campaign concluded (final report). Post-primary report not required for candidate whose name will appear on general election ballot or from continuing political committee. Continuing political committees also file monthly reports by 10th day if total contributions or expenditures since last report exceed $200. Candidates and political committees may file only post-election reports if they qualify for abbreviated campaign reporting or candidates may file only the registration statement if they qualify for mini-campaign reporting. (r) |
| West Virginia | Candidates, financial agents, party committee treasurers, and persons, associations or persons and organizations (including corporations) that support or oppose a candidate or issue, and their treasurers or equivalent officer. | Secy. of state: state, legislative, and multi-county political subdivision offices. Clerk of the county commission: all other offices. Electronic filing and online reporting system is being finalized. | Last Saturday in March or within 15 days thereafter before the primary; seven-10 days before and 25-30 days after a primary, general or special election; and annually on last Saturday in March or within 15 days thereafter if contributions or expenditures exceed $5,000 or any loan is outstanding; and on last Saturday in September or within 15 days thereafter or next preceding general election day if financial transactions exceed $500 or any loan is outstanding. (s) |

# CAMPAIGN FINANCE LAWS: GENERAL FILING REQUIREMENTS — Continued

| State or other jurisdiction | Statements required from | Statements filed with | Time for filing |
|---|---|---|---|
| Wisconsin | Candidates and personal campaign committees, political committees, political groups, individuals and conduits that meet minimum criteria concerning contributions, disbursements, obligations, or transfers. A political committee, political group, or individual, if other than a candidate or personal campaign committee is exempted from registration and reporting if it does not make or accept contributions, make disbursements, or incur obligations of over $25 in a calendar year. Elections for presidential elector, convention delegate, and precinct committeeman are exempted from registration and reporting. Persons, political committees and political groups (except political committees and individuals required to file a statement under oath concerning independent candidate-related disbursements) that do not anticipate aggregate contributions, disbursements, or obligations of over $1,000 in a calendar year and receipt of single-source contributions of over $100 in a calendar year are exempt from reporting. | State Elections Board: political party committees, state office candidates and committees, committees and individuals in both state and local office elections, and political groups and individuals involved with statewide referenda. Clerk of the most populous jurisdiction: local office candidates and committees (and duplicates of certain reports required to be filed with State Elections Board) and committees and individuals involved with local referenda only. City clerk: city school district elections. School district clerk: other district school elections. | Eighth-14 days before a primary or general election: continuing semi-annual reports between January 1 and 31 and July 1 and 20 until a termination report is filed. An unreported cumulative contribution of $500 or more by a state office candidate, committee, or individual within 15 days before an election must be reported within 24 hours of receipt. A candidate-related disbursement of more than $20 cumulatively within 15 days before an election must be reported within 24 hours of making. |
| Wyoming | Candidates, candidates' campaign committees, political action committees, state and county political party central committees, and referendum/initiative organizations. | Secretary of state: statewide, state legislative, and supreme court and district judgeship candidates and their supporting committees; PACs or organizations supporting or opposing statewide initiative or referendum petition drive or statewide ballot proposition; and political party state central committees. Both secretary of state and county clerk: district attorney candidates and supporting committees and political party county central committees. County clerk: other office candidates and supporting committees, and PACs supporting or opposing municipal initiatives or referenda. | Candidates: within 10 days after an election. Non-party political action committees: within 10 days after an election; PACs and candidates' campaign committees formed after an election to defray campaign expenses and any ongoing committees also report semi-annually on July 1 and December 31 of each odd-numbered year until committee terminates. Party committees: 10 days after general or special election. Political action committees or organizations supporting or opposing initiative or referendum petition drive: within 10 days after petition submitted and, if PAC or organization supports petition drive, 30-45 days before election. Political action committees and organizations supporting or opposing ballot proposition: within 10 days after election. |
| Dist. of Columbia | Candidates spending more than $250 in any one election; political committees; persons making independent expenditures of $50 or more. | Director of campaign finance. | Each year: January 31. Election years: 10th day of March, June, August, October and December; 8 days before an election. Non-election years: July 31. Contributions of $200 or more received after closing date for last pre-election report must be reported within 24 hours. |
| American Samoa | Candidates, committees, and parties. | Campaign Spending Commission. | Organizational report: not later than the earliest of on or before day of filing for nomination or election; at least 45 days before the general or special election; or by the 10th day after receiving contributions aggregating $100 or more or making or incurring a reportable expenditure. Preliminary report: 15th calendar day before election or primary. Final report: 20th calendar day after general, special, or runoff election. Deficit reports: 5th day after last day of election year and every three months thereafter until no deficit. |

See footnotes at end of table.

# CAMPAIGN FINANCE LAWS: GENERAL FILING REQUIREMENTS — Continued

| State or other jurisdiction | Statements required from | Statements filed with | Time for filing |
|---|---|---|---|
| Guam | Candidates, political committees, and parties. | Guam Election Commission . | Organizational report: not later than the earliest of on or before day of filing for nomination or election; or by the 10th day after receiving contributions aggregating $100,000 or more or making or incurring expenditures of more than $100,000. Preliminary report: 10th day before election or primary. Final primary report: 10th day after general, special, or runoff election. Final general election report: 20th calendar day after general, special, or runoff election. Surplus reports: 60 days after election and every six months thereafter until individual becomes candidate again. Deficit reports: 60 days after election and every three months thereafter until no deficit. |
| No. Mariana Islands | Candidates for commonwealth office. | Board of Elections. | Within 50 days after general election. |
| Puerto Rico | Political parties, candidates, persons, and independent political groups. | Commonwealth Election Commission. | Generally every three months. Cumulative statement due for period up to May 31st of the year prior to the general election year. Monthly reports beginning September 1st of the year prior to the general election year, and then every 1st and 15th day from October 1 through the last day of the election year. Last statement due 90 days after election. |
| U.S. Virgin Islands | Political committees, including candidates' principal committees. | Supervisor of Elections. | (t) |

*Source:* Edward D. Feigenbaum, J.D. and James A. Palmer, J.D., INGroup, Noblesville, Indiana. March 2000; *Finance Law 2000: A Summary of State Campaign Finance Laws with Quick Reference Charts.*

*Note:* This table deals with filing requirements for state and local offices in general terms. For detailed legal requirements, state statutes should be consulted.

(a) Short forms may be used by candidates and officeholders who raise and spend less than $1,000 in calendar year. There are three types of committees: (1) recipient committees which receive $1,000 or more in contributions in a year; (2) independent expenditure committees, which make independent expenditures of $1,000 or more in a year; and (3) major donor committees, which make contributions of $10,000 or more in a year.

(b) Statewide officers, candidates, and committees: Original and one copy with the secy. of state, two copies with the registrar-recorder of Los Angeles County, two copies with the registrar of voters of the County of San Francisco, and two copies with the filer's county of domicile. State legislature, Board of Equalization, appellate and superior court elections: Original and one copy with the Secy. of state, two copies with the county clerk with the largest number of registered voters in the district affected, and two copies with the filer's county of domicile. Other multi-county elections: original and one copy with the county clerk with the largest number of registered voters in the district affected, two copies with the filer's county of domicile. County offices and municipal courts: original and one copy with the county clerk, two copies with the filer's county of domicile. City elections: original and one copy with the city clerk.

(c) Late contributions received or made and late independent expenditures of $1,000 or more made during the 16 days before an election must be reported by special methods within 24 hours.

(d) Also required from corporations and labor organizations making expenditures in referenda, and of certain persons making independent expenditures. Public utilities file a special report with Indiana Utility Regulatory Commission. Certain Hoosier Lottery vendors, riverboat gaming license holders and suppliers, and parimutuel horse-racing license holders file reports with regulatory entities and Election Division.

(e) General Assembly candidates file duplicate with board of candidate's county of residence. State office candidate filings available online in searchable form. Local candidates and committees file with county election board of each county in district. Referenda reports filed with appropriate county election board and State Election Commission. Public utilities file a special report with the Indiana Utility Regulatory Commission. Gaming interest reports are filed with the appropriate regulatory agency (Indiana Gaming Commission or Indiana Horse Racing Commission) and the Election Division.

(f) Any contribution or loan to a statewide candidate of $2,000, or more than $400 to any legislative or district court candidate received between the closing date and the last pre-election report and the election must be reported within 48 hours after receipt, and in next required report.

(g) Contributions of more than $250 received by any committee after the closing date of the last pre-election disclosure report but before election day must be reported within 48 hours after receipt. Supplemental reports are required each January 15 if contributions or expenditures of $1,000 or more were made or received since the last report. A supplemental report is required if post-election report shows outstanding debts greater than $5,000; this report must be filed until the deficit is less than $5,000.

(h) Incidental committees: two days before deadline for statewide ballot issue committee; except if involved with state district candidate or local candidate/issue, then two days before deadline for state district office candidate (excluding closing-report filing). Report required for all candidates and related political committees within 24 hours if contribution of $500 or more received for statewide office or statewide ballot issue, between the 10th day before election and day of election, or within 48 hours if contribution of $100 or more received for state district offices within 17 days before election.

(i) An existing committee that does not anticipate contributions or expenditures of more than $1,000 in an election year may exempt itself from regular reporting.

(j) Report of contributions of $1,000 or more received within 14 days before election is required to be filed within five days after receipt.

(k) Notice of a contribution greater than $500 received at second Wednesday before election is to be filed within 24 hours. Political committee report of independent expenditures to be filed within 24 hours after aggregate expenditures greater than $500 are made, and thereafter each time $500 more is spent.

(l) Single-source contribution of over $600 received by a continuing political committee, political party committee, or legislative leadership committee after final day of quarterly reporting period and on or before election day to be reported within 48 hours. Single-source contributions of more than $600 received by a candidate committee, joint candidates committee, or political committee between the 13th day before and election day to be reported within 48 hours.

Expenditure of over $600 by political committee between 13th day before and election day or by a continuing political committee between March 31st and primary election day or after September 20th and general election day to be reported within 48 hours.

# CAMPAIGN FINANCE LAWS: GENERAL FILING REQUIREMENTS — Continued

(m) Candidates and political committees in non-municipal elections: quarterly reports—by 7 working days after each quarter in even-numbered year if involved in election except first quarter report covers through 17th day before primary and is due 7 days after that date, and 3rd quarter report covers through 17th day before general election and is due 7 days after that date; semi-annual reports—by last Friday in July and January if contributions received or expenditures made and no other report required; 48-hour report (political committee, political party, or referendum committee)—within 48 hours if contribution or transfer of more than $1,000 received after last pre-election report before an election; final; report when all funds are disbursed, loans repaid or forgiven, and committee bank account closed. Candidates and political committees in municipal elections: Election conducted on partisan basis: pre-primary by 10th day before primary; pre-election report—10 days prior to election unless a second primary is held and the candidate appeared on the ballot in the second primary, then 10 days before the second primary; annual report if contributions are received or expenditures made during a calendar year for which no reports are otherwise required—by the last Friday in January of following year. Election conducted under nonpartisan election and run-off basis: pre-election report—by 10 days prior to election; annual report if contributions are received or expenditures made during a calendar year for which no reports are otherwise required—by Friday in January of following year. Election conducted under nonpartisan primary method: pre-primary report—10 days prior to primary if the candidate is in primary or 10 days prior to election. If the candidate is not in a primary; annual report if no contributions are received or expenditures made during a calendar year for which no reports are otherwise required—by last Friday in January of following year. Election conducted under nonpartisan plurality method: pre-election report—10 days prior to election; annual report if contributions received or expenditures made during a calendar year for which no reports are otherwise required—by last Friday in January of the following year. Referendum committees: no later than 10th day before referendum and no later than 10th day after referendum, with additional reports due if not a final report. Report of otherwise unreported contribution or independent expenditure of $100 or more 30 days after exceeding $100 or 10 days before election, whichever is earlier.

(n) If large contribution, loan, or transfer of funds received within 10 days of election ($5,000 if it concerns a state office candidate; $2,500 if it concerns a local office candidate), report must be filed within 72 hours. Any report due in December to is to be filed by January 31st.

(o) Texas Ethics Commission: candidate for statewide office, district office filled by voters of more than one county, state senator or representative, or state board of education; specific-purpose committee supporting or opposing candidate filing with Commission; officeholder and specific-purpose political committee for assisting an officeholder if a candidate for the office files with the Commission; specific-purpose political committee involved with a statewide measure; specific-purpose political committee required to file with more than one filing officer; and a general-purpose political committee. County clerk: candidate for county office, precinct office, or an office filled by voters of one county; specific-purpose political committees supporting or opposing a candidate who files with the county clerk; officeholder and specific- purpose political committee for assisting an officeholder if a candidate for the office files with the county clerk; and specific-purpose political committee involved with a county measure. Texas Ethics Comm'n and county clerk: candidate for a judicial office filled by voters of only one county; specific-purpose committee for supporting or opposing a candidate for or assisting a holder of a judicial district office filled by voters of only one county ; and a holder of a judicial office filled by voters of only one county. Clerk or Secretary of non-county political subdivision: candidates for local office; specific-purpose political committee supporting or opposing a local office candidate; officeholder and specific- purpose political committee for assisting an office-holder files with the clerk/secretary; and specific-purpose political committee involved with a local measure. Filers with Texas Ethics Comm'n required to file by electronic transfer unless exempted.

(p) Report due dates: semiannual reports (by July 15 and January 31) and pre-election reports (by 30th and 8th day before each election, and if run-off election, by 8th day before election). Candidates: semiannual reports, pre-election reports if opposed and aggregate contributions exceed $500, and final report when no more reportable activity. Officeholders: pre-appointment of treasurer report (due by 15th day after appointment of campaign treasurer) semi-annual reports (except local officeholders whose aggregate contributions and expenditures do not exceed $500), and final report when no more reportable activity. Specific-purpose political committees: semiannual reports, pre-election reports if supporting opposed candidates and aggregate contributions and expenditures exceed $500 (non-officeholder committees only) or dissolution report (officeholder committees) when no more reportable activity, and termination report when campaign treasurer appointment terminated. General-purpose committees: semiannual reports (all committees) and pre-election reports (non-officeholder committees only) but non-officeholder committee may elect to file alternative monthly reports in lieu of semiannual and pre-election reports (by 5th of month). Additional information must be reported by judicial candidates, holders of judicial office, and specific-purpose committees for supporting or opposing candidate for or assisting a holder of a judicial office. All recipients of large aggregate pre- election direct expenditures between Th 2nd and 2nd day before election: reported within 48 hours.

(q) Candidates in counties and in 1st, 2nd, and 3rd class cities with population of 10,000 or more are required to file pursuant to local ordinance.

(r) Contributions of over $500 received by a candidate or political committee or made by a political committee within 21 days of the general election are to be reported within 24 hours (contribution made) or 48 hours (contribution received). From July 1 to general election, reports of bank deposits during previous 7 days due each Friday.

(s) Independent expenditure of $1,000 or more for a statewide, legislative, or multi-county judicial candidate, or $500 or more for an county-office candidate, single-county judicial candidate, committee supporting or opposing a candidate or an issue on the ballot, or municipal candidate or municipal issue that is made after the 11th day but more than 12 hours before the day of any election must be reported within 24 hours after the expenditure is made or debt for the communication is incurred.

(t) (1) Quarterly Reports. Not later than 10 days after the close of each calendar quarter in which contributions were received or expenditures made in such quarter of over $500. Amounts received or expended in a quarter that are not sufficient to be reported in that quarter are cumulative and reported in the next regular reporting period in which the receipts or expenditures, including the cumulative receipts and expenditures, are $500 or more. (2) Pre-Election Reports. Not later than the 10th day before the date of an election in which a candidate supported or opposed by the committee is running. This report is for the reporting period commencing the day after the close of the preceding reporting period and closing on the 30th day preceding the election. (3) Post-Election Reports. Not later than 30 days after the date of an election in which a candidate supported or opposed by the committee is running. This report is for the reporting period commencing the day after the close of the preceding reporting period and closing on the 20th day after the day of the election. The Supervisor of Elections may waive the requirement for the filing of a quarterly report if a pre-election or post-election report is required to be filed in that quarter; however, if a quarterly report is waived, any period of time in that quarter not included in a pre-election or post-election report must be included in the reporting period of the next regular quarterly filing. For a run-off election, the Supervisor of Elections may adjust the dates of the reporting period and filing deadlines for reports to ensure timely receipt.

**Table 5.10**
## CAMPAIGN FINANCE LAWS: LIMITATIONS ON CONTRIBUTIONS BY ORGANIZATIONS
### (As of December 1999)

| State or other jurisdiction | Corporate | Labor union | Separate segregated fund-political action committee (PAC) | Regulated industry | Political party |
|---|---|---|---|---|---|
| Alabama | Limited to $500 to any candidate, political committee or political party per election. | Unlimited. | Unlimited. | Public utility regulated by Public Service Commission may only contribute through a PAC. Special instructions on soliciting lobbyists. | Unlimited. |
| Alaska | Prohibited. | Prohibited. | Limited to $1,000 per candidate per year. | Prohibited. | Limited to: $100,000 to candidates for Governor/Lt. Gov., $15,000 to candidates for state senate, $10,000 to candidates for state house of reps., $5,000 to all other candidates. |
| Arizona | Prohibited. | Prohibited. | Limited to $760 for statewide candidates and $300 for local candidates; combined total for all PACs is $75,610 statewide and $7,560 local. Committees certified to give at the upper limits are limited to $3,790 statewide and $1,510 local. | Prohibited. | . . . |
| Arkansas | Limited to $1,000 per candidate per election. | Limited to $1,000 per candidate per election. | Limited to $1,000 per candidate per election from approved political action committee. | Limited to $1,000 per candidate per election. | Limited to $2,500 per candidate per election. |
| California | Limits of $1,000 per candidate per special election or special runoff election only. Certain jurisdictions have local limits on contributions to candidates. | Limits of $5,000 for a broad-based political committee; and $2,500 for a political committee  per candidate per special election or special runoff election only. Certain jurisdictions have local limits on contributions to candidates. | Limits of $5,000 for a broad-based political committee; and $2,500 for a political committee per candidate per special election or special runoff election only. Certain jurisdictions have local limits on contributions to candidates. | Limits of $5,000 for a broad-based political committee; $2,500 for a political committee; and $1,000 per person per candidate per special election or special runoff election only. Certain jurisdictions have local limits on contributions to candidates. | Limits of $5,000 per candidate per special election or special runoff election only. |
| Colorado | Prohibited. | Prohibited. | Political committee contributions are subject to aggregate limits of: $400,000 for governor; $80,000 for secretary of state, attorney general, or state treasurer; $20,000 for lt. governor; $15,000 for the state senate; and $10,000 for the house of representatives, state board of education, and regent of the University of Colorado. | Prohibited. | Political committee contributions are subject to aggregate limits of: $400,000 for governor; $80,000 for secretary of state, attorney general, or state treasurer; $20,000 for lt. governor; $15,000 for the state senate; and $10,000 for the house of representatives, state board of education, and regent of the University of Colorado. |

See footnotes at end of table.

# LIMITATIONS ON CONTRIBUTIONS BY ORGANIZATIONS - Continued

| State or other jurisdiction | Corporate | Labor union | Separate segregated fund-political action committee (PAC) | Regulated industry | Political party |
|---|---|---|---|---|---|
| Connecticut | Prohibited. | Prohibited. | Corporate PAC: limited to aggregate of $100,000/election and twice individual limits per candidate. Labor PAC: limited to aggregate of $50,000 per election and same limits per candidate as individuals. | Prohibited. | Unlimited. |
| Delaware | Limited to $1,200 per statewide candidate per election and $600 per nonstatewide candidate per election. | Limited to $1,200 per statewide candidate per election and $600 per nonstatewide candidate per election. | Limited to $1,200 per statewide candidate per election and $600 per nonstatewide candidate per election. | Limited to $1,200 per statewide candidate per election and $600 per nonstatewide candidate per election. | Limited by office |
| Florida | Limited to $500 per candidate per election. | Limited to $500 per candidate per election. | Limited to $500 per candidate per election. | Limited to $500 per candidate. Investment and law firms and their officers, directors, and employees making contributions or engaged in fundraising for gubernatorial or cabinet candidates can't compete for business from Florida Housing Finance Agency. Food outlets and convenience stores cannot solicit or make contributions of more than $100 to a candidate for omm'r of agriculture, and certain officials and employees of that office may not solicit contributions. Similar restrictions apply to the Treasurer and candidates for Treasurer and Treasurer office employees with respect to insurer and affiliated contributions, and the Comptroller and candidates for Comptroller and Comptroller office employees with respect to those licensed or authorized to do business by the comptroller (or applying for the same) and affiliated contributions. | Party may not contribute to candidate for judicial office (enforcement enjoined). Party limited in contributions to candidates receiving public financing. Generally, $50,000 limit, with no more than $25,000 in last 28 days before general election. |
| Georgia | Limited to $5,000 in the aggregate to statewide candidates in an election year, and $1,000 in the aggregate in a non-election year. Limited to $2,000 in the aggregate to general assembly and other candidates in an election year, and $1,000 in the aggregate in a non-election year. | Limited to $5,000 in the aggregate to statewide candidates in an election year, and $1,000 in the aggregate in a non-election year. Limited to $2,000 in the aggregate to general assembly and other candidates in an election year, and $1,000 in the aggregate in a non-election year. | Limited to $5,000 in the aggregate to statewide candidates in an election year, and $1,000 in the aggregate in a non election year. Limited to $2,000 in the aggregate to general assembly and other candidates in an election year, and $1,000 in the aggregate in a non-election year. | Certain public utilities regulated by Public Service Commission may not contribute. Regulated industries may not contribute to candidates nor public officers for the office regulating the entity. | Limited to $5,000 in the aggregate to statewide candidates in an election year, and $1,000 in the aggregate in a non-election year. Limited to $2,000 in the aggregate to general assembly and other candidates in an election year, and $1,000 in the aggregate in a non-election year. |

## LIMITATIONS ON CONTRIBUTIONS BY ORGANIZATIONS - Continued

| State or other jurisdiction | Corporate | Labor union | Separate segregated fund-political action committee (PAC) | Regulated industry | Political party |
|---|---|---|---|---|---|
| Hawaii | Limited to $1,000 in any election period; no limit to ballot issue committees. | Limited to $1,000 in any election period; no limit to ballot issue committes | Limited to $2,000 for two-year offices; $4,000 for four-year offices; $6,000 for statewide offices in any election period; $1,000 to a noncandidate committee; no limit to ballot issue cmtes. | Limited to $2,000 for two-year offices; $4,000 for four-year offices; $6,000 for statewide offices in any election period; $1,000 to a noncandidate committee; no limit to ballot issue committees. Certain state contractors required to file special statements of contributions. Some restrictions on corporations with foreign ties. | Limited to $50,000 for governor; $40,000 for lieutenant governor; $25,000 for partisan mayor and prosecuting attorney; $20,000 for state senate and partisan offices of county council; $15,000 for state representative. |
| Idaho | Limited to $5,000 each for a candidate in a primary or general election, or $1,000 each for other candidates per election . | Limited to $5,000 each for a candidate in a primary or general election, or $1,000 each for other candidates per election . | Limited to $5,000 each for a candidate in a primary or general election, or $1,000 each for other candidates per election . | Limited to $5,000 each for a candidate in a primary or general election, or $1,000 each for other candidates per election . | Limited to $10,000 each for a candidate in a primary or general election, or $2,000 each for other candidates per election. |
| Illinois | Unlimited. | Unlimited. | Unlimited. | Unlimited. | Unlimited. |
| Indiana | Limited to an aggregate of $5,000 for statewide candidates, an aggregate of $5,000 for state party central committees; $6,000 for other offices; $4,000 for state legislative caucuses; and $2,000 for other party committees. | Limited to an aggregate of $5,000 for statewide candidates, an aggregate of $5,000 for state party central committees; $6,000 for other offices; $4,000 for state legislative caucuses; and $2,000 for other party committees. Unlimited if through a union PAC; up to $500 per calendar year if there is no PAC. | Unlimited. | No contributions to state candidates by major lottery vendors or by persons (individuals and entities) holding certain riverboat gaming, parimutuel horse racing and related suppliers licenses. Limited to aggregates of $5,000 for statewide candidates; $5,000 for state party central committees; $6,000 for other offices; $4,000 for state legislative caucuses; and $2,000 for other party committees. | Unlimited. |
| Iowa | Prohibited. | Unlimited if through a union PAC; up to $500 per calendar year if there is no PAC. | Unlimited. | Prohibited for banks, insurance companies, savings & loans and credit unions, statewide notification center, and for not-for-profit organizations involved in riverboat gambling. | Unlimited. |
| Kansas | Limited to $2,000 per statewide candidate per election; $1,000 per election for Senate seats; $500 per election for House seats, local office, district judge, district magistrate judge, district attorney and state school board. | Limited to $2,000 per statewide candidate per election; $1,000 per election for Senate seats; $500 per election for House seats, local office, district judge, district magistrate judge, district attorney and state school board. | Limited to $2,000 per statewide candidate per election; $1,000 per election for Senate seats; $500 per election for House seats, local office, district judge, district magistrate judge, district attorney and state school board. | Limited to $2,000 per statewide candidate per election; $1,000 per election for Senate seats; $500 per election for House seats, local office, district judge, district magistrate judge, district attorney and state school board. | Unlimited in uncontested primaries and general election. |

See footnotes at end of table.

# LIMITATIONS ON CONTRIBUTIONS BY ORGANIZATIONS - Continued

| State or other jurisdiction | Corporate | Labor union | Separate segregated fund-political action committee (PAC) | Regulated industry | Political party |
|---|---|---|---|---|---|
| Kentucky | Prohibited. | Limited to $1,000 per candidate per election. | Limited to $1,000 per candidate per election. | Prohibited. No contributions in violation of law by major lottery venders and lottery auditors. | Limited to $1,000 per slate per election. |
| Louisiana | Limited to $5,000 for major office candidates, $2,500 for district office candidates, and $1,000 for any other offices, per candidate, per election. During any four-year period, may not contribute greater than $100,000 to any political committee other than a candidate committee. | Limited to $5,000 for major office candidates, $2,500 for district office candidates, and $1,000 for any other offices, per candidate, per election. During any four-year period, may not contribute greater than $100,000 to any political committee other than a candidate committee. | Limited to $5,000 for major office candidates, $2,500 for district office candidates, and $1,000 for any other offices, per candidate, per election. During any four-year period, may not contribute greater than $100,000 to any political committee other than a candidate committee. PACs with greater than 250 members who contributed at least $50 to the PAC during the preceding calendar year may give twice the limits. Aggregate limits from all PACs combined that candidates may receive for primary and general elections: $50,000 for major office; $48,195 for district office; $10,000 for other office. | Those associated with certain specified gaming interests may not contribute (although restrictions on certain truck stop owners with video poker machines and video draw poker machine licensees have been ruled unconstitutional). Others limited to $5,000 for major office candidates, $2,500 for district office candidates, and $1,000 for any other offices, per candidate, per election. | Unlimited. |
| Maine | Limited to $500 per gubernatorial candidate per election and $250 per other candidates per election. | Limited to $500 per gubernatorial candidate per election and $250 per other candidates per election. | Limited to $500 per gubernatorial candidate per election and $250 per other candidates per election. | Limited to $500 per gubernatorial candidate per election and $250 per other candidates per election. | Limited to $5,000 per candidate per election. |
| Maryland | Limited to an aggregate of $10,000 per four-year election cycle and $4,000 per candidate or political committee. | Limited to an aggregate of $10,000 per four-year election cycle and $4,000 per candidate or political committee. | Limited to an aggregate of $6,000 per four-year election cycle per candidate or political committee. | Limited to an aggregate of $10,000 per four-year election cycle and $4,000 per candidate or political committee. | Unlimited. |
| Massachusetts | Prohibited. | Limited to $500 per candidate per year if exceed aggregate contributions of $15,000 or 10% of gross revenues, whichever is less. | Limited to $500 per candidate, with aggregate annual limits depending upon office sought. | Prohibited. If business or corporation or professional corporation. Registered lobbyists limited to $200 per candidate per year. | State party committees limited to contributions of not more than $3,000 per candidate, per year. In-kind contributions are not limited. |
| Michigan | Prohibited for candidate elections (except from a separate segregated fund). | Prohibited for candidate elections (except from a separate segregated fund). | Limited to $3,400 for a statewide office, $1,000 for state Senate and $500 for state representative candidates per election cycle. A PAC that qualifies as an independent committee may contribute ten times these amounts. Lawyer PAC limited to $100 per judicial candidate. | Prohibited except through a PAC. Domestic dependent sovereign( Indian tribe) may not contribute directly. Certain individuals and entities with casino and casino supplier interest prohibited. | State central: $68,000 for governor/ lt. governor; $10,000 for Senate, $5,000 for House, $68,000 for all other state elective offices. |

# LIMITATIONS ON CONTRIBUTIONS BY ORGANIZATIONS - Continued

| State or other jurisdiction | Corporate | Labor union | Separate segregated fund- political action committee (PAC) | Regulated industry | Political party |
|---|---|---|---|---|---|
| Minnesota | Prohibited. | From a political fund: Governor/lt. governor: limited to $2,000 per election year and $500 in a non-election year. Attorney general: limited to $1,000 per election year and $200 in a non-election year. Other statewide offices: limited to $500 per election year and $100 in a non-election year. State senate/state representative: limited to $500 per election year and $100 in a non-election year. | Governor/lt. governor: limited to $2,000 per election year and $500 in a non-election year. Attorney general: limited to $1,000 per election year and $200 in a non-election year. Other statewide offices: limited to $500 per election year and $100 in a non-election year. State Senate/state representative: limited to $500 per election year and $100 in a non-election year. | Prohibited; including for insurance companies. | Governor/lt. governor: limited to $20,000 per election year and $5,000 in a non-election year. Attorney general: limited to $10,000 per election year and $2,000 in a non-election year. Other statewide offices: limited to $5,000 per election year and $1,000 in a non-election year. State Senate/state representative: limited to $5,000 per election year and $1,000 in a non-election year. |
| Mississippi | Limited to $1,000 per candidate per election. | Unlimited | Unlimited. | Prohibited for regulated industries, companies, corporations, stock holders, their agents or representatives with respect to campaigns for Public Service Commissioner. | Unlimited; except to nonpartisan judicial candidates. |
| Missouri | Unlimited. | Unlimited. | Unlimited. Pending a decision by the U.S. Supreme Court. | Unlimited. | Unlimited, pending a decision by the U.S. Supreme Court. |
| Montana | Prohibited, except for ballot issues. | As an independent committee, limited for each contested primary and general election in a campaign to $400 for governor/lieutenant governor, $200 for other statewide candidates, and $100 for all other candidates. | As an independent committee, limited for each contested primary and general election in a campaign to $400 for governor/lieutenant governor, $200 for other statewide candidates, and $100 for all other candidates. | Prohibited. | All political committees of a political party on the ballot at most recent gubernatorial election, limited for all elections in a campaign to aggregate of $15,000 for governor/lt. governor, $5,000 for other statewide candidates, $2,000 for public service commissioner, $800 for state senator, and $500 for other candidates. Contributions to judicial candidates prohibited. |

See footnotes at end of table.

# LIMITATIONS ON CONTRIBUTIONS BY ORGANIZATIONS - Continued

| State or other jurisdiction | Corporate | Labor union | Separate segregated fund-political action committee (PAC) | Regulated industry | Political party |
|---|---|---|---|---|---|
| Nebraska | Legislative candidates and candidates for other state offices if designated as eligible for public funding during an election period: limited to maximum amount of aggregate contributions in election period that may be accepted from independent committees; businesses (including corporations); labor unions; industry, trade, or professional associations; and political parties: Gov—$750,000; Sec'y of State, Treas, Att'y Gen'l, Auditor of Public Acc'ts— 75,000; Public Service Commission, Board of Regents of Univ. of Nebraska & State Board of Education $25,000; Legislature—$36,500. | Legislative candidates and candidates for other state offices if designated as eligible for public funding during an election period: limited to maximum amount of aggregate contributions in election period that may be accepted from independent committees; businesses (including corporations); labor unions; industry, trade, or professional associations; and political parties: Gov—$750,000; Sec'y of State, Treas, Att'y Gen'l, Auditor of Public Acc'ts— 75,000; Public Service Commission, Board of Regents of Univ. of Nebraska & State Board of Education $25,000; Legislature—$36,500. | Legislative candidates and candidates for other state offices if designated as eligible for public funding during an election period: limited to maximum amount of aggregate contributions in election period that may be accepted from independent committees; businesses (including corporations); labor unions; industry, trade, or professional associations; and political parties: Gov— $750,000; Sec'y of State, Treas, Att'y Gen'l, Auditor of Public Acc'ts— 75,000; Public Service Commission, Board of Regents of Univ. of Nebraska & State Board of Education— $25,000; Legislature—$36,500. | Legislative candidates and candidates for other state offices if designated as eligible or public funding during an election period: limited to maximum amount of aggregate contributions in election period that may be accepted from independent committees; businesses (including corporations); labor unions; industry, trade, or professional associations; and political parties: Gov— $750,000; Sec'y of State, Treas, Att'y Gen'l, Auditor of Public Acc'ts— 75,000; Public Service Commission, Board of Regents of Univ. of Nebraska & State Board of Education— $25,000; Legislature—$36,500. | Legislative candidates and candidates for other state offices if designated as eligible or public funding during an election period: limited to maximum amount of aggregate contributions in election period that may be accepted from independent committees; businesses (including corporations); labor unions; industry, trade, or professional associations; and political parties: Gov— $750,000; Sec'y of State, Treas, Att'y Gen'l, Auditor of Public Acc'ts— 75,000; Public Service Commission, Board of Regents of Univ. of Nebraska & State Board of Education— $25,000; Legislature—$36,500. |
| Nevada | Any candidate: $5,000 per primary and general election. | Any candidate: $5,000 per primary and general election. | Any candidate: $5,000 per primary and general election. | Any candidate: $5,000 per primary and general election. | Any candidate: $5,000 per each primary and general election; otherwise unlimited. |
| New Hampshire | Pending final outcome of federal-court litigation, limited to $5,000 per candidate, per election, except limited to $1,000 per election if to candidate or political committee working on behalf of a candidate who does not voluntarily agree to limit campaign expenditures. | Prohibited. | Limited to $1,000 per election if to candidate or political committee working on behalf of a candidate who does not voluntarily agree to limit campaign expenditures; otherwise unlimited. | Prohibited. | Political party political committee limited to $1,000 per election if to candidate or political committee working on behalf of a candidate who does not voluntarily agree to limit campaign expenditures; otherwise unlimited. |
| New Jersey | Limited to $1,800 per non-governor candidate per primary or general election; $30,000 to political party state committee or county committee or legislative leadership committee per year; $5,900 to municipal party committee per year. Unlimited to political committee or continuing political committee. | Limited to $1,800 per non-governor candidate per primary or general election; $30,000 to political party state committee or county committee or legislative leadership committee per year; $5,900 to municipal party committee per year. Unlimited to political committee or continuing political committee. | Limited to $5,900 per non-governor candidate per primary or general election; or general election; $30,000 to political party state committee or county committee or legislative leadership committee per year; $5,900 to municipal party committee per year. $5,900 per political committee per primary or general election, and $5,900 per continuing political committee per year. | Prohibited for certain bank, utility, and insurance corporations or associations; governor candidate per primary or general election: $2,100 per governor candidate per primary or general election; $30,000 to political party state committee or county committee or legislative leadership committee per year; $5,900 to municipal party committee per year. Unlimited to political committee or continuing political committee. | Political party state committee limited to $2,100 per candidate for governor unlimited for candidates for non- governor office. County and municipal committees may not contribute to candidate for governor; also limited in contributions to municipal party committee ($5,000 per year), candidates in other counties, and candidates in certain legislative districts containing county of county committee. Political party national committee limited to $59,000 per year to state party committee; otherwise, subject to PAC limits. |

# LIMITATIONS ON CONTRIBUTIONS BY ORGANIZATIONS - Continued

| State or other jurisdiction | Corporate | Labor union | Separate segregated fund-political action committee (PAC) | Regulated industry | Political party |
|---|---|---|---|---|---|
| New Mexico | Unlimited. | Unlimited. | Unlimited. | Unlimited. Solicitation by state regulatory office or candidate for the office of directly regulated entity or persons prohibited if charges for service set by or license issued by the regulatory office. | Unlimited. |
| New York | Same maximum aggregate limit per office per election and per party committee or constituted committee per calendar year as individuals, but limited to an aggregate of $5,000 in political contributions and expenditures per calendar year. | Same maximum aggregate limit per office per election and per party committee or constituted committee per calendar year as individuals. | Same maximum aggregate limit per office per election and per party committee or constituted committee per calendar year as individuals. | Same maximum aggregate limit per office per election and per party committee or constituted committee per calendar year as individuals, and if a corporation, also limited to an aggregate of $5,000 in contributions and expenditures per calendar year. | Prohibited in primary, unlimited in general election. |
| North Carolina | Prohibited, except independent, non-profit corporation that promotes social, educational, or political ideas, which are limited to $4,000 per candidate campaign or other political committee per primary, second primary, and general election. | Prohibited. | Limited to $4,000 per candidate campaign or other political committee per primary, second primary, and general election. | Prohibited. | Unlimited. |
| North Dakota | Prohibited. | Prohibited. | Unlimited. | Prohibited. | Unlimited. |
| Ohio | Prohibited, except for nonpartisan activities, gift to party building fund, sponsoring corporation's PAC, or involvement with ballot issue. | Prohibited, except for nonpartisan activities, gift to party building fund, sponsoring labor union's PAC, or involvement with ballot issue. | PACs or political contributing entities limited to $2,500 to campaign committee of statewide or general assembly candidate in primary or general election; $5,000 to county political party for the party's state candidate fund or to legislative campaign fund in calendar year; $16,000 to state political party for the party's state candidate fund in calendar year; and $2,500 to another political action committee or political contributing entity, except political action committee or entity affiliated with contributing committee, in calendar year. | Prohibited, except for nonpartisan activities, gift to party building fund, sponsoring corporation's PAC, or involvement with ballot issue. | Political party (national, state, and county): limited to $2,500 to PAC or political contributing entity in a calendar year. State candidate fund of state political party: cash transfers limited to $523,000 to designated state campaign committee of statewide candidate in primary or general election; $104,500 to designated state campaign committee of state senator candidate in primary or general election; and $52,000 to designated state campaign committee of state representative candidate in primary or general election; unlimited to state candidate fund of state or county political party and legislative campaign fund. (a) |

See footnotes at end of table.

## LIMITATIONS ON CONTRIBUTIONS BY ORGANIZATIONS - Continued

| State or other jurisdiction | Corporate | Labor union | Separate segregated fund-political action committee (PAC) | Regulated industry | Political party |
|---|---|---|---|---|---|
| Oklahoma | Prohibited, except to ballot measure campaign or PAC used for political purposes by corporation. | Limited per person or family to $5,000 to a political party committee or political action committee in a calendar year, $5,000 to a candidate/candidate committee for state office or municipal office in a municipality of 250,000 or more, for election campaign, and $1,000 to any other local candidate/candidate committee for election campaign. | Limited per person or family to $5,000 to a political party committee or political action committee in a calendar year, $5,000 to a candidate/candidate committee for state office or municipal office in a municipality of 250,000 or more, for election campaign, and $1,000 to any other local candidate/candidate committee for election campaign. | Prohibited. | Limited to $5,000 to a political party or organization in a calendar year, $5,000 to a candidate/ candidate committee for state office, county office in a county of 250,000 or more, or municipal office in a municipality of 250,000 or more, and $1,000 to any other office candidate/candidate committee. |
| Oregon | Unlimited. | Unlimited. | Unlimited. | Unlimited. | Unlimited. |
| Pennsylvania | Prohibited. | Prohibited. | Prohibited. | Prohibited. | Unlimited. |
| Rhode Island | Prohibited. | Prohibited. | $1,000 per recipient per calendar year and maximum of $25,000 for all recipients, except per recipient limit doubles to $2,000 if recipient is a candidate for general office who has qualified for public funding, and an additional $10,000 may be contributed to a political party committee for organizational and party-building activities. Limited to $3,500 per statewide candidate per election; $1,000 per other candidate per election; $3,500 per committee per calendar year. | Prohibited. | $25,000 to any one party candidate (no limit on allowable in-kind contributions); unlimited for aggregate contributions to all party candidates; $10,000 to a party committee for organizational and party-building activities. |
| South Carolina | Limited to $3,500 per statewide candidate per election; $1,000 per other candidate per election; $3,500 per committee per calendar year. Corporation or corporate committee may solicit contributions to the corporation or corporate committee only from shareholders, employees, and families; however, a non-profit corporation or its committee may solicit the general public for contributions for ballot measures. | Limited to $3,500 per statewide candidate per election; $1,000 per other candidate per election; $3,500 per committee per calendar year. Organization or organization committee may solicit contributions to the organization only from members and families. | Limited to $3,500 per statewide candidate per election; $1,000 per other candidate per election; $3,500 per committee per calendar year. | Limited to $3,500 per statewide candidate per election; $1,000 per other candidate per election; $3,500 per committee per calendar year. Public utility may not include contributions or expenditures to influence election or operate PAC in its operating expenses. Lobbyist and contractors may not contribute. | Limited to $50,000 per statewide candidate per election, $5,000 per other candidate per election. |

# LIMITATIONS ON CONTRIBUTIONS BY ORGANIZATIONS - Continued

| State or other jurisdiction | Corporate | Labor union | Separate segregated fund-political action committee (PAC) | Regulated industry | Political party |
|---|---|---|---|---|---|
| **South Dakota** | Prohibited. | Prohibited if union is corporation; permitted if an association but not out of dues or treasury funds. | Unlimited. | Prohibited. | Unlimited. |
| **Tennessee** | Prohibited. | Limited to $2,500 for state office candidate and $1,000 for other candidate in aggregate per election. Limited to $1,000 for judicial candidate. | Limited to $7,500 for statewide office or state senate and $5,000 for other office in the aggregate per election. Candidate for statewide office limited to 50 percent of total contributions in aggregate from committees. Candidates for other office limited to $75,000 in aggregate from all committees. Limited to $1,000 for judicial candidate. Prohibited within 10 days before election. | Prohibited; public service commissioner or candidate for that office may not accept a contribution from a regulated party during contested case. | Unlimited, except to $1,000 for judicial candidate. |
| **Texas** | Unlimited to political parties, except during 60 days before election, and to political committees to support or oppose a measure. | Unlimited to political parties, except during 60 days before election, and to political committees to support or oppose a measure. | Unlimited, but may not be made from mandatory assessments from corporation employees or labor organization members. Contributions from an out-of-state political committee are subject to special notification and reporting requirements. | Unlimited to political parties, except during 60 days before election, and to political committees to support or oppose a measure. | Unlimited. |
| **Utah** | Unlimited, except for insurers. | Unlimited. | Unlimited. | Insurers prohibited from making political contributions, if they do not have security surplus. | Unlimited. |
| **Vermont** | Contributions from one source limited in 2-year general election cycle to candidate for governor, lieutenant governor, secretary of state, state treasurer, auditor of accounts, or attorney general—$400; candidate for state senator or county office—$300; candidate for state representative or local office—$200; and political committee (other than a political committee of a candidate) or political party—$2,000. | Contributions from one source limited in 2-year general election cycle to candidate for governor, lieutenant governor, secretary of state, state treasurer, auditor of accounts, or attorney general—$400; candidate for state senator or county office—$300; candidate for state representative or local office—$200; and political committee (other than a political committee of a candidate) or political party—$2,000. | Contributions from one source limited in 2-year general election cycle to candidate for governor, lieutenant governor, secretary of state, state treasurer, auditor of accounts, or attorney general—$400; candidate for state senator or county office—$300; candidate for state representative or local office—$200; and political committee (other than a political committee of a candidate) or political party—$2,000. | Contributions from one source limited in 2-year general election cycle to candidate for governor, lieutenant governor, secretary of state, state treasurer, auditor of accounts, or attorney general—$400; candidate for state senator or county office—$300; candidate for state representative or local office—$200; and political committee (other than a political committee of a candidate) or political party—$2,000. | Contributions from one source limited in 2-year general election cycle to candidate for governor, lieutenant governor, secretary of state, state treasurer, auditor of accounts, or attorney general—$400; candidate for state senator or county office—$300; candidate for state representative or local office—$200; and political committee (other than a political committee of a candidate) or political party—$2,000. |
| **Virginia** | Unlimited. | Unlimited. | Unlimited. | Pari-mutuel betting licensees cannot contribute to candidates. | Unlimited. |

See footnotes at end of table.

# LIMITATIONS ON CONTRIBUTIONS BY ORGANIZATIONS - Continued

| State or other jurisdiction | Corporate | Labor union | Separate segregated fund-political action committee (PAC) | Regulated industry | Political party |
|---|---|---|---|---|---|
| Washington | Aggregate contributions per election to state office candidates limited to $600 for state legislative office candidate and $1,200 for state executive office candidate. Aggregate contributions within 21 days of a general election may not exceed $5,000 for a campaign for other than statewide office. Aggregate contributions in calendar year to each political party state organization and to each major party county central committee or legislative district committee limited to $3,000 and to a caucus of the state legislature limited to $600. | Aggregate contributions per election to state office candidates limited to $600 for state legislative office candidate and $1,200 for state executive office candidate. Aggregate contributions within 21 days of a general election may not exceed $5,000 for a campaign for other than statewide office. Aggregate contributions in calendar year to each political party state organization and to each major party county central committee or legislative district committee limited to $3,000 and to a caucus of the state legislature limited to $600. Labor organization may not make contributions from agency shop fees paid by non-member's authorization. | Aggregate contributions per election to state office candidates limited to $600 for state legislative office candidate and $1,200 for state executive office candidate. Aggregate contributions within 21 days of a general election may not exceed $5,000 for a campaign for other than statewide office. Aggregate contributions in calendar year to each political party state organization and to each major party county central committee or legislative district committee limited to $3,000 and to a caucus of the state legislature limited to $600. | Aggregate contributions per election to state office candidates limited to $600 for state legislative office candidate and $1,200 for state executive office candidate. Aggregate contributions within 21 days of a general election may not exceed $5,000 for a campaign for other than statewide office. Aggregate contributions in calendar year to each political party state organization and to each major party county central committee or legislative district committee limited to $3,000 and to a caucus of the state legislature limited to $600. Insurer or fraternal benefit may not contribute to insurance commissioner candidate. | Aggregate contributions per election cycle to state office candidates by a political party or a caucus of the state legislature are limited to 60¢ per voter in district (state legislative office candidate) or state (state executive office candidate) and by a major party county central committee or legislative district committee limited to 30¢ per voter in district (state legislative office candidate) or state (state executive office candidate). County central committees and legislative district committees may contribute for only those state legislative offices that include their jurisdiction. Aggregate contributions made by a single contributor other than a major political party state organization within 21 days of a general election may not exceed $50,000 for a statewide office campaign or $5,000 for any other campaign. |
| West Virginia | Prohibited. | Limited to $1,000 per candidate, per primary or general election. | Limited to $1,000 per candidate, per primary or general election. | Prohibited. | Limited to $1,000 per candidate, per primary or general election, and $1,000 to state party executive committee per calendar year. National party committee may contribute $50,000 per year to state party executive committee or to state party legislative caucus political committee. |

# LIMITATIONS ON CONTRIBUTIONS BY ORGANIZATIONS - Continued

| State or other jurisdiction | Corporate | Labor union | Separate segregated fund-political action committee (PAC) | Regulated industry | Political party |
|---|---|---|---|---|---|
| **Wisconsin** | Prohibited except concerning a referendum. | Prohibited if labor union is a chapter 185 association, except concerning a referendum. | Limited to 4 percent of authorized disbursement level for statewide office candidate, $1,000 for state senator, $500 for assembly representative, varying amounts for other offices, and $6,000 in a calendar year for a political party. | Prohibited; also may not offer special privileges to candidates, political committees, and individuals making independent disbursements. | Unlimited; however, a political party or legislative campaign committee that files a statement under oath concerning independent candidate-related disbursements becomes subject to the limits for PACs. A candidate may not receive more than 65 percent of authorized disbursement level from all political committees. Political party may not receive more than $150,000 in any biennium from all political committees other than political party and legislative campaign committees. Contributions from committees (other than political party or legislative campaign committees) limited to $6,000 in a calendar year. |
| **Wyoming** | Prohibited for candidates and political parties. | Prohibited for candidates and political parties. | Unlimited. | Prohibited for candidates and political parties. | Prohibited in party's primary elections; otherwise unlimited. |
| **Dist. of Columbia** | Limited to an aggregate of $8,500 per election and $2,000 for mayor; $1,500 for council chair or councilmember-at-large; $500 for council member from a district or board of education member at-large; $200 for board of education member from a district or party official; and $25 for a neighborhood advisory committee member. | Limited to an aggregate of $8,500 per election and $2,000 for mayor; $1,500 for council chair or councilmember-at-large; $500 for council member from a district or board of education member at-large; $200 for board of education member from a district or party official; and $25 for a neighborhood advisory committee member. | Limited to an aggregate of $8,500 per election and $2,000 for mayor; $1,500 for council chair or councilmember-at-large; $500 for council member from a district or board of education member at-large; $200 for board of education member from a district or party official; and $25 for a neighborhood advisory committee member. | Limited to an aggregate of $8,500 per election and $2,000 for mayor; $1,500 for council chair or councilmember-at-large; $500 for council member from a district or board of education member at-large; $200 for board of education member from a district or party official; and $25 for a neighborhood advisory committee member. | Limited to maximum of $5,000 to any one political committee in any one election. |
| **American Samoa** | Limited to no more than $250 in aggregate to a candidate, committee, or party. | Limited to no more than $250 in aggregate to a candidate, committee, or party. | Limited to no more than $250 in aggregate to a candidate, committee, or party. | Limited to no more than $250 in aggregate to a candidate, committee, or party. | Limited to no more than $250 in aggregate to a candidate, committee, or party. |
| **Guam** | Limited to no more than $1,000 per candidate or political party, with a per event limit applicable. | Prohibited. | Limited to no more than $1,000 per candidate or political party. | Banks may not contribute. | Limited to no more than $1,000 per candidate or political party. |

See footnotes at end of table.

# LIMITATIONS ON CONTRIBUTIONS BY ORGANIZATIONS - Continued

| State or other jurisdiction | Corporate | Labor union | Separate segregated fund-political action committee (PAC) | Regulated industry | Political party |
|---|---|---|---|---|---|
| Northern Marianas ......... | No Restriction. | No Restriction. | No Restriction. | No Restriction. | No restriction. |
| Puerto Rico ................... | (1) In a non-election year: (a) to a candidate of a political party, a municipal or central directing body of a party, or an independent candidate—up to $1,000 per year and (b) to all candidates and parties— maximum total annual amount of $5,000; (2) in an election year: (a) to a candidate for governor, a political party, or a combination of both—$2,500 per year, (b) to any other candidate—$1,000 per year but not to exceed $2,500 per year for all other candidates, (c) to an independent group or committee that supports a candidate or political party—$500 per year, and (d) to all independent committees or candidates maximum total annual amount of $5,000; and (3) in a primary election: to any candidate—$200. | (1) In a non-election year: (a) to a candidate of a political party, a municipal or central directing body of a party, or an independent candidate—up to $1,000 per year and (b) to all candidates and parties— maximum total annual amount of $5,000; (2) in an election year: (a) to a candidate for governor, a political party, or a combination of both—$2,500 per year, (b) to any other candidate—$1,000 per year but not to exceed $2,500 per year for all other candidates, (c) to an independent group or committee that supports a candidate or political party—$500 per year, and (d) to all independent committees or candidates—maximum total annual amount of $5,000; and (3) in a primary election: to any candidate—$200. | (1) In a non-election year: (a) to a candidate of a political party, a municipal or central directing body of a party, or an independent candidate—up to $1,000 per year and (b) to all candidates and parties— maximum total annual amount of $5,000; (2) in an election year: (a) to a candidate for governor, a political party, or a combination of both—$2,500 per year, (b) to any other candidate—$1,000 per year but not to exceed $2,500 per year for all other candidates, (c) to an independent group or committee that supports a candidate or political party—$500 per year, and (d) to all independent committees or candidates—maximum total annual amount of $5,000; and (3) in a primary election: to any candidate—$200. | Banks may not contribute. | Municipal and district political bodies may not contribute in excess of specified contribution limits to their party's general funds. |
| U.S. Virgin Islands.......... | Limited to $1,000 in the aggregate per election to a candidate or candidate's authorized political committee (or, if made to a multicandidate committee, $1,000 multiplied by the number of candidates). | Limited to $1,000 in the aggregate per election to a candidate or candidate's authorized political committee (or, if made to a multicandidate committee, $1,000 multiplied by the number of candidates). | Limited to $1,000 in the aggregate per election to a candidate or candidate's authorized political committee (or, if made to a multicandidate committee, $1,000 multiplied by the number of candidates). | Limited to $1,000 in the aggregate per election to a candidate or candidate's authorized political committee (or, if made to a multicandidate committee, $1,000 multiplied by the number of candidates). | Limited to $1,000 in the aggregate per election to a candidate or candidate's authorized political committee (or, if made to a multicandidate committee, $1,000 multiplied by the number of candidates). |

County political party with no state candidate fund and located in a county under 150,000 population: limited to $2,500 from other accounts to designated state campaign committee in primary or general election. Legislative campaign fund: limited to $52,000 in primary and $104,500 in general election to designated state campaign committee of state senator candidate and $26,500 in a primary and $52,000 in general election to designated state campaign committee of state representative candidate; unlimited to state candidate fund of a state or local political party. Prohibited to another legislative campaign fund or PAC or political contributing entity.

*Source:* Edward D. Feigenbaum, J.D. and James A. Palmer, J.D., INGroup, Noblesville, Indiana, March 2000; Finance Law 2000: A Summary of State Campaign Finance Laws with Quick Reference Charts.

*Note:* For detailed legal requirements, state statutes should be consulted.

(a) State candidate fund of county political party: cash transfers limited to $2,500 to campaign committee of a statewide or general assembly candidate not a designated state campaign in primary or general election; cash transfers limited to $523,000 to designated state campaign committee of statewide candidate in primary or general election; $104,500 to designated state campaign committee of state senator candidate in primary or general election; and $52,000 to designated state campaign committee of state representative candidate in primary or general election.

**Table 5.11**

**CAMPAIGN FINANCE LAWS: LIMITATIONS ON CONTRIBUTIONS BY INDIVIDUALS**
**(As of December 1999)**

| State or other jurisdiction | Individual | Candidate | Government employees | Anonymous or in name of another |
|---|---|---|---|---|
| Alabama | Unlimited. | Unlimited. | ... | Anonymous or in name of another Contribution in the name of another prohibited. |
| Alaska | Limited to $500 per office per year. | Candidate: unlimited, except must not exceed $5,000 within 33 days before election; caps also exist on how much a candidate may repay personal loans. Family: limited to $500 per office per year. | Contribution may not be required of state employees. Judges and judicial office candidates may not contribute. | Prohibited. |
| Arizona | Limited to $760 per statewide candidate; $300 per other offices; and a maximum of $2,820 in total contributions per calendar year. | Candidate: Unlimited, but may trigger new limits for opponent. Family: Certain family members may contribute under candidate's unlimited aegis. | ... | Prohibited. |
| Arkansas | Limited to $1,000 per candidate per election. | Candidate: unlimited. Family : Limited to $1,000 per candidate per election. | Certain state employees are prohibited from soliciting, as are certain judges (for campaigns other than their own). Contribution may not be required of state employees. | Anonymous contribution must be less than $50 per year. Contribution in the name of another prohibited. |
| California | Limits of $1,000 per person per candidate per special election or special runoff election only. Certain jurisdictions have local limits on contributions to candidates. | Candidate: Generally unlimited. Family: Limits of $1,000 per person per candidate per special election or special runoff election only. Certain jurisdictions have local limits on contributions to candidates. | Local agency employees may not solicit employees of agency except incidentally through a large solicitation. | Anonymous contribution must not exceed $100. Contribution in the name of another prohibited. |
| Colorado | Unlimited (as a result of court ruling). | Candidates: contributions by candidates abiding by voluntary campaign spending limits to their own campaigns are treated as political committee contributions and are subject to aggregate limits of: $400,000 for governor; $80,000 for secretary of state, attorney general, or state treasurer; $20,000 for lt. governor; $15,000 for the state senate; and $10,000 for the house of representatives, state board of education, and regent of the University of Colorado. | Judges and employees subject to their direction and control should not solicit funds for a political organization or candidate. Judges and employees subject to their direction and control should not pay an assessment or contribute to apolitical organization or candidate (other than the specific judicial candidate). | Contributions in the name of another are prohibited. Earmarking of contributions through political parties also prohibited. |
| Connecticut | Limit to an aggregate of $15,000 per election and $2,500 for governor; $1,500 for other statewide office; $1,000 for sheriff or local chief executive; $500 for state senate, or probate judge; $250 for state representative or other local office; and $5,000 per year to state party. | Candidates: unlimited Family : limited to aggregate of $15,000 per election, and $2,500 for governor; $1,500 for other statewide office; $1,000 for sheriff or local chief executive; $500 for state senate, or pro-bate judge; $250 for state representative or other local offices; and $5,000 per year to state party. | State department heads and deputies may not solicit. | Anonymous contribution must be less than $15. Contributions in the name of another are prohibited. |

See footnotes at end of table.

# LIMITATIONS ON CONTRIBUTIONS BY INDIVIDUALS — Continued

| State or other jurisdiction | Individual | Candidate | Government employees | Anonymous or in name of another |
|---|---|---|---|---|
| Delaware | Limited to $1,200 per statewide candidate per election and $600 per non-statewide candidate per election. | Limited to $1,200 per statewide candidate per election and $600 per non-statewide candidate per election. | ... | Anonymous or in name of another prohibited. |
| Florida | Limited to $500 per candidate per election. Unemancipated child under 18 limited to $100 per candidate per election. Some restrictions on judges and judicial personnel. | Unlimited, except candidates accepting public financing are limited to $25,000 to their own campaigns. Some restrictions on candidates for judge. Family: each family member limited to $500 per candidate per election. | Solicitation generally prohibited for state employees during working hours, or within a building owned by a state entity. Judges may not solicit contributions. Judges should not make contributions. | Prohibited. |
| Georgia | Limited to $5,000 in the aggregate to statewide candidates in an election year, and $1,000 in the aggregate in a non-election year. Limited to $2,000 in the aggregate to general assembly and other candidates in an election year, and $1,000 in the aggregate in a non-election year. | Candidate: unlimited. Spouse and children: unlimited. Other family members: same as individual limits. | Prohibited for state employees to coerce another state employee. | Prohibited. |
| Hawaii | Limited to $2,000 for two-year offices; $4,000 for four-year offices; $6,000 for statewide offices in an election period; $50,000 to a political party; $1,000 to a noncandidate committee; no limit to ballot issue committees. | Limited to $50,000, including the candidate's family, in any election period. This figure includes loans from the candidate's immediate family members to the candidate. | Solicitation of contributions prohibited. Contributions to other employees are prohibited. | Prohibited. |
| Idaho | Limited to $5,000 each for a candidate in a primary or general election, or $1,000 each for other candidates perelection. | Candidates unlimited Family limited to $5,000 each for a candidate in a primary or general election, or $1,000 each for other candidates per election. | Prohibited for state employee to coerce another state employee. Contribution permitted. | Anonymous contribution must be $50 or less. Contribution in the name of another prohibited. |
| Illinois | Unlimited, but generally prohibited for judicial candidates and judicial employees. | Unlimited, but generally prohibited for judicial candidates and judicial employees. | Solicitation and contribution by employees prohibited under certain circumstances; for certain specified state and local employees, including contributions from all state employees under the governor's control to the governor's campaign committee. Generally prohibited for judges and judicial employees. | Prohibited. |

# LIMITATIONS ON CONTRIBUTIONS BY INDIVIDUALS — Continued

| State or other jurisdiction | Individual | Candidate | Government employees | Anonymous or in name of another |
|---|---|---|---|---|
| **Indiana** | Unlimited, except foreign nationals may not contribute to public question campaigns. | Unlimited. | Certain law enforcement personnel/ firefighters may not solicit on duty or in uniform; state employees cannot solicit (1) when on duty, (2) acting in official capacity, (3) from those employees known to have a business relationship with the employee's agency, and (4) from state employees directly supervised by the employee. Judges may not personally solicit. Contribution may not be required. Judges should not contribute, and their employees, are subject to the same constraints. | Contribution in the name of another prohibited. |
| **Iowa** | Unlimited. | Unlimited. | Prohibited for state employee to coerce another state employee. Prohibited for judges and certain judicial employees. | Prohibited. |
| **Kansas** | Limited to $2,000 per statewide candidate per election; $1,000 per election for senate seats; $500 per election for house seats, local office, district judge, district magistrate judge, district attorney, and state school board. | Candidate: unlimited Family: limited to $2,000 per statewide candidate per election; $1,000 per election for senate seats; $500 per election for house seats and local office, district judge, district magistrate judge, district attorney, and state school board. | Certain employees cannot compel contributions. | Anonymous contribution must be $10 or less, and may not exceed an aggregate of: $1,000 per election for statewide candidates; $500 per senate candidates; and $250 per election for all other candidates. Contribution in the name of another prohibited. |
| **Kentucky** | Limited to $500 per candidate per election (lower limits for school board), $500 to a political issues committee, $1,500 to PAC, and $2,500 to all state/local political parties. Minors limited to $100. No more than $1,500 in total contributions to all permanent committees and contributing organizations in any year (but unlimited to inaugural committees). | Candidates: direct contributions are unlimited. Loans are limited to $50,000 per joint slate for governor and lt. governor; $25,000 per statewide candidate; and $10,000 for other candidates. Family: limited to $1,000 per candidate per election. Minors limited to $100. | Solicitations are generally prohibited except as part of a larger solicitation not specifically targeted at state employees. Assessments and coercion of state employees prohibited. Prohibited for judges. May not be required of state employees. School district employees may not contribute to school board candidates in their districts. | Anonymous contribution must be $50 or less with any excess aggregating more than $1,000 escheating to the commonwealth. Contribution in the name of another prohibited. (note: court held this statute to be unconstitutional ). |
| **Louisiana** | Limited to $5,000 for major office candidates, $2,500 for district office candidates, and $1,000 for any other offices, per candidate, per election. During any four-year period, may not contribute more than $100,000 to any political committee other than a candidate committee. | Candidate: unlimited. Family: limited to $5,000 for major office candidates, $2,500 for district office candidates, and $1,000 for any other offices, per candidate, per election. During any 4-year period, may not contribute more than $100,000 to any political committee other than a candidate committee. | Solicitation and contribution generally prohibited. | Prohibited. |

See footnotes at end of table.

# LIMITATIONS ON CONTRIBUTIONS BY INDIVIDUALS — Continued

| State or other jurisdiction | Individual | Candidate | Government employees | Anonymous or in name of another |
|---|---|---|---|---|
| Maine | Limited to an aggregate of $25,000 in a calendar year and $500 per gubernatorial candidate per election and $250 per other candidates per election. Special limits on public finance-qualifying (seed) contributions. | Candidate: unlimited. Spouse: unlimited. | Prohibited for state employee to coerce another state employee. | Anonymous contribution prohibited over $10. Contribution in the name of another prohibited. |
| Maryland | Limited to an aggregate of $10,000 per 4-year election cycle and $4,000 per candidate or political committee. | Candidate: unlimited. Spouse: unlimited. | Contribution may not be required. | Prohibited. |
| Massachusetts | Limited to $500 per candidate per year, with an aggregate limit of $12,500 per year. Minors limited to $25 per year. | Candidate: unlimited, except for loans, which are limited depending upon office sought. Family: limited to $500 per candidate per year. Minors limited to $25 per year. | Solicitation generally prohibited. Contribution may not be required. | Prohibited. |
| Michigan | Limited to $3,400 for a statewide office, $1,000 for state senate, and $500 for state representative candidates per election cycle; lawyers limited to $100 for candidate for judicial office. Differing local limits dependent upon population. | Unlimited, except to $50,000 per gubernatorial campaign from candidate and family per election cycle. Certain large contributions from candidate's family in gubernatorial race may trigger lift of expenditure limit for other candidates. | Prohibited for judges and employees under direction and control of a judge for that judge's candidacy. Contribution may not be required. | Prohibited. |
| Minnesota | Governor/lt. governor: limited to $2,000 per election year and $500 in a non-election year. Attorney general: limited to $1,000 per election year and $200 in a non-election year. Other statewide offices: limited to $500 per election year and $100 in a non-election year. State senate/state representative: limited to $500 per election year and $100 in a non-election year. Elective judgeship no limit. | Candidate: unlimited, except limited to 10 times election year limit if accepting a public subsidy. Family: Governor/Lt. Governor: Limited to $2,000 per election year and $500 in a non-election year. Attorney General: Limited to $1,000 per election year and $200 in a non-election year. Other statewide offices: Limited to $500 per election year and $100 in a non-election year. State Senate/State Representative: Limited to $500 per election year and $100 in a non-election year. Elective judgeships: no limit | Solicitation prohibited during hours of employment. Prohibited for judges and their employees, and judicial candidates. Contribution may not be required. | Anonymous contributions must be less than $20. Contribution in the name of another prohibited. |
| Mississippi | Unlimited. | Unlimited. | Solicitation prohibited for employees of certain specified agencies. Contribution may not be required. Employees of certain specified agencies may not contribute. | ... |

# LIMITATIONS ON CONTRIBUTIONS BY INDIVIDUALS — Continued

| State or other jurisdiction | Individual | Candidate | Government employees | Anonymous or in name of another |
|---|---|---|---|---|
| Missouri | Unlimited, pending a decision by the U.S. Supreme Court. | Candidate: unlimited. Family: unlimited, pending a decision by the U.S. Supreme Court. | Judge and judge's employees may not solicit for party. Merit system employees may not receive or be solicited for contributions. Members of the Missouri Ethics Commission may not contribute. Judge and judicial candidates should not contribute to party, unless judge a candidate. | Anonymous contribution must be $25 or less. Contribution in the name of another prohibited. |
| Montana | Limited for each contested primary and general election in a campaign to $400 for governor/ lieutenant governor, $200 for other statewide candidates, and $100 for all other candidates. | Candidate: unlimited Family: each individual limited for each contested primary and general election in a campaign to $400 for governor/ lt. governor, $200 for other state wide candidates, and $100 for all other candidates. | Solicitation by municipal government employees prohibited while on job or at place of employment. Ethics Commission members are prohibited from contributing. | Prohibited. |
| Nebraska | Unlimited. | Candidate: Unlimited, except that candidate committee cannot contribute to another candidate committee other than in fundraising event. Family: unlimited. | Contribution unlimited. | Anonymous contribution prohibited. Contribution in the name of another prohibited, except earmarked contributions permitted if disclosure requirements met. |
| Nevada | Any candidate: $5,000 per primary and general election. | Any candidate: $5,000 per primary and general election. | May not solicit funds for a political organization or candidate. | If anonymous contribution $100 or more, must be delivered to state treasurer or donated to nonprofit entity. Contributions in the name of another are prohibited. |
| New Hampshire | Limited to $5,000 per candidate, per election, except limited to $1,000 per election if to candidate or political committee working on behalf of a candidate who does not voluntarily agree to limit campaign expenditures. | Candidate: unlimited Family: limited to $5,000 per candidate, per election, except limited to $1,000 per election if to candidate or political committee working on behalf of a candidate who does not voluntarily agree to limit campaign expenditures. | Cannot coerce classified state employee to contribute. | Prohibited. |
| New Jersey | Limited to $1,500 per non-governor candidate per primary or general election; $2,100 per governor candidate per primary or general election; $30,000 to political party state committee or county committee or legislative leadership committee per year; $5,900 to municipal party committee per year. Unlimited to political committee or continuing political committee. | Candidate for non-governor office unlimited. Candidate for governor accepting public funds limited to $25,000 per primary or general election from personal funds; if not accepting public funds, unlimited. $30,000 to political party state committee or county committee or legislative leadership committee per year. $5,900 to politica committee per election; $5,900 to continuing political committee or municipal party committee per year. Family: spouse of candidate for governor and presumably other family members limited to $2,100 per primary or general election; unlimited for spouse, child, parent, or sibling residing in same household of candidate for non-governor office. | Prohibited to demand from other public employees. | Prohibited. |

See footnotes at end of table.

# LIMITATIONS ON CONTRIBUTIONS BY INDIVIDUALS — Continued

| State or other jurisdiction | Individual | Candidate | Government employees | Anonymous or in name of another |
|---|---|---|---|---|
| New Mexico | Unlimited. | Unlimited. | Elected office, public officer or employee with regulatory office, candidate for regulatory office, or agent of candidate may not solicit contributions from regulated entities and persons. Non-probationary state employees cannot be dismissed for failure to contribute. | Anonymous contributions prohibited if over $100. Aggregate anonymous contributions received during primary or general election limited to $2,000 for statewide races and $500 for other races. Excess over limit must be donated to general fund or to a Section 170(b)(1)(A) organization. In the name of another person prohibited if recipient knows contribution is from third person that directed that contribution not be publicly reported. |
| New York | Limited to an aggregate of $150,000 per year and maximum aggregate per office. Statewide office: primary product of number of enrolled voters in candidate's party in state x $0.05, but not less than $4,900 or more than $14,700; general election - $30,700. State senator: primary - $4,900; general election - $7,700. Member of assembly: primary - $3,100; general election - $3,100. New York City mayor, public advocate, comptroller: primary election - greater of $4,500 or product of number of enrolled voters in candidate's party in city x $.05, but not more than $14,700; general election - $30,700. Other public office: primary - greater of $1,000 or product of number of enrolled voters in candidate's party in district x $.05, but not more than $50,000. Party of constituted committee limited to aggregate of $76,500 per year. | Candidate: unlimited to own campaign. Family: Candidate's spouse is unlimited. Other family members (candidate's child, parent, grandparent, brother, sister, and their spouses together) limited to maximum aggregate per office. Statewide office: primary— product of number of enrolled voters in candidate's party in state x $.025; general election— product of number of registered voters x $.025; state senator: primary— greater of $20,000 or product of number of enrolled voters in candidate's party in district multiplied by $0.25, but not more than $100,000; general election— greater of $20,000 or product of number of registered voters in district x $0.25, but not more than $100,000. Member of assembly: primary— greater of $12,500 or product of number of enrolled voters in candidate's party in district x $0.25, but not more than $100,000; general election—greater of $12,500 or product of number of registered voters in district x $0.25, but not more than $100,000. Other public office and New York City mayor, public advocate, comptroller, greater of $1,250 or product of enrolled voters in candidate's party in district or city x $0.25, but not more than $100,000; general election—greater of $1,250 or product of number of enrolled voters in district x $.25, but not more than $100,000. | Solicitation prohibited for police force members and judicial candidates. Contribution permitted, but may not be required. | Anonymous prohibited. In the name of another prohibited, except contributions of not more than $2,500 in name of partnership does not violate prohibition. |
| North Carolina | Limited to $4,000 per committee or candidate per primary, second primary, and general election. | Unlimited. | Judge or judicial candidate should not solicit or make contributions . No person may coerce a state employee or applicant for a state position subject to the Personnel Act to make a contribution by threatening adverse or preferential personnel actions. | Prohibited. |

# LIMITATIONS ON CONTRIBUTIONS BY INDIVIDUALS — Continued

| State or other jurisdiction | Individual | Candidate | Government employees | Anonymous or in name of another |
|---|---|---|---|---|
| **North Dakota** ............. | Unlimited. | Unlimited. | Full-time judges and judicial candidates may not solicit contributions. Full-time judges and judicial candidates may not make contributions to political organizations and candidates. State officers and employees may not solicit campaign funds while on duty or in uniform. Political subdivision may extend prohibition to local public employees. | Prohibited. |
| **Ohio** ................ | Limited to $2,500 to campaign committee of statewide or general assembly candidate in primary or general election; $5,000 to county political party for party's state candidate fund or to legislative campaign funds in calendar year; $16,000 to state political party for the party's state candidate fund in calendar year; and $5,000 to political action committee or political contributing entity in calendar year. | Candidate and family: Unlimited to own campaign, but if candidate for statewide or general assembly receives or expends personal funds of more than $100,000 in primary or $150,000 in general election for statewide office or more than $25,000 per election for general assembly, a personal funds notice must be filed; otherwise, the use of personal funds is limited to the above reporting threshold by the candidate's campaign committee is limited to the above reporting threshold amounts.  Candidate campaign committee: $2,500 to campaign committee of statewide or general assembly in a primary or general election; $2,500 to political action committee or political contributing entity in calendar year; except designated state campaign committee, $16,000 to state political party for party's state candidate fund in calendar year; except designated state campaign committee, $5,000 to designated state campaign committee fund in calendar year; and except a designated state campaign committee, $5,000 to county political party for the state candidate fund in calendar year. | May not solicit or be solicited if in classified service or public employee. Judge may not solicit or receive campaign funds. Employees of state elected officers may not contribute to the officer for whom the employee works or to candidates for that office. | Prohibited. |

See footnotes at end of table.

# LIMITATIONS ON CONTRIBUTIONS BY INDIVIDUALS — Continued

| State or other jurisdiction | Individual | Candidate | Government employees | Anonymous or in name of another |
|---|---|---|---|---|
| Oklahoma | Limited per person or family to $5,000 to a political party committee or political action committee in a calendar year, $5,000 to a candidate/ candidate committee for state office, county office in a county of 250,000 or more, or municipal office in a municipality of 250,000 or more for election campaign, and $1,000 to any other local candidate/candidate committee for election campaign. | Unlimited to own campaign; otherwise subject to individuals' limits. Candidate committee may not contribute or make independent expenditure for another candidate; principal campaign committee for federal-office candidate may not contribute or make independent expenditure to candidate committee for state-office candidate. Family: limited per person or family to $5,000 to a political party committee or political action committee in a calendar year, $5,000 to a candidate/candidate committee for state office, county office in a county of 250,000 or more, or municipal office in a municipality of 250,000 or more for state office, county office in a county of 250,000 or more, or municipal office in a municipality of 250,000 or more for election campaign, and $1,000 to any other local candidate/ candidate committee for election campaign. | State officials and employees may not solicit or receive contributions. Judges should not solicit. Prohibited for state highway patrol members and supernumerary tax consultants. Judges should not contribute. | Anonymous contributions prohibited. Contributions in the name of another are prohibited. |
| Oregon | Unlimited. | Unlimited. | Solicitation prohibited during hours of employment. Contribution may not be demanded to pay a political assessment. | Prohibited. |
| Pennsylvania | Unlimited. | Unlimited. | Public officers and employees may not demand a political assessment. Judges should not solicit funds. State classified service, state crime commission, public utility commission, community action agency, and county board of health personnel may not solicit. Workplace contributions by state classified service employees are restricted. Judges and judicial candidates should not make candidate contributions. | Prohibited. |
| Rhode Island | $1,000 per recipient per calendar year and maximum of $10,000 for all recipients, except per-recipient limit doubles to $2,000 if recipient is a candidate for general office who has qualified to receive public funding and an additional $10,000 may be contributed to a political party committee for organizational and party-building activities. | Candidate: to own campaign, generally unlimited; however, for a candidate for general office who has qualified and elected to receive public funding contributions (and loans) by the candidate may not exceed 5% of the total the candidate is permitted to spend in the campaign. Family: $1,000 per recipient per calendar year and maximum of $10,000 for all recipients, except per-recipient limit doubles to $2,000 if recipient is a candidate for general office who has qualified to receive public funding, and an additional $10,000 may be contributed to a political party committee for organizational and party-building activities . | State classified employees may not solicit. State or municipal officials may not solicit contribution with understanding that official will be influenced. Full-time judge or candidate for judicial office should not solicit. State classified employees may not be solicited. | Prohibited. Must be returned to donor if identity can be ascertained; if it cannot, escheats to state. |

# LIMITATIONS ON CONTRIBUTIONS BY INDIVIDUALS — Continued

| State or other jurisdiction | Individual | Candidate | Government employees | Anonymous or in name of another |
|---|---|---|---|---|
| **South Carolina** .......... | Limited to $3,500 per statewide candidate per election; $1,000 per other candidate per election; $3,500 per committee per calendar year. | Candidate: unlimited. Family: limited to $3,500 per statewide candidate per election; $1,000 per other candidate per election; $3,500 per committee per calendar year. | Employer cannot give preference to employees who contribute; must inform them of right to refuse without penalty. No one may solicit uniformed law enforcement officer, judge, judicial candidate, solicitor and staff, and attorney general and staff except for own campaign. Judge and judicial candidate should not solicit. Contribution prohibited by state ethics commission personnel; judges and judicial candidates should not contribute, except in elective office may contribute to a political party or organization. Employees and officers of the Judicial Department may not coerce or command political contributions from state officers and employees. | Anonymous contribution prohibited generally. Must give to children's trust fund. |
| **South Dakota** .......... | Limited to any calendar year to $1,000 for a statewide office candidate; $250 for a legislative or county office candidate; and $3,000 to a political party. | Unlimited. | Judge or judicial candidate may not solicit. Judge or judicial candidate may not contribute to a political organization or candidate. | ... |
| **Tennessee** .......... | Limited to $2,500 for state office candidate and $1,000 for other candidate in aggregate per election. Limited to $1,000 for a judicial candidate. | Limited to $250,000 for statewide office, $40,000 for state senate, or $20,000 for other office, in aggregate per election. Unlimited to judicial candidate from family of candidate and spouse. | Prohibited for state government superiors to solicit their employees. Prohibited to solicit persons who receive government benefits. State career service employees may not solicit. Judges should not solicit. Employees of sheriff's department under civil service law may not solicit. Judges expressly permitted to contribute only to political party or candidate. | ... |
| **Texas** .......... | Unlimited. | Unlimited. | Texas Lottery Commission members cannot receive or advise persons to make contribution for political purposes. State employee cannot coerce or restrict political contributions. County election administrator prohibited. Contributions made in state capitol prohibited. | Prohibited. |

See footnotes at end of table.

# LIMITATIONS ON CONTRIBUTIONS BY INDIVIDUALS — Continued

| State or other jurisdiction | Individual | Candidate | Government employees | Anonymous or in name of another |
|---|---|---|---|---|
| Utah ............... | Unlimited. | Unlimited. | Prohibited to solicit executive branch employees during hours of employment. Judges should not solicit funds. Judges are not permitted to make contributions to a political party or organization. | ... |
| Vermont ............... | Contributions from one source limited in 2-year general election cycle to candidate for governor, lieutenant governor, secretary of state, state treasurer, auditor of accounts, or attorney general—$400; candidate for state senator or county office—$300; candidate for state representative or local office—$200; and political committee (other than a political committee of a candidate) or political party—$2,000. | Unlimited, except federal office candidate limited to $1,000 to another candidate or committee per election. Family: unlimited | Solicitation prohibited. | Prohibited. |
| Virginia ............... | Unlimited. | Unlimited. | Contribution by judges prohibited. | ... |
| Washington ............... | Aggregate contributions per election to state office candidates limited to $600 for state legislative office candidate and $1,200 for state executive office candidate. Aggregate contributions within 21 days of a general election may not exceed $5,000 for a campaign for other than statewide office. | Unlimited using their own personal funds or portion of jointly held funds, but may not make aggregate contributions within 21 days of a general election to own campaign exceeding $50,000 for statewide office or $5,000 for other than statewide office. Candidates for state office may not accept aggregate contributions per election cycle from all political party county central committees and legislative district committees combined that exceed 25 per voter in district (state legislative office candidate) or state (state executive office candidate). Candidates may not accept contributions that exceed limits. Otherwise, same as for individuals. Family member: aggregate contributions per election to state office candidates limited to $600 for state legislative office candidate and $1,200 for state executive office candidate. Aggregate contributions within 21 days of a general election may not exceed $5,000 for a campaign for other than statewide office. | Solicitation on government property is prohibited. State or local official or official's agent may not solicit from employees in officials agency. Judges may not solicit. Contribution prohibited if city with commission form of government. Judges may not contribute to a political party, political organization, or non-judicial candidate. | Contribution may not be made so as to conceal the source. Anonymous contribution limited to greater of one percent of total accumulated contributions received or $300. Contribution in the name of another prohibited. |
| West Virginia ............... | Limited to $1,000 per candidate, per primary or general election and $1,000 to state party executive committee per calendar year. | Limited to $1,000 per candidate, per primary or general election and $1,000 to state party executive committee per calendar year. | State classified service employees and judges and judicial candidates may not solicit. Non-elective salaried government employees may not be solicited. | Anonymous contribution prohibited. Contributor disclosure required for contribution in the name of another. |

See footnotes at end of table.

# LIMITATIONS ON CONTRIBUTIONS BY INDIVIDUALS — Continued

| State or other jurisdiction | Individual | Candidate | Government employees | Anonymous or in name of another |
|---|---|---|---|---|
| Wisconsin | Limited to an aggregate of $10,000 in a calendar year. Limits for campaign: $10,000 for statewide office, $1,000 for state senator, $500 for state assembly representative, $2,500 or $3,000 for court of appeals judge (depending on population of district), $1,000 or $3,000 for circuit judge (depending on population of circuit), and for local office, the greater of $250 or 1¢ x number of inhabitants ($3,000 maximum). | Unlimited as to candidate's own personal funds and property or personal funds and property owned jointly or as marital property with spouse. State office candidate who receives election campaign fund grant is limited to 200 percent of the amount that an individual may contribute. Family member: aggregate contributions per election to state office candidates limited to $600 for state legislative office candidate and $1,200 for state executive office candidate. Aggregate contributions within 21 days of a general election may not exceed $5,000 for a campaign for other than statewide office. | Solicitation and contribution prohibited during hours of employment or while engaged in official duties. Judges may not solicit or contribute for political party. | Anonymous contribution must be $10 or less. Contribution in the name of another prohibited. |
| Wyoming | Limited to $1,000 per candidate, per primary, general, or special election, and to $25,000 total contributions in 2-year period of general election year and the preceding year. | Limited to candidate; otherwise subject to $25,000 limit in 2-year period of general election year and the preceding year. | Judges may not solicit funds for candidates. Intradepartmental solicitation of contributions from municipal police or fire civil service personnel in communities of 4,000 or more is prohibited. | ... |
| Dist. of Columbia | Limited to an aggregate of $8,500 per election and $2,000 for mayor; $1,500 for council chair or councilmember at-large; $500 for council-member from a district or board of education member at-large; $200 for board of education member from a district or party official; and $25 for a neighborhood advisory committee member. | Limited to an aggregate of $8,500 per election and $2,000 for mayor; $1,500 for council chair or councilmember at-large; $500 for council-member from a district or board of education member at-large; $200 for board of education member from a district or party official; and $25 for a neighborhood advisory committee member. | Contribution permitted but employees may not solicit or collect political contributions. | Anonymous contributions prohibited. Contributions in the name of another are prohibited. |
| American Samoa | Limited to no more than $100 in aggregate to a candidate, committee, or party. | Limited to no more than $100 in aggregate to a candidate, committee, or party. | ... | Prohibited, except for amounts that aggregate less than $250 when obtained by multiple contributions made by 10 or more persons at the same event. |
| Guam | Limited to no more than $1,000 in any calendar year to any one candidate in a primary election and then again in any general election. | Limited to no more than $1,000 in any calendar year to any one candidate in a primary election and then again in any general election. | Prohibited for judges. | Anonymous contributions are Prohibited, except for amounts that aggregate less than $250 when obtained by multiple contributions made by 10 or more persons at the same event, and at certain events with ticket price or cost of not more than $25 per person. Contributions in the name of another are prohibited. |

# LIMITATIONS ON CONTRIBUTIONS BY INDIVIDUALS — Continued

| State or other jurisdiction | Individual | Candidate | Government employees | Anonymous or in name of another |
|---|---|---|---|---|
| Northern Marianas ...... | No restrictions. | No restrictions. | Solicitation is generally prohibited. Contributions may not be required. | ... |
| Puerto Rico .................. | (1) In a non-election year: (a) to a candidate of a political party, a municipal or central directing body of a party, or an independent candidate—up to $1,000 per year and (b) to all candidates and parties—maximum total annual amount of $5,000; (2) in an election year: (a) to a candidate for governor, a political party, or a combination of both—$2,500 per year, (b) to any other candidate—$1,000 per year but not to exceed $2,500 per year for all other candidates—maximum total annual amount of $5,000; and (3) in a primary election: to any candidate—$200. | (1) In a non-election year: (a) to a candidate of a political party, a municipal or central directing body of a party, or an independent candidate—up to $1,000 per year and (b) to all candidates and parties— maximum total annual amount of $5,000; (2) in an election year: (a) to a candidate for governor, a political party, or a combination of both—$2,500 per year, (b) to any other candidate—$1,000 per year but not to exceed $2,500 per year for all other candidates, (c) to an independent group or committee that supports a candidate or political party—$500 per year, and (d) to independent committees or candidates— maximum total annual amount of $5,000; and (3) in a primary election: to any candidate—$500. | Solicitation is generally prohibited. Special restrictions for those involved in granting of permits and franchises. Contributions may not be required. Judges should not make contributions. | Anonymous contributions are prohibited, in amounts in excess of $100; $25 in PAC's. Contributions in the name of another are prohibited. |
| U.S. Virgin Islands ....... | Limited to $1,000 in the aggregate per election to a candidate or candidate's authorized political committee (or, if made to a multicandidate committee, $1,000 multiplied by the number of candidates); otherwise, unlimited. | Candidate's personal funds to own campaign: unlimited. | ... | Anonymous contributions are prohibited if over $100. Special attribution requirements applicable. |

*Source:* Edward D. Feigenbaum, J.D. and James A. Palmer, J.D., INGroup, Noblesville, Indiana, March 2000; Finance Law 2000: A Summary of State Campaign Finance Laws with Quick Reference Charts.
*Note:* For detailed legal requirements, state statutes should be consulted.

*Key:*
... — No reference to contributions in the law.

**Table 5.12**
## CAMPAIGN FINANCE LAWS: LIMITATIONS ON EXPENDITURES
(As of December 31, 1999)

| State or other jurisdiction | Who may make expenditures | Total expenditures allowed | Expenditures before first filing | Post-election use of surplus funds (a) | For certain purposes | Personal use of candidate |
|---|---|---|---|---|---|---|
| **Alabama** | Only committee named and designated by candidate. | ... | ... | Unlimited as to officeholder expenses, contributions to charity, transfers to another committee, donations to state agencies or funds, or uses for other non-personal lawful purposes. | Limited to necessary and and ordinary campaign and officeholding expenses, or charitable contributions. | Generally prohibited. Not permitted for judges and judicial candidates. Not permitted for surplus funds. |
| **Alaska** | Candidate, treasurer, or deputy treasurer. | ... | No expenditures permitted before filing date except personal travel expenses and public opinion polls or surveys. | Surplus may be given to charity; used to repay contributors; spent on a future campaign; used to repay candidate up to a limited amount; donated to a party, the state, or a municipality; or may be transferred to an office allowance fund up to a limited amount. | Use of campaign funds must reasonably relate to election campaign. Funds may not be used to knowingly pay in excess of fair market value for campaign goods/services; to pay a criminal fine or penalty; or to make contributions to another candidate or to a group. | Prohibited. |
| **Arizona** | Treasurer or authorized agent. | ... | Limited to less than $500 prior to registering committee. | May be retained for a future campaign; returned to contributors; donated to a party committee, certain charitable organizations, political organizations within limits. | ... | Surplus funds may not be used for personal use of the candidate |
| **Arkansas** | ... | ... | ... | After setting aside any funds needed to pay debts, and an amount equal to the yearly salary for the office sought, surplus funds must either be turned over to the state treasurer for the benefit of the general revenue fund, to a nonprofit organization under the Internal Revenue Code, to an organized political party or political party caucus, or to contributors to the candidate's campaign. Special requirements cover specifically defined carryover funds. | ... | A candidate who takes a leave of absence without pay from primary place of employment may take campaign funds during the campaign and before the election as personal income, up to the amount of income lost due to the leave of absence. |

See footnotes at end of table.

# LIMITATIONS ON EXPENDITURES — Continued

| State or other jurisdiction | Who may make expenditures | Total expenditures allowed | Expenditures before first filing | Post-election use of surplus funds (a) | For certain purposes | Personal use of candidate |
|---|---|---|---|---|---|---|
| California | Candidate or treasurer. | ... | ... | May be used for debts or charitable contributions; contributed to a political party, candidate for federal office or ballot measure committee; contributed to an out-of-state campaign, or used to defray certain legal or professional expenses associated with the election and aftermath; or used to purchase home or office security system subject to restrictions. | Must be directly related to political, legislative, or governmental purpose if candidate or elected officer receives substantial personal benefit. Certain expenditures must be directly related regardless of benefit received. | Prohibited. |
| Colorado | Professional lobbyists may not dispense certain party funds. | Voluntary campaign spending limits of: $2 million for governor; $400,000 for secretary of state, state treasurer & attorney general; $100,00 for lt. governor; $75,000 for state senate; $50,000 for state house of representatives, state board of education, or regent of the University of Colorado | Prohibited. | May be contributed to a political party subject to aggregate limits; donated to an Internal Revenue Service-recognized charitable organization; returned to contributors; or retained for use in a subsequent election; officeholders may use surplus for certain specified purposes related to office. | Must be reasonably related to supporting the election of the candidate. May not be used to encourage another candidate's withdrawal from race. | Prohibited. |
| Connecticut | Treasurer or those authorized by treasurer. | ... | No expenditures permitted until treasurer and campaign depository have been designated. | May be donated to another committee (except one established to further the candidate's future campaigns), distributed pro rata to contributors, or used for transition expenses. Ballot question committees may also distribute surplus to government agencies or tax-exempt organizations. | Polls, meeting halls, rally expenses, printing and advertising, professional service fees, travel, staff salaries, rent, supplies, voter transportation, communications, petition-related expenses, and other expenses permitted by the Commission. | Prohibited. |
| Delaware | Candidate committee. | ... | ... | May be contributed to a tax-exempt religious, charitable, educational, or scientific organization, volunteer fire department, or a successful committee. | Staff salaries, travel expenses, filing fees, communications and printing, food, office supplies, voter lists and canvasses, poll watchers, rent advertising, rallies, or legal counsel. | ... |

# LIMITATIONS ON EXPENDITURES — Continued

| State or other jurisdiction | Who may make expenditures | Total expenditures allowed | Expenditures before first filing | Post-election use of surplus funds (a) | For certain purposes | Personal use of candidate |
|---|---|---|---|---|---|---|
| Florida ............... | Only campaign treasurers or deputy treasurers. | Publicly financed candidates and those agreeing to voluntary limits: $5 million for governor and lt. governor; $2 million for cabinet. Limits may be increased under certain circumstances. | ... | Funds remaining after an election are to be used to pay remaining obligations incurred prior to or on election day. Surplus funds may be used to reimburse a candidate for candidate's contributions; transferred to a public officeholder account in various amounts dependent upon office; returned pro rata to contributors; given to a candidate's political party (limited to $10,000 after 01/01/99); donated to a nonprofit or charitable organization; or given to the state for the general fund or the election campaign financing trust fund (by a state candidate) or political subdivision (by a local candidate). | Expenditures may only be used to influence the results of an election. | Prohibited. |
| Georgia ............... | Candidate, chair, treasurer, or designated agents. | ... | ... | May be donated to any charitable organization and nonprofit organization; transferred to any future campaign for elective office for which they were received; used for repayment of any prior campaign obligation incurred as a candidate; or transferred to any national, state, or local committee of any political party or to any candidate. | May only be used to defray ordinary and necessary campaign expenses incurred in connection with the candidate's campaign for elective office, or the public officer's fulfillment or retention of that office. | Prohibited. |

See footnotes at end of table.

# LIMITATIONS ON EXPENDITURES — Continued

| State or other jurisdiction | Who may make expenditures | Total expenditures allowed | Expenditures before first filing | Post-election use of surplus funds (a) | For certain purposes | Personal use of candidate |
|---|---|---|---|---|---|---|
| **Hawaii** | Only campaign treasurer or deputy treasurer. | Voluntary election year limits: governor - $2.50 x qualified voters; lt. governor - $1.40 x qualified voters; mayor - $2.00 x qualified voters; House/ Senate/council prosecutor - $1.40 x qualified voters; others - 20¢ x qualified voters. | Limited, as certain expenditures trigger filing requirement. | May be used for fundraising; candidate-sponsored, politically related activity; ordinary and necessary office-holder expenses; donations to any community service, scientific, education, youth, recreation, charitable, or literary organization. | Must be related to a campaign purpose, including donations to community, youth, social or recreational organizations; reports, surveys, and polls. | Prohibited. |
| **Idaho** | ... | ... | ... | Surplus may only be used for ordinary and necessary office-holder expenses; unlimited transfers to any party committee; donations to charitable organizations; or any lawful purpose other than personal use. | ... | Prohibited. |
| **Illinois** | Must be authorized by chair, treasurer, or their designated agents. | May be limited for Citizens Utility Board candidates in exchange for listing in state-sponsored voter's pamphlet. | ... | ... | Only for nomination, election or retention of a person in public office, or in connection with a public policy question. Law limits certain types of illegal or questionable expenditures/transactions. | Comprehensive list of expenditures prohibited. |
| **Indiana** | Only treasurer may make expenditures. | ... | ... | May be transferred to candidate committees, political committees, or state election commission, political parties, certain tax-exempt organizations, used for continuing political activity or officeholder expenses reasonably related to the expenses of holding elective office, or returned pro rata to contributors. | Must be used for campaign, for continuing political activity related to service in an elected office, or contributions to party committees or other candidate committees. | Prohibited except that a candidate may, under a written contract with the candidate's committee, receive a salary or reimbursemet for lost wages or salary payments from other employment incurred by the candidate as a result of services provided to the committee. |

# LIMITATIONS ON EXPENDITURES — Continued

| State or other jurisdiction | Who may make expenditures | Total expenditures allowed | Expenditures before first filing | Post-election use of surplus funds (a) | For certain purposes | Personal use of candidate |
|---|---|---|---|---|---|---|
| Iowa | Must be through sole depository account. | ... | Initial report must account for all funds raised and spent for current election activity, even if in different calendar year. | Public checkoff funds received by a political party may not be used to lease or purchase any item whose benefits extend beyond the time in which the funds must be spent. Candidates' campaign funds may not generally be used to pay civil/criminal penalties; personal debts or expenses; for personal services unrelated to the campaign; most motor vehicle leases and payments; professional organization and most service organization memberships; mortgage or rental payments for the candidate; meals, groceries, and other food not for campaign uses; payments clearly in excess of the fair market value of the service or item. | Generally prohibited. Public checkoff funds received by a political party may only be used for legitimate campaign purposes in general elections, including salaries, rent, advertising, supplies, travel, campaign paraphernalia, contributions to other candidates or committees, and the like. Candidate campaign funds may only be used for legitimate campaign purposes, including salaries, rent, advertising, supplies, travel, campaign paraphernalia, or for constituency services or office-holder expenses. | Prohibited. |
| Kansas | Must be by or through treasurer. | ... | No expenditures permitted until registration form properly filed. | Residual funds must be contributed to a charitable organization, a party committee, to the state general fund, or returned in whole or pro rata to contributors. | Must be for legitimate campaign or officeholding expenses. | Prohibited. |
| Kentucky | Treasurer must make or authorize all expenditures on behalf of a candidate. | Candidates accepting public financing limited to $1.8 million in a primary election; $300,000 in a primary runoff election; and $1.8 million in a general election, adjusted for inflation. | No expenditures permitted until primary campaign depository is designated. | Any unexpended balance may be returned pro rata to all contributors, transferred to the candidate's party executive committee, retained for election to the same office, be donated to a Section 501(c)(3) charity, or escheat to the state treasury. | Political parties receiving tax money may use these funds to support their party's candidates in a general election, and for administrative costs of maintaining a party headquarters. Case law suggests limited expenditure categories. | Prohibited. |

See footnotes at end of table.

# LIMITATIONS ON EXPENDITURES — Continued

| State or other jurisdiction | Who may make expenditures | Total expenditures allowed | Expenditures before first filing | Post-election use of surplus funds (a) | For certain purposes | Personal use of candidate |
|---|---|---|---|---|---|---|
| Louisiana | Any person, upon proper notification to treasurer. | ... | No expenditures aggregating in excess of $500 may be made by a political committee until statement of organization is properly filed. | May be returned pro rata to contributors; given to a charitable organization; spent for or against a candidate, political party, or a proposition; used in future political campaigns; or activity related to a future campaign. Special restrictions on retention and disbursement of funds by judges and judicial candidates. | Must be related to a political campaign or holding of office. | Prohibited except to replace items stolen, lost, or damaged in connection with a campaign, or for interest to candidate on repayment of a loan to the campaign. |
| Maine | ... | PAC is limited to expenditures of $5,000 per candidate or political committee per election. Publicly financed candidates for governor, state senate, and house of representatives are limited in total spending. | ... | Returned pro rata to contributors, used for the candidate's future campaigns or transferred to other committees, unrestricted gift to the state; gift to charitable or educational organization; loan repayment or debt retirement of campaign expenses; or payment for expenses incurred in performance of office to which elected; unspent funds revert to state. | Public funds may only be used for campaign-related purposes. | ... |
| Maryland | Public funds may only be spent upon authority of candidate or treasurer. Other expenditures must be made through treasurer. | Publicly financed candidates for governor/lt. governor limited to 30 x qualified voters, adjusted annually on January 1. | No expenditures permitted until registration form is properly filed. | Public funds must be repaid not later than 60 days after the election for which the funds are granted. Other surplus funds must be returned on a pro rata basis to contributors; paid to a party central committee; donated to a local board of education, recognized non-profit educational or charitable organization; or given to a higher education institution for scholarships. | Public contributions may only be used to further the candidate's nomination or election, for legal purposes, and for expenses not incurred later than 30 days after the election. | ... |

# LIMITATIONS ON EXPENDITURES — Continued

| State or other jurisdiction | Who may make expenditures | Total expenditures allowed | Expenditures before first filing | Post-election use of surplus funds (a) | For certain purposes | Personal use of candidate |
|---|---|---|---|---|---|---|
| Massachusetts | Candidate, committee treasurer, or designee. | Limits for candidates certified to receive clean election funds, beginning with 2002 election, with differing limits per office and per primary and general election. | No committee expenditures permitted until committee is properly organized. Certain testing the waters expenditures permitted. | ... | Public financing funds must be spent for expenses directly related to campaign. Other candidates may make expenditures for enhancement of their political future. | Prohibited. |
| Michigan | An expenditure may only be made with the authorization of the treasurer or the treasurer's designee. | Gubernatorial candidates who accept public funds limited to $2 million per election; additional expenditures are authorized in response to editorials, endorsements, etc. Cap may be lifted under certain circumstances. | ... | Public funds must be promptly repaid and may not be used in a subsequent election. Other funds may be transferred to another committee of same candidate (with restrictions), party, legislative caucus committees, tax-exempt charitable institution, or returned to contributors. Judicial candidate surplus funds must be returned to contributors or donated to state bar client security fund. | Public funds may only be spent on services, facilities, materials, or other things of value to further the candidate's election during the election year. | Public funds cannot be used to pay a candidate. No campaign funds may be used to personally benefit a candidate. |
| Minnesota | Must be authorized by treasurer or deputy treasurer of the committee or fund | Candidates accepting public subsidies are limited as follows in election years (adjusted each election year based on Consumer Price Index; 1998 figures shown): governor/lt. governor: $1,926,127; attorney general: $321,023; other statewide office: $160,514; state senate: $43,150 (1992 figure; to be refined in March 2000) state representative: $24,083. Limits in non-election years are 20 percent of election year limits. Under certain conditions, expenditures may increase. | ... | ... | Limited to salaries, wages, and fees; communications, mailing, and transportation and travel; advertising and printing; office space and furnishings; supplies; and other expenses reasonably related to the election. Certain expenditures may be designated as permissible noncampaign disbursements by law and Campaign Finance and Public Disclose Board Rule. | Prohibited. |

See footnotes at end of table.

# LIMITATIONS ON EXPENDITURES — Continued

| State or other jurisdiction | Who may make expenditures | Total expenditures allowed | Expenditures before first filing | Post-election use of surplus funds (a) | For certain purposes | Personal use of candidate |
|---|---|---|---|---|---|---|
| **Mississippi** | ... | ... | Prohibited for judicial candidates. | ... | ... | Discouraged for Judicial candidates. |
| **Missouri** | All expenditures must be made by or through the treasurer | Voluntary limitations ruled unconstitutional. | Limitations placed on exploratory comittees. | ... | May only be used for specified expenses. | Prohibited except for attorney's fees in defending certain actions. |
| **Montana** | Campaign treasurer and deputy campaign treasurer. | ... | ... | ... | Voluntary expenditure limit of $150,000 per year by political committees favoring or opposing a ballot issue. | ... |
| **Nebraska** | Treasurers or assistant treasurers; however, candidates and their agents are also permitted to make expenditures. | ... | Expenditure may not be made by a committee raising, receiving, or disbursing more than $5,000 in a calendar year until it files a statement of organization and has a treasurer. | After an election, a committee may expend or transfer funds for continued operation of campaign offices; social events for workers, volunteers, and constituents; obtaining public input and opinion; repayment of campaign loans; newsletters and other political communications; gifts of acknowledgment; and office-holder related meals, lodging and travel. After termination of a candidate committee, unexpended funds may be transferred to another candidate committee, a political party committee, a tax-exempt charitable organization, the Campaign Finance Limitation Act Cash Fund; the state or certain political subdivisions; or returned to contributors. | A committee other than a political party may not expend or transfer funds except for goods, materials, services, or facilities to assist or oppose a candidate for ballot question. | A committee may not make expenditures for the payment of a candidate's clothes, or medical or dental expenses; mortgage or rental payments for the candidate's permanent residence; installment payments for an auto owned by the candidate; satisfaction of personal debts (excluding reportable campaign loans); or personal services (such as legal legal or accounting services). |

# LIMITATIONS ON EXPENDITURES — Continued

| State or other jurisdiction | Who may make expenditures | Total expenditures allowed | Expenditures before first filing | Post-election use of surplus funds (a) | For certain purposes | Personal use of candidate |
|---|---|---|---|---|---|---|
| Nevada | ... | ... | ... | Elected and defeated candidates and non-candidate officeholders are required to dispose of unspent contributions in a statutorily authorized manner, including return to contributors, contribution for political purpose, and donation to tax-exempt nonprofit entity. Elected candidates may use for present or future campaign expenses or public office expenses. Judicial office candidates are subject to the Code of Judicial Conduct requirements as to the disposition of unspent contributions. Execess of any contribution over $5,000 must be returned to the contibutor by candidate defeated in primary. | ... | Prohibited. |
| New Hampshire | Candidates or candidate's fiscal agent. | Candidate may agree to limit campaign expenditures made by candidate and by committees, political party and immediate family on candidate's behalf in a primary or general election in accordance with a maximum expenditure schedule. | Before a non-party political committee may receive contributions or make expenditures of more than $500, a registration statement must be filed. If the political committee is organized to support a candidate, written consent of the candidate or candidate's fiscal agent must be secured and filed before making expenditures. | Contributions may be used after general or special election for fundraising or other politically related activity sponsored by the candidate, or for donations to charitable organizations. | ... | ... |

See footnotes at end of table.

# LIMITATIONS ON EXPENDITURES — Continued

| State or other jurisdiction | Who may make expenditures | Total expenditures allowed | Expenditures before first filing | Post-election use of surplus funds (a) | For certain purposes | Personal use of candidate |
|---|---|---|---|---|---|---|
| New Jersey ............ | Treasurer or deputy treasurer of a candidate, political party committee, political committee, and continuing political committee. | Spending limits for gubernatorial candidates (excluding travel expenses) for 1997 election: $3.1 million in primary and $6.9 million in general election. Spending limits subject to adjustment prior to election year to reflect changes in campaign costs. Governor candidate receiving public funding is limited to $25,000 in primary and $25,000 in general election from candidate's personal funds. | . . . | . . . | Contributions may be used for the payment of campaign expenses; contributions to any charitable organization described in Section 170(c) of Internal Revenue Code, or non-profit organization that is exempt from taxation under Section 501(c) of the Internal Revenue Code; transmittal to another candidate, candidate committee, or joint candidates committee or to a political committee continuing political committee, legislative leadership committee, or political party committee for the lawful use by such other candidate or committee; the payment of the overhead and administrative expenses related to the operation of the candidate committee or joint candidates committee of a candidate or a legislative leadership committee; the pro-rata repayment of contributors; or the payment of ordinary and necessary expenses of holding public office. Gubernatorial candidates limited as to use of public funds. | Prohibited. |
| New Mexico ............ | Treasurer of candidate or political committee. | Treasurer must be appointed and separate bank account established before candidate or political committee may make an expenditure. | . . . | Judicial candidates must return unused funds to contributors or donate to charitable organization. | Prohibited. | Prohibited. |

# LIMITATIONS ON EXPENDITURES — Continued

| State or other jurisdiction | Who may make expenditures | Total expenditures allowed | Expenditures before first filing | Post-election use of surplus funds (a) | For certain purposes | Personal use of candidate |
|---|---|---|---|---|---|---|
| New York | Candidate or treasurer of candidate or political committee. | ... | Expenditures may not be made by a political committee until the designation of a treasurer and depository have been filed. | May be used for any lawful purpose, including transfer to political party committee, return to donor, or holding for use in subsequent campaign. | Contributions may be expended for any lawful purpose. | Contributions may not be converted to personal use not related to political campaign or holding public office or party position. |
| North Carolina | Except for independent expenditures, candidate-related expenditures may be made only through the treasurer or assistant treasurer of a candidate or political committee. | Candidates for state constitutional office in general election who qualify for and receive public matching funds are subject to expenditure limit depending on office involved. | Except for independent expenditures, candidate-related expenditures may not be made until a treasurer is appointed and certified. | ... | ... | ... |
| North Dakota | ... | ... | ... | ... | ... | Judicial candidates may not permit use of campaign funds for private benefit. |
| Ohio | For a campaign committee, only the campaign treasurer and deputy campaign treasurer. | Campaign committee of a statewide or general assembly candidate that fails to file a personal-funds notice when receipt or expenditure of candidate's personal funds exceeds reporting threshold (statewide candidate—$100,000 in primary and $150,000 in general election; general assembly candidate - $25,000 per election) may not expend personal funds in excess of threshold amount. | Candidate must designate a treasurer before candidate's campaign committee may receive contributions or make expenditures.Statewide and general assembly candidates my not make expenditures of personal funds exceeding $500 unless funds are deposited into campaign fund of candidates campaign committee. | ... | Candidate expenditures must be legitimate, verifiable, ordinary, and necessary. | Prohibited. |

See footnotes at end of table.

# LIMITATIONS ON EXPENDITURES — Continued

| State or other jurisdiction | Who may make expenditures | Total expenditures allowed | Expenditures before first filing | Post-election use of surplus funds (a) | For certain purposes | Personal use of candidate |
|---|---|---|---|---|---|---|
| Oklahoma | Treasurer and deputy treasurer of candidate committees and other committees. | ... | ... | Surplus funds of state candidate/candidate committee may be disposed of by return to contributors, donation to charitable organization, retention for a future campaign, deposit with the state, defense of campaign legal actions, community activity, political activity, or transfer to political party committee. Other committees and local candidates/committees are authorized to dispose of surplus campaign funds for permitted purposes. | Candidates may use contributions only to defray campaign expenditures or ordinary and necessary expenses incurred in connection with duties of public officeholder. | Prohibited. |
| Oregon | Expenditures must be made by or through the treasurer of a political committee. | ... | ... | A candidate or candidate's principal campaign committee may dispose of excess contributions by using them to defray any ordinary and necessary expenses incurred with duties as an officeholder; transferring them to a political committee of a political party; contributing them to a charitable organization; or using them for any other lawful purpose. | ... | ... |
| Pennsylvania | For a political committee, the treasurer, or appointed assistant treasurer. | ... | No expenditure may be made by a political committee until a chair and treasurer have been appointed. | After financial activity is terminated, residual funds may be used for lawful expenditures, or returned pro rata to contributors. | No candidate, political committee chair, or treasurer may make an expenditure except as provided by law. | Judicial candidate should not use contributions for private benefit. |

# LIMITATIONS ON EXPENDITURES — Continued

| State or other jurisdiction | Who may make expenditures | Total expenditures allowed | Expenditures before first filing | Post-election use of surplus funds (a) | For certain purposes | Personal use of candidate |
|---|---|---|---|---|---|---|
| **Rhode Island** | Campaign treasurer or deputy campaign treasurer. | Unlimited, except for candidate for general office who accepts public funding. | No expenditures may be made before the appointment of a treasurer and the filing of such designation. | Campaign funds not used to pay for the expenses of gaining or holding public office may be maintained in campaign accounts; be donated to a candidate for public office, a political organization, or a PAC, subject to the statutory limitations on contributions; be transferred in whole or in part to a newly established PAC; be donated to a tax-exempt charitable organization; be donated to the state; or be returned to the donor. | Contributions may not be used to repay more than $200,000 during an election cycle of any cumulative personal loans to campaign by the candidate. | Prohibited. |
| **South Carolina** | Candidates or duly authorized officer of a committee. | . . . | . . . | Disposition of excess funds of a candidate or committee is restricted to specific recipients and uses. | . . . | Prohibited. |
| **South Dakota** | . . . | . . . | . . . | . . . | Necessary expenditure of money for ordinary or usual expense of conducting a political campaign unless expressly forbidden. Judicial candidates may not use or permit use of contributions for private benefit. | Judicial office candidate should not use for private benefit. |
| **Tennessee** | Political treasurer of candidate and political campaign committee. | . . . | Candidate and political committee are required to certify name and address of political treasurer before making an expenditure in an election. | . . . | Clerical/office force; dissemination of literature; public speakers; newspaper announcements of candidacy; and transportation of voters unable to go to the polls. | Prohibited. |

See footnotes at end of table.

# LIMITATIONS ON EXPENDITURES — Continued

| State or other jurisdiction | Who may make expenditures | Total expenditures allowed | Expenditures before first filing | Post-election use of surplus funds (a) | For certain purposes | Personal use of candidate |
|---|---|---|---|---|---|---|
| **Texas** | Candidate for candidate's own election; political committee; campaign treasurer or assistant campaign treasurer acting in an official capacity; and an individual who makes independent, unreimbursed expenditures. | Voluntary limits on aggregate expenditures per election for judicial candidates; statewide judicial office - $2 million; office or chief justice of the court of appeals - $500,000 if the population of the judicial district is more than one million, or $350,000 if the population of the judicial district is one million or less; and other non-statewide judicial offices - $350,000 if the population of the judicial district is more than one million, $200,000 if the population of the judicial district is 250,000 to one million, and $100,000 if the population of the judicial district is less than 250,000. | Candidates may not make or authorize expenditures before filing a campaign treasurer appointment. Specific-purpose political committees may not make expenditures that exceed $500 without filing a campaign treasurer appointment. Specific-purpose and general-purpose political committees, other than political party county executive committees, may not make expenditures totaling more than $500 to support or oppose a candidate for statewide office, state legislature, state board of education, or multi-county district office unless a campaign treasurer appointment was filed at least 30 days before the election. General purpose political committees, other than political party county executive, may not make expenditures exceeding $500 unless a campaign treasurer appointment was filed at least 60 days before the expenditures and the committee has accepted contributions from at least 10 people. | . . . | Use of public funds for political advertising prohibited. Payment from contributions for personal services of candidate, officeholder, or family restricted. Reimbursement of personal funds for expenditures by and repayment of loans made by relatives of a candidate or officeholder limited to an aggregate of $500,000 per election for governor and $250,000 per election for other statewide office. | Contributions may not be converted to the personal use of a candidate or officeholder. Specific purpose political committee contributions to the personal use of a former candidate or officeholder. Expenditures from personal funds may be reimbursed from contributions. |

# LIMITATIONS ON EXPENDITURES — Continued

| State or other jurisdiction | Who may make expenditures | Total expenditures allowed | Expenditures before first filing | Post-election use of surplus funds (a) | For certain purposes | Personal use of candidate |
|---|---|---|---|---|---|---|
| Utah ............ | Candidate and the secretary of a personal campaign committee in the case of a candidate for state executive office. A committee member may not make an expenditure over $1,000 without written authorization by candidate or committee secretary. | ... | State office candidate must file a statement of appointment of personal campaign committee before the committee may make expenditures. | ... | Expenditures prohibited by law may not be made. | Judicial candidates may not use contributions for candidate's private benefit. |
| Vermont ............ | Designated treasurer. | Expenditures are limited in 2-year general election cycle: governor non-incumbent-$300,000, incumbent-$225,000; lt. Governor non-incumbent-$100,000, incumbent-$85,000; secretary of state, state treasurer, auditor of accounts, att'y gen'l non-incumbent-$45,000, incumbent-$38,250; state senator non-incumbent-$4,000 plus $2,500 for each add'l seat in the senate district, incumbent-$3,600 plus $2,250 for each add'tl seat in the senate district, state rep (single-member district) non-incumbent $2,000, incumbent-$1,800; state rep (two-member district) non-incumbent-$3,000, incumbent-$2,700; county office (all candidates)-$4,000 | ... | ... | Existing surplus may be contributed and existing debts assigned to new fund. | Conversion of surplus funds to personal use of candidate is prohibited, but the candidate may use such funds to reduce personal campaign debts. |

See footnotes at end of table.

# LIMITATIONS ON EXPENDITURES — Continued

| State or other jurisdiction | Who may make expenditures | Total expenditures allowed | Expenditures before first filing | Post-election use of surplus funds (a) | For certain purposes | Personal use of candidate |
|---|---|---|---|---|---|---|
| Virginia ............... | ... | ... | Candidate must appoint one campaign treasurer not later than upon acceptance of a contribution. | After filing of final report, surplus funds may be used in a succeeding election; returned to contributors; donated to a Section 170 organization; contributed to other candidates or committees, including a political party committee; or used to defray unreimbursable elective office expenses of candidate. | Prohibited. | Prohibited. |
| Washington ............... | Campaign treasurer, candidate, or person on authority of campaign treasurer or candidate. | ... | ... | May be disposed of by return to the contributors in an amount not to exceed the original contributions, transfer to the candidate's personal account for reimbursement for lost earnings during the campaign, donation to a registered charitable organization, transmittal to the state, retention for a future campaign for the same office, transferred to a political party or caucus political committee, or payment of non-reimbursed public office-related expenses. | ... | Contributions may be transferred to the personal account of a candidate or expended for candidate's personal use for reimbursement for loans to cover lost earnings while campaigning or performing services for the political committee and for direct out-of-pocket expenses for repayment of loans made to political committee. Candidates may not be reimbursed more than $3,800 per election for loans made to their own campaigns. |

# LIMITATIONS ON EXPENDITURES — Continued

| State or other jurisdiction | Who may make expenditures | Total expenditures allowed | Expenditures before first filing | Post-election use of surplus funds (a) | For certain purposes | Personal use of candidate |
|---|---|---|---|---|---|---|
| West Virginia | Candidates, financial agents and political committee treasurers. | … | No person may act as treasurer or financial agent before filing designation. Political party may not disburse money for election expenses unless treasurer is appointed. | Excess campaign assets may be disposed of by transfer to new candidate committee; contribution to political party committee or candidate; or returned to contributors on a pro rata basis. Per statute, excess funds may be transferred by a terminating political committee to another committee for the same candidate. Per statute, excess contributions may be used in connection with duties as a public officeholder; contributed to a charitable organization; or transferred to a political party committee, or, effective 7/2/00, to any candidate for public office. | Generally, lawful payments for political expenses; rent, maintenance, and furnishing of political headquarters or office; payment of support staff; political advertising and advertising agency services; public meeting-related expenses; travel, lodging and administrative expenses; nominating petition costs; prevention of unlawful registration of voters; voter transportation; public polls; non-cash post-election expressions of appreciation; political party dues/subscriptions; and contributions to in-state party committees. Judicial candidates may not use or permit use of contributions for private benefit. | Personal use of funds by candidate prohibited, except for reimbursement of election expenses. Use of excess campaign assets for personal economic benefit is prohibited. |
| Wisconsin | Treasurer of a candidate, political committee, political group, or individual. | State office candidates who receive election campaign fund grant may not expend more for a campaign than amount specified in the authorized disbursement schedule unless opponents not accepting grant do not agree to comply with the limit voluntarily. | Disbursements may not be made by candidate or personal campaign committee, political committee, political group, or individual before registration statement is filed and campaign depository account established. | Residual funds may be used for any political purpose not prohibited by law, returned to the donor, or donated to a charitable organization or the common school fund. | Expenditures may be made for any lawful purpose. Contributions must be used for a political purpose. | … |
| Wyoming | … | … | … | Permissable use disposition of excess campaign funds not specified. | … | Candidate for judicial office may not use contributions for private benefit of candidate. |
| Dist. of Columbia | Only the chair, treasurer, or designated agents may make an expenditure. | … | … | May be donated to a political party for political purposes; returned to donors; transferred to a scientific, technical, or literacy or educational organization; or used for constituent services with certain limits. | … | … |

See footnotes at end of table.

## LIMITATIONS ON EXPENDITURES — Continued

| State or other jurisdiction | Who may make expenditures | Total expenditures allowed | Expenditures before first filing | Post-election use of surplus funds (a) | For certain purposes | Personal use of candidate |
|---|---|---|---|---|---|---|
| American Samoa | Requires written authorization of treasurer. | ... | Triggers organizational report filing. | Surplus must be returned pro rata to contributors if their identities are known. If no donors are found, surplus may be contributed to another candidate's fund, party, charity, or nonprofit organization, or surplus escheats to the territory. | Must be related to the campaign. | ... |
| Guam | Requires written authorization of treasurer. | ... | Permissible, as long as not greater than $100,000. | Candidates who withdraw or cease to be candidates must return contributions to their party, or to another candidate of the same party. | ... | ... |
| No. Marianas Islands | ... | ... | ... | ... | ... | ... |
| Puerto Rico | ... | Limited for candidates for governor and parties using public funding. | ... | ... | ... | ... |
| U.S. Virgin Islands | May not be made in absence of treasurer and requires authorization by certain officials. | ... | Triggers organizational report filing. | ... | Must be related to the campaign. | ... |

Source: Edward D. Feigenbaum, J.D. and James A. Palmer, J.D., INGroup, Noblesville, Indiana, March 2000; Finance Law 2000: A Summary of State Campaign Finance Laws with Quick Reference Charts.
Note: For detailed legal requirements, state statutes should be consulted.
Key:
... — No reference in the law.
(a) Post election.
(b) Unopposed candidate may not take any campaign funds for personal use or for income for spouse or dependent children after the filing deadline (or if opposed in the primary but not in the general election, after the date of winning the nomination).

**Table 5.13**

**FUNDING OF STATE ELECTIONS: TAX PROVISIONS AND PUBLIC FINANCING**

**(As of December 31, 1999)**

| State | Tax provisions relating to individuals | | | | Public financing | |
|---|---|---|---|---|---|---|
| | Credit | Deduction | Checkoff | Surcharge | Source of funds | Distribution of funds |
| Alabama | ... | ... | ... | $1 (a) | Surcharge | To political party designated by taxpayer. |
| Alaska | ... | ... | ... | ... | ... | ... |
| Arizona (f) | ... | $100 (a). Money designated as surcharge is deductible. | ... | $2, $5, or $10 (c) | Surcharge and donated amounts. | To political party designated by taxpayer. |
| Arkansas | $50 for contributions to candidates; small donor PAC; approved PAC; or organized political party [a] | ... | ... | ... | ... | ... |
| California | ... | ... | ... | $1, $5, $10, or $25 (b) | Surcharge and an equal amount matched by state. | To political parties for party activities and distribution to statewide general election candidates. |
| Colorado | ... | ... | ... | ... | ... | ... |
| Connecticut | ... | ... | ... | ... | ... | ... |
| Delaware | ... | ... | ... | ... | ... | ... |
| Florida | ... | ... | ... | $5 (d) | Direct appropriations; candidate filing fees; donated surplus funds; and voluntary surcharge on intangibles tax return, motor vehicle registration, driver's license application, boat registration, and annual reports for corporations. | To candidates for governor and lieutenant governor and members of the cabinet. |
| Georgia | ... | ... | ... | ... | ... | ... |
| Hawaii | ... | $100 for contributions to central or county party committees, or $500 for contributions to candidates who abide by expenditure limits, with deductible maximum of $100 of a total contribution to a single candidate. | $2 (a) | ... | Checkoff, appropriated funds, other moneys. | To candidates for all non-federal elective offices. |
| Idaho | ... | ... | $1 | ... | Checkoff | To political party designated by taxpayer. |
| Illinois | ... | ... | ... | ... | Revenues from personalized motor vehicle license plates. | Percentage divided equally between the qualified political parties for state and county party use. |
| Indiana | ... | ... | ... | ... | Checkoff | To political party designated by taxpayer or divided among qualified parties as specified by taxpayer. |
| Iowa | ... | ... | $1.50 (a) | ... | Checkoff | To political party designated by taxpayer for party activities and distribution to general election candidates. |
| Kansas | ... | ... | ... | ... | ... | ... |
| Kentucky | ... | ... | $2 (a) | ... | Checkoff | To political party designated by taxpayer |
| Louisiana | ... | ... | ... | ... | (1) Surcharge | (1) To political party designated by taxpayer |
| Maine | ... | ... | $3 (a) | ... | (2) Checkoff, general fund, surplus candidate seed money, unspent candidate funds, voluntary donations and fines | (2) To candidates for governor, state senate, and house of representatives in primary and general elections. |

# FUNDING OF STATE ELECTIONS

| State | Tax provisions relating to individuals | | | | Public financing | |
|---|---|---|---|---|---|---|
| | Credit | Deduction | Checkoff | Surcharge | Source of funds | Distribution of funds |
| Maryland | ... | ... | ... | Add-on not to exceed $500 per tax filer. | Direct appropriations; fines; and tax add-ons. | To candidates for governor and lieutenant governor only. |
| Massachusetts | ... | ... | $1 (a) | ... | Direct appropriations; checkoff; monies from former public campaign finance fund. | To candidates for certain offices abiding by expenditure limits and raising specified qualifying contributions in statewide primary and general elections. |
| Michigan | ... | ... | $3 (a) | ... | Checkoff | To candidates in gubernatorial primaries and candidates for governor and lieutenant governor in general election. |
| Minnesota | Refund up to $50 for contributions to political parties and qualified candidates. (a) | ... | $5 (a) | ... | Direct appropriations, checkoff, anonymous contributions to candidates and committees | To qualifying candidates for governor, lt. governor, attorney general, other statewide offices, and state senator and state representative, after primary and general elections; to the state committee of a political party for multi-candidate expenditures; and to state general fund for administrative purposes. |
| Mississippi | ... | ... | ... | ... | ... | ... |
| Missouri | ... | ... | ... | ... | ... | ... |
| Montana | ... | $100 (a) | ... | ... | ... | ... |
| Nebraska | ... | ... | ... | $2 of income tax refund. | Direct appropriations, taxpayer contribution of income tax refund, amounts repaid to campaign finance limitation cash fund by candidates, civil penalties, and late filing fees. | If highest estimated maximum expenditure of opponents not agreeing to abide by the statutory spending limitation for the office is greater than the spending limitation, the difference to otherwise qualified candidates for governor, lieutenant governor, secretary of state, attorney general, auditor of public accounts, legislature, public service commission, board of regents of the University of Nebraska, and state board of education who agree to abide by the statutory spending limitation. Applicable only to legislative offices in 1998 general election. |
| Nevada | ... | ... | ... | ... | ... | ... |
| New Hampshire | ... | ... | $1 (a) | ... | ... | ... |
| New Jersey | ... | ... | $2 (a) | ... | Direct appropriations and checkoff. | To qualified gubernatorial candidates. |
| New Mexico | ... | ... | ... | ... | Checkoff | To political party designated by taxpayer. |
| New York | ... | ... | ... | ... | ... | ... |
| North Carolina | $25 for political contribution or newsletter fund contribution. Income tax surcharge for candidates is intended to be deductible. | ... | $1 (a) | Up to amount of income tax refund due. | Checkoff for political parties fund; surcharge for candidates fund. | Political parties fund divided among political parties according to registration. In non-general election years, not more than 50% in election campaign fund to state party and 50% to presidential election year candidates fund. In general election year, 100% in election campaign fund to state party (with 50% to special party committee). If presidential election year, 100% in presidential election year candidates fund to state party (with 50% to special party committee). Candidates fund divided among opposed candidates for governor who agree to abide by the expenditure limit and raise matching funds equal to 5% of expenditure limit. Matching funds are provided on a one-to-one basis for general election campaign. |

See footnotes at end of table.

# FUNDING OF STATE ELECTIONS

| State | Tax provisions relating to individuals | | | | Public financing | |
|---|---|---|---|---|---|---|
| | Credit | Deduction | Checkoff | Surcharge | Source of funds | Distribution of funds |
| North Dakota | ... | ... | ... | ... | ... | ... |
| Ohio | $50 for contributions to statewide candidates. (a) | $1 (a) | ... | ... | Checkoff | Divided equally among major political parties each calendar quarter. Party allocation divided: 50 percent to state executive committee of party, and 50 percent to county executive committees of party according to proportion of income from tax return checkoffs in each county to total checkoff income. |
| Oklahoma | ... | $100 | ... | ... | ... | ... |
| Oregon | Lesser of (1) total contributions with a maximum of $50 [a], or (2) the taxpayer's liability for contribution to a major or minor party, a candidate for any office, or registered political committee. | ... | ... | ... | ... | ... |
| Pennsylvania | ... | ... | ... | ... | ... | ... |
| Rhode Island | ... | ... | $5 (a) | ... | Checkoff ("credit") | First $2 ($4 for a joint return) of checkoff allocated to major political parties. Distributed to eligible political party designated by taxpayer. If a party is not designated, 5% of the amount is allocated to each party for each state officer elected, and the remainder to each party in proportion to the votes its candidate for governor received in previous election. Maximum of $200,000 allocated to all political parties. Remainder to qualifying candidates in general election for governor, lt. governor, secretary of state, attorney general, and general treasurer as state matching funds (maximum for 1994 was $750,000 for governor and $187,500 for other candidates). |
| South Carolina | ... | ... | ... | ... | ... | ... |
| South Dakota | ... | ... | ... | ... | ... | ... |
| Tennessee | ... | ... | ... | ... | ... | ... |
| Texas | ... | ... | ... | ... | ... | ... |
| Utah | ... | ... | $1 | ... | Checkoff (although funds actually are revenue from sales and use taxes). | To political party designated by taxpayer: 50 percent to state central committee, and 50 percent to county central committee in proportion to the number of taxpayers designating the party in each county to the total number of taxpayers in the state who designate the party. |
| Vermont | ... | ... | ... | Up to amount of income tax refund or overpayment $25 (a) of income tax refund. | Surcharge, public funding penalties, unexpended campaign finance grants, portion of corporation annual reporting fees, tax on lobbying expenditures, gifts, and state appropriations. | To qualifying candidates for governor and lt. governor. Governor candidates: Non-incumbent—$75,000 minus qualifying contributions for primary: $250,000 for general election. Incumbent—$63,750 minus qualifying contributions for primary and $191,250 for general election. Lt. Governor candidates: Non-incumbent—$25,000 minus qualifying contributions for primary; $75,000 for general election. Incumbent—$21,250 minus qualifying contributions for primary; $63,750 for general election. |

See footnotes at end of table.

# FUNDING OF STATE ELECTIONS

| State | Tax provisions relating to individuals | | | | Source of funds | Public financing |
| --- | --- | --- | --- | --- | --- | --- |
| | Credit | Deduction | Checkoff | Surcharge | | Distribution of funds |
| Virginia | $25 for contributions to candidates (a) | ... | ... | $25 (a) of income tax refund. | Surcharge | To designated political party. |
| Washington | ... | ... | ... | ... | ... | ... |
| West Virginia | ... | ... | ... | ... | ... | ... |
| Wisconsin | ... | ... | $1 (a) | ... | Checkoff | According to formula, to state legislative office and state Supreme Court candidates in a spring, general, or special election. (e) |
| Wyoming | ... | ... | ... | ... | ... | ... |
| District of Columbia | 50% of contributions to a maximum of $50 (a) | ... | ... | ... | ... | ... |
| American Samoa | ... | ... | ... | ... | ... | ... |
| Guam | ... | ... | ... | ... | ... | ... |
| No. Mariana Islands | ... | ... | ... | ... | ... | ... |
| Puerto Rico | ... | ... | ... | ... | Commonwealth treasury | To political parties and gubernatorial candidates. In non-general election years, participating political parties may draw not more than $300,000 from a special electoral fund. In a general election year, political parties may draw against the surplus left from preceding years, and each participating political party and its candidate for governor have the right to draw on the fund not more than $600,000. The political parties and candidates for governor that avail themselves of the benefits of the electoral fund in an election year may incur additional campaign expenses up to a maximum of $5 million. In general election year, political parties whose gubernatorial candidates opt for public funding share equally in additional funding ($1.50 x total registered voters). In general election year, all political parties and independent candidates receive pro rata share of $1.2 million provided for voter transportation (minimum $25,000). |
| U.S. Virgin Islands | ... | ... | ... | ... | ... | ... |

Source: Edward D. Feigenbaum, J.D. and James A. Palmer, J.D., INGroup, Noblesville, Indiana, March 2000; Finance Law 2000: A Summary of State Campaign Finance Laws with Quick Reference Charts.

Note: Table details only those states that have a tax provision relating to individuals or a provision for public financing of state elections.

Credits and deductions may be allowed only for certain types of candidates and/or political parties. Consult state statutes for further details.

Key:

... — No provision.
(a) For joint returns, amount indicated may be doubled.
(b) And a separate designation of $1, $5, $10, or $25.
(c) Additional amounts may be donated.
(d) On intangibles tax return.
(e) Candidates must meet certain qualifications.
(f) Arizona's Clean Elections Act has been ruled unconstitutional; its provisions are not included here.

## Table 5.14
## STATEWIDE INITIATIVE AND REFERENDUM

| State or other jurisdiction | Changes to constitution | | | Changes to statutes | | | |
|---|---|---|---|---|---|---|---|
| | Initiative | | Referendum | Initiative | | Referendum | |
| | Direct (a) | Indirect (a) | Legislative (b) | Direct (c) | Indirect (c) | Legislative | Citizen petition (d) |
| Alabama | . . . | . . . | . . . | . . . | . . . | . . . | . . . |
| Alaska | . . . | . . . | ★ | . . . | ★ | . . . | ★ |
| Arizona | ★ | . . . | ★ | ★ | . . . | ★ | ★ |
| Arkansas | ★ | . . . | ★ | ★ | . . . | ★ | ★ |
| California | ★ | . . . | ★ | ★ | . . . | ★ | ★ |
| Colorado | ★ | . . . | ★ | ★ | . . . | ★ | ★ |
| Connecticut | . . . | . . . | ★ | . . . | . . . | . . . | . . . |
| Delaware* | . . . | . . . | ★ | . . . | . . . | ★ | . . . |
| Florida | ★ | . . . | ★ | . . . | . . . | . . . | . . . |
| Georgia | . . . | . . . | ★ | . . . | . . . | . . . | . . . |
| Hawaii | . . . | . . . | ★ | . . . | . . . | . . . | . . . |
| Idaho | . . . | . . . | ★ | ★ | . . . | ★ | ★ |
| Illinois | ★ | . . . | ★ | ★ | . . . | ★ | . . . |
| Indiana* | . . . | . . . | ★ | . . . | . . . | . . . | . . . |
| Iowa | . . . | . . . | ★ | . . . | . . . | . . . | . . . |
| Kansas | . . . | . . . | ★ | . . . | . . . | . . . | . . . |
| Kentucky* | . . . | . . . | ★ | . . . | . . . | ★ | ★ |
| Louisiana | . . . | . . . | ★ | . . . | . . . | . . . | . . . |
| Maine | . . . | . . . | ★ | . . . | ★ | ★ | ★ |
| Maryland | . . . | . . . | ★ | . . . | . . . | ★ | ★ |
| Massachusetts* | . . . | ★ | ★ | . . . | ★ | ★ | ★ |
| Michigan | ★ | . . . | ★ | . . . | ★ | ★ | ★ |
| Minnesota | . . . | . . . | ★ | . . . | . . . | . . . | . . . |
| Mississippi | . . . | ★ | ★ | . . . | . . . | . . . | . . . |
| Missouri | ★ | . . . | ★ | ★ | . . . | ★ | ★ |
| Montana | ★ | . . . | ★ | ★ | . . . | ★ | ★ |
| Nebraska | ★ | . . . | ★ | ★ | . . . | . . . | ★ |
| Nevada* | ★ | . . . | ★ | ★ | ★ | ★ | ★ |
| New Hampshire | . . . | . . . | ★ | . . . | . . . | . . . | . . . |
| New Jersey | . . . | . . . | ★ | . . . | . . . | . . . | . . . |
| New Mexico | . . . | . . . | ★ | . . . | . . . | ★ | ★ |
| New York | . . . | . . . | ★ | . . . | . . . | . . . | . . . |
| North Carolina* | . . . | . . . | ★ | . . . | . . . | . . . | . . . |
| North Dakota | ★ | . . . | ★ | ★ | . . . | ★ | ★ |
| Ohio | ★ | . . . | ★ | ★ | ★ | ★ | ★ |
| Oklahoma | ★ | . . . | ★ | ★ | . . . | ★ | ★ |
| Oregon | ★ | . . . | ★ | ★ | . . . | ★ | ★ |
| Pennsylvania | . . . | . . . | ★ | . . . | . . . | . . . | . . . |
| Rhode Island | . . . | . . . | ★ | . . . | . . . | . . . | . . . |
| South Carolina | . . . | . . . | ★ | . . . | . . . | . . . | . . . |
| South Dakota | ★ | . . . | ★ | ★ | . . . | . . . | ★ |
| Tennessee | . . . | . . . | ★ | . . . | . . . | . . . | . . . |
| Texas | . . . | . . . | ★ | . . . | . . . | . . . | . . . |
| Utah | . . . | . . . | ★ | ★ | ★ | ★ | ★ |
| Vermont | . . . | . . . | ★ | . . . | . . . | . . . | . . . |
| Virginia | . . . | . . . | ★ | . . . | . . . | . . . | . . . |
| Washington | . . . | . . . | ★ | ★ | ★ | ★ | ★ |
| West Virginia* | . . . | . . . | ★ | . . . | . . . | . . . | . . . |
| Wisconsin | . . . | . . . | ★ | . . . | . . . | . . . | . . . |
| Wyoming | . . . | . . . | ★ | . . . | ★ | . . . | ★ |
| U.S. Virgin Islands | . . . | ★ | ★ | . . . | ★ | ★ | ★ |

*Sources*: State election administration offices, state constitutions and statutes, except where noted by * where data are from *The Book of the States, 1998-99.*

*Note*: This table summarizes state provisions for initiatives and referenda. Initiatives may propose constitutional amendments or develop state legislation and may be formed either directly or indirectly. The direct initiative allows a proposed measure to be placed on the ballot after a specific number of signatures have been secured on a citizen petition. The indirect initiative must be submitted to the legislature for a decision after the required number of signatures has been secured on a petition and prior to placing the proposed measure on the ballot. Referendum refers to the process whereby a state law or constitutional amendment passed by the legislature may be referred to the voters before it goes into effect. Three forms of referenda exist: (1) citizen petition, whereby the people may petition for a referendum on legislation

which has been considered by the legislature;

(2) submission by the legislature (designated in table as "Legislative"), whereby the legislature may voluntarily submit laws to the voters for their approval; and

(3) constitutional requirement, whereby the state constitution may require that certain questions be submitted to the voters.

*Key*:
★ — State Provision.
. . . — No state provision.
(a) See Table 1.3, "Constitutional Amendment Procedure: By Initiative," for more detail.
(b) See Table 1.2, "Constitutional Amendment Procedure: By the Legislature," for more detail.
(c) See Tables 5.15 through 5.18 on State Initiatives, for more detail.
(d) See Tables 5.19 through 5.22 on State Referenda, for more detail.

## Table 5.15
## STATE INITIATIVES: REQUESTING PERMISSION TO CIRCULATE A PETITION

| State or other jurisdiction | Applied to (a) | | Signatures required to request a petition (b) | | Request submitted to | Request form furnished by (c) | Restricted subject matter (d) | Individual responsible for petition | | Financial contributions reported (e) | Deposits required (f) |
|---|---|---|---|---|---|---|---|---|---|---|---|
| | Const. amdt. | Statute | Const. amdt. | Statute | | | | Title | Summary | | |
| Alabama | ... | ... | ... | ... | ... | ... | ... | ... | ... | ... | ... |
| Alaska | ... | I | ... | 100 | LG | SP | Y | LG | LG | Y | $100 |
| Arizona | D | D | 15% (g) | 10% (g) | SS | ST | N | ... | ... | Y | ... |
| Arkansas | D | D | 10% | 8% | AG | SP | N | AG | AG | Y | ... |
| California | D | D | ... | ... | AG | SP | N | AG | AG | Y | $200 |
| Colorado | D | D | ... | ... | ... | ... | N | (h) | (h) | Y | ... |
| Connecticut | ... | ... | ... | ... | ... | ... | ... | ... | ... | ... | ... |
| Delaware* | ... | ... | ... | ... | ... | ... | ... | ... | ... | ... | ... |
| Florida | D | ... | ... | ... | SS | SP | N | P | P | Y | ... |
| Georgia | ... | ... | ... | ... | ... | ... | ... | ... | ... | ... | ... |
| Hawaii | ... | ... | ... | ... | ... | ... | ... | ... | ... | ... | ... |
| Idaho | ... | D | ... | 20 | SS | SP | N | AG | AG | Y | ... |
| Illinois | D | ... | ... | ... | ... | ... | Y | ... | ... | ... | ... |
| Indiana | ... | ... | ... | ... | ... | ... | ... | ... | ... | ... | ... |
| Iowa | ... | ... | ... | ... | ... | ... | ... | ... | ... | ... | ... |
| Kansas | ... | ... | ... | ... | ... | ... | ... | ... | ... | ... | ... |
| Kentucky* | ... | ... | ... | ... | ... | ... | ... | ... | ... | ... | ... |
| Louisiana | ... | ... | ... | ... | ... | ... | ... | ... | ... | ... | ... |
| Maine | ... | I | ... | 5 (i) | ... | SS | Y | P | SS | Y | ... |
| Maryland | ... | ... | ... | ... | ... | ... | ... | ... | ... | ... | ... |
| Massachusetts* | I | I | 10 | 10 | AG | SS | Y | AG | AG | Y | ... |
| Michigan | D | I | ... | ... | ... | ... | Y | P | P | Y | ... |
| Minnesota | ... | ... | ... | ... | ... | ... | ... | ... | ... | ... | ... |
| Mississippi | I | ... | ... | ... | SS | ... | Y | AG | AG | Y | ... |
| Missouri | D | D | ... | ... | SS | SP | Y | SS,AG | ... | Y | N |
| Montana | D | D | ... | ... | SS | SP | Y | AG | AG | Y (j) | ... |
| Nebraska | D | D | ... | ... | SS | SP | Y | AG | AG | Y | N |
| Nevada* | D | I | ... | ... | SS | SP | Y | P | P | N | N |
| New Hampshire | ... | ... | ... | ... | ... | ... | ... | ... | ... | ... | ... |
| New Jersey | ... | ... | ... | ... | ... | ... | ... | ... | ... | ... | ... |
| New Mexico | ... | ... | ... | ... | ... | ... | ... | ... | ... | ... | ... |
| New York* | ... | ... | ... | ... | ... | ... | ... | ... | ... | ... | ... |
| North Carolina* | ... | ... | ... | ... | ... | ... | ... | ... | ... | ... | ... |
| North Dakota | D | D | 25 (k) | 25 (k) | SS | SP | N | SS,AG | SS,AG | Y (e) | ... |
| Ohio | D | I | ... | ... | SS | SP | Y | ... | AG | Y | ... |
| Oklahoma (l) | D | D | ... | ... | SS | SP | N | AG | AG | Y | ... |
| Oregon | D | D | 25 | 25 | SS | SS | N | AG | AG | Y | ... |
| Pennsylvania | ... | ... | ... | ... | ... | ... | ... | ... | ... | ... | ... |
| Rhode Island | ... | ... | ... | ... | ... | ... | ... | ... | ... | ... | ... |
| South Carolina | ... | ... | ... | ... | ... | ... | ... | ... | ... | ... | ... |
| South Dakota | D | D | ... | ... | SS | SP | N | P | ... | Y | ... |
| Tennessee | ... | ... | ... | ... | ... | ... | ... | ... | ... | ... | ... |
| Texas | ... | ... | ... | ... | ... | ... | ... | ... | ... | ... | ... |
| Utah | ... | I,D | ... | 5% | LG | SP | N | SP | ... | Y (m) | N |
| Vermont | ... | ... | ... | ... | ... | ... | ... | ... | ... | ... | ... |
| Virginia | ... | ... | ... | ... | ... | ... | ... | ... | ... | ... | ... |
| Washington | ... | I,D | ... | 1 | SS | SP | N | AG | AG | Y | N |
| West Virginia* | ... | ... | ... | ... | ... | ... | ... | ... | ... | ... | ... |
| Wisconsin | ... | ... | ... | ... | ... | ... | ... | ... | ... | ... | ... |
| Wyoming | ... | D | ... | 100 | SS | SS | Y | AG,SS | AG,SS | Y | $500 |
| U.S. Virgin Islands | ... | D | ... | 10% EV | (n) | (n) | Y | (h) | (h) | Y | ... |

*Source*: State election administration offices, state constitutions and statutes, except where noted by * where data are from *The Book of the States, 1998-99*.

Key:
... — Not applicable
D — Direct initiative
I — Indirect initiative
EV — Eligible voters
LG — Lieutenant Governor
SS — Secretary of State
SBE - State Board of Elections

(a) An initiative may provide a constitutional amendment or develop a new statute, and may be formed either directly or indirectly. The direct initiative allows a proposed measure to be placed on the ballot after a specific number of signatures have been secured on a petition. The indirect initiative must first be submitted to the legislature for decision after the required number of signatures have been secured on a petition, prior to placing the proposed measure on the ballot.

(b) Prior to circulating a statewide petition, a request for permission to do so must first be submitted to a specified state officer.

(c) The form on which the request for petition is submitted may be the responsibility of the sponsor or may be furnished by the state.

# Table 5.15
## STATE INITIATIVES: REQUESTING PERMISSION TO CIRCULATE A PETITION - Continued

(d) Restrictions may exist regarding the subject matter to which an initiative may be applied. The majority of these restrictions pertain to the dedication of state revenues and appropriations, and laws that maintain the preservation of public peace, safety, and health. In Illinois, amendments are restricted to "structural and procedural subjects contained in" the legislative article.

(e) In some states, a list of financial contributors and the amount of their contributions must be submitted to the specified state officer with whom the petition is filed. In North Dakota, if over $100 in aggregate for calendar year.

(f) A deposit may be required after permission to circulate a petition has been granted. This amount is refunded when the completed petition has been filed correctly.

(g) The total number of votes cast for governor in last election.

(h) Title Setting Board–secretary of state, attorney general, director of legislative legal services.

(i) The name and address of five voters.

(j) Contributions reported to Commissioner of Political Practices; petitions filed with Secretary of State.

(k) Petition needs 25 people who act as a sponsoring committee. Their names and addresses appear on the front of the petition.

(l) In Oklahoma, a person is not required to obtain permission to circulate a petition. Information provided by Oklahoma refers to procedural requirements for filing a petition only.

(m) Political issues committees must report if contributions or expenditures exceed $750 in a calendar year.

(n) In the U.S. Virgin Islands, the Supervisor of Elections is responsible.

## Table 5.16
## STATE INITIATIVES: CIRCULATING THE PETITION

| State or other jurisdiction | Basis for signatures (see key below) Const. amdt. | Statute | Maximum time period allowed for petition circulation (a) | Can signatures be removed from petition (b) | Completed petition filed with | Days prior to election Const. amdt. | Statute |
|---|---|---|---|---|---|---|---|
| Alabama | ... | ... | ... | ... | ... | ... | ... |
| Alaska | 15% VG | 10% TV from 2/3 ED | 1 yr. | Y | (c) | ... | 4 mos. |
| Arizona | 10% VG | 10% VG | 2 yr. | Y | SS | 4 mos. | 4 mos. |
| Arkansas | 8% VG | 8% VG | ... | N | SS | 4 mos. | 4 mos. |
| California | 5% VG | 5% VG | 150 days | Y | SS (d) | 131 days | 131 days |
| Colorado | 5% VSS | 5% VSS | 6 mos. | N | SS | 3 mos. | 3 mos. |
| Connecticut | ... | ... | ... | ... | ... | ... | ... |
| Delaware* | ... | ... | ... | ... | ... | ... | ... |
| Florida | 8% VEP, 8% from 1/2 CD | ... | 4 yr. | ... | SS | 91 days | ... |
| Georgia | ... | ... | ... | ... | ... | ... | ... |
| Hawaii | ... | ... | ... | ... | ... | ... | ... |
| Idaho | 6% EV | ... | (e) | Y | SS | ... | 4 mos. |
| Illinois | 8% VG | ... | 2 yr. | Y | SS | 6 mos. | ... |
| Indiana* | ... | ... | ... | ... | ... | ... | ... |
| Iowa | ... | ... | ... | ... | ... | ... | ... |
| Kansas | ... | ... | ... | ... | ... | ... | ... |
| Kentucky* | ... | ... | ... | ... | ... | ... | ... |
| Louisiana | ... | ... | ... | ... | ... | ... | ... |
| Maine | 10% VG | ... | 1 yr. | ... | SS | ... | (f) |
| Maryland | ... | ... | ... | ... | ... | ... | ... |
| Massachusetts* | 3% VG, no more than 25% from 1 county | 3% VG, no more than 25% from 1 county (g) | ... | Y | SS | (i) | (i) |
| Michigan | 10% VG | 8% VG | (h) | N | SS | (i) | ... |
| Minnesota | ... | ... | ... | ... | ... | ... | ... |
| Mississippi | 12% VG | ... | 1 yr. | ... | SS (d) | 90 days prior to LS | ... |
| Missouri | 8% VG, 8% each from 2/3 CD | 5% VG, 5% each from 2/3 CD | 2 yrs. | Y | SS | 6 mos. | 6 mos. |
| Montana | 10% VG, 10% each from 2/5 SLD | 5% VG, 5% each from 1/3 SLD | 1 yr. | Y | SS | (j) | (j) |
| Nebraska | 10% EV, 5% each from 2/5 counties | 7% EV, 5% each from 2/5 counties | ... | Y | SS | 4 mos. | 4 mos. |
| Nevada* | 10% TV, 10% each from 3/4 counties | 10% TV, 10% each from 3/4 counties | (k) | ... | SS | 90 days | 30 days prior to LS |
| New Hampshire | ... | ... | ... | ... | ... | ... | ... |
| New Jersey | ... | ... | ... | ... | ... | ... | ... |
| New Mexico | ... | ... | ... | ... | ... | ... | ... |
| New York | ... | ... | ... | ... | ... | ... | ... |
| North Carolina* | ... | ... | ... | ... | ... | ... | ... |
| North Dakota | 4% resident population | 2% resident population | 1 yr. | N | SS | 90 days | 90 days |
| Ohio | 10% VG, 1.5% each from 1/2 counties | 3% VG, 1.5% each from 1/2 counties (l) | ... | N | SS | 90 days | 90 days |
| Oklahoma | 15% VH | 8% VH | 90 days | N | SS | ... | ... |
| Oregon | 8% VG | 6% VG | ... | N (m) | SS | 4 mos. | 4 mos. |
| Pennsylvania | ... | ... | ... | ... | ... | ... | ... |
| Rhode Island | ... | ... | ... | ... | ... | ... | ... |
| South Carolina | ... | ... | ... | ... | ... | ... | ... |

See footnotes at end of table.

# STATE INITIATIVES: CIRCULATING THE PETITION — Continued

| State or other jurisdiction | Basis for signatures (see key below) | | Maximum time period allowed for petition circulation (a) | Can signatures be removed from petition (b) | Completed petition filed with | Days prior to election | |
|---|---|---|---|---|---|---|---|
| | Const. amdt. | Statute | | | | Const. amdt. | Statute |
| South Dakota | 10% VG | 5% VG | 1 yr. | N | SS | 1 yr. | May, 1st. T |
| Tennessee | ... | ... | ... | ... | ... | ... | ... |
| Texas | ... | 10% VG, 10% each from 20 counties | 2 election cycles | Y | LG | ... | June 1 |
| Utah | ... | ... | ... | ... | ... | ... | ... |
| Vermont | ... | ... | ... | ... | ... | ... | ... |
| Virginia | ... | 8% VG | (l) | Y | SS | ... | (n) |
| Washington* | ... | ... | ... | ... | ... | ... | ... |
| West Virginia* | ... | ... | ... | ... | ... | ... | ... |
| Wisconsin | ... | 15% TV, from 2/3 counties | 18 mos. | Y | SS | ... | 120 days |
| Wyoming | ... | ... | ... | ... | ... | ... | ... |
| U.S. Virgin Islands | ... | 10 % ED | 180 days | ... | SBE | ... | 90 days |

*Sources:* State election administration offices, except where noted by * where data are from *The Book of the States, 1998-99.*

Key:
... — Not applicable.
VG — Total votes cast for the position of governor in the last election.
EV — Eligible voters.
VH — Total votes cast for the office receiving the highest number of votes in last general election.
TV — Total voters in last election.
VSS — Total votes cast for all candidates for the office of secretary of state at the previous general election.
VEP — Total votes cast in the state as a whole on the last presidential election.
ED — Election district.
CD — Congressional district.
SBE - State Board of Elections.
SLD — State legislative district.
LG — Lieutenant Governor
SS — Secretary of State
LS — Legislative session
Y — Yes
N — No
T—Tuesday

(a) The petition circulation period begins when petition forms have been approved and provided to sponsors. Sponsors are those individuals granted permission to circulate a petition, and are therefore responsible for the validity of each signature on a given petition.
(b) Should an individual wish to remove his/her name from a petition, a request to do so must be submitted in writing to the state officer with whom the petition is filed.
(c) Director of elections.
(d) Petitions first must be submitted to county circuit clerks for signature certification.
(e) 6% of qualified voters at most recent general election including 6% each from 22 counties. 18 months from receipt of ballot title or April 30 of year of election on initiative, whichever occurs earlier.
(f) To be placed on November ballot, petitions must be submitted to SS by 5:00 p.m. on 50th day after convening of Legislature in 1st regular session, or by 5:00 p.m. on 25th day in 2nd regular session.
(g) First Wednesday in December.
(h) In Michigan, signatures dated more than 180 days prior to the filing date are ruled invalid.
(i) Constitutional amendment–not less than 120 days prior to the next general election; statute–160 days prior to the next general election.
(j) Third Friday of the fourth month prior to election (3 months).
(k) Constitutional amendment–276 days; Amend or create a statute–291 days.
(l) Direct–6 months; Indirect–10 months.
(m) Not after petition has been filed.
(n) Direct–4 months; Indirect–2 weeks prior to legislative session.

**Table 5.17**

## STATE INITIATIVES: PREPARING THE INITIATIVE TO BE PLACED ON THE BALLOT

| State or other jurisdiction | Signatures verified by: (a) | Within how many days after filing | Number of days to amend/appeal a petition that is: | | Penalty for falsifying petition (denotes fine, jail term) | Petition certified by: (d) |
| --- | --- | --- | --- | --- | --- | --- |
| | | | Incomplete (b) | Not Accepted (c) | | |
| Alabama | ... | ... | ... | ... | ... | ... |
| Alaska | Director of elections | 60 days | ... | 30 days | Class B misdemeanor | LG |
| Arizona | County recorder | 10 days | ... | ... | Class 1 misdemeanor | SS |
| Arkansas | SS | 30 days | 30 days | 15 days | Class D felony | SS |
| California | Clerk or registrar of voters | 30 days | 15 days | ... | (e) | SS |
| Colorado | SS | 30 days | ... | ... | ... | SS |
| Connecticut | ... | ... | ... | ... | ... | ... |
| Delaware* | ... | ... | ... | ... | ... | ... |
| Florida | Supervisor of elections | ... | ... | ... | ... | SS |
| Georgia | ... | ... | ... | ... | ... | ... |
| Hawaii | ... | ... | ... | ... | ... | ... |
| Idaho | County clerk | 60 days | ... | 10 days | ... | SS |
| Illinois | SBE and election authority | Approx. 45 days | ... | ... | $5,000, 2 yrs. | SBE |
| Indiana* | ... | ... | ... | ... | ... | ... |
| Iowa | ... | ... | ... | ... | ... | ... |
| Kansas | ... | ... | ... | ... | ... | ... |
| Kentucky* | ... | ... | ... | ... | ... | ... |
| Louisiana | ... | ... | ... | ... | ... | ... |
| Maine | Registrar of voters, SS | ... | ... | ... | ... | SS |
| Maryland | ... | ... | ... | ... | ... | ... |
| Massachusetts* | Local board of registrar | 2 weeks | 4 weeks (f) | ... | ... | SS |
| Michigan | SS, local election officials | ... | ... | ... | $1,000, 1 yr. | BSC |
| Minnesota | ... | ... | ... | ... | $500, 90 days | ... |
| Mississippi | Circuit clerk | ... | ... | ... | $1,000, 1 yr. | SS |
| Missouri | SS, local election authority | 93 days | ... | ... | Class A misdemeanor | SS |
| Montana | County clerk and recorder | 4 weeks | ... | ... | $500, 6 mos. | SS |
| Nebraska | County clerk or election commissioner | 40 days | ... | ... | Calss IV felony | SS |
| Nevada* | County clerk or registrar | 20-50 days | ... | 10 days | $10,000, 1-10 yrs. | SS |
| New Hampshire | ... | ... | ... | ... | ... | ... |
| New Jersey | ... | ... | ... | ... | ... | ... |
| New Mexico | ... | ... | ... | ... | ... | ... |
| New York | ... | ... | ... | ... | ... | ... |
| North Carolina* | ... | ... | ... | ... | ... | ... |
| North Dakota | SS | 35 days | 20 days | ... | $1,000, 6 mos. | SS |
| Ohio | County board of elections | ... | 10 days | ... | ... | SS |
| Oklahoma | ... | ... | ... | ... | $1,000, 1 yr. | ... |
| Oregon | SS, county elections official | 15 days | (g) | ... | Class C felony (possible) | SS |
| Pennsylvania | ... | ... | ... | ... | ... | ... |
| Rhode Island | ... | ... | ... | ... | ... | ... |
| South Carolina | ... | ... | ... | ... | ... | ... |

See footnotes at end of table.

# STATE INITIATIVES: PREPARING THE INITIATIVE TO BE PLACED ON THE BALLOT - Continued

| State or other jurisdiction | Signatures verified by: (a) | Within how many days after filing | Number of days to amend/appeal a petition that is: | | Penalty for falsifying petition (denotes fine, jail term) | Petition certified by: (d) |
|---|---|---|---|---|---|---|
| | | | Incomplete (b) | Not Accepted (c) | | |
| South Dakota .......... | SS | ... | ... | ... | ... | SS |
| Tennessee .......... | ... | ... | ... | ... | ... | ... |
| Texas .......... | ... | ... | ... | ... | ... | ... |
| Utah .......... | County clerk | ... | ... | ... | Class A misdemeanor | LG |
| Vermont .......... | ... | ... | ... | ... | ... | ... |
| Virginia .......... | SS | ... | ... | ... | ... | SS |
| Washington .......... | SS | (h) | ... | 10 days (i) | Class C felony | SS |
| West Virginia* .......... | ... | ... | ... | ... | ... | ... |
| Wisconsin .......... | SS | 60 days | 30 days | 30 days | $1,000, 1 yr. | SS |
| Wyoming .......... | ... | 60 days | 30 days | 30 days | ... | ... |
| U.S. Virgin Islands .......... | Supervisor of elections | ... | ... | ... | ... | SBE |

Sources: State election administration offices, except where data are from *The Book of the States, 1998-99.*

Key:
... — Not applicable.
SS — Secretary of State.
LG — Lieutenant Governor.
BSC — Board of State Canvassers.
SBE — State Board of Elections.

(a) The validity of the signatures, as well as the correct number of required signatures must be verified before the initiative is allowed on the ballot.

(b) If an insufficient number of signatures is submitted, sponsors may amend the original petition by filing additional signatures within a given number of days after filing. If the necessary number of signatures has not been submitted by this date, the petition is declared void.

(c) In some cases, the state officer will not accept a valid petition. In such a case, sponsors may appeal this decision to the Supreme Court, where the sufficiency of the petition will be determined. If the petition is determined to be sufficient, the initiative is required to be placed on the ballot.

(d) A petition is certified for the ballot when the required number of signatures has been submitted by the filing deadline, and are determined to be valid.

(e) No more than $500, one year in county jail, or both.

(f) Applies to statutory initiatives.

(g) If an initiative petition is submitted not less than 165 days before the election and if the secretary of state determines there are insufficient signatures, but the deadline for filing the signatures has not passed, the petitioners may submit additional signatures.

(h) Direct—no specific limit; Indirect—45 days.

(i) In Washington, a petition that is not accepted may be appealed within 10 days.

## Table 5.18
## STATE INITIATIVES: VOTING ON THE INITIATIVE

| Stae or other jurisdiction | Ballot (a) Title by: | Summary by: | Election where initiative voted on | Effective date of approved initiative (b) Const. amdt. | Statute | Days to contest election results (c) | Can an approved initiative be: Amended? | Vetoed? | Repealed? | Can a defeated initiative be refiled? |
|---|---|---|---|---|---|---|---|---|---|---|
| Alabama | ... | ... | ... | ... | ... | ... | ... | ... | ... | ... |
| Alaska | LG,AG | LG,AG | (d) | ... | 90 days (e) | 10 | Y | N | after 2 yrs. | Y |
| Arizona | ... | ... | GE | IM (f) | IM (f) | 5 | Y (g) | N (f) | Y (g) | Y |
| Arkansas | AG | AG | GE | 30 days | 30 days | 60 | Y | N | Y | Y |
| California | AG | AG | GE,PR or SP | 1 day | IM | 5 | Y (h) | N | Y | Y |
| Colorado | SS,AG,LSS | SS,AG,LSS | (i) | 30 days | 30 days | ... | Y | N | Y | Y |
| Connecticut | ... | ... | ... | ... | ... | ... | ... | ... | ... | ... |
| Delaware* | ... | ... | ... | ... | ... | ... | ... | ... | ... | ... |
| Florida | P,AG | P,AG | GE | (j) | ... | 10 | Y | N | N | Y |
| Georgia | ... | ... | ... | ... | ... | ... | ... | ... | ... | ... |
| Hawaii | ... | ... | ... | ... | ... | ... | ... | ... | ... | ... |
| Idaho | AG | AG | GE | ... | 30 days | 20 | Y | N | Y | Y |
| Illinois | (k) | (k) | GE | 20 days | ... | 15 | ... | ... | ... | ... |
| Indiana* | ... | ... | ... | ... | ... | ... | ... | ... | ... | ... |
| Iowa | ... | ... | ... | ... | ... | ... | ... | ... | ... | ... |
| Kansas | ... | ... | ... | ... | ... | ... | ... | ... | ... | ... |
| Kentucky* | ... | ... | ... | ... | ... | ... | ... | ... | ... | ... |
| Louisiana | ... | ... | ... | ... | ... | ... | ... | ... | ... | ... |
| Maine | ... | ... | REG or SP | ... | 30 days (f) | ... | Y | N | Y | ... |
| Maryland | ... | ... | ... | ... | ... | ... | ... | ... | ... | ... |
| Massachusetts* | AG | AG | GE | 30 days | 30 days | 10 | Y | Y | Y | after 2 biennial elections |
| Michigan | BSC | BSC | GE | 45 days | 10 days | 2 (l) | Y | N | Y | Y |
| Minnesota | ... | ... | ... | ... | ... | ... | ... | ... | ... | ... |
| Mississippi | AG | AG | GE | 30 days | ... | ... | Y | N | Y | after 2 yrs. |
| Missouri | SS,AG | ... | GE | 30 days | IM | 30 | Y (m) | N | Y (m) | Y |
| Montana | ... | AG | GE | 1-Jul | Oct. 1 | ... | ... | N | ... | ... |
| Nebraska | AG | AG | GE 4 mos. after filing | 10 days | 10 days | 40 | ... | N | ... | Y |
| Nevada* | SS,AG | SS,AG | GE | 10 days (n) | 10 days (n) | 14 (o) | N | N | N | ... |
| New Hampshire | ... | ... | ... | ... | ... | ... | ... | ... | ... | ... |
| New Jersey | ... | ... | ... | ... | ... | ... | ... | ... | ... | ... |
| New Mexico | ... | ... | ... | ... | ... | ... | ... | ... | ... | ... |
| New York | ... | ... | ... | ... | ... | ... | ... | ... | ... | ... |
| North Carolina* | ... | ... | ... | ... | ... | ... | ... | ... | ... | ... |
| North Dakota | AG,SS | AG,SS | PR,SP or GE | 30 days | 30 days | 14 | w/i 7 yrs. (p) | N | w/i 7 yrs. (p) | Y |
| Ohio | SS | Ohio Ballot Board | (q) | 30 days | 30 days | 15 | ... | N | ... | Y |
| Oklahoma | P,AG | P,AG | REG or SP | IM | IM | ... | ... | N | Y | after 3 yrs. |
| Oregon | AG | AG | GE even yrs. | 30 days | 30 days | 40 | Y | N | Y | Y |
| Pennsylvania | ... | ... | ... | ... | ... | ... | ... | ... | ... | ... |
| Rhode Island | ... | ... | ... | ... | ... | ... | ... | ... | ... | ... |
| South Carolina | ... | ... | ... | ... | ... | ... | ... | ... | ... | ... |
| South Dakota | AG | AG | GE | 1 day | 1 day | 10 | Y | N | Y | Y |
| Tennessee | ... | ... | ... | ... | ... | ... | ... | ... | ... | ... |
| Texas | ... | ... | ... | ... | ... | ... | ... | ... | ... | ... |
| Utah | LC | LC | GE | ... | 5 days (r) | 40 | Y | N | Y | Y |
| Vermont | ... | ... | ... | ... | ... | ... | ... | ... | ... | ... |
| Virginia | ... | ... | ... | ... | ... | ... | ... | ... | ... | ... |
| Washington | AG | AG | GE | ... | IM | 3 | after 2 yrs. | ... | after 2 yrs. | Y |
| West Virginia* | ... | ... | ... | ... | ... | ... | ... | ... | ... | ... |
| Wisconsin | ... | ... | ... | ... | ... | ... | ... | ... | ... | ... |
| Wyoming | SS | SS,AG | GE 120 days after LS | ... | 90 days | ... | Y | N | after 2 yrs. | after 5 yrs. |
| U.S. Virgin Islands | TB | TB | LC | IM | IM | 30 | Y | N | N | Y |

See footnotes at end of table.

## STATE INITIATIVES: VOTING ON THE INITIATIVE — Continued

*Sources*: State election administration offices, except where noted by *
where data are from *The Book of the States 1998-99*.

*Key*:

. . . — Not applicable.
LG — Lieutenant Governor.
SS — Secretary of State.
AG — Attorney General.
P — Proponent.
LC — Legislative Council.
LSS — Legislative Legal Services.
PR — Primary election.
GE — General election.
REG — Regular election.
SP — Special election.
TB — Title board.
IM — Immediately.
LS — Legislative session.
Y — Yes.
N — No.
w/i — Within.
BSC — Board of State Canvassers.
SBE — State Board of Elections.

(a) In some states, the ballot title and summary will differ from that on the petition.

(b) A majority of the popular vote is required to enact a measure. In Massachusetts and Nebraska, apart from satisfying the requisite majority vote, the measure must receive, respectively, 30% and 35% of the total votes cast in favor. An initiative approved by the voters may be put into effect immediately after the approving votes have been canvassed. In California and Nebraska, the measure may specify an enacting date. In Colorado, measures take effect from the date of proclamation by governor, but no later than 30 days after votes have been canvassed and certified by secretary of state. In Nebraska, 10 days after completion of canvass by the State Board of Canvassers.

(c) Individuals may contest the results of a vote on an initiative within a certain number of days after the election including the measure proposed.

(d) First statewide election at least 120 days after the legislative session.

(e) After certification of election.

(f) Upon governor's proclamation.

(g) Unless measure was approved by a majority vote of qualified electors.

(h) As specified.

(i) Ballot issues shall be decided in a state general election, biennial local district election or on the first Tuesday in November of odd-numbered years.

(j) First Tuesday after the first Monday in January following the general election.

(k) Title and summary provided in petition or, if initiated by General Assembly, in the legislation.

(l) After election is certified.

(m) By vote of people for constitutional change.

(n) Fourth Wednesday in November.

(o) After election; if a recount is done, contest must be filed within five days of recount.

(p) Except by a two-thirds vote by both houses of the legislature.

(q) General election at least 90 days after filing.

(r) Effective date may be written in the initiative, otherwise it takes place within five days

## Table 5.19
## STATE REFERENDUMS: REQUESTING PERMISSION TO CIRCULATE A CITIZEN PETITION

| State or other jurisdiction | Citizen petition (a) | Signatures required to request a petition (b) | Request submitted to: | Request forms furnished by: (c) | Restricted subject matter (d) | Individual responsible for petiton | | Financial contributions reported (e) | Deposit required (f) |
|---|---|---|---|---|---|---|---|---|---|
| | | | | | | Title | Summary | | |
| Alabama | ... | ... | ... | ... | ... | ... | ... | ... | ... |
| Alaska | Y | 100 | LG | SP | Y | LG | LG | Y | $100 |
| Arizona | Y | 5% VG | SS | ST | N | Y | Y | Y | ... |
| Arkansas | Y | 6% VG | AG | SP | N | AG | AG | Y | ... |
| Calforina | Y | ... | AG | SP | N | AG | AG | Y | N |
| Colorado | Y | ... | ... | ... | N | (g) | (g) | Y | ... |
| Connecticut | ... | ... | ... | ... | ... | ... | ... | ... | ... |
| Delaware* | ... | ... | ... | ... | ... | ... | ... | ... | ... |
| Florida | ... | ... | ... | ... | ... | ... | ... | ... | ... |
| Georgia | ... | ... | ... | ... | ... | ... | ... | ... | ... |
| Hawaii | ... | ... | ... | ... | ... | ... | ... | ... | ... |
| Idaho | Y | ... | SS | SP | N | AG | AG | Y | ... |
| Illinois | ... | ... | ... | ... | Y | ... | ... | ... | ... |
| Indiana* | ... | ... | ... | ... | ... | ... | ... | ... | ... |
| Iowa | ... | ... | ... | ... | ... | ... | ... | ... | ... |
| Kansas | ... | ... | ... | ... | ... | ... | ... | ... | ... |
| Kentucky* | Y | ... | SS | ... | Y | ... | ... | ... | ... |
| Louisiana | ... | ... | ... | ... | ... | ... | ... | ... | ... |
| Maine | Y | 5 (h) | SS | SS | Y | SP | SS | Y | ... |
| Maryland | Y | N | ... | SBE | Y | SS | SS | Y | N |
| Massachusetts* | Y | 10 | SS | SS | ... | AG | AG | Y | ... |
| Michigan | Y | ... | ... | ... | Y | P | P | Y | ... |
| Minnesota | ... | ... | ... | ... | ... | ... | ... | ... | ... |
| Mississippi | ... | ... | ... | ... | ... | ... | ... | ... | ... |
| Missouri | Y | ... | SS | SP | Y | SS,AG | ... | Y | N |
| Montana | Y | ... | SS | SP | Y | AG | AG | Y | N |
| Nebraska | Y | ... | SS | SP | Y | AG | AG | Y | N |
| Nevada* | Y | ... | SS | SP | N | P | P | (i) | N |
| New Hampshire | ... | ... | ... | ... | ... | ... | ... | ... | ... |
| New Jersey | ... | ... | ... | ... | ... | ... | ... | ... | ... |
| New Mexico | Y | ... | SS | ... | ... | SS | SS | ... | ... |
| New York | ... | ... | ... | ... | ... | ... | ... | ... | ... |
| North Carolina* | ... | ... | ... | ... | ... | ... | ... | ... | ... |
| North Dakota | Y | 25 EV | SS | SP | N | SS,AG | SS,AG | Y (e) | N |
| Ohio | Y | ... | SS | SP | Y | ... | AG | Y | N |
| Oklahoma (j) | Y | ... | SS | SP | N | SP,AG | SP,AG | Y | ... |
| Oregon | Y | ... | SS | SS | N | AG | AG | Y | ... |
| Pennsylvania | ... | ... | ... | ... | ... | ... | ... | ... | ... |
| Rhode Island | ... | ... | ... | ... | ... | ... | ... | ... | ... |
| South Carolina | ... | ... | ... | ... | ... | ... | ... | ... | ... |
| South Dakota | Y | ... | SS | SP | Y | P | ... | Y | N |
| Tennessee | ... | ... | ... | ... | ... | ... | ... | ... | ... |
| Texas | ... | ... | ... | ... | ... | ... | ... | ... | ... |
| Utah | Y | 5 | LG | SP | N | SP | ... | Y (k) | ... |
| Vermont | ... | ... | ... | ... | ... | ... | ... | ... | ... |
| Virginia | ... | ... | ... | ... | ... | ... | ... | ... | ... |
| Washington | Y | 1 | SS | SP | Y | AG | AG | Y | N |
| West Virginia* | ... | ... | ... | ... | ... | ... | ... | ... | ... |
| Wisconsin | ... | ... | ... | ... | ... | ... | ... | ... | ... |
| Wyoming | Y | 100 | SS | SS | Y | SS | SS | Y | $500 |
| U.S. Virgin Islands | N | 10% | (l) | Y | ... | (h) | (h) | Y | N |

*Sources:* State election administration offices, except where noted by * where data are from *The Book of the States, 1998-99.*

*Key:*
... — Not applicable.
EV — Eligible voters.
VG — Total votes cast for the position
VG — of governor in the last election.
LG — Lieutenant governor.
SS — Secretary of state.
SBE - State Board of Elections

AG — Attorney general.
P — Proponent.
ST — State.
SP — Sponsor.
Y — Yes.
N — No.

(a) Three forms of referenda exist: citizen petition, submission by the legislature, and constitutional requirement. This table outlines the steps necessary to enact a citizen's petition.

(b) Prior to circulating a statewide petition, a request for permission to do so must first be submitted to a specified state officer. Some states require such signatures to only be those of eligible voters.

(c) The form on which the request for petition is submitted may be the responsibility of the sponsor or may be furnished by the state.

(d) Restrictions may exist regarding the subject matter to which a referendum may be applied. The majority of these restrictions pertain to the dedication of state revenues and appropriations, and laws that maintain the preservation of public peace, safety and health. In Kentucky, referenda are only permitted for the establishment of soil and water and watershed conservation districts.

## STATE REFERENDUMS: REQUESTING PERMISSION TO CIRCULATE A CITIZEN PETITION - Continued

(e) In some states, a list of individuals who contribute financially to the referendum campaign must be submitted to the specified state officer with whom the petition is filed. In North Dakota, if over $100 in aggregate for calendar year.

(f) A deposit may be required after permission to circulate a petition has been granted. This amount is refunded when the completed petition has been filed correctly.

(g) Title Setting Board secretary of state, attorney general, director of legislative legal services.

(h) The name and address of five voters.

(i) Expenditures advocating defeat or passage of the question in excess of $500 must be reported.

(j) In Oklahoma, a person is not required to receive permission to circulate a petition. The individual must, however, file the petition with the secretary of state. The circulation period is 90 days.

(k) If more than $750 is spent to influence the vote.

(l) In the U.S. Virgin Islands, the Supervisor of Elections has responsibility.

## Table 5.20
## STATE REFERENDUMS: CIRCULATING THE CITIZEN PETITION

| State or other jurisdiction | Basis for signatures | Maximum time period allowed for petition circulation (a) | Can signatures be removed from petition (b) | Completed petition filed: With | Completed petition filed: Days after legislative session |
|---|---|---|---|---|---|
| Alabama | ... | ... | ... | ... | ... |
| Alaska | 10% TV, from 2/3 ED | w/i 90 days of LS | Y | LG | 90 days |
| Arizona | 5% VG | w/i 90 days after LS | Y | SS | 90 days |
| Arkansas | 6% VG | ... | N | SS | 90 days |
| California | 5% VG | 90 days | Y | SS | 90 days |
| Colorado | 5% VSS | 6 mos. | ... | SS | 90 days |
| Connecticut | ... | ... | ... | ... | ... |
| Delaware* | ... | ... | ... | ... | ... |
| Florida | ... | ... | ... | ... | ... |
| Georgia | ... | ... | ... | ... | ... |
| Hawaii | ... | ... | ... | ... | ... |
| Idaho | 6% EV (d) | w/i 60 days after LS | ... | SS | 60 days |
| Illinois | 10% EV | 24 mos. prior to election | Y | SBE | 6 mos. before election |
| Indiana* | ... | ... | ... | ... | ... |
| Iowa | ... | ... | ... | ... | ... |
| Kansas | ... | ... | ... | ... | ... |
| Kentucky* | 5% VG | ... | ... | SS | 4 mos. |
| Louisiana | ... | ... | ... | ... | ... |
| Maine | 10% VG | 90 days of LS (c) | ... | SS | 90 days |
| Maryland | 3 % VG | ... | Y | SS | ... |
| Massachusetts* | 3% VG | 90 days | ... | SS | 90 days after signed by governor |
| Michigan | 5% VG | 90 days after LS | N | SS | 90 days |
| Minnesota | ... | ... | ... | ... | ... |
| Mississippi | ... | ... | ... | ... | ... |
| Missouri | 5% VG, from 2/3 ED | w/i 90 days after LS | N | SS | 90 days |
| Montana | 5% VG, 5% each from 1/3 ED | ... | Y | SS | 6 mos. |
| Nebraska | 5% VG, 5% from 2/5 county | ... | Y | SS | 90 days |
| Nevada* | 10% EV last GE | approx. 6 mos. | ... | SS | 120 prior to next GE |
| New Hampshire | ... | ... | ... | ... | ... |
| New Jersey | ... | ... | ... | ... | ... |
| New Mexico | 10% EV last GE, from 3/4 county | ... | ... | ... | 4 mos. prior to next GE |
| New York | ... | ... | ... | ... | ... |
| North Carolina* | ... | ... | ... | ... | ... |
| North Dakota | 2% total population | 90 days | ... | SS | 90 days after receiving |
| Ohio | 6% VG, 3% each from 1/2 county | ... | ... | SS | 90 days |
| Oklahoma | 5% vh | w/i 90 days of LS | N | SS | 90 days |
| Oregon | 4% VG | w/i 90 days of LS | N | SS | 90 days |
| Pennsylvania | ... | ... | ... | ... | ... |
| Rhode Island | ... | ... | ... | ... | ... |
| South Carolina | ... | ... | ... | ... | ... |
| South Dakota | 5% VG | ... | N | SS | 90 days |
| Tennessee | ... | ... | ... | ... | ... |
| Texas | ... | ... | ... | ... | ... |
| Utah | 10% VG | ... | Y | LG | 60 days |
| Vermont | ... | ... | ... | ... | ... |
| Virginia | ... | ... | ... | ... | ... |
| Washington | 4% VG | w/i 90 days after LS | Y | SS | 90 days |
| West Virginia* | ... | ... | ... | ... | ... |
| Wisconsin | ... | ... | ... | ... | ... |
| Wyoming | 15% TV, from 2/3 county | w/i 90 days after LS | Y | SS | 90 days |
| U.S. Virgin Islands | 10% EV,D | 180 | Y | SBE | 60 days |

*Sources*: State election administration offices, except where noted by *
where data are from *The Book of the States 1998-99*.

*Key*:

. . . — Not applicable.

VG — Total votes cast for the position of governor in the last election.

EV — Eligible voters.

TV — Total voters in the last general election.

VH — Total votes cast for the office receiving the highest number of votes in last general election.

VSS — Total votes cast for all candidates for the office of secretary of state at the previous general election.

ED — Election district.

GE — General election.

LS — Legislative session.

LG — Lieutenant governor.

SBE - State Board of Elections.

SS — Secretary of state.

Y — Yes

N — No

w/i — Within

(a) The petition circulation period begins when petition forms have been approved and provided to or by the sponsors. Sponsors are those individuals granted permission to circulate a petition, and are therefore responsible for the validity of each signature on a given petition.

(b) Should an individual wish to remove his/her name from a petition, a request to do so must first be submitted in writing to the state officer with whom the petition is filed.

(c) Request for petition must be submitted within 10 days of adjournment of legislative session.

(d) In Idaho, this figure includes 6% each from 22 counties.

## Table 5.21
## STATE REFERENDUMS: PREPARING THE CITIZEN PETITION REFERENDUM TO BE PLACED ON BALLOT

| State or other jurisdiction | Signatures verified by: (a) | Within how many days after filing | No. of days to amend/appeal petition that is: Incomplete (b) | Not accepted (c) | Penalty for falsifying petition (denotes fine, jail term) | Petition certified by: (d) |
|---|---|---|---|---|---|---|
| Alabama | ... | ... | ... | ... | ... | ... |
| Alaska | Director of elections | 60 | 10 (e) | 30 days | Class B misdemeanor | LG |
| Arizona | SS, county recorder | 20 (f) | ... | 10 | Class 1 misdemeanor | SS |
| Arkansas | SS | ... | 30 | 15 | Class D felony | SS |
| California | County clerk or registrar of voters | ... | ... | ... | ... | SS |
| Colorado | SS | 30 | 15 (g) | ... | (h) | SS |
| Connecticut | ... | ... | ... | ... | ... | ... |
| Delaware* | ... | ... | ... | ... | ... | ... |
| Florida | ... | ... | ... | ... | ... | ... |
| Georgia | ... | ... | ... | ... | ... | ... |
| Hawaii | ... | ... | ... | ... | ... | ... |
| Idaho | County clerk | ... | ... | 10 | $5,000, 2 yrs. | SS |
| Illinois | SBE and election authorities | Approx. 45 | ... | ... | ... | SBE |
| Indiana* | ... | ... | ... | ... | ... | ... |
| Iowa | ... | ... | ... | ... | ... | ... |
| Kansas | ... | ... | ... | ... | ... | ... |
| Kentucky* | ... | ... | ... | ... | ... | ... |
| Louisiana | ... | ... | ... | ... | ... | ... |
| Maine | SS, registrars of voters | 30 | ... | ... | ... | ... |
| Maryland | County board of elections | 20 | ... | ... | Misdemeanor | SBE,SS |
| Massachusetts* | Local boards of registrars | ... | ... | ... | $1,000, 1 year | SS |
| Michigan | SS, local election officials | 60 | ... | ... | $500, 90 days | BSC |
| Minnesota | ... | ... | ... | ... | ... | ... |
| Mississippi | ... | ... | ... | ... | ... | ... |
| Missouri | SS, local election authorities | (n) | ... | ... | Class A misdemeanor | SS |
| Montana | County clerk, recorder | 28 | ... | ... | $500, 6 mos. | SS |
| Nebraska | SS, county clerk, election commr. | 40 | ... | ... | Class IV felony | SS |
| Nevada* | County clerk, registrar | 20-50 | ... | ... | $10,000, 1-10 yrs. | SS |
| New Hampshire | ... | ... | ... | ... | ... | ... |
| New Jersey | ... | ... | ... | ... | ... | ... |
| New Mexico | ... | ... | 30 | 15 | ... | ... |
| New York | ... | ... | ... | ... | ... | ... |
| North Carolina* | ... | ... | ... | ... | ... | ... |
| North Dakota | SS | 35 | 20 (i) | ... | ... | SS |
| Ohio | County board of elections | ... | 10 | ... | $1,000, 6 months | SS |
| Oklahoma | ... | ... | ... | ... | $500, 2 yrs. | ... |
| Oregon | SS, county elections officials | 15 | ... | ... | Class C felony (possible) | SS |
| Pennsylvania | ... | ... | ... | ... | ... | ... |
| Rhode Island | ... | ... | ... | ... | ... | ... |
| South Carolina | ... | ... | ... | ... | ... | ... |
| South Dakota | SS | ... | ... | ... | ... | SS |
| Tennessee | ... | ... | ... | ... | ... | ... |
| Texas | ... | ... | ... | ... | ... | ... |
| Utah | County clerks | 55 | ... | ... | $500, 2 yrs. | LG |
| Vermont | ... | ... | ... | ... | ... | ... |
| Virginia | ... | ... | ... | ... | ... | ... |
| Washington | SS | (j) | ... | 10 (k) | ... | SS |
| West Virginia* | ... | ... | ... | ... | ... | ... |
| Wisconsin | ... | ... | ... | ... | ... | ... |
| Wyoming | SS | 60 | 60 | 60 | $1,000, 1 yr. | SS |
| U.S. Virgin Islands | Supervisor of Elections | 60 | 30 | 30 | ... | (l) |

*Sources*: State election administration offices, except where noted by * where data are from *The Book of the States 1998-99.*

*Key:*
... — Not applicable.
SS — Secretary of State.
LG — Lieutenant Governor.
BSC — Board of State Canvassers.
SBE — State Board of Elections.

(a) The validity of the signatures, as well as the correct number of required signatures must be verified before the referendum is allowed on the ballot.

(b) If an insufficient number of signatures are submitted, sponsors may amend the original petition by filing additional signatures within a given number of days after filing. If the necessary number of signatures have not been submitted by this date, the petition is declared void.

(c) In some cases, the state officer will not accept a valid petition. In such cases, sponsors may appeal this decision to the Supreme Court, where the sufficiency of the petition will be determined. If the petition is determined to be sufficient, the referendum is required to be placed on the ballot.

(d) A petition is certified for the ballot when the required number of signatures have been submitted by the filing deadline, and are determined to be valid.

(e) If within 90 days of the legislative session.

(f) The secretary of state has 15 days to count signatures and to complete random sample; the county recorder then has 10 days to verify signatures.

(g) At least 3 months prior to general election.

(h) Not more than $500 or one year in city jail, or both.

(i) No additional signatures may be added. Sponsors have 20 days to correct insufficient signatures which already have been gathered.

(j) No specified time.

(k) A petition that is not accepted may be appealed in 10 days.

(l) Legislature.

(m) Must be certified as sufficient or insufficient by the 13th Tuesday prior to the general election.

## Table 5.22
## STATE REFERENDUMS: VOTING ON THE CITIZEN PETITION REFERENDUM

| State or other jurisdiction | Ballot (a) | | Election where referendum voted on | Effective date of approved referendum (b) | Days to contest election results (c) |
|---|---|---|---|---|---|
| | Title by: | Summary by: | | | |
| Alabama | ... | ... | ... | ... | ... |
| Alaska | LG, AG | LG, AG | 1st statewide election 180 days after LS | 30 days | 10 |
| Arizona | ... | ... | GE | IM | 5 |
| Arkansas | AG | AG | GE or SP | 30 days | 60 |
| California | AG | AG | GE or SP 31 days after LS | IM | ... |
| Colorado | SS, AG, LSS | SS, AG, LSS | (d) | 30 days | ... |
| Connecticut | ... | ... | ... | ... | ... |
| Delaware* | ... | ... | ... | ... | ... |
| Florida | ... | ... | ... | ... | ... |
| Georgia | ... | ... | ... | ... | ... |
| Hawaii | ... | ... | ... | ... | ... |
| Idaho | AG | AG | GE | 30 days | 20 (e) |
| Illinois | ... | ... | GE | ... | 30 |
| Indiana* | ... | ... | ... | ... | ... |
| Iowa | ... | ... | ... | ... | ... |
| Kansas | ... | ... | ... | ... | ... |
| Kentucky* | ... | ... | GE or SP | IM | ... |
| Louisiana | ... | ... | ... | ... | ... |
| Maine | ... | ... | PR, GE or SP more than 60 days after filing | 30 days | ... |
| Maryland | SS, AG | LSS | GE | 30 days | 3 (e) |
| Massachusetts* | ... | ... | GE more than 60 days after filing | 30 days | ... |
| Michigan | BSC | BSC | GE | 10 days | 2 (e) |
| Minnesota | ... | ... | ... | ... | ... |
| Mississippi | ... | ... | ... | ... | ... |
| Missouri | SS, AG | ... | GE | IM | 30 |
| Montana | AG | AG | GE | Oct. 1 (f) | ... |
| Nebraska | AG | AG | GE not less than 30 days after filing | 10 days | 40 |
| Nevada* | SS, AG | SS, AG | GE | Nov., 4th Wed. | 19 (g) |
| New Hampshire | ... | ... | ... | ... | ... |
| New Jersey | ... | ... | ... | ... | ... |
| New Mexico | SS | ... | GE | IM | ... |
| New York | ... | ... | ... | ... | ... |
| North Carolina* | ... | ... | ... | ... | ... |
| North Dakota | SS, AG | SS, AG | PR, SP or GE | 30 days | 14 (e) |
| Ohio | ... | Ohio Ballot Bd. | GE more than 60 days after filing | 30 days | 15 |
| Oklahoma | SS | ... | GE or SP | IM | ... |
| Oregon | AG | AG | GE (h) | 30 days | 40 |
| Pennsylvania | ... | ... | ... | ... | ... |
| Rhode Island | ... | ... | ... | ... | ... |
| South Carolina | ... | ... | ... | ... | ... |
| South Dakota | AG | AG | GE | 1 day | 10 |
| Tennessee | ... | ... | ... | ... | ... |
| Texas | ... | ... | ... | ... | ... |
| Utah | LC | LC | GE | 5 days (f) | 40 |
| Vermont | ... | ... | ... | ... | ... |
| Virginia | ... | ... | ... | ... | ... |
| Washington | AG | AG | GE | IM | 3 |
| West Virginia* | ... | ... | ... | ... | ... |
| Wisconsin | ... | ... | ... | ... | ... |
| Wyoming | SS | SS, AG | GE more than 120 days after LS | 90 days | 30 |
| U.S. Virgin Islands | (i) | (i) | GE | IM | 7 |

See footnotes at end of table.

## STATE REFERENDUMS: VOTING ON THE CITIZEN PETITION REFERENDUM - Continued

*Sources*: State election administration offices, except where noted by * where data are from *The Book of the States, 1998-99.*

*Key:*

. . . — Not applicable.

LG — Lieutenant Governor.

AG — Attorney General.

SS — Secretary of State.

BSC — Board of State Canvassers.

LC — Legislative Counsel.

LSS — Legislative Legal Services.

SBE — State Board of Elections .

(a) In some states, the ballot title and summary will differ from that on the petition.

(b) A majority of the popular vote is required to enact a measure in every state. In Arizona, a referendum approved by the voters becomes effective upon the governor's proclamation. In Nebraska, a referendum may be put into effect immediately after the approving votes have been canvassed by the Board of State Canvassers and upon the governor's proclamation. In Colorado measures take effect from the date of proclamation by governor, but no later than 30 days after votes have been canvassed and certified by secretary of state. In Massachusetts the measure must also receive at lease 30 percent of the total ballots cast in the last election.

(c) Individuals may contest the results of a vote on a referendum within a certain number of days after the election including this matter. In Alaska, five days to request recount with appeal to the court within five days after recount.

(d) In Colorado, ballot issues shall be decided in state general election, biennial local district election or on the first Tuesday in November of odd-numbered years.

(e) After election is certified.

(f) Unless otherwise specified.

(g) In Nevada, 14 days after election or 5 days after recount.

(h) In Oregon, a state referendum initiated by citizen petition can only be voted on in a general election. A referral by the legislature can be voted on in a general election, a primary, or on any date determined necessary.

(i) In the U.S. Virgin Islands, the Supervisor of Elections has responsibility.

## Table 5.23
## STATE RECALL PROVISIONS: APPLICABILITY TO STATE OFFICIALS AND PETITION CIRCULATION

| State or other jurisdiction | Officers to whom recall is applicable (a) | No. of times recall can be attempted | Recall may be initiated after official has been in office | Recall may not be initiated with days remaining in term | Basis for signatures (b) (see key below) Statewide officers | Others | Maximum time allowed for petition circulation (c) |
|---|---|---|---|---|---|---|---|
| Alabama | ... | ... | ... | ... | ... | ... | ... |
| Alaska | All but judicial officers | ... | 120 days | 180 | 25% VO | 25% VO | ... |
| Arizona | All | (d) | 6 mos./5 days legislators | ... | 25% VO | 25% VO | 120 days |
| Arkansas | All | ... | No limit | ... | ... | ... | ... |
| California | All | (e) | ... | ... | 12% VO, 1% from 5 counties | 20% VO | 160 days |
| Colorado | All but judicial officers | (f) | 6 mos./5 days legislators | 6 mos. | 25% VO | 25% VO | 60 days |
| Connecticut* | ... | ... | ... | ... | ... | ... | ... |
| Delaware* | ... | ... | ... | ... | ... | ... | ... |
| Florida | ... | ... | ... | ... | ... | ... | ... |
| Georgia | All | ... | 180 days | 180 | 15% EV (g), 1/15 from each congressional district | 30% EV (g) | 90 days |
| Hawaii | ... | ... | ... | ... | ... | ... | ... |
| Idaho | All but judicial officers | (d) | 90 days | ... | 20% EVg | 20% EV | 60 days |
| Illinois* | ... | ... | ... | ... | ... | ... | ... |
| Indiana* | ... | ... | ... | ... | ... | ... | ... |
| Iowa* | ... | ... | ... | ... | ... | ... | ... |
| Kansas | All but judicial officers | 1 | 120 days | 200 | 40% VO | 40% VO | 90 days |
| Kentucky* | ... | ... | ... | ... | ... | ... | ... |
| Louisiana | All but judicial officers of records | (h) | ... | 6 mos. | 33 1/3% EV (i) | 33 1/3% EV (i) | 180 days |
| Maine | ... | ... | ... | ... | ... | ... | ... |
| Maryland | ... | ... | ... | ... | ... | ... | ... |
| Massachusetts* | ... | ... | ... | ... | ... | ... | ... |
| Michigan | All but judicial officers of records | ... | 6 mos. | 6 mos. | 25% VG | 25% VG | (j) |
| Minnesota | All state level officials | No limit | No limit | 6 mos. | 25% VO | 25% VO | 90 days |
| Mississippi | ... | ... | ... | ... | ... | ... | ... |
| Missouri | ... | ... | ... | ... | ... | ... | ... |
| Montana | All public officers elected or appt. | (d) | 2 mos. | ... | 10% EV | (k) | 3 mos. |
| Nebraska | ... | ... | ... | ... | ... | ... | ... |
| Nevada* | All public officers | (d) | 6 mos. (l) | ... | 25% VO in given jurisdiction | 25% VO in given jurisdiction | 60 days |
| New Hampshire | ... | ... | ... | ... | ... | ... | ... |
| New Jersey | All elected officials | (t) | (u) | (v) | 25% VO in given jurisdiction | 25% VO in given jurisdiction | (w) |
| New Mexico | All county officials | 1 | ... | 180 | ... | ... | ... |
| New York | ... | ... | ... | ... | ... | 33 1/3% VO | ... |
| North Carolina* | ... | ... | ... | ... | ... | ... | ... |
| North Dakota | All but U.S. Congress | 1 | ... | ... | ... | ... | ... |
| Ohio | ... | ... | ... | ... | 25% EVg | 25% EVg | ... |
| Oklahoma | ... | ... | ... | ... | ... | ... | ... |
| Oregon | All but U.S. Congress | (d) | 6 mos./5 days legislators | ... | 15% (m) | 15% (m) | 90 days |
| Pennsylvania | ... | ... | ... | ... | ... | ... | ... |
| Rhode Island | G,LG,SS,AG,T | ... | 1 yr. | ... | 15% (n) | ... | 90 days |
| South Carolina | ... | ... | 6 mos. | ... | ... | ... | ... |

See footnotes at end of table.

# STATE RECALL PROVISIONS: APPLICABILITY TO STATE OFFICIALS AND PETITION CIRCULATION — Continued

| State or other jurisdiction | Officers to whom recall is applicable (a) | No. of times recall can be attempted | Recall may be initiated after official has been in office | Recall may not be initiated with days remaining in term | Basis for signatures (b) (see key below) — Statewide officers | Others | Maximum time allowed for petition circulation (c) |
|---|---|---|---|---|---|---|---|
| South Dakota | Municipal only (1st and 2nd class) | ... | ... | ... | ... | 15% EV | ... |
| Tennessee | ... | ... | ... | ... | ... | ... | ... |
| Texas | ... | ... | ... | ... | ... | ... | ... |
| Utah | ... | ... | ... | ... | ... | ... | ... |
| Vermont | ... | ... | ... | ... | ... | ... | ... |
| Virginia | ... | ... | ... | ... | ... | ... | (o) |
| Washington | All but judges of courts of records | ... | IM | 180 | 25% VO | 35% VO | ... |
| West Virginia* | ... | 1 | 1 yr. (p) | ... | ... | ... | ... |
| Wisconsin | All | ... | 1 yr. | ... | 25% VG (q) | 25% VP (r) | 60 days (s) |
| Wyoming | ... | ... | ... | ... | ... | ... | ... |
| U.S. Virgin Islands | All | ... | 1 yr. | 1 yr. | 30% VO | 30% VO | 180 days |

*Sources:* State election administration offices, except where noted by * where data are from *The Book of the States 1998-99.*

Key:
... — Not applicable.
All — All elective officials.
VO — Number of votes cast in the last election for the office or official being recalled.
EVg — Number of eligible voters in the last general election for governor.
EV — Eligible voters.
VG — Total votes cast for the position of governor in the last election.
VP — Total votes cast for position of president in last presidential election.
IM — Immediately.

(a) An elective official may be recalled by qualified voters entitled to vote for the recalled official's successor. An appointed official may be recalled by qualified voters entitled to vote for the successor(s) of the elective officer(s) authorized to appoint an individual to the position.

(b) Signature requirements for recall of those other than state elective officials are based on votes in the jurisdiction to which the said official has been elected.

(c) The petition circulation period begins when petition forms have been approved and provided to sponsors. Sponsors are those individuals granted permission to circulate a petition, and are therefore responsible for the validity of each signature on a given petition.

(d) Additional recall attempts can be made provided that the state treasury is reimbursed the cost of the previous recall attempt(s).

(e) Must wait until 6 months after the first recall attempt.

(f) If signatures are obtained at least equal in number to 50% of those voting in the last general election.

(g) Eligible voters for office at last general election to fill office.

(h) Must wait at least until 18 months after the first recall attempt.

(i) Basis for signatures 33 1/3% if over 1,000 EV; 40% if under EV.

(j) In Michigan, signatures dated more than 90 days prior to the filing deadline are ruled invalid.

(k) 15% EV for district or county officials, 20% EV for municipal or school officials.

(l) Six months or 10 days after legislative session begins for legislators.

(m) 15% of the total votes cast in the public officer's electoral district for all candidates for governor at the election next preceding the filing of the petition at which a candidate for governor was elected for a four-year term.

(n) In Rhode Island, a recall may be instituted by filing with the state board of elections an application for issuance of a recall petition against said general officer which is signed by duly qualified electors equal to three percent of the total number of votes cast at the last preceding general election for that office. If, upon verification, the application is determined to contain signatures of the required number of electors, the state board of elections shall issue a recall petition for circulation amongst the electors of the state. Within 90 days of issuance, recall petitions containing the signatures of duly qualified electors consisting of 15% of the total number of votes cast in the last preceding general election for said office must be filed with the sate elections board.

(o) Statewide officials 270 days; others 180 days.

(p) Petition may be filed after official has been in office one year.

(q) State, congressional, judicial, legislative and county offices.

(r) For city, village, town and school district elected officials.

(s) For statewide offices, 30 days for local offices (city, town and village).

(t) An elected official sought to be recalled who is not recalled as the result of a recall election shall not again be subject to recall until after having served one year of a term calculated from the date of the recall election.

(u) The recall drive may not commence before the 50th day preceding the completion of the elected official's first year of the current term.

(v) No election to recall an elected official shall be held after the date occurring six months prior to the general election for that office , as appropriate, in the final year of the official's term.

(w) The maximum time allowed for petition circulation is 320 days for a governor or 160 days for other elected officials.

# Table 5.24
## STATE RECALL PROVISIONS: PETITION REVIEW, APPEAL AND ELECTION

| State or other jurisdiction | Signatures verified (a) by: | Days to amend/appeal a petition that is: Incomplete (b) | Not accepted (c) | Penalty for falsifying petition (denotes fines, jail time) | Days allowed for petition to be certified (d) | Days to step down after certification (e) | Voting on the recall (f) Election held | Election type | Days to contest election results (g) |
|---|---|---|---|---|---|---|---|---|---|
| Alabama | ... | ... | ... | ... | ... | ... | ... | ... | ... |
| Alaska | Director of elections | 20 | 30 | Class B misdemeanor | 30 | ... | 60-90 days after cert. | SP, GE or PR | 10 |
| Arizona | SS, county recorder | ... | ... | Class 1 misdemeanor | 70 | 5 | 75-120 days after cert. | SP | 5 |
| Arkansas | ... | ... | ... | ... | ... | ... | ... | ... | ... |
| California | County clerk/registrar of voters | ... | ... | ... | ... | ... | 60-80 days after cert. | SP | ... |
| Colorado | SS,county clerk | 60 | ... | $1,000/1 yr. | 10 | 5 | 45-75 days after cert. | SP OR GE | ... |
| Connecticut | ... | ... | ... | ... | ... | ... | ... | ... | ... |
| Delaware* | ... | ... | ... | ... | ... | ... | ... | ... | ... |
| Florida | ... | ... | ... | $1,000, 12 mos. | ... | ... | ... | ... | ... |
| Georgia | Election Supervisor | Not allowed | 10 | ... | 30-45 | ... | 30-45 days after cert. | SP, PR or GE | 5 |
| Hawaii | ... | ... | ... | ... | ... | ... | ... | ... | ... |
| Idaho | County clerk | 30 | 10 | $5,000, 2 yrs. | 10 | 5 | 45+ days after cert. (h) | SP or GE (h) | 20 (i) |
| Illinois | ... | ... | ... | ... | ... | ... | ... | ... | ... |
| Indiana* | ... | ... | ... | ... | ... | ... | ... | ... | ... |
| Iowa | ... | ... | ... | ... | ... | ... | ... | ... | ... |
| Kansas | County election officer | ... | ... | Class B misdemeanor | 30 | ... | 60-90 days after cert. | SP or GE | 30 |
| Kentucky* | ... | ... | ... | $100-1,000, 30-90 days | 10 | ... | (j) | SP | 30 |
| Louisiana | Registrar of voters | ... | ... | ... | ... | ... | ... | ... | ... |
| Maine | ... | ... | ... | ... | ... | ... | ... | ... | ... |
| Maryland | ... | ... | ... | ... | ... | ... | ... | ... | ... |
| Massachusetts* | SS, local election officials (k) | ... | ... | $500, 90 days | 35 | ... | w/i 60 days after cert. | SP | 2 (i) |
| Michigan | SS | ... | ... | ... | 10 | ... | ... | SP | 7 |
| Minnesota | ... | ... | ... | ... | ... | ... | ... | ... | ... |
| Mississippi | ... | ... | ... | ... | ... | ... | ... | ... | ... |
| Missouri | ... | ... | ... | ... | ... | ... | ... | ... | ... |
| Montana | County clerk, recorder | 10 | ... | $500, 6 mos. | 30 | 5 | 3 mos. after cert. | SP or GE | ... |
| Nebraska | ... | ... | ... | ... | ... | ... | ... | ... | ... |
| Nevada* | County clerk, registrar | ... | ... | $10,000, 1-10 yrs. | 25-50 | 5 | (l) | SP | 10 |
| New Hampshire | ... | ... | ... | ... | ... | 5 | ... | ... | ... |
| New Jersey | Recall elections official | ... | ... | Crime of the 4th degree | 10 | ... | (u) | SP or GE | (v) |
| New Mexico | County clerk | ... | ... | ... | ... | ... | 90 day after cert. | SP | ... |
| New York | ... | ... | ... | ... | ... | ... | ... | ... | ... |
| North Carolina* | ... | ... | ... | ... | ... | ... | ... | ... | ... |
| North Dakota | SS | 20 (m) | ... | ... | 35 | 10 (n) | ... | SP, GE or PR | 14 (o) |
| Ohio | ... | ... | ... | ... | ... | ... | ... | ... | ... |
| Oklahoma | ... | ... | ... | ... | ... | ... | ... | ... | ... |
| Oregon | SS or county clerk | ... | ... | Class C felony (possible) | 10 | 5 | w/i 40 days after cert. | SP | 40 |
| Pennsylvania | ... | ... | ... | ... | ... | ... | ... | ... | ... |
| Rhode Island | ... | ... | ... | ... | ... | ... | ... | ... | ... |
| South Carolina | ... | ... | ... | ... | ... | ... | ... | ... | ... |

See footnotes at end of table.

# STATE RECALL PROVISIONS: PETITION REVIEW, APPEAL AND ELECTION — Continued

| State or other jurisdiction | Signatures verified (a) by: | Days to amend/appeal a petition that is: Incomplete (b) | Not accepted (c) | Penalty for falsifying petition (denotes fines, jail time) | Days allowed for petition to be certified (d) | Days to step down after certification (e) | Voting on the recall (f) Election held | Election type | Days to contest election results (g) |
|---|---|---|---|---|---|---|---|---|---|
| **South Dakota** | Municipal finance officer | ... | ... | ... | ... | ... | (l) | SP | ... |
| **Tennessee** | ... | ... | ... | ... | ... | ... | ... | ... | ... |
| **Texas** | ... | ... | ... | ... | ... | ... | ... | ... | ... |
| **Utah** | ... | ... | ... | ... | ... | ... | ... | ... | ... |
| **Vermont** | ... | ... | ... | ... | ... | ... | ... | ... | ... |
| **Virginia** | SS, county auditor | ... | ... | Felony | w/i 10 | IM | 45-50 days after cert. | SP | 3 |
| **Washington** | ... | ... | 10 (p) | ... | ... | ... | ... | SP | 3 |
| **West Virginia*** | ... | ... | ... | ... | ... | ... | ... | ... | ... |
| **Wisconsin** | Filing offices (q) | 5 | 7 (r) | Not more than $1,000, not more than 3 yrs. or both. | 31 | 10 | 6 weeks after cert. | SP (s) | 3 (t) |
| **Wyoming** | ... | ... | ... | ... | ... | ... | ... | ... | ... |
| **U.S. Virgin Islands** | Supervisor of Elections | ... | ... | ... | 60 | ... | ... | GE | 7 |

*Sources:* State election administration offices, except where noted by * where data are from *The Book of the States 1998-99.*

Key:
... — Not applicable.
SBE - State Board of Elections.
SS — Secretary of State.
SP — Special election.
GE — General election.
PR — Primary election.
IM — Immediate and automatic removal from office.
w/i — Within

(a) The validity of the signatures, as well as the correct number of required signatures must be verified before the recall is allowed on the ballot.

(b) If an insufficient number of signatures are submitted, sponsors may amend the original petition by filing additional signatures within a given number of days. If the necessary number of signatures have not been submitted by this date, the petition is declared void.

(c) In some cases, the state officer will not accept a valid petition. In such a case, sponsors may appeal this decision to the Supreme Court, where the sufficiency of the petition will be determined. When this is declared, the recall is required to be placed on the ballot.

(d) A petition is certified for the ballot when the required number of signatures has been submitted by the filing deadline, and are determined to be valid.

(e) The official to whom a recall is proposed has a certain number of days to step down from his position before a recall election is initiated, if he desires to do so.

(f) A majority of the popular vote is required to recall an official in each state.

(g) Individuals may contest the results of a vote on a recall within a certain number of days after the results are certified. In Alaska, an appeal to courts must be filed within five days of the recount.

(h) In Idaho, the dates on which elections may be conducted are the first Tuesday in February, the fourth Tuesday in May, the first Tuesday in August, or the Tuesday following the first Monday in November. In addition, an emergency election may be called upon motion of the governing board of a political subdivision. Recall elections conducted by any political subdivision shall be held on the nearest of these dates which falls more than 45 days after the clerk of the political subdivision orders that the recall election shall be held.

(i) After election is certified.

(j) The election must not be held on the next available date of six dates per year allowed by the election committee.

(k) In Michigan, the registration status of each signer is verified by the city and township clerks. The Board of State Canvassers certifies the petition as having adequate number of valid signatures. Both of these procedures fall under the auspices of the secretary of state. The governor determines the sufficiency of recall petitions for secretary of state.

(l) In Nevada, a recall election is held 10-20 days after the court determines a recall election is to be held. In South Dakota, a recall election is held 30-50 days after the governing board orders a recall election. The governing board must meet within 10 days after the petition is filed.

(m) Only signatures already collected can be amended such as adding addresses or correcting some other flaw which makes the signatures unverifiable.

(n) After petition is filed with the secretary of state.

(o) Fourteen days after the canvas board has certified the results.

(p) In Washington, a petition that is not accepted may be appealed in 10 days.

(q) Where declaration of candidacy is filed.

(r) After certificate.

(s) May be held on general election but is still considered special election.

(t) Business days.

(u) New Jersey Permanent Statutes, 19:27A-13. In the case of an office which is ordinarily filled at the general election, a recall election shall be held at the next general election occurring at least 55 days following the fifth business day after service of certification, unless it was indicated in the notice of intention to recall that the recall election shall be held at a special election in which case the recall election official shall order and fix the date for holding the recall election to be the next Tuesday occurring during the period beginning with the 55th day and ending on the 61st day following the fifth business day after service of the certification of the petition

(v) New Jersey Permanent Statutes, 19:27A-16.

# Chapter Six

# STATE
# FINANCES

*With significant changes in fiscal federalism anticipated and new responsibilities devolving from Washington to the states, the importance of state finances has rarely been so critical — includes information on state budgetary procedures and fund management, revenues and expenditures, state debt, taxes, federal government grants and payments to states, and federal program spending by state.*

For additional information on Chapter Six contact
The States Information Center, at The Council of State Governments,
(859) 244-8253 or E-mail: sic@csg.org.

## Table 6.1
## STATE BUDGETARY CALENDARS

| State | Budget guidelines to agencies | Agency requests submitted to governor | Agency hearings held | Governor's budget sent to legislature | Legislature adopts budget | Fiscal year begins | Frequency of legislative/ budget cycles |
|---|---|---|---|---|---|---|---|
| Alabama | September | November | January | February | Feb/May | October | Annual/Annual |
| Alaska | July | October | November | December | May | July | Annual/Annual |
| Arizona | June 1 | September 1 | Nov/Dec | January | Jan/April | July | Annual/ Biennial |
| Arkansas | March | July | August | Sept/Dec | Jan/April | July | Biennial/Biennial |
| California | April/Nov | September | Sept/Nov | January 10 | June 15 | July | Biennial/Annual |
| Colorado | June | August 15 | August/Sept | November 1 | May | July | Annual/Annual |
| Connecticut | July | September | February | February | June/ May(a) | July | Annual/Biennial |
| Delaware | August | Oct/Nov | Oct/Nov | January | June 30 | July | Annual/Annual |
| Florida | June | September | November (b) | January | April/May | July | Annual/Annual |
| Georgia | June | September | Nov/Dec | January | March | July | Annual/Annual |
| Hawaii | July/Aug | September | November | December | April | July | Annual/Biennial |
| Idaho | June | September | . . . | January | March | July | Annual/Annual |
| Illinois | September | Oct/Nov | Nov/Dec | February | May | July | Annual/Annual |
| Indiana | May | August | Sept/Nov | January | April | July | Annual/Biennial |
| Iowa | June | October 1 | Nov/Dec | January | April/May | July | Annual/Annual |
| Kansas | June | September | November | January | May | July | Annual/Annual, |
| Kentucky | July | October | Nov/Dec | January | April | July | Biennial/Biennial |
| Louisiana | September | November | February | February | June | July | Annual/Annual |
| Maine | July | September | Oct/Dec | January | June | July | Biennial/Biennial |
| Maryland | June | August 31 | Oct/Nov | January | April | July | Annual/Annual |
| Massachusetts | August | October | October | January | June | July | Annual/Annual |
| Michigan | August | November | December | (d) | June/July | October | Annual/Annual |
| Minnesota | May/June | October 15 | Sept/Dec | Nov/Jan (f) | May | July | Annual/Biennial |
| Mississippi | June | August | . . . | Nov/Jan (f) | . . . | July | Annual/Annual |
| Missouri | July | October | . . . | January | April/May | July | Annual/Annual (g) |
| Montana(h) | Jan 31/Aug 1 | May/Sept 1 | May-June Sept-Oct | January | April | July | Biennial/Biennial |
| Nebraska | July | September | Jan/Feb | January | April | July | Annual/Biennial |
| Nevada | Jan/June | August | Sept/Dec | January | May | July | Biennial/Biennial |
| New Hampshire | August | October 1 | November | February 15 | May | July | Annual/Biennial |
| New Jersey | July/August | October | . . . | January | June | July | Annual/Annual |
| New Mexico | July | September | Sept/Dec | January | Feb/March | July | Annual/Annual |
| New York | July | September | Oct/Nov | January | March | April | Annual/Annual |
| North Carolina | January | August | Sept/Nov | February | June | July | Biennial/Biennial(i) |
| North Dakota | March | June/July | July/Oct | December | Jan/April | July | Biennial/Biennial |
| Ohio | July | Sept/Oct | Oct/Nov | February (j) | June | July | Annual/Biennial |
| Oklahoma | July | October | Oct/Dec | February (k) | May (l) | July | Annual/Annual |
| Oregon | Jan/July | September | Sept/Nov | January | Jan/June | July | Biennial/Biennial |
| Pennsylvania | August | October | Dec/Jan | February (m) | May/June | July | Annual/Annual |
| Rhode Island | July | October | Nov/Dec | February | June | July | Annual/Annual |
| South Carolina | August | October | . . . | January | June | July | Annual/Annual |
| South Dakota | June/July | September | Sept/Oct | December | March | July | Annual/Annual |
| Tennessee | August | October | November | Feb 1 (n) | April/May | July | Annual/Annual |
| Texas | March | July/Nov | July/Sept | January | May | September | Biennial/Biennial |
| Utah | July | September | Oct/Nov | December | February | July | Annual/Annual |
| Vermont | October | November | Nov/Dec | January | May | July | Annual(o)/Annual |
| Virginia | April/August | June/Oct | Sept/Oct | December | March/April | July | Annual/Biennial |
| Washington | April | September | . . . | December | April/May | July | Annual/Biennial |
| West Virginia | July | September | Oct/Nov | January | March | July | Annual/Annual |
| Wisconsin | June | September | . . . | January | June/July | July | Biennial/Biennial |
| Wyoming | 15-May | September | (p) | December | March | July | Annual/Biennial |
| Puerto Rico | March | Sept/Dec | Aug/Sept Dec-Jan | February | June | July | Annual/Annual |

See footnotes at end of table.

## STATE BUDGETARY CALENDARS — Continued

*Source*: National Association of State Budget Officers, *Budget Processes in the States, October 1999.*

Key:

. . . — Not applicable

(a) Legislature adopts budget during June of odd years, May of even years.

(b) Agency hearings on legislative budget requests must be prior to the governor's recommendations. Historically these hearings occur in November. In his or her first year of office a new governor may request, subject to approval of the President of the Senate or the Speaker of the House of Representatives, that his or her recommended balanced budget be submitted at a later time prior to the governor's first session.

(c) Nineteen agencies are on a biennial budget cycle. The rest are on an annual cycle.

(d) Within 30 days after legislature convenes in regular session, except when a newly elected governor is inaugurated when presentation must occur within 60 days after legislature convenes.

(e) Fourth Tuesday.

(f) The executive budget is submitted in January during the first year of a governor's term,

(g) There is a constitutional authority to do annual and biennial budgeting. Beginning in fiscal 1994, the operating budget has been on an annual basis while the capital budget has been on a biennial basis.

(h) Montana uses an Executive Planning Process (EPP) for proposals to provide new services, add FTE, change program services or alter funding sources. The earlier dates reflect this process which is linked with the regular budget in the September 1 submittal.

(i) The Constitution requires the preparation of a biennial budget, the General Assembly routinely conducts a short session for adjustments to the second year of the biennium.

(j) Budget submission delayed to mid-March for new governors.

(k) First Monday.

(l) Last Friday.

(m) Budget is submitted in March when governor has been elected for first full term.

(n) The budget may be submitted by March 1 during the first year of a governor's term.

(o) State Constitution prescribes a biennial legislature; in practice, legislature meets annually, in regular and adjourned sessions.

(p) By November 20.

## Table 6.2
## OFFICIALS OR AGENCIES RESPONSIBLE FOR BUDGET PREPARATION, REVIEW AND CONTROLS

| State or other jurisdiction | Official/agency(ies) responsible for preparing budget document | Special budget review agency in legislative branch | Official/agency(ies) responsible for budgetary and related accounting controls |
|---|---|---|---|
| Alabama | State Finance Director | Legislative Fiscal Ofc. | State Finance Director |
| Alabama | State Finance Director | Legislative Fiscal Ofc. | State Finance Director |
| Alaska | Director, Ofc. of Mgmt. & Budget | Div. Of Legislative Audit | Director, Div. Of Finance, Dept. of Administration |
| Arizona | Director, Ofc. of Strategic Planning & Budgeting | Jt. Legislative Budget Cmte. | Assistant Director, Finance Div., Dept. of Administration |
| Arkansas | Administrator, Ofc. of Budget, Dept. of Finance & Admn. | Fiscal & Tax Research Services, Bur. Of Legislative Research | Director, Dept. of Finance & Administration |
| California | Director, Dept. of Finance | Ofc. Of the Legislative Analyst; Senate Cmte. On Budget & Fiscal Review; Assembly Cmte. On Appropriations | Director, Dept. of Finance |
| Colorado | Executive Director, Ofc. of State Planning & Budgeting, Ofc. of the Governor | Jt. Budget Cmte. | State Controller, Ofc. Of the State Controller, Support Services |
| Connecticut | Executive Budget Officer, Budget & Finance Div., Ofc. of Policy & Mgmt. | Ofc. of Fiscal Analysis | Senior Economic Advisor to the Governor, Ofc. Of Policy Management |
| Delaware | Director, Ofc. of the Budget | Legislative Info. Services; Ofc. Of the Controller General | Secretary, Dept. of Finance |
| Florida | Director, Ofc. of Planning & Budgeting, Executive Ofc. of the Governor | Fiscal Responsibility Council; Budget Cmte. | Director, Div. Of Finance, Dept. of Banking & Finance |
| Georgia | Director, Ofc. of Planning & Budget | Legislative Budget Ofc. | Treasurer, Ofc. Of Treasury & Fiscal Services |
| Hawaii | Director of Finance, Dept. of Budget and Finance | Ofc. Of the Legislative Auditor | Director of Finance, Dept. of Budget & Finance |
| Idaho | Administrator, Div. of Financial Mgmt., Ofc. of the Governor | Jt. Finance Appropriations Cmte.; Budget & Policy Analysis, Legislative Services Ofc. | Administrator, Div. Of Financial Mgmt., Ofc. Of the Governor |
| Illinois | Director, Bur. of the Budget, Ofc. of the Governor | Economic & Fiscal Comm. | Director, Bur. Of the Budget, Ofc. of the Governor |
| Indiana | Director, Budget Agcy. | Fiscal & Mgmt. Analysis Ofc., Legislative Services Agency | Director, Budget Agency |
| Iowa | Director, Dept. of Mgmt., Ofc. of the Governor | Legislative Fiscal Bur. | Director, Dept. of Revenue & Finance; Director, Dept. of Mgmt. |
| Kansas | Director, Div. of the Budget, Dept. of Admn. | Legislative Research Dept. | |
| Kentucky | State Budget Director, Governor's Ofc. | Ofc. Of Budget Review, Legislative Research Comm. | Secretary, Finance & Administration Cabinet |
| Louisiana | Budget Director, Div. of Admn., Ofc. of the Governor | State Fiscal Services; Legislative Fiscal Ofc.; Fiscal Div., House Legislative Services | Commissioner, Div. Of Administration |
| Maine | State Budget Officer, Bur. of the Budget, Dept. of Admn. & Financial Services | Ofc. Of Fiscal & Program Review, Legislative Council | Commissioner, Dept. of Adm. & Financial Services |
| Maryland | Secretary, Ofc. of the Secretary, Dept. of Budget & Mgmt. | Ofc. Of Policy Analysis, Dept. of Legislative Services | Secretary, Ofc. Of the Secretary, Dept. of Budget & Mgmt. |
| Massachusetts | Budget Director, Executive Ofc. for Admn. & Finance | Senate, House Ways & Means Cmtes. | Secretary, Executive Ofc. For Administration & Finance |
| Michigan | State Budget Director, Dept. of Mgmt. & Budget | Senate, House Fiscal Agencies | State Budget Director, Dept. of Mgmt. & Budget |
| Minnesota | Commissioner, Dept. of Finance | Senate, House Chief Fiscal Analysts | Commissioner, Dept. of Finance |
| Mississippi | Director, Ofc of Budget & Fund Mgmt., Dept. of Finance & Admn. | Jt. Legislative Budget Ofc. | Director, Dept. of Finance & Administration |
| Missouri | Director, Div. of Budget & Planning, Ofc. of Admn. | Senate, House Appropriations Cmtes.; Budget Cmte.; Jt. Legislative Research Cmte., Oversight Div. | Commissioner, Administration, Ofc. Of Administration |
| Montana | Director, Ofc. of Budget & Program Planning | Legislative Fiscal Div. | Director, Ofc. Of Budget & Program Planning |

## BUDGET OFFICIALS OR AGENCIES — Continued

| State or other jurisdiction | Official/agency responsible for preparing budget document | Special budget review agency in legislative branch | Agency(ies) responsible for budgetary and related accounting controls |
|---|---|---|---|
| Nebraska | Administrator, Budget Div., Dept. of Adm. Services | Legislative Fiscal Ofc. | Budget Div., Dept. of Administrative Services; Auditor of Public Accounts; Dept. of Revenue |
| Nebraska | Administrator, Budget Div., Dept. of Adm. Services | Legislative Fiscal Ofc. | State Tax Commissioner, Dept. of Revenue; Administrator, Budget Div., Dept. of Adm. Services; Auditor of Public Accounts |
| Nevada | Director, Dept. of Admn. | Legislative Counsel Bur., Fiscal Analysis Div. | |
| New Hampshire | Commissioner, Commissioner's Ofc., Dept. of Adm. Services; Asst. Commissioner & Budget Officer, Budget Ofc., Adm. Services | Ofc. Of Legislative Budget Assistant | Commissioner, Commissioner's Ofc., Dept. of Adm. Services |
| New Jersey | Director, Ofc. of Mgmt. & Budget; Dept. of Treasury | Assembly Majority Staff; Ofc. Of Legislative Services; Budget & Fiscal Analysis, Assembly and Senate Minority Staff; Central Staff, Revenue, Finance & Appropriations | Director, Ofc. Of Mgmt. & Budget, Dept. of Treasury |
| New Mexico | Director, Budget Div., Dept.of Finance & Admn. | Jt. Legislative Finance Cmte. | Secretary, Finance & Administration |
| New York | Director, Div. of Budget, Executive Dept. | Ways & Means Cmte. | Comptroller |
| North Carolina | State Budget Officer, Ofc. of State Budget | Fiscal Research Div. | State Budget Officer, Ofc. Of the State Budget |
| North Dakota | Director, Budget Analyst, Ofc. Of Mgmt. & Budget | Legislative Council | Director, Ofc. Of Mgmt. & Budget, |
| Ohio | Director, Ofc. of Budget & Mgmt. | Legislative Budget Ofc. | Director, Ofc. Of Budget & Mgmt. |
| Oklahoma | Director, Ofc. of State Finance | Fiscal Div.; Senate Fiscal Staff Div. | Director, Ofc. Of State Finance |
| Oregon | Dpty. Director, Dept. of Adm. Services | Legislative Fiscal Ofc. | Deputy Director, Dept. of Adm. Services |
| Pennsylvania | Cabinet Secretary, Ofc. Of the Budget, Budget Dept. | Appropriations Cmte.; Legislative Budget & Finance Comm.; Democratic Appropriations Cmte. | Cabinet Secretary, Ofc. Of the Budget, Budget Dept. |
| Rhode Island | Executive Director/State Budget Officer, State Budget Ofc., Dept. of Admn. | Senate Finance Cmte. | Executive Director/State Budget Officer, State Budget Ofc., Dept. of Administration |
| South Carolina | Director, Ofc. of State Budget, Budget & Control Bd. | Ways & Means Cmte.; Budget & Control Board; Finance Cmte. | Executive Director, Budget & Control Board |
| South Dakota | Commissioner, Bur. of Finance & Mgmt. | Fiscal Research & Budget Analysis, Legislative Research Council | Commissioner, Bur. Of Finance & Mgmt. |
| Tennessee | Assistant Commissioner, Budget Div., Dept. of Finance & Admn. | Fiscal Review Cmte. | Commissioner, Finance & Administration |
| Texas | Director, Budget & Planning, Ofc. of the Governor | Legislative Budget Bd. | Comptroller, Comptroller of Public Accounts |
| Utah | Director, Ofc. Of Planning & Budget, Governor's Ofc. | Ofc. of Legislative Fiscal Analyst | Director, Div. Of Finance, Dept. of Adm. Services |
| Vermont | Commissioner, Agency of Admn., Dept. of Finance & Mgmt. | Jt. Fiscal Ofc. | Commissioner, Agency of Administration, Dept. of Finance & Mgmt. |
| Virginia | Director, Dept. of Planning & Budget | Senate Finance Cmte.; House Appropriations Cmte. | Secretary of Finance, Governor's Cabinet |
| Washington | Director, Ofc. of Financial Mgmt. | Legislative Transportation Cmte.; Senate Ways & Means Cmte.; House Appropriations Cmte. | Director, Ofc. Of Financial Mgmt. |
| West Virginia | Director, Budget Div., Dept. of Finance & Admn. | Budget Div., Legislative Auditor's Ofc.; Jt. Standing Cmte. On Finance | Cabinet Secretary, Dept. of Administration |
| Wisconsin | Director, Div. Of Executive Budget & Finance, Dept. of Admn. | Legislative Fiscal Bur. | Administrator, DOA/Div. Of Technical Mgmt. |
| Wyoming | Administrator, Budget Div. | Legislative Services Ofc. | State Auditor |
| Dist. of Columbia | Director, Dept. of Finance & Revenue | Budget Ofc. | Chief Financial Officer, Ofc. Of the Chief Financial Officer |
| American Samoa | Director, Program Planning & Budget | Legislative Financial Ofc.; Budget & Appropriations Cmte. | Treasurer, Dept. of the Treasury |
| Guam | Director, Bur. of Budget & Mgmt. Research | Legislative Accounting Div. | Director, Dept. of Administration |
| No. Mariana Islands | Special Assistant for Mgmt. & Budget, Ofc. of Mgmt. & Budget, Ofc. of the Governor | Finance & Accounting Div. | Secretary of Finance, Finance & Accounting, Dept. of Finance |

## BUDGET OFFICIALS OR AGENCIES — Continued

| State or other jurisdiction | Official/agency responsible for preparing budget document | Special budget review agency in legislative branch | Agency(ies) responsible for budgetary and related accounting controls |
|---|---|---|---|
| **Puerto Rico** .......................... | Director, Ofc. of Budget & Mgmt. | Secretary of Administration; Speaker's Ofc. | Director, Ofc. Of Budget & Mgmt. |
| **U.S. Virgin Islands** ............. | Director, Ofc. of Mgmt. & Budget | Business & Financial Management, Legislature of U.S. Virgin Islands | Commissioner, Dept. of Finance |

*Sources:* The Council of State Governments, *State Legislative Leadership, Committees and Staff: 1999* and *State Administrative Officials Classified by Function: 1999.*

## Table 6.3
## STATE BALANCED BUDGETS: CONSTITUTIONAL AND STATUTORY PROVISIONS, GUBERNATORIAL AND LEGISLATIVE AUTHORITY

| State or other jurisdiction | Constitutional and Statutory Provisions | | | Gubernatorial Authority | | | Legislative Authority | |
|---|---|---|---|---|---|---|---|---|
| | Governor must submit a balanced budget | Legislature must pass a balanced budget | Governor must sign a balanced budget | Governor has line item veto | Can reduce budget without legislative approval | Restrictions on budget reductions | Votes required to pass revenue increase | Votes required to pass budget |
| Alabama | C,S | S | ... | (a) | ★ | ATB | Majority | Majority |
| Alaska | S | S | S | ★ | ... | ... | Majority | Majority (c) |
| Arizona | C,S | C,S | C,S | ★ | ... | ... | 2/3 elected | Majority |
| Arkansas | S | S | S | ★ | (d) | ATB | 3/4 elected (b) | 3/4 elected (oo) |
| California | C | ... | S | ★ | ... | ... | 2/3 elected | 2/3 elected (pp) |
| Colorado | C | C | C | ★ | ★ | ... | Majority (e) | Majority elected |
| Connecticut | S | C,S | C | ★ | ★ | MR | Majority | Majority (f) |
| Delaware | C,S | C,S | C,S | ★ | ... | ★ | 3/5 elected | Majority |
| Florida | C,S | C,S | C,S | ★ | ★ (g) | MR | 2/3 elected | Majority |
| Georgia | C | C | C | ★ | ★ | (h) | Majority | Majority |
| Hawaii | C,S | ... | C,S | ★ | ★ (i) | ... | Majority (j) | Majority elected (qq) |
| Idaho | ... | C (k) | ... | ★ | ★ (l) | ★ (l) | Majority | Majority |
| Illinois | C,S | C | S | ★ (m) | ... | ... | Majority | Majority elected (n) |
| Indiana | ... | ... | ... | ... | ★ | ... | Majority | Majority |
| Iowa | C,S | S | ... | ★ | ★ | ATB | Majority | Majority |
| Kansas | S | C,S | ... | ★ | ... | ATB | Majority | Majority |
| Kentucky | C,S | C,S | C,S | ★ | ... | ... | 2/5 elected | Majority elected |
| Louisiana | C,S | C,S | C,S | ★ | ★ | MR | 2/3 elected | Majority |
| Maine | C,S | C | C,S | ★ | ★ | ATB | Majority | Majority (rr) |
| Maryland | C | C | (o) | ... | ★(p) | ★(q) | Majority | Majority elected |
| Massachusetts | C,S | C,S | C,S | ★ | ★ | ... | Majority | Majority (s) |
| Michigan | C,S | C | C,S | ★ | ... | (t) | Majority | Majority |
| Minnesota | C,S | C,S | C,S | ★ | ★ | MR | Majority | Majority elected |
| Mississippi | S | S | ... | ★ | ★ | ATB | 3/5 elected | Majority elected (ss) |
| Missouri | C | ... | C | ★ | ★ | ... | Majority | Majority elected |
| Montana | S | C | ... | ★ | ★ | MR(u) | Majority | Majority |
| Nebraska | C | S | ... | ★ | ... | ★ | Majority | Majority elected (tt) |
| Nevada | S | C | C | ... | ★ | MR | 3/5 elected | Majority |
| New Hampshire | S | ... | ... | ... | ... | ... | Majority | Majority |
| New Jersey | C | C | C | ★ | ★ | ... | Majority | Majority |
| New Mexico | C | C | C | ★ | ... | ... | Majority | Majority |
| New York | C | ... | (v) | ★ (w) | ★ (x) | (x) | Majority | Majority |
| North Carolina | C,S | S | ... | ... | ★ (z) | ... | Majority | Majority |
| North Dakota | C | C | C | ★ | ★ | ATB | Majority | Majority (uu) |
| Ohio | C | C | C | ★ (aa) | ★ | ★ | Majority | Majority |
| Oklahoma | S | C (bb) | C (bb) | ★ | ★ (cc) | ★ | 3/4 elected | Majority elected |
| Oregon | C | C | C | ★ | ★ | MR | 2/3 elected | Majority elected |
| Pennsylvania | C,S | ... | C,S | ★ | ★ (dd) | ... | Majority elected | Majority elected |
| Rhode Island | C | C | S | ... | ★ | ★ | Majority | 2/3 elected |
| South Carolina | C | C | C | ★ | ★ (ee) | ★ | Majority | Majority |
| South Dakota | C | C | C | ★ | ... | ★ | 2/3 elected | Majority elected (vv) |
| Tennessee | C | C | C | ★ | ... | ... | Majority | Majority |
| Texas | ... | C,S | C | ★ | ★ | ... | Majority | Majority |
| Utah | S | C,S | (ff) | ★ | ★ | ATB (gg) | Majority | Majority elected |
| Vermont | ... | ... | ... | ... | ★ (hh) | ★ (hh) | Majority | Majority |
| Virginia | (ii) | ... | C (ii) | ★(jj) | ★ (nn) | MR | Majority (ll) | Majority elected |
| Washington | S | ... | ... | ★ | ★ | ATB | Majority | Majority |
| West Virginia | ... | C | C | ★ | ★ (mm) | ★ (mm) | Majority | Majority elected |
| Wisconsin | C | C | C,S | ★ | ★ (nn) | ... | Majority | Majority |
| Wyoming | C | C | ... | ★ | ★ | ... | Majority | Majority |
| Puerto Rico | C | C | C | ★ | ★ | ... | Majority | Majority |

*Sources:* The Council of State Governments, the National Association of State Budget Officers, *Budgetary Processes in the States, 1999,* and the National Conference of State Legislatures.

*Key:*
C — Constitutional
S — Statutory
ATB — Across the board
MR — Maximum reduction dictated
★ — Yes
... — No

(a) The governor may return a bill without limit for recommended amendments for amount and language, as long as the legislature is still in session.

(b) For revenue and appropriation bills. Joint session.

(c) A simple majority is required to pass the budget. In Alaska, a simple majority is required for most annual appropriations, but if expenditures are expected to exceed the appropriation level in the prior year's budget and a withdrawal form the budget reserve fund is needed to make up the difference, a three-fourths vote is required. Since the provision became effective in 1991, the supermajority has been necessary for few appropriation items in each budget.

## STATE BALANCED BUDGETS - Continued

(d) The governor and chief fiscal officer of the state have the authority to reduce general revenue funding to agencies should shortfalls occur in revenue collections.

(e) All tax increases must be approved by a vote of the people.

(f) Appropriations require a simple majority of members elected, unless the general fund expenditure ceiling is exceeded. In that case, the Legislature must obtain a three-fifths majority.

(g) The elected cabinet (Administrative Commission) for the Executive Branch and the Chief Justice of the Supreme Court for the Judicial Branch are authorized to resolve deficits under $300 million. Deficits over $300 million shall be resolved by the legislature.

(h) The governor, during the first six months of a fiscal year in which the current revenue estimate on which appropriations are based is expected to exceed actual revenues, is authorized to require state agencies to reserve such appropriations as specified by the governor for budget reductions to be recommended to the general assembly at its next regular session.

(i) The governor's authority to reduce, expand and reorganize budgets can be done only pursuant to existing statutes.

(j) If general fund expenditure ceiling is exceeded, two-thirds vote required; otherwise majority of elected members.

(k) The constitution requires that the legislature pass a balanced budget. The governor, as the chief budget officer of the state, has always insured that expenditures do not exceed revenues.

(l) The governor's authority to reduce budgets is temporary. The State Board of Examiners (Governor, Attorney General and Secretary of State) has permanent appropriation reduction authority.

(m) The governor can veto appropriation items entirely (Item Veto) or merely reduce an item of appropriation to a lesser amount (Reduction Veto).
If the governor reduces an item of appropriation, the remaining items in the bill are not affected and can become law immediately.

(n) A majority vote is required to pass the budget until June 1. After that date, the required vote increases to three-fifths majority.

(o) The budget bill when and as passed by both houses, shall be a law immediately without further action by the governor.

(p) With the approval of the Board of Public Works, the governor may reduce by not more than 25 percent any appropriation that the governor considers unnecessary.

(q) The governor may not, however, reduce an appropriation to the legislative or judicial branches of government; for the payment of principal and interest on state debt; the funding for public schools (K-12); or the salary of a public officer during the term of office.

(r) Governor has no veto power over the budget bill.

(s) For capital budget, two-thirds votes required.

(t) There are both statutory and constitutional restrictions on executive branch authority to make budget reductions, involving approval by both House and Senate appropriations committees.

(u) Additional restrictions on budget reductions exclude principle and interest on state debt, legislative and judicial branches, school equalization aid and salaries of elected officials.

(v) The governor is not technically required to sign a balanced budget, but the governor, legislative leaders and the comptroller must certify the budget is in balance in order to meet borrowing requirements.

(w) Any appropriation added to the governor's budget by the legislature is subject to line item veto.

(x) May reduce budget without approval only for state operations; only restriction on reductions is that reductions in aid to localities cannot be made without legislative approval.

(y) The governor has no veto power over the budget bill, except for appropriations for the legislature and judiciary and items added to the governor's original budget proposal. In these cases, two-thirds of elected members in each chamber can vote to override the gubernatorial veto.

(z) Except for certain block grants. The Governor is required to maintain a balanced budget for the fiscal period and has the authority through the Constitution and General Statutes to make reductions to insure there is no overdraft or deficit.

(aa) Line item veto in appropriation act only.

(bb) Legislature could pass and the governor could sign a budget where appropriations exceed cash and estimated revenues, but consitutional and statutory provisions reduce the appropriations so that the budget is balanced.

(cc) Would require agreement of agency governing boards and or CEO.

(dd) The governor may reduce budgets selectively; he must provide 10 days prior notice and the reasons for so doing before lapsing current year grant and subsidy money.

(ee) The Budget and Control Board can authorize an across-the-board agency reduction when there is a revenue shortfall. When in session, the General Assembly has five statewide session days to take action to prevent the reduction.

(ff) Governor may allow balanced budget to go into law without signature.

(gg) Statutorily required to include requests from legislature , courts and other elected officials.

(hh) Reductions based on revenue shortfalls of greater than 1 percent require legislative approval.

(ii) Requirement applies only to budget execution. The governor is required to insure that actual expenditures do not exceed actual revenues.

(jj) Governor may return bill without limit for recommended amendments for amount and language. For purposes of a veto, a line item is defined as an indivisible sum of money that may or may not coincide with the way in which items are displayed in an appropriation act.

(kk) The governor has power to withhold allotments of appropriations, but cannot reduce legislative appropriations.

(ll) Two-thirds of members present includes a majority of the members elected.

(mm) The governor can reduce expenditures but not appropriations. Public education has priority.

(nn) Cannot reduce appropriations, but can withhold allotments.

(oo) A majority vote is required for education and highways; a three-fourths vote of the elected members is required on all others.

(pp) A two-thirds majority is required for appropriations from the general fund, except for public school appropriations, which require a simple majority.

(qq) If the general fund expenditure ceiling is exceeded, a two-thirds vote is required, otherwise, the majority of elected members is required.

(rr) For emergency enactment, a two-thirds vote is required.

(ss) A majority is required to pass the agency appropriations bill, unless a bill is considered a donation (e.g., a donation to the Mississippi Burn Center). In this case, Joint Rule 66 requires a two-thirds vote of the elected members.

(tt) Main budget bills typically have the "e" (emergency) clause attached, thus requiring a two-thirds vote. The "e" clause is necessary for the budget to be operative by the beginning of the fiscal year.

(uu) Emergency measures and measures that amend a statute that has been referred or enacted through an initiated measure within the last seven years must pass both houses by a two-thirds majority.

(vv) A two-thirds majority is required for individual spending bills.

## Table 6.4
## REVENUE ESTIMATING PRACTICES

| State or other jurisdiction | Primary authority for revenue estimate | Estimates bind the budget | Frequency of estimates updates | Multi-year forecasting | Economic Advisory Boards |
|---|---|---|---|---|---|
| Alabama | I | ... | Annual | CY + 1 | Executive Budget Office |
| Alaska | AO | ... | Semi-annual (a) | CY | Office of Management & Budget, Dept. of Revenue, Dept. of Labor |
| Arizona | ... | ... | Annual | CY | Office of Strategic Planning & Budgeting |
| Arkansas | I | ★ | Annual | CY | Fiscal Officer; Budget Office; Economic Analysis; Tax Research |
| California | I | ... | Semi-annual | CY | Dept. of Finance |
| Colorado | S | ... | Quarterly | CY | Governor's Revenue Estimating Advisory Committee |
| Connecticut | S | ... | Monthly | CY + 3 | Office of Policy & Management |
| Delaware | EO | ★ | Quarterly, Monthly (b) | CY + 5 | Economic and Financial Advisory Council |
| Florida | S | ★ | Semi-annual | CY | Consensus Revenue Estimating Conference |
| Georgia | ... | ★ | Annual | CY + 1 | Office of Planning & Budget |
| Hawaii | ... | ★(c) | Quarterly | CY + 4 | Council on Revenues; State Economist |
| Idaho | ... | ... | Semi-annual | CY | Division of Financial Management |
| Illinois | ... | ... | Annual | CY + 1 | Budget Agency |
| Indiana | EO | ★ | Annual | FY | Budget Agency |
| Iowa | ... | ★ | Quarterly | CY + 4 | Dept. of Management |
| Kansas | I | ... | Semi-annual | CY + 3 | Budget Office; Revenue Dept.; Legislative Research Dept. |
| Kentucky | ... | ★ | Biennial | CY + 4 | Finance Secretary, Legislative Research Commission |
| Louisiana | C,S | ★ | Quarterly | CY + 4 | Governor, Legislature, Revenue Estimating Conference |
| Maine | ... | ★ | Semi-annual | CY + 2 | State Budget Officer; Consensus Economic Forecasting Commission |
| Maryland | I | ... | Annual (d) | CY + 3 | Expenditures- Dept. of Budget and Management; Revenues-board of Revenue Estimates |
| Massachusetts | I | ★ | Quarterly (e) | CY + 1 | Revenue Dept./ Budget Bureau |
| Michigan | ... | ★ | Semi-annual | CY + 1 | Office of Revenue and Tax Analysis- Dept. of Treasury |
| Minnesota | EO | ★ | Semi-annual (f) | CY + 4 | Dept. of Finance |
| Mississippi | S | ★ | ... | CY | Office of Budget & Fund Management |
| Missouri | ... | ... | Annual | CY + 4 | Budget Office |
| Montana | ... | ... | Biennially | CY | Contract with forecasting firm- Wharton Economic Forecasting Assoc. |
| Nebraska | S | ★ | Semi-annual | CY + 2 | Revenue Dept. and Economic Forecasting Advisory Board |
| Nevada | S | ★ | Biennially | CY + 4-10 | Economic Forum |
| New Hampshire | ... | ★ | Annual | CY | Budget Office & Dept. of Revenue Administration |
| New Jersey | S | ★ | Semi-annual | CY + 2 | Council of Economic Advisors |
| New Mexico | S | ... | Annual | CY | Economic Analysis Bureau; Dept. of Finance & Administration |
| New York | ... | ★ | Quarterly | CY + 2 | Division of the Budget |
| North Carolina | ... | ★ | Annual | CY + 4 | Office of State Budget & Management |
| North Dakota | EO | ★ | Biennially | CY | OMB contracts with econometrics forecasting firm |
| Ohio | I | ... | Biennially/Monthly (g) | CY | Office of Budget & Management |
| Oklahoma | ... | ★ | Semi-annual (h) | CY + 2 | Oklahoma Tax Commission; Office of State Finance |
| Oregon | EO | ★ | Quarterly | CY + 2 | Office of Economic Analysis within Dept. of Administrative Services |
| Pennsylvania | ... | ★ | Annual (i) | CY + 4 | Budget Office & Revenue Dept. |
| Rhode Island | ... | ★ | Quarterly (j) | CY + 4 | Revenue Estimating Conference |
| South Carolina | S, Proviso | ... | Semi-annual | CY | Board of Economic Advisors |
| South Dakota | EO | ★ | Annual | CY + 3 | Bureau of Finance & Management |
| Tennessee | S | ... | Semi-annual | CY | Center of Business & Economic Research- Univ. of Tennessee |
| Texas | ... | ★ | Biennially | CY | Comptroller's Office |
| Utah | S | ★ | Annual | CY + 5 | Office of Planning & Budget & Tax Commission |
| Vermont | I | ... | Semi-annual | CY | Dept. of Finance & Management |
| Virginia | S | ★ | Semi-annual | CY + 4 | Dept. of Taxation |
| Washington | EO | ... | Quarterly | CY + 8 | Economic and Revenue Forecast Council |
| West Virginia | ... | ★ | Monthly | CY + 4 | Dept. of Tax & Revenue |
| Wisconsin | ... | ... | Annual | CY | Dept. of Revenue |
| Wyoming | S | ... | ... | CY | Economic Analysis Division |
| Dist. of Columbia* | E | ★ | Three times a year | CY + 5 | (k) |
| American Samoa* | E | ★ | Semi-annual | CY + 2 | ... |
| Puerto Rico | EO | ★ | Annual | CY | Planning Board; Government Development Bank |

See footnotes at end of table.

# REVENUE ESTIMATING PRACTICES

*Source*: The National Association of State Budget Officers, *Budget Processes in the States, October 1999*, except where noted by * where data are from *The Book of the States, 1998-99*.

Key:

★ — Yes.

. . . — No.

S- Statutory

C- Constitutional

EO- Executive Order

I- Informal

AO- Administrative Order

CY — Current year

FY - Fiscal year

(a) Revenue estimates must be published annually but traditionally are published semi-annually.

(b) Statutes require that estimates "shall be considered."

(c) Quarterly estimates are done for Sept., Dec., and May; monthly estimates are done for April, May and June.

(d) The statute requires the Board of Revenue Estimates to provide the governor with an annual estimate. In practice, the official estimate is provided in December and updated in March. Informal estimates are provided throughout the year.

(e) Dept. of Revenue publishes estimates 3 times a year. Secretary for Administration and Finance and the legislature agree on revenue estimates in the spring for the fiscal year beginning in July.

(f) Five-year revenue estimates are formally published twice a year in November and February.

(g) The governor must publish revenue estimates in the biennial executive budget submitted to the general assembly. A monthly financial report prepared for the governor by the Office of Budget and Management contains revenue estimates for the current fiscal year and reflects any revisions to those estimates made during the fiscal year.

(h) Revenue estimates are made by various agencies. The State Finance Office reviews, consolidates and presents the estimates to the State Equalization Board late in December and again in mid-February. The Board certifies an official estimate that is only revised if laws affecting it are passed by the general assembly.

(i) Revenue estimates are updated when new legislation affects current year revenues.

(j) Per state statute, a Consensus Revenue Estimating Conference must be held within the first ten days of November and May.

(k) Advisory board planned.

## Table 6.5
## ALLOWABLE STATE INVESTMENTS

| State or other jurisdiction | Certificates of deposits (in state) | Certificates of deposits (nationally) | Other time deposits | Bankers acceptance | Commercial paper | Corporate notes/bonds | Mutuals | State and local government obligations | U.S. Treasury obligations | U.S. agency obligations | Eurodollars (CDs or TDs) | Repurchase agreements |
|---|---|---|---|---|---|---|---|---|---|---|---|---|
| Alabama | ★ | | ★ | | | ★ | | ★ | ★ | ★ | | ★ |
| Alaska | | | | | | | | | | | | ★ |
| Arizona | ★ | ★ | | ★ | ★ | | | | ★ | ★ | | ★ |
| Arkansas | ★ | | ★ | | | | | | | | | ★ |
| California | ★ | ★ | ★ | ★ | ★ | ★ | ★ (a) | ★ | ★ | ★ | | ★ |
| Colorado | ★ | | ★ | ★ | ★ | ★ | ★ (a) | | ★ | ★ | | ★ |
| Connecticut | ★ | ★ | ★ | ★ | ★ | ★ | ★ | ★ | ★ | ★ | ★ | ★ |
| Delaware | ★ | ★ | ★ | ★ | ★ | ★ | ★ | ★ | ★ | ★ | | ★ |
| Florida | ★ | ★ | ★ | ★ | ★ | ★ | ★ | ★ | ★ | ★ | | ★ |
| Georgia | ★ | ★ | ★ | ★ | ★ | ★ | | ★ | ★ | ★ | | ★ |
| Hawaii | ★ | ★ | ★ | | | | ★ | | ★ | ★ | | ★ |
| Idaho | ★ | | ★ | | ★ | ★ | | | ★ | ★ | | ★ |
| Illinois | ★ | | | ★ | ★ | | ★ | ★ | ★ | ★ | | ★ |
| Indiana | ★ | | | ★ | ★ | ★ | | ★ | ★ | ★ | ★ | ★ |
| Iowa | ★ | | ★ | ★ | ★ | ★ | ★ | ★ | ★ | ★ | | ★ |
| Kansas | ★ | | | | | | | ★ | ★ | ★ | | ★ |
| Kentucky | ★ | ★ | ★ | ★ | ★ | ★ | | ★ | ★ | ★ | | ★ |
| Louisiana | ★ | ★ | ★ | ★ | ★ | | ★ | ★ | ★ | ★ | | ★ |
| Maine | ★ | ★ | | | | | | ★ | ★ | ★ | | ★ |
| Maryland | ★ | | ★ | ★ | ★ | ★ | ★ | ★ | ★ | ★ | | ★ |
| Massachusetts | ★ | ★ | | ★ | ★ | | ★ | | ★ | ★ | | ★ |
| Michigan | ★ | ★ | | ★ | ★ | ★ | | | ★ | ★ | ★ | ★ |
| Minnesota | | | | | ★ (b) | ★ (b) | | | | | | ★ |
| Mississippi | ★ | | | | (b) | (b) | | | | | | |
| Missouri | ★ | | | ★ | ★ | ★ | ★ | ★ | ★ | ★ | | ★ |
| Montana | | | | | | | | | | | | |
| Nebraska | ★ | ★ | ★ | ★ | ★ | ★ | | ★ | ★ | ★ | ★ | ★ |
| Nevada | ★ | ★ | | ★ | ★ | ★ | | ★ | ★ | ★ | | ★ |
| New Hampshire | ★ | | | | | | | | ★ | ★ | ★ | ★ |
| New Jersey | ★ | | | ★ | ★ | | ★ | | ★ | ★ | | ★ |
| New Mexico | ★ | | | ★ | ★ | ★ | | ★ | ★ | ★ | | ★ |
| New York | ★ | | ★ | ★ | ★ | | | | ★ | ★ | | ★ |
| North Carolina | ★ | | | ★ | ★ | | ★ | | ★ | ★ | | ★ |
| North Dakota | ★ | | | | | | | | | | | ★ |
| Ohio | ★ | ★ | ★ | | | | ★ (c) | | | | | ★ |
| Oklahoma | ★ | ★ | ★ | ★ | ★ | ★ | ★ (c) | ★ | ★ | ★ | ★ | ★ |
| Oregon | ★ | ★ | ★ | ★ | ★ | ★ | | ★ | ★ | ★ | ★ | ★ |
| Pennsylvania | ★ | ★ | ★ | ★ | ★ | ★ | | ★ | ★ | ★ | ★ | ★ |
| Rhode Island | ★ | ★ | | | | | | | ★ | ★ | ★ | ★ |
| South Carolina | ★ | ★ | ★ | | | | | ★ | ★ | ★ | | ★ |

See footnotes at end of table.

# ALLOWABLE STATE INVESTMENTS — Continued

| State or other jurisdiction | Certificates of deposits (in state) | Certificates of deposits (nationally) | Other time deposits | Bankers acceptance | Commercial paper | Corporate notes/bonds | Mutuals | State and local government obligations | U.S. Treasury obligations | U.S. agency obligations | Eurodollars (CDs or TDs) | Repurchase agreements |
|---|---|---|---|---|---|---|---|---|---|---|---|---|
| South Dakota | ★ (d) | ★ | ★ | ★ | ★ | ★ (e) | ★ (f) | ★ | ★ | ★ | ... | ★ |
| Tennessee | ★ | ... | ★ | ★ | ★ | ... | ... | ... | ★ | ★ | ... | ★ |
| Texas | ... | ★ (g) | ... | ★ | ★ | ... | ... | ★ | ★ | ★ | ... | ★ |
| Utah | ★ | ★ | ... | ★ | ★ | ★ | ... | ★ | ★ | ★ | ... | ★ |
| Vermont | ★ | ... | ★ | ★ | ★ | ... | ★ | ★ | ★ | ... | ... | ... |
| Virginia | ★ | ... | ★ | ★ | ★ | ★ | ★ | ... | ★ | ★ | ... | ★ |
| Washington | ★ | ... | ... | ★ | ★ | ... | ... | ★ | ★ | ★ | ... | ★ |
| West Virginia | ... | ★ | ★ | ... | ... | ★ | ... | ... | ... | ★ | ★ | ... |
| Wisconsin | ★ | ... | ★ | ★ | ★ | ★ | ... | ... | ★ | ★ | ★ | ★ |
| Wyoming | ★ | | ★ | ★ | ★ | ... | ... | ★ | ★ | ★ | ... | ★ |
| Dist. of Columbia | ★ | ... | ★ | ... | ... | ... | ... | ★ | ★ | ★ | ... | ★ |
| Puerto Rico | ★ | ★ | ★ | ★ | ... | ... | ★ | ★ | ★ | ★ | ★ | ★ |

*Source:* National Association of State Treasurers' *State Treasury Activities & Functions, 1997.*

*Key:*
★ — Investment allowed.
... — Investment not allowed.
(a) Money market funds only.
(b) Funds invested by outside money managers can invest up to 30 percent of total portfolio, if desired.
(c) Money market funds only.
(d) Must be collateralized 110 percent
(e) Above triple B only.
(f) Limited to those in which the state has beneficial interest.
(g) With rating restrictions.

## Table 6.6
## CASH MANAGEMENT PROGRAMS AND SERVICES

| State or other jurisdiction | Reviews of cash management programs | | | | Agency preparing cash management services | | | | | |
| | Banking relations | | Investment practices | | | | | | | |
| | Reviewing agency | Frequency of review | Reviewing agency | Frequency of review | Lock boxes | Wire transfers | Zero balance accounts | Information services | Account reconciliation services | Automated clearinghouse |
|---|---|---|---|---|---|---|---|---|---|---|
| Alabama | ... | ... | ... | ... | OF | OF | ... | IH | IH | OF |
| Alaska | SE | Annually | SE | Ongoing | OF | IH | ... | IH | IH | OF |
| Arizona | SE | Monthly | SE | Monthly | ... | IH,OF | OF | Y | IH,OF | IH,OF |
| Arkansas | SE | As Needed | SE | Monthly | ... | OF | ... | IH | IH | OF |
| California | SE | Biannually | SE | Quarterly | OF | IH,OF | OF | IH,OF | IH,OF | OF |
| Colorado | SE | Weekly | SE | Periodically | OF | OF | OF | OF | OF | IH,OF |
| Connecticut | SE | Quarterly | OF | Weekly | OF | IH,OF | OF | IH,OF | IH,OF | IH,OF |
| Delaware | (a) | 5-7 years | (a) | Annually | OF | IH | OF | IH,OF | IH | IH |
| Florida | SE | 4 years | SE | Annually | IH,OF | OF | OF | IH | IH | OF |
| Georgia | SE | Annually | SE | Daily | OF | IH,OF | OF | OF | OF | IH |
| Hawaii | SE | (b) | SE | (c) | OF | OF | IH | OF | IH | OF |
| Idaho | SE | Ongoing | SE | Ongoing | ... | IH | OF | IH,OF | IH | OF |
| Illinois | SE | Annually | SE | Annually | OF | IH,OF | OF | IH | IH | IH |
| Indiana | SE | Annually | SE | Annually | OF | OF | OF | IH | ... | OF |
| Iowa | SE | 4 years | SE (g) | Monthly | OF | IH,OF (d) | OF | OF (e) | ... | IH (f) |
| Kansas | SE | 3 years | SE | Annually | OF | IH | OF | IH,OF | ... | IH,OF |
| Kentucky | SE | (h) | SE | Quarterly/Annually | ... | OF | OF | OF | IH,OF | OF |
| Louisiana | SE | As Needed | SE | As Needed | OF | OF | OF | OF | OF | OF |
| Maine | SE | 2 years | SE | Quarterly | OF | OF | OF | IH,OF | IH,OF | OF |
| Maryland | SE | Annually | SE | Annually | IH,OF | IH | IH,OF | IH | IH,OF | IH |
| Massachusetts | SE | Daily | SE | Daily | OF | OF | ... | OF | IH,OF | OF |
| Michigan | SE | Annually | SE | Annually | OF | OF | OF | IH | ... | OF |
| Minnesota | SE | Ongoing (i) | SE | Ongoing (j) | OF | IH | OF | IH | ... | IH,OF |
| Mississippi | SE | Ongoing | SE | Ongoing | ... | OF | OF | ... | ... | OF |
| Missouri | SE | 4 Years | SE | 4 Years | IH | OF | OF | IH,OF | IH,OF | IH,OF |
| Montana | SE | Monthly | SE | Monthly/Annually | ... | IH,OF | ... | IH | IH | IH,OF |
| Nebraska | SE | Ongoing | SE | Ongoing | ... | OF | IH,OF | IH,OF | IH | IH,OF |
| Nevada | SE | Quarterly | SE | Quarterly/Monthly | OF | IH,OF | OF | ... | IH,OF | OF |
| New Hampshire | SE | As Needed | SE | Monthly | OF | OF | OF | OF | OF | OF |
| New Jersey | SE | Ongoing | SE | Daily | OF | IH,OF | OF | IH,OF | IH,OF | IH,OF |
| New Mexico | SE | Periodically | SE | Periodically | OF | OF | OF | IH | IH | IH,OF |
| New York | SE | ... | SE | Annually (k) | Y | Y | Y | IH | Y | ... |
| North Carolina | SE | Annually | SE | Quarterly | IH,OF | IH | OF | IH | IH | IH,OF |
| North Dakota | SE | Daily | SE | Daily | OF | OF | OF | IH | IH | OF |
| Ohio | SE | Biannually | SE | (l) | IH,OF | OF | ... | IH | OF | IH,OF |
| Oklahoma | SE | Ongoing | SE | Ongoing | OF | OF | OF | IH,OF | IH | IH,OF |
| Oregon | SE/OF | Periodically | SE/OF | Periodically | OF | IH,OF | OF | IH | Y | IH,OF |
| Pennsylvania | SE | Daily | SE | Daily | OF | IH | ... | IH,OF | IH | IH |
| Rhode Island | SE | Quarterly | SE | Weekly | OF | IH,OF | ... | IH,OF | IH | IH,OF |
| South Carolina | SE | Annually | SE/OF | Annually | OF | IH,OF | IH,OF | ... | IH,OF | OF |

See footnotes at end of table.

# CASH MANAGEMENT PROGRAMS AND SERVICES — Continued

| State or other jurisdiction | Reviews of cash management programs | | | | Agency preparing cash management services | | | | | |
| | Banking relations | | Investment practices | | Lock boxes | Wire transfers | Zero balance accounts | Information services | Account reconciliation services | Automated clearinghouse |
| | Reviewing agency | Frequency of review | Reviewing agency | Frequency of review | | | | | | |
|---|---|---|---|---|---|---|---|---|---|---|
| **South Dakota** | SE (m) | Ongoing | SE (m) | Annually (n) | (o) | IH | OF | IH,OF | IH,OF (p) | IH,OF |
| **Tennessee** | SE | Monthly | SE | Quarterly | IH | IH | ... | IH | IH | IH |
| **Texas** | SE | Ongoing | SE | Ongoing | IH | IH,OF | IH | OF (q) | IH | OF |
| **Utah** | SE | Monthly | SE | Monthly | OF | IH | IH | IH | IH | IH |
| **Vermont** | SE | 3 Years | SE | Annually | IH,OF | IH,OF | OF | IH,OF | IH | IH,OF |
| **Virginia** | SE | Annually | SE/OF | Periodically | IH,OF | OF | OF | IH,OF | IH,OF | IH,OF |
| **Washington** | SE | Ongoing | SE | Annually | OF | OF | OF | IH,OF | IH | IH,OF |
| **West Virginia*** | N.A. | N.A. | N.A. | Annually | IH,OF | OF | OF | N.A. | IH,OF | IH,OF |
| **Wisconsin** | SE | 6 Years | SE/OF | ... | OF | IH,OF | IH | IH,OF | IH,OF | IH,OF |
| **Wyoming** | SE | Annually | SE/OF | Annually | ... | IH,OF | IH | ... | IH | OF |
| **Dist. of Columbia** | SE/OF | Annually | SE/OF | Annually | IH,OF | IH,OF | OF | IH | IH | IH,OF |
| **Puerto Rico** | SE | ... | SE | ... | OF | OF | IH | IH,OF | IH,OF | OF |

*Source:* National Association of State Treasurers, *State Treasury Activities & Functions, 1997,* except where noted by * where data are from 1996.

*Key:*
SE — State employee or board.
OF — Outside firm.
IH — Within treasurer's office.
Y — Utilizes services, performance not specified.
... — Service not utilized.
N.A. — Not available.
(a) Cash management policy board.
(b) Reviewed when contract expires.
(c) No set period for review.
(d) Treasurer initiated wires by phone and the use of software.

(e) Treasury uses bank software to access balance and ACH information.
(f) State agencies create the files.
(g) Board also reviews.
(h) Contract renewed on a two-year cycle.
(i) Bid every three years.
(j) Quarterly formal reviews.
(k) Sooner if required by changing market conditions.
(l) Weekly, strategic meetings; annual, policy meetings.
(m) Daily by treasurer; quarterly by treasurer and Finance Office; annually by treasurer and Department of Legislative Audit.
(n) And as necessary.
(o) Service provided by outside firm, but currently not in use.
(p) Initiated by bank; verified by state.
(q) Balance reporting.

## Table 6.7
## DEMAND DEPOSITS

| State or other jurisdiction | Method for selecting depository | | | | | | | Selection of depository made by | Compensation for demand deposits | | Collateralization required above the federal insurance level | Percentage requiring collateral |
|---|---|---|---|---|---|---|---|---|---|---|---|---|
| | Competitive bid | Application | Negotiation | Depositor's convenience | Compensating balances | Agency's convenience | Treasurer's approval | | Procedure Used | Method for determining compensation | | |
| Alabama | | | | ★ | | ★ | ★ | Treasurer | CMB | Account analysis | Yes | 100 (a) |
| Alaska | | | | ★ | ★ | ★ | ★ | Treasurer | CMB, FS | Competitive bid, account analysis | Yes | 100 |
| Arizona | ★ | | | ★ | | | | Treasurer | CMB | Account analysis | Yes | 102 |
| Arkansas | ★ | | | ★ | | ★ | ★ | Treasurer | MB | Account negotiation | Yes | 100 |
| California | | ★ | | ★ | ★ | ★ | ★ | Treasurer | CMB | Account negotiation | Yes | 110 |
| Colorado | ★ | ★ | ★ | ★ | | ★ | ★ | Treasurer Controller | CMB, FS, MB | Competitive bid | Yes | 100 |
| Connecticut | ★ | ★ | ★ | ★ | | ★ | ★ | Treasurer | CMB, FS, MB | Competitive bid, account analysis, annual negotiation | Yes | (b) |
| Delaware | ★ | | ★ | | | | | Treasurer, Board | CMB, FS | Account analysis | (c) | (c) |
| Florida | ★ | | | | | | | Treasurer | FS | Competitive bid | Yes | 25-200 |
| Georgia | | | | | | ★ (d) | | (e) | FS | Account analysis | No | ... |
| Hawaii | ★ | ★ | ★ | | | | ★ | Treasurer | CMB, FS | Competitive bid, account analysis | Yes | 100 |
| Idaho | | ★ | ★ | ★ | | | | Treasurer | FS | Annual negotiation | No | ... |
| Illinois | | ★ | ★ | ★ | | | ★ | (f) | CMB, FS | Account analysis (g) | Yes | 110 |
| Indiana | ★ | | | ★ | | ★ | | Treasurer | CMB | Account analysis | No | 0 |
| Iowa | ★ | | | ★ | | | | Treasurer | CMB, FS | Competitive bid | Yes | (a) |
| Kansas | ★ | | | | | ★ | | Board | CMB, FS | Competitive bid, annual negotiation | Yes | (a) |
| Kentucky | ★ | | | | | ★ | ★ | (i) | CMB, FS | Competitive bid | Yes | 1 |
| Louisiana | ★ | ★ | | | | | | Treasurer | FS | Competitive bid | Yes | 100 |
| Maine | ★ | | ★ | ★ | | ★ | ★ | Treasurer | CMB | Account analysis | Yes | (h) |
| Maryland | ★ | | | | | ★ | | Treasurer | FS | Account analysis | Yes | 100 |
| Massachusetts | ★ | | | ★ | | ★ | ★ | Treasurer and agency | CMB, FS | Account analysis | No | 0 |
| Michigan | | | | ★ | ★ | | | Treasurer | CMB | Annual negotiation, account analysis | Yes | 100 |
| Minnesota | ★ | | | ★ | | | | Comm. of Finance | CMB, FS | Competitive bid, account analysis | Yes | 110 |
| Mississippi | | ★ | | | | ★ | ★ | Treasurer | CMB, FS | Account analysis | Yes | (a) |
| Missouri | ★ | | | ★ | | ★ | ★ | Treasurer | CB | (j) | Yes | 100 |
| Montana | ★ | | | | | | | Treasurer | FS | Competitive bid | Yes | 50 |
| Nebraska | ★ | | | ★ | | ★ | ★ | Treasurer | CMB | Account analysis | Yes | 110 |
| Nevada | ★ | | | | | | | Treasurer | CMB, FS | Competitive bid, account analysis | Yes | 102 |
| New Hampshire | ★ | ★ | ★ | ★ | | ★ | ★ | Treasurer | CMB, FS | Account analysis | No | 0 |
| New Jersey | ★ | | | ★ | ★ | ★ | | Treasurer | CMB, FS | Competitive bid, account analysis | Yes | 100-120 |

See footnotes at end of table.

# DEMAND DEPOSITS — Continued

| State or other jurisdiction | Method for selecting depository | | | | | | | Selection of depository made by | Compensation for demand deposits | | Collateralization required above the federal insurance level | Percentage requiring collateral |
|---|---|---|---|---|---|---|---|---|---|---|---|---|
| | Competitive bid | Application | Negotiation | Depositor's convenience | Compensating balances | Agency's convenience | Treasurer's approval | | Procedure used | Method for determining compensation | | |
| New Mexico | | | | | | ★ | ★ | Treasurer (k) | CMB | Account analysis | Yes | (l) |
| New York | ★ | | ★ | | | ★ | ★ | Treasurer | CMB, FS | Account analysis | Yes | 100 |
| North Carolina | | | | ★ | | ★ | | Treasurer | CMB | Account analysis, annual negotiation | Yes | 100 |
| North Dakota | | | | | | | | State Constitution | (m) | State Constitution | No | |
| Ohio | ★ (n) | | | ★ | | ★ | | Board | CMB, FS | Account analysis | Yes | 100 |
| Oklahoma | | | | ★ | | | ★ | Treasurer | CMB, FS | Account analysis | Yes | 110 |
| Oregon | | ★ | | ★ | | | ★ | Board | CMB | Negotiation | Yes | 25 |
| Pennsylvania | | ★ | ★ | | | | | Treasurer | CMB, FS | Account analysis | No (o) | 120 |
| Rhode Island | | | ★ | | | | ★ | Treasurer | CMB | Account analysis | Yes | 0 |
| South Carolina | | ★ | ★ | ★ | | | ★ | Treasurer | CMB | Account analysis | Yes | 100 |
| South Dakota | (p) | ★ | | | | | | Treasurer | CB, FS (q) | Competitive bid | Yes | 110 |
| Tennessee | | ★ | | | | | | Treasurer | CMB/FS | Account analysis, Competitive bid | Yes | 105 |
| Texas | ★ | | ★ | | | ★ | | Board | CMB, FS | Account analysis | Yes | 105 (r) |
| Utah | ★ | | ★ | ★ | | ★ | ★ | Treasurer | FS | Competitive bid, account analysis | No | |
| Vermont | ★ | | | | | | ★ | Treasurer | FS | Competitive bid | Yes | 102 |
| Virginia | ★ | | ★ | ★ | | ★ | ★ | Treasurer | CMB, FS | Competitive bid, account analysis | Yes | 50-100 (s) |
| Washington | ★ | | ★ | ★ | | ★ | ★ | Treasurer, state agencies | CMB, FS | Account analysis, competitive bid annual negotiation | Yes | 10 |
| West Virginia* | ★ | | | ★ | | ★ | | Board | CB,FS | Competitive bid, account analysis | Yes | 88.6 |
| Wisconsin | ★ | | | | | | | Board | FS | Account analysis | No | N.A. |
| Wyoming | ★ | | | | | | | Treasurer | FS | Account analysis, competitive bid | Yes | 100 |
| Dist. of Columbia | ★ | | | | | | | Treasurer | CMB | Competitive bid | Yes | 102 |
| Puerto Rico | ★ | | | | | | ★ | Treasurer | CMB, FS | Account analysis | Yes | 100 |

Source: National Association of State Treasurers, *State Treasury Activities & Functions, 1997*, except where noted by * where data are from 1996.

Key:

★ — Method utilized.
··· — Method not utilized.
N.A. — Not available.
CB — Competitive bid.
CMB — Compensating balances.
FS — Fee for service.
MB — Minimum balance.

(a) Public funds in excess of FDIC must be collateralized.
(b) Depends upon Risk Based Capital Ratio.
(c) Banks must meet certain financial criteria. If they do not meet the criteria they must collateralize to 102 percent MTM.
(d) With approval of State Depository Board.
(e) Agencies with approval of State Depository Board.
(f) Banks/savings and loans request funds in writing, and Treasurer's staff base deposits on safety and soundness review.
(g) Based on fee schedule negotiated in contract.
(h) Demand deposits that exceed 25 percent of a bank's retained earnings must be collateralized.
(i) Treasurer, Finance Secretary and a selection committee are responsible for the selection of institutions.
(j) Prices are established based on market rates.
(k) Treasurer approves agency's selection.
(l) Minimum 50 percent collateral required on all deposits
(m) Fees through interest rates.
(n) Approval by State Board of Deposits.
(o) Only under special circumstances.
(p) Competitive bid for treasury's primary account, auditor's warrant imprest account and college accounts. Auditor and treasurer jointly approve local account service.
(q) State agencies pay electronic banking service fees. Daily account analysis with earning credit determination.
(r) Requires 125 percent if mortgage backed securities are pledged.
(s) Fifty percent, all banks pool risk for remaining 50 percent. One hundred percent, saving banks and those banks rated low.

## Table 6.8
## SUMMARY OF FINANCIAL AGGREGATES, BY STATE: 1997
(In millions of dollars)

| State | Revenue | | | | Expenditure | | | | Debt outstanding at end of fiscal year | Cash and security holdings at end of fiscal year |
| --- | --- | --- | --- | --- | --- | --- | --- | --- | --- | --- |
| | Total | General | Utilities and liquor store | Insurance trust | Total | General | Utilities and liquor store | Insurance trust | | |
| United States .......... | $1,039,423 | $814,382 | $7,337 | $217,703 | $893,827 | $788,176 | $10,479 | $95,172 | $455,697 | $1,784,947 |
| Alabama ..................... | 14,008 | 11,487 | 139 | 2,382 | 12,945 | 11,669 | 142 | 1,134 | 3,780 | 21,639 |
| Alaska ....................... | 9,439 | 7,425 | 21 | 1,993 | 5,722 | 5,160 | 24 | 539 | 3,291 | 34,320 |
| Arizona ..................... | 13,692 | 11,499 | 25 | 2,168 | 12,419 | 11,266 | 28 | 1,124 | 2,742 | 25,615 |
| Arkansas ................... | 8,844 | 7,290 | 0 | 1,554 | 7,685 | 7,103 | 0 | 582 | 2,248 | 11,899 |
| California ................... | 131,349 | 103,929 | 151 | 27,269 | 117,643 | 102,853 | 74 | 14,716 | 45,337 | 226,142 |
| Colorado ................... | 12,780 | 9,945 | 0 | 2,835 | 10,861 | 9,381 | 5 | 1,475 | 3,402 | 23,591 |
| Connecticut ............... | 14,520 | 13,015 | 22 | 1,483 | 13,826 | 11,952 | 217 | 1,657 | 17,051 | 22,887 |
| Delaware ................... | 4,211 | 3,469 | 8 | 733 | 3,404 | 3,098 | 39 | 266 | 3,434 | 7,510 |
| Florida ...................... | 41,432 | 34,281 | 5 | 7,146 | 37,464 | 34,658 | 80 | 2,726 | 16,022 | 65,401 |
| Georgia ..................... | 24,028 | 19,714 | 0 | 4,315 | 21,975 | 20,448 | 0 | 1,527 | 6,186 | 36,320 |
| Hawaii ...................... | 6,701 | 5,527 | 0 | 1,174 | 6,093 | 5,421 | 0 | 672 | 5,253 | 10,843 |
| Idaho ........................ | 4,289 | 3,402 | 48 | 839 | 3,674 | 3,251 | 39 | 385 | 1,598 | 7,294 |
| Illinois ...................... | 39,038 | 32,068 | 0 | 6,970 | 35,302 | 31,266 | 0 | 4,036 | 23,801 | 59,776 |
| Indiana ..................... | 17,537 | 15,992 | 0 | 1,545 | 16,370 | 15,400 | 0 | 970 | 6,140 | 23,269 |
| Iowa ......................... | 9,509 | 8,360 | 90 | 1,059 | 9,348 | 8,622 | 62 | 664 | 2,014 | 18,889 |
| Kansas ...................... | 7,950 | 7,264 | 0 | 685 | 7,496 | 6,875 | 0 | 621 | 1,211 | 8,826 |
| Kentucky ................... | 15,033 | 12,431 | 0 | 2,601 | 12,949 | 11,634 | 9 | 1,306 | 7,120 | 24,059 |
| Louisiana .................. | 15,929 | 13,529 | 4 | 2,396 | 14,286 | 12,790 | 3 | 1,493 | 7,030 | 26,722 |
| Maine ....................... | 5,215 | 4,059 | 70 | 1,086 | 4,441 | 3,961 | 47 | 433 | 3,203 | 6,400 |
| Maryland .................. | 20,128 | 14,800 | 92 | 5,236 | 16,200 | 14,002 | 358 | 1,840 | 9,873 | 40,443 |
| Massachusetts ............ | 26,538 | 23,811 | 69 | 2,658 | 25,791 | 23,589 | 95 | 2,106 | 29,386 | 35,435 |
| Michigan ................... | 45,509 | 33,857 | 483 | 11,169 | 36,092 | 32,546 | 374 | 3,172 | 14,431 | 60,166 |
| Minnesota ................. | 22,882 | 17,207 | 0 | 5,674 | 18,443 | 16,796 | 0 | 1,647 | 4,862 | 36,925 |
| Mississippi ................ | 9,400 | 7,895 | 142 | 1,363 | 9,006 | 8,014 | 114 | 877 | 2,455 | 14,574 |
| Missouri .................... | 16,601 | 13,774 | 0 | 2,827 | 14,230 | 13,082 | 0 | 1,148 | 7,579 | 32,267 |
| Montana .................... | 3,524 | 2,879 | 33 | 612 | 3,204 | 2,826 | 29 | 349 | 2,056 | 6,727 |
| Nebraska ................... | 5,537 | 4,740 | 0 | 797 | 4,802 | 4,548 | 0 | 254 | 1,494 | 6,895 |
| Nevada ...................... | 6,494 | 4,386 | 26 | 2,082 | 5,130 | 4,328 | 46 | 755 | 2,769 | 12,360 |
| New Hampshire .............. | 3,561 | 2,796 | 240 | 525 | 3,324 | 2,891 | 209 | 223 | 5,848 | 9,090 |
| New Jersey ................. | 36,087 | 26,963 | 469 | 8,655 | 29,430 | 23,053 | 1,562 | 4,815 | 26,591 | 63,138 |
| New Mexico ................. | 8,188 | 6,963 | 0 | 1,225 | 7,059 | 6,486 | 0 | 572 | 2,458 | 18,665 |
| New York .................... | 95,442 | 75,383 | 2,176 | 17,884 | 83,243 | 70,017 | 4,299 | 8,927 | 74,078 | 153,766 |
| North Carolina ............. | 25,527 | 21,696 | 0 | 3,831 | 22,864 | 20,955 | 0 | 1,910 | 5,677 | 42,723 |
| North Dakota .............. | 2,818 | 2,427 | 0 | 391 | 2,426 | 2,222 | 0 | 204 | 900 | 4,562 |
| Ohio ......................... | 45,250 | 30,792 | 389 | 14,069 | 37,407 | 30,705 | 263 | 6,439 | 13,437 | 113,511 |
| Oklahoma .................. | 11,328 | 8,704 | 267 | 2,356 | 9,593 | 8,286 | 252 | 1,055 | 3,795 | 16,869 |
| Oregon ...................... | 15,004 | 11,286 | 191 | 3,528 | 12,388 | 10,367 | 116 | 1,905 | 5,841 | 24,103 |
| Pennsylvania .............. | 49,318 | 35,212 | 733 | 13,372 | 39,296 | 33,709 | 677 | 4,911 | 15,368 | 77,929 |
| Rhode Island .............. | 4,229 | 3,501 | 9 | 719 | 4,002 | 3,373 | 37 | 593 | 5,302 | 9,587 |
| South Carolina ........... | 13,805 | 10,750 | 700 | 2,355 | 12,847 | 11,127 | 640 | 1,080 | 5,350 | 20,140 |
| South Dakota .............. | 2,316 | 1,920 | 0 | 395 | 2,070 | 1,947 | 0 | 123 | 1,841 | 5,697 |
| Tennessee .................. | 15,696 | 13,366 | 0 | 2,330 | 14,284 | 13,304 | 4 | 976 | 3,315 | 22,632 |
| Texas ........................ | 63,864 | 45,546 | 0 | 18,318 | 48,887 | 44,124 | 0 | 4,763 | 12,462 | 121,587 |
| Utah ......................... | 7,724 | 5,903 | 96 | 1,725 | 6,818 | 6,285 | 72 | 461 | 2,451 | 12,538 |
| Vermont .................... | 2,370 | 2,053 | 27 | 290 | 2,123 | 1,971 | 28 | 125 | 2,037 | 3,672 |
| Virginia ..................... | 24,322 | 18,089 | 258 | 5,975 | 19,287 | 17,807 | 231 | 1,249 | 9,941 | 42,855 |
| Washington ................ | 26,841 | 18,213 | 271 | 8,358 | 22,207 | 18,803 | 230 | 3,174 | 9,493 | 47,230 |
| West Virginia ............. | 7,467 | 6,038 | 47 | 1,381 | 7,145 | 6,099 | 44 | 1,003 | 3,040 | 7,478 |
| Wisconsin .................. | 23,592 | 16,649 | 0 | 6,943 | 18,200 | 16,229 | 0 | 1,971 | 9,832 | 53,026 |
| Wyoming ................... | 2,559 | 2,095 | 36 | 427 | 2,127 | 1,877 | 31 | 219 | 872 | 6,955 |

Source: U.S. Department of Commerce, Bureau of the Census.

Note: Detail may not add to totals due to rounding. Data presented are statistical in nature and do not represent an accounting statement. Therefore, a difference between an individual government's total revenues and expenditures does not necessarily indicate a budget surplus or deficit.

## Table 6.9
## SUMMARY OF FINANCIAL AGGREGATES, BY STATE: 1998
### (In millions of dollars)

| State | Revenue | | | | Expenditure | | | | Debt outstanding at end of fiscal year | Cash and security holdings at end of fiscal year |
|---|---|---|---|---|---|---|---|---|---|---|
| | Total | General | Utilities and liquor store | Insurance trust | Total | General | Utilities and liquor store | Insurance trust | | |
| United States .............. | $1,095,862 | $864,863 | $7,687 | $223,311 | $930,037 | $827,654 | $11,185 | $63,087 | $483,117 | $2,061,508 |
| Alabama .......................... | 14,844 | 12,433 | 142 | 2,269 | 137,288 | 12,476 | 146 | 919 | 4,167 | 23,466 |
| Alaska .......................... | 9,039 | 7,973 | 22 | 1,044 | 58,038 | 5,230 | 25 | 438 | 3,800 | 41,008 |
| Arizona .......................... | 16,582 | 11,812 | 21 | 4,748 | 13,328 | 12,070 | 27 | 924 | 2,807 | 31,571 |
| Arkansas .......................... | 9,487 | 7,724 | 0 | 1,763 | 8,104 | 7,572 | 0 | 349 | 2,384 | 13,344 |
| California .......................... | 144,985 | 111,088 | 160 | 33,738 | 120,330 | 106,681 | 85 | 8,582 | 50,251 | 269,125 |
| Colorado .......................... | 13,514 | 10,953 | 0 | 2,561 | 11,278 | 10,105 | 5 | 1,000 | 3,637 | 25,068 |
| Connecticut .................... | 16,520 | 14,452 | 24 | 2,045 | 14,516 | 12,681 | 200 | 1,131 | 17,727 | 26,339 |
| Delaware .......................... | 4,594 | 3,883 | 9 | 702 | 3,465 | 3,203 | 43 | 153 | 3,770 | 9,544 |
| Florida .......................... | 51,752 | 36,780 | 5 | 14,966 | 39,214 | 36,662 | 69 | 1,739 | 16,969 | 77,359 |
| Georgia .......................... | 25,707 | 20,165 | 0 | 5,542 | 21,735 | 20,281 | 0 | 1,206 | 6,040 | 51,019 |
| Hawaii .......................... | 6,761 | 5,474 | 0 | 1,287 | 5,860 | 5,261 | 0 | 452 | 5,710 | 11,719 |
| Idaho .......................... | 4,705 | 3,592 | 50 | 1,063 | 3,786 | 3,377 | 40 | 207 | 1,883 | 9,829 |
| Illinois .......................... | 40,460 | 33,787 | 0 | 6,674 | 35,685 | 32,005 | 0 | 2,593 | 25,314 | 66,723 |
| Indiana .......................... | 18,508 | 17,113 | 0 | 1,395 | 17,223 | 16,278 | 0 | 747 | 6,704 | 26,047 |
| Iowa .......................... | 10,029 | 8,821 | 94 | 1,114 | 9,729 | 9,030 | 65 | 481 | 2,029 | 22,073 |
| Kansas .......................... | 8,444 | 7,785 | 0 | 659 | 7,681 | 7,040 | 0 | 508 | 1,411 | 10,057 |
| Kentucky .......................... | 15,989 | 12,969 | 0 | 3,020 | 13,541 | 12,284 | 8 | 882 | 6,814 | 28,007 |
| Louisiana .......................... | 17,605 | 13,649 | 6 | 3,950 | 14,919 | 13,423 | 3 | 1,343 | 7,093 | 29,631 |
| Maine .......................... | 5,690 | 4,567 | 71 | 1,052 | 4,606 | 4,173 | 48 | 300 | 3,474 | 6,704 |
| Maryland .......................... | 20,559 | 15,589 | 95 | 4,875 | 16,578 | 14,481 | 368 | 1,077 | 10,536 | 42,235 |
| Massachusetts .................. | 28,235 | 25,801 | 76 | 2,357 | 27,194 | 25,153 | 110 | 1,214 | 32,833 | 46,252 |
| Michigan .......................... | 40,069 | 36,084 | 514 | 3,471 | 37,410 | 34,066 | 395 | 2,082 | 16,147 | 66,027 |
| Minnesota .......................... | 24,509 | 17,856 | 0 | 6,653 | 18,418 | 16,662 | 0 | 1,341 | 5,333 | 44,816 |
| Mississippi .......................... | 10,611 | 1,400 | 148 | 2,063 | 9,336 | 8,526 | 119 | 590 | 2,674 | 16,484 |
| Missouri .......................... | 19,021 | 14,884 | 0 | 4,137 | 15,313 | 14,191 | 0 | 849 | 8,091 | 35,726 |
| Montana .......................... | 3,626 | 2,980 | 34 | 611 | 3,262 | 2,890 | 30 | 222 | 2,259 | 7,240 |
| Nebraska .......................... | 5,636 | 4,829 | 0 | 806 | 4,754 | 4,565 | 0 | 148 | 1,908 | 8,301 |
| Nevada .......................... | 7,320 | 4,615 | 27 | 2,679 | 5,398 | 4,696 | 83 | 357 | 2,881 | 14,245 |
| New Hampshire.............. | 4,010 | 2,968 | 255 | 788 | 3,477 | 3,039 | 220 | 161 | 5,367 | 8,522 |
| New Jersey.......................... | 37,007 | 28,357 | 4,709 | 8,180 | 31,702 | 25,974 | 1,414 | 2,820 | 27,214 | 68,959 |
| New Mexico .......................... | 9,059 | 7,127 | 0 | 1,932 | 7,540 | 6,944 | 0 | 523 | 2,572 | 23,850 |
| New York.......................... | 96,131 | 80,720 | 2,279 | 13,133 | 87,338 | 73,869 | 4,954 | 5,474 | 73,254 | 168,410 |
| North Carolina .............. | 33,327 | 23,950 | 0 | 9,377 | 24,605 | 22,671 | 0 | 1,565 | 6,877 | 59,153 |
| North Dakota ................ | 3,128 | 2,533 | 0 | 595 | 2,527 | 2,327 | 0 | 79 | 857 | 5,321 |
| Ohio .......................... | 48,133 | 32,300 | 429 | 15,404 | 39,209 | 31,943 | 262 | 4,823 | 14,183 | 123,272 |
| Oklahoma .......................... | 12,186 | 9,411 | 274 | 2,501 | 9,953 | 8,693 | 255 | 794 | 3,951 | 18,712 |
| Oregon .......................... | 15,688 | 11,273 | 201 | 4,215 | 13,466 | 10,967 | 123 | 1,628 | 5,729 | 26,707 |
| Pennsylvania .................... | 48,503 | 36,833 | 776 | 10,894 | 40,804 | 35,603 | 717 | 2,921 | 16,394 | 86,783 |
| Rhode Island .................. | 4,438 | 3,781 | 10 | 646 | 3,964 | 3,413 | 38 | 264 | 5,352 | 9,787 |
| South Carolina ................ | 15,203 | 11,415 | 728 | 3,060 | 13,575 | 11,846 | 659 | 821 | 5,191 | 22,234 |
| South Dakota .................. | 2,874 | 2,098 | 0 | 776 | 2,245 | 2,120 | 0 | 107 | 2,068 | 6,342 |
| Tennessee .......................... | 16,675 | 14,086 | 0 | 2,589 | 14,775 | 13,875 | 4 | 600 | 3,192 | 25,329 |
| Texas .......................... | 57,807 | 48,066 | 0 | 9,741 | 51,065 | 46,405 | 0 | 3,822 | 14,408 | 145,605 |
| Utah .......................... | 8,762 | 6,627 | 103 | 2,032 | 7,470 | 6,927 | 77 | 309 | 3,435 | 14,363 |
| Vermont .......................... | 2,373 | 2,196 | 28 | 148 | 2,295 | 2,154 | 30 | 69 | 2,110 | 4,276 |
| Virginia .......................... | 25,918 | 19,268 | 259 | 6,392 | 20,529 | 19,037 | 242 | 1,079 | 10,828 | 48,807 |
| Washington .................... | 27,980 | 19,079 | 295 | 8,606 | 22,880 | 19,671 | 243 | 1,265 | 10,289 | 54,731 |
| West Virginia .................. | 7,808 | 6,206 | 47 | 1,556 | 7,149 | 6,210 | 44 | 347 | 3,433 | 8,203 |
| Wisconsin .......................... | 21,395 | 18,169 | 0 | 3,226 | 19,101 | 16,980 | 0 | 1,656 | 10,721 | 64,258 |
| Wyoming .......................... | 2,653 | 2,337 | 39 | 278 | 2,172 | 1,920 | 34 | 125 | 1,043 | 7,915 |

Source: U.S. Department of Commerce, Bureau of the Census.

Note: Detail may not add to totals due to rounding. Data presented are statistical in nature and do not represent an accounting statement. Therefore, a difference between an individual government's total revenues and expenditures does not necessarily indicate a budget surplus or deficit.

## Table 6.10
## NATIONAL TOTALS OF STATE GOVERNMENT FINANCES FOR SELECTED YEARS: 1995-1997

| Item | 1997 | 1996 | 1995 | Per capita 1997 | Per capita 1996 | Per capita 1995 | Percent change 1996 to 1997 | Percent change 1995 to 1996 |
|---|---|---|---|---|---|---|---|---|
| **Population (in thousands)** | 267,107,000 | 264,740,570 | 262,201,000 | | | | | |
| **Revenue total** | $1,039,422,594 | $967,005,172 | $903,755,501 | $3,891.41 | $3,652.65 | $3,446.80 | 7.5 | 7.0 |
| General revenue | 814,382,150 | 770,713,150 | 739,015,866 | 3,048.90 | 2911.20 | 2818.51 | 5.7 | 4.3 |
| Taxes | 443,335,463 | 418,970,791 | 399,147,521 | 1,659.77 | 1582.57 | 1522.30 | 5.8 | 5.0 |
| Intergovernmental revenue | 230,592,191 | 221,469,370 | 215,558,360 | 863.30 | 836.55 | 822.11 | 4.1 | 2.7 |
| From Federal Government | 215,420,924 | 208,099,676 | 202,485,216 | 806.50 | 786.05 | 772.25 | 3.5 | 2.8 |
| Public welfare | 123,087,017 | 118,153,874 | 114,944,717 | 460.82 | 446.30 | 438.38 | 4.2 | 2.8 |
| Education | 33,663,410 | 34,054,557 | 31,943,573 | 126.03 | 128.63 | 121.83 | -1.1 | 6.6 |
| Highways | 19,346,121 | 18,809,418 | 19,418,924 | 72.43 | 71.05 | 74.06 | 2.9 | -3.1 |
| Employment security administration | 3,656,898 | 3,787,030 | 3,972,476 | 13.69 | 14.30 | 15.15 | -3.4 | -4.7 |
| Other | 35,667,478 | 33,294,797 | 32,205,526 | 133.53 | 125.76 | 122.83 | 7.1 | 3.4 |
| From local government | 15,171,267 | 13,369,694 | 13,073,144 | 56.80 | 50.50 | 49.86 | 13.5 | 2.3 |
| Charges and miscellaneous revenue | 140,454,496 | 130,272,989 | 124,309,985 | 525.84 | 492.08 | 474.10 | 7.8 | 4.8 |
| Liquor stores revenue | 3,291,509 | 3,159,573 | 3,073,404 | 12.32 | 11.93 | 11.72 | 4.2 | 2.8 |
| Utility revenue | 4,045,724 | 3,919,223 | 3,845,228 | 15.15 | 14.80 | 14.67 | 3.2 | 1.9 |
| Insurance trust revenue | 217,703,211 | 189,213,226 | 157,821,003 | 815.04 | 714.71 | 601.91 | 15.1 | 19.9 |
| Employee retirement | 168,184,443 | 33,684,503 | 37,040,879 | 629.65 | 127.24 | 141.27 | 399.3 | -9.1 |
| Unemployment compensation | 34,881,959 | 139,316,425 | 104,450,918 | 130.59 | 526.24 | 398.36 | -75.0 | 33.4 |
| Other | 14,636,809 | 16,212,298 | 16,329,206 | 54.80 | 61.24 | 62.28 | -9.7 | -0.7 |
| **Expenditure and debt redemption** | 935,207,917 | 902,353,282 | 874,365,113 | 3,501.25 | 3408.44 | 3334.71 | 3.6 | 3.2 |
| Debt redemption | 41,381,094 | 42,394,650 | 37,471,443 | 154.92 | 160.14 | 142.91 | -2.4 | 13.1 |
| Expenditure total | 893,826,823 | 859,958,632 | 836,893,670 | 3,346.32 | 3248.31 | 3191.80 | 3.9 | 2.8 |
| General expenditure | 788,175,737 | 755,276,699 | 724,564,751 | 2,950.79 | 2852.89 | 2763.39 | 4.4 | 4.2 |
| Education | 275,820,952 | 263,519,202 | 249,670,340 | 1,032.62 | 995.39 | 952.21 | 4.7 | 5.5 |
| Intergovernmental expenditure | 164,147,715 | 156,954,115 | 148,160,436 | 614.54 | 592.86 | 565.06 | 4.6 | 5.9 |
| State institutions of higher education | 96,881,264 | 92,976,045 | 89,458,449 | 362.71 | 351.20 | 341.18 | 4.2 | 3.9 |
| Other education | 178,939,688 | 170,543,157 | 160,211,891 | 669.92 | 644.19 | 611.03 | 4.9 | 6.4 |
| Public welfare | 203,204,283 | 195,730,925 | 194,786,516 | 760.76 | 739.33 | 742.89 | 3.8 | 0.5 |
| Intergovernmental expenditure | 35,754,024 | 35,053,889 | 34,365,957 | 133.86 | 132.41 | 131.07 | 2.0 | 2.0 |
| Cash assistance, categorical program | 33,997,491 | 34,998,902 | 36,034,099 | 127.28 | 132.20 | 137.43 | -2.9 | -2.9 |
| Cash assistance, other | 1,959,671 | 2,213,536 | 2,375,958 | 7.34 | 8.36 | 9.06 | -11.5 | -6.8 |
| Other public welfare | 167,247,121 | 158,518,487 | 156,376,459 | 626.14 | 598.77 | 596.40 | 5.5 | 1.4 |
| Highways | 60,203,916 | 58,254,885 | 57,374,450 | 225.39 | 220.05 | 218.82 | 3.3 | 1.5 |
| Intergovernmental expenditure | 11,431,270 | 10,707,338 | 10,481,616 | 42.80 | 40.44 | 39.98 | 6.8 | 2.2 |
| Regular state highway facilities | 56,658,718 | 54,955,528 | 54,028,210 | 212.12 | 207.58 | 206.06 | 3.1 | 1.7 |
| State toll highways/facilities | 3,545,198 | 3,299,357 | 3,346,240 | 13.27 | 12.46 | 12.76 | 7.5 | -1.4 |
| Health and hospitals | 63,192,929 | 62,033,317 | 60,003,203 | 236.58 | 234.32 | 228.84 | 1.9 | 3.4 |
| State hospitals and institutions for handicapped | 28,798,274 | 29,063,252 | 28,882,739 | 107.82 | 109.78 | 110.15 | -0.9 | 0.6 |
| Other | 34,394,655 | 32,970,065 | 31,120,464 | 128.77 | 124.54 | 118.69 | 4.3 | 5.9 |
| Natural resources | 12,908,623 | 12,861,853 | 12,533,912 | 48.33 | 48.58 | 47.80 | 0.4 | 2.6 |
| Corrections | 29,042,709 | 27,324,135 | 26,069,038 | 108.73 | 103.21 | 99.42 | 6.3 | 4.8 |
| Financial administration | 13,697,685 | 12,493,783 | 12,761,394 | 51.28 | 47.19 | 48.67 | 9.6 | -2.1 |
| Employment security administration | 3,995,714 | 3,917,577 | 3,932,011 | 14.96 | 14.80 | 15.00 | 2.0 | -0.4 |
| Police protection | 7,500,993 | 7,173,419 | 6,451,364 | 28.08 | 27.10 | 24.60 | 4.6 | 11.2 |
| Interest on general debt | 26,310,095 | 25,402,062 | 24,485,426 | 98.50 | 95.95 | 93.38 | 3.6 | 3.7 |
| Veterans' services | 241,120 | 225,645 | 206,109 | 0.90 | 0.85 | 0.79 | 6.9 | 9.5 |
| Utility expenditure | 7,782,506 | 8,043,307 | 7,585,965 | 29.14 | 30.38 | 28.93 | -3.2 | 6.0 |
| Insurance trust expenditure | 95,171,612 | 94,045,406 | 93,281,908 | 356.31 | 355.24 | 355.76 | 1.2 | 0.8 |
| Employee retirement | 56,570,417 | 53,082,851 | 47,541,349 | 211.79 | 200.51 | 181.32 | 6.6 | 11.7 |
| Unemployment compensation | 27,475,379 | 29,337,402 | 35,032,015 | 102.86 | 110.82 | 133.61 | -6.3 | -16.3 |
| Other | 11,125,816 | 11,625,153 | 10,708,544 | 41.65 | 43.91 | 40.84 | -4.3 | 8.6 |
| **Total expenditure by character and object** | 893,826,823 | 859,958,632 | 836,893,670 | 3,346.32 | 3248.31 | 3191.80 | 3.9 | 2.8 |
| Direct expenditure | 629,619,614 | 607,856,174 | 595,915,542 | 2,357.18 | 2296.05 | 2272.74 | 3.6 | 2.0 |
| Current operation | 425,898,730 | 405,415,661 | 396,035,029 | 1,594.49 | 1531.37 | 1510.43 | 5.1 | 2.4 |
| Capital outlay | 59,657,707 | 58,915,152 | 57,828,938 | 223.35 | 222.54 | 220.55 | 1.3 | 1.9 |
| Construction | 46,991,379 | 46,924,479 | 46,113,125 | 175.93 | 177.25 | 175.87 | 0.1 | 1.8 |
| Other capital outlay structures | 12,666,328 | | | 47.42 | | | | |

## NATIONAL TOTALS OF STATE GOVERNMENT FINANCES FOR SELECTED YEARS: 1995-1997 - Continued

| Item | 1997 | 1996 | 1995 | Per capita 1997 | Per capita 1996 | Per capita 1995 | Percent change 1996 to 1997 | Percent change 1995 to 1996 |
|---|---|---|---|---|---|---|---|---|
| **Revenue total** ................................. | $1,039,422,594 | $967,005,172 | $903,755,501 | $3,891.41 | $3,652.65 | $3,446.80 | 7.5 | 7.0 |
| Assistance and subsidies ........... | 21,866,744 | 23,312,951 | 23,511,134 | 81.87 | 88.06 | 89.67 | -6.2 | -0.8 |
| Interest on debt ......................... | 27,024,821 | 26,167,004 | 25,258,533 | 101.18 | 98.84 | 96.33 | 3.3 | 3.6 |
| Insurance benefits and .............. repayments ............................. | 95,171,612 | 94,045,406 | 93,281,908 | 356.31 | 355.24 | 355.76 | 1.2 | 0.8 |
| Intergovernmental expenditure .... | 264,207,209 | 252,102,458 | 240,978,128 | 989.14 | 952.26 | 919.06 | 4.8 | 4.6 |
| **Cash and security holdings at end of fiscal year** .................................. | 1,784,947,182 | 1,558,248,670 | 1,388,001,038 | 6,682.52 | 5885.95 | 5293.65 | 14.5 | 12.3 |
| Insurance trust .............................. | 1,288,725,273 | 1,103,605,750 | 962,445,729 | 4,824.75 | 4168.63 | 3670.64 | 16.8 | 14.7 |
| Unemployment fund balance .... | 40,025,974 | 36,868,099 | 36,736,602 | 149.85 | 139.26 | 140.11 | 8.6 | 0.4 |
| Debt offsets ................................. | 231,162,757 | 226,280,807 | 215,791,447 | 865.43 | 854.73 | 823.00 | 2.2 | 4.9 |

*Source:* U.S. Department of Commerce, Bureau of the Census.

## Table 6.11
## STATE GENERAL REVENUE, BY SOURCE AND BY STATE: 1997
(In thousands of dollars)

| State | Total general revenue (a) | Taxes Total | Sales and gross receipts Total (b) | General | Motor fuels | Licenses Total (b) | Motor vehicle | Individual income | Corporation net income | Intergovernmental revenue | Charges and miscellaneous general revenue |
|---|---|---|---|---|---|---|---|---|---|---|---|
| United States | $814,382,150 | $443,335,463 | $215,737,108 | $147,068,715 | $27,131,805 | $28,216,617 | $12,965,303 | $144,668,011 | $30,661,951 | $230,592,191 | $140,454,496 |
| Alabama | 11,487,011 | 5,484,161 | 2,866,477 | 1,505,713 | 472,814 | 424,165 | 170,633 | 1,687,599 | 226,616 | 3,553,541 | 2,449,309 |
| Alaska | 7,424,923 | 1,619,110 | 96,014 | 0 | 35,578 | 77,924 | 28,827 | 0 | 331,337 | 1,042,225 | 4,763,588 |
| Arizona | 11,499,078 | 6,833,806 | 3,803,450 | 2,855,234 | 504,906 | 437,200 | 323,079 | 1,668,414 | 600,890 | 3,237,414 | 1,427,858 |
| Arkansas | 7,290,031 | 3,776,600 | 2,017,650 | 1,429,445 | 351,525 | 221,790 | 97,100 | 1,246,600 | 229,982 | 2,264,482 | 1,248,949 |
| California | 103,929,227 | 61,666,886 | 25,222,055 | 19,973,609 | 2,822,335 | 2,962,520 | 1,510,949 | 23,272,871 | 5,803,652 | 30,345,109 | 11,917,232 |
| Colorado | 9,944,905 | 5,290,131 | 2,178,700 | 1,412,903 | 490,847 | 261,406 | 139,184 | 2,560,337 | 224,275 | 2,595,939 | 2,058,835 |
| Connecticut | 13,014,623 | 8,145,787 | 4,164,892 | 2,598,337 | 544,005 | 341,262 | 210,777 | 2,807,391 | 530,430 | 2,943,626 | 1,925,210 |
| Delaware | 3,469,482 | 1,743,234 | 253,405 | 0 | 102,388 | 578,563 | 27,602 | 663,111 | 172,562 | 672,129 | 1,054,119 |
| Florida | 34,280,835 | 21,080,120 | 16,081,231 | 12,068,290 | 1,480,898 | 1,370,177 | 809,031 | 0 | 1,232,731 | 8,297,195 | 4,903,520 |
| Georgia | 19,713,921 | 10,897,538 | 4,905,464 | 3,915,761 | 553,026 | 405,025 | 202,056 | 4,741,200 | 726,321 | 6,007,066 | 2,809,317 |
| Hawaii | 5,526,957 | 3,087,946 | 1,925,971 | 1,457,274 | 75,143 | 89,876 | 61,447 | 976,579 | 67,570 | 1,302,690 | 1,136,321 |
| Idaho | 3,401,841 | 1,960,505 | 923,985 | 622,192 | 211,528 | 147,586 | 45,651 | 711,657 | 138,277 | 849,475 | 591,861 |
| Illinois | 32,068,167 | 18,544,570 | 8,796,140 | 5,295,943 | 1,221,422 | 1,215,100 | 769,224 | 6,286,770 | 1,803,931 | 8,713,602 | 4,809,995 |
| Indiana | 15,991,546 | 9,100,842 | 4,131,854 | 3,042,874 | 617,109 | 193,720 | 115,619 | 3,750,826 | 904,265 | 3,859,176 | 3,031,528 |
| Iowa | 8,360,300 | 4,686,244 | 2,228,431 | 1,500,162 | 385,652 | 421,385 | 262,488 | 1,719,566 | 221,041 | 2,007,968 | 1,666,088 |
| Kansas | 7,264,375 | 4,229,721 | 2,007,052 | 1,475,825 | 302,657 | 211,755 | 128,781 | 1,512,816 | 291,080 | 1,839,813 | 1,194,841 |
| Kentucky | 12,431,136 | 6,818,992 | 3,194,113 | 1,882,682 | 406,573 | 427,137 | 152,787 | 2,205,023 | 292,753 | 3,463,950 | 2,148,194 |
| Louisiana | 13,529,327 | 5,646,255 | 2,759,050 | 1,828,434 | 494,604 | 435,603 | 96,045 | 1,560,048 | 380,155 | 4,329,084 | 3,553,988 |
| Maine | 4,059,117 | 2,019,491 | 964,667 | 683,152 | 155,917 | 117,339 | 56,078 | 771,810 | 97,146 | 1,299,070 | 740,556 |
| Maryland | 14,799,832 | 8,604,406 | 3,695,153 | 2,095,319 | 613,840 | 349,632 | 190,265 | 3,768,560 | 343,499 | 3,411,382 | 2,784,044 |
| Massachusetts | 23,810,978 | 13,305,471 | 4,217,418 | 2,876,066 | 602,840 | 431,012 | 244,911 | 7,181,821 | 1,213,366 | 5,808,872 | 4,696,635 |
| Michigan | 33,857,435 | 19,855,941 | 8,871,817 | 7,132,110 | 840,977 | 1,016,050 | 652,888 | 5,930,404 | 2,228,753 | 8,267,080 | 5,734,414 |
| Minnesota | 17,207,455 | 11,223,269 | 4,775,726 | 3,114,600 | 539,399 | 821,373 | 510,434 | 4,778,972 | 699,234 | 3,625,727 | 2,358,459 |
| Mississippi | 7,895,021 | 4,016,549 | 2,665,109 | 1,916,461 | 356,414 | 266,271 | 116,986 | 791,009 | 225,924 | 2,904,204 | 974,268 |
| Missouri | 13,773,787 | 7,815,966 | 3,701,961 | 2,592,460 | 648,619 | 562,367 | 237,057 | 3,038,167 | 411,045 | 3,719,819 | 2,238,002 |
| Montana | 2,878,900 | 1,308,855 | 274,367 | 0 | 175,418 | 151,322 | 49,406 | 406,276 | 81,999 | 959,197 | 610,848 |
| Nebraska | 4,740,329 | 2,548,174 | 1,281,350 | 865,708 | 277,127 | 164,907 | 74,352 | 937,297 | 137,338 | 1,164,360 | 1,027,795 |
| Nevada | 4,386,336 | 3,034,156 | 2,601,308 | 1,698,714 | 216,534 | 302,637 | 98,298 | 0 | 0 | 829,530 | 522,650 |
| New Hampshire | 2,795,550 | 914,847 | 458,732 | 0 | 110,758 | 120,568 | 56,304 | 52,682 | 208,388 | 988,193 | 892,510 |
| New Jersey | 26,963,004 | 14,414,778 | 7,192,382 | 4,415,428 | 464,676 | 742,208 | 399,809 | 4,825,411 | 1,263,979 | 6,362,916 | 6,185,310 |
| New Mexico | 6,963,118 | 3,322,410 | 1,806,516 | 1,345,759 | 236,696 | 133,707 | 86,661 | 747,813 | 173,205 | 1,973,080 | 1,667,628 |
| New York | 75,382,513 | 34,864,623 | 12,139,863 | 7,353,097 | 474,202 | 945,142 | 612,900 | 17,554,367 | 3,042,094 | 30,470,368 | 10,047,522 |
| North Carolina | 21,695,686 | 12,678,199 | 5,316,289 | 3,056,831 | 997,217 | 774,753 | 345,984 | 5,458,963 | 981,378 | 6,318,006 | 2,699,481 |
| North Dakota | 2,426,989 | 1,064,010 | 606,113 | 311,433 | 104,270 | 76,787 | 38,458 | 163,316 | 75,223 | 812,005 | 550,974 |
| Ohio | 30,792,152 | 16,417,761 | 8,055,125 | 5,234,151 | 1,368,232 | 1,355,317 | 557,388 | 6,141,212 | 737,363 | 8,992,850 | 5,381,541 |

See footnotes at end of table.

# STATE GENERAL REVENUE, BY SOURCE AND BY STATE: 1997 — Continued

| State | Total general revenue (a) | Taxes Total | Sales and gross receipts Total (b) | General | Motor fuels | Licenses Total (b) | Motor vehicle | Individual income | Corporation net income | Intergovernmental revenue | Charges and miscellaneous general revenue |
|---|---|---|---|---|---|---|---|---|---|---|---|
| Oklahoma | 8,703,926 | 5,060,601 | 1,940,658 | 1,272,606 | 347,258 | 700,643 | 545,620 | 1,697,600 | 221,172 | 2,169,755 | 1,473,570 |
| Oregon | 11,285,810 | 4,946,304 | 673,827 | 0 | 421,427 | 512,339 | 333,843 | 3,272,594 | 384,073 | 3,517,946 | 2,821,560 |
| Pennsylvania | 35,212,460 | 19,377,456 | 9,221,017 | 6,054,540 | 789,522 | 1,919,706 | 505,700 | 5,574,994 | 1,575,707 | 9,420,286 | 6,414,718 |
| Rhode Island | 3,500,923 | 1,644,047 | 813,403 | 489,624 | 123,662 | 79,856 | 47,314 | 639,703 | 89,198 | 1,108,615 | 748,261 |
| South Carolina | 10,750,064 | 5,381,412 | 2,735,295 | 2,032,134 | 327,777 | 411,179 | 95,938 | 1,932,992 | 239,350 | 3,161,523 | 2,207,129 |
| South Dakota | 1,920,419 | 768,491 | 609,401 | 410,928 | 95,148 | 93,625 | 30,050 | 0 | 36,888 | 673,220 | 478,708 |
| Tennessee | 13,365,828 | 6,616,361 | 5,087,032 | 3,839,914 | 723,413 | 737,935 | 201,217 | 128,189 | 479,660 | 5,065,016 | 1,684,451 |
| Texas | 45,546,186 | 23,024,628 | 18,403,991 | 11,361,888 | 2,383,040 | 3,265,491 | 785,558 | 0 | 0 | 13,800,422 | 8,721,136 |
| Utah | 5,903,010 | 3,010,696 | 1,579,769 | 1,265,084 | 216,992 | 90,381 | 47,696 | 1,127,712 | 177,415 | 1,592,311 | 1,300,003 |
| Vermont | 2,052,541 | 899,161 | 409,267 | 183,836 | 58,419 | 67,621 | 38,687 | 323,140 | 45,327 | 666,942 | 486,438 |
| Virginia | 18,089,498 | 9,627,591 | 3,766,542 | 2,118,945 | 734,541 | 430,751 | 263,540 | 4,727,791 | 425,154 | 3,544,685 | 4,917,222 |
| Washington | 18,212,938 | 11,202,296 | 8,289,331 | 6,572,213 | 685,238 | 509,656 | 244,433 | 0 | 0 | 4,112,300 | 2,898,342 |
| West Virginia | 6,038,200 | 2,905,947 | 1,514,674 | 831,239 | 228,038 | 151,441 | 75,486 | 786,190 | 251,230 | 2,040,033 | 1,092,220 |
| Wisconsin | 16,649,037 | 10,186,768 | 4,231,265 | 2,864,982 | 693,975 | 614,352 | 226,204 | 4,538,218 | 638,975 | 3,636,662 | 2,825,607 |
| Wyoming | 2,095,423 | 662,350 | 281,806 | 214,815 | 47,209 | 78,055 | 44,558 | 0 | 0 | 851,332 | 581,741 |

Source: U.S. Department of Commerce, Bureau of the Census.

Note: Detail may not add to totals due to rounding.

(a) Total general revenue equals total taxes plus intergovernmental revenue plus charges and miscellaneous revenue.

(b) Total includes other taxes not shown separately in this table.

**Table 6.12**
**STATE GENERAL REVENUE, BY SOURCE AND BY STATE: 1998**
(In thousands of dollars)

| State | Total general revenue (a) | Taxes Total | Sales and gross receipts Total (b) | Sales and gross receipts General | Sales and gross receipts Motor fuels | Licenses Total (b) | Licenses Motor vehicle | Individual income | Corporation net income | Intergovernmental revenue | Charges and miscellaneous general revenue |
|---|---|---|---|---|---|---|---|---|---|---|---|
| United States | $864,863,438 | $474,392,344 | $227,342,553 | $155,970,891 | $28,345,059 | $29,667,576 | $13,666,561 | $160,746,478 | $31,093,725 | $240,788,817 | $149,682,277 |
| Alabama | 12,433,410 | 5,739,128 | 2,993,580 | 1,570,650 | 486,059 | 434,433 | 176,657 | 1,793,561 | 248,803 | 4,021,037 | 2,673,245 |
| Alaska | 7,973,315 | 1,186,237 | 116,803 | 0 | 34,894 | 94,334 | 38,360 | 0 | 275,758 | 1,079,799 | 5,707,279 |
| Arizona | 11,813,762 | 6,949,370 | 4,008,203 | 3,050,111 | 534,344 | 233,167 | 133,519 | 1,863,196 | 528,161 | 3,329,995 | 1,534,397 |
| Arkansas | 7,724,459 | 4,056,582 | 2,101,805 | 1,513,673 | 348,534 | 237,372 | 103,702 | 1,390,304 | 252,870 | 2,368,339 | 1,299,538 |
| California | 111,087,737 | 67,713,613 | 26,511,610 | 21,301,860 | 2,875,306 | 3,135,510 | 1,643,332 | 27,784,407 | 5,587,671 | 30,893,821 | 12,480,303 |
| Colorado | 10,953,476 | 5,890,211 | 2,318,437 | 1,530,832 | 503,060 | 277,802 | 152,816 | 2,881,537 | 271,143 | 2,788,627 | 2,274,638 |
| Connecticut | 14,452,190 | 9,393,604 | 4,720,531 | 3,031,699 | 569,880 | 360,017 | 221,952 | 3,405,916 | 534,939 | 3,016,337 | 2,042,249 |
| Delaware | 3,883,087 | 1,981,473 | 254,920 | 0 | 98,987 | 649,097 | 30,997 | 761,445 | 205,274 | 724,706 | 1,176,908 |
| Florida | 36,780,333 | 22,521,069 | 16,927,929 | 12,923,644 | 1,497,169 | 1,451,319 | 836,471 | 0 | 1,271,261 | 8,301,851 | 5,957,413 |
| Georgia | 20,164,786 | 11,589,495 | 4,992,011 | 3,993,493 | 557,922 | 396,748 | 170,113 | 5,317,375 | 739,738 | 5,676,362 | 2,898,929 |
| Hawaii | 5,473,742 | 3,176,246 | 1,911,751 | 1,425,352 | 73,594 | 92,647 | 62,350 | 1,083,388 | 61,755 | 1,175,599 | 1,121,897 |
| Idaho | 3,591,719 | 2,057,378 | 952,713 | 652,843 | 207,292 | 196,047 | 97,381 | 778,909 | 117,694 | 862,978 | 671,363 |
| Illinois | 33,786,763 | 19,771,284 | 9,111,575 | 5,596,046 | 1,300,658 | 1,207,679 | 750,977 | 6,986,995 | 1,961,566 | 8,958,993 | 5,056,486 |
| Indiana | 17,112,711 | 9,747,426 | 4,408,797 | 3,156,272 | 639,819 | 216,632 | 133,718 | 4,065,074 | 928,218 | 3,943,070 | 3,422,215 |
| Iowa | 8,821,047 | 4,802,531 | 2,214,369 | 1,528,824 | 325,732 | 452,880 | 295,248 | 1,838,498 | 196,841 | 2,215,812 | 1,802,704 |
| Kansas | 7,784,967 | 4,661,846 | 2,190,421 | 1,619,246 | 332,810 | 213,835 | 126,880 | 1,743,983 | 305,914 | 1,862,929 | 1,260,192 |
| Kentucky | 12,968,961 | 7,115,149 | 3,257,523 | 1,981,290 | 414,119 | 446,730 | 172,233 | 2,418,144 | 333,666 | 3,602,966 | 2,250,846 |
| Louisiana | 13,648,882 | 6,082,026 | 3,199,028 | 1,981,231 | 530,943 | 456,721 | 100,999 | 1,450,814 | 359,510 | 4,026,348 | 3,540,508 |
| Maine | 4,566,877 | 2,369,820 | 1,140,703 | 830,758 | 157,324 | 118,536 | 60,225 | 906,374 | 107,125 | 1,411,320 | 785,737 |
| Maryland | 15,589,078 | 9,190,482 | 3,842,769 | 2,161,233 | 676,650 | 350,854 | 169,534 | 4,139,159 | 378,714 | 3,533,711 | 2,864,885 |
| Massachusetts | 25,801,142 | 14,488,496 | 4,370,666 | 2,962,535 | 621,291 | 450,609 | 244,379 | 8,031,943 | 1,354,899 | 6,458,265 | 4,854,381 |
| Michigan | 36,084,560 | 21,215,742 | 9,501,447 | 7,572,789 | 1,041,328 | 1,104,998 | 725,101 | 6,316,125 | 2,354,764 | 8,557,047 | 6,311,771 |
| Minnesota | 17,856,170 | 11,503,928 | 4,933,013 | 3,243,611 | 553,758 | 875,040 | 546,680 | 4,749,801 | 753,188 | 3,938,396 | 2,413,846 |
| Mississippi | 8,399,929 | 4,242,525 | 2,798,071 | 2,034,804 | 388,632 | 300,255 | 127,006 | 847,075 | 244,301 | 2,947,073 | 1,210,331 |
| Missouri | 14,884,052 | 8,221,876 | 3,799,626 | 2,627,839 | 668,078 | 574,521 | 241,097 | 3,371,717 | 357,904 | 4,246,338 | 2,415,838 |
| Montana | 2,980,419 | 1,327,652 | 274,745 | 0 | 178,170 | 156,932 | 49,157 | 444,161 | 77,928 | 1,047,919 | 604,848 |
| Nebraska | 4,829,306 | 2,633,216 | 1,317,506 | 919,750 | 265,546 | 169,034 | 72,883 | 973,905 | 142,150 | 1,282,063 | 914,027 |
| Nevada | 4,614,860 | 3,113,000 | 2,626,396 | 1,656,749 | 247,771 | 335,993 | 102,395 | 0 | 0 | 911,731 | 590,129 |
| New Hampshire | 2,968,123 | 1,008,518 | 497,958 | 0 | 115,446 | 124,730 | 58,712 | 61,799 | 236,193 | 1,023,619 | 935,986 |
| New Jersey | 28,357,336 | 15,604,971 | 7,650,366 | 4,766,195 | 476,158 | 753,229 | 403,947 | 5,590,579 | 1,178,053 | 6,391,527 | 6,360,828 |
| New Mexico | 7,127,032 | 3,574,537 | 1,950,744 | 1,454,913 | 240,945 | 187,971 | 122,985 | 799,006 | 180,021 | 1,846,136 | 1,706,359 |
| New York | 80,720,172 | 36,154,533 | 12,422,939 | 7,615,370 | 494,577 | 966,735 | 614,100 | 18,289,070 | 3,127,524 | 33,790,935 | 10,774,704 |
| North Carolina | 23,949,838 | 13,869,426 | 5,735,162 | 3,272,774 | 1,114,316 | 841,745 | 389,436 | 6,124,709 | 999,759 | 6,817,303 | 3,263,109 |
| North Dakota | 2,533,365 | 1,078,375 | 610,006 | 309,139 | 105,863 | 79,755 | 39,630 | 177,873 | 82,544 | 892,685 | 562,305 |
| Ohio | 32,299,884 | 17,642,836 | 8,311,164 | 5,531,207 | 1,328,277 | 1,456,872 | 579,971 | 6,967,816 | 765,883 | 8,953,346 | 5,703,702 |

See footnotes at end of table.

# STATE GENERAL REVENUE, BY SOURCE AND BY STATE: 1998 — Continued

| State | Total general revenue (a) | Taxes Total | Sales and gross receipts Total (b) | General | Motor fuels | Licenses Total (b) | Motor vehicle | Individual income | Corporation net income | Intergovernmental revenue | Charges and miscellaneous general revenue |
|---|---|---|---|---|---|---|---|---|---|---|---|
| Oklahoma | 9,411,095 | 5,300,829 | 2,009,614 | 1,328,295 | 354,842 | 746,669 | 587,481 | 1,885,237 | 222,621 | 2,516,285 | 1,593,981 |
| Oregon | 11,273,159 | 4,999,361 | 671,587 | 0 | 382,195 | 505,870 | 309,536 | 3,438,600 | 279,197 | 3,364,556 | 2,909,242 |
| Pennsylvania | 36,833,236 | 20,629,483 | 9,687,694 | 6,313,056 | 811,126 | 2,180,733 | 695,012 | 6,024,816 | 1,562,856 | 9,608,658 | 6,595,095 |
| Rhode Island | 3,781,200 | 1,821,305 | 900,202 | 525,672 | 125,378 | 87,653 | 51,695 | 735,639 | 69,714 | 1,146,311 | 813,584 |
| South Carolina | 11,415,166 | 5,683,148 | 2,894,288 | 2,162,858 | 339,163 | 404,915 | 104,932 | 2,087,461 | 213,622 | 3,442,418 | 2,289,600 |
| South Dakota | 2,098,360 | 833,662 | 661,363 | 442,549 | 113,560 | 104,911 | 31,264 | 0 | 38,269 | 764,232 | 500,466 |
| Tennessee | 14,086,340 | 6,996,120 | 5,320,654 | 4,027,787 | 752,233 | 656,281 | 209,533 | 160,836 | 607,418 | 5,264,984 | 1,825,236 |
| Texas | 48,065,757 | 24,629,000 | 19,883,534 | 12,474,161 | 2,506,029 | 3,533,965 | 838,627 | 0 | 0 | 14,605,424 | 8,831,333 |
| Utah | 6,627,390 | 3,500,583 | 1,772,731 | 1,311,955 | 306,574 | 120,317 | 69,917 | 1,374,525 | 184,584 | 1,689,850 | 1,436,957 |
| Vermont | 2,196,423 | 957,656 | 424,012 | 194,501 | 56,185 | 65,560 | 36,417 | 365,616 | 45,886 | 729,547 | 509,220 |
| Virginia | 19,267,867 | 10,542,966 | 3,911,261 | 2,225,021 | 760,721 | 455,443 | 284,253 | 5,405,468 | 445,659 | 3,780,977 | 4,943,924 |
| Washington | 19,079,085 | 11,806,170 | 8,682,790 | 6,909,239 | 708,185 | 528,840 | 256,496 | 0 | 0 | 4,247,049 | 3,025,866 |
| West Virginia | 6,205,724 | 3,011,990 | 1,557,852 | 856,276 | 232,667 | 158,994 | 81,974 | 866,107 | 221,528 | 2,096,294 | 1,097,440 |
| Wisconsin | 18,168,632 | 11,149,754 | 4,586,948 | 3,047,406 | 845,528 | 637,496 | 269,934 | 5,047,515 | 680,639 | 3,794,650 | 3,224,228 |
| Wyoming | 2,336,524 | 855,716 | 402,736 | 335,383 | 45,421 | 79,150 | 44,547 | 0 | 0 | 838,599 | 642,209 |

Source: U.S. Department of Commerce, Bureau of the Census.
Note: Detail may not add to totals due to rounding.
(a) Total general revenue equals total taxes plus intergovernmental revenue plus charges and miscellaneous revenue.
(b) Total includes other taxes not shown separately in this table.

# Table 6.13
## STATE EXPENDITURE, BY CHARACTER AND OBJECT AND BY STATE: 1997
### (In thousands of dollars)

| State | Intergovernmental expenditure | Total | Direct expenditures Current operation | Capital outlay Total | Construction | Other | Assistance and subsidies | Interest on debt | Insurance benefits and repayments | Exhibit: Total salaries and wages |
|---|---|---|---|---|---|---|---|---|---|---|
| United States ........ | $264,207,209 | $629,619,614 | $425,898,730 | $59,657,707 | $46,991,379 | $12,666,328 | $21,866,744 | $27,024,821 | $95,171,612 | $135,597,841 |
| Alabama .............. | 3,292,491 | 9,652,376 | 7,241,270 | 770,809 | 596,985 | 173,824 | 282,494 | 223,666 | 1,134,137 | 2,468,794 |
| Alaska ................. | 1,015,071 | 4,707,384 | 3,309,084 | 439,775 | 347,737 | 92,038 | 176,749 | 243,028 | 538,748 | 976,442 |
| Arizona ............... | 4,528,382 | 7,890,299 | 5,480,384 | 768,110 | 491,728 | 276,382 | 354,768 | 162,844 | 1,124,193 | 2,139,788 |
| Arkansas ............. | 1,967,398 | 5,717,254 | 4,224,063 | 655,413 | 520,448 | 134,965 | 134,506 | 121,553 | 581,719 | 1,483,034 |
| California ............ | 49,635,672 | 68,007,601 | 45,977,063 | 3,708,494 | 2,788,287 | 920,207 | 1,121,672 | 2,484,498 | 14,715,874 | 14,104,634 |
| Colorado ............. | 3,017,473 | 7,843,755 | 5,302,956 | 742,649 | 543,477 | 199,172 | 84,129 | 239,340 | 1,474,681 | 2,083,044 |
| Connecticut ......... | 2,480,762 | 11,345,259 | 7,379,375 | 859,196 | 732,605 | 126,591 | 501,572 | 948,060 | 1,657,056 | 2,621,209 |
| Delaware ............. | 575,892 | 2,827,727 | 1,935,447 | 353,323 | 269,903 | 83,420 | 64,111 | 208,863 | 265,983 | 786,149 |
| Florida ................ | 11,899,912 | 25,563,946 | 17,817,600 | 3,135,668 | 2,212,176 | 923,492 | 980,124 | 904,603 | 2,725,951 | 7,393,143 |
| Georgia ............... | 6,141,128 | 15,834,244 | 11,348,238 | 1,811,415 | 1,489,320 | 322,095 | 761,713 | 385,469 | 1,527,409 | 3,248,447 |
| Hawaii ................ | 156,055 | 5,937,320 | 3,902,225 | 833,357 | 683,468 | 149,889 | 201,247 | 328,297 | 672,194 | 1,678,578 |
| Idaho .................. | 1,067,190 | 2,607,020 | 1,746,045 | 296,889 | 220,963 | 75,926 | 76,800 | 102,251 | 385,035 | 580,651 |
| Illinois ................ | 9,148,129 | 26,153,745 | 17,059,582 | 2,088,073 | 1,684,748 | 403,325 | 1,443,970 | 1,526,401 | 4,035,719 | 4,293,559 |
| Indiana ............... | 5,507,860 | 10,862,576 | 8,140,034 | 1,248,981 | 1,049,405 | 199,576 | 215,206 | 288,138 | 970,217 | 2,479,639 |
| Iowa ................... | 2,869,259 | 6,478,509 | 4,674,318 | 758,059 | 608,771 | 149,288 | 268,090 | 114,458 | 663,584 | 1,694,243 |
| Kansas ................ | 2,325,562 | 5,170,519 | 3,526,523 | 793,521 | 651,126 | 142,395 | 157,644 | 71,450 | 621,381 | 1,383,492 |
| Kentucky ............. | 2,918,190 | 10,030,828 | 6,885,246 | 1,121,177 | 897,677 | 223,500 | 333,938 | 384,328 | 1,306,139 | 2,405,426 |
| Louisiana ............ | 3,170,676 | 11,115,028 | 7,790,851 | 1,050,891 | 842,481 | 208,410 | 236,093 | 544,082 | 1,493,111 | 2,755,139 |
| Maine ................. | 772,724 | 3,668,560 | 2,646,772 | 226,281 | 186,055 | 40,226 | 189,218 | 172,911 | 433,378 | 608,061 |
| Maryland ............. | 3,536,070 | 12,663,475 | 8,524,965 | 1,150,434 | 952,426 | 198,008 | 546,602 | 601,837 | 1,839,637 | 2,792,968 |
| Massachusetts ...... | 5,636,518 | 20,154,142 | 12,943,968 | 2,536,074 | 2,203,143 | 332,931 | 779,822 | 1,788,002 | 2,106,276 | 3,331,581 |
| Michigan ............. | 14,145,451 | 21,946,724 | 15,462,769 | 1,502,725 | 1,128,013 | 374,712 | 1,022,686 | 786,993 | 3,171,551 | 5,170,072 |
| Minnesota ........... | 6,942,130 | 11,501,134 | 7,943,828 | 916,841 | 674,437 | 242,404 | 683,820 | 309,277 | 1,647,368 | 3,238,279 |
| Mississippi .......... | 2,685,689 | 6,320,051 | 4,236,392 | 925,187 | 541,174 | 384,013 | 129,454 | 151,531 | 877,487 | 1,294,145 |
| Missouri .............. | 3,944,195 | 10,285,519 | 6,932,243 | 1,332,136 | 961,327 | 370,809 | 430,471 | 442,955 | 1,147,714 | 2,423,225 |
| Montana .............. | 714,924 | 2,488,973 | 1,596,989 | 346,100 | 303,629 | 42,471 | 65,991 | 130,989 | 348,904 | 518,166 |
| Nebraska ............. | 1,210,235 | 3,591,510 | 2,656,228 | 506,517 | 420,520 | 85,997 | 84,320 | 90,200 | 254,245 | 1,006,978 |
| Nevada ................ | 1,771,680 | 3,357,945 | 1,982,203 | 388,360 | 326,871 | 61,489 | 57,699 | 174,559 | 755,124 | 820,068 |
| New Hampshire...... | 413,800 | 2,909,738 | 2,007,845 | 206,272 | 156,847 | 49,425 | 92,814 | 379,797 | 223,010 | 573,454 |
| New Jersey ........... | 6,382,582 | 23,047,004 | 14,281,256 | 2,283,969 | 1,868,717 | 415,252 | 281,949 | 1,385,208 | 4,814,622 | 4,995,846 |
| New Mexico .......... | 2,075,053 | 4,983,640 | 3,754,132 | 336,186 | 230,236 | 105,950 | 197,242 | 123,798 | 572,282 | 1,261,303 |
| New York.............. | 25,637,864 | 57,605,426 | 38,115,857 | 5,486,691 | 4,671,679 | 815,012 | 906,287 | 4,169,682 | 8,926,909 | 10,061,908 |
| North Carolina...... | 7,314,766 | 15,549,685 | 10,910,123 | 1,858,322 | 1,369,139 | 489,183 | 574,277 | 297,042 | 1,909,921 | 4,199,642 |
| North Dakota........ | 540,154 | 1,885,506 | 1,415,722 | 163,749 | 133,543 | 30,206 | 44,871 | 57,476 | 203,688 | 433,968 |
| Ohio ................... | 10,441,531 | 26,965,353 | 15,427,292 | 2,748,621 | 2,176,466 | 572,155 | 1,485,611 | 864,726 | 6,439,103 | 4,742,992 |

See footnotes at end of table.

# STATE EXPENDITURE, BY CHARACTER AND OBJECT AND BY STATE: 1997 — Continued

| State | Intergovernmental expenditure | Direct expenditures Total | Current operation | Capital outlay Total | Capital outlay Construction | Capital outlay Other | Assistance and subsidies | Interest on debt | Insurance benefits and repayments | Exhibit: Total salaries and wages |
|---|---|---|---|---|---|---|---|---|---|---|
| Oklahoma | 2,625,134 | 6,967,577 | 4,816,147 | 664,013 | 472,453 | 191,560 | 190,727 | 241,936 | 1,054,754 | 1,759,516 |
| Oregon | 3,207,793 | 9,180,455 | 5,765,526 | 722,782 | 623,724 | 99,058 | 425,690 | 361,039 | 1,905,418 | 1,759,333 |
| Pennsylvania | 9,844,265 | 29,451,979 | 20,237,663 | 1,678,474 | 1,298,935 | 379,539 | 1,444,466 | 1,180,679 | 4,910,697 | 5,031,283 |
| Rhode Island | 506,349 | 3,495,427 | 2,173,040 | 267,401 | 221,425 | 45,976 | 162,110 | 300,298 | 592,578 | 716,969 |
| South Carolina | 2,929,143 | 9,918,078 | 7,332,158 | 844,018 | 388,889 | 455,129 | 287,892 | 373,661 | 1,080,349 | 2,554,208 |
| South Dakota | 435,456 | 1,635,026 | 1,107,435 | 255,530 | 210,868 | 44,662 | 31,975 | 116,907 | 123,179 | 350,540 |
| Tennessee | 3,645,098 | 10,639,203 | 7,653,205 | 1,390,238 | 1,109,670 | 280,568 | 416,778 | 202,611 | 976,371 | 2,417,814 |
| Texas | 12,805,943 | 36,081,427 | 25,788,698 | 3,151,034 | 2,437,822 | 713,212 | 1,535,654 | 843,072 | 4,762,969 | 6,508,824 |
| Utah | 1,673,127 | 5,144,623 | 3,574,290 | 815,931 | 710,201 | 105,730 | 163,936 | 129,698 | 460,768 | 1,377,198 |
| Vermont | 312,333 | 1,810,936 | 1,373,997 | 109,952 | 76,174 | 33,778 | 90,370 | 111,735 | 124,882 | 438,859 |
| Virginia | 5,337,239 | 13,949,267 | 9,811,241 | 1,592,604 | 1,329,726 | 262,878 | 697,621 | 598,667 | 1,249,134 | 3,471,333 |
| Washington | 5,681,708 | 16,525,177 | 10,076,673 | 1,871,716 | 1,571,869 | 299,847 | 866,745 | 536,156 | 3,173,887 | 3,633,267 |
| West Virginia | 1,625,623 | 5,519,856 | 3,639,386 | 602,210 | 505,393 | 96,817 | 96,550 | 179,047 | 1,002,663 | 935,000 |
| Wisconsin | 6,993,213 | 11,206,320 | 7,133,735 | 1,063,181 | 856,544 | 206,637 | 454,575 | 584,032 | 1,970,797 | 2,331,572 |
| Wyoming | 702,317 | 1,424,488 | 836,648 | 278,358 | 242,159 | 36,199 | 33,695 | 56,971 | 218,816 | 324,058 |

Source: U.S. Department of Commerce, Bureau of the Census.
Note: Detail may not add to totals due to rounding.

## Table 6.14
## STATE EXPENDITURE, BY CHARACTER AND OBJECT AND BY STATE: 1998
(In thousands of dollars)

| State | Intergovernmental expenditure | Total | Direct expenditures | | | | | | | Exhibit: Total salaries and wages |
|---|---|---|---|---|---|---|---|---|---|---|
| | | | Current operation | Capital outlay | | | Assistance and subsidies | Interest on debt | Insurance benefits and repayments | |
| | | | | Total | Construction | Other | | | | |
| United States | $278,853,409 | $651,183,158 | $446,439,710 | $64,441,178 | $50,541,874 | $13,899,304 | $21,514,628 | $27,589,595 | $91,198,047 | $139,969,688 |
| Alabama | 3,419,845 | 10,308,586 | 7,575,449 | 755,486 | 582,930 | 172,556 | 668,076 | 202,507 | 1,107,068 | 2,522,557 |
| Alaska | 983,153 | 4,820,020 | 3,486,538 | 382,310 | 320,283 | 62,027 | 161,433 | 241,349 | 548,390 | 977,778 |
| Arizona | 5,023,261 | 8,304,706 | 5,660,035 | 888,544 | 567,187 | 321,357 | 370,625 | 154,790 | 1,230,712 | 2,280,083 |
| Arkansas | 2,109,996 | 5,993,519 | 4,457,537 | 753,271 | 612,772 | 140,499 | 127,559 | 123,705 | 531,447 | 1,543,261 |
| California | 51,053,075 | 69,276,430 | 48,496,657 | 3,620,157 | 2,748,592 | 871,565 | 1,168,977 | 2,426,583 | 13,564,056 | 14,268,096 |
| Colorado | 3,159,458 | 8,118,243 | 5,720,705 | 899,355 | 723,607 | 175,748 | 89,695 | 240,926 | 1,167,562 | 2,235,670 |
| Connecticut | 2,627,781 | 11,888,492 | 7,845,322 | 846,824 | 719,214 | 127,610 | 578,243 | 983,022 | 1,635,081 | 2,687,424 |
| Delaware | 591,279 | 2,874,149 | 2,027,100 | 346,528 | 267,352 | 79,176 | 68,604 | 212,958 | 218,959 | 830,022 |
| Florida | 12,537,431 | 26,676,579 | 18,993,077 | 3,325,318 | 2,308,708 | 1,016,610 | 836,943 | 1,038,346 | 2,482,895 | 7,014,591 |
| Georgia | 6,310,697 | 15,424,764 | 10,891,834 | 2,003,708 | 1,578,378 | 425,330 | 689,045 | 385,903 | 1,454,274 | 3,364,822 |
| Hawaii | 147,059 | 5,713,366 | 3,926,361 | 650,864 | 520,535 | 130,329 | 191,599 | 345,596 | 598,946 | 1,511,263 |
| Idaho | 1,104,201 | 2,681,412 | 1,816,872 | 305,630 | 226,508 | 79,122 | 79,335 | 110,813 | 368,762 | 646,011 |
| Illinois | 9,862,059 | 25,823,199 | 17,103,170 | 2,008,264 | 1,617,264 | 391,000 | 1,417,828 | 1,614,009 | 3,679,928 | 4,405,492 |
| Indiana | 5,883,074 | 11,340,108 | 8,658,561 | 1,223,934 | 1,008,735 | 215,199 | 222,824 | 289,692 | 945,097 | 2,605,913 |
| Iowa | 2,794,519 | 6,934,652 | 5,138,217 | 795,715 | 624,705 | 171,010 | 250,040 | 116,786 | 633,894 | 1,592,413 |
| Kansas | 2,508,870 | 5,172,144 | 3,552,824 | 766,392 | 623,716 | 142,676 | 133,281 | 78,796 | 640,851 | 1,415,457 |
| Kentucky | 3,006,904 | 10,534,169 | 7,399,034 | 1,161,168 | 920,914 | 240,254 | 297,873 | 426,497 | 1,249,597 | 2,508,150 |
| Louisiana | 3,451,053 | 11,467,665 | 8,084,666 | 1,196,247 | 970,990 | 225,257 | 269,767 | 424,507 | 1,492,478 | 3,158,727 |
| Maine | 851,942 | 3,754,529 | 2,837,904 | 198,502 | 159,416 | 39,086 | 164,741 | 168,070 | 385,312 | 614,576 |
| Maryland | 3,710,641 | 12,867,842 | 8,655,036 | 1,236,463 | 1,028,748 | 207,715 | 632,884 | 614,261 | 1,729,198 | 2,844,779 |
| Massachusetts | 6,215,380 | 20,978,936 | 13,642,119 | 2,915,829 | 2,622,967 | 292,862 | 690,824 | 1,799,050 | 1,931,114 | 3,508,022 |
| Michigan | 15,430,418 | 21,979,373 | 15,534,549 | 1,624,034 | 1,215,831 | 408,203 | 998,553 | 873,563 | 2,948,674 | 5,378,975 |
| Minnesota | 6,022,123 | 12,396,179 | 8,610,822 | 1,108,448 | 817,765 | 290,683 | 611,656 | 309,287 | 1,755,966 | 3,047,451 |
| Mississippi | 2,876,187 | 6,459,649 | 4,452,290 | 1,013,915 | 587,600 | 426,315 | 146,971 | 156,053 | 690,420 | 1,504,935 |
| Missouri | 4,176,567 | 11,136,677 | 7,853,817 | 1,233,932 | 905,662 | 328,270 | 449,358 | 477,658 | 1,121,912 | 2,533,149 |
| Montana | 712,620 | 2,549,547 | 1,666,753 | 346,427 | 310,275 | 36,152 | 59,621 | 134,338 | 342,408 | 534,686 |
| Nebraska | 1,291,135 | 3,462,378 | 2,587,584 | 487,741 | 394,653 | 93,088 | 91,291 | 106,831 | 188,931 | 1,043,884 |
| Nevada | 1,915,179 | 3,482,405 | 2,169,743 | 443,335 | 353,484 | 89,851 | 55,076 | 195,946 | 618,305 | 912,214 |
| New Hampshire | 454,682 | 3,022,498 | 2,092,744 | 240,612 | 186,455 | 54,157 | 86,046 | 385,471 | 217,625 | 593,020 |
| New Jersey | 7,176,343 | 24,525,531 | 15,943,789 | 2,721,046 | 2,336,709 | 384,337 | 311,751 | 1,235,420 | 4,313,525 | 5,621,886 |
| New Mexico | 2,186,948 | 5,352,671 | 4,007,079 | 391,074 | 297,320 | 93,754 | 206,420 | 152,309 | 595,789 | 1,277,138 |
| New York | 27,271,351 | 60,066,941 | 39,982,970 | 6,454,288 | 4,646,330 | 1,807,958 | 935,442 | 4,179,077 | 8,515,164 | 10,309,890 |
| North Carolina | 7,928,480 | 16,676,462 | 11,756,082 | 2,073,446 | 1,491,663 | 581,783 | 527,132 | 385,485 | 1,934,317 | 4,204,380 |
| North Dakota | 541,455 | 1,985,368 | 1,440,271 | 256,639 | 227,912 | 28,727 | 36,538 | 52,318 | 199,602 | 448,383 |
| Ohio | 11,214,371 | 27,994,895 | 15,839,114 | 2,919,070 | 2,390,481 | 528,589 | 1,382,987 | 849,710 | 7,004,014 | 4,989,041 |

See footnotes at end of table.

# STATE EXPENDITURE, BY CHARACTER AND OBJECT AND BY STATE: 1998 — Continued

| State | Intergovernmental expenditure | Total | Direct expenditures Current operation | Capital outlay Total | Capital outlay Construction | Capital outlay Other | Assistance and subsidies | Interest on debt | Insurance benefits and repayments | Exhibit: Total salaries and wages |
|---|---|---|---|---|---|---|---|---|---|---|
| Oklahoma | $2,802,808 | $7,149,925 | $5,064,655 | $660,558 | $471,422 | $189,136 | $178,688 | $240,878 | $1,005,146 | $1,804,590 |
| Oregon | 3,706,815 | 9,758,876 | 5,976,117 | 779,549 | 684,479 | 95,070 | 302,050 | 325,140 | 2,376,020 | 1,903,691 |
| Pennsylvania | 10,157,714 | 30,645,826 | 21,381,277 | 2,192,504 | 1,818,365 | 374,139 | 1,385,627 | 1,203,126 | 4,483,292 | 5,176,778 |
| Rhode Island | 548,018 | 3,416,319 | 2,239,177 | 228,411 | 167,676 | 60,735 | 166,825 | 269,232 | 512,674 | 751,378 |
| South Carolina | 3,142,089 | 10,432,837 | 7,852,702 | 865,033 | 612,886 | 252,147 | 255,985 | 389,442 | 1,069,675 | 2,694,447 |
| South Dakota | 493,167 | 1,751,647 | 1,158,976 | 315,360 | 258,836 | 56,524 | 35,323 | 117,230 | 124,758 | 359,860 |
| Tennessee | 3,923,819 | 10,851,359 | 7,975,087 | 1,419,360 | 1,216,149 | 203,211 | 356,005 | 204,657 | 896,250 | 2,351,934 |
| Texas | 14,026,888 | 37,037,885 | 26,233,907 | 3,672,504 | 2,719,408 | 953,096 | 1,563,511 | 908,244 | 4,659,719 | 7,006,120 |
| Utah | 1,716,976 | 5,753,306 | 3,772,561 | 1,187,032 | 1,075,752 | 111,280 | 166,418 | 160,620 | 466,675 | 1,417,352 |
| Vermont | 355,608 | 1,939,702 | 1,486,838 | 129,860 | 94,674 | 35,186 | 90,168 | 121,907 | 110,929 | 440,753 |
| Virginia | 5,660,133 | 14,869,143 | 10,470,565 | 1,780,894 | 1,500,421 | 280,473 | 708,806 | 658,677 | 1,250,201 | 3,653,279 |
| Washington | 6,048,013 | 16,831,888 | 10,754,012 | 1,666,146 | 1,366,752 | 299,394 | 900,789 | 544,405 | 2,966,536 | 3,839,701 |
| West Virginia | 1,530,110 | 5,618,700 | 3,740,317 | 621,045 | 523,804 | 97,241 | 108,411 | 254,554 | 894,373 | 907,797 |
| Wisconsin | 7,481,155 | 11,620,196 | 7,559,513 | 1,044,879 | 867,523 | 177,356 | 257,551 | 636,959 | 2,121,294 | 2,432,060 |
| Wyoming | 710,559 | 1,461,465 | 867,381 | 283,527 | 248,066 | 35,461 | 29,433 | 62,892 | 218,232 | 295,809 |

*Source:* U.S. Department of Commerce, Bureau of the Census.
*Note:* Detail may not add to totals due to rounding.

## Table 6.15
## STATE GENERAL EXPENDITURE, BY FUNCTION AND BY STATE: 1997
### (In thousands of dollars)

| State | Total general expenditure (a) | Education | Public welfare | Highways | Hospitals | Natural resources | Health | Corrections | Financial administration | Employment security administration | Police |
|---|---|---|---|---|---|---|---|---|---|---|---|
| United States ...... | $788,175,737 | $275,820,952 | $203,204,283 | $60,203,916 | $29,313,344 | $12,908,623 | $33,879,585 | $29,042,709 | $13,697,685 | $3,995,714 | $7,500,993 |
| Alabama ............ | 11,668,841 | 5,175,279 | 2,537,627 | 837,255 | 882,613 | 175,948 | 566,651 | 233,870 | 116,413 | 61,526 | 93,163 |
| Alaska .............. | 5,159,684 | 1,198,832 | 742,419 | 589,804 | 28,220 | 288,928 | 159,454 | 152,126 | 123,758 | 29,804 | 56,722 |
| Arizona ............ | 11,266,376 | 4,033,411 | 2,688,434 | 1,167,477 | 54,907 | 167,453 | 558,780 | 564,150 | 142,293 | 48,978 | 132,094 |
| Arkansas .......... | 7,102,933 | 2,819,359 | 1,666,931 | 762,961 | 362,721 | 137,542 | 261,311 | 206,131 | 139,720 | 39,286 | 60,085 |
| California .......... | 102,852,991 | 35,546,384 | 30,205,384 | 4,581,485 | 2,917,670 | 2,011,381 | 6,083,766 | 3,967,874 | 1,896,619 | 402,368 | 1,038,589 |
| Colorado .......... | 9,381,494 | 4,192,249 | 2,220,679 | 809,696 | 145,875 | 151,918 | 247,006 | 455,517 | 145,314 | 41,049 | 55,270 |
| Connecticut ...... | 11,951,814 | 2,894,082 | 2,914,519 | 756,474 | 977,504 | 76,163 | 402,219 | 493,772 | 241,685 | 85,384 | 109,559 |
| Delaware .......... | 3,098,351 | 1,070,248 | 500,817 | 262,472 | 60,422 | 54,850 | 166,892 | 123,147 | 85,205 | 8,968 | 52,294 |
| Florida ............. | 34,657,577 | 11,599,453 | 7,692,925 | 3,158,547 | 551,166 | 1,103,741 | 1,850,393 | 1,849,198 | 660,260 | 37,727 | 319,706 |
| Georgia ............ | 20,447,963 | 8,938,020 | 5,334,599 | 1,083,616 | 652,117 | 373,421 | 691,605 | 881,856 | 285,257 | 107,909 | 172,147 |
| Hawaii ............. | 5,420,946 | 1,557,019 | 983,336 | 321,658 | 237,641 | 71,097 | 276,988 | 127,535 | 51,472 | 35,323 | 7,019 |
| Idaho .............. | 3,250,563 | 1,345,736 | 599,005 | 396,677 | 37,764 | 115,910 | 92,562 | 102,510 | 44,066 | 24,585 | 32,247 |
| Illinois ............. | 31,266,155 | 9,160,030 | 9,163,553 | 2,596,833 | 846,042 | 268,294 | 1,702,964 | 951,277 | 677,629 | 215,284 | 303,309 |
| Indiana ............ | 15,400,219 | 6,410,821 | 3,221,243 | 1,648,038 | 227,424 | 162,330 | 406,647 | 418,649 | 202,326 | 91,436 | 152,953 |
| Iowa ............... | 8,621,990 | 3,594,533 | 1,737,531 | 1,094,526 | 493,587 | 212,175 | 185,579 | 200,491 | 123,545 | 85,132 | 58,567 |
| Kansas ............. | 6,874,700 | 3,037,234 | 1,124,166 | 1,013,022 | 303,263 | 165,039 | 301,760 | 206,167 | 118,002 | 18,810 | 41,166 |
| Kentucky .......... | 11,634,331 | 4,398,379 | 3,207,075 | 1,090,645 | 447,971 | 215,328 | 302,747 | 260,235 | 187,042 | 73,203 | 121,365 |
| Louisiana ......... | 12,789,619 | 4,558,193 | 2,959,999 | 850,034 | 1,063,310 | 312,996 | 395,194 | 416,981 | 148,073 | 64,340 | 191,760 |
| Maine .............. | 3,961,074 | 1,121,825 | 1,336,834 | 362,137 | 53,917 | 116,478 | 207,689 | 66,013 | 64,816 | 29,319 | 39,036 |
| Maryland .......... | 14,001,947 | 4,400,969 | 3,023,036 | 1,245,276 | 319,502 | 316,791 | 779,238 | 741,403 | 331,693 | 35,942 | 250,796 |
| Massachusetts ... | 23,588,935 | 4,956,373 | 5,881,466 | 2,144,031 | 886,275 | 202,166 | 1,325,680 | 811,276 | 332,769 | 74,885 | 266,975 |
| Michigan .......... | 32,546,413 | 14,308,911 | 6,722,557 | 2,058,795 | 1,420,141 | 325,276 | 2,046,674 | 1,291,102 | 263,374 | 168,387 | 253,342 |
| Minnesota ........ | 16,795,896 | 6,175,744 | 4,458,650 | 1,255,439 | 428,811 | 360,387 | 501,351 | 325,355 | 232,967 | 103,384 | 89,160 |
| Mississippi ....... | 8,013,965 | 2,751,842 | 1,891,305 | 775,672 | 422,071 | 162,509 | 247,910 | 212,029 | 62,703 | 49,400 | 56,158 |
| Missouri ........... | 13,082,000 | 5,051,366 | 3,066,313 | 1,264,747 | 441,048 | 263,132 | 569,282 | 368,118 | 200,458 | 69,007 | 155,908 |
| Montana ........... | 2,825,746 | 1,019,932 | 500,598 | 343,808 | 28,715 | 145,817 | 162,858 | 73,189 | 90,169 | 5,955 | 32,673 |
| Nebraska .......... | 4,547,500 | 1,587,703 | 1,030,428 | 596,154 | 328,258 | 130,593 | 215,305 | 105,630 | 72,366 | 24,998 | 45,551 |
| Nevada ............ | 4,328,082 | 1,677,034 | 653,902 | 369,988 | 67,089 | 66,134 | 89,068 | 180,483 | 122,919 | 38,024 | 39,307 |
| New Hampshire .. | 2,891,458 | 624,135 | 904,665 | 306,495 | 41,250 | 30,082 | 138,275 | 59,804 | 59,907 | 20,854 | 29,158 |
| New Jersey ....... | 23,053,317 | 7,281,765 | 4,825,740 | 1,592,629 | 974,484 | 244,520 | 754,228 | 1,002,137 | 384,999 | 85,526 | 236,487 |
| New Mexico ...... | 6,486,411 | 2,515,590 | 1,253,017 | 643,909 | 320,578 | 84,891 | 269,931 | 186,491 | 105,891 | 37,431 | 58,008 |
| New York .......... | 70,016,990 | 16,243,287 | 27,594,459 | 2,763,965 | 3,311,633 | 299,091 | 2,147,669 | 2,287,303 | 1,650,007 | 406,892 | 344,324 |
| North Carolina ... | 20,954,530 | 8,560,989 | 4,732,991 | 1,888,358 | 781,710 | 407,759 | 899,998 | 935,287 | 194,374 | 75,296 | 219,378 |
| North Dakota ..... | 2,221,972 | 773,326 | 452,311 | 230,119 | 44,984 | 102,804 | 56,870 | 21,323 | 36,011 | 5,817 | 8,617 |
| Ohio ............... | 30,704,822 | 11,232,590 | 7,960,889 | 2,468,029 | 875,478 | 316,243 | 1,352,057 | 1,263,203 | 707,988 | 196,160 | 204,209 |
| Oklahoma ......... | 8,286,451 | 3,691,186 | 1,723,463 | 806,319 | 290,809 | 153,846 | 324,915 | 351,976 | 180,256 | 31,590 | 52,558 |
| Oregon ............ | 10,367,237 | 3,603,278 | 2,389,844 | 1,024,093 | 438,214 | 256,943 | 366,493 | 429,292 | 451,179 | 40,544 | 146,405 |
| Pennsylvania ..... | 33,708,562 | 10,512,893 | 10,018,793 | 2,492,658 | 1,697,003 | 435,759 | 1,379,050 | 1,077,853 | 523,130 | 217,912 | 647,215 |
| Rhode Island ..... | 3,372,641 | 913,835 | 869,066 | 191,541 | 79,877 | 24,557 | 248,079 | 119,698 | 80,914 | 34,294 | 32,843 |
| South Carolina ... | 11,127,158 | 3,902,910 | 2,621,547 | 664,814 | 611,090 | 173,793 | 703,186 | 429,244 | 123,127 | 62,795 | 159,579 |

See footnotes at end of table.

# STATE GENERAL EXPENDITURE, BY FUNCTION AND BY STATE: 1997 — Continued

| State | Total general expenditure (a) | Education | Public welfare | Highways | Hospitals | Natural resources | Health | Corrections | Financial administration | Employment security administration | Police |
|---|---|---|---|---|---|---|---|---|---|---|---|
| South Dakota........ | 1,947,303 | 581,493 | 389,031 | 282,217 | 39,703 | 83,810 | 58,861 | 59,877 | 45,157 | 15,196 | 16,203 |
| Tennessee .......... | 13,304,143 | 4,669,507 | 3,986,728 | 1,298,659 | 544,800 | 168,567 | 572,837 | 469,241 | 120,946 | 80,327 | 95,724 |
| Texas .............. | 44,124,401 | 18,303,434 | 11,524,742 | 3,290,971 | 1,961,616 | 571,590 | 1,331,742 | 2,252,637 | 591,912 | 231,821 | 293,623 |
| Utah ............... | 6,285,397 | 3,025,148 | 989,944 | 583,568 | 319,921 | 166,595 | 172,481 | 175,358 | 104,202 | 29,005 | 57,567 |
| Vermont ........... | 1,970,740 | 644,872 | 522,923 | 190,741 | 8,714 | 62,352 | 49,852 | 43,703 | 46,238 | 9,063 | 30,086 |
| Virginia ........... | 17,806,854 | 7,047,584 | 3,233,825 | 2,140,430 | 1,163,248 | 140,872 | 540,595 | 823,949 | 463,696 | 76,737 | 326,050 |
| Washington ........ | 18,802,561 | 7,803,155 | 4,059,165 | 1,558,220 | 564,674 | 464,108 | 1,009,328 | 562,335 | 276,506 | 161,055 | 202,081 |
| West Virginia ...... | 6,098,674 | 2,386,272 | 1,603,186 | 782,897 | 82,939 | 145,098 | 134,349 | 94,905 | 152,719 | 25,598 | 41,030 |
| Wisconsin ......... | 16,228,736 | 6,285,567 | 3,223,178 | 1,276,706 | 446,159 | 298,185 | 497,319 | 573,642 | 192,572 | 65,526 | 59,168 |
| Wyoming .......... | 1,877,294 | 637,411 | 259,445 | 289,311 | 28,416 | 123,361 | 73,897 | 37,367 | 43,041 | 15,862 | 13,759 |

Source: U.S. Department of Commerce, Bureau of the Census.
Note: Detail may not add to totals due to rounding.
(a) Does not represent some of detail.

## Table 6.16
## STATE GENERAL EXPENDITURE, BY FUNCTION AND BY STATE: 1998
(In thousands of dollars)

| State | Total general expenditure (a) | Education | Public welfare | Highways | Hospitals | Natural resources | Health | Corrections | Financial administration | Employment security administration | Police |
|---|---|---|---|---|---|---|---|---|---|---|---|
| United States | $827,653,545 | $294,813,967 | $207,926,206 | $63,619,723 | $28,928,103 | $13,540,517 | $35,066,884 | $30,600,550 | $14,532,331 | $4,120,610 | $8,038,265 |
| Alabama | 12,475,614 | 5,362,196 | 3,027,120 | 882,080 | 948,312 | 180,408 | 554,980 | 257,214 | 125,488 | 66,714 | 102,178 |
| Alaska | 5,230,194 | 1,207,913 | 758,931 | 549,996 | 26,311 | 264,689 | 161,108 | 158,809 | 140,943 | 30,874 | 57,963 |
| Arizona | 12,069,852 | 4,392,711 | 2,648,198 | 1,192,360 | 62,466 | 155,794 | 656,826 | 717,458 | 203,619 | 43,524 | 134,753 |
| Arkansas | 7,572,068 | 3,019,425 | 1,796,670 | 779,160 | 371,271 | 161,955 | 271,451 | 205,929 | 154,297 | 40,714 | 63,150 |
| California | 106,680,820 | 38,139,544 | 30,411,684 | 4,631,083 | 2,431,517 | 2,082,181 | 6,388,493 | 3,437,824 | 1,918,523 | 341,145 | 1,145,727 |
| Colorado | 10,104,647 | 4,333,068 | 2,401,070 | 989,106 | 150,831 | 156,021 | 282,136 | 619,477 | 140,319 | 41,135 | 62,578 |
| Connecticut | 12,680,829 | 3,143,491 | 3,036,491 | 685,700 | 1,054,818 | 73,103 | 402,252 | 480,406 | 292,486 | 86,541 | 114,216 |
| Delaware | 3,203,423 | 1,071,578 | 501,377 | 287,672 | 56,801 | 42,599 | 184,013 | 142,219 | 106,722 | 11,563 | 54,276 |
| Florida | 36,662,429 | 12,594,739 | 8,159,979 | 3,254,239 | 502,081 | 1,067,914 | 1,840,385 | 1,931,914 | 718,663 | 43,355 | 337,665 |
| Georgia | 20,281,187 | 9,191,987 | 4,691,784 | 1,282,449 | 700,255 | 417,590 | 681,884 | 857,067 | 279,691 | 118,624 | 150,635 |
| Hawaii | 5,261,479 | 1,636,140 | 919,329 | 248,700 | 231,668 | 87,103 | 269,974 | 120,854 | 50,964 | 40,725 | 6,966 |
| Idaho | 3,376,692 | 1,402,567 | 594,902 | 397,106 | 45,164 | 117,740 | 93,361 | 123,853 | 49,851 | 30,674 | 36,034 |
| Illinois | 32,005,330 | 9,865,236 | 8,905,100 | 2,475,229 | 806,842 | 285,842 | 1,733,954 | 1,066,498 | 684,728 | 224,065 | 332,364 |
| Indiana | 16,278,085 | 6,833,269 | 3,298,261 | 1,721,220 | 216,860 | 167,774 | 421,808 | 447,358 | 254,784 | 107,221 | 179,143 |
| Iowa | 9,030,380 | 3,744,201 | 1,937,222 | 1,055,929 | 537,465 | 220,096 | 194,559 | 227,326 | 146,627 | 90,394 | 65,801 |
| Kansas | 7,040,163 | 3,237,140 | 1,092,556 | 936,852 | 285,042 | 158,056 | 293,522 | 254,981 | 118,313 | 23,941 | 45,021 |
| Kentucky | 12,283,555 | 4,574,047 | 3,291,011 | 1,172,164 | 444,045 | 242,064 | 318,865 | 304,348 | 189,333 | 79,072 | 129,274 |
| Louisiana | 13,423,227 | 4,827,916 | 2,957,958 | 981,487 | 1,212,424 | 359,124 | 380,552 | 447,672 | 158,640 | 63,083 | 207,625 |
| Maine | 4,173,227 | 1,171,467 | 1,397,211 | 325,590 | 49,431 | 117,838 | 251,644 | 72,311 | 74,083 | 34,488 | 40,455 |
| Maryland | 14,481,262 | 4,770,296 | 3,254,774 | 1,198,105 | 336,751 | 306,531 | 773,271 | 742,354 | 324,679 | 35,603 | 273,975 |
| Massachusetts | 25,152,926 | 5,477,503 | 6,181,247 | 2,386,682 | 524,659 | 251,467 | 1,396,566 | 861,816 | 354,453 | 80,893 | 306,873 |
| Michigan | 34,066,033 | 15,405,529 | 6,835,409 | 2,186,323 | 1,118,566 | 376,934 | 2,200,499 | 1,314,740 | 287,717 | 150,688 | 255,842 |
| Minnesota | 16,662,336 | 6,481,515 | 4,558,705 | 1,240,704 | 231,861 | 396,474 | 467,222 | 332,410 | 248,757 | 104,470 | 114,120 |
| Mississippi | 8,526,198 | 3,041,818 | 1,887,879 | 867,780 | 466,143 | 190,599 | 248,810 | 220,605 | 69,948 | 46,712 | 55,715 |
| Missouri | 14,191,332 | 5,450,817 | 3,301,240 | 1,278,170 | 460,591 | 247,236 | 603,186 | 461,253 | 208,117 | 68,854 | 154,872 |
| Montana | 2,889,840 | 1,058,894 | 465,737 | 349,196 | 39,852 | 148,188 | 188,941 | 86,907 | 121,811 | 8,753 | 34,833 |
| Nebraska | 4,564,582 | 1,683,083 | 1,108,310 | 572,780 | 140,758 | 135,993 | 217,079 | 118,779 | 70,240 | 28,865 | 46,980 |
| Nevada | 4,696,321 | 1,835,050 | 723,363 | 389,074 | 82,491 | 62,445 | 92,485 | 205,550 | 139,222 | 45,326 | 43,838 |
| New Hampshire | 3,039,479 | 693,769 | 924,685 | 318,049 | 46,904 | 32,827 | 122,456 | 60,588 | 64,099 | 21,989 | 32,784 |
| New Jersey | 25,974,058 | 8,460,330 | 5,234,703 | 1,864,700 | 1,022,082 | 303,203 | 813,249 | 1,066,895 | 551,711 | 107,232 | 252,699 |
| New Mexico | 6,943,830 | 2,622,644 | 1,276,673 | 875,468 | 319,694 | 85,318 | 267,416 | 196,329 | 110,896 | 40,359 | 54,659 |
| New York | 73,869,205 | 17,402,994 | 28,537,685 | 2,772,205 | 3,346,194 | 343,235 | 2,351,440 | 2,372,095 | 1,692,753 | 386,915 | 419,160 |
| North Carolina | 22,670,625 | 9,495,500 | 4,885,953 | 2,075,677 | 829,645 | 451,922 | 961,591 | 980,517 | 198,953 | 87,830 | 255,059 |
| North Dakota | 2,327,221 | 809,866 | 462,372 | 322,002 | 45,006 | 83,178 | 45,534 | 31,602 | 34,724 | 6,794 | 10,772 |
| Ohio | 31,943,277 | 11,602,317 | 8,146,684 | 2,631,239 | 1,014,384 | 308,937 | 1,480,747 | 1,369,457 | 667,203 | 205,604 | 207,888 |
| Oklahoma | 8,693,045 | 3,922,300 | 1,748,808 | 861,893 | 257,278 | 153,353 | 340,508 | 415,996 | 180,879 | 35,976 | 27,361 |
| Oregon | 10,967,163 | 4,209,031 | 2,351,201 | 994,968 | 467,787 | 264,394 | 371,130 | 472,231 | 436,084 | 68,330 | 138,279 |
| Pennsylvania | 35,603,075 | 11,013,141 | 10,516,078 | 3,069,182 | 1,538,005 | 505,277 | 1,360,888 | 1,229,494 | 568,405 | 228,668 | 703,188 |
| Rhode Island | 3,413,431 | 982,103 | 1,017,366 | 189,681 | 77,953 | 37,752 | 129,777 | 126,578 | 59,356 | 38,155 | 25,495 |
| South Carolina | 11,845,862 | 4,208,554 | 2,955,074 | 711,195 | 707,356 | 185,264 | 627,252 | 422,760 | 143,313 | 67,647 | 170,145 |

See footnotes at end of table.

# STATE GENERAL EXPENDITURE, BY FUNCTION AND BY STATE: 1998 — Continued

| State | Total general expenditure (a) | Education | Public welfare | Highways | Hospitals | Natural resources | Health | Corrections | Financial administration | Employment security administration | Police |
|---|---|---|---|---|---|---|---|---|---|---|---|
| South Dakota ............. | 2,120,056 | 642,539 | 409,795 | 347,399 | 40,654 | 79,741 | 59,841 | 57,511 | 46,567 | 16,736 | 17,140 |
| Tennessee ................ | 13,875,109 | 4,919,897 | 4,196,566 | 1,374,234 | 555,729 | 176,907 | 522,405 | 441,404 | 132,462 | 80,283 | 103,110 |
| Texas ...................... | 46,405,054 | 19,769,645 | 10,833,211 | 3,520,271 | 2,305,130 | 642,634 | 1,450,106 | 2,598,309 | 629,987 | 234,429 | 291,058 |
| Utah ....................... | 6,926,890 | 3,179,399 | 1,041,917 | 934,933 | 353,279 | 132,780 | 183,665 | 187,668 | 128,479 | 33,495 | 61,277 |
| Vermont .................. | 2,154,062 | 679,263 | 565,386 | 220,338 | 8,672 | 64,189 | 58,618 | 39,099 | 55,959 | 9,409 | 32,053 |
| Virginia .................. | 19,036,655 | 7,489,643 | 3,420,433 | 2,231,629 | 1,274,442 | 148,678 | 535,124 | 933,078 | 515,381 | 85,270 | 348,330 |
| Washington ............. | 19,670,796 | 8,198,270 | 4,339,781 | 1,527,968 | 587,524 | 498,543 | 1,081,493 | 564,964 | 291,074 | 166,312 | 215,955 |
| West Virginia ........... | 6,210,754 | 2,301,476 | 1,647,612 | 806,824 | 78,360 | 140,556 | 131,488 | 120,013 | 153,734 | 24,927 | 43,660 |
| Wisconsin ............... | 16,980,057 | 6,595,328 | 3,007,116 | 1,352,012 | 487,563 | 308,614 | 524,385 | 654,545 | 196,154 | 67,117 | 61,316 |
| Wyoming ................ | 1,919,710 | 662,818 | 263,589 | 300,920 | 29,186 | 119,457 | 77,945 | 41,485 | 41,140 | 19,117 | 14,005 |

Source: U.S. Department of Commerce, Bureau of the Census.
Note: Detail may not add to totals due to rounding.
(a) Does not represent sum of state figures because total includes miscellaneous expenditures not shown.

## Table 6.17
## STATE DEBT OUTSTANDING AT END OF FISCAL YEAR, BY STATE: 1997
(In thousands of dollars. Per capita in dollars.)

| State | Total | Per capita | Long-term Total | Full faith and credit | Nonguaranteed | Short-term | Net long-term (a) Total | Full faith and credit |
|---|---|---|---|---|---|---|---|---|
| United States ................. | $455,697,359 | $1,706.05 | $453,555,597 | $119,513,779 | $334,041,818 | $ 2,141,762 | $222,392,840 | $109,513,292 |
| Alabama ............................. | 3,780,493 | 875.32 | 3,780,094 | 871,389 | 2,908,705 | 399 | 1,902,530 | 813,439 |
| Alaska ................................. | 3,290,599 | 5,403.28 | 3,290,599 | 393,424 | 2,897,175 | 0 | 795,404 | 385,335 |
| Arizona ............................... | 2,741,940 | 601.96 | 2,741,940 | 268,295 | 2,473,645 | 0 | 2,432,801 | 268,295 |
| Arkansas ............................ | 2,247,810 | 890.93 | 2,247,018 | 305,819 | 1,941,199 | 792 | 721,315 | 305,819 |
| California ........................... | 45,336,911 | 1,405.01 | 45,261,188 | 15,321,978 | 29,939,210 | 75,723 | 26,144,951 | 15,289,573 |
| Colorado ............................ | 3,402,235 | 873.94 | 3,402,228 | 4,821 | 3,397,407 | 7 | 313,818 | 4,821 |
| Connecticut ....................... | 17,050,816 | 5,214.32 | 17,050,816 | 10,631,465 | 6,419,351 | 0 | 9,617,985 | 9,178,703 |
| Delaware ............................ | 3,434,196 | 4,691.52 | 3,429,865 | 657,614 | 2,772,251 | 4,331 | 1,380,010 | 640,636 |
| Florida ............................... | 16,021,603 | 1,093.33 | 16,021,165 | 746,225 | 15,274,940 | 438 | 11,088,568 | 430,935 |
| Georgia .............................. | 6,185,586 | 826.29 | 6,185,586 | 4,725,235 | 1,460,351 | 0 | 4,580,880 | 4,706,205 |
| Hawaii ................................ | 5,252,711 | 4,425.20 | 5,246,578 | 3,102,288 | 2,144,290 | 6,133 | 4,293,180 | 3,094,664 |
| Idaho .................................. | 1,598,125 | 1,320.76 | 1,598,025 | 0 | 1,598,025 | 100 | 185,989 | 0 |
| Illinois ................................ | 23,800,807 | 2,000.74 | 23,796,802 | 6,912,695 | 16,884,107 | 4,005 | 7,856,338 | 6,300,014 |
| Indiana ............................... | 6,140,051 | 1,047.08 | 6,071,414 | 0 | 6,071,414 | 68,637 | 2,454,998 | 0 |
| Iowa ................................... | 2,013,891 | 706.13 | 1,995,282 | 0 | 1,995,282 | 18,609 | 757,622 | 0 |
| Kansas ............................... | 1,211,295 | 466.78 | 1,200,697 | 0 | 1,200,697 | 10,598 | 1,181,220 | 0 |
| Kentucky ............................ | 7,120,354 | 1,821.99 | 7,120,354 | 0 | 7,120,354 | 0 | 4,186,074 | -2,849 |
| Louisiana ........................... | 7,030,252 | 1,615.41 | 7,008,551 | 2,186,612 | 4,821,939 | 21,701 | 2,765,362 | 1,924,340 |
| Maine .................................. | 3,202,599 | 2,578.58 | 3,202,599 | 438,620 | 2,763,979 | 0 | 514,941 | 412,290 |
| Maryland ............................ | 9,873,357 | 1,938.23 | 9,873,357 | 3,030,190 | 6,843,167 | 0 | 4,826,694 | 3,018,905 |
| Massachusetts ................... | 29,386,049 | 4,803.21 | 29,049,500 | 13,369,651 | 15,679,849 | 336,549 | 14,218,874 | 12,985,641 |
| Michigan ............................ | 14,431,375 | 1,476.51 | 14,423,284 | 1,794,600 | 12,628,684 | 8,091 | 4,682,781 | 1,794,600 |
| Minnesota .......................... | 4,862,084 | 1,037.58 | 4,862,084 | 2,116,586 | 2,745,498 | 0 | 2,223,187 | 1,782,843 |
| Mississippi ........................ | 2,454,627 | 898.80 | 2,454,627 | 1,410,753 | 1,043,874 | 0 | 1,465,510 | 1,399,528 |
| Missouri ............................. | 7,579,129 | 1,403.02 | 7,573,629 | 1,017,490 | 6,556,139 | 5,500 | 1,265,817 | 907,559 |
| Montana ............................. | 2,055,644 | 2,338.62 | 2,048,979 | 103,640 | 1,945,339 | 6,665 | 408,005 | 100,781 |
| Nebraska ............................ | 1,494,425 | 901.89 | 1,494,288 | 0 | 1,494,288 | 137 | 142,026 | 0 |
| Nevada ............................... | 2,769,136 | 1,651.24 | 2,765,326 | 1,743,396 | 1,021,930 | 3,810 | 1,909,189 | 1,702,016 |
| New Hampshire .................. | 5,848,446 | 4,985.89 | 5,848,446 | 768,020 | 5,080,426 | 0 | 961,017 | 609,465 |
| New Jersey ......................... | 26,590,636 | 3,301.95 | 26,543,538 | 3,437,450 | 23,106,088 | 47,098 | 14,298,040 | 3,437,450 |
| New Mexico ........................ | 2,458,248 | 1,420.95 | 2,419,231 | 347,138 | 2,072,093 | 39,017 | 840,104 | 347,138 |
| New York ............................ | 74,078,490 | 4,084.38 | 73,565,040 | 10,522,288 | 63,042,752 | 513,450 | 37,621,025 | 8,805,818 |
| North Carolina ................... | 5,677,453 | 764.64 | 5,677,453 | 1,514,477 | 4,162,976 | 0 | 2,106,801 | 1,514,477 |
| North Dakota ..................... | 900,079 | 1,404.18 | 900,079 | 0 | 900,079 | 0 | 32,608 | 0 |
| Ohio ................................... | 13,437,403 | 1,201.27 | 13,281,900 | 3,043,290 | 10,238,610 | 155,503 | 7,022,670 | 2,903,153 |
| Oklahoma .......................... | 3,795,206 | 1,144.17 | 3,795,134 | 326,540 | 3,468,594 | 72 | 2,277,870 | 326,540 |
| Oregon ............................... | 5,840,879 | 1,801.07 | 5,840,879 | 3,308,717 | 2,532,162 | 0 | 2,751,565 | 1,770,680 |
| Pennsylvania ...................... | 15,367,631 | 1,278.51 | 14,988,308 | 4,820,898 | 10,167,410 | 379,323 | 6,671,580 | 4,168,116 |
| Rhode Island ...................... | 5,301,681 | 5,371.51 | 5,282,246 | 1,106,068 | 4,176,178 | 19,435 | 2,205,767 | 1,106,068 |
| South Carolina ................... | 5,349,807 | 1,422.82 | 5,145,034 | 1,050,451 | 4,094,583 | 204,773 | 3,693,198 | 1,050,451 |
| South Dakota ..................... | 1,840,686 | 2,494.15 | 1,840,296 | 0 | 1,840,296 | 390 | 311,643 | 0 |
| Tennessee .......................... | 3,314,928 | 617.54 | 3,164,828 | 981,984 | 2,182,844 | 150,100 | 1,240,665 | 978,707 |
| Texas .................................. | 12,461,867 | 641.08 | 12,432,461 | 6,256,028 | 6,176,433 | 29,406 | 9,075,687 | 4,260,473 |
| Utah ................................... | 2,450,730 | 1,190.25 | 2,431,811 | 367,160 | 2,064,651 | 18,919 | 740,918 | 340,883 |
| Vermont ............................. | 2,037,435 | 3,459.14 | 2,028,453 | 543,800 | 1,484,653 | 8,982 | 588,747 | 543,800 |
| Virginia .............................. | 9,940,870 | 1,476.22 | 9,940,870 | 537,299 | 9,403,571 | 0 | 2,762,557 | 537,299 |
| Washington ........................ | 9,493,472 | 1,692.24 | 9,493,398 | 6,191,859 | 3,301,539 | 74 | 6,342,845 | 6,136,734 |
| West Virginia ..................... | 3,039,506 | 1,673.74 | 3,036,511 | 150,790 | 2,885,721 | 2,995 | 1,532,329 | 145,211 |
| Wisconsin .......................... | 9,831,858 | 1,901.71 | 9,831,858 | 3,086,736 | 6,745,122 | 0 | 4,905,990 | 3,086,736 |
| Wyoming ............................ | 871,948 | 1,816.56 | 871,948 | 0 | 871,948 | 0 | 93,145 | 0 |

Source: U.S. Department of Commerce, Bureau of the Census.
Note: Detail may not add to totals due to rounding.
(a) Long-term debt outstanding minus long-term debt offsets.

## Table 6.18
## STATE DEBT OUTSTANDING AT END OF FISCAL YEAR, BY STATE: 1998
### (Amounts in thousands. Per capita amounts in dollars)

| State | Total | Per capita | Long-term Total | Full faith and credit | Nonguaranteed | Short-term | Net long-term (a) Total | Full faith and credit |
|---|---|---|---|---|---|---|---|---|
| United States ............ | $483,117,137 | 1787.3 | $480,947,787 | $124,653,314 | $356,294,473 | $2,169,350 | $237,106,827 | $114,890,436 |
| Alabama ........................... | 4,166,572 | 957.4 | 4,165,972 | 768,709 | 3,397,263 | 600 | 2,133,475 | 702,307 |
| Alaska ............................. | 3,799,708 | 6188.4 | 3,799,708 | 627,449 | 3,172,259 | 0 | 1,027,497 | 627,060 |
| Arizona ............................ | 2,806,922 | 601.2 | 2,806,922 | 253,852 | 2,553,070 | 0 | 2,354,084 | 253,852 |
| Arkansas ........................ | 2,384,116 | 939.4 | 2,384,046 | 406,379 | 1,977,667 | 70 | 911,962 | 406,379 |
| California ....................... | 50,250,539 | 1538.3 | 50,250,539 | 15,963,790 | 34,286,749 | 0 | 28,488,313 | 15,854,163 |
| Colorado ........................ | 3,637,200 | 915.9 | 3,637,200 | 2,475 | 3,634,725 | 0 | 292,242 | 2,475 |
| Connecticut .................... | 17,727,048 | 5414.5 | 17,727,048 | 10,701,142 | 7,025,906 | 0 | 9,101,428 | 9,134,331 |
| Delaware ........................ | 3,770,259 | 5067.6 | 3,762,010 | 688,324 | 3,073,686 | 8,249 | 1,459,587 | 667,444 |
| Florida ............................ | 16,969,289 | 1137.7 | 16,968,662 | 633,955 | 16,334,707 | 627 | 12,346,818 | 414,343 |
| Georgia ........................... | 6,039,633 | 790.3 | 6,039,633 | 4,594,795 | 1,444,838 | 0 | 4,399,508 | 4,576,874 |
| Hawaii ............................ | 5,709,739 | 4786.0 | 5,709,739 | 3,387,988 | 2,321,751 | 0 | 4,580,312 | 3,384,992 |
| Idaho .............................. | 1,883,221 | 1532.3 | 1,883,011 | 0 | 1,883,011 | 210 | 209,625 | 0 |
| Illinois ............................ | 25,314,532 | 2101.7 | 25,311,498 | 7,025,210 | 18,286,288 | 3,034 | 7,926,804 | 6,281,408 |
| Indiana ........................... | 6,704,287 | 1136.5 | 6,655,053 | 0 | 6,655,053 | 49,234 | 2,347,009 | 0 |
| Iowa ............................... | 2,029,300 | 709.0 | 2,005,870 | 0 | 2,005,870 | 23,430 | 722,302 | 0 |
| Kansas ............................ | 1,411,135 | 536.8 | 1,401,729 | 0 | 1,401,729 | 9,406 | 1,378,097 | 0 |
| Kentucky ........................ | 6,813,880 | 1731.2 | 6,813,880 | 0 | 6,813,880 | 0 | 4,055,340 | -3,410 |
| Louisiana ........................ | 7,093,467 | 1623.6 | 7,092,126 | 2,155,922 | 4,936,204 | 1,341 | 2,718,168 | 1,889,862 |
| Maine .............................. | 3,474,244 | 2792.8 | 3,473,788 | 361,550 | 3,112,238 | 456 | 518,330 | 335,220 |
| Maryland ........................ | 10,536,254 | 2051.9 | 10,536,254 | 3,275,320 | 7,260,934 | 0 | 5,058,031 | 3,263,433 |
| Massachusetts ................ | 32,833,163 | 5341.3 | 32,494,516 | 14,485,530 | 18,008,986 | 338,647 | 16,422,304 | 14,156,437 |
| Michigan ........................ | 16,147,205 | 1644.8 | 16,139,632 | 1,988,800 | 14,150,832 | 7,573 | 5,150,044 | 1,988,800 |
| Minnesota ...................... | 5,332,686 | 1128.6 | 5,332,686 | 2,462,811 | 2,869,875 | 0 | 2,422,666 | 2,008,698 |
| Mississippi ..................... | 2,673,577 | 971.5 | 2,673,577 | 1,637,855 | 1,035,722 | 0 | 1,707,647 | 1,629,911 |
| Missouri ......................... | 8,091,313 | 1487.6 | 8,086,413 | 1,089,608 | 6,996,805 | 4,900 | 1,608,056 | 971,733 |
| Montana ......................... | 2,258,784 | 2566.8 | 2,247,217 | 193,014 | 2,054,203 | 11,567 | 515,628 | 186,840 |
| Nebraska ........................ | 1,908,357 | 1147.5 | 1,908,249 | 2,938 | 1,905,311 | 108 | 121,003 | 2,938 |
| Nevada ........................... | 2,880,506 | 1648.8 | 2,877,272 | 1,762,121 | 1,115,151 | 3,234 | 1,919,850 | 1,723,645 |
| New Hampshire ............... | 5,367,479 | 4529.5 | 5,367,479 | 721,092 | 4,646,387 | 0 | 922,419 | 557,343 |
| New Jersey ..................... | 27,213,664 | 3353.5 | 27,208,430 | 3,606,963 | 23,601,467 | 5,234 | 15,520,775 | 3,606,963 |
| New Mexico .................... | 2,571,766 | 1480.6 | 2,558,173 | 338,067 | 2,220,106 | 13,593 | 892,796 | 338,067 |
| New York ........................ | 73,254,370 | 4030.5 | 72,711,720 | 10,448,614 | 62,263,106 | 542,650 | 38,913,022 | 8,617,588 |
| North Carolina ............... | 6,877,271 | 911.4 | 6,877,271 | 2,123,944 | 4,753,327 | 0 | 2,751,238 | 2,123,944 |
| North Dakota ................. | 857,474 | 1344.0 | 857,468 | 0 | 857,468 | 6 | 23,156 | 0 |
| Ohio ............................... | 14,182,878 | 1265.3 | 14,049,437 | 2,913,680 | 11,135,757 | 133,441 | 7,506,710 | 2,796,148 |
| Oklahoma ....................... | 3,951,153 | 1180.5 | 3,951,071 | 318,095 | 3,632,976 | 82 | 2,241,974 | 318,095 |
| Oregon ........................... | 5,729,123 | 1745.6 | 5,729,123 | 2,964,990 | 2,764,133 | 0 | 2,701,371 | 1,680,723 |
| Pennsylvania .................. | 16,393,928 | 1366.0 | 16,039,102 | 4,820,172 | 11,218,930 | 354,826 | 7,536,984 | 4,652,542 |
| Rhode Island .................. | 5,351,703 | 5416.7 | 5,332,199 | 954,102 | 4,378,097 | 19,504 | 2,150,450 | 954,102 |
| South Carolina ............... | 5,191,423 | 1353.3 | 4,949,773 | 1,033,490 | 3,916,283 | 241,650 | 3,579,093 | 1,033,490 |
| South Dakota ................. | 2,067,990 | 2802.2 | 2,067,192 | 0 | 2,067,192 | 798 | 317,472 | 0 |
| Tennessee ...................... | 3,191,892 | 587.7 | 3,052,792 | 945,175 | 2,107,617 | 139,100 | 1,118,723 | 942,758 |
| Texas .............................. | 14,408,011 | 729.2 | 14,252,994 | 6,655,071 | 7,597,923 | 155,017 | 10,731,553 | 4,552,882 |
| Utah ............................... | 3,435,168 | 1635.8 | 3,414,378 | 1,202,310 | 2,212,068 | 20,790 | 1,648,704 | 1,173,023 |
| Vermont ......................... | 2,109,788 | 3569.9 | 2,102,915 | 581,990 | 1,520,925 | 6,873 | 642,950 | 581,990 |
| Virginia .......................... | 10,828,138 | 1594.5 | 10,764,138 | 498,554 | 10,265,584 | 64,000 | 2,829,969 | 498,554 |
| Washington ..................... | 10,289,381 | 1808.6 | 10,289,301 | 6,608,542 | 3,680,759 | 80 | 6,740,298 | 6,553,563 |
| West Virginia .................. | 3,433,365 | 1895.8 | 3,424,345 | 114,780 | 3,309,565 | 9,020 | 1,888,744 | 114,780 |
| Wisconsin ....................... | 10,720,738 | 2052.2 | 10,720,738 | 3,334,146 | 7,386,592 | 0 | 4,464,002 | 3,334,146 |
| Wyoming ........................ | 1,043,498 | 2169.4 | 1,043,498 | 0 | 1,043,498 | 0 | 88,294 | 0 |

Source: U.S. Department of Commerce, Bureau of the Census.
Note: Detail may not add to totals due to rounding.
(a) Long-term debt outstanding minus long-term debt offsets.

## Table 6.19
## AGENCIES ADMINISTERING MAJOR STATE TAXES
### (As of February 2000)

| State or other jurisdiction | Income | Sales | Gasoline | Motor vehicle |
|---|---|---|---|---|
| Alabama | Dept. of Revenue | Dept. of Revenue | Dept. of Revenue | Dept. of Revenue |
| Alaska | Dept. of Revenue | . . . | Dept. of Revenue | Dept. of Public Safety |
| Arizona | Dept. of Revenue | Dept. of Revenue | Dept. of Transportation | Dept. of Transportation |
| Arkansas | Dept. of Fin. & Admin. | Dept. of Fin. & Admin. | Dept. of Fin. & Admin. | Dept. of Fin. & Admin. |
| California | Franchise Tax Bd. | Bd. of Equalization | Bd. of Equalization | Dept. of Motor Vehicles |
| Colorado | Dept. of Revenue | Dept. of Revenue | Dept. of Revenue | Dept. of Revenue |
| Connecticut | Dept. of Revenue Serv. | Dept. of Revenue Serv. | Dept. of Revenue Serv. | Dept. of Motor Vehicles |
| Delaware | Div. of Revenue | . . . | Dept. of Transportation | Dept. of Public Safety |
| Florida | Dept. of Revenue | Dept. of Revenue | Dept. of Revenue | Dept. of Motor Vehicles |
| Georgia | Dept. of Revenue | Dept. of Revenue | Dept. of Revenue | Dept. of Revenue |
| Hawaii | Dept. of Taxation | Dept. of Taxation | Dept. of Taxation | County Treasurer |
| Idaho | Dept. of Revenue & Tax. | Dept. of Revenue & Tax. | Dept. of Revenue & Tax. | Dept. of Transportation |
| Illinois | Dept. of Revenue | Dept. of Revenue | Dept. of Revenue | Secretary of State |
| Indiana | Dept. of Revenue | Dept. of Revenue | Dept. of Revenue | Bur. of Motor Vehicles |
| Iowa | Dept. of Revenue & Finance | Dept. of Revenue & Finance | Dept. of Revenue & Finance | Local |
| Kansas | Dept. of Revenue | Dept. of Revenue | Dept. of Revenue | Local (a) |
| Kentucky | Revenue Cabinet | Revenue Cabinet | Revenue Cabinet | Transportation Cabinet |
| Louisiana | Dept. of Revenue & Tax. | Dept. of Revenue & Tax. | Dept. of Revenue & Tax. | Dept. of Public Safety |
| Maine | Revenue Services | Revenue Services | Revenue Services | Secretary of State |
| Maryland | Comptroller | Comptroller | Comptroller | Dept. of Transportation |
| Massachusetts | Dept. of Revenue | Dept. of Revenue | Dept. of Revenue | Reg. of Motor Vehicles |
| Michigan | Dept. of Treasury | Dept. of Treasury | Dept. of Treasury | Secretary of State |
| Minnesota | Dept. of Revenue | Dept. of Revenue | Dept. of Revenue | Dept. of Public Safety |
| Mississippi | Tax Comm. | Tax Comm. | Tax Comm. | Tax Comm. |
| Missouri | Dept. of Revenue | Dept. of Revenue | Dept. of Revenue | Dept. of Revenue |
| Montana | Dept. of Revenue | . . . | Dept. of Transportation | Local |
| Nebraska | Dept. of Revenue | Dept. of Revenue | Dept. of Revenue | Dept. of Motor Vehicles |
| Nevada | . . . | Dept. of Taxation | Dept. of Taxation | Dept. of Motor Vehicles |
| New Hampshire | Dept. of Revenue Admin. | . . . | Dept. of Safety | Dept. of Safety |
| New Jersey | Dept. of Treasury | Dept. of Treasury | Dept. of Treasury | Dept. of Law & Public Safety |
| New Mexico | Tax & Revenue Dept. | Tax & Revenue Dept. | Tax & Revenue Dept. | Tax & Revenue Dept. |
| New York | Dept. of Tax. & Finance | Dept. of Tax. & Finance | Dept. of Tax. & Finance | Dept. of Motor Vehicles |
| North Carolina | Dept. of Revenue | Dept. of Revenue | Dept. of Revenue | Dept. of Transportation |
| North Dakota | Tax. Commr. | Tax Commr. | Tax Commr. | Dept. of Transportation |
| Ohio | Dept. of Taxation | Dept. of Taxation | Dept. of Taxation | Bur. of Motor Vehicles |
| Oklahoma | Tax Comm. | Tax Comm. | Tax Comm. | Tax Comm. |
| Oregon | Dept. of Revenue | . . . | Dept. of Transportation | Dept. of Transportation |
| Pennsylvania | Dept. of Revenue | Dept. of Revenue | Dept. of Revenue | Dept. of Transportation |
| Rhode Island | Dept. of Administration | Dept. of Administration | Dept. of Administration | Dept. of Administration |
| South Carolina | Dept. of Revenue | Dept. of Revenue | Dept. of Revenue | Dept. of Public Safety |
| South Dakota | . . . | Dept. of Revenue | Dept. of Revenue | Dept. of Revenue |
| Tennessee | Dept. of Revenue | Dept. of Revenue | Dept. of Revenue | Dept. of Safety |
| Texas | . . . | Comptroller | Comptroller | Dept. of Transportation |
| Utah | Tax Comm. | Tax Comm. | Tax Comm. | Tax Comm. |
| Vermont | Commr. of Taxes | Commr. of Taxes | Commr. of Motor Vehicles | Commr. of Motor Vehicles |
| Virginia | Dept. of Taxation | Dept. of Taxation | Dept. of Motor Vehicles | Dept. of Motor Vehicles |
| Washington | . . . | Dept. of Revenue | Dept. of Licensing | Dept. of Licensing |
| West Virginia | Dept. of Tax & Revenue | Dept. of Tax & Revenue | Dept. of Tax & Revenue | Div. of Motor Vehicles |
| Wisconsin | Dept. of Revenue | Dept. of Revenue | Dept. of Revenue | Dept. of Transportation |
| Wyoming | . . . | Dept. of Revenue | Dept. of Revenue | Dept. of Transportation |
| Dist. of Columbia | Dept. of Fin. & Revenue | Dept. of Fin. & Revenue | Dept. of Fin. & Revenue | Dept. of Fin. & Revenue |

See footnotes at end of table.

# AGENCIES ADMINISTERING MAJOR STATE TAXES — Continued

| State or other jurisdiction | Tobacco | Death | Alcoholic beverage | Numb. admin. |
|---|---|---|---|---|
| Alabama | Dept. of Revenue | Dept. of Revenue | Alcoh. Bev. Control Bd. | |
| Alaska | Dept. of Revenue | Dept. of Revenue | Dept. of Revenue | |
| Arizona | Dept. of Revenue | Dept. of Revenue | Dept. of Revenue | |
| Arkansas | Dept. of Fin. & Admin. | Dept. of Fin. & Admin. | Dept. of Fin. & Admin. | |
| California | Bd. of Equalization | Controller | Bd. of Equalization | 4 |
| Colorado | Dept. of Revenue | Dept. of Revenue | Dept. of Revenue | 1 |
| Connecticut | Dept. of Revenue Serv. | Dept. of Revenue Serv. | Dept. of Revenue Serv. | 2 |
| Delaware | Div. of Revenue | Div. of Revenue | Dept. of Public Safety | 3 |
| Florida | Dept. of Business Reg. | Dept. of Revenue | Dept. of Business Reg. | 3 |
| Georgia | Dept. of Revenue | Dept. of Revenue | Dept. of Revenue | 1 |
| Hawaii | Dept. of Taxation | Dept. of Taxation | Dept. of Taxation | 2 |
| Idaho | Dept. of Revenue & Tax. | Dept. of Revenue & Tax. | Dept. of Revenue & Tax. | 2 |
| Illinois | Dept. of Revenue | Attorney General | Dept. of Revenue | 3 |
| Indiana | Dept. of Revenue | Dept. of Revenue | Dept. of Revenue | 2 |
| Iowa | Dept. of Revenue & Finance | Dept. of Revenue & Finance | Dept. of Revenue & Finance | 2 |
| Kansas | Dept. of Revenue | Dept. of Revenue | Dept. of Revenue | 2 |
| Kentucky | Revenue Cabinet | Revenue Cabinet | Revenue Cabinet | 2 |
| Louisiana | Dept. of Revenue & Tax | Dept. of Revenue & Tax. | Dept. of Revenue & Tax. | 2 |
| Maine | Revenue Services | Revenue Services | Bureau of Liquor Enf. | 3 |
| Maryland | Comptroller | Local | Comptroller | 3 |
| Massachusetts | Dept. of Revenue | Dept. of Revenue | Dept. of Revenue | 2 |
| Michigan | Dept. of Treasury | Dept. of Treasury | Liquor Control Comm. | 3 |
| Minnesota | Dept. of Revenue | Dept. of Revenue | Dept. of Revenue | 2 |
| Mississippi | Tax Comm. | Tax Comm. | Tax Comm. | 1 |
| Missouri | Dept. of Revenue | Dept. of Revenue | Dept. of Revenue | 1 |
| Montana | Dept. of Revenue | Dept. of Revenue | Dept. of Revenue | 3 |
| Nebraska | Dept. of Revenue | Dept. of Revenue | Liquor Control Comm. | 3 |
| Nevada | Dept. of Taxation | Dept. of Taxation | Dept. of Taxation | 2 |
| New Hampshire | Dept. of Revenue Admin. | Dept. of Revenue Admin. | Liquor Comm. | 3 |
| New Jersey | Dept. of Treasury | Dept. of Treasury | Dept. of Treasury | 2 |
| New Mexico | Tax & Revenue Dept. | Tax & Revenue Dept. | Tax & Revenue Dept. | 1 |
| New York | Dept. of Tax. & Finance | Dept. of Tax. & Finance | Dept. of Tax & Finance | 2 |
| North Carolina | Dept. Revenue | Dept. of Revenue | Dept. of Revenue | 2 |
| North Dakota | Tax Commr. | Tax Commr. | Treasurer | 3 |
| Ohio | Dept. of Taxation | Dept. of Taxation | State Treasurer | 3 |
| Oklahoma | Tax Comm. | Tax Comm. | Tax Comm. | 1 |
| Oregon | Dept. of Revenue | Dept. of Revenue | Liquor Control Comm. | 3 |
| Pennsylvania | Dept. of Revenue | Dept. of Revenue | Dept. of Revenue | 2 |
| Rhode Island | Dept. of Administration | Dept. of Administration | Dept. of Administration | 1 |
| South Carolina | Dept. of Revenue | Dept. of Revenue | Dept. of Revenue | 2 |
| South Dakota | Dept. of Revenue | Dept. of Revenue | Dept. of Revenue | 1 |
| Tennessee | Dept. of Revenue | Dept. of Revenue | Dept. of Revenue | 2 |
| Texas | Comptroller | Comptroller | Comptroller | 2 |
| Utah | Tax Comm. | Tax Comm. | Tax Comm. | 1 |
| Vermont | Commr. of Taxes | Commr. of Taxes | Commr. of Taxes | 2 |
| Virginia | Dept. of Taxation | Dept. of Taxation | Alcoh. Bev. Control | 3 |
| Washington | Dept. of Revenue | Dept. of Revenue | Liquor Control Board | 3 |
| West Virginia | Dept. of Tax & Revenue | Dept. of Tax & Revenue | Dept. of Tax & Revenue | 2 |
| Wisconsin | Dept. of Revenue | Dept. of Revenue | Dept. of Revenue | 2 |
| Wyoming | Dept. of Revenue | Dept. of Revenue | Dept. of Revenue | 2 |
| Dist. of Columbia | Dept. of Fin. & Revenue | Dept. of Fin. & Revenue | Dept. of Fin. & Revenue | 1 |

Source: The Federation of Tax Administrators.
Key:
... — Not applicable

(a) Joint state and local administration. State level functions are performed by the Department of Revenue in Kansas.

## Table 6.20
## STATE TAX AMNESTY PROGRAMS
## November 22, 1982 - Present

| State or other jurisdiction | Amnesty period | Legislative authorization | Major taxes covered | Accounts receivable included | Collections ($ millions) (a) | Installment arrangements permitted (b) |
|---|---|---|---|---|---|---|
| Alabama | 1/20/84 - 4/1/84 | No (c) | All | No | 3.2 | No |
| Arizona | 11/22/82 - 1/20/83 | No (c) | All | No | 6.0 | Yes |
| Arkansas | 9/1/87 - 11/30/87 | Yes | All | No | 1.7 | Yes |
| California | 12/10/84 - 3/15/85 | Yes | Individual income | Yes | 154.0 | Yes |
| | | Yes | Sales | No | 43.0 | Yes |
| Colorado | 9/16/85 - 11/15/85 | Yes | All | No | 6.4 | Yes |
| Connecticut | 9/1/90 - 11/30/90 | Yes | All | Yes | 54.0 | Yes |
| | 9/1/95 - 11/30/95 | Yes | All | Yes | 46.2 | Yes |
| Florida | 1/1/87 -6/30/87 | Yes | Intangibles | No | 13.0 | No |
| | 1/1/88 - 6/30/88 | Yes (d) | All | No | 8.4 (d) | No |
| Georgia | 10/1/92 - 12/5/92 | Yes | All | Yes | 51.3 | No |
| Idaho | 5/20/83 - 8/30/83 | No (c) | Individual income | No | 0.3 | No |
| Illinois | 10/1/84 - 11/30/84 | Yes | All | Yes | 160.5 | No |
| Iowa | 9/2/86 - 10/31/86 | Yes | All | Yes | 35.1 | N.A. |
| Kansas | 7/1/84 - 9/30/84 | Yes | All | No | 0.6 | No |
| Kentucky | 9/15/88 - 9/30/88 | Yes (c) | All | No | 61.1 | No |
| Louisiana | 10/1/85 - 12/31/85 | Yes | All | No | 1.2 | Yes (f) |
| | 10/1/87 - 12/15/87 | Yes | All | No | 0.3 | Yes (f) |
| Maine | 11/1/90 - 12/31/90 | Yes | All | Yes | 29.0 | Yes |
| Maryland | 9/1/87 - 11/2/87 | Yes | All | Yes | 34.6 (g) | No |
| Massachusetts | 10/17/83 - 1/17/84 | Yes | All | Yes | 86.5 | Yes (h) |
| Michigan | 5/12/86 - 6/30/86 | Yes | All | Yes | 109.8 | No |
| Minnesota | 8/1/84 - 10/31/84 | Yes | All | Yes | 12.1 | No |
| Mississippi | 9/1/86 - 11/30/86 | Yes | All | No | 1.0 | No |
| Missouri | 9/1/83 - 10/31/83 | No (c) | All | No | 0.9 | No |
| New Jersey | 9/10/87 - 12/8/87 | Yes | All | Yes | 186.5 | Yes |
| | 3/15/96 - 6/1/96 | Yes | All | Yes | 359.0 | No |
| New Mexico | 8/15/85 - 11/13/85 | Yes | All (i) | No | 13.6 | Yes |
| New York | 11/1/85 - 1/31/86 | Yes | All (j) | Yes | 401.3 | Yes |
| | 11/1/96 - 1/31/97 | Yes | All | Yes | N.A. | Yes (o) |
| North Carolina | 9/1/89 - 12/1/89 | Yes | All (k) | Yes | 37.6 | No |
| North Dakota | 9/1/83 - 11/30/83 | No (c) | All | No | 0.2 | Yes |
| Oklahoma | 7/1/84 - 12/31/84 | Yes | Income, Sales | Yes | 13.9 | No (l) |
| Pennsylvania | 10/13/95 - 1/10/96 | Yes | All | Yes | N.A. | No |
| Rhode Island | 10/15/86 - 1/12/87 | Yes | All | No | 0.7 | Yes |
| | 4/15/96 - 6/28/96 | Yes | All | Yes | 7.9 | Yes |
| South Carolina | 9/1/85 - 11/30/85 | Yes | All | Yes | 7.1 | Yes |
| Texas | 2/1/84 - 2/29/84 | No (c) | All (m) | No | 0.5 | No |
| Vermont | 5/15/90 - 6/25/90 | Yes | All | Yes | 1.0 (e) | No |
| Virginia | 2/1/90 - 3/31/90 | Yes | All | Yes | 32.2 | No |
| West Virginia | 10/1/86 - 12/31/86 | Yes | All | Yes | 15.9 | Yes |
| Wisconsin | 9/15/85 - 11/22/85 | Yes | All | Yes (n) | 27.3 | Yes |
| Dist. of Columbia | 7/1/87 - 9/30/87 | Yes | All | Yes | 24.3 | Yes |
| | 7/10/95 - 8/31/95 | Yes | All (p) | N.A. | 19.5 | Yes (p) |

See footnotes at end of table.

# STATE TAX AMNESTY PROGRAMS — Continued

*Source*: The Federation of Tax Administrators, February 1997.
*Key:*

N.A. — Not available

(a) Where applicable, figure indicates local portions of certain taxes collected under the state tax amnesty program.

(b) "No" indicates requirement of full payment by the expiration of the amnesty period. "Yes" indicates allowance of full payment after the expiration of the amnesty period.

(c) Authority for amnesty derived from pre-existing statutory powers permitting the waiver of tax penalties.

(d) Does not include intangibles tax and drug taxes. Gross collections totaled $22.1 million, with $13.7 million in penalties withdrawn.

(e) Preliminary figure.

(f) Amnesty taxpayers were billed for the interest owed, with payment due within 30 days of notification.

(g) Figure includes $1.1 million for the separate program conducted by the Department of Natural Resources for the boat excise tax.

(h) The amnesty statute was construed to extend the amnesty to those who applied to the department before the end of the amnesty period, and permitted them to file overdue returns and pay back taxes and interest at a later date.

(i) The severance taxes, including the six oil and gas severance taxes, the resources excise tax, the corporate franchise tax, and the special fuels tax were not subject to amnesty.

(j) Availability of amnesty for the corporation tax, the oil company taxes, the transporation and transmissions companies tax, the gross receipts oil tax and the unincorporated business tax restricted to entities with 500 or fewer employees in the United States on the date of application. In addition, a taxpayer principally engaged in aviation, or a utility subject to the supervision of the State Department of Public Service was also ineligible.

(k) Local taxes and real property taxes were not included.

(l) Full payment of tax liability required before the end of the amnesty period to avoid civil penalties.

(m) Texas does not impose a corporate or individual income tax. In practical effect, the amnesty was limited to the sales tax and other excises.

(n) Waiver terms varied depending upon the date the tax liability was assessed.

(o) Installment arrangements were permitted if applicant demonstrated that payment would present a severe financial hardship.

(p) Does not include real property taxes. All interest was waived on tax payments made before July 31, 1995. After this date, only 50% of the interest was waived..

## Table 6.21
## STATE EXCISE TAX RATES
### (As of January 1, 2000)

| State or other jurisdiction | General sales and gross receipts tax (percent) | Cigarettes (cents per pack of 20) | Distilled spirits ($ per gallon) | Motor fuel (c) (cents per gallon) Gasoline | Diesel | Gasohol |
|---|---|---|---|---|---|---|
| Alabama | 4 | 16.5 (d) | (h) | 18 (k) | 19 (k) | 18 (k) |
| Alaska | . . . | 100 | $5.60 (j) | 8 | 8 | . . . |
| Arizona | 5 | 58 | 3.00 | 18 (m) | 18 (m) | 18 (m) |
| Arkansas | 4.625 | 31.5 (e) | 2.50 (j) | 19.7 (r) | 20.7 (r) | 19.7 (r) |
| California | 6 | 87 | 3.30 (j) | 18 | 18 | 18 |
| Colorado | 3 | 20 | 2.28 | 22 | 20.5 | 22 |
| Connecticut | 6 | 50 | 4.50 (j) | 32 | 18 | 31 |
| Delaware | . . . | 24 | 3.75 (j) | 23 (o) | 23 (o) | 23 (o) |
| Florida | 6 | 33.9 | 6.50 (j) | 13.1 (l) | 25.1 | 13.1 (l) |
| Georgia | 4 | 12 | 3.79 (j) | 7.5 | 7.5 | 7.5 |
| Hawaii | 4 | 100 | 5.92 | 16 (k) | 16 (k) | 16 (k) |
| Idaho | 5 (a) | 28 | (h) | 26 (q) | 26 (q) | 23.5 (q) |
| Illinois | 6.25 (b) | 58 (d) | 4.50(j) | 19.3 (k, m) | 21.5 (m) | 19 |
| Indiana | 5 | 15.5 | 2.68 (j) | 15 (m) | 16 (m) | 15 (m) |
| Iowa | 5 | 36 | (h) | 20 | 22.5 | 19 |
| Kansas | 4.9 (a) | 24 | 2.50 (j) | 20 | 22 | 20 |
| Kentucky | 6 | 3 (e) | 1.92 (i, j) | 16.4 (m, n) | 13.4 (m, n) | 16.4 (n) |
| Louisiana | 4 | 20 | 2.50 (j) | 20 | 20 | 20 |
| Maine | 5.5 (s) | 74 | (h) | 22 | 23 | 22 |
| Maryland | 5 | 66 | 1.50 | 23.5 | 24.3 | 23.5 |
| Massachusetts | 5 | 76 | 4.05 (i, j) | 21 (n) | 21 (n) | 21 (n) |
| Michigan | 6 | 75 | (h) | 19 | 15 | 19 |
| Minnesota | 6.5 | 48 | 5.03 (j) | 20 | 20 | 20 |
| Mississippi | 7 | 18 | (h) | 18.4 | 18.4 | 18.4 |
| Missouri | 4.225 | 17 (d) | 2.00 | 17.05 | 17.05 | 15.05 |
| Montana | . . . | 18 | (h) | 27 | 27.75 | 27 |
| Nebraska | 5 | 34 | 3.00 | 24.8 (o) | 24.8 (o) | 24.8 (o) |
| Nevada | 6.5 | 35 | 2.05 (j) | 24 (k) | 27 (k) | 24 (k) |
| New Hampshire | . . . | 52 | (h) | 18.7 | 18.7 | 18.7 |
| New Jersey | 6 | 80 | 4.40 | 10.5 | 13.5 | 10.5 |
| New Mexico | 5 | 21 | 6.06 | 18 | 19 | 18 |
| New York | 4 | 56 (d, g) | 6.44 (j) | 8 (m, n) | 8 (m, n) | 8 (n) |
| North Carolina | 4 | 5 | (h, i) | 22.25 (n) | 22.25 (n) | 22.25 (n) |
| North Dakota | 5 | 44 | 2.50 (j) | 21 | 21 | 21 |
| Ohio | 5 | 24 | (h) | 22 | 22 | 22 |
| Oklahoma | 4.5 | 23 | 5.56 (j) | 17 | 14 | 17 |
| Oregon | . . . | 68 | (h) | 29 (k) | 29 (k) | 29 (k) |
| Pennsylvania | 6 | 31 | (h) | 25.9 | 30.8 | 25.9 |
| Rhode Island | 7 | 71 | 3.75 | 29 | 29 | 29 |
| South Carolina | 5 | 7 | 2.72 (j) | 16 | 16 | 16 |
| South Dakota | 4 (a) | 33 | 3.93 (j) | 22 (k) | 22 (k) | 20 (k) |
| Tennessee | 6 | 13 (d, e) | 4.00 (j) | 21.4 (k) | 18.4 (k) | 21.4 (k) |
| Texas | 6.25 | 41 | 2.40 (j) | 20 | 20 | 20 |
| Utah | 4.75 | 51.5 | (h) | 24.75 | 24.75 | 24.75 |
| Vermont | 5 (a) | 44 | (f,h) | 20 (p) | 17 (p) | 20 (p) |
| Virginia | 3.5 | 2.5 (d) | (h) | 17.5 (k, p) | 16 (k, p) | 17.5 (k, p) |
| Washington | 6.5 | 82.5 | (h, i) | 23 | 23 | 23 |
| West Virginia | 6 | 17 | (h) | 25.35 | 25.35 | 25.35 |
| Wisconsin | 5 | 59 | 3.25 | 25.8 (o) | 25.8 (o) | 25.8 (o) |
| Wyoming | 4 (a, c) | 12 | (h) | 14 | 14 | 14 |
| Dist. of Columbia | 5.75 | 65 | 1.50 (j) | 20 | 20 | 20 |

See footnotes at end of table.

# STATE EXCISE TAX RATES — Continued

*Source*: Compiled by The Federation of Tax Administrators from various sources.

*Key*:

. . . — Tax is not applicable.

(a) Some states tax food, but allow an (income) tax credit to compensate poor households. They are Idaho, Kansas, South Dakota, Vermont and Wyoming.

(b) 1.25 percent of the tax in Illinois is distributed to local governments.

(c) Tax rate may be adjusted annually according to a formula based on balances in the unappropriated general fund and the school foundation fund.

(d) Counties and cities may impose an additional tax on a pack of cigarettes in Alabama, 1-6 cents; Illinois, 10-15 cents; Missouri, 4-7 cents; Tennessee, 1 cent; and Virginia, 2-15 cents.

(e) Dealers pay an additional enforcement and administrative fee of 0.1 cents per pack in Kentucky and 0.05 cents in Tennessee. In Arkansas, a fee of $1.25/1,000 cigarettes fee is imposed.

(f) 10 percent on-premise sales tax.

(g) The tax rate will increase to $1.11 per pack on March 1, 2000.

(h) In 18 states, the government directly controls the sales of distilled spirits. Revenue in these states is generated from various taxes, fees and net liquor profits.

(i) Sales tax is applied to on-premise sales only.

(j) Other taxes in addition to excise taxes for the following states: Alaska, under 21 percent - $0.85/gallon; Arkansas, under 5 percent - $0.50/gallon, under 21 percent - $1.00/gallon, $0.20/case and 3 percent off - 14 percent on-premise retail taxes; California, over 50 percent - $6.60/gallon; Connecticut, under 7 percent - $2.05/gallon; Delaware, under 25 percent - $2.50/gallon; Florida, under 17.259 percent - $2.25/gallon, over 55.780 percent - $9.53/gallon, 6.67cents/ounce on-premise retail tax; Georgia, $0.83/gallon local tax; Illinois, under 20 percent - $0.73/gallon, $0.50/gallon in Chicago and $1.00/gallon in Cook County; Indiana, under 15 percent - $0.47/gallon; Kansas, 8 percent off- and on-premise retail tax; Kentucky, under 6 percent - $0.25/gallon, $0.05/case and 9 percent wholesale tax; Louisiana, under 6 percent - $0.32/gallon; Massachusetts, under 15 percent - $1.10/gallon, over 50 percent alcohol - $4.05/proof gallon, 0.57 percent on private club sales; Minnesota, $0.01/bottle (except miniatures) and 8.5 percent sales tax; Nevada, under 14 percent - $0.40/gallon and under 21 percent - $0.75/gallon; New York, under 24 percent - $2.54/gallon, $1.00/gallon New York City; North Dakota, 7 percent state sales tax; Oklahoma, $1.00/bottle on-premise and 12 percent on-premise; South Carolina, $5.36/case and 9 percent surtax; South Dakota, under 14 percent - $0.93/gallon, 2 percent wholesale tax; Tennessee, $0.15/case and 15 percent on-premise, under 7 percent - $1.10/gallon; Texas, 14 percent on-premise and $0.05/drink on airline sales; and District of Columbia, 8 percent off- and 10 percent on-premise sales tax.

(k) Tax rates do not include local option taxes. In Alabama, 1-3 cents; Hawaii, 8-11.5 cents; Illinois, 5 cents in Chicago and 6 cents in Cook County (gasoline only); Nevada1.75 to7.75 cents; Oregon, 1-2 cents; South Dakota, 1 cent; Tennessee, 1 cent; and Virginia, 2 percent.

(l) Local taxes for gasoline and gasohol vary from 5.5 cents to 17 cents. Plus a 2.07 cents/gallon pollution tax.

(m) Carriers pay an additional surcharge equal to Arizona, 8 cents; Illinois, 6.3 cents (gasoline) and 6.0 cents (diesel); Indiana, 11 cents; Kentucky, 2 percent (gasoline) and 4.7 percent (diesel); New York, 22.21 cents (gasoline) and 23.21 cents (diesel).

(n) Tax rate is based on the average wholesale price and is adjusted quarterly. The actual rates are: Kentucky, 9 percent; Massachusetts, 19.1 percent; and North Carolina, 7 percent.

(o) A portion of the rate is adjustable based on maintenance costs, sales volume, or cost of fuel to state government.

(p) Large trucks pay a higher tax, Vermont, total of 25 cents/gallon; Virginia, additional 3.5 cents.

(q) Tax rate is reduced by the percentage of ethanol used in blending (reported rate assumes the maximum 10 percent ethanol).

(r) Tax rate will increase to 20.5 cents on July 1, 2000.

(s ) Tax rate is scheduled to decrease to 5.0% on 7/1/00.

## Table 6.22
## FOOD AND DRUG SALES TAX EXEMPTIONS
### (As of January 1, 2000)

| State or other jurisdiction | Tax rate (percentage) | Exemptions Food (a) | Prescription drugs | Nonprescription drugs |
|---|---|---|---|---|
| Alabama | 4 | ... | ★ | ... |
| Alaska | none | ... | ... | ... |
| Arizona | 5 | ★ | ★ | ... |
| Arkansas | 4.625 | ... | ★ | ... |
| California | 6 | ★ | ★ | ... |
| Colorado | 3 | ★ | ★ | ... |
| Connecticut | 6 | ★ | ★ | ... |
| Delaware | none | ... | ... | ... |
| Florida | 6 | ★ | ★ | ★ |
| Georgia | 4 | ★ | ★ | ... |
| Hawaii | 4 | ... | ★ | ... |
| Idaho (a) | 5 | ... | ★ | ... |
| Illinois(b) | 6.25 | 1 percent | 1 percent | 1 percent |
| Indiana | 5 | ★ | ★ | ... |
| Iowa | 5 | ★ | ★ | ... |
| Kansas (a) | 4.9 | ... | ★ | ... |
| Kentucky | 6 | ★ | ★ | ... |
| Louisiana | 4 | 3.0(e) | ★ | ... |
| Maine | 5.5 (f) | ★ | ★ | ... |
| Maryland | 5 | ★ | ★ | ★ |
| Massachusetts | 5 | ★ | ★ | ... |
| Michigan | 6 | ★ | ★ | ... |
| Minnesota | 6.5 | ★ | ★ | ★ |
| Mississippi | 7 | ... | ★ | ... |
| Missouri | 4.225 | ... | ★ | ... |
| Montana | none | ... | ... | ... |
| Nebraska | 5 | ★ | ★ | ... |
| Nevada | 6.5 | ★ | ★ | ... |
| New Hampshire | none | ... | ... | ... |
| New Jersey | 6 | ★ | ★ | ★ |
| New Mexico | 5 | ... | ★ | ... |
| New York | 4 | ★ | ★ | ★ |
| North Carolina | 4 | (e) | ★ | ... |
| North Dakota | 5 | ★ | ★ | ... |
| Ohio | 5 | ★ | ★ | ... |
| Oklahoma | 4.5 | ... | ★ | ... |
| Oregon | none | ... | ... | ... |
| Pennsylvania | 6 | ★ | ★ | ★ |
| Rhode Island | 7 | ★ | ★ | ★ |
| South Carolina | 5 | ... | ★ | ... |
| South Dakota (a) | 4 | ... | ★ | ... |
| Tennessee | 6 | ... | ★ | ... |
| Texas | 6.25 | ★ | ★ | ... |
| Utah | 4.75 | ... | ★ | ... |
| Vermont (a) | 5 | ★ | ★ | ... |
| Virginia | 3.5 | 3.0(d) | ★ | ★ |
| Washington | 6.5 | ★ | ★ | ... |
| West Virginia | 6 | ... | ★ | ... |
| Wisconsin | 5 | ★ | ★ | ... |
| Wyoming (a) (c) | 4 | ... | ★ | ... |
| Dist. of Columbia | 5.75 | ★ | ★ | ★ |

*Source*: The Federation of Tax Administrators, January 2000.
*Key*:
★ — Yes
... — No

(a) Some states tax food, but allow an (income) tax credit to compensate poor households. They are: Idaho, Kansas, South Dakota, Vermont and Wyoming.

(b) 1.25 percent of the tax in Illinois is distributed to local governments.

(c) The tax rate may be adjusted annually according to a formula based on balances in the unappropriated general fund and the school foundation fund.

(d) Tax rate on food is scheduled to decrease to 2.5 percent on 4/1/00

(e) Food sales are subject to local sales tax. In Louisiana, food sales are scheduled to be exempt on 7/1/00.

(f) Tax rate scheduled to decrease to 5 percent on 7/1/00.

## Table 6.23
## STATE INDIVIDUAL INCOME TAXES
### (Tax rate for the year 2000 - as of January 1, 2000)

| State or other jurisdiction | Tax rate range (in percents) Low | High | Number of brackets | Income brackets Lowest | Highest | Personal exemptions Single | Married | Dependents | Federal income tax deductible |
|---|---|---|---|---|---|---|---|---|---|
| Alabama | 2.0 - | 5.0 | 3 | 500 (b) - | 3,000 (b) | 1,500 | 3,000 | 300 | ★ |
| Alaska | ------(aa)------ | | | | | | | | |
| Arizona | 2.8 - | 5.04 | 5 | 10,000 (b) - | 150,000 (b) | 2,100 | 4,200 | 2,300 | |
| Arkansas | 1.0 - | 7.0 (e) | 6 | 2,999 - | 25,000 | 20 (c) | 40 (c) | 20 (c) | |
| California (a) | 1.0 - | 9.3 | 6 | 5,264(b) - | 34,548 (b) | 72 (c) | 142 (c) | 227 (c) | |
| Colorado | 4.8 | | 1 | ------Flat rate------ | | ------None------ | | | |
| Connecticut | 3.0 - | 4.5 | 2 | 10,000 (b) - | 10,000 (b) | 12,000 (f) | 24,000 (f) | 0 | |
| Delaware | 2.2 - | 5.95 | 7 | 5,000 - | 60,000 | 110 (c) | 220 (c) | 110 (c) | |
| Florida | ------(aa)------ | | | | | | | | |
| Georgia | 1.0 - | 6.0 | 6 | 750 (g) - | 7,000 (g) | 2,700 | 5,400 | 2,700 | |
| Hawaii (h) | 1.6 - | 8.75 | 8 | 2,000(b) - | 40,000 (b) | 1,040 | 2,080 | 1,040 | |
| Idaho | 2.0 - | 8.2 | 8 | 1,000 (i) - | 20,000 (i) | 2,750 (d) | 5,500 (d) | 2,750 (d) | |
| Illinois | 3.0 | | 1 | ------Flat rate------ | | 2,000 | 4,000 | 2,000 | |
| Indiana | 3.4 | | 1 | ------Flat rate------ | | 1,000 | 2,000 | 1,000 | |
| Iowa (a) | 0.36 - | 8.98 | 9 | 1,162 - | 52,290 | 40 (c) | 80 (c) | 40 (c) | ★ |
| Kansas | 3.5 - | 6.45 | 3 | 15,000 (b) - | 30,000 (b) | 2,250 | 4,500 | 2,250 | |
| Kentucky | 2.0 - | 6.0 | 5 | 3,000 - | 8,000 | 20 (c) | 40 (c) | 20 (c) | |
| Louisiana | 2.0 - | 6.0 | 3 | 10,000 (b) - | 50,000 (b) | 4,500 (j) | 9,000 (j) | 1,000 (j) | ★ |
| Maine (a) | 2.0 - | 8.5 | 4 | 4,150 (b) - | 16,500 (b) | 2,850 | 5,600 | 2,850 | |
| Maryland (k) | 2.0 - | 4.8 | 4 | 1,000 - | 3,000 | 1,850 | 3,700 | 1,850 | |
| Massachusetts | 5.95 | | 1 | ------Flat rate------ | | 4,400 | 8,800 | 1,000 | |
| Michigan (a) | 4.3(l) | | 1 | ------Flat rate------ | | 2,800 | 5,600 | 2,800 | |
| Minnesota (a) | 5.5 - | 8 | 3 | 17,250 (b) - | 56,680 (b) | 2,750 (d) | 5,500 (d) | 2,750 (d) | |
| Mississippi | 3.0 - | 5.0 | 3 | 5,000 - | 10,000 | 6,000 | 9,500 | 1,500 | |
| Missouri | 1.5 - | 6.0 | 10 | 1,000 - | 9,000 | 2,100 | 4,200 | 2,100 | ★ (m) |
| Montana (a) | 2.0 - | 11.0 | 10 | 2,000 - | 70,400 | 1,610 | 3,220 | 1,610 | ★ |
| Nebraska (a) | 2.51 - | 6.68 | 4 | 2,400 (n) - | 26,500 (n) | 91(c) | 182 (c) | 91 (c) | |
| Nevada | ------(aa)------ | | | | | | | | |
| New Hampshire | ------(bb)------ | | | | | | | | |
| New Jersey | 1.4 - | 6.37 | 6 | 20,000 (o) - | 75,000 (o) | 1,000 | 2,000 | 1,500 | |
| New Mexico | 1.7 - | 8.2 | 7 | 5,500 (p) - | 65,000 (p) | 2,750 (d) | 5,500 (d) | 2,750 (d) | |
| New York | 4.0 - | 6.85 | 5 | 8,000 (b) - | 20,000 (b) | 0 | 0 | 1,000 | |
| North Carolina | 6.0 - | 7.75 | 3 | 12,750 (q) - | 60,000 (q) | 2,500(d) | 5,000 (d) | 2,500 (d) | |
| North Dakota | 2.67 - | 12.0 (r) | 8 | 3,000 - | 50,000 | 2,750 (d) | 5,500 (d) | 2,750 (d) | ★ (r) |
| Ohio (a) | 0.716- | 7.228 (s) | 9 | 5,000 - | 200,000 | 1,050 (s) | 2,100 (s) | 1,050 (s) | |
| Oklahoma | 0.5 - | 6.75 (t) | 8 | 1,000 - | 10,000 | 1,000 | 2,000 | 1,000 | ★ (t) |
| Oregon (a) | 5.0 - | 9.0 | 3 | 2,350 (b) - | 5,850 (b) | 132 (c) | 264(c) | 132 (c) | ★ (u) |
| Pennsylvania | 2.8 | | 1 | ------Flat rate------ | | ------None------ | | | |
| Rhode Island | ------(v)------ | | | | | | | | |
| South Carolina (a) | 2.5 - | 7.0 | 6 | 2,310 - | 11,550 | 2,750 (d) | 5,500 (d) | 2,750 (d) | |
| South Dakota | ------(aa)------ | | | | | | | | |
| Tennessee | State Income Tax is Limited to Dividends and Interest Income Only. | | | | | | | | |
| Texas | ------(aa)------ | | | | | | | | |
| Utah | 2.3 - | 7.0 | 6 | 750 (b) - | 3,750 (b) | 2,063 (d) | 4,125 (d) | 2,063 (d) | ★ (v) |
| Vermont | ------(w)------ | | | | | | | | |
| Virginia | 2.0 - | 5.75 | 4 | 3,000 - | 17,000 | 800 | 1,600 | 800 | |
| Washington | ------(aa)------ | | | | | | | | |
| West Virginia | 3.0 - | 6.5 | 5 | 10,000 - | 60,000 | 2,000 | 4,000 | 2,000 | |
| Wisconsin | 4.73 - | 6.75 (y) | 4 | 7,790 - | 116,890 | 600 | 1,200 | 600 | |
| Wyoming | ------(aa)------ | | | | | | | | |
| Dist. of Columbia | 5.0 - | 9.5 (z) | 3 | 10,000 - | 20,000 | 1,370 | 2,740 | 1,370 | |

See footnotes at end of table.

## STATE INDIVIDUAL INCOME TAXES — Continued

*Source*: The Federation of Tax Administrators from various sources.

(a) Seven states have statutory provision for automatic adjustment of tax brackets, personal exemption or standard deductions to the rate of inflation. Nebraska indexes the personal exemption amounts only.

(b) For joint returns, the taxes are twice the tax imposed on half the income.

(c) Tax credits.

(d) These states allow personal exemption or standard deductions as provided in the Internal Revenue Code. Utah allows a personal exemption equal to three-fourths the federal exemptions.

(e) A special tax table is available for low income taxpayers reducing their tax payments.

(f) Combined personal exemptions and standard deduction. An additional tax credit is allowed ranging from 75 percent to 0 percent based on state adjusted gross income. Exemption amounts are phased out for higher income taxpayers until they are eliminated for households earning over $52,500.

(g) The tax brackets reported are for single individuals. For married households filing separately, the same rates apply to income brackets ranging from $500 to $5,000; and the income brackets range from $1,000 to $10,000 for joint filers.

(h) For tax years beginning after 2000, the tax rates range from 1.5 percent to 8.5 percent for the same tax brackets.

(i) For joint returns, the tax is twice the tax imposed on half the income. A $10 filing fee is charged for each return and a $15 credit is allowed for each exemption.

(j) Combined personal exemption and standard deduction.

(k)Top rate is scheduled to decrease to 4.75% for tax years beginning after 2001.

(l) Tax rate scheduled to decrease to 4.2% for tax year 2001.

(m) Limited to $10,000 for joint returns and $5,000 for individuals.

(n) The tax brackets reported are for single individuals. For married couples filing jointly, the same rates apply for income under $4,000 to over $46,750.

(o) The tax brackets reported are for single individuals. A separate schedule is provided for married individuals filing jointly which ranges from 1.4 percent under $20,000 to 6.37 percent for income over $150,000.

(p) The tax brackets reported are for single individuals. For married individuals filing jointly, the rate ranges from 1.7 percent under $8,000 to 8.2 percent over $100,000. Married households filing separately pay the tax imposed on half the income.

(q) The tax brackets reported are for single individuals. For married taxpayers, the same rates apply to income brackets ranging from $21,250 to $100,000. Lower exemption amounts allowed for high income taxpayers.

(r) An additional $300 personal exemption is allowed for joint returns or unmarried head of households. Taxpayers have the option of paying 14 percent of the adjusted federal income tax liability, without a deduction of federal taxes.

(s) Plus an additional $20 per exemption tax credit. Rates are for tax year 1999, the 2000 rates will not be determined until July, 2000.

(t) The rate range reported is for single persons not deducting federal income tax. For married persons filing jointly, the same rates apply to income brackets ranging from $2,000 to $21,000. Separate schedules, with rates ranging from 0.5 percent to 10 percent, apply to taxpayers deducting federal income taxes.

(u) Limited to $3,000.

(v) Current federal tax liability is 26 percent. Tax rate scheduled to decrease to 25.5 percent of federal tax liability for tax year 2001.

(w) Current federal tax liability is 24 percent. One half of the federal income taxes are deductible.

(x) If Vermont tax liability for any taxable year exceeds the tax liability determinable under federal tax law in effect on December 31, 1998, the taxpayer will be entitled to a credit of 106 percent of the excess tax.

(y) The tax brackets reported are for single individuals. For married taxpayers, the same rates apply to income ranging from $10,390 to $155,850. Tax rates scheduled to decrease for tax years 2001 and beyond (ranging from 4.6% to 6.75). Personal exemption amounts scheduled to increase to $700 for tax year 2001.

(z) Tax rate decreases are scheduled for tax years 2001 and 2002.

(aa) No state income tax.

(bb) State income tax is limited to dividends and interest income only.

## Table 6.24
## STATE PERSONAL INCOME TAXES: FEDERAL STARTING POINTS

| State or other jurisdiction | Relation to Internal Revenue Code | Tax base |
|---|---|---|
| Alabama | . . . | . . . |
| Alaska | (a) | |
| Arizona | 1/1/98 | Federal adjusted gross income |
| Arkansas | . . . | . . . |
| California | 1/1/98 | Federal adjusted gross income |
| Colorado | Current | Federal taxable income |
| Connecticut | Current | Federal adjusted gross income |
| Delaware | Current | Federal adjusted gross income |
| Florida | (a) | . . . |
| Georgia | 1/1/98 | Federal adjusted gross income |
| Hawaii | 12/31/97 | Federal taxable income |
| Idaho | 1/1/99 | Federal taxable income |
| Illinois | Current | Federal adjusted gross income |
| Indiana | 1/1/98 | Federal adjusted gross income |
| Iowa | 1/1/99 | Federal adjusted gross income |
| Kansas | Current | Federal adjusted gross income |
| Kentucky | 12/31/97 | Federal adjusted gross income |
| Louisiana | Current | Federal adjusted gross income |
| Maine | 12/31/97 | Federal adjusted gross income |
| Maryland | Current | Federal adjusted gross income |
| Massachusetts | Current | Federal adjusted gross income |
| Michigan | Current (b) | Federal adjusted gross income |
| Minnesota | 12/31/97 | Federal taxable income |
| Mississippi | . . . | . . . |
| Missouri | Current | Federal adjusted gross income |
| Montana | Current | Federal adjusted gross income |
| Nebraska | Current | Federal adjusted gross income |
| Nevada | (a) | . . . |
| New Hampshire | (c) | . . . |
| New Jersey | . . . | . . . |
| New Mexico | Current | Federal adjusted gross income |
| New York | Current | Federal adjusted gross income |
| North Carolina | 6/1/99 | Federal taxable income |
| North Dakota | Current | Federal liability (d) |
| Ohio | Current | Federal adjusted gross income |
| Oklahoma | Current | Federal adjusted gross income |
| Oregon | Current (e) | Federal taxable income |
| Pennsylvania | . . . | . . . |
| Rhode Island | Current | Federal liability |
| South Carolina | 12/31/98 | Federal taxable income |
| South Dakota | (a) | . . . |
| Tennessee | (c) | . . . |
| Texas | (a) | . . . |
| Utah | Current | Federal taxable income |
| Vermont | Current (f) | Federal liability |
| Virginia | Current | Federal adjusted gross income |
| Washington | (a) | . . . |
| West Virginia | 1/1/97 | Federal adjusted gross income |
| Wisconsin | 12/31/98 | Federal adjusted gross income |
| Wyoming | (a) | . . . |
| Dist. of Columbia | 4/5/97 | Federal adjusted gross income |

*Source:* Compiled by the Federation of Tax Administrators from various sources, January 1, 2000.

*Key:*

. . . — State does not employ a federal starting point.

Current — Indicates state has adopted the Internal Revenue Code as currently in effect. Dates indicate state has adopted the IRC as amended to that date.

(a) No state income tax.
(b) Or 1/1/96, taxpayer's option.
(c) On interest and dividends only.
(d) Or federal taxable income based on current Internal Revenue Code.
(e) Certain sections conform to the Internal Revenue Code as of 12/31/96.
(f) Not to exceed tax computed using Internal Revenue Code as of 12/31/98.

## Table 6.25
## RANGE OF STATE CORPORATE INCOME TAX RATES
### (As of January 1, 2000)

| State or other jurisdiction | Tax rate (percent) | Tax brackets Lowest | Tax brackets Highest | Number of brackets | Tax rate (a) (percent) financial institution | Federal income tax deductible |
|---|---|---|---|---|---|---|
| Alabama | 5.0 | —————Flat Rate————— | | 1 | 6.0 | ★ |
| Alaska | 1.0 - 9.4 | 10,000 | 90,000 | 10 | 1.0 - 9.4 | ... |
| Arizona | 8.0 (z) | —————Flat Rate————— | | 1 | 8.0 (z) | ... |
| Arkansas | 1.0 - 6.5 | 3,000 | 100,000 | 6 | 1.0 - 6.5 | ... |
| California | 8.84 (c) | —————Flat Rate————— | | 1 | 10.84(c ) | ... |
| Colorado | 4.75 | —————Flat Rate————— | | 1 | 4.8 | ... |
| Connecticut | 7.5 (d) | —————Flat Rate————— | | 1 | 7.5 (d) | ... |
| Delaware | 8.7 | —————Flat Rate————— | | 1 | 8.7 - 1.7 (e) | ... |
| Florida | 5.5 (f) | —————Flat Rate————— | | 1 | 5.5 (f) | ... |
| Georgia | 6.0 | —————Flat Rate————— | | 1 | 6.0 | ... |
| Hawaii | 4.4 - 6.4 (g) | 25,000 | 100,000 | 3 | 7.92 (g) | ... |
| Idaho | 8.0 (h) | —————Flat Rate————— | | 1 | 8.0 (h) | ... |
| Illinois | 7.3 (i) | —————Flat Rate————— | | 1 | 7.3 (i) | ... |
| Indiana | 7.9 (j) | —————Flat Rate————— | | 1 | 8.5 | ... |
| Iowa | 6.0 - 12.0 | 25,000 | 250,000 | 4 | 5.0 | ★ (k) |
| Kansas | 4.0 (l) | —————Flat Rate————— | | 1 | 2.25 (l) | ... |
| Kentucky | 4.0 - 8.25 | 25,000 | 250,000 | 5 | (a) | ... |
| Louisiana | 4.0 - 8.0 | 25,000 | 200,000 | 5 | (a) | ★ |
| Maine | 3.5 - 8.93 (m) | 25,000 | 250,000 | 4 | 1.0 | ... |
| Maryland | 7.0 | —————Flat Rate————— | | 1 | 7.0 | ... |
| Massachusetts | 9.5 (n) | —————Flat Rate————— | | 1 | 10.5 (n) | ... |
| Michigan | | _____ See Note _____ | | | | |
| Minnesota | 9.8 (o) | —————Flat Rate————— | | 1 | 9.8 (o) | ... |
| Mississippi | 3.0 - 5.0 | 5,000 | 10,000 | 3 | 3.0 - 5.0 | ... |
| Missouri | 6.25 | —————Flat Rate————— | | 1 | 7 | ★ (k) |
| Montana | 6.75 (p) | —————Flat Rate————— | | 1 | 6.75 (p) | ... |
| Nebraska | 5.58 - 7.81 | 50,000 | | 2 | (a) | ... |
| Nevada | | _____ See Note _____ | | | | |
| New Hampshire | 8.0 (q) | —————Flat Rate————— | | 1 | 8.0 (q) | ... |
| New Jersey | 9.0 (r) | —————Flat Rate————— | | 1 | 9.0 (r) | ... |
| New Mexico | 4.8 - 7.6 | 500,000 | 1 million | 3 | 4.8 - 7.6 | ... |
| New York | 8.5 (s) | —————Flat Rate————— | | 1 | 8.5 (s) | ... |
| North Carolina | 6.9 (t) | —————Flat Rate————— | | 1 | 6.9 (t) | ... |
| North Dakota | 3.0 - 10.5 | 3,000 | 50,000 | 6 | 7.0 (b) | ★ |
| Ohio | 5.1 - 8.5 (u) | 50,000 | | 2 | (u) | ... |
| Oklahoma | 6.0 | —————Flat Rate————— | | 1 | 6.0 | ... |
| Oregon | 6.6 (b) | —————Flat Rate————— | | 1 | 6.6 (b) | ... |
| Pennsylvania | 9.99 | —————Flat Rate————— | | 1 | (a) | ... |
| Rhode Island | 9 | —————Flat Rate————— | | 1 | 9.0 (v) | ... |
| South Carolina | 5.0 | —————Flat Rate————— | | 1 | 4.5 (w) | ... |
| South Dakota | ... | ... | | ... | 6.0 - 1.0 (b) | ... |
| Tennessee | 6.0 | —————Flat Rate————— | | 1 | 6.0 | ... |
| Texas | | _____ See Note _____ | | | | |
| Utah | 5.0 (b) | —————Flat Rate————— | | ... | 5.0 (b) | ... |
| Vermont | 7.0 - 9.75 (b) | 10,000 | 250,000 | 4 | 7.0 - 9.75 (b) | ... |
| Virginia | 6.0 | —————Flat Rate————— | | 1 | 6.0 (x) | ... |
| Washington | | _____ See Note _____ | | | | |
| West Virginia | 9.0 | —————Flat Rate————— | | 1 | 9.0 | ... |
| Wisconsin | 7.9 | —————Flat Rate————— | | 1 | 7.9 | ... |
| Wyoming | | _____ See Note _____ | | | | |
| Dist. of Columbia | 9.975 (y) | —————Flat Rate————— | | | 9.975 (y) | ... |

See footnotes at end of table.

# RANGE OF STATE CORPORATE INCOME TAX RATES — Continued

*Source:* Compiled by the Federation of Tax Administrators from various sources. February 2000.

★ — Yes

. . . — No

*Note:* Michigan imposes a single business tax (sometimes described as a business activities tax or value added tax) of 2.2% on the sum of federal taxable income of the business, compensation paid to employees, dividends, interest, royalties paid and other items. Similarly, Texas imposes a franchise tax of 4.5% of earned surplus. Nevada, Washington, and Wyoming do not have state corporate income taxes.

(a) Rates listed include the corporate tax rate applied to financial institutions or excise taxes based on income. Some states have other taxes based upon the value of deposits or shares.

(b) Minimum tax is $50. In North Dakota (banks), $10 in Oregon, $250 in Rhode Island, $500 per location in South Dakota (banks), $100 in Utah, $250 in Vermont.

(c) Minimum tax is $800. The tax rate on S-Corporations is 1.5% (3.5% for banks).

(d) Or 3.1 mills per dollar of capital stock and surplus (maximum tax $1 million or $250.

(e) The marginal rate decreases over 4 brackets ranging from $20 to $650 million in taxable income. Building and loan associations are taxed at a flat 8.7%.

(f) Or 3.3% Alternative Minimum Tax. An exemption of $5,000 is allowed.

(g) Capital gains are taxed at 4%. There is also an alternative tax of 0.5% of gross annual sales.

(h) Minimum tax is $20. An additional tax of $10 is imposed on each return.

(i) Includes a 2.5% personal property replacement tax.

(j) Consists of 3.4% on income from sources within the state plus a 4.5% supplemental income tax.

(k) Fifty percent of the federal income tax is deductible.

(l) Plus a surtax of 3.35% (2.125% for banks) taxable income in excess of $50,000 ($25,000).

(m) Or a 27% tax on Federal Alternative Minimum Taxable Income.

(n) Rate includes a 14% surtax, as does the following: an additional tax of $7.00 per $1,000 on taxable tangible property (or net worth allocable to state, for intangible property corporations); minimum tax of $456.

(o) Plus a 5.8% tax on any Alternative Minimum Taxable Income over the base tax.

(p) A 7% tax on taxpayers using water's edge combination. Minimum tax is $50.

(q) Plus a 0.50 percent tax on the enterprise base (total compensation, interest and dividends paid). Business profits tax imposed on both corporations and unincorporated associations.

(r) The rate reported in the table is the business franchise tax rate. The minimum tax is $200. Corporations not subject to the franchise tax are subject to a 7.25% income tax. Banks other than savings institutions are subject to the franchise tax. S-Corporations are subject to an entity level tax of 2.0%. Corporations with net income under $100,000 are taxed at 7.5%.

(s) Or 1.78 (0.1 for banks) mills per dollar of capital (up to $350,000; or 3.0% of the minimum taxable income); or a minimum of $100 to $1,500 depending on payroll size ($250 plus 2.5% surtax for banks); if any of these is greater than the tax computed on net income. An additional tax of 0.9 mills per dollar of subsidiary capital is imposed on corporations. Small corporations with income under $200,000 pay tax of 7.5% on all income.

(t) Financial institutions are also subject to a tax equal to $30 per one million in assets.

(u) Or 4.0 mills times the value of the taxpayer's issued and outstanding share of stock with a maximum payment of $150,000. An additional litter tax is imposed equal to 0.11% on the first $50,000 of taxable income, 0.22% on income over $50,000; or 0.14 mills on net worth.

(v) For banks, the alternative tax is $2.50 per $10,000 of capital stock ($100 minimum).

(w) Savings and Loans are taxed at a 6% rate.

(x) State and national banks subject to the state's franchise tax on net capital is exempt from the income tax.

(y)Minimum tax is $100. Includes surtax. Tax rate scheduled to decrease to 9.0% for tax years beginning after 2002.

(z) Minimum tax of $50. Tax rate scheduled to fall for tax years 2001 and beyond, if revenue meets certain targeted levels.

## Table 6.26
## STATE SEVERANCE TAXES: 2000

| State | Title and application of tax (a) | Rate |
|---|---|---|
| Alabama | Iron Ore Mining Tax | $.03/ton |
| | Forest Products Severance Tax | Varies by species and ultimate use. |
| | Oil and Gas Conservation & Regulation of Production Tax | 2% of gross value at point of production, of all oil and gas produced. 1% of the gross value (for a 5-year period from the date production begins) for well, for which the initial permit issued by the Oil and Gas Board is dated on or after July 1, 1996 and before July 1, 2002, except a replacement well for which the initial permit was dated before July 1, 1996 |
| | Oil and Gas Privilege Tax on Production | 8% of gross value at point of production; 4% of gross value at point of incremental production resulting from a qualified enhanced recovery project; 4% if wells produce 25 bbl. or less oil per day or 200,000 cu. ft. or less gas per day; 6% of gross value at point of production for certain on-shore and off-shore wells. A 50% rate reduction for wells permitted by the oil and gas board on or after July 1, 1996 and before July 1, 2002 for 5 years from initial production, except for replacement wells for which the initial permit was dated before July 1, 1996. |
| | Coal Severance Tax | $.135/ton |
| | Coal and Lignite Severance Tax | $.20/ton in addition to coal severance tax. |
| Alaska | Fisheries Business Tax | 1% to 5% of fish value based on type of fish and processing. |
| | Fishery Resource Landing Tax | 3% of the value of the fishery resource at the place of landing for a established commercial fish species; 1% of the value of the of the fishery resource at the place of landing for a developing commercial fish species. |
| | Seafood Marketing Assessment | .03% on all commercial fish species. |
| | Oil and Gas Properties Production Tax | (Oil) The greater of either $0.80/bbl for old crude oil ($0.60 for some older fields) or 15% of gross value at the production point, multiplied by the Economic Limit Factor; (Gas) The greater of either $0.64/1000 cu. ft. of gas or 10% of gross value at the production point, multiplied by the Economic Limit Factor; and conservation surcharges of $.03 cents per barrel, with an additional $.05 cents per barrel as needed to maintain a $50 million balance in the oil and hazardous substance response fund. |
| | Salmon Marketing Tax | 1% of the value of salmon that is removed or transferred. |
| Arizona* | Severance Tax (b) | 2.5% of net severance base for mining; $1.50/1000 board ft. ($2.13 for pondersoa pine) for timbering. |
| Arkansas | Natural Resources Severance Tax | Separate rate for each substance. |
| | Oil and Gas Conservation Tax | Maximum 25 mills/bbl. of oil and 5 mills/1,000 cu. ft. of gas. (c) |
| California | Oil and Gas Production Tax | Rate determined annually by Department of Conservation. (d) |
| Colorado | Severance Tax (e) | Taxable years commencing prior to July 1, 1999, 2.25% of gross income exceeding $11 million for metallic minerals and taxable years commencing after July 1,1999, 2.25% of gross income exceeding $19 million for metallic minerals; on or after July 1,1999, $.05/ton for each ton exceeding 625,000 tons each quarter for molybdenum ore; 2% to 5% based on gross income for oil, gas, CO2, and coalbed methane; after July 1,1999, $.36/ton adjusted by the producers' prices index for each ton exceeding 300,000 tons each quarter for coal; and 4% of gross proceeds on production exceeding 15,000 tons per day for oil shale. |
| Florida | Oil and Gas Conservation Levy | Maximum 1.5 mills/$1 of market value at wellhead. (f) |
| | Oil, Gas and Sulfur Production Tax | 5% of gross value for small well oil, and 8% of gross value for all other, and an additional 12.5% for escaped oil; the gas base rate times the gas base adjustment rate each fiscal year for gas; and the sulfur base rate times the sulfur base rate adjustment each fiscal year for sulfur. (g) |
| | Solid Minerals Tax (h) | 8% of the value of the minerals severed, except phosphate rock (rate computed annually at $1.08/ton times the changes in the producer price index) and heavy minerals (rate computed annually at a base rate of $1.34/ton times the base rate adjustment). |
| Idaho | Ore Severance Tax | 2% of net value |
| | Oil and Gas Production Tax | Maximum of 5 mills/bbl. of oil and 5 mills/50,000 cu. ft. of gas. (c) |
| | Additional Oil and Gas Production Tax | 2% of market value at site of production. |
| Illinois | Timber Fee | 4% of purchase price (i) |

See footnotes at end of table.

# STATE SEVERANCE TAXES — Continued

| State | Title and application of tax (a) | Rate |
|-------|-------------------------------|------|
| Indiana | Petroleum Production Tax (j) | 1% of value or $.24 per barrel for oil or $.03 per 1000 cu. ft. of gas, whichever is greater. |
| Kansas | Severance Tax (k) | 8% of gross value of oil and gas, less property tax credit of 3.67%; $1/ton of coal. |
| | Oil and Gas Conservation Tax | 27.27 mills/bbl. crude oil or petroleum marketed or used each month; 5.83 mills/1,000 cu. ft. of gas sold or marketed each month. |
| | Mined-Land Conservation & Reclamation Tax | $50, plus per ton fee of between $.03 and $.10. |
| Kentucky | Oil Production Tax | 4.5% of market value |
| | Coal Severance Tax | 4.5% of gross value, less transportation expenses |
| | Natural Resource Severance Tax (l) | 4.5% of gross value, less transportation expenses |
| Louisiana | Natural Resources Severance Tax | Rate varies according to substance. |
| | Oil Field Site Restoration Fee | Rate varies according to type of well and production. |
| | Freshwater Mussel Tax | 5% of revenues from the sale of whole freshwater mussels, at the point of first sale. |
| Maine | Mining Excise Tax | The greater of a tax on facilities and equipment or a tax on gross proceeds. |
| Maryland | Mine Reclamation Surcharge | $.15/ton of coal removed by open-pit, strip or deep mine methods. Of the $.15, $.06 is remitted to the county from which the coal was removed. |
| Michigan | Gas and Oil Severance Tax | 5% (gas), 6.6% (oil) and 4% (oil from stripper wells and marginal properties) of gross cash market value of the total production. Maximum additional fee of 1% of gross cash market value on all oil and gas produced in state in previous year. |
| Minnesota | Taconite and Iron Sulfides | $2.141 per ton of concentrates or pellets |
| | Direct Reduced Iron | 2.141 per ton of concentrates plus an additional $.03 per ton for each 1% that the iron content exceeds 72% |
| Mississippi | (m) Oil and Gas Severance Tax | 6% of value at point of gas production; 3.5% of gross value of occluded natural gas from coal seams at point of production for well's first five years; also, maximum 35 mills/bbl. oil or 4 mills/1,000 cu. ft. gas (Oil and Gas Board maintenance tax). 6% of value at point of oil production; 3% of value at production when enhanced oil recovery method used. |
| | Timber Severance Tax | Varies depending on type of wood and ultimate use. |
| | Salt Severance Tax | 3% of value of entire production in state. |
| Missouri | Assessment on Surface Coal Mining Permittees | $.45/ton for first 50,000 tons sold, shipped or otherwise disposed of in calendar year, and $.30/ton for next 50,000 tons. Whenever Coal Mine Land Reclamation Fund balance is less than $7 million, $.25/ton for first 50,000 tons and $.15/ton for second 50,000 tons. Whenever Fund is less than $2 million, $.30/ton for first 50,000 tons and $.20 for the second 50,000 tons. |
| Montana* | Coal Severance Tax | Varies by quality of coal and type of mine. |
| | Metalliferous Mines License Tax (n) | Progressive rate, taxed on amounts in excess of $250,000. For concentrate shipped to smelter, mill or reduction work, 1.81%. Gold, silver or any platinum group metal shipped to refinery, 1.6%. |
| | Oil or Gas Conservation Tax | Maximum 0.3% on the market value of each barrel of crude petroleum oil or 10,000 cu. ft. of natural gas produced, saved and marketed or stored within or exported from the state. (O) |
| | Oil and Natural Gas Production Tax | Varies according to the type of well and type of production. |
| | Micaceous Minerals License Tax | $.05/ton |
| | Cement License Tax (p) | $.22/ton of cement, $.05/ton of cement, plaster, gypsum or gypsum products. |
| | Mineral Mining Tax | $25 plus 0.5% of gross value greater than $5,000. For talc, $25 plus 4% of gross value greater than $625. For coal, $25 plus 0.40% of gross value greater than $6,250. For vermiculite, $25 plus 2% of gross value greater than $1,250. For limestone, $25 plus 10% of gross value greater than $250. For industrial garnets, $25 plus 1% of gross value greater than $2,500.00 |
| Nebraska | Oil and Gas Severance Tax | 3% of value of nonstripper oil and natural gas; 2% of value of stripper oil. |
| | Oil and Gas Conservation Tax | Maximum 7 mills/$1 of value at wellhead, as of January 1, 2000 (c) |
| | Uranium Tax | 2% of gross value over $5 million. |

See footnotes at end of table.

## STATE SEVERANCE TAXES — Continued

| State | Title and application of tax (a) | Rate |
|---|---|---|
| Nevada* | Minerals Extraction Tax | Between 2% and 5% of net proceeds of each geographically separate extractive operation, based on ratio of net proceeds to gross proceeds of whole operation. |
| | Oil and Gas Conservation Tax | $50/mills/bbl. of oil and 50 mills/50,000 cu. ft. of gas. |
| New Hampshire | Refined Petroleum Products Tax | 0.1% of fair market value |
| | Excavation Tax | $.02 per cubic yard of earth excavated. |
| | Excavation Activity Tax | Replaces real property tax on the land area that has been excavated and not reclaimed. The assessed per acre value and tax varies depending upon municipality. |
| | Timber Tax | 10% of stumpage value |
| New Mexico* | Resources Excise Tax (q) | Varies according to substance. |
| | Severance Tax (q) | Varies according to substance. |
| | Oil and Gas Severance Tax | 3.75% of value of oil, other liquid hydrocarbons, natural gas and carbon dioxide. 1.875% of value of oil and other liquid hydrocarbons produced from a qualified enhanced recovery project. |
| | Oil and Gas Privilege Tax | 3.15% of value of oil, other liquid hydrocarbons and carbon dioxide. 4% of value of natural gas. |
| | Natural Gas Processor's Tax | 0.45% of value of products. |
| | Oil and Gas Ad Valorem Production Tax | Varies, based on property tax in district of production. |
| | Oil and Gas Conservation Tax (r) | 0.19% of value. |
| North Carolina | Oil and Gas Conservation Tax | Maximum 5 mills/barrel of oil and 0.5 mill/1,000 cu. ft. of gas. |
| | Primary Forest Product Assessment Tax | Varies according to species. |
| North Dakota | Oil Gross Production Tax | 5% of gross value at well. |
| | Gas Gross Production Tax | $.04/1000 cu.ft. of gas produced (the rate is subject to a a gas rate adjustment each fiscal year). |
| | Coal Severance Tax | $.75/ton plus $.02/ton. (s) |
| | Oil Extraction Tax | 6.5% of gross value at well (with exceptions due to date of well completion, production volumes and production incentives). |
| Ohio | Resource Severance Tax | $.10/bbl. of oil; $.025/1,000 cu. ft. of natural gas; $.04/ton of salt; $.02/ ton of sand, gravel, limestone and dolomite; $.09/ton of coal; and $0.01/ ton of clay, sandstone or conglomerate, shale, gypsum or quartzite. |
| Oklahoma | Title and application of tax (a) Oil, Gas and Mineral Gross Production Tax and Petroleum Excise Tax (t) | Rate; 0.75% levied on asphalt and metals. 7% casinghead gas and natural gas , as well as 0.95% being levied on crude oil, casinghead gas and natural gas. Oil Gross Production Tax is now a variable rate tax, beginning with January 1999 production, at the following rates based on the average price of Oklahoma oil: a) If the average price equals or exceeds $17/bbl, the tax shall be 7%; b) If the average price is less than $17/bbl, but is equal to or exceeds $14/bbl, the tax shall be 4%; c) If the average price is less than $14/bbl, the tax shall be 1%. |
| Oregon | Forest Products Harvest Tax | $3.19/1000 board ft. harvested from public and private land. |
| | Oil and Gas Production Tax | 6% of gross value at well. |
| | Privilege Tax on Eastern Oregon Timber | 1.1% of immediate harvest value from privately owned land. |
| | Privilege Tax on Western Oregon Timber | 1.8% of stumpage value from privately owned land. |
| South Dakota | Precious Metals Severance Tax | $4 per ounce of gold severed plus additional tax depending on price of gold; 10% on net profits or royalties from sale of precious metals, and 8% of royalty value. |
| | Energy Minerals Severance Tax (u) | 4.5% of taxable value of any energy minerals. |
| | Conservation Tax | 2.4 mills of taxable value of any energy minerals. |
| Tennessee | Oil and Gas Severance Tax | 3% of sales price |
| | Coal Severance Tax | $.20/ton |
| | (v) | |
| Texas | Gas Production Tax | 7.5% of market value. |
| | Oil Production Tax | The greater of 4.6% of market value or $.046/bbl. 2.3% of market value for oil produced from qualified enhanced recovery projects. |
| | Sulphur Production Tax | $1.03/long ton or fraction thereof. |
| | Cement Production Tax | $.0275/100 lbs. or fraction thereof. |
| | Oil-Field Cleanup Regulatory Fees | 5/16 of $.01/barrel; 1/30 of $.01/1000 cubic feet of gas. (w) |
| Utah | Metalliferous Minerals Tax | 2.6% of taxable value for metals. |
| | Oil and Gas Tax | 3% of value for the first $13 per barrel of oil, 5% from $13.01 and above; 3% of value for first $1.50/mcf, 5% from $1.51 and above; and 4% of taxable value of natural gas liquids. |
| | Oil and Gas Conservation Tax | $.2 of market value at wellhead. |

# STATE SEVERANCE TAXES — Continued

| State | Title and application of tax (a) | Rate |
|---|---|---|
| Virginia* | Forest Products Tax | Varies by species and ultimate use. |
| | Coal Surface Mining Reclamation Tax (x) | Varies depending on balance of Coal Surface Mining Reclamation Fund. |
| Washington | Uranium and Thorium Milling Tax | $0.02/per kilogram. |
| | Enhanced Food Fish Tax | 0.09% to 5.65% of value (depending on species) at point of landing. |
| | Timber Excise Tax | 5% of stumpage value for harvests on public and private lands. |
| West Virginia | Natural Resource Severance Taxes | Coal, state rate is greater of 4.65% or $.75 per ton. Local rate is .35%. Special state rates for coal from new low seam mines. For seams between 37" and 45" the rate is greater of 1.65% or $.75/ton. For seams less than 37" the rate is greater of .65% or $.75/ton. Limestone or sandstone quarried or mined, 5% of gross value. Oil, 5% of gross value. Natural gas, 5% of gross value. Timber, 3.22% of gross value. Other natural resources, 5% of gross value. |
| Wisconsin | Mining Net Proceeds Tax | Progressive net proceeds tax ranging from 3% to 15%. |
| | Oil and Gas Severance Tax | 7% of market value of oil or gas at the mouth of the well. |
| Wyoming | Severance Tax | Severance Tax is defined as an excise tax imposed on the present and continuing privilege of removing, extracting, severing or producing any mineral in this state. Except as otherwise provided by W.S. 39-14-205 (Tax Exemptions), The total Severance Tax on crude oil, lease condensate or natural gas shall be six percent (6%), comprising one and one-half percent (1.5% ) imposed by the Wyoming constitution article 15, section 19 and four and one-half percent (4.5%) imposed by Wyoming statute. The tax shall be distributed as as provided in W.S. 39-14-211 and is imposed as follows: i. One and one-half percent (1.5%);plus ii. One-half percent (.5%); plus iii. Two percent (2%); plus iv. Two percent (2%). Severance Tax is applied to the taxable value of crude oil, lease condensate or natural gas. The taxable value is the gross sales value of the product less Federal, State or Tribal Royalties paid and less allowable transportation deductions. If the product produced is natural gas, an additional deduction is allowed for processing. Rates vary from 1.50% to 6.0% on different grades of oil. Taxes on coal and other minerals varies from 2% |

*Source*: The Council of State Governments' survey, January 2000, except as noted by * where information is from *The Book of the States 1998-99*.

(a) Application of tax is same as that of title unless otherwise indicated by a footnote.

(b) Timber, metalliferous minerals.

(c) Actual rate set by administrative actions.

(d) For 1999, $.0326159/bbl of oil or 10,000 cu. ft. of natural gas.

(e) Metallic minerals, molybdenum ore, coal, oil shale, oil and gas.

(f) As of January 31, 2000, set at 1.2 mills/$1.

(g) Through June 30, 1997, the gas production tax was $.106/mcf of gas and the sulfur production tax was $2.72/long ton of sulfur.

(h) Clay, gravel, phosphate rock, lime, shells, stone, sand, heavy minerals and rare earths.

(i) Buyer deducts amount from payment to grower; amount forwarded to Department of Conservation.

(j) Petroleum, oil, gas and other hydrocarbons.

(k) Coal, oil and gas.

(l) Coal and oil excepted.

(m) State also has two related taxes; Mining Occupation Tax and Net Proceeds Tax. Also selected counties must impose an Aggregate Materials Tax of $.10/cubic yard or $.07/ton on materials produced in the county.

(n) Metals, precious and semi-precious stones and gems.

(o) Currently, the tax is levied at the rate of 0.3%.

(p) Cement and gypsum or allied products.

(q) Natural resources except oil, natural gas, liquid hydrocarbons or carbon dioxide.

(r) Oil, coal, gas, liquid hydrocarbons, geothermal energy, carbon dioxide and uranium.

(s) Rate reduced by 50 percent if burned in cogeneration facility using renewable resources as fuel to generate at least 10 percent of its energy output. Between June 30, 1995 and July 1, 2000, the rate is reduced by 50% for coal mined for out-of-state shipment. Between June 30, 1999 and July 1, 2003, the rate is reduced by 50% for coal burned in coal-fired boilers where the generating station has a total capacity of not more than 210 megawatts.

(t) Asphalt and ores bearing lead, zinc, jack, gold, silver, copper or petroleum or other crude oil or other mineral oil, natural gas or casinghead gas and uranium ore.

(u) Any mineral fuel used in the production of energy, including coal, lignite, petroleum, oil, natural gas, uranium and thorium.

(v) Counties and municipalities also authorized to levy severance taxes on sand, gravel, sandstone, chert and limestone and a privilege tax on nuclear materials.

(w) Fees will not be collected when Oil-Field Cleanup Fund reaches $10 million, but will again be collected when fund falls below $6 million.

(x) Until 2003, any county and city may adopt a license tax at a rate not over 1% of gross receipts on persons engaged in the business of severing coal or gases.

(y) Currently, rate is .7 mills/$1.

## Table 6.27
## NATIONAL SUMMARY OF STATE GOVERNMENT TAX REVENUE, BY TYPE OF TAX: 1996 to 1998

| Tax source | Amount (in thousands of dollars) | | | Percent change year-to-year | | Percent distribution, 1997 | Per capita, 1997 (in dollars) |
|---|---|---|---|---|---|---|---|
| | 1998 | 1997 | 1996 | 1997 to 1998 | 1996 to 1997 | | |
| Total Collections ...................... | $474,990,564 | $443,335,463 | $418,970,791 | 6.7 | 5.5 | 100.0 | $1,659.8 |
| Sales & gross receipts tax ............. | 227,404,841 | 215,737,108 | 205,687,307 | 5.1 | 4.7 | 47.9 | 807.7 |
| General .......................................... | 156,061,702 | 147,068,715 | 139,278,702 | 5.8 | 4.3 | 32.9 | 550.6 |
| Selective ....................................... | 71,343,139 | 68,668,393 | 66,408,605 | 3.7 | 3.3 | 15.0 | 257.1 |
| Motor fuels sales ....................... | 28,330,413 | 27,131,805 | 25,981,234 | 4.2 | 5.2 | 6.0 | 101.6 |
| Insurance premium .................... | 9,150,229 | 9,219,106 | 9,057,273 | -0.8 | 1.8 | 1.9 | 34.5 |
| Public utilities .......................... | 8,792,973 | 8,604,806 | 8,600,938 | 2.1 | 0.0 | 1.9 | 32.2 |
| Tobacco products ...................... | 7,746,662 | 7,451,157 | 7,337,848 | 3.8 | 1.5 | 1.6 | 27.9 |
| Alcoholic beverage sales .......... | 3,767,473 | 3,697,849 | 3,666,690 | 1.8 | 0.8 | 0.8 | 13.8 |
| Amusement ................................. | 2,130,240 | 1,899,362 | 1,862,391 | 10.8 | 1.9 | 0.4 | 7.1 |
| Parimutuels ................................ | 405,298 | 423,526 | 458,866 | 4.5 | -8.3 | 0.1 | 1.6 |
| Other selective sales ................. | 11,019,851 | 10,240,782 | 9,443,365 | 7.1 | 7.8 | 2.3 | 38.3 |
| Licenses ......................................... | 29,682,659 | 28,216,617 | 27,036,285 | 4.9 | 4.2 | 6.2 | 105.6 |
| Motor vehicle .............................. | 13,672,480 | 12,965,303 | 12,740,349 | 5.2 | 1.7 | 2.9 | 48.5 |
| Occupation and business, NEC ... | 6,179,621 | 5,822,580 | 5,610,852 | 5.8 | 3.6 | 1.3 | 21.8 |
| Corporation in general ................ | 6,127,611 | 5,882,411 | 5,158,425 | 4.0 | 12.3 | 1.3 | 22.0 |
| Motor vehicle operators ............. | 1,260,931 | 1,183,609 | 1,166,843 | 6.1 | 1.4 | 0.3 | 4.4 |
| Hunting and fishing .................... | 1,037,831 | 1,014,527 | 989,955 | 2.2 | 2.4 | 0.2 | 3.8 |
| Public utility .............................. | 358,560 | 343,414 | 372,725 | 4.2 | 8.5 | 0.1 | 1.3 |
| Alcoholic beverage ..................... | 302,257 | 305,801 | 307,061 | 1.2 | -0.4 | 0.1 | 1.1 |
| Amusement .................................. | 299,858 | 277,407 | 240,872 | 7.5 | 13.2 | 0.1 | 1.0 |
| Other ............................................ | 443,510 | 421,565 | 449,203 | 4.9 | 6.6 | 0.1 | 1.6 |
| Individual income .......................... | 161,249,928 | 144,668,011 | 134,683,257 | 10.3 | 6.9 | 33.9 | 541.6 |
| Corporation net income .................. | 31,108,628 | 30,661,951 | 29,315,684 | 1.4 | 4.4 | 6.5 | 114.8 |
| Property .......................................... | 10,661,670 | 10,297,108 | 9,973,524 | 3.4 | 3.1 | 2.2 | 38.6 |
| Death and gift ................................. | 6,940,007 | 5,913,125 | 5,320,098 | 14.8 | 10.0 | 1.5 | 22.1 |
| Documentary and stock transfer .... | 3,544,117 | 2,698,557 | 2,559,338 | 23.9 | 5.2 | 0.7 | 10.1 |
| Severance ....................................... | 4,158,897 | 4,863,877 | 4,112,485 | -17.0 | 15.4 | 0.9 | 18.2 |
| Other ............................................... | 239,817 | 279,109 | 282,813 | -16.4 | -1.3 | 0.1 | 1.0 |

*Source:* U.S. Department of Commerce, Bureau of the Census.
*Note:* Because of rounding, detail may not add to totals. Population figures as of July 1, 1997 were used to calculate per capita amounts; see Table 6.32.

## Table 6.28
## SUMMARY OF STATE GOVERNMENT TAX REVENUE, BY STATE:
## 1995 TO 1997

| | Amount (in thousands of dollars) | | | Percent change year-to-year | | |
| | | | | 1996 to | 1995 to | Per capita, 1997 |
| State | 1997 | 1996 | 1995 | 1997 | 1996 | (in dollars) |
|---|---|---|---|---|---|---|
| United States ................ | $443,335,463 | $418,970,791 | $399,147,521 | 5.5 | 4.7 | $1,659.8 |
| Alabama ........................... | 5,484,161 | 5,257,771 | 5,077,827 | 4.1 | 3.4 | 1,269.8 |
| Alaska .............................. | 1,619,110 | 1,519,082 | 1,922,463 | 6.2 | -26.6 | 2,658.6 |
| Arizona ............................ | 6,833,806 | 6,409,395 | 6,223,489 | 6.2 | 2.9 | 1,500.3 |
| Arkansas .......................... | 3,776,600 | 3,708,744 | 3,391,785 | 1.8 | 8.5 | 1,496.9 |
| California ......................... | 61,666,886 | 57,746,664 | 53,269,075 | 6.4 | 7.8 | 1,911.1 |
| Colorado .......................... | 5,290,131 | 4,820,163 | 4,531,366 | 8.9 | 6.0 | 1,358.9 |
| Connecticut ...................... | 8,145,787 | 7,830,171 | 7,474,119 | 3.9 | 4.5 | 2,491.1 |
| Delaware .......................... | 1,743,234 | 1,688,349 | 1,594,818 | 3.1 | 5.5 | 2,381.5 |
| Florida ............................. | 21,080,120 | 19,699,255 | 18,564,650 | 6.6 | 5.8 | 1,438.5 |
| Georgia ............................ | 10,897,538 | 10,292,371 | 9,486,639 | 5.6 | 7.8 | 1,455.7 |
| Hawaii ............................. | 3,087,946 | 3,079,404 | 2,874,496 | 0.3 | 6.7 | 2,601.5 |
| Idaho ............................... | 1,960,505 | 1,857,006 | 1,733,120 | 5.3 | 6.7 | 1,620.3 |
| Illinois ............................. | 18,544,570 | 17,277,319 | 16,589,789 | 6.8 | 4.0 | 1,558.9 |
| Indiana ............................ | 9,100,842 | 8,437,031 | 8,045,753 | 7.3 | 4.6 | 1,552.0 |
| Iowa ................................ | 4,686,244 | 4,440,540 | 4,403,428 | 5.2 | 0.8 | 1,643.1 |
| Kansas .............................. | 4,229,721 | 3,978,761 | 3,765,488 | 5.9 | 5.4 | 1,630.0 |
| Kentucky .......................... | 6,818,992 | 6,489,256 | 6,284,623 | 4.8 | 3.2 | 1,744.9 |
| Louisiana ......................... | 5,646,255 | 4,906,283 | 4,676,969 | 13.1 | 4.7 | 1,297.4 |
| Maine .............................. | 2,019,491 | 1,896,564 | 1,812,574 | 6.1 | 4.4 | 1,626.0 |
| Maryland ......................... | 8,604,406 | 8,166,692 | 8,060,982 | 5.1 | 1.3 | 1,689.1 |
| Massachusetts ................. | 13,305,471 | 12,455,370 | 11,601,135 | 6.4 | 6.9 | 2,174.8 |
| Michigan ......................... | 19,855,941 | 19,128,687 | 17,723,494 | 3.7 | 7.3 | 2,031.5 |
| Minnesota ........................ | 11,223,269 | 10,242,646 | 9,327,886 | 8.7 | 8.9 | 2,395.1 |
| Mississippi ...................... | 4,016,549 | 3,860,523 | 3,599,244 | 3.9 | 6.8 | 1,470.7 |
| Missouri .......................... | 7,815,966 | 7,210,351 | 6,751,959 | 7.7 | 6.4 | 1,446.9 |
| Montana .......................... | 1,308,855 | 1,256,416 | 1,214,152 | 4.0 | 3.4 | 1,489.0 |
| Nebraska .......................... | 2,548,174 | 2,369,462 | 2,219,725 | 7.0 | 6.3 | 1,537.8 |
| Nevada ............................ | 3,034,156 | 2,889,254 | 2,698,343 | 4.8 | 6.6 | 1,809.3 |
| New Hampshire .............. | 914,847 | 837,092 | 918,461 | 8.5 | -9.7 | 779.9 |
| New Jersey ....................... | 14,414,778 | 14,384,897 | 13,606,950 | 0.2 | 5.4 | 1,790.0 |
| New Mexico ..................... | 3,322,410 | 3,060,637 | 2,844,484 | 7.9 | 7.1 | 1,920.5 |
| New York ........................ | 34,864,623 | 34,150,039 | 34,294,492 | 2.0 | -0.4 | 1,922.3 |
| North Carolina ................ | 12,678,199 | 11,882,318 | 11,425,714 | 6.3 | 2.8 | 1,707.5 |
| North Dakota .................. | 1,064,010 | 985,327 | 958,725 | 7.4 | 2.7 | 1,659.9 |
| Ohio ................................ | 16,417,761 | 15,649,492 | 15,186,174 | 4.7 | 3.0 | 1,467.7 |
| Oklahoma ........................ | 5,060,601 | 4,617,688 | 4,416,463 | 8.8 | 4.4 | 1,525.7 |
| Oregon ............................ | 4,946,304 | 4,415,725 | 4,286,038 | 10.7 | 2.9 | 1,525.2 |
| Pennsylvania ................... | 19,377,456 | 18,295,012 | 18,262,139 | 5.6 | 0.2 | 1,612.1 |
| Rhode Island ................... | 1,644,047 | 1,549,195 | 1,490,340 | 5.8 | 3.8 | 1,665.7 |
| South Carolina ................ | 5,381,412 | 5,113,034 | 4,763,097 | 5.0 | 6.8 | 1,431.2 |
| South Dakota ................... | 768,491 | 730,251 | 694,037 | 5.0 | 5.0 | 1,041.3 |
| Tennessee ........................ | 6,616,361 | 6,184,562 | 5,907,721 | 6.5 | 4.5 | 1,232.6 |
| Texas ............................... | 23,024,628 | 21,270,839 | 20,288,774 | 7.6 | 4.6 | 1,184.5 |
| Utah ................................ | 3,010,696 | 2,913,960 | 2,675,502 | 3.2 | 8.2 | 1,462.2 |
| Vermont .......................... | 899,161 | 841,029 | 801,376 | 6.5 | 4.7 | 1,526.6 |
| Virginia ........................... | 9,627,591 | 8,900,413 | 8,783,939 | 7.6 | 1.3 | 1,429.7 |
| Washington ...................... | 11,202,296 | 10,586,463 | 10,195,584 | 5.5 | 3.7 | 1,996.8 |
| West Virginia .................. | 2,905,947 | 2,770,888 | 2,731,907 | 4.6 | 1.4 | 1,600.2 |
| Wisconsin ........................ | 10,186,768 | 10,292,434 | 9,029,488 | -1.0 | 12.3 | 1,970.4 |
| Wyoming ......................... | 662,350 | 625,966 | 666,725 | 5.5 | -6.5 | 1,379.9 |

*Source:* U.S. Department of Commerce, Bureau of the Census.

**Table 6.29**
**STATE GOVERNMENT TAX REVENUE, BY TYPE OF TAX: 1997**
**(In thousands of dollars)**

| State | Total | Sales and gross receipts | Licenses | Individual income | Corporation net income | Severance | Property | Death and gift | Documentary and stock transfer | Other |
|---|---|---|---|---|---|---|---|---|---|---|
| United States | $443,335,463 | $215,737,108 | $28,216,617 | $144,668,011 | $30,661,951 | $4,863,877 | 10,297,108 | $5,913,125 | $2,698,557 | $279,109 |
| Alabama | 5,484,161 | 2,866,477 | 424,165 | 1,687,599 | 226,616 | 80,238 | 131,229 | 44,511 | 23,326 | 0 |
| Alaska | 1,619,110 | 96,014 | 77,924 | 0 | 331,337 | 1,058,602 | 53,567 | 1,666 | 0 | 0 |
| Arizona | 6,833,806 | 3,803,450 | 437,200 | 1,668,414 | 600,890 | 0 | 256,879 | 66,973 | 0 | 0 |
| Arkansas | 3,776,600 | 2,017,650 | 221,790 | 1,246,600 | 229,982 | 13,450 | 8,355 | 18,555 | 16,831 | 3,387 |
| California | 61,666,886 | 25,222,055 | 2,962,520 | 23,272,871 | 5,803,652 | 37,416 | 3,611,595 | 756,777 | 0 | 0 |
| Colorado | 5,290,131 | 2,178,700 | 261,406 | 2,560,337 | 224,275 | 30,274 | 0 | 34,641 | 0 | 498 |
| Connecticut | 8,145,787 | 4,164,892 | 341,262 | 2,807,391 | 530,430 | 0 | 1 | 226,837 | 74,974 | 0 |
| Delaware | 1,743,234 | 253,405 | 578,563 | 663,111 | 172,562 | 0 | 0 | 31,755 | 43,838 | 0 |
| Florida | 21,080,120 | 16,081,231 | 1,370,177 | 0 | 1,232,731 | 75,844 | 787,614 | 536,523 | 996,000 | 0 |
| Georgia | 10,897,538 | 4,905,464 | 405,025 | 4,741,200 | 726,321 | 0 | 38,155 | 60,296 | 190 | 20,887 |
| Hawaii | 3,087,946 | 1,925,971 | 89,876 | 976,579 | 67,570 | 0 | 0 | 22,169 | 5,781 | 0 |
| Idaho | 1,960,505 | 923,985 | 147,586 | 711,657 | 138,277 | 3,021 | 0 | 4,052 | 0 | 31,927 |
| Illinois | 18,544,570 | 8,796,140 | 1,215,100 | 6,286,770 | 1,803,931 | 0 | 204,263 | 199,423 | 38,943 | 0 |
| Indiana | 9,100,842 | 4,131,854 | 193,720 | 3,750,826 | 904,265 | 611 | 4,203 | 115,363 | 0 | 0 |
| Iowa | 4,686,244 | 2,228,431 | 421,385 | 1,719,566 | 221,041 | 0 | 0 | 88,213 | 7,608 | 0 |
| Kansas | 4,229,721 | 2,007,052 | 211,755 | 1,512,816 | 291,080 | 87,185 | 43,804 | 76,029 | 0 | 0 |
| Kentucky | 6,818,992 | 3,194,113 | 427,137 | 2,205,023 | 292,753 | 186,642 | 414,857 | 95,287 | 3,180 | 0 |
| Louisiana | 5,646,255 | 2,759,050 | 435,603 | 1,560,048 | 380,155 | 408,340 | 25,324 | 77,735 | 0 | 0 |
| Maine | 2,019,491 | 964,667 | 117,339 | 771,810 | 97,146 | 0 | 42,216 | 14,771 | 11,542 | 0 |
| Maryland | 8,604,406 | 3,695,153 | 349,632 | 3,768,560 | 343,499 | 0 | 236,099 | 105,967 | 78,126 | 27,370 |
| Massachusetts | 13,305,471 | 4,217,418 | 431,012 | 7,181,821 | 1,213,366 | 0 | 128 | 202,707 | 59,019 | 0 |
| Michigan | 19,855,941 | 8,871,817 | 1,016,050 | 5,930,404 | 2,228,753 | 41,154 | 1,688,279 | 79,484 | 0 | 0 |
| Minnesota | 11,223,269 | 4,775,726 | 821,373 | 4,778,972 | 699,234 | 3,218 | 9,748 | 48,465 | 86,533 | 0 |
| Mississippi | 4,016,549 | 2,665,109 | 266,271 | 791,009 | 225,924 | 32,933 | 22,816 | 12,487 | 0 | 0 |
| Missouri | 7,815,966 | 3,701,961 | 562,367 | 3,038,167 | 411,045 | 114 | 15,532 | 81,160 | 0 | 5,620 |
| Montana | 1,308,855 | 274,367 | 151,322 | 406,276 | 81,999 | 93,907 | 234,906 | 14,562 | 0 | 51,516 |
| Nebraska | 2,548,174 | 1,281,350 | 164,907 | 937,297 | 137,338 | 1,806 | 4,923 | 15,231 | 5,322 | 0 |
| Nevada | 3,034,156 | 2,601,308 | 302,637 | 0 | 0 | 38,892 | 61,293 | 27,666 | 2,360 | 0 |
| New Hampshire | 914,847 | 458,732 | 120,568 | 52,682 | 208,388 | 0 | 588 | 40,557 | 33,332 | 0 |
| New Jersey | 14,414,778 | 7,192,382 | 742,208 | 4,825,411 | 1,263,979 | 0 | 2,540 | 313,447 | 74,811 | 0 |
| New Mexico | 3,322,410 | 1,806,516 | 133,707 | 747,813 | 173,205 | 409,516 | 33,815 | 17,838 | 0 | 0 |
| New York | 34,864,623 | 12,139,863 | 945,142 | 17,554,367 | 3,042,094 | 0 | 0 | 889,323 | 293,834 | 51,516 |
| North Carolina | 12,678,199 | 5,316,289 | 774,753 | 5,458,963 | 981,378 | 1,970 | 0 | 144,846 | 33,332 | 0 |
| North Dakota | 1,064,010 | 606,113 | 76,787 | 163,316 | 75,223 | 135,552 | 2,212 | 4,807 | 0 | 0 |
| Ohio | 16,417,761 | 8,055,125 | 1,355,317 | 6,141,212 | 737,363 | 9,155 | 17,614 | 101,975 | 0 | 0 |

# STATE GOVERNMENT TAX REVENUE, BY TYPE OF TAX: 1997 — Continued

| State | Total | Sales and gross receipts | Licenses | Individual income | Corporation net income | Severance | Property | Death and gift | Documentary and stock transfer | Other |
|---|---|---|---|---|---|---|---|---|---|---|
| Oklahoma | 5,060,601 | 1,940,658 | 700,643 | 1,697,600 | 221,172 | 404,050 | 0 | 80,514 | 6,885 | 9,079 |
| Oregon | 4,946,304 | 673,827 | 512,339 | 3,272,594 | 384,073 | 52,898 | 79 | 33,856 | 16,638 | 0 |
| Pennsylvania | 19,377,456 | 9,221,017 | 1,919,706 | 5,574,994 | 1,575,707 | 0 | 203,497 | 615,495 | 237,201 | 29,839 |
| Rhode Island | 1,644,047 | 813,403 | 79,856 | 639,703 | 89,198 | 0 | 4,115 | 12,614 | 5,084 | 74 |
| South Carolina | 5,381,412 | 2,735,295 | 411,179 | 1,932,992 | 239,350 | 0 | 13,604 | 28,174 | 20,818 | 0 |
| South Dakota | 768,491 | 609,401 | 93,625 | 0 | 36,888 | 6,958 | 0 | 21,488 | 131 | 0 |
| Tennessee | 6,616,361 | 5,087,032 | 737,935 | 128,189 | 479,660 | 1,124 | 0 | 60,558 | 94,926 | 26,937 |
| Texas | 23,024,628 | 18,403,991 | 3,265,491 | 0 | 0 | 1,147,660 | 0 | 207,486 | 0 | 0 |
| Utah | 3,010,696 | 1,579,769 | 90,381 | 1,127,712 | 177,415 | 25,137 | 0 | 10,282 | 0 | 11,803 |
| Vermont | 899,161 | 409,267 | 67,621 | 323,140 | 45,327 | 0 | 10,296 | 18,015 | 13,692 | 11,803 |
| Virginia | 9,627,591 | 3,766,542 | 430,751 | 4,727,791 | 425,154 | 1,715 | 21,600 | 92,163 | 102,774 | 59,101 |
| Washington | 11,202,296 | 8,289,331 | 509,656 | 0 | 0 | 82,170 | 1,926,666 | 88,469 | 306,004 | 0 |
| West Virginia | 2,905,947 | 1,514,674 | 151,441 | 786,190 | 251,230 | 176,947 | 2,780 | 17,367 | 5,318 | 0 |
| Wisconsin | 10,186,768 | 4,231,265 | 614,352 | 4,538,218 | 638,975 | 2,181 | 76,345 | 50,825 | 33,536 | 1,071 |
| Wyoming | 662,350 | 281,806 | 78,055 | 0 | 0 | 213,197 | 85,571 | 3,721 | 0 | 0 |

Source: U.S. Department of Commerce, Bureau of the Census.

# Table 6.30
## STATE GOVERNMENT SALES AND GROSS RECEIPTS TAX REVENUE: 1997
### (In thousands of dollars)

| State | Total | General sales or gross receipts | Selective sales and gross receipts Total | Motor fuels | Public utilities | Tobacco products | Insurance | Alcoholic beverages | Parimutuels | Amusements | Other |
|---|---|---|---|---|---|---|---|---|---|---|---|
| United States | $215,737,108 | $147,068,715 | $68,668,393 | $27,131,805 | $8,604,806 | $7,451,157 | $9,219,106 | $3,697,849 | $423,526 | $1,899,362 | $10,240,782 |
| Alabama | 2,866,477 | 1,505,713 | 1,360,764 | 472,814 | 414,052 | 69,882 | 155,989 | 117,004 | 4,272 | 81 | 126,670 |
| Alaska | 96,014 | 0 | 96,014 | 35,578 | 2,739 | 15,908 | 28,365 | 11,553 | 0 | 1,871 | 0 |
| Arizona | 3,803,450 | 2,855,234 | 948,216 | 504,906 | 88,138 | 169,037 | 137,661 | 45,093 | 2,607 | 774 | 0 |
| Arkansas | 2,017,650 | 1,429,445 | 588,205 | 351,525 | 0 | 94,709 | 66,150 | 26,218 | 7,211 | 577 | 41,815 |
| California | 25,222,055 | 19,973,609 | 5,248,446 | 2,822,335 | 42,642 | 672,735 | 1,284,081 | 269,613 | 90,213 | 0 | 66,827 |
| Colorado | 2,178,700 | 1,412,903 | 765,797 | 490,847 | 7,057 | 67,395 | 113,875 | 24,397 | 7,396 | 0 | 54,830 |
| Connecticut | 4,164,892 | 2,598,337 | 1,566,555 | 544,005 | 179,296 | 125,554 | 185,777 | 39,671 | 11,118 | 209,514 | 271,620 |
| Delaware | 253,405 | 0 | 253,405 | 102,388 | 23,450 | 21,705 | 42,691 | 10,868 | 203 | 0 | 52,100 |
| Florida | 16,081,231 | 12,068,290 | 4,012,941 | 1,480,898 | 575,701 | 442,224 | 486,594 | 553,520 | 64,907 | 0 | 409,097 |
| Georgia | 4,905,464 | 3,915,761 | 989,703 | 553,026 | 0 | 89,930 | 221,728 | 125,019 | 0 | 0 | 0 |
| Hawaii | 1,925,971 | 1,457,274 | 468,697 | 75,143 | 114,364 | 36,427 | 77,174 | 38,347 | 0 | 0 | 127,242 |
| Idaho | 923,985 | 622,192 | 301,793 | 211,528 | 2,974 | 30,729 | 47,202 | 5,372 | 0 | 0 | 3,988 |
| Illinois | 8,796,140 | 5,295,943 | 3,500,197 | 1,221,422 | 888,593 | 428,480 | 126,556 | 56,650 | 40,302 | 276,905 | 461,289 |
| Indiana | 4,131,854 | 3,042,874 | 1,088,980 | 617,109 | 4,912 | 90,717 | 138,086 | 32,433 | 3,485 | 0 | 202,238 |
| Iowa | 2,228,431 | 1,500,162 | 728,269 | 385,652 | 0 | 99,814 | 105,957 | 12,479 | 2,961 | 121,406 | 0 |
| Kansas | 2,007,052 | 1,475,825 | 531,227 | 302,657 | 900 | 56,034 | 89,604 | 63,025 | 4,090 | 1,055 | 13,862 |
| Kentucky | 3,194,113 | 1,882,682 | 1,311,431 | 406,573 | 0 | 19,790 | 275,681 | 61,466 | 18,614 | 207 | 529,100 |
| Louisiana | 2,759,050 | 1,828,434 | 930,616 | 494,604 | 12,711 | 88,262 | 250,460 | 50,041 | 4,695 | 917 | 28,926 |
| Maine | 964,667 | 683,152 | 281,515 | 155,917 | 491 | 45,377 | 43,362 | 32,254 | 4,114 | 0 | 0 |
| Maryland | 3,695,153 | 2,095,319 | 1,599,834 | 613,840 | 156,196 | 103,281 | 165,868 | 23,378 | 2,893 | 9,107 | 525,271 |
| Massachusetts | 4,217,418 | 2,876,066 | 1,341,352 | 602,840 | 0 | 281,708 | 297,756 | 60,880 | 10,185 | 7,439 | 80,544 |
| Michigan | 8,871,817 | 7,132,110 | 1,739,707 | 840,977 | 0 | 555,849 | 185,873 | 118,243 | 11,733 | 0 | 27,032 |
| Minnesota | 4,775,726 | 3,114,600 | 1,661,126 | 539,399 | 46 | 189,341 | 181,103 | 56,054 | 828 | 62,233 | 632,122 |
| Mississippi | 2,665,109 | 1,916,461 | 748,648 | 356,414 | 0 | 56,733 | 103,397 | 38,918 | 0 | 193,186 | 0 |
| Missouri | 3,701,961 | 2,592,460 | 1,109,501 | 648,619 | 300 | 114,032 | 185,707 | 23,514 | 0 | 120,946 | 16,383 |
| Montana | 274,367 | 0 | 274,367 | 175,418 | 18,779 | 14,949 | 36,813 | 16,311 | 157 | 0 | 11,940 |
| Nebraska | 1,281,350 | 865,708 | 415,642 | 277,127 | 2,575 | 48,148 | 39,625 | 16,155 | 528 | 8,093 | 23,391 |
| Nevada | 2,601,308 | 1,698,714 | 902,594 | 216,534 | 5,760 | 57,554 | 97,290 | 14,232 | 0 | 493,223 | 18,001 |
| New Hampshire | 458,732 | 0 | 458,732 | 110,758 | 56,797 | 50,421 | 53,220 | 11,104 | 5,196 | 1,946 | 169,290 |
| New Jersey | 7,192,382 | 4,415,428 | 2,776,954 | 464,676 | 1,161,544 | 249,586 | 294,155 | 76,111 | 1,270 | 309,043 | 220,569 |
| New Mexico | 1,806,516 | 1,345,759 | 460,757 | 236,696 | 7,037 | 25,037 | 61,143 | 34,658 | 760 | 3,772 | 91,654 |
| New York | 12,139,863 | 7,353,097 | 4,786,766 | 474,202 | 1,683,018 | 664,197 | 680,785 | 186,845 | 41,617 | 504 | 1,055,598 |
| North Carolina | 5,316,289 | 3,056,831 | 2,259,458 | 997,217 | 311,723 | 46,677 | 247,233 | 170,985 | 0 | 0 | 485,623 |
| North Dakota | 606,113 | 311,433 | 294,680 | 104,270 | 27,031 | 23,873 | 20,797 | 5,162 | 0 | 11,100 | 102,447 |
| Ohio | 8,055,125 | 5,234,151 | 2,820,974 | 1,368,232 | 712,893 | 298,407 | 346,355 | 79,689 | 15,379 | 0 | 19 |

# STATE GOVERNMENT SALES AND GROSS RECEIPTS TAX REVENUE: 1997 — Continued

| State | Total | General sales or gross receipts Total | Selective sales and gross receipts Total | Motor fuels | Public utilities | Tobacco products | Insurance | Alcoholic beverages | Parimutuels | Amusements | Other |
|---|---|---|---|---|---|---|---|---|---|---|---|
| Oklahoma | 1,940,658 | 1,272,606 | 668,052 | 347,258 | 14,810 | 77,836 | 142,534 | 56,195 | 3,773 | 13,427 | 12,219 |
| Oregon | 673,827 | 0 | 673,827 | 421,427 | 8,876 | 154,562 | 75,936 | 11,753 | 1,140 | 133 | 0 |
| Pennsylvania | 9,221,017 | 6,054,540 | 3,166,477 | 789,522 | 717,508 | 335,530 | 377,273 | 155,912 | 23,991 | 418 | 766,323 |
| Rhode Island | 813,403 | 489,624 | 323,779 | 123,662 | 69,381 | 54,282 | 33,445 | 8,594 | 5,647 | 0 | 28,768 |
| South Carolina | 2,735,295 | 2,032,134 | 703,161 | 327,777 | 37,607 | 30,510 | 77,704 | 117,793 | 0 | 27,358 | 84,412 |
| South Dakota | 609,401 | 410,928 | 198,473 | 95,148 | 1,536 | 20,981 | 33,671 | 9,874 | 707 | 25 | 36,531 |
| Tennessee | 5,087,032 | 3,839,914 | 1,247,118 | 723,413 | 6,773 | 85,903 | 244,000 | 67,591 | 0 | 0 | 119,438 |
| Texas | 18,403,991 | 11,361,888 | 7,042,103 | 2,383,040 | 368,488 | 654,770 | 672,674 | 431,652 | 13,510 | 23,506 | 2,494,463 |
| Utah | 1,579,769 | 1,265,084 | 314,685 | 216,992 | 0 | 31,922 | 45,367 | 20,404 | 0 | 0 | 0 |
| Vermont | 409,267 | 183,836 | 225,431 | 58,419 | 7,650 | 13,841 | 18,552 | 13,375 | 3 | 0 | 113,611 |
| Virginia | 3,766,542 | 2,118,945 | 1,647,597 | 734,541 | 124,427 | 16,198 | 219,032 | 108,943 | 0 | 34 | 444,422 |
| Washington | 8,289,331 | 6,572,213 | 1,717,118 | 685,238 | 241,342 | 277,595 | 212,184 | 139,090 | 3,891 | 11 | 157,767 |
| West Virginia | 1,514,674 | 831,239 | 683,435 | 228,038 | 193,053 | 33,989 | 77,254 | 7,748 | 10,013 | 0 | 133,340 |
| Wisconsin | 4,231,265 | 2,864,982 | 1,366,283 | 693,975 | 311,656 | 213,346 | 102,347 | 40,556 | 3,852 | 551 | 0 |
| Wyoming | 281,806 | 214,815 | 66,991 | 47,209 | 0 | 5,390 | 13,020 | 1,107 | 265 | 0 | 0 |

*Source:* U.S. Department of Commerce, Bureau of the Census.

## Table 6.31
## STATE GOVERNMENT LICENSE TAX REVENUE: 1997
### (In thousands of dollars)

| State or other jurisdiction | Total | Motor vehicle | Motor vehicle operators | Corporations in general | Occupations and businesses, n.e.c. | Hunting and fishing | Alcoholic beverages | Public utilities | Amusements | Other |
|---|---|---|---|---|---|---|---|---|---|---|
| United States | $28,216,617 | $12,965,303 | $1,183,609 | $5,882,411 | $5,822,580 | $1,014,527 | $305,801 | $343,414 | $277,407 | $421,565 |
| Alabama | 424,165 | 170,633 | 16,113 | 109,504 | 99,876 | 17,318 | 2,301 | 8,261 | 0 | 159 |
| Alaska | 77,924 | 28,827 | 0 | 1,188 | 30,519 | 16,089 | 1,096 | 29 | 91 | 85 |
| Arizona | 437,200 | 323,079 | 10,723 | 5,681 | 49,966 | 14,639 | 4,153 | 0 | 0 | 28,945 |
| Arkansas | 221,790 | 97,100 | 16,165 | 7,863 | 65,737 | 20,455 | 1,575 | 8,316 | 316 | 4,263 |
| California | 2,962,520 | 1,510,949 | 111,056 | 40,978 | 1,121,598 | 74,157 | 34,340 | 62,056 | 169 | 7,217 |
| Colorado | 261,406 | 139,184 | 14,796 | 4,370 | 41,225 | 53,553 | 3,757 | 0 | 4,116 | 405 |
| Connecticut | 341,262 | 210,777 | 27,503 | 11,343 | 78,260 | 3,175 | 5,763 | 0 | 222 | 4,219 |
| Delaware | 578,563 | 27,602 | 161 | 390,739 | 148,505 | 939 | 861 | 3,063 | 171 | 6,522 |
| Florida | 1,370,177 | 809,031 | 98,776 | 121,853 | 251,101 | 15,315 | 28,303 | 27,399 | 8,745 | 9,654 |
| Georgia | 405,025 | 202,056 | 35,750 | 30,691 | 69,966 | 20,648 | 10,619 | 0 | 0 | 35,295 |
| Hawaii | 89,876 | 61,447 | 376 | 2,433 | 16,938 | 228 | 0 | 8,088 | 0 | 366 |
| Idaho | 147,586 | 45,651 | 6,112 | 949 | 38,517 | 23,271 | 1,116 | 27,907 | 0 | 4,063 |
| Illinois | 1,215,100 | 769,224 | 50,546 | 124,104 | 237,460 | 23,704 | 4,386 | 0 | 2,412 | 3,264 |
| Indiana | 193,720 | 115,619 | 0 | 4,726 | 44,913 | 15,023 | 7,783 | 0 | 5,174 | 482 |
| Iowa | 421,385 | 262,488 | 11,512 | 35,131 | 69,657 | 17,682 | 8,400 | 8,320 | 5,082 | 3,113 |
| Kansas | 211,755 | 128,781 | 9,416 | 21,303 | 32,258 | 12,338 | 2,074 | 3,360 | 170 | 2,055 |
| Kentucky | 427,137 | 152,787 | 8,222 | 148,378 | 90,041 | 17,266 | 1,996 | 4,704 | 439 | 3,304 |
| Louisiana | 435,603 | 96,045 | 9,350 | 247,804 | 54,534 | 21,886 | 2,100 | 2,628 | 0 | 1,256 |
| Maine | 117,339 | 56,078 | 8,811 | 2,648 | 33,146 | 12,234 | 3,090 | 0 | 690 | 642 |
| Maryland | 349,632 | 190,265 | 15,950 | 13,086 | 116,715 | 10,887 | 520 | 0 | 12 | 2,197 |
| Massachusetts | 431,012 | 244,911 | 62,310 | 20,206 | 56,279 | 6,284 | 1,159 | 0 | 563 | 39,300 |
| Michigan | 1,016,050 | 652,888 | 38,539 | 10,850 | 216,180 | 44,799 | 11,703 | 16,556 | 710 | 23,825 |
| Minnesota | 821,373 | 510,434 | 26,503 | 3,426 | 228,375 | 37,473 | 820 | 0 | 368 | 13,974 |
| Mississippi | 266,271 | 116,986 | 13,676 | 75,063 | 40,487 | 11,226 | 3,288 | 4,162 | 1,383 | 0 |
| Missouri | 562,367 | 237,057 | 18,660 | 89,174 | 155,466 | 27,109 | 3,552 | 16,512 | 850 | 13,987 |
| Montana | 151,322 | 49,406 | 5,034 | 997 | 27,209 | 28,772 | 1,569 | 0 | 37,135 | 1,192 |
| Nebraska | 164,907 | 74,352 | 7,045 | 5,614 | 50,982 | 10,431 | 249 | 0 | 0 | 16,234 |
| Nevada | 302,637 | 98,298 | 10,721 | 15,284 | 94,569 | 454 | 0 | 0 | 79,794 | 3,517 |
| New Hampshire | 120,568 | 56,304 | 8,420 | 4,181 | 35,668 | 6,412 | 3,140 | 3,395 | 423 | 2,625 |
| New Jersey | 742,208 | 399,809 | 28,885 | 129,743 | 110,903 | 12,026 | 5,498 | 2,248 | 49,554 | 3,542 |
| New Mexico | 133,707 | 86,661 | 3,995 | 2,334 | 25,418 | 10,850 | 3,772 | 53 | 0 | 624 |
| New York | 945,142 | 612,900 | 95,200 | 67,187 | 72,011 | 31,191 | 28,331 | 34,448 | 374 | 3,500 |
| North Carolina | 774,753 | 345,984 | 68,698 | 230,081 | 98,368 | 15,017 | 5,863 | 0 | 8,021 | 2,721 |
| North Dakota | 76,787 | 38,458 | 3,160 | 0 | 27,421 | 7,280 | 243 | 0 | 225 | 0 |
| Ohio | 1,355,317 | 557,388 | 34,557 | 481,155 | 219,739 | 29,574 | 27,027 | 1,036 | 0 | 4,841 |

# STATE GOVERNMENT LICENSE TAX REVENUE: 1997 — Continued

| State or other jurisdiction | Total | Motor vehicle | Motor vehicle operators | Corporations in general | Occupations and businesses, n.e.c. | Hunting and fishing | Alcoholic beverages | Public utilities | Amusements | Other |
|---|---|---|---|---|---|---|---|---|---|---|
| Oklahoma | 700,643 | 545,620 | 5,580 | 39,680 | 88,466 | 12,078 | 5,394 | 4 | 3,482 | 339 |
| Oregon | 512,339 | 333,843 | 17,802 | 5,331 | 114,747 | 25,895 | 1,816 | 9,921 | 742 | 2,242 |
| Pennsylvania | 1,919,706 | 505,700 | 52,173 | 970,851 | 279,612 | 44,708 | 13,953 | 42,785 | 84 | 9,840 |
| Rhode Island | 79,856 | 47,314 | 359 | 9,705 | 19,589 | 1,474 | 9 | 0 | 265 | 1,141 |
| South Carolina | 411,179 | 95,938 | 17,242 | 39,619 | 96,501 | 13,689 | 10,461 | 0 | 58,107 | 79,622 |
| South Dakota | 93,625 | 30,050 | 2,009 | 1,134 | 41,446 | 12,388 | 258 | 0 | 134 | 6,206 |
| Tennessee | 737,935 | 201,217 | 36,546 | 400,840 | 71,935 | 19,106 | 1,967 | 4,565 | 0 | 1,759 |
| Texas | 3,265,491 | 785,558 | 83,896 | 1,830,595 | 229,080 | 64,672 | 24,110 | 14,416 | 6,425 | 26,739 |
| Utah | 90,381 | 47,696 | 9,664 | 3,679 | 13,077 | 14,178 | 749 | 0 | 0 | 1,338 |
| Vermont | 67,621 | 38,687 | 3,217 | 1,161 | 16,708 | 4,861 | 454 | 0 | 134 | 2,399 |
| Virginia | 430,751 | 263,540 | 24,705 | 25,708 | 87,326 | 18,730 | 6,385 | 0 | 0 | 4,357 |
| Washington | 509,656 | 244,433 | 24,472 | 11,349 | 149,966 | 29,368 | 9,026 | 11,569 | 151 | 29,322 |
| West Virginia | 151,441 | 75,486 | 3,657 | 6,400 | 25,004 | 14,927 | 10,318 | 15,439 | 0 | 210 |
| Wisconsin | 614,352 | 226,204 | 22,663 | 70,912 | 236,149 | 49,495 | 446 | 0 | 660 | 7,823 |
| Wyoming | 78,055 | 44,558 | 2,883 | 5,380 | 2,967 | 19,253 | 8 | 2,166 | 0 | 840 |

*Source:* U.S. Department of Commerce, Bureau of the Census.

## Table 6.32
## FISCAL YEAR, POPULATION AND PERSONAL INCOME, BY STATE

| State | Date of close of fiscal year in 1997 | Total population (excluding armed forces overseas) (in thousands) | | | Personal income, calendar year 1996 | |
|---|---|---|---|---|---|---|
| | | July 1, 1997 | July 1, 1996 | July 1, 1995 | Amount (in millions) | Per capita (in dollars) |
| United States .................. | . . . | 267,107 | 264,640 | 262,208 | $6,079,436 | $22,972 |
| Alabama .............................. | September 30 | 4,319 | 4,287 | 4,262 | 81,578 | 19,029 |
| Alaska ................................. | June 30 | 609 | 605 | 602 | 14,488 | 23,947 |
| Arizona ............................... | June 30 | 4,555 | 4,434 | 4,308 | 86,420 | 19,490 |
| Arkansas ............................. | June 30 | 2,523 | 2,506 | 2,481 | 44,958 | 17,940 |
| California ............................ | June 30 | 32,268 | 31,858 | 31,558 | 760,431 | 23,869 |
| Colorado ............................. | June 30 | 3,893 | 3,816 | 3,742 | 89,771 | 23,525 |
| Connecticut ........................ | June 30 | 3,270 | 3,267 | 3,267 | 104,056 | 31,851 |
| Delaware ............................. | June 30 | 732 | 723 | 716 | 18,843 | 26,062 |
| Florida ................................ | June 30 | 14,654 | 14,419 | 14,181 | 326,668 | 22,655 |
| Georgia ............................... | June 30 | 7,486 | 7,334 | 7,192 | 156,555 | 21,346 |
| Hawaii ................................. | June 30 | 1,187 | 1,183 | 1,179 | 29,184 | 24,669 |
| Idaho ................................... | June 30 | 1,210 | 1,188 | 1,165 | 21,993 | 18,513 |
| Illinois ................................ | June 30 | 11,896 | 11,845 | 11,795 | 298,413 | 25,193 |
| Indiana ................................ | June 30 | 5,864 | 5,828 | 5,788 | 124,384 | 21,342 |
| Iowa .................................... | June 30 | 2,852 | 2,848 | 2,841 | 59,453 | 20,875 |
| Kansas ................................. | June 30 | 2,595 | 2,579 | 2,570 | 56,028 | 21,725 |
| Kentucky ............................. | June 30 | 3,908 | 3,882 | 3,856 | 72,762 | 18,743 |
| Louisiana ............................ | June 30 | 4,352 | 4,341 | 4,329 | 82,422 | 18,987 |
| Maine .................................. | June 30 | 1,242 | 1,239 | 1,234 | 24,957 | 20,143 |
| Maryland ............................. | June 30 | 5,094 | 5,060 | 5,027 | 132,784 | 26,242 |
| Massachusetts .................... | June 30 | 6,118 | 6,085 | 6,061 | 170,185 | 27,968 |
| Michigan ............................. | September 30 | 9,774 | 9,731 | 9,655 | 228,369 | 23,468 |
| Minnesota ........................... | June 30 | 4,686 | 4,649 | 4,607 | 110,494 | 23,767 |
| Mississippi .......................... | June 30 | 2,731 | 2,711 | 2,691 | 44,998 | 16,598 |
| Missouri .............................. | June 30 | 5,402 | 5,364 | 5,325 | 116,154 | 21,654 |
| Montana .............................. | June 30 | 879 | 877 | 869 | 16,052 | 18,303 |
| Nebraska ............................. | June 30 | 1,657 | 1,649 | 1,636 | 35,161 | 21,323 |
| Nevada ................................ | June 30 | 1,677 | 1,601 | 1,530 | 37,319 | 23,310 |
| New Hampshire ................... | June 30 | 1,173 | 1,160 | 1,146 | 29,381 | 25,328 |
| New Jersey .......................... | June 30 | 8,053 | 8,002 | 7,956 | 237,155 | 29,637 |
| New Mexico ......................... | June 30 | 1,730 | 1,711 | 1,686 | 30,685 | 17,934 |
| New York ............................. | March 31 | 18,137 | 18,134 | 18,146 | 501,965 | 27,681 |
| North Carolina .................... | June 30 | 7,425 | 7,309 | 7,187 | 151,841 | 20,775 |
| North Dakota ...................... | June 30 | 641 | 643 | 641 | 11,945 | 18,577 |
| Ohio .................................... | June 30 | 11,186 | 11,163 | 11,133 | 251,037 | 22,488 |
| Oklahoma ........................... | June 30 | 3,317 | 3,295 | 3,271 | 60,901 | 18,483 |
| Oregon ................................ | June 30 | 3,243 | 3,196 | 3,143 | 67,870 | 21,236 |
| Pennsylvania ....................... | June 30 | 12,020 | 12,040 | 12,046 | 284,386 | 23,620 |
| Rhode Island ...................... | June 30 | 987 | 988 | 990 | 23,601 | 23,888 |
| South Carolina .................... | June 30 | 3,760 | 3,717 | 3,683 | 69,786 | 18,775 |
| South Dakota ...................... | June 30 | 738 | 738 | 735 | 14,272 | 19,339 |
| Tennessee ........................... | June 30 | 5,368 | 5,307 | 5,235 | 110,579 | 20,836 |
| Texas ................................... | August 31 | 19,439 | 19,091 | 18,738 | 397,067 | 20,799 |
| Utah .................................... | June 30 | 2,059 | 2,018 | 1,974 | 35,577 | 17,630 |
| Vermont .............................. | June 30 | 589 | 586 | 583 | 12,415 | 21,186 |
| Virginia ............................... | June 30 | 6,734 | 6,666 | 6,601 | 158,669 | 23,803 |
| Washington ......................... | June 30 | 5,610 | 5,520 | 5,436 | 129,117 | 23,391 |
| West Virginia ...................... | June 30 | 1,816 | 1,820 | 1,822 | 32,333 | 17,765 |
| Wisconsin ............................ | June 30 | 5,170 | 5,146 | 5,113 | 114,042 | 22,161 |
| Wyoming ............................. | June 30 | 480 | 480 | 479 | 9,932 | 20,692 |

*Source:* U.S. Department of Commerce, Bureau of the Census.
*Key:*
... — Not applicable

## Table 6.33
## SUMMARY DISTRIBUTION OF FEDERAL FUNDS, BY STATE AND TERRITORY:
## FISCAL YEAR 1998
### (In millions of dollars)

| State or other jurisdiction | Total | Direct Payments Total | Retirement and Disability | Other Direct Payments | Grants | Procurement | Salaries and Wages |
|---|---|---|---|---|---|---|---|
| United States ................... | $1,484,177 | $835,619 | $507,202 | $328,417 | $269,128 | $209,260 | $170,171 |
| Alabama ............................... | 25,297 | 15,089 | 9,483 | 5,606 | 4,161 | 3,104 | 2,944 |
| Alaska ................................... | 4,767 | 1,194 | 756 | 438 | 1,427 | 863 | 1,282 |
| Arizona ................................. | 24,067 | 13,595 | 9,086 | 4,509 | 4,147 | 3,793 | 2,533 |
| Arkansas ............................... | 13,016 | 9,048 | 5,607 | 3,441 | 2,440 | 475 | 1,054 |
| California ............................. | 161,571 | 86,771 | 49,217 | 37,554 | 32,090 | 25,365 | 17,344 |
| Colorado .............................. | 21,009 | 10,164 | 6,648 | 3,516 | 3,048 | 4,300 | 3,496 |
| Connecticut ......................... | 19,424 | 10,600 | 6,245 | 4,355 | 3,653 | 3,814 | 1,357 |
| Delaware .............................. | 3,553 | 2,293 | 1,479 | 814 | 678 | 215 | 367 |
| Florida .................................. | 83,558 | 58,414 | 36,235 | 22,179 | 10,320 | 7,128 | 7,696 |
| Georgia ................................. | 37,144 | 20,324 | 12,764 | 7,560 | 6,233 | 4,603 | 5,984 |
| Hawaii .................................. | 8,442 | 3,641 | 2,348 | 1,293 | 1,190 | 1,053 | 2,557 |
| Idaho .................................... | 5,961 | 3,235 | 2,135 | 1,100 | 1,055 | 1,019 | 652 |
| Illinois .................................. | 55,467 | 35,246 | 20,579 | 14,667 | 10,156 | 4,576 | 5,490 |
| Indiana ................................. | 26,098 | 17,796 | 10,750 | 7,046 | 4,152 | 2,233 | 1,917 |
| Iowa ...................................... | 14,535 | 10,241 | 5,571 | 4,670 | 2,424 | 930 | 941 |
| Kansas .................................. | 13,426 | 8,497 | 5,086 | 3,411 | 1,934 | 1,316 | 1,680 |
| Kentucky .............................. | 23,161 | 12,588 | 7,984 | 4,604 | 4,236 | 3,850 | 2,488 |
| Louisiana ............................. | 22,900 | 13,839 | 7,622 | 6,217 | 4,708 | 2,351 | 2,002 |
| Maine ................................... | 7,463 | 4,088 | 2,659 | 1,429 | 1,602 | 1,025 | 748 |
| Maryland ............................. | 41,565 | 18,083 | 10,508 | 7,575 | 5,022 | 10,417 | 8,042 |
| Massachusetts ..................... | 37,173 | 20,864 | 11,484 | 9,380 | 8,019 | 5,451 | 2,840 |
| Michigan .............................. | 41,917 | 28,613 | 17,544 | 11,069 | 8,618 | 1,871 | 2,814 |
| Minnesota ............................ | 20,399 | 12,701 | 7,572 | 5,129 | 4,199 | 1,795 | 1,704 |
| Mississippi ........................... | 15,314 | 9,176 | 5,443 | 3,733 | 3,025 | 1,613 | 1,500 |
| Missouri ............................... | 32,682 | 18,221 | 10,842 | 7,379 | 5,065 | 6,341 | 3,055 |
| Montana ............................... | 5,465 | 3,337 | 1,809 | 1,528 | 1,139 | 376 | 614 |
| Nebraska .............................. | 8,253 | 5,292 | 3,187 | 2,105 | 1,511 | 487 | 963 |
| Nevada.................................. | 7,566 | 4,846 | 3,287 | 1,559 | 1,081 | 805 | 835 |
| New Hampshire .................... | 5,272 | 3,258 | 2,232 | 1,026 | 1,042 | 524 | 448 |
| New Jersey ........................... | 40,373 | 25,715 | 15,174 | 10,541 | 7,108 | 4,091 | 3,458 |
| New Mexico ......................... | 12,933 | 5,036 | 3,375 | 1,661 | 2,547 | 3,769 | 1,581 |
| New York............................... | 99,766 | 58,464 | 33,295 | 25,169 | 28,066 | 5,995 | 7,240 |
| North Carolina ..................... | 35,677 | 21,645 | 14,346 | 7,299 | 7,133 | 2,064 | 4,833 |
| North Dakota ....................... | 4,131 | 2,253 | 1,169 | 1,084 | 1,067 | 258 | 554 |
| Ohio ..................................... | 52,006 | 33,663 | 21,075 | 12,588 | 9,733 | 4,368 | 4,242 |
| Oklahoma ............................ | 18,205 | 11,128 | 7,038 | 4,090 | 3,059 | 1,381 | 2,637 |
| Oregon .................................. | 15,119 | 9,646 | 6,307 | 3,339 | 3,275 | 728 | 1,471 |
| Pennsylvania ....................... | 67,350 | 44,501 | 26,507 | 17,994 | 12,381 | 5,163 | 5,306 |
| Rhode Island ....................... | 6,039 | 3,644 | 2,129 | 1,515 | 1,368 | 313 | 715 |
| South Carolina ..................... | 19,870 | 11,611 | 7,785 | 3,826 | 3,525 | 2,489 | 2,246 |
| South Dakota ....................... | 4,319 | 2,487 | 1,414 | 1,073 | 1,007 | 317 | 508 |
| Tennessee ............................ | 30,497 | 17,238 | 10,656 | 6,582 | 5,510 | 5,116 | 2,633 |
| Texas .................................... | 92,019 | 51,152 | 30,388 | 20,764 | 15,809 | 13,893 | 11,164 |
| Utah ..................................... | 8,728 | 4,430 | 3,069 | 1,361 | 1,727 | 1,180 | 1,392 |
| Vermont ............................... | 2,895 | 1,659 | 1,066 | 593 | 803 | 154 | 278 |
| Virginia ................................ | 55,830 | 21,525 | 14,769 | 6,756 | 4,423 | 18,523 | 11,360 |
| Washington .......................... | 31,186 | 16,232 | 10,716 | 5,516 | 5,422 | 4,920 | 4,612 |
| West Virginia ....................... | 10,697 | 6,870 | 4,498 | 2,372 | 2,480 | 488 | 859 |
| Wisconsin ............................. | 21,883 | 14,426 | 9,330 | 5,096 | 4,697 | 1,295 | 1,464 |
| Wyoming .............................. | 2,743 | 1,343 | 909 | 434 | 850 | 175 | 376 |
| Dist. of Columbia ............... | 24,034 | 3,298 | 1,683 | 1,615 | 4,101 | 5,200 | 11,436 |
| American Samoa ................. | 135 | 35 | 29 | 6 | 91 | 7 | 3 |
| Guam .................................... | 998 | 221 | 155 | 66 | 266 | 167 | 344 |
| No. Mariana Islands ......... | 63 | 19 | 11 | 8 | 39 | 3 | 2 |
| Puerto Rico ........................ | 11,119 | 6,111 | 4,031 | 2,080 | 3,895 | 374 | 739 |
| U.S. Virgin Islands ............. | 482 | 175 | 104 | 71 | 256 | 11 | 40 |
| U.S. undistributed ............. | 28,615 | 38 | 11 | 27 | 116 | 25,126 | 3,336 |

*Source:* U.S. Department of Commerce, Bureau of the Census.
*Key:*
. . . — Not applicable

## Table 6.34
## FEDERAL GOVERNMENT GRANTS TO STATE AND LOCAL GOVERNMENTS BY AGENCY AND FOR SELECTED PROGRAMS, BY STATE AND TERRITORY: FISCAL YEAR 1997
### (In thousands of dollars)

| State or other jurisdiction | Total | Child nutrition programs | Food Stamp administration (a) | Special supplemental food program (WIC) | State and private forestry | Economic development administration | Corporation for Public Broadcasting | National Guard centers — construction |
|---|---|---|---|---|---|---|---|---|
| United States ......... | $ 229,777,577 | $ 8,062,688 | $ 3,449,049 | $ 3,861,647 | $ 61,090 | $ 407,729 | $ 267,589 | $ 185,521 |
| Alabama ...................... | 3,483,041 | 157,596 | 32,056 | 64,812 | 1,824 | 7,030 | 2,182 | 3,509 |
| Alaska ........................... | 1,303,464 | 23,320 | 7,856 | 17,811 | 1,766 | 3,642 | 4,369 | 193 |
| Arizona ......................... | 3,355,424 | 149,273 | 18,430 | 79,291 | 795 | 2,106 | 2,353 | 676 |
| Arkansas ...................... | 2,283,436 | 95,229 | 18,596 | 44,662 | 688 | 6,978 | 1,112 | 95 |
| California ..................... | 27,013,531 | 1,071,241 | 376,206 | 665,863 | 1,380 | 78,308 | 21,170 | 2,729 |
| Colorado ...................... | 2,444,273 | 85,790 | 30,734 | 38,821 | 1,616 | 8,226 | 3,830 | 180 |
| Connecticut ................. | 2,904,793 | 65,518 | 13,686 | 33,485 | 70 | 2,280 | 2,213 | 5,085 |
| Delaware ...................... | 629,290 | 24,570 | 7,285 | 8,324 | 415 | 353 | 0 | 0 |
| Florida .......................... | 8,504,474 | 429,208 | 86,276 | 189,240 | 777 | 11,613 | 10,661 | 7,439 |
| Georgia ......................... | 5,468,540 | 286,832 | 54,439 | 107,042 | 1,319 | 13,555 | 3,947 | 07 |
| Hawaii .......................... | 1,184,441 | 35,150 | 11,715 | 27,438 | 41 | 2,980 | 2,075 | 577 |
| Idaho ............................ | 936,091 | 31,367 | 6,822 | 15,504 | 1,029 | 3,892 | 1,479 | 240 |
| Illinois .......................... | 9,295,980 | 305,867 | 74,439 | 140,507 | 2,380 | 14,911 | 8,166 | 225 |
| Indiana ......................... | 3,539,159 | 124,177 | 34,099 | 66,416 | 440 | 4,861 | 4,938 | 17,702 |
| Iowa ............................. | 1,976,615 | 70,402 | 13,626 | 33,123 | 856 | 7,780 | 2,273 | 915 |
| Kansas .......................... | 1,620,412 | 92,181 | 11,284 | 26,607 | 775 | 4,903 | 2,145 | 5,874 |
| Kentucky ...................... | 3,702,442 | 137,604 | 31,787 | 57,555 | 2,141 | 5,873 | 3,439 | 12,692 |
| Louisiana ..................... | 4,456,619 | 238,906 | 44,594 | 76,110 | 1,075 | 4,854 | 2,699 | 1,988 |
| Maine ........................... | 1,377,516 | 33,223 | 6,490 | 12,436 | 670 | 8,115 | 1,774 | 167 |
| Maryland ...................... | 3,949,751 | 119,644 | 21,830 | 47,531 | 1,512 | 5,038 | 3,193 | 3,976 |
| Massachusetts ............. | 6,365,437 | 142,392 | 40,123 | 54,409 | 448 | 6,058 | 16,027 | 1,510 |
| Michigan ...................... | 7,237,216 | 213,032 | 228,702 | 112,426 | 1,888 | 13,293 | 6,376 | 1,228 |
| Minnesota .................... | 3,951,952 | 145,562 | 45,327 | 46,588 | 2,069 | 8,346 | 7,442 | 6,226 |
| Mississippi ................... | 2,625,642 | 146,909 | 23,098 | 49,313 | 635 | 6,543 | 1,366 | 21,120 |
| Missouri ....................... | 4,231,480 | 145,240 | 32,525 | 64,333 | 1,006 | 20,839 | 3,408 | 3,115 |
| Montana ....................... | 990,627 | 26,662 | 8,381 | 11,936 | 1,239 | 3,804 | 683 | 14,213 |
| Nebraska ...................... | 1,227,434 | 56,618 | 8,154 | 20,352 | 984 | 633 | 4,580 | 1,684 |
| Nevada ......................... | 983,247 | 30,189 | 6,505 | 18,370 | 461 | 1,920 | 1,487 | 8,600 |
| New Hampshire. ........... | 842,376 | 16,936 | 2,797 | 10,114 | 995 | 6,182 | 1,082 | 0 |
| New Jersey .................... | 6,601,731 | 151,124 | 81,653 | 72,616 | 1,166 | 6,581 | 2,857 | 2,349 |
| New Mexico .................. | 2,152,210 | 93,564 | 16,520 | 30,157 | 926 | 5,153 | 2,134 | 2,311 |
| New York ...................... | 24,383,648 | 542,181 | 191,639 | 261,610 | 2,115 | 14,575 | 21,037 | 1,459 |
| North Carolina ............. | 6,284,021 | 237,272 | 40,717 | 89,166 | 1,631 | 7,647 | 3,289 | 2,003 |
| North Dakota ............... | 1,074,270 | 24,144 | 5,889 | 11,599 | 263 | 4,217 | 1,295 | 1,801 |
| Ohio ............................. | 8,326,504 | 233,068 | 103,684 | 126,945 | 1,041 | 6,460 | 9,248 | 3,174 |
| Oklahoma .................... | 2,510,011 | 121,982 | 33,680 | 53,230 | 2,424 | 3,000 | 1,969 | 2,959 |
| Oregon ......................... | 2,853,070 | 91,223 | 30,350 | 43,707 | 726 | 6,613 | 2,487 | 6,154 |
| Pennsylvania ................ | 10,267,937 | 245,948 | 96,682 | 131,437 | 2,243 | 7,950 | 9,063 | 2,644 |
| Rhode Island ................ | 1,143,642 | 22,128 | 7,035 | 10,840 | 317 | 6,196 | 601 | 75 |
| South Carolina ............. | 2,987,166 | 141,203 | 19,521 | 58,442 | 1,313 | 9,047 | 5,521 | 9,294 |
| South Dakota ............... | 981,851 | 27,514 | 7,866 | 12,820 | 484 | 3,371 | 1,541 | 2,917 |
| Tennessee .................... | 4,554,942 | 163,829 | 32,851 | 84,036 | 1,021 | 6,671 | 3,816 | 10,988 |
| Texas ........................... | 13,183,815 | 758,035 | 139,383 | 296,873 | 1,417 | 20,509 | 8,927 | 1,557 |
| Utah ............................. | 1,354,900 | 71,486 | 30,067 | 29,443 | 281 | 1,418 | 2,780 | 1,212 |
| Vermont ....................... | 600,940 | 14,185 | 10,617 | 8,936 | 4,364 | 941 | 855 | 8 |
| Virginia ........................ | 3,517,818 | 117,348 | 54,454 | 67,902 | 1,472 | 4,639 | 34,606 | 40 |
| Washington .................. | 4,495,543 | 135,116 | 36,675 | 76,688 | 1,522 | 7,079 | 4,588 | 917 |
| West Virginia ................ | 2,100,291 | 61,347 | 8,154 | 28,493 | 2,190 | 6,808 | 1,690 | 4,329 |
| Wisconsin ..................... | 3,616,885 | 102,924 | 40,174 | 56,002 | 1,918 | 5,093 | 4,415 | 499 |
| Wyoming ...................... | 761,974 | 14,495 | 3,427 | 6,512 | 709 | 515 | 520 | 1,986 |
| Dist. of Columbia .......... | 2,739,718 | 22,395 | 7,909 | 11,430 | 249 | 1,364 | 4,992 | 265 |
| America Samoa ............. | 120,762 | 9,292 | 4,837 | 3,781 | 4 | 130 | 339 | 0 |
| Guam ........................... | 124,798 | 4,087 | 1,806 | 4,983 | 0 | 1,251 | 537 | 367 |
| No. Mariana Islands ..... | 35,133 | 0 | 0 | 0 | 0 | 1,029 | 0 | 0 |
| Puerto Rico .................. | 3,718,583 | 144,997 | 1,140,169 | 138,159 | 0 | 4,414 | 3,004 | 0 |
| U.S. Virgin Islands ........ | 371,096 | 11,160 | 5,427 | 5,421 | 0 | 142 | 449 | 4,262 |
| U.S. undistributed ......... | 1,031,545 | 0 | 0 | 0 | 0 | 0 | 8,558 | 0 |

See footnotes at end of table.

## FEDERAL GOVERNMENT GRANTS — Continued

| State or other jurisdiction | Education for the disadvantaged | School improvement programs | Education for the handicapped | Vocational and adult education | Construction of wastewater treatment facilities | FEMA disaster relief | Support payments (AFDC) | Children and family services |
|---|---|---|---|---|---|---|---|---|
| United States | $ 7,159,360 | $ 1,641,752 | $ 3,399,308 | $ 1,356,923 | $ 2,679,072 | $ 5,186,055 | $ 9,700,264 | $ 1,840,839 |
| Alabama | 130,002 | 35,713 | 52,868 | 27,852 | 31,265 | 31,787 | 57,930 | 28,183 |
| Alaska | 25,666 | 12,781 | 12,083 | 4,514 | 18,829 | 16,322 | 57,467 | 23,545 |
| Arizona | 113,107 | 31,407 | 43,073 | 21,689 | 22,873 | 34,916 | 80,404 | 31,371 |
| Arkansas | 81,047 | 14,823 | 31,712 | 15,065 | 21,834 | 33,886 | 99,601 | 19,031 |
| California | 836,491 | 172,583 | 324,012 | 160,653 | 245,200 | 2,023,633 | 1,706,109 | 177,794 |
| Colorado | 70,875 | 18,421 | 42,969 | 21,993 | 17,379 | 12,671 | 182,211 | 24,367 |
| Connecticut | 54,620 | 19,952 | 42,582 | 11,463 | 30,353 | 9,862 | 72,869 | 20,263 |
| Delaware | 17,631 | 7,656 | 10,063 | 5,473 | 18,693 | 89 | 36,728 | 6,294 |
| Florida | 294,290 | 74,488 | 164,777 | 55,912 | 71,204 | 95,415 | 367,467 | 93,888 |
| Georgia | 175,414 | 31,454 | 72,673 | 39,022 | 42,885 | 273,226 | 188,323 | 40,103 |
| Hawaii | 19,977 | 16,928 | 13,158 | 9,812 | 17,338 | 23,527 | 93,131 | 14,956 |
| Idaho | 25,615 | 7,704 | 13,614 | 6,308 | 16,475 | 44,915 | 33,842 | 17,587 |
| Illinois | 339,093 | 69,460 | 139,839 | 45,600 | 123,977 | 110,901 | 607,648 | 70,805 |
| Indiana | 113,251 | 28,712 | 89,297 | 30,375 | 45,347 | 19,835 | 42,260 | 33,796 |
| Iowa | 51,531 | 11,246 | 33,256 | 15,363 | 38,956 | 18,188 | 66,155 | 21,523 |
| Kansas | 60,514 | 18,451 | 38,352 | 12,547 | 27,407 | 2,523 | 61,295 | 17,383 |
| Kentucky | 135,792 | 28,078 | 59,480 | 24,676 | 43,093 | 126,333 | 69,061 | 25,007 |
| Louisiana | 203,662 | 30,114 | 51,188 | 26,943 | 32,959 | 16,832 | 62,004 | 35,703 |
| Maine | 29,143 | 10,289 | 18,324 | 7,759 | 19,698 | 12,635 | 29,840 | 10,519 |
| Maryland | 62,176 | 23,013 | 59,549 | 19,279 | 48,202 | 2,516 | 452,911 | 30,874 |
| Massachusetts | 152,770 | 46,097 | 97,738 | 28,290 | 236,473 | 50,544 | 139,872 | 39,106 |
| Michigan | 309,622 | 69,752 | 99,146 | 71,223 | 145,467 | 31,230 | 127,116 | 65,022 |
| Minnesota | 86,401 | 23,331 | 62,832 | 21,761 | 42,064 | 290,835 | 234,690 | 30,759 |
| Mississippi | 125,430 | 22,010 | 35,576 | 18,380 | 24,454 | 4,471 | 49,290 | 19,857 |
| Missouri | 154,261 | 27,316 | 64,226 | 31,745 | 50,273 | 12,771 | 122,854 | 37,091 |
| Montana | 28,384 | 8,666 | 14,467 | 7,794 | 13,977 | 3,678 | 27,018 | 8,760 |
| Nebraska | 32,579 | 7,380 | 19,863 | 7,935 | 19,890 | 019,035 | 70,429 | 13,085 |
| Nevada | 19,376 | 8,894 | 14,277 | 6,795 | 10,625 | 40,525 | 36,368 | 11,504 |
| New Hampshire | 16,587 | 5,292 | 14,667 | 6,252 | 12,332 | 7,305 | 16,108 | 9,049 |
| New Jersey | 146,043 | 46,930 | 140,031 | 31,417 | 67,815 | 24,122 | 248,970 | 81,624 |
| New Mexico | 597,255 | 151,039 | 216,880 | 60,835 | 317,982 | 137,701 | 1,535,266 | 104,661 |
| New York | 62,926 | 16,955 | 29,718 | 12,088 | 24,735 | 2,325 | 143,645 | 16,964 |
| North Carolina | 148,214 | 35,960 | 94,649 | 41,207 | 54,227 | 409,679 | 283,351 | 46,487 |
| North Dakota | 17,069 | 6,570 | 8,388 | 7,434 | 12,021 | 287,122 | 23,402 | 8,492 |
| Ohio | 291,106 | 63,775 | 127,823 | 43,059 | 69,090 | 92,843 | 219,284 | 70,602 |
| Oklahoma | 86,576 | 29,265 | 38,500 | 21,632 | 26,329 | 2,714 | 141,875 | 32,559 |
| Oregon | 75,513 | 22,776 | 47,553 | 13,634 | 20,394 | 50,180 | 69,646 | 22,700 |
| Pennsylvania | 309,399 | 55,344 | 110,172 | 55,995 | 89,195 | 34,530 | 549,081 | 81,101 |
| Rhode Island | 23,652 | 6,744 | 13,404 | 6,502 | 15,352 | 3,159 | 83,821 | 8,591 |
| South Carolina | 95,631 | 18,412 | 49,943 | 17,649 | 26,647 | 15,092 | 45,496 | 22,340 |
| South Dakota | 20,469 | 7,994 | 10,251 | 5,202 | 22,252 | 102,153 | 9,700 | 11,709 |
| Tennessee | 121,505 | 25,001 | 73,852 | 32,234 | 43,419 | 18,682 | 67,450 | 32,956 |
| Texas | 609,608 | 107,458 | 235,251 | 85,892 | 99,963 | 31,602 | 346,757 | 110,048 |
| Utah | 31,793 | 11,788 | 30,134 | 13,171 | 12,457 | 363 | 26,999 | 10,605 |
| Vermont | 15,522 | 6,705 | 10,373 | 5,064 | 8,759 | 5,843 | 10,372 | 8,579 |
| Virginia | 96,269 | 17,558 | 82,256 | 31,800 | 49,410 | 40,779 | 104,563 | 38,160 |
| Washington | 123,924 | 30,838 | 66,646 | 27,716 | 49,636 | 150,131 | 245,423 | 39,527 |
| West Virginia | 72,427 | 12,124 | 25,111 | 12,126 | 32,243 | 43,157 | 58,120 | 14,561 |
| Wisconsin | 124,923 | 36,253 | 63,706 | 30,688 | 59,118 | 36,788 | 102,688 | 31,411 |
| Wyoming | 16,170 | 6,284 | 8,277 | 4,890 | 20,199 | 46 | 9,485 | 8,199 |
| Dist. of Columbia | 19,977 | 9,824 | 102,612 | 4,145 | 8,181 | 39 | 55,732 | 26,097 |
| American Samoa | 0 | 0 | 2,360 | 0 | 0 | 37,481 | 0 | 3,290 |
| Guam | 0 | 48 | 9,341 | 674 | 4,869 | 01,339 | 4,706 | 3,215 |
| No. Mariana Islands | 49 | 98 | 5,591 | 123 | 431 | 0 | 0 | 459 |
| Puerto Rico | 287,976 | 32,338 | 36,893 | 23,967 | 45,229 | 182,108 | 117,210 | 25,317 |
| U.S. Virgin Islands | 0 | 1,160 | 20,928 | 0 | 1,579 | 144,397 | 6,218 | 3,283 |
| U.S. undistributed | 57 | 499 | 3,005 | 5,307 | 8,020 | 1,928 | 0 | 79 |

See footnotes at end of table.

## FEDERAL GOVERNMENT GRANTS — Continued

| State or other jurisdiction | Low income home energy assistance | Medicaid | Centers for Disease Control | Substance abuse and mental health | Supplemental Security Income | Section 8 housing assistance grants | Public housing grants | Office of Justice Assistance-Justice programs |
|---|---|---|---|---|---|---|---|---|
| United States .......... | $ 1,249,124 | $ 95,552,288 | $ 435,708 | $ 1,585,527 | $ 28,368,000 | $ 8,153,497 | $ 3,862,576 | $ 2,432,959 |
| Alabama ............................. | 11,137 | 1,565,263 | 8,019 | 21,917 | 633,000 | 76,922 | 88,688 | 31,053 |
| Alaska ................................. | 6,734 | 231,863 | 385 | 2,396 | 30,000 | 18,060 | 84,058 | 7,531 |
| Arizona .............................. | 5,737 | 1,247,708 | 3,530 | 23,106 | 316,000 | 65,744 | 104,756 | 57,645 |
| Arkansas ............................ | 7,515 | 1,014,109 | 4,897 | 11,327 | 335,000 | 56,264 | 27,412 | 17,579 |
| California ........................... | 62,955 | 9,423,671 | 28,393 | 216,384 | 5,513,000 | 1,144,588 | 179,216 | 569,064 |
| Colorado ............................ | 19,319 | 840,137 | 5,934 | 22,335 | 230,000 | 104,005 | 24,124 | 30,581 |
| Connecticut ....................... | 27,250 | 1,339,549 | 3,670 | 17,710 | 195,000 | 164,559 | 50,654 | 17,056 |
| Delaware ............................ | 2,876 | 226,408 | 1,150 | 4,300 | 46,000 | 24,721 | 9,816 | 9,654 |
| Florida ............................... | 13,392 | 3,536,257 | 10,732 | 66,198 | 1,499,000 | 312,286 | 85,657 | 138,024 |
| Georgia .............................. | 10,949 | 2,302,418 | 24,946 | 35,235 | 744,000 | 149,280 | 97,946 | 50,671 |
| Hawaii ................................ | 1,263 | 352,352 | 3,103 | 7,380 | 89,000 | 53,874 | 23,887 | 7,001 |
| Idaho .................................. | 6,306 | 295,176 | 2,040 | 5,748 | 69,000 | 21,719 | 3,295 | 9,683 |
| Illinois ............................... | 75,565 | 3,509,696 | 12,861 | 66,433 | 1,145,000 | 398,272 | 274,699 | 95,014 |
| Indiana ............................... | 30,409 | 1,565,614 | 6,590 | 36,098 | 370,000 | 118,918 | 33,350 | 35,532 |
| Iowa ................................... | 23,716 | 839,306 | 5,102 | 14,224 | 153,000 | 58,211 | 4,920 | 18,497 |
| Kansas ................................ | 10,871 | 643,108 | 3,033 | 12,443 | 146,000 | 41,019 | 14,548 | 14,737 |
| Kentucky ............................ | 17,578 | 1,816,017 | 6,445 | 19,485 | 676,000 | 100,513 | 54,461 | 21,938 |
| Louisiana ........................... | 10,070 | 2,463,810 | 8,942 | 25,875 | 728,000 | 94,323 | 55,842 | 29,490 |
| Maine ................................. | 16,347 | 708,948 | 2,655 | 6,136 | 100,000 | 57,061 | 7,879 | 7,351 |
| Maryland ............................ | 17,714 | 1,456,044 | 10,624 | 32,135 | 364,000 | 188,337 | 55,231 | 44,009 |
| Massachusetts ................. | 47,066 | 2,484,608 | 12,830 | 36,772 | 740,000 | 414,693 | 115,182 | 52,443 |
| Michigan ............................ | 77,768 | 3,380,325 | 17,002 | 62,513 | 945,000 | 211,309 | 87,575 | 48,976 |
| Minnesota .......................... | 53,828 | 1,639,385 | 7,965 | 24,025 | 253,000 | 136,468 | 47,560 | 25,478 |
| Mississippi ........................ | 8,935 | 1,264,111 | 6,502 | 13,272 | 518,000 | 68,734 | 25,252 | 15,699 |
| Missouri ............................. | 30,583 | 1,915,552 | 8,646 | 26,136 | 453,000 | 128,838 | 84,676 | 45,061 |
| Montana ............................. | 10,024 | 286,162 | 2,205 | 4,462 | 54,000 | 20,628 | 22,078 | 8,966 |
| Nebraska ............................ | 10,643 | 465,177 | 4,991 | 7,133 | 81,000 | 36,268 | 25,393 | 13,310 |
| Nevada ............................... | 2,018 | 260,416 | 2,596 | 8,212 | 88,000 | 33,896 | 39,453 | 11,931 |
| New Hampshire ................. | 10,100 | 378,477 | 3,653 | 5,568 | 44,000 | 40,934 | 5,230 | 8,285 |
| New Jersey ......................... | 40,293 | 2,845,394 | 10,139 | 46,531 | 628,000 | 368,865 | 146,886 | 58,175 |
| New Mexico ....................... | 5,359 | 757,280 | 3,543 | 7,944 | 177,000 | 33,782 | 47,449 | 18,603 |
| New York ........................... | 149,111 | 12,547,834 | 57,286 | 103,581 | 2,932,000 | 985,879 | 688,025 | 236,948 |
| North Carolina ................. | 17,989 | 3,127,616 | 12,102 | 34,211 | 699,000 | 144,976 | 64,812 | 44,255 |
| North Dakota ................... | 10,641 | 226,897 | 1,312 | 3,002 | 30,000 | 19,871 | 13,460 | 6,706 |
| Ohio ................................... | 58,756 | 3,909,281 | 14,871 | 72,344 | 1,111,000 | 338,403 | 137,879 | 63,244 |
| Oklahoma .......................... | 9,451 | 899,572 | 7,427 | 16,872 | 283,000 | 73,299 | 103,106 | 20,106 |
| Oregon ............................... | 46,234 | 990,773 | 4,573 | 17,068 | 198,000 | 98,029 | 23,710 | 28,993 |
| Pennsylvania ..................... | 92,025 | 4,585,439 | 17,323 | 64,828 | 1,235,000 | 343,848 | 242,879 | 70,945 |
| Rhode Island ................... | 7,399 | 503,067 | 2,556 | 5,309 | 109,000 | 86,935 | 21,203 | 9,891 |
| South Carolina ................ | 6,850 | 1,554,660 | 6,090 | 19,063 | 410,000 | 86,385 | 26,890 | 25,974 |
| South Dakota ................... | 10,831 | 223,900 | 2,365 | 2,848 | 49,000 | 20,062 | 37,376 | 8,523 |
| Tennessee ........................... | 17,697 | 2,332,900 | 5,961 | 25,199 | 658,000 | 114,965 | 67,177 | 37,480 |
| Texas .................................. | 21,896 | 6,199,211 | 20,313 | 102,038 | 1,491,000 | 363,601 | 114,119 | 166,898 |
| Utah ................................... | 7,953 | 485,369 | 3,283 | 11,949 | 86,000 | 29,028 | 4,918 | 17,813 |
| Vermont ............................. | 7,949 | 240,412 | 1,395 | 3,036 | 50,000 | 24,497 | 1,084 | 6,531 |
| Virginia .............................. | 22,076 | 1,223,374 | 8,943 | 35,942 | 507,000 | 165,963 | 39,422 | 42,388 |
| Washington ........................ | 25,465 | 1,757,021 | 9,749 | 34,072 | 432,000 | 112,577 | 63,092 | 48,640 |
| West Virginia ..................... | 8,517 | 944,718 | 3,811 | 9,665 | 297,000 | 58,284 | 12,141 | 13,668 |
| Wisconsin ........................... | 48,553 | 1,617,128 | 8,661 | 27,462 | 370,000 | 122,021 | 35,573 | 28,953 |
| Wyoming ............................ | 2,110 | 135,357 | 872 | 1,958 | 23,000 | 9,144 | 3,317 | 5,079 |
| Dist. of Columbia ........... | 3,005 | 481,055 | 4,639 | 3,779 | 85,000 | 75,408 | 45,168 | 4,243 |
| American Samoa ............ | 0 | 2,687 | 197 | 268 | 0 | 0 | 0 | 1,869 |
| Guam .................................. | 55 | 4,337 | 1,483 | 748 | 0 | 5,925 | 2,166 | 2,703 |
| No. Mariana Islands ...... | 0 | 1,464 | 133 | 252 | 3,000 | 735 | 0 | 1,163 |
| Puerto Rico ...................... | 174 | 127,771 | 4,841 | 19,782 | 0 | 121,973 | 169,278 | 17,079 |
| U.S. Virgin Islands ......... | 51 | 4,695 | 986 | 572 | 0 | 8,596 | 18,607 | 3,804 |
| U.S. undistributed ......... | 15 | 371,409 | 1,415 | 80,249 | 0 | 0 | 0 | 26 |

See footnotes at end of table.

## FEDERAL GOVERNMENT GRANTS — Continued

| State or other jurisdiction | Job Training Partnership Act | State unemployment insurance & services | State justice institute grants | Highway trust fund | FAA0 airport trust fund | Federal transit administration | All other grants |
|---|---|---|---|---|---|---|---|
| United States | $ 3,214,576 | $ 1,997,534 | $ 6,520 | $ 20,466,500 | $ 1,489,298 | $ 4,554,647 | $ 34,307,219 |
| Alabama | 46,713 | 28,891 | 64 | 299,281 | 14,146 | 10,190 | 613,873 |
| Alaska | 10,811 | 13,351 | 74 | 239,943 | 81,022 | 1,746 | 294,898 |
| Arizona | 62,281 | 25,539 | 115 | 333,602 | 29,229 | 35,297 | 485,582 |
| Arkansas | 23,894 | 21,672 | 1 | 285,241 | 16,975 | 9,194 | 302,965 |
| California | 595,260 | 346,825 | 309 | 2,096,697 | 143,980 | 675,397 | 3,626,713 |
| Colorado | 29,528 | 30,715 | 347 | 207,335 | 41,870 | 20,243 | 470,810 |
| Connecticut | 33,287 | 42,573 | 18 | 368,379 | 3,700 | 71,769 | 378,934 |
| Delaware | 5,349 | 5,224 | 1 | 85,585 | 915 | 5,545 | 104,170 |
| Florida | 139,682 | 75,291 | 86 | 736,401 | 66,272 | 154,438 | 1,208,448 |
| Georgia | 56,163 | 37,042 | 53 | 472,968 | 32,408 | 118,576 | 746,950 |
| Hawaii | 18,562 | 10,187 | 9 | 206,736 | 5,614 | 9,653 | 196,012 |
| Idaho | 14,979 | 12,459 | 1 | 160,888 | 6,847 | 3,865 | 151,228 |
| Illinois | 115,202 | 98,159 | 14 | 703,522 | 76,934 | 280,554 | 1,527,410 |
| Indiana | 44,679 | 20,107 | 6 | 428,835 | 20,814 | 40,036 | 502,454 |
| Iowa | 23,552 | 17,590 | 32 | 228,999 | 17,092 | 19,544 | 318,149 |
| Kansas | 17,694 | 14,162 | 0 | 186,091 | 9,776 | 5,395 | 259,605 |
| Kentucky | 41,813 | 24,329 | 53 | 292,543 | 37,863 | 16,054 | 490,289 |
| Louisiana | 62,579 | 17,825 | 40 | 255,912 | 28,268 | 48,358 | 522,577 |
| Maine | 19,529 | 13,239 | 166 | 117,926 | 6,748 | 3,445 | 197,613 |
| Maryland | 53,585 | 16,819 | 164 | 419,054 | 14,771 | 89,899 | 648,070 |
| Massachusetts | 68,423 | 52,221 | 1 | 1,025,055 | 15,472 | 225,391 | 761,901 |
| Michigan | 89,166 | 85,205 | 362 | 605,237 | 54,932 | 67,928 | 933,068 |
| Minnesota | 30,858 | 38,891 | 9 | 302,237 | 24,253 | 12,689 | 517,176 |
| Mississippi | 33,025 | 14,877 | 3 | 194,984 | 3,422 | 7,133 | 398,115 |
| Missouri | 44,366 | 34,634 | 1 | 444,225 | 45,293 | 62,096 | 547,832 |
| Montana | 12,622 | 7,528 | 3 | 171,466 | 9,498 | 2,515 | 206,245 |
| Nebraska | 9,993 | 6,302 | 3 | 167,314 | 10,351 | 5,513 | 212,185 |
| Nevada | 17,716 | 16,235 | 25 | 148,487 | 46,769 | 22,378 | 143,113 |
| New Hampshire | 12,980 | 8,898 | 111 | 104,797 | 8,349 | 3,448 | 125,819 |
| New Jersey | 91,278 | 80,673 | 10 | 644,146 | 13,801 | 351,890 | 797,916 |
| New Mexico | 23,667 | 13,064 | 75 | 201,149 | 4,657 | 11,413 | 461,020 |
| New York | 233,902 | 122,056 | 249 | 1,201,396 | 92,459 | 751,645 | 3,051,918 |
| North Carolina | 62,411 | 35,817 | 21 | 447,951 | 33,094 | 35,350 | 715,328 |
| North Dakota | 8,309 | 8,326 | 0 | 141,366 | 7,054 | 4,340 | 145,680 |
| Ohio | 100,443 | 73,535 | 42 | 763,143 | 37,056 | 93,737 | 1,202,347 |
| Oklahoma | 41,581 | 18,790 | 0 | 270,128 | 8,157 | 13,357 | 377,630 |
| Oregon | 40,323 | 32,212 | 57 | 339,589 | 13,399 | 164,125 | 521,850 |
| Pennsylvania | 150,634 | 110,438 | 24 | 934,182 | 66,290 | 255,912 | 1,549,541 |
| Rhode Island | 17,476 | 15,461 | 2 | 105,970 | 8,716 | 7,044 | 142,754 |
| South Carolina | 42,005 | 26,571 | 23 | 251,914 | 17,095 | 10,452 | 376,019 |
| South Dakota | 7,400 | 4,693 | 10 | 145,641 | 16,496 | 4,896 | 147,350 |
| Tennessee | 41,426 | 30,416 | 239 | 378,314 | 27,453 | 39,604 | 717,431 |
| Texas | 221,140 | 88,569 | 59 | 1,179,467 | 127,474 | 173,122 | 1,544,497 |
| Utah | 13,003 | 22,335 | 0 | 153,257 | 17,190 | 43,100 | 266,084 |
| Vermont | 8,543 | 6,648 | 44 | 89,290 | 2,046 | 7,357 | 90,984 |
| Virginia | 54,097 | 27,661 | 217 | 441,798 | 33,790 | 36,750 | 640,249 |
| Washington | 84,867 | 55,798 | 57 | 466,878 | 24,753 | 91,574 | 623,406 |
| West Virginia | 35,270 | 10,444 | 6 | 218,506 | 13,752 | 12,982 | 375,631 |
| Wisconsin | 31,932 | 45,372 | 12 | 329,108 | 16,034 | 39,643 | 536,805 |
| Wyoming | 6,870 | 4,366 | 1 | 134,039 | 8,408 | 1,369 | 342,656 |
| Dist. of Columbia | 25,284 | 10,420 | 0 | 94,186 | 85 | 116,671 | 1,573,756 |
| American Samoa | 475 | 0 | 0 | 13,062 | 2,155 | 192 | 38,342 |
| Guam | 2,627 | 50 | 0 | 11,037 | 7,349 | 312 | 51,462 |
| No. Mariana Islands | 594 | 0 | 0 | 0 | 2,475 | 0 | 20,537 |
| Puerto Rico | 130,276 | 15,894 | 5 | 79,484 | 13,058 | 55,956 | 781,231 |
| U.S. Virgin Islands | 1,687 | 1,133 | 0 | 20,334 | 1,283 | 9 | 104,913 |
| U.S. undistributed | 2,769 | 0 | 3,297 | 121,425 | 135 | 203,551 | 219,707 |

*Source*: U.S. Department of Commerce, Bureau of the Census.
*Note*: Detail may not add to totals due to rounding. All amounts in this table represent actual expenditures of the federal government during the fiscal year.

(a) For Puerto Rico, amounts shown is for nutritional assistance grant program. All other amounts are grant payments for food stamp administration.

## Table 6.35
## FEDERAL GOVERNMENT EXPENDITURES FOR SALARIES AND WAGES,
## BY STATE AND TERRITORY: FISCAL YEAR 1997
(In thousands of dollars)

| State or other jurisdiction | Total | Department of Defense Total | Military Total | Active | Inactive | Civilian | Postal service | All other federal agencies |
|---|---|---|---|---|---|---|---|---|
| United States | $166,144,639 | $66,719,191 | $39,012,729 | $33,995,971 | $5,016,758 | $27,706,462 | $43,834,999 | $55,590,449 |
| Alabama | 2,901,554 | 1,481,022 | 719,480 | 468,309 | 251,171 | 761,542 | 540,273 | 880,259 |
| Alaska | 1,284,377 | 748,083 | 575,116 | 500,590 | 74,526 | 172,967 | 118,802 | 417,492 |
| Arizona | 2,574,026 | 1,077,042 | 780,056 | 617,866 | 162,190 | 296,986 | 631,774 | 865,210 |
| Arkansas | 1,067,316 | 374,275 | 260,067 | 157,495 | 102,572 | 114,208 | 352,401 | 340,640 |
| California | 17,587,324 | 8,536,282 | 4,930,841 | 4,493,790 | 437,051 | 3,605,441 | 4,745,111 | 4,305,931 |
| Colorado | 3,385,896 | 1,410,679 | 1,031,930 | 931,557 | 100,373 | 378,749 | 760,859 | 1,214,358 |
| Connecticut | 1,353,146 | 403,546 | 300,794 | 256,757 | 44,037 | 102,752 | 633,139 | 316,461 |
| Delaware | 382,745 | 196,845 | 142,390 | 113,508 | 28,882 | 54,455 | 122,988 | 62,912 |
| Florida | 7,665,537 | 3,592,984 | 2,414,050 | 2,230,179 | 183,871 | 1,178,934 | 2,227,204 | 1,845,349 |
| Georgia | 5,707,084 | 3,031,157 | 1,917,597 | 1,728,243 | 189,354 | 1,113,560 | 1,083,094 | 1,592,833 |
| Hawaii | 2,330,499 | 2,009,508 | 1,286,547 | 1,261,531 | 25,016 | 722,961 | 140,915 | 180,076 |
| Idaho | 626,790 | 189,130 | 143,434 | 121,431 | 22,003 | 45,696 | 149,515 | 288,145 |
| Illinois | 5,404,479 | 1,520,379 | 963,984 | 815,459 | 148,525 | 556,395 | 2,297,821 | 1,586,279 |
| Indiana | 1,781,224 | 465,444 | 111,138 | 38,022 | 73,116 | 354,306 | 867,240 | 448,540 |
| Iowa | 943,091 | 118,696 | 72,698 | 14,220 | 58,478 | 45,998 | 558,655 | 265,740 |
| Kansas | 1,588,609 | 669,953 | 492,905 | 445,937 | 46,968 | 177,048 | 468,928 | 449,728 |
| Kentucky | 2,273,057 | 1,147,275 | 921,914 | 851,661 | 70,253 | 225,361 | 536,769 | 589,013 |
| Louisiana | 2,065,655 | 870,429 | 600,724 | 495,287 | 105,437 | 269,705 | 561,567 | 633,659 |
| Maine | 754,952 | 392,943 | 148,396 | 105,069 | 43,327 | 244,547 | 230,642 | 131,367 |
| Maryland | 7,556,326 | 2,567,724 | 1,085,598 | 957,192 | 128,406 | 1,482,126 | 918,883 | 4,069,719 |
| Massachusetts | 2,823,810 | 509,952 | 197,593 | 126,631 | 70,962 | 312,359 | 1,304,499 | 1,009,359 |
| Michigan | 2,741,173 | 434,428 | 122,370 | 37,758 | 84,612 | 312,058 | 1,559,120 | 747,625 |
| Minnesota | 1,637,522 | 184,193 | 99,470 | 26,770 | 72,700 | 84,723 | 888,397 | 564,932 |
| Mississippi | 1,542,393 | 896,864 | 532,350 | 442,034 | 90,316 | 364,514 | 286,653 | 358,876 |
| Missouri | 3,032,668 | 927,416 | 525,006 | 392,733 | 132,273 | 402,410 | 1,059,980 | 1,045,272 |
| Montana | 594,997 | 151,396 | 112,709 | 94,263 | 18,446 | 38,687 | 135,000 | 308,601 |
| Nebraska | 974,000 | 459,911 | 335,066 | 298,355 | 36,711 | 124,845 | 294,525 | 219,564 |
| Nevada | 823,553 | 338,075 | 260,639 | 248,155 | 12,484 | 77,436 | 224,044 | 261,434 |
| New Hampshire | 479,561 | 110,656 | 61,618 | 21,102 | 40,516 | 49,038 | 243,018 | 125,887 |
| New Jersey | 3,475,852 | 1,149,237 | 352,667 | 262,975 | 89,692 | 796,570 | 1,618,544 | 708,071 |
| New Mexico | 1,595,408 | 731,200 | 433,925 | 409,911 | 24,014 | 297,275 | 217,856 | 646,352 |
| New York | 7,038,642 | 1,086,541 | 681,589 | 497,458 | 184,131 | 404,952 | 3,499,807 | 2,452,294 |
| North Carolina | 4,887,127 | 3,061,734 | 2,466,883 | 2,269,763 | 197,120 | 594,851 | 1,089,691 | 735,702 |
| North Dakota | 575,450 | 318,309 | 261,800 | 239,883 | 21,917 | 56,509 | 110,020 | 147,121 |
| Ohio | 4,297,891 | 1,472,201 | 486,971 | 336,930 | 150,041 | 985,230 | 1,804,140 | 1,021,550 |
| Oklahoma | 2,628,873 | 1,581,944 | 885,601 | 788,725 | 96,876 | 696,343 | 470,157 | 576,772 |
| Oregon | 1,422,319 | 186,408 | 84,970 | 28,443 | 56,527 | 101,438 | 483,534 | 752,377 |
| Pennsylvania | 5,266,876 | 1,354,419 | 296,336 | 114,505 | 181,831 | 1,058,083 | 2,272,750 | 1,639,707 |
| Rhode Island | 709,140 | 399,404 | 156,681 | 135,741 | 20,940 | 242,723 | 208,984 | 100,752 |
| South Carolina | 2,076,815 | 1,320,370 | 954,361 | 838,906 | 115,455 | 366,009 | 418,241 | 338,204 |
| South Dakota | 510,859 | 153,484 | 114,138 | 87,446 | 26,692 | 39,346 | 117,346 | 240,029 |
| Tennessee | 2,624,136 | 367,516 | 160,339 | 62,609 | 97,730 | 207,177 | 829,474 | 1,427,146 |
| Texas | 10,897,258 | 5,053,040 | 3,399,871 | 3,077,572 | 322,299 | 1,653,169 | 2,733,806 | 3,110,412 |
| Utah | 1,387,834 | 642,492 | 193,577 | 149,505 | 44,072 | 448,915 | 276,188 | 469,154 |
| Vermont | 267,369 | 39,535 | 22,082 | 5,053 | 17,029 | 17,453 | 115,662 | 112,172 |
| Virginia | 11,311,843 | 8,023,889 | 4,121,590 | 4,034,229 | 87,361 | 3,902,299 | 1,146,340 | 2,141,614 |
| Washington | 4,573,778 | 2,692,382 | 1,629,846 | 1,511,903 | 117,943 | 1,062,536 | 820,192 | 1,061,204 |
| West Virginia | 862,846 | 151,900 | 95,426 | 15,500 | 79,926 | 56,474 | 279,328 | 431,618 |
| Wisconsin | 1,363,475 | 187,010 | 91,853 | 21,737 | 70,116 | 95,157 | 753,124 | 423,341 |
| Wyoming | 375,137 | 151,354 | 118,828 | 100,486 | 18,342 | 32,526 | 68,524 | 155,259 |
| Dist. of Columbia | 11,597,515 | 1,165,664 | 493,282 | 450,040 | 43,242 | 672,382 | 363,640 | 10,068,211 |
| American Samoa | 2,408 | 28 | 0 | 0 | 0 | 28 | 0 | 0 |
| Guam | 359,165 | 337,222 | 195,168 | 191,646 | 3,522 | 142,054 | 7,007 | 14,936 |
| No. Mariana Islands | 1,931 | 21 | 0 | 0 | 0 | 21 | 592 | 1,318 |
| Puerto Rico | 730,070 | 271,440 | 167,310 | 72,367 | 94,943 | 104,130 | 173,948 | 284,682 |
| U.S. Virgin Islands | 40,687 | 4,160 | 1,155 | 734 | 421 | 3,005 | 14,287 | 22,240 |
| U.S. undistributed | 1,380,568 | 0 | 0 | 0 | 0 | 0 | 0 | 0 |

Source: U.S. Department of Commerce, Bureau of the Census.    Note: Detail may not add to totals due to rounding.

## Table 6.36
## FEDERAL GOVERNMENT DIRECT PAYMENTS FOR INDIVIDUALS BY PROGRAM, STATE AND TERRITORY: FISCAL YEAR 1998
### (In thousands of dollars)

| State or other jurisdiction | Total | Social Security Retirement insurance payments | Social Security Survivors insurance payments | Social Security Disability insurance payments | Medicare Hospital insurance payments | Medicare Supplementary medical insurance payments | Federal retirement & disability payments Civilian | Federal retirement & disability payments Military | Payments for unemployment compensation |
|---|---|---|---|---|---|---|---|---|---|
| United States ........ | $835,618,293 | $248,982,887 | $76,127,791 | $50,062,611 | $134,969,613 | $74,539,239 | $43,833,664 | $30,457,015 | $18,494,426 |
| Alabama .................... | 15,088,890 | 3,739,375 | 1,462,274 | 1,134,927 | 2,528,251 | 1,212,225 | 1,050,524 | 784,940 | 190,923 |
| Alaska ...................... | 1,194,098 | 242,676 | 99,927 | 65,830 | 112,794 | 51,954 | 134,353 | 109,365 | 107,094 |
| Arizona ................... | 13,594,246 | 4,477,728 | 1,136,908 | 824,452 | 1,948,259 | 1,211,666 | 870,953 | 845,066 | 134,963 |
| Arkansas ................. | 9,047,606 | 2,427,331 | 822,766 | 734,761 | 1,348,576 | 682,504 | 419,438 | 371,812 | 177,587 |
| California ................. | 86,771,558 | 24,037,917 | 6,751,535 | 4,389,714 | 14,772,357 | 9,197,082 | 4,213,225 | 3,572,550 | 2,430,070 |
| Colorado ................. | 10,164,366 | 2,787,272 | 867,237 | 641,091 | 1,347,739 | 763,394 | 801,200 | 837,657 | 149,243 |
| Connecticut ............. | 10,600,387 | 3,907,495 | 933,982 | 544,816 | 1,957,518 | 1,063,609 | 274,334 | 163,897 | 325,448 |
| Delaware ................. | 2,293,605 | 772,768 | 222,575 | 138,660 | 343,430 | 190,239 | 114,220 | 102,001 | 62,710 |
| Florida .................... | 58,414,143 | 18,936,327 | 4,538,244 | 2,905,548 | 10,194,916 | 6,898,969 | 2,953,095 | 3,238,956 | 618,792 |
| Georgia ................... | 20,324,131 | 5,186,940 | 1,888,074 | 1,493,358 | 3,145,197 | 1,632,373 | 1,285,485 | 1,179,540 | 244,017 |
| Hawaii .................... | 3,641,808 | 1,090,326 | 228,085 | 128,940 | 399,632 | 259,054 | 461,962 | 247,915 | 144,949 |
| Idaho ...................... | 3,234,958 | 1,039,193 | 299,385 | 191,620 | 388,874 | 214,412 | 203,912 | 164,116 | 93,984 |
| Illinois .................... | 35,246,082 | 11,222,749 | 3,525,877 | 1,879,648 | 6,137,257 | 3,101,789 | 1,182,553 | 476,254 | 1,070,876 |
| Indiana ................... | 17,796,288 | 5,890,259 | 1,842,426 | 1,124,764 | 2,753,583 | 1,387,869 | 621,484 | 287,966 | 214,339 |
| Iowa ....................... | 10,240,526 | 3,197,197 | 950,262 | 455,019 | 1,186,302 | 747,234 | 358,047 | 127,093 | 150,364 |
| Kansas .................... | 8,496,575 | 2,630,994 | 783,796 | 399,203 | 1,183,454 | 698,292 | 428,570 | 302,492 | 118,792 |
| Kentucky ................. | 12,588,304 | 3,162,071 | 1,262,933 | 1,299,396 | 1,954,562 | 968,862 | 570,280 | 335,053 | 216,907 |
| Louisiana ................ | 13,839,025 | 3,038,188 | 1,523,147 | 946,795 | 2,867,807 | 1,234,959 | 453,911 | 420,825 | 129,446 |
| Maine ..................... | 4,088,409 | 1,244,331 | 358,726 | 304,134 | 562,621 | 293,521 | 255,379 | 164,612 | 84,004 |
| Maryland ................. | 18,083,063 | 4,084,762 | 1,346,539 | 687,397 | 2,442,856 | 1,408,032 | 2,677,858 | 761,362 | 301,345 |
| Massachusetts .......... | 20,863,646 | 6,223,366 | 1,656,697 | 1,240,013 | 4,377,942 | 1,960,063 | 854,982 | 290,907 | 685,960 |
| Michigan ................. | 28,612,695 | 9,721,339 | 3,101,103 | 1,979,392 | 4,830,266 | 2,903,059 | 711,778 | 319,046 | 947,278 |
| Minnesota ............... | 12,701,664 | 4,242,601 | 1,213,892 | 644,596 | 1,769,384 | 943,407 | 455,681 | 193,897 | 324,387 |
| Mississippi .............. | 9,176,203 | 2,123,864 | 834,588 | 782,049 | 1,492,211 | 684,927 | 428,191 | 359,535 | 100,232 |
| Missouri .................. | 18,220,610 | 5,432,957 | 1,701,030 | 1,156,137 | 2,948,290 | 1,546,355 | 933,009 | 476,545 | 253,210 |
| Montana .................. | 3,336,298 | 828,681 | 257,452 | 172,658 | 340,474 | 192,013 | 196,700 | 105,166 | 51,921 |
| Nebraska ................. | 5,291,903 | 1,644,221 | 488,644 | 232,696 | 619,092 | 366,249 | 235,232 | 207,308 | 41,056 |
| Nevada ................... | 4,845,370 | 1,565,097 | 381,947 | 296,545 | 635,653 | 388,782 | 331,797 | 415,381 | 177,787 |
| New Hampshire ........ | 3,258,075 | 1,164,472 | 287,921 | 218,331 | 462,986 | 230,125 | 222,162 | 159,392 | 24,192 |
| New Jersey .............. | 25,715,503 | 8,947,492 | 2,356,064 | 1,326,913 | 4,488,536 | 2,615,882 | 1,024,914 | 317,119 | 1,046,446 |
| New Mexico ............ | 5,036,235 | 1,323,098 | 441,231 | 311,203 | 561,703 | 340,809 | 459,141 | 362,747 | 74,785 |
| New York ................ | 58,463,799 | 18,521,866 | 4,951,756 | 3,629,540 | 10,763,800 | 6,012,950 | 1,767,030 | 437,561 | 1,498,774 |
| North Carolina ........ | 21,645,350 | 6,823,829 | 1,987,399 | 1,772,906 | 3,183,474 | 1,615,169 | 1,029,136 | 1,125,369 | 378,140 |
| North Dakota ........... | 2,252,427 | 594,311 | 207,025 | 84,385 | 270,803 | 155,161 | 107,378 | 49,174 | 27,741 |
| Ohio ....................... | 33,663,105 | 10,752,628 | 3,810,174 | 2,065,076 | 5,649,828 | 3,065,637 | 1,377,222 | 583,016 | 653,613 |
| Oklahoma ............... | 11,127,796 | 3,072,616 | 1,068,439 | 630,022 | 1,805,367 | 813,544 | 882,764 | 494,135 | 87,038 |
| Oregon ................... | 9,645,871 | 3,363,025 | 873,978 | 535,850 | 1,230,585 | 744,036 | 563,364 | 321,209 | 387,053 |
| Pennsylvania ............ | 44,500,710 | 14,310,278 | 4,439,450 | 2,232,028 | 8,458,789 | 4,443,332 | 1,982,960 | 648,094 | 1,353,104 |
| Rhode Island ........... | 3,643,869 | 1,167,331 | 269,570 | 214,886 | 612,843 | 301,012 | 182,680 | 95,070 | 140,287 |
| South Carolina ......... | 11,610,887 | 3,343,892 | 1,067,101 | 963,486 | 1,555,943 | 838,045 | 696,819 | 808,103 | 152,420 |
| South Dakota ........... | 2,486,393 | 702,517 | 221,782 | 111,686 | 297,554 | 164,434 | 154,123 | 79,099 | 13,686 |
| Tennessee ................ | 17,238,481 | 4,738,267 | 1,657,463 | 1,345,693 | 3,116,934 | 1,310,803 | 839,054 | 660,742 | 300,726 |
| Texas ...................... | 51,152,631 | 13,234,766 | 5,097,231 | 2,575,984 | 8,492,531 | 4,101,755 | 2,698,672 | 3,063,144 | 844,309 |
| Utah ....................... | 4,429,178 | 1,336,994 | 397,482 | 218,587 | 531,011 | 270,130 | 639,855 | 189,130 | 79,621 |
| Vermont .................. | 1,659,272 | 568,055 | 160,260 | 116,376 | 240,921 | 115,133 | 70,170 | 46,506 | 41,474 |
| Virginia ................... | 21,524,622 | 5,224,488 | 1,708,678 | 1,254,478 | 2,481,754 | 1,387,795 | 2,619,142 | 2,442,909 | 166,812 |
| Washington .............. | 16,232,299 | 5,022,019 | 1,336,647 | 877,719 | 1,985,592 | 1,182,946 | 1,141,203 | 1,146,728 | 735,687 |
| West Virginia ........... | 6,870,206 | 1,815,099 | 775,040 | 739,687 | 1,053,897 | 543,302 | 259,936 | 127,989 | 120,801 |
| Wisconsin ................ | 14,426,404 | 5,468,772 | 1,498,411 | 840,367 | 2,069,584 | 1,165,578 | 432,768 | 207,427 | 443,663 |
| Wyoming ................. | 1,342,157 | 422,532 | 132,763 | 80,256 | 175,690 | 89,775 | 98,286 | 64,027 | 23,384 |
| Dist. of Columbia ..... | 3,297,459 | 359,887 | 126,161 | 81,457 | 375,108 | 212,690 | 886,884 | 58,548 | 66,556 |
| American Samoa ...... | 34,929 | 6,932 | 7,381 | 6,690 | 0 | 0 | 116 | 4,957 | 0 |
| Guam ...................... | 220,971 | 39,078 | 23,118 | 6,925 | 715 | 373 | 51,609 | 26,888 | 0 |
| No. Mariana Islands .. | 19,339 | 2,743 | 3,516 | 730 | 0 | 0 | 69 | 638 | 0 |
| Puerto Rico ............. | 6,111,331 | 1,701,136 | 722,433 | 1,016,201 | 501,790 | 609,284 | 153,237 | 74,071 | 281,781 |
| U.S. Virgin Islands ... | 174,933 | 56,730 | 19,259 | 10,989 | 12,579 | 6,694 | 12,670 | 1,966 | 4,653 |
| U.S. undistributed .... | 37,603 | 0 | 0 | 0 | 0 | 0 | 2,145 | 0 | 0 |

See footnotes at end of table.

## FEDERAL GOVERNMENT DIRECT PAYMENTS—Continued

| State or other jurisdiction | Veterans benefits programs | Supplemental security income payments | Food stamps | Housing assistance | Agricultural assistance | Excess earned income tax credit | Federal employee health insurance programs | All other |
|---|---|---|---|---|---|---|---|---|
| United States .............. | $18,594,777 | $27,641,736 | $16,943,877 | $21,518,553 | $12,385,798 | $24,062,259 | $10,704,892 | $26,299,105 |
| Alaska ..................... | 440,751 | 663,259 | 357,318 | 198,702 | 97,241 | 650,959 | 180,190 | 397,032 |
| Alabama .................. | 61,312 | 30,521 | 49,747 | 42,129 | 7,292 | 27,197 | 1,431 | 50,477 |
| Arizona ................... | 385,721 | 351,589 | 253,455 | 162,030 | 52,008 | 440,538 | 130,808 | 368,102 |
| Arkansas ................. | 337,566 | 343,859 | 205,780 | 138,318 | 392,144 | 344,487 | 58,135 | 242,542 |
| California ................ | 1,483,152 | 3,950,692 | 2,071,639 | 3,439,983 | 346,269 | 2,955,666 | 784,674 | 2,375,032 |
| Colorado ................. | 298,245 | 245,509 | 156,917 | 264,440 | 223,039 | 258,938 | 155,266 | 367,180 |
| Connecticut .............. | 138,596 | 211,305 | 161,194 | 483,449 | 41,941 | 154,611 | 58,338 | 179,855 |
| Delaware ................. | 46,388 | 50,498 | 33,610 | 72,222 | 9,770 | 61,918 | 13,672 | 58,924 |
| Florida ................... | 1,383,462 | 1,588,883 | 847,775 | 820,931 | 54,405 | 1,597,677 | 454,661 | 1,381,494 |
| Georgia .................. | 616,282 | 816,317 | 538,294 | 401,934 | 150,359 | 943,840 | 218,896 | 583,224 |
| Hawaii ................... | 80,771 | 85,544 | 178,216 | 118,840 | 1,974 | 62,314 | 94,261 | 59,027 |
| Idaho .................... | 87,096 | 73,475 | 46,693 | 59,171 | 134,721 | 96,789 | 24,162 | 117,354 |
| Illinois .................. | 414,816 | 1,264,202 | 844,102 | 1,009,075 | 854,248 | 907,254 | 212,063 | 1,143,318 |
| Indiana .................. | 283,116 | 403,666 | 263,189 | 359,155 | 343,436 | 435,000 | 106,484 | 1,479,552 |
| Iowa ..................... | 156,894 | 165,245 | 109,460 | 159,938 | 1,926,488 | 162,327 | 61,475 | 327,181 |
| Kansas ................... | 172,594 | 154,170 | 82,783 | 110,126 | 912,217 | 169,008 | 43,579 | 306,508 |
| Kentucky ................. | 330,074 | 727,736 | 344,941 | 245,566 | 118,909 | 363,609 | 186,922 | 500,485 |
| Louisiana ................ | 350,060 | 739,206 | 467,295 | 264,916 | 234,159 | 726,127 | 88,621 | 353,563 |
| Maine .................... | 162,930 | 110,353 | 100,233 | 174,332 | 26,687 | 83,957 | 32,026 | 130,563 |
| Maryland ................. | 302,803 | 393,200 | 281,553 | 484,674 | 34,971 | 387,883 | 2,086,997 | 400,830 |
| Massachusetts ............ | 448,505 | 644,185 | 221,816 | 1,255,290 | 3,596 | 279,718 | 168,137 | 552,468 |
| Michigan ................. | 423,620 | 1,003,656 | 588,474 | 500,486 | 154,536 | 667,753 | 132,798 | 628,111 |
| Minnesota ................ | 270,854 | 278,942 | 173,315 | 331,564 | 953,429 | 222,035 | 119,956 | 563,726 |
| Mississippi ............... | 272,061 | 537,846 | 254,346 | 177,456 | 283,272 | 539,125 | 63,680 | 242,822 |
| Missouri ................. | 371,348 | 468,366 | 345,485 | 342,954 | 380,190 | 473,474 | 810,545 | 580,714 |
| Montana .................. | 87,736 | 58,298 | 52,374 | 65,026 | 662,731 | 73,512 | 21,016 | 170,541 |
| Nebraska ................. | 136,966 | 86,728 | 67,738 | 88,781 | 624,003 | 106,178 | 38,507 | 308,504 |
| Nevada ................... | 132,553 | 97,068 | 63,225 | 81,778 | 5,600 | 140,232 | 29,285 | 102,643 |
| New Hampshire ........... | 105,328 | 48,246 | 30,212 | 115,374 | 6,683 | 56,522 | 39,458 | 86,670 |
| New Jersey ............... | 357,031 | 611,688 | 383,612 | 1,020,449 | 6,875 | 514,985 | 133,042 | 564,455 |
| New Mexico .............. | 190,830 | 191,807 | 144,405 | 92,119 | 54,310 | 228,083 | 70,539 | 189,426 |
| New York ................ | 861,345 | 2,630,312 | 1,487,290 | 2,244,956 | 64,497 | 1,458,013 | 347,839 | 1,786,271 |
| North Carolina ........... | 648,174 | 759,202 | 421,099 | 364,797 | 104,707 | 830,626 | 121,523 | 479,800 |
| North Dakota ............. | 42,301 | 31,825 | 25,123 | 58,993 | 430,134 | 40,220 | 17,586 | 110,267 |
| Ohio ..................... | 630,749 | 1,217,463 | 615,553 | 872,243 | 229,081 | 802,252 | 189,066 | 1,149,505 |
| Oklahoma ................ | 461,879 | 305,969 | 230,900 | 190,663 | 288,911 | 357,429 | 121,206 | 316,912 |
| Oregon ................... | 282,282 | 215,227 | 197,719 | 222,586 | 93,400 | 227,596 | 108,922 | 279,039 |
| Pennsylvania ............. | 728,931 | 1,214,300 | 764,939 | 890,176 | 57,065 | 771,473 | 571,745 | 1,634,039 |
| Rhode Island ............. | 83,883 | 98,148 | 57,179 | 223,503 | 2,040 | 64,171 | 33,939 | 97,327 |
| South Carolina ........... | 339,408 | 449,776 | 263,759 | 204,412 | 61,828 | 508,016 | 82,004 | 275,874 |
| South Dakota ............. | 68,669 | 53,886 | 36,923 | 58,888 | 326,981 | 54,857 | 11,318 | 129,992 |
| Tennessee ................ | 464,307 | 707,043 | 437,308 | 310,168 | 125,827 | 607,837 | 122,638 | 493,669 |
| Texas .................... | 1,474,286 | 1,599,280 | 1,424,903 | 939,075 | 823,330 | 2,616,510 | 533,306 | 1,633,549 |
| Utah ..................... | 89,074 | 89,864 | 75,252 | 75,309 | 25,622 | 129,525 | 61,935 | 219,787 |
| Vermont .................. | 43,111 | 42,513 | 33,758 | 59,108 | 8,884 | 36,386 | 6,910 | 69,707 |
| Virginia .................. | 580,233 | 553,300 | 306,853 | 442,518 | 52,130 | 540,989 | 805,663 | 956,879 |
| Washington .............. | 522,683 | 443,470 | 319,371 | 300,215 | 213,597 | 327,391 | 197,276 | 479,948 |
| West Virginia ............ | 204,249 | 318,258 | 224,257 | 130,317 | 15,557 | 164,753 | 49,728 | 327,338 |
| Wisconsin ................ | 298,633 | 398,430 | 130,104 | 281,725 | 282,823 | 286,241 | 71,376 | 550,503 |
| Wyoming ................. | 36,250 | 23,829 | 20,871 | 23,944 | 28,708 | 37,845 | 14,385 | 69,612 |
| Dist. Of Columbia ........ | 50,248 | 90,799 | 84,857 | 164,237 | 41,679 | 66,462 | 553,778 | 78,107 |
| American Samoa ........... | 2,710 | 0 | 5,300 | 0 | 0 | 0 | 0 | 843 |
| Guam .................... | 6,061 | 0 | 34,413 | 15,849 | 1 | 0 | 12,228 | 3,715 |
| No. Mariana Islands ........ | 390 | 2,979 | 5,100 | 2,445 | 0 | 0 | 0 | 728 |
| Puerto Rico ............... | 343,723 | 0 | 0 | 342,886 | 7,252 | 1,951 | 50,899 | 304,687 |
| Virgin Islands ............ | 1,737 | 0 | 21,851 | 18,330 | 4,243 | 0 | 0 | 3,232 |
| U.S. undistributed .......... | 0 | 0 | 0 | 0 | 0 | 0 | 0 | 35,458 |

*Source*: U.S. Department of Commerce, Bureau of the Census.

*Note*: Detail may not add to totals due to rounding. Amounts represent actual expenditures during the fiscal year.

## Table 6.37
## FEDERAL GOVERNMENT PROCUREMENT CONTRACTS—
## VALUE OF AWARDS, BY STATE AND TERRITORY: FISCAL YEAR 1996
### (In thousands of dollars)

| State or other jurisdiction | Total | Department of Defense | Postal Service | All other |
|---|---|---|---|---|
| United States | $200,543,115 | $128,628,822 | $10,436,999 | $61,477,294 |
| Alabama | 2,936,599 | 1,838,999 | 129,647 | 967,953 |
| Alaska | 803,901 | 565,149 | 28,632 | 210,120 |
| Arizona | 3,485,395 | 2,921,102 | 144,453 | 419,840 |
| Arkansas | 453,019 | 249,336 | 85,073 | 118,610 |
| California | 27,723,583 | 19,971,914 | 1,141,751 | 6,609,918 |
| Colorado | 4,656,320 | 3,010,286 | 175,269 | 1,470,765 |
| Connecticut | 3,122,527 | 2,684,617 | 152,345 | 285,565 |
| Delaware | 153,775 | 101,565 | 27,956 | 24,254 |
| Florida | 8,125,596 | 5,880,491 | 538,551 | 1,706,554 |
| Georgia | 4,741,012 | 3,981,794 | 254,093 | 505,125 |
| Hawaii | 1,027,398 | 907,306 | 35,713 | 84,379 |
| Idaho | 945,045 | 131,993 | 35,060 | 777,992 |
| Illinois | 3,165,199 | 1,184,500 | 550,621 | 1,430,078 |
| Indiana | 2,090,255 | 1,574,180 | 206,884 | 309,191 |
| Iowa | 777,558 | 371,832 | 134,590 | 271,136 |
| Kansas | 1,109,643 | 779,583 | 114,391 | 215,669 |
| Kentucky | 2,004,606 | 858,782 | 125,538 | 1,020,286 |
| Louisiana | 2,086,487 | 1,076,852 | 135,817 | 873,818 |
| Maine | 907,359 | 791,913 | 54,009 | 61,437 |
| Maryland | 8,521,750 | 4,090,160 | 223,491 | 4,208,099 |
| Massachusetts | 6,080,621 | 4,696,131 | 306,627 | 1,077,863 |
| Michigan | 2,188,854 | 1,249,599 | 372,470 | 566,785 |
| Minnesota | 1,534,730 | 963,700 | 215,677 | 355,353 |
| Mississippi | 2,326,200 | 1,962,533 | 68,680 | 294,987 |
| Missouri | 10,593,615 | 9,218,323 | 249,139 | 1,126,153 |
| Montana | 262,931 | 89,622 | 32,032 | 141,277 |
| Nebraska | 584,873 | 366,759 | 71,607 | 146,507 |
| Nevada | 1,406,672 | 290,489 | 49,686 | 1,066,497 |
| New Hampshire | 671,585 | 566,876 | 55,045 | 49,664 |
| New Jersey | 3,750,337 | 2,577,472 | 398,242 | 774,623 |
| New Mexico | 3,676,231 | 679,539 | 52,343 | 2,944,349 |
| New York | 6,319,855 | 3,558,545 | 834,111 | 1,927,199 |
| North Carolina | 2,293,304 | 1,655,034 | 244,770 | 393,500 |
| North Dakota | 209,820 | 106,140 | 26,706 | 76,974 |
| Ohio | 4,583,274 | 2,735,950 | 435,509 | 1,411,815 |
| Oklahoma | 1,205,250 | 776,660 | 112,747 | 315,843 |
| Oregon | 610,417 | 201,403 | 113,682 | 295,332 |
| Pennsylvania | 5,530,752 | 3,772,681 | 539,992 | 1,218,079 |
| Rhode Island | 422,850 | 328,714 | 48,031 | 46,105 |
| South Carolina | 2,504,519 | 1,016,216 | 97,998 | 1,390,305 |
| South Dakota | 248,588 | 109,537 | 28,778 | 110,273 |
| Tennessee | 4,317,302 | 1,131,991 | 198,361 | 2,986,950 |
| Texas | 13,840,351 | 9,073,887 | 639,645 | 4,126,819 |
| Utah | 1,072,486 | 393,157 | 62,870 | 616,459 |
| Vermont | 295,096 | 225,427 | 28,159 | 41,510 |
| Virginia | 14,528,576 | 10,345,629 | 271,949 | 3,910,998 |
| Washington | 4,603,131 | 2,380,798 | 185,593 | 2,036,740 |
| West Virginia | 513,725 | 203,059 | 67,779 | 242,887 |
| Wisconsin | 1,161,640 | 555,972 | 182,215 | 423,453 |
| Wyoming | 153,196 | 91,558 | 16,539 | 45,099 |
| District of Columbia | 4,579,905 | 1,197,256 | 90,714 | 3,291,935 |
| American Samoa | 4,161 | 3,014 | 0 | 1,147 |
| Guam | 112,399 | 109,817 | 0 | 2,582 |
| No. Marianas Islands | 1,471 | 579 | 146 | 746 |
| Puerto Rico | 404,700 | 267,117 | 41,771 | 95,812 |
| U.S. Virgin Islands | 22,287 | 13,658 | 3,502 | 5,127 |
| Undistributed (a) | 19,090,384 | 12,741,626 | 0 | 6,348,758 |

*Source:* U.S. Department of Commerce, Bureau of the Census.
*Note:* Amounts shown for U.S. Postal Service represent actual outlays for contractual commitments, while all other amounts shown represent the value of contract actions, and do not reflect Federal Government expenditures. Nonpostal data generally involve only current year contract actions; however, multiple-year obligations may be reflected for contract actions of less than 3 years duration. Foreign procurement contract awards are excluded from United States totals.
Foreign award total equals $7,499,710,000, including $6,367,932,000 for the Department of Defenseand $1,131,778,000 for all other Federal agencies.
(a) Includes awards under $25,000 and classified location awards (Department of Defense).

## Table 6.38
## FEDERAL GOVERNMENT PROCUREMENT CONTRACTS—VALUE OF AWARDS,
## BY STATE AND TERRITORY: FISCAL YEAR 1997
### (In thousands of dollars)

| State or other jurisdiction | Total | Department of Defense | Department of Energy | Postal service | National Aeronautics and Space Administration | All other Federal agencies |
|---|---|---|---|---|---|---|
| United States ........... | $193,071,377 | $119,855,710 | $15,128,399 | $11,037,998 | $11,000,404 | $36,048,866 |
| Alabama ........................... | 3,230,792 | 2,158,777 | 1,466 | 136,045 | 574,633 | 359,871 |
| Alaska ............................. | 855,730 | 644,868 | 46 | 29,915 | 11,161 | 169,740 |
| Arizona ........................... | 2,635,632 | 1,970,420 | 6,781 | 159,086 | 39,780 | 459,565 |
| Arkansas ......................... | 454,611 | 192,045 | 1,422 | 88,737 | 0 | 172,407 |
| California ....................... | 26,246,986 | 18,507,768 | 1,859,659 | 1,194,856 | 2,661,415 | 2,023,288 |
| Colorado ........................ | 3,493,767 | 1,895,847 | 624,425 | 191,590 | 157,737 | 624,168 |
| Connecticut ..................... | 2,918,223 | 2,517,044 | 9,889 | 159,430 | 84,975 | 146,885 |
| Delaware ......................... | 156,606 | 105,288 | 0 | 30,969 | 3,056 | 17,293 |
| Florida ........................... | 8,082,879 | 6,303,598 | 81,113 | 560,828 | 432,967 | 704,373 |
| Georgia ........................... | 4,773,688 | 3,902,308 | 11,838 | 272,732 | 11,397 | 575,413 |
| Hawaii ............................ | 1,077,348 | 925,848 | 0 | 35,484 | 6,224 | 109,792 |
| Idaho .............................. | 887,793 | 143,376 | 607,560 | 37,649 | 283 | 98,925 |
| Illinois ........................... | 3,190,459 | 1,250,427 | 754,763 | 578,609 | 5,156 | 601,504 |
| Indiana ........................... | 2,328,930 | 1,739,133 | 10,352 | 218,378 | 40,736 | 320,331 |
| Iowa ............................... | 805,527 | 438,227 | 25,843 | 140,674 | 2,341 | 198,442 |
| Kansas ............................ | 988,592 | 681,025 | -330 | 118,080 | 1 | 189,816 |
| Kentucky ......................... | 2,754,616 | 1,139,256 | 166,281 | 135,163 | -12 | 1,313,928 |
| Louisiana ........................ | 2,776,529 | 1,743,025 | 224,018 | 141,407 | 356,725 | 311,354 |
| Maine ............................. | 1,018,013 | 917,691 | 441 | 58,077 | 236 | 41,568 |
| Maryland ........................ | 8,476,741 | 3,868,519 | 99,708 | 231,382 | 1,167,492 | 3,109,640 |
| Massachusetts ................. | 6,120,867 | 4,885,005 | 23,913 | 328,483 | 90,656 | 792,810 |
| Michigan ......................... | 2,010,223 | 1,097,663 | 2,070 | 392,599 | 12,149 | 505,742 |
| Minnesota ....................... | 1,683,924 | 1,090,046 | 2,225 | 223,705 | 3,307 | 364,641 |
| Mississippi ...................... | 1,727,232 | 1,361,702 | 216 | 72,181 | 134,187 | 158,946 |
| Missouri ......................... | 6,324,370 | 4,748,635 | 413,544 | 266,911 | 15,033 | 880,247 |
| Montana .......................... | 260,152 | 80,174 | 33,784 | 33,994 | 1,478 | 110,722 |
| Nebraska ......................... | 521,066 | 261,655 | 151 | 74,164 | 337 | 184,759 |
| Nevada. ........................... | 550,310 | 255,889 | 133,873 | 56,416 | 1,905 | 102,227 |
| New Hampshire ............... | 486,851 | 388,128 | 221 | 61,194 | 8,094 | 29,214 |
| New Jersey ....................... | 4,097,316 | 2,970,610 | 95,434 | 407,562 | 158,457 | 465,253 |
| New Mexico ..................... | 3,534,180 | 494,446 | 2,697,543 | 54,858 | 51,221 | 236,112 |
| New York ........................ | 5,777,954 | 3,157,301 | 669,803 | 881,279 | 20,601 | 1,048,970 |
| North Carolina ................ | 1,960,363 | 1,082,834 | 2,193 | 274,393 | 6,616 | 594,327 |
| North Dakota .................. | 229,320 | 120,067 | 578 | 27,704 | 70 | 80,901 |
| Ohio ............................... | 4,604,567 | 2,711,822 | 635,861 | 454,297 | 294,883 | 507,704 |
| Oklahoma ........................ | 1,187,700 | 737,869 | 27,438 | 118,389 | 5,137 | 298,867 |
| Oregon ............................ | 579,939 | 164,352 | 2,649 | 121,758 | 6,044 | 285,136 |
| Pennsylvania ................... | 5,125,983 | 3,035,609 | 467,021 | 572,296 | 56,869 | 994,188 |
| Rhode Island ................... | 355,592 | 257,410 | 0 | 52,624 | 143 | 45,415 |
| South Carolina ................ | 2,404,143 | 901,394 | 1,295,349 | 105,316 | 131 | 101,953 |
| South Dakota .................. | 252,629 | 86,735 | 4,804 | 29,549 | 542 | 130,999 |
| Tennessee ........................ | 4,385,680 | 1,164,321 | 1,647,197 | 208,868 | 14,495 | 1,350,799 |
| Texas .............................. | 13,292,575 | 7,347,347 | 318,522 | 688,394 | 3,587,420 | 1,350,892 |
| Utah ............................... | 1,205,982 | 433,428 | 8,169 | 69,546 | 429,384 | 265,455 |
| Vermont .......................... | 149,548 | 97,900 | 110 | 29,125 | 604 | 21,809 |
| Virginia .......................... | 16,253,703 | 11,037,794 | 775,289 | 288,657 | 351,495 | 3,800,468 |
| Washington ..................... | 4,601,097 | 2,586,195 | 1,290,917 | 206,531 | 117,214 | 400,240 |
| West Virginia .................. | 502,168 | 150,376 | 41,190 | 70,337 | 11,980 | 228,285 |
| Wisconsin ....................... | 1,306,988 | 564,623 | 1,333 | 189,643 | 13,048 | 538,341 |
| Wyoming ......................... | 148,602 | 48,401 | 2,634 | 17,255 | 715 | 79,597 |
| Dist. of Columbia ........... | 4,184,367 | 1,139,184 | 49,082 | 91,567 | 49,886 | 2,854,648 |
| American Samoa ............. | 4,165 | 1,589 | 0 | 0 | 0 | 2,576 |
| Guam. ............................. | 120,759 | 113,948 | 0 | 1,764 | 0 | 5,047 |
| No. Marianas Islands ..... | 3,956 | 2,972 | 0 | 149 | 0 | 835 |
| Puerto Rico ..................... | 317,700 | 205,222 | 11 | 43,802 | 0 | 68,665 |
| U.S. Virgin Islands. ........ | 7,825 | 1,593 | 0 | 3,598 | 0 | 2,634 |
| Undistributed (a) ........... | 19,641,120 | 14,029,981 | 0 | 0 | 0 | 5,611,139 |

*Source*: U.S. Department of Commerce, Bureau of the Census.

*Note*: Amounts shown for U.S. Postal Service represent actual outlays for contractual commitments, while all other amounts shown represent the value of contract actions, and do not reflect Federal Government expenditures. Nonpostal data generally involve only current year contract actions; however, multiple-year obligations may be reflected for contract actions of less than 3 years duration. Foreign procurement contract awards are excluded from United States totals. Foreign award total equals $7,523,052,000, including $6,081,301,000 for the Department of Defense and $1,441,751,000 for all other Federal agencies.

(a) Includes awards under $25,000 and classified location awards (Department of Defense).

## Table 6.39
## FEDERAL GOVERNMENT EXPENDITURES FOR OTHER PROGRAMS, BY STATE AND TERRITORY: FISCAL YEAR 1997
(In thousands of dollars)

| State or other jurisdiction | Total | Grants Total | Department of Health & Human Service research grants | National Science Foundation | NASA-space program research grants | National Endowment for the Arts Arts | National Endowment for the Arts Humanities | Corporation for National and Community Service (a) | All other programs |
|---|---|---|---|---|---|---|---|---|---|
| United States .......... | $57,941,609 | $29,736,874 | $16,930,325 | $2,123,986 | $929,416 | $114,190 | $89,523 | $413,349 | $9,136,085 |
| Alabama ..................... | 771,137 | 473,548 | 270,344 | 9,170 | 34,871 | 957 | 652 | 6,399 | 151,155 |
| Alaska ........................ | 201,261 | 152,007 | 26,821 | 6,316 | 7,546 | 893 | 582 | 1,444 | 108,405 |
| Arizona ...................... | 671,451 | 439,574 | 247,451 | 49,920 | 16,313 | 1,164 | 1,154 | 3,318 | 120,255 |
| Arkansas .................... | 524,086 | 149,151 | 82,550 | 5,662 | 572 | 442 | 468 | 4,310 | 55,148 |
| California ................... | 5,935,767 | 4,044,154 | 2,274,163 | 314,900 | 367,411 | 11,011 | 8,123 | 35,117 | 1,033,430 |
| Colorado ................... | 1,045,913 | 615,035 | 288,100 | 144,068 | 22,486 | 1,529 | 1,412 | 6,944 | 150,496 |
| Connecticut ............... | 642,826 | 472,369 | 298,663 | 21,369 | 3,870 | 1,555 | 953 | 5,472 | 140,487 |
| Delaware ................... | 96,810 | 60,572 | 17,765 | 10,773 | 1,654 | 570 | 648 | 1,520 | 27,642 |
| Florida ...................... | 1,582,717 | 757,831 | 384,895 | 47,513 | 17,728 | 1,412 | 861 | 16,540 | 288,883 |
| Georgia ..................... | 989,299 | 515,804 | 300,659 | 34,100 | 14,471 | 2,281 | 1,106 | 9,557 | 153,631 |
| Hawaii ....................... | 243,669 | 132,703 | 46,318 | 18,418 | 5,220 | 861 | 1,530 | 1,309 | 59,047 |
| Idaho ........................ | 250,942 | 86,467 | 38,047 | 2,058 | 444 | 532 | 476 | 2,219 | 42,692 |
| Illinois ....................... | 2,034,659 | 975,304 | 575,256 | 114,104 | 13,122 | 4,426 | 5,138 | 6,632 | 256,626 |
| Indiana. ..................... | 1,724,320 | 351,162 | 175,779 | 44,485 | 2,450 | 649 | 799 | 8,174 | 118,825 |
| Iowa .......................... | 1,829,466 | 236,752 | 146,265 | 15,125 | 5,545 | 573 | 866 | 5,146 | 63,231 |
| Kansas ....................... | 1,022,965 | 193,770 | 77,668 | 12,369 | 2,260 | 547 | 569 | 5,020 | 95,338 |
| Kentucky .................... | 757,790 | 254,681 | 149,414 | 7,347 | 1,693 | 1,114 | 1,339 | 5,645 | 88,129 |
| Louisiana .................. | 686,347 | 330,306 | 177,380 | 20,752 | 6,088 | 969 | 838 | 5,550 | 118,730 |
| Maine ....................... | 193,296 | 123,138 | 61,895 | 8,908 | 674 | 686 | 686 | 3,594 | 46,712 |
| Maryland ................... | 3,405,276 | 1,195,143 | 847,425 | 49,279 | 53,895 | 2,621 | 2,550 | 9,212 | 230,162 |
| Massachusetts ............ | 2,351,706 | 1,944,340 | 1,222,435 | 185,647 | 40,860 | 4,234 | 9,059 | 19,111 | 462,993 |
| Michigan .................. | 1,291,531 | 869,548 | 517,370 | 63,991 | 19,112 | 1,097 | 1,336 | 9,712 | 256,928 |
| Minnesota .................. | 1,571,525 | 498,538 | 313,876 | 34,477 | 3,515 | 4,759 | 1,248 | 9,452 | 131,211 |
| Mississippi ................. | 540,767 | 253,079 | 162,190 | 5,026 | 3,242 | 666 | 822 | 7,016 | 74,117 |
| Missouri .................... | 1,744,237 | 533,785 | 358,691 | 22,640 | 5,552 | 2,586 | 916 | 7,537 | 135,862 |
| Montana .................... | 761,753 | 129,345 | 71,125 | 8,526 | 3,684 | 574 | 457 | 3,965 | 41,015 |
| Nebraska ................... | 702,519 | 169,500 | 67,942 | 7,383 | 2,285 | 571 | 527 | 3,394 | 87,397 |
| Nevada ..................... | 216,337 | 147,039 | 43,045 | 9,277 | 774 | 460 | 569 | 2,045 | 90,870 |
| New Hampshire ........... | 210,840 | 133,177 | 54,627 | 20,672 | 7,567 | 978 | 762 | 4,913 | 43,657 |
| New Jersey ................ | 837,028 | 501,280 | 238,245 | 52,520 | 7,147 | 1,153 | 1,972 | 14,201 | 186,041 |
| New Mexico .............. | 479,797 | 328,173 | 130,156 | 13,984 | 8,904 | 886 | 901 | 3,775 | 169,566 |
| New York ................... | 3,257,976 | 2,300,133 | 1,479,084 | 203,161 | 29,527 | 29,036 | 12,008 | 31,943 | 515,374 |
| North Carolina ............ | 1,301,334 | 817,983 | 573,114 | 35,863 | 11,371 | 2,044 | 2,138 | 7,216 | 186,236 |
| North Dakota ............. | 624,308 | 98,234 | 34,489 | 3,146 | 1,293 | 500 | 462 | 1,000 | 57,344 |
| Ohio ......................... | 1,292,856 | 753,291 | 523,993 | 36,201 | 25,687 | 1,914 | 1,223 | 12,783 | 151,491 |
| Oklahoma ................. | 784,906 | 346,667 | 242,481 | 10,845 | 1,783 | 552 | 627 | 4,560 | 85,820 |
| Oregon ..................... | 670,661 | 431,479 | 224,783 | 31,035 | 4,166 | 1,376 | 707 | 7,759 | 161,653 |
| Pennsylvania .............. | 2,367,734 | 1,422,784 | 899,254 | 101,307 | 18,352 | 4,636 | 3,320 | 16,003 | 379,911 |
| Rhode Island ............. | 227,829 | 151,053 | 78,383 | 15,638 | 3,411 | 665 | 2,187 | 5,018 | 45,751 |
| South Carolina ............ | 460,118 | 281,794 | 126,833 | 17,019 | 3,514 | 854 | 978 | 3,122 | 129,474 |
| South Dakota .............. | 369,924 | 86,572 | 46,036 | 3,207 | 2,286 | 595 | 533 | 1,103 | 32,812 |
| Tennessee ................. | 784,422 | 440,557 | 282,111 | 15,087 | 7,636 | 696 | 720 | 5,284 | 129,023 |
| Texas ........................ | 3,123,824 | 1,379,376 | 922,641 | 64,544 | 53,181 | 3,368 | 2,731 | 31,789 | 301,121 |
| Utah ......................... | 363,038 | 233,141 | 116,926 | 16,925 | 2,949 | 978 | 660 | 2,691 | 92,012 |
| Vermont .................... | 129,463 | 93,322 | 43,932 | 6,866 | 515 | 618 | 425 | 2,398 | 38,567 |
| Virginia ..................... | 1,798,036 | 748,952 | 308,647 | 32,805 | 25,119 | 1,544 | 2,863 | 4,549 | 373,425 |
| Washington ............... | 1,355,093 | 842,729 | 550,321 | 44,653 | 9,541 | 2,469 | 840 | 5,395 | 229,509 |
| West Virginia .............. | 294,580 | 196,717 | 60,714 | 40,977 | 16,104 | 475 | 610 | 3,331 | 74,507 |
| Wisconsin .................. | 1,037,002 | 500,428 | 300,337 | 37,073 | 7,992 | 1,174 | 1,966 | 5,781 | 146,105 |
| Wyoming ................... | 107,806 | 65,696 | 11,496 | 5,615 | 634 | 528 | 416 | 1,168 | 45,837 |
| Dist. of Columbia .......... | 1,745,522 | 1,098,843 | 215,760 | 37,178 | 21,252 | 5,927 | 3,378 | 25,398 | 789,951 |
| American Samoa ........... | 17,818 | 17,801 | 1,802 | 0 | 0 | 267 | 212 | 539 | 14,980 |
| Guam ........................ | 38,759 | 25,072 | 2,407 | 100 | 0 | 248 | 236 | 491 | 21,591 |
| No. Marianas Islands .... | 10,337 | 10,287 | 211 | 0 | 0 | 272 | 229 | 0 | 9,574 |
| Puerto Rico ................. | 403,635 | 275,351 | 209,150 | 3,929 | 2,150 | 444 | 500 | 4,828 | 54,349 |
| U.S. Virgin Islands ......... | 56,491 | 51,330 | 8,864 | 32 | 0 | 269 | 235 | 955 | 40,975 |
| Undistributed ................ | 89 | 0 | 0 | 0 | 0 | 0 | 0 | 0 | 0 |

See footnotes at end of table.

## FEDERAL GOVERNMENT EXPENDITURES FOR OTHER PROGRAMS — Continued

| State or other jurisdiction | Total | Direct payments – other than for individuals | | | | | | All other programs |
|---|---|---|---|---|---|---|---|---|
| | | Department of Agriculture | | | | | | |
| | | Feed grain production stabilization payments | Conservation Reserve Program | Crop insurance claims & payments | Wheat production stabilization paymemts | Other agricultural programs | All other programs | |
| United States | $28,204,735 | $2,402,539 | $1,671,801 | $2,106,704 | $1,721,500 | $1,625,678 | $18,676,513 |
| Alabama | 297,589 | 6,807 | 23,174 | 1,969 | 6,539 | 33,240 | 225,861 |
| Alaska | 49,254 | 115 | 899 | 60 | 1 | 4,143 | 44,035 |
| Arizona | 231,877 | 1,981 | 1 | 86 | 5,719 | 38,635 | 185,455 |
| Arkansas. | 374,935 | 10,236 | 11,747 | 6,797 | 34,497 | 219,405 | 92,254 |
| California | 1,891,613 | 14,315 | 8,438 | 10,912 | 35,877 | 204,146 | 1,617,924 |
| Colorado | 430,878 | 33,107 | 77,730 | 1,310 | 59,439 | 19,000 | 240,292 |
| Connecticut | 170,456 | 891 | 0 | 45,664 | 1 | 571 | 123,330 |
| Delaware | 36,238 | 3,443 | 63 | 409 | 1,204 | 1,012 | 30,107 |
| Florida | 824,886 | 2,956 | 5,193 | 7,600 | 1,135 | 12,396 | 795,607 |
| Georgia | 473,495 | 16,905 | 26,313 | 21,110 | 17,561 | 56,786 | 334,820 |
| Hawaii | 110,966 | 0 | 0 | 68 | 0 | 960 | 109,937 |
| Idaho | 164,474 | 15,621 | 37,371 | 1,345 | 58,546 | 6,254 | 45,338 |
| Illinois | 1,059,355 | 335,404 | 60,896 | 56,764 | 45,738 | 18,723 | 541,830 |
| Indiana | 1,373,158 | 170,363 | 31,919 | 1,154 | 24,285 | 4,683 | 1,140,754 |
| Iowa | 1,592,715 | 384,429 | 166,857 | 882,386 | 2,033 | 8,489 | 148,521 |
| Kansas | 829,195 | 122,658 | 149,614 | 191,526 | 273,813 | 10,448 | 81,137 |
| Kentucky | 503,109 | 39,631 | 23,211 | 6,070 | 12,627 | 7,874 | 413,696 |
| Louisiana | 356,041 | 9,401 | 6,507 | 4,237 | 7,518 | 143,334 | 185,044 |
| Maine | 70,159 | 744 | 1,604 | 699 | 12 | 2,770 | 64,330 |
| Maryland | 2,210,133 | 11,375 | 1,508 | 826 | 3,800 | 2,274 | 2,190,351 |
| Massachusetts | 407,366 | 528 | 6 | 657 | 2 | 2,238 | 403,936 |
| Michigan | 421,983 | 63,167 | 19,994 | 6,753 | 19,783 | 5,910 | 306,376 |
| Minnesota | 1,072,986 | 182,840 | 94,996 | 353,933 | 80,850 | 17,318 | 343,048 |
| Mississippi | 287,688 | 6,561 | 35,654 | 5,598 | 12,454 | 115,560 | 111,861 |
| Missouri | 1,210,453 | 83,016 | 106,059 | 7,964 | 54,148 | 49,908 | 909,357 |
| Montana | 632,408 | 26,639 | 99,899 | 330,816 | 115,441 | 4,307 | 55,304 |
| Nebraska | 533,019 | 247,238 | 73,186 | 4,002 | 68,632 | 5,264 | 134,698 |
| Nevada | 69,298 | 419 | 94 | 76 | 920 | 1,095 | 66,693 |
| New Hampshire | 77,664 | 417 | 1 | 87 | 0 | 953 | 76,206 |
| New Jersey. | 335,748 | 1,883 | 31 | 1,071 | 603 | 813 | 331,346 |
| New Mexico | 151,624 | 7,926 | 17,672 | 1,697 | 8,495 | 14,627 | 101,207 |
| New York | 957,843 | 22,922 | 3,110 | 3,775 | 3,663 | 8,369 | 916,004 |
| North Carolina | 483,351 | 28,331 | 6,291 | 1,245 | 14,194 | 35,183 | 398,107 |
| North Dakota | 526,073 | 55,564 | 103,357 | 92 | 235,152 | 10,643 | 121,265 |
| Ohio | 539,565 | 106,147 | 25,196 | 5,799 | 34,861 | 4,082 | 363,482 |
| Oklahoma | 438,239 | 9,850 | 47,632 | 7,732 | 134,356 | 40,033 | 198,636 |
| Oregon | 239,182 | 4,231 | 24,969 | 902 | 36,191 | 6,948 | 165,941 |
| Pennsylvania | 944,950 | 19,163 | 5,830 | 1,562 | 2,321 | 5,736 | 910,338 |
| Rhode Island | 76,776 | 31 | 0 | 7 | 0 | 712 | 76,026 |
| South Carolina | 178,324 | 10,057 | 11,285 | 3,148 | 8,717 | 13,300 | 131,817 |
| South Dakota | 283,352 | 87,370 | 66,738 | 333 | 73,378 | 15,957 | 39,577 |
| Tennessee | 343,865 | 16,903 | 21,594 | 4,090 | 12,552 | 51,101 | 237,625 |
| Texas. | 1,744,449 | 113,923 | 155,379 | 31,365 | 104,091 | 333,530 | 1,006,161 |
| Utah | 129,897 | 2,365 | 8,554 | 235 | 4,849 | 3,002 | 110,893 |
| Vermont | 36,141 | 1,301 | 11 | 295 | 12 | 2,148 | 32,374 |
| Virginia | 1,049,084 | 13,340 | 3,772 | 1,378 | 7,028 | 15,753 | 1,007,812 |
| Washington | 512,364 | 14,399 | 51,851 | 906 | 88,833 | 16,527 | 339,849 |
| West Virginia | 97,863 | 1,846 | 29 | 310 | 210 | 4,293 | 91,175 |
| Wisconsin | 536,574 | 90,301 | 46,038 | 67,275 | 4,010 | 4,031 | 324,919 |
| Wyoming | 42,111 | 3,483 | 9,495 | 29 | 5,409 | 2,515 | 21,180 |
| Dist. of Columbia | 646,679 | 0 | 0 | 0 | 0 | 36,242 | 610,437 |
| American Samoa | 17 | 0 | 0 | 0 | 0 | 6 | 11 |
| Guam. | 13,687 | 0 | 0 | 0 | 0 | 82 | 13,605 |
| No. Marianas Islands | 50 | 0 | 0 | 0 | 0 | 1 | 48 |
| Puerto Rico | 128,285 | 0 | 33 | 22,580 | 0 | 1,956 | 103,715 |
| U.S. Virgin Islands | 5,161 | 0 | 0 | 0 | 0 | 301 | 4,860 |
| Undistributed | 89 | 0 | 0 | 0 | 0 | 89 | 0 |

See footnotes at end of table.

## FEDERAL GOVERNMENT EXPENDITURES FOR OTHER PROGRAMS—Continued

| State or other jurisdiction | Federal employees life and health insurance program | Postal service | Legal service corportion grants | National flood insurance claims payments | Other |
|---|---|---|---|---|---|
| United States ............ | $10,671,636 | $2,193,998 | $274,213 | $939,387 | $4,597,279 |
| Alabama ...................... | 175,111 | 27,041 | 5,683 | 9,222 | 8,803 |
| Alaska. ........................ | 1,077 | 5,946 | 956 | 26 | 36,029 |
| Arizona ....................... | 127,107 | 31,621 | 7,212 | 95 | 19,420 |
| Arkansas ..................... | 51,622 | 17,638 | 3,292 | 2,039 | 17,662 |
| California .................... | 821,215 | 237,499 | 29,234 | 45,546 | 484,430 |
| Colorado .................... | 135,486 | 38,082 | 2,970 | 557 | 63,198 |
| Connecticut ................ | 50,716 | 31,689 | 1,707 | 4,166 | 35,052 |
| Delaware .................... | 15,040 | 6,156 | 422 | 36 | 8,453 |
| Florida ....................... | 444,337 | 111,474 | 12,599 | 123,311 | 103,885 |
| Georgia ...................... | 206,146 | 54,210 | 7,250 | 1,411 | 65,804 |
| Hawaii ........................ | 95,541 | 7,053 | 955 | 1,169 | 5,219 |
| Idaho .......................... | 21,558 | 7,483 | 1,078 | 1,316 | 13,903 |
| Illinois. ....................... | 218,080 | 115,009 | 10,460 | 10,058 | 188,223 |
| Indiana ....................... | 97,157 | 43,406 | 4,505 | 11,261 | 984,424 |
| Iowa ........................... | 54,831 | 27,961 | 2,415 | 2,294 | 61,020 |
| Kansas ........................ | 41,636 | 23,470 | 2,157 | 844 | 13,030 |
| Kentucky ..................... | 226,186 | 26,866 | 5,371 | 79,056 | 76,218 |
| Louisiana .................... | 87,437 | 28,107 | 7,595 | 26,295 | 35,610 |
| Maine ......................... | 30,021 | 11,544 | 1,081 | 2,154 | 19,530 |
| Maryland .................... | 2,119,458 | 45,991 | 3,046 | 6,215 | 15,640 |
| Massachusetts .............. | 157,846 | 65,292 | 4,147 | 8,092 | 168,559 |
| Michigan .................... | 126,863 | 78,036 | 9,467 | 1,604 | 90,406 |
| Minnesota ................... | 101,869 | 44,465 | 3,704 | 58,010 | 135,000 |
| Mississippi .................. | 58,754 | 14,347 | 5,023 | 11,154 | 22,583 |
| Missouri ..................... | 785,181 | 53,053 | 5,249 | 2,432 | 63,441 |
| Montana ..................... | 19,429 | 6,757 | 1,088 | 1,769 | 26,262 |
| Nebraska .................... | 33,785 | 14,741 | 1,367 | 1,516 | 83,290 |
| Nevada ....................... | 30,198 | 11,214 | 1,046 | 19,517 | 4,718 |
| New Hampshire .............. | 36,951 | 12,163 | 535 | 2,260 | 24,297 |
| New Jersey .................. | 125,396 | 81,010 | 4,502 | 21,545 | 98,893 |
| New Mexico ................. | 68,554 | 10,904 | 2,562 | 26 | 19,161 |
| New York ..................... | 359,055 | 175,170 | 17,886 | 18,437 | 345,456 |
| North Carolina .............. | 111,260 | 54,540 | 6,671 | 183,681 | 41,955 |
| North Dakota ............... | 15,801 | 5,507 | 782 | 90,610 | 8,565 |
| Ohio .......................... | 188,483 | 90,300 | 10,504 | 24,909 | 49,285 |
| Oklahoma ................... | 106,999 | 23,532 | 4,295 | 1,545 | 62,265 |
| Oregon ....................... | 96,717 | 24,201 | 2,857 | 9,840 | 32,326 |
| Pennsylvania ............... | 544,241 | 113,754 | 10,145 | 16,939 | 225,259 |
| Rhode Island ............... | 34,508 | 10,460 | 728 | 260 | 30,071 |
| South Carolina ............. | 73,844 | 20,933 | 4,067 | 4,312 | 28,661 |
| South Dakota ............... | 9,870 | 5,873 | 1,583 | 7,659 | 14,591 |
| Tennessee ................... | 111,160 | 41,516 | 5,851 | 3,248 | 75,850 |
| Texas ......................... | 528,814 | 136,831 | 23,743 | 40,009 | 276,765 |
| Utah ........................... | 58,746 | 13,824 | 1,547 | 22 | 36,755 |
| Vermont ...................... | 5,666 | 5,789 | 419 | 363 | 20,136 |
| Virginia ...................... | 898,639 | 57,376 | 4,804 | 21,715 | 25,279 |
| Washington .................. | 199,756 | 41,052 | 4,262 | 7,896 | 86,884 |
| West Virginia ............... | 39,333 | 13,981 | 2,710 | 24,317 | 10,834 |
| Wisconsin .................... | 68,849 | 37,695 | 4,104 | 7,427 | 206,845 |
| Wyoming ..................... | 12,157 | 3,430 | 550 | 225 | 4,818 |
| Dist. of Columbia ........... | 578,954 | 18,201 | 1,456 | 112 | 11,713 |
| American Samoa .............. | ... | ... | ... | 18 | ... |
| Guam ......................... | 13,064 | 351 | 149 | ... | 41 |
| No. Mariana Islands ........ | ... | 30 | ... | ... | 18 |
| Puerto Rico ................. | 51,134 | 8,706 | 16,159 | 17,410 | 10,306 |
| U.S. Virgin Islands ........... | ... | 715 | 265 | 3,437 | 443 |
| Undistributed ............... | ... | ... | ... | ... | ... |

*Source*: U.S. Department of Commerce, Bureau of the Census.

*Note*: Because of rounding, detail may not add to totals. Amounts represent a mix of value of awards and actual expenditures during the fiscal year. Grant amounts are other than those for State and local governments which are shown in table 2. See text for additional information.

*Key*:

... — Not applicable

(a) Corporation for National and Community Service grants include the following federal domestic assistance programs; the Foster Grandparent Program; Retired Senior Volunteer Program; Volunteer Demonstration Program; Literacy Corps (VISTA); Learn and Serve America; Americorps; Planning and Program Development; Training and Technical Assistance; and Points of Light Foundation.

## Table 6.40
## FEDERAL GOVERNMENT EXPENDITURES FOR OTHER PROGRAMS, BY STATE AND TERRITORY: FISCAL YEAR 1998
(In thousands of dollars)

| State or other jurisdiction | Total | Department of Health & Human Service research grants | Department of Transportation | Department of Education | Department of Agriculture | Housing and Urban Development | Department of Labor | Department of Justice | Environmental Protection Agency |
|---|---|---|---|---|---|---|---|---|---|
| United States | $269,127,647 | $153,469,298 | $26,442,809 | $22,915,951 | $19,275,492 | $11,080,969 | $9,163,114 | $4,727,433 | $4,192,988 |
| Alabama | 4,160,938 | 2,249,484 | 469,163 | 375,337 | 320,048 | 219,435 | 133,168 | 63,942 | 59,058 |
| Alaska | 1,427,344 | 450,330 | 313,289 | 151,039 | 77,170 | 77,134 | 57,020 | 23,352 | 50,927 |
| Arizona | 4,147,037 | 2,090,441 | 335,872 | 507,595 | 320,069 | 168,640 | 137,175 | 92,568 | 58,927 |
| Arkansas | 2,439,749 | 1,397,890 | 282,809 | 212,980 | 240,843 | 79,462 | 94,087 | 36,546 | 32,056 |
| California | 32,090,102 | 18,405,203 | 2,779,768 | 2,606,809 | 2,398,366 | 993,501 | 1,428,309 | 746,148 | 334,830 |
| Colorado | 3,048,054 | 1,526,490 | 338,810 | 215,404 | 187,766 | 91,753 | 94,679 | 67,982 | 78,122 |
| Connecticut | 3,652,835 | 2,291,756 | 459,562 | 231,448 | 155,495 | 159,120 | 114,208 | 49,218 | 56,933 |
| Delaware | 677,862 | 320,843 | 100,396 | 62,787 | 49,489 | 22,108 | 28,191 | 21,718 | 22,513 |
| Florida | 10,319,617 | 5,615,609 | 1,235,074 | 1,046,611 | 794,704 | 338,150 | 327,525 | 269,749 | 149,071 |
| Georgia | 6,233,180 | 3,342,014 | 863,110 | 533,828 | 611,323 | 221,245 | 195,648 | 119,957 | 42,116 |
| Hawaii | 1,190,375 | 551,436 | 115,931 | 136,901 | 96,924 | 76,566 | 55,093 | 26,791 | 42,385 |
| Idaho | 1,055,268 | 471,161 | 211,231 | 54,976 | 107,837 | 25,561 | 45,695 | 20,217 | 28,455 |
| Illinois | 10,155,664 | 5,742,573 | 991,640 | 896,995 | 662,279 | 746,744 | 305,611 | 211,427 | 129,701 |
| Indiana. | 4,151,859 | 2,347,030 | 543,411 | 370,942 | 278,549 | 157,030 | 140,012 | 59,825 | 68,865 |
| Iowa | 2,424,071 | 1,352,130 | 264,081 | 167,935 | 177,681 | 58,615 | 81,641 | 31,803 | 77,905 |
| Kansas | 1,933,840 | 1,012,096 | 257,334 | 227,666 | 154,796 | 58,916 | 61,150 | 31,374 | 40,959 |
| Kentucky | 4,235,505 | 2,467,430 | 441,869 | 368,237 | 339,949 | 149,083 | 147,443 | 56,155 | 47,389 |
| Louisiana | 4,708,002 | 2,793,979 | 365,152 | 473,957 | 438,992 | 194,866 | 122,630 | 74,137 | 92,980 |
| Maine | 1,601,918 | 1,016,030 | 121,554 | 111,283 | 83,193 | 38,739 | 56,825 | 18,412 | 42,112 |
| Maryland | 5,022,359 | 3,169,352 | 359,979 | 352,551 | 229,788 | 163,082 | 223,647 | 91,974 | 87,470 |
| Massachusetts | 8,018,927 | 5,042,836 | 778,274 | 483,473 | 273,367 | 327,177 | 181,388 | 100,538 | 162,134 |
| Michigan | 8,618,073 | 5,334,206 | 665,504 | 808,715 | 526,818 | 321,401 | 223,015 | 125,876 | 225,514 |
| Minnesota | 4,198,564 | 2,476,677 | 361,355 | 339,887 | 309,597 | 152,415 | 97,755 | 58,078 | 105,803 |
| Mississippi | 3,024,990 | 1,781,550 | 257,326 | 310,986 | 307,008 | 91,883 | 76,631 | 38,121 | 39,339 |
| Missouri | 5,064,914 | 3,053,135 | 631,420 | 429,810 | 340,770 | 172,902 | 138,612 | 79,732 | 87,518 |
| Montana | 1,138,555 | 447,748 | 203,992 | 132,796 | 82,206 | 36,815 | 40,877 | 19,290 | 35,974 |
| Nebraska | 1,511,118 | 834,806 | 178,652 | 146,051 | 115,335 | 48,824 | 38,831 | 25,778 | 29,258 |
| Nevada | 1,080,506 | 463,478 | 184,329 | 92,631 | 80,307 | 49,238 | 54,499 | 32,870 | 36,804 |
| New Hampshire | 1,041,749 | 560,222 | 113,905 | 75,433 | 47,910 | 30,979 | 32,832 | 26,350 | 37,538 |
| New Jersey | 7,107,729 | 4,195,948 | 804,101 | 547,078 | 356,951 | 392,235 | 277,108 | 131,386 | 166,716 |
| New Mexico | 2,546,652 | 1,140,329 | 213,552 | 316,835 | 184,675 | 70,626 | 86,121 | 46,150 | 41,408 |
| New York | 28,066,441 | 19,573,911 | 1,764,451 | 1,688,031 | 1,252,326 | 1,652,933 | 714,727 | 431,854 | 226,947 |
| North Carolina | 7,133,457 | 4,444,808 | 708,413 | 548,930 | 491,760 | 206,095 | 198,188 | 110,865 | 115,845 |
| North Dakota | 1,067,323 | 375,424 | 182,696 | 99,168 | 58,646 | 26,794 | 32,062 | 16,862 | 41,528 |
| Ohio | 9,732,737 | 6,118,013 | 847,475 | 826,101 | 634,050 | 428,981 | 267,429 | 126,978 | 169,482 |
| Oklahoma | 3,059,375 | 1,657,301 | 322,444 | 322,824 | 268,044 | 137,750 | 94,427 | 49,552 | 63,785 |
| Oregon | 3,274,913 | 1,714,756 | 319,469 | 263,618 | 398,342 | 76,701 | 126,655 | 51,625 | 66,478 |
| Pennsylvania | 12,381,019 | 7,500,271 | 1,292,944 | 895,247 | 604,333 | 712,701 | 412,968 | 136,513 | 138,516 |
| Rhode Island | 1,367,504 | 762,624 | 239,076 | 93,870 | 49,085 | 53,511 | 45,298 | 18,370 | 35,333 |
| South Carolina | 3,524,548 | 2,096,151 | 367,767 | 326,065 | 281,163 | 91,993 | 101,777 | 60,206 | 36,357 |
| South Dakota | 1,007,203 | 394,393 | 145,937 | 118,867 | 70,169 | 32,648 | 27,508 | 19,906 | 22,438 |
| Tennessee | 5,510,315 | 3,361,935 | 528,048 | 435,115 | 340,218 | 178,509 | 160,550 | 91,339 | 50,239 |
| Texas | 15,809,020 | 9,002,659 | 1,608,986 | 1,819,046 | 1,429,081 | 562,581 | 558,639 | 261,476 | 128,520 |
| Utah | 1,727,197 | 835,705 | 245,869 | 170,239 | 132,979 | 30,940 | 56,094 | 40,788 | 40,379 |
| Vermont | 803,416 | 419,918 | 112,729 | 70,469 | 49,743 | 15,547 | 30,742 | 17,834 | 29,488 |
| Virginia | 4,422,961 | 2,079,906 | 540,129 | 470,012 | 358,091 | 141,651 | 302,341 | 124,024 | 79,318 |
| Washington | 5,422,486 | 3,145,816 | 481,934 | 437,242 | 381,635 | 173,427 | 238,488 | 96,992 | 90,656 |
| West Virginia | 2,480,131 | 1,334,998 | 344,570 | 195,089 | 149,755 | 57,922 | 78,753 | 41,150 | 49,659 |
| Wisconsin | 4,697,205 | 2,807,540 | 490,831 | 405,973 | 298,905 | 142,753 | 135,716 | 57,433 | 117,842 |
| Wyoming | 849,802 | 207,617 | 139,641 | 70,417 | 37,525 | 14,857 | 24,717 | 11,648 | 23,924 |
| Dist. of Columbia | 4,101,064 | 1,011,187 | 372,641 | 279,102 | 50,200 | 159,669 | 179,643 | 71,311 | 116,242 |
| American Samoa | 90,667 | 11,057 | 9,690 | 16,104 | 13,265 | 1,666 | 1,684 | 4,234 | 368 |
| Guam | 265,829 | 25,188 | 30,336 | 21,461 | 15,575 | 5,772 | 32,791 | 3,969 | 1,867 |
| No. Marianas Islands | 39,288 | 2,702 | 12,144 | 10,233 | 1,722 | 1,380 | 949 | 6,750 | 336 |
| Puerto Rico | 3,894,546 | 609,856 | 68,947 | 520,025 | 1,541,042 | 403,872 | 232,828 | 68,003 | 36,533 |
| U.S. Virgin Islands | 255,946 | 31,352 | 23,197 | 23,727 | 17,634 | 36,072 | 10,714 | 10,288 | 861 |
| Undistributed | 115,897 | 0 | 0 | 0 | 0 | 0 | 0 | 1 | 0 |

See footnotes at end of table.

## FEDERAL GOVERNMENT EXPENDITURES FOR OTHER PROGRAMS—Continued

| State or other jurisdiction | National Science Foundation | Department of Interior | Federal Emergency Management | NASA space program research grants | Department of Energy | Department of Commerce | Corporation for National and Community Service | Corporation for Public Broadcasting |
|---|---|---|---|---|---|---|---|---|
| United States | $3,334,002 | $2,819,801 | $2,399,938 | $1,036,702 | $1,555,291 | $948,027 | $486,969 | $264,560 |
| Alabama | 21,653 | 24,091 | 57,226 | 35,760 | 28,865 | 7,249 | 5,745 | 1,837 |
| Alaska | 14,812 | 131,393 | 4,279 | 4,770 | 19,961 | 22,123 | 5,666 | 4,049 |
| Arizona | 136,777 | 180,126 | 16,288 | 20,311 | 8,015 | 8,023 | 6,678 | 2,885 |
| Arkansas | 6,774 | 8,549 | 7,013 | 1,561 | 2,348 | 3,739 | 4,409 | 1,014 |
| California | 532,881 | 126,538 | 592,922 | 423,431 | 155,422 | 121,506 | 48,615 | 19,518 |
| Colorado | 159,797 | 103,757 | 6,372 | 24,815 | 38,502 | 61,001 | 5,339 | 2,498 |
| Connecticut | 34,029 | 6,120 | 3,900 | 4,817 | 31,115 | 6,929 | 6,378 | 2,604 |
| Delaware | 14,905 | 3,975 | 4,097 | 2,362 | 3,668 | 5,133 | 1,427 | 0 |
| Florida | 87,172 | 19,843 | 226,190 | 21,181 | 43,274 | 31,247 | 16,871 | 10,163 |
| Georgia | 58,503 | 7,411 | 87,231 | 15,720 | 35,248 | 15,126 | 7,886 | 3,744 |
| Hawaii | 17,689 | 7,714 | 13,675 | 13,698 | 3,614 | 6,101 | 2,782 | 993 |
| Idaho | 4,134 | 35,022 | 5,549 | 783 | 13,520 | 8,217 | 2,899 | 1,003 |
| Illinois | 175,603 | 31,977 | 58,246 | 10,869 | 50,751 | 18,734 | 14,264 | 8,896 |
| Indiana | 57,025 | 18,775 | 17,326 | 4,180 | 31,852 | 4,714 | 7,383 | 4,566 |
| Iowa | 21,001 | 10,594 | 28,203 | 6,182 | 98,074 | 4,371 | 4,340 | 1,994 |
| Kansas | 17,279 | 16,537 | 13,963 | 3,145 | 3,852 | 6,205 | 5,469 | 1,850 |
| Kentucky | 14,640 | 61,177 | 48,296 | 1,831 | 8,167 | 18,490 | 8,346 | 3,117 |
| Louisiana | 25,582 | 13,244 | 16,127 | 5,273 | 8,818 | 21,726 | 6,126 | 2,358 |
| Maine | 8,012 | 15,752 | 45,194 | 2,396 | 3,169 | 12,337 | 3,338 | 1,290 |
| Maryland | 82,308 | 10,659 | 5,661 | 58,010 | 32,736 | 22,925 | 18,183 | 4,018 |
| Massachusetts | 260,423 | 6,515 | 41,013 | 40,126 | 105,042 | 30,201 | 18,774 | 10,587 |
| Michigan | 109,217 | 30,455 | 52,839 | 26,746 | 54,904 | 33,088 | 11,064 | 5,417 |
| Minnesota | 42,914 | 51,098 | 100,662 | 3,636 | 17,139 | 12,124 | 9,259 | 8,585 |
| Mississippi | 11,773 | 20,013 | 6,501 | 6,397 | 9,595 | 10,539 | 12,022 | 1,304 |
| Missouri | 36,326 | 23,767 | 6,785 | 5,278 | 11,099 | 4,788 | 7,226 | 3,652 |
| Montana | 14,461 | 89,792 | 6,786 | 2,295 | 1,777 | 9,284 | 4,427 | 782 |
| Nebraska | 10,064 | 14,134 | 38,531 | 2,333 | 2,243 | 2,157 | 3,412 | 4,041 |
| Nevada | 10,927 | 38,804 | 4,006 | 661 | 15,706 | 2,886 | 2,106 | 1,599 |
| New Hampshire | 34,939 | 5,266 | 13,616 | 8,954 | 2,624 | 15,377 | 2,654 | 946 |
| New Jersey | 87,013 | 3,171 | 11,654 | 8,066 | 26,424 | 21,341 | 14,221 | 2,077 |
| New Mexico | 23,188 | 290,347 | 4,633 | 11,536 | 76,100 | 9,039 | 4,277 | 2,240 |
| New York | 267,046 | 16,242 | 93,316 | 38,489 | 106,046 | 42,183 | 34,437 | 20,065 |
| North Carolina | 43,261 | 15,617 | 73,891 | 9,872 | 17,139 | 33,086 | 9,727 | 18,458 |
| North Dakota | 6,964 | 70,269 | 127,172 | 3,124 | 6,284 | 10,348 | 1,071 | 1,101 |
| Ohio | 62,903 | 32,887 | 36,295 | 27,797 | 31,370 | 20,825 | 10,428 | 7,779 |
| Oklahoma | 18,186 | 73,633 | 4,838 | 2,204 | 4,412 | 10,269 | 4,602 | 1,557 |
| Oregon | 41,631 | 94,795 | 28,678 | 4,513 | 9,569 | 32,278 | 8,793 | 2,645 |
| Pennsylvania | 145,283 | 122,932 | 31,126 | 16,845 | 170,851 | 27,439 | 15,644 | 8,674 |
| Rhode Island | 23,952 | 5,152 | 1,982 | 3,734 | 3,908 | 5,293 | 4,495 | 483 |
| South Carolina | 25,035 | 8,091 | 5,195 | 2,667 | 28,650 | 34,282 | 4,238 | 3,763 |
| South Dakota | 6,731 | 129,517 | 15,871 | 2,930 | 60 | 8,980 | 1,688 | 1,088 |
| Tennessee | 27,336 | 14,574 | 60,789 | 4,597 | 27,311 | 11,056 | 10,307 | 3,352 |
| Texas | 119,540 | 27,167 | 25,849 | 46,477 | 42,882 | 36,262 | 25,775 | 8,693 |
| Utah | 30,399 | 70,008 | 7,539 | 4,660 | 11,570 | 8,350 | 3,557 | 2,972 |
| Vermont | 7,737 | 5,147 | 20,130 | 475 | 2,674 | 3,317 | 2,705 | 1,055 |
| Virginia | 59,376 | 24,398 | 14,138 | 26,281 | 26,111 | 24,352 | 11,254 | 40,140 |
| Washington | 72,541 | 101,827 | 33,773 | 12,101 | 37,882 | 37,403 | 22,239 | 4,568 |
| West Virginia | 84,515 | 32,911 | 25,028 | 19,579 | 9,967 | 13,396 | 5,006 | 1,226 |
| Wisconsin | 61,101 | 43,767 | 27,986 | 9,325 | 26,729 | 13,482 | 6,313 | 4,289 |
| Wyoming | 9,332 | 284,995 | 1,480 | 659 | 3,910 | 82 | 4,332 | 575 |
| Dist. of Columbia | 75,325 | 14,455 | 6,034 | 17,613 | 42,549 | 6,398 | 22,433 | 6,988 |
| American Samoa | 0 | 22,950 | 8,276 | 0 | 144 | 1,085 | 0 | 298 |
| Guam | 160 | 36,536 | 88,864 | 80 | 166 | 714 | 0 | 442 |
| No. Marianas Islands | 0 | 1,032 | 505 | 0 | 164 | 807 | 0 | 0 |
| Puerto Rico | 13,822 | 3,318 | 64,262 | 5,560 | 1,159 | 9,229 | 5,187 | 2,681 |
| U.S. Virgin Islands | 8 | 46,722 | 52,137 | 0 | 158 | 890 | 1,150 | 385 |
| Undistributed | 0 | 114,243 | 0 | 0 | 0 | 0 | 0 | 1,653 |

## FEDERAL GOVERNMENT EXPENDITURES FOR OTHER PROGRAMS — Continued

| State or other jurisdiction | Tennessee Valley Authority | Institute of Museum and Library Service | National Endowment for the Arts | Humanities | Equal Employment Opportunity | Small Business Administration | Other |
|---|---|---|---|---|---|---|---|
| United States ................. | $263,659 | $185,574 | $86,834 | $94,380 | $26,460 | $25,579 | $4,331,817 |
| Alabama ............................. | 64,609 | 2,597 | 685 | 599 | 0 | 117 | 20,270 |
| Alaska. .............................. | 0 | 1,285 | 1,157 | 1,122 | 196 | 258 | 16,012 |
| Arizona ............................. | 0 | 3,165 | 1,601 | 943 | 77 | 382 | 50,479 |
| Arkansas ........................... | 0 | 1,869 | 521 | 689 | 0 | 171 | 24,419 |
| California ........................... | 0 | 18,902 | 8,438 | 5,607 | 2,570 | 657 | 340,161 |
| Colorado ........................... | 0 | 3,187 | 1,765 | 693 | 464 | 122 | 38,736 |
| Connecticut ....................... | 0 | 1,964 | 1,279 | 1,826 | 551 | 0 | 33,583 |
| Delaware ........................... | 0 | 971 | 561 | 907 | 91 | 33 | 11,687 |
| Florida ............................... | 0 | 9,602 | 1,133 | 1,912 | 1,010 | 384 | 73,142 |
| Georgia ............................. | 3,755 | 4,648 | 2,188 | 3,224 | 157 | 341 | 58,757 |
| Hawaii ............................... | 0 | 1,487 | 819 | 1,195 | 132 | 0 | 18,449 |
| Idaho ................................. | 0 | 1,324 | 520 | 454 | 258 | 59 | 16,393 |
| Illinois. .............................. | 232 | 7,191 | 2,814 | 5,643 | 1,240 | 10 | 82,224 |
| Indiana .............................. | 0 | 4,845 | 810 | 1,485 | 426 | 34 | 32,774 |
| Iowa .................................. | 0 | 2,128 | 673 | 719 | 654 | 226 | 33,121 |
| Kansas ............................... | 0 | 1,798 | 618 | 574 | 434 | 180 | 17,645 |
| Kentucky ........................... | 15,550 | 2,217 | 820 | 985 | 245 | 399 | 33,670 |
| Louisiana ........................... | 0 | 2,381 | 1,164 | 585 | 10 | 75 | 47,840 |
| Maine ................................ | 0 | 1,439 | 598 | 773 | 249 | 480 | 18,743 |
| Maryland ........................... | 0 | 2,927 | 2,223 | 2,943 | 680 | 359 | 100,884 |
| Massachusetts .................... | 0 | 4,956 | 5,349 | 6,244 | 1,134 | 481 | 138,895 |
| Michigan ........................... | 0 | 5,546 | 1,317 | 2,260 | 1,463 | 567 | 52,141 |
| Minnesota .......................... | 0 | 3,116 | 2,860 | 1,870 | 418 | 414 | 42,902 |
| Mississippi ........................ | 13,707 | 1,741 | 674 | 478 | 0 | 84 | 27,318 |
| Missouri ............................ | 0 | 3,855 | 1,934 | 922 | 684 | 507 | 24,692 |
| Montana ............................ | 0 | 1,184 | 706 | 614 | 267 | 305 | 6,177 |
| Nebraska ........................... | 0 | 1,564 | 847 | 450 | 498 | 28 | 13,281 |
| Nevada .............................. | 0 | 1,338 | 900 | 555 | 551 | 263 | 6,048 |
| New Hampshire .................. | 0 | 1,197 | 701 | 832 | 1,256 | 522 | 27,696 |
| New Jersey ......................... | 0 | 5,646 | 1,598 | 2,299 | 554 | 349 | 51,793 |
| New Mexico ....................... | 0 | 2,080 | 829 | 874 | 191 | 294 | 21,328 |
| New York ........................... | 0 | 12,343 | 14,039 | 13,031 | 164 | 953 | 102,907 |
| North Carolina ................... | 955 | 5,139 | 1,245 | 3,845 | 67 | 2,232 | 74,019 |
| North Dakota ..................... | 0 | 772 | 610 | 620 | 137 | 324 | 5,347 |
| Ohio .................................. | 0 | 7,607 | 1,763 | 1,763 | 1,912 | 554 | 70,345 |
| Oklahoma .......................... | 0 | 2,100 | 586 | 514 | 373 | 395 | 19,579 |
| Oregon .............................. | 0 | 1,913 | 1,035 | 1,347 | 628 | 229 | 29,215 |
| Pennsylvania ...................... | 0 | 8,538 | 2,788 | 3,179 | 1,418 | 4,527 | 128,282 |
| Rhode Island ...................... | 0 | 1,193 | 952 | 1,819 | 93 | 0 | 17,281 |
| South Carolina ................... | 0 | 2,867 | 902 | 1,376 | 542 | 2,573 | 42,888 |
| South Dakota ..................... | 0 | 1,255 | 544 | 445 | 216 | 219 | 5,793 |
| Tennessee .......................... | 164,222 | 3,051 | 715 | 769 | 301 | 0 | 35,982 |
| Texas ................................. | 0 | 10,422 | 2,641 | 3,480 | 923 | 730 | 87,191 |
| Utah .................................. | 0 | 1,471 | 1,001 | 630 | 296 | 253 | 31,498 |
| Vermont ............................ | 0 | 1,176 | 680 | 1,301 | 40 | 355 | 10,154 |
| Virginia ............................. | 629 | 4,465 | 1,277 | 2,839 | 271 | 626 | 91,332 |
| Washington ........................ | 0 | 4,214 | 1,418 | 1,074 | 725 | 116 | 46,415 |
| West Virginia ..................... | 0 | 1,410 | 539 | 429 | 174 | 2,269 | 31,786 |
| Wisconsin .......................... | 0 | 3,476 | 683 | 1,271 | 1,338 | 542 | 39,910 |
| Wyoming ........................... | 0 | 628 | 536 | 457 | 64 | 0 | 12,406 |
| Dist. of Columbia ............... | 0 | 1,101 | 3,235 | 2,215 | 94 | 357 | 1,662,272 |
| American Samoa ................. | 0 | 115 | 257 | 209 | 0 | 0 | 1 |
| Guam ................................ | 0 | 98 | 266 | 361 | 0 | 0 | 1,183 |
| No. Mariana Islands .......... | 0 | 59 | 267 | 238 | 0 | 0 | 0 |
| Puerto Rico ....................... | 0 | 1,879 | 489 | 669 | 199 | 224 | 304,762 |
| U.S. Virgin Islands ............. | 0 | 133 | 265 | 226 | 27 | 0 | 0 |
| Undistributed ..................... | 0 | 0 | 0 | 0 | 0 | 0 | 0 |

*Source*: U.S. Department of Commerce, Bureau of the Census.
*Note*: Because of rounding, detail may not add to totals.

## Table 6.41
## FEDERAL GOVERNMENT LOAN AND INSURANCE PROGRAMS — VOLUME OF ASSISTANCE PROVIDED, BY STATE AND TERRITORY: FISCAL YEAR 1997
### (In thousands of dollars)

| State or other jurisdiction | Total | *Direct loans* Commodity loans-price supports | Farmers Home Administration rural housing loans | Federal Direct student loans | Housing for the elderly or handicapped | Other direct loans |
|---|---|---|---|---|---|---|
| United States ................. | $20,954,495 | $5,383,367 | $3,514,204 | $9,320,876 | $560,423 | $2,175,625 |
| Alabama ............................ | 383,587 | 28,176 | 75,411 | 233,594 | 4,797 | 41,609 |
| Alaska ............................... | 27,228 | 34 | 21,328 | 1,022 | 2,967 | 1,877 |
| Arizona ............................. | 245,398 | 2,076 | 74,048 | 145,430 | 3,133 | 20,712 |
| Arkansas ........................... | 492,998 | 283,211 | 85,807 | 75,837 | 1,873 | 46,270 |
| California ........................... | 1,359,147 | 124,795 | 161,027 | 816,588 | 65,166 | 191,572 |
| Colorado ........................... | 317,740 | 44,577 | 63,634 | 180,369 | 11,174 | 17,986 |
| Connecticut ....................... | 141,498 | 186 | 5,822 | 116,171 | 13,015 | 6,304 |
| Delaware ........................... | 17,071 | 2,613 | 4,998 | 6,514 | 311 | 2,635 |
| Florida ............................... | 471,881 | 86,034 | 96,355 | 211,443 | 33,948 | 44,101 |
| Georgia ............................. | 654,136 | 166,012 | 116,615 | 336,399 | 11,600 | 23,510 |
| Hawaii ............................... | 50,372 | . . . | 41,900 | 107 | 4,074 | 4,291 |
| Idaho. ............................... | 208,081 | 32,353 | 54,867 | 101,570 | 1,582 | 17,710 |
| Illinois ............................... | 1,048,491 | 362,875 | 105,666 | 487,743 | 27,203 | 65,003 |
| Indiana ............................. | 670,488 | 195,869 | 90,013 | 322,603 | 9,221 | 52,781 |
| Iowa ................................. | 1,056,306 | 646,396 | 71,087 | 303,870 | 3,761 | 31,193 |
| Kansas ............................... | 249,536 | 118,835 | 57,431 | 51,362 | 5,097 | 16,812 |
| Kentucky ........................... | 438,137 | 32,921 | 95,310 | 152,692 | 2,677 | 154,537 |
| Louisiana ........................... | 354,678 | 188,691 | 63,840 | 58,881 | 16,942 | 26,324 |
| Maine ............................... | 94,639 | 74 | 49,193 | 20,182 | 2,615 | 22,574 |
| Maryland ........................... | 267,495 | 13,247 | 61,856 | 168,369 | 12,127 | 11,895 |
| Massachusetts ................... | 620,420 | 113 | 52,761 | 523,036 | 17,853 | 26,656 |
| Michigan ........................... | 827,390 | 59,289 | 155,674 | 537,979 | 16,962 | 57,486 |
| Minnesota ......................... | 999,105 | 594,220 | 122,097 | 132,109 | 13,255 | 137,424 |
| Mississippi ......................... | 591,218 | 475,679 | 46,781 | 39,651 | 2,125 | 26,982 |
| Missouri ............................. | 495,101 | 115,685 | 105,005 | 245,556 | 7,736 | 21,120 |
| Montana ............................ | 147,707 | 75,286 | 54,027 | 3,738 | 602 | 14,054 |
| Nebraska ........................... | 464,890 | 353,799 | 49,713 | 49,375 | 2,283 | 9,720 |
| Nevada ............................. | 110,132 | 60 | 15,814 | 63,691 | . . . | 30,566 |
| New Hampshire ................. | 40,142 | . . . | 24,033 | 4,927 | 6,221 | 4,961 |
| New Jersey ........................ | 380,533 | 3,466 | 43,853 | 303,878 | 9,481 | 19,856 |
| New Mexico ...................... | 72,983 | 6,008 | 26,812 | 28,104 | 2,197 | 9,862 |
| New York ........................... | 1,142,783 | 28,703 | 92,827 | 900,422 | 73,464 | 47,365 |
| North Carolina ................... | 519,242 | 90,195 | 120,053 | 174,125 | 10,463 | 124,406 |
| North Dakota ..................... | 481,037 | 232,192 | 46,093 | 1,815 | . . . | 200,936 |
| Ohio ................................. | 897,397 | 91,359 | 113,014 | 557,807 | 56,843 | 78,375 |
| Oklahoma ......................... | 176,643 | 27,510 | 64,635 | 53,326 | 6,673 | 24,498 |
| Oregon ............................. | 271,865 | 7,883 | 49,402 | 149,470 | 5,260 | 59,849 |
| Pennsylvania ..................... | 336,211 | 16,308 | 112,849 | 135,357 | 13,057 | 58,639 |
| Rhode Island ..................... | 80,415 | . . . | 8,354 | 61,467 | 9,797 | 797 |
| South Carolina ................... | 207,436 | 7,515 | 59,937 | 110,468 | 873 | 28,644 |
| South Dakota ..................... | 266,466 | 177,291 | 50,894 | 4,255 | 4,757 | 29,269 |
| Tennessee ......................... | 380,239 | 118,205 | 95,737 | 114,271 | 8,988 | 43,038 |
| Texas ................................. | 606,093 | 233,469 | 171,257 | 101,598 | 17,537 | 82,232 |
| Utah ................................. | 234,934 | 196,659 | 32,106 | 1,848 | 853 | 3,468 |
| Vermont ............................. | 77,530 | 111 | 16,514 | 54,721 | 797 | 5,386 |
| Virginia ............................. | 630,417 | 29,722 | 66,245 | 491,405 | 3,999 | 39,047 |
| Washington ....................... | 346,920 | 48,489 | 75,323 | 154,346 | 7,541 | 61,221 |
| West Virginia ..................... | 207,658 | 1,880 | 29,529 | 141,683 | 3,520 | 31,047 |
| Wisconsin ......................... | 336,816 | 61,144 | 87,217 | 139,190 | 10,952 | 38,313 |
| Wyoming ........................... | 27,975 | 2,153 | 21,040 | 2,266 | 733 | 1,782 |
| Dist. of Columbia ............... | 108,263 | . . . | . . . | 102,475 | 4,762 | 1,027 |
| American Samoa ................. | 37 | . . . | . . . | . . . | . . . | 37 |
| Guam ............................... | 28,933 | . . . | 2,672 | 24,913 | . . . | 1,349 |
| No. Marianas Islands ........ | 304 | . . . | 294 | . . . | . . . | 10 |
| Puerto Rico ....................... | 270,952 | . . . | 100,265 | 113,598 | 5,527 | 51,562 |
| U.S. Virgin Islands ............. | 19,400 | . . . | 5,170 | 7,259 | 2,027 | 4,944 |
| Unrestricted ....................... | . . . | . . . | . . . | . . . | . . . | . . . |

See footnotes at end of table.

## FEDERAL GOVERNMENT LOAN AND INSURANCE PROGRAMS — Continued

| | | Guaranteed loans | | | | | | | |
|---|---|---|---|---|---|---|---|---|---|
| State or other jurisdiction | Total | Mortgage insurance for homes | Guaranteed student loans | Veterans housing guaranteed & insured loans (a) | Mortgage insurance condominiums | Farmers Home Administration programs | Small business loans | Other guaranteed loans | Total insurance |
| United States ......... | $118,522,601 | $61,877,918 | $21,193,659 | $8,631,675 | $4,801,256 | $2,487,135 | $7,227,674 | $12,303,284 | $458,180,365 |
| Alabama ...................... | 1,065,678 | 540,608 | 154,559 | 135,806 | 10,171 | 27,156 | 61,412 | 135,967 | 3,211,883 |
| Alaska ......................... | 515,477 | 343,842 | 15,698 | 69,922 | 20,300 | 13,498 | 15,070 | 37,148 | 246,604 |
| Arizona ....................... | 3,158,076 | 1,722,674 | 573,602 | 250,249 | 50,734 | 25,368 | 250,247 | 285,203 | 2,528,593 |
| Arkansas ..................... | 877,429 | 431,586 | 181,135 | 74,582 | 2,643 | 74,891 | 45,559 | 67,033 | 1,135,340 |
| California .................... | 17,779,744 | 10,260,181 | 2,228,752 | 944,904 | 1,080,868 | 101,190 | 1,438,149 | 1,725,700 | 37,846,870 |
| Colorado ..................... | 3,726,269 | 2,238,537 | 298,475 | 324,820 | 327,163 | 51,052 | 183,098 | 303,123 | 2,077,198 |
| Connecticut ................. | 1,462,628 | 735,042 | 305,827 | 46,253 | 102,016 | 8,248 | 160,538 | 104,705 | 3,408,076 |
| Delaware ..................... | 293,117 | 179,030 | 38,220 | 33,492 | 1,293 | 2,521 | 21,109 | 17,452 | 1,854,065 |
| Florida ........................ | 6,346,646 | 3,352,147 | 1,160,574 | 582,949 | 289,226 | 42,439 | 283,296 | 636,017 | 189,911,823 |
| Georgia ....................... | 4,359,453 | 2,024,761 | 419,400 | 386,920 | 81,233 | 89,354 | 250,016 | 1,107,770 | 7,223,600 |
| Hawaii ........................ | 379,047 | 100,132 | 64,110 | 17,725 | 111,483 | 21,807 | 15,987 | 47,803 | 5,368,361 |
| Idaho .......................... | 562,403 | 373,397 | 21,299 | 60,622 | 3,796 | 26,644 | 52,766 | 23,879 | 1,474,855 |
| Illinois ........................ | 5,072,755 | 2,959,452 | 757,422 | 199,298 | 367,531 | 82,488 | 173,181 | 533,383 | 6,254,346 |
| Indiana ....................... | 2,112,899 | 1,138,020 | 497,853 | 146,178 | 18,687 | 55,923 | 61,403 | 194,836 | 2,614,118 |
| Iowa ........................... | 679,974 | 208,644 | 211,797 | 32,842 | 13,892 | 86,552 | 51,571 | 74,676 | 3,564,238 |
| Kansas ........................ | 828,960 | 342,996 | 213,865 | 84,817 | 3,222 | 54,908 | 60,256 | 68,897 | 2,096,927 |
| Kentucky ..................... | 1,076,520 | 485,338 | 210,333 | 100,318 | 19,269 | 77,590 | 44,763 | 138,910 | 1,566,222 |
| Louisiana .................... | 1,568,950 | 619,262 | 574,212 | 102,283 | 6,999 | 69,828 | 69,304 | 127,063 | 32,370,362 |
| Maine ......................... | 466,688 | 190,556 | 125,630 | 32,154 | 5,185 | 31,446 | 29,487 | 52,229 | 680,585 |
| Maryland ..................... | 4,412,757 | 2,806,571 | 289,097 | 427,904 | 388,785 | 14,609 | 113,943 | 371,848 | 4,514,449 |
| Massachusetts ............. | 2,047,751 | 876,493 | 627,656 | 92,262 | 63,032 | 15,227 | 150,467 | 222,612 | 4,300,620 |
| Michigan ..................... | 2,635,646 | 1,623,149 | 333,065 | 169,292 | 52,662 | 79,034 | 150,989 | 227,456 | 2,559,140 |
| Minnesota ................... | 2,658,153 | 1,340,735 | 413,288 | 138,748 | 154,935 | 93,718 | 138,617 | 378,112 | 3,423,424 |
| Mississippi .................. | 876,518 | 430,181 | 226,616 | 62,708 | 528 | 28,946 | 48,959 | 78,580 | 3,791,737 |
| Missouri ...................... | 2,121,751 | 1,036,122 | 528,598 | 137,415 | 23,326 | 64,497 | 113,251 | 218,543 | 2,432,343 |
| Montana ...................... | 505,360 | 187,547 | 96,381 | 27,218 | 4,972 | 74,124 | 61,278 | 53,840 | 1,384,163 |
| Nebraska ..................... | 787,633 | 368,253 | 199,195 | 69,143 | 899 | 73,609 | 33,045 | 43,489 | 2,842,794 |
| Nevada ....................... | 1,503,835 | 1,055,490 | 43,649 | 166,373 | 66,985 | 17,791 | 53,145 | 100,401 | 1,368,274 |
| New Hampshire............. | 646,117 | 297,200 | 181,934 | 37,846 | 31,480 | 1,668 | 44,051 | 51,938 | 400,386 |
| New Jersey .................. | 3,479,652 | 2,258,323 | 222,659 | 132,719 | 230,903 | 8,204 | 277,644 | 349,200 | 19,064,560 |
| New Mexico ................. | 682,630 | 335,777 | 87,403 | 88,456 | 6,740 | 29,096 | 53,580 | 81,578 | 806,137 |
| New York ..................... | 6,062,200 | 2,736,486 | 1,994,424 | 131,483 | 22,260 | 59,341 | 389,012 | 729,195 | 11,498,404 |
| North Carolina ............. | 2,556,226 | 1,242,456 | 468,387 | 364,298 | 67,750 | 94,759 | 96,507 | 222,070 | 10,360,356 |
| North Dakota ............... | 359,707 | 119,533 | 101,079 | 14,916 | 3,755 | 62,898 | 20,538 | 36,988 | 2,560,550 |
| Ohio ........................... | 3,612,608 | 1,854,060 | 827,812 | 223,689 | 118,434 | 56,141 | 207,228 | 325,244 | 2,958,103 |
| Oklahoma ................... | 1,502,190 | 602,170 | 330,282 | 132,174 | 7,790 | 89,215 | 69,186 | 271,374 | 1,354,001 |
| Oregon ....................... | 1,090,837 | 607,674 | 148,695 | 119,739 | 15,493 | 32,002 | 92,414 | 74,820 | 2,554,150 |
| Pennsylvania ............... | 4,217,471 | 1,657,367 | 1,763,952 | 182,519 | 67,878 | 56,036 | 202,265 | 287,454 | 5,644,152 |
| Rhode Island ............... | 606,175 | 239,179 | 146,718 | 21,996 | 10,631 | 5,380 | 58,203 | 124,067 | 1,234,365 |
| South Carolina ............. | 1,052,942 | 346,487 | 301,858 | 116,032 | 10,471 | 26,799 | 45,420 | 205,876 | 14,481,902 |
| South Dakota ............... | 386,226 | 112,630 | 114,166 | 19,767 | 571 | 60,564 | 19,034 | 59,495 | 1,386,742 |
| Tennessee ................... | 2,561,294 | 1,563,609 | 434,269 | 209,706 | 40,699 | 35,613 | 95,447 | 181,951 | 1,357,648 |
| Texas .......................... | 7,910,134 | 3,869,827 | 1,562,042 | 677,344 | 62,050 | 155,414 | 762,846 | 820,610 | 33,740,544 |
| Utah ........................... | 1,605,607 | 1,055,987 | 162,036 | 77,262 | 76,251 | 26,837 | 81,304 | 125,929 | 271,473 |
| Vermont ...................... | 175,497 | 25,000 | 91,407 | 6,599 | 3,059 | 14,291 | 28,500 | 6,641 | 206,030 |
| Virginia ....................... | 3,793,080 | 2,136,846 | 273,226 | 613,622 | 365,146 | 18,299 | 94,981 | 290,960 | 7,686,605 |
| Washington .................. | 2,620,202 | 1,356,022 | 329,691 | 355,437 | 152,845 | 29,787 | 143,854 | 252,566 | 3,228,821 |
| West Virginia ............... | 236,536 | 84,983 | 50,123 | 21,248 | 174 | 36,845 | 30,144 | 13,019 | 1,013,139 |
| Wisconsin .................... | 1,197,622 | 255,814 | 380,899 | 108,831 | 5,182 | 120,808 | 126,951 | 199,137 | 1,407,142 |
| Wyoming ..................... | 256,758 | 114,174 | 49,148 | 20,745 | 464 | 18,217 | 17,921 | 36,088 | 469,768 |
| Dist. of Columbia ......... | 680,769 | 120,074 | 328,719 | 9,816 | 21,847 | 0 | 39,177 | 161,135 | 47,428 |
| American Samoa ........... | 0 | 0 | 0 | 0 | 0 | 0 | 0 | 0 | 1,634 |
| Guam .......................... | 12,916 | 6,328 | 149 | 1,017 | 171 | 3,500 | 1,405 | 346 | 19,065 |
| No. Marianas Islands .... | 94 | 0 | 0 | 0 | 0 | 0 | 0 | 94 | 0 |
| Puerto Rico .................. | 1,326,825 | 905,210 | 32,263 | 26,638 | 206,797 | 40,965 | 97,131 | 17,822 | 2,144,395 |
| U.S. Virgin Islands ........ | 8,131 | 3,959 | 10 | 581 | 578 | 0 | 1,933 | 1,071 | 231,856 |
| Undistributed ............... | 0 | 0 | 0 | 0 | 0 | 0 | 0 | 0 | 0 |

Source: U.S. Department of Commerce, Bureau of the Census.
Note: Detail may not add to totals due to rounding. Amounts represent dollar volume of direct loans made and loans guaranteed, or the face value of insurance coverage provided during the fiscal year.

Key:
. . . — Not applicable
(a) Represents only the federal government's contingent liability which is the lesser of $36,000 or 40 percent of the loan (minimum $22,500). Amount shown does not represent the full value of closed loans, as shown in the federal budget.

Table 6.42
## FEDERAL GOVERNMENT LOAN AND INSURANCE PROGRAMS — VOLUME OF ASSISTANCE PROVIDED, BY STATE AND TERRITORY: FISCAL YEAR 1998
(In thousands of dollars)

| State or other jurisdiction | Total | Commodity loans-price supports | Farmers Home Administration rural housing loans | Federal Direct student loans | Housing for the elderly or handicapped | Other direct loans |
|---|---|---|---|---|---|---|
| United States ................. | $23,716,470 | $7,276,154 | $5,696,858 | $9,320,876 | $551,037 | $871,546 |
| Alabama ............................ | 382,204 | 10,026 | 98,039 | 233,594 | 3,617 | 36,928 |
| Alaska. ............................... | 38,496 | 31 | 31,555 | 1,022 | 3,439 | 2,449 |
| Arizona ............................. | 278,441 | 2,531 | 124,097 | 145,430 | 5,098 | 1,286 |
| Arkansas ........................... | 475,976 | 265,608 | 127,583 | 75,837 | 4,856 | 2,091 |
| California .......................... | 1,483,129 | 292,197 | 202,467 | 816,588 | 63,221 | 108,656 |
| Colorado .......................... | 337,010 | 65,600 | 85,573 | 180,369 | 3,042 | 2,426 |
| Connecticut ...................... | 140,743 | 415 | 19,011 | 116,171 | 4,395 | 750 |
| Delaware .......................... | 39,646 | 2,493 | 19,997 | 6,514 | 3,450 | 7,192 |
| Florida .............................. | 512,442 | 21,043 | 171,178 | 211,443 | 40,462 | 68,316 |
| Georgia ............................ | 762,936 | 181,300 | 182,592 | 336,399 | 11,067 | 51,579 |
| Hawaii .............................. | 52,575 | 0 | 50,066 | 107 | 2,001 | 401 |
| Idaho ................................ | 244,264 | 57,120 | 83,653 | 101,570 | 1,050 | 870 |
| Illinois .............................. | 1,205,273 | 465,811 | 174,432 | 487,743 | 25,957 | 51,330 |
| Indiana ............................. | 727,660 | 245,154 | 149,429 | 322,603 | 6,332 | 4,142 |
| Iowa ................................. | 1,216,037 | 771,068 | 129,162 | 303,870 | 5,386 | 6,551 |
| Kansas .............................. | 351,405 | 219,971 | 74,512 | 51,362 | 2,277 | 3,282 |
| Kentucky ........................... | 598,514 | 256,911 | 179,776 | 152,692 | 264 | 8,872 |
| Louisiana .......................... | 306,369 | 111,249 | 114,782 | 58,881 | 18,692 | 2,765 |
| Maine ............................... | 107,553 | 79 | 77,758 | 20,182 | 1,208 | 8,326 |
| Maryland .......................... | 300,358 | 9,055 | 119,266 | 168,369 | 3,429 | 239 |
| Massachusetts ................... | 638,723 | 137 | 74,518 | 523,036 | 11,554 | 29,478 |
| Michigan ........................... | 985,533 | 164,775 | 252,938 | 537,979 | 16,733 | 13,108 |
| Minnesota ......................... | 1,149,835 | 773,609 | 188,939 | 132,109 | 7,078 | 48,100 |
| Mississippi ........................ | 633,015 | 501,017 | 85,678 | 39,651 | 1,940 | 4,730 |
| Missouri ............................ | 568,379 | 144,559 | 166,309 | 245,556 | 11,060 | 895 |
| Montana ............................ | 216,653 | 132,103 | 77,414 | 3,738 | 2,605 | 794 |
| Nebraska ........................... | 534,409 | 413,817 | 69,436 | 49,375 | 1,549 | 231 |
| Nevada ............................. | 94,125 | 0 | 29,266 | 63,691 | 0 | 1,168 |
| New Hampshire ................. | 43,476 | 0 | 30,986 | 4,927 | 6,528 | 1,034 |
| New Jersey ........................ | 402,092 | 3,485 | 67,110 | 303,878 | 20,805 | 6,814 |
| New Mexico ...................... | 88,021 | 8,209 | 49,668 | 28,104 | 1,956 | 84 |
| New York ........................... | 1,176,780 | 29,764 | 128,900 | 900,422 | 87,972 | 29,720 |
| North Carolina .................. | 882,898 | 435,771 | 242,467 | 174,125 | 13,700 | 16,836 |
| North Dakota ..................... | 357,200 | 258,690 | 76,233 | 1,815 | 1,222 | 19,240 |
| Ohio ................................. | 993,114 | 144,354 | 194,909 | 557,807 | 54,136 | 41,909 |
| Oklahoma ......................... | 238,978 | 85,704 | 94,483 | 53,326 | 3,416 | 2,048 |
| Oregon ............................. | 267,086 | 11,257 | 96,253 | 149,470 | 5,849 | 4,256 |
| Pennsylvania ..................... | 401,345 | 13,577 | 223,375 | 135,357 | 23,592 | 5,443 |
| Rhode Island ..................... | 82,439 | 0 | 12,723 | 61,467 | 8,249 | 0 |
| South Carolina .................. | 237,627 | 7,583 | 112,765 | 110,468 | 3,839 | 2,972 |
| South Dakota ..................... | 356,480 | 258,798 | 85,571 | 4,255 | 3,925 | 3,931 |
| Tennessee ......................... | 454,028 | 130,778 | 174,403 | 114,271 | 9,251 | 25,325 |
| Texas ................................ | 732,635 | 389,774 | 216,238 | 101,598 | 12,289 | 12,736 |
| Utah ................................. | 252,058 | 191,264 | 55,976 | 1,848 | 2,945 | 26 |
| Vermont ............................ | 85,296 | 138 | 26,024 | 54,721 | 143 | 4,270 |
| Virginia ............................ | 689,522 | 25,868 | 147,067 | 491,405 | 4,151 | 21,031 |
| Washington ....................... | 365,499 | 73,367 | 108,255 | 154,346 | 10,037 | 19,494 |
| West Virginia ..................... | 213,865 | 1,614 | 58,190 | 141,683 | 1,177 | 11,201 |
| Wisconsin .......................... | 382,547 | 95,776 | 123,785 | 139,190 | 9,461 | 14,334 |
| Wyoming ........................... | 33,357 | 2,703 | 27,652 | 2,266 | 632 | 104 |
| Dist. of Columbia .............. | 103,620 | 0 | 0 | 102,475 | 584 | 562 |
| American Samoa ............... | 0 | 0 | 0 | 0 | 0 | 0 |
| Guam ............................... | 185,050 | 0 | 10,554 | 24,913 | 0 | 149,583 |
| No. Marianas Islands ........ | 12,859 | 0 | 1,757 | 0 | 0 | 11,101 |
| Puerto Rico ....................... | 279,717 | 0 | 163,606 | 113,598 | 2,176 | 337 |
| U.S. Virgin Islands ............. | 17,180 | 0 | 8,481 | 7,259 | 1,240 | 201 |

See footnotes at end of table.

**Table 6.43**
**STATE GAMING**

| State or other jurisdiction | Charitable bingo | Charitable games | Card rooms | Casinos & gaming | Non-casino devices | Indian casinos | Indian bingo | Sports betting | Video lottery | Keno-style games | Instant/pulltabs | Lotto games | Numbers games | Greyhound | Jai alai | Harness | Quarter horse | Thorough-bred | Inter-track wagering | Off track wagering | Telephone wagering |
|---|---|---|---|---|---|---|---|---|---|---|---|---|---|---|---|---|---|---|---|---|---|
| Alabama | ● | ● | | | | | ● | | | | | | | ● | | | | | | | |
| Alaska | ● | ● | | | | ● | ● | | | | ● | | | | | | ● | ● | ● | ● | |
| Arizona | ● | ● | ● | ● | | ● | ● | | | ● | ● | ● | ● | ● | ● | | ● | ● | ● | ● | |
| Arkansas | ● | ● | ● | | | | | | | | ● | | | | | | ● | ● | ● | ● | ● |
| California | ● | ● | ● | ● | | ● | ● | | | | ● | ● | ● | | | | ● | ● | ● | ● | |
| Colorado | ● | ● | ● | ● | | ● | ● | | | ● | ● | ● | | | | | ● | ● | ● | ● | |
| Connecticut | ● | ● | ● | | | ● | ● | | | ● | ● | ● | ● | ● | ● | | ● | ● | ● | ● | |
| Delaware | ● | ● | | | | | | | | | ● | ● | ● | | | ● | ● | ● | ● | ● | |
| Florida | ● | ● | ● | | | ● | ● | | | | ● | ● | ● | ● | ● | ● | ● | ● | ● | | |
| Georgia | | | | | | | ● | | | | ● | ● | | | | | | | | | |
| Hawaii | | | | | | | | | | | | | | | | | | | | | |
| Idaho | ● | ● | | | | ● | ● | | | | ● | ● | | | | | ● | ● | ● | ● | |
| Illinois | ● | ● | | ● | ● | ● | ● | | | | ● | ● | ● | | | ● | ● | ● | ● | ● | |
| Indiana | ● | ● | | ● | | ● | ● | | | | ● | ● | ● | | | ● | ● | ● | ● | ● | |
| Iowa | ● | ● | ● | ● | ● | ● | ● | | | | ● | ● | | ● | | ● | ● | ● | ● | | |
| Kansas | ● | ● | | | | ● | ● | | | | ● | ● | | ● | | | ● | ● | ● | | |
| Kentucky | ● | ● | | | | | | | | | ● | ● | | | | ● | ● | ● | ● | ● | ● |
| Louisiana | ● | ● | ● | ● | ● | ● | ● | | | ● | ● | ● | ● | ● | | ● | ● | ● | ● | ● | |
| Maine | ● | ● | ● | | | | | | | | ● | ● | | | | | ● | ● | ● | ● | |
| Maryland | ● | ● | ● | | ● | | | | | | ● | ● | ● | | | ● | ● | ● | ● | ● | |
| Massachusetts | ● | ● | ● | | | ● | ● | | | ● | ● | ● | ● | ● | | ● | ● | ● | ● | ● | ● |
| Michigan | ● | ● | ● | ● | ● | ● | ● | | | | ● | ● | ● | ● | | ● | ● | ● | ● | | |
| Minnesota | ● | ● | ● | ● | ● | ● | ● | | | | ● | ● | | | | ● | ● | ● | ● | | |
| Mississippi | ● | ● | | ● | ● | ● | ● | | | | ● | | | | | | ● | ● | ● | | |
| Missouri | ● | ● | | ● | ● | | ● | | | | ● | ● | ● | | | | ● | ● | ● | | |
| Montana | ● | ● | ● | ● | ● | ● | ● | ● | | ● | ● | ● | | ● | ● | ● | ● | ● | ● | ● | ● |
| Nebraska | ● | ● | | ● | ● | ● | ● | ● | | | ● | ● | ● | ● | ● | | ● | ● | ● | ● | ● |
| Nevada | ● | ● | ● | ● | ● | ● | ● | ● | | | | | | | | | ● | ● | ● | ● | ● |
| New Hampshire | ● | ● | | | | | | | | | ● | ● | | ● | | | ● | ● | ● | ● | |
| New Jersey | ● | ● | ● | ● | ● | | | ● | | | ● | ● | ● | | | ● | ● | ● | ● | ● | ● |
| New Mexico | ● | ● | | | | ● | ● | | | | ● | ● | | | | | ● | ● | ● | ● | ● |
| New York | ● | ● | ● | | | ● | ● | | | | ● | ● | ● | | | ● | ● | ● | ● | ● | |
| North Carolina | | | | | ● | ● | | | | | | | | | | | | ● | | | |
| North Dakota | ● | ● | ● | | ● | ● | ● | | | | ● | ● | | | | | ● | ● | ● | ● | ● |
| Ohio | ● | ● | | | | | | | | | ● | ● | | | | ● | ● | ● | ● | ● | |

# STATE GAMING - Continued

| State or other jurisdiction | Charitable bingo | Charitable games | Card rooms | Casinos & gaming | Non-casino devices | Indian casinos | Indian bingo | Sports betting | Lottery Operated Games | | | | | Parimutuel Wagering | | | | | | | |
|---|---|---|---|---|---|---|---|---|---|---|---|---|---|---|---|---|---|---|---|---|---|
| | | | | | | | | | Video lottery | Keno-style games | Instant/ pulltabs | Lotto games | Numbers games | Greyhound | Jai alai | Harness | Quarter horse | Thorough-bred | Inter-track wagering | Off track wagering | Telephone wagering |
| Oklahoma | ♦ | ♦ | ♦ | | | ★ | ♦ | | | | ♦ | ♦ | ♦ | ♦ | | | ♦ | ♦ | | | |
| Oregon | ♦ | ♦ | ♦ | | | ♦ | ♦ | ♦ | ♦ | ♦ | ♦ | ♦ | ♦ | ♦ | ♦ | | ♦ | ♦ | ♦ | ♦ | ♦ |
| Pennsylvania | ♦ | ♦ | | | | | ♦ | | | | ♦ | ♦ | ♦ | | | | ♦ | ♦ | ♦ | ♦ | ♦ |
| Rhode Island | ♦ | ♦ | | ♦ | ♦ | | | | ♦ | ♦ | ♦ | ♦ | ♦ | ♦ | ♦ | ♦ | | ♦ | ♦ | | |
| South Carolina | ♦ | | | | | | | | | | | | | | | | | | | | |
| South Dakota | ♦ | ♦ | ♦ | ♦ | | ♦ | ♦ | | ♦ | | ♦ | ♦ | ♦ | ♦ | | | ♦ | ♦ | ♦ | ♦ | |
| Tennessee | ♦ | | | | | | | | | | | | | | | | ♦ | ♦ | ♦ | | |
| Texas | ♦ | ♦ | | | | ♦ | ♦ | | | | ♦ | ♦ | ♦ | ♦ | | | ■ | ♦ | ♦ | | |
| Utah | ♦ | | | | | | | | | | | | | | | | | | | | |
| Vermont | ♦ | ♦ | | | | | | | | | ♦ | ♦ | ♦ | | | ♦ | ♦ | ♦ | | |
| Virginia | ♦ | ♦ | | | | | ♦ | | | | ♦ | ♦ | ♦ | ♦ | | | ♦ | ♦ | ♦ | | |
| Washington | ♦ | ♦ | ♦ | ♦: | | ♦: | ♦ | | ♦ | ♦ | ♦ | ♦ | ♦ | ♦ | | | ♦ | ♦ | ♦ | | |
| West Virginia | ♦ | ♦ | | | | | ♦ | | ♦ | | ♦ | ♦ | ♦ | ♦ | | | ♦ | ♦ | ♦ | | |
| Wisconsin | ♦ | ♦ | | ♦ | | ♦ | ♦ | | | | ♦ | ♦ | ♦ | ♦ | | | ♦ | ♦ | ♦ | | |
| Wyoming | ♦ | ♦ | ♦ | ♦ | | | | | | | | | | | | | ♦ | ♦ | ♦ | | |
| Dist. of Columbia | ♦ | | | | | | | | | | | ♦ | ♦ | ♦ | | | | | | | |
| Puerto Rico | | | | ♦ | ♦ | | | | | | | ♦ | ♦ | ♦ | | | ♦ | ♦ | ♦ | ♦ | ♦ |
| U.S. Virgin Islands | | | | | | | | | | | | | | | | | | | | | |

*Source: International Gaming & Wagering Business, September 1999.*

Key:
♦ Legal and operative.
♦ Implemented since June 1996.
: Table games only (no slots).
★ Authorized but not yet implemented.
† Commerical bingo, keno or pull tabs only.
♦ Permitted by law and previously operative.
■ Operative but no parimutuel wagering.
† † Previously operative but now not permitted.
★ Compacts signed for non-casino gaming, such as parimutuel wagering and lottery; however, casino games may be operating.

# Chapter Seven

# MANAGEMENT, REGULATION AND PERSONNEL

*Staffing the states — includes information on personnel systems, information resource management, and regulatory activities. Also: statistics on employment, payrolls and retirement systems, and tables on licensing and regulation of selected non-health occupations and professions.*

For additional information on Chapter Seven contact
The States Information Center, at The Council of State Governments,
(859) 244-8253 or E-mail: sic@csg.org.

# Table 7.1
# THE OFFICE OF STATE PERSONNEL EXECUTIVE: SELECTION, PLACEMENT AND STRUCTURE

| State or other jurisdiction | Method of selection | Reports to: Governor | Reports to: Personnel board | Reports to: Other | Directs departmental employees | Legal basis for personnel department | Organizational status: Separate agency | Organizational status: Part of a larger agency |
|---|---|---|---|---|---|---|---|---|
| Alabama | B | ... | ★ | ... | ★ | S | ★ | ... |
| Alaska | D (a) | ... | ... | ★(b) | ★ | S | ... | ★ |
| Arizona | D | ... | ... | ★(b) | ★ | C (d) | ... | ★ |
| Arkansas | D (c) | ★ | ... | ★(b) | ★ | S | ... | ... |
| California | G | ★ | ... | ★(b) | ★ | R, C | ★ | ... |
| Colorado | G | ★ | ... | ★(b) | ... | C, S | ... | ★ |
| Connecticut | D (e) | ... | ... | ★(b) | ★ | S | ... | ★ |
| Delaware | G | ★ | ... | ... | ★ | S | ★ | ... |
| Florida | D (f) | ... | ... | ★(b) | ... | C, S (g) | ... | ★ |
| Georgia | G | ★ | ... | ... | ★ | C, S | ★ | ... |
| Hawaii | G | ★ | ... | ... | ★ | S | ★ | ... |
| Idaho | G | ★ | ... | ... | ★ | S | ... | ★ |
| Illinois | D (h) | ... | ... | ★(b) | ★ | S | ... | ★ |
| Indiana | G | ★ | ... | ... | ★ | S | ★ | ... |
| Iowa | G | ★ | ... | ... | ★ | S | ★ | ... |
| Kansas | D (a) | ... | ... | ★(b) | ★ | S | ... | ★ |
| Kentucky | G | ★ | ... | ... | ★ | S | ★ | ... |
| Louisiana | B, (i) | ... | ... | ★(b) | ★ | C | ★ | ... |
| Maine | ... | ... | ... | ... | ... | ... | ... | ... |
| Maryland | D (j) | ... | ... | ★(b) | ★ | S | ... | ★ |
| Massachusetts | ... | ... | ... | ... | ... | ... | ... | ... |
| Michigan | (k) | ... | ... | ★(k) | ★ | C, E (l) | ★ | ... |
| Minnesota | G | ★ | ... | ... | ★ | S | ★ | ... |
| Mississippi | B | ... | ★ | ... | ★ | S | ★ | ... |
| Missouri | G | ... | ... | ★(b, m) | ★ | C, S | ... | ★ |
| Montana | D (a) | ... | ... | ★(b) | ★ | S | ... | ★ |
| Nebraska | D (n) | ... | ... | ★(b) | ★ | S | ... | ★ |
| Nevada | G | ★ | ... | ... | ... | S | ★ | ... |
| New Hampshire | (o) | ... | ... | ★(b, n) | ★ | S | ... | ★ |
| New Jersey | G (p) | ★ | ... | ... | ★ | C, S | ★ | ... |
| New Mexico | G | ... | ★ | ... | ★ | S | ★ | ... |
| New York | G (q) | ★ | ... | ... | ★ | S | ★ | ... |
| North Carolina | G | ★ | ... | ... | ★ | S | ★ | ... |
| North Dakota | D (r) | ... | ... | ★(b) | ★ | S | ... | ★ |
| Ohio | D (n) | ... | ... | ★(b) | ★ | S | ... | ★ |
| Oklahoma | G | ★ | ... | ... | ★ | S | ★ | ... |
| Oregon | D (n, s) | ... | ... | ... | ... | S | ... | ★ |
| Pennsylvania | G, D (m) | ... | ... | ★(b) | ★ | E | ... | ★ |
| Rhode Island | ... | ... | ... | ... | ... | ... | ... | ... |
| South Carolina | D (t) | ... | ... | ★(u) | ★ | S | ... | ★ |
| South Dakota | ... | ... | ... | ... | ... | ... | ... | ... |
| Tennessee | G | H | ... | ... | ★ | S | ★ | ... |
| Texas | ... | ... | ... | ... | ... | ... | ... | ... |
| Utah | G | ★ | ... | ★(v) | ★ | S | ★ | ... |
| Vermont | G | ... | ... | ★(w, x) | ★ | S | ... | ★ |
| Virginia | G | ... | ... | ★(y) | ★ | S | ★ | ... |
| Washington | G | ★ | ... | ... | ★ | S | ★ | ... |
| West Virginia | D (a) | ... | ... | ★(b) | ★ | S, E | ... | ★ |
| Wisconsin | G | ★ | ... | ... | ★ | S | ★ | ... |
| Wyoming | D (z) | ... | ... | ★(b) | ... | S | ... | ★ |

See footnotes at end of table.

# THE OFFICE OF STATE PERSONNEL EXECUTIVE — Continued

*Source*: National Association of State Personnel Executives, *State Personnel Office: Roles and Functions*, Fourth Edition, 1999.

*Note*: See above referenced source for more detailed information.

*Key*:

★ — Yes

. . . — No; or state/jurisdiction did not respond to survey.

B — Appointment by personnel board.

D — Appointment by department head.

G — Appointment by governor.

C — Constitution.

S — Statute.

E — Executive Order.

R — Rules.

N.A. — Not available.

(a) Department of Administration.

(b) Reports to department head.

(c) Finance and Administration.

(d) In California, personnel rules ARS 41-783 are used in the legal basis for the central personnel agency. The legal basis for the state personnel board is constitutional.

(e) Administrative Services.

(f) Department of Management Services.

(g) The state personnel executive directs the employees of the workforce program (human resource management). Human resource management administers the state personnel system, which is comprised of the Career Service (CS), Selected Exempt Service (SES), and Senior Management Service (SMS) pay plans.

(h) Central Management Services.

(i) Appointment also by State Civil Service Commission.

(j) Department of Budget and Management.

(k) Civil Service Commission.

(l) The legal basis for the civil service commission and the state personnel director is constitutional. The legal basis for state agencies is executive order.

(m) Office of Administration.

(n) Department of Administrative Services.

(o) Governor, Department Head, Nominated by Commissioner of Administrative Services, Appointed by Governor & Council.

(p) With approval of the Senate.

(q) With consent of the state Senate.

(r) Office of Management and Budget.

(s) With approval of the Governor.

(t) Budget and Control Board.

(u) Division Director.

(v) Chief of Staff.

(w) Agency of Administration.

(x) Agency Head.

(y) Secretary of Administration.

(z) Department of Administration and Information.

# Table 7.2
## STATE PERSONNEL ADMINISTRATION: FUNCTIONS

| State or other jurisdiction | Administers merit tests (a) | Establishes qualifications | Provides human resource information system (a) | Human resource planning | Classification | Position allocation | Compensation (a) | Recruitment | Selection | Performance evaluation (a) | Position audits | Other personnel function audits | Employee promotion | Employee assistance & counseling | Human resource development |
|---|---|---|---|---|---|---|---|---|---|---|---|---|---|---|---|
| Alabama | CPA | CPA | ... | CPA | CPA | CPA | CPA | SR | SR | DA | CPA | CPA | DA | DA | SR |
| Alaska | CPA | CPA | SR | SR | CPA | CPA | CPA | CPA | DA | DA | CPA | CPA | DA | DA | SR |
| Arizona | ... | ... | ... | SR | ... | ... | ... | DA | DA | ... | ... | ... | ... | ... | ... |
| Arkansas | CPA | CPA | CPA | SR | CPA | CPA | CPA | DA | DA | DA | CPA | DA | DA | DA | SR |
| California | CPA | SR | DA | SR | CPA | CPA | CPA | SR | SR | SR | SR | SR | SR | SR | SR |
| Colorado | SR | CPA | CPA | SR | CPA | DA | SR | SR | SR | SR | DA | CPA | DA | CPA | SR |
| Connecticut | CPA | CPA | CPA | CPA | CPA | SR | CPA | CPA, SR | CPA | CPA | SR | SR | SR | SR | SR |
| Delaware | CPA | CPA | CPA | ... | CPA | DA | CPA | DA | DA | DA | ... | CPA | DA | DA | DA |
| Florida | ... | CPA | CPA | SR | DA | DA | CPA | SR | DA | DA | DA | CPA | DA | DA | DA |
| Georgia | SR | SR | ... | SR | CPA | DA | SR | SR | DA | DA | DA | CPA | DA | SR | SR |
| Hawaii | CPA | CPA | CPA | CPA | CPA | SR | CPA | SR | DA | DA | CPA | SR | SR | SR | CPA |
| Idaho | SR | SR | ... | SR | SR | ... | SR | SR | DA | DA | SR | CPA | DA | CPA | SR |
| Illinois | CPA | CPA | SR | SR | SR | SR | SR | SR | SR | DA | CPA | SR | DA | SR | SR |
| Indiana | CPA | CPA | CPA | SR | CPA | SR | CPA | SR | DA | DA | SR | SR | DA | DA | SR |
| Iowa | CPA | CPA | CPA | SR | CPA | CPA | CPA | SR | SR | SR | CPA | CPA | SR | CPA | SR |
| Kansas | ... | CPA | CPA | SR | SR | SR | CPA | SR | SR | CPA | CPA | CPA | SR | SR | SR |
| Kentucky | CPA | CPA | CPA | SR | CPA | CPA | CPA | SR | SR | SR | CPA | SR | SR | CPA | SR |
| Louisiana | CPA | CPA | SR | SR | SR | SR | SR | SR | SR | SR | SR | SR | ... | SR | CPA |
| Maine | ... | ... | ... | ... | ... | ... | ... | ... | ... | ... | ... | ... | ... | ... | ... |
| Maryland | SR | CPA | CPA | SR | SR | SR | SR | SR | SR | SR | CPA | CPA | SR | CPA | SR |
| Massachusetts | ... | DA | SR | SR | CPA | CPA | CPA | ... | DA | DA | CPA | CPA | SR | DA | ... |
| Michigan | CPA | SR | CPA | SR | SR | SR | CPA | SR | DA | DA | SR | SR | DA | SR | SR |
| Minnesota | SR | CPA | SR | SR | SR | SR | SR | SR | DA | DA | SR | SR | DA | DA | SR |
| Mississippi | SR | CPA | SR | SR | CPA | SR | CPA | SR | SR | SR | SR | SR | SR | SR | SR |
| Missouri | CPA | CPA | CPA | SR | CPA | CPA | SR | SR | CPA | SR | CPA | DA | SR | SR | SR |
| Montana | DA | DA | CPA | DA | CPA | SR | SR | DA | DA | DA | CPA | DA | DA | SR | SR |
| Nebraska | ... | SR | SR | SR | SR | SR | CPA | CPA | DA | SR | CPA | DA | DA | SR | SR |
| Nevada | SR | CPA | SR | SR | SR | CPA | SR | SR | SR | SR | SR | SR | SR | SR | CPA |
| New Hampshire | SR | CPA | CPA | SR | CPA | ... | CPA | SR | SR | SR | CPA | CPA | SR | SR | SR |
| New Jersey | CPA | CPA | CPA | SR | CPA | CPA | CPA | SR | SR | SR | CPA | CPA | SR | CPA | SR |
| New Mexico | CPA | SR | CPA | SR | CPA | SR | CPA | SR | SR | SR | CPA | CPA | DA | DA | SR |
| New York | CPA | CPA | SR | DA | SR | DA | SR | SR | DA | DA | SR | ... | DA | DA | DA |
| North Carolina | ... | CPA | CPA | DA | SR | SR | CPA | DA | DA | DA | SR | SR | DA | DA | DA |
| North Dakota | ... | CPA | DA | DA | CPA | CPA | SR | DA | DA | DA | CPA | DA | DA | DA | DA |
| Ohio | SR | CPA | CPA | SR | CPA | SR | SR | SR | SR | SR | CPA | CPA | SR | DA | SR |

See footnotes at end of table.

# STATE PERSONNEL ADMINISTRATION: FUNCTIONS — Continued

| State or other jurisdiction | Administers merit tests (a) | Establishes qualifications | Provides human resource information system (a) | Human resource planning | Classification | Position allocation | Compensation (a) | Recruitment | Selection | Performance evaluation (a) | Position audits | Other personnel function audits | Employee promotion | Employee assistance & counseling | Human resource development |
|---|---|---|---|---|---|---|---|---|---|---|---|---|---|---|---|
| Oklahoma | CPA | CPA | CPA | DA | CPA | CPA | CPA | CPA | DA | CPA | CPA | CPA | DA | SR | SR |
| Oregon | ... | SR | CPA | SR | CPA | DA | CPA | SR | DA | DA | CPA | CPA | DA | CPA | SR |
| Pennsylvania | CPA | CPA | CPA | SR | CPA | CPA | CPA | SR | DA | CPA | SR | CPA | DA | DA | SR |
| Rhode Island | ... | ... | ... | ... | ... | ... | ... | ... | ... | ... | ... | ... | ... | ... | ... |
| South Carolina | DA | CPA | CPA | SR | SR | ... | SR | SR | DA | SR | SR | SR | DA | DA | SR |
| South Dakota | ... | ... | ... | ... | ... | ... | ... | ... | ... | ... | ... | ... | ... | ... | ... |
| Tennessee | CPA | CPA | CPA | SR | CPA | CPA | CPA | DA | CPA | CPA | CPA | SR | CPA | ... | SR |
| Texas | DA | SR | DA | DA | DA | DA | SR | DA | SR | DA | SR | CPA | DA | DA | DA |
| Utah | ... | SR | CPA | CPA | CPA | SR | SR | SR | SR | DA | CPA | CPA | DA | DA | CPA |
| Vermont | ... | CPA | CPA | SR | CPA | CPA | CPA | CPA, SR | DA | DA | CPA | CPA | DA | CPA | CPA, DA, SR |
| Virginia | ... | SR | CPA | SR | CPA | SR | CPA | SR | DA | SR | SR | DA | DA | SR | DA |
| Washington | SR | SR | CPA | SR | SR | DA | CPA | SR | SR | CPA | SR | CPA | DA | CPA | SR |
| West Virginia | CPA | CPA | SR | ... | CPA | CPA | CPA | ... | ... | CPA | CPA | CPA | ... | ... | ... |
| Wisconsin | CPA | SR | SR | SR | SR | SR | SR | SR | SR | DA | SR | CPA | SR | DA | SR |
| Wyoming | ... | SR | SR | ... | SR | CPA | SR | SR | SR | SR | CPA | ... | DA | ... | ... |

*Key:*

CPA — Functions performed in central personnel agency.
DA — Functions performed in a decentralized agency.
O — Functions performed by other agency.
SR — Functions are a shared responsibility.
... — Not applicable; or state did not respond to survey.

# STATE PERSONNEL ADMINISTRATION: FUNCTIONS—Continued

| State or other jurisdiction | Employee health & wellness program | Affirmative action | Labor & employee relations | Collective bargaining/labor negotiations | Grievance & appeals | Retirement | Employee incentive | Productivity system | Employee attitude survey | Child care/ elder care | Workers compensation | Group health insurance | Deferred compensation | Drug testing | Budget recommendations to legislature |
|---|---|---|---|---|---|---|---|---|---|---|---|---|---|---|---|
| Alabama | SR | (b) | DA | DA | (b) | SR | DA | DA | ... | (b) | (b) | (b) | DA | DA | (b) |
| Alaska | SR | DA | SR | CPA | (c) | ... | ... | DA | ... | DA | (c) | (c) | SR | CPA | (c) |
| Arizona | CPA, SR | CPA, SR | DA | CPA | DA | CPA, DA | CPA, DA | CPA, DA | CPA, DA | DA | CPA | CPA | DA | CPA | CPA |
| Arkansas | SR | SR | DA | CPA | DA | SR | SR | SR | SR | CPA | CPA | CPA | DA | SR | CPA |
| California | SR | ... | ... | CPA | DA | DA | ... | ... | ... | CPA | CPA | CPA | CPA | CPA | CPA |
| Colorado | SR | DA | DA | ... | ... | DA | DA | SR | SR | SR | CPA | CPA | DA | CPA | CPA |
| Connecticut | SR | SR | SR | ... | ... | SR | SR | SR | CPA | CPA | CPA | CPA | CPA | CPA | ... |
| Delaware | SR | CPA | SR | CPA | CPA | SR | DA | DA | SR | CPA | DA | DA | DA | DA | DA |
| Florida | SR | DA | SR | SR | ... | DA | DA | SR | SR | DA | CPA | CPA | SR | DA | CPA |
| Georgia | SR | SR | SR | ... | CPA | SR | SR | SR | SR | ... | CPA | CPA | SR | SR | CPA |
| Hawaii | SR | CPA | SR | CPA | DA | SR | SR | SR | DA | SR | CPA | CPA | SR | CPA | CPA |
| Idaho | SR | SR | SR | ... | DA | CPA | SR | SR | SR | SR | CPA | CPA | DA | CPA | CPA |
| Illinois | SR | SR | SR | SR | SR | CPA | DA | DA | SR | CPA | CPA | SR | DA | SR | CPA |
| Indiana | SR | SR | SR | SR | SR | SR | SR | SR | SR | CPA | CPA | CPA | SR | CPA | CPA |
| Iowa | SR | SR | SR | SR | CPA | SR | SR | SR | SR | CPA | CPA | CPA | SR | CPA | CPA |
| Kansas | SR | CPA | SR | CPA | DA | SR | SR | SR | DA | CPA | CPA | CPA | CPA | CPA | CPA |
| Kentucky | SR | CPA | SR | CPA | DA | SR | SR | SR | SR | CPA | CPA | SR | DA | SR | SR |
| Louisiana | SR | SR | SR | SR | SR | SR | SR | SR | SR | SR | SR | SR | DA | SR | SR |
| Maine | ... | ... | ... | ... | ... | ... | ... | ... | ... | ... | ... | ... | ... | ... | ... |
| Maryland | SR | CPA | ... | CPA | DA | SR | DA | SR | DA | DA | CPA | DA | CPA | CPA | ... |
| Massachusetts | SR | ... | SR | SR | DA | SR | DA | SR | DA | DA | DA | DA | SR | DA | DA |
| Michigan | SR | DA | SR | CPA | DA | DA | DA | SR | DA | SR | DA | DA | DA | DA | ... |
| Minnesota | SR | SR | SR | SR | SR | DA | SR | DA | DA | SR | CPA | SR | DA | SR | DA |
| Mississippi | SR | DA | DA | DA | ... | DA | SR | SR | DA | CPA | SR | SR | DA | SR | DA |
| Missouri | CPA, DA | SR | DA | CPA | DA | CPA | SR | CPA | ... | DA | CPA | DA | DA | CPA, SR | DA |
| Montana | SR | CPA | SR | CPA | DA | SR | DA | DA | DA | DA | CPA | CPA | DA | CPA | CPA |
| Nebraska | SR | DA | CPA | SR | DA | DA | DA | DA | DA | SR | CPA | CPA | DA | DA | CPA |
| Nevada | SR | O | SR | SR | O | SR | SR | SR | ... | SR | SR | ... | DA | O | ... |
| New Hampshire | SR | SR | SR | CPA | DA | SR | SR | SR | DA | CPA | SR | CPA | SR | CPA | ... |
| New Jersey | SR | SR | DA | SR | SR | SR | SR | CPA | ... | DA | CPA | DA | SR | CPA | ... |
| New Mexico | SR | DA | SR | DA | DA | SR | DA | DA | DA | SR | DA | DA | DA | SR | DA |
| New York | DA | SR | CPA | DA | DA | DA | DA | DA | DA | SR | CPA | CPA | DA | DA | CPA |
| North Carolina | SR | DA | SR | ... | DA | SR | SR | SR | DA | SR | SR | SR | DA | SR | CPA |
| North Dakota | SR | DA | DA | DA | DA | DA | DA | DA | DA | DA | DA | DA | DA | SR | DA |
| Ohio | SR | SR | DA | SR | SR | SR | DA | DA | SR | CPA | CPA | DA | CPA | SR | ... |

See footnotes at end of table.

# STATE PERSONNEL ADMINISTRATION: FUNCTIONS—Continued

| State or other jurisdiction | Employee health & wellness program | Affirmative action | Labor & employee relations | Collective bargaining/labor negotiations | Grievance & appeals | Retirement | Employee incentive | Productivity system | Employee attitude survey | Child care/ elder care | Workers compensation | Group health insurance | Deferred compensation | Drug testing | Budget recommendations to legislature |
|---|---|---|---|---|---|---|---|---|---|---|---|---|---|---|---|
| Oklahoma | SR | DA | SR | CPA | DA | SR | SR | SR | CPA | DA | DA | DA | DA | DA | DA |
| Oregon | SR | CPA | CPA | CPA | CPA | SR | CPA | SR | DA | CPA | CPA | CPA | SR | CPA | CPA |
| Pennsylvania | SR | DA | SR | SR | CPA | … | … | DA | CPA | CPA | CPA | CPA | SR | CPA | … |
| Rhode Island | … | … | … | … | … | … | … | … | … | … | … | … | … | … | … |
| South Carolina | SR | … | SR | SR | CPA | SR | SR | CPA | DA | DA | CPA | CPA | DA | CPA | CPA |
| South Dakota | … | … | … | … | … | … | … | … | … | … | … | … | … | … | … |
| Tennessee | SR | … | SR | SR | … | SR | SR | CPA | … | … | SR | DA | … | SR | SR |
| Texas | DA | DA | DA | DA | SR | DA | DA | DA | … | SR | CPA | CPA | … | SR | … |
| Utah | SR | CPA | DA | CPA | CPA | CPA | … | … | CPA | CPA | CPA | CPA | CPA | CPA | CPA |
| Vermont | CPA, DA, SR | CPA | CPA | CPA | CPA | DA | … | CPA, DA, SR | CPA | CPA | CPA | CPA | CPA, SR | CPA, SR | … |
| Virginia | SR | SR | … | … | SR | SR | … | SR | … | SR | CPA | SR | DA | CPA | … |
| Washington | SR | DA | SR | SR | … | DA | SR | DA | SR | DA | DA | DA | DA | CPA | … |
| West Virginia | … | … | … | … | CPA | … | … | … | … | CPA | CPA | CPA | … | … | … |
| Wisconsin | SR | DA | SR | SR | CPA | DA | DA | DA | DA | SR | CPA | CPA | DA | CPA | … |
| Wyoming | SR | DA | … | DA | … | … | … | CPA | … | DA | DA | DA | … | … | … |

*Source:* National Association of State Personnel Executives, *State Personnel Office: Roles and Functions, Fourth Edition,* 1999.

*Note:* See above referenced source for more detailed information.

Key:

CPA — Functions performed in centralized personnel agency.

DA — Functions performed in a decentralized agency.

O — Functions performed by other agency.

SR — Functions are a shared responsibility.

… — Not applicable; or state did not respond to survey.

(a) Other functions are as follows: Iowa, SR: Safety, Records, ADA, FMLA & Other leave programs, CPA: Unemployment Insurance, Pre-tax Accounts; Kansas, CPA: State Civil Service Board; Kentucky, CPA: Section 125 Flexible Spending Account;

Vermont, CPA: Tuition reimbursements; West Virginia, CPA: Layoffs.

(b) In Alabama, employee health & wellness programs, retirement, workers' compensation, group health insurance, deferred compensation, and cafeteria benefits are part of a centralized agency but not the personnel department.

(c) In Alaska, retirement, group health insurance, deferred compensation, and cafeteria benefits are designated to an agency or division within the department of administration but not connected with the division personnel.

## Table 7.3
## CLASSIFICATION AND COMPENSATION PLANS

| State or other jurisdiction | Legal basis for classification | Current number of classifications in state | Requirement for periodic comprehensive classification review plan | Date of most recent comprehensive review of classification | Legal basis for compensation plan | Compensation schedules determined by: |
|---|---|---|---|---|---|---|
| Alabama | S | 1,362 | ★ | 1989 (d) | J, M | P |
| Alaska | C, S, CB | 994 | ... | ... | J, M, G, F, V | L |
| Arizona | S, R | 1,450 | ... | (e) | J, M | P |
| Arkansas | S | 1,619 | ... | 1991 | J, M | L |
| California | C, S | 4,000 | ... | (f) | J, M, G, F, V | P |
| Colorado | C, S, R | 793 (b) | ... | (g) | J, M, F, V | P, (aa) |
| Connecticut | S, R | 4,050 | ★ | (h) | J (x) | P, (bb), CB |
| Delaware | S | 1,400 | ... | 1987 | J, M, F | GV, L |
| Florida | S | 3,142 (c) | ★ | 1994 (i) | J, M, G | P (c) |
| Georgia | C, S, R, EO | 3,258 | ... | ... | J, M, F | P, (cc), (dd) |
| Hawaii | S | 1,700 | ... | ... | J | CB, (ee) |
| Idaho | S | 1,231 | ... | ... | J, M, F | L |
| Illinois | S, CB | 990 | ... | (d) | J, M, G, F, V | P |
| Indiana | S | 1,400 | ... | (j) | (y) | P |
| Iowa | S, R | 814 | ... | (k) | J, M, F, V | CB |
| Kansas | S | 739 | ★ | 1994 | M, F, V | GV, P |
| Kentucky | S | 1,542 | ... | (l) | J, M, V | GV, P |
| Louisiana | C | 2,889 | ... | (m) | J, M, G, F | GV, P |
| Maine | ... | ... | ... | ... | ... | ... |
| Maryland | S | 2,000 | ... | ... | J, M, F | S |
| Massachusetts | ... | ... | ... | ... | ... | ... |
| Michigan | C (a) | 1,633 | ... | (f) | J, M, F, V | (a) |
| Minnesota | S | 2,000 | ... | ... | J, M, F | CB |
| Mississippi | S | 2,582 | ... | (e) | J, M, G, F, V | (ff) |
| Missouri | S, R | 1,308 | ... | ... | M, V | GV, P, L |
| Montana | S | 1,500 | ... | ... | J, M, V | L |
| Nebraska | S | 1,655 | ... | (n) | J, M | P |
| Nevada | S, R | 1,351 | ... | (o) | J, M, F, V | GV, L, (gg) |
| New Hampshire | S, CB | 1,000 | ... | (p) | J, M, CB | P, L, CB |
| New Jersey | S, R | 8,300 | ... | (q) | J, F | P, CB |
| New Mexico | S | 1,176 | ★ | (r) | J, F | (cc) |
| New York | S | 4,738 | ... | (s) | J, M, G, V | (hh), CB |
| North Carolina | S, R | 3,015 | ... | (f) | J, M, G, F, V | GV, P, L |
| North Dakota | S | 977 | ... | (e) | J, M | P |
| Ohio | S, CB | 2,500 | ... | (f) | (z) | L, CB |
| Oklahoma | S | 370 | ... | (f) | J, M, V | P |
| Oregon | S | 800 | ... | (t) | J, M, V | P, CB |
| Pennsylvania | S, R, EO, CB | 2,800 | ... | (e) | J, M, V | GV |
| Rhode Island | ... | ... | ... | ... | ... | ... |
| South Carolina | S, R | 450 | ★ | (e) | J, M, F | P |
| South Dakota | ... | ... | ... | ... | ... | ... |
| Tennessee | S | 1,766 | ... | (f) | J, M | P |
| Texas | S | 870 | ★ | (u) | J, M | L |
| Utah | S | 2,577 | ... | (e) | J, M | L |
| Vermont | S, CB | 1,300 | ... | 1985 (i) | J, V | CB (ii) |
| Virginia | S | 1,638 | ★ | (v) | J, M, G | GV, P, L |
| Washington | S, R | 1,733 | ... | ... | J, M, F, V | P |
| West Virginia | S | 790 | ... | (h) | J, M, F, V | P |
| Wisconsin | S | 2,028 | ... | (d) | J, M, V | L |
| Wyoming | ... | 475 | ... | (w) | J, M | P |

See footnotes at end of table.

# CLASSIFICATION AND COMPENSATION PLANS — Continued

*Source*: National Association of State Personnel Executives, *State Personnel Office: Roles and Functions, Fourth Edition*, 1999.

*Note*: See above referenced source for more detailed information.

*Key*:

★— Yes

. . . — No; or state did not respond to survey.

C — Constitution.

F — Performance.

G — Geographic.

J — Job Analysis.

L — Legislature.

M — Market.

P — Personnel Department.

S — Statute.

R — Regulation.

V — Longevity/Seniority.

CB — Collective Bargaining.

GV — Governor.

EO — Executive Order.

N.A. — Not available.

(a) In Michigan, the civil service commission, appointed by the governor, must approve collective bargaining agreements for exclusively represented employers. The employee relations board makes recommendations for non-exclusively represented employers.

(b) In Colorado, as of July 1, 1999, the number of classifications should have dropped to 681.

(c) In Florida, Career Service has 1,658 classifications, Selected Exempt Service has 1,066, and Senior Management Service has 418.

(d) Continually or ongoing.

(e) As evidence of need arises.

(f) Not on a schedule.

(g) No mandate to review the system in its entirety, but periodically certain groups are studied each year.

(h) Every 5 years.

(i) Undergoing a review currently.

(j) Periodically.

(k) A review has not been done in 30 years.

(l) A review is under consideration.

(m) The goal for the next review is 3-5 years.

(n) Nebraska is reviewing their system now after 25 years.

(o) Approximately every 10 years.

(p) Every 5-10 years.

(q) Periodically, based on need, review specific occupational categories.

(r) Determined by executive management.

(s) Infrequently.

(t) Review by occupational families.

(u) Every 2 years.

(v) Bi-annually.

(w) Try to do occupational reviews on a 5-year basis.

(x) Objective job evaluation point system.

(y) Equitable distribution of funds allocated by the legislature.

(z) Point factor evaluation system.

(aa) Annual Salary Survey.

(bb) Office of Policy & Management.

(cc) State Personnel Board.

(dd) In Georgia, the 38 schedules in the compensation plan include 12 for special occupational plans such as teachers and physicians, 2 for hourly paid employees and 19 for agencies with independent salary authority such as the general assembly, law department and authorities.

(ee) Legislative approval.

(ff) Duties, labor market.

(gg) Personnel commission.

(hh) Negotiations.

(ii) Then funded/approved by Legislature.

## Table 7.4
## SELECTED EMPLOYEE LEAVE POLICIES

| State or other jurisdiction | Annual leave | | | Sick leave | | | |
|---|---|---|---|---|---|---|---|
| | Accrual 1st year (in days/year) | Accrual 5th year (in days/year) | Employees reimbursed for unused leave | Accrual 1st year (in days/year) | Employees reimbursed for unused leave | Types of leave reimbursed | Child care offered on state property |
| Alabama | 13 | 16.25 | ★ | 13 | . . . | A | . . . |
| Alaska | 15 | 24 | ★ | 15 | . . . | P, A (v) | . . . |
| Arizona | 12 | 15 | ★(k) | 12 | (k) | V, C (w) | ★ |
| Arkansas | 12 | 15 | ★(l) | 12 | (l) | A | . . . |
| California | 17 | 22 | ★ | 12 | . . . | V, A, P, (x) | ★ |
| Colorado | 12 | 15 | ★(m) | 10 | (m) | A | ★ |
| Connecticut | (a) | (a) | ★ | . . . | ★ | V | ★ |
| Delaware | 15 | 15 | ★ | 15 | ★ | A (y) | . . . |
| Florida | 13 | 15.5 | ★(n) | 13 | ★(n) | A, C (z) | ★ |
| Georgia | 15 | 18 | ★ | 15 | . . . | A (aa) | ★ |
| Hawaii | 21 | 21 | ★(o) | 21 | (o) | V, C (bb) | . . . |
| Idaho | 12 | 15 | . . . | 12 | . . . | . . . | ★ |
| Illinois | 10 | 10 | ★ | 12 | ★ | V | ★ |
| Indiana | 15 | 18 | ★ | 9 | . . . | V (cc) | ★ |
| Iowa | 10 | 15 | . . . | 18 | ★(u) | . . . | . . . |
| Kansas | 12 (b) | 15.3 (b) | ★ | 12 | ★ | A | . . . |
| Kentucky | 12 (c) | 15 (c) | ★ | 12 | . . . | A, C | . . . |
| Louisiana | (d) | (d) | ★(p) | (s) | (p) | A (dd) | . . . |
| Maine | . . . | . . . | . . . | . . . | . . . | . . . | . . . |
| Maryland | (e) | (e) | ★ | 15 (t) | . . . | A | . . . |
| Massachusetts | . . . | . . . | . . . | . . . | . . . | . . . | . . . |
| Michigan | 19 (f) | 17.225 (f) | ★(q) | 13 | (q) | A (ee), P | . . . |
| Minnesota | 13 | 16.25 | ★ | 13 | ★ | V | . . . |
| Mississippi | 18 | 21 | ★ | 12 | . . . | P | . . . |
| Missouri | 15 | 15 | ★ | 15 | . . . | A | . . . |
| Montana | 15 | 15 | ★ | 12 | ★ | V | . . . |
| Nebraska | 12 | 12 | ★ | 12 | . . . | V | . . . |
| Nevada | 15 | 15 | ★ | 15 | ★ | A, C | . . . |
| New Hampshire | 12 | 15 | ★ | 15 | ★ | A, (ff), (gg) | . . . |
| New Jersey | 12 | 15 | ★ | 12 | ★ | V (hh) | ★ |
| New Mexico | 10 to 12 | 12 to 15 | ★ | 12 | . . . | A | . . . |
| New York | 13 | 18 | ★ | 13 | . . . | A, (ii) | ★ |
| North Carolina | 11.75 | 16.75 | ★ | 12 | . . . | V | . . . |
| North Dakota | 8 | 10 | . . . | 8 | ★ | . . . | . . . |
| Ohio | 10 | 15 | ★ | 10 | ★ | P, V, (jj) | ★ |
| Oklahoma | 10 | 15 | ★ | 15 | . . . | A | ★ |
| Oregon | 12 | 15 | ★ | 12 | . . . | V | . . . |
| Pennsylvania | 7 (g) | 15 | ★ | 13 | ★ | A, P | ★ |
| Rhode Island | . . . | . . . | . . . | . . . | . . . | . . . | . . . |
| South Carolina | 15 | 15 | . . . | 15 | . . . | . . . | ★ |
| South Dakota | . . . | . . . | . . . | . . . | . . . | . . . | . . . |
| Tennessee | 12 (h) | 18 (h) | ★ | 12 | . . . | A, C | ★ |
| Texas | 10.5 | 13.5 | ★ | 12 | . . . | A | . . . |
| Utah | 13 | 16.25 | ★ | 13 | ★ | (kk) | ★ |
| Vermont | . . . | . . . | . . . | . . . | . . . | . . . | . . . |
| Virginia | 4 hours (i) | 5 hours (i) | ★ | 64 hours | . . . | A | . . . |
| Washington | 12 | 15 | ★ | 12 | ★ | A | ★ |
| West Virginia | 15 | 18 | ★(r) | 18 | (r) | A (r) | ★ |
| Wisconsin | (j) | (j) | . . . | 16.25 | . . . | . . . | . . . |
| Wyoming | 12 | 15 | ★ | 12 | ★ | V | ★ |

See footnotes at end of table.

## SELECTED EMPLOYEE LEAVE POLICIES — Continued

*Source*: National Association of State Personnel Executives, *State Personnel Office: Roles and Functions, Fourth Edition*, 1999.

*Note*: See above referenced source for more detailed information.

*Key*:

★ — Yes

. . . — No; or state did not respond to survey.

A — Annual leave.

C — Compensatory leave.

P — Personal leave.

V — Vacation leave.

(a) In Connecticut, 120 total vacation days can be carried over from year to year.

(b) In Kansas, annual leave can be carried over according to the following: Less than 5 years, 18 days; 5-10 years, 22 days; 10-less than 15 years, 26 days; and more than 15 years, 30 days.

(c) In Kentucky, the amount of annual leave that can be carried over from year to year varies with years of service, but the maximum is 440 hours.

(d) In Louisiana, the accrual rate is as follows: 1st year, .0461 hr./hrs. worked; and 5th year, .0692 hr./hrs. worked.

(e) In Maryland, the accrual rate is as follows: 1st year and 5th year, 1 hr./ 26 hrs. worked. The maximum number of hours of annual leave can be accrued according to the following: 1-5 years, 80 hours maximum; 10-15 years, 120 hours maximum; and 20 years, 160 hours maximum.

(f) In Michigan, annual leave can be carried over according to the following: 1-5 years, 30 days; 5-10 years, 31.88 days; 10-15 years, 33.75 days; and 15-20 years, 35.63 days.

(g) In Pennsylvania, management gets 10 days.

(h) In Tennessee, annual leave can be carried over according to the following: 1-5 years, 30 days; 5-10 years, 36 days; 10-20 years, 39 days; and 20+ years, 42 days.

(i) In Virginia, annual leave can be carried over according to the following: 1-5 years, 24 days; 5-10 years, 30 days; 10-20 years, 36 days; and 20+ years, 42 days.

(j) In Wisconsin, annual leave can be carried over according to the following: 1 year, 8 days; 6 years, 15 days; 11 years, 17 days; 16 years, 20 days; and 21 years, 22 days.

(k) In Arizona, sick leave in excess of 500 hours is reimbursed on a partial basis at retirement only.

(l) In Arkansas, as of July 1, 1999, sick leave not used is reimbursed upon retirement.

(m) In Colorado, sick leave not used is reimbursed upon retirement only and then only one-fourth of the accrued time.

(n) In Florida, the state reimburses employees for sick leave not used upon separation of employment if they have 10 years of service. Twenty-five percent of sick leave is paid up to 480 hours.

(o) In Hawaii, if employee is vested in retirement system, sick leave is used as additional service time.

(p) In Louisiana, sick leave can be converted to retirement benefit upon retirement.

(q) In Michigan, for employees hired on or after October 1, 1980, unused sick leave is not paid. For employees hired before October 1, 1980, 50 percent of unused sick leave is paid at death or retirement.

(r) In West Virginia, sick leave can be converted to either service credit or insurance premium payment on retirement.

(s) In Louisiana, .0461 hr./hrs. worked.

(t) In Maryland, an employee cannot exceed 120 hours of sick leave each year.

(u) In Iowa, employees are reimbursed for unused sick leave up to $2,000.

(v) In Alaska, annual leave for other bargaining units.

(w) In Arizona, compensatory time for overtime earned.

(x) Holiday.

(y) Paid in full.

(z) Special compensatory time.

(aa) Up to 45 days.

(bb) All by exception.

(cc) In Indiana, up to 30 days vacation (unused at time of expiration).

(dd) In Louisiana, can be paid for up to 300 hours of annual leave; upon retirement, balance can be applied.

(ee) Unused.

(ff) Floating holidays.

(gg) Bonus.

(hh) Earned and unused.

(ii) Overtime compensation.

(jj) Sick leave.

(kk) Comp hours, Excess hours, Converted sick, Vacation hours.

# Table 7.5
## STATE EMPLOYEES: PAID HOLIDAYS

| State or other jurisdiction | Major holidays (a) | Martin Luther King's Birthday (b) | Lincoln's Birthday | President's Day (c) | Washington's Birthday (c) | Good Friday | Memorial Day (d) | Columbus Day (e) | Veteran's Day | Day after Thanksgiving | Day before or after Christmas | Day before or after New Year's | Election Day (f) | Other (g) |
|---|---|---|---|---|---|---|---|---|---|---|---|---|---|---|
| Alabama | ★ | ★(h) | | | ★(i) | | ★ | ★ | ★ | | | | | ★ |
| Alaska | ★ | ★ | (j) | ★ | | | ★ | | ★ | | | | | ★ |
| Arizona (k) | ★ | ★ | | ★ | ★ | | ★ | ★ | ★ | | | | | |
| Arkansas | ★ | ★ | ★ | | ★★ | | ★ | | ★ | (l)★ | Before | | | ★ |
| California | ★ | ★ | ★ | | ★ | ★ | ★ | ★ | ★ | ★ | | | ★ | ★ |
| Colorado (m) | ★ | ★ | | ★ | | | ★ | ★ | ★ | | | | | |
| Connecticut* (k) | ★ | ★ | ★ | ★ | | ★★ | ★ | ★ | ★ | ★ | | | ★ | ★ |
| Delaware | ★ | ★ | | ★ | | ★ | ★ | ★ | ★ | ★ | | | ★ | ★ |
| Florida (k) | ★ | ★ | | ★ | (n) | | ★ | | ★ | (n) | (n) | | | ★ |
| Georgia* (k) | ★ | ★ | | ★ | | | ★ | ★ | ★ | | (o) | | | ★ |
| Hawaii | ★ | ★ | | ★ | | | ★ | ★ | ★ | | | | ★ | ★ |
| Idaho | ★ | ★ | | ★ | | | ★ | ★ | ★ | | | | | ★ |
| Illinois | ★ | ★ | ★(o) | ★ | | | ★ | ★ | ★ | (o)★ | (o) | | | ★ |
| Indiana | ★ | ★(l) | | ★ | (m,o) | | ★ | ★ | ★ | (o)★ | | | | ★ |
| Iowa | ★ | ★ | | | | | ★ | ★ | ★ | | | | | |
| Kansas (k) | ★ | ★ | | ★ | | | ★ | ★ | ★ | (l) | ★(l) | ★(l) | | ★ |
| Kentucky (k) | ★ | ★(l) | | | | ★(p) | (l)★ | | | ★(l) | ★(l) | ★(l) | ★ | ★ |
| Louisiana | ★ | ★ | ★ | ★ | | ★ | ★ | ★ | ★ | ★★ | | | ★ | ★ |
| Maine (k) | ★ | ★ | | ★ | | | ★ | ★ | ★ | | | | | |
| Maryland | ★ | ★ | | | | | ★ | ★ | ★ | | | | ★ | ★ |
| Massachusetts | ★ | ★ | | ★ | ★ | | ★ | ★ | ★ | ★ | Before | Before | | ★ |
| Michigan | ★ | ★ | | ★ | | | ★ | | ★ | ★ | | | | ★ |
| Minnesota | ★ | ★ | | ★ | | | ★ | ★ | ★ | ★ | | Before | | |
| Mississippi (k) | ★ | ★ | | | | | ★ | | ★ | | | | | ★ |
| Missouri | ★ | ★ | ★ | | | | ★ | ★ | ★ | | | | | ★ |
| Montana* (k) | ★ | ★ | | ★ | | | ★ | ★ | ★ | (l) | | | | ★ |
| Nebraska (k) | ★ | ★ | | ★ | | | ★ | ★ | ★ | ★ | | | | ★ |
| Nevada (k) | ★ | ★ | | ★ | | | ★ | ★ | ★ | ★ | | | | ★ |
| New Hampshire* (k) | H | ★ | | | | | ★ | | ★ | | | | | |
| New Jersey | ★ | ★ | ★ | | | ★ | ★ | ★ | ★ | | | | ★ | ★ |
| New Mexico | ★ | ★ | | (q) | ★ | | ★ | | ★ | (q) | | | | ★ |
| New York | ★ | ★ | (j) | ★ | | | ★ | ★ | ★ | | | | ★ | ★ |
| North Carolina* | ★ | ★ | | | ★ | | ★ | | ★ | ★(l) | ★ | | | |
| North Dakota (k) | ★ | ★ | | | | (l)★★ | ★ | ★ | ★ | | (r) | | | ★ |
| Ohio (k) | ★ | ★ | | ★ | | ★★ | ★ | ★ | ★ | (q) | (r) | | (l) | |

See footnotes at end of table.

# STATE EMPLOYEES: PAID HOLIDAYS — Continued

| State or other jurisdiction | Major holidays (a) | Martin Luther King's Birthday (b) | Lincoln's Birthday | President's Day (c) | Washington's Birthday (c) | Good Friday | Memorial Day (d) | Columbus Day (e) | Veteran's Day | Day after Thanksgiving | Day before or after Christmas | Day before or after New Year's | Election Day (f) | Other (g) |
|---|---|---|---|---|---|---|---|---|---|---|---|---|---|---|
| Oklahoma (k) | ★ | ★ | … | ★ | … | … | ★ | … | ★ | ★ | (i) | (i) | … | … |
| Oregon (k) | ★ | ★ | … | ★ | … | … | ★ | … | ★ | ★ | (i) | (i) | … | ★ |
| Pennsylvania | ★ | ★ | … | ★ | ★ | … | ★ | ★ | ★ | … | (i) | (i) | … | … |
| Rhode Island | ★ | ★ | … | … | … | … | ★ | ★ | ★ | ★ | (i) | … | ★(s) | ★ |
| South Carolina (k) | ★ | … | ★ | … | … | … | ★ | … | ★ | ★ | (i) | … | … | ★ |
| South Dakota | ★ | ★ | … | ★ | ★ | … | ★ | (t) | ★ | (t) | ★ | … | … | ★ |
| Tennessee | ★ | ★ | … | ★ | ★ | ★ | ★ | ★ | ★ | ★ | ★ | … | … | … |
| Texas (u) | ★ | (w) | … | … | (v) | (v) | ★ | … | ★ | ★ | ★ | … | … | ★ |
| Utah | ★ | (i) | … | ★ | … | … | ★ | (i) | ★ | … | (i) | (i) | … | … |
| Vermont (k) | ★ | (x) | … | ★ | ★ | … | ★ | (i) | ★ | ★ | (i) | … | … | … |
| Virginia* | ★ | (x) | … | … | ★ | … | ★ | … | ★ | ★ | (y) | (y) | … | ★ |
| Washington* | ★ | ★ | … | ★ | … | … | ★ | ★ | ★ | ★ | … | … | … | ★ |
| West Virginia | ★ | ★ | ★ | … | … | … | ★ | ★ | ★ | … | (y) | (y) | ★(z) | ★ |
| Wisconsin | ★ | ★ | … | … | … | ★(p) | ★ | … | … | … | Before | Before | … | ★ |
| Wyoming | ★ | ★(aa) | … | ★ | … | … | ★ | ★ | ★ | … | … | … | … | ★ |
| Dist. of Columbia | ★ | ★ | … | ★ | ★ | … | ★ | ★ | ★ | ★ | … | … | … | … |

** Holidays in addition to any other authorized paid personal leave granted state employees.

Source: The Council of State Governments' survey of state personnel offices, January 2000, except where * denotes information from The Book of The States, 1998-1999.

Note: In some states, the governor may proclaim additional holidays or select from a number of holidays for observance by state employees. In some states, the list of paid holidays is determined by the personnel department at the beginning of each year; as a result, the number of holidays may change from year to year. Number of paid holidays may also vary across some employee classifications. Dates are given for 2000 and may change slightly for 2001. If a holiday falls on a weekend, generally employees get the day preceding or following.

Key:

★ — Paid holiday granted.

. . . — Paid holiday not granted.

(a) New Year's Day, Independence Day, Labor Day, Thanksgiving Day, and Christmas Day.

(b) Third Monday in January.

(c) Generally, third Monday in February; Washington's Birthday or President's Day. In some states the holiday is called President's Day or Washington-Lincoln Day. Most frequently, this day recognizes George Washington and Abraham Lincoln.

(d) Last Monday in May in all states indicated, except Vermont where holiday is observed on May 30. Generally, states follow the federal government's observance (last Monday in May) rather than the traditional Memorial Day (May 30).

(e) Second Monday in October.

(f) General election day only, unless otherwise indicated. In Indiana, primary and general election days.

(g) Additional holidays:

Alabama–Mardi Gras Day (day before Ash Wednesday) in Baldwin and Mobile Counties only; in other counties, state employees receive one floating holiday. Confederate Memorial Day (fourth Monday in April), Jefferson Davis' Birthday (first Monday in June).

Alaska–Seward's Day (last Monday in March), Alaska Day (October 18).

Arkansas–Employee's birthday.

California–One personal day.

Delaware–Return Day, after 12 noon (Thursday after a general election) in Sussex County only.

Florida–One personal day.

Georgia–Confederate Memorial Day (April 26).

Hawaii–Prince Johan Kuhio Kalanianaole Day (March 26), King Kamehameha I Day (June 11), Admissions Day (third Friday in August).

Illinois– Three personal holidays per year.

Iowa–Two floating holidays.

Kansas–Discretionary day (taken whenever employee chooses with supervisor's approval).

Louisiana–Mardi Gras Day (day before Ash Wednesday), Inauguration Day (every four years), in Baton Rouge only).

Maine–Patriot's Day (third Monday in April).

Massachusetts–Patriot's Day (third Monday in April), Evacuation Day (March 17) and Bunker Hill Day (June 17).

Minnesota–One floating holiday.

Mississippi–Confederate's Memorial Day (last Monday in April).

Missouri–Harry Truman's Birthday (May 8).

Nebraska–Arbor Day (last Friday in April).

Nevada–Nevada Day (last Friday in October).

New Mexico–One personal holiday to permanent incumbents who have completed the one year probationary period.

Oregon–Two discretionary days.

Rhode Island–Victory Day (second Monday in August).

South Carolina–One floating holiday.

# STATE EMPLOYEES: PAID HOLIDAYS — Continued

South Dakota–Native American's Day (second Monday in October).

Texas–Confederate Heroes Day (January 19), Texas Independence Day (March 2), Cesar Chavez Day ( March 31), San Jacinto Day (April 21), Emancipation Day (June 19) and Lyndon Johnson's Birthday (August 27). A state employee may observe Rosh Hashanah, Yom Kippur and Good Friday in lieu of any state holiday on which the employee's agency is required to be open.

Utah–Pioneer Day (July 24).

Vermont–Town Meeting Day (first Tuesday in March), Battle of Bennington Day (August 16).

Washington–One floating holiday.

West Virginia–West Virginia Day (June 20).

District of Columbia–Inauguration Day (January 20, every four years).

(h) Also for Robert E. Lee's Birthday.

(i) Also for Thomas Jefferson's Birthday.

(j) Floating holiday; employee may take the holiday on another day. State offices are open.

(k) If a holiday falls on a Saturday, it is observed on the Friday before. If it falls on a Sunday, observed on the following Monday. In Oregon, it is rescheduled if it falls on someone's scheduled day off.

(l) At the discretion of the governor. In South Carolina, the day after Christmas is an established holiday.

(m) In Colorado, agencies have the discretion to observe an alternate holiday schedule in lieu of statutory holidays.

(n) In Georgia, Robert E. Lee's Birthday is observed on the day after Thanksgiving, and Washington's birthday is observed the day after Christmas.

(o) In Indiana, Lincoln's Birthday is observed on the day after Thanksgiving, and Washington's birthday is observed the day before Christmas.

(p) In Kentucky half day. In Wisconsin not a paid holiday. Employees have an additional half-day of personal leave time each calendar year.

(q) In New Mexico, President's Day is observed on the day after Thanksgiving.

(r) In North Dakota, if the day before Christmas is a weekday, state offices close at noon.

(s) In South Carolina, election day is a holiday in even-numbered years.

(t) In Tennessee, state employees have selected by ballot to observe Columbus Day on the day after Thanksgiving during the past few years.

(u) In Texas, a holiday is not observed if it falls on Saturday or Sunday.

(v) In Texas, a state employee may observe Good Friday in lieu of any state holiday on which the employee's agency is required to be open.

(w) Called Human Rights Day; celebrates Martin Luther King, Jr. and others who worked for human rights.

(x) Called Lee/Jackson/King Day, after Robert E. Lee, Stonewall Jackson and Martin Luther King, Jr.

(y) Half day on Christmas Eve and New Year's Eve if they fall on Monday, Tuesday, Wednesday or Thursday.

(z) In West Virginia, both general and primary elections are holidays.

(aa) Called Martin Luther King, Jr./Wyoming Equality Day.

## Table 7.6
## CIVIL SERVICE REFORM IN THE STATES

| State or other jurisdiction | Extent of reform | Initiator of reform | Merit testing | Classification | Compensation | Recruitment | Selection | Performance evaluation | Training | Employee relations | Benefits | Layoffs |
|---|---|---|---|---|---|---|---|---|---|---|---|---|
| | | | *Personnel functions under reform or considered for reform* | | | | | | | | | |
| Alabama | I | P | ... | ... | ... | ... | ... | ★ | ... | ... | ... | ... |
| Alaska | I | N.A. | ... | ★ | ★ | ★ | ★ | ★ | ★ | ★ | ★ | ... |
| Arizona | I | G (a) | ... | ★ | ★ | ★ | ★ | ★ | ★ | ★ | ★ | ★ |
| Arkansas | I | G | ... | ★ | ★ | ★ | ... | ★ | ★ | ... | ★ | ... |
| California | I | G,P | ★ | ... | ... | ... | ★ | ... | ... | ... | ... | ... |
| Colorado | W | G,L,P | ★ | ★ | ★ | ★ | ★ | ★ | ★ | ★ | ★ | ★ |
| Connecticut* | I | L,P | ★ | ★ | ★ | ... | ★ | ★ | ... | ★ | ... | ... |
| Delaware | N.A. | N.A. | ★ | ★ | ★ | ★ | ★ | ★ | ★ | ★ | ★ | ... |
| Florida | W | G,P | ★ | ★ | ★ | ★ | ★ | ★ | ★ | ★ | ★ | ★ |
| Georgia* | I | G | ★ | ★ | ★ | ★ | ★ | ★ | ... | ★ | ... | .. |
| Hawaii | W | G,P | ★ | ★ | ★ | ★ | ★ | ★ | ★ | ★ | ★ | ★ |
| Idaho | I | (a) | ★ | ★ | ★ | ★ | ★ | ★ | ★ | ★ | ★ | ★ |
| Illinois | (c) | G | ★ | ★ | ★ | ★ | ★ | ... | ★ | ★ | ★ | ... |
| Indiana | I | G,P | ★ | ★ | ★ | ★ | ★ | ★ | ★ | ★ | ★ | ... |
| Iowa | I | G,P | ★ | ★ | ★ | I | I | ★ | I | ... | ... | ★ |
| Kansas | I | G,L,P | I | I | ★ | I | I | ★ | I | ... | I | I |
| Kentucky | I | G,L,P | ... | ★ | ★ | ... | ... | ★ | ★ | ... | ... | ★ |
| Louisiana | N.A. | G,L,P | ★ | ★ | ★ | ★ | ★ | ★ | ... | ★ | ... | ... |
| Maine | I | G,L,P | ★ | ... | ... | ... | ... | ★ | ... | ... | ... | ... |
| Maryland | W | G,L,P | ★ | ★ | ★ | ★ | ★ | ★ | ★ | ★ | ★ | ★ |
| Massachusetts | W | G,P (a) | ★ | ★ | ★ | ★ | ★ | ★ | ★ | ★ | ★ | ★ |
| Michigan | I | G,P | ★ | ★ | ★ | ★ | ★ | ★ | ★ | ★ | ★ | ... |
| Minnesota | W | P | ★ | ★ | ... | ★ | ★ | ... | ... | ... | ... | ... |
| Mississippi | N.A. | N.A. | ... | ... | ... | ... | ... | ... | ... | ... | ... | ... |
| Missouri | N.A. | G | ★ | ★ | ★ | ★ | ★ | ★ | ★ | ... | ★ | ★ |
| Montana* | W | G,P | ... | ★ | ★ | ... | ... | ★ | ... | ★ | ... | ... |
| Nebraska | I | P | ... | ★ | ★ | ★ | ★ | ★ | ★ | ★ | ★ | ★ |
| Nevada | I | G,P | ★ | ★ | ★ | ★ | ★ | ... | ★ | ★ | ... | ... |
| New Hampshire* | | | | | | | ----(g)---- | | | | | |
| New Jersey | W | G,P | ★ | ★ | ★ | ★ | ★ | ★ | ★ | ... | ★ | ★ |
| New Mexico | (e) | ... | ... | (e) | (e) | ... | ... | ... | ... | ... | ... | ... |
| New York | I | G,P | ★ | ★ | ... | ... | ★ | ★ | ... | ... | ... | ★ |
| North Carolina* | I | G,P | N.A. | ★ | ★ | ★ | ★ | ★ | ... | ★ | ★ | ... |
| North Dakota | I | G,P | ... | I | I | I | I | I | I | I | I | I |
| Ohio | W | G,P | ★ | ★ | ★ | ★ | ★ | ★ | ★ | ★ | ★ | ... |
| Oklahoma | I | G,L | ... | ★ | ★ | ★ | ... | ★ | ... | ... | ... | ... |
| Oregon | I | G,P | ★ | ★ | ★ | ★ | ★ | ★ | ... | ... | ★ | ... |
| Pennsylvania | I | B,L,P | ★ | ... | ... | I | ... | ... | ... | ... | ... | ... |
| Rhode Island | I | G | ★ | ★ | ★ | ★ | ★ | ★ | ... | ★ | ★ | ... |
| South Carolina | | | | | | | ----(d)---- | | | | | |
| South Dakota | | | | | | No reform underway/planned | | | | | | |
| Tennessee | I | N.A. | ★ | ... | ★ | ★ | ★ | ★ | ★ | ... | ... | ... |
| Texas | | | | | | | ----(f)---- | | | | | |
| Utah | | | | | | No reform underway/planned | | | | | | |
| Vermont | I | G,L,P | ★ | ★ | ★ | ★ | ★ | ★ | ... | ★ | ★ | ★ |
| Virginia* | I | P | ... | ★ | ★ | ★ | ... | ★ | ... | ... | ★ | ★ |
| Washington* | I | N.A. | ★ | ★ | ★ | ★ | ★ | ★ | ... | ... | ... | ... |
| West Virginia | I | P | ★ | ★ | ★ | ★ | ★ | ★ | ★ | ★ | ... | ... |
| Wisconsin | I | G,P,L | ★ | ★ | ★ | ★ | ★ | ... | ... | ... | ... | ... |
| Wyoming | I | G,P | ... | ★ | ★ | ... | ... | ... | ... | ... | ... | ... |
| Dist. of Columbia | I | G | ... | ... | ★ | ... | ... | ★ | ★ | ★ | ★ | ★ |
| U.S. Virgin Islands | W | P | ★ | ★ | ★ | ★ | ★ | ★ | ★ | ★ | ★ | ★ |

See footnotes at end of table.

# CIVIL SERVICE REFORM IN THE STATES - Continued

*Source*: The Council of State Governments survey, January 2000,except where noted by *where data are from *The Book of The States, 1998-99*.
*Key*:
★ — Function is being reformed or considered for reform.
. . . — No reform.
I — Incremental reform.
W — Wholesale reform.
G — Governor.
L — Legislature.
P — Personnel agency.
N.A. — Not available.
(a) Other initiators: Arizona, Idaho–various state agencies; Massachusetts–various groups dedicated to improving the effectiveness and efficiency of the delivery of state government services.
(b) Reform is being planned or under consideration by the state personnel executives in Delaware and Louisiana; no further information available.

(c) Extent of reform unknown until review process has been completed.
(d) South Carolina has recently completed reform in the areas of merit testing, classification, compensation, recruitment, selection, performance evaluation, training, and employee relations. Currently the Office of Human Resources is undergoing a comprehensive revision of the State Human Resources Regulations.
(e) Streamlining classification and compensation system to include class consolidation and wider salary grades.
(f) Data not available.
(g) Division of Personnel instituted a Certified Public Manager Program in 1996.

## Table 7.7
## ALTERNATIVE WORKING ARRANGEMENTS FOR STATE EMPLOYEES

| State | Flextime | Share leave | Telecommute | Job sharing | Incentives/credits for not using sick leave |
|---|---|---|---|---|---|
| Alabama | ★ | ★ | . . . | . . . | . . . |
| Alaska | ★ | ★ | ★ | ★ | . . . |
| Arizona | ★ | ★ | ★ | ★ | ★ |
| Arkansas | ★ | ★ | ★ | ★ | ★ |
| California | ★ | ★ | ★ | ★ | . . . |
| Colorado | ★ | ★ | ★ | ★ | ★ |
| Connecticut* | ★ | ★ | . . . | ★ | . . . |
| Delaware | ★ | . . . | . . . | . . . | . . . |
| Florida | ★ | ★ | ★ | ★ | . . . |
| Georgia* | ★ | ★ | ★ | ★ | ★ |
| Hawaii | ★ | ★ | ★ | ★ | ★ |
| Idaho | ★ | ★ | ★ | ★ | ★ |
| Illinois | ★ | ★ | ★ | ★ | ★ |
| Indiana | ★ | . . . | ★ | ★ | . . . |
| Iowa | ★ | ★ | ★ | ★ | ★ |
| Kansas | ★ | ★ | ★ | ★ | ★ |
| Kentucky | ★ | ★ | ★ | N.A. | ★ |
| Louisiana | ★ | . . . | ★ | ★ | . . . |
| Maine | ★ | . . . | . . . | ★ | . . . |
| Maryland | ★ | ★ | ★ | ★ | ★ |
| Massachusetts | ★ | ★ | ★ | ★ | . . . |
| Michigan | N.A. | ★ | N.A. | ★ | . . . |
| Minnesota | ★ | . . . | ★ | . . . | . . . |
| Mississippi | ★ | ★ | . . . | . . . | . . . |
| Missouri | ★ | ★ | ★(limited) | ★ | . . . |
| Montana* | ★ | ★ | ★ | ★ | ★ |
| Nebraska | ★ | . . . | ★ | ★ | . . . |
| Nevada | ★ | ★ | ★ | ★ | ★ |
| New Hampshire* | ★ | . . . | . . . | ★ | ★ |
| New Jersey | | | ----- (a) ----- | | |
| New Mexico | ★ | ★ | ★ | ★ | ★ |
| New York | ★(d) | ★ | ★ | ★ | . . . |
| North Carolina* | ★ | ★ | N.A. | ★ | . . . |
| North Dakota | ★ | ★ | ★ | ★ | ★ |
| Ohio | ★ | ★ | . . . | . . . | ★ |
| Oklahoma | ★ | ★ | . . . | . . . | . . . |
| Oregon | ★ | ★ | ★ | ★ | ★ |
| Pennsylvania | ★ | . . . | . . . | ★ | ★ |
| Rhode Island | ★ | . . . | ★ | ★ | ★ |
| South Carolina | ★ | ★ | ★ | ★ | (b) |
| South Dakota | ★ | ★ | . . . | ★ | . . . |
| Tennessee | ★ | ★ | ★ | ★ | . . . |
| Texas | ★ | . . . | ★ | ★ | . . . |
| Utah | ★ | ★ | ★ | ★ | ★ |
| Vermont | ★ | ★ | ★ | ★ | ★ |
| Virginia* | ★ | ★ | ★ | ★ | ★ |
| Washington* | ★ | ★ | ★ | ★ | ★ |
| West Virginia | ★ | ★ | ★ | ★ | ★ |
| Wisconsin | ★ | ★ | ★ | ★ | ★ |
| Wyoming | ★ | ★ | ★ | ★ | . . . |

*Source*: The Council of State Governments survey, January 2000, except where * denotes information from *1998-1999 Book of the States*.

*Key*:
★ — Yes
. . . — No
N.A. — Not applicable.
(a) Information not available.
(b) 90 days may be credited towards retirement.
(c ) New York has two types of alternative work schedules, compressed workweeks and compressed pay periods.
(d) Not currently in use.

## Table 7.8
## INFORMATION RESOURCE MANAGEMENT: CHIEF INFORMATION OFFICERS

| State | Chief information officer's title and division (a) | Officer's decisions are binding | Has authority to approve: State IRM plans | State IRM policies | State IRM standards | State-level IRM acquisitions |
|---|---|---|---|---|---|---|
| Alabama | Chief Information Officer, Information Services Division | ... | ★ | ★ | ★ | ★(e) |
| Alaska* | Chief Technology Officer, Information Technology Agency | N.A. | N.A. | N.A. | N.A. | N.A. |
| Arizona | Chief Information Officer, Government Information Technology Agency | (b) | ★ | ★ | ★ | ★ (f) |
| Arkansas* | Director, Department of Information Services (c) | ★ | ... | ★ | ★ | ★ |
| California | Chief Information Officer, Dept. of Information Technology | ★ | ★ | ★(g) | ★ | ★(h) |
| Colorado* | Chief Information Officer, Information Mgmt. Commission Department of Personnel/General Support Services | N.A. | N.A. | N.A. | N.A. | N.A. |
| Connecticut | Chief Information Officer, Department of Information Technology | ★ | ★ | ★ | ★ | ★ (i) |
| Delaware | Executive Director, Office of Information Services (OIS) | (b) | ★ | ★ | ★ | ★ |
| Florida | Statewide CIO | ★ | ★ | ★ | ... | ... |
| Georgia | Chief Information Officer, Information Technology Policy Council | (j) | (j) | ★ | (j) | (j) |
| Hawaii | Administrator (Special Advisor on Technology to the Governor), Information & Communication Services Division, Department of Accounting & General Services | ... | ... | ... | ... | ... |
| Idaho | Project Team Manager, Information Technology Resource Management Council | ★ | N.A. | N.A. | N.A. | N.A. |
| Illinois | Director, Illinois Tecnology Office | ★ | ★ | ★(k) | ★ | ★(k) |
| Indiana | Director, Division of Information Technology, Department of Administration | (l) | ... | ... | ... | ★(m) |
| Iowa | Chief Information Officer, Information Technology Services | ★ | ... | ... | ★ | ★(n) |
| Kansas | Chief Information Technology Officer, Exec. Branch/ Chief Information Technology Architect | ★ | (o) | (o) | (o) | ★(p) |
| Kentucky | Chief Information Officer Governor's Office for Technology | ★ | ★ | ★ | ★ | ★ |
| Louisiana | Assistant Commissioner, Office of Information Services Department of Administration | (q) | ★ | ★ | ★ | ★ |
| Maine | Chief Information Officer, Bureau of Information Services | ★ | ★ | ... | ... | ★(r) |
| Maryland | Chief Information Officer, Department of Budget & Management | ★ | ★ | ★ | ★ | ★ |
| Massachusetts | Chief Information Officer, Information Technology Division | ... | ★(s) | ★(s) | ★(s) | ... |
| Michigan | Chief Information Officer & Deputy Director for IT Department of Management & Budget | ★ | ★ | ★ | ★ | ★ |
| Minnesota | Commissioner, Dept. of Administration and Office of Technology | ★ | ★ | ★ | ★ | ★ (t) |
| Mississippi | Executive Director, Department of Information Technology Services | ★ | ★ | ★ | ★ | ★ (u) |
| Missouri | Chief Information Officer, Office of Information Technology | N.A. | ★ | ★ | ★ | ★ |
| Montana* | Administrator, Information Services Division Department of Administration | (b) | ★ | ★ | ★ | ★ |
| Nebraska | Chief Information Officer | ... | ... | ... | ... | ... |
| Nevada | Director, Department of InformationTechnology | ★ | ★ | ★ | ★ | ★(v) |
| New Hampshire | Director, Division of Information Technology Mgmt. | ★ | ★ | ★ | ★ | ★(w) |
| New Jersey | Chief Information Officer , Office of the Governor | ★ | ★ | ★ | ★ | ★ |
| New Mexico | Chief Information Officer, Information Technology Management Office | ★ | ★ | ★ | ★ | ★(x) |
| New York | Executive Deputy Commissioner, Office for Technology | N.A. | (y) | (y) | (y) | (y,z) |
| North Carolina | CIO/Asst. Secretary for InformationTechnology Information Technology Services, Department of Commerce | ★ | ... | ... | ★ | ★ |
| North Dakota | Chief Information Officer, Information Technology Dept. | ★ | ★ | ★ | ★ | ★(aa) |
| Ohio | State CIO and Assistant Director Department of Administrative Services | ★ | ★ | ★ | ★ | ★ |
| Oklahoma | Director of Information Services Office of State Finance | ... | ★ | ... | ★ | ★ |
| Oregon* | Chief Information Officer, Information Resources Management Division, Department of Administrative Services (d) | ★ | ★ | ★ | ★ | ★ |
| Pennsylvania | Chief Information Officer Commonwealth Technology Center | ★ | ★ | ★ | ★ | ★ |

See footnotes at end of table.

## FEDERAL GOVERNMENT LOAN AND INSURANCE PROGRAMS — Continued

| State or other jurisdiction | Total | Guaranteed loans | | | | | | |
|---|---|---|---|---|---|---|---|---|
| | | Mortgage insurance for homes | Guaranteed student loans | Veterans housing guaranteed & insured loans (a) | Mortgage insurance condominiums | Farmers Home Administration programs | Small business loans | Other guaranteed loans |
| United States ......... | $145,089,152 | $84,314,615 | $22,071,776 | $11,753,255 | $7,403,361 | $4,152,515 | $6,521,807 | $8,871,823 |
| Alabama ........................... | 1,185,248 | 644,416 | 165,275 | 164,276 | 11,014 | 47,170 | 56,676 | 96,420 |
| Alaska .............................. | 637,141 | 413,653 | 22,085 | 93,341 | 35,439 | 21,647 | 10,791 | 40,185 |
| Arizona ............................ | 3,864,100 | 2,402,308 | 601,767 | 400,822 | 74,044 | 45,934 | 194,808 | 144,416 |
| Arkansas ......................... | 2,886,823 | 2,081,069 | 176,761 | 96,345 | 246,461 | 161,582 | 51,818 | 72,788 |
| California ........................ | 25,230,882 | 16,428,279 | 2,324,637 | 1,451,729 | 2,023,916 | 181,875 | 1,250,686 | 1,569,760 |
| Colorado ......................... | 3,095,742 | 1,599,408 | 314,223 | 469,192 | 244,520 | 111,670 | 162,740 | 193,988 |
| Connecticut ..................... | 1,634,218 | 910,849 | 298,702 | 57,124 | 125,562 | 16,971 | 116,732 | 108,278 |
| Delaware ......................... | 430,569 | 236,214 | 43,114 | 40,240 | 1,661 | 4,853 | 15,993 | 88,493 |
| Florida ............................. | 7,400,310 | 4,265,809 | 1,196,174 | 803,239 | 392,398 | 68,239 | 310,604 | 363,847 |
| Georgia ........................... | 4,164,381 | 2,523,367 | 427,974 | 471,707 | 91,398 | 203,688 | 235,401 | 210,846 |
| Hawaii ............................. | 498,584 | 141,580 | 65,660 | 23,988 | 196,917 | 26,282 | 13,151 | 31,006 |
| Idaho ............................... | 638,980 | 457,448 | 17,639 | 57,435 | 2,675 | 25,762 | 53,124 | 24,896 |
| Illinois ............................ | 6,699,085 | 4,450,346 | 827,200 | 295,883 | 577,853 | 94,324 | 164,605 | 288,873 |
| Indiana ............................ | 2,723,202 | 1,747,421 | 515,418 | 195,793 | 31,011 | 93,729 | 67,792 | 72,038 |
| Iowa ................................ | 797,911 | 270,246 | 216,631 | 46,529 | 11,393 | 140,040 | 46,459 | 66,612 |
| Kansas ............................ | 1,010,447 | 450,505 | 214,330 | 100,183 | 5,280 | 132,281 | 56,368 | 51,501 |
| Kentucky ......................... | 1,244,774 | 586,154 | 216,922 | 124,880 | 24,216 | 211,131 | 42,501 | 38,969 |
| Louisiana ........................ | 1,621,417 | 718,174 | 533,982 | 106,250 | 10,891 | 99,799 | 63,337 | 88,984 |
| Maine .............................. | 521,501 | 243,595 | 137,588 | 43,708 | 7,807 | 25,861 | 20,814 | 42,127 |
| Maryland ......................... | 6,421,118 | 4,506,447 | 309,051 | 630,255 | 634,845 | 18,498 | 79,004 | 243,018 |
| Massachusetts ................. | 2,531,875 | 1,232,449 | 639,655 | 136,147 | 102,000 | 19,919 | 121,214 | 280,491 |
| Michigan ......................... | 3,201,880 | 2,185,631 | 350,715 | 195,464 | 88,491 | 81,167 | 132,420 | 167,992 |
| Minnesota ....................... | 3,078,408 | 1,639,534 | 427,000 | 215,221 | 171,041 | 187,613 | 143,027 | 294,972 |
| Mississippi ...................... | 1,007,010 | 494,747 | 241,926 | 81,260 | 531 | 62,724 | 69,172 | 56,650 |
| Missouri .......................... | 2,647,000 | 1,433,803 | 569,265 | 199,608 | 33,144 | 150,300 | 95,228 | 165,652 |
| Montana .......................... | 481,213 | 212,405 | 91,028 | 30,332 | 4,381 | 69,609 | 43,248 | 30,209 |
| Nebraska ......................... | 835,864 | 393,937 | 200,541 | 89,587 | 1,565 | 90,752 | 28,806 | 30,676 |
| Nevada ............................ | 2,068,341 | 1,533,988 | 43,735 | 250,480 | 102,255 | 8,562 | 70,225 | 59,096 |
| New Hampshire ............... | 740,348 | 361,941 | 178,119 | 55,366 | 43,509 | 6,516 | 42,965 | 51,931 |
| New Jersey ...................... | 3,695,720 | 2,591,703 | 241,758 | 144,910 | 282,035 | 14,688 | 246,601 | 174,025 |
| New Mexico ..................... | 827,082 | 442,156 | 91,824 | 110,964 | 8,828 | 85,047 | 41,650 | 46,613 |
| New York ......................... | 6,988,946 | 3,299,727 | 2,042,012 | 149,681 | 41,508 | 85,995 | 327,578 | 1,042,444 |
| North Carolina ................ | 3,049,210 | 1,648,385 | 489,380 | 495,962 | 92,358 | 132,170 | 84,502 | 106,453 |
| North Dakota ................... | 472,889 | 170,127 | 109,731 | 21,020 | 6,683 | 120,273 | 20,758 | 24,297 |
| Ohio ................................ | 4,551,694 | 2,674,373 | 854,533 | 353,995 | 136,279 | 142,630 | 168,821 | 221,063 |
| Oklahoma ........................ | 1,449,107 | 672,119 | 345,378 | 169,183 | 9,050 | 95,729 | 72,232 | 85,417 |
| Oregon ............................ | 1,232,515 | 728,171 | 159,256 | 141,538 | 22,653 | 34,972 | 79,391 | 66,535 |
| Pennsylvania ................... | 4,676,438 | 1,993,989 | 1,930,114 | 215,046 | 75,848 | 75,911 | 199,044 | 186,485 |
| Rhode Island ................... | 637,553 | 337,244 | 148,878 | 31,196 | 14,355 | 8,258 | 62,054 | 35,568 |
| South Carolina ................ | 1,140,291 | 378,173 | 316,943 | 156,995 | 13,309 | 110,905 | 50,099 | 113,867 |
| South Dakota ................... | 458,105 | 148,658 | 122,072 | 26,434 | 586 | 113,444 | 19,121 | 27,790 |
| Tennessee ....................... | 2,859,431 | 1,831,257 | 452,072 | 228,612 | 55,943 | 127,241 | 68,108 | 96,198 |
| Texas ............................... | 9,334,170 | 4,871,474 | 1,624,949 | 834,278 | 72,584 | 220,326 | 724,721 | 985,839 |
| Utah ................................ | 1,969,765 | 1,326,488 | 207,928 | 81,482 | 111,668 | 25,995 | 64,458 | 151,747 |
| Vermont ........................... | 189,289 | 32,772 | 97,959 | 11,097 | 4,340 | 12,796 | 26,480 | 3,845 |
| Virginia ........................... | 5,132,544 | 2,980,908 | 305,572 | 940,311 | 583,580 | 53,387 | 93,479 | 175,308 |
| Washington ...................... | 3,310,164 | 1,930,715 | 319,928 | 470,565 | 226,539 | 47,297 | 160,433 | 154,687 |
| West Virginia ................... | 251,538 | 99,813 | 46,932 | 24,902 | 328 | 33,677 | 32,316 | 13,570 |
| Wisconsin ........................ | 1,228,201 | 370,123 | 381,641 | 158,271 | 7,876 | 129,332 | 108,680 | 72,278 |
| Wyoming ......................... | 260,740 | 126,787 | 50,804 | 25,360 | 816 | 18,640 | 18,713 | 19,622 |
| Dist. of Columbia .......... | 649,699 | 184,735 | 332,384 | 13,835 | 39,560 | 0 | 8,992 | 70,193 |
| American Samoa ........... | 0 | 0 | 0 | 0 | 0 | 0 | 0 | 0 |
| Guam .............................. | 12,677 | 3,750 | 72 | 991 | 431 | 3,770 | 3,662 | 0 |
| No. Marianas Islands .... | 0 | 0 | 0 | 0 | 0 | 0 | 0 | 0 |
| Puerto Rico ..................... | 1,403,193 | 901,818 | 32,540 | 19,601 | 299,401 | 49,833 | 78,083 | 21,917 |
| U.S. Virgin Islands ......... | 9,821 | 3,424 | 0 | 643 | 583 | 1,700 | 2,121 | 1,350 |

*Source:* U.S. Department of Commerce, Bureau of the Census.
*Note:* Detail may not add to totals due to rounding. Amounts represent dollar volume of direct loans made and loans guaranteed, or the face value of insurance coverage provided during the fiscal year.

## INFORMATION RESOURCE MANAGEMENT: CHIEF INFORMATION OFFICERS - Continued

| | | | Has authority to approve: | | | |
|---|---|---|---|---|---|---|
| State | Chief information officer's title and division (a) | Officer's decisions are binding | State IRM plans | State IRM policies | State IRM standards | State-level IRM acquisitions |
| **Rhode Island** ............. | Chief Information Officer, Office of Library & Information Services, Department of Administration | ★ | ★ | ★ | ★ | ★ |
| **South Carolina** .......... | Director, (bb) Office of Information Resources, State Budget & Control Board | (bb) | (bb) | (bb) | (bb) | (bb) |
| **South Dakota** ............. | Chief Information Officer | ★ | ★ | ★ | ★ | ★ |
| **Tennessee** ................... | Chief Information Oficer, Finance & Administration | ★ | ★ | ★ | ★ | ★ |
| **Texas** ........................... | Executive Director, Department of Information Resources | ★ | ... | ★ | ★ | ... |
| **Utah** ............................. | Chief Information Officer, Governor's Office | ★ | ★ | ★ | ★ | ★ |
| **Vermont** ...................... | Chief Information Officer, Agency of Administration | ... | ★ | ★ | ★ | ★(cc) |
| **Virginia** ...................... | Secretary of Technology, Office of Technology | ★ | ★ | ★ | ★ | ★(dd) |
| **Washington** ................ | Director/CIO Washington State Department of Information Services | ★ | (ee) | (ee) | (ee) | (ee,ff) |
| **West Virginia** ............. | Chief Technology Officer, Governor's Office of Technology | ★ | ★ | ★ | ★ | ★ (cc) |
| **Wisconsin** ................... | Director, Bureau of Technology Policy & Planning | (gg) | (hh) | (hh) | (hh) | (hh) |
| **Wyoming** ..................... | Administrator, Division of Information Technology | (ii) | ★(jj) | ... | ★(jj) | ... |

*Source*: National Association of State Information Resource Executives, January 2000, except where * denotes data are from *The Book of The States 1998-99*.

*Key*:
★ — Yes
... — No
N.A. — Not available

(a) The state's chief information officer is the individual with the highest level of authority for managing information resources and services.

(b) Decisions are binding in some cases, but not in others, depending on the situaton.

(c) For centralized services only.

(d) Only for the Department of Administrative Services.

(e) $500 threshold.

(f) Threshold - $25,000 and above. Over $1 million, a board action is required.

(g) The CIO engages with the Governor's office in developing strategy alignment relative to Information Technology policy and governance

(h) Threshold varies by department according to size, IT experience and function.

(i) Threshold- greater than $20,000.

(j) Yes, for Y2K.

(k) For policy issues, any dollar amount. For state level IRM acquisitions, all procurements $1 million and above.

(l) Within certain boundaries. The approval of the chair of the Data Processing Oversight Commission may be required.

(m) $750,000 annual incremental increase in expenditure.

(n) Less than $15,000 can be exempt.

(o) These responsibilities are handled by a chief Information Technology Architect who reports to an Information Technology Executive Counsel. Today the CITO for the Executive Branch also serves as the Chief Information Technology Architect.

(p) Threshold- $250,000 or greater.

(q) The authority of the CIO is restricted to the Executive Branch of Government.

(r) The standards of approval are different for small versus large purchases.

(s) Threshold is $200,000.

(t) The threshold is $100,000 and above on acquisitions. IRM is done on all projects.

(u) $250,000 (Acquisitions over $250,000 require board approval)

(v) Threshold amount is $50,000.

(w) Threshold amount is $5,000.

(x) Threshold is based on legislative approval, it varies.

(y) The CIO advises and assists with state IRM plans, establishes statewide technology policies including but not limited to technology standards and reviews and coordinates the purchase of technology by state agencies.

(z) Threshold- Notification is required for software over $20,000; for all other technology purchases over $50,000.

(aa) Threshold - $25,000.

(bb) South Carolina does not have a CIO.

(cc) Threshold-$10,000.

(dd) Threshold-$100,000.

(ee) The Information Services Board approves ( The CIO is a member).

(ff) Threshold depends on a risk/severity assessment.

(gg) Since 1995, Wisconsin has operated under an enterprise management concept for technology and has in effect, two CIOs. The Administrator for the Division of Technology Management in DOA is responsible for state planning, standards and telecommunications networks. The Administrator of the Division of Info-Tech Services is responsible for the state's primary data center that provides mainframe and other platform services to state agencies.

(hh) The Division of Technology Management drafts the state IT standards and policies. Final decisions rest with the Secretary of the Department of Administration.

(ii) The CIO's decisions are a cooperative effort of the Governor, Cabinet and the CIO.

(jj) The threshold will vary by product/project as per procurement guidelines.

## Table 7.9
## INFORMATION RESOURCE MANAGEMENT: STATE COMMISSIONS, CENTRAL ORGANIZATIONS AND BUDGETS

| State | State commissions | | Central IRM organization (b) | IRM budget as a percentage of total state budget |
|---|---|---|---|---|
| | IRM commission (a) | Authority to approve: | | |
| Alabama | . . . | . . . | ★ | 2-3% |
| Alaska* | ★ | A,B,C,D | N.A. | N.A. |
| Arizona | . . . | D | ★ | 3% |
| Arkansas* | . . . | . . . | ★ | N.A. |
| California | . . . | . . . | . . . | 3% |
| Colorado* | ★ | A,B,C,D | N.A. | N.A. |
| Connecticut | . . . | . . . | ★ | 1.70% |
| Delaware | ★ | B | ★ | (c) |
| Florida | ★ | . . . | ★ | 5% |
| Georgia | ★ | B | ★ | 2.70% |
| Hawaii | . . . | . . . | ★ | (d) |
| Idaho | ★ | A,B,C,D | ★(e) | (f) |
| Illinois | ★ | A,B,C,D | ★ | 3.50% |
| Indiana | ★ | A,B,C,D | ★ | .009%(g) |
| Iowa | ★ | . . . | ★ | Approx. .8% |
| Kansas | ★(h) | A,B,C | ★ | (i) |
| Kentucky | . . . | . . . | ★(j) | <1% |
| Louisiana | . . . | . . . | ★(k) | 1.76% |
| Maine | ★ | B,C | ★(l) | 1% |
| Maryland | ★ | . . . | ★ | 13% |
| Massachusetts | . . . | . . . | ★ | N.A. |
| Michigan | . . . | . . . | ★ | 1.20% |
| Minnesota | . . . | . . . | ★ | Estimate 15-20% |
| Mississippi | ★ | A,B,C,D(m) | ★ | 5% |
| Missouri | . . . | . . . | . . . | 3% |
| Montana* | ★ | B,C (w) | ★ | N.A. |
| Nebraska | ★ | A,B,C | ★ | 0% |
| Nevada | ★(n) | A,B,C,D | ★ | N.A. |
| New Hampshire | . . . | . . . | . . . | N.A. |
| New Jersey | ★ | . . . | ★ | Approx. 3% |
| New Mexico | ★ | A,B,C,D | ★ | 10% |
| New York | ★ | A,B,C (o) | ★ | N.A. |
| North Carolina | ★ | A,B | ★ | (p) |
| North Dakota | . . . | . . . | ★ | 2.50% |
| Ohio | ★ | . . . | ★ | 6% |
| Oklahoma | . . . | . . . | ★ | 0.03% |
| Oregon* | ★ | A,B,C | ★ | N.A. |
| Pennsylvania | . . . | . . . | ★ | Approx.5% (q) |
| Rhode Island | ★ | A,B,C | ★ | Approx. 3% |
| South Carolina | ★ | B,C | ★(r) | N.A. |
| South Dakota | . . . | . . . | ★ | 2.10% |
| Tennessee | ★(s) | A,B,C,D | ★ | 1.75% |
| Texas | ★ | B,C | ★ | 2.80% |
| Utah | ★ | B,C | ★ | Approx. 2.5% |
| Vermont | ★ | B,C | . . . | (t) |
| Virginia | ★ | (u) | ★ | Approx. 2% |
| Washington | ★ | A,B,C,D | ★ | N.A. |
| West Virginia | ★ | A,B,D | ★ | 2% |
| Wisconsin | . . . | . . . | ★(v) | N.A. |
| Wyoming | ★ | B,D | . . . | N.A. |

Source: National Association of State Information Resource Executives, January 2000, except as noted by * where data are from *The Book of the States, 1998-99*

Key:

★ — Organization exists in the state

. . . . — Organization does not exist in the state

A — State IRM plans

B — State IRM policies

C — State IRM standards

D — State-level IRM acquisitions

N.A. — Not available

(a) Formal board, commission, committee or authority established for the purpose of directing or managing the planning and implementation of information processing resources, policies, standards and services within the state.

(b) A department or agency with state-level authority over information management; usually sets policy and standards; possibly subject to approval of an IRM commission; and may have influence over day-to-day IRM operations.

(c) For fiscal year 1999 OIS' budget represented 1% of the total state budget; statewide, IRM expenditures( exclusive of personnel costs)were approx. 7.5% of total. With staff costs, guestimate that amount to double.

(d) Percentage of total budget not available .3% for IRM organization.

(e) IT is not centrally managed. The Department of Administration handles central issues; i.e: WAN administration and services. Each agency is responsible for its IT organization and operation.

(f) Department of Administration's IT budget is approx. 2% of the state's overall expenditures for IT. Administration's IT budget is approx. 0.28% of the state's overall state budget.

(g) The DPOC budget is $663,203 out of a total $7,251,318,370 General

## INFORMATION RESOURCE MANAGEMENT: STATE COMMISSIONS, CENTRAL ORGANIZATIONS AND BUDGETS - continued

Fund Appropriations.

(h) For planning and IT architecture.

(i) Base budget = 1.9% for IT. New iniatives average about 1.5% additional per year.

(j) Governor's Office for Technology ( Note that IRM terminology is no longer used.)

(k) This office is in the formative stages. The CIO shall manage and direct the Department of Information Technology established within the Executive Dept., Office of the Governor, Div. of Admin. The authority of the CIO is restricted to the Executive Branch of government.

(l) There is a central agency. It controls the operations and services that it provides to other state agencies. It does not have a general control function over other state agencies.

(m) Over $250,000.

(n) Advisory.

(o) The Commission provides guidance and support for state IRM plans and review and comment for state IRM policies and standards.

(p) The total including agency IT expenditures for fiscal year 1997-98

was 1.69%.

(q) The central IT budget as compared to the overall budget.

(r ) Shared responsibility between Office of Information Resources (operations) and Office of Research & Statistical Services( IT planning).

(s) The Council looks at policy and major direction issues. OIR and the CIO are staff and carry out the decisions.

(t) There is no IRM budget.

(u) Council on Technology Services is advisory to the CIO on plans, policies & standards.

(v) The Division of Technology Management drafts the state IT plan, working in concert with the Division of Info-Tech Services and state agencies. The Division is also responsible for the preparation of state IT standards and policies. Final decisions rest with the Secretary of the Department of Administration.

(w) Montana does not currently have an IRM: however, Information Technology Advisory Council does develop and approve a statewide strategic plan and information tehnology plan.

## Table 7.10
## STATE AID FOR LIBRARIES
### (Fiscal Year 1997)

| State or other jurisdiction | Number of public libraries (a) | Individual public libraries | Public library systems | Other individual libraries | Multitype library systems | Single agency or library (b) | Library construction | Other assistance | Total |
|---|---|---|---|---|---|---|---|---|---|
| Alabama | 205 | $4,651,000 | $1,072,000 | $0 | $0 | $0 | $463,000 | $0 | $6,185,000 |
| Alaska | 85 | 906,000 | 0 | 54,000 | 0 | 491,000 | 130,000 | 0 | 1,582,000 |
| Arizona | 40 | 1,613,000 | 0 | 13,000 | 0 | 479,000 | 468,000 | 0 | 2,573,000 |
| Arkansas | 37 | 785,000 | 3,062,000 | 0 | 0 | 3,000 | 315,000 | 3,000 | 4,168,000 |
| California | 171 | 32,328,000 | 3,078,000 | 406,000 | 3,162,000 | 279,000 | 1,374,000 | 108,000 | 40,734,000 |
| Colorado | 108 | 562,000 | 14,000 | 89,000 | 1,891,000 | 1,252,000 | 141,000 | 162,000 | 4,110,000 |
| Connecticut | 195 | 1,331,000 | 0 | 25,000 | 882,000 | 46,000 | 3,056,000 | 0 | 5,340,000 |
| Delaware | 30 | 1,332,000 | 322,000 | 9,000 | 0 | 0 | 483,000 | 0 | 2,146,000 |
| Florida | 98 | 30,393,000 | 0 | 0 | 1,750,000 | 185,000 | 2,248,000 | 12,000 | 34,588,000 |
| Georgia | 55 | 25,188,000 | 0 | 0 | 0 | 0 | 12,654,000 | 0 | 37,841,000 |
| Hawaii | 1 | 0 | 0 | 0 | 0 | 0 | 0 | 0 | 0 |
| Idaho | 106 | 487,000 | 0 | 0 | 30,000 | 0 | 0 | 3,000 | 520,000 |
| Illinois | 617 | 15,971,000 | 0 | 1,082,000 | 22,151,000 | 2,477,000 | 5,915,000 | 2,646,000 | 50,241,000 |
| Indiana | 238 | 4,380,000 | 0 | 150,000 | 3,131,000 | 0 | 224,000 | 13,000 | 7,896,000 |
| Iowa | 529 | 196,000 | 0 | 50,000 | 30,000 | 10,000 | 136,000 | 98,000 | 520,000 |
| Kansas | 324 | 2,268,000 | 824,000 | 40,000 | 0 | 0 | 124,000 | 535,000 | 3,790,000 |
| Kentucky | 116 | 5,120,000 | 0 | 0 | 0 | 0 | 706,000 | 0 | 5,826,000 |
| Louisiana | 65 | 684,000 | 0 | 0 | 0 | 0 | 513,000 | 0 | 1,197,000 |
| Maine | 268 | 44,000 | 0 | 0 | 210,000 | 0 | 100,000 | 0 | 354,000 |
| Maryland | 24 | 17,958,000 | 1,443,000 | 0 | 0 | 5,519,000 | 304,000 | 2,401,000 | 27,624,000 |
| Massachusetts | 370 | 7,545,000 | 8,302,000 | 11,000 | 2,888,000 | 5,820,000 | 13,384,000 | 506,000 | 38,457,000 |
| Michigan | 383 | 17,018,000 | 5,347,000 | 394,000 | 572,000 | 0 | 553,000 | 0 | 23,884,000 |
| Minnesota | 130 | 4,426,000 | 4,697,000 | 0 | 835,000 | 56,000 | 1,286,000 | 0 | 11,300,000 |
| Mississippi | 47 | 0 | 5,506,000 | 0 | 2,000 | 0 | 363,000 | 0 | 5,871,000 |
| Missouri | 148 | 3,435,000 | 0 | 0 | 0 | 0 | 29,000 | 94,000 | 3,558,000 |
| Montana | 82 | 40,000 | 301,000 | 11,000 | 158,000 | 19,000 | 101,000 | 300,000 | 929,000 |
| Nebraska | 230 | 607,000 | 0 | 25,000 | 596,000 | 147,000 | 128,000 | 19,000 | 1,522,000 |
| Nevada | 23 | 386,000 | 0 | 44,000 | 40,000 | 0 | 161,000 | 0 | 631,000 |
| New Hampshire | 229 | 0 | 0 | 0 | 77,000 | 0 | 141,000 | 0 | 217,000 |
| New Jersey | 307 | 8,889,000 | 280,000 | 194,000 | 1,744,000 | 758,000 | 0 | 0 | 11,864,000 |
| New Mexico | 72 | 262,000 | 48,000 | 0 | 0 | 0 | 329,000 | 0 | 639,000 |
| New York | 740 | 42,935,000 | 27,431,000 | 5,006,000 | 6,445,000 | 529,000 | 1,579,000 | 6,924,000 | 90,850,000 |
| North Carolina | 75 | 14,769,000 | 0 | 81,000 | 0 | 197,000 | 325,000 | 0 | 15,372,000 |
| North Dakota | 79 | 440,000 | 0 | 37,000 | 0 | 0 | 126,000 | 0 | 602,000 |
| Ohio | 250 | 1,104,000 | 822,000 | 148,000 | 1,119,000 | 11,407,000 | 0 | 0 | 14,601,000 |
| Oklahoma | 114 | 572,000 | 1,585,000 | 0 | 0 | 0 | 264,000 | 0 | 2,421,000 |
| Oregon | 124 | 765,000 | 547,000 | 37,000 | 40,000 | 15,000 | 105,000 | 0 | 1,508,000 |
| Pennsylvania | 460 | 23,069,000 | 1,503,000 | 4,065,000 | 8,389,000 | 1,092,000 | 1,825,000 | 0 | 39,943,000 |
| Rhode Island | 50 | 594,000 | 0 | 2,000 | 0 | 947,000 | 1,798,000 | 0 | 3,341,000 |
| South Carolina | 40 | 5,579,000 | 0 | 3,000 | 0 | 36,000 | 438,000 | 0 | 6,056,000 |
| South Dakota | 112 | 17,000 | 0 | 42,000 | 0 | 13,000 | 65,000 | 0 | 136,000 |
| Tennessee | 141 | 1,763,000 | 4,786,000 | 0 | 0 | 419,000 | 256,000 | 0 | 7,224,000 |
| Texas | 500 | 1,833,000 | 7,718,000 | 0 | 1,837,000 | 0 | 1,041,000 | 41,000 | 12,470,000 |
| Utah | 70 | 2,540,000 | 0 | 178,000 | 0 | 0 | 253,000 | 5,000 | 2,976,000 |
| Vermont | 197 | 0 | 0 | 0 | 0 | 20,000 | 81,000 | 0 | 101,000 |
| Virginia | 90 | 14,101,000 | 0 | 0 | 0 | 0 | 220,000 | 575,000 | 14,895,000 |
| Washington | 69 | 609,000 | 0 | 62,000 | 114,000 | 1,185,000 | 664,000 | 151,000 | 2,785,000 |
| West Virginia | 97 | 3,835,000 | 3,268,000 | 0 | 0 | 0 | 0 | 0 | 7,102,000 |
| Wisconsin | 381 | 554,000 | 12,040,000 | 46,000 | 0 | 904,000 | 167,000 | 2,000 | 13,712,000 |
| Wyoming | 23 | 132,000 | 166,000 | 36,000 | 0 | 10,000 | 92,000 | 0 | 436,000 |
| Dist. of Columbia | 1 | 0 | 0 | 0 | 0 | 0 | 0 | 0 | 0 |

*Source*: U.S. Department of Education, National Center for Education Statistics, State Library Agencies Survey, Fiscal Year 1997.

(a) Source for this column: U.S. Department of Education, National Center for Education Statistics, Federal-State Cooperative System for Public Library Data (FSCS), Public Libraries Survey, Fiscal Year 1996.

(b) Financial assistance to a single agency or library providing a statewide service.

## Table 7.11
## STATE PURCHASING: BUY-AMERICAN LAWS AND OTHER PRACTICES

| | | | Preference to specified products | | | |
|---|---|---|---|---|---|---|
| *State* | *Buy-American laws affecting public procurement* | *Small business* | *Recycled plastic* | *Recycled paper* | *Other products with recycled content* | *Other* |
| Alabama | ... | ... | ... | ... | ... | ... |
| Alaska | (a) | ... | ★ | ★ | ★ | ★ |
| Arizona | ... | ★ | ... | ★ | ★ | ★ |
| Arkansas | ... | ... | ... | ★ | ... | ... |
| California | ★(b) | ★ | ★ | ★ | ★ | ... |
| Colorado | ... | ... | ... | ... | ... | |
| Connecticut | ... | ★(c) | ★ | ★ | ★ | ★ |
| Delaware | ... | ... | ... | ... | ... | ... |
| Florida | ... | ... | ★ | ★ | ★ | ... |
| Georgia | ... | ... | ... | ... | ... | ... |
| Hawaii | ... | ... | ★ | ★ | ★ | ★ |
| Idaho | ... | ... | ... | ... | ... | ... |
| Illinois | ★(d) | ... | ★ | ... | ★ | ★ |
| Indiana | ★ | ★ | ★ | ★ | ★ | ... |
| Iowa | ★(e) | ★ | ... | ★ | ... | ★ |
| Kansas | ★(f) | ... | ... | ★ | ... | ... |
| Kentucky | ... | ... | ★ | ★ | ★ | ★ |
| Louisiana | ★(e) | ★ | ★ | ★ | ★ | ★ (g) |
| Maine | ... | ... | ... | ★ | ... | ... |
| Maryland | ★(e) | ★ | ★ | ★ | ★ | ... |
| Massachusetts | ... | ... | ... | ... | ... | ★ |
| Michigan | ... | ... | ★ | ★ | ★ | ... |
| Minnesota | ★ | ★ | ★ | ★ | ★ | ... |
| Mississippi | ★(h) | ... | ★ | ★ | ★ | ... |
| Missouri | ★ | ... | ★ | ... | ... | ... |
| Montana | ... | ... | ... | ... | ... | ... |
| Nebraska | ... | ... | ... | ... | ... | ... |
| Nevada | ... | ... | ... | ... | ... | ... |
| New Hampshire | ... | ... | ... | ... | ... | ... |
| New Jersey | ★(i) | ★ | ★ | ★ | ★ | ... |
| New Mexico | ★(e) | ... | ★ | ★ | (j) | ... |
| New York | ★(d) | ... | ★ | ★ | (k) | ... |
| North Carolina | ... | ... | ★ | ... | ★ | ... |
| North Dakota | ... | ... | ... | ... | ... | ... |
| Ohio | ★ | ... | ... | ★ | ★ | ★ |
| Oklahoma | (c) | ... | ... | ... | ... | ... |
| Oregon | ... | ... | ★ | ★ | ★ | ... |
| Pennsylvania | ★(d,e) | ... | ★ | ★ | ... | ... |
| Rhode Island | ★ | ... | ... | ★ | ... | ... |
| South Carolina | ★(l) | ... | ... | ★ | ... | ... |
| South Dakota | ... | ... | ★ | ★ | ★ | ★ |
| Tennessee | ... | ... | ... | ... | ★ | ... |
| Texas | ★(m) | ★ | ★ | ★ | ★ | ★ |
| Utah | ... | ... | ... | ★ | ... | ... |
| Vermont | ★(n) | ... | ★ | ★ | ★ | ... |
| Virginia | ... | ... | ... | ★ | ... | ... |
| Washington | ... | ... | ★ | ★ | ★(o) | ... |
| West Virginia | ★(d) | ... | ★ | ★ | ★ | ... |
| Wisconsin | ★(p) | ... | ... | ... | (q) | ... |
| Wyoming | ★(e,r) | ... | ... | ... | ★(s) | ... |

*Source*: National Association of State Purchasing Officials, *State and Local Government Purchasing,* 5th Edition (1997).

*Key:*

★ — Yes

. . . — No

(a) No "Buy American" but have "Buy Alaska" laws.

(b) For some automobile purchases. However, "Buy American" was ruled unconstitutional in a 1971 court case, and "Buy California" was determined to be unconstitutional by the Attorney General.

(c) Minority small businesses share a part of the overall preference for all small businesses.

(d) Steel. In Maryland, 10,000 pounds or more for public work projects. In New York, steel for public works projects only. Also aluminium in Pennsylvania. In West Virginia, over 50,000 pounds, glass and aluminium.

(e) Vehicles only.

(f) Optional for director.

(g) In-state vendor will be given some preference that competitor received in competitor's home state.

(h) Only meat.

(i) Materials used in conjunction with public works contracts.

(j) Provides a 5% bidders preference to qualified New Mexico businesses; manufacturers and contractors.

(k) All products.

(l) Two percent preference on made in U.S.A.

(m) Preferal for U.S. made steel and federal funded highway projects (25%) and in the event of a tie bid (U.S. or foreign).

(n) Steel for AOT.

(o) Tires, vehicle lubricants, latex paints, lead acid batteries, compost, insulation, and panel board.

(p) The state will purchase materials that are manufactured to the greatest extent in the United States in case of tie bids.

(q) State agencies must buy recycled products if practical.

(r) Beef.

(s) Paper.

## Table 7.12
## STATE PURCHASING OF RECYCLED PRODUCTS

| State | Purchases of recycled products required by law | State purchases | | | | Restrictions on purchasing | |
|---|---|---|---|---|---|---|---|
| | | Recycled oil | Alternative fuels | Alternative fuel vehicles | Soybean ink | Foam cups and plates | Products with CFCs |
| Alabama | ... | ... | ... | (a) | ... | ... | ... |
| Alaska | ★ | ... | S | ... | ★ | ... | ... |
| Arizona | ... | ★ | S | ★ | ★ | ... | ... |
| Arkansas | ... | ... | R | ★ | ★ | ... | ★ |
| California | ★ | ★ | O | ★ | ★ | ... | ... |
| Colorado | ★ | N/A | N/A | N/A | ... | ... | ... |
| Connecticut | ★ | ★ | R (b) | ★ | ... | ... | ★ |
| Delaware | ... | ... | O | ★ | ... | ... | ... |
| Florida | ★ | ★ | S | ★ | ★ | ... | ★ |
| Georgia | ... | ... | O | ★ | ... | ... | ... |
| Hawaii | ★ | ... | ... | ... | ... | ... | ★ |
| Idaho | ... | ... | R | ★ | ... | ... | ... |
| Illinois | ... | ★ | O | ★ | ★ | ... | ... |
| Indiana | ... | ★ | S | ★ | ... | ... | ... |
| Iowa | ... | ★ | O | ★ | ★ | ... | ★ |
| Kansas | ★ | ... | S | ★ | ... | ... | ... |
| Kentucky | ★ | ★ | R | ★ | ... | ... | ... |
| Louisiana | ★ | ... | R | ★ | ★ | ... | ... |
| Maine | ★ | ★ | R | ★ | ★ | ★ | ★ |
| Maryland | ... | ... | R | ★ | ★ | ... | ... |
| Massachusetts | ... | ... | R | ★ | ★ | ★ | ★ |
| Michigan | ... | ★ | S | ★ | ★ | ... | ★ |
| Minnesota | ... | ★ | S | ★ | ★ | ... | ★ |
| Mississippi | ... | ★ | R | ★ | ★ | ... | ... |
| Missouri | ★ | ★ | S | ★ | ★ | ★ | ★ |
| Montana | ... | ... | ... | ... | ... | ... | ... |
| Nebraska | ... | ★ | O | ★ | ★ | ★ | ★ |
| Nevada | ... | ... | R | ★ | ... | ... | ... |
| New Hampshire | ★ | ★ | S | ★ | ... | ... | ★ |
| New Jersey | ★ | ★ | R | ★ | ★ | ... | ... |
| New Mexico | ... | ... | O (c) | ★(d) | ★ | ... | ... |
| New York | ... | ★ | R | ★ | ★ | ... | ★ |
| North Carolina | ★ | ... | ... | ... | ★ | ... | ★ |
| North Dakota | ★ | ... | ... | ... | ★ | ... | ... |
| Ohio | ... | ★ | ★ | ★ | ★ | ... | ... |
| Oklahoma | ... | ... | ★ | ... | ★ | ... | ... |
| Oregon | ★ | ★ | S | ★ | ★ | ★ | ... |
| Pennsylvania | ... | ★ | R | ★(e) | ★ | ... | ... |
| Rhode Island | ★ | ... | R | ★ | ... | ... | ★ |
| South Carolina | ... | ... | S | ★ | ★ | ... | ... |
| South Dakota | ... | ★ | S | ★ | ★ | ... | ... |
| Tennessee | ★ | ★ | S | ★ | ★ | ... | ... |
| Texas | ★ | ★ | S | ★ | ★ | ... | ★ |
| Utah | ... | ★ | S | ★ | ★ | ... | ... |
| Vermont | ★ | ★ | ... | ★ | ★ | ... | ... |
| Virginia | ... | ... | R | ★ | ... | ★ | ★ |
| Washington | ★ | ★ | R | ★ | ... | ★ | ... |
| West Virginia | ★ | ★ | R | ★ | ★ | ★ | ... |
| Wisconsin | ... | ★ | S | ★ | ★ | ... | ★ |
| Wyoming | ★ | ... | R | ★ | ... | ... | ... |

*Source*: National Association of State Purchasing Officials, *State and Local Government Purchasing*, 5th Edition (1997).

Key:
★ — Yes
... — No
O = Often
S = Sometimes
R = Rarely
N/A = Not Applicable

(a) Used in test vehicles only.
(b) Pilot program.
(c) Test programs only - unable to get bids.
(d) Most are done by conversion rather than as original equipment.
(e) Beginning in 1996 (7).

## Table 7.13
## SUMMARY OF STATE GOVERNMENT EMPLOYMENT: 1953-1998

| | Employment (in thousands) | | | | | | Monthly payrolls (in millions of dollars) | | | Average monthly earnings of full-time employees | | |
| | Total, full-time and part-time | | | Full-time equivalent | | | | | | | | |
| Year (October) | All | Education | Other | All | Education | Other | All | Education | Other | All | Education | Other |
|---|---|---|---|---|---|---|---|---|---|---|---|---|
| 1953 | 1,082 | 294 | 788 | 966 | 211 | 755 | $278.6 | $73.5 | $205.1 | $289 | $320 | $278 |
| 1954 | 1,149 | 310 | 839 | 1,024 | 222 | 802 | 300.7 | 78.9 | 221.8 | 294 | 325 | 283 |
| 1955 | 1,199 | 333 | 866 | 1,081 | 244 | 837 | 325.9 | 88.5 | 237.4 | 302 | 334 | 290 |
| 1956 | 1,268 | 353 | 915 | 1,136 | 250 | 886 | 366.5 | 108.8 | 257.7 | 321 | 358 | 309 |
| 1957 (April) .. | 1,300 | 375 | 925 | 1,153 | 257 | 896 | 372.5 | 106.1 | 266.4 | 320 | 355 | 309 |
| 1958 | 1,408 | 406 | 1,002 | 1,259 | 284 | 975 | 446.5 | 123.4 | 323.1 | 355 | 416 | 333 |
| 1959 | 1,454 | 443 | 1,011 | 1,302 | 318 | 984 | 485.4 | 136.0 | 349.4 | 373 | 427 | 352 |
| 1960 | 1,527 | 474 | 1,053 | 1,353 | 332 | 1,021 | 524.1 | 167.7 | 356.4 | 386 | 439 | 365 |
| 1961 | 1,625 | 518 | 1,107 | 1,435 | 367 | 1,068 | 586.2 | 192.4 | 393.8 | 409 | 482 | 383 |
| 1962 | 1,680 | 555 | 1,126 | 1,478 | 389 | 1,088 | 634.6 | 201.8 | 432.8 | 429 | 518 | 397 |
| 1963 | 1,775 | 602 | 1,173 | 1,558 | 422 | 1,136 | 696.4 | 230.1 | 466.3 | 447 | 545 | 410 |
| 1964 | 1,873 | 656 | 1,217 | 1,639 | 460 | 1,179 | 761.1 | 257.5 | 503.6 | 464 | 560 | 427 |
| 1965 | 2,028 | 739 | 1,289 | 1,751 | 508 | 1,243 | 849.2 | 290.1 | 559.1 | 484 | 571 | 450 |
| 1966 | 2,211 | 866 | 1,344 | 1,864 | 575 | 1,289 | 975.2 | 353.0 | 622.2 | 522 | 614 | 483 |
| 1967 | 2,335 | 940 | 1,395 | 1,946 | 620 | 1,326 | 1105.5 | 406.3 | 699.3 | 567 | 666 | 526 |
| 1968 | 2,495 | 1,037 | 1,458 | 2,085 | 694 | 1,391 | 1256.7 | 477.1 | 779.6 | 602 | 687 | 544 |
| 1969 | 2,614 | 1,112 | 1,501 | 2,179 | 746 | 1,433 | 1430.5 | 554.5 | 876.1 | 655 | 743 | 597 |
| 1970 | 2,755 | 1,182 | 1,573 | 2,302 | 803 | 1,499 | 1612.2 | 630.3 | 981.9 | 700 | 797 | 605 |
| 1971 | 2,832 | 1,223 | 1,609 | 2,384 | 841 | 1,544 | 1741.7 | 681.5 | 1,060.2 | 731 | 826 | 686 |
| 1972 | 2,957 | 1,267 | 1,690 | 2,487 | 867 | 1,619 | 1936.6 | 746.9 | 1,189.7 | 778 | 871 | 734 |
| 1973 | 3,013 | 1,280 | 1,733 | 2,547 | 887 | 1,660 | 2158.2 | 822.2 | 1,336.0 | 843 | 952 | 805 |
| 1974 | 3,155 | 1,357 | 1,798 | 2,653 | 929 | 1,725 | 2409.5 | 932.7 | 1,476.9 | 906 | 1,023 | 855 |
| 1975 | 3,271 | 1,400 | 1,870 | 2,744 | 952 | 1,792 | 2652.7 | 1,021.7 | 1,631.1 | 964 | 1,080 | 909 |
| 1976 | 3,343 | 1,434 | 1,910 | 2,799 | 973 | 1,827 | 2893.7 | 1,111.5 | 1,782.1 | 1,031 | 1,163 | 975 |
| 1977 | 3,491 | 1,484 | 2,007 | 2,903 | 1,005 | 1,898 | 3194.6 | 1,234.4 | 1,960.1 | 1,096 | 1,237 | 1,031 |
| 1978 | 3,539 | 1,508 | 2,032 | 2,966 | 1,016 | 1,950 | 3483.0 | 1,332.9 | 2,150.2 | 1,167 | 1,311 | 1,102 |
| 1979 | 3,699 | 1,577 | 2,122 | 3,072 | 1,046 | 2,026 | 3869.3 | 1,451.4 | 2,417.9 | 1,257 | 1,399 | 1,193 |
| 1980 | 3,753 | 1,599 | 2,154 | 3,106 | 1,063 | 2,044 | 4284.7 | 1,608.0 | 2,676.6 | 1,373 | 1,523 | 1,305 |
| 1981 | 3,726 | 1,603 | 2,123 | 3,087 | 1,063 | 2,024 | 4667.5 | 1,768.0 | 2,899.5 | 1,507 | 1,671 | 1,432 |
| 1982 | 3,747 | 1,616 | 2,131 | 3,083 | 1,051 | 2,032• | 5027.7 | 1,874.0 | 3,153.7 | 1,625 | 1,789 | 1,551 |
| 1983 | 3,816 | 1,666 | 2,150 | 3,116 | 1,072 | 2,044 | 5345.5 | 1,989.0 | 3,357.0 | 1,711 | 1,850 | 1,640 |
| 1984 | 3,898 | 1,708 | 2,190 | 3,177 | 1,091 | 2,086 | 5814.9 | 2,178.0 | 3,637.0 | 1,825 | 1,991 | 1,740 |
| 1985 | 3,984 | 1,764 | 2,220 | 2,990 | 945 | 2,046 | 6328.6 | 2,433.7 | 3,884.9 | 1,935 | 2,155 | 1,834 |
| 1986 | 4,068 | 1,800 | 2,267 | 3,437 | 1,256 | 2,181 | 6801.4 | 2,583.4 | 4,226.9 | 2,052 | 2,263 | 1,956 |
| 1987 | 4,115 | 1,804 | 2,310 | 3,491 | 1,264 | 2,227 | 7297.8 | 2,758.3 | 4,539.5 | 2,161 | 2,396 | 2,056 |
| 1988 | 4,236 | 1,854 | 2,381 | 3,606 | 1,309 | 2,297 | 7842.3 | 2,928.6 | 4,913.7 | 2,260 | 2,490 | 2,158 |
| 1989 | 4,365 | 1,925 | 2,440 | 3,709 | 1,360 | 2,349 | 8443.1 | 3,175.0 | 5,268.1 | 2,372 | 2,627 | 2,259 |
| 1990 | 4,503 | 1,984 | 2,519 | 3,840 | 1,418 | 2,432 | 9083.0 | 3,426.0 | 5,657.0 | 2,472 | 2,732 | 2,359 |
| 1991 | 4,521 | 1,999 | 2,522 | 3,829 | 1,375 | 2,454 | 9437.0 | 3,550.0 | 5,887.0 | 2,479 | 2,530 | 2,433 |
| 1992 | 4,595 | 2,050 | 2,545 | 3,856 | 1,384 | 2,472 | 9828.0 | 3,774.0 | 6,054.0 | 2,562 | 2,607 | 2,521 |
| 1993 | 4,673 | 2,112 | 2,562 | 3,891 | 1,436 | 2,455 | 10288.2 | 3,999.3 | 6,288.9 | 2,722 | 3,034 | 2,578 |
| 1994 | ... | ... | ... | 3,917 | 1,442 | 2,475 | 10666.3 | 4,176.8 | 6,489.3 | ... | ... | ... |
| 1995 | ... | ... | ... | 3,971 | 1,469 | 2,502 | 10926.5 | 4,173.3 | 6,753.2 | ... | ... | ... |
| 1996 | (a) | (a) | (a) | (a) | (a) | (a) | (a) | (a) | (a) | (a) | (a) | (a) |
| 1997 (March) | 4,733 | 2,114 | 2,619 | 3,987 | 1,484 | 2,503 | 11413.1 | 4,372.0 | 7,041.1 | ... | ... | ... |
| 1998 (March) | 4,758 | 2,173 | 2,585 | 3,985 | 1,511 | 2,474 | 11845.2 | 4,632.1 | 7,213.1 | ... | ... | ... |

*Source*: U.S. Department of Commerce, Bureau of the Census.
*Note*: Detail may not add to totals due to rounding.
*Key*:
... — Not applicable
(a) Due to a change in the reference period, from October to March, the October 1996 Annual Survey of Government Employment and Payroll was not conducted. This change in collection period was effective, beginning with the March 1997 survey.

## Table 7.14
## EMPLOYMENT AND PAYROLLS OF STATE AND LOCAL GOVERNMENTS, BY FUNCTION: MARCH 1997

| Functions | All employees, full-time and part-time (in thousands) | | | March payrolls (in millions of dollars) | | | Average March earnings of full-time employees |
|---|---|---|---|---|---|---|---|
| | Total | State governments | Local governments | Total | State governments | Local governments | |
| All functions ........................................ | 16,733 | 4,733 | 12,000 | $39,412 | $11,413 | $27,999 | $2,882 |
| Education: ........................................... | | | | | | | |
| Higher education ............................. | 2,451 | 1,965 | 486 | 4,800 | 3,994 | 806 | 3,281 |
| Instructional personnel only ........ | 870 | 634 | 236 | 2,398 | 1,949 | 449 | 4,627 |
| Elementary/Secondary schools ...... | 6,408 | 50 | 6,358 | 14,713 | 119 | 14,594 | 2,788 |
| Instructional personnel only ....... | 4,320 | 34 | 4,286 | 11,667 | 94 | 11,573 | 3,105 |
| Libraries ......................................... | 156 | 1 | 155 | 234 | 1 | 232 | 2,383 |
| Other Education ............................. | 99 | 99 | 0 | 259 | 259 | 0 | 2,883 |
| Selected functions: ........................... | | | | | | | |
| Streets and Highways ...................... | 548 | 252 | 297 | 1,396 | 677 | 719 | 2,653 |
| Public Welfare ................................ | 498 | 225 | 273 | 1,172 | 561 | 612 | 2,505 |
| Hospitals ......................................... | 1,060 | 495 | 565 | 2,603 | 1,239 | 1,364 | 2,658 |
| Police protection ............................. | 856 | 94 | 762 | 2,645 | 307 | 2,338 | 3,382 |
| Police Officers ............................. | 623 | 56 | 567 | 2,160 | 203 | 1,957 | 3,614 |
| Fire protection ................................ | 356 | 0 | 356 | 990 | 0 | 990 | 3,673 |
| Firefighters only ........................... | 329 | 0 | 329 | 929 | 0 | 929 | 3,724 |
| Natural Resources ........................... | 206 | 165 | 40 | 496 | 409 | 86 | 2,795 |
| Correction ....................................... | 679 | 458 | 220 | 1,776 | 1,183 | 592 | 2,751 |
| Social Insurance ............................. | 96 | 96 | 0 | 259 | 259 | 0 | 2,813 |
| Financial Admin. ............................. | 394 | 172 | 221 | 968 | 464 | 504 | 2,716 |
| Judicial and Legal .......................... | 366 | 139 | 228 | 1,071 | 467 | 604 | 3,148 |
| Other Government Admin. ............ | 384 | 60 | 323 | 694 | 157 | 537 | 2,795 |
| Utilities .......................................... | 451 | 26 | 425 | 1,440 | 110 | 1,331 | 3,374 |
| State Liquor stores ......................... | 9 | 9 | 0 | 16 | 16 | 0 | 2,428 |
| Other and unallocable ................... | 1,716 | 427 | 1,289 | 3,880 | 1,191 | 2,689 | 2,745 |

*Source*: U.S. Department of Commerce, Bureau of the Census.

*Note*: Due to a change in the collection period the data in this table are reported for March 1997 instead of October1996.

## Table 7.15
## EMPLOYMENT AND PAYROLLS OF STATE AND LOCAL GOVERNMENTS, BY FUNCTION: MARCH 1998

| Functions | All employees, full-time and part-time (in thousands) | | | March payrolls (in millions of dollars) | | | Average March earnings of full-time employees |
|---|---|---|---|---|---|---|---|
| | Total | State governments | Local governments | Total | State governments | Local governments | |
| All functions ............................................. | 17,089 | 4,758 | 12,331 | $41,453 | $11,845 | $29,608 | $2,979 |
| Education: ................................................. | | | | | | | |
| Higher education ................................. | 2,516 | 2,011 | 505 | 5,098 | 4,209 | 889 | 3,416 |
| Higher Education-Instruc. ................. | 891 | 651 | 240 | 2,531 | 2,043 | 488 | 4,761 |
| Elementary/Secondary schools .......... | 6,652 | 55 | 6,597 | 15,648 | 139 | 15,509 | 2,865 |
| Elem & Sec School Instruction ........ | 4,488 | 38 | 4,450 | 12,367 | 111 | 12,256 | 3,180 |
| Libraries .............................................. | 160 | 1 | 159 | 243 | 1 | 242 | 2,436 |
| Other Education ................................... | 107 | 107 | 0 | 285 | 285.00 | 0 | 3,022 |
| Selected functions: ................................... | | | | | | | |
| Streets & Highways ............................. | 550 | 246 | 304 | 1,463 | 705 | 758 | 2,784 |
| Public Welfare ..................................... | 500 | 228 | 272 | 1,214 | 591 | 623 | 2,581 |
| Hospitals .............................................. | 1,013 | 453 | 560 | 2,570 | 1,182 | 1,388 | 2,755 |
| Police protection ................................. | 877 | 95 | 782 | 2,788 | 319 | 2,469 | 3,482 |
| Police Protection-Officers ................. | 638 | 56 | 582 | 2,279 | 210 | 2,069 | 3,727 |
| Fire protection .................................... | 363 | 0 | 363 | 1,055 | 0 | 1,055 | 3,849 |
| Firefighters ......................................... | 337 | 0 | 337 | 991 | 0 | 991 | 3,902 |
| Natural Resources ............................... | 205 | 163 | 42 | 506 | 413 | 93 | 2,909 |
| Correction ........................................... | 693 | 467 | 226 | 1,865 | 1,239 | 626 | 2,828 |
| Social Insurance Administration ........ | 93 | 93 | 0 | 262 | 262 | 0 | 2,948 |
| Financial Administration ................... | 398 | 170 | 228 | 1,020 | 478 | 542 | 2,844 |
| Judicial and Legal .............................. | 379 | 144 | 235 | 1,146 | 493 | 653 | 3,246 |
| Other Government Administration ... | 395 | 59 | 336 | 737 | 160 | 577 | 2,928 |
| Utilities ............................................... | 454 | 25 | 429 | 1,468 | 110 | 1,358 | 2,865 |
| State Liquor Stores ............................. | 9 | 9 | 0 | 16 | 16 | 0 | 2,513 |
| Other & Unallocable .......................... | 1,725 | 432 | 1,293 | 4,069 | 1,243 | 2,826 | 2,847 |

*Source:* U.S. Department of Commerce, Bureau of the Census.

*Note:* Statistics for local governments are estimates subject to sampling variation. Detail may not add to totals due to rounding.

## Table 7.16
## STATE AND LOCAL GOVERNMENT EMPLOYMENT, BY STATE: MARCH 1997

| State or other jurisdiction | All employees (full-time and part-time) State | All employees (full-time and part-time) Local | Full-time equivalent employment Number Total | Full-time equivalent employment Number State | Full-time equivalent employment Number Local | Number per 10,000 population Total | Number per 10,000 population State | Number per 10,000 population Local | 1997 Population |
|---|---|---|---|---|---|---|---|---|---|
| United States ................. | 4,732,608 | 12,000,351 | 14,214,109 | 3,986,680 | 10,227,429 | 531 | 149 | 382 | 267,636 |
| Alabama ............................. | 95,490 | 191,238 | 256,458 | 81,089 | 175,369 | 594 | 188 | 406 | 4,319 |
| Alaska ................................. | 25,244 | 28,081 | 45,490 | 22,358 | 23,132 | 747 | 367 | 380 | 609 |
| Arizona ............................... | 74,710 | 194,329 | 226,563 | 61,232 | 165,331 | 497 | 134 | 363 | 4,555 |
| Arkansas ............................ | 54,806 | 106,086 | 139,367 | 48,561 | 90,806 | 552 | 192 | 360 | 2,523 |
| California ........................... | 406,554 | 1,439,385 | 1,529,599 | 335,430 | 1,194,169 | 474 | 104 | 370 | 32,268 |
| Colorado ............................ | 76,385 | 188,405 | 212,578 | 59,432 | 153,146 | 546 | 153 | 393 | 3,893 |
| Connecticut ....................... | 69,370 | 119,350 | 164,112 | 59,774 | 104,338 | 502 | 183 | 319 | 3,270 |
| Delaware ............................ | 26,182 | 20,861 | 40,741 | 21,876 | 18,865 | 557 | 299 | 258 | 732 |
| Florida ................................ | 226,884 | 631,590 | 730,982 | 187,457 | 543,525 | 499 | 128 | 371 | 14,654 |
| Georgia ............................... | 131,240 | 359,584 | 435,945 | 111,465 | 324,480 | 582 | 149 | 433 | 7,486 |
| Hawaii ................................ | 66,365 | 15,248 | 65,995 | 51,676 | 14,319 | 556 | 435 | 121 | 1,187 |
| Idaho .................................. | 26,609 | 59,109 | 68,572 | 22,537 | 46,035 | 567 | 186 | 380 | 1,210 |
| Illinois ............................... | 165,981 | 562,108 | 600,920 | 141,027 | 459,893 | 505 | 119 | 387 | 11,896 |
| Indiana ............................... | 106,778 | 256,091 | 307,385 | 86,638 | 220,747 | 524 | 148 | 376 | 5,864 |
| Iowa ................................... | 62,637 | 144,949 | 168,531 | 55,864 | 112,667 | 591 | 196 | 395 | 2,852 |
| Kansas ................................ | 55,255 | 150,710 | 162,776 | 44,474 | 118,302 | 627 | 171 | 456 | 2,595 |
| Kentucky ............................ | 85,126 | 148,174 | 206,356 | 71,616 | 134,740 | 528 | 183 | 345 | 3,908 |
| Louisiana ........................... | 110,652 | 184,500 | 264,467 | 94,491 | 169,976 | 608 | 217 | 391 | 4,352 |
| Maine ................................. | 24,775 | 58,814 | 66,387 | 20,127 | 46,260 | 535 | 162 | 372 | 1,242 |
| Maryland ............................ | 92,510 | 194,389 | 251,703 | 80,068 | 171,635 | 494 | 157 | 337 | 5,094 |
| Massachusetts ................... | 107,279 | 243,545 | 303,665 | 89,748 | 213,917 | 496 | 147 | 350 | 6,118 |
| Michigan ............................ | 174,093 | 424,209 | 470,613 | 137,942 | 332,671 | 481 | 141 | 340 | 9,774 |
| Minnesota .......................... | 86,442 | 248,283 | 260,244 | 71,399 | 188,845 | 555 | 152 | 403 | 4,686 |
| Mississippi ........................ | 57,995 | 138,514 | 173,591 | 51,335 | 122,256 | 636 | 188 | 448 | 2,731 |
| Missouri ............................. | 107,403 | 235,546 | 290,454 | 88,845 | 201,609 | 538 | 164 | 373 | 5,402 |
| Montana ............................. | 23,617 | 42,779 | 50,924 | 18,248 | 32,676 | 579 | 208 | 372 | 879 |
| Nebraska ............................ | 35,518 | 91,556 | 105,101 | 29,724 | 75,377 | 634 | 179 | 455 | 1,657 |
| Nevada ............................... | 25,440 | 65,572 | 79,577 | 22,970 | 56,607 | 475 | 137 | 338 | 1,677 |
| New Hampshire ................. | 22,262 | 48,268 | 55,859 | 17,029 | 38,830 | 476 | 145 | 331 | 1,173 |
| New Jersey ......................... | 137,159 | 345,712 | 421,282 | 122,919 | 298,363 | 523 | 153 | 370 | 8,053 |
| New Mexico ....................... | 50,039 | 78,586 | 110,980 | 41,039 | 69,941 | 642 | 237 | 404 | 1,730 |
| New York ............................ | 275,696 | 972,370 | 1,110,246 | 250,078 | 860,168 | 612 | 138 | 474 | 18,137 |
| North Carolina ................... | 139,309 | 343,859 | 415,803 | 122,298 | 293,505 | 560 | 165 | 395 | 7,425 |
| North Dakota ..................... | 21,022 | 34,999 | 36,605 | 15,384 | 21,221 | 571 | 240 | 331 | 641 |
| Ohio ................................... | 179,122 | 495,388 | 561,229 | 140,137 | 421,092 | 502 | 125 | 376 | 11,186 |
| Oklahoma .......................... | 84,532 | 147,750 | 201,550 | 72,088 | 129,462 | 608 | 217 | 390 | 3,317 |
| Oregon ............................... | 66,294 | 150,234 | 171,712 | 53,713 | 117,999 | 529 | 166 | 364 | 3,243 |
| Pennsylvania ..................... | 180,983 | 426,135 | 515,927 | 150,371 | 365,556 | 429 | 125 | 304 | 12,020 |
| Rhode Island ..................... | 23,923 | 32,438 | 49,279 | 20,177 | 29,102 | 499 | 204 | 295 | 987 |
| South Carolina .................. | 88,780 | 158,044 | 221,735 | 77,783 | 143,952 | 590 | 207 | 383 | 3,760 |
| South Dakota ..................... | 16,942 | 38,365 | 39,837 | 13,270 | 26,567 | 540 | 180 | 360 | 738 |
| Tennessee .......................... | 93,641 | 216,021 | 276,033 | 81,759 | 194,274 | 514 | 152 | 362 | 5,368 |
| Texas .................................. | 291,940 | 947,232 | 1,112,355 | 261,975 | 850,380 | 572 | 135 | 437 | 19,439 |
| Utah ................................... | 53,389 | 85,781 | 109,028 | 45,144 | 63,884 | 530 | 219 | 310 | 2,059 |
| Vermont ............................. | 14,229 | 23,351 | 30,266 | 12,425 | 17,841 | 514 | 211 | 303 | 589 |
| Virginia .............................. | 130,978 | 289,315 | 358,733 | 105,514 | 253,219 | 533 | 157 | 376 | 6,734 |
| Washington ........................ | 133,250 | 220,503 | 293,245 | 108,093 | 185,152 | 523 | 193 | 330 | 5,610 |
| West Virginia ..................... | 37,744 | 66,096 | 92,275 | 32,349 | 59,926 | 508 | 178 | 330 | 1,816 |
| Wisconsin .......................... | 77,230 | 254,154 | 266,342 | 64,709 | 201,633 | 515 | 125 | 390 | 5,170 |
| Wyoming ............................ | 12,824 | 35,474 | 38,446 | 11,023 | 27,423 | 801 | 230 | 571 | 480 |
| Dist. of Columbia .............. | 0 | 47,271 | 46,246 | 0 | 46,246 | 874 | 0 | 874 | 529 |

*Source:* U.S. Department of Commerce, Bureau of the Census.
*Note:* Statistics for local governments are estimates subject to sampling variation. Detail may not add to totals due to rounding.

## Table 7.17
## STATE AND LOCAL GOVERNMENT EMPLOYMENT, BY STATE: MARCH 1998

| State or other jurisdiction | All employees (full-time and part-time) | | Full-time equivalent employment | | | | | | 1998 Population |
|---|---|---|---|---|---|---|---|---|---|
| | | | Number | | | Number per 10,000 population | | | |
| | State | Local | Total | State | Local | Total | State | Local | |
| United States ................. | 4,758,427 | 12,330,767 | 14,490,645 | 3,985,350 | 10,505,295 | 536 | 147 | 389 | 270,299,000 |
| Alabama .............................. | 96,206 | 192,230 | 257,286 | 82,483 | 174,803 | 591 | 190 | 402 | 4,351,999 |
| Alaska ................................. | 25,540 | 27,151 | 44,216 | 22,147 | 22,069 | 720 | 361 | 359 | 614,010 |
| Arizona ............................... | 76,191 | 192,027 | 226,937 | 61,904 | 165,033 | 486 | 133 | 353 | 4,668,631 |
| Arkansas ............................. | 56,662 | 109,984 | 143,004 | 49,351 | 93,653 | 563 | 194 | 369 | 2,538,303 |
| California ............................ | 413,550 | 1,462,618 | 1,549,461 | 335,353 | 1,214,108 | 474 | 103 | 372 | 32,666,550 |
| Colorado ............................. | 78,151 | 191,651 | 220,910 | 61,476 | 159,434 | 556 | 155 | 401 | 3,970,971 |
| Connecticut ........................ | 70,754 | 118,954 | 164,057 | 60,853 | 103,204 | 501 | 186 | 315 | 3,274,069 |
| Delaware ............................ | 26,924 | 20,200 | 40,656 | 22,080 | 18,576 | 547 | 297 | 250 | 743,603 |
| Florida ................................ | 216,942 | 651,976 | 736,151 | 176,953 | 559,198 | 494 | 119 | 375 | 14,915,980 |
| Georgia ............................... | 133,376 | 365,839 | 440,950 | 112,373 | 328,577 | 577 | 147 | 430 | 7,642,207 |
| Hawaii ................................ | 67,376 | 15,399 | 67,053 | 52,615 | 14,438 | 562 | 441 | 121 | 1,193,001 |
| Idaho .................................. | 26,671 | 61,402 | 70,684 | 22,041 | 48,643 | 575 | 179 | 396 | 1,228,684 |
| Illinois ................................ | 165,747 | 574,072 | 607,768 | 138,539 | 469,229 | 505 | 115 | 390 | 12,045,326 |
| Indiana ............................... | 107,010 | 262,814 | 307,905 | 82,850 | 225,055 | 522 | 140 | 382 | 5,899,195 |
| Iowa ................................... | 63,398 | 148,756 | 167,883 | 53,032 | 114,851 | 587 | 185 | 401 | 2,862,447 |
| Kansas ................................ | 54,939 | 156,588 | 167,295 | 44,395 | 122,900 | 636 | 169 | 467 | 2,629,067 |
| Kentucky ............................ | 86,124 | 156,448 | 211,610 | 72,606 | 139,004 | 538 | 184 | 353 | 3,936,499 |
| Louisiana ........................... | 112,163 | 193,167 | 272,267 | 94,349 | 177,918 | 623 | 216 | 407 | 4,368,967 |
| Maine ................................. | 24,297 | 64,262 | 68,140 | 19,982 | 48,158 | 548 | 161 | 387 | 1,244,250 |
| Maryland ............................ | 95,604 | 205,874 | 267,915 | 88,627 | 179,288 | 522 | 173 | 349 | 5,134,808 |
| Massachusetts .................... | 102,136 | 248,315 | 301,433 | 84,073 | 217,360 | 490 | 137 | 354 | 6,147,132 |
| Michigan ............................ | 171,071 | 425,875 | 472,678 | 135,996 | 336,682 | 481 | 139 | 343 | 9,817,242 |
| Minnesota .......................... | 78,689 | 262,553 | 268,139 | 69,199 | 198,940 | 567 | 146 | 421 | 4,725,419 |
| Mississippi ......................... | 58,769 | 142,315 | 177,123 | 51,817 | 125,306 | 644 | 188 | 455 | 2,752,092 |
| Missouri ............................. | 103,814 | 248,015 | 297,864 | 86,633 | 211,231 | 548 | 159 | 388 | 5,438,559 |
| Montana ............................. | 23,466 | 42,994 | 52,644 | 19,264 | 33,380 | 598 | 219 | 379 | 880,453 |
| Nebraska ............................ | 34,759 | 93,174 | 106,997 | 29,176 | 77,821 | 644 | 175 | 468 | 1,662,719 |
| Nevada ............................... | 26,639 | 67,238 | 82,871 | 24,132 | 58,739 | 474 | 138 | 336 | 1,746,898 |
| New Hampshire .................. | 22,304 | 48,232 | 57,200 | 17,061 | 40,139 | 483 | 144 | 339 | 1,185,048 |
| New Jersey ......................... | 138,137 | 354,914 | 431,350 | 123,098 | 308,252 | 532 | 152 | 380 | 8,115,011 |
| New Mexico ........................ | 52,740 | 81,448 | 114,200 | 42,784 | 71,416 | 657 | 246 | 411 | 1,736,931 |
| New York ............................ | 277,154 | 1,005,966 | 1,149,858 | 251,587 | 898,271 | 633 | 138 | 494 | 18,175,301 |
| North Carolina ................... | 139,833 | 357,254 | 421,648 | 123,329 | 298,319 | 559 | 163 | 395 | 7,546,493 |
| North Dakota ...................... | 20,719 | 34,984 | 36,512 | 15,297 | 21,215 | 572 | 240 | 332 | 638,244 |
| Ohio ................................... | 172,204 | 500,478 | 564,029 | 135,824 | 428,205 | 503 | 121 | 382 | 11,209,493 |
| Oklahoma ........................... | 84,135 | 152,840 | 204,451 | 71,325 | 133,126 | 611 | 213 | 398 | 3,346,713 |
| Oregon ............................... | 68,235 | 150,875 | 175,673 | 55,605 | 120,068 | 535 | 169 | 366 | 3,281,974 |
| Pennsylvania ...................... | 178,614 | 441,754 | 528,692 | 149,185 | 379,507 | 441 | 124 | 316 | 12,001,451 |
| Rhode Island ...................... | 24,303 | 32,754 | 49,844 | 20,232 | 29,612 | 504 | 205 | 300 | 988,480 |
| South Carolina ................... | 95,572 | 174,247 | 236,671 | 80,022 | 156,649 | 617 | 209 | 408 | 3,835,962 |
| South Dakota ...................... | 16,652 | 39,336 | 40,311 | 13,056 | 27,255 | 546 | 177 | 369 | 738,171 |
| Tennessee ........................... | 92,438 | 229,996 | 285,698 | 80,727 | 204,971 | 526 | 149 | 377 | 5,430,621 |
| Texas .................................. | 301,513 | 971,223 | 1,140,226 | 268,005 | 872,221 | 577 | 136 | 441 | 19,759,614 |
| Utah ................................... | 56,213 | 89,168 | 113,811 | 46,485 | 67,326 | 542 | 221 | 321 | 2,099,758 |
| Vermont ............................. | 14,154 | 24,011 | 31,283 | 12,530 | 18,753 | 529 | 212 | 317 | 590,883 |
| Virginia .............................. | 141,463 | 298,125 | 368,717 | 110,675 | 258,042 | 543 | 163 | 380 | 6,791,345 |
| Washington ........................ | 137,317 | 227,419 | 296,020 | 106,432 | 189,588 | 520 | 187 | 333 | 5,689,263 |
| West Virginia ..................... | 37,818 | 68,468 | 93,730 | 32,004 | 61,726 | 518 | 177 | 341 | 1,811,156 |
| Wisconsin ........................... | 76,983 | 264,434 | 276,493 | 64,703 | 211,790 | 529 | 124 | 405 | 5,223,500 |
| Wyoming ............................ | 12,958 | 35,667 | 38,626 | 11,085 | 27,541 | 803 | 231 | 573 | 480,907 |
| Dist. of Columbia .............. | 0 | 45,283 | 43,705 | 0 | 43,705 | 837 | 0 | 837 | 523,000 |

Source U.S. Department of Commerce, Bureau of the Census.
Note: Statistics for local governments are estimates subject to sampling variation. Detail may not add to totals due to rounding.

## Table 7.18
## STATE AND LOCAL GOVERNMENT PAYROLLS AND AVERAGE EARNINGS
## OF FULL-TIME EMPLOYEES, BY STATE: MARCH 1997

| State or other jurisdiction | Amount of payroll (in thousands of dollars) | | | Percentage of March payroll | | Average earnings of full-time state and local government employees (dollars) | | |
|---|---|---|---|---|---|---|---|---|
| | Total | State government | Local governments | State government | Local government | All | Education employees | Other |
| United States ................. | $39,411,694 | $11,413,088 | $27,998,606 | 29 | 71 | $2,882 | $2,882 | $2,882 |
| Alabama ............................... | 564,271 | 198,863 | 365,408 | 35 | 65 | 2,243 | 2,252 | 2,234 |
| Alaska ................................... | 163,984 | 80,796 | 83,188 | 49 | 51 | 3,751 | 3,703 | 3,790 |
| Arizona ................................. | 577,933 | 154,233 | 423,700 | 27 | 73 | 2,685 | 2,620 | 2,749 |
| Arkansas .............................. | 288,603 | 114,425 | 174,178 | 40 | 60 | 2,120 | 2,181 | 2,049 |
| California ............................. | 5,263,693 | 1,232,997 | 4,030,696 | 23 | 77 | 3,674 | 3,507 | 3,801 |
| Colorado .............................. | 601,724 | 200,695 | 401,029 | 33 | 67 | 2,906 | 2,849 | 2,963 |
| Connecticut ......................... | 564,180 | 203,465 | 360,715 | 36 | 64 | 3,567 | 3,671 | 3,459 |
| Delaware .............................. | 110,764 | 59,287 | 51,476 | 54 | 46 | 2,820 | 3,017 | 2,638 |
| Florida .................................. | 1,855,324 | 496,647 | 1,358,677 | 27 | 73 | 2,596 | 2,417 | 2,738 |
| Georgia ................................. | 1,002,193 | 276,656 | 725,537 | 28 | 72 | 2,335 | 2,351 | 2,319 |
| Hawaii .................................. | 182,755 | 137,283 | 45,472 | 75 | 25 | 2,780 | 2,677 | 2,857 |
| Idaho .................................... | 152,003 | 51,545 | 100,458 | 34 | 66 | 2,278 | 2,139 | 2,439 |
| Illinois ................................. | 1,791,137 | 421,328 | 1,369,809 | 24 | 76 | 3,135 | 3,068 | 3,199 |
| Indiana ................................. | 746,681 | 221,168 | 525,513 | 30 | 70 | 2,508 | 2,725 | 2,243 |
| Iowa ..................................... | 425,677 | 165,190 | 260,487 | 39 | 61 | 2,672 | 2,693 | 2,646 |
| Kansas .................................. | 378,890 | 113,190 | 265,699 | 30 | 70 | 2,429 | 2,446 | 2,410 |
| Kentucky .............................. | 469,016 | 183,556 | 285,461 | 39 | 61 | 2,353 | 2,400 | 2,289 |
| Louisiana ............................. | 574,703 | 239,657 | 335,045 | 42 | 58 | 2,204 | 2,237 | 2,171 |
| Maine ................................... | 158,750 | 52,847 | 105,903 | 33 | 67 | 2,493 | 2,459 | 2,539 |
| Maryland .............................. | 757,726 | 234,640 | 523,086 | 31 | 69 | 3,115 | 3,398 | 2,866 |
| Massachusetts ..................... | 912,770 | 272,495 | 640,275 | 30 | 70 | 3,118 | 3,114 | 3,123 |
| Michigan .............................. | 1,478,401 | 454,455 | 1,023,946 | 31 | 69 | 3,350 | 3,517 | 3,148 |
| Minnesota ............................ | 750,312 | 220,170 | 530,142 | 29 | 71 | 3,109 | 3,063 | 3,161 |
| Mississippi .......................... | 341,380 | 119,190 | 222,190 | 35 | 65 | 1,995 | 2,015 | 1,975 |
| Missouri ............................... | 664,929 | 203,429 | 461,500 | 31 | 69 | 2,356 | 2,447 | 2,263 |
| Montana ............................... | 114,425 | 43,863 | 70,562 | 38 | 62 | 2,388 | 2,477 | 2,292 |
| Nebraska .............................. | 245,104 | 66,517 | 178,587 | 27 | 73 | 2,443 | 2,375 | 2,508 |
| Nevada .................................. | 242,104 | 67,918 | 174,186 | 28 | 72 | 3,184 | 2,947 | 3,352 |
| New Hampshire .................... | 142,690 | 42,999 | 99,691 | 30 | 70 | 2,683 | 2,699 | 2,665 |
| New Jersey ........................... | 1,502,837 | 435,363 | 1,067,474 | 29 | 71 | 3,720 | 3,947 | 3,482 |
| New Mexico .......................... | 245,388 | 96,929 | 148,459 | 40 | 60 | 2,251 | 2,179 | 2,335 |
| New York .............................. | 3,740,259 | 861,857 | 2,878,402 | 23 | 77 | 3,524 | 3,712 | 3,404 |
| North Carolina ..................... | 1,009,009 | 320,620 | 688,389 | 32 | 68 | 2,484 | 2,545 | 2,423 |
| North Dakota ....................... | 87,772 | 37,030 | 50,741 | 42 | 58 | 2,543 | 2,780 | 2,270 |
| Ohio ..................................... | 1,534,747 | 406,235 | 1,128,512 | 26 | 74 | 2,858 | 2,959 | 2,765 |
| Oklahoma ............................ | 408,242 | 143,983 | 264,259 | 35 | 65 | 2,079 | 2,148 | 2,007 |
| Oregon ................................. | 482,939 | 151,436 | 331,502 | 31 | 69 | 2,953 | 2,960 | 2,946 |
| Pennsylvania ....................... | 1,510,172 | 452,816 | 1,057,357 | 30 | 70 | 3,045 | 3,325 | 2,779 |
| Rhode Island ....................... | 153,881 | 63,345 | 90,537 | 41 | 59 | 3,244 | 3,358 | 3,128 |
| South Carolina ..................... | 512,006 | 183,971 | 328,035 | 36 | 64 | 2,352 | 2,458 | 2,252 |
| South Dakota ....................... | 86,727 | 31,380 | 55,347 | 36 | 64 | 2,259 | 2,280 | 2,231 |
| Tennessee ............................ | 621,991 | 197,786 | 424,204 | 32 | 68 | 2,304 | 2,311 | 2,298 |
| Texas .................................... | 2,609,460 | 672,488 | 1,936,972 | 26 | 74 | 2,396 | 2,367 | 2,431 |
| Utah ..................................... | 266,462 | 113,716 | 152,746 | 43 | 57 | 2,593 | 2,547 | 2,653 |
| Vermont ............................... | 71,927 | 30,952 | 40,975 | 43 | 57 | 2,480 | 2,451 | 2,520 |
| Virginia ................................ | 903,852 | 273,503 | 630,349 | 30 | 70 | 2,652 | 2,670 | 2,632 |
| Washington .......................... | 896,429 | 307,272 | 589,157 | 34 | 66 | 3,298 | 3,409 | 3,223 |
| West Virginia ....................... | 208,456 | 75,294 | 133,162 | 36 | 64 | 2,312 | 2,513 | 2,035 |
| Wisconsin ............................ | 773,460 | 204,267 | 569,193 | 26 | 74 | 3,060 | 3,200 | 2,898 |
| Wyoming .............................. | 85,926 | 23,340 | 62,586 | 27 | 73 | 2,354 | 2,446 | 2,270 |
| Dist. of Columbia ............... | 177,629 | 0 | 177,629 | 0 | 100 | 3,878 | 3,411 | 4,023 |

*Source:* U.S. Department of Commerce, Bureau of the Census.
*Note:* Statistics for local governments are estimates subject to sampling variation. Detail may not add to totals due to rounding.

## Table 7.19
## STATE AND LOCAL GOVERNMENT PAYROLLS AND AVERAGE EARNINGS
## OF FULL-TIME EMPLOYEES, BY STATE: MARCH 1998

| State or other jurisdiction | Amount of payroll (in thousands of dollars) | | | Percentage of March payroll | | Average earnings of full-time state and local government employees (dollars) | | |
|---|---|---|---|---|---|---|---|---|
| | Total | State government | Local governments | State government | Local government | All | Education employees | Other |
| United States .............. | $41,453,515 | $11,845,219 | $29,608,296 | 29 | 71 | $2,979 | $2,971 | $2,986 |
| Alabama ............................ | 582,062 | 203,885 | 378,177 | 35 | 65 | 2,304 | 2,316 | 2,291 |
| Alaska ............................... | 162,717 | 81,433 | 81,285 | 50 | 50 | 3,789 | 3,683 | 3,871 |
| Arizona ............................. | 608,117 | 169,375 | 438,742 | 28 | 72 | 2,828 | 2,709 | 2,951 |
| Arkansas .......................... | 310,199 | 125,027 | 185,172 | 40 | 60 | 2,209 | 2,266 | 2,141 |
| California .......................... | 5,524,144 | 1,264,415 | 4,259,728 | 23 | 77 | 3,795 | 3,603 | 3,946 |
| Colorado ........................... | 649,408 | 210,094 | 439,314 | 32 | 68 | 3,044 | 3,004 | 3,083 |
| Connecticut ...................... | 578,326 | 218,099 | 360,227 | 38 | 62 | 3,672 | 3,751 | 3,588 |
| Delaware .......................... | 119,004 | 62,444 | 56,560 | 52 | 48 | 3,035 | 3,340 | 2,756 |
| Florida .............................. | 1,926,189 | 495,118 | 1,431,070 | 26 | 74 | 2,674 | 2,467 | 2,845 |
| Georgia ............................. | 1,067,504 | 294,531 | 772,972 | 28 | 72 | 2,458 | 2,493 | 2,422 |
| Hawaii ............................... | 190,657 | 143,750 | 46,908 | 75 | 25 | 2,860 | 2,799 | 2,907 |
| Idaho ................................. | 166,468 | 59,662 | 106,806 | 36 | 64 | 2,424 | 2,349 | 2,514 |
| Illinois .............................. | 1,869,618 | 422,754 | 1,446,864 | 23 | 77 | 3,240 | 3,111 | 3,371 |
| Indiana ............................. | 764,494 | 219,547 | 544,946 | 29 | 71 | 2,557 | 2,755 | 2,306 |
| Iowa .................................. | 433,009 | 160,234 | 272,775 | 37 | 63 | 2,737 | 2,760 | 2,709 |
| Kansas .............................. | 409,465 | 121,426 | 288,039 | 30 | 70 | 2,554 | 2,531 | 2,581 |
| Kentucky ........................... | 486,671 | 190,557 | 296,114 | 39 | 61 | 2,387 | 2,389 | 2,385 |
| Louisiana .......................... | 607,694 | 227,273 | 380,421 | 37 | 63 | 2,272 | 2,301 | 2,245 |
| Maine ................................ | 165,124 | 54,033 | 111,091 | 33 | 67 | 2,534 | 2,471 | 2,623 |
| Maryland ........................... | 814,906 | 264,514 | 550,392 | 32 | 68 | 3,154 | 3,434 | 2,883 |
| Massachusetts .................. | 947,063 | 270,969 | 676,094 | 29 | 71 | 3,244 | 3,176 | 3,313 |
| Michigan ........................... | 1,504,890 | 450,988 | 1,053,903 | 30 | 70 | 3,463 | 3,642 | 3,243 |
| Minnesota ......................... | 806,098 | 235,005 | 571,092 | 29 | 71 | 3,245 | 3,204 | 3,293 |
| Mississippi ........................ | 366,060 | 125,411 | 240,649 | 34 | 66 | 2,105 | 2,141 | 2,071 |
| Missouri ............................ | 708,265 | 210,762 | 497,503 | 30 | 70 | 2,462 | 2,574 | 2,350 |
| Montana ............................ | 118,181 | 46,188 | 71,993 | 39 | 61 | 2,370 | 2,399 | 2,336 |
| Nebraska ........................... | 254,586 | 66,679 | 187,907 | 26 | 74 | 2,510 | 2,378 | 2,637 |
| Nevada .............................. | 261,967 | 73,339 | 188,628 | 28 | 72 | 3,326 | 3,119 | 3,470 |
| New Hampshire ................. | 145,626 | 42,762 | 102,864 | 29 | 71 | 2,666 | 2,654 | 2,680 |
| New Jersey ........................ | 1,578,534 | 451,679 | 1,126,855 | 29 | 71 | 3,828 | 4,084 | 3,544 |
| New Mexico ....................... | 261,195 | 102,295 | 158,899 | 39 | 61 | 2,341 | 2,342 | 2,339 |
| New York ........................... | 3,953,861 | 893,241 | 3,060,620 | 23 | 77 | 3,617 | 3,757 | 3,523 |
| North Carolina .................. | 1,068,873 | 332,673 | 736,200 | 31 | 69 | 2,604 | 2,718 | 2,488 |
| North Dakota ..................... | 89,494 | 37,275 | 52,219 | 42 | 58 | 2,588 | 2,828 | 2,328 |
| Ohio .................................. | 1,598,090 | 406,015 | 1,192,074 | 25 | 75 | 2,963 | 3,083 | 2,851 |
| Oklahoma .......................... | 416,977 | 142,157 | 274,819 | 34 | 66 | 2,101 | 2,176 | 2,020 |
| Oregon .............................. | 510,652 | 161,177 | 349,475 | 32 | 68 | 3,063 | 3,005 | 3,113 |
| Pennsylvania ..................... | 1,598,540 | 458,535 | 1,140,005 | 29 | 71 | 3,167 | 3,474 | 2,860 |
| Rhode Island ..................... | 156,530 | 64,062 | 92,468 | 41 | 59 | 3,266 | 3,372 | 3,158 |
| South Carolina .................. | 551,649 | 194,583 | 357,066 | 35 | 65 | 2,389 | 2,448 | 2,329 |
| South Dakota ..................... | 89,487 | 31,727 | 57,760 | 35 | 65 | 2,310 | 2,299 | 2,324 |
| Tennessee ......................... | 676,360 | 202,450 | 473,910 | 30 | 70 | 2,425 | 2,422 | 2,426 |
| Texas ................................ | 2,768,954 | 745,437 | 2,023,517 | 27 | 73 | 2,480 | 2,432 | 2,541 |
| Utah .................................. | 284,484 | 119,149 | 165,335 | 42 | 58 | 2,668 | 2,594 | 2,759 |
| Vermont ............................ | 78,758 | 34,289 | 44,470 | 44 | 56 | 2,659 | 2,587 | 2,758 |
| Virginia ............................. | 979,602 | 321,662 | 657,940 | 33 | 67 | 2,779 | 2,816 | 2,736 |
| Washington ....................... | 950,879 | 328,577 | 622,302 | 35 | 65 | 3,435 | 3,483 | 3,403 |
| West Virginia .................... | 212,084 | 75,763 | 136,320 | 36 | 64 | 2,310 | 2,496 | 2,048 |
| Wisconsin .......................... | 833,681 | 207,996 | 625,686 | 25 | 75 | 3,185 | 3,314 | 3,041 |
| Wyoming ........................... | 90,023 | 24,201 | 65,822 | 27 | 73 | 2,468 | 2,579 | 2,370 |
| Dist. of Columbia ............. | 156,299 | 0 | 156,299 | 0 | 100 | 3,610 | 3,320 | 3,694 |

Source: U.S. Department of Commerce, Bureau of the Census.
Note: Statistics for local governments are estimates subject to sampling variation. Detail may not add to totals due to rounding.

## Table 7.20
## STATE GOVERNMENT EMPLOYMENT (FULL-TIME EQUIVALENT), FOR SELECTED FUNCTIONS, BY STATE: MARCH 1997

| State | All functions | Education — Higher education (a) | Education — Other education (b) | Highways | Public welfare | Hospitals | Corrections | Police protection | Natural resources | Financial and other governmental administration | Judicial and legal administration |
|---|---|---|---|---|---|---|---|---|---|---|---|
| United States ......... | 3,986,680 | 1,352,247 | 131,865 | 247,717 | 220,862 | 468,654 | 435,655 | 92,246 | 150,053 | 221,495 | 134,980 |
| Alabama ...................... | 81,089 | 20,908 | 3,423 | 3,954 | 4,023 | 11,703 | 4,197 | 1,247 | 2,478 | 3,005 | 2,841 |
| Alaska ......................... | 22,358 | 4,246 | 3,430 | 2,667 | 1,871 | 322 | 1,272 | 427 | 2,100 | 1,550 | 1,178 |
| Arizona ...................... | 61,232 | 23,403 | 2,731 | 2,996 | 5,881 | 667 | 8,156 | 1,708 | 2,328 | 4,419 | 1,190 |
| Arkansas .................... | 48,561 | 15,494 | 2,740 | 3,649 | 3,663 | 4,857 | 3,601 | 932 | 2,219 | 2,496 | 382 |
| California ................... | 335,430 | 114,513 | 4,720 | 16,432 | 3,666 | 31,905 | 44,193 | 12,337 | 15,946 | 20,983 | 2,750 |
| Colorado ..................... | 59,432 | 33,227 | 1,346 | 3,074 | 1,480 | 3,980 | 4,551 | 1,126 | 1,343 | 2,533 | 2,980 |
| Connecticut ................ | 59,774 | 13,463 | 2,903 | 3,857 | 4,828 | 10,733 | 8,131 | 1,690 | 549 | 3,574 | 3,549 |
| Delaware ..................... | 21,876 | 6,817 | 268 | 1,503 | 1,388 | 2,261 | 2,022 | 840 | 475 | 1,012 | 1,323 |
| Florida ....................... | 187,457 | 0 | 0 | 11,557 | 9,100 | 17,016 | 37,676 | 3,973 | 7,617 | 10,424 | 13,941 |
| Georgia ....................... | 111,465 | 43,809 | 1,945 | 5,941 | 7,589 | 12,859 | 17,223 | 2,210 | 5,246 | 4,161 | 1,184 |
| Hawaii ......................... | 51,676 | 35,902 | 5,497 | 832 | 1,092 | 3,311 | 2,156 | 0 | 1,413 | 1,964 | 2,061 |
| Idaho .......................... | 22,537 | 6,755 | 23,033 | 1,661 | 1,860 | 882 | 1,594 | 421 | 1,979 | 1,347 | 432 |
| Illinois ....................... | 141,027 | 8,610 | 520 | 7,953 | 13,298 | 15,197 | 14,362 | 4,089 | 3,994 | 8,610 | 2,977 |
| Indiana ....................... | 86,638 | 52,760 | 3,004 | 4,308 | 5,119 | 5,819 | 6,199 | 1,996 | 3,517 | 4,097 | 1,047 |
| Iowa ........................... | 55,864 | 47,671 | 1,159 | 2,975 | 3,242 | 7,761 | 2,399 | 963 | 2,901 | 2,224 | 2,263 |
| Kansas ........................ | 44,474 | 26,301 | 1,177 | 3,780 | 1,705 | 5,646 | 3,504 | 976 | 1,580 | 2,787 | 2,044 |
| Kentucky ..................... | 71,616 | 17,834 | 709 | 5,561 | 4,664 | 5,192 | 5,100 | 1,820 | 3,534 | 4,430 | 3,839 |
| Louisiana .................... | 94,491 | 25,449 | 4,010 | 5,753 | 5,973 | 21,116 | 6,789 | 1,093 | 4,847 | 4,197 | 1,728 |
| Maine .......................... | 20,127 | 27,863 | 3,851 | 2,770 | 2,280 | 526 | 1,152 | 393 | 1,270 | 1,485 | 577 |
| Maryland ..................... | 80,068 | 5,393 | 1,004 | 4,700 | 7,268 | 6,050 | 10,796 | 2,300 | 2,009 | 5,321 | 3,756 |
| Massachusetts ............ | 89,748 | 17,826 | 1,993 | 4,415 | 7,381 | 17,840 | 6,114 | 2,040 | 1,336 | 6,401 | 6,502 |
| Michigan ..................... | 137,942 | 21,798 | 729 | 3,375 | 13,542 | 14,381 | 16,701 | 2,993 | 4,636 | 4,431 | 2,701 |
| Minnesota ................... | 71,399 | 63,342 | 550 | 4,979 | 2,346 | 4,666 | 3,518 | 852 | 2,958 | 3,886 | 1,978 |
| Mississippi ................. | 51,335 | 37,539 | 1,583 | 3,335 | 3,201 | 9,387 | 4,114 | 979 | 3,621 | 1,646 | 415 |
| Missouri ..................... | 88,845 | 15,254 | 1,794 | 6,533 | 7,455 | 13,642 | 9,038 | 2,304 | 2,804 | 3,825 | 3,374 |
| Montana ...................... | 18,248 | 27,480 | 2,125 | 1,826 | 1,471 | 1,259 | 827 | 426 | 1,253 | 1,335 | 199 |
| Nebraska ..................... | 29,724 | 6,597 | 834 | 2,313 | 2,783 | 4,626 | 1,958 | 655 | 1,693 | 1,099 | 724 |
| Nevada ........................ | 22,970 | 10,055 | 676 | 1,510 | 1,094 | 1,800 | 3,014 | 633 | 990 | 1,924 | 448 |
| New Hampshire .......... | 17,029 | 7,238 | 97 | 1,918 | 1,307 | 866 | 1,147 | 413 | 456 | 784 | 896 |
| New Jersey ................. | 122,919 | 5,158 | 318 | 7,748 | 5,402 | 16,475 | 8,363 | 3,550 | 2,497 | 6,813 | 12,414 |
| New Mexico ................ | 41,039 | 26,942 | 17,909 | 2,412 | 1,395 | 5,390 | 3,955 | 567 | 1,671 | 1,910 | 2,037 |
| New York ..................... | 250,078 | 15,205 | 924 | 14,146 | 7,216 | 49,959 | 34,197 | 5,405 | 3,108 | 23,387 | 16,621 |
| North Carolina ........... | 122,298 | 45,214 | 4,778 | 12,332 | 1,360 | 15,808 | 19,248 | 3,288 | 4,257 | 4,687 | 5,598 |
| North Dakota .............. | 15,384 | 42,588 | 2,897 | 929 | 283 | 1,163 | 424 | 225 | 1,232 | 930 | 397 |
| Ohio ............................ | 140,137 | 6,638 | 329 | 7,857 | 2,201 | 15,954 | 16,290 | 2,439 | 3,807 | 9,541 | 2,336 |
| Oklahoma ................... | 72,088 | 64,542 | 2,225 | 4,175 | 5,847 | 5,827 | 10,590 | 1,678 | 1,551 | 3,144 | 2,090 |
| Oregon ........................ | 53,713 | 24,787 | 2,179 | 3,410 | 6,959 | 6,959 | 3,547 | 1,370 | 2,853 | 5,249 | 2,721 |
| Pennsylvania .............. | 150,371 | 15,211 | 1,064 | 13,761 | 12,055 | 15,576 | 13,828 | 6,473 | 7,372 | 11,223 | 2,445 |
| Rhode Island .............. | 20,177 | 49,191 | 2,887 | 884 | 1,861 | 1,251 | 1,649 | 254 | 549 | 1,383 | 1,096 |
| South Carolina ........... | 77,783 | 6,167 | 1,008 | 5,026 | 4,990 | 9,607 | 8,412 | 2,156 | 2,502 | 3,609 | 645 |
| South Dakota .............. | 13,270 | 24,339 | 2,841 | 1,254 | 928 | 1,025 | 761 | 266 | 838 | 708 | 504 |
| Tennessee ................... | 81,759 | 4,941 | 388 | 4,819 | 4,517 | 10,547 | 7,296 | 1,760 | 3,475 | 3,204 | 1,868 |
| Texas .......................... | 261,975 | 34,324 | 1,830 | 14,031 | 21,875 | 40,708 | 42,986 | 3,464 | 12,275 | 12,171 | 4,836 |
| Utah ............................ | 45,144 | 80,877 | 4,802 | 1,779 | 3,069 | 4,875 | 2,600 | 700 | 1,072 | 1,737 | 1,469 |
| Vermont ...................... | 12,425 | 22,607 | 963 | 1,106 | 1,079 | 180 | 881 | 469 | 620 | 786 | 544 |
| Virginia ...................... | 105,514 | 4,353 | 388 | 9,788 | 2,015 | 13,085 | 13,154 | 2,428 | 2,987 | 4,822 | 3,002 |
| Washington ................. | 108,093 | 39,576 | 2,814 | 6,353 | 7,634 | 7,514 | 7,071 | 1,931 | 5,119 | 4,012 | 1,660 |
| West Virginia .............. | 32,349 | 48,899 | 699 | 5,910 | 78 | 1,912 | 1,006 | 940 | 1,916 | 1,628 | 1,141 |
| Wisconsin ................... | 64,709 | 11,916 | 1,422 | 1,937 | 1,099 | 7,635 | 7,188 | 853 | 2,612 | 4,050 | 1,905 |
| Wyoming ..................... | 11,023 | 27,554 | 1,206 | 1,933 | 607 | 934 | 705 | 194 | 648 | 551 | 372 |

*Source:* U.S. Department of Commerce, Bureau of the Census.
(a) Includes instructional and other personnel.

(b) Includes instructional and other personnel in elementary and secondary schools.

## Table 7.21
## STATE GOVERNMENT EMPLOYMENT (FULL-TIME EQUIVALENT), FOR SELECTED FUNCTIONS, BY STATE: MARCH 1998

| State | All functions | Education — Higher education (a) | Education — Other education (b) | Highways | Public welfare | Hospitals | Corrections | Police protection | Natural resources | Financial and other governmental administration | Judicial and legal administration |
|---|---|---|---|---|---|---|---|---|---|---|---|
| United States ........ | 3,998,617 | 1,370,485 | 140,891 | 241,896 | 224,397 | 430,763 | 444,711 | 93,156 | 146,569 | 217,779 | 139,678 |
| Alabama ...................... | 82,483 | 32,752 | 3,376 | 3,748 | 3,842 | 11,369 | 4,382 | 1,236 | 2,418 | 3,138 | 2,987 |
| Alaska ......................... | 23,114 | 4,134 | 3,522 | 2,629 | 1,883 | 223 | 1,284 | 430 | 2,001 | 1,502 | 1,179 |
| Arizona ....................... | 61,904 | 24,034 | 2,838 | 3,034 | 5,832 | 667 | 8,159 | 1,712 | 2,417 | 4,131 | 1,359 |
| Arkansas ..................... | 49,351 | 16,387 | 4,739 | 3,577 | 3,663 | 4,480 | 3,518 | 1,082 | 2,207 | 2,372 | 396 |
| California .................... | 335,353 | 114,706 | 1,229 | 16,838 | 3,688 | 31,246 | 45,686 | 12,295 | 13,826 | 22,078 | 3,087 |
| Colorado ..................... | 61,476 | 34,547 | 6,465 | 3,068 | 1,837 | 3,815 | 4,910 | 1,319 | 1,322 | 2,574 | 3,091 |
| Connecticut ................ | 61,722 | 12,323 | 299 | 3,553 | 4,533 | 9,940 | 8,569 | 1,624 | 582 | 3,845 | 3,644 |
| Delaware ..................... | 22,080 | 6,820 | 1,920 | 1,411 | 1,540 | 2,201 | 2,152 | 842 | 474 | 1,024 | 1,416 |
| Florida ........................ | 176,953 | 42,881 | 6,704 | 10,025 | 12,228 | 10,350 | 32,147 | 3,875 | 7,442 | 9,904 | 15,769 |
| Georgia ....................... | 112,373 | 37,677 | 23,681 | 6,092 | 9,064 | 11,982 | 17,963 | 2,117 | 4,505 | 3,579 | 1,192 |
| Hawaii ......................... | 57,888 | 6,778 | 565 | 879 | 910 | 3,072 | 2,263 | | 1,224 | 1,812 | 2,162 |
| Idaho .......................... | 22,041 | 8,228 | 2,993 | 1,620 | 1,732 | 930 | 1,624 | 421 | 1,926 | 1,532 | 431 |
| Illinois ........................ | 138,539 | 52,289 | 1,261 | 7,745 | 12,563 | 14,941 | 14,803 | 3,981 | 4,006 | 8,237 | 3,030 |
| Indiana ........................ | 82,850 | 44,863 | 1,144 | 4,329 | 5,126 | 5,711 | 6,169 | 2,034 | 3,495 | 2,988 | 1,054 |
| Iowa ............................ | 53,032 | 23,488 | 783 | 2,975 | 2,751 | 7,703 | 2,727 | 944 | 2,931 | 2,110 | 2,344 |
| Kansas ........................ | 44,395 | 17,679 | 3,982 | 3,420 | 2,138 | 4,819 | 3,425 | 992 | 1,659 | 2,488 | 2,074 |
| Kentucky ..................... | 72,606 | 26,150 | 3,702 | 5,604 | 4,590 | 4,824 | 5,362 | 1,811 | 3,686 | 4,488 | 3,946 |
| Louisiana .................... | 94,349 | 28,785 | 1,128 | 5,694 | 6,104 | 20,451 | 6,789 | 1,098 | 4,863 | 4,162 | 1,697 |
| Maine .......................... | 20,012 | 5,759 | 1,990 | 2,579 | 1,933 | 472 | 1,152 | 362 | 1,226 | 1,529 | 616 |
| Maryland ..................... | 88,627 | 26,511 | 724 | 4,633 | 7,057 | 5,979 | 11,095 | 2,364 | 2,180 | 5,011 | 3,778 |
| Massachusetts ............ | 84,073 | 22,339 | 466 | 4,448 | 7,307 | 8,697 | 6,152 | 2,675 | 1,282 | 6,392 | 6,611 |
| Michigan ..................... | 136,001 | 64,382 | 3,841 | 2,951 | 12,597 | 12,724 | 17,484 | 2,993 | 4,563 | 4,403 | 2,017 |
| Minnesota ................... | 69,199 | 32,358 | 1,552 | 5,019 | 2,429 | 4,809 | 3,585 | 859 | 2,997 | 3,835 | 2,058 |
| Mississippi .................. | 51,817 | 16,434 | 2,101 | 3,282 | 3,110 | 9,653 | 4,136 | 927 | 3,327 | 1,628 | 463 |
| Missouri ...................... | 86,633 | 24,419 | 583 | 6,533 | 7,708 | 12,981 | 10,458 | 2,380 | 2,714 | 3,741 | 3,376 |
| Montana ...................... | 19,264 | 8,068 | 610 | 1,872 | 1,475 | 598 | 884 | 429 | 1,313 | 1,209 | 193 |
| Nebraska ..................... | 29,176 | 9,626 | 119 | 2,325 | 2,783 | 4,626 | 1,907 | 667 | 1,700 | 1,086 | 673 |
| Nevada ........................ | 24,132 | 7,238 | 319 | 1,542 | 939 | 1,847 | 3,091 | 627 | 1,078 | 1,782 | 513 |
| New Hampshire ........... | 17,061 | 5,158 | 18,017 | 1,905 | 1,317 | 815 | 1,152 | 415 | 466 | 774 | 906 |
| New Jersey .................. | 129,107 | 26,803 | 880 | 7,421 | 5,689 | 15,827 | 9,335 | 3,637 | 2,499 | 6,685 | 12,381 |
| New Mexico ................ | 42,784 | 16,978 | 4,114 | 2,347 | 1,315 | 5,586 | 3,789 | 633 | 1,569 | 1,994 | 2,228 |
| New York ..................... | 251,587 | 47,730 | 2,985 | 13,045 | 8,221 | 47,660 | 35,053 | 5,460 | 3,197 | 23,352 | 17,228 |
| North Carolina ............ | 123,329 | 43,483 | 329 | 12,266 | 1,323 | 14,266 | 19,089 | 3,311 | 4,350 | 4,417 | 5,982 |
| North Dakota .............. | 15,297 | 6,577 | 2,186 | 913 | 288 | 1,148 | 448 | 223 | 1,210 | 869 | 405 |
| Ohio ............................ | 135,824 | 63,413 | 2,153 | 7,562 | 2,139 | 12,308 | 17,085 | 2,439 | 3,899 | 9,279 | 2,675 |
| Oklahoma ................... | 71,325 | 25,583 | 1,102 | 4,104 | 5,992 | 3,668 | 10,730 | 1,714 | 1,538 | 3,398 | 2,248 |
| Oregon ........................ | 55,605 | 15,211 | 2,806 | 3,857 | 5,139 | 6,995 | 4,020 | 1,394 | 2,888 | 5,399 | 2,695 |
| Pennsylvania .............. | 149,185 | 49,889 | 1,057 | 13,637 | 12,102 | 15,125 | 14,164 | 5,391 | 7,267 | 11,065 | 2,445 |
| Rhode Island .............. | 20,346 | 5,864 | 2,841 | 881 | 1,861 | 1,251 | 1,719 | 279 | 558 | 1,455 | 1,075 |
| South Carolina ........... | 80,022 | 26,189 | 374 | 4,881 | 4,985 | 9,131 | 8,970 | 2,747 | 2,619 | 3,306 | 668 |
| South Dakota .............. | 13,056 | 4,679 | 1,987 | 961 | 929 | 929 | 859 | 273 | 827 | 740 | 511 |
| Tennessee ................... | 80,727 | 34,163 | 4,684 | 4,769 | 5,150 | 9,987 | 6,066 | 1,760 | 3,462 | 3,244 | 1,865 |
| Texas .......................... | 268,005 | 87,115 | 1,003 | 13,783 | 21,044 | 39,474 | 46,166 | 3,579 | 11,681 | 11,462 | 4,768 |
| Utah ............................ | 46,485 | 23,150 | 416 | 1,762 | 3,136 | 4,850 | 2,833 | 724 | 1,128 | 1,781 | 1,556 |
| Vermont ...................... | 12,530 | 4,293 | 2,829 | 990 | 1,123 | 189 | 902 | 469 | 635 | 885 | 558 |
| Virginia ....................... | 110,675 | 44,852 | 3,006 | 9,933 | 1,972 | 11,695 | 13,640 | 2,504 | 3,072 | 4,795 | 3,219 |
| Washington ................. | 106,432 | 44,985 | 1,398 | 6,205 | 7,541 | 7,462 | 7,816 | 2,132 | 5,061 | 3,855 | 1,665 |
| West Virginia .............. | 32,004 | 12,007 | 1,199 | 5,579 | 76 | 1,723 | 961 | 951 | 1,963 | 1,690 | 1,112 |
| Wisconsin ................... | 64,703 | 27,554 | 150 | 1,920 | 1,074 | 7,462 | 7,312 | 836 | 2,671 | 4,058 | 1,951 |
| Wyoming ..................... | 11,085 | 3,174 | 150 | 1,750 | 619 | 960 | 726 | 189 | 645 | 696 | 381 |

*Source:* U.S. Department of Commerce, Bureau of the Census.
(a) Includes instructional and other personnel.

(b) Includes instructional and other personnel in elementary and secondary schools.

**Table 7.22**
**STATE GOVERNMENT PAYROLLS FOR SELECTED FUNCTIONS,**
**BY STATE: MARCH 1997**
**(In thousands of dollars)**

| | | | | | | | | | | | |
|---|---|---|---|---|---|---|---|---|---|---|---|
| | | | | | | | _Selected functions_ | | | | |
| | | _Education_ | | | | | | | | _Financial and other_ | _Judicial_ |
| _State_ | _All functions_ | _Higher education (a)_ | _Other education (b)_ | _Highways_ | _Public welfare_ | _Hospitals_ | _Corrections_ | _Police protection_ | _Natural resources_ | _governmental administration_ | _and legal administration_ |
| United States ........ | $11,413,088 | $3,993,986 | $377,986 | $677,286 | $560,730 | $1,239,459 | $1,183,205 | $306,667 | $409,456 | $620,570 | $466,917 |
| Alabama ..................... | 198,863 | 81,463 | 9,680 | 9,165 | 9,905 | 24,038 | 10,199 | 4,054 | 6,378 | 8,190 | 8,191 |
| Alaska ...................... | 80,796 | 14,068 | 11,633 | 10,464 | 5,863 | 1,056 | 5,140 | 1,986 | 7,782 | 5,577 | 4,772 |
| Arizona ..................... | 154,233 | 66,069 | 6,128 | 7,576 | 11,207 | 1,510 | 18,451 | 5,554 | 5,769 | 10,229 | 4,236 |
| Arkansas .................. | 114,425 | 41,500 | 6,618 | 9,334 | 7,092 | 9,447 | 6,289 | 2,456 | 5,140 | 5,626 | 1,718 |
| California ................. | 1,232,997 | 407,733 | 16,093 | 62,762 | 12,317 | 120,721 | 168,495 | 48,489 | 51,216 | 70,160 | 13,268 |
| Colorado .................. | 200,695 | 116,479 | 4,069 | 9,797 | 4,947 | 11,973 | 13,272 | 3,325 | 4,958 | 8,109 | 10,212 |
| Connecticut .............. | 203,465 | 49,722 | 8,714 | 13,903 | 15,469 | 37,801 | 25,666 | 6,360 | 1,832 | 11,067 | 11,296 |
| Delaware .................. | 59,287 | 20,823 | 927 | 3,290 | 3,448 | 4,693 | 5,235 | 3,023 | 1,209 | 2,594 | 3,607 |
| Florida ..................... | 496,647 | 127,026 | 5,551 | 25,974 | 17,820 | 38,049 | 105,822 | 10,920 | 18,513 | 28,922 | 44,207 |
| Georgia ..................... | 276,656 | 100,112 | 15,940 | 9,243 | 16,133 | 28,625 | 37,637 | 6,132 | 12,564 | 11,393 | 5,048 |
| Hawaii ...................... | 137,283 | 24,377 | 55,642 | 2,175 | 3,143 | 8,076 | 5,259 | 0 | 4,573 | 5,009 | 6,394 |
| Idaho ........................ | 51,545 | 16,385 | 1,226 | 4,528 | 4,485 | 2,207 | 3,707 | 1,263 | 5,118 | 3,453 | 1,731 |
| Illinois ..................... | 421,328 | 145,937 | 9,340 | 28,794 | 41,065 | 42,654 | 43,454 | 15,306 | 10,464 | 24,102 | 14,228 |
| Indiana ..................... | 221,168 | 134,590 | 2,997 | 8,939 | 10,253 | 10,949 | 14,141 | 6,195 | 7,083 | 8,403 | 3,862 |
| Iowa ......................... | 165,190 | 81,012 | 3,246 | 8,135 | 8,875 | 21,818 | 7,078 | 3,031 | 5,488 | 7,113 | |
| Kansas ...................... | 113,190 | 74,898 | 298,201 | 9,401 | 3,966 | 13,671 | 9,147 | 2,641 | 4,398 | 5,881 | 5,352 |
| Kentucky .................. | 183,556 | 71,300 | 11,007 | 12,992 | 10,562 | 11,757 | 10,966 | 4,956 | 8,402 | 10,838 | 9,632 |
| Louisiana ................. | 239,657 | 91,259 | 9,441 | 12,083 | 13,918 | 43,713 | 13,036 | 2,532 | 10,868 | 9,321 | 5,537 |
| Maine ....................... | 52,847 | 14,385 | 2,522 | 6,797 | 5,505 | 1,361 | 2,952 | 1,190 | 3,371 | 3,879 | 1,862 |
| Maryland .................. | 234,640 | 64,012 | 6,002 | 13,339 | 16,973 | 15,026 | 29,719 | 7,614 | 5,858 | 15,118 | 10,766 |
| Massachusetts .......... | 272,495 | 65,180 | 2,367 | 15,179 | 22,825 | 44,799 | 20,569 | 7,287 | 4,687 | 19,754 | 20,346 |
| Michigan .................. | 454,455 | 200,032 | 2,071 | 11,843 | 43,236 | 53,353 | 55,805 | 10,354 | 15,284 | 14,404 | 9,200 |
| Minnesota ................ | 220,170 | 109,989 | 5,449 | 17,162 | 6,590 | 14,128 | 11,012 | 3,407 | 9,320 | 12,311 | 7,546 |
| Mississippi ............... | 119,190 | 40,882 | 4,275 | 6,738 | 6,013 | 20,937 | 7,330 | 2,344 | 8,051 | 4,095 | 1,805 |
| Missouri ................... | 203,429 | 71,223 | 4,742 | 16,402 | 14,124 | 27,898 | 17,091 | 6,250 | 6,271 | 7,378 | 9,194 |
| Montana ................... | 43,863 | 15,682 | 2,096 | 4,601 | 3,460 | 2,553 | 1,885 | 1,064 | 3,015 | 3,117 | 842 |
| Nebraska .................. | 66,517 | 21,329 | 1,871 | 5,506 | 5,893 | 9,508 | 4,324 | 1,698 | 3,250 | 2,574 | 2,603 |
| Nevada ..................... | 67,918 | 20,486 | 335 | 4,680 | 2,954 | 5,263 | 9,128 | 1,869 | 2,655 | 5,847 | 1,869 |
| New Hampshire ........ | 42,999 | 13,058 | 806 | 4,977 | 3,058 | 2,002 | 2,961 | 1,358 | 1,035 | 1,952 | 2,569 |
| New Jersey ................ | 435,363 | 103,795 | 64,836 | 28,045 | 18,076 | 47,076 | 31,380 | 16,647 | 9,144 | 22,554 | 41,531 |
| New Mexico .............. | 96,929 | 36,507 | 2,251 | 5,916 | 3,166 | 11,510 | 8,872 | 1,349 | 4,328 | 5,053 | 5,700 |
| New York .................. | 861,857 | 148,998 | 16,006 | 41,922 | 22,867 | 156,711 | 115,507 | 20,594 | 11,199 | 69,826 | 76,138 |
| North Carolina ......... | 320,620 | 115,587 | 8,421 | 27,228 | 3,542 | 40,387 | 46,561 | 10,734 | 11,361 | 12,137 | 17,044 |
| North Dakota ........... | 37,030 | 16,735 | 716 | 2,238 | 568 | 2,181 | 914 | 545 | 2,704 | 2,522 | 1,216 |
| Ohio ......................... | 406,235 | 176,571 | 7,768 | 26,225 | 7,437 | 39,345 | 47,907 | 8,705 | 10,544 | 30,407 | 8,240 |
| Oklahoma ................. | 143,983 | 53,770 | 4,920 | 6,776 | 10,177 | 13,378 | 14,338 | 4,120 | 3,139 | 6,380 | 5,898 |
| Oregon ..................... | 151,436 | 49,829 | 2,932 | 8,274 | 12,545 | 14,350 | 10,121 | 4,701 | 7,445 | 14,481 | 7,617 |
| Pennsylvania ............ | 452,816 | 162,546 | 8,616 | 38,050 | 35,204 | 38,172 | 39,629 | 21,752 | 22,903 | 31,715 | 9,628 |
| Rhode Island ............ | 63,345 | 16,648 | 3,916 | 2,647 | 6,096 | 4,103 | 7,265 | 1,181 | 1,735 | 3,341 | 3,773 |
| South Carolina ......... | 183,971 | 64,697 | 7,077 | 9,449 | 10,568 | 16,478 | 17,196 | 5,380 | 6,593 | 8,973 | 2,260 |
| South Dakota ............ | 31,380 | 12,387 | 864 | 3,103 | 1,917 | 1,971 | 1,449 | 657 | 1,886 | 1,722 | 1,359 |
| Tennessee ................. | 197,786 | 85,875 | 4,464 | 10,199 | 10,686 | 25,178 | 15,105 | 4,690 | 7,778 | 8,115 | 6,623 |
| Texas ........................ | 672,488 | 233,070 | 11,523 | 31,612 | 44,900 | 116,389 | 86,964 | 9,698 | 32,262 | 31,247 | 15,939 |
| Utah ......................... | 113,716 | 55,852 | 2,508 | 5,225 | 7,418 | 10,632 | 6,462 | 2,056 | 2,945 | 4,657 | 4,380 |
| Vermont ................... | 30,952 | 10,919 | 1,098 | 2,671 | 1,898 | 375 | 2,045 | 1,621 | 1,646 | 1,926 | 1,617 |
| Virginia .................... | 273,503 | 108,266 | 7,906 | 26,815 | 5,346 | 25,352 | 29,179 | 7,320 | 8,345 | 12,721 | 9,644 |
| Washington .............. | 307,272 | 134,713 | 2,294 | 21,850 | 23,044 | 21,436 | 14,590 | 6,701 | 12,990 | 12,061 | 6,607 |
| West Virginia ........... | 75,294 | 31,629 | 3,450 | 13,131 | 103 | 2,822 | 1,800 | 2,462 | 4,529 | 3,390 | 2,872 |
| Wisconsin ................. | 204,267 | 96,351 | 3,589 | 6,259 | 2,935 | 20,301 | 18,698 | 2,580 | 7,058 | 11,174 | 8,747 |
| Wyoming .................. | 23,340 | 6,281 | 351 | 3,869 | 1,139 | 1,729 | 1,454 | 516 | 1,646 | 1,378 | 1,079 |

_Source:_ U.S. Department of Commerce, Bureau of the Census.
(a) Includes instructional and other personnel.

(b) Includes instructional and other personnel in elementary and secondary schools.

## Table 7.23
## STATE GOVERNMENT PAYROLLS FOR SELECTED FUNCTIONS, BY STATE: MARCH 1998
(In thousands of dollars)

| State | All functions | Education Higher education (a) | Education Other education (b) | Highways | Public welfare | Hospitals | Corrections | Police protection | Natural resources | Financial and other governmental administration | Judicial and legal administration |
|---|---|---|---|---|---|---|---|---|---|---|---|
| United States ....... | $11,872,746 | $4,208,926 | $284,658 | $705,475 | $590,726 | $1,182,401 | $1,238,805 | $319,003 | $413,184 | $637,979 | $493,307 |
| Alabama .................. | 203,886 | 84,749 | 9,582 | 9,093 | 9,449 | 23,788 | 10,485 | 4,333 | 6,269 | 8,646 | 8,711 |
| Alaska ..................... | 84,053 | 14,059 | 1,673 | 10,686 | 5,952 | 761 | 5,224 | 2,028 | 7,621 | 5,520 | 4,882 |
| Arizona ................... | 169,376 | 73,107 | 6,516 | 8,571 | 12,950 | 1,510 | 20,621 | 5,568 | 6,576 | 10,457 | 4,741 |
| Arkansas ................. | 125,025 | 48,570 | 6,941 | 9,153 | 7,092 | 10,508 | 7,055 | 2,788 | 5,078 | 5,611 | 1,809 |
| California ................ | 1,264,415 | 416,374 | 16,232 | 84,645 | 12,467 | 117,656 | 172,645 | 47,094 | 46,652 | 73,947 | 14,869 |
| Colorado ................. | 210,093 | 121,615 | 3,913 | 9,946 | 6,036 | 10,920 | 15,037 | 4,433 | 5,174 | 8,339 | 10,757 |
| Connecticut ............. | 219,822 | 47,317 | 8,556 | 12,797 | 15,863 | 38,203 | 28,199 | 6,739 | 1,981 | 13,110 | 11,715 |
| Delaware ................. | 62,444 | 21,633 | 1,011 | 3,185 | 3,924 | 4,820 | 5,795 | 3,032 | 1,249 | 2,680 | 4,042 |
| Florida .................... | 495,117 | 133,838 | 5,726 | 26,338 | 26,035 | 22,270 | 94,103 | 11,429 | 16,692 | 28,010 | 51,624 |
| Georgia ................... | 294,531 | 111,816 | 20,417 | 9,963 | 20,517 | 28,017 | 39,686 | 6,102 | 11,305 | 10,374 | 5,364 |
| Hawaii ..................... | 153,789 | 24,061 | 404 | 2,353 | 2,347 | 7,757 | 5,509 | | 3,783 | 4,627 | 6,845 |
| Idaho ...................... | 59,660 | 23,715 | 1,578 | 4,210 | 4,214 | 2,153 | 4,064 | 1,263 | 4,795 | 4,102 | 1,817 |
| Illinois .................... | 422,752 | 146,370 | 9,823 | 25,883 | 39,989 | 42,406 | 45,938 | 15,654 | 11,037 | 24,458 | 14,788 |
| Indiana ................... | 219,545 | 132,209 | 3,403 | 9,067 | 10,574 | 11,279 | 14,045 | 6,156 | 7,205 | 7,434 | 3,947 |
| Iowa ....................... | 160,235 | 75,506 | 3,342 | 8,135 | 7,181 | 22,880 | 7,250 | 3,144 | 8,500 | 5,525 | 7,185 |
| Kansas .................... | 121,426 | 49,645 | 2,412 | 9,655 | 6,498 | 12,415 | 8,060 | 2,689 | 4,789 | 6,629 | 5,549 |
| Kentucky ................. | 190,557 | 73,569 | 11,587 | 13,694 | 10,531 | 11,481 | 11,863 | 5,057 | 8,572 | 11,650 | 10,677 |
| Louisiana ................ | 227,274 | 77,249 | 9,653 | 12,436 | 14,455 | 44,717 | 13,036 | 2,546 | 10,915 | 10,009 | 5,614 |
| Maine ..................... | 54,074 | 15,633 | 2,782 | 6,665 | 4,824 | 1,600 | 2,952 | 1,239 | 3,459 | 3,995 | 1,976 |
| Maryland ................. | 264,515 | 87,697 | 6,191 | 13,357 | 17,982 | 14,968 | 30,868 | 8,348 | 6,935 | 14,526 | 10,976 |
| Massachusetts .......... | 270,968 | 70,840 | 2,679 | 15,579 | 22,912 | 23,461 | 20,025 | 9,409 | 4,878 | 21,446 | 21,551 |
| Michigan ................. | 450,994 | 209,617 | 1,692 | 10,709 | 40,745 | 39,819 | 59,557 | 10,353 | 15,461 | 14,617 | 7,635 |
| Minnesota ............... | 235,006 | 110,537 | 12,860 | 17,736 | 7,063 | 15,201 | 11,641 | 3,452 | 9,829 | 12,832 | 8,281 |
| Mississippi .............. | 125,412 | 46,060 | 3,972 | 6,936 | 6,091 | 21,970 | 7,409 | 2,508 | 7,235 | 4,501 | 2,184 |
| Missouri .................. | 210,762 | 71,108 | 5,081 | 17,186 | 15,209 | 27,270 | 20,269 | 6,576 | 6,493 | 8,134 | 9,603 |
| Montana .................. | 46,187 | 18,714 | 1,415 | 4,965 | 3,535 | 1,222 | 2,021 | 1,086 | 3,435 | 2,836 | 768 |
| Nebraska ................. | 66,680 | 20,393 | 1,905 | 6,616 | 5,893 | 9,508 | 4,319 | 1,724 | 3,275 | 2,679 | 2,175 |
| Nevada .................... | 73,341 | 20,486 | 394 | 5,001 | 2,611 | 5,580 | 9,715 | 2,312 | 2,919 | 5,154 | 2,279 |
| New Hampshire ........ | 42,763 | 13,058 | 826 | 4,466 | 3,184 | 1,918 | 2,976 | 1,434 | 1,053 | 1,929 | 2,645 |
| New Jersey ............... | 464,567 | 110,071 | 13,682 | 27,977 | 19,545 | 46,812 | 35,489 | 17,028 | 9,449 | 22,869 | 42,693 |
| New Mexico .............. | 102,294 | 42,270 | 2,040 | 5,630 | 2,957 | 11,642 | 8,614 | 2,154 | 4,110 | 4,963 | 6,174 |
| New York .................. | 893,238 | 162,526 | 14,436 | 40,185 | 27,446 | 155,328 | 121,012 | 23,120 | 11,571 | 71,813 | 77,618 |
| North Carolina ......... | 332,673 | 121,718 | 8,783 | 28,341 | 3,965 | 38,678 | 48,932 | 10,819 | 11,656 | 11,805 | 18,456 |
| North Dakota ........... | 37,276 | 16,979 | 754 | 2,214 | 574 | 2,228 | 968 | 567 | 2,667 | 2,213 | 1,258 |
| Ohio ....................... | 406,016 | 180,043 | 7,762 | 25,083 | 7,482 | 30,402 | 51,486 | 8,710 | 10,865 | 30,847 | 9,348 |
| Oklahoma ............... | 142,160 | 57,225 | 4,970 | 6,705 | 10,225 | 6,628 | 14,553 | 4,192 | 3,155 | 6,656 | 6,459 |
| Oregon .................... | 161,177 | 49,829 | 3,112 | 12,750 | 14,649 | 14,513 | 11,035 | 4,713 | 7,887 | 15,690 | 7,970 |
| Pennsylvania ........... | 458,536 | 163,421 | 8,617 | 38,110 | 36,580 | 38,628 | 41,940 | 20,350 | 23,333 | 32,277 | 9,628 |
| Rhode Island ........... | 64,269 | 15,741 | 2,627 | 2,838 | 6,096 | 4,103 | 7,274 | 1,258 | 1,775 | 3,604 | 3,947 |
| South Carolina ......... | 194,584 | 70,561 | 7,115 | 9,524 | 10,854 | 16,026 | 18,786 | 7,154 | 6,852 | 8,952 | 2,382 |
| South Dakota ........... | 31,727 | 11,909 | 871 | 2,477 | 1,950 | 1,921 | 1,660 | 708 | 1,900 | 1,880 | 1,418 |
| Tennessee ................ | 202,451 | 87,341 | 4,951 | 10,199 | 12,465 | 27,450 | 12,204 | 4,690 | 7,923 | 8,769 | 6,891 |
| Texas ...................... | 745,437 | 276,525 | 12,445 | 36,075 | 45,994 | 122,969 | 97,830 | 10,206 | 33,545 | 32,047 | 17,276 |
| Utah ....................... | 119,148 | 56,563 | 2,655 | 5,438 | 7,757 | 11,736 | 7,054 | 2,248 | 3,165 | 4,951 | 4,696 |
| Vermont .................. | 34,290 | 11,014 | 1,207 | 2,811 | 2,971 | 463 | 2,177 | 1,621 | 1,868 | 2,709 | 1,766 |
| Virginia ................... | 321,663 | 147,204 | 8,048 | 26,086 | 5,235 | 29,541 | 31,202 | 7,926 | 9,160 | 13,450 | 10,002 |
| Washington .............. | 328,580 | 132,849 | 10,562 | 22,485 | 23,601 | 22,746 | 23,059 | 7,434 | 15,304 | 11,741 | 7,037 |
| West Virginia ........... | 75,760 | 32,959 | 3,484 | 11,192 | 99 | 2,787 | 1,832 | 2,494 | 4,717 | 3,752 | 2,843 |
| Wisconsin ................ | 207,996 | 96,351 | 3,603 | 6,417 | 2,937 | 19,995 | 19,770 | 2,570 | 7,440 | 11,545 | 9,327 |
| Wyoming ................. | 24,202 | 6,282 | 368 | 3,912 | 1,221 | 1,747 | 1,561 | 545 | 1,677 | 1,669 | 1,109 |

*Source:* U.S. Department of Commerce, Bureau of the Census.

(a) Includes instructional and other personnel.

(b) Includes instructional and other personnel in elementary and secondary schools.

## Table 7.24
## NUMBER, MEMBERSHIP AND MONTHLY BENEFIT PAYMENTS OF STATE-ADMINISTERED
## EMPLOYEE RETIREMENT SYSTEMS: 1995 THROUGH 1997

| Item | 1997 | 1996 | 1995 |
|---|---|---|---|
| **Number of systems** | N.A. | N.A. | N.A. |
| **Membership, last month of fiscal year:** | | | |
| Total membership | 13,502,159 | 13,169,559 | 13,083,119 |
| Active members | 11,210,405 | 11,121,200 | 10,967,868 |
| Inactive members | 2,291,754 | 2,048,359 | 2,115,251 |
| Percent distribution | 100.0 | 100.0 | 100.0 |
| Active members | 83.0 | 84.4 | 83.8 |
| Inactive members | 17.0 | 15.6 | 16.2 |
| | | | |
| **Beneficiaries receiving periodic benefits:** | | | |
| Total number of retired/survivors | 4,253,036 | 4,166,221 | 4,024,628 |
| Former active members, retired service | 3,661,670 | 3,599,888 | 3,483,053 |
| Former active members, retired disability | 241,303 | 225,521 | 220,309 |
| Survivors of former active members | 350,063 | 340,812 | 321,266 |
| Percent distribution | 100.0 | 100.0 | 100.0 |
| Percent former active members, retired service | 86.1 | 86.4 | 86.5 |
| Percent former active members, retired disability | 5.7 | 5.4 | 5.5 |
| Percent survivors of former active members | 8.2 | 8.2 | 8.0 |
| | | | |
| **Recurrent benefit payments for last month of fiscal year:** | | | |
| Total amount of benefit for retired/survivors | $4,277,792,550 | $4,142,330,275 | $3,781,984,022 |
| Amount former active members, retired service | $3,853,280,996 | $3,751,445,046 | $3,412,094,819 |
| Amount former active members, retired disability | $220,712,545 | $209,156,037 | $193,334,198 |
| Amount survivors of former active members | $203,799,009 | $181,729,192 | $176,555,005 |
| Percent distribution | 100.0 | 100.0 | 100.0 |
| For former active members, retired service | 90.1 | 90.6 | 90.2 |
| For former active members, retired disability | 5.2 | 5.0 | 5.1 |
| For survivors of former active members | 4.8 | 4.4 | 4.7 |
| | | | |
| **Average monthly payment for beneficiaries:** | | | |
| Average for all beneficiaries (in dollars) | $1,006 | $994 | $940 |
| For former active members, retired service | $1,052 | $1,042 | $980 |
| For former active members, retired disability | $915 | $927 | $878 |
| For survivors of former active members | $582 | $533 | $550 |

*Source:* U.S. Department of Commerce, Bureau of the Census.
*Note:* Detail may not add to totals due to rounding.
N.A. — Not available.

## Table 7.25
## NATIONAL SUMMARY OF FINANCES OF STATE-ADMINISTERED EMPLOYEE
## RETIREMENT SYSTEMS: SELECTED YEARS, 1995-1997

| | Amount (in millions of dollars) | | | Percentage distribution | | |
|---|---|---|---|---|---|---|
| | 1997 | 1996 | 1995 | 1997 | 1996 | 1995 |
| **Receipts** .................................... | $188,404,549 | $156,305,752 | $123,293,015 | 100.0 | 100.0 | 100.0 |
| Employee contributions .................... | 17,424,513 | 16,406,926 | 15,721,701 | 9.2 | 10.5 | 12.8 |
| Government contributions ............... | 36,975,418 | 32,972,747 | 31,603,697 | 19.6 | 21.1 | 25.6 |
| From State Government ................ | 20,192,916 | 16,882,464 | 16,225,237 | 10.7 | 10.8 | 13.2 |
| From Local Government ............. | 16,782,502 | 16,090,283 | 15,378,460 | 8.9 | 10.3 | 12.5 |
| Earnings on investments ................... | 134,004,618 | 106,926,079 | 75,967,617 | 71.1 | 68.4 | 61.6 |
| | | | | | | |
| **Payments** .................................... | 58,925,673 | 55,298,781 | 49,523,895 | 100.0 | 100.0 | 100.0 |
| Benefits paid ..................................... | 53,729,462 | 50,507,371 | 45,759,560 | 91.2 | 91.3 | 92.4 |
| Withdrawals ...................................... | 2,840,955 | 2,644,613 | 2,191,399 | 4.8 | 4.8 | 4.4 |
| Administration .................................. | 2,355,256 | 2,146,797 | 1,572,936 | 4.0 | 3.9 | 3.2 |
| | | | | | | |
| **Total cash and securities** .................... | 1,220,527,088 | 1,044,650,139 | 913,930,491 | 100.0 | 100.0 | 100.0 |
| Cash and deposits ............................. | 57,325,477 | 49,367,394 | 54,163,156 | 4.7 | 4.7 | 5.9 |
| Cash on hand and demand .......... | 4,674,679 | 3,777,329 | 2,714,016 | 0.4 | 0.4 | 0.3 |
| Time and saving deposits ............ | 1,006,355 | 1,555,274 | 913,545 | 0.1 | 0.1 | 0.1 |
| All other short term ...................... | 51,644,443 | 44,034,791 | 50,535,595 | 4.2 | 4.2 | 5.5 |
| **Securities** ..................................... | 1,089,349,314 | 927,183,387 | 804,715,181 | 89.3 | 88.8 | 88.0 |
| Government securities ..................... | 219,784,346 | 216,325,590 | 201,045,924 | 18.0 | 20.7 | 22.0 |
| Federal government securities ...... | 219,584,946 | 215,929,452 | 200,515,333 | 18.0 | 20.7 | 21.9 |
| Federal securities ...................... | 164,944,185 | 167,050,802 | 160,717,961 | 13.5 | 16.0 | 17.6 |
| Federal agency securities .......... | 54,640,761 | 48,878,650 | 39,797,372 | 4.5 | 4.7 | 4.4 |
| State and Local Governments ...... | 199,400 | 396,138 | 530,591 | 0.0 | 0.0 | 0.1 |
| Nongovernment securities ............... | 869,564,968 | 710,857,797 | 603,669,257 | 71.2 | 68.0 | 66.1 |
| Corporate bonds .......................... | 185,259,386 | 175,830,923 | 164,324,545 | 15.2 | 16.8 | 18.0 |
| Corporate stocks .......................... | 424,794,006 | 350,140,658 | 300,547,610 | 34.8 | 33.5 | 32.9 |
| Mortgages .................................... | 12,160,708 | 23,576,186 | 16,665,236 | 1.0 | 2.3 | 1.8 |
| Funds held in trust ....................... | 57,797,055 | 34,209,754 | 28,457,760 | 4.7 | 3.3 | 3.1 |
| Foreign and international securities | 130,681,334 | 0 | 0 | 10.7 | 0.0 | 0.0 |
| Other securities ........................... | 58,872,479 | 127,100,276 | 93,674,106 | 4.8 | 12.2 | 10.2 |
| Other investments ........................... | 73,852,297 | 68,099,358 | 55,052,154 | 6.1 | 6.5 | 6.0 |
| Real property ............................... | 28,538,000 | 26,783,244 | 24,510,964 | 2.3 | 2.6 | 2.7 |
| Other investments ....................... | 45,314,297 | 41,316,114 | 30,541,190 | 3.7 | 4.0 | 3.3 |

*Source:* U.S. Department of Commerce, Bureau of the Census.

## Table 7.26
## MEMBERSHIP AND BENEFIT OPERATIONS OF STATE-ADMINISTERED EMPLOYEE RETIREMENT SYSTEMS: LAST MONTH OF FISCAL YEAR 1996-97

| State | Membership, last month of the fiscal year | Beneficiaries receiving periodic benefit payments | | | | Benefit Operations, last month of fiscal year — Periodic benefit payment for the month (in thousands of dollars) | | | |
|---|---|---|---|---|---|---|---|---|---|
| | | Total (a) | Persons retired on account of age or length of service | Persons retired on account of disability | Survivors of deceased former members | Total (a) | Persons retired on account of age or length of service | Persons retired on account of disability | Survivors of deceased former members |
| United States | 13,502,159 | 4,253,036 | 3,661,670 | 241,303 | 350,063 | 4,277,792,550 | 3,853,280,996 | 220,712,545 | 203,799,009 |
| Alabama | 218,311 | 64,300 | 55,322 | 4,274 | 4,704 | 68,787,838 | 63,303,078 | 2,996,660 | 2,488,100 |
| Alaska | 53,101 | 16,100 | 16,100 | 0 | 0 | 27,856,647 | 27,856,647 | 0 | 0 |
| Arizona | 188,170 | 59,026 | 55,444 | 2,718 | 864 | 64,377,982 | 58,801,141 | 3,817,118 | 1,759,723 |
| Arkansas | 182,552 | 30,165 | 26,508 | 2,356 | 1,301 | 25,027,448 | 22,784,848 | 1,565,922 | 676,678 |
| California | 1,267,608 | 497,206 | 382,935 | 53,359 | 60,912 | 585,376,356 | 522,955,307 | 54,268,875 | 8,152,174 |
| Colorado | 221,741 | 49,451 | 40,353 | 7,164 | 1,934 | 64,967,436 | 49,408,700 | 8,371,736 | 7,187,000 |
| Connecticut | 113,314 | 52,292 | 46,032 | 2,821 | 3,439 | 78,105,154 | 72,406,444 | 3,288,031 | 2,410,679 |
| Delaware | 36,348 | 15,434 | 11,300 | 1,707 | 2,427 | 11,794,793 | 9,705,360 | 1,004,627 | 1,084,806 |
| Florida | 625,367 | 155,702 | 133,676 | 8,623 | 13,403 | 23,672,035 | 9,965,847 | 4,900,021 | 8,806,167 |
| Georgia | 428,053 | 74,201 | 61,136 | 5,250 | 7,815 | 86,125,559 | 75,934,936 | 4,817,202 | 5,373,421 |
| Hawaii | 59,500 | 27,174 | 25,084 | 1,066 | 1,024 | 36,079,992 | 35,066,865 | 884,959 | 128,168 |
| Idaho | 65,042 | 21,412 | 20,539 | 393 | 480 | 12,810,266 | 12,288,121 | 234,952 | 287,193 |
| Illinois | 550,428 | 186,528 | 150,513 | 5,609 | 30,406 | 194,025,838 | 176,559,846 | 4,834,305 | 12,631,687 |
| Indiana | 285,436 | 77,041 | 73,304 | 3,305 | 432 | 53,711,797 | 51,759,787 | 1,089,755 | 862,255 |
| Iowa | 236,216 | 63,235 | 61,416 | 932 | 887 | 29,766,555 | 27,687,992 | 1,482,290 | 596,273 |
| Kansas | 159,100 | 48,559 | 44,057 | 567 | 3,935 | 32,123,895 | 29,633,706 | 623,598 | 1,866,591 |
| Kentucky | 216,673 | 67,774 | 65,395 | 1,397 | 982 | 66,536,559 | 63,882,510 | 1,845,759 | 808,290 |
| Louisiana | 248,398 | 91,496 | 73,478 | 6,160 | 11,858 | 94,066,017 | 82,254,071 | 4,494,226 | 7,317,720 |
| Maine | 98,860 | 27,309 | 21,770 | 1,645 | 3,894 | 23,916,883 | 19,710,423 | 2,003,328 | 2,203,132 |
| Maryland | 201,787 | 72,644 | 59,816 | 7,578 | 5,250 | 78,976,302 | 69,392,520 | 6,636,215 | 2,947,567 |
| Massachusetts | 237,074 | 74,071 | 64,263 | 3,262 | 6,546 | 70,252,928 | 62,752,363 | 4,122,708 | 3,377,857 |
| Michigan | 411,893 | 164,023 | 139,096 | 8,314 | 16,613 | 155,579,054 | 132,954,566 | 7,553,396 | 15,071,092 |
| Minnesota | 320,286 | 89,972 | 81,291 | 2,818 | 5,863 | 88,309,378 | 81,490,962 | 2,672,632 | 4,145,784 |
| Mississippi | 238,385 | 48,194 | 38,655 | 3,222 | 6,317 | 36,502,312 | 32,416,000 | 1,686,312 | 2,400,000 |
| Missouri | 225,909 | 68,646 | 59,550 | 1,855 | 7,241 | 60,183,823 | 55,599,010 | 1,162,011 | 3,422,802 |
| Montana | 69,028 | 22,678 | 21,287 | 639 | 752 | 16,062,472 | 15,245,395 | 369,851 | 447,226 |
| Nebraska | 67,489 | 9,110 | 8,703 | 261 | 146 | 5,827,103 | 5,516,336 | 168,947 | 141,820 |
| Nevada | 74,750 | 18,835 | 15,134 | 950 | 2,751 | 26,183,823 | 22,976,805 | 1,039,145 | 2,167,873 |
| New Hampshire | 44,750 | 13,096 | 11,263 | 1,179 | 654 | 9,987,009 | 8,589,164 | 899,105 | 498,740 |
| New Jersey | 435,281 | 159,576 | 144,544 | 0 | 15,032 | 197,499,680 | 178,028,716 | 0 | 19,470,964 |
| New Mexico | 122,123 | 32,973 | 28,249 | 1,311 | 3,413 | 36,013,639 | 32,527,220 | 1,244,660 | 2,241,759 |
| New York | 787,229 | 372,521 | 345,063 | 1,723 | 25,735 | 411,995,258 | 387,189,217 | 1,846,521 | 22,959,520 |
| North Carolina | 449,444 | 121,667 | 101,457 | 8,686 | 11,524 | 112,282,703 | 97,868,999 | 7,437,037 | 6,976,667 |
| North Dakota | 29,522 | 8,736 | 7,744 | 252 | 740 | 5,499,592 | 5,052,943 | 97,572 | 349,077 |
| Ohio | 898,627 | 283,812 | 231,085 | 27,734 | 24,993 | 384,344,373 | 335,098,431 | 35,208,976 | 14,036,966 |

See footnotes at end of table.

# MEMBERSHIP AND BENEFIT OPERATIONS, FISCAL YEAR 1996-97 — Continued

| State | Membership, last month of the fiscal year | Benefit Operations, last month of fiscal year | | | | | | | |
| --- | --- | --- | --- | --- | --- | --- | --- | --- | --- |
| | | Beneficiaries receiving periodic benefit payments | | | | Periodic benefit payment for the month (in thousands of dollars) | | | |
| | | Total (a) | Persons retired on account of age or length of service | Persons retired on account of disability | Survivors of deceased former members | Total (a) | Persons retired on account of age or length of service | Persons retired on account of disability | Survivors of deceased former members |
| Oklahoma | 144,106 | 57,994 | 50,497 | 3,025 | 4,472 | 55,951,289 | 49,885,599 | 2,876,495 | 3,189,195 |
| Oregon | 185,111 | 70,058 | 65,879 | 4,179 | 0 | 73,447,750 | 69,524,610 | 3,923,140 | 0 |
| Pennsylvania | 385,892 | 204,775 | 181,707 | 9,845 | 13,223 | 170,478,189 | 160,807,429 | 3,793,940 | 5,876,820 |
| Rhode Island | 85,386 | 15,420 | 15,420 | 0 | 0 | 21,531,833 | 21,531,833 | 0 | 0 |
| South Carolina | 340,636 | 60,689 | 48,589 | 6,735 | 5,365 | 53,886,546 | 45,757,733 | 4,872,500 | 3,256,313 |
| South Dakota | 39,773 | 13,778 | 11,310 | 401 | 2,067 | 7,634,370 | 6,709,897 | 269,339 | 655,134 |
| Tennessee | 190,837 | 66,662 | 58,132 | 3,237 | 5,293 | 45,548,436 | 41,477,636 | 1,356,935 | 2,713,865 |
| Texas | 1,127,417 | 227,824 | 191,745 | 12,587 | 23,492 | 245,434,109 | 218,201,308 | 9,364,348 | 17,868,453 |
| Utah | 97,969 | 24,863 | 24,048 | 815 | 0 | 22,460,845 | 21,652,481 | 808,364 | 0 |
| Vermont | 24,176 | 7,079 | 6,134 | 369 | 576 | 5,292,878 | 4,789,000 | 225,008 | 278,870 |
| Virginia | 272,011 | 84,240 | 71,019 | 11,992 | 1,229 | 77,405,000 | 67,116,000 | 9,761,000 | 528,000 |
| Washington | 272,119 | 90,116 | 90,116 | 0 | 0 | 93,313,017 | 93,313,017 | 0 | 0 |
| West Virginia | 99,133 | 39,402 | 28,130 | 3,364 | 7,908 | 15,406,339 | 12,011,752 | 1,364,631 | 2,029,956 |
| Wisconsin | 332,068 | 92,198 | 85,418 | 5,423 | 1,357 | 106,342,378 | 98,564,630 | 7,213,544 | 564,204 |
| Wyoming | 37,760 | 12,979 | 11,964 | 201 | 814 | 9,031,072 | 7,273,795 | 214,849 | 1,542,428 |

Source: U.S. Department of Commerce, Bureau of the Census.
(a) Detail may not add to totals due to rounding.

## Table 7.27
## FINANCES OF STATE—ADMINISTERED EMPLOYEE RETIREMENT SYSTEMS, BY STATE: FISCAL 1996-97
### (In thousands of dollars)

| | | | Receipts during fiscal year | | | | Payments during fiscal year | | |
| | | | Government contributions | | | | | | |
| State | Total | Employee contributions | From states | From local governments | Earnings on investments | Total | Benefits | Withdrawals | Other |
|---|---|---|---|---|---|---|---|---|---|
| United States | $188,404,549 | $17,424,513 | $20,192,916 | $16,782,502 | $134,004,618 | $58,925,673 | $53,729,462 | $2,840,955 | $2,355,256 |
| Alabama | 2,559,638 | 293,504 | 411,872 | 72,667 | 1,781,595 | 866,077 | 799,981 | 54,697 | 11,399 |
| Alaska | 1,906,306 | 135,586 | 101,799 | 106,291 | 1,562,630 | 409,720 | 383,472 | 15,155 | 11,093 |
| Arizona | 1,465,204 | 275,506 | 72,836 | 242,943 | 873,919 | 685,274 | 640,387 | 41,261 | 3,626 |
| Arkansas | 1,387,505 | 44,930 | 110,566 | 154,260 | 1,077,749 | 371,064 | 307,332 | 6,055 | 57,677 |
| California | 21,229,398 | 2,934,323 | 1,629,929 | 2,530,903 | 14,134,243 | 8,184,840 | 7,559,018 | 410,161 | 215,661 |
| Colorado | 2,195,363 | 316,407 | 208,926 | 307,740 | 1,362,290 | 1,053,886 | 818,226 | 69,159 | 166,501 |
| Connecticut | 1,037,711 | 219,081 | 508,017 | 22,116 | 288,497 | 954,706 | 938,275 | 15,427 | 1,004 |
| Delaware | 680,844 | 26,171 | 76,346 | 2,225 | 576,102 | 159,454 | 142,843 | 1,886 | 14,725 |
| Florida | 6,895,209 | 25,773 | 779,140 | 2,257,839 | 3,832,457 | 1,666,759 | 1,574,507 | 1,762 | 90,490 |
| Georgia | 4,460,193 | 306,742 | 778,509 | 199,779 | 3,175,163 | 1,166,518 | 1,076,979 | 48,003 | 41,536 |
| Hawaii | 1,165,903 | 54,365 | 236,836 | 85,285 | 789,417 | 483,673 | 410,522 | 26,175 | 46,976 |
| Idaho | 581,481 | 115,807 | 66,028 | 129,069 | 270,577 | 208,097 | 169,859 | 19,095 | 19,143 |
| Illinois | 6,028,019 | 893,787 | 762,139 | 367,025 | 4,005,068 | 2,569,490 | 2,328,067 | 88,975 | 152,448 |
| Indiana | 1,736,575 | 203,888 | 644,263 | 158,476 | 729,948 | 696,225 | 641,678 | 41,857 | 12,690 |
| Iowa | 833,509 | 230,590 | 44,229 | 133,330 | 425,360 | 435,900 | 401,054 | 25,627 | 9,219 |
| Kansas | 656,322 | 166,121 | 113,434 | 42,500 | 334,267 | 465,528 | 396,661 | 36,762 | 32,105 |
| Kentucky | 2,515,899 | 365,980 | 465,526 | 145,203 | 1,539,190 | 878,644 | 809,703 | 50,831 | 18,110 |
| Louisiana | 2,651,222 | 410,677 | 674,392 | 64,798 | 1,501,355 | 1,394,295 | 1,190,655 | 77,407 | 126,233 |
| Maine | 1,167,769 | 100,683 | 251,561 | 0 | 815,525 | 317,802 | 284,139 | 15,717 | 17,946 |
| Maryland | 5,010,124 | 84,444 | 694,933 | 56,827 | 4,173,920 | 1,214,073 | 980,684 | 40,060 | 193,329 |
| Massachusetts | 1,816,422 | 467,514 | 880,323 | 451 | 468,134 | 1,071,422 | 905,297 | 162,007 | 4,118 |
| Michigan | 9,995,571 | 315,816 | 573,227 | 1,205,619 | 7,900,909 | 1,934,511 | 1,871,990 | 29,059 | 33,462 |
| Minnesota | 5,117,966 | 398,603 | 132,712 | 366,271 | 4,220,380 | 1,136,687 | 1,054,845 | 43,273 | 38,569 |
| Mississippi | 1,328,179 | 245,292 | 139,569 | 214,667 | 728,651 | 584,969 | 511,528 | 50,319 | 23,122 |
| Missouri | 2,583,119 | 294,721 | 275,561 | 340,517 | 1,672,320 | 803,870 | 722,895 | 36,981 | 43,994 |
| Montana | 442,766 | 98,685 | 38,068 | 71,750 | 234,263 | 211,575 | 192,240 | 14,715 | 4,620 |
| Nebraska | 748,431 | 85,182 | 44,008 | 64,169 | 555,072 | 194,570 | 105,406 | 85,023 | 4,141 |
| Nevada | 1,309,102 | 38,199 | 119,411 | 357,038 | 794,454 | 320,015 | 300,322 | 8,867 | 10,826 |
| New Hampshire | 474,452 | 73,669 | 35,439 | 19,900 | 345,444 | 196,183 | 126,512 | 15,603 | 54,068 |
| New Jersey | 9,128,063 | 898,309 | 3,055,466 | 286,798 | 4,887,490 | 2,675,133 | 2,547,020 | 101,272 | 26,841 |
| New Mexico | 1,211,157 | 227,716 | 150,778 | 145,996 | 686,667 | 478,141 | 417,053 | 46,171 | 14,917 |
| New York | 13,686,386 | 488,920 | 561,409 | 1,089,995 | 11,546,062 | 5,272,662 | 5,063,952 | 100,819 | 107,891 |
| North Carolina | 4,027,003 | 604,774 | 602,127 | 146,951 | 2,673,151 | 1,395,725 | 1,282,448 | 106,779 | 6,498 |
| North Dakota | 211,341 | 33,742 | 10,952 | 23,805 | 142,842 | 82,857 | 63,053 | 6,111 | 13,693 |
| Ohio | 11,103,058 | 1,673,387 | 834,224 | 1,411,257 | 7,184,190 | 4,025,753 | 3,760,662 | 162,109 | 102,982 |
| Oklahoma | 2,274,436 | 230,543 | 359,359 | 121,464 | 1,563,070 | 814,411 | 722,885 | 41,345 | 50,181 |
| Oregon | 2,433,764 | 303,724 | 135,072 | 298,966 | 1,696,002 | 1,097,653 | 856,508 | 52,542 | 188,603 |
| Pennsylvania | 9,378,707 | 685,103 | 393,613 | 796,565 | 7,503,426 | 2,805,646 | 2,658,769 | 30,285 | 116,592 |
| Rhode Island | 494,735 | 133,500 | 160,800 | 5,880 | 194,555 | 264,000 | 264,000 | 0 | 0 |
| South Carolina | 2,125,834 | 346,895 | 183,296 | 253,056 | 1,342,587 | 752,515 | 681,480 | 60,010 | 11,025 |
| South Dakota | 388,058 | 50,525 | 16,744 | 30,920 | 289,869 | 109,291 | 90,724 | 10,386 | 8,181 |
| Tennessee | 2,168,492 | 143,656 | 278,417 | 59,168 | 1,687,251 | 549,029 | 521,339 | 23,833 | 3,857 |
| Texas | 18,025,532 | 1,568,294 | 1,131,796 | 465,747 | 14,859,695 | 3,478,348 | 3,075,653 | 351,910 | 50,785 |
| Utah | 1,453,960 | 27,790 | 102,445 | 206,166 | 1,117,559 | 288,069 | 269,617 | 10,587 | 7,865 |
| Vermont | 247,358 | 24,058 | 42,154 | 3,026 | 178,120 | 77,889 | 60,667 | 1,596 | 15,626 |
| Virginia | 5,953,176 | 58,164 | 361,462 | 493,663 | 5,039,887 | 1,127,983 | 928,861 | 77,349 | 121,773 |
| Washington | 6,614,332 | 528,335 | 623,064 | 256,446 | 5,206,487 | 1,211,012 | 1,114,296 | 66,726 | 29,990 |
| West Virginia | 658,620 | 107,257 | 60,578 | 232,297 | 258,690 | 306,532 | 291,299 | 12,236 | 2,997 |
| Wisconsin | 6,474,758 | 22,396 | 250,914 | 686,792 | 5,514,656 | 1,354,942 | 1,309,076 | 36,883 | 8,983 |
| Wyoming | 365,375 | 45,379 | 8,647 | 47,886 | 263,463 | 122,255 | 105,023 | 10,087 | 7,145 |

*Source:* U.S. Department of Commerce, Bureau of the Census.

## Table 7.28
## COMPARATIVE STATISTICS FOR STATE-ADMINISTERED PUBLIC EMPLOYEE RETIREMENT SYSTEMS: FISCAL 1995-96

| State | Percent of receipts paid by | | | Annual benefit payments as a percentage of | | Average benefit payments (a) | Investments earnings as a percentage of cash and security holdings | Percentage distribution of cash and investment holdings | | | |
| --- | --- | --- | --- | --- | --- | --- | --- | --- | --- | --- | --- |
| | | | | | | | | | Governmental securities | | |
| | Employee contribution | State government | Local government | Annual receipts | Cash and investments | | | Cash and deposits | Federal | State and local | Nongovernmental securities and other investments |
| United States | 9.2 | 10.7 | 8.9 | 28.5 | 4.4 | 1,006 | 11 | 4.7 | 18 | 0 | 77.3 |
| Alabama | 11.5 | 16.1 | 2.8 | 31.3 | 4.6 | 1,070 | 10.3 | 6.8 | 13.4 | 0.0 | 79.8 |
| Alaska | 7.1 | 5.3 | 5.6 | 20.1 | 4.6 | 1,730 | 18.6 | 1.9 | 31.8 | 0.0 | 66.3 |
| Arizona | 18.8 | 5.0 | 16.6 | 43.7 | 3.4 | 1,091 | 4.6 | 5.5 | 22.7 | 0.0 | 71.9 |
| Arkansas | 3.2 | 8.0 | 11.1 | 22.1 | 3.8 | 830 | 13.4 | 11.2 | 17.1 | 0.3 | 71.4 |
| California | 13.8 | 7.7 | 11.9 | 35.6 | 4.3 | 1,177 | 8.0 | 3.0 | 14.6 | 0.0 | 82.3 |
| Colorado | 14.4 | 9.5 | 14.0 | 37.3 | 4.9 | 1,314 | 8.2 | 3.9 | 5.1 | 0.1 | 91.0 |
| Connecticut | 21.1 | 49.0 | 2.1 | 90.4 | 7.1 | 1,494 | 2.2 | 4.8 | 0.1 | 0.0 | 95.1 |
| Delaware | 3.8 | 11.2 | 0.3 | 21.0 | 4.4 | 764 | 17.6 | 7.8 | 0.0 | 0.0 | 92.2 |
| Florida | 0.4 | 11.3 | 32.7 | 22.8 | 3.2 | 152 | 7.7 | 7.8 | 11.5 | 0.0 | 80.6 |
| Georgia | 6.9 | 17.5 | 4.5 | 24.1 | 3.8 | 1,161 | 11.3 | 1.9 | 47.9 | 0.0 | 50.2 |
| Hawaii | 4.7 | 20.3 | 7.3 | 35.2 | 5.8 | 1,328 | 11.2 | 7.7 | 12.2 | 0.0 | 80.1 |
| Idaho | 19.9 | 11.4 | 22.2 | 29.2 | 4.4 | 598 | 7.0 | 5.0 | 15.2 | 0.0 | 79.8 |
| Illinois | 14.8 | 12.6 | 6.1 | 38.6 | 6.3 | 1,040 | 10.8 | 10.8 | 9.5 | 0.0 | 79.7 |
| Indiana | 11.7 | 37.1 | 9.1 | 37.0 | 5.8 | 697 | 6.6 | 3.6 | 63.4 | 0.0 | 33.0 |
| Iowa | 27.7 | 5.3 | 16.0 | 48.1 | 2.7 | 471 | 2.8 | 1.1 | 4.7 | 0.0 | 94.2 |
| Kansas | 25.3 | 17.3 | 6.5 | 60.4 | 6.2 | 662 | 5.2 | 0.7 | 7.1 | 0.0 | 92.2 |
| Kentucky | 14.5 | 18.5 | 5.8 | 32.2 | 5.2 | 982 | 9.9 | 6.7 | 13.4 | 0.0 | 79.9 |
| Louisiana | 15.5 | 25.4 | 2.4 | 44.9 | 6.8 | 1,028 | 8.6 | 5.7 | 16.1 | 0.0 | 78.2 |
| Maine | 8.6 | 21.5 | 0.0 | 24.3 | 8.7 | 876 | 24.9 | 3.7 | 3.0 | 0.0 | 93.2 |
| Maryland | 1.7 | 13.9 | 1.1 | 19.6 | 3.3 | 1,087 | 14.0 | 3.5 | 19.5 | 0.0 | 77.0 |
| Massachusetts | 25.7 | 48.5 | 0.0 | 49.8 | 5.4 | 948 | 2.8 | 5.9 | 6.9 | 0.0 | 87.3 |
| Michigan | 3.2 | 5.7 | 12.1 | 18.7 | 4.3 | 949 | 18.3 | 9.5 | 10.9 | 0.0 | 79.6 |
| Minnesota | 7.8 | 2.6 | 7.2 | 20.6 | 3.8 | 982 | 15.0 | 0.4 | 3.4 | 0.0 | 96.2 |
| Mississippi | 18.5 | 10.5 | 16.2 | 38.5 | 4.8 | 757 | 6.9 | 10.8 | 32.4 | 0.4 | 56.4 |
| Missouri | 11.4 | 10.7 | 13.2 | 28.0 | 3.5 | 877 | 8.1 | 4.5 | 19.4 | 0.0 | 76.1 |
| Montana | 22.3 | 8.6 | 16.2 | 43.4 | 6.4 | 708 | 7.8 | 4.2 | 21.2 | 0.0 | 74.6 |
| Nebraska | 11.4 | 5.9 | 8.6 | 14.1 | 2.7 | 640 | 14.3 | 1.0 | 37.2 | 0.0 | 61.7 |
| Nevada | 2.9 | 9.1 | 27.3 | 22.9 | 4.0 | 1,390 | 10.5 | 3.5 | 29.7 | 0.0 | 66.8 |
| New Hampshire | 15.5 | 7.5 | 4.2 | 26.7 | 3.9 | 763 | 10.6 | 20.7 | 6.8 | 0.0 | 72.5 |
| New Jersey | 9.8 | 33.5 | 3.1 | 27.9 | 6.3 | 1,238 | 12.1 | 0.0 | 3.7 | 0.0 | 96.3 |
| New Mexico | 18.8 | 12.4 | 12.1 | 34.4 | 5.2 | 1,092 | 8.5 | 5.4 | 36.9 | 0.0 | 57.8 |
| New York | 3.6 | 4.1 | 8.0 | 37.0 | 4.9 | 1,106 | 11.2 | 2.4 | 22.0 | 0.0 | 75.6 |
| North Carolina | 15.0 | 15.0 | 3.6 | 31.8 | 4.2 | 923 | 8.8 | 32.1 | 0.0 | 0.0 | 67.9 |
| North Dakota | 16.0 | 5.2 | 11.3 | 29.8 | 3.7 | 630 | 8.5 | 1.5 | 5.6 | 0.0 | 92.9 |
| Ohio | 15.1 | 7.5 | 12.7 | 33.9 | 4.7 | 1,354 | 9.0 | 4.2 | 29.4 | 0.0 | 66.3 |

See footnotes at end of table.

# COMPARATIVE STATISTICS: FISCAL 1995-96 — Continued

| State | Percent of receipts paid by | | | Annual benefit payments as a percentage of | | Average benefit payments (a) | Investments earnings as a percentage of cash and security holdings | Percentage distribution of cash and investment holdings | | | |
|---|---|---|---|---|---|---|---|---|---|---|---|
| | | | | | | | | | Governmental securities | | |
| | Employee contribution | State government | Local government | Annual receipts | Cash and investments | | | Cash and deposits | Federal | State and local | Nongovernmental securities and other investments |
| Oklahoma | 10.1 | 15.8 | 5.3 | 31.8 | 7.0 | 965 | 15.1 | 3.6 | 20.3 | 0.9 | 75.2 |
| Oregon | 12.5 | 5.5 | 12.3 | 35.2 | 6.1 | 1,048 | 12.1 | 5.6 | 17.5 | 0.0 | 76.8 |
| Pennsylvania | 7.3 | 4.2 | 8.5 | 28.3 | 4.6 | 833 | 12.9 | 1.6 | 12.2 | 0.0 | 86.2 |
| Rhode Island | 27.0 | 32.5 | 1.2 | 53.4 | 4.8 | 1,396 | 3.5 | 0.2 | 30.5 | 0.0 | 69.3 |
| South Carolina | 16.3 | 8.6 | 11.9 | 32.1 | 4.3 | 888 | 8.4 | 3.8 | 41.1 | 0.0 | 55.2 |
| South Dakota | 13.0 | 4.3 | 8.0 | 23.4 | 2.6 | 554 | 8.3 | 10.8 | 11.3 | 0.0 | 77.9 |
| Tennessee | 6.6 | 12.8 | 2.7 | 24.0 | 2.8 | 683 | 9.2 | 4.9 | 29.8 | 0.0 | 65.3 |
| Texas | 8.7 | 6.3 | 2.6 | 17.1 | 3.5 | 1,077 | 16.8 | 3.1 | 22.6 | 0.0 | 74.3 |
| Utah | 1.9 | 7.0 | 14.2 | 18.5 | 3.0 | 903 | 12.3 | 3.0 | 11.0 | 0.0 | 86.0 |
| Vermont | 9.7 | 17.0 | 1.2 | 24.5 | 3.6 | 748 | 10.5 | 2.5 | 0.0 | 0.0 | 97.5 |
| Virginia | 1.0 | 6.1 | 8.3 | 15.6 | 3.3 | 919 | 18.0 | 0.5 | 10.1 | 0.0 | 89.4 |
| Washington | 8.0 | 9.4 | 3.9 | 16.8 | 3.4 | 1,035 | 15.7 | 2.0 | 28.4 | 0.0 | 69.6 |
| West Virginia | 16.3 | 9.2 | 35.3 | 44.2 | 9.9 | 391 | 8.8 | 6.2 | 89.1 | 0.0 | 4.7 |
| Wisconsin | 0.3 | 3.9 | 10.6 | 20.2 | 3.1 | 1,153 | 13.2 | 3.7 | 17.0 | 0.0 | 79.4 |
| Wyoming | 12.4 | 2.4 | 13.1 | 28.7 | 4.0 | 696 | 10.1 | 5.9 | 39.3 | 0.0 | 54.9 |

*Source:* U.S. Department of Commerce, Bureau of the Census.

. . . — Not available.

(a) Average benefit payment for the last month of fiscal year.

## Table 7.29
## STATE REGULATION OF SELECTED NON-HEALTH OCCUPATIONS AND PROFESSIONS: 2000

| State or other jurisdiction | Accountant, Certified Public | Architect | Auctioneer | Barber | Cosmetologist | Embalmer (a) | Engineer, Professional (b) | Funeral Director | Insurance Agent | Insurance Broker | Landscape Architect | Polygraph Examiner | Real Estate Agent | Real Estate Broker | Surveyor, Land |
|---|---|---|---|---|---|---|---|---|---|---|---|---|---|---|---|
| Alabama | L | L | L | … | L | L | L | L | L | L | L | L | L | L | L |
| Alaska | L | L | … | L | L | L | L | L | L | … | … | … | L | L | L |
| Arizona | L | L | … | L | L | L | L | L | L | L | L | … | L | L | L |
| Arkansas | L | L | L | L | L | L | L | L | L | … | L | L | L | L | L |
| California | L | L | … | L | L | L | L | L | L | … | L | … | L | L | L |
| Colorado | L | L | … | L | L | … | L | … | L | L | … | … | L | L | L |
| Connecticut | L | L | … | L | L | L | L | L | L | L | C | … | L | L | L |
| Delaware | L | L | L | L | L | … | L | L | L | L | L | … | L | L | L |
| Florida | L | L | L | L | L | L | L | L | L | … | L | L | L | L | L |
| Georgia | L | L | L | L | L | L | L | L | L | … | L | L | L | L | L |
| Hawaii | L | L | … | L | L | L | L | L | L | … | L | … | L | L | L |
| Idaho | L | L | … | L | L | … | L | … | L | L | L | … | L | L | L |
| Illinois | L | L | … | L | L | L | L | L | L | … | … | L | L | L | L |
| Indiana | L | L | L | L | L | … | L | L | L | L | … | L | L | L | L |
| Iowa | L | L | … | L | L | … | L | L | L | … | C | L | L | L | L |
| Kansas | L | L | … | L | L | L | L | L | L | L | L | … | L | L | L |
| Kentucky | L | L | L | L | L | L | L | L | L | … | L | L | L | L | L |
| Louisiana | L | L | L | L | L | L | L | L | L | L | L | L | L | L | C |
| Maine | L | L | L | L | L | L | L | L | L | L | L | L | L | L | L |
| Maryland | L | L | … | L | L | … | L | L | L | L | L | … | L | L | L |
| Massachusetts | L | L | L | L | L | L | L | L | L | … | L | … | L | L | L |
| Michigan | L | L | … | L | L | … | L | L | L | … | C | L | L | L | L |
| Minnesota | L | L | … | L | L | … | L | L | L | … | L | … | L | L | L |
| Mississippi | L | L | … | L | L | L | L | L | L | … | L | … | L | L | L |
| Missouri | L | L | … | L | L | L | L | L | L | L | C | … | L | L | L |
| Montana | L | L | … | L | L | … | L | L | L | … | L | L | L | L | L |
| Nebraska | L | L | … | L | L | L | L | L | L | L | L | L | L | L | L |
| Nevada | L | L | … | L | L | L | L | L | L | L | L | L | L | L | L |
| New Hampshire | L | L | L | L | L | L | L | L | L | L | … | L | L | L | L |
| New Jersey | L | L | … | … | L | … | L | L | L | … | C | … | L | L | L |
| New Mexico | L | L | … | L | L | … | L | L | L | L | L | L | L | L | L |
| New York | L | L | … | L | L | L | L | L | L | L | L | … | L | L | L |
| North Carolina | L | L | L | L | L | L | L | L | L | L | C | L | L | L | L |
| North Dakota | L | L | L | L | L | L | L | L | L | L | L | … | L | L | L |
| Ohio | L | L | L | L | L | L | L | L | L | L | L | … | L | L | L |
| Oklahoma | L | L | … | L | L | L | L | L | L | … | L | L | L | L | L |
| Oregon | L | L | … | L | L | L | L | L | L | … | L | L | L | L | L |
| Pennsylvania | L | L | L | L | L | … | L | L | L | L | L | … | L | L | L |
| Rhode Island | L | L | L | L | L | L | L | L | L | L | L | … | L | L | L |
| South Carolina | L | L | L | L | L | L | L | L | L | L | L | L | L | L | L |
| South Dakota | L | L | … | L | L | L | L | L | L | L | L | L | L | L | L |
| Tennessee | L | L | L | L | L | L | L | L | L | L | … | L | L | L | L |
| Texas | L | L | L | L | L | L | L | L | L | L | … | L | L | L | L |
| Utah | L | L | … | L | L | … | L | L | L | L | L | L | L | L | L |
| Vermont | L | L | L | L | L | L | L | L | L | L | … | L | L | L | L |
| Virginia | L | L | L | L | L | … | L | L | L | L | C | L | L | L | L |
| Washington | L | L | L | L | L | … | L | L | L | C | C | … | L | L | L |
| West Virginia | L | L | L | L | L | L | L | L | L | L | C | … | L | L | L |
| Wisconsin | L | L | L | L | L | … | L | L | L | L | … | … | L | L | L |
| Wyoming | L | L | … | L | L | L | L | L | L | L | … | … | L | L | L |
| Dist. of Columbia | L | L | L | L | L | … | L | L | L | L | L | … | L | L | … |

*Source:* Council on Licensure, Enforcement and Regulation, January 2000, and various national associations of state boards.

Key:
C — Certification
L — Licensure
R — Regulation

(a) In some states, embalmers are not licensed separately from funeral directors; embalming is part of the funeral director's job.

(b) In addition to licensing professional engineers, some states regulate engineers by specific areas of expertise, such as civil engineers.

# Table 7.30
# STATE REGULATION OF HEALTH OCCUPATIONS AND PROFESSIONS: 2000

| State and other jurisdiction | Acupuncturist | Chiropractor | Counselor, Professional | Counselor, Alcoholism | Counselor, Drug | Counselor, Pastoral | Counselor, Substance Abuse | Dentist | Dental Assistant | Dental Hygienist | Denturist | Dietitian | Emergency Medical Technician (a) | Hearing Aid Dealer & Fitter |
|---|---|---|---|---|---|---|---|---|---|---|---|---|---|---|
| Alabama | ... | L | L | ... | ... | ... | ... | L | ... | L | ... | L | L | L |
| Alaska | L | L | ... | ... | ... | ... | ... | L | ... | L | ... | ... | L | L |
| Arizona | ... | L | C | C | C | ... | C | L | C | L | L | ... | L | L |
| Arkansas | ... | L | L | C | ... | ... | ... | L | R | L | ... | L | L | L |
| California | L | L | L | C | C | ... | ... | L | L | L | ... | C | L | L |
| Colorado | R | L | L | ... | ... | ... | ... | L | ... | L | ... | ... | L | L |
| Connecticut | ... | L | L | L | L | ... | L | L | ... | L | ... | L | L | L |
| Delaware | L | L | L | ... | ... | ... | ... | L | ... | L | ... | L | L | L |
| Florida | L | L | L | ... | ... | ... | ... | L | C | L | ... | L | L | L |
| Georgia | L | L | L | ... | ... | ... | ... | L | ... | L | ... | ... | L | L |
| Hawaii | L | L | ... | C | C | ... | C | L | ... | L | ... | L | L | L |
| Idaho | ... | L | L | ... | ... | ... | ... | L | ... | L | L | L | L | L |
| Illinois | ... | L | L | ... | ... | ... | ... | L | ... | L | ... | ... | L | L |
| Indiana | ... | L | L | L | L | ... | L | L | ... | L | ... | L | L | L |
| Iowa | ... | L | C | C | ... | ... | ... | L | C | L | ... | C | L | L |
| Kansas | ... | L | L | L | L | ... | ... | L | ... | L | ... | L | L | L |
| Kentucky | L | L | C | C | C | ... | C | L | ... | L | ... | C | L | L |
| Louisiana | L | L | L | L | L | L | L | L | L | L | ... | L | L | L |
| Maine | L | L | C | L | L | ... | ... | L | ... | L | L | L | L | L |
| Maryland | L | L | C | ... | ... | ... | ... | L | L | L | ... | L | L | L |
| Massachusetts | ... | L | L | ... | ... | ... | ... | L | ... | L | ... | ... | L | L |
| Michigan | ... | L | L | ... | ... | ... | ... | L | L | L | ... | L | L | L |
| Minnesota | ... | L | L | ... | ... | ... | ... | L | L | L | ... | L | L | L |
| Mississippi | ... | L | L | ... | ... | ... | ... | L | ... | L | ... | L | L | L |
| Missouri | ... | L | L | ... | ... | ... | ... | L | L | L | ... | ... | L | L |
| Montana | L | L | C | C | C | ... | C | L | ... | L | L | L | L | L |
| Nebraska | L | L | L | C | ... | ... | ... | L | ... | L | ... | L | L | L |
| Nevada | ... | L | C | C | C | C | C | L | R | L | L | L | L | L |
| New Hampshire | L | L | L | ... | ... | ... | ... | L | ... | L | ... | L | L | L |
| New Jersey | L | L | L | L | L | ... | ... | L | C | L | ... | ... | L | L |
| New Mexico | L | L | C | ... | L | ... | ... | L | ... | L | ... | L | L | L |
| New York | L | L | L | ... | L | ... | ... | L | ... | L | ... | L | L | L |
| North Carolina | ... | L | L | ... | L | ... | ... | L | L | L | ... | L | L | L |
| North Dakota | ... | L | L | ... | L | ... | ... | L | C | L | L | ... | L | L |
| Ohio | ... | L | L | ... | ... | ... | ... | L | ... | L | ... | L | L | L |

See footnotes at end of table.

Key:
C — Certification
L — Licensure
R — Regulation
* — Enabling legislation
... — Not regulated

# STATE REGULATION OF HEALTH OCCUPATIONS AND PROFESSIONS: 2000 — Continued

| State and other jurisdiction | Acupuncturist | Chiropractor | Counselor, Professional | Counselor, Alcoholism | Counselor, Drug | Counselor, Pastoral | Counselor, Substance Abuse | Dentist | Dental Assistant | Dental Hygienist | Denturist | Dietitian | Emergency Medical Technician (a) | Hearing Aid Dealer & Fitter |
|---|---|---|---|---|---|---|---|---|---|---|---|---|---|---|
| Oklahoma | ... | L | L | ... | ... | ... | ... | L | C | L | ... | L | L | L |
| Oregon | L | L | L | ... | ... | ... | ... | L | ... | L | L | L | L | L |
| Pennsylvania | R | L | L | ... | ... | ... | ... | L | ... | L | ... | ... | L | L |
| Rhode Island | L | L | ... | ... | ... | ... | C | L | ... | L | ... | ... | L | L |
| South Carolina | ... | L | L | ... | ... | ... | ... | L | ... | L | ... | ... | L | L |
| South Dakota | L | L | L | ... | ... | ... | ... | L | L | L | ... | ... | L | L |
| Tennessee | L | L | L | ... | L | ... | ... | L | L | L | ... | C | L | L |
| Texas | L | L | L | ... | ... | ... | ... | L | L | L | ... | L | L | L |
| Utah | L | L | L | ... | ... | ... | ... | L | L | L | ... | ... | L | ... |
| Vermont | L | L | L | ... | ... | ... | ... | L | ... | L | ... | ... | L | L |
| Virginia | L | L | L | C | C | ... | L | L | ... | L | ... | L | L | L |
| Washington | L | L | C | ... | ... | ... | ... | L | ... | L | ... | ... | L | L |
| West Virginia | ... | L | C | ... | ... | ... | ... | L | L | L | ... | ... | L | L |
| Wisconsin | L | L | C | ... | ... | ... | L | L | ... | L | ... | ... | L | L |
| Wyoming | ... | L | L | ... | ... | ... | ... | L | ... | L | ... | ... | L | L |
| Dist. of Columbia | L | L | L | ... | ... | ... | ... | L | ... | L | ... | L | L | ... |
| Puerto Rico | ... | L | ... | ... | ... | ... | ... | L | L | L | ... | ... | L | ... |

Key:
C — Certification
L — Licensure
R — Regulation
* — Enabling legislation
. . . — Not regulated

# STATE REGULATION OF HEALTH OCCUPATIONS AND PROFESSIONS: 2000 — Continued

| State and other jurisdiction | Homeopath | Massage Therapist | Nurse, Licensed Practical (b) | Nurse, Midwife (b) | Nurse Practitioner (b) | Nurse, Registered (b) | Nursing Home Administrator | Occupational Therapist | Occupational Therapy Assistant | Optician | Optometrist | Osteopath | Pharmacist | Physical Therapist |
|---|---|---|---|---|---|---|---|---|---|---|---|---|---|---|
| Alabama | ... | ... | L | L | L | L | L | L | L | ... | L | L | L | L |
| Alaska | L | ... | L | L | L | L | L | L | L | L | L | L | L | L |
| Arizona | L | ... | L | L | L | L | L | L | L | L | L | L | L | L |
| Arkansas | ... | L | L | L | L | L | L | L | L | L | L | L | L | L |
| California | ... | ... | ... | ... | L | L | L | C | ... | C | L | L | L | L |
| Colorado | L | ... | L | L | L | L | L | L | L | ... | L | L | L | L |
| Connecticut | L | ... | L | L | L | L | L | L | L | L | L | L | L | L |
| Delaware | ... | L | L | L | L | L | L | L | L | L | L | L | L | L |
| Florida | ... | L | L | L | L | L | L | L | L | L | L | L | L | L |
| Georgia | ... | ... | L | L | L | L | L | L | L | L | L | L | L | L |
| Hawaii | ... | L | L | L | L | L | L | L | L | L | L | L | L | L |
| Idaho | ... | ... | L | ... | L | L | C | C | C | ... | L | L | L | C |
| Illinois | ... | ... | L | L | L | L | L | L | L | L | L | L | L | L |
| Indiana | ... | L | L | L | L | L | C | L | L | L | L | L | L | L |
| Iowa | ... | ... | L | L | L | L | L | L | L | ... | L | L | L | C |
| Kansas | ... | ... | L | L | L | L | L | C | C | ... | L | L | L | L |
| Kentucky | ... | ... | L | L | L | L | L | L | L | L | L | L | L | L |
| Louisiana | ... | L | L | L | L | L | L | L | L | ... | L | L | L | L |
| Maine | ... | R | L | L | L | L | L | L | L | ... | L | L | L | L |
| Maryland | ... | ... | L | ... | L | L | L | C | C | ... | L | L | L | L |
| Massachusetts | ... | ... | L | L | L | L | L | L | L | L | L | L | L | L |
| Michigan | ... | ... | L | C | C | L | L | R | R | ... | L | L | L | C |
| Minnesota | ... | L | L | L | L | L | L | L | L | ... | L | L | L | L |
| Mississippi | ... | L | L | L | L | L | L | C | C | ... | L | L | L | L |
| Missouri | ... | L | L | L | L | L | L | L | L | L | L | L | L | L |
| Montana | ... | ... | L | L | L | L | L | L | L | ... | L | L | L | L |
| Nebraska | L | L | L | L | L | L | L | L | L | ... | L | L | L | L |
| Nevada | L | L | L | L | L | L | L | L | L | R | L | L | L | L |
| New Hampshire | ... | ... | L | L | L | L | L | L | L | L | L | L | L | L |
| New Jersey | ... | ... | L | L | L | L | L | ... | ... | ... | L | L | L | L |
| New Mexico | L | L | L | L | L | L | L | L | L | ... | L | L | L | L |
| New York | L | L | L | L | L | L | L | L | L | ... | L | L | L | L |
| North Carolina | ... | L | L | L | L | L | L | L | L | L | L | L | L | L |
| North Dakota | L | L | L | L | L | L | L | L | L | ... | L | L | L | L |
| Ohio | ... | ... | L | L | L | L | L | L | L | L | L | L | L | L |

See footnotes at end of table.

*Key:*
C — Certification
L — Licensure
R — Regulation
* — Enabling legislation
. . . — Not regulated

## STATE REGULATION OF HEALTH OCCUPATIONS AND PROFESSIONS: 2000 — Continued

| State and other jurisdiction | Homeopath | Massage Therapist | Nurse, Licensed Practical (b) | Nurse Midwife (b) | Nurse Practitioner (b) | Nurse, Registered (b) | Nursing Home Administrator | Occupational Therapist | Occupational Therapy Assistant | Optician | Optometrist | Osteopath | Pharmacist | Physical Therapist |
|---|---|---|---|---|---|---|---|---|---|---|---|---|---|---|
| Oklahoma | ... | ... | L | C | C | L | L | L | L | ... | L | L | L | L |
| Oregon | ... | L | L | C | C | L | L | L | L | ... | L | L | L | L |
| Pennsylvania | ... | ... | L | L | L | L | L | L | L | ... | L | L | L | L |
| Rhode Island | ... | L | L | L | L | L | L | L | ... | L | L | L | L | L |
| South Carolina | ... | ... | L | L | L | L | L | L | L | L | L | L | L | L |
| South Dakota | ... | ... | L | L | L | L | L | L | L | ... | L | L | L | L |
| Tennessee | ... | L | L | L | L | L | L | L | L | L | L | L | L | L |
| Texas | ... | L | L | L | L | L | L | L | L | L | L | L | L | L |
| Utah | ... | ... | L | ... | ... | L | (c) | L | L | ... | L | L | L | L |
| Vermont | ... | ... | L | L | L | L | L | L | L | L | L | L | L | L |
| Virginia | ... | ... | L | L | ... | L | L | C | ... | L | L | L | L | L |
| Washington | ... | L | L | L | ... | L | L | L | L | L | L | L | L | L |
| West Virginia | ... | ... | L | L | ... | L | L | L | L | ... | L | L | L | L |
| Wisconsin | ... | ... | L | L | ... | L | L | C | C | ... | L | L | L | L |
| Wyoming | ... | ... | L | L | L | L | L | L | L | ... | L | L | L | L |
| Dist. of Columbia | ... | ... | L | L | L | L | L | L | L | ... | L | L | L | L |
| Puerto Rico | ... | ... | L | L | L | L | (c) | L | L | L | L | ... | L | L |

Key:
C — Certification
L — Licensure
R — Regulation
* — Enabling legislation
... — Not regulated

# STATE REGULATION OF HEALTH OCCUPATIONS AND PROFESSIONS: 2000 — Continued

| State and other jurisdiction | Physical Therapy Assistant | Physician | Physician Assistant | Podiatrist | Psychologist | Radiologic Technologist | Radiation Therapist | Respiratory Therapist | Sanitarian | Social Worker | Speech-Language Pathologist & Aud. | Therapist, Marriage & Family | Veterinarian | Veterinary Technician |
|---|---|---|---|---|---|---|---|---|---|---|---|---|---|---|
| Alabama | L | L | L | L | L | … | … | … | … | L | L | … | L | L |
| Alaska | L | L | L | L | L | … | … | … | … | C | … | C | L | L |
| Arizona | L | L | C | L | L | C | C | C | R | … | L | … | L | L |
| Arkansas | L | L | C | L | L | C | … | L | … | L | L | … | L | R |
| California | L | L | L | L | L | C | L | L | … | … | … | L | L | … |
| Colorado | … | L | C | L | L | … | … | … | … | … | L | L | L | … |
| Connecticut | R | L | L | L | L | L | L | … | … | … | L | L | L | … |
| Delaware | L | L | L | L | L | L | L | L | … | … | L | … | L | … |
| Florida | L | L | L | L | L | L | L | L | L | … | L | L | L | L |
| Georgia | L | L | L | L | L | … | … | … | L | … | L | L | L | … |
| Hawaii | … | L | L | L | L | L | L | R | … | L | L | … | L | … |
| Idaho | L | L | L | L | L | … | … | … | R | L | L | L | L | … |
| Illinois | L | L | C | L | L | L | L | C | … | L | L | L | L | L |
| Indiana | L | L | L | L | C | L | L | L | … | L | L | … | L | … |
| Iowa | L | L | L | L | L | L | … | L | … | L | L | L | L | … |
| Kansas | R | L | C | L | L | … | * | C | L | L | L | … | L | L |
| Kentucky | L | L | L | L | L | L | L | L | L | L | L | L | L | L |
| Louisiana | L | L | L | L | L | L | L | L | L | L | L | C | L | L |
| Maine | L | L | L | L | L | L | … | L | … | L | L | … | L | L |
| Maryland | L | L | L | L | L | … | … | C | … | L | L | L | L | … |
| Massachusetts | L | L | L | L | L | L* | … | L | L | L | L | … | L | L |
| Michigan | … | L | L | L | L | … | … | … | C | C | C | L | L | R |
| Minnesota | … | L | L | L | L | … | … | C | C | L | … | L | L | L |
| Mississippi | L | L | … | L | L | … | … | L | L | L | C | C | L | L |
| Missouri | … | L | L | L | L | … | … | C | C | … | L | … | L | … |
| Montana | C | L | L | L | L | … | … | L | … | L | L | L | L | … |
| Nebraska | C | L | L | L | L | L | … | L | L | C | L | L | L | L |
| Nevada | L | L | L | L | L | … | … | … | R | L | L | L | L | … |
| New Hampshire | C | L | L | L | L | … | … | … | … | L | L | L | L | L |
| New Jersey | L | L | L | L | L | … | … | L | … | L | L | L | L | … |
| New Mexico | L | L | L | L | L | C | L | L | … | L | L | … | L | L |
| New York | L | L | L | L | C | L | L | … | … | C | L | … | L | … |
| North Carolina | L | L | L | L | L | … | … | L | L | C | L | C | L | L |
| North Dakota | L | L | L | L | L | … | … | … | L | L | L | L | L | … |
| Ohio | L | L | L | L | L | … | … | L | L | L | L | C | L | L |

See footnotes at end of table.

Key:
C — Certification
L — Licensure
R — Regulation
* — Enabling legislation
. . . — Not regulated

# STATE REGULATION OF HEALTH OCCUPATIONS AND PROFESSIONS: 2000 — Continued

| State and other jurisdiction | Physical Therapy Assistant | Physician | Physician Assistant | Podiatrist | Psychologist | Radiologic Technologist | Radiation Therapist | Respiratory Therapist | Sanitarian | Social Worker | Speech-Language Pathologist & Aud. | Therapist, Marriage & Family | Veterinarian | Veterinary Technician |
|---|---|---|---|---|---|---|---|---|---|---|---|---|---|---|
| Oklahoma | L | L | L | L | L | ... | ... | ... | L | L | L | L | L | L |
| Oregon | R | L | L | L | L | L | ... | L | L | ... | L | L | L | L |
| Pennsylvania | L | L | C | L | L | ... | ... | ... | L | ... | L | L | L | R |
| Rhode Island | L | L | L | L | L | ... | ... | L | L | L | L | L | L | ... |
| South Carolina | L | L | L | L | L | ... | ... | L | L | L | L | L | L | L |
| South Dakota | L | L | L | L | L | ... | ... | ... | C | L | L | ... | L | ... |
| Tennessee | L | L | L | L | L | ... | ... | L | L | L | L | L | L | ... |
| Texas | ... | L | L | L | L | L* | L | L | L | L | L | L | L | ... |
| Utah | L | L | L | L | L | L | ... | ... | ... | L | L | L | L | ... |
| Vermont | ... | L | L | L | L | ... | ... | ... | ... | ... | L | ... | L | ... |
| Virginia | L | L | L | L | L | C | ... | C | L | L | L | L | L | L |
| Washington | ... | L | L | L | L | C | ... | L | L | L | ... | L | L | ... |
| West Virginia | L | L | L | L | L | L | ... | ... | L | L | L | ... | L | L |
| Wisconsin | ... | L | L | L | L | ... | ... | L | L | C | L | C | L | L |
| Wyoming | ... | L | L | L | L | L | L | ... | L | L | L | L | L | ... |
| Dist. of Columbia | L | L | L | L | L | L | ... | ... | ... | ... | ... | ... | L | ... |
| Puerto Rico | L | L | ... | L | L | L | ... | L | ... | L | L | ... | L | ... |

Source: Council on Licensure, Enforcement and Regulation, January 2000, and various national associations of state boards.

Key:
C — Certification
L — Licensure
R — Regulation
* — Enabling legislation
... — Not regulated

(a) There are eight categories of emergency medical technicians, from basic to paramedic to task-specific certifications. No state regulates all categories, but every state regulates at least one category.

(b) Some states recognize various categories of advanced practice nurses (e.g. geriatric, school health, and women's health).

(c) In Indiana, Utah and Puerto Rico, nursing home administrators are not licensed as such, but they are licensed more broadly as health facility administrators.

## Table 7.31
## STATUS OF MANDATORY CONTINUING EDUCATION
## FOR SELECTED PROFESSIONS: 1999

| State or other jurisdiction | Architects | Certified Public Accountants | Dentists | Professional Engineer | Lawyers | Nurses | Nursing Home Administrator | Optometry | Pharmacy | Physical Therapist | Physicians | Psychology | Real Estate | Social Work | Veterinary Medicine |
|---|---|---|---|---|---|---|---|---|---|---|---|---|---|---|---|
| Alabama | ★ | ★ | ★ | ★ | ★ | ★ | ★ | ★ | ★ | ★ | ★ | ★ | ★ | ★ | ★ |
| Alaska | ... | ★ | ★ | ... | ... | ★ | ... | ★ | ★ | ★ | ★ | ★ | ★ | ★ | ★ |
| Arizona | ... | ★ | ★ | E | ★ | ... | ★ | ★ | ★ | ... | ★ | ★ | ★ | ★ | ★ |
| Arkansas | ★ | ★ | ★ | ★ | ★ | ... | ★ | ★ | ★ | ★ | E | ★ | ★ | ★ | ★ |
| California | ... | ★ | ★ | E | ★ | ★ | ★ | ★ | ★ | ... | ★ | ★ | ★ | ★ | ... |
| Colorado | ... | ★ | ... | ... | ★ | ... | ... | ★ | ... | ... | ... | ... | ★ | ... | ★ |
| Connecticut | ... | ★ | ... | ... | ... | ... | ... | ★ | ★ | ... | ... | ... | ... | ... | ... |
| Delaware | E | ★ | ★ | ... | ★ | ★ | ★ | ★ | ★ | ★ | ★ | ★ | ★ | ★ | ★ |
| Florida | ★ | ★ | ★ | ... | ★ | ★ | ★ | ★ | ★ | ★ | ★ | ★ | ★ | ★ | ★ |
| Georgia | ... | ★ | ★ | ★ | ★ | ... | ★ | ★ | ★ | ★ | ★ | ★ | ★ | ★ | ★ |
| Hawaii | ... | ★ | ... | ... | ... | ... | ... | ★ | ... | ... | ★ | ... | ★ | ... | ... |
| Idaho | ... | ★ | ★ | ... | ★ | S | ★ | ★ | ★ | ... | ★ | ... | ★ | E | ★ |
| Illinois | ... | ★ | ★ | ... | ... | ... | ★ | ★ | ★ | ... | ★ | ... | ★ | ★ | ★ |
| Indiana | ... | ★ | ★ | E | ★ | S | ★ | ★ | ★ | ... | ... | ★ | ★ | E | ★ |
| Iowa | ★ | ★ | ★ | ★ | ★ | ★ | ★ | ★ | ★ | ★ | ★ | ★ | ★ | ★ | ★ |
| Kansas | ★ | ★ | ★ | ★ | ★ | ★ | ★ | ★ | ★ | ★ | ★ | ★ | ★ | ★ | ★ |
| Kentucky | ★ | ★ | ★ | ... | ★ | ★ | ★ | ★ | ★ | ★ | ★ | ★ | ★ | ... | ★ |
| Louisiana | ★ | ★ | ★ | ... | ★ | ★ | ★ | ★ | ★ | ★ | ★ | ★ | ★ | ★ | ★ |
| Maine | ... | ★ | ★ | ... | ... | ... | ★ | ★ | ★ | ... | ... | ★ | ★ | ★ | ★ |
| Maryland | ... | ★ | ★ | ... | ... | ★ | ★ | ★ | ★ | ★ | ... | ★ | ★ | ★ | ★ |
| Massachusetts | ... | ★ | ★ | ... | ... | ★ | ★ | ★ | ★ | ★ | ... | ★ | ★ | ★ | ★ |
| Michigan | E | ★ | ★ | E | ... | ... | ★ | ★ | ★ | ... | ★ | E | ★ | ... | E |
| Minnesota | E | ★ | ★ | E | ★ | ★ | ★ | ★ | ★ | ★ | ★ | ★ | ★ | ★ | ★ |
| Mississippi | ... | ★ | ★ | ... | ★ | ★ | ★ | ★ | ★ | ★ | ... | ★ | ★ | ★ | ★ |
| Missouri | ... | ★ | ★ | ... | ★ | ... | ★ | ★ | ★ | ... | ★ | ★ | ★ | E | ★ |
| Montana | E | ★ | ★ | ★ | ★ | ... | ★ | ★ | ★ | E | ... | ★ | ★ | ★ | ★ |
| Nebraska | E | ★ | ★ | E | ... | ★ | ★ | ★ | ★ | ... | E | ★ | ★ | ★ | ★ |
| Nevada | E | ★ | ★ | E | ★ | ★ | ★ | ★ | ★ | ★ | ★ | ★ | ★ | ★ | ★ |
| New Hampshire | ... | ★ | ★ | ★ | ★ | ★ | ★ | ★ | ★ | ★ | ★ | ★ | ★ | ★ | ★ |
| New Jersey | E | ★ | ★ | ... | S | ... | ★ | ★ | ★ | ... | ... | ... | ... | E | ... |
| New Mexico | ... | ★ | ★ | ★ | ★ | ★ | ★ | ★ | ★ | ★ | ★ | ★ | ★ | ★ | ★ |
| New York | ... | ★ | ★ | ... | ... | ... | ★ | S | ★ | ... | ... | ★ | ... | ... | ... |
| North Carolina | E | ★ | ★ | ★ | ★ | ... | ★ | ★ | ★ | ... | ★ | E | ★ | ★ | ★ |
| North Dakota | ... | ★ | ★ | ... | ★ | ... | ★ | ★ | ★ | ★ | ... | ★ | ★ | ★ | ★ |
| Ohio | E | ★ | ★ | ... | ★ | ★ | ★ | ★ | ★ | ★ | ★ | ★ | ★ | ★ | ★ |
| Oklahoma | ... | ★ | ★ | E | ★ | ★ | ★ | ★ | ★ | ... | ★ | ★ | ★ | S | ★ |
| Oregon | ... | ★ | ★ | E | ★ | ★ | ★ | ★ | ★ | ... | ★ | ★ | ★ | ★ | ★ |
| Pennsylvania | ... | ★ | E | ... | ★ | ... | ★ | ★ | ★ | ... | S | ★ | ★ | E | ★ |
| Rhode Island | ... | ★ | ★ | ... | ★ | S | ★ | ★ | ★ | ... | ★ | ★ | ★ | ★ | ★ |
| South Carolina | ... | ★ | ★ | ★ | ★ | ... | ★ | ★ | ★ | ... | ★ | ★ | ★ | ★ | ★ |
| South Dakota | ★ | ★ | ★ | ★ | ... | ... | ★ | ★ | ★ | ... | ... | ★ | ★ | ★ | ★ |
| Tennessee | ★ | ★ | ★ | ★ | ★ | ... | ★ | ★ | ★ | ... | ★ | ★ | ★ | ★ | ★ |
| Texas | E | ★ | ★ | ... | ★ | ★ | ★ | ★ | ★ | ★ | ★ | ★ | ★ | ★ | ★ |
| Utah | E | ★ | ★ | E | ★ | ★ | ★ | ★ | ★ | ... | ★ | ★ | ★ | ★ | ★ |
| Vermont | ... | ★ | ... | E | ★ | ... | ★ | ★ | ★ | ... | ... | ★ | ★ | ... | E |
| Virginia | ... | ★ | ★ | E | ★ | ... | ★ | ★ | ★ | ... | ... | ★ | ★ | ... | ★ |
| Washington | ... | ★ | ... | ... | ★ | S | ★ | ★ | ★ | ★ | ★ | ★ | ★ | E | ★ |
| West Virginia | ★ | ★ | ★ | ★ | ★ | ★ | ★ | ★ | ★ | ★ | ★ | ★ | ★ | ★ | ★ |
| Wisconsin | ... | ... | ... | ... | ★ | ... | ★ | S | ... | ... | ★ | ★ | ★ | E | ... |
| Wyoming | E | ★ | ... | ★ | ★ | ★ | ★ | ★ | ★ | ... | ... | ★ | ★ | ★ | ★ |
| Dist. of Columbia | E | ★ | ★ | ... | ... | ★ | ★ | ★ | ★ | ★ | E | ★ | ★ | E | ★ |

*Source:* Louis Phillips & Associates, Duluth, GA.
*Key:*
★ — Required.
E — Enabling legislation.
S — Under certain circumstances.
... — No requirements.

## Table 7.32
## MINIMUM AGE FOR SPECIFIED ACTIVITIES

| State or other jurisdiction | Age of majority (b) | Minimum age for marriage with consent (a) | | Minimum age for making a will | Minimum age for buying alcohol | Minimum age for serving on a jury | Minimum age for leaving school (c) |
|---|---|---|---|---|---|---|---|
| | | Male | Female | | | | |
| Alabama | 18 | 14 (d,e) | 14 (d,e) | 18 | 21 | 19 | 16 |
| Alaska | 18 | 16 (f) | 16 (f) | 18 | 21 | 18 | 16 |
| Arizona | 18 | 16 (f) | 16 (f) | 18 | 21 | 18 | 16 (g) |
| Arkansas | 18 | 17 (f,h) | 16 (f,h) | 18 | 21 | 18 | 17 |
| California | 18 | (i) | (i) | 18 | 21 | 18 | 18 |
| Colorado | 18 | 16 (f) | 16 (f) | 18 | 21 | 18 | 16 |
| Connecticut | 18 | 16 (f) | 16 (f) | 18 | 21 | 18 | 16 |
| Delaware | 18 | 18 (h) | 16 (h) | 18 | 21 | 18 | 16 |
| Florida | 18 | 16 (d,h ) | 16 (d,h ) | 18 | 21 | 18 | 16 |
| Georgia | 16 | 16 (h) | 16 (h) | 14 | 21 | 18 | 16 |
| Hawaii | 16 | 15 (f) | 15 (f) | 18 | 21 | 18 | 18 (j) |
| Idaho | 18 | 16 (f) | 16 (f) | 18 (k) | 21 | 18 | 16 |
| Illinois | 18 | 16 (l) | 16 (l) | 18 | 21 | 18 | 16 |
| Indiana | 18 | 18 (f,h) | 18 (f,h) | 18 (m) | 21 | 18 | 18 (n) |
| Iowa | 18 | 18 (f) | 18 (f) | 18 | 21 | 18 | 16 |
| Kansas | 18 | 14 | 12 | 18 | 21 | 18 | 18 |
| Kentucky | 18 | 18 (f) | 18 (f) | 18 | 21 | 18 | 16 (n) |
| Louisiana | 18 | 18 (f) | 18 (f) | 18 | 21 | 18 | 17 |
| Maine | 18 | 18 (f) | 18 (f) | 18 | 21 | 18 | 17 |
| Maryland | 18 | 18 (h,o) | 18 (h,o) | 18 | 21 | 18 | 16 |
| Massachusetts | 18 | 14 (p) | 12 (p) | 18 | 21 | 18 | 16 |
| Michigan | 18 | 16 | 16 | 18 | 21 | 18 | 16 |
| Minnesota | 18 | 16 (f) | 16 (f) | 18 | 21 | 18 | 16 (r) |
| Mississippi | (q) | (i,p) | (i,p) | 18 | 21 | 21 | 17 |
| Missouri | 18 | 15 (s) | 15 (s) | 18 (t) | 21 | 21 | 16 |
| Montana | 18 | 16 (f) | 16 (f) | 18 | 21 | 18 | 16 (u) |
| Nebraska | 17 | 17 | 17 | 18 | 21 | 19 | 16 |
| Nevada | 18 | 16 (f) | 16 (f) | 18 | 21 | 18 | 17 |
| New Hampshire | 18 | 18 (v) | 18 (v) | 18 (w) | 21 | 18 | 16 |
| New Jersey | 18 | 16 (f,h) | 16 (f,h) | 18 | 21 | 18 | 16 |
| New Mexico | 18 | 16 (h,s) | 16 (h,s) | 18 | 21 | 18 | 18 |
| New York | 18 | 16 (v) | 16 (v) | 18 | 21 | 18 | 16 (x) |
| North Carolina | 18 | 16 (h) | 16 (h) | 18 | 21 | 18 | 16 |
| North Dakota | 18 | 16 | 16 | 18 | 21 | 18 | 16 |
| Ohio | 18 | 18 (f,h) | 16 (f,h) | 18 | 21 | 18 | 18 |
| Oklahoma | 18 | 16 (f,h) | 16 (f,h) | 18 | 21 | 18 | 18 |
| Oregon | 18 | 17 (y) | 17 (y) | 18 (z) | 21 | 18 | 18 |
| Pennsylvania | 18 | 16 (s) | 16 (s) | 18 | 21 | 18 | 17 |
| Rhode Island | 18 | 18 (s) | 16 (s) | 18 | 21 | 18 | 16 |
| South Carolina | 18 | 16 (h) | 14 (h) | 18 (aa) | 21 | 18 | 17 |
| South Dakota | 18 | 16 | 16 | 18 | 21 | 18 | 16 (u) |
| Tennessee | 18 | 16 (s) | 16 (s) | 18 | 21 | 18 | 17 |
| Texas | 18 | 14(p,v) | 14 (p,v) | 18 (bb) | 21 | 18 | 17 |
| Utah | 18 (cc) | 16 (d,f) | 16 (d,f) | 18 | 21 | 18 | 18 |
| Vermont | 18 | 16 (f) | 16 (f) | 18 | 21 | 18 | 16 |
| Virginia | 18 | 16 (h) | 16 (h) | 18 | 21 | 18 | 18 |
| Washington | 18 | 17 (s) | 17 (s) | 18 | 21 | 18 | 18 (dd) |
| West Virginia | 18 | 18 (h) | 18 (h) | 18 | 21 | 18 | 16 |
| Wisconsin | 18 | 16 | 16 | 18 | 21 | 18 | 18 |
| Wyoming | 18 | 16 (s) | 16 (s) | 18 | 21 | 18 | 16 |
| Dist. of Columbia | 18 | 16 (d ) | 16 (d) | 18 | 21 | 18 | 18 |
| Puerto Rico | 21 (h) | 18 (h,s) | 16 (h,s) | N.A. | N.A. | 18 | 18 |

See footnotes at end of table.

# MINIMUM AGE FOR SPECIFIED ACTIVITIES — Continued

*Sources*: The Century Council; Education Commission of the States, *Clearinghouse Notes*, March 2000, www.ecs.org ; National Center for State Courts; Gary Skoloff, Skoloff & Wolfe; state statutes.

N.A. — Not available

(a) With parental consent. Minimum age for marrying without consent is 18 years in all states, except in Nebraska where the minimum age is 17 and Puerto Rico where the minimum age is 21.

(b) Generally, the age at which an individual has legal control over own actions and business (e.g., ability to contract) except as otherwise provided by statute. In many states, age of majority is arrived at upon marriage if minimum legal marrying age is lower than prescribed age of majority.

(c) Without graduating.

(d) Parental consent not required if minor was previously married.

(e) Other statutory requirements apply.

(f) Younger persons may marry with parental consent and/or permission of judge. In Connecticut judicial approval.

(g) Or completed 10th grade.

(h) Younger persons may obtain license in case of pregnancy or birth of child.

(i) No age limits.

(j) Students over the age of 16 can withdraw with the approval of both the principal and the student's guardian, and if an alternative education program exists.

(k) Or any emancipated minor

(l) Judicial consent may be given when parents refuse to consent.

(m) Or who is younger and a member of the armed forces, or of the merchant marine of the United States, or its allies, may make a will

(n) An individual in Indiana is required to stay in school until he or she: is between 16 and 18 and meets the requirement for an exit interview; or reaches at least 18 years of age. Withdrawal before 18 requires guardian's and principal's written permission. In Kentucky, must have parental signature for leaving school between the ages of 16 and 18.

(o) If parties are at least 16, proof of age and the consent of parents in person is required. If a parent is ill, an affidavit by the incapacitated parent and a physician's affidavit required.

(p) Parental consent and/or permission of judge required. In Massachusetts, under 18 requires court authority.

(q) Age of consent 17 for males and 15 for females.

(r) Beginning in the 2000-2001 school year " every child between 7 and 18 years of age shall receive instruction..."

(s) Younger parties may obtain license in special circumstances.

(t) Or any minor emancipated by adjudication, marriage or entry into active military duty.

(u) Montana and South Dakota require that a child shall remain in school until the later of either the child's 16th birthday or the date of completion of the work of the eighth grade.

(v) Below age of consent parties need parental consent and permission of judge, no younger than 14 for males and 13 for females (14 in New York).

(w) Married persons under 18.

(x) Age 17 in New York City and Buffalo.

(y) If a party has no parent residing within state, and one party has residence within state for 6 months no permission required.

(z) Or lawfully married.

(aa) Or married or emancipated as decreed by family court.

(bb) Or who is or has been lawfully married, or who is a member of the armed forces of the United States or of the auxiliaries thereof or of the maritime service.

(cc) Authorizes counties to provide for premarital counseling as a requisite to issuance of license to persons under 19 and persons previously divorced.

(dd) Early withdrawal possible if the student is age 16 or older, is regularly and lawfully employed, has met graduation requirements, or has received a certificate of educational competence.

## Table 7.33
## STATE MOTOR VEHICLE REGISTRATIONS: 1998

| State or other jurisdiction | (a) Automobiles | (a,b) Buses | Trucks | (a) Motorcycles | Total registrations 1996 | Total registrations 1998 | Percentage change |
|---|---|---|---|---|---|---|---|
| United States ............. | 131,838,538* | 715,540* | 79,062,475* | 3,879,450 | 210,236,393* | 215,496,003* | 2.4 |
| Alabama ....................... | 2,062,734 | 8,641 | 1,787,553 | 44,540 | 3,360,389 | 3,903,468 | 13.9 |
| Alaska ......................... | 232,170 | 2,196 | 311,499 | 13,695 | 544,139 | 559,560 | 2.8 |
| Arizona ....................... | 1,728,185 | 4,454 | 1,211,377 | 54,373 | 3,054,396 | 2,998,389 | -1.9 |
| Arkansas ..................... | 928,958 | 5,995 | 819,262 | 21,070 | 1,649,833 | 1,775,285 | 7.1 |
| California ..................... | 16,174,220 | 45,426 | 9,380,604 | 403,971 | 25,727,755 | 26,004,221 | 1.1 |
| Colorado ...................... | 1,843,385 | 5,720 | 1,616,989 | 97,236 | 3,527,504 | 3,563,330 | 1.1 |
| Connecticut .................. | 1,998,457 | 9,739 | 692,437 (c) | 50,594 | 2,657,159 | 2,751,227 | 3.4 |
| Delaware ...................... | 416,709 | 2,011 | 197,772 | 10,174 | 602,992 | 626,666 | 3.8 |
| Florida ......................... | 7,437,597 | 43,077 | 3,795,715 | 221,966 | 11,091,930 | 11,498,355 | 3.6 |
| Georgia ........................ | 4,032,998 | 17,068 | 2,843,253 | 85,552 | 6,356,164 | 6,978,871 | 9 |
| Hawaii ......................... | 449,731 | 4,107 | 249,998 | 20,445 | 811,031 | 724,281 | -11.9 |
| Idaho ........................... | 501,509 | 3,604 | 613,780 | 34,530 | 1,095,159 | 1,153,423 | 5.1 |
| Illinois ......................... | 6,425,276 | 17,508 | 2,863,926 | 204,225 | 8,987,967 | 9,510,935 | 5.5 |
| Indiana ........................ | 3,273,026 | 25,905 | 2,072,722 | 102,848 | 5,312,090 | 5,474,501 | 3 |
| Iowa ............................ | 1,737,582 | 8,103 | 1,307,450 | 128,540 | 3,001,296 | 3,181,675 | 5.7 |
| Kansas ......................... | 1,127,367 | 3,804 | 990,239 | 47,634 | 2,158,649 | 2,169,044 | 0.5 |
| Kentucky ...................... | 1,715,524 | 12,034 | 1,117,054 | 39,901 | 2,732,588 | 2,884,513 | 5.3 |
| Louisiana ..................... | 1,966,954 | 20,926 | 1,442,837 | 39,638 | 3,334,328 | 3,470,355 | 4 |
| Maine .......................... | 565,338 | 2,899 | 361,368 | 28,117 | 985,427 | 957,722 | -2.8 |
| Maryland ...................... | 2,621,923 | 11,736 | 1,116,616 | 42,636 | 3,672,515 | 3,792,911 | 3.2 |
| Massachusetts ............... | 3,782,940 | 11,554 | 1,364,674 | 99,583 | 4,793,293 | 5,258,751 | · 8.9 |
| Michigan ...................... | 5,104,781 | 25,142 | 2,998,227 | 154,358 | 8,160,367 | 8,282,508 | 1.5 |
| Minnesota ..................... | 2,412,412 | 14,719 | 1,750,710 | 128,097 | 3,977,083 | 4,305,938 | 7.7 |
| Mississippi ................... | 1,250,200 | 10,185 | 995,359 | 31,138 | 2,211,889 | 2,286,882 | 3.3 |
| Missouri ....................... | 2,600,722 | 13,166 | 1,763,632 | 53,653 | 4,404,558 | 4,431,173 | 0.7 |
| Montana ....................... | 458,116 | 2,798 | 527,363 | 21,582 | 993,942 | 1,009,859 | 1.6 |
| Nebraska ...................... | 834,188 | 5,559 | 686,251 | 18,662 | 1,497,154 | 1,544,660 | 3.1 |
| Nevada ......................... | 665,940 | 1,706 | 552,631 | 24,709 | 1,118,147 | 1,244,986 | 10.2 |
| New Hampshire .............. | 687,770 | 1,735 | 348,960 (c) | 46,040 | 1,164,003 | 1,084,505 | -7.3 |
| New Jersey .................... | 4,215,195 | 19,581 | 1,545,560 (c) | 100,564 | 5,913,531 | 5,880,900 | -0.5 |
| New Mexico ................... | 821,031 | 3,632 | 770,129 | 32,364 | 1,576,211 | 1,627,156 | 3.2 |
| New York ...................... | 7,664,320 | 48,636 | 2,709,077 (c) | 138,846 | 10,771,848 | 10,560,879 | -1.9 |
| North Carolina ............... | 3,530,711 | 30,739 | 2,300,380 | 75,002 | 5,827,089 | 5,936,832 | 1.9 |
| North Dakota ................. | 330,275 | 2,299 | 339,584 | 16,167 | 695,441 | 688,325 | -1 |
| Ohio ............................ | 6,664,356 | 35,530 | 3,339,602 | 229,306 | 9,990,203 | 10,268,794 | 2.8 |
| Oklahoma ..................... | 1,548,949 | 15,935 | 1,354,302 | 53,326 | 3,140,933 | 2,972,512 | -5.6 |
| Oregon ......................... | 1,588,313 | 12,755 | 1,378,996 | 64,506 | 2,911,889 | 3,044,570 | 4.4 |
| Pennsylvania ................. | 6,131,725 | 35,309 | 2,811,780 (c) | 191,073 | 8,758,765 | 9,169,887 | 4.5 |
| Rhode Island ................. | 522,292 | 1,831 | 190,894 (c) | 17,673 | 712,976 | 732,690 | 2.7 |
| South Carolina ............... | 1,822,640 | 15,399 | 1,055,022 | 41,116 | 2,829,794 | 2,934,177 | 3.6 |
| South Dakota ................. | 381,752 | 2,696 | 384,059 | 25,210 | 775,805 | 793,717 | 2.3 |
| Tennessee ..................... | 2,695,539 | 17,576 | 1,755,950 | 59,620 | 4,909,351 | 4,528,685 | -8.4 |
| Texas ........................... | 7,455,714 | 80,091 | 5,788,362 | 149,175 | 13,635,683 | 13,473,342 | -1.2 |
| Utah ............................ | 850,487 | 1,232 | 680,534 | 24,470 | 1,468,259 | 1,556,723 | 5.7 |
| Vermont ....................... | 295,664 | 1,931 | 198,558 | 16,684 | 521,395 | 512,837 | -1.6 |
| Virginia ........................ | 3,774,372 | 17,783 | 2,026,139 | 57,582 | 5,633,643 | 5,875,876 | 4.2 |
| Washington ................... | 2,776,482 | 9,088 | 2,038,417 | 106,352 | 4,707,100 | 4,930,339 | 4.6 |
| West Virginia ................. | 776,583 | 3,299 | 597,953 | 22,496 | 1,422,360 | 1,400,331 | -1.5 |
| Wisconsin ..................... | 2,544,109 | 13,438 | 1,645,772 | 170,329 | 4,141,144 | 4,373,648 | 5.4 |
| Wyoming ...................... | 219,220 | 2,661 | 337,110 | 15,799 | 577,002 | 574,790 | -0.3 |
| Dist. of Columbia ............ | 192,097 | 2,582 | 34,037 | 1,562 | 239,015 | 230,278 | -3.7 |
| Puerto Rico ................... | 1,962,378 | 3,418 | 27,869 | 33,502 | N.A. | 2,027,167 | N.A. |

*Source*: Federal Highway Administration. U.S. Department of Transportation (1998). Compiled for the calendar year ending Dec. 31, 1998 from reports of state authorities.
*Figures do not include Puerto Rico.
N.A. = Not available
(a) Includes federal, state, county and municipal vehicles. Vehicles owned by the military services are not included.
(b) The numbers of private and commercial buses given here are estimates by the Federal Highway Administration of the numbers in operation, rather than registration counts of the states.

(c) The following farm trucks, registered at a nominal fee and restricted to use in the vicinity of the owner's farm, are not included in this table: Connecticut, 5,546; New Hampshire, 5,163; New Jersey, 6,730; New York, 30,509; Pennsylvania, 22,852; and Rhode Island, 1,137.

## Table 7.34
## MOTOR VEHICLE OPERATORS LICENSES: 1998

| State or other jurisdiction | Years for which issued | Renewal date | Amount of fee | Total licensed drivers during 1998 (in thousands) |
|---|---|---|---|---|
| Alabama | 4 | Issuance | $20.00 (a) | 3,434,117 |
| Alaska | 5 | Birthday | 15.00 | 456,891 |
| Arizona | until 60th Birthday | Birthday | 10.00 - 25.00 | 3,198,276 |
| Arkansas | 4 | Birthday | 14.00 | 1,918,451 |
| California | 5 | Birthday | 15.00 | 20,498,902 |
| Colorado | 5 | Birthday | 15.00 | 2,946,476 |
| Connecticut | 4 | Birthday | 28.75 - 43.50 | 2,349,28 |
| Delaware | 5 | Birthday | 12.50 | 545,872 |
| Florida | 4 or 6 | Birthday | 20.00 (b) | 12,026,947 |
| Georgia | 4 | Birthday | 10.00-15.00 | 5,315,739 |
| Hawaii | 2, 4, 6 (c) | Birthday | (d) | 746,329 |
| Idaho | 4 | Birthday | 20.50 | 862,674 |
| Illinois | 4 and 5 | Birthday | 10.00 | 7,700,880 |
| Indiana | 3 and 4 (d) | Birth month | 6.00 (d) | 3,976,241 |
| Iowa | 2 and 4 (d) | Birthday | 16.00 (d) | 1,950,374 |
| Kansas | 4 and 6 | Birthday | 8.00 - 18.00 (a) | 1,851,449 |
| Kentucky | 4 | Birth month | 8.00 | 2,640,335 |
| Louisiana | 4 | Birthday | 18.00 | 2,736,305 |
| Maine | 6 | Birthday | 30.00 | 912,506 |
| Maryland | 5 | Birthday | 30.00 | 3,177,783 |
| Massachusetts | 5 | Birthday | 33.75 (a) | 4,394,355 |
| Michigan | 4 | Birthday | 13.00 | 6,802,704 |
| Minnesota | 4 | Birthday | 18.50 - 37.50 | 2,868,002 |
| Mississippi | 4 and 1 (e) | Birthday | 20.00 | 1,758,293 |
| Missouri | 3 | Issuance | 7.50 | 3,798,096 |
| Montana | 4 and 8 | Birthday | 16.00 - 32.00 | 646,512 |
| Nebraska | 5 | Birthday | 18.75 | 1,185,794 |
| Nevada | 4 | Birthday | 15.50 - 20.50 | 1,245,905 |
| New Hampshire | 4 | Birthday | 32.00 | 907,479 |
| New Jersey | 4 | Issuance | 16.00 - 18.00 | 5,563,492 |
| New Mexico | 4 | Birthday | 16.00 | 1,203,869 |
| New York | 5 | Birthday | 28.00 | 10,554,098 |
| North Carolina | 5 | Birthday | 12.50 | 5,534,284 |
| North Dakota | 4 | Birthday | 10.00 | 454,933 |
| Ohio | 4 | Birthday | 10.75 | 7,941,479 |
| Oklahoma | 4 | Issuance | 19.00 | 2,305,361 |
| Oregon | 4 | Birthday | 26.25 | 2,417,002 |
| Pennsylvania | 4 | Birth month | 29.00 (d) | 8,404,689 |
| Rhode Island | 5 | Birthday | 30.00 | 681,832 |
| South Carolina | 5 | Birthday | 12.50 | 2,679,131 |
| South Dakota | 5 | Birthday | 8.00 | 535,339 |
| Tennessee | 5 | Birthday | 19.50 | 4,072,836 |
| Texas | 4,5,6 | Birthday (f) | 16.00 - 24.00 (f) | 13,322,911 |
| Utah | 5 | Birthday | 15.00 - 20.00 | 1,393,242 |
| Vermont | 2 or 4 | Birthday | 12.00 - 20.00 | 497,172 |
| Virginia | 5 | Birth month | 12.00 | 4,787,150 |
| Washington | 4 | Birthday | 14.00 | 4,078,895 |
| West Virginia | 5 | Birthday | 13.00 | 1,280,539 |
| Wisconsin | 8 | Birthday | 18.00 - 64.00 | 3,709,957 |
| Wyoming | 4 | Birthday | 20.00 | 359,158 |
| Dist. of Columbia | 4 | Birthday | 20.00 | 349,835 |

*Sources*: AAA, *Digest of Motor Laws* (1999); U.S. Department of Transportation, *Federal Highway Administration, Highway Statistics, 1998*. Status of requirements as of January 1, 1999.

(a) The following examination fees are in addition to the fee shown for a license: Alabama-$5; Kansas-$3; Massachusetts-$20.

(b) Original license is $20. Renewal fee is $20 for six years if no moving violation convictions within past three years.

(c) Licenses issued for two years to persons 72 years and over. Fee for two-year licenses: $6; four-year licenses: $6. Six-year licenses $18. Four-year licenses issued to persons 15-17 years.

(d) Indiana three-year renewal license for persons 75 years and older; Iowa- $8 for two-year license for persons over 18 and under 70; Pennsylvania-$14 for two-year license for persons 65 years and over.

(e) Under 18 years, licenses expire after 1 year and cost $5.00.

(f) Licenses issued to those under 18 expire on 18th birthday. License fee is prorated with a $5 minimum.

## Table 7.35
## MOTOR VEHICLE LAWS
### (As of January 1, 2000)

| State or other jurisdiction | Plates transfer to new owner | Minimum age for driver's license Regular | Minimum age for driver's license Learner's | Child restraints mandatory for passengers under ___ years (d) | Mandatory seat belt law (e) | Liability laws (f) | Vehicle inspection (g) |
|---|---|---|---|---|---|---|---|
| Alabama | ... | 16 | 15 | 6 | ★ | S | (spot) (h) |
| Alaska | ★ | 16 | 14 | 7 | ★ | S | (spot) (h) (i) |
| Arizona | ★ | 16 (c) | 15 + 7 mo. | 5 | ★ | C | (i) |
| Arkansas | ... | 16 | 14-18 | 4 | ★ | S, NF | (h) |
| California | ★ | 18 (c) | 15 | 4 | ★ | C | (i) |
| Colorado | ... | 21 | 15 | 4 | ★ | S,NF | (i) |
| Connecticut | ... | 16 | 16 | 4 | ★ | S | ★ |
| Delaware | ★ | 16 (b) | 15 +10 mo. | 4 | ★ | S,NF | ★ |
| Florida | ... | 16 | 15 | 6 | ★ | NF | (i) |
| Georgia | ... | 16 | 15 | 4 | ★ | C | (i) |
| Hawaii | ★ | 15 | 15 | 4 | ★ | S, NF | (h) |
| Idaho | ... | 17 | 15 | 4 | ★ | S,C | (i) |
| Illinois | ... | 18 | 15 | 4 | ★ | S | ★ |
| Indiana | ... | 16.5 | 16 | 4 | ★ | C | (i) |
| Iowa | ... | 18 (c) | 14 | 3 | ★ | S | (spot) (h) (i) |
| Kansas | ... | 16 | 14 | 4 | ★ | NF,UM | (spot) (h) |
| Kentucky | ★ | 16 | 16 | (d) | ★ | C,NF | (i) |
| Louisiana | ... | 15 | 15 | 5 | ★ | C | ★ |
| Maine | ... | 21 | 15 | 4 | ★ | C | ★ |
| Maryland | ... | 16 + 1 mo. | 15 + 9 mo. | 4 | ★ | C,NF | ★ |
| Massachusetts | ... | 16 | 16 | 12 | ★ | C,NF | ★ |
| Michigan | ... | 18 (c) | 16 | 4 | ★ | C,NF | (spot) (h) |
| Minnesota | ★ | 18 | 15 | 4 | ★ | C,NF | (spot) (h) (i) |
| Mississippi | ... | 16 | 15 | 4 | ★ | S,F | (h) |
| Missouri | ... | 16 | 15 | 4 | ★ | C | ★ |
| Montana | ... | 16 | ... | 4 | ★ | C | ... |
| Nebraska | ... | 17 | 15 | 4 | ★ | F | ... |
| Nevada | ... | 16 | 15 | 5 | ★ | F,C | ★ |
| New Hampshire | ... | 18 | ... | 4 | ★ | S,F | (h) |
| New Jersey | ... | 17 | 16 + 5 mo. | 5 | ★ | S,NF,UJ | ★ |
| New Mexico | ... | 16 | 15 | 11 | ★ | C | ... |
| New York | ... | 18 | 16 | 4 | ★ | S,C,NF | ★ |
| North Carolina | ... | 16 (c) | 15 | 3 | ★ | S,C | ★ |
| North Dakota | ... | 16 | 14 | 4 | ★ | S,NF,UM,UJ,C | (spot) (h) |
| Ohio | ... | 18 | 15 1/2 | 4 | ★ | C | (spot) (h) (i) |
| Oklahoma | ★ | 16 | 15 1/2 | 4 | ★ | S,C | ★ |
| Oregon | ★ | 16 | 15 | 4 | ★ | F,C,NF | (spot) (h) (i) |
| Pennsylvania | ... | 16 | 16 | 4 | ★ | C | ★ |
| Rhode Island | ... | 16 | 16 | 4 | ★ | S | ★ |
| South Carolina | ★ | 16 | 15 | 6 | ★ | C,UM | ... |
| South Dakota | ★ | 16 | 14 | 5 | ★ | C,UM | ... |
| Tennessee | ... | 16 | 15 | 4 | ★ | S,F | ★ |
| Texas | ★ | 18 | 15 | 2 | ★ | S,F,C,UM | ★ |
| Utah | ... | 16 | 15+9 mo. | 10 | ★ | S,UM | ★ |
| Vermont | ... | 18 | 15 | 5 | ★ | S | ★ |
| Virginia | ... | 18 | 15 | 4 | ★ | S,UM | ★ |
| Washington | ★ | 18 | 15 + 6 mo. | 3 | ★ | S,F,C | (i) |
| West Virginia | ... | 16 | 15 | 9 | ★ | S,C | (h) |
| Wisconsin | ... | 18 | 15 + 6 mo. | 4 | ★ | S | (spot) (h) (i) |
| Wyoming | ... | 16 | 15 | 5 | ★ | S,C | ... |
| Dist. of Columbia | ... | 16 | 16 | 3 | ★ | C | ★ |
| American Samoa | ★ | 16 | 16 | ★ | ★ | C | (h) |
| Guam | ... | 16 | 15 | 2 | ★ | S | ★ |
| Puerto Rico | ★ | 16 | 16 | 4 | ★ | C | ★ |
| U.S. Virgin Islands | ★ | 18 | ... | 5 | ★ | UJ | (h) |

See footnotes at end of table.

# MOTOR VEHICLE LAWS — Continued

*Source*: AAA, *Digest of Motor Laws* (2000) edition.

Key:

★ — Provision.

. . . — No provision.

(a) Some states reduce the minimun age requirement if applicants meet certain criteria (e.g., they have completed a driver education course or financial hardship). Generally, this table lists the minimum age requirement without such exceptions.

(b) New drivers or permit holders are typically required to have a guardian or parental consent to get their license or permit. They may be required to be enrolled in or have completed a driver education course. When they drive, they may be required to be accompanied by a licensed operator or an adult over 21. New drivers may also be restricted from driving between certain hours (e.g., 11 p.m. - 6 a.m.) and carrying a certain number of passengers.

(c) Graduated driver's license system.

(d) The type of child restraint (safety seat or seat belt) required typically depends on the age of the child. It can mean a federally approved child's safety seat. The majority of states allow for substituting adult safety belts by age 5. Other restrictions include height or weight requirements; typically children under 40 pounds or 40 inches tall.

(e) These states have enacted mandatory seat belt legislation. These laws vary as to whether they cover front seat occupants, back seat occupants or both. There are exceptions for the age, weight or height of the occupants in a vehicle and the type of vehicle (e.g., taxicabs).

(f) Most jurisidictions have a non-resident service of process law. Some have a guest suit law. In this column only: S–"Security-type" financial responsibility law (following accident report, each driver/owner of the vehicles involved must show ability to pay damages which may be charged in subsequent legal actions arising from accident); F–"Future-proof type" financial responsibility law (persons who have been convicted of certain serious traffic offenses or who have failed to pay a judgement against them for damages arising from an accident must make a similar showing of financial responsibility); C–"Compulsory insurance" law (typically, motorists must show proof of financial responsibility liability insurance usually as a condition of vehicle registration); NF–"No-fault insurance" law (vehicle owner looks to own insurance company for reimbursement for accident damages, rather than having to prove in court that the other party was responsible); UJ–"Unsatisfied judgement funds" law (state-operated funds financed with fees from motorists unable to provide evidence of insurance or from assessments levied on auto insurance companies to cover pedestrians and others who do not have no-fault insurance); UM–"Uninsured motorist" law (insurance companies must offer coverage against potential damage by uninsured motorists).

(g) "Spot" indicates spot check, usually for reasonable cause, or random roadside inspection for defective or missing equipment.

(h) Safety inspection. Inspections can be limited to certain counties or municipalities. Inspections can be limited to certain vehicles (e.g., commercial trucks) and certain vehicle model years.

(i) Emission inspections. Inspections can be limited to certain counties or municipalities. Inspections can be limited to certain vehicles (e.g., commercial trucks) and certain vehicle model years.

## Table 7.36
## STATE NO-FAULT MOTOR VEHICLE INSURANCE PROVISIONS

| State or other jurisdiction | Purchase of Personal Injury Protection (PIP) | Minimum tort liablity threshold (a) | Maximum first-party benefits | | | |
|---|---|---|---|---|---|---|
| | | | Medical | Income loss | Replacement services | Survivors/funeral/ death benefits |
| Colorado ......... | M | $2,500 | $50,000 within 5 years (additional $50,000 for rehabilitation expenses incurred within 10 yrs. of accident). | Up to $400/wk for up to 52 weeks | Up to $25/day for up to 52 wks. | $1,000 |
| Florida .............. | M | No dollar threshold. | ----------------$10,000 overal max. on first party benefits---------------- 80% of all costs. | 60% of lost income. | Limited only by total benefits limit. | Funeral benefit: $5,000 |
| Hawaii .............. | M | $5,000 | ------------------generally, $10,000 per person aggregate---------------- | Optional PIP - $500/ mo. or $3,000/ accident up to $2,000/ mo.or $12,000/ accident | | Optional PIP - death benefits: $25,000 up to $100,000. Funeral: $2,000 |
| Kansas .............. | M | $2,000 | $4,500 (additional $4,500 for rehabilitation). | Up to $900/mo. for one yr. (if benefits not subject to taxes, max. 85% of lost income). | $25/day for 365days. | Up to $900/mo. for lost income and replacement services for up to one yr., less disability payments received before death. Funeral benefit: $2,000. |
| Kentucky .......... | M | $1,000 | ----------------$10,000 overall max. on first-party benefits--------------- Limited only by total benefits limit. | Up to $200/wk. (If not subject to taxes, benefits can be reduced max. 15%). | Up to $200/wk. | Up to $200/wk. each for survivors' economic loss and survivors' replacement services loss. Funeral benefit: $1,000 |
| Massachusetts . | M | $2,000 | ----------------$8,000 overall max. on first-party benefits--------------- Limited only by total benefits limit, if incurred within 2 yrs. | Up to 75% of lost income. | Up to 75% of actual loss. | Funeral benefit: limited only by total benefits limit. |
| Michigan .......... | M | No dollar threshold. | No dollar limits. | Up to 85% up to $3,760 /mo up to 3 yrs. | $20/day for up to 3 yrs. | Up to 85% up to $3,760/mo up to 3 yrs. for survivors. Funeral benefits: $1,750 - $5,000 |
| Minnesota ........ | M | $4,000 | --------$20,000 max. for first-party benefits other than medical-------- $20,000 | 85% of lost income up to $250/wk. | $200/wk., beginning 8 days after accident. | Up to $200/wk. ea. for survivors' economic loss and survivors' replacement service loss. Funeral benefit: $2,000. |
| New Jersey ....... | M | (b) | Max $250,000. Subject to $250 deductible and 20% co-payment for the first $5,000. | Up to $100/wk. for one year, to a maximum total benefit of $2,500 | Up to $12/day for a max. of $4,380 | Death benefits equal to the income loss that would have been paid had the injured party not died. Funeral benefit: $1,000 |
| New York .......... | M | No dollar threshold. | ----------------$50,000 overall max. on first-party benefits--------------- Limited only by total benefits limit. | 80% of lost income up to $2,000/mo. for up to 3 yrs. | $25/day for up to one yr. | $2,000 in addition to other benefits. |
| North Dakota ... | M | $2,500 | ----------------$30,000 overall max. on first-party benefits--------------- Limited only by total benefits limit. | 85% of lost income up to $150/wk. | Up to $15/day. | Up to $150/wk. for survivors' income loss and $15/day for survivors' replacement services. Funeral benefit: $3,500. |

## STATE NO-FAULT MOTOR VEHICLE INSURANCE PROVISIONS — Continued

| State or other jurisdiction | Purchase of Personal Injury Protection (PIP) | Minimum tort liablity threshold (a) | Maximum first-party benefits | | | |
|---|---|---|---|---|---|---|
| | | | Medical | Income loss | Replacement services | Survivors/funeral/ death benefits |
| Utah ................. | M | $3,000 | $3,000 | 85% of lost income up to $250/wk. for up to 52 wks., subject to 3-day elimination period | $20/day for up to 365 days subject to 3-day elimination period | $3,000 survivors benefit. Funeral benefit: $1,500. |
| Puerto Rico ...... | | No dollar threshold. | All reasonable medical expenses within 2 yrs. | Between $50 and 100/ wk for up to 52 weeks | | $10,000 for death within 1 yr. of accident. Funeral benefit: $1,000 |

*Source:* This Table was compiled from 1998 and 1999 material provided by the the National Association of Insurance Commissioners , NAIC's No Fault Study, 1999, used with permission; the Alliance of American Insurers, Compendium of Insurance Charts-Automobile-Property, © 1999 by Alliance of American Insurers, used with permission, all rights reserved and the Insurance Information Institute, Insurance Issues Update, December 1998.

*Definitions:* The December 1998 *Insurance Issues Update* declares "the term 'no-fault' auto insurance is used loosely to denote any auto insurance program that allows policyholders to recover financial losses from their own insurance companies, regardless of fault. But, in its strictest form, no-fault applies only to states laws that provide for the payment of no-fault first party benefits and restrict the right to sue. Under current no-fault laws, motorists may sue for severe injuries and for pain and suffering only if the case meets certain conditions. These conditions,known as a threshold, relate to the severity of the injury. They may be expressed in verbal terms (a descriptive or verbal threshold) or in dollar amounts of medical bills, a monetary threshold. Some laws also include the days of disablity incurred as a result of the accident."

Using this definition, the Insurance Information Institute and the NAIC report that 13 states and Puerto Rico had true no-fault insurance laws as of 1999. The 13 states are Colorado, Florida, Hawaii, Kansas, Kentucky, Massachusetts, Michigan, Minnesota, New Jersey, New York, North Dakota, Pennsylvania and Utah.

The NAIC reports that Hawaii replaced its No-Fault insurance law with Act 275 of 1998. The only remnant of no-fault in Hawaii's system is the PIP component. Certain coverages that were once mandatory are now optional, including wage loss, death benefits, funeral benefits, collision and uninsured motorists.

The Insurance Institute says Florida, Michigan, New Jersey, New York and Pennsylvania have verbal thresholds. Colorado, Hawaii, Kansas, Kentucky, Massachusetts, Minnesota, North Dakota and Utah use a monetary threshold. The Institute reports that three states have a "choice" no-fault law. In New Jersey, Pennsylvania and Kentucky, motorists may reject the lawsuit threshold and retain the right to sue for any auto-related injury.

*Key:*
O - Optional
M - Mandatory

(a) Generally, this refers to minimum amount of medical expenses necessary before victim can sue for general damages (e.g. "pain and suffering"). In some states, a victim cannot recover unless economic loss exceeds a specific amount or an injury results in conditions that are cited in state law, (e.g., permanent disfigurement, disability, dismemberment, fractures, etc.).

(b) Motorists choose one of two optional limitations.

## Table 7.37
## STATE PUBLIC UTILITY COMMISSIONS

| State or other jurisdiction | Regulatory authority | Members Number | Members Selection | Selection of Chair | Length of commissioners' terms (in years) | Number of full-time employees |
|---|---|---|---|---|---|---|
| Alabama | Public Service Commission | 3 | E | E | 4 | 130 |
| Alaska | Regulatory Commission of Alaska | 5 | GL | G | 6 | 55 |
| Arizona | Corporation Commission | 3 | E | C | 6 | 296.5 |
| Arkansas** | Public Service Commission | 3 | GS | G | 6 | 100 |
| California | Public Utilities Commission | 5 | GS | G | 6 | 891 |
| Colorado | Public Utilities Commission | 3 | GS | G | 4 | 95 |
| Connecticut | Department of Public Utility Control | 5 | GL | C | 4 | 153 |
| Delaware** | Public Service Commission | 5 | GS | G | 5 | 24 |
| Florida | Public Service Commission | 5 | GS (a) | C | 4 | 401 |
| Georgia** | Public Service Commission | 5 | E | (b) | 6 | 135 |
| Hawaii* | Public Utilities Commission | 3 | GS | G | 6 | 31 |
| Idaho** | Public Utilities Commission | 3 | GS | C | 6 | 57 |
| Illinois | Commerce Commission | 7 | GS | G | 5 | 325 |
| Indiana | Utility Regulatory Commission | 5 | G | G | 4 | 70 |
| Iowa | Utilities Board | 3 | GS | GS | 6 | 75 |
| Kansas | State Corporation Commission | 3 | GS | C | 4 | 215 |
| Kentucky | Public Service Commission | 3 | GS | G | 4 | 127 |
| Louisiana** | Public Service Commission | 5 | E | C | 6 | 108 |
| Maine | Public Utilities Commission | 3 | GS | G | 6 | 64.5 |
| Maryland** | Public Service Commission | 5 | GS | G | 5 | 135 |
| Massachusetts | Department of Telecommunications | 5 | G | G | staggered | 140 |
| Michigan | Public Service Commission | 3 | GS | G | 6 | 139 |
| Minnesota | Public Utilities Commission | 5 | GS | G | 6 | 45 |
| Mississippi | Public Service Commission | 3 | E | C | 4 | 139 |
| Missouri** | Public Service Commission | 5 | GS | G | 6 | 203 |
| Montana** | Public Service Commission | 5 | E | C | 4 | 46 |
| Nebraska | Public Service Commission | 5 | E | C | 6 | 45 |
| Nevada** | Public Service Commission | 3 | G | G | 4 | 97 |
| New Hampshire** | Public Utilities Commission | 3 | GC | GC | 6 | 70 |
| New Jersey | Board of Public Utilities | 3 | GS | G | 6 | 388 |
| New Mexico | Public Regulation Commission | 5 | E | C | 4 | 243 |
| New York | Public Service Commission | 5 | GS | G | 6 | 620 |
| North Carolina | Utilities Commission | 7 | GL | G | 8 | 140(e) |
| North Dakota | Public Service Commission | 3 | E | C | 6 | 42 |
| Ohio | Public Utilities Commission | 5 | GS (c) | G | 5 | 353 |
| Oklahoma | Corporation Commission | 3 | E | C | 6 | 454 |
| Oregon | Public Utility Commission | 3 | GS | G | 4 | 118 |
| Pennsylvania | Public Utility Commission | 5 | GS | G | 5 | 538 |
| Rhode Island | Public Utilities Commission | 3 | GS | G | 6 | 11 |
| South Carolina** | Public Service Commission | 7 | E | (b) | 4 | 128 |
| South Dakota | Public Utilities Commission | 3 | E | C | 6 | 24 |
| Tennessee | Tennessee Regulatory Authority | 3 | G, L, L | C | 6 | 84 |
| Texas | Public Utility Commission | 3 | GS | G | 6 | 242 |
| Utah | Public Service Commission (e) | 3 | GS | G | 6 | 15 |
| Vermont** | Public Service Board | 3 | GS | G | 6 | 14 |
| Virginia | State Corporation Commission | 3 | L | (b) | 6 | 560 |
| Washington | Utilities & Transportation Commission | 3 | GS | G | 6 | 160 |
| West Virginia | Public Service Commission | 3 | GS | G | 6 | 240 |
| Wisconsin | Public Service Commission | 3 | GS | G | 6 | 184.5 |
| Wyoming | Public Service Commission | 3 | GS | C | 6 | 30 |
| Dist. of Columbia** | Public Service Commission | 3 | MC | MC | 4 | 89 |
| Puerto Rico | Public Service Commission | 5 | GS | GS | 4 | 264 |
| U.S. Virgin Islands | Public Service Commission | 7(d) | G | E | 3 (d) | 4 |

*Source:* Survey by The Council of State Governments, January 2000, except as noted by * where data is from *The Book of the States 1998-99;* ** denotes information obtained from state web site.

*Note:* See Table 7.44, "Selected Regulatory Functions of State Public Utility Commissions," for information on commissions' authority.

*Key:*
G — Appointed by Governor.
GC — Appointed by Governor, with consent of the Governor's Council.
C — Elected by the Commission.
GS — Appointed by the Governor, with consent of Senate.
L — Appointed by the Legislature.
GL — Appointed by Governor, with consent of entire Legislature.
MC — Appointed by the Mayor, with consent of City Council.

E — Elected by the public.
(a) Governor chooses candidates from a list developed by a nine member nominating committee.
(b) Chairmanship rotates annually.
(c) Applicants are screened by PUC Nominating Council. Four names then provided to governor.
(d) 7 voting members; 2 non-voting members are appointed for indefinite terms.
(e) Utah has 3 separate governmental agencies involved in the regulation of public utilities.
(f) Employee numbers are authorized positions and include employees of a separate public advocacy body.

## Table 7.38
## SELECTED REGULATORY FUNCTIONS OF STATE PUBLIC UTILITY COMMISSIONS

| | Agency has authority to: | | | | | | | | | |
| State or other jurisdiction | Controls rates of privately owned utilities on sales to ultimate consumers of | | Prescribe temporary rates, pending investigation | | Require prior authorization of the changes | | Suspend proposed rate changes | | Initiate rate investigation on its own motion | |
| | Electric | Gas | Electric | Gas | Electric | Gas | Electric | Gas | Electric | Gas |
|---|---|---|---|---|---|---|---|---|---|---|
| Alabama | ★ | ★ | ★ | ★ | ★ | ★ | ★ | ★ | ★ | ★ |
| Alaska | ★ | ★ | ★ | ★ | ★ | ★ | ★ | ★ | ★ | ★ |
| Arizona | ★ | ★ | ★ | ★ | ★ | ★ | . . . | . . . | ★ | |
| Arkansas | ★ | ★ | ★ | ★ | ★ | ★ | ★ | ★ | ★ | ★ |
| California | ★ | ★ | ★ | ★ (a) | ★ | ★ | ★ | ★ | ★ | ★ |
| Colorado | ★ | ★ | ★ (b) | ★ (b) | ★ | ★ | ★ | ★ | ★ | ★ |
| Connecticut | ★ | ★ | ★ | ★ | ★ | ★ | ★ | ★ | ★ | ★ |
| Delaware | ★ | ★ | ★ | ★ | ★ | ★ | ★ | ★ | ★ | ★ |
| Florida | ★ | ★ | ★(c) | ★(c) | ★ | ★ | ★ | ★ | ★ | ★ |
| Georgia | ★ | ★ | ★ | ★ | ★ | ★ | ★ | ★ | ★ | ★ |
| Hawaii | ★ | ★ | ★ | ★ | ★ | ★ | ★ | ★ | ★ | ★ |
| Idaho | ★ | ★ | ★ | ★ | ★(d) | ★(d) | ★ | ★ | ★ | ★ |
| Illinois | ★ | ★ | ★ | ★ | ★ | ★ | ★ | ★ | ★ | ★ |
| Indiana | ★ | ★ | ★ | ★ | ★ | ★ | ★ | ★ | ★ | ★ |
| Iowa | ★ | ★ | ★ | ★ | ★ | ★ | ★ | ★ | ★ | ★ |
| Kansas | ★ | ★ | ★ | ★ | ★ | ★ | ★ | ★ | ★ | ★ |
| Kentucky | ★ | ★ | ★ | ★ | ★ | ★ | ★ | ★ | ★ | ★ |
| Louisiana | ★ | ★(e) | ★ | ★ | ★ | ★ | ★ | ★ | ★ | ★ |
| Maine | ★ | ★ | ★ | ★ | ★ | ★ | ★ | ★ | ★ | ★ |
| Maryland | ★ | ★ | ★ | ★ | ★ | ★ | ★ | ★ | ★ | ★ |
| Massachusetts | ★ | ★ | ★ | ★ | ★ | ★ | ★ | ★ | ★ | ★ |
| Michigan | ★ | ★ | ★(f) | ★(f) | ★ | ★ | (g) | (g) | ★ | ★ |
| Minnesota | ★ | ★(h) | ★ | ★ | ★ | ★ | ★ | ★ | ★ | ★ |
| Mississippi | ★ | ★ | ★ | ★ | ★ | ★ | ★ | ★ | ★ | ★ |
| Missouri | ★ | ★ | ★ | ★ | ★ | ★ | ★ | ★ | ★ | ★ |
| Montana | ★ | ★ | ★ | ★ | ★ | ★ | ★ | ★ | ★ | ★ |
| Nebraska (i) | . . . | . . . | . . . | . . . | . . . | . . . | . . . | . . . | . . . | . . . |
| Nevada | ★ | ★ | ★ | ★ | ★ | ★ | ★ | ★ | ★ | ★ |
| New Hampshire | ★ | ★ | ★ | ★ | ★ | ★ | ★ | ★ | ★ | ★ |
| New Jersey | ★ | ★ | ★ | ★ | ★ | ★ | ★ | ★ | ★ | ★ |
| New Mexico | ★ | ★ | ★(j) | ★(j) | ★ | ★ | ★ | ★ | ★ | ★ |
| New York | ★ | ★ | ★ | ★ | ★ | ★ | ★ | ★ | ★ | ★ |
| North Carolina | ★ | ★ | ★ | ★ | ★ | ★ | ★ | ★ | ★ | ★ |
| North Dakota | ★ | ★ | ★ | ★ | ★ | ★ | ★ | ★ | ★ | ★ |
| Ohio | ★ | ★ | ★ | ★ | ★ | ★ | ★ | ★ | ★ | ★ |
| Oklahoma | ★ | ★ | ★ | ★ | ★ | ★ | ★ | ★ | ★ | ★ |
| Oregon | ★ | ★ | ★ | ★ | ★ | ★ | ★ | ★ | ★ | ★ |
| Pennsylvania | ★(k) | ★(l) | ★ | ★ | ★ | ★ | ★ | ★ | ★ | ★ |
| Rhode Island | ★ | ★ | ★ | ★ | ★ | ★ | ★ | ★ | ★ | ★ |
| South Carolina | ★ | ★ | ★ | . . . | ★ | ★ | . . . | . . . | ★ | ★ |
| South Dakota | ★ | ★ | ★ | ★ | ★ | ★ | ★ | ★ | ★ | ★ |
| Tennessee | ★ | ★ | ★(j) | ★(j) | ★ | ★ | ★ | ★ | ★ | ★ |
| Texas | | | | | | | | | | |
| Public Utilities Comm. | ★ | . . . | ★ | . . . | ★ | . . . | ★ | . . . | ★ | . . . |
| Railroad Comm. | . . . | ★ | . . . | ★ | . . . | ★ | . . . | ★ | . . . | ★ |
| Utah | ★ | ★ | ★ | ★ | ★ | ★ | ★ | ★ | ★ | ★ |
| Vermont | ★ | ★ | ★ | ★ | ★ | ★ | ★ | ★ | ★ | ★ |
| Virginia | ★ | ★ | ★ | ★ | ★ | ★ | ★ | ★ | ★ | ★ |
| Washington | ★ | ★ | ★ | ★ | ★ | ★ | ★ | ★ | ★ | ★ |
| West Virginia | ★ | ★ | ★ | ★ | ★ | ★ | ★ | ★ | ★ | ★ |
| Wisconsin | ★ | ★ | ★ | ★ | ★ | ★ | (g) | (g) | ★ | ★ |
| Wyoming | ★ | ★ | ★ | ★ | ★ | ★ | ★ | ★ | ★ | ★ |
| Dist. of Columbia | ★ | ★ | ★ | ★ | ★ | ★ | ★ | ★ | ★ | ★ |
| Puerto Rico | . . . | ★ | . . . | . . . | . . . | . . . | . . . | . . . | . . . | . . . |
| U.S. Virgin Islands | . . . | . . . | ★ | . . . | ★ | . . . | . . . | . . . | . . . | . . . |

See footnotes at end of table.

## SELECTED REGULATORY FUNCTIONS OF STATE PUBLIC UTILITY COMMISSIONS — Continued

*Source*: Survey by The Council of State Governments, January 2000.
*Note*: Full names of commissions are shown on Table 7.37, "State Public Utility Commissions."

*Key*:
★ — No new data.
★— Yes
. . . — No
(a) Authority is not exercised.
(b) No specific statutory authority.
(c) Under Florida statute, utility may apply for interim increase, which must be granted if it proves that it is currently earning below the range of its last authorized rate of return.
(d) Rates become effective after expiration of suspension period if Commission does not take action.
(e) Except no authority over rates charged to industrial customers by any gas company.

(f) Interim rates may be prescribed after statutory requirements are met.
(g) Rate changes do not go into effect until approved by Commission.
(h) Rates not regulated for gas utilities serving fewer than 650 customers.
(i) Telephone is the only regulated utility with jurisdiction limited to rate increases for basic exchange service of more than 10 percent during a 12-month period. State has no private power companies. Natural gas is provided by private companies through franchise granted by each local jurisdiction.
(j) Emergency only.
(k) The Commission regulates only the distribution rates of the electric distribution company and the generation charges of the provider of last resort.
(l) The Commission regulates only the distribution rates of the natural gas distribution company and the gas supply charges of the supplier of last resort.

## Table 7.39
## LOBBYISTS: DEFINITIONS AND PROHIBITED ACTIVITIES

| State or other jurisdiction | Definition of a lobbyist includes | | | | | | | Prohibited activities involving lobbyists | | | | | |
|---|---|---|---|---|---|---|---|---|---|---|---|---|---|
| | Legislative lobbying | Administrative agency lobbying | Elective officials as lobbyists | Public employees as lobbyists | Compensation standard | Expenditure standard | Time standard | Making campaign contributions at any time | Making campaign contributions during legislative sessions | Making expenditures in excess of $ per official per year | Solicitation by officials or employees for contributions or gifts | Contingent compensation | Other |
| Alabama | ★ | ★ | ... | ★ | ... | ★ | ★ | ★ | ... | ... | ★ | ★ | ... |
| Alaska | ★ | ★ | ... | ... | ... | ... | ★ | (hh) | ★ | ... | ★ | ★ | ... |
| Arizona | ★ | ★ | ... | ... | ... | ... | ... | ... | ★ | ... | ... | ★ | (r) |
| Arkansas | ★ | ★ | ★ | ★ | ... | ★ | ... | ... | ... | ... | ... | ... | (d) |
| California | ★ | ★ | ... | ★ | ★ | ... | ★ | (a) | (b) | ... | (c) | ★ | (d) |
| Colorado | ★ | ... | ★ | ... | ★ | ★ | ... | ★ | ★ | ... | ... | ★ | ... |
| Connecticut* | ★ | ★ | ... | ... | ★ | ★ | ★ | ... | ★ | ... | (o) | ★ | (d,e) |
| Delaware | ★ | ★ | ... | ... | ★ | ... | ... | ... | ... | ... | (o) | ... | ... |
| Florida | ★ | ★ | ... | ★ | ★ | ★ | ... | ★ | ... | ... | ★ | ★ | ... |
| Georgia | ★ | ... | ... | ★ | ★ | ★ | ... | ... | ★ | ... | ... | ★ | (f) |
| Hawaii | ★ | ★ | ... | ... | ★ | ★ | ★ | ... | ... | ... | ... | ★ | ... |
| Idaho | ★ | ... | ★ | ★ | ★ | ... | ... | ... | ... | ... | ★ | ★ | (g) |
| Illinois | ★ | ★ | ... | ... | ... | ... | ... | ... | ... | ... | ... | ★ | (g,f,h) |
| Indiana | ★ | ... | ... | ... | ★ | ★ | ... | ... | ... | ... | ... | ... | ... |
| Iowa | ★ | ★ | ... | ... | ... | ... | ... | ... | ★ | (i) | ★ | ★ | ... |
| Kansas | ★ | ★ | ... | ... | ... | ★ | ... | ... | ★ | $40 (j) | ★ | ★ | ... |
| Kentucky | ★ | ★ | ... | ... | ★ | ★ | ... | ★ | ★ | $100 | ★ | ★ | ... |
| Louisiana | ★ | ... | ... | ... | ★ | ★ | ... | ★(k) | ... | ... | ★ | ... | (l) |
| Maine | ★ | (m) | ... | (n) | ★ | ★ | ★ | ★ | ... | ... | (o) | ★ | ... |
| Maryland | ★ | ★ | ... | ... | ★ | ★ | ★ | ... | ... | ... | ... | ★ | (p) |
| Massachusetts | ★ | ★ | ... | ... | ★ | ★ | ... | ... | ... | ... | ... | ★ | (d) |
| Michigan | ★ | ★ | ... | ★ | ★ | ★ | ... | ... | ★ | ★ | (s) | ★ | (d,q,r) |
| Minnesota | ★ | ★ | ... | ★ | ... | ★ | ★ | ... | ... | ... | ... | ★ | (t) |
| Mississippi* | ★ | ★ | ... | ★ | ... | ★ | ★ | ... | ... | ... | ★ | ... | ... |
| Missouri* | ★ | ★ | ★ | ★ | ★ | ★ | ★ | ... | ... | ... | ... | ... | (u) |
| Montana | ★ | ★ | ... | ★ | ... | ★ | ... | ... | ... | ... | ★(w) | ★ | (v) |
| Nebraska | ★ | ... | ... | ... | ... | ... | ... | ... | ... | ... | ... | ... | ... |
| Nevada | ★ | ... | ★ | ★ | ... | ... | ... | ... | ★ | $100 | ★ | ★ | (x) |
| New Hampshire | ★ | ... | ... | ... | ★ | ... | ... | ... | ... | ... | ... | ... | ... |
| New Jersey | ★ | ★ | ... | ... | ★ | ★ | ★ | ... | ... | ... | ... | ... | ... |
| New Mexico | ★ | ★ | ... | ... | ... | ... | ... | ... | ★ | ... | ... | ★ | ★ |
| New York | ★ | ★ | ... | ... | ★ | ★ | ★ | ... | ★ | ... | ... | ★ | ... |
| North Carolina | ★ | ... | ... | (y) | ... | ... | ... | ... | ★ | ... | ... | ★ | ... |
| North Dakota | ★ | ... | ... | ... | ... | ... | ... | ... | ... | ... | ... | ... | ... |
| Ohio | ★ | ★ | ... | ★ | ★ | ★ | ... | ... | ... | ... | ★ | ★ | (y,z,aa) |
| Oklahoma | ★ | ... | ... | ... | ★ | ... | ... | ... | ... | ★ | ★ | ... | (bb) |
| Oregon | ★ | ... | ★ | ★ | ... | ★ | ★ | ★ | ... | ★ | (cc) | ★ | ... |
| Pennsylvania | ★ | ★ | ... | ... | ★ | ★ | ... | ★ | ... | ... | ... | ★ | ... |
| Rhode Island* | ★ | ... | ... | ★ | ... | ... | ... | ... | ... | ... | ... | ★ | ... |
| South Carolina | ★ | ★ | ★ | ... | ... | ★ | ★ | ★ | ★ | (dd) | ★ | ★ | (d,dd) |
| South Dakota | ★ | ... | ... | ★ | ... | ... | ★ | ... | ... | ... | ★ | ★ | ... |
| Tennessee | ★ | ★ | ★ | ★ | ... | ... | ... | ... | ★ | ★ | ★ | ... | ... |
| Texas | ★ | ★ | ... | ★ | ★ | ★ | ★ | ... | ★ | (ee) | ... | ★ | (e,f,ff) |
| Utah | ★ | ★ | ★(ii) | ★(jj) | (kk) | ... | ... | ... | ★ | ... | (ll) | ★ | ★ (mm) |
| Vermont | ★ | ★ | ... | ★ | ★ | ★ | ... | ★ | ★ | ... | ★ | ★ | ... |
| Virginia | ★ | ... | ... | ... | ... | ... | ... | ... | ... | ... | ... | ★ | ... |
| Washington | ★ | ★ | ★ | ★ | ★ | ★ | ★ | ... | ★ | ... | ... | ★ | ... |
| West Virginia | ★ | ★ | ... | ... | ★ | ★ | ... | ... | ... | ... | (gg) | ★ | ... |
| Wisconsin | ★ | ★ | ... | ★ | ★ | ... | ★ | ... | ★ | ... | ★ | ... | ... |
| Wyoming | ★ | ... | ... | ★ | ... | ... | ... | ... | ... | ... | ... | ... | (z) |
| Dist. of Columbia | ★ | ★ | ... | ... | ★ | ★ | ★ | ... | ... | $100 | ... | ... | ... |

See footnotes at end of table.

# LOBBYISTS: DEFINITIONS AND PROHIBITED ACTIVITIES — Continued

*Source*: The Council of State Governments' survey, January 2000 , except as noted by * where data is from *The Book of the States, 1998-99*.

*Key:*

★— Application exists.

. . . — Not applicable.

(a) Cannot deliver a contribution in the state capitol or any state building.

(b) Does not apply to campaign contributions. Cannot act as an agent or intermediary in the making of any gift or to arrange for the making of any gift by any other person.

(c) No prohibition on officials soliciting but officials may only accept gifts from a single source in any calendar year with a total value of $250.

(d) Lobbyists making gifts in excess of the following thresholds to state officials: California, $10. per year; Connecticut, $50 for gifts per year, $150 for food and drink per year; Michigan, $44 per month per official; South Carolina, anything of value.

(e) Giving of fees and honoraria banned; "necessary expenses" allowed.

(f) Offering or proposing anything which may be reasonably construed to improperly influence a legislator's official acts, decisions or votes. Lobbying without registering.

(g) Expenditures without full disclosure; lobbying without registering.

(h) Legislative officials, full-time public officials or employees may not receive compensation for lobbying. Lobbying without registering, if compensated.

(i) Expenditures in excess of $3 per official in any one calendar day.

(j) The $40. limit applies to all elected, state office holders.

(k) Only if the contribution is made during an undisclosed fundraiser.

(l) State employees prohibited from lobbying.

(m) Governor only.

(n) Only registration required (no fee).

(o) Prohibited in criminal code.

(p) Lobbyist cannot solicit, serve on committees or transmit funds relating to legislative elections. By order of the speaker of the House and president of the Senate, legislators cannot hold fund-raisers during the legislative session. Legislators are prohibited from receiving certain nominal gifts from regulated lobbyists if the cost exceeds $15. Regulated lobbyists are prohibited from making a gift to an official or employee that cannot be accepted by that official or employee. Lobbyist campaign finance activity limitation was extended to also include elections for governor, lt. gov., attorney general and comptroller. Fundraising restrictions during session were extended to include governor, lt. gov., attorney general and comptroller.

(q) State senators or representatives may not lobby for balance of term when they resign from office. This prohibition does not apply to other public officials.

(r) The Campaign Finance Act prohibits state senators or representatives from accepting payment for an appearance, speech, article, or any activity related to or associated with the performance of duties as an elected official.

(s) Officials can solicit contributions but may not accept gifts.

(t) A district court overturned provisions prohibiting commercial use of information on all disclosure programs filed with the Campaign Finance and Public Disclosure Board.

(u) Employment of non-registered lobbyists.

(v) A state officer or employee may not lobby on behalf of an organization while on the job. A public officer, legislator, or public employee may not accept a gift worth $50 or more that would influence "a reasonable person's" professional judgement, or that would serve as a reward for a professional decision.

(w) If over $50 per month.

(x) Instigating the introduction of legislation for the purpose of obtaining employment to lobby in opposition thereto. Making false statements or misrepresentation to legislators or in a registration report concerning lobbying activities. Except during specified periods, acting as a lobbyists without being registered.

(y) State government agency liaisons lobbying on issues concerning their agency (no fee).

(z) Lobbying without registering.

(aa) A legislator is prohibited from accepting the following from a legislative agent: travel or lodging, over $75 aggregated/year for meals, and $75 aggregated year for gifts.

(bb) May not knowingly make a false statement or representation of fact to legislative, judicial or executive branches; nor knowingly provide, to same, a copy of a document which contains a false statement without written notification of such; nor appear, during session, on the floor of the House or Senate in the absence of an express invitation.

(cc) During regular or special session.

(dd) Lobbyists' principals cannot offer to pay for lodging, transportation, meals, entertainment, beverages, etc, unless all members of the General Assembly, the House or the Senate, or one of the Committees, subcommittees, legislative caucuses or county legislative delegations are invited.

(ee) Expenditures in excess of $500 per year for entertainment or gifts.

(ff) Lobbying without registering; giving loans or gifts of cash to legislators; pleasure trips; appearing, during session, on the floor of the House or Senate without an invitation; knowingly making a false statement or misrepresentation of fact to a member of legislative or executive branch; giving awards or mementos that exceed $500.

(gg) Officials can only solicit for charitable purposes.

(hh) Alaska law prohibits lobbyists from giving campaign contributions to candidates for the legislature other than to the candidate(s) that are campaigning to represent the district in which the lobbyist is registered to vote.

(ii) An elected official is not considered a lobbyist when acting in his official capacity on matters pertaining to their office.

(jj) A state official is not considered a lobbyist when acting within the scope of employment.

(kk) An individual is not required to make expenditures to be considered a lobbyist.

(ll) There is no law prohibiting the solicitation of contributions.

(mm) Other prohibited activities: 1. Lobbyists may not seek to influence an official by communicating with the official's employer. 2. Lobbyists may not intentionally communicate to a public official any false information that is materially related to a matter within the responsibility of the official.

## Table 7.40
## LOBBYISTS: REGISTRATION AND REPORTING

| State or other jurisdiction | Agency which administers registration and reports requirements for lobbyists | Frequency | Legislation/administrative action seeking to influence | Expenditures benefiting public officials or employees | Compensation received [broken down by employer(s)] | Total compensations received | Categories of expenditures | Total expenditures | Contributions received from other for lobbying purposes | Other |
|---|---|---|---|---|---|---|---|---|---|---|
| Alabama | Ethics Comm. | Quarterly | ★ | ... | ... | ... | ★ | ... | ... | ... |
| Alaska | Public Offices Comm. | Monthly (b) | ★ | ★ | ★ | ★ | ★ | ★ | ★ | ★ (c) |
| Arizona | Secretary of State | Annually | ... | ★ | ... | ... | (mm) | ★ | ... | (c) |
| Arkansas | Ethics Comm. (d) | Monthly and quarterly | ... | ★ | ... | ... | ★ | ★ | ... | (c) |
| California | Political Reform Division, Secretary of State | Quarterly | ★ | ★ | ★ | ★ | ... | ★ | ★ | (e) |
| Colorado | Secretary of State | Monthly | ★ | ★ | ★ | ★ | ★ | ★ | ... | ... |
| Connecticut* | State Ethics Comm. | Monthly (a,f) | ★ | (g) | ★ | ★ | ★ | ★ | ... | (h) |
| Delaware | Public Integrity Comm. | Quarterly | ★ | ★ | ... | ... | ★ | ★ | ★ | ... |
| Florida | Jt. Legislative Mgt. Cmte. | Quarterly | ... | ★ | ... | ... | ★ | ★ | ★ | ... |
| Georgia | Ethics Comm. | Monthly (b) | ★ | ★ | ... | ... | ... | ... | ... | ... |
| Hawaii | State Ethics Comm. | Jan., March, May | ★ | ★ | ★ | ★ | ★ | ★ | ★ | ... |
| Idaho | Secretary of State | Monthly (a) and annually | ★ | ★ | ... | ... | ★ | ★ | ... | ... |
| Illinois | Secretary of State | Semi-annually and annually | ... | ★ | ... | ... | ★ | ★ | ... | (c,i,j,k) |
| Indiana | Lobby Registration Comm. | Semi-annually | ★ | ★ | ... | ... | ★ | ★ | ... | (l) |
| Iowa | Secretary of Senate, Clerk of House | Monthly (m) | ★ | ★ | ... | ... | ... | ★ | ... | ... |
| Kansas | Ethics Comm. | (n) | ★ | ★ | ... | ... | ★ | ★ | ... | ... |
| Kentucky | Legislative Ethics Comm. | (o) | ★ | ★ | ★ | ... | ★ | ★ | ... | ... |
| Louisiana | Board of Ethics | Annually-registration Semi-annual reporting | ★ | ★(p) | ... | ... | ... | ★ | ... | (q) |
| Maine | Comm. on Govt'l. Ethics | Monthly (a) and after session | ★ | ★ | ★ | ★ | ★ | ★ | ★ | ... |
| Maryland | Ethics Comm. | Semi-annually | ★ | ★ | ★ | ★ | ★ | ★ | (r) | ... |
| Massachusetts | Secretary of State | Semi-annually | ★ | ★ | ★ | ★ | ★ | ★ | ★ | ... |
| Michigan | Secretary of State | Semi-annually | ★ | ★(s) | ... | ... | ★ | ★ | ... | (t) |
| Minnesota | Campaign Finance & Public Disclosure Board | Three times a year | ★ | ★ | ... | ... | ★ | ★ | ★ | (u) |
| Mississippi* (v) | Secretary of State | Annually and 2 times per session | ★ | ★ | ★ | ★ | ★ | ★ | ★ | ... |
| Missouri* | Ethics Comm. | Semi-annually and annually (a) | ★ | ★ | ... | ... | ★ | ★ | ... | (r,w) |
| Montana | Commr. of Political Practices | ... | ... | ★ | ★ | ★ | ★ | ★ | (x) | ... |
| Nebraska | Accountability & Disclosure Comm. | Quarterly | ★ | ★ | ... | ★ | ★ | ★ | (y) | (j) |
| Nevada | Legislative Counsel Bureau | Monthly (a) and after session | ... | ★ | ... | ... | ★ | ★ | ... | ... |
| New Hampshire | Secretary of State | April, Aug., Dec. | ★ | ★ | ★ | ★ | ★ | ★ | ... | ... |
| New Jersey | Election Law Enforcement Comm. | Annually and quarterly | ★ | ★ | ★ | ★ | ★ | ★ | ★ | ... |
| New Mexico | Secretary of State | Before, during & after session | ★ | ★ | ... | ... | ★ | ★ | ★ | ... |
| New York | Temporary State Comm. on Lobbying | Bi-monthly and semi-annually | ★(nn) | ★ | ★ | ★ | ★ | ★ | ... | ... |
| North Carolina | Secretary of State | After session and year end | ... | ... | (z) | ... | ★ | ... | ... | (bb) |
| North Dakota | Secretary of State | (aa) | ... | ... | ... | ... | ... | ★ | ... | ... |
| Ohio | Office of the Legislative Inspector General | Every four months | ★ | ★ | ... | ... | ★ | ★ | ... | ... |
| Oklahoma | Ethics Comm. | Biennially | ... | ★ | ... | ... | ... | ... | ... | (cc) |
| Oregon | Gov't standards & Practices Comm. | (dd) | ★ | ... | ... | ... | ★ | ★ | ... | ... |
| Pennsylvania | State Ethics Comm. | Quarterly | ★ | ★ | ★ | ★ | ★ | ★ | ... | ... |
| Rhode Island* | Secretary of State | (ee) | ★ | ★ | ★ | ★ | ★ | ★ | ... | ... |
| South Carolina | Ethics Comm. | Apr.10, Oct. 10 and year end | ★ | ★ | ★ | ★ | ★ | ★ | ★ | ★ (ff) |

See footnotes at end of table.

## LOBBYISTS: REGISTRATION AND REPORTING — Continued

| State or other jurisdiction | Agency which administers registration and reports requirements for lobbyists | Frequency | Legislation/administrative action seeking to influence | Expenditures benefiting public officials or employees | Compensation received [broken down by employer(s)] | Total compensations received | Categories of expenditures | Total expenditures | Contributions received from other for lobbying purposes | Other |
|---|---|---|---|---|---|---|---|---|---|---|
| South Dakota ............... | Secretary of State | After session | ★ | . . . | . . . | . . . | ★ | ★ | . . . | . . . |
| Tennessee .................... | Registry of Election Finance | Semi-annually | . . . | ★(oo) | . . . | . . . | . . . | . . . | . . . | . . . |
| Texas ........................... | Ethics Comm. | Monthly and annually | ★ | ★(gg) | ★ | ★ | ★ | ★ | . . . | . . . |
| Utah ............................. | Lieutenant Governor | (hh) | ★ | ★ | . . . | . . . | (pp) | ★ | . . . | . . . |
| Vermont ...................... | Secretary of State | March 25, July 25 and year end (ii) | ★ | ★ | ★ | ★ | . . . | ★ | . . . | (jj) |
| Virginia ...................... | Secretary of State | Yearly | ★ | . . . | ★ | ★ | ★ | ★ | . . . | ★ |
| Washington ................ | Public Disclosure Comm. | Monthly | ★ | ★ | ★ | ★ | ★ | ★ | ★ | . . . |
| West Virginia .............. | Ethics Comm. | After session, annually, and mid-session | . . . | ★ | . . . | . . . | ★ | ★ | . . . | . . . |
| Wisconsin ................... | Ethics Board | Biennially | ★ | (kk) | ★ | ★ | ★ | ★ | . . . | (ll) |
| Wyoming .................... | Secretary of State | Yearly | . . . | ★ | . . . | . . . | ★ | ★ | . . . | . . . |
| Dist. of Columbia ........... | Office of Campaign Finance | Biennially | ★ | ★ | ★ | ★ | ★ | ★ | ★ | . . . |

*Source*: The Council of State Governments' survey, January 2000, except as noted by * where data are from *The Book of the States, 1998-99*.

*Key*:

★ — Application exists.

. . . — Not applicable.

(a) During legislative session. In Missouri, filed with the secretary of Senate and clerk of the House.

(b) During legislative session, quarterly thereafter.

(c) Must make separate disclosure report.

(d) Reporting forms are filed with the secretary of state.

(e) Campaign contributions made; lump sum reporting of overhead and other payments in connection with lobbying activities.

(f) Also, first, second and fourth quarters.

(g) In detail, if over $10 per person.

(h) Fundamental terms of lobbying contracts.

(i) Entertainment expense.

(j) Disclosure of honoraria or other money loaned, promised or paid to official or staff of legislative or executive branches of state government.

(k) Categories of expenditures exceeding thresholds.

(l) Compensation and reimbursement to others, receptions, and entertainment. Compensated lobbyists must report on behalf of each client by filing an activity report naming the client.

(m) In the Senate, reports are required only if $15 or more is provided to senators or their staff on any one day.

(n) February, March, April, May, September, and January.

(o) Initial registration begins seven days after engagement to lobby. Updated registration forms are due not later than the 15th day of January, February, March, April, May and September of even-numbered years; the 15th day of January, May and September of odd-numbered years.

(p) Reporting applies to expenditures made with respect to legislators only.

(q) Expenditures for individual legislators which exceed $50 on an occasion or $250 in a reporting period, expenditures for recognized groups of legislators, and expenditures for individual legislators for out-of-state speaking engagements.

(r) To a limited extent.

(s) Food and beverage expenditures for public officials are disclosed. Expenditures for persons who are not public officials are not disclosed. Travel and lodging in excess of $575 provided to a public official must be disclosed.

(t) Financial transactions of $900 or more are disclosed. Gifts in excess of $44 to a single public official are prohibited.

(u) Metropolitan governmental unit action seeking to influence.

(v) Effective January 1, 1995, Mississippi will require lobbyists to disclose the name of the government official whenever anything of value is given by a lobbyist.

(w) Business relationships with public officials, if over $50

(x) If over $250.

(y) Must report names and addresses of persons giving more than $100.

(z) In North Carolina, the principal shall estimate and report the compensation paid or promised directly or indirectly, to all lobbyists based on estimated time, effort and expense in connection with lobbying activities on behalf of the principal. If a lobbyist is a full-time employee of the principal, or is compensated by means of an annual fee or retainer, the principal shall estimate and report the portion of all such lobbyists' salaries or retainers that compensate the lobbyists for lobbying.

(aa) As a result of a law change by the 1995 Legislative Assembly, the registration period is now from July 1 to June 30 of following year. The reporting requirements are for the same period of time.

(bb) Any expenditure over $25 per occasion.

(cc) By whom the lobbyist is reimbursed, retained or employed to lobby, and on whose behalf the lobbying is done.

(dd) Even-numbered years: January 31, July 31; odd-numbered years: January 31, April 30, July 31.

(ee) At specified times during legislative session and at end of legislative session.

(ff) Reports required from lobbyist's principal.

(gg) In detail, if over $50 per person.

(hh) After the session, annually, seven days before a general election, and seven days after the end of a special session or veto override session.

(ii) January 20 for preceding year; March 10 for January and February.

(jj) A lobbyist who is compensated, in whole or in part, by an employer for the purpose of lobbying on behalf of another person, group or coalition is required to provide the name of the employer, the name of the person, group or coalition on whose behalf he/she lobbies and a description of the matters for which lobbying has been engaged by the employer.

(kk) Prohibited.

(ll) Daily record of time spent on lobbying on each reported bill, budget topic and administrative rule. Reports filed by lobbyist's employer.

(mm) Food and beverage expenditures for public officials are disclosed. Expenditures for persons who are not public officials are not disclosed.

(nn) New York's Lobbying Act of 2000 requires a description of the subject lobbied or expected to be lobbied, as well as listing the legislative bill number and the rule, regulation, and ratemaking number lobbied or expected to be lobbied.

(oo) Lobbyist only have to disclose campaign contributions exceeding $100 made to benefit legislative and executive branch officials or candidates for state public office.

(pp) Lobbyist must break down their expenditures into three categories: travel expenditures; expenditures not exceeding $50 per person; expenditures exceeding $50 per person( lobbyist must report the name of the official benefited).

# PROGRAMS AND ISSUES

*Includes information on public school attendance, higher education institutions and their full-time faculty salaries, fees and room rates at higher education institutions, prison populations, child labor laws, and health care and highway spending.*

For additional information on Chapter Eight contact
The States Information Center, at The Council of State Governments,
(859) 244-8253 or E-mail: sic@csg.org.

## Table 8.1
## MEMBERSHIP AND ATTENDANCE IN PUBLIC ELEMENTARY AND SECONDARY SCHOOLS, BY STATE: 1996-97 AND 1998-99

| State or other jurisdiction | 1996-97 (est.) | | | 1998-99 | | |
|---|---|---|---|---|---|---|
| | Estimated average daily membership (ADM) | Estimated average daily attendance (ADA) | ADA as a percent of ADM | Estimated average daily membership (ADM) | Estimated average daily attendance (ADA) | ADA as a percent of ADM |
| United States .................. | ... | 42,089,312 | ... | ... | 42,970,027 | ... |
| Alabama ............................... | 739,635 | 710,969 | 96.1 | 738,809 | 704,001 | 95.3 |
| Alaska .................................. | 127,754 | 111,256 | 87.1 | 132,905 | 112,809 | 84.9 |
| Arizona ................................ | 778,449 | 728,730 | 93.6 | 775,089 | 769,459 | 99.3 |
| Arkansas ............................. | 449,871 | 423,366 | 94.1 | 454,503 | 438,312 | 96.4 |
| California ............................ | ... | 5,545,212 | ... | ... | 5,671,448 | ... |
| Colorado ............................ | ... | 624,546 | ... | ... | 648,378 | ... |
| Connecticut ....................... | 528,000 | 499,410 | 94.6 | 545,200 | 522,580 | 95.9 |
| Delaware ............................. | 108,880 | 101,860 | 93.6 | 112,030 | 105,206 | 93.9 |
| Florida ................................. | 2,163,914 | 2,010,709 | 92.9 | 2,260,414 | 2,100,377 | 92.9 |
| Georgia ................................ | 1,321,239 | 1,223,575 | 92.6 | 1,401,291 | 1,306,137 | 93.2 |
| Hawaii .................................. | 186,290 | 173,584 | 93.2 | 187,543 | 174,373 | 93 |
| Idaho ................................... | ... | 233,056 | ... | ... | 230,155 | ... |
| Illinois ................................. | 1,902,376 | 1,769,060 | 93 | 1,969,415 | 1,835,104 | 93.2 |
| Indiana ................................ | 943,332 | 899,201 | 95.3 | 952,234 | 910,695 | 95.6 |
| Iowa ..................................... | 497,869 | 474,486 | 95.3 | 94,898 | 471,655 | 95.3 |
| Kansas ................................. | 440,788 | 417,813 | 94.8 | 442,222 | 419,656 | 94.9 |
| Kentucky ............................. | 628,391 | 573,133 | 91.2 | 627,646 | 568,877 | 90.6 |
| Louisiana ............................ | 777,546 | 730,078 | 94.9 | 754,481 | 704,567 | 93.4 |
| Maine .................................. | 214,293 | 203,433 | 93.9 | 208,146 | 197,739 | 95 |
| Maryland ............................ | 813,672 | 759,970 | 93.4 | 839,374 | 786,575 | 93.7 |
| Massachusetts .................... | 932,833 | 861,654 | 92.4 | 953,538 | 882,155 | 92.5 |
| Michigan ............................. | ... | 1,531,341 | ... | ... | 1,560,757 | ... |
| Minnesota ........................... | 838,197 | 784,102 | 93.5 | 857,770 | 801,333 | 93.4 |
| Mississippi .......................... | 495,296 | 469,601 | 94.8 | 496,762 | 472,086 | 95 |
| Missouri .............................. | ... | 813,982 | ... | ... | 831,185 | ... |
| Montana .............................. | 162,854 | 148,289 | 91.1 | 157,598 | 142,078 | 90.2 |
| Nebraska ............................. | 286,284 | 272,089 | 95 | 287,257 | 255,619 | 89 |
| Nevada ................................ | 277,039 | 254,572 | 91.9 | 293,721 | 273,700 | 93.2 |
| New Hampshire .................. | 190,696 | 180,470 | 94.6 | 198,040 | 187,191 | 94.5 |
| New Jersey .......................... | 1,212,931 | 1,133,579 | 93.5 | 1,234,156 | 1,155,489 | 93.6 |
| New Mexico ......................... | 308,555 | 277,700 | 90 | 328,753 | 295,878 | 90 |
| New York ............................. | 2,790,753 | 2,528,660 | 90.6 | 2,836,253 | 2,570,037 | 90.6 |
| North Carolina ................... | 1,169,855 | 1,110,558 | 94.9 | 1,208,386 | 1,146,519 | 94.9 |
| North Dakota ..................... | 118,830 | 114,116 | 96 | 118,011 | 111,989 | 94.9 |
| Ohio ..................................... | 1,845,601 | 1,724,144 | 93.4 | 1,803,900 | 1,681,773 | 93.2 |
| Oklahoma ........................... | 612,000 | 574,400 | 93.9 | 627,550 | 599,210 | 95.5 |
| Oregon ................................ | 527,500 | 488,000 | 92.5 | 512,726 | 474,754 | 92.6 |
| Pennsylvania ...................... | 1,790,415 | 1,661,500 | 92.8 | 1,805,800 | 1,683,800 | 93.2 |
| Rhode Island ...................... | 152,088 | 140,482 | 92.4 | 153,004 | 141,923 | 92.8 |
| South Carolina ................... | 644,019 | 622,995 | 96.7 | 651,321 | 623,763 | 95.8 |
| South Dakota ..................... | 134,064 | 127,563 | 95.2 | 132,739 | 126,388 | 95.2 |
| Tennessee ........................... | 885,473 | 828,271 | 93.5 | 894,013 | 836,215 | 93.5 |
| Texas ................................... | ... | 3,506,844 | ... | ... | 3,661,146 | ... |
| Utah ..................................... | 474,386 | 448,864 | 94.6 | 472,978 | 447,532 | 94.6 |
| Vermont .............................. | 98,000 | 92,826 | 94.7 | 96,664 | 91,456 | 94.6 |
| Virginia ............................... | 1,083,232 | 1,018,658 | 94 | 1,100,921 | 1,037,205 | 94.2 |
| Washington ........................ | 972,198 | 910,949 | 93.7 | 998,940 | 936,007 | 93.7 |
| West Virginia ...................... | 300,710 | 281,290 | 93.5 | 294,229 | 275,994 | 93.8 |
| Wisconsin ........................... | 861,157 | 806,043 | 93.6 | 882,860 | 830,417 | 94.1 |
| Wyoming ............................. | 97,591 | 92,159 | 94.4 | 93,066 | 88,025 | 94.6 |
| Dist. of Columbia .............. | 77,186 | 70,164 | 90.9 | 76,672 | 70,300 | 91.7 |

*Source*: Adapted from National Education Association, *Rankings & Estimates: Rankings of the States 1999 and Estimates of School Statistics 2000.* © NEA, Washington, D.C. 2000. All rights reserved.

*Note*: Average Daily Membership (ADM) for the school year is an average obtained by dividing the aggregate days of membership by the number of days in which school is in session. Pupils are "members" of a school from the date they are placed on the current roll until they leave permanently.

Membership is the total number of pupils belonging–the sum of those present and those absent. Average Daily Attendance (ADA) for the school year is the aggregate days pupils were actually present in school divided by the number of days school was actually in session.

*Key:*

... — Not available.

## Table 8.2
## ENROLLMENT, AVERAGE DAILY ATTENDANCE AND CLASSROOM TEACHERS
## IN PUBLIC ELEMENTARY AND SECONDARY SCHOOLS, BY STATE: 1998-99

| State or other jurisdiction | Total enrollment (a) | Estimated average daily attendance (a) | Classroom teachers (a) | Pupils per teacher based on enrollment | Pupils per teacher based on average daily attendance |
|---|---|---|---|---|---|
| United States .............. | 46,286,051 | 42,970,027 | 2,792,406 | 16.6 | 15.4 |
| Alabama ................................ | 739,956 | 704,001 | 46,177 | 16.0 | 15.2 |
| Alaska ................................ | 135,373 | 112,809 | 7,696 | 17.6 | 14.7 |
| Arizona ................................ | 823,040 | 769,459 | 43,219 | 19.0 | 17.8 |
| Arkansas ................................ | 456,710 | 438,312 | 28,108 | 16.2 | 15.6 |
| California ................................ | 5,844,111 | 5,671,448 | 260,539 | 22.4 | 21.8 |
| Colorado ................................ | 699,135 | 648,378 | 38,089 | 18.4 | 17.0 |
| Connecticut ................................ | 545,663 | 522,580 | 39,209 | 13.9 | 13.3 |
| Delaware ................................ | 113,082 | 105,206 | 7,073 | 16.0 | 14.9 |
| Florida ................................ | 2,333,570 | 2,100,377 | 129,731 | 18.0 | 16.2 |
| Georgia ................................ | 1,401,291 | 1,306,137 | 88,654 | 15.8 | 14.7 |
| Hawaii ................................ | 187,395 | 174,373 | 11,019 | 17.0 | 15.8 |
| Idaho ................................ | 244,623 | 230,155 | 13,399 | 18.3 | 17.2 |
| Illinois ................................ | 2,011,530 | 1,835,104 | 122,122 | 16.5 | 15.0 |
| Indiana ................................ | 988,094 | 910,695 | 57,840 | 17.1 | 15.7 |
| Iowa ................................ | 502,570 | 471,655 | 33,415 | 15.0 | 14.1 |
| Kansas ................................ | 469,758 | 419,656 | 31,899 | 14.7 | 13.2 |
| Kentucky ................................ | 638,830 | 568,877 | 39,000 | 16.4 | 14.6 |
| Louisiana ................................ | 764,939 | 704,567 | 48,721 | 15.7 | 14.5 |
| Maine ................................ | 210,927 | 197,739 | 15,086 | 14.0 | 13.1 |
| Maryland ................................ | 841,671 | 786,575 | 49,249 | 17.1 | 16.0 |
| Massachusetts ................................ | 948,313 | 882,155 | 64,985 | 14.6 | 13.6 |
| Michigan ................................ | 1,696,475 | 1,560,757 | 91,233 | 18.6 | 17.1 |
| Minnesota ................................ | 856,421 | 801,333 | 54,035 | 15.8 | 14.8 |
| Mississippi ................................ | 502,379 | 472,086 | 29,939 | 16.8 | 15.8 |
| Missouri ................................ | 895,304 | 831,185 | 62,281 | 14.4 | 13.3 |
| Montana ................................ | 159,988 | 142,078 | 10,221 | 15.7 | 13.9 |
| Nebraska ................................ | 289,981 | 255,619 | 20,100 | 14.4 | 12.7 |
| Nevada ................................ | 311,063 | 273,700 | 16,653 | 18.7 | 16.4 |
| New Hampshire ................................ | 203,127 | 187,191 | 13,290 | 15.3 | 14.1 |
| New Jersey ................................ | 1,240,874 | 1,155,489 | 93,090 | 13.3 | 12.4 |
| New Mexico ................................ | 328,753 | 295,878 | 19,897 | 16.5 | 14.9 |
| New York ................................ | 2,838,554 | 2,570,037 | 201,168 | 14.1 | 12.8 |
| North Carolina ................................ | 1,245,608 | 1,146,519 | 78,627 | 15.8 | 14.6 |
| North Dakota ................................ | 114,597 | 111,989 | 7,955 | 14.4 | 14.1 |
| Ohio ................................ | 1,842,067 | 1,681,773 | 111,452 | 16.5 | 15.1 |
| Oklahoma ................................ | 628,510 | 599,210 | 40,559 | 15.5 | 14.8 |
| Oregon ................................ | 542,809 | 474,754 | 29,317 | 18.5 | 16.2 |
| Pennsylvania ................................ | 1,816,566 | 1,683,800 | 111,065 | 16.4 | 15.2 |
| Rhode Island ................................ | 153,710 | 141,923 | 11,859 | 13.0 | 12.0 |
| South Carolina ................................ | 654,993 | 623,763 | 42,202 | 15.5 | 14.8 |
| South Dakota ................................ | 131,764 | 126,388 | 9,070 | 14.5 | 13.9 |
| Tennessee ................................ | 903,319 | 836,215 | 53,593 | 16.9 | 15.6 |
| Texas ................................ | 3,971,267 | 3,661,146 | 261,275 | 15.2 | 14.0 |
| Utah ................................ | 477,061 | 447,532 | 21,585 | 22.1 | 20.7 |
| Vermont ................................ | 106,691 | 91,456 | 8,084 | 13.2 | 11.3 |
| Virginia ................................ | 1,124,022 | 1,037,205 | 79,803 | 14.1 | 13.0 |
| Washington ................................ | 999,616 | 936,007 | 49,500 | 20.2 | 18.9 |
| West Virginia ................................ | 296,562 | 275,994 | 20,623 | 14.4 | 13.4 |
| Wisconsin ................................ | 879,535 | 830,417 | 56,592 | 15.5 | 14.7 |
| Wyoming ................................ | 94,420 | 88,025 | 6,646 | 14.2 | 13.2 |
| Dist. of Columbia .............. | 79,434 | 70,300 | 5,462 | 14.5 | 12.9 |

*Source*: Adapted from National Education Association, *Rankings & Estimates: Rankings of the States 1999 and Estimates of School Statistics 2000*.
© NEA, Washington, D.C. 2000. All rights reserved.

*Key*:

(a) Estimated.

## Table 8.3
## AVERAGE ANNUAL SALARY OF INSTRUCTIONAL STAFF IN PUBLIC
## ELEMENTARY AND SECONDARY SCHOOLS: 1959-60 TO 1998-99

| State or other jurisdiction | Average annual salary for: (in unadjusted dollars) | | | | | | | |
|---|---|---|---|---|---|---|---|---|
| | 1959-60 | 1969-70 | 1979-80 | 1989-90 | 1994-95 | 1995-96 | 1996-97 | 1998-99 |
| Alabama | $4,002 | $6,954 | $13,338 | $26,200 | $32,597 | $32,459 | $33,744 | $35,820 |
| Alaska | 6,859 | 10,993 | 27,697 | 43,161 | 48,929 | 50,516 | 52,033 | 46,845 |
| Arizona | 5,590 | 8,975 | 16,180 | 33,529 | 41,325 | 42,870 | 44,157 | 35,025 |
| Arkansas | 3,295 | 6,445 | 12,704 | 23,296 | 29,677 | 30,607 | 31,526 | 32,350 |
| California | 6,600 | 9,980 | 18,626 | 39,309 | 42,538 | 44,027 | 45,349 | 45,400 |
| Colorado | 4,997 | 7,900 | 16,840 | 31,832 | 35,712 | 36,353 | 37,445 | 38,025 |
| Connecticut | 6,008 | 9,400 | 16,989 | 41,888 | 53,020 | 51,951 | 52,067 | 51,584 |
| Delaware | 5,800 | 9,300 | 16,845 | 34,620 | 40,668 | 42,177 | 43,085 | 43,164 |
| Florida | 5,080 | 8,600 | 14,875 | 30,275 | 33,617 | 34,411 | 34,983 | 35,916 |
| Georgia | 3,904 | 7,372 | 14,547 | 29,541 | 34,507 | 35,786 | 37,933 | 39,675 |
| Hawaii | 5,390 | 9,829 | 20,436 | 32,956 | 37,319 | 37,057 | 36,986 | 40,377 |
| Idaho | 4,216 | 7,257 | 14,110 | 24,758 | 31,063 | 32,285 | 33,277 | 34,063 |
| Illinois | 5,814 | 9,950 | 18,271 | 33,912 | 42,448 | 42,411 | 44,235 | 45,569 |
| Indiana | 5,542 | 9,574 | 16,256 | 31,905 | 37,569 | 38,832 | 39,998 | 41,163 |
| Iowa | 4,030 | 8,200 | 15,776 | 27,619 | 32,622 | 33,529 | 34,480 | 34,927 |
| Kansas | 4,450 | 7,811 | 14,513 | 30,154 | 36,709 | 37,626 | 38,379 | 37,405 |
| Kentucky | 3,327 | 7,624 | 15,350 | 27,482 | 34,232 | 33,115 | 34,109 | 35,526 |
| Louisiana | 4,978 | 7,220 | 14,020 | 25,036 | 27,629 | 28,167 | 29,013 | 32,510 |
| Maine | 3,694 | 8,059 | 13,743 | 27,831 | 33,182 | 33,994 | 35,015 | 34,906 |
| Maryland | 5,557 | 9,885 | 18,308 | 37,520 | 42,300 | 42,958 | 42,988 | 42,526 |
| Massachusetts | 5,545 | 9,175 | 18,900 | 40,175 | 48,543 | 52,663 | 54,244 | 45,075 |
| Michigan | 5,654 | 10,125 | 20,682 | 37,286 | 48,507 | 50,764 | 52,288 | 48,207 |
| Minnesota | 5,275 | 9,957 | 16,654 | 33,340 | 38,615 | 37,680 | 38,811 | 39,458 |
| Mississippi | 3,314 | 6,012 | 12,274 | 25,079 | 27,870 | 28,712 | 28,648 | 29,530 |
| Missouri | 4,536 | 8,091 | 14,543 | 28,166 | 32,466 | 33,870 | 34,887 | 34,746 |
| Montana | 4,425 | 8,100 | 15,080 | 29,526 | 30,052 | 30,908 | 31,836 | 31,356 |
| Nebraska | 3,876 | 7,855 | 14,236 | 27,024 | 32,803 | 34,023 | 35,045 | 32,880 |
| Nevada | 5,693 | 9,689 | 17,290 | 31,970 | 36,553 | 37,879 | 39,179 | 38,883 |
| New Hampshire | 4,455 | 8,018 | 13,508 | 29,798 | 39,564 | 42,188 | 43,455 | 37,405 |
| New Jersey | 5,871 | 9,500 | 18,851 | 37,485 | 49,196 | 50,435 | 51,949 | 51,193 |
| New Mexico | 5,382 | 8,125 | 15,406 | 25,790 | 28,866 | 29,389 | 30,271 | 32,398 |
| New York | 6,537 | 10,200 | 20,400 | 40,000 | 48,300 | 48,754 | 50,218 | 49,437 |
| North Carolina | 4,178 | 7,744 | 14,445 | 28,952 | 32,360 | 31,622 | 32,571 | 36,098 |
| North Dakota | 3,695 | 6,900 | 13,684 | 23,788 | 26,515 | 27,153 | 27,905 | 28,976 |
| Ohio | 5,124 | 8,594 | 16,100 | 32,467 | 37,867 | 39,038 | 40,087 | 40,566 |
| Oklahoma | 4,659 | 7,139 | 13,500 | 23,944 | 28,928 | 30,584 | 31,000 | 31,149 |
| Oregon | 5,535 | 9,200 | 16,996 | 32,100 | 40,100 | 40,980 | 42,210 | 42,883 |
| Pennsylvania | 5,308 | 9,000 | 17,060 | 34,110 | 45,422 | 47,087 | 48,500 | 48,457 |
| Rhode Island | 5,499 | 8,900 | 18,425 | 36,704 | 41,464 | 42,900 | 44,188 | 45,650 |
| South Carolina | 3,450 | 7,000 | 13,670 | 28,453 | 31,512 | 33,155 | 34,219 | 34,506 |
| South Dakota | 3,725 | 6,700 | 13,010 | 22,120 | 25,726 | 27,354 | 27,767 | 28,552 |
| Tennessee | 3,929 | 7,290 | 14,193 | 27,949 | 32,452 | 34,412 | 35,093 | 36,500 |
| Texas | 4,708 | 7,503 | 14,729 | 28,549 | 31,444 | 33,861 | 35,217 | 35,041 |
| Utah | 5,096 | 8,049 | 17,403 | 24,591 | 29,672 | 31,780 | 33,000 | 32,950 |
| Vermont | 4,466 | 8,225 | 13,300 | 29,012 | 36,681 | 37,054 | 38,167 | 36,800 |
| Virginia | 4,312 | 8,200 | 14,655 | 31,656 | 34,587 | 35,535 | 36,602 | 37,475 |
| Washington | 5,643 | 9,500 | 19,735 | 31,828 | 37,752 | 39,594 | 39,591 | 38,692 |
| West Virginia | 3,952 | 7,850 | 14,395 | 23,842 | 33,051 | 33,296 | 34,360 | 34,244 |
| Wisconsin | 4,870 | 9,150 | 16,335 | 32,445 | 37,534 | 39,212 | 40,389 | 40,657 |
| Wyoming | 4,937 | 8,532 | 16,830 | 29,047 | 32,300 | 32,493 | 32,626 | 33,500 |
| Dist. of Columbia | 6,280 | 11,075 | 23,027 | 32,638 | 42,088 | 39,663 | 40,854 | 47,150 |

*Sources*: U.S. Department of Education, National Center for Education Statistics, Statistics of State School Systems; National Education Association, *Rankings & Estimates: Rankings of the States 1999 and Estimates of School Statistics 2000.* © NEA, Washington, D.C. 2000. All rights reserved

*Note*: Instructional staff includes supervisors, principals, classroom teachers, librarians and other related instructional staff. Information for the years 1992-93 and 1993-94 can be located in *The Book of the States*, Volume 32, 1998-99.

## Table 8.4
# STATE COURSE REQUIREMENTS FOR HIGH SCHOOL GRADUATION

| State or other jurisdiction | All courses | English/ language arts | Social studies | Mathe- matics | Science | Physical education/ health | Electives | Other courses | Last known revision or effective date |
|---|---|---|---|---|---|---|---|---|---|
| | | | | | | *Years of instruction in . . .* | | | |
| **Alabama (a)** | 24 | 4 | 4 | 4 | 4 | 1.5 | 5.5 | .5 fine arts, .5 computer applications | 1995 |
| **Alaska (b)** | 21 | 4 | 3 | 2 | 2 | 1 | 9 | . . . | 1997 |
| **Arizona (c)** | 20 | 4 | 2.5 | 2 | 2 | . . . | 8 | .5 free enterprise, 1 fine arts or vocational education | 1996 |
| **Arkansas (d)** | | | | | | | | | |
| College prep diploma | 21 | 4 | 3 | 3 | 3 | 1 | 4 | 2 foreign language | 2002 |
| Technical diploma | 21 | 4 | 2 | 3 | 3 | 1 | . . . | 6 vocational courses | 2002 |
| **California (e)** | 13 | 3 | 3 | 2 | 2 | 2 | As prescribed locally | 1 (includes foreign language, or visual performing arts) | 1990 |
| **Colorado (f)** | . . . | . . . | . . . | . . . | . . . | . . . | . . . | | 1998 |
| **Connecticut (g)** | 20 | 4 | 3 | 3 | 2 | 1 | 6 | 1 arts or vocational education | 1996 |
| **Delaware (h)** | | | | | | | | | |
| Standard diploma | 20 | 4 | 3 | 2 | 2 | 1.5 | 6.5 | 1 computer literacy | 1999 |
| Standard diploma | 22 | 4 | 3 | 3 | 3 | 1.5 | . . . | 1 computer literacy, 3 Career Pathway, 3.5 additional academic coursework | 2000 |
| Standard diploma | 22 | 4 | 3 | 3 | 3 | 1.5 | . . . | 1 computer literacy, 1 visual and performing arts, 3 Career Pathway, 2.5 additional academic coursework | 2001 |
| **Florida (i)** | 24 | 4 | 2.5 | 3 | 3 | 1 | 9 | .5 economics, 1 practical arts career education or exploratory career education (f) | 1997 |
| **Georgia (j)** | | | | | | | | | |
| Vocational diploma | 21 | 4 | 3 | 3 | 3 | 1 | 2 | 1 computer technology, 4 vocational diploma units | 1997 |
| College prep. diploma | 21 | 4 | 3 | 3 | 3 | 1 | 4 | 2 foreign languange, 1 fine arts, vocational education, computer technology or junior ROTC | |
| **Hawaii (k)** | | | | | | | | | |
| Standard diploma | 22 | 4 | 4 | 3 | 3 | 2 | 6 | . . . | 1997 |
| Recognition Diploma | 24 | 4 | 4 | 3 | 3 | 2 | 6 | 2 foreign language, performing/fine arts or vocational education | 1997 |
| **Idaho (l)** | 21 | 4 | 2.5 | 2 | 2 | 1.5 | 6 | .5 reading, .5 speech or debate, 2 humanities | 2001 |
| **Illinois (m)** | 16 | 3 | 2 | 2 | 1 | 4.5 | 2.25 | 1 music, art, foreign language or vocational education, .25 consumer education | 1995 |
| **Indiana (n)** | 19.5 | 4 | 2 | 2 | 2 | 1.5 | 8 | . . . | 1995 |
| **Iowa (o)** | . . . | . . . | . . . | . . . | . . . | . . . | . . . | . . . | 1998 |
| **Kansas (p)** | 21 | 4 | 3 | 2 | 2 | 1 | 9 | . . . | |
| **Kentucky (q)** | 22 | 4 | 3 | 3 | 3 | 1 | 7 | 1 visual and performing arts | 1997 |
| **Louisiana (r)** | | | | | | | | | |
| Standard diploma | 23 | 4 | 3 | 3 | 3 | 2 | 8 | . . . | 1998 |
| Regents diploma | 24 | 4 | 4 | 4 | 3 | 2 | 4 | 3 foreign language, 1 fine arts | 1998 |
| **Maine (s)** | 16 | 4 | 2 | 2 | 2 | 1.5 | 3.5 | 1 fine arts | 1992 |
| **Maryland (t)** | 21 | 4 | 3 | 3 | 3 | 1 | 3 | 1 fine arts, 2 foreign language or advanced technology | 1997 |
| **Massachusetts (u)** | . . . | . . . | 1 | . . . | . . . | 4 | . . . | local boards determine remaining requirements | 1994 |
| **Michigan (v)** | . . . | . . . | . . . | . . . | . . . | . . . | . . . | 1 civics | 1997 |
| **Minnesota (w)** | . . . | . . . | . . . | . . . | . . . | . . . | . . . | . . . | 2000 |
| **Mississippi (x)** | 20 | 4 | 3 | 3 | 2 | 0.5 | 6 | 1 arts, .5 computer education | 1998 |
| | 20 | 4 | 3 | 3 | 3 | 0.5 | 4.5 | 1 arts, .5 computer education, .5 keyboarding | 2002 |
| **Missouri (y)** | 22 | 3 | 2 | 2 | 2 | 1 | 10 | 1 fine arts, 1 practical arts | 1993 |
| **Montana (z)** | 20 | 4 | 2 | 2 | 2 | 1 | 7 | 1 fine arts, 1 practical/vocational arts | 1993 |
| **Nebraska (aa)** | 200 high school credit hours | . . . | . . . | . . . | . . . | . . . | . . . | . . . | 1996 |
| **Nevada (bb)** | 22.5 | 4 | 2 | 2 | 2 | 2.5 | 8.5 | 1 arts/humanities, .5 computer literacy | 1997 |
| **New Hampshire(cc)** | 19.75 | 4 | 2 | 2 | 2 | 1.25 | 7 | .5 arts, .5 computer education, .5 business/economics | 1993 |
| **New Jersey (dd)** | 22 | 4 | 3 | 3 | 3 | 4 | 4.5 | 1 fine, practical or performing arts; .5 consumer education | 1996 |

See footnotes at end of table.

## STATE COURSE REQUIREMENTS — Continued

| State or other jurisdiction | All courses | English/ language arts | Social studies | Mathe-matics | Science | Physical education/ health | Electives | Other courses | Last known revision or effective date |
|---|---|---|---|---|---|---|---|---|---|
| New Mexico (ee) ........ | 23 | 4 | 3 | 3 | 2 | 1 | 9 | 1 communication skills | 1997 |
| New York (ff) ............. | | | | | | | | | |
|   Local diploma ........... | 18.5 | 4 | 4 | 2 | 2 | 2.5 | 5 | 1 | 1996 |
|   Regents diploma ....... | 18.5 | 4 | 4 | 2 | 2 | 2.5 | 5 | 1 art and/or music, 3 second language | 2000 |
| North Carolina (gg) ... | 20 | 4 | 3 | 3 | 3 | 1 | 6 | . . . | 1993 |
| North Dakota (hh) ..... | 17 | 4 | 3 | 2 | 2 | 1 | 5 | . . . | 1994 |
| Ohio (ii) ...................... | 18 | 3 | 2 | 2 | 1 | 1 | 9 | . . . | 1998 |
| | 21 | 4 | 3 | 3 | 2 | 1 | 8 | . . . | 2001 |
| | 21 | 4 | 3 | 3 | 3 | 1 | 7 | . . . | 2003 |
| Oklahoma (jj) ............ | 20 | 4 | 2 | 2 | 2 | . . . | 8 | 1 visual arts, 1 general music | 1996 |
| | 21 | 4 | 2 | 3 | 2 | . . . | 8 | 1 visual arts, 1 general music | 2000 |
| Oregon (kk) ............... | 22 | 3 | 3 | 2 | 2 | 2 | 9 | 1 applied arts, fine arts or foreign language | 1997 |
| Pennsylvania (ll) ........ | 21 | 4 | 3 | 3 | 3 | 1 | 5 | 2 arts/humanities or computer science | 1993 |
| Rhode Island (mm) .... | | | | | | | | | |
|   Standard diploma ..... | 16 | 4 | 2 | 2 | 2 | . . . | 6 | . . . | 1989 |
|   College preparatory .. | 18 | 4 | 2 | 3 | 2 | . . . | 4 | 2 foreign language, .5 computer literacy, .5 arts | . . . |
| South Carolina (nn) ... | | | | | | | | | |
|   Tech prep ................. | 20 | 4 | 3 | 3 | 2 | 1 | 7 | . . . | 2000 |
|   Tech prep ................. | 24 | 4 | 3 | 4 | 3 | 1 | 7 | 1 computer science, 1 vocational unit | 2001 |
|   College prep ............. | 24 | 4 | 3 | 4 | 3 | 1 | 7 | 1 computer science, 1 foreign language | 2001 |
| South Dakota (oo) ...... | 20 | 4 | 3 | 2 | 2 | . . . | 8 | .5 computer studies, .5 fine arts | 1996 |
| Tennessee (pp) ............ | | | | | | | | | |
|   Technical preparatory | 20 | 4 | 3 | 3 | 3 | 1 | 2 | 4 units in particular technical area | 1994 |
|   University preparatory | 20 | 4 | 3 | 3 | 3 | 1 | 3 | 2 foreign language, 1 fine arts | 1994 |
| Texas (qq) .................... | 22 | 4 | 2.5 | 3 | 2 | 2 | 5.5 | 1 world history/geography or approved science, .5 economics, .5 speech, 1 technology application | 1997 |
| Utah (rr) ...................... | 24 | 3 | 3 | 2 | 2 | 2 | 9.5 | 1.5 arts, 1 applied technical education | 1997 |
| Vermont (ss) ............... | 14.5 | 4 | 3 | 2 | 2 | . . . | 1.5 | 1 arts, 1 additional unit in science or math | 1997 |
| Virginia (tt) ................. | | | | | | | | | |
|   Standard diploma ..... | 22 | 4 | 3 | 3 | 3 | 2 | 6 | 1 fine or practical arts | 1998 |
|   Advanced studies ...... | 24 | 4 | 4 | 4 | 4 | 2 | 2 | 3 foreign language, 1 fine or practical arts | 1998 |
| Washington (uu) ........ | 19 | 3 | 2.5 | 2 | 2 | 2 | 5.5 | 1 occupational education, 1 fine/ visual or performing arts | 1998 |
| West Virginia (vv) ...... | 21 | 4 | 3 | 2 | 2 | 2 | 7 | 1 foreign language, performing arts or fine arts | . . . |
| | 24 | 4 | 4 | 4 | 4 | 2 | 2 | 3 foreign language, 1 fine or practical arts | 1999 |
| Wisconsin (ww) .......... | 21.5 | 4 | 3 | 2 | 2 | 2 | 8 | . . . | 1995 |
| Wyoming (xx) ............. | 13 (xx) | 4 | 3 | 3 | 3 | . . . | (xx) | . . . | 1997 |
| Dist. of Columbia (yy) | 23.5 | 4 | 3.5 | 3 | 3 | 1.5 | 3.5 | 2 foreign language, 1 social values/ life skills, 1 career/vocational, 5 art, .5 music | 1996 |

See footnotes at end of table.

# STATE COURSE REQUIREMENTS — Continued

*Source*: Education Commission of the States, *Clearinghouse Notes*, November 1998., www.ecs.org

Key:

. . . — No requirement.

(a) In Alabama, passing graduation exams in reading, language, math, science, and social studies is required. Math requirement include algebra I and geometry. Science includes 1 biology and 1 physical science. Physical education requirement consists of 1 in PE and .5 in health. Demonstration of computer literacy through related coursework is required.

(b) In Alaska, students must pass a competency exam in reading, writing and math. Electives are established by the local board of education.

(c) In Arizona, The state board of education adopts competency tests in reading, writing and math. Language arts requirement must include .5 of speech/debate. Social studies requirement consist of 1 world history/geography and 1.5 in U.S./Arizona history and constitutions.

(d) In Arkansas, basic competencies are tested in grades 4, 8, and 11 or 12 in science, math, English, history and social studies. Science includes 1 life science and one physical science. Physical education consists of .5 in PE and .5 in health and safety. Arkansas also issues a college preparatory and technical diploma beyond the basic diploma. The college prep diploma maintains the total units required but defines courses which must be taken in social studies, math and science. The technical diploma also defines courses which must be completed in social studies, math and science; eliminates electives; and adds 6 units in sequential and related vocational credits to the other category. Legislation in 1997 eliminates the three diploma types and creates a common core curriculum for all students beginning with the graduating class of 2002. Requirements remain the same as the current basic diploma. Math requirement then includes 1 in algebra or equivalent and 1 in geometry or equivalent. Science requirement then includes 1 in biology or equivalent and 1 in physical science.

(e) In California, electives are left to the discretion of the local board of education. Social studies consists of 1 U.S. history and geography; 1 world history, culture and geography; .5 American government and .5 in economics. Science includes biological and physical sciences.

(f) In Colorado, legislation in 1998 implemented a statewide assessment program as part of the indicators for state accreditation. Beginning with the spring semester of 2001, the program requires all 10th graders to take an assessment in reading, writing and math. Beginning with the spring semester of 2003, 12th graders scoring below proficient on the 10th grade assessment will retake the assessment. Results of the retake exam will be included as accreditation indicators. Colorado is a local control state where the curriculum and other graduation requirements are left to the discretion of the individual local districts.

(g) In Connecticut, 50 hours of community service may be used for .5 credits towards graduation requirements.

(h) In Delaware, the student testing program assesses performance of 10th graders in reading, writing and math. In June of 2000, only those students passing exams will be eligible for a diploma. Requirements for the graduating class of 2000 increases the total to 22, increases both math and science to 3 units, eliminates electives and changes the other requirement to 7.5 to consist of 3 in career pathways (academic, visual and performing arts, foreign language or vocational education program), 1 in computer literacy and 3.5 in additional academic, visual and performing arts, foreign languages and/or vocational technical education program units. The graduating classes of 2001 and beyond retain these same requirements except that 1 unit of visual and performing arts will be required as part of the 7.5 other course requirement.

(i) In Florida, all 11th grade students must pass competency tests. Social studies requirement consists of 1 American history, 1 world history and .5 in American government. Two of the science units must be in laboratory sciences. Physical education consists of .5 in PE and .5 in life management skills. Beginning in the 1997-98 school year, 1 math credit must be in algebra 1 or higher. School boards may award .5 credits for 75 hours of community service. Students must achieve a 2.0 GPA to graduate.

(j) In Georgia, all 11th grade students must pass a curriculum based assessment exam prior to graduation. Georgia issues a college preparatory or vocational diploma. The math requirement includes 1 algebra unit. The vocational diploma other requirement consists of 4 vocational diploma units and 1 in computer technology. For the college preparatory diploma the other requirement consists of 2 in foreign language and 1 in computer technology and/or fine arts and/or vocational education and/or junior ROTC and/or foreign language.

(k) In Hawaii, the state test of essential competencies (HSTEC) is administered to 10th grade students. Passing is required to graduate. Physical education requirement consists of 1 in PE, .5 in health and .5 in guidance. For a diploma with a board of education recognition endorsement, students must add 2 units in foreign language, performing/fine arts or vocational education (total 24 units) and maintain a 3.0 GPA.

(l) In Idaho, to qualify for graduation the state board of education requires either a C average in core subjects, demonstrated competency on statewide achievement test and direct writing assessment in the 11th grade or validation of student achievement through an approved, locally developed, core competency plan. Science requirement includes 1 in laboratory science. Physical education requirement consists of 1 in PE and .5 in health. The social studies requirement includes 1 U.S. history and 1 in American government. Effective July 1, 2000, the requirement is increased to 2.5 adding .5 in economics.

(m) In Illinois, passing end of course exam in American history and government is required to graduate. Social studies requirement includes 1 in U.S. history and .5 in American government. Science requirement may include 1 unit in computer technology. Physical education requirement consists of 4 in PE and .5 in health. Students may test out of consumer education requirement.

(n) In Indiana, obtaining the educational proficiency standard through the Indiana statewide testing for educational progress program is required for graduation. Statute requires state board to determine grade level for the test, but it must be given higher than 9th grade. Students must successfully complete a course concerning the constitutions of the U.S. and Indiana to graduate. Social studies requirement includes 1 in U.S. history and 1 in U.S. government. Physical education requirement is 1 in PE and .5 in health and safety.

(o) In Iowa, legislation in 1998 requires the establishment of a set of core academic indicators in reading, math, and science for grade 11. Graduation requirements are determined on a local level guided by an established minimum education program which must be offered in public schools. Requirements include 1 unit of U.S. history and .5 in American government. All students must participate in physical education each semester unless they are specifically excused.

(p) In Kansas, passing a course in Kansas history and government between the 7th and 12th grade is required for graduation. The language arts requirement includes 3 English units. The social studies requirement includes 1 American history and .5 in American government. The physical education requirement may include .5 units in health.

(q) In Kentucky, an assessment exam is given in reading, math, science, social studies, and writing during 11th grade. A writing portfolio is required in 12th grade. Passing is not tied to graduation. Social studies units incorporate U.S. history, economics, government, world geography and world civilization. Math requirements include algebra 1 and geometry. Physical education requirement consists of .5 in PE and .5 in health.

(r) In Louisiana, passing state graduation test is required. Social studies requirement consist of 1 in American history, 1 in world history/geography/ civilization, .5 in civics and .5 in free enterprise. Math requirement includes algebra. Science requirement includes biology. Physical education requirement is 1.5 in PE and .5 in health. Louisiana honors curriculum (to receive a Regent's diploma) increases the total unit requirement to 24. Social studies and math are increased to 4, electives are reduced to 4 and the other requirement is increased to 3 which consists of 2 in foreign language and 1 in fine arts.

(s) In Maine, students must pass computer proficiency standards. Social studies requirement includes 1 in American history and government. Science requirement includes 1 year of laboratory study. Physical education requirement consists of 1 in PE and .5 in health.

(t) In Maryland, passage of English, math and government exams is required for graduation. Biology may be included at the discretion of the local district. Completion of a state approved career and technology program may substitute for the advanced technology units. Additionally, 75 clock hours of student community service is required for graduation.

(u) In Massachusetts, competency determination in math, science and technology, history and social studies, foreign languages, and English, at the 10th grade level based on comprehensive diagnostic assessment is required for graduation. Social studies unit requirement is in American history. Local boards determine all remaining requirements.

(v) In Michigan, state assessment tests are administered in communications skills, math, science and social studies. Students passing tests receive a state endorsement on their diplomas. Local boards may issue diploma for completion of their established requirements regardless of whether the student receives the state endorsement. All remaining requirements are established by the local board. The state board establishes academic curriculum content standards model setting forth desired learning objectives in math, science, reading, history, geography, economics, American governance and writing.

(w) In Minnesota, students must pass a state test, or approved alternative test, in writing composition, reading and math. Testing usually begins in the 10th grade depending on the district. A "profile of learning" requirement has been enacted which requires students to complete 24 of 48 standards in broad academic areas prior to graduation.

## STATE COURSE REQUIREMENTS — Continued

(x) In Mississippi, students must demonstrate minimum performance standards in reading, writing and math on state examination. Social studies requirement consists of 1 in U.S. history, 1 in world history, .5 in U.S. government and .5 in Mississippi studies. PE requirement is in health. For the graduating class of 2002, electives are reduced to 4.5 units, science is increased to 3 units and other is increased to 2 units with the addition of a .5 unit of keyboarding.

(y) In Missouri, students must pass an end of course exam in the principles of the constitutions of the U.S. and Missouri prior to graduation. Social studies requirement includes .5 in U.S. and state government.

(z) In Montana, PE requirement is in health.

(aa) In Nebraska, all students are required to complete a minimum of 200 high school credit hours prior to graduation. A minimum of 80 percent of these hours must be completed in core curriculum subjects. Local boards determine requirements.

(bb) In Nevada, students must pass the Nevada high school proficiency examinations in reading, math and writing for graduation. Social studies requirements consist of 1 in American history and 1 in American government. Physical education requirement is 2 in PE and .5 in health. Computer literacy may be waived by demonstration of competency.

(cc) In New Hampshire, social studies requirement includes 1 U.S. and New Hampshire history and government. Science requirement is 1 physical science and 1 biological science. Physical education requirement is 1 PE and .25 health. Computer education requirement may be met through examination or course prior to high school.

(dd) In New Jersey, passing statewide proficiency examination in the 11th grade in reading, writing, and math is required for graduation. Social studies requirement consists of 2 U.S. history and 1 world history/cultures. Science requirement must be fulfilled with natural or physical sciences.

(ee) In New Mexico, students must pass a state competency exam in order to receive a diploma. If exam is not passed, student receives a certificate of completion upon exit at the completion of 12th grade. Social studies requirement consists of government and economics, world and U.S. history and geography. Science requirement includes 1 lab component.

(ff) In New York, passage of comprehensive exams in English, math, U.S. history and government, science and global studies is required for graduation. Within an established range, local districts may determine passing scores. New York issues either a local or Regent's diploma. Requirements for a Regent's diploma include more stringent course difficulty sequencing and additional exams. A minimum sequence of three units in a second language is required for the Regent's diploma. Physical education requirement includes .5 of health. Only the health unit may be counted towards total graduation credit.

(gg) In North Carolina, state competency examination is required for graduation. Social studies requirement consists of 1 in government and economics, 1 in U.S. history and 1 in world studies. Math requirement includes 1 in algebra I. Science requirement includes 1 in biology and 1 in physical science.

(hh) In North Dakota, Social Studies requirement includes 1 in world history and 1 in U.S. history, both with strong geography components. The math requirement may include business math. The state department of public instruction sets the state minimum of 17 total units. State recommends that school districts establish their requirements at a minimum of 20 units.

(ii) In Ohio, passage of exams for proficiency in reading, writing, math, science and citizenship are required for graduation. Social studies requirement includes .5 in U.S. history and .5 in U.S. government. Physical education requirement consists of .5 in PE and .5 in health. A graduation requirement exists to complete 3 units in a subject other than English and are considered a minor.

(jj) In Oklahoma, competency tests are administered in math, science, English, history, geography and culture, and the arts during the 11th grade. However, they are not tied to graduation requirements. Social studies requirement includes U.S. and Oklahoma history. For the graduating class of 2000 total units increase to 21 by increasing math to 3.

(kk) In Oregon, certificates of initial mastery are issued to sophomores for demonstrated proficiency in core subject areas. Certificates of initial mastery are not required to graduate. A statewide assessment is given to 10th graders in math, English, science and history. Physical education requirement consists of 1 in PE and 1 in health.

(ll) In Pennsylvania, students must achieve 52 state academic performance standards and locally developed student learning outcomes. Students must also complete a project in one or more areas of concentrated studies. Pennsylvania is phasing out the required units in individual subject system. Graduation requirements are now based on the local districts' submission of a strategic plan, fulfillment of the state performance standards and local student learning outcomes.

(mm) In Rhode Island, students are required to take educational assessment examinations in reading, writing, and math during 10th grade. The social studies requirement includes 1 in U.S. history and government.

(nn) In South Carolina, passage of an exit examination in reading, writing, and math is required for graduation. Students are allowed four opportunities to pass the examination. South Carolina uses a technical preparation track and a college preparation track to fulfill course requirements. Technical track students who will graduate in the year 2000 must use electives to complete a career major which consists of four sequential units in an occupational program. Social studies requirement includes 1 in U.S. history, .5 in U.S. government and .5 in Economics. Physical education requirement may be met with junior ROTC.

(oo) In South Dakota, Language Arts requirement includes 1.5 in writing, 1 in literature (of which .5 is American literature) and .5 in speech. The social studies requirement includes .5 in U.S. history, .5 in U.S. government, and .5 in geography. Science requirement is in laboratory sciences. Students may complete the computer studies requirement through demonstrated mastery of basic course content.

(pp) In Tennessee, passage of the Tennessee comprehensive assessment program tests are required to obtain a full diploma. Certificates of attendance or unsatisfactory performance are issued to students not passing the examination. Math requirement includes algebra. Science includes biology. Tennessee issues a university preparation or a technical preparation diploma.

(qq) In Texas, students must pass the secondary exit level assessment instruments in English and math or pass the end of course instruments in algebra I and English II and either biology I or U.S. history. Social studies requirement consists of 1 in world history or world geography, 1 in U.S. history and .5 in U.S. government. Math requirement must include algebra I. Science requirement must include 1 from biology I, chemistry I or physics I. Physical education requirement consists of 1.5 in PE and .5 in health.

(rr) In Utah, assessment of student mastery of required core subjects occurs at the completion of 8th, 10th and 12th grade. Implementation is the responsibility of local districts. The state does not require passage to graduate. Required elective areas are divided into college entry or applied technology clusters.

(ss) In Vermont, statewide academic examinations are administered in math, science, English and social studies in order to qualify for a "governor's diploma." Social studies requirement includes 1 U.S. history and 1 world history. Science requirement consists of 1 physical and 1 natural science.

(tt) In Virginia, students must pass all components of the literacy passport test in order to graduate. End of course standards of learning tests for certain courses are also required. The science requirement for both the standard and advanced studies diploma is in laboratory courses.

(uu) In Washington, assessment tests are given to 11th graders to assess strengths and weaknesses. Beginning with the 2000-2001 school year, passing assessment examinations result in issuance of a certificate of mastery which is required for graduation. Social studies requirement consists of 1 U.S. history and government, .5 Washington state history and government and 1 world history. Science requires 1 laboratory course.

(vv) In West Virginia, students in grades 9-11 take the Stanford Achievement Test to assess basic skills. Physical education requirement consists of 1 in PE and 1 in health. For the freshman class entering in fall of 1999, total units increase to 24. Math (to include algebra and 1 higher math) is increased to 3. Science (to include coordinated and thematic science and 1 higher science) is increased to 3. Electives are reduced to 4. Students must also graduate with "work base learning" requirements which are determined by local boards.

(ww) In Wyoming, legislation in 1997 requires the state board of education to establish, through testing or other means, a requirement for each student to demonstrate mastery of the common core of knowledge and skills in order to earn a high school diploma. The means and process to establish this requirement have not been implemented. Social studies requirement includes history and American government. Electives are determined by the local school board. Thirteen units are required plus the elective units as determined by the school board in order to obtain the total units.

## Table 8.5
## NUMBER OF INSTITUTIONS OF HIGHER EDUCATION AND BRANCHES,
## BY TYPE, CONTROL OF INSTITUTION AND STATE: 1996-97

| State or other jurisdiction | Total | Public 4-Year institutions | | | | | Private 4-Year institutions | | | |
|---|---|---|---|---|---|---|---|---|---|---|
| | | Research | Doctoral | Master | Baccalaureate | Other 4-Year | Research | Doctoral | Master | Baccalaureate |
| United States .......... | 4,009 | 85 | 66 | 278 | 113 | 72 | 40 | 49 | 291 | 659 |
| Alabama ........................... | 82 | 2 | 2 | 13 | 1 | 0 | 0 | 0 | 4 | 10 |
| Alaska .............................. | 7 | 0 | 1 | 2 | 0 | 0 | 0 | 0 | 1 | 1 |
| Arizona ............................ | 67 | 2 | 1 | 1 | 0 | 1 | 0 | 0 | 2 | 8 |
| Arkansas .......................... | 47 | 1 | 0 | 6 | 2 | 1 | 0 | 0 | 1 | 8 |
| California ......................... | 383 | 9 | 1 | 19 | 0 | 3 | 3 | 9 | 33 | 33 |
| Colorado .......................... | 69 | 2 | 3 | 2 | 5 | 2 | 0 | 1 | 3 | 8 |
| Connecticut ..................... | 42 | 1 | 0 | 4 | 0 | 1 | 1 | 0 | 7 | 6 |
| Delaware .......................... | 9 | 1 | 0 | 1 | 0 | 0 | 0 | 0 | 2 | 1 |
| Florida ............................. | 134 | 3 | 3 | 3 | 0 | 1 | 1 | 2 | 11 | 24 |
| Georgia ............................ | 102 | 2 | 1 | 12 | 1 | 3 | 1 | 2 | 2 | 21 |
| Hawaii .............................. | 20 | 1 | 0 | 0 | 2 | 0 | 0 | 0 | 2 | 1 |
| Idaho ................................ | 14 | 1 | 1 | 1 | 1 | 0 | 0 | 0 | 0 | 3 |
| Illinois .............................. | 173 | 3 | 2 | 7 | 0 | 0 | 2 | 3 | 15 | 30 |
| Indiana ............................. | 96 | 2 | 3 | 7 | 2 | 0 | 1 | 0 | 6 | 22 |
| Iowa ................................. | 64 | 2 | 0 | 1 | 0 | 0 | 0 | 0 | 5 | 27 |
| Kansas .............................. | 58 | 2 | 1 | 4 | 1 | 2 | 0 | 0 | 5 | 13 |
| Kentucky .......................... | 65 | 1 | 1 | 6 | 0 | 0 | 0 | 0 | 4 | 16 |
| Louisiana ......................... | 77 | 1 | 3 | 9 | 0 | 1 | 1 | 0 | 3 | 3 |
| Maine ............................... | 34 | 0 | 1 | 1 | 5 | 1 | 0 | 1 | 1 | 7 |
| Maryland .......................... | 56 | 1 | 1 | 9 | 1 | 1 | 1 | 0 | 4 | 6 |
| Massachusetts ................. | 124 | 1 | 1 | 8 | 2 | 3 | 6 | 3 | 12 | 26 |
| Michigan .......................... | 110 | 3 | 2 | 10 | 0 | 0 | 0 | 2 | 6 | 21 |
| Minnesota ........................ | 116 | 1 | 0 | 6 | 4 | 1 | 0 | 1 | 4 | 15 |
| Mississippi ....................... | 44 | 2 | 1 | 3 | 2 | 1 | 0 | 0 | 2 | 5 |
| Missouri ........................... | 109 | 1 | 3 | 6 | 2 | 2 | 2 | 0 | 9 | 19 |
| Montana ........................... | 29 | 0 | 2 | 3 | 1 | 0 | 0 | 0 | 0 | 4 |
| Nebraska .......................... | 37 | 1 | 0 | 4 | 1 | 1 | 0 | 0 | 2 | 9 |
| Nevada ............................. | 13 | 0 | 1 | 1 | 0 | 0 | 0 | 0 | 0 | 1 |
| New Hampshire ............... | 29 | 0 | 1 | 2 | 2 | 0 | 0 | 2 | 2 | 5 |
| New Jersey ....................... | 58 | 1 | 2 | 7 | 3 | 1 | 1 | 2 | 5 | 6 |
| New Mexico ..................... | 44 | 2 | 0 | 3 | 0 | 1 | 0 | 0 | 1 | 6 |
| New York ......................... | 310 | 3 | 3 | 19 | 8 | 9 | 8 | 9 | 29 | 46 |
| North Carolina ................ | 121 | 2 | 1 | 9 | 3 | 1 | 1 | 1 | 7 | 28 |
| North Dakota ................... | 23 | 0 | 2 | 1 | 3 | 0 | 0 | 0 | 1 | 1 |
| Ohio ................................. | 178 | 4 | 6 | 1 | 11 | 2 | 1 | 1 | 11 | 32 |
| Oklahoma ........................ | 45 | 2 | 0 | 6 | 4 | 2 | 0 | 1 | 4 | 4 |
| Oregon ............................. | 51 | 2 | 1 | 2 | 1 | 2 | 0 | 0 | 4 | 10 |
| Pennsylvania ................... | 249 | 3 | 2 | 16 | 21 | 3 | 3 | 3 | 19 | 44 |
| Rhode Island ................... | 12 | 1 | 0 | 1 | 0 | 0 | 1 | 0 | 1 | 3 |
| South Carolina ................ | 60 | 2 | 0 | 6 | 3 | 1 | 0 | 0 | 2 | 17 |
| South Dakota ................... | 27 | 0 | 1 | 2 | 2 | 3 | 0 | 0 | 0 | 8 |
| Tennessee ........................ | 83 | 1 | 3 | 5 | 0 | 2 | 1 | 0 | 5 | 25 |
| Texas ............................... | 187 | 4 | 6 | 22 | 2 | 6 | 1 | 3 | 14 | 20 |
| Utah ................................. | 21 | 2 | 0 | 1 | 2 | 0 | 1 | 0 | 2 | 1 |
| Vermont ........................... | 25 | 1 | 0 | 2 | 2 | 0 | 0 | 0 | 3 | 10 |
| Virginia ............................ | 92 | 3 | 3 | 6 | 3 | 0 | 0 | 0 | 13 | 20 |
| Washington ...................... | 72 | 2 | 0 | 5 | 1 | 0 | 0 | 0 | 11 | 3 |
| West Virginia ................... | 37 | 1 | 0 | 1 | 9 | 2 | 0 | 0 | 3 | 6 |
| Wisconsin ........................ | 66 | 2 | 0 | 11 | 0 | 0 | 0 | 1 | 5 | 15 |
| Wyoming .......................... | 9 | 1 | 0 | 0 | 0 | 0 | 0 | 0 | 0 | 0 |
| U.S. Service Schools | 12 | 0 | 0 | 0 | 0 | 11 | 0 | 0 | 0 | 0 |
| District of Columbia ...... | 17 | 0 | 0 | 1 | 0 | 1 | 3 | 2 | 3 | 1 |
| American Samoa ............. | 1 | 0 | 0 | 0 | 0 | 0 | 0 | 0 | 0 | 0 |
| Guam ............................... | 2 | 0 | 0 | 1 | 0 | 0 | 0 | 0 | 0 | 0 |
| Northern Marianas ........ | 1 | 0 | 0 | 0 | 0 | 0 | 0 | 0 | 0 | 0 |
| Puerto Rico ..................... | 66 | 0 | 1 | 1 | 5 | 4 | 0 | 0 | 6 | 19 |

*Source*: U.S. Department of Education, National Center for Education Statistics, Integrated Postsecondary Education Data System (IPEDS), "Institutional Characteristics, 1996-97" survey. (This table was prepared December 1998.)

*Note*:—New institutions which do not have sufficient data to report by detailed level are included under other 4-year or depending on level reported by institution.

# NUMBER OF INSTITUTIONS OF HIGHER EDUCATION AND BRANCHES, BY TYPE, CONTROL OF INSTITUTION AND STATE: 1996-97 - Continued

*Note*:-Research institutions are commited to graduate education through the doctorate, give high priority to research and receive more than $15.5 million in federal research funds annually.

Doctoral institutions offer a full range of baccalaureate programs and are committed to eduation through the doctorate. They award at least 40 doctoral degrees annually in 5 or more disciplines.

Master's institutions offer a full range of baccalaureate programs and are committed to education through the master's degree. They award at least 20 master's degrees per year.

Baccalaureate institutions primarily emphasize undergraduate education.

Other specialized 4-year institutions awarding degrees primarily in single fields of study, such as medicine, business, fine arts, theology and engineering. Also, includes some institutions which have 4-year programs, but have not reported sufficient data to identify program category.

## Table 8.6
## AVERAGE SALARY OF FULL-TIME INSTRUCTIONAL FACULTY IN INSTITUTES OF HIGHER EDUCATION, BY TYPE AND CONTROL OF INSTITUTION AND STATE: 1996-97

| State or other jurisdiction | All Institutions | Public institutions | | | | | Private institutions | | | | |
|---|---|---|---|---|---|---|---|---|---|---|---|
| | | Total | 4-year institutions | | | 2-year | Total | 4-year institutions | | | 2-year |
| | | | Total | University | 4-year | | | Total | University | Other 4-year | |
| United States ............ | $50,829 | $50,303 | $52,718 | $57,047 | $49,836 | $44,584 | $52,112 | $52,443 | $67,457 | $45,938 | $32,628 |
| Alabama ....................... | 42,006 | 42,843 | 44,785 | 48,913 | 42,219 | 37,708 | 37,530 | 37,701 | ... | 37,701 | 25,023 |
| Alaska ......................... | 50,091 | 50,725 | 50,657 | 50,914 | 50,494 | 59,281 | 38,307 | 38,307 | ... | 38,307 | ... |
| Arizona ....................... | 52,605 | 52,681 | 54,206 | 57,275 | 45,889 | 49,601 | 50,636 | 50,636 | ... | 50,636 | ... |
| Arkansas ..................... | 39,488 | 39,915 | 42,800 | 48,836 | 40,820 | 31,780 | 37,269 | 38,059 | ... | 38,059 | 16,681 |
| California ..................... | 59,870 | 59,543 | 63,276 | 75,604 | 60,987 | 54,529 | 61,172 | 61,394 | 75,175 | 54,043 | 36,992 |
| Colorado ..................... | 50,095 | 49,784 | 52,336 | 58,381 | 47,221 | 37,225 | 52,270 | 52,270 | 55,228 | 48,623 | ... |
| Connecticut .................. | 61,592 | 61,598 | 64,695 | 70,883 | 58,855 | 52,640 | 61,584 | 62,293 | 79,548 | 55,058 | 35,069 |
| Delaware ..................... | 56,948 | 57,203 | 59,872 | 62,295 | 46,688 | 43,846 | 54,483 | 54,483 | ... | 54,483 | ... |
| Florida ........................ | 47,598 | 47,576 | 52,100 | 57,386 | 49,010 | 41,436 | 47,685 | 47,718 | 59,180 | 43,449 | 26,720 |
| Georgia ....................... | 47,193 | 47,721 | 49,929 | 55,990 | 48,444 | 37,663 | 45,767 | 46,227 | 69,677 | 39,794 | 30,492 |
| Hawaii ........................ | 52,175 | 52,488 | 57,364 | 58,846 | 48,142 | 44,264 | 48,572 | 48,572 | ... | 48,572 | ... |
| Idaho .......................... | 44,016 | 44,179 | 45,201 | 49,095 | 43,360 | 37,295 | 43,460 | 40,100 | ... | 40,100 | 44,970 |
| Illinois ........................ | 52,548 | 50,970 | 51,532 | 55,988 | 47,655 | 50,034 | 55,292 | 55,746 | 72,650 | 44,627 | 28,830 |
| Indiana ....................... | 48,588 | 48,299 | 50,719 | 53,481 | 45,021 | 34,590 | 49,193 | 49,429 | 71,279 | 43,084 | 30,265 |
| Iowa ........................... | 47,191 | 51,033 | 57,503 | 60,581 | 49,273 | 36,710 | 40,880 | 40,897 | 51,200 | 39,593 | 29,025 |
| Kansas ........................ | 41,655 | 43,272 | 47,067 | 49,907 | 40,890 | 35,437 | 31,478 | 31,768 | ... | 31,768 | 25,910 |
| Kentucky ..................... | 43,410 | 45,097 | 47,773 | 54,298 | 43,871 | 35,627 | 37,369 | 37,369 | ... | 37,369 | ... |
| Louisiana ..................... | 44,884 | 43,530 | 44,635 | 52,901 | 42,521 | 34,416 | 51,281 | 51,340 | 58,881 | 38,830 | 48,630 |
| Maine .......................... | 45,199 | 43,882 | 45,874 | 49,583 | 43,866 | 35,831 | 48,616 | 49,255 | ... | 49,255 | 28,944 |
| Maryland ..................... | 50,802 | 49,781 | 52,144 | 59,221 | 48,566 | 45,594 | 54,379 | 54,441 | 71,669 | 45,791 | 25,000 |
| Massachusetts .............. | 58,697 | 51,427 | 55,611 | 64,374 | 52,029 | 41,536 | 62,790 | 63,061 | 71,789 | 53,799 | 35,212 |
| Michigan ..................... | 54,248 | 56,393 | 56,869 | 63,355 | 51,451 | 54,698 | 43,242 | 43,459 | 47,513 | 42,919 | 20,074 |
| Minnesota .................... | 48,877 | 50,390 | 53,763 | 64,476 | 48,163 | 45,176 | 45,347 | 45,591 | ... | 45,591 | 36,638 |
| Mississippi ................... | 39,644 | 40,232 | 43,302 | 45,240 | 42,010 | 36,257 | 34,896 | 35,749 | ... | 35,749 | 23,554 |
| Missouri ...................... | 47,063 | 47,579 | 49,568 | 58,603 | 47,753 | 40,596 | 46,023 | 46,424 | 62,112 | 37,842 | 29,963 |
| Montana ...................... | 40,589 | 41,731 | 43,338 | 45,089 | 39,402 | 31,758 | 33,714 | 34,360 | ... | 34,360 | 26,100 |
| Nebraska ..................... | 44,701 | 46,030 | 49,374 | 56,249 | 44,649 | 34,332 | 40,574 | 40,574 | 47,592 | 36,828 | ... |
| Nevada ........................ | 51,959 | 52,050 | 55,194 | 58,997 | 52,647 | 44,829 | 37,946 | 37,946 | ... | 37,946 | ... |
| New Hampshire ............ | 49,425 | 47,339 | 50,127 | 51,630 | 47,545 | 36,029 | 52,143 | 52,991 | ... | 52,991 | 27,236 |
| New Jersey ................... | 61,538 | 61,419 | 64,359 | 71,997 | 61,765 | 54,694 | 61,850 | 61,989 | 75,071 | 51,694 | 25,845 |
| New Mexico .................. | 43,322 | 43,552 | 47,244 | 49,782 | 40,250 | 32,627 | 38,532 | 38,532 | ... | 38,532 | ... |
| New York ..................... | 56,996 | 55,913 | 58,051 | 62,459 | 57,349 | 52,120 | 58,092 | 58,546 | 69,356 | 51,389 | 29,503 |
| North Carolina ............. | 47,462 | 49,096 | 51,803 | 62,388 | 47,500 | 32,153 | 43,687 | 43,978 | 61,504 | 37,234 | 31,300 |
| North Dakota ............... | 36,366 | 37,103 | 38,347 | 39,434 | 36,099 | 32,190 | 31,158 | 32,623 | ... | 32,623 | 23,785 |
| Ohio ........................... | 50,240 | 51,914 | 54,747 | 56,462 | 48,586 | 42,722 | 46,526 | 46,769 | 67,470 | 44,502 | 29,678 |
| Oklahoma .................... | 41,961 | 42,514 | 44,841 | 50,253 | 40,482 | 35,991 | 39,830 | 40,329 | 50,222 | 35,806 | 25,654 |
| Oregon ........................ | 44,506 | 44,212 | 45,121 | 47,702 | 42,250 | 43,161 | 45,546 | 45,546 | ... | 45,546 | ... |
| Pennsylvania ................ | 55,132 | 56,029 | 57,330 | 62,407 | 54,469 | 48,938 | 54,040 | 54,457 | 73,122 | 48,846 | 31,440 |
| Rhode Island ............... | 54,797 | 52,382 | 55,721 | 60,085 | 48,226 | 42,341 | 56,582 | 56,582 | ... | 56,582 | ... |
| South Carolina ............. | 42,246 | 43,199 | 48,228 | 53,983 | 42,235 | 32,486 | 38,030 | 38,169 | ... | 38,169 | 31,540 |
| South Dakota ............... | 36,482 | 37,279 | 37,382 | 38,107 | 36,391 | 26,212 | 33,685 | 33,738 | ... | 33,738 | 28,800 |
| Tennessee ................... | 45,532 | 45,994 | 49,315 | 56,243 | 46,955 | 35,625 | 44,488 | 44,636 | 67,787 | 35,955 | 23,582 |
| Texas .......................... | 46,434 | 45,576 | 48,678 | 55,528 | 43,062 | 39,963 | 50,117 | 50,292 | 59,321 | 43,378 | 26,395 |
| Utah ........................... | 46,735 | 45,037 | 47,232 | 51,683 | 39,984 | 36,352 | 50,704 | 50,859 | 51,750 | 39,229 | 37,370 |
| Vermont ....................... | 44,722 | 46,461 | 46,461 | 49,695 | 38,167 | ... | 43,140 | 44,403 | ... | 44,403 | 20,261 |
| Virginia ....................... | 48,468 | 49,391 | 52,734 | 57,209 | 49,924 | 38,940 | 45,405 | 45,503 | ... | 45,503 | 28,018 |
| Washington .................. | 46,038 | 46,051 | 51,042 | 54,807 | 44,925 | 39,662 | 45,989 | 45,989 | ... | 45,989 | ... |
| West Virginia ............... | 40,929 | 41,942 | 42,570 | 49,056 | 39,510 | 33,520 | 35,534 | 35,534 | ... | 35,534 | ... |
| Wisconsin .................... | 49,325 | 50,747 | 52,106 | 63,364 | 48,066 | 48,694 | 43,320 | 43,320 | 54,490 | 40,117 | ... |
| Wyoming ..................... | 39,855 | 39,855 | 46,743 | 46,743 | ... | 33,007 | ... | ... | ... | ... | ... |
| U.S. Service Schools .... | 61,536 | 61,536 | 61,536 | ... | 61,536 | ... | ... | ... | ... | ... | ... |
| District of Columbia .... | 59,385 | ... | ... | ... | ... | ... | 59,385 | 59,385 | 60,978 | 45,531 | ... |
| American Samoa .......... | 29,072 | 29,072 | ... | ... | ... | 29,072 | ... | ... | ... | ... | ... |
| Guam .......................... | 47,679 | 47,679 | 51,109 | ... | 51,109 | 43,155 | ... | ... | ... | ... | ... |
| Northern Marianas ..... | 35,628 | 35,628 | ... | ... | ... | 35,628 | ... | ... | ... | ... | ... |
| Puerto Rico ................. | 32,030 | 33,641 | 33,495 | 36,820 | 31,389 | 36,361 | 21,412 | 21,412 | ... | 21,412 | ... |
| Virgin Islands ............. | 44,976 | 44,976 | 44,976 | ... | 44,976 | ... | ... | ... | ... | ... | ... |

*Source*: U.S. Department of Education, National Center for Education Statistics, Integrated Postsecondary Education Data System (IPEDS), "Salaries, Tenure, and Fringe Benefits of Full-Time Instructional Faculty, 1996-97" survey. (This table was prepared February 1998).

*Note*:—Data include imputations for nonrespondent institutions.
Includes 2-year and 4-year degree-granting institutions that were eligible to participate in title IV federal financial aid programs.
*Key*:
. . . Data not reported or not applicable.

**Table 8.7**

**ESTIMATED UNDERGRADUATE TUITION AND FEES AND ROOM AND BOARD RATES IN INSTITUTIONS OF HIGHER EDUCATION, BY CONTROL OF INSTITUTION AND STATE: 1997-98**

| State or other jurisdiction | Public 4-year 1996-97 | | Public 4-year 1997-98 (a) | | | | Private 4-year 1996-97 | | Private 4-year 1997-98 (a) | | | | Public 2-year tuition only (in-state) | |
|---|---|---|---|---|---|---|---|---|---|---|---|---|---|---|
| | Total | Tuition (in state) | Total | Tuition (in state) | Room | Board | Total | Tuition | Total | Tuition | Room | Board | 1996-97 | 1997-98 (a) |
| United States | $7,334 | $2,987 | $7,628 | $3,110 | $2,314 | $2,204 | $18,442 | $12,881 | $19,143 | $13,392 | $3,002 | $2,750 | $1,276 | $1,318 |
| Alabama | 6,002 | 2,362 | 6,354 | 2,487 | 1,888 | 1,979 | 12,164 | 8,002 | 12,724 | 8,350 | 1,958 | 2,416 | 1,359 | 1,343 |
| Alaska | 6,892 | 2,550 | 7,131 | 2,609 | 2,585 | 1,937 | 12,707 | 8,131 | 13,214 | 8,377 | 2,008 | 2,828 | 1,850 | 1,900 |
| Arizona | 6,314 | 2,009 | 6,669 | 2,058 | 2,403 | 2,208 | 12,330 | 7,886 | 11,388 | 6,992 | 2,042 | 2,354 | 783 | 820 |
| Arkansas | 5,402 | 2,258 | 5,890 | 2,451 | 1,879 | 1,560 | 10,784 | 7,037 | 11,506 | 7,581 | 1,630 | 2,296 | 937 | 942 |
| California | 8,304 | 2,720 | 8,491 | 2,709 | 3,164 | 2,619 | 20,760 | 14,429 | 19,745 | 13,469 | 3,258 | 3,018 | 371 | 379 |
| Colorado | 7,321 | 2,561 | 7,552 | 2,622 | 2,249 | 2,680 | 18,137 | 12,003 | 18,882 | 12,661 | 2,900 | 3,321 | 1,395 | 1,449 |
| Connecticut | 9,256 | 4,111 | 9,652 | 4,273 | 2,855 | 2,524 | 23,916 | 17,458 | 25,083 | 18,345 | 3,814 | 2,924 | 1,722 | 1,814 |
| Delaware | 8,886 | 4,170 | 9,165 | 4,318 | 2,589 | 2,257 | 12,602 | 7,444 | 13,354 | 7,829 | 2,950 | 2,575 | 1,330 | 1,380 |
| Florida | 6,559 | 1,789 | 6,890 | 1,909 | 2,621 | 2,360 | 16,029 | 11,112 | 17,057 | 11,687 | 2,792 | 2,577 | 1,151 | 1,252 |
| Georgia | 6,508 | 2,241 | 6,924 | 2,356 | 2,298 | 2,270 | 16,409 | 10,942 | 17,133 | 11,374 | 3,233 | 2,527 | 1,093 | 1,153 |
| Hawaii | .... | 2,294 | .... | 2,790 | .... | .... | 14,151 | 6,541 | 14,448 | 6,748 | 3,000 | 4,700 | 789 | 956 |
| Idaho | 5,681 | 1,979 | 6,074 | 2,201 | 1,615 | 2,258 | 15,722 | 12,210 | 15,167 | 11,661 | 1,312 | 2,195 | 1,043 | 1,102 |
| Illinois | 8,193 | 3,522 | 8,537 | 3,701 | 2,237 | 2,600 | 17,606 | 12,376 | 18,580 | 13,105 | 2,963 | 2,513 | 1,290 | 1,347 |
| Indiana | 8,110 | 3,198 | 8,494 | 3,344 | 2,112 | 3,037 | 17,670 | 13,234 | 18,625 | 13,986 | 2,186 | 2,452 | 2,331 | 2,415 |
| Iowa | 6,174 | 2,655 | 6,426 | 2,761 | 1,865 | 1,800 | 16,562 | 12,403 | 17,472 | 13,094 | 2,010 | 2,368 | 1,845 | 1,885 |
| Kansas | 5,895 | 2,219 | 6,098 | 2,311 | 1,833 | 1,953 | 12,995 | 9,129 | 13,737 | 9,688 | 1,685 | 2,364 | 1,248 | 1,285 |
| Kentucky | 5,460 | 2,241 | 5,662 | 2,328 | 1,473 | 1,861 | 12,085 | 8,138 | 12,885 | 8,570 | 1,941 | 2,374 | 1,215 | 1,232 |
| Louisiana | 5,637 | 2,233 | 5,710 | 2,269 | 1,573 | 1,868 | 18,407 | 12,885 | 18,928 | 13,212 | 2,922 | 2,794 | 1,047 | 1,080 |
| Maine | 8,262 | 3,648 | 8,576 | 3,880 | 2,319 | 2,378 | 22,619 | 16,956 | 24,505 | 18,645 | 2,764 | 3,096 | 2,545 | 2,594 |
| Maryland | 9,179 | 3,849 | 9,717 | 4,135 | 2,976 | 2,606 | 21,967 | 15,332 | 23,079 | 16,209 | 3,755 | 3,116 | 2,102 | 2,171 |
| Massachusetts | 9,045 | 4,272 | 8,894 | 3,981 | 2,564 | 2,350 | 24,339 | 17,188 | 25,620 | 18,149 | 4,095 | 3,376 | 2,341 | 2,221 |
| Michigan | 8,645 | 3,988 | 8,947 | 4,131 | 2,190 | 2,625 | 13,930 | 9,580 | 14,459 | 10,018 | 2,210 | 2,230 | 1,576 | 1,618 |
| Minnesota | 7,148 | 3,546 | 7,617 | 3,776 | 2,193 | 1,649 | 17,980 | 13,623 | 18,559 | 14,046 | 2,220 | 2,293 | 2,187 | 2,245 |
| Mississippi | 5,532 | 2,499 | 5,534 | 2,568 | 1,526 | 1,440 | 10,482 | 7,210 | 11,226 | 7,725 | 1,773 | 1,729 | 954 | 958 |
| Missouri | 7,204 | 3,245 | 7,520 | 3,394 | 2,303 | 1,824 | 14,763 | 9,990 | 15,504 | 10,475 | 2,430 | 2,598 | 1,281 | 1,311 |
| Montana | 6,511 | 2,490 | 6,855 | 2,607 | 1,987 | 2,260 | 11,701 | 7,858 | 12,476 | 8,469 | 1,716 | 2,291 | 1,610 | 1,713 |
| Nebraska | 5,722 | 2,269 | 6,100 | 2,414 | 1,563 | 2,123 | 13,748 | 9,797 | 14,456 | 10,308 | 1,989 | 2,159 | 1,227 | 1,267 |
| Nevada | 7,707 | 1,815 | 7,295 | 1,884 | 3,231 | 2,179 | .... | 7,731 | 12,707 | 7,391 | 3,000 | 2,316 | 1,010 | 1,106 |
| New Hampshire | 9,123 | 4,641 | 9,846 | 5,193 | 2,821 | 1,831 | 21,436 | 15,839 | 21,129 | 15,729 | 3,160 | 2,240 | 2,858 | 3,177 |
| New Jersey | 9,661 | 4,269 | 10,235 | 4,562 | 3,374 | 2,299 | 20,984 | 14,371 | 21,825 | 15,125 | 3,521 | 3,180 | 1,949 | 2,033 |
| New Mexico | 5,428 | 2,014 | 5,459 | 2,068 | 1,659 | 1,732 | 14,823 | 9,944 | 14,490 | 9,408 | 2,460 | 2,622 | 659 | 679 |
| New York | 9,294 | 3,802 | 9,460 | 3,844 | 3,124 | 2,492 | 21,528 | 14,544 | 22,569 | 15,246 | 4,058 | 3,265 | 2,519 | 2,576 |
| North Carolina | 5,440 | 1,841 | 5,919 | 1,895 | 1,926 | 2,098 | 16,311 | 11,651 | 17,177 | 12,342 | 2,337 | 2,499 | 581 | 584 |
| North Dakota | 5,924 | 2,381 | 6,264 | 2,545 | 1,130 | 2,590 | 10,437 | 7,434 | 10,794 | 7,705 | 1,356 | 1,732 | 1,783 | 1,798 |
| Ohio | 8,490 | 3,841 | 9,022 | 4,009 | 2,668 | 2,345 | 17,905 | 12,980 | 18,681 | 13,559 | 2,541 | 2,581 | 2,335 | 2,388 |

See footnotes at end of table.

# ESTIMATED UNDERGRADUATE TUITION AND FEES AND ROOM AND BOARD RATES IN INSTITUTIONS OF HIGHER EDUCATION, BY CONTROL OF INSTITUTION AND STATE: 1997-98 — Continued

| State or other jurisdiction | Public 4-year 1996-97 | | Public 4-year 1997-98 | | | | Private 4-year 1996-97 | | Private 4-year 1997-98 | | | | Public 2-year tuition only (in-state) | |
|---|---|---|---|---|---|---|---|---|---|---|---|---|---|---|
| | Total | Tuition (in state) | Total | Tuition (in state) | Room | Board | Total | Tuition | Total | Tuition | Room 1997-98 (a) | Board | 1996-97 | 1997-98 (a) |
| Oklahoma | 5,076 | 1,937 | 5,301 | 2,054 | 1,330 | 1,917 | 11,563 | 7,622 | 12,960 | 8,881 | 1,924 | 2,155 | 1,268 | 1,285 |
| Oregon | 7,988 | 3,408 | 8,394 | 3,496 | 1,963 | 2,935 | 19,869 | 14,769 | 21,096 | 15,796 | 2,473 | 2,827 | 1,526 | 1,573 |
| Pennsylvania | 9,501 | 4,994 | 9,769 | 5,188 | 2,419 | 2,162 | 20,887 | 14,927 | 21,684 | 15,569 | 3,213 | 2,901 | 2,013 | 2,098 |
| Rhode Island | 9,648 | 3,903 | 9,962 | 4,013 | 3,100 | 2,848 | 22,490 | 15,675 | 23,209 | 16,263 | 3,881 | 3,066 | 1,736 | 1,746 |
| South Carolina | 7,238 | 3,205 | 7,160 | 3,414 | 2,153 | 1,594 | 14,125 | 10,207 | 14,847 | 10,755 | 1,994 | 2,098 | 1,114 | 1,162 |
| South Dakota | 5,814 | 2,722 | 5,993 | 2,900 | 1,335 | 1,758 | 13,756 | 9,617 | 14,538 | 9,950 | 1,766 | 2,822 | 3,430 | 3,930 |
| Tennessee | 5,498 | 2,052 | 5,788 | 2,296 | 1,807 | 1,685 | 14,970 | 10,450 | 15,684 | 11,047 | 2,380 | 2,257 | 1,047 | 1,133 |
| Texas | 5,911 | 2,028 | 6,313 | 2,273 | 2,093 | 1,946 | 13,684 | 9,373 | 14,554 | 9,970 | 2,230 | 2,355 | 791 | 820 |
| Utah | 5,559 | 2,011 | 5,953 | 2,113 | 1,524 | 2,316 | 7,697 | 3,094 | 7,787 | 3,183 | 1,436 | 3,167 | 1,390 | 1,439 |
| Vermont | 11,360 | 6,533 | 11,469 | 6,492 | 3,259 | 1,718 | 22,855 | 16,474 | 23,917 | 17,158 | 3,774 | 2,985 | 2,516 | 2,616 |
| Virginia | 8,450 | 3,968 | 8,627 | 4,045 | 2,390 | 2,192 | 15,775 | 11,165 | 16,612 | 11,809 | 2,288 | 2,515 | 1,466 | 1,475 |
| Washington | 7,320 | 2,933 | 7,704 | 3,036 | 2,379 | 2,289 | 18,461 | 13,656 | 19,198 | 14,072 | 2,645 | 2,482 | 1,447 | 1,516 |
| West Virginia | 6,348 | 2,091 | 6,558 | 2,168 | 2,134 | 2,256 | 15,184 | 10,774 | 15,673 | 11,166 | 1,941 | 2,567 | 1,373 | 1,404 |
| Wisconsin | 6,075 | 2,748 | 6,409 | 2,958 | 1,861 | 1,590 | 16,864 | 12,478 | 17,430 | 12,948 | 2,021 | 2,462 | 1,947 | 2,061 |
| Wyoming | 6,016 | 2,144 | 6,450 | 2,326 | 1,724 | 2,400 | ... | ... | ... | ... | ... | ... | 1,048 | 1,157 |
| District of Columbia | ... | 1,502 | ... | 1,910 | ... | ... | 22,599 | 15,586 | 23,807 | 16,496 | 4,361 | 2,949 | ... | ... |

*Source:* U.S. Department of Education, National Center for Education Statistics, Integrated Postsecondary Education Data System (IPEDS), "Fall Enrollment" and "Institutional Characteristics" surveys. (This table was prepared November 1998.)

*Note:*—Data are for the entire academic year and are average charges. Tuition and fees were weighted by the number of full-time-equivalent undergraduates in 1996, but are not adjusted to reflect student residency. Room and board are based on full-time students. Because of rounding, details may not add to totals.

Key:
(a) Preliminary data based on fall 1996 enrollments.
. . . Data not reported or not applicable.

**Table 8.8**
**GENERAL REVENUE OF PUBLIC SCHOOL SYSTEMS, BY SOURCE: 1996-97**
**(In thousands of dollars)**

| State or other jurisdiction | Total (a) | Intergovernmental | | | | | Total | From own sources | | | | |
| --- | --- | --- | --- | --- | --- | --- | --- | --- | --- | --- | --- | --- |
| | | Total | Directly from federal government | From state | | From other local governments | | Taxes | Parent government contributions | Current charges | | Other |
| | | | | Federal aid distributed by state | Other | | | | | School lunch | Other | |
| United States | $307,471,283 | $172,903,365 | $1,658,902 | $18,077,641 | $149,946,399 | $3,220,423 | $134,567,918 | $93,394,202 | $22,952,188 | $4,494,412 | $3,669,534 | $10,057,582 |
| Alabama | 3,978,735 | 3,172,719 | 20,165 | 356,035 | 2,498,847 | 297,672 | 806,016 | 409,067 | 0 | 95,800 | 134,635 | 166,514 |
| Alaska | 1,131,950 | 837,927 | 85,968 | 59,595 | 692,364 | 0 | 294,023 | 0 | 226,758 | 10,289 | 24,175 | 32,801 |
| Arizona | 4,324,648 | 2,435,928 | 107,293 | 297,998 | 1,907,516 | 123,121 | 1,888,720 | 1,553,756 | 0 | 69,947 | 48,178 | 216,839 |
| Arkansas | 2,337,173 | 1,606,935 | 20,265 | 197,872 | 1,387,107 | 1,691 | 730,238 | 561,410 | 0 | 39,340 | 77,806 | 51,682 |
| California | 35,068,873 | 23,537,684 | 252,460 | 2,598,306 | 20,560,730 | 126,188 | 11,531,189 | 8,475,789 | 447,948 | 367,181 | 146,878 | 2,093,393 |
| Colorado | 4,121,482 | 1,990,790 | 23,063 | 181,975 | 1,784,304 | 1,448 | 2,130,692 | 1,722,345 | 0 | 67,849 | 70,285 | 270,213 |
| Connecticut | 4,704,352 | 2,067,060 | 14,737 | 143,716 | 1,719,703 | 188,904 | 2,637,292 | 0 | 2,575,381 | 49,057 | 4,834 | 8,020 |
| Delaware | 875,305 | 632,577 | 7,686 | 49,036 | 575,855 | 0 | 242,728 | 201,650 | 0 | 11,410 | 0 | 29,668 |
| Florida | 14,363,029 | 8,014,787 | 83,266 | 908,960 | 7,022,561 | 0 | 6,348,242 | 5,255,697 | 0 | 216,861 | 420,950 | 454,734 |
| Georgia | 8,245,609 | 5,137,998 | 17,121 | 517,842 | 4,471,781 | 131,254 | 3,107,611 | 2,715,119 | 0 | 139,968 | 40,554 | 211,970 |
| Hawaii | 1,213,792 | 1,184,421 | 25,270 | 70,525 | 1,088,410 | 216 | 29,371 | 0 | 0 | 15,690 | 5,539 | 8,142 |
| Idaho | 1,199,202 | 828,084 | 7,635 | 73,119 | 747,250 | 80 | 371,118 | 308,176 | 0 | 19,007 | 2,506 | 41,429 |
| Illinois | 13,547,390 | 5,396,521 | 25,246 | 822,572 | 4,532,935 | 15,768 | 8,150,869 | 7,297,507 | 0 | 175,900 | 130,940 | 546,522 |
| Indiana | 7,691,458 | 4,143,618 | 8,283 | 296,842 | 3,783,388 | 55,105 | 3,547,840 | 2,988,606 | 0 | 147,800 | 98,597 | 312,837 |
| Iowa | 3,136,328 | 1,804,538 | 7,731 | 145,429 | 1,646,498 | 4,880 | 1,331,790 | 1,082,271 | 0 | 71,284 | 99,578 | 78,657 |
| Kansas | 3,008,676 | 1,940,826 | 13,062 | 139,393 | 1,682,302 | 106,069 | 1,067,850 | 879,862 | 0 | 64,029 | 20,108 | 103,851 |
| Kentucky | 3,841,751 | 2,736,341 | 19,689 | 322,212 | 2,381,664 | 12,776 | 1,105,410 | 915,097 | 0 | 73,646 | 9,265 | 107,402 |
| Louisiana | 4,104,155 | 2,579,681 | 34,617 | 443,391 | 2,087,903 | 13,770 | 1,524,474 | 1,355,330 | 0 | 41,570 | 22,235 | 105,339 |
| Maine | 1,477,358 | 743,990 | 4,986 | 69,517 | 669,487 | 0 | 733,368 | 286,198 | 405,852 | 10,907 | 5,335 | 25,076 |
| Maryland | 6,036,752 | 2,636,188 | 11,259 | 281,001 | 2,343,928 | 0 | 3,400,564 | 0 | 3,144,155 | 94,620 | 76,742 | 85,047 |
| Massachusetts | 7,528,326 | 4,157,534 | 22,908 | 314,972 | 3,341,044 | 478,610 | 3,370,792 | 0 | 3,163,887 | 82,222 | 48,613 | 76,070 |
| Michigan | 13,282,583 | 9,550,691 | 49,803 | 756,910 | 8,728,340 | 15,638 | 3,731,892 | 2,940,917 | 0 | 166,149 | 104,214 | 520,612 |
| Minnesota | 6,107,786 | 3,732,474 | 14,057 | 237,153 | 3,321,859 | 159,405 | 2,375,312 | 1,798,493 | 0 | 122,108 | 113,146 | 341,565 |
| Mississippi | 2,270,907 | 1,563,097 | 13,025 | 292,491 | 1,253,204 | 4,377 | 707,810 | 514,569 | 2,236 | 38,733 | 39,616 | 112,656 |
| Missouri | 5,509,756 | 3,170,611 | 13,609 | 322,843 | 2,695,581 | 138,578 | 2,339,145 | 1,943,343 | 0 | 99,166 | 141,486 | 155,150 |
| Montana | 985,403 | 646,558 | 32,624 | 57,941 | 465,343 | 90,650 | 338,845 | 267,576 | 0 | 13,128 | 29,781 | 28,360 |
| Nebraska | 1,948,173 | 760,171 | 19,139 | 96,644 | 630,765 | 13,623 | 1,188,002 | 1,041,978 | 0 | 38,381 | 58,350 | 49,293 |
| Nevada | 1,698,144 | 1,157,256 | 4,070 | 64,061 | 1,089,122 | 3 | 540,888 | 410,625 | 0 | 21,004 | 41,151 | 68,108 |
| New Hampshire | 1,281,998 | 139,108 | 3,627 | 40,712 | 94,550 | 219 | 1,142,890 | 873,283 | 217,445 | 25,735 | 6,914 | 19,513 |
| New Jersey | 12,566,665 | 5,226,977 | 17,266 | 409,994 | 4,799,701 | 16 | 7,339,688 | 6,008,142 | 719,705 | 138,867 | 39,127 | 433,847 |
| New Mexico | 1,768,105 | 1,518,434 | 87,903 | 143,368 | 1,287,163 | 0 | 249,671 | 177,078 | 0 | 20,402 | 14,657 | 37,534 |
| New York | 26,564,345 | 12,285,254 | 11,488 | 1,435,203 | 10,477,889 | 360,674 | 14,279,091 | 9,257,285 | 4,180,381 | 211,621 | 46,279 | 583,525 |
| North Carolina | 6,826,598 | 4,729,275 | 33,745 | 437,513 | 4,258,017 | 3 | 2,097,323 | | 1,739,370 | 180,770 | 41,910 | 135,273 |
| North Dakota | 649,318 | 353,752 | 27,041 | 48,275 | 270,361 | 8,075 | 295,566 | 233,896 | 0 | 14,796 | 19,405 | 27,469 |
| Ohio | 12,552,152 | 5,867,220 | 62,484 | 666,267 | 5,124,101 | 14,368 | 6,684,932 | 5,696,096 | 0 | 238,786 | 398,305 | 351,745 |

# GENERAL REVENUE OF PUBLIC SCHOOL SYSTEMS, BY SOURCE: 1996-97 — Continued

| State or other jurisdiction | Total (a) | Intergovernmental | | | | | From own sources | | | | | |
| | | Total | Directly from federal government | From state | | From other local governments | Total | Taxes | Current charges | | | Other |
| | | | | Federal aid distributed by state | Other | | | | Parent government contributions | School lunch | Other | |
|---|---|---|---|---|---|---|---|---|---|---|---|---|
| Oklahoma | 3,387,387 | 2,322,024 | 39,085 | 239,124 | 1,974,522 | 69,293 | 1,065,363 | 776,958 | 0 | 53,038 | 138,053 | 97,314 |
| Oregon | 3,461,270 | 2,021,044 | 3,585 | 188,075 | 1,826,329 | 3,055 | 1,440,226 | 1,109,838 | 0 | 46,805 | 96,663 | 186,920 |
| Pennsylvania | 14,529,225 | 6,584,344 | 38,069 | 743,424 | 5,695,856 | 106,995 | 7,944,881 | 7,284,587 | 0 | 228,970 | 80,409 | 350,915 |
| Rhode Island | 1,178,635 | 580,252 | 4,860 | 58,354 | 470,876 | 46,162 | 598,383 | 0 | 576,734 | 15,125 | 844 | 5,680 |
| South Carolina | 3,864,925 | 2,413,890 | 3,223 | 300,017 | 2,027,332 | 83,318 | 1,451,035 | 1,169,257 | 0 | 58,558 | 110,983 | 112,237 |
| South Dakota | 742,716 | 346,122 | 27,549 | 43,019 | 265,354 | 10,200 | 396,594 | 357,128 | 0 | 16,188 | 3,745 | 19,533 |
| Tennessee | 4,369,537 | 2,821,346 | 14,356 | 344,835 | 2,114,799 | 347,356 | 1,548,191 | 0 | 1,207,142 | 90,232 | 175,827 | 74,990 |
| Texas | 23,024,288 | 11,653,243 | 120,245 | 1,568,730 | 9,878,849 | 85,419 | 11,371,045 | 10,016,112 | 0 | 392,009 | 260,506 | 702,418 |
| Utah | 2,186,190 | 1,510,130 | 12,990 | 127,054 | 1,367,806 | 2,280 | 676,060 | 536,174 | 0 | 40,818 | 18,217 | 80,851 |
| Vermont | 797,194 | 270,433 | 626 | 37,005 | 232,557 | 245 | 526,761 | 488,334 | 0 | 11,130 | 4,549 | 22,748 |
| Virginia | 7,258,836 | 3,295,383 | 49,167 | 307,600 | 2,938,616 | 0 | 3,963,453 | 0 | 3,713,499 | 130,368 | 23,496 | 96,090 |
| Washington | 6,620,434 | 4,848,213 | 86,844 | 301,279 | 4,443,435 | 16,655 | 1,772,221 | 1,370,795 | 0 | 78,769 | 125,367 | 197,290 |
| West Virginia | 2,052,224 | 1,459,482 | 5,978 | 164,242 | 1,286,247 | 3,015 | 592,742 | 505,778 | 0 | 25,736 | 7,259 | 53,969 |
| Wisconsin | 6,680,590 | 4,003,595 | 22,111 | 266,475 | 3,681,682 | 33,327 | 2,676,995 | 2,393,083 | 0 | 100,733 | 38,356 | 144,823 |
| Wyoming | 657,930 | 413,662 | 6,346 | 36,825 | 320,566 | 49,925 | 244,268 | 214,997 | 0 | 11,340 | 755 | 17,176 |
| Dist. of Columbia | 711,625 | 73,177 | 21,277 | 51,900 | 0 | 0 | 638,448 | 0 | 631,695 | 570 | 2,411 | 3,772 |

Source: U.S. Department of Commerce, Bureau of the Census.

Note: Revenue from state sources for state cependent school systems is included as intergovernmental revenue from state rather than as parent government contributions. Detail may not add to totals due to rounding.

(a) To avoid duplication, interschool system transactions are excluded.

## Table 8.9
## SUMMARY OF STATE GOVERNMENT DIRECT EXPENDITURES FOR EDUCATION, BY STATE: 1997
### (In thousands of dollars)

| State | Total (a) | Elementary and secondary: Total | Current operation | Capital outlay: Total | Construction | Higher education: Total | Current operation | Capital outlay: Total | Construction | Other education: Total | Current operation | Capital outlay: Total | Construction | Assistance & subsidies |
|---|---|---|---|---|---|---|---|---|---|---|---|---|---|---|
| United States | $111,673,237 | $2,809,577 | $2,269,141 | $540,436 | $444,134 | $90,472,130 | $80,685,017 | $9,787,113 | $5,871,620 | $18,391,530 | $9,066,352 | $587,312 | $314,257 | $8,737,866 |
| Alabama | 2,347,003 | 0 | 0 | 0 | 0 | 1,979,473 | 1,769,013 | 210,460 | 133,762 | 367,530 | 256,730 | 3,067 | 203 | 107,733 |
| Alaska | 578,372 | 214,152 | 198,442 | 15,710 | 9,922 | 304,638 | 300,101 | 4,537 | 0 | 59,582 | 52,370 | 1,662 | 0 | 5,550 |
| Arizona | 1,689,372 | 0 | 0 | 0 | 0 | 1,395,577 | 1,253,082 | 142,495 | 67,276 | 293,795 | 177,200 | 4,860 | 922 | 111,735 |
| Arkansas | 1,190,953 | 59 | 59 | 0 | 0 | 914,356 | 798,208 | 116,148 | 72,660 | 276,538 | 201,545 | 12,546 | 5,294 | 62,447 |
| California | 11,296,208 | 143,531 | 143,531 | 0 | 0 | 9,079,534 | 8,185,896 | 893,638 | 513,568 | 2,073,143 | 947,854 | 3,617 | 0 | 1,121,672 |
| Colorado | 2,212,908 | 0 | 0 | 0 | 0 | 2,033,590 | 1,829,187 | 204,403 | 126,158 | 179,318 | 87,785 | 7,404 | 4,754 | 84,129 |
| Connecticut | 1,128,156 | 179 | 179 | 0 | 0 | 909,575 | 889,541 | 20,034 | 1,803 | 218,402 | 141,140 | 6,209 | 3,581 | 71,053 |
| Delaware | 614,020 | 0 | 0 | 0 | 0 | 498,589 | 459,371 | 39,218 | 36,742 | 115,431 | 82,616 | 1,531 | 0 | 31,284 |
| Florida | 3,175,108 | 0 | 0 | 0 | 0 | 2,484,960 | 2,124,390 | 360,570 | 232,012 | 690,148 | 272,415 | 25,798 | 18,552 | 391,935 |
| Georgia | 3,464,996 | 0 | 0 | 0 | 0 | 2,539,760 | 2,118,266 | 421,494 | 249,272 | 925,236 | 416,040 | 131,343 | 99,032 | 377,853 |
| Hawaii | 1,557,019 | 946,734 | 763,531 | 183,203 | 153,333 | 589,625 | 546,739 | 42,886 | 20,456 | 20,660 | 15,589 | 194 | 0 | 4,877 |
| Idaho | 521,112 | 0 | 0 | 0 | 0 | 453,453 | 389,546 | 63,907 | 46,657 | 67,659 | 42,482 | 7,297 | 6,359 | 17,880 |
| Illinois | 3,845,999 | 356 | 0 | 356 | 356 | 2,860,213 | 2,564,083 | 296,130 | 147,958 | 985,430 | 427,623 | 35,822 | 25,067 | 521,985 |
| Indiana | 3,340,964 | 0 | 0 | 0 | 0 | 2,954,836 | 2,615,492 | 339,344 | 223,344 | 386,128 | 175,215 | 5,638 | 2,278 | 205,275 |
| Iowa | 1,550,396 | 0 | 0 | 0 | 0 | 1,298,523 | 1,199,933 | 98,590 | 35,541 | 251,873 | 104,344 | 702 | 133 | 146,827 |
| Kansas | 1,121,367 | 0 | 0 | 0 | 0 | 977,075 | 904,700 | 72,375 | 20,825 | 144,292 | 81,822 | 3,181 | 1,911 | 59,289 |
| Kentucky | 1,945,348 | 0 | 0 | 0 | 0 | 1,560,128 | 1,378,140 | 181,988 | 103,862 | 385,220 | 250,093 | 17,773 | 2,219 | 117,354 |
| Louisiana | 1,994,478 | 37,442 | 37,442 | 0 | 0 | 1,642,488 | 1,526,805 | 115,683 | 39,629 | 314,548 | 217,188 | 4,129 | 1,208 | 93,231 |
| Maine | 507,880 | 8,959 | 8,841 | 118 | 0 | 404,826 | 370,021 | 34,805 | 20,500 | 94,095 | 66,216 | 691 | 5 | 27,188 |
| Maryland | 2,138,497 | 0 | 0 | 0 | 0 | 1,768,569 | 1,619,067 | 149,502 | 91,217 | 369,928 | 188,770 | 2,383 | 129 | 178,775 |
| Massachusetts | 2,172,304 | 0 | 0 | 0 | 0 | 1,669,912 | 1,559,749 | 110,163 | 53,493 | 502,392 | 348,424 | 1,827 | 50 | 152,141 |
| Michigan | 4,825,370 | 0 | 0 | 0 | 0 | 4,317,147 | 3,825,898 | 491,249 | 330,444 | 508,223 | 188,411 | 1,811 | 113 | 318,001 |
| Minnesota | 2,391,772 | 0 | 0 | 0 | 0 | 2,022,356 | 1,837,498 | 184,858 | 113,783 | 369,416 | 152,802 | 2,055 | 37 | 214,559 |
| Mississippi | 1,108,704 | 0 | 0 | 0 | 0 | 905,871 | 778,022 | 127,849 | 88,428 | 202,833 | 110,413 | 10,117 | 0 | 82,303 |
| Missouri | 1,821,036 | 0 | 0 | 0 | 0 | 1,507,534 | 1,313,466 | 194,068 | 96,411 | 313,502 | 168,764 | 5,829 | 357 | 138,909 |
| Montana | 480,703 | 0 | 0 | 0 | 0 | 396,463 | 343,375 | 53,088 | 36,308 | 84,240 | 56,794 | 798 | 12 | 26,648 |
| Nebraska | 831,371 | 0 | 0 | 0 | 0 | 743,046 | 676,948 | 66,098 | 30,477 | 88,325 | 53,015 | 2,605 | 435 | 32,705 |
| Nevada | 583,075 | 0 | 0 | 0 | 0 | 534,567 | 482,466 | 52,101 | 21,839 | 48,508 | 32,274 | 281 | 21 | 15,953 |
| New Hampshire | 437,938 | 0 | 0 | 0 | 0 | 383,712 | 358,811 | 24,901 | 13,104 | 54,226 | 14,974 | 1,711 | 299 | 37,541 |
| New Jersey | 3,278,022 | 765,525 | 708,168 | 57,357 | 45,933 | 2,080,624 | 1,883,211 | 197,413 | 122,052 | 431,873 | 146,687 | 3,237 | 2,235 | 281,949 |
| New Mexico | 1,026,488 | 0 | 0 | 0 | 0 | 914,853 | 815,642 | 99,211 | 47,865 | 111,635 | 66,702 | 2,173 | 446 | 42,760 |
| New York | 5,751,584 | 0 | 0 | 0 | 0 | 4,438,165 | 3,956,309 | 481,856 | 351,973 | 1,313,419 | 387,679 | 19,453 | 17,319 | 906,287 |
| North Carolina | 3,379,751 | 98,825 | 50,512 | 48,313 | 0 | 2,841,886 | 2,508,951 | 332,935 | 191,633 | 439,040 | 246,877 | 9,333 | 4,006 | 182,830 |
| North Dakota | 449,093 | 0 | 0 | 0 | 0 | 393,583 | 358,745 | 34,838 | 21,699 | 55,510 | 40,137 | 969 | 300 | 14,404 |
| Ohio | 5,181,681 | 0 | 0 | 0 | 0 | 4,236,634 | 3,637,130 | 599,504 | 383,262 | 945,047 | 229,396 | 161,748 | 85,892 | 553,903 |

# SUMMARY OF STATE GOVERNMENT DIRECT EXPENDITURES FOR EDUCATION, BY STATE: 1997 — Continued

| State | Total (a) | Elementary and secondary | | | | Higher education | | | | Other education | | | | |
|---|---|---|---|---|---|---|---|---|---|---|---|---|---|---|
| | | Total | Current operation | Capital outlay | | Total | Current operation | Capital outlay | | Total | Current operation | Capital outlay | | Assistance & subsidies |
| | | | | Total | Construction | | | Total | Construction | | | Total | Construction | |
| Oklahoma | 1,559,883 | 17,994 | 17,994 | 0 | 0 | 1,367,707 | 1,245,683 | 122,024 | 41,550 | 174,182 | 87,107 | 9,615 | 5,031 | 77,460 |
| Oregon | 1,361,123 | 0 | 0 | 0 | 0 | 1,146,267 | 1,029,409 | 116,858 | 98,363 | 214,856 | 136,144 | 85 | 0 | 78,627 |
| Pennsylvania | 4,990,852 | 22,166 | 0 | 22,166 | 22,166 | 3,631,009 | 3,269,790 | 361,219 | 205,722 | 1,337,677 | 825,052 | 16,857 | 4,810 | 495,768 |
| Rhode Island | 472,481 | 23,036 | 23,036 | 0 | 0 | 339,838 | 324,091 | 15,747 | 3,672 | 109,607 | 70,933 | 6,564 | 5,791 | 32,110 |
| South Carolina | 1,889,672 | 61,153 | 60,364 | 789 | 0 | 1,558,528 | 1,404,395 | 154,133 | 108,667 | 269,991 | 157,812 | 15,498 | 7,322 | 96,681 |
| South Dakota | 283,277 | 0 | 0 | 0 | 0 | 242,398 | 211,313 | 31,085 | 16,301 | 40,879 | 33,525 | 467 | 3 | 6,887 |
| Tennessee | 2,236,446 | 248,106 | 248,106 | 0 | 0 | 1,990,089 | 1,627,010 | 363,079 | 259,458 | 246,357 | 159,466 | 2,681 | 769 | 84,210 |
| Texas | 7,122,844 | 0 | 0 | 0 | 0 | 6,174,656 | 5,501,296 | 673,360 | 416,984 | 700,082 | 356,884 | 4,326 | 97 | 338,872 |
| Utah | 1,456,811 | 0 | 0 | 0 | 0 | 1,314,161 | 1,165,149 | 149,012 | 88,448 | 142,650 | 98,212 | 1,632 | 240 | 42,806 |
| Vermont | 392,190 | 0 | 0 | 0 | 0 | 319,672 | 294,599 | 25,073 | 14,116 | 72,518 | 35,259 | 407 | 0 | 36,852 |
| Virginia | 3,190,930 | 8,936 | 8,936 | 0 | 0 | 2,776,235 | 2,499,687 | 276,548 | 139,993 | 405,759 | 182,901 | 8,085 | 343 | 214,773 |
| Washington | 3,383,592 | 212,424 | 0 | 212,424 | 212,424 | 2,723,308 | 2,375,459 | 347,849 | 247,466 | 447,860 | 182,134 | 5,428 | 3,020 | 260,298 |
| West Virginia | 855,051 | 0 | 0 | 0 | 0 | 690,299 | 646,945 | 43,354 | 13,769 | 164,752 | 115,502 | 10,532 | 1,038 | 38,718 |
| Wisconsin | 2,316,775 | 0 | 0 | 0 | 0 | 1,982,425 | 1,745,122 | 237,303 | 127,024 | 334,350 | 154,425 | 4,539 | 2,624 | 175,386 |
| Wyoming | 222,262 | 0 | 0 | 0 | 0 | 179,397 | 167,267 | 12,130 | 4,074 | 42,865 | 22,610 | 802 | 0 | 19,453 |

*Source:* U.S. Department of Commerce, Bureau of Census.

*Note:* Detail may not add to totals due to rounding.

(a) To avoid duplication, interschool systems transactions are excluded.

# Table 8.10
## SUMMARY OF STATE GOVERNMENT DIRECT EXPENDITURES FOR EDUCATION, BY STATE: 1998
### (In thousands of dollars)

| State | Total (a) | Elementary and secondary Total | Current operation | Capital outlay Total | Construction | Higher education Total | Current operation | Capital outlay Total | Construction | Other education Total | Current operation | Capital outlay Total | Construction | Assistance & subsidies |
|---|---|---|---|---|---|---|---|---|---|---|---|---|---|---|
| United States | $118,562,969 | $2,886,270 | $2,451,211 | $435,059 | $318,122 | $96,250,706 | $85,260,475 | $10,990,231 | $7,066,446 | $19,425,993 | $9,471,382 | $544,626 | $279,830 | $9,409,985 |
| Alabama | 2,419,676 | 0 | 0 | | | 2,031,555 | 1,847,494 | 184,061 | 103,292 | 388,121 | 267,396 | 3,681 | 308 | 117,044 |
| Alaska | 588,527 | 213,893 | 198,202 | 15,691 | 9,910 | 315,672 | 314,526 | 1,146 | 0 | 58,962 | 53,783 | 834 | 31 | 4,345 |
| Arizona | 1,733,867 | 0 | 0 | | | 1,486,991 | 1,343,916 | 143,075 | 52,116 | 246,876 | 119,768 | 4,954 | 571 | 122,154 |
| Arkansas | 1,306,308 | 635 | 635 | | | 1,027,537 | 832,752 | 194,785 | 146,476 | 278,136 | 182,213 | 16,827 | 8,754 | 79,096 |
| California | 12,142,434 | 153,955 | 153,955 | | | 9,817,227 | 8,700,242 | 1,116,985 | 859,063 | 2,171,252 | 998,524 | 3,751 | 0 | 1,168,977 |
| Colorado | 2,249,758 | 0 | 0 | | | 2,074,671 | 1,921,302 | 153,369 | 84,953 | 175,087 | 81,784 | 3,608 | 924 | 89,695 |
| Connecticut | 1,259,703 | 1,931 | 1,931 | | | 1,010,379 | 933,937 | 76,442 | 30,950 | 247,393 | 146,816 | 13,507 | 9,903 | 87,070 |
| Delaware | 616,028 | 0 | 0 | | | 496,120 | 480,422 | 15,698 | 8,062 | 119,908 | 78,237 | 1,188 | 0 | 40,483 |
| Florida | 3,451,155 | 0 | 0 | | | 2,730,282 | 2,271,847 | 458,435 | 328,545 | 720,873 | 286,942 | 26,457 | 14,945 | 407,474 |
| Georgia | 3,606,850 | 0 | 0 | | | 2,760,130 | 2,274,953 | 485,177 | 311,407 | 846,720 | 357,108 | 54,484 | 42,680 | 435,128 |
| Hawaii | 1,636,140 | 973,182 | 812,702 | 160,480 | 127,229 | 640,078 | 582,009 | 58,069 | 31,724 | 22,880 | 17,322 | 960 | 0 | 4,598 |
| Idaho | 549,907 | 0 | | | | 479,547 | 403,572 | 75,975 | 47,017 | 70,360 | 45,228 | 5,577 | 4,684 | 19,555 |
| Illinois | 4,012,238 | 0 | | | | 2,970,536 | 2,636,395 | 334,141 | 172,981 | 1,041,702 | 453,092 | 22,119 | 13,860 | 566,491 |
| Indiana | 3,584,954 | 0 | | | | 3,178,601 | 2,870,607 | 307,994 | 181,118 | 406,353 | 180,860 | 3,672 | 1,833 | 221,821 |
| Iowa | 1,712,459 | 0 | | | | 1,381,011 | 1,263,776 | 117,235 | 52,915 | 331,448 | 184,459 | 4,104 | 3,078 | 142,885 |
| Kansas | 1,160,307 | 0 | | | | 1,017,786 | 904,581 | 113,205 | 46,884 | 142,521 | 74,987 | 2,742 | 1,507 | 64,792 |
| Kentucky | 2,068,533 | 0 | | | | 1,671,462 | 1,461,301 | 210,161 | 120,394 | 397,071 | 262,916 | 14,284 | 3,563 | 119,871 |
| Louisiana | 2,049,597 | 0 | | | | 1,696,515 | 1,563,109 | 133,406 | 44,238 | 353,082 | 245,700 | 8,931 | 4,393 | 98,451 |
| Maine | 500,510 | 8,284 | 8,284 | | | 413,223 | 379,582 | 33,641 | 21,395 | 79,003 | 49,758 | 1,640 | 58 | 27,605 |
| Maryland | 2,195,451 | 11 | | 11 | 11 | 1,828,445 | 1,704,547 | 123,898 | 122,711 | 366,995 | 170,392 | 6,964 | 2,469 | 189,639 |
| Massachusetts | 2,347,969 | 0 | | | | 1,822,028 | 1,713,018 | 109,010 | 50,579 | 525,941 | 361,239 | 2,569 | 4 | 162,133 |
| Michigan | 5,164,773 | 0 | | | | 4,629,002 | 4,077,329 | 551,673 | 383,624 | 535,771 | 188,448 | 1,576 | 74 | 345,747 |
| Minnesota | 2,726,482 | 0 | | | | 2,307,748 | 2,106,565 | 201,183 | 120,811 | 418,734 | 198,516 | 3,462 | 0 | 216,756 |
| Mississippi | 1,250,485 | 0 | | | | 1,006,668 | 815,941 | 190,727 | 102,506 | 243,817 | 115,259 | 9,486 | 1 | 119,072 |
| Missouri | 1,982,475 | 0 | | | | 1,620,141 | 1,404,949 | 215,192 | 121,080 | 362,334 | 201,349 | 6,960 | 115 | 154,025 |
| Montana | 468,631 | 0 | | | | 378,599 | 344,014 | 34,585 | 19,039 | 90,032 | 60,615 | 431 | 210 | 28,986 |
| Nebraska | 896,954 | 0 | | | | 803,505 | 723,237 | 80,268 | 52,547 | 93,449 | 51,585 | 3,675 | 400 | 38,189 |
| Nevada | 640,920 | 0 | | | | 583,462 | 522,006 | 61,456 | 25,192 | 57,458 | 38,406 | 431 | 30 | 18,621 |
| New Hampshire | 470,543 | 0 | | | | 412,765 | 375,168 | 37,597 | 23,278 | 57,778 | 15,888 | 2,751 | 154 | 39,139 |
| New Jersey | 3,615,805 | 905,955 | 829,399 | 76,556 | 42,958 | 2,203,024 | 1,978,778 | 224,246 | 149,775 | 506,826 | 190,436 | 4,639 | 2,163 | 311,751 |
| New Mexico | 1,059,033 | 0 | | | | 936,845 | 842,248 | 94,597 | 50,315 | 122,188 | 68,645 | 1,605 | 362 | 51,938 |
| New York | 6,172,682 | 0 | | | | 4,810,530 | 4,113,097 | 697,433 | 502,674 | 1,362,152 | 385,382 | 41,328 | 34,872 | 935,442 |
| North Carolina | 3,661,523 | 82,902 | 39,567 | 43,335 | | 3,097,951 | 2,714,175 | 383,776 | 235,311 | 480,670 | 276,287 | 8,642 | 2,704 | 195,741 |
| North Dakota | 470,592 | 0 | | | | 418,197 | 383,519 | 34,678 | 17,049 | 52,395 | 36,419 | 636 | 259 | 15,340 |
| Ohio | 5,125,591 | 0 | | | | 4,152,138 | 3,571,634 | 580,504 | 413,774 | 973,453 | 197,878 | 153,077 | 84,114 | 622,498 |

# SUMMARY OF STATE GOVERNMENT DIRECT EXPENDITURES FOR EDUCATION, BY STATE: 1998 — Continued

| State | Total (a) | Elementary and secondary | | Capital outlay | | Higher education | | Capital outlay | | Other education | | Capital outlay | | Assistance & subsidies |
| | | Total | Current operation | Total | Construction | Total | Current operation | Total | Construction | Total | Current operation | Total | Construction | |
|---|---|---|---|---|---|---|---|---|---|---|---|---|---|---|
| Oklahoma | 1,669,712 | 17,071 | 17,071 | 0 | 0 | 1,454,613 | 1,364,928 | 89,685 | 28,718 | 198,028 | 106,805 | 5,219 | 1,588 | 86,004 |
| Oregon | 1,474,149 | 0 | 0 | 0 | 0 | 1,224,559 | 1,084,527 | 140,032 | 103,027 | 249,590 | 169,398 | 55 | 54 | 80,137 |
| Pennsylvania | 5,287,851 | 20,164 | 0 | 20,164 | 20,164 | 3,815,985 | 3,388,718 | 427,267 | 294,705 | 1,451,702 | 909,077 | 20,934 | 9,029 | 521,691 |
| Rhode Island | 500,587 | 46,429 | 46,429 | 0 | 0 | 348,596 | 333,750 | 14,846 | 3,955 | 105,562 | 70,918 | 2,255 | 1,660 | 32,389 |
| South Carolina | 2,043,570 | 77,589 | 76,617 | 972 | 0 | 1,677,798 | 1,498,860 | 178,938 | 105,579 | 288,183 | 156,778 | 28,530 | 21,130 | 102,875 |
| South Dakota | 292,642 | 0 | 0 | 0 | 0 | 248,339 | 221,413 | 26,926 | 6,950 | 44,303 | 34,680 | 1,099 | 7 | 8,524 |
| Tennessee | 2,289,233 | 0 | 0 | 0 | 0 | 2,041,683 | 1,669,437 | 372,246 | 280,775 | 247,550 | 157,909 | 1,752 | 625 | 87,889 |
| Texas | 7,594,637 | 239,836 | 239,836 | 0 | 0 | 6,597,020 | 5,907,002 | 690,018 | 415,089 | 757,781 | 383,182 | 3,664 | 285 | 370,935 |
| Utah | 1,578,631 | 0 | 0 | 0 | 0 | 1,428,876 | 1,226,951 | 201,925 | 140,183 | 149,755 | 102,905 | 1,043 | 72 | 45,807 |
| Vermont | 398,009 | 0 | 0 | 0 | 0 | 320,841 | 300,328 | 20,513 | 10,725 | 77,168 | 37,147 | 513 | 0 | 39,508 |
| Virginia | 3,474,618 | 26,583 | 26,583 | 0 | 0 | 3,002,455 | 2,652,942 | 349,513 | 214,437 | 445,580 | 207,167 | 10,008 | 351 | 228,405 |
| Washington | 3,502,246 | 117,850 | 0 | 117,850 | 117,850 | 2,889,415 | 2,522,013 | 367,402 | 278,547 | 494,981 | 203,166 | 6,822 | 4,536 | 284,993 |
| West Virginia | 883,229 | 0 | 0 | 0 | 0 | 716,088 | 668,027 | 48,061 | 19,717 | 167,141 | 109,804 | 19,163 | 297 | 38,174 |
| Wisconsin | 2,453,033 | 0 | 0 | 0 | 0 | 2,092,727 | 1,874,774 | 217,953 | 127,541 | 360,306 | 158,446 | 1,777 | 1,173 | 200,083 |
| Wyoming | 221,962 | 0 | 0 | 0 | 0 | 181,340 | 170,257 | 11,083 | 2,703 | 40,622 | 20,363 | 240 | 0 | 20,019 |

Source: U.S. Department of Commerce, Bureau of the Census.
Note: Detail may not add to totals due to rounding.
(a) To avoid duplication, interschool system transactions are excluded.

## Table 8.11
## TRENDS IN STATE PRISON POPULATION, 1997-98

| State or other jurisdiction | Total population 1998(a) | Total population 1997 | Percentage change 1997-98 | More than a year 1998 (f) | More than a year 1997 | Percentage change 1997-98 | Incarceration rate 1998 (a) | Year or less and unsentenced 1996 | Year or less and unsentenced 1995 | Percentage change |
|---|---|---|---|---|---|---|---|---|---|---|
| United States .......... | 1,302,019 | 1,242,153 | 4.8 | 1,252,830 | 1,195,498 | 4.8 | 461 | 43,848 | | 7.3 |
| Alabama ......................... | 23,326 | 22,290 | 4.6 | 22,655 | 21,680 | 4.5 | 519 | 652 | 588 | 10.9 |
| Alaska (b) ..................... | 4,097 | 4,165 | -1.6 | 2,541 | 2,571 | -1.2 | 413 | 1,140 | 1,240 | -8.1 |
| Arizona (d) ..................... | 25,311 | 23,484 | 7.8 | 23,955 | 22,353 | 7.2 | 507 | 970 | 1,050 | -7.6 |
| Arkansas ........................ | 10,638 | 10,021 | 6.2 | 10,561 | 9,936 | 6.3 | 415 | 78 | 390 | -80 |
| California ....................... | 161,904 | 155,790 | 3.9 | 159,109 | 152,739 | 4.2 | 483 | 3,184 | 3,901 | -18.4 |
| Colorado ........................ | 14,312 | 13,461 | 6.3 | 14,312 | 13,461 | 6.3 | 357 | N.D. | N.D. | N.D. |
| Connecticut (b) ............. | 17,605 | 17,241 | 2.1 | 12,193 | 11,920 | 2.3 | 372 | 4,899 | 4,351 | 12.6 |
| Delaware (b) ................... | 5,558 | 4,435 | 2.3 | 3,211 | 3,264 | -1.6 | 429 | 1,991 | 1,822 | 9.3 |
| Florida (d) ..................... | 67,224 | 64,626 | 4.0 | 67,193 | 64,574 | 4.1 | 447 | 17 | 13 | 30.8 |
| Georgia (d) ..................... | 39,262 | 36,505 | 7.6 | 38,758 | 35,787 | 8.3 | 502 | 811 | 98 | 727.6 |
| Hawaii (b) ...................... | 4,924 | 4,978 | -1.1 | 3,670 | 3,448 | 6.4 | 307 | 985 | 883 | 11.6 |
| Idaho ............................. | 4,083 | 3,911 | 4.4 | 4,083 | 3,911 | 4.4 | 330 | N.D. | N.D. | N.D. |
| Illinois (d)(e) ................. | 43,051 | 40,788 | 5.5 | 43,051 | 40,788 | 5.5 | 357 | 0 | 0 | N.D. |
| Indiana .......................... | 19,197 | 17,903 | 7.2 | 19,016 | 17,730 | 7.3 | 321 | 169 | 79 | 113.9 |
| Iowa (d)(e) ..................... | 7,394 | 6,938 | 6.6 | 7,394 | 6,938 | 6.6 | 258 | N.D. | N.D. | N.D. |
| Kansas (e) ...................... | 8,183 | 7,911 | 3.4 | 8,183 | 7,911 | 3.4 | 310 | N.D. | N.D. | N.D. |
| Kentucky ........................ | 14,987 | 14,600 | 2.7 | 14,987 | 14,600 | 2.7 | 379 | 0 | 0 | N.D. |
| Louisiana ....................... | 32,227 | 29,265 | 10.1 | 32,227 | 29,265 | 10.1 | 736 | N.D. | N.D. | N.D. |
| Maine ............................. | 1,612 | 1,620 | -0.5 | 1,562 | 1,542 | 1.3 | 125 | 55 | 25 | 120 |
| Maryland ........................ | 22,572 | 22,232 | 1.5 | 21,540 | 21,088 | 2.1 | 418 | 1,055 | 989 | 6.7 |
| Massachusetts (c) .......... | 11,832 | 11,947 | -1.0 | 10,739 | 10,847 | -1.0 | 275 | 862 | 1,248 | -30.9 |
| Michigan ........................ | 45,879 | 44,771 | 2.5 | 45,879 | 44,771 | 2.5 | 466 | N.D. | 0 | N.D. |
| Minnesota ...................... | 5,572 | 5,326 | 4.6 | 5,557 | 5,306 | 4.7 | 117 | 5 | 0 | N.D. |
| Mississippi ..................... | 16,678 | 14,296 | 16.7 | 15,855 | 13,676 | 15.9 | 574 | 319 | 134 | 138.1 |
| Missouri ......................... | 24,974 | 23,998 | 4.1 | 24,949 | 23,998 | 4.0 | 457 | 4 | 0 | N.D. |
| Montana ......................... | 2,734 | 2,517 | 8.6 | 2,734 | 2,517 | 8.6 | 310 | N.D. | N.D. | N.D. |
| Nebraska ........................ | 3,676 | 3,402 | 8.1 | 3,588 | 3,329 | 7.8 | 215 | 87 | 90 | -3.3 |
| Nevada ........................... | 9,651 | 9,024 | 6.9 | 9,651 | 9,024 | 6.9 | 542 | 137 | 166 | -17.5 |
| New Hampshire.............. | 2,169 | 2,168 | 0.0 | 2,169 | 2,168 | 0.0 | 182 | 49 | 29 | 69 |
| New Jersey (e) ................ | 31,121 | 28,361 | 9.7 | 31,121 | 28,361 | 9.7 | 382 | N.D. | N.D. | N.D. |
| New Mexico .................... | 4,985 | 4,688 | 6.3 | 4,732 | 4,450 | 6.3 | 271 | 279 | 323 | -13.6 |
| New York........................ | 72,638 | 70,295 | 3.3 | 72,289 | 70,021 | 3.2 | 397 | 0 | N.D. | N.D. |
| North Carolina .............. | 31,811 | 31,612 | 0.6 | 27,193 | 27,567 | -1.4 | 358 | 3,087 | 1,102 | 180.1 |
| North Dakota ................. | 915 | 797 | 14.8 | 814 | 715 | 13.8 | 128 | 75 | 64 | 17.2 |
| Ohio (e) .......................... | 48,450 | 48,016 | 0.9 | 48,450 | 48,016 | 0.9 | 432 | 0 | 0 | N.D. |
| Oklahoma (e) .................. | 20,892 | 20,542 | 1.7 | 20,892 | 20,542 | 1.7 | 622 | N.D. | N.D. | N.D. |
| Oregon ........................... | 8,927 | 7,999 | 11.6 | 8,596 | 7,589 | 13.3 | 260 | 1,327 | 1,361 | -2.5 |
| Pennsylvania .................. | 36,377 | 34,964 | 4.0 | 36,373 | 34,957 | 4.1 | 303 | 2 | 6 | -66.7 |
| Rhode Island (b) ............ | 3,445 | 3,371 | 2.2 | 2,175 | 2,100 | 3.6 | 220 | 1,225 | 1,031 | 18.8 |
| South Carolina ............... | 22,115 | 21,173 | 4.4 | 21,236 | 20,264 | 4.8 | 550 | 663 | 547 | 21.2 |
| South Dakota ................. | 2,435 | 2,242 | 8.6 | 2,430 | 242 | 8.4 | 329 | N.D. | N.D. | N.D. |
| Tennessee (e) .................. | 17,738 | 16,659 | 6.5 | 17,738 | 16,659 | 6.5 | 325 | N.D. | N.D. | N.D. |
| Texas (e) ......................... | 144,510 | 140,351 | 3.0 | 144,510 | 140,351 | 3.0 | 724 | 4345 | 4,417 | -1.6 |
| Utah .............................. | 4,391 | 4,301 | 2.1 | 4,337 | 4,280 | 1.3 | 205 | 111 | 91 | 22 |
| Vermont (b) .................... | 1,426 | 1,270 | 12.3 | 1,110 | 828 | 34.1 | 188 | 318 | 231 | 37.7 |
| Virginia .......................... | 28,560 | 28,385 | 0.6 | 27,191 | 27,524 | -1.2 | 399 | 352 | 83 | 324.1 |
| Washington .................... | 14,161 | 13,214 | 7.2 | 14,154 | 13,214 | 7.1 | 247 | 87 | 91 | N.D. |
| West Virginia ................. | 3,478 | 3,148 | 10.5 | 3,478 | 3,148 | 10.5 | 192 | 24 | 29 | -17.2 |
| Wisconsin ....................... | 18,451 | 16,277 | 13.4 | 17,477 | 15,639 | 11.8 | 334 | 588 | 862 | -31.8 |
| Wyoming ........................ | 1,571 | 1,549 | 1.4 | 1,571 | 1,549 | 1.4 | 327 | 0 | 0 | N.D. |
| Dist. of Columbia (b) ..... | 9,949 | 9,353 | 6.4 | 9,949 | 9,353 | 6.4 | 1,913 | 708 | 758 | -6.6 |

*Sources*: U.S. Department of Justice, Bureau of Justice Statistics, *Bulletin, Prisoners in 1998* (August 1999) and the Sourcebook of Criminal Justice Statistics 1998.

*Key*:

N.D. — Not defined.

(a) The number of prisoners with sentences of more than one year per 100,000 resident populations.

(b) Prisons and jails form one integrated system. Data include total jail and prison population.

(c) The incarceration rate includes an estimated 6,200 inmates sentenced to more than 1 year but held in local jails or houses of corrections.

(d) Population figures are based on custody counts.

(e) Includes some inmates sentenced to 1 year or less.

(f) Advance count of prisoners may be revised by BJS.

(g) Data for inmates sentenced to one year or less may include some inmates for whom sentence is unknown.

(h) Data for inmates sentenced to more than 1 year may include some inmates sentenced to 1 year or less and may be estimated in some states.

## Table 8.12
## ADULTS ADMITTED TO STATE PRISONS, 1996

| State or other jurisdiction | Prisoner population (1/1/96) | Total | Number of sentenced prisoners admitted during 1996 | | | | | |
|---|---|---|---|---|---|---|---|---|
| | | | New court commitments | Parole or other conditional release violators returned | Escapees and AWOLs returned | Returns from appeal or bond | Transfers from other jurisdictions | Other admissions |
| United States ............... | 1,085,644 | 555,992 | 353,893 | 175,305 | 9,808 | 627 | 3,327 | 13,032 |
| Alabama ......................... | 20,130 | 9,750 | 7,477 | 1,840 | 265 | 85 | 20 | 63 |
| Alaska (a) ...................... | 2,042 | 2,377 | 1,549 | 782 | 41 | 5 | 0 | 0 |
| Arizona (b) .................... | 20,291 | 9,090 | 7,014 | 2,005 | 30 | 0 | 41 | 0 |
| Arkansas ........................ | 8,522 | 5,215 | 3,234 | 1,878 | 7 | 11 | 50 | 35 |
| California ....................... | 131,745 | 123,876 | 46,465 | 75,785 | 390 | . . . | 1,236 | 0 |
| Colorado ........................ | 11,063 | 6,098 | 4,346 | 1,360 | 371 | 7 | 14 | 0 |
| Connecticut (a) .............. | 10,418 | 1,227 | 404 | 238 | 121 | 4 | 3 | 457 |
| Delaware (a,c,h) ............. | 3,014 | 1,481 | 936 | 363 | 39 | 0 | 0 | 143 |
| Florida (b) ...................... | 63,866 | 24,209 | 19,972 | 3,722 | 244 | . . . | 15 | 256 |
| Georgia (b) ..................... | 34,085 | 15,714 | 12,533 | 3,042 | 79 | 2 | 56 | 2 |
| Hawaii (a,d) ................... | 2,590 | 2,356 | 1,353 | 916 | 80 | 0 | 0 | 7 |
| Idaho .............................. | 3,328 | 2,526 | 1,971 | 542 | 13 | 0 | . . . | 0 |
| Illinois (b,c) ................... | 37,658 | 24,541 | 18,290 | 5,224 | 1,012 | 15 | . . . | 0 |
| Indiana (e) ..................... | 16,046 | 8,847 | 8,016 | 769 | 8 | . . . | 54 | 0 |
| Iowa (b) .......................... | 5,906 | 4,156 | 2,604 | 792 | 596 | 32 | 78 | 54 |
| Kansas (e) ...................... | 7,054 | 4,244 | 2,859 | 1,298 | 12 | . . . | 0 | 75 |
| Kentucky ........................ | 12,060 | 7,685 | 5,672 | 1,854 | 117 | . . . | 0 | 42 |
| Louisiana ....................... | 25,195 | 14,175 | 6,206 | 7,435 | 84 | 225 | 28 | 197 |
| Maine ............................. | 1,401 | 803 | 528 | 267 | 8 | 0 | 0 | 0 |
| Maryland (d,e,h) ............ | 20,450 | 9,715 | 7,974 | 1,623 | 103 | . . . | 13 | 2 |
| Massachusetts (f,h) ........ | 10,427 | 3,412 | 2,201 | 883 | 15 | . . . | 313 | 0 |
| Michigan (b) ................... | 41,112 | 13,731 | 8,049 | 3,606 | 1,011 | 0 | 13 | 1,052 |
| Minnesota ...................... | 4,846 | 3,304 | 2,478 | 826 | . . . | . . . | . . . | 0 |
| Mississippi (e) ............... | 12,251 | 5,467 | 4,762 | 322 | 39 | . . . | 0 | 344 |
| Missouri ......................... | 19,134 | 13,462 | 7,916 | 3,36 | 1,215 | 19 | 39 | 937 |
| Montana (d) .................... | 1,837 | 1,005 | 663 | 341 | . . . | . . . | 1 | 0 |
| Nebraska ........................ | 3,045 | 1,724 | 1,370 | 335 | 19 | . . . | 0 | 0 |
| Nevada (c,e) ................... | 7,713 | 4,272 | 2,975 | 636 | 42 | . . . | . . . | 619 |
| New Hampshire (e) ........ | 2,015 | 996 | 641 | 340 | 15 | . . . | 0 | 0 |
| New Jersey (c,e) ............. | 27,066 | 15,001 | 9,382 | 5,617 | 2 | . . . | . . . | 0 |
| New Mexico .................... | 3,925 | 2,845 | 1,642 | 1,153 | 20 | 0 | 30 | 0 |
| New York (e) ................... | 68,486 | 32,152 | 21,192 | 8,240 | 2,091 | 116 | 498 | 15 |
| North Carolina (c) ......... | 27,914 | 14,359 | 9,601 | 4,579 | 179 | 0 | 0 | 0 |
| North Dakota .................. | 544 | 585 | 488 | 92 | 5 | 0 | 0 | 0 |
| Ohio (c) ........................... | 44,663 | 21,727 | 17,948 | 3,742 | 10 | 18 | 9 | 0 |
| Oklahoma (c,e) ............... | 18,151 | 7,433 | 6,867 | 225 | 341 | 0 | 0 | 0 |
| Oregon ........................... | 6,515 | 3,712 | 2,141 | 1,469 | 75 | 27 | . . . | 0 |
| Pennsylvania ................. | 32,410 | 9,918 | 5,744 | 3,770 | 124 | 22 | 79 | 179 |
| Rhode Island (a,c) ......... | 1,833 | 1,036 | 715 | 283 | 24 | 4 | 10 | 0 |
| South Carolina .............. | 19,015 | 8,243 | 5,830 | 2,259 | 60 | 8 | . . . | 86 |
| South Dakota ................. | 1,871 | 1,143 | 891 | 192 | 7 | 0 | 8 | 45 |
| Tennessee (c) .................. | 15,206 | 8,320 | 4,578 | 3,623 | 87 | . . . | 32 | 0 |
| Texas (c,d) ...................... | 127,766 | 38,716 | 24,468 | 7,566 | 0 | 0 | . . . | 6,682 |
| Utah ............................... | 3,447 | 2,587 | 1,353 | 1,224 | 8 | 2 | 0 | 0 |
| Vermont (a,b) ................. | 1,048 | 803 | 204 | 249 | 50 | . . . | 11 | 289 |
| Virginia .......................... | 27,260 | 9,823 | 8,191 | 1,632 | . . . | . . . | . . . | 0 |
| Washington .................... | 11,608 | 6,462 | 5,532 | 774 | 132 | 24 | 0 | 0 |
| West Virginia ................. | 2,483 | 1 | 876 | 168 | 5 | 0 | 0 | 0 |
| Wisconsin ...................... | 10,337 | 7,019 | 4,619 | 1,385 | . . . | . . . | 0 | 1,015 |
| Wyoming (e) ................... | 1,395 | 614 | 523 | 82 | 6 | 0 | 3 | 0 |
| Dist. of Columbia (a,c,h) | 9,794 | 6,706 | 3,304 | 1,949 | 606 | 1 | 631 | 215 |

*Source*: U.S. Department of Justice, Bureau of Justice Statistics, *Correctional Populations in the United States 1996*, (April 1999).

Key:

. . . — Not available.

(a) Figures include both jail and prison inmates; jails and prisons are combined in one system.

(b) Data are for custody rather than jurisdiction counts.

(c) Data by sentence length may be slightly incorrect.

(d) Some or all data for the admission categories are estimated.

(e) New court commitments may include a small number of other admissions.

(f) Figures include all inmates in Massachusetts custody, regardless of jurisdiction, as well as Massachusetts inmates housed in other states.

(g) Include inmates housed in local jails or other facilities.

(h) Unconditional releases may include some releases to probation or appeal/bond.

## Table 8.13
## STATE PRISON CAPACITIES, 1998

| State or other jurisdiction | Rated capacity | Operational capacity | Design capacity | Population as a percent of capacity: (a) | |
|---|---|---|---|---|---|
| | | | | Highest capacity | Lowest capacity |
| Alabama | 21,800 | 21,800 | 21,800 | 100 | 100 |
| Alaska | 2,603 | 2,691 | 2,603 | 119 | 123 |
| Arizona | . . . | 23,036 | 23,036 | 110 | 110 |
| Arkansas | 10,208 | 10,208 | 10,208 | 100 | 100 |
| California | . . . | . . . | 79,875 | 203 | 203 |
| Colorado | . . . | 9,842 | 8,037 | 118 | 144 |
| Connecticut (b) | . . . | . . . | . . . | . . . | . . . |
| Delaware | . . . | 4,206 | 3,192 | 125 | 165 |
| Florida | 77,370 | 70,785 | 52,407 | 87 | 128 |
| Georgia | . . . | 39,320 | . . . | 100 | 100 |
| Hawaii | . . . | 3,122 | 2,197 | 120 | 171 |
| Idaho | 3,167 | 3,991 | 3,167 | 95 | 120 |
| Illinois | 32,062 | 32,062 | 27,342 | 134 | 157 |
| Indiana | 13,983 | 17,119 | . . . | 101 | 123 |
| Iowa | 5,701 | 5,701 | 5,701 | 130 | 130 |
| Kansas | 8,189 | . . . | . . . | 100 | 100 |
| Kentucky | 11,428 | 11,180 | 7,421 | 122 | 187 |
| Louisiana | 19,016 | 18,975 | . . . | 100 | 100 |
| Maine | 1,460 | 1,629 | 1,460 | 99 | 110 |
| Maryland | . . . | 22,688 | . . . | 99 | 99 |
| Massachusetts | . . . | . . . | 9,162 | 122 | 122 |
| Michigan | . . . | 44,804 | . . . | 99 | 99 |
| Minnesota | 5,567 | 5,724 | 5,724 | 96 | 99 |
| Mississippi | . . . | 13,916 | 14,649 | 103 | 108 |
| Missouri | . . . | 26,302 | . . . | 95 | 95 |
| Montana | . . . | 1,748 | 1244 | 126 | 178 |
| Nebraska | . . . | 2,963 | 2,371 | 124 | 155 |
| Nevada | 9,251 | . . . | 6,820 | 104 | 142 |
| New Hampshire | 1,841 | 1,864 | 1,744 | 109 | 117 |
| New Jersey | . . . | . . . | 17,282 | 158 | 158 |
| New Mexico | . . . | 3,447 | . . . | 109 | 109 |
| New York | 60,879 | 65,717 | 53,409 | 107 | 132 |
| North Carolina | 27,866 | . . . | 27,866 | 113 | 113 |
| North Dakota | 1005 | 952 | 1005 | 84 | 89 |
| Ohio | 37,245 | . . . | . . . | 130 | 130 |
| Oklahoma | . . . | 21,578 | . . . | 93 | 93 |
| Oregon | . . . | 8,646 | . . . | 102 | 102 |
| Pennsylvania | 24247 | 30,992 | 24,247 | 117 | 150 |
| Rhode Island | 3,858 | 3,858 | 3,858 | 89 | 89 |
| South Carolina | . . . | 22,595 | 21,265 | 96 | 102 |
| South Dakota | . . . | 2,470 | . . . | 99 | 99 |
| Tennessee | 16130 | 15,778 | . . . | 97 | 99 |
| Texas | 148,756 | 148,756 | 151,430 | 95 | 97 |
| Utah | . . . | 4,280 | 4,462 | 81 | 84 |
| Vermont | 1,140 | 1,140 | 1,023 | 103 | 115 |
| Virginia | 29,171 | 29,171 | 29,171 | 90 | 90 |
| Washington | 8,902 | 11,575 | 11,575 | 122 | 159 |
| West Virginia | 2,698 | 2,827 | 2,695 | 100 | 105 |
| Wisconsin | . . . | 11,136 | . . . | 136 | 136 |
| Wyoming | 1231 | 1,243 | 1,047 | 115 | 137 |
| Dist. of Columbia | 7,973 | 7,289 | . . . | 91 | 100 |

*Source:* U.S. Department of Justice, Bureau of Justice Statistics, *Prisoners in 1998* (August 1999).

Key:

. . . — Not available.

(a) Population counts exclude jail backups and inmates held in other states.

(b) Connecticut no longer reports capacity due to a law passed in 1995.

## Table 8.14
## ADULTS ON PROBATION, 1998

| State or other jurisdiction | Probation population 1/1/98 | 1998 Entries | 1998 Exits | Probation population 12/31/98 | Percent change in probation population during 1998 | Probation population Under intensive supervision 1997 | Probation population Under electronic monitoring 1997 |
|---|---|---|---|---|---|---|---|
| Alabama (b,g,j) | 38,720 | 17,279 | 15,626 | 44,047 | 13.8 | 920 | 75 |
| Alaska (a,h) | 4,212 | 1,745 | 1,501 | 4,456 | 5.8 | 51 | NA |
| Arizona (e,f,g,j) | 44,813 | 28,944 | 21,944 | 52,580 | 17.3 | 3,174 | 200 |
| Arkansas (a) | 28,294 | 13,668 | 8,379 | 33,583 | 7.3 | 0 | 0 |
| California (a) | 304,531 | 167,106 | 147,210 | 324,427 | 6.5 | . . . | . . . |
| Colorado (b,g,j) | 45,499 | 26,477 | 21,337 | 47,792 | 5.0 | . . . | . . . |
| Connecticut (e) | 55,989 | 32,318 | 30,797 | 57,510 | 2.7 | 1,549 | 250 |
| Delaware (e,f,g) | 18,837 | 11,013 | 9,820 | 20,030 | 6.3 | 4,265 | 531 |
| Florida (b,g,j) | 239,694 | 144,384 | 142,007 | 239,021 | -0.3 | 25,919 | 1,338 |
| Georgia (j) | 149,963 | 60,206 | 58,304 | 151,865 | 1.3 | 5,355 | NA |
| Hawaii | 15,401 | 7,443 | 7,133 | 15,711 | 2.0 | 81 | 10 |
| Idaho | 6,367 | 3,138 | 1,828 | 7,677 | 20.6 | 126 | 57 |
| Illinois | 119,481 | 68,232 | 55,863 | 131,850 | 10.4 | 1,270 | . . . |
| Indiana | 96,752 | 84,946 | 79,798 | 101,900 | 5.3 | . . . | . . . |
| Iowa | 16,834 | 17,184 | 15,571 | 18,447 | 9.6 | 757 | 18 |
| Kansas(h,i) | 16,339 | 19,306 | 19,482 | 16,163 | -1.1 | NA | 46 |
| Kentucky | 12,093 | 6,554 | 5,755 | 12,892 | 6.6 | 294 | NA |
| Louisiana | 35,453 | 16,136 | 18,561 | 33,028 | -6.8 | NA | NA |
| Maine (b) | 7,178 | . . . | . . . | 6,953 | -3.1 | NA | NA |
| Maryland | 74,612 | 40,179 | 36,740 | 78,051 | 4.6 | 1,416 | NA |
| Massachusetts | 46,430 | 40,165 | 40,028 | 46,567 | 0.3 | . . . | . . . |
| Michigan (b,g,j) | 165,449 | 61,755 | 58,729 | 172,147 | 4.0 | 1,944 | 2,972 |
| Minnesota | 94,920 | 54,671 | 58,618 | 90,973 | -4.2 | NA | NA |
| Mississippi(h,i,l) | 10,997 | 6,461 | 5,928 | 11,530 | 4.8 | NA | NA |
| Missouri (e,f,g,j) | 46,301 | 17,815 | 16,110 | 48,006 | 3.7 | 943 | 197 |
| Montana (a,b) | 4,683 | . . . | . . . | 5,133 | 9.6 | 25 | 100 |
| Nebraska | 16,439 | 12,560 | 13,062 | 15,937 | -3.1 | 652 | 220 |
| Nevada (e,f,g) | 11,670 | 5,794 | 4,903 | 12,561 | 7.6 | 374 | 250 |
| New Hampshire | 4,876 | 3,760 | 3,461 | 5,175 | 6.1 | 37 | 4 |
| New Jersey(g) | 130,565 | 58,200 | 55,538 | 133,227 | 2.0 | 1,373 | NA |
| New Mexico(g,j) | 8,905 | 8,926 | 7,371 | 10,460 | 17.5 | 414 | 23 |
| New York | 181,105 | 48,384 | 38,971 | 190,518 | 5.2 | 6,945 | NA |
| North Carolina | 105,416 | 59,436 | 60,154 | 104,698 | -0.7 | 9,536 | 887 |
| North Dakota (e,f) | 2,700 | 1,622 | 1,664 | 2,658 | -1.6 | 20 | 10 |
| Ohio (b,g,j) | 113,493 | 74,298 | 70,719 | 117,618 | 3.6 | 9,030 | 2,664 |
| Oklahoma (g,j) | 28,790 | 13,912 | 13,760 | 28,942 | 0.5 | 343 | . . . |
| Oregon (e,f) | 43,980 | 16,876 | 16,047 | 44,809 | 1.9 | 502 | 315 |
| Pennsylvania (g) | 108,230 | 43,091 | 30,227 | 121,094 | 11.9 | 13,564 | . . . |
| Rhode Island(g) | 19,648 | 7,099 | 6,404 | 20,343 | 3.5 | 224 | NA |
| South Carolina | 43,095 | 15,280 | 17,066 | 41,309 | -4.1 | 2,384 | . . . |
| South Dakota (b,i,k) | 3,730 | 4,098 | 3,958 | 3,480 | -6.7 | 50 | NA |
| Tennessee(g,j) | 35,836 | 23,368 | 21,796 | 37,408 | 4.4 | 1,775 | 596 |
| Texas | 438,232 | 196,385 | 190,859 | 443,758 | 1.3 | 2,991 | 1,127 |
| Utah | 9,519 | 4,130 | 4,174 | 9,475 | -0.5 | 241 | 23 |
| Vermont | 7,686 | 5,503 | 3,892 | 9,297 | 21.0 | NA | NA |
| Virginia (f) | 30,002 | 24,687 | 24,113 | 30,576 | 1.9 | 765 | 32 |
| Washington (b,g,j) | 145,547 | 45,839 | 41,123 | 152,609 | 4.9 | 814 | 77 |
| West Virginia (a,b) | 6,298 | . . . | . . . | 6,362 | 1.0 | NA | NA |
| Wisconsin | 53,848 | 24,752 | 23,324 | 55,276 | 2.7 | . . . | . . . |
| Wyoming | 3,486 | 3,074 | 2,735 | 3,825 | 9.7 | 49 | 20 |
| Dist. of Columbia (c) | 10,043 | 9,840 | 9,278 | 10,605 | 5.6 | 78 | . . . |

*Sources:* U.S. Department of Justice, Bureau of Justice Statistics, *Probation and Parole in the United States, 1998,* (August 1999).

Key:

NA — Not applicable.

. . . — Number not known.

(a) All data are estimated.

(b) Because of nonresponsive or incomplete data, the population on December 31, 1998, does not equal the population on January 1, 1998, plus entries, minus exits.

(c) Intensive supervision probationers could not be separated from electronic monitoring probationers and were therefore reported together

(d) Total entries are estimated.

(e) Detailed data are estimated for electronic monitoring.

(f) Detailed data are estimated for intensive supervision

(g) Some date are estimated.

(h) Data do not include absconders.

(i) Data do not include out-of state cases.

(j) Multiple agencies reporting.

(k) Data are for year beginning July 1,1997, and ending June 30,1998.

(l) Data do not include inactive cases.

## Table 8.15
## ADULTS ON PAROLE, 1998

| State or other jurisdiction | Parole population 1/1/98 | 1998 Entries | 1998 Exits | Parole population 12/31/98 | Percent change in parole population during 1998 | Parole population Under intensive supervision 1997 | Parole population Under electronic monitoring 1997 |
|---|---|---|---|---|---|---|---|
| Alabama (a,b,c,i) ............ | 6,356 | 2,423 | 2,059 | 6,785 | 6.7 | 100 | 40 |
| Alaska (a) ...................... | 472 | 313 | 293 | 492 | 4.2 | 21 | NA |
| Arizona ......................... | 3,378 | 6,207 | 5,843 | 3,742 | 10.8 | . . . | 120 |
| Arkansas (a,b,c,j) .......... | 4,685 | 5,415 | 4,763 | 6,371 | 11.4 | 46 | 57 |
| California(g,i) ................ | 104,412 | 140,724 | 134,519 | 110,617 | 5.9 | 10,641 | 12 |
| Colorado(d) ................... | 4,139 | 4,421 | 3,356 | 5,204 | 25.7 | 504 | NA |
| Connecticut ................... | 996 | 1,449 | 1,260 | 1,185 | 19 | 20 | 17 |
| Delaware (a,c) ............... | 591 | . . . | 192 | 572 | -3.2 | 203 | 9 |
| Florida (d) .................... | 8,477 | 4,315 | 5,371 | 7,421 | -12.5 | 10 | NA |
| Georgia (b) .................... | 21,915 | 10,360 | 11,749 | 20,482 | -6.5 | 1,206 | 1,100 |
| Hawaii ........................... | 1,827 | 791 | 609 | 2,009 | 10 | 84 | 4 |
| Idaho (c) ....................... | 820 | 832 | 378 | 1,274 | 55.4 | 61 | 19 |
| Illinois .......................... | 30,348 | 23,773 | 23,689 | 30,432 | 0.3 | 446 | 337 |
| Indiana(g,h) .................. | 4,044 | 4,681 | 4,467 | 4,258 | 5.3 | 50 | 21 |
| Iowa .............................. | 2,037 | 2,608 | 2,451 | 2,194 | 7.7 | 387 | 17 |
| Kansas(g,e) .................... | 6,150 | 4,982 | 5,107 | 6,025 | -2 | NA | 35 |
| Kentucky ....................... | 4,233 | 2,938 | 2,663 | 4,508 | 6.5 | 272 | NA |
| Louisiana ...................... | 19,927 | 13,533 | 14,701 | 18,759 | -5.9 | 150 | 54 |
| Maine(f) ........................ | 67 | 2 | 4 | 65 | -3 | NA | NA |
| Maryland ....................... | 15,763 | 8,459 | 8,694 | 15,528 | -1.5 | 2,495 | 71 |
| Massachusetts (a,e) .......... | 4,596 | 3,718 | 3,443 | 4,489 | -2.3 | 70 | 10 |
| Michigan ....................... | 14,351 | 10,503 | 9,523 | 15,331 | 6.8 | 3,835 | 242 |
| Minnesota(e) .................. | 2,446 | 3,011 | 2,462 | 2,995 | 22.4 | 369 | 75 |
| Mississippi (g,h,k) .......... | 1,378 | 1,094 | 983 | 1,489 | 8.1 | NA | NA |
| Missouri (a,e) ................. | 12,514 | 5,034 | 7,182 | 10,366 | -17.2 | NA | 208 |
| Montana (a,b,e) .............. | 755 | . . . | . . . | 667 | -11.7 | 31 | 31 |
| Nebraska ....................... | 688 | 710 | 774 | 624 | -9.3 | 79 | NA |
| Nevada (f,e) ................... | 3,463 | 2,606 | 2,014 | 4,055 | 17.1 | 102 | 50 |
| New Hampshire .............. | 1,083 | 565 | 507 | 1,141 | 5.4 | 124 | 17 |
| New Jersey(f) ................. | 16,903 | 16,281 | 18,627 | 14,557 | -13.9 | 1,039 | 68 |
| New Mexico ................... | 1,626 | 1,671 | 1,524 | 1,773 | 9 | 198 | 55 |
| New York ....................... | 59,670 | 25,096 | 25,218 | 59,548 | -0.2 | NA | 69 |
| North Carolina(f) ........... | 8,148 | 6,923 | 9,331 | 5,740 | -29.6 | 1,098 | 151 |
| North Dakota(c) ............. | 116 | 338 | 279 | 175 | 50.9 | 5 | 3 |
| Ohio .............................. | 6,803 | 9,275 | 4,774 | 11,304 | 66.2 | NA | NA |
| Oklahoma(f) .................. | 1,928 | 317 | 713 | 1,532 | -20.5 | 73 | NA |
| Oregon (c) ..................... | 16,815 | 7,010 | 6,555 | 17,270 | 2.7 | 308 | 193 |
| Pennsylvania(f) .............. | 78,264 | 24,726 | 19,822 | 83,168 | 6.3 | 10,749 | . . . |
| Rhode Island ................. | 526 | 532 | 589 | 469 | -10.8 | NA | 50 |
| South Carolina ............... | 4,813 | 939 | 1,393 | 4,359 | -9.4 | 455 | . . . |
| South Dakota ................. | 823 | 825 | 560 | 1,088 | 32.2 | 100 | NA |
| Tennessee (c) ................. | 8,693 | 3,086 | 4,174 | 7,605 | -12.5 | 1,213 | 10 |
| Texas (a,c) ..................... | 109,437 | 32,189 | 29,604 | 112,022 | 2.4 | 1,931 | 767 |
| Utah ............................. | 3,281 | 2,686 | 2,195 | 3,772 | 15 | 514 | 83 |
| Vermont ........................ | 677 | 257 | 243 | 691 | 2.1 | NA | NA |
| Virginia (a,b,c) .............. | 10,710 | 5,115 | 9,125 | 6,700 | -37.4 | 1,150 | 84 |
| Washington (a,b) ............ | 480 | 23 | 155 | 375 | -21.9 | NA | NA |
| West Virginia ................. | 894 | 675 | 594 | 975 | 9.1 | . . . | NA |
| Wisconsin (b) ................. | 9,540 | 4,058 | 4,671 | 8,927 | -6.4 | . . . | . . . |
| Wyoming (f) ................... | 422 | 272 | 246 | 448 | 6.2 | 17 | 8 |
| Dist. of Columbia(a,b) ....... | 7,761 | 1,553 | 2,975 | 6,625 | -14.6 | NA | NA |

*Sources*: U.S. Department of Justice, Bureau of Justice Statistics, *Probation and Parole in the United States*, 1998,( August 1999).

Key:
NA— Not Available
. . . — Number not known.
(a) All data are estimated.
(b) Because of nonresponse, or incomplete data, the population on December 31, 1998, does not equal the population on January 1, 1998, plus entries, minus exits.
(c) Detailed data are estimated for intensive supervision and electronic monitoring.
(d) Intensive supervision and electronic monitoring are combined program.

(e) Detailed data are estimated for electronic monitoring.
(f) Some data are estimated
(g) Data do not include absconders.
(h) Data do not include out-of state cases.
(i) Multiple agencies reporting.
(j) Data are for year beginning March 30,1998, and ending December 31, 1998.
(k) Data do not include inactive cases.

## Table 8.16
## CAPITAL PUNISHMENT
### (As of December 1999)

| State or other jurisdiction | Capital offenses | Minimum age | Prisoners under sentence of death (1) | Method of execution |
|---|---|---|---|---|
| Alabama | Capital murder with a finding of at least 1 of 9 aggravating circumstances. | 16 | 185 | Electrocution |
| Alaska | . . . | . . . | . . . | . . . |
| Arizona | First degree murder accompanied by at least 1 of 10 aggravating factors. | . . . | 121 | Lethal gas or lethal injection (a) |
| Arkansas | Capital murder with a finding of at least 1 of 10 aggravating circumstances; treason. | 14 | 40 | Lethal injection or electrocution (b) |
| California | First-degree murder with special circumstances; train-wrecking; treason; perjury causing execution. | 18 | 561 | Lethal gas or lethal injection |
| Colorado | First-degree murder with at least 1 of 13 aggravating factors; treason. Capital sentencing excludes persons determined to be mentally retarded. | 18 | 5 | Lethal injection |
| Connecticut | Capital felony with 9 categories of aggravated homicide. | 18 | 7 | Lethal injection |
| Delaware | First-degree murder with aggravating circumstances. | 16 | 18 | Hanging or lethal injection (c) |
| Florida | First-degree murder; felony murder; capital drug-trafficking. | 16 | 389 | Electrocution or lethal injection |
| Georgia | Murder; kidnapping with bodily injury or ransom where the victim dies; aircraft hijacking; treason. | 17 | 134 | Electrocution |
| Hawaii | . . . | . . . | . . . | . . . |
| Idaho | First-degree murder; aggravated kidnapping. | None | 21 | Firing Squad or lethal injection |
| Illinois | First-degree murder with 1 of 15 aggravating circumstances. | 18 | 160 | Lethal injection |
| Indiana | Murder with 16 aggravating circumstances. Capital sentencing excludes persons determined to be mentally retarded. | 16 | 43 | Lethal injection |
| Iowa | . . . | . . . | . . . | . . . |
| Kansas | Capital murder, with 7 aggravating circumstances. Capital sentencing excludes persons determined to be mentally retarded. | 18 | 3 | Lethal injection |
| Kentucky | Murder with aggravating factors; kidnapping with aggravating factors. | 16 | 39 | Electrocution or lethal injection |
| Louisiana | First-degree murder; aggravated rape of victim under age 12; treason. | None | 87 | Lethal injection |
| Maine | . . . | . . . | . . . | . . . |
| Maryland | First-degree murder, either premeditated or during the commission of a felony, provided that certain death eligibility requirements are satisfied. | 18 | 17 | Lethal injection |
| Massachusetts | . . . | . . . | . . . | . . . |
| Michigan | . . . | . . . | . . . | . . . |
| Minnesota | . . . | . . . | . . . | . . . |
| Mississippi | Capital murder; aircraft piracy. | 16 (d) | 63 | Lethal gas or lethal injection (e) |
| Missouri | First-degree murder. | 16 | 83 | Lethal injection or lethal gas |
| Montana | Capital murder with 1 of 9 aggravating circumstances; capital sexual assault. | None | 6 | Lethal injection |
| Nebraska | First-degree murder with a finding of at least 1 statutorily-defined aggravating circumstance. statutorily-defined aggravating circumstance. | 18 | 9 | Electrocution |
| Nevada | First-degree murder with 13 aggravating circumstances. | 16 | 89 | Lethal injection |
| New Hampshire | Six categories of capital murder. | 17 | 0 | Lethal injection or hanging (f) |
| New Jersey | Purposeful or knowing murder by one's own conduct; contract murder; solicitation by command or threat in furtherance of a narcotics conspiracy. | 18 | 16 | Lethal injection |
| New Mexico | First-degree murder in conjunction with a finding of at least 1 of 7 aggravating circumstances. | 18 | 5 | Lethal injection |
| New York | First-degree murder with 1 of 12 aggravating factors. Capital sentencing excludes persons determined to be mentally retarded. | 18 | 5 | Lethal injection |
| North Carolina | First-degree murder. | 17 (h) | 224 | Lethal injection or lethal gas |
| North Dakota | . . . | . . . | . . . | . . . |
| Ohio | Aggravated murder with at least 1 of 8 aggravating circumstances. | 18 | 199 | Electrocution or lethal injection |

## CAPITAL PUNISHMENT— Continued

| State or other jurisdiction | Capital offenses | Minimum age | Prisoners under sentence of death (l) | Method of execution |
|---|---|---|---|---|
| Oklahoma | First-degree murder in conjunction with a finding of at least 1 of 8 statutorily defined aggravating circumstances. | 16 | 149 | Lethal injection, electrocution or firing squad (h) |
| Oregon | Aggravated murder. | 18 | 27 | Lethal injection |
| Pennsylvania | First-degree murder with 18 aggravating circumstances. | None | 232 | Lethal injection |
| Rhode Island | . . . | . . . | . . . | . . . |
| South Carolina | Murder with 1 of 10 aggravating circumstances. Mental retardation is a mitigating factor. | None | 67 | Electrocution or lethal injection |
| South Dakota | First-degree murder with 1 of 10 aggravating circumstances; aggravated kidnapping. | None (i) | 3 | Lethal injection |
| Tennessee | First-degree murder. | 18 | 101 | Lethal injection |
| Texas | Criminal homicide with 1 of 8 aggravating circumstances. | 17 | 462 | Lethal injection |
| Utah | Aggravated murder. | None | 11 | Lethal injection or firing squad |
| Vermont | . . . | . . . | . . . | . . . |
| Virginia | First-degree murder with 1 of aggravating circumstances. | 14 (j) | 31 | Electrocution or lethal injection |
| Washington | Aggravated first-degree murder. | 18 | 17 | Lethal injection or hanging |
| West Virginia | . . . | . . . | . . . | . . . |
| Wisconsin | . . . | . . . | . . . | . . . |
| Wyoming | First-degree murder. | 16 | 2 | Lethal injection or lethal gas (k) |
| Dist. of Columbia | . . . | . . . | . . . | . . . |

*Source*: U.S. Department of Justice, Bureau of Justice Statistics, *Capital Punishment* 1998 (December 1999). The Council of State Governments. NAACP Legal Defense and Educational Fund Inc., *Death Row, U.S.A.* Winter 2000 (January 1, 2000).

*Key:*

. . . — No capital punishment statute.

(a) Arizona authorizes lethal injection for persons sentenced after 11/15/92; those sentenced before that date may select lethal injection or lethal gas.

(b) Arkansas authorizes lethal injection for persons committing a capital offense on or after 7/4/83; those who committed the offense before that date may select lethal injection or electrocution.

(c) Delaware authorizes lethal injection for those whose capital offense occurred after 6/13/86; those who committed the offense before that date may select lethal injection or hanging.

(d) Minimum age defined by statute is 13, but the effective age is 16, based on Mississippi Supreme Court decision.

(e) Mississippi authorizes lethal injection for those convicted after 7/1/84 and lethal gas for those convicted earlier.

(f) New Hampshire authorizes hanging only if lethal injection cannot be given.

(g) The age required is 17 unless the murderer was incarcerated for murder when a subsequent murder occurred; then the age may be 14.

(h) Oklahoma authorizes electrocution if lethal injection is ever held to be unconstitutional and firing squad if both lethal injection and electrocution are held unconstitutional.

(i) Juveniles may be transferred to adult court. Age can be a mitigating factor.

(j) The minimum age for transfer to adult court is age 14 by statute, but the effective age for capital sentence is 16 based on interpretation of a U.S. Supreme Court decision by the State attorney general's office.

(k) Wyoming authorizes lethal gas if lethal injection is ever held to be unconstitutional.

(l) When added, states totals are slightly higher because some inmates are sentanced in more than one state.

## Table 8.17
## MAXIMUM BENEFITS FOR TEMPORARY TOTAL DISABILITY
## PROVIDED BY WORKERS' COMPENSATION STATUTES
### (As of December 1999)

| State or other jurisdiction | Maximum percentage of wages | Maximum payment per week | | Maximum period | | Total maximum stated in law |
|---|---|---|---|---|---|---|
| | | Amount | Based on | Duration of disability | Number of weeks | |
| **United States (a)** | | | | | | |
| FECA | 66-2/3 (b) | $1,359.91 | (b) | ★ | . . . | . . . |
| LHWCA | 66-2/3 | 835.74 | 200% of NAWW | ★ | . . . | . . . |
| **Alabama** | 66-2/3 | 493.00 | 100% of SAWW | ★ | . . . | . . . |
| **Alaska** | 80 of worker's spendable earnings | 700.00 (c) | . . . | ★ (d) | . . . | . . . |
| **Arizona** | 66-2/3 | 323.10 (e) | . . . | ★ | . . . | . . . |
| **Arkansas** | 66-2/3 | 375.00 | 85% of SAWW | . . . | 450 | . . . |
| **California** | 66-2/3 | 490.00 | . . . | ★ | . . . | . . . |
| **Colorado** | 66-2/3 | 519.61 (f) | 91% of SAWW | ★ | . . . | . . . |
| **Connecticut** | 75 of worker's spendable earnings | 764.00 (c) | 100% of SAWW | ★ | . . . | . . . |
| **Delaware** | 66-2/3 | 411.11 | 66-2/3% of SAWW | ★ | . . . | . . . |
| **Florida** | 66-2/3 | 522.00 (g) | 100% of SAWW | . . . | 104 | . . . |
| **Georgia** | 66-2/3 | 325.00 (h) | . . . | . . . | 400 | . . . |
| **Hawaii** | 66-2/3 | 519.00 | 100% of SAWW | ★ | . . . | . . . |
| **Idaho** | 67 | 410.40 | 90% of SAWW | . . . | 52 (i) | . . . |
| **Illinois** | 66-2/3 | 862.80 | 133-1/3% of SAWW | ★ | . . . | . . . |
| **Indiana** | 66-2/3 | 468.00 | . . . | . . . | 500 | $234,000 |
| **Iowa** | 80 of worker's spendable earnings | 947.00 | 200% of SAWW | ★ | . . . | . . . |
| **Kansas** | 66-2/3 | 366.00 (g) | 75% of SAWW | ★ | . . . | 100,000 |
| **Kentucky** | 66-2/3 | 487.20 (j) | 100% of SAWW | ★ | . . . | . . . |
| **Louisiana** | 66-2/3 | 367.00 (k) | 75% of SAWW | ★ | . . . | . . . |
| **Maine** | 80 of worker's after tax earnings | 441.00 (l) | 90% of SAWW | ★ | . . . | . . . |
| **Maryland** | 66-2/3 | 602.00 | 100% of SAWW | ★ | . . . | . . . |
| **Massachusetts** | 60 | 699.91 (m) | 100% of SAWW | . . . | 156 | . . . |
| **Michigan** | 80 of worker's spendable earnings | 580.00 (n) | 90% of SAWW | ★ | . . . | . . . |
| **Minnesota** | 66-2/3 | 615.00 (o) | . . . | . . . | 104 (p) | . . . |
| **Mississippi** | 66-2/3 | 292.86 | 66-2/3% of SAWW | . . . | 450 | 131,787 |
| **Missouri** | 66-2/3 | 562.67 | 105% of SAWW | . . . | 400 | . . . |
| **Montana** | 66-2/3 | 411.00 (c) | 100% of SAWW | ★ | . . . | . . . |
| **Nebraska** | 66-2/3 | 468.00 | 100% of SAWW | ★ | . . . | . . . |
| **Nevada** | 66-2/3 | 532.63 | 100% of SAWW | ★ | . . . | . . . |
| **New Hampshire** | 60 | 840.00 | 150% of SAWW | ★ | . . . | . . . |
| **New Jersey** | 70 | 539.00 | 75% of SAWW | . . . | 400 | . . . |
| **New Mexico** | 66-2/3 | 392.05 | 85% of SAWW | ★ | . . . | . . . |
| **New York** | 66-2/3 | 400.00 | . . . | ★ | . . . | . . . |
| **North Carolina** | 66-2/3 | 560.00 | 110% of SAWW | ★ | . . . | . . . |
| **North Dakota** | 66-2/3 | 417.00 (q) | 100% of SAWW | ★ | . . . | . . . |
| **Ohio** | 72 for first 12 weeks; 66-2/3 thereafter | 567.00 (r) | 100% of SAWW | ★ | . . . | . . . |
| **Oklahoma** | 70 | 426.00 | 100% of SAWW | . . . | 156 (s) | . . . |
| **Oregon** | 66-2/3 | 576.64 | 100% of SAWW | ★ | . . . | . . . |
| **Pennsylvania** | 66-2/3 | 588.00 (t) | 100% of SAWW | . . . | 90 days | . . . |
| **Rhode Island** | 75 of worker's spendable earnings | 544.00 (u) | 100% of SAWW | ★ | . . . | . . . |
| **South Carolina** | 66-2/3 | 483.47 | 100% of SAWW | . . . | 500 | . . . |
| **South Dakota** | 66-2/3 | 408.00 | 100% of SAWW | ★ | . . . | . . . |
| **Tennessee** | 66-2/3 | 515.00 | . . . | . . . | 400 | 206,000 |
| **Texas** | 70 of worker's earnings over $8.50 per hour; 75 for all others | 523.00 | 100% of SAWW | . . . | 104 (v) | . . . |
| **Utah** | 66-2/3 | 487.00 (w) | 100% of SAWW | . . . | 312 | . . . |
| **Vermont** | 66-2/3 | 727.00 (x) | 150% of SAWW | ★ | . . . | . . . |

See footnotes at end of table.

## MAXIMUM BENEFITS — Continued

| State or other jurisdiction | Maximum percentage of wages | Maximum payment per week | | Maximum period | | Total maximum stated in law |
|---|---|---|---|---|---|---|
| | | Amount | Based on | Duration of disability | Number of weeks | |
| Virginia ..................... | 66-2/3 | 534.00 | 100% of SAWW | . . . | 500 | . . . |
| Washington ................ | 60-75 | 692.70 (c) | 110% of SAMW | ★ | . . . | . . . |
| West Virginia ............. | 70 | 466.11 | 100% of SAWW | . . . | 208 | . . . |
| Wisconsin ................... | 66-2/3 | 538.00 (c) | 100% of SAWW | ★ | . . . | . . . |
| Wyoming .................... | 66-2/3 of actual monthly earnings | 465.00 | 103% of SAMW | ★ | . . . | . . . |
| Dist. of Columbia ....... | 66-2/3 or 80 of worker's spendable earnings; whichever is less | 834.82 | 100% of SAWW | ★ | . . . | . . . |
| Puerto Rico ............... | 66-2/3 | 65.00 | . . . | . . . | 312 | . . . |
| U.S. Virgin Islands ....... | 66-2/3 | 311.00 | 66-2/3% of SAWW | ★ | | |

*Source*: U.S. Department of Labor, Branch of Planning, Policy and Review, Division of Planning, Policy and Standards, Office of Workers' Compensation Programs, Employment Standards Administration.

*Key*:

★ — Yes

. . . — Not applicable.

SAWW — State's average weekly wage.

SAMW — State's average monthly wage.

NAWW — National average weekly wage.

(a) Federal Employees Compensation Act (FECA) and the Longshore and Harbor Worker's Compensation Act (LS/HWCA).

(b) Benefits under FECA are computed at a maximum of 75 percent of the pay of a specific grade level in the federal civil service.

(c) Benefits are subject to Social Security benefit offsets.

(d) Benefits payable for duration of disability until date of medical stability is reached.

(e) Additional $25 monthly added to benefits of dependents residing in the U.S.

(f) Benefits are subject to Social Security benefit offsets and to reduction by benefits under an employer pension or disability plan.

(g) Benefits are subject to Social Security and Unemployment Insurance benefit offsets.

(h) Maximum weekly benefit in catastrophic cases shall be paid until such time as employee undergoes a change in condition for the better.

(i) After 52 weeks, benefits are 60 percent of SAWW for duration of disability.

(j) Benefits terminate when employee qualifies for Social Security benefits.

(k) Payments are subject to Unemployment Insurance benefit offsets.

(l) Benefits subject to Unemployment Insurance benefits offsets, except if benefits started prior to date of injury, or if benefits are a spouse's entitlement.

(m) Additional $6 will be added per dependent if weekly benefits are below $150.

(n) Benefits subject to reduction by Unemployment Insurance and Social Security benefits, and those under an employer disability, retirement or pension plan.

(o) Compensation stops if employee withdraws from labor market, is released to work without any physical restrictions, or refuses offer to work that is consistent with a rehabilitation plan.

(p) Payments made for 104 weeks, or 90 days after maximum medical improvement.

(q) Additional $10 per week payable for each dependent child, not to exceed worker's net wage. Benefits are reduced by 50 percent of Social Security benefits.

(r) Benefits are subject to Social Security benefit offset and if concurrent and/or duplicate with those under employer non-occupational benefits plan.

(s) Period of disability can be extended to 300 weeks by the WC Court for good cause.

(t) Benefits are subject to Social Security benefit offsets, and by those under an employer-funded pension plan as well as severance pay.

(u) An additional $9 for each dependent, including a non-working spouse; aggregate not to exceed 80 percent of the worker's average weekly wage.

(v) Maximum is 104 weeks, or upon reaching maximum medical improvements, whichever is sooner.

(w) Additional $5 for dependent spouse and each dependent child up to 4, under age 18, but not to exceed 100 percent of the state average weekly wage.

(x) Additional $10 is paid for each dependent under 21 years of age.

**Table 8.18**

**SELECTED STATE CHILD LABOR STANDARDS AFFECTING MINORS UNDER 18 IN NON-FARM EMPLOYMENT**

**(As of January 1, 2000)**

**(Occupational coverage, exemptions and deviations usually omitted)**

| State or other jurisdiction | Maximum daily and weekly hours and days per week for minors (a) | | Nightwork prohibited for minors (a) | |
|---|---|---|---|---|
| | Under 16 years of age | 16 and 17 years of age | Under 16 years of age | 16 and 17 years of age |
| Federal (FLSA) | 8-40, non-schoolday period Schoolday/week: 3-18 (b) | | 7 p.m. (9 p.m. June 1 through Labor Day) to 7 a.m. | |
| Alabama | 8-40-6 Schoolday/week: 3-18 | | 7 p.m. (9 p.m. during summer vacation) to 7 a.m. | 10 p.m. before schoolday to 5 a.m., if enrolled in school |
| Alaska | 6-day week Schoolday/week: 9 (c)-23 | 6-day week | 9 p.m. to 5 a.m. | |
| Arizona | 8-40 Schoolday/week: 3-18 | | 9:30 p.m. (11 p.m. before non-schoolday) to 6 a.m. 7 p.m. to 6 a.m. in door-to-door sales or deliveries | |
| Arkansas | 8-48-6 | 10-54-6 | 7 p.m. (9 p.m. before non-schoolday) to 6 a.m. | 11 p.m. before schoolday to 6 a.m. |
| California | 8-40-6 Schoolday/week: 3-18 | 8-48-6 Schoolday/week: 4-28 (d) except before 8 non-schoolday | 7 p.m. (9 p.m. June 1 through Labor Day) to 7 a.m. | 10 p.m. (12:30 a.m. before non-schoolday) to 5 a.m. |
| Colorado | 8-40 Schoolday: 6 | 8-40 | 9:30 p.m. to 5 a.m. before schoolday | |
| Connecticut | 8-40-6 In mercantile during periods of school vacation of 5 days or more | Enrolled in and not graduated from a secondary institution. 8-48-6, non-school weeks. Schoolday/week: 6 (8 on Friday, Saturday and Sunday) - 32 in restaurant, recreational, amusement, theater, manufacturing, mechanical, retail, hairdressing, bowling alley, pool hall, or photography gallery establishments. Not enrolled in and not graduated from a secondary institution. 8-48-6 in retail/mercantile establishments. 9-48-6 in restaurant, manufacturing, mechanical, recreation, amusement and theatre establishments. | 7 p.m. (9 p.m. July 1 to the first Monday in September) to 7 a.m. | 11:00 p.m. (midnight if school vacation, not prior to a schoolday, or not attending school) to 6 a.m. in restaurants, recreational, amusement and theater establishments. 10 p.m. (11 p.m. if school vacation, not prior to a school day, or not attending school; midnight in a supermarket of 3,500 quare feet or more when no school the next day) to 6 a.m. in manufacturing, mechanical and retail establishments. 10 p.m. to 6 a.m. in hairdressing, bowling alley, pool hall, or photography gallery establishments. |

See footnotes at end of table.

# SELECTED STATE CHILD LABOR STANDARDS — Continued

| State or other jurisdiction | Maximum daily and weekly hours and days per week for minors (a) | | Nightwork prohibited for minors (a) | |
|---|---|---|---|---|
| | Under 16 years of age | 16 and 17 years of age | Under 16 years of age | 16 and 17 years of age |
| Delaware .......... | 8-40-6 Schoolday/week: 4-18 (d) | 12 (c) | 7 p.m. (9 p.m. June 1 through Labor Day) to 7 a.m. | 8 hours of non-work, non-school time required in each 24-hour day |
| Florida .......... | 8-40-6 Schoolday: 3 when followed by schoolday, except if enrolled in vocational program Schoolweek: 15 | 8-30-6 during schoolyear | 7 p.m. before schoolday to 7 a.m. on schoolday (9 p.m. during holidays and summer vacations to 7 a.m.) | 11 p.m. to 6:30 a.m., before schoolday |
| Georgia .......... | 8-40 Schoolday: 4 | | 9 p.m. to 6 a.m. | |
| Hawaii .......... | 8-40-6 Schoolday: 10 (c) | | 7 p.m. to 7 a.m. (9 p.m. to 6 a.m. June 1 through day before Labor Day) | |
| Idaho .......... | 9-54 | | 9 p.m. to 6 a.m. | |
| Illinois .......... | 8-48-6 Schoolday/week: 3[8 (c)] (e)-23 (d) | | 7 p.m. (9 p.m. June 1 through Labor Day) to 7 a.m. (f) | |
| Indiana .......... | 8-40 Schoolday/week: 3 | 8-30 (40 with parental permission)-6, except if not enrolled in school; 9-30 (48 with parental permission) non-school weeks, minors enrolled in school | 7 p.m. (9 p.m. June 1 through Labor Day) to 7 a.m. | 10 p.m. (midnight before non-schoolday with written parental permission) to 6 a.m., minors of 16 enrolled in school 10 p.m. to 6 a.m. before schoolday, minors of 17 enrolled in grades 9 through 12 (11:30 p.m. with written parental permission or 1 a.m. with written parental permission up to 2 non-consecutive nights per week) |
| Iowa .......... | 8-40 Schoolday/week: 4-28 | | 7 p.m. (9 p.m. June 1 through Labor Day) to 7 a.m. | |
| Kansas .......... | 8-40 | | 10 p.m. before schoolday to 7 a.m. | |
| Kentucky .......... | 8-40 Schoolday/week: 3-18 | 6 (8 Saturday and Sunday) 40, if attending school | 7 p.m. (9 p.m. June 1 through Labor Day) to 7 a.m. | 11:30 p.m. (1 a.m. Friday and Saturday) to 6 a.m. when school is in session |
| Louisiana .......... | 8-40-6 Schoolday/week: 3-18 | | 7 p.m. (9 p.m. June 1 through Labor Day) to 7 a.m. | |
| Maine .......... | 8-40-6 Schoolday/week: 3-18 (g) | 10-50-6 if enrolled in school; schoolday/week: 4-20, except 8 before non-schoolday, if enrolled in school (28 hours in a week with multiple days of school closure) (g) | 7 p.m. (9 p.m. during summer school vacation) to 7 a.m. | 10 p.m. (12 a.m. before non-schoolday) to 7 a.m. if enrolled in school 5 a.m. before non-schoolday |

# SELECTED STATE CHILD LABOR STANDARDS — Continued

| State or other jurisdiction | Maximum daily and weekly hours and days per week for minors (a) | | Nightwork prohibited for minors (a) | |
|---|---|---|---|---|
| | Under 16 years of age | 16 and 17 years of age | Under 16 years of age | 16 and 17 years of age |
| Maryland .......... | 8-40<br>Schoolday/week: 4-23 (d) | 12 (c) | 8 p.m. (9 p.m. Memorial Day thorough Labor Day) to 7 a.m. | 8 hours of non-work, non-schoolday time required in each 24-hour day |
| Massachusetts .......... | 8-48-6<br>4-24 in farm work, under 14 | 9-48-6 | 7 p.m. (9 p.m. July 1 through Labor Day) to 6:30 a.m. | 10 p.m. (midnight in restaurants and at race tracks on Friday, Saturday and vacation) to 6 a.m. |
| Michigan .......... | 10-48-6<br>Schoolweek: 48 (c) | 10-48-6<br>Schoolweek: 48 (c) | 9 p.m. to 7 a.m. | 10:30 p.m. to 6 a.m., if attending school<br>11:30 p.m. to 6 a.m., if not attending school |
| Minnesota .......... | 8-40 | 8-40 | 9 p.m. to 7 a.m. | 11 p.m. to 5 a.m. before schoolday (11:30 p.m. to 4:30 a.m., with written parental permission) |
| Mississippi .......... | 8-44 in factory, mill, cannery or workshop | | 7 p.m. to 6 a.m. in factory, mill, cannery or workshop | |
| Missouri .......... | 8-40-6<br>Schoolday: 3 | | 7 p.m. (9 p.m. June 1 through Labor Day (10:30 p.m. at regional Fairs or expositions)) to 7 a.m. | |
| Montana .......... | 8-40<br>Schoolday/week: 3-18 (b) | | 7 p.m. (9 p.m. during periods outside the school year (June 1 through Labor Day, depending on local standards)) to 7 a.m. | |
| Nebraska .......... | 8-48 | | 8 p.m. to 6 a.m., under 14<br>10 p.m. (beyond 10 p.m. before non-schooday with special permit) to 6 a.m., 14 and 15 | |
| Nevada .......... | 8-48 | | | |
| New Hampshire .......... | 8 on non-schoolday, 48-hour week during vacation, if enrolled in school<br>Schoolday/week: 3-23 if enrolled in school | 48-hour week, 6-day week, during vacation if enrolled in school<br>30-hour week, 6-day week, if enrolled in school | 9 p.m. to 7 a.m. | |
| New Jersey .......... | 8-40-6<br>10-hour day, 6-day week in agriculture<br>Schoolday/week: 3-18 | 8-40-6 | 7 p.m. (9 p.m. during summer vacation with parental permission) to 7 a.m. | 11 p.m. to 6 a.m. during school term, with specified variations |
| New Mexico .......... | 8-44 (48 in special cases), under 14 | | 9 p.m. to 7 a.m., under 14 | |
| New York .......... | 8-40-6<br>Schoolday/week: 3-18 (b) | 8-48-6<br>Schoolday/week: 4 before schoolday, 8 Friday, Saturday, Sunday or holiday-28, if enrolled in school | 7 p.m. (9 p.m. June 21 through Labor Day) to 7 a.m. | 10 p.m. (midnight before schooldays with written permission from both parent and school and before non-schoolday with written parental consent) to 6 a.m., while school is in session; midnight to 6 a.m. while school is not in session |

See footnotes at end of table.

# SELECTED STATE CHILD LABOR STANDARDS — Continued

| State or other jurisdiction | Maximum daily and weekly hours and days per week for minors (a) | | Nightwork prohibited for minors (a) | |
|---|---|---|---|---|
| | Under 16 years of age | 16 and 17 years of age | Under 16 years of age | 16 and 17 years of age |
| **North Carolina** | 8-40 Schoolday/week: 3-18 (b) | | 7 p.m. (9 p.m. during summer vacation) to 7 a.m. | 11 p.m. to 5 a.m. before schoolday while school is in session. Not applicable with written permission from both parent and school |
| **North Dakota** | 8-40-6 Schoolday/week: 3-18 if not exempted from school attendance | 8-48-6 | 7 p.m. (9 p.m. June 1 through Labor Day) to 7 a.m. | |
| **Ohio** | 8-40 Schoolday/week: 3-18 | | 7 p.m. (9 p.m. June 1 to Sept. 1 and during school holidays of 5 schooldays or more) to 7 a.m., 7 p.m. to 7 a.m. in door-to-door sales | 11 p.m. before schoolday to 7 a.m. on schoolday (6 a.m. if not employed after 8 p.m. previous night) if required to attend school. 8 p.m. to 7 a.m. in door-to-door sales |
| **Oklahoma** | 8-40 Schoolday/week: 3-18 8 hours on schooldays before non-schooldays if employer not covered by FLSA | | 7 p.m. (9 p.m. June 1 through Labor Day) to 7 a.m. 9 p.m. before non-schooldays if employer not covered by FLSA | |
| **Oregon** | 8-40 Schoolday/week: 3-18 (b) | 44-hour week: (emergency overtime with permit) | 7 p.m. (9 p.m. June 1 through Labor Day) to 7 a.m. | |
| **Pennsylvania** | 8-44-6 Schoolday/week: 4-26 (d) | 8-44-6 28 in schoolweek, if enrolled in regular day school | 7 p.m. (10 p.m. during vacation from June to Labor Day) to 7 a.m. | 11 p.m. (midnight before non-schoolday) to 6 a.m., if enrolled in regular day school |
| **Rhode Island** | 8-40 | 9-48, during school year | 7 p.m. (9 p.m. during school vacation) to 6 a.m. | 11:30 p.m. (1:30 a.m. before non-schoolday) to 6 a.m. if regularly attending school |
| **South Carolina** | 8-40 Schoolday/week: 3-18 | | 7 p.m. (9 p.m. June 1 through Labor Day) to 7 a.m. | |
| **South Dakota** | 8-40 Schoolday/week: 4-20 | | After 10 p.m. before schoolday | |
| **Tennessee** | 8-40 Schoolday/week: 3-18 | | 7 p.m. to 7 a.m. (9 p.m. to 6 a.m. before non-schooldays) | 10 p.m. to 6 a.m. (Sunday-Thursday before schooldays) (midnight, with parental permission, up to 3 nights a week) |
| **Texas** | 8-48 | | 10 p.m. (midnight before non-schoolday or in summer if not enrolled in summer school) to 5 a.m. | |
| **Utah** | 8-40 Schoolday: 4 | | 9:30 p.m. to 5 a.m. before schoolday | |
| **Vermont** | 8-48-6 | 9-50 | 7 p.m. to 6 a.m. | |

# SELECTED STATE CHILD LABOR STANDARDS — Continued

| State or other jurisdiction | Maximum daily and weekly hours and days per week for minors (a) | | Nightwork prohibited for minors (a) | |
|---|---|---|---|---|
| | Under 16 years of age | 16 and 17 years of age | Under 16 years of age | 16 and 17 years of age |
| Virginia | 8-40, non-school period Schoolday/week: 3-18 | | 7 p.m. (9 p.m. June 1 through Labor Day) to 7 a.m. | |
| Washington | 8-40-6 Schoolday/week: 3 (8 Friday, Saturday and Sunday ) - 16 | 8-48-6 Schoolday/week: 4 (8 Saturday and Sunday) -20 6-28 with special variance agreed to by parent, employer, student and school | 7 p.m. (9 p.m. Friday and Saturday when school is not in session) to 7 a.m. | 10 p.m. Sunday-Thursday (midnight Friday and Saturday and when school is not in session) to 7 a.m. (5 a.m. when school is not in session). 9 a.m. to 7 a.m. in door-to-door sales. |
| West Virginia | 8-40-6 | | 8 p.m. to 5 a.m. | |
| Wisconsin | 8-40-6 Schoolday/week: 4 (8 last schoolday and non-schoolday) 18 (d) | (h) - 50 - 6 Schoolday/week: 5 (8 last schoolday of week and non-schoolday)-26 (d) | 8 p.m. (11 p.m. before non-schoolday) to 7 a.m. | 11 p.m. (12:30 a.m. before non-schoolday) to 7 a.m. 5 a.m. on non-schoolday during school week (h). |
| Wyoming | 8-56 | | 10 p.m. (midnight before non-schoolday and for minors not enrolled in school) to 5 a.m. | Midnight to 5 a.m., female |
| Dist. of Columbia | 8-48-6 | 8-48-6 | 7 p.m. (9 p.m. June 1 through Labor Day) to 7 a.m. | 10 p.m. to 6 a.m. |
| Guam | 8-40-6 Schoolday: 9(c) | 8-40-6 Schoolday: 9 (c) | 10 p.m. (midnight on non-school nights) to 6 a.m. | 10 p.m. (midnight on non-school nights) to 6 a.m. |
| Puerto Rico | 8-40-6 Schoolday: 8 (c) | 8-40-6 | 6 p.m. to 8 a.m. | 10 p.m. to 6 a.m. |

*Source:* U.S. Department of Labor, Office of External Affairs, Wage and Hour Division, Employment Standards Administration.

(a) State hours limitations on a schoolday and in a schoolweek usually apply only to those enrolled in school. Several states exempt high school graduates from the hours and/or nightwork or other provisions, or have less restrictive provisions for minors participating in various school-work programs. Separate nightwork standards in messenger service and street trades are common, but are not displayed in table.

(b) Students of 14 and 15 enrolled in approved Work Experience and Career Exploration programs may work during school hours up to 3 hours on a schoolday and 23 hours in a schoolweek.

(c) Combined hours of work and school.

(d) More hours are permitted when school is in session less than 5 days.

(e) Illinois. Eight hours are permitted on both Saturday and Sunday if minor does not work outside school hours more than 6 consecutive days in a week and total hours worked outside school does not exceed 24.

(f) Illinois. Minors age 14 or older, employed in recreational or educational activities by a park district or municipal parks and recreation department may work up to 3 hours per school day twice a week until 9 p.m., while school is in session, if the number of hours worked does not exceed 24 a week. Work is permitted until 10 p.m. during summer vacation.

(g) Minors under age 18 enrolled in school may work up to 50 hours during any week that school is in session less than 3 days or during the first or last week of the school calendar, regardless of how many days school is in session for the week.

(h) Wisconsin has no limit during non-school week on daily hours or nightwork for 16- and 17-year-olds. However, they must be paid time and one-half for work in excess of 10 hours per day or 40 hours per week, whichever is greater. Also, 8 hours rest is required between end of work and start of work the next day, and any work between 12:30 a.m. and 5 a.m. must be directly supervised by an adult.

## Table 8.19
### CHANGES IN BASIC MINIMUM WAGES IN NON-FARM EMPLOYMENT UNDER STATE LAW: SELECTED YEARS 1970 TO 2000

| State or other jurisdiction | 1970(a) | 1972 | 1976(a) | 1979 | 1981 | 1988 | 1991 | 1992 | 1994 | 1996 | 1997 | 1998 | 2000 |
|---|---|---|---|---|---|---|---|---|---|---|---|---|---|
| Federal (FLSA) | $1.30 & $1.60 | 1.60 | $2.20 & $2.30 | 2.90 | 3.35 | 3.35 | 3.80 | 4.25 | 4.25 | 4.25 | 4.75 | 5.15 | 5.15 |
| Alabama | … | … | … | … | … | … | … | … | … | … | … | … | … |
| Alaska | 2.10 | 2.10 | 2.80 | 3.40 | 3.85 | 3.85 | 4.30 | 4.75 | 4.75 | 4.75 | 5.25 | 5.65 | 5.65 |
| Arizona | 18.72-26.40/ wk. (b) | 18.72-26.40/ wk. (b) | … | … | … | … | … | … | … | … | … | … | … |
| Arkansas | 1.10 wk. (b) | 1.20 | 1.90 | 2.30 | 2.70 | 3.25 | 3.35 | 3.65 | 4.25 | 4.25(c) | 4.25(c) | 5.15(c) | 5.15(c) |
| California | 1.65 (b) | 1.65 (b) | 2.00 | 2.90 | 3.35 | 3.35 | 4.25 | 4.25 | 4.25 | 4.25 | 4.75 | 5.15 | 5.15 |
| Colorado | 1.00-1.25 (b) | 1.00-1.25 (b) | 1.00-1.25 (b) | 1.90 | 1.90 | 3.00 | 3.00 | 3.00 | 3.00 | 3.00 | | 5.15 | 5.15 |
| Connecticut | 1.60 | 1.85 | 2.21 & 2.31 | 2.91 | 3.37 | 3.75 | 4.25 | 4.27 | 4.27 | 4.27 | 4.77 | 5.18 | 5.18 |
| Delaware | 1.25 | 1.60 | 2.00 | 2.00 | 2.00 | 3.35 | 3.80 | 4.25 | 4.25 | 4.65 | 5.00 | 5.15 | 5.15 |
| Florida | … | … | … | … | … | … | … | … | … | … | … | … | … |
| Georgia | … | 1.25 | 1.25 | 1.25 | 1.25 | 3.25 | 3.25 | 3.25 | 3.25 | 3.25(d) | 3.25(d) | 3.25(d) | 3.25(d) |
| Hawaii | 1.60 | 1.60 | 2.40 | 2.65 | 3.10 | 3.85 | 3.85 | 3.85 | 5.25 | 5.25 | 5.25 | 5.25 | 5.25 |
| Idaho | 1.25 | 1.40 | 1.60 | 2.30 | 2.30 | 2.30 | 3.80 | 4.25 | 4.25 | 4.25 | 4.25 | 5.15 | 5.15 |
| Illinois | … | 1.40 | 2.10 | 2.30 | 2.30 | 3.35 | 3.80 | 4.25 | 4.25 | 4.25(c) | 4.75(c) | 5.15(c) | 5.15(c) |
| Indiana | 1.25 | 1.25 | 1.25 | 2.00 | 2.00 | 2.00 | 3.35 | 3.35 | 3.35 | 3.35(e) | 3.35(e) | 3.35(e) | 3.35(e) |
| Iowa | … | … | … | … | … | … | 4.25 | 4.65 | 4.65 | 4.65 | 4.75 | 5.15 | 5.15 |
| Kansas | .65-.75 (b) | .65-.75 (b) | 1.60 | 1.60 | 1.60 | 1.60 | 2.65 | 2.65 | 2.65 | 2.65 | 2.65 | 2.65 | 2.65 |
| Kentucky | … | … | 1.60 | 2.00 | 2.15 | 3.35 | 3.80 | 4.25 | 4.25 | 4.25 | 4.25 | 4.25 | 4.25 |
| Louisiana | … | … | … | … | … | … | … | … | … | … | … | … | … |
| Maine | 1.60 | 1.40-1.80 | 2.30 | 2.90 | 3.35 | 3.65 | 3.85 | 4.25 | 4.25 | 4.25 | 4.75 | 5.15 | 5.15 |
| Maryland | 1.30 | 1.60 | 2.20 & 2.30 | 2.90 | 3.35 | 3.35 | 3.80 | 4.25 | 4.25 | 4.25 | 4.75 | 5.15 | 5.15 |
| Massachusetts | 1.60 | 1.75 | 2.10 | 2.90 | 3.35 | 3.65 | 3.75 | 4.25 | 4.25 | 4.75 | 5.25 | 5.25 | 5.25 |
| Michigan | 1.25 | 1.60 | 2.20 | 2.90 | 3.35 | 3.35 | 3.35 | 3.35 | 3.35 | 3.35(e) | 3.35(e) | 5.15(e) | 5.15(e) |
| Minnesota | .70-1.15 (b) | .75-1.60 | 1.80 | 2.30 | 3.10 | 3.55 & 3.50 (f) | 4.25 (g) | 4.25 (g) | 4.25 (g) | 4.25(g) | 4.25(g) | 5.15(g) | 5.15(g) |
| Mississippi | … | … | … | … | … | … | … | … | … | … | … | … | … |
| Missouri | … | … | … | … | … | … | 3.80 | 4.25 | 4.25 | 4.25 | 4.75 | 5.15 | 5.15 |
| Montana | … | 1.60 | 1.80 | 2.00 | 2.00 | 3.35 | 3.80 | 4.25 (g) | 4.25 (g) | 4.25(c) | 4.75(g) | 5.15(g) | 5.15(g) |
| Nebraska | 1.00 | 1.00 | 1.60 | 1.60 | 1.60 | 3.35 | 3.35 | 4.25 | 4.25 | 4.25(c) | 4.25(c) | 5.15(c) | 5.15(c) |
| Nevada | 1.30 | 1.60 | 2.20 & 2.30 | 2.75 | 2.75 | 3.35 | 3.80 | 4.25 | 4.25 | 4.25 | 4.75 | 5.15 | 5.15 |
| New Hampshire | 1.45 & 1.60 | 1.60 | 2.20-2.30 | 2.90 | 3.35 | 3.55 | 3.85 | 4.25 | 4.25 | 4.25 | 4.75 | 5.15 | 5.15 |
| New Jersey | 1.50 | 1.50 | 2.20 | 2.50 | 3.35 | 3.35 | 3.80 | 4.25 | 5.05 | 5.05 | 5.05 | 5.05 | 5.05 |
| New Mexico | 1.30-1.60 | 1.30-1.60 | 2.00 | 2.30 | 2.90 | 3.35 | 3.35 | 3.35 | 4.25 | 4.25 | 4.25 | 4.25 | 4.25 |
| New York | 1.60 | 1.85 | 2.30 | 2.90 | 3.35 | 3.35 | 3.80 | 4.25 | 4.25 | 4.25 | 4.25 | 4.25 | 4.25 |
| North Carolina | 1.25 | 1.45 | 2.00 | 2.50 | 2.90 | 3.35 | 3.35 | 3.80 | 4.25 | 4.25 | 4.25 | 5.15 | 5.15 |
| North Dakota | 1.00-1.45 | 1.00-1.45 | 2.00-2.20 | 2.10-2.30 | 2.80-3.10 | 2.80-3.10 | 3.40 | 4.25 | 4.25 | 4.25 | 4.25 | 5.15 | 5.15 |
| Ohio | .75-1.25 (b) | .75-1.25 (b) | 1.60 | 2.30 | 2.30 | 2.30 | 3.80 (g) | 4.25 (g) | 4.25 (g) | 4.25(g) | 4.25(g) | 4.25(g) | 4.25(g) |
| Oklahoma | 1.00 | 1.40 | 1.80 | 2.00 | 3.10 | 3.35 | 3.80 (g) | 4.25 (g) | 4.25 (g) | 4.25(g) | 4.75(g) | 5.15(g) | 5.15(g) |
| Oregon | 1.25 | 1.25 | 2.30 | 2.30 | 3.10 | 3.35 | 4.75 | 4.75 | 4.75 | 4.75 | 5.50 | 6.00 | 6.00 |
| Pennsylvania | 1.30 | 1.60 | 2.20 | 2.90 | 3.35 | 3.35 | 3.80 | 4.25 | 4.25 | 4.25 | 4.75 | 5.15 | 5.15 |
| Rhode Island | 1.60 | 1.60 | 2.30 | 2.30 | 2.90 | 3.65 | 4.25 | 4.45 | 4.45 | 4.45 | 5.15 | 5.15 | 5.15 |
| South Carolina | … | … | … | … | … | … | … | … | … | … | … | … | … |

See footnotes at end of table.

# CHANGES IN BASIC MINIMUM WAGES — Continued

| State or other jurisdiction | 1970 (a) | 1972 | 1976 (a) | 1979 | 1981 | 1988 | 1991 | 1992 | 1994 | 1996 | 1997 | 1998 | 2000 |
|---|---|---|---|---|---|---|---|---|---|---|---|---|---|
| South Dakota | 1.00 | 1.00 | 2.00 | 2.30 | 2.30 | 2.80 | 3.80 | 4.25 | 4.25 | 4.25 | 4.25 | 5.15 | 5.15 |
| Tennessee | ... | ... | ... | ... | ... | ... | ... | ... | ... | ... | ... | ... | ... |
| Texas | ... | 1.40 | 1.40 | 1.40 | 1.40 | 3.35 | 3.35 | 3.35 | 3.35 | 3.35 | 3.35 | 3.35 | 3.35 |
| Utah | 1.00-1.15 (b) | 1.20-1.35 (b) | 1.55-1.70 (b) | 2.20-2.45 (b) | 2.50-2.75 (b) |  | 3.80 | 4.25 | 4.25 | 4.25 | 4.75 | 5.15 | 5.15 |
| Vermont | 1.60 | 1.60 | 2.30 | 2.90 | 2.50-2.75 (b) | 3.55 | 3.85 | 4.25 | 4.25 | 4.75(e) | 5.00(e) | 5.25(e) | 5.25(e) |
| Virginia | ... | ... | 2.00 | 2.35 | 2.65 | 2.65 | 2.65 | 3.65 | 4.25 | 4.25(c) | 4.75(c) | 5.15(c) | 5.15(c) |
| Washington | 1.60 | 1.60 | 2.20-2.30 | 2.30 | 2.30 | 2.30 | 4.25 | 4.25 | 4.25 | 4.90 | 4.90 | 4.90 | 4.90 |
| West Virginia | 1.00 | 1.20 | 2.00 | 2.20 | 2.75 | 3.35 | 3.35 | 3.80 | 4.25 | 4.25(d) | 4.25(d) | 4.75(d) | 4.75(d) |
| Wisconsin | 1.30 (b) | 1.45 (b) | 2.10 | 2.80 | 3.25 | 3.35 | 3.80 | 3.80 | 4.25 | 4.25 | 4.75 | 5.15 | 5.15 |
| Wyoming | 1.30 (b) | 1.50 | 1.60 | 1.60 | 1.60 | 1.60 | 1.60 | 1.60 | 1.60 | 1.60 | 1.60 | 1.60 | 1.60 |
| Dist. of Columbia | 1.60-2.00 | 1.60-2.25 | 2.25-2.75 | 2.46-3.00 | 2.50-3.75 | 3.50-4.85 | 3.70-4.85 | 3.90-5.45 | 4.25 | 5.25 (h) | 5.75 | 6.15 | 6.15 |
| Guam | 1.60 | 1.90 | 2.30 | 2.90 | 3.35 | 3.35 | 3.80 | 4.25 | 4.25 | 4.25 | 4.75 | 5.15 | 5.15 |
| Puerto Rico | .43-1.60 | .65-1.60 | .76-2.50 | 1.20-2.50 | 1.20-3.10 | 1.20-3.35 | 1.20-4.25 (h) | 1.20-4.25 (h) | 1.20-4.25 (h) | 1.20-4.25 (i) | 1.20-4.75 (i) | 1.20-5.15 (i) | 1.20-5.15 (i) |
| U.S. Virgin Islands | N.A. | N.A. | N.A. | 2.90 | 3.35 | 3.35 | 4.65 (g,j) | 4.65 (g,j) | 4.65 (g,j) | 4.65 (g) | 4.65 (g,j) | 4.65 (g,j) | 4.65 (g,j) |

*Source:* U.S. Department of Labor, Office of State Standards Programs, Wage and Hour Division, Employment Standards Administration.

*Note:* Rates are for January 1 of each year, except 1972, which show rates as of February. A range of rates, as in Puerto Rico, reflects rates which differ by industry, occupation or other factors, as established under a wage-board type law.

*Key:*
... — Not applicable.
N.A. — Not available.

(a) Under the Federal Fair Labor Standards Act (FLSA), the two rates shown in 1970 and 1976 reflect the former multiple-track minimum wage system: in effect from 1961 to 1978. The lower rate applied to newly covered persons brought under the act by amendments, whose rates were gradually phased in. A similar dual-track system was also in effect in certain years under the laws in Connecticut, Maryland and Nevada.

(b) For the years indicated, the laws in Arizona, Arkansas, California, Colorado, Kentucky, Minnesota, Ohio, Utah and Wisconsin applied only to women and minors.

(c) Applicable to employers of four or more.

(d) Applicable to employers of six or more. In West Virginia, applicable to employers of six or more in one location.

(e) Applicable to employers of two or more.

(f) For the years 1988-1990, Minnesota had a two-tier wage schedule with the higher rate applicable to employers covered by the FLSA and the lower rate to employers not covered by the FLSA.

(g) Minnesota sets a lower rate for enterprises with annual receipts of less than $500,000 ($4.90, January 1, 1998-January 1, 2000). The dollar amount prior to September 1, 1997 was $362,500 ($4.00, January 1, 1991-January 1, 1997); Montana sets a lower rate for businesses with gross annual sales of $110,000 or less ($4.00, January 1, 1992-January 1, 2000); Ohio sets a lower rate for employers with gross annual sales from $150,000 to $500,000 ($3.35, January 1, 1991-January 1, 2000) and for employers with gross annual sales under $150,000 ($2.80, January 1, 2000); Oklahoma sets a lower rate for employers of fewer than 10 full-time employees at any one location and for those with annual gross sales of less than $100,000 ($2.00, January 1, 1991-January 1, 2000); and the U.S. Virgin Islands sets a lower rate for businesses with gross annual receipts of less than $150,000 ($4.30, January 1, 1991-January 1, 2000).

(h) In the District of Columbia wage orders were replaced by a statutory minimum wage on October 1, 1993. A $5.45 minimum rate remained in effect for the laundry and dry cleaning industry as the result of the grandfather clause.

(i) In Puerto Rico, separate minimum rates are in effect for almost 350 non-farm occupations by industry Mandatory Decrees. Rates higher than those in the range listed in effect in a few specific occupations.

(j) In the U.S. Virgin Islands, implementation of an indexed rate, which was to have started January 1, 1991, has been delayed.

## Table 8.20
## STATUS OF APPROVED STATE PLANS DEVELOPED IN ACCORDANCE WITH
## THE FEDERAL OCCUPATIONAL SAFETY AND HEALTH ACT
### (As of January 12, 2000)

| State or other jurisdiction | Status of state plan | | | | | | |
|---|---|---|---|---|---|---|---|
| | Operational status agreement (a) | Different standards (b) | 21(d) On-site consultation agreement (c) | On-shore maritime coverage | Date of initial approval | Date certified (d) | Date of 18(e) final approval (e) |
| Alaska | ... | ... | ★ | ... | 7/31/73 | 9/9/77 | 9/28/84 |
| Arizona | ... | ... | ... | ... | 10/29/74 | 9/18/81 | 6/20/85 |
| California | ★ | ★ | ★ | ★ | 4/24/73 | 8/12/77 | ... |
| Connecticut (f) | ... | ... | ★ | ... | 10/2/73 | 8/19/86 | ... |
| Hawaii | ... | ★ | ★ | ... | 12/28/73 | 4/26/78 | 4/30/84 |
| Indiana | ... | ... | ... | ... | 2/25/74 | 9/24/81 | 9/26/86 |
| Iowa | ... | ... | ★ | ... | 7/20/73 | 9/14/76 | 7/2/85 |
| Kentucky | ... | ... | ... | ... | 7/23/73 | 2/8/80 | 6/13/85 |
| Maryland | ... | ... | ★ | ... | 6/28/73 | 2/15/80 | 7/18/85 |
| Michigan | ★ | ★ | ★ | ... | 9/24/73 | 1/16/81 | ... |
| Minnesota | ... | ... | ★ | ★ | 5/29/73 | 9/28/76 | 7/30/85 |
| Nevada | ★ | ... | ... | ... | 12/4/73 | 8/13/81 | ... |
| New Mexico | ★ | ... | ... | ... | 12/4/75 | 12/4/84 | ... |
| New York (f) | ... | ... | ★ | ... | 6/1/84 | ... | ... |
| North Carolina | ... | ... | ★ | ... | 1/26/73 | 9/29/76 | 12/10/96 |
| Oregon | ★ | ★ | ★ | ★ | 12/22/72 | 9/15/82 | ... |
| South Carolina | ... | ... | ★ | ... | 11/30/72 | 7/28/76 | 12/15/87 |
| Tennessee | ... | ... | ★ | ... | 6/28/73 | 5/3/78 | 7/22/85 |
| Utah | ... | ... | ★ | ... | 1/4/73 | 11/11/76 | 7/16/85 |
| Vermont | ★ | ... | ★ | ★ | 10/1/73 | 3/4/77 | ... |
| Virginia | ... | ... | ★ | ... | 9/23/76 | 8/15/84 | 11/30/88 |
| Washington | ★ | ★ | ... | ★ | 1/19/73 | 1/26/82 | ... |
| Wyoming | ... | ... | ★ | ... | 4/25/74 | 12/18/80 | 6/27/85 |
| Puerto Rico | ★ | ... | ... | ... | 8/15/77 | 9/7/82 | ... |
| U.S. Virgin Islands (g) | ... | ... | ... | ... | 8/31/73 | 9/22/81 | 04/17/84 (h) |

Source: U.S. Department of Labor, Directorate of Federal-State Operations, Office of State Programs, Occupational Safety and Health Administration.

Key:
★ — Yes
... — No

(a) Concurrent federal jurisdiction suspended.
(b) Standards frequently not identical to the federal.
(c) On-site consultation is available in all states either through 21(d) Agreement or under a State Plan.
(d) Developmental steps satisfactorily completed.
(e) Concurrent federal jurisdiction relinquished (superseded Operational Status Agreement).
(f) Plan covers only state and local government employees.
(g) Plan covers only safety issues.
(h) Final approval suspended 11/13/95.

## Table 8.21
## HEALTH INSURANCE COVERAGE
## PERSONS WITH OR WITHOUT HEALTH INSURANCE COVERAGE BY STATE: 1998

| State or other jurisdiction | Total (a) | Persons covered (a) | Persons not covered (a) | Percent not covered |
|---|---|---|---|---|
| United States ..................... | 271,743 | 227,462 | 44,281 | 16.3 |
| Alabama ................................. | 4,201 | 3,487 | 714 | 17.0 |
| Alaska .................................... | 647 | 535 | 112 | 17.3 |
| Arizona .................................. | 4,905 | 3,719 | 1,187 | 24.2 |
| Arkansas ................................ | 2,563 | 2,084 | 478 | 18.7 |
| California ............................... | 33,375 | 26,002 | 7,373 | 22.1 |
| Colorado ................................ | 3,971 | 3,371 | 599 | 15.1 |
| Connecticut ............................ | 3,283 | 2,871 | 412 | 12.6 |
| Delaware ................................ | 783 | 668 | 115 | 14.7 |
| Florida ................................... | 14,678 | 12,114 | 2,564 | 17.5 |
| Georgia .................................. | 7,666 | 6,325 | 1,341 | 17.5 |
| Hawaii ................................... | 1,201 | 1,080 | 121 | 10.0 |
| Idaho ..................................... | 1,274 | 1049 | 225 | 17.7 |
| Illinois ................................... | 12,295 | 10,453 | 1,842 | 15.0 |
| Indiana .................................. | 5,840 | 5,001 | 839 | 14.4 |
| Iowa ...................................... | 2,837 | 2,572 | 265 | 9.3 |
| Kansas ................................... | 2,616 | 2,346 | 270 | 10.3 |
| Kentucky ................................ | 3,865 | 3,320 | 545 | 14.1 |
| Louisiana ............................... | 4,310 | 3,493 | 817 | 19.0 |
| Maine ..................................... | 1,266 | 1,106 | 161 | 12.7 |
| Maryland ............................... | 5,046 | 4,209 | 837 | 16.6 |
| Massachusetts ....................... | 6,117 | 5,490 | 627 | 10.3 |
| Michigan ................................ | 10,041 | 8,712 | 1,328 | 13.2 |
| Minnesota .............................. | 4,833 | 4,385 | 448 | 9.3 |
| Mississippi ............................. | 2,761 | 2,208 | 554 | 20.0 |
| Missouri ................................. | 5,405 | 4,836 | 570 | 10.5 |
| Montana ................................. | 925 | 744 | 181 | 19.6 |
| Nebraska ................................ | 1,716 | 1,561 | 155 | 9.0 |
| Nevada ................................... | 1,862 | 1,468 | 394 | 21.2 |
| New Hampshire ..................... | 1,224 | 1,086 | 138 | 11.3 |
| New Jersey ............................. | 8,092 | 6,763 | 1,329 | 16.4 |
| New Mexico ........................... | 1,829 | 1,443 | 386 | 21.1 |
| New York ............................... | 18,420 | 15,243 | 3,177 | 17.3 |
| North Carolina ...................... | 7,427 | 6,316 | 1,111 | 15.0 |
| North Dakota ........................ | 646 | 554 | 92 | 14.2 |
| Ohio ...................................... | 11,225 | 10,055 | 1,169 | 10.4 |
| Oklahoma .............................. | 3,269 | 2,670 | 599 | 18.3 |
| Oregon ................................... | 3,356 | 2,875 | 481 | 14.3 |
| Pennsylvania ......................... | 11,912 | 10,664 | 1,248 | 10.5 |
| Rhode Island ......................... | 968 | 872 | 96 | 10.0 |
| South Carolina ...................... | 3,851 | 3,257 | 594 | 15.4 |
| South Dakota ........................ | 711 | 610 | 102 | 14.3 |
| Tennessee .............................. | 5,572 | 4,849 | 724 | 13.0 |
| Texas ..................................... | 19,945 | 15,065 | 4,880 | 24.5 |
| Utah ...................................... | 2,106 | 1,812 | 293 | 13.9 |
| Vermont ................................. | 593 | 535 | 58 | 9.9 |
| Virginia .................................. | 6,688 | 5,742 | 946 | 14.1 |
| Washington ............................ | 5,747 | 5,042 | 706 | 12.3 |
| West Virginia ........................ | 1,750 | 1,448 | 302 | 17.2 |
| Wisconsin .............................. | 5,129 | 4,525 | 604 | 11.8 |
| Wyoming ................................ | 486 | 404 | 82 | 16.9 |
| Dist. of Columbia ................. | 512 | 425 | 87 | 17.0 |

*Source:* U.S. Census Bureau, March 1999 Current Population Survey.
*Key:*
(a) In thousands.

## Table 8.22
## TOTAL ROAD AND STREET MILEAGE: 1998
### (Classified by jurisdiction)

| State or other jurisdiction | Rural mileage | | | | Urban mileage | | | | Total rural and urban mileage |
|---|---|---|---|---|---|---|---|---|---|
| | Under state control (a) | Under local control | Under federal control (b) | Total rural roads | Under state control (a) | Under local control | Under federal control (b) | Total urban mileage | |
| United States .......... | 880,538 | 2,073,365 | 118,369 | 3,072,272 | 655,011 | 192,211 | 1,485 | 848,707 | 3,920,979 |
| Alabama .......................... | 14,563 | 58,308 | 727 | 73,598 | 20,343 | 277 | 10 | 20,630 | 94,228 |
| Alaska ............................ | 7,324 | 2,099 | 1,447 | 10,870 | 481 | 1,327 | 1 | 1,809 | 12,679 |
| Arizona .......................... | 7,806 | 17,046 | 11,798 | 36,650 | 15,377 | 1,891 | 51 | 17,319 | 53,969 |
| Arkansas ........................ | 19,541 | 63,446 | 2,136 | 85,123 | 9,491 | 496 | . . . | 9,987 | 95,110 |
| California ........................ | 16,158 | 53,577 | 12,679 | 82,414 | 71,239 | 12,291 | 7 | 83,537 | 165,951 |
| Colorado ........................ | 12,128 | 52,184 | 6,959 | 71,271 | 10,692 | 3,309 | . . . | 14,001 | 85,272 |
| Connecticut .................... | 2,139 | 6,842 | 4 | 8,985 | 1,837 | 9,905 | . . . | 11,742 | 20,727 |
| Delaware ........................ | 3,742 | . . . | 7 | 3,749 | 1,983 | . . . | . . . | 1,983 | 5,732 |
| Florida ............................ | 7,192 | 58,240 | 1,647 | 67,079 | 45,105 | 3,232 | . . . | 48,337 | 115,416 |
| Georgia .......................... | 15,162 | 69,937 | 1,084 | 86,183 | 3,353 | 23,975 | 41 | 27,369 | 113,552 |
| Hawaii ............................ | 770 | 1,475 | 101 | 2,346 | 267 | 1,589 | 17 | 1,873 | 4,219 |
| Idaho .............................. | 18,590 | 14,424 | 9,177 | 42,191 | 2,394 | 1,510 | 12 | 3,916 | 46,107 |
| Illinois ............................ | 19,544 | 82,282 | 231 | 102,057 | 30,077 | 5,802 | 26 | 35,905 | 137,962 |
| Indiana .......................... | 12,756 | 60,728 | . . . | 73,484 | 14,190 | 5,670 | . . . | 19,860 | 93,344 |
| Iowa .............................. | 14,839 | 88,393 | 114 | 103,346 | 8,602 | 859 | 4 | 9,465 | 112,811 |
| Kansas ............................ | 12,587 | 111,042 | 116 | 123,745 | 10,081 | . . . | . . . | 10,081 | 133,826 |
| Kentucky ........................ | 26,802 | 34,953 | 856 | 62,611 | 7,801 | 3,076 | 147 | 11,024 | 73,635 |
| Louisiana ........................ | 17,237 | 28,958 | 623 | 46,818 | 10,595 | 3,332 | 2 | 13,929 | 60,747 |
| Maine ............................ | 8,230 | 11,610 | 169 | 20,009 | 2,618 | 8 | 4 | 2,630 | 22,639 |
| Maryland ........................ | 4,327 | 11,588 | 39 | 15,954 | 5,456 | 8,384 | 395 | 14,235 | 30,189 |
| Massachusetts ................ | 1,651 | 10,450 | 90 | 12,191 | 9,425 | 13,614 | 21 | 23,060 | 35,251 |
| Michigan ........................ | 11,239 | 78,423 | 2083 | 91,745 | 19,020 | 10,717 | . . . | 29,737 | 121,482 |
| Minnesota ...................... | 17,555 | 96,229 | 1,656 | 115,440 | 13,692 | 2,055 | . . . | 15,747 | 131,187 |
| Mississippi ...................... | 9,829 | 54,712 | 830 | 65,371 | 858 | 7,044 | 22 | 7,924 | 73,295 |
| Missouri ........................ | 36,385 | 69,159 | 936 | 106,480 | 14,563 | 1,804 | . . . | 16,367 | 122,847 |
| Montana ........................ | 9,183 | 44,386 | 13,836 | 67,405 | 1,965 | 520 | . . . | 2,485 | 69,890 |
| Nebraska ........................ | 13,279 | 74,174 | 159 | 87,612 | 4,652 | 480 | . . . | 5,132 | 92,744 |
| Nevada .......................... | 5,562 | 21,756 | 2,401 | 29,719 | 3,699 | 1,971 | 22 | 5,692 | 35,411 |
| New Hampshire .............. | 5,498 | 6,559 | 137 | 12,194 | 2,748 | 182 | . . . | 2,930 | 15,124 |
| New Jersey ...................... | 4,104 | 7,578 | 27 | 11,709 | 18,661 | 5,549 | 2 | 24,212 | 35,921 |
| New Mexico .................... | 11,161 | 35,051 | 7,557 | 53,769 | 2,635 | 3,509 | . . . | 6,144 | 59,913 |
| New York........................ | 13,861 | 57,813 | 27 | 71,701 | 20,985 | 19,799 | 39 | 40,823 | 112,524 |
| North Carolina ................ | 73,597 | . . . | 1,921 | 75,518 | 22,833 | . . . | 258 | 23,091 | 98,609 |
| North Dakota ................ | 9,542 | 74,687 | 539 | 84,768 | 1,682 | 153 | . . . | 1,835 | 86,603 |
| Ohio .............................. | 21,186 | 61,543 | 26 | 82,755 | 25,344 | 8,115 | 5 | 33,464 | 116,219 |
| Oklahoma ...................... | 12,600 | 86,747 | 19 | 99,366 | 12,834 | 322 | 2 | 13,158 | 112,524 |
| Oregon .......................... | 13,060 | 31,598 | 13,133 | 57,791 | 8,430 | 2,227 | 33 | 10,690 | 68,481 |
| Pennsylvania .................. | 83,889 | 266 | 988 | 85,143 | 32,862 | 1,276 | . . . | 34,138 | 119,281 |
| Rhode Island .................. | 325 | 1,011 | 9 | 1,345 | 903 | 3,802 | . . . | 4,705 | 6,050 |
| South Carolina .............. | 35,276 | 18,019 | 991 | 54,286 | 8,522 | 2,086 | . . . | 10,608 | 64,894 |
| South Dakota ................ | 9,470 | 69,980 | 1,982 | 81,432 | 1,778 | 201 | 1 | 1,980 | 83,412 |
| Tennessee ...................... | 15,444 | 53,157 | 410 | 69,011 | 15,246 | 2,340 | 7 | 17,593 | 86,604 |
| Texas ............................ | 81,996 | 131,386 | 913 | 214,295 | 75,662 | 6,596 | 28 | 82,286 | 296,581 |
| Utah .............................. | 7,546 | 21,868 | 4,680 | 34,094 | 6,045 | 1,189 | 15 | 7,249 | 41,343 |
| Vermont ........................ | 2,797 | 9,998 | 86 | 12,881 | 1,217 | 130 | 24 | 1,371 | 14,252 |
| Virginia .......................... | 49,264 | 28 | 1,740 | 51,032 | 17,045 | 1,531 | 252 | 18,828 | 69,860 |
| Washington .................... | 20,020 | 35,270 | 7,285 | 62,575 | 12,426 | 5,225 | . . . | 17,651 | 80,226 |
| West Virginia ................ | 31,961 | . . . | 677 | 32,638 | 3,192 | . . . | . . . | 3,192 | 35,830 |
| Wisconsin ...................... | 14,813 | 79,622 | 1,286 | 95,721 | 13,660 | 2,571 | . . . | 16,231 | 111,952 |
| Wyoming ........................ | 9,386 | 14,763 | 2,031 | 26,180 | 2,007 | 270 | 1 | 2,278 | 28,458 |
| Dist. of Columbia .......... | . . . | . . . | . . . | . . . | 1,385 | . . . | 36 | 1,421 | 1,421 |
| Puerto Rico .................... | 7,622 | . . . | . . . | . . . | 7,053 | . . . | . . . | 7,053 | 14,675 |

*Source*: U.S. Department of Transportation, *Federal Highway Administration, Highway Statistics,* 1998.

*Key:*

. . . — Not applicable.

(a) Includes state highway agency, state park, state toll and other state agency roadways.

(b) Mileage in federal parks, forests and reservations that are not part of the state and local highway systems.

## Table 8.23
## STATE RECEIPTS FOR HIGHWAYS: 1998
(In thousands of dollars)

| State or other jurisdiction | State highway user tax revenues (a) | Road and crossing tolls (a) | Other state imposts, general fund revenues (b) | Miscellaneous income | Federal highway administration | Transfers from local governments | Bond proceeds (c) | Total receipts |
|---|---|---|---|---|---|---|---|---|
| United States | $40,505,704 | $4,097,318 | 4,459,720 | $2,542,222 | $19,222,231 | $1,206,907 | $6,044,543 | $78,078,645 |
| Alabama | 676,349 | . . . | 11,854 | 4,267 | 305,648 | 15,391 | . . . | 1,013,509 |
| Alaska | 47,225 | 14,900 | 119,802 | 22,100 | 199,759 | . . . | . . . | 403,786 |
| Arizona | 671,331 | . . . | 181,430 | 30,428 | 270,257 | 212,254 | . . . | 1,365,700 |
| Arkansas | 450,715 | . . . | 13,530 | 16,981 | 285,375 | 7,242 | . . . | 773,753 |
| California | 4,140,963 | 208,710 | 517,247 | 231,621 | 1,753,093 | 298,992 | . . . | 7,150,626 |
| Colorado | 645,744 | . . . | 334,967 | 22,427 | 253,935 | 21,107 | . . . | 1,278,180 |
| Connecticut | 509,990 | 160 | 7 | 82,970 | 339,132 | 2,107 | 161,039 | 1,095,405 |
| Delaware | 141,579 | 110,587 | 71,562 | 63,393 | 108,110 | . . . | 81,147 | 576,378 |
| Florida | 1,863,427 | 471,951 | 96,622 | 140,865 | 696,797 | 74,212 | 953,336 | 4,297,210 |
| Georgia | 597,580 | 20,464 | 237,709 | 52,204 | 688,543 | 6,819 | 179,660 | 1,782,979 |
| Hawaii | 93,022 | . . . | 1,708 | 13,028 | 127,228 | . . . | 1,149 | 236,135 |
| Idaho | 290,067 | . . . | . . . | . . . | 118,286 | 2,433 | . . . | 410,786 |
| Illinois | 1,828,826 | 323,409 | 111,281 | 66,308 | 658,633 | 32,204 | 31,635 | 3,052,296 |
| Indiana | 931,905 | 79,161 | 54,289 | 149,577 | 449,640 | 23,525 | 181,876 | 1,869,973 |
| Iowa | 674,440 | . . . | 210,461 | 13,500 | 217,535 | . . . | . . . | 1,115,936 |
| Kansas | 428,350 | 60,107 | 201,967 | 63,221 | 230,303 | 18,855 | 1,617 | 1,004,420 |
| Kentucky | 988,863 | 13,087 | 21,013 | 94,834 | 326,643 | 119 | . . . | 1,444,379 |
| Louisiana | 676,937 | 36,839 | 404,636 | 29,160 | 280,567 | . . . | . . . | 1,428,139 |
| Maine | 214,546 | 44,953 | 2,156 | 5,050 | 124,692 | . . . | 33,265 | 424,662 |
| Maryland | 812,300 | 138,114 | 82,945 | 23,774 | 342,679 | . . . | 500 | 1,400,312 |
| Massachusetts | 644,028 | 188,652 | 865 | 132,212 | 840,188 | 70 | 616,820 | 2,422,835 |
| Michigan | 1,577,287 | 25,611 | 148,956 | 41,958 | 534,392 | 30,048 | 18,551 | 2,376,803 |
| Minnesota | 1,032,255 | . . . | . . . | 58,567 | 296,315 | 39,563 | 27,810 | 1,454,510 |
| Mississippi | 471,922 | . . . | 107,401 | 10,730 | 203,594 | 5,331 | 2,500 | 801,478 |
| Missouri | 822,671 | . . . | 189,651 | 32,383 | 386,945 | 23,733 | . . . | 1,455,383 |
| Montana | 203,679 | . . . | . . . | 2,862 | 177,476 | 1,016 | . . . | 385,033 |
| Nebraska | 318,140 | . . . | 125,586 | 8,502 | 165,471 | 19,118 | . . . | 636,817 |
| Nevada | 369,582 | . . . | 1,333 | 18,272 | 120,844 | 11,892 | . . . | 521,923 |
| New Hampshire | 179,938 | 54,388 | . . . | 9,962 | 94,063 | 9,344 | . . . | 347,695 |
| New Jersey | 468,738 | 577,118 | . . . | 139,170 | 487,445 | . . . | 716,252 | 2,388,723 |
| New Mexico | 321,630 | . . . | . . . | 10,813 | 184,480 | 1,308 | . . . | 518,231 |
| New York | 1,540,303 | 750,840 | 1,276 | 307,424 | 1,018,767 | 24,418 | 1,225,837 | 4,868,865 |
| North Carolina | 1,356,661 | 1,674 | 284,747 | 52,953 | 559,594 | 4,358 | 250,000 | 2,509,987 |
| North Dakota | 141,380 | . . . | 5,129 | 688 | 148,757 | 15,228 | . . . | 311,182 |
| Ohio | 1,806,624 | 159,435 | 57,228 | 124,518 | 677,314 | 47,797 | 332,052 | 3,204,968 |
| Oklahoma | 525,403 | 125,482 | 31,905 | 23,453 | 246,890 | 10,689 | 685,425 | 1,649,247 |
| Oregon | 633,333 | . . . | 25,496 | 11,171 | 342,150 | . . . | . . . | 1,012,150 |
| Pennsylvania | 2,350,323 | 403,889 | 67,716 | 117,610 | 834,492 | 14,633 | 30,614 | 3,819,277 |
| Rhode Island | 147,541 | 11,390 | . . . | 1,806 | 88,227 | . . . | 51,761 | 300,725 |
| South Carolina | 447,093 | . . . | 8,369 | 23,250 | 248,106 | 2,261 | 47,222 | 776,301 |
| South Dakota | 139,539 | . . . | 44,357 | 522 | 160,793 | 10,935 | . . . | 356,146 |
| Tennessee | 860,535 | 50 | 106,212 | 21,859 | 483,604 | 20,692 | . . . | 1,492,952 |
| Texas | 2,901,801 | 59,584 | 25,178 | 131,978 | 1,105,185 | 86,474 | 100,660 | 4,410,860 |
| Utah | 369,154 | 270 | 146,353 | 2,319 | 169,380 | 4,400 | 251,235 | 943,111 |
| Vermont | 106,439 | . . . | 1,368 | 6,198 | 89,392 | 1,696 | 650 | 205,743 |
| Virginia | 1,293,021 | 77,828 | 367,320 | 54,929 | 441,631 | 31,718 | 34,930 | 2,301,377 |
| Washington | 1,181,128 | 86,421 | 222 | 39,171 | 448,136 | 10,743 | . . . | 1,765,821 |
| West Virginia | 498,360 | 52,244 | 20,204 | 15,103 | 304,619 | 145 | . . . | 890,675 |
| Wisconsin | 943,708 | . . . | . . . | 7,967 | 302,810 | 61,085 | . . . | 1,315,570 |
| Wyoming | 91,178 | . . . | 17,528 | 6,013 | 208,218 | 2,952 | . . . | 325,889 |
| Dist. of Columbia | 78,331 | . . . | 134 | 2,241 | 76,098 | . . . | 27,000 | 183,804 |

*Source*: U.S. Department of Transportation, *Federal Highway Administration, Highway Statistics, 1998.* (December 1999)

*Note*: Detail may not add to totals due to rounding.

Key:

. . . - Not applicable.

(a) Amounts shown represent only those highway-user revenues that were expended on state or local roads. Amounts expended on non-highway purposes are excluded.

(b) Amounts shown represent gross general fund appropriations for highways reduced by the amount of highway-user revenues placed in the state general fund.

(c) Bonds issued for and redeemed by refunding are excluded.

## Table 8.24
## STATE DISBURSEMENTS FOR HIGHWAYS: 1998
### (In thousands of dollars)

| State or other jurisdiction | Capital outlay | | | | Maintenance & traffic services | Administration & highway police | Interest | Grants-in-aid to local governments | Bond retirement (b) | Total disbursements |
|---|---|---|---|---|---|---|---|---|---|---|
| | Federal-aid highways | | | | | | | | | |
| | National highway system (a) | Other federal aid systems | Other roads & streets | Total | | | | | | |
| United States .. | $23,752,592 | $10,676,639 | $4,105,436 | $38,534,667 | $11,556,843 | $9,782,619 | $2,745,172 | $11,184,615 | $2,886,341 | $76,690,257 |
| Alabama | 232,922 | 138,710 | 163,650 | 535,282 | 173,483 | 139,743 | 2,202 | 199,364 | 3,205 | 1,053,279 |
| Alaska | 119,189 | 25,454 | 79,964 | 224,607 | 122,800 | 49,549 | 149 | 4,089 | 2,592 | 403,786 |
| Arizona | 361,442 | 70,841 | 217,144 | 649,427 | 80,569 | 99,406 | 77,760 | 397,160 | 126,170 | 1,430,492 |
| Arkansas | 310,304 | 169,793 | 11,720 | 491,817 | 130,053 | 63,599 | . . . | 129,545 | . . . | 815,014 |
| California | 2,113,660 | 382,717 | 173,203 | 2,669,580 | 721,065 | 1,586,554 | 1,054 | 1,589,303 | 6,880 | 6,574,436 |
| Colorado | 471,383 | 89,747 | 48,693 | 609,823 | 161,402 | 117,284 | . . . | 277,074 | . . . | 1,165,583 |
| Connecticut | 349,188 | 130,425 | 22,528 | 502,141 | 79,536 | 111,326 | 182,141 | 22,909 | 252,014 | 1,150,067 |
| Delaware | 111,265 | 55,550 | 81,705 | 248,520 | 100,737 | 76,553 | 45,134 | 4,000 | 45,134 | 526,209 |
| Florida | 1,322,828 | 1,089,367 | 35,849 | 2,448,044 | 423,879 | 364,055 | 215,655 | 246,659 | 63,491 | 3,761,783 |
| Georgia | 351,875 | 745,417 | 13,822 | 1,111,114 | 139,499 | 157,465 | 141,178 | 164 | 64,026 | 1,613,446 |
| Hawaii | 151,170 | 43,222 | 354 | 194,746 | 21,958 | 34,589 | 11,568 | 18,740 | 25,948 | 307,549 |
| Idaho | 84,994 | 74,564 | 49,561 | 209,119 | 55,062 | 37,918 | . . . | 112,176 | . . . | 414,275 |
| Illinois | 794,932 | 544,623 | 132,847 | 1,472,402 | 369,965 | 318,523 | 155,630 | 485,772 | 144,155 | 2,946,447 |
| Indiana | 440,916 | 337,542 | 7,046 | 785,504 | 300,951 | 145,957 | 36,792 | 366,327 | 16,690 | 1,652,221 |
| Iowa | 313,509 | 146,136 | 45,921 | 505,566 | 119,699 | 120,794 | . . . | 431,096 | . . . | 1,777,155 |
| Kansas | 391,280 | 178,147 | 67,738 | 637,165 | 115,699 | 95,988 | 57,863 | 141,070 | 15,595 | 1,063,380 |
| Kentucky | 363,592 | 254,837 | 159,290 | 777,719 | 204,984 | 167,423 | 81,072 | 146,455 | 103,025 | 1,480,678 |
| Louisiana | 280,388 | 263,133 | 99,512 | 643,033 | 150,762 | 214,477 | 31,689 | 46,629 | 313,728 | 1,400,318 |
| Maine | 88,903 | 74,370 | 24,418 | 187,691 | 131,544 | 32,425 | 14,106 | 17,084 | 25,975 | 408,825 |
| Maryland | 399,817 | 123,922 | 64,485 | 588,224 | 180,052 | 171,500 | 20,520 | 396,524 | 21,843 | 1,378,663 |
| Massachusetts | 1,457,279 | 241,791 | 154,898 | 1,853,968 | 209,644 | 324,064 | 252,415 | 188,723 | 133,630 | 2,962,444 |
| Michigan | 691,115 | 178,970 | 95,638 | 965,723 | 194,985 | 257,005 | 47,867 | 886,701 | 29,715 | 2,381,996 |
| Minnesota | 337,322 | 113,808 | 110,864 | 561,994 | 233,789 | 164,544 | 5,542 | 405,981 | 5,195 | 1,377,045 |
| Mississippi | 341,279 | 164,977 | 58,079 | 564,335 | 73,354 | 105,494 | 261 | 97,639 | 261 | 843,443 |
| Missouri | 389,820 | 362,524 | 39,328 | 791,672 | 253,895 | 152,629 | . . . | 240,155 | . . . | 1,438,351 |
| Montana | 113,660 | 87,638 | 10,269 | 211,567 | 66,663 | 53,642 | 3,424 | 30,508 | 11,795 | 377,599 |
| Nebraska | 176,425 | 95,041 | 3 | 271,469 | 63,146 | 48,734 | . . . | 205,777 | . . . | 589,126 |
| Nevada (d) | 191,805 | 25,504 | 1,598 | 218,907 | 78,158 | 72,891 | 1,040 | 56,842 | 17,700 | 445,538 |
| New Hampshire | 100,279 | 28,954 | 39,703 | 168,936 | 87,629 | 58,074 | 19,184 | 14,629 | 22,461 | 370,913 |
| New Jersey | 538,166 | 182,264 | 55,218 | 775,648 | 362,205 | 501,105 | 358,728 | 198,400 | 316,589 | 2,512,675 |
| New Mexico | 137,767 | 74,852 | 57,043 | 269,662 | 62,266 | 179,014 | 4,969 | 49,677 | 4,845 | 570,433 |
| New York | 2,128,539 | 288,375 | 134,951 | 2,551,865 | 841,014 | 489,228 | 430,646 | 317,001 | 532,578 | 5,162,332 |
| North Carolina | 396,184 | 452,460 | 506,520 | 1,355,164 | 565,572 | 341,823 | 5,482 | 83,745 | . . . | 2,351,786 |
| North Dakota | 91,348 | 72,064 | 26,486 | 189,898 | 25,694 | 35,567 | . . . | 54,560 | . . . | 305,979 |
| Ohio | 1,309,183 | 152,709 | 2,669 | 1,464,561 | 309,543 | 272,207 | 54,688 | 810,578 | 116,375 | 3,027,952 |
| Oklahoma | 194,503 | 136,685 | 128,629 | 459,817 | 138,663 | 95,207 | 43,323 | 12,630 | 193,993 | 943,633 |
| Oregon | 285,342 | 81,885 | 83,594 | 450,821 | 169,911 | 122,674 | 878 | 295,015 | 11,620 | 1,050,919 |
| Pennsylvania | 918,064 | 456,404 | 171,603 | 1,546,071 | 1,194,673 | 443,926 | 183,741 | 183,937 | 186,246 | 3,738,594 |
| Rhode Island | 86,584 | 63,807 | 29,782 | 180,173 | 47,010 | 23,097 | 18,523 | . . . | 31,643 | 300,446 |
| South Carolina | 164,430 | 271,105 | 29,899 | 465,434 | 143,806 | 119,178 | 4,399 | 30,563 | 2,405 | 765,785 |
| South Dakota | 148,620 | 14,615 | 40,443 | 203,678 | 40,208 | 31,892 | . . . | 29,488 | . . . | 305,266 |
| Tennessee | 358,885 | 388,079 | 25,557 | 772,521 | 223,131 | 162,278 | . . . | 262,088 | . . . | 1,420,018 |
| Texas | 1,480,609 | 561,789 | 325,660 | 2,368,058 | 820,661 | 669,036 | 39,575 | 368,665 | 29,124 | 4,295,119 |
| Utah | 654,896 | 160,600 | 4,642 | 820,138 | 88,408 | 77,000 | 6,800 | 110,423 | 26,400 | 1,129,169 |
| Vermont | 34,180 | 48,705 | 16,988 | 99,873 | 49,327 | 45,244 | 1,091 | 2,025 | 21,600 | 219,160 |
| Virginia | 524,914 | 415,402 | 303,997 | 1,244,313 | 676,989 | 289,415 | 58,208 | 200,102 | 10,879 | 2,479,906 |
| Washington | 491,987 | 200,382 | 1 | 692,370 | 239,368 | 286,355 | 59,030 | 465,152 | 63,090 | 1,805,365 |
| West Virginia | 345,480 | 143,920 | 10,033 | 499,433 | 271,228 | 74,850 | 13,621 | 310 | 33,260 | 892,702 |
| Wisconsin | 470,096 | 198,308 | 40,724 | 709,128 | 144,673 | 133,264 | 46,498 | 328,006 | 36,074 | 1,397,701 |
| Wyoming | 123,002 | 43,049 | 34,508 | 200,559 | 78,300 | 28,266 | . . . | 14,327 | . . . | 321,452 |
| Dist. of Columbia | 17,272 | 31,456 | 66,659 | 115,387 | 18,971 | 19,788 | 10,726 | . . . | 18,932 | 183,804 |

*Source*: U.S. Department of Transportation, Federal Highway Administration, Highway Statistics, 1998. Compiled from reports of state authorities.

*Key*:
. . . — Not applicable.

(a) In 1995, Congress approved the official National Highway System (NHS). Prior to approval, the NHS consisted of the entire principal arterial system.

b) Bonds issued for and redeemed by funding are excluded.

## Table 8.25
## APPORTIONMENT OF FEDERAL-AID HIGHWAY FUNDS: FISCAL YEAR 1999
(In thousands of dollars)

| State or other jurisdiction | National highway system | Surface transportation program | Interstate maintenance | Bridge program | Highway safety | Total (a) |
|---|---|---|---|---|---|---|
| United States (b) .... | $4,607,463 | $5,376,526 | $3,758,769 | $3,210,979 | $165,601 | $17,119,338 |
| Alabama ...................... | 85,449 | 109,903 | 74,889 | 61,717 | 2,006 | 333,964 |
| Alaska ......................... | 25,167 | 26,883 | 20,208 | 13,503 | 850 | 86,611 |
| Arizona ....................... | 79,610 | 89,142 | 74,706 | 9,258 | 3,434 | 256,150 |
| Arkansas ..................... | 66,886 | 77,280 | 48,922 | 36,525 | 1,784 | 231,397 |
| California .................... | 438,478 | 530,519 | 336,416 | 253,894 | 17,360 | 1,576,667 |
| Colorado ..................... | 69,644 | 75,845 | 56,575 | 20,783 | 1,794 | 224,641 |
| Connecticut ................ | 37,751 | 51,909 | 39,920 | 63,016 | 1,798 | 194,394 |
| Delaware ..................... | 34,679 | 26,883 | 6,991 | 14,008 | 1,069 | 83,630 |
| Florida ........................ | 205,447 | 238,167 | 144,000 | 51,362 | 8,287 | 647,263 |
| Georgia ....................... | 138,500 | 187,793 | 142,484 | 57,916 | 5,174 | 531,867 |
| Hawaii ......................... | 35,080 | 26,883 | 6,590 | 18,047 | 785 | 87,385 |
| Idaho .......................... | 39,037 | 33,298 | 29,531 | 10,396 | 2,095 | 114,357 |
| Illinois ........................ | 147,022 | 199,250 | 170,154 | 113,654 | 9,827 | 639,907 |
| Indiana ....................... | 111,156 | 136,300 | 106,674 | 40,237 | 3,318 | 397,685 |
| Iowa ........................... | 73,442 | 78,331 | 52,795 | 48,822 | 2,525 | 255,915 |
| Kansas ........................ | 68,864 | 86,792 | 50,517 | 55,959 | 2,548 | 264,680 |
| Kentucky ..................... | 77,778 | 87,349 | 70,455 | 40,710 | 2,169 | 278,461 |
| Louisiana .................... | 64,335 | 88,004 | 65,934 | 78,588 | 1,772 | 298,633 |
| Maine .......................... | 24,189 | 28,536 | 20,465 | 22,370 | 1,043 | 96,603 |
| Maryland ..................... | 68,542 | 85,585 | 63,864 | 51,718 | 2,423 | 272,132 |
| Massachusetts ............. | 64,584 | 91,392 | 63,077 | 106,614 | 2,091 | 327,758 |
| Michigan ..................... | 137,662 | 191,491 | 113,349 | 87,103 | 6,243 | 535,848 |
| Minnesota ................... | 81,438 | 104,769 | 68,122 | 27,433 | 3,488 | 285,250 |
| Mississippi .................. | 63,561 | 76,187 | 47,085 | 46,297 | 2,605 | 235,735 |
| Missouri ...................... | 110,121 | 139,394 | 105,824 | 101,363 | 3,302 | 460,004 |
| Montana ...................... | 56,080 | 35,196 | 41,155 | 13,856 | 670 | 146,957 |
| Nebraska ..................... | 58,056 | 54,405 | 34,040 | 27,951 | 1,510 | 175,962 |
| Nevada ........................ | 37,355 | 37,074 | 32,393 | 8,027 | 1,186 | 116,035 |
| New Hampshire ........... | 27,806 | 26,883 | 13,864 | 17,980 | 981 | 87,514 |
| New Jersey ................... | 101,571 | 118,811 | 68,521 | 146,982 | 3,653 | 439,538 |
| New Mexico ................. | 57,797 | 47,357 | 52,623 | 6,557 | 1,250 | 165,584 |
| New York ..................... | 168,849 | 215,190 | 131,061 | 321,098 | 9,339 | 845,537 |
| North Carolina ............ | 114,371 | 145,171 | 95,301 | 86,453 | 3,638 | 444,934 |
| North Dakota .............. | 61,692 | 34,020 | 22,684 | 6,557 | 1,196 | 126,149 |
| Ohio ........................... | 149,829 | 198,455 | 161,410 | 112,627 | 7,734 | 630,055 |
| Oklahoma ................... | 79,707 | 103,662 | 64,764 | 59,056 | 2,280 | 309,469 |
| Oregon ........................ | 67,177 | 72,760 | 52,674 | 9,670 | 2,742 | 205,023 |
| Pennsylvania ............... | 158,378 | 193,117 | 140,125 | 315,208 | 7,064 | 813,892 |
| Rhode Island ............... | 33,101 | 26,883 | 8,569 | 26,878 | 529 | 95,960 |
| South Carolina ........... | 65,307 | 91,499 | 63,721 | 35,284 | 2,671 | 258,482 |
| South Dakota .............. | 52,606 | 37,888 | 27,532 | 10,551 | 1,014 | 129,591 |
| Tennessee .................... | 99,510 | 120,818 | 96,793 | 61,608 | 2,085 | 380,814 |
| Texas .......................... | 347,568 | 422,473 | 283,715 | 122,955 | 7,550 | 1,184,261 |
| Utah ............................ | 36,385 | 43,804 | 51,294 | 8,825 | 1,171 | 141,479 |
| Vermont ...................... | 26,462 | 26,883 | 15,209 | 19,416 | 667 | 88,637 |
| Virginia ....................... | 108,779 | 143,095 | 108,924 | 80,469 | 4,262 | 445,529 |
| Washington ................. | 82,490 | 105,328 | 73,632 | 97,293 | 4,221 | 362,964 |
| West Virginia .............. | 31,961 | 41,824 | 32,450 | 59,901 | 763 | 166,899 |
| Wisconsin .................... | 103,473 | 112,283 | 65,975 | 35,249 | 3,119 | 320,099 |
| Wyoming ..................... | 61,455 | 26,883 | 38,254 | 6,557 | 595 | 133,744 |
| Dist. of Columbia ........ | 39,132 | 26,883 | 2,538 | 21,801 | 1,030 | 91,384 |
| American Samoa .......... | 3,214 | ... | ... | ... | 263 | 3,477 |
| Guam .......................... | 12,856 | ... | ... | ... | 328 | 13,184 |
| No. Mariana Islands ... | 3,214 | ... | ... | ... | 337 | 3,551 |
| Puerto Rico ................. | (b) | ... | ... | ... | 1,739 | 1,739 |
| U.S. Virgin Islands ...... | 12,856 | ... | ... | ... | 210 | 13,066 |

*Source*: U.S. Department of Transportation, Federal Highway Administration, Highway Statistics 1999.

*Note*: Apportioned pursuant to the Transportation Efficiency Act of 1998 (TEA-21) does not include funds from the Mass Transit Account of the Highway Trust Fund or the NationalRecreational Trails Trust Fund.

(a) Does not include funds from the following programs: emergency relief, Federal lands highway programs, Commonwealth of Puerto Rico highway programs, high priority projects, Woodrow Wilson Bridge, National Byways, construction of ferry boats and ferry terminal facilities, and intelligent vehicle-system, among others. These funds are allocated from the Highway Trust Fund.

(b) Under TEA-21, Puerto Rico received a stand-alone authorization of $92,075,874 for FY 1999.

# Chapter Nine

# INTERGOVERNMENTAL AFFAIRS

*State-federal and state-local relations in an era of federalism reform — includes information on state intergovernmental revenue from and expenditures to the federal government and local governments and data on state intergovernmental expenditures per capita.*

For additional information on Chapter Nine contact
The States Information Center, at The Council of State Governments,
(859) 244-8253 or E-mail: sic@csg.org.

## Table 9.1
## TOTAL FEDERAL GRANTS TO STATE AND LOCAL GOVERNMENTS
## BY STATE: 1989-1998
## (In thousands of dollars)

| State or other jurisdiction | 1998 | 1997 | 1996 | 1995 | 1994 | 1993 | 1992 | 1991 | 1990 | 1989 |
|---|---|---|---|---|---|---|---|---|---|---|
| United States ..... | $269,128 | $229,778 | $227,542 | $228,936 | $214,239 | $195,201 | $178,000 | $153,350 | $134,457 | $121,079 |
| Alabama ...................... | 4,161 | 3,483 | 3,325 | 3,419 | 3,209 | 3,081 | 2,795 | 2,347 | 2,101 | 1,802 |
| Alaska ........................ | 1,427 | 1,303 | 1,051 | 1,125 | 1,063 | 948 | 837 | 738 | 717 | 663 |
| Arizona ...................... | 4,147 | 3,355 | 3,095 | 3,150 | 2,996 | 2,640 | 2,235 | 1,810 | 1,620 | 1,305 |
| Arkansas .................... | 2,440 | 2,283 | 2,131 | 2,019 | 1,966 | 1,855 | 1,691 | 1,439 | 1,250 | 1,106 |
| California .................... | 32,090 | 27,014 | 26,413 | 26,934 | 26,219 | 21,635 | 19,738 | 16,885 | 13,932 | 11,936 |
| Colorado .................... | 3,048 | 2,444 | 2,410 | 2,391 | 2,102 | 2,109 | 1,905 | 1,707 | 1,429 | 1,359 |
| Connecticut ................ | 3,653 | 2,905 | 3,080 | 3,195 | 3,028 | 2,691 | 2,593 | 2,393 | 1,973 | 1,771 |
| Delaware .................... | 678 | 629 | 600 | 560 | 472 | 455 | 425 | 386 | 313 | 313 |
| Florida ....................... | 10,320 | 8,504 | 8,442 | 9,078 | 5,028 | 4,408 | 4,028 | 3,553 | 3,136 | 3,089 |
| Georgia ...................... | 6,233 | 5,469 | 5,359 | 5,461 | 1,088 | 984 | 839 | 739 | 598 | 528 |
| Hawaii ....................... | 1,190 | 1,184 | 1,126 | 1,162 | 778 | 712 | 694 | 590 | 569 | 501 |
| Idaho ......................... | 1,055 | 936 | 887 | 849 | 8,506 | 7,845 | 6,937 | 5,954 | 5,280 | 4,989 |
| Illinois ....................... | 10,156 | 9,296 | 9,229 | 9,487 | 3,553 | 3,732 | 3,242 | 2,767 | 2,423 | 2,115 |
| Indiana ...................... | 4,152 | 3,539 | 3,657 | 3,546 | 2,015 | 1,737 | 1,660 | 1,475 | 1,289 | 1,183 |
| Iowa .......................... | 2,424 | 1,977 | 2,030 | 2,074 | 1,666 | 1,608 | 1,376 | 1,165 | 1,021 | 912 |
| Kansas ....................... | 1,934 | 1,620 | 1,700 | 1,649 | 3,096 | 3,041 | 2,951 | 2,493 | 2,044 | 1,853 |
| Kentucky .................... | 4,236 | 3,702 | 3,355 | 3,437 | 5,233 | 4,817 | 4,417 | 3,249 | 2,658 | 2,304 |
| Louisiana ................... | 4,708 | 4,457 | 4,734 | 5,291 | 1,269 | 1,166 | 1,047 | 926 | 762 | 688 |
| Maine ........................ | 1,602 | 1,378 | 1,389 | 1,315 | 3,637 | 3,310 | 2,940 | 2,557 | 2,350 | 2,156 |
| Maryland .................... | 5,022 | 3,950 | 3,544 | 3,594 | 6,261 | 5,520 | 5,218 | 4,709 | 3,857 | 3,688 |
| Massachusetts ............. | 8,019 | 6,365 | 6,813 | 6,829 | 7,117 | 6,654 | 6,004 | 5,426 | 4,751 | 4,553 |
| Michigan .................... | 8,618 | 7,237 | 7,194 | 7,589 | 3,515 | 3,297 | 2,894 | 2,559 | 2,366 | 2,269 |
| Minnesota .................. | 4,199 | 3,952 | 3,535 | 3,685 | 2,507 | 2,285 | 2,193 | 1,822 | 1,595 | 1,366 |
| Mississippi ................. | 3,025 | 2,626 | 2,754 | 2,738 | 3,971 | 3,566 | 3,498 | 2,827 | 2,177 | 2,031 |
| Missouri ..................... | 5,065 | 4,231 | 4,091 | 4,159 | 906 | 831 | 765 | 687 | 591 | 559 |
| Montana ..................... | 1,139 | 991 | 964 | 933 | 1,114 | 1,108 | 997 | 868 | 779 | 709 |
| Nebraska .................... | 1,511 | 1,227 | 1,232 | 1,440 | 797 | 767 | 669 | 544 | 442 | 389 |
| Nevada ...................... | 1,081 | 983 | 876 | 882 | 956 | 652 | 935 | 540 | 427 | 411 |
| New Hampshire........... | 1,042 | 842 | 890 | 866 | 6,163 | 6,189 | 5,217 | 4,517 | 3,977 | 3,570 |
| New Jersey .................. | 7,108 | 6,602 | 6,506 | 6,639 | 1,714 | 1,534 | 1,379 | 1,118 | 959 | 907 |
| New Mexico ................ | 2,547 | 2,152 | 1,942 | 1,866 | 22,445 | 21,166 | 19,305 | 17,226 | 15,761 | 13,700 |
| New York.................... | 28,066 | 24,384 | 24,560 | 24,348 | 4,862 | 4,498 | 3,971 | 3,447 | 2,942 | 2,498 |
| North Carolina ........... | 7,133 | 6,284 | 5,227 | 5,487 | 702 | 640 | 603 | 533 | 471 | 431 |
| North Dakota .............. | 1,067 | 1,074 | 734 | 768 | 8,366 | 7,716 | 7,064 | 6,220 | 5,388 | 4,965 |
| Ohio .......................... | 9,733 | 8,327 | 8,776 | 9,115 | 2,359 | 2,111 | 2,066 | 1,788 | 1,568 | 1,508 |
| Oklahoma .................. | 3,059 | 2,510 | 2,435 | 2,472 | 2,355 | 2,099 | 2,050 | 1,694 | 1,708 | 1,426 |
| Oregon ...................... | 3,275 | 2,853 | 2,797 | 2,763 | 9,705 | 8,517 | 8,293 | 6,870 | 6,125 | 6,390 |
| Pennsylvania .............. | 12,381 | 10,268 | 10,117 | 10,354 | 1,100 | 1,107 | 986 | 908 | 773 | 684 |
| Rhode Island .............. | 1,368 | 1,144 | 1,176 | 1,276 | 2,726 | 2,521 | 2,393 | 2,078 | 1,892 | 1,455 |
| South Carolina ........... | 3,525 | 2,987 | 3,032 | 3,027 | 724 | 654 | 601 | 539 | 511 | 464 |
| South Dakota .............. | 1,007 | 982 | 867 | 813 | 3,940 | 3,925 | 3,658 | 3,129 | 2,717 | 2,353 |
| Tennessee .................. | 5,510 | 4,555 | 4,476 | 4,531 | 12,669 | 11,035 | 9,645 | 7,837 | 6,889 | 5,974 |
| Texas ......................... | 15,809 | 13,184 | 13,287 | 13,338 | 1,209 | 1,173 | 1,042 | 839 | 838 | 822 |
| Utah .......................... | 1,727 | 1,355 | 1,446 | 1,318 | 546 | 557 | 503 | 409 | 377 | 356 |
| Vermont ..................... | 803 | 601 | 641 | 625 | 3,180 | 2,945 | 2,773 | 2,432 | 2,237 | 2,119 |
| Virginia ...................... | 4,423 | 3,518 | 3,403 | 3,504 | 3,924 | 3,722 | 3,374 | 2,832 | 2,568 | 2,294 |
| Washington ................ | 5,422 | 4,496 | 4,152 | 4,351 | 2,166 | 1,884 | 1,668 | 1,284 | 1,009 | 952 |
| West Virginia .............. | 2,480 | 2,100 | 2,088 | 2,074 | 3,450 | 3,397 | 3,127 | 2,799 | 2,538 | 2,312 |
| Wisconsin .................. | 4,697 | 3,617 | 3,679 | 3,729 | 714 | 645 | 593 | 597 | 568 | 484 |
| Wyoming .................... | 850 | 762 | 708 | 748 | 2,222 | 1,961 | 1,951 | 1,847 | 1,718 | 1,523 |
| Dist. of Columbia ........ | 4,101 | 2,740 | 2,578 | 2,238 | 8,018 | 7,579 | 6,187 | 5,209 | 4,576 | 4,095 |
| American Samoa ......... | 91 | 121 | 71 | 73 | 67 | 59 | 107 | 51 | 79 | 75 |
| Guam ........................ | 266 | 125 | 134 | 162 | 154 | 161 | 139 | 116 | 100 | 116 |
| No. Mariana Islands ... | 39 | 35 | 31 | 41 | 52 | 47 | 65 | 75 | 62 | 60 |
| Puerto Rico ................ | 3,895 | 3,719 | 3,387 | 3,535 | 3,388 | 3,132 | 3,084 | 2,916 | 3,082 | 2,515 |
| U.S. Virgin Islands...... | 256 | 371 | 373 | 217 | 191 | 181 | 158 | 175 | 273 | 116 |
| Undistributed ............. | 116 | 1,032 | 3,009 | 592 | 1,059 | 592 | 475 | 711 | 302 | 366 |

*Source:* U.S. Department of Commerce, Bureau of the Census.
*Key:*
. . .— Not applicable.

## Table 9.2
## SUMMARY OF STATE INTERGOVERNMENTAL PAYMENTS: 1944 TO 1998
(In thousands, except per capita)

| | Total | | | To local governments | | | | | |
|---|---|---|---|---|---|---|---|---|---|
| | | | | | For specified purposes | | | | |
| Fiscal year | Amount | Per capita | To federal government (a) | Total | For general local government support | Education | Public welfare | Highways | All other |
| 1944 | $1,842,000 | $13.95 | ... | $1,842,000 | $274,000 | $861,000 | $368,000 | $298,000 | $41,000 |
| 1946 | 2,092,000 | 15.03 | ... | 2,092,000 | 357,000 | 953,000 | 376,000 | 339,000 | 67,000 |
| 1948 | 3,283,000 | 22.60 | ... | 3,283,000 | 428,000 | 1,554,000 | 648,000 | 507,000 | 146,000 |
| 1950 | 4,217,000 | 28.13 | ... | 4,217,000 | 482,000 | 2,054,000 | 792,000 | 610,000 | 279,000 |
| 1952 | 5,044,000 | 32.57 | ... | 5,044,000 | 549,000 | 2,523,000 | 976,000 | 728,000 | 268,000 |
| 1953 | 5,384,000 | 34.20 | ... | 5,384,000 | 592,000 | 2,737,000 | 981,000 | 803,000 | 271,000 |
| 1954 | 5,679,000 | 35.41 | ... | 5,679,000 | 600,000 | 2,930,000 | 1,004,000 | 871,000 | 274,000 |
| 1955 | 5,986,000 | 36.61 | ... | 5,986,000 | 591,000 | 3,150,000 | 1,046,000 | 911,000 | 288,000 |
| 1956 | 6,538,000 | 39.26 | ... | 6,538,000 | 631,000 | 3,541,000 | 1,069,000 | 984,000 | 313,000 |
| 1957 | 7,440,000 | 43.87 | ... | 7,440,000 | 668,000 | 4,212,000 | 1,136,000 | 1,082,000 | 342,000 |
| 1958 | 8,089,000 | 46.65 | ... | 8,089,000 | 687,000 | 4,598,000 | 1,247,000 | 1,167,000 | 390,000 |
| 1959 | 8,689,000 | 49.26 | ... | 8,689,000 | 725,000 | 4,957,000 | 1,409,000 | 1,207,000 | 391,000 |
| 1960 | 9,443,000 | 52.88 | ... | 9,443,000 | 806,000 | 5,461,000 | 1,483,000 | 1,247,000 | 446,000 |
| 1962 | 10,906,000 | 58.97 | ... | 10,906,000 | 839,000 | 6,474,000 | 1,777,000 | 1,327,000 | 489,000 |
| 1963 | 11,885,000 | 63.34 | ... | 11,885,000 | 1,012,000 | 6,993,000 | 1,919,000 | 1,416,000 | 545,000 |
| 1964 | 12,968,000 | 68.15 | ... | 12,968,000 | 1,053,000 | 7,664,000 | 2,108,000 | 1,524,000 | 619,000 |
| 1965 | 14,174,000 | 73.57 | ... | 14,174,000 | 1,102,000 | 8,351,000 | 2,436,000 | 1,630,000 | 655,000 |
| 1966 | 16,928,000 | 86.94 | ... | 16,928,000 | 1,361,000 | 10,177,000 | 2,882,000 | 1,725,000 | 783,000 |
| 1967 | 19,056,000 | 96.94 | ... | 19,056,000 | 1,585,000 | 11,845,000 | 2,897,000 | 1,861,000 | 868,000 |
| 1968 | 21,950,000 | 110.56 | ... | 21,950,000 | 1,993,000 | 13,321,000 | 3,527,000 | 2,029,000 | 1,080,000 |
| 1969 | 24,779,000 | 123.56 | ... | 24,779,000 | 2,135,000 | 14,858,000 | 4,402,000 | 2,109,000 | 1,275,000 |
| 1970 | 28,892,000 | 142.64 | ... | 28,892,000 | 2,958,000 | 17,085,000 | 5,003,000 | 2,439,000 | 1,407,000 |
| 1971 | 32,640,000 | 158.39 | ... | 32,640,000 | 3,258,000 | 19,292,000 | 5,760,000 | 2,507,000 | 1,823,000 |
| 1972 | 36,759,246 | 176.27 | ... | 36,759,246 | 3,752,327 | 21,195,345 | 6,943,634 | 2,633,417 | 2,234,523 |
| 1973 | 40,822,135 | 193.81 | ... | 40,822,135 | 4,279,646 | 23,315,651 | 7,531,738 | 2,953,424 | 2,741,676 |
| 1974 | 45,941,111 | 216.07 | $341,194 | 45,599,917 | 4,803,875 | 27,106,812 | 7,028,750 | 3,211,455 | 3,449,025 |
| 1975 | 51,978,324 | 242.03 | 974,780 | 51,003,544 | 5,129,333 | 31,110,237 | 7,136,104 | 3,224,861 | 4,403,009 |
| 1976 | 57,858,242 | 266.79 | 1,179,580 | 56,678,662 | 5,673,843 | 34,083,711 | 8,307,411 | 3,240,806 | 5,372,891 |
| 1977 | 62,459,903 | 285.10 | 1,386,237 | 61,073,666 | 6,372,543 | 36,964,306 | 8,756,717 | 3,631,108 | 5,348,992 |
| 1978 | 67,287,260 | 303.88 | 1,472,378 | 65,814,882 | 6,819,438 | 40,125,488 | 8,585,558 | 3,821,135 | 6,463,263 |
| 1979 | 75,962,980 | 339.25 | 1,493,215 | 74,469,765 | 8,224,338 | 46,195,698 | 8,675,473 | 4,148,573 | 7,225,683 |
| 1980 | 84,504,451 | 374.07 | 1,746,301 | 82,758,150 | 8,643,789 | 52,688,101 | 9,241,551 | 4,382,716 | 7,801,993 |
| 1981 | 93,179,549 | 406.89 | 1,872,980 | 91,306,569 | 9,570,248 | 57,257,373 | 11,025,445 | 4,751,449 | 8,702,054 |
| 1982 | 98,742,976 | 426.78 | 1,793,284 | 96,949,692 | 10,044,372 | 60,683,583 | 11,965,123 | 5,028,072 | 9,228,542 |
| 1983 | 100,886,902 | 431.77 | 1,764,821 | 99,122,081 | 10,364,144 | 63,118,351 | 10,919,847 | 5,277,447 | 9,442,292 |
| 1984 | 108,373,188 | 459.49 | 1,722,115 | 106,651,073 | 10,744,740 | 67,484,926 | 11,923,430 | 5,686,834 | 10,811,143 |
| 1985 | 121,571,151 | 510.56 | 1,963,468 | 119,607,683 | 12,319,643 | 74,936,970 | 12,673,123 | 6,019,069 | 13,658,898 |
| 1986 | 131,966,258 | 548.76 | 2,105,831 | 129,860,427 | 13,383,912 | 81,929,467 | 14,214,613 | 6,470,049 | 13,862,386 |
| 1987 | 141,278,672 | 581.88 | 2,455,362 | 138,823,310 | 14,245,089 | 88,253,298 | 14,753,727 | 6,784,699 | 14,786,497 |
| 1988 | 151,661,866 | 618.55 | 2,652,981 | 149,008,885 | 14,896,991 | 95,390,536 | 15,032,315 | 6,949,190 | 16,739,853 |
| 1989 | 165,415,415 | 667.98 | 2,929,622 | 162,485,793 | 15,749,681 | 104,601,291 | 16,697,915 | 7,376,173 | 18,060,733 |
| 1990 | 175,027,632 | 705.46 | 3,243,634 | 171,783,998 | 16,565,106 | 109,438,131 | 18,403,149 | 7,784,316 | 19,593,296 |
| 1991 | 186,398,234 | 740.91 | 3,464,364 | 182,933,870 | 16,977,032 | 116,179,860 | 20,903,400 | 8,126,477 | 20,747,101 |
| 1992 | 201,313,434 | 791.04 | 3,608,911 | 197,704,523 | 16,368,139 | 124,919,686 | 25,942,234 | 8,480,871 | 21,993,593 |
| 1993 | 214,094,882 | 832.00 | 3,625,051 | 210,469,831 | 17,690,986 | 131,179,517 | 31,339,777 | 9,298,624 | 20,960,927 |
| 1994 | 225,635,410 | 868.50 | 3,603,447 | 222,031,963 | 18,044,015 | 135,861,024 | 30,624,514 | 9,622,849 | 27,879,561 |
| 1995 | 240,978,128 | 919.10 | 3,616,831 | 237,361,297 | 18,996,435 | 148,160,436 | 30,772,525 | 10,481,616 | 28,926,886 |
| 1996 | 252,102,458 | 952.30 | 3,896,667 | 248,205,791 | 20,019,771 | 156,954,115 | 31,180,345 | 10,707,338 | 29,321,099 |
| 1997 | 264,207,209 | 989.10 | 3,839,942 | 260,367,267 | 21,808,828 | 164,147,715 | 35,754,024 | 11,431,270 | 27,225,430 |
| 1998 | 278,853,409 | 1031.6 | 3,515,734 | 275,337,675 | 22,693,158 | 176,250,998 | 32,327,325 | 11,648,853 | 32,417,341 |

*Source:* U.S. Department of Commerce, Bureau of the Census.
*Key:*
. . . — Not available.

(a) Represents primarily state reimbursements for the supplemental security income program. This column also duplicates some funds listed under "Public welfare" and "All other" columns.

## Table 9.3
## STATE INTERGOVERNMENTAL EXPENDITURE, BY STATE: 1995-98
### (Amounts are in thousands of dollars and per capitas are in whole dollars)

| State | Amount (in thousands) | | | | Per capita amounts | | | | Percentage change in per capita amounts | | |
|---|---|---|---|---|---|---|---|---|---|---|---|
| | 1998 | 1997 | 1996 | 1995 | 1998 | 1997 | 1996 | 1995 | 1997 to 1998 | 1996 to 1997 | 1995 to 1996 |
| United States ........ | $278,853,409 | $264,207,209 | $252,102,458 | $240,978,128 | $1,031.6 | $989.1 | $952.3 | $919.1 | 5.5 | 4.8 | 4.6 |
| Alabama ..................... | 3,419,845 | 3,292,491 | 3,076,820 | 2,619,713 | 785.8 | 762.3 | 720.0 | 616.0 | 3.9 | 7.0 | 17.4 |
| Alaska ....................... | 983,153 | 1,015,071 | 1,057,577 | 1,095,556 | 1,601.2 | 1,666.8 | 1,742.3 | 1,813.8 | -3.1 | -4.0 | -3.5 |
| Arizona ...................... | 5,023,261 | 4,528,382 | 4,255,135 | 3,992,499 | 1,075.9 | 994.2 | 960.9 | 946.5 | 10.9 | 6.4 | 6.6 |
| Arkansas .................... | 2,109,996 | 1,967,398 | 1,636,037 | 1,585,671 | 831.4 | 779.8 | 651.9 | 638.4 | 7.2 | 20.3 | 3.2 |
| California ................... | 51,053,075 | 49,635,672 | 48,758,607 | 44,892,639 | 1,562.8 | 1,538.2 | 1,529.5 | 1,421.1 | 2.9 | 1.8 | 8.6 |
| Colorado .................... | 3,159,458 | 3,017,473 | 2,849,915 | 2,702,979 | 795.6 | 775.1 | 745.5 | 721.4 | 4.7 | 5.9 | 5.4 |
| Connecticut ............... | 2,627,781 | 2,480,762 | 2,424,347 | 2,408,985 | 802.6 | 758.6 | 740.4 | 735.6 | 5.9 | 2.3 | 0.6 |
| Delaware .................... | 591,279 | 575,892 | 511,314 | 509,719 | 794.7 | 786.7 | 705.4 | 710.9 | 2.7 | 12.6 | 0.3 |
| Florida ....................... | 12,537,431 | 11,899,912 | 11,139,772 | 10,949,733 | 840.5 | 812.1 | 773.6 | 773.0 | 5.4 | 6.8 | 1.7 |
| Georgia ...................... | 6,310,697 | 6,141,128 | 5,285,164 | 4,849,875 | 825.8 | 820.3 | 718.8 | 673.5 | 2.8 | 16.2 | 9.0 |
| Hawaii ....................... | 147,059 | 156,055 | 144,333 | 144,145 | 123.3 | 131.5 | 121.9 | 121.4 | -5.8 | 8.1 | 0.1 |
| Idaho ......................... | 1,104,201 | 1,067,190 | 999,289 | 943,526 | 898.5 | 882.0 | 840.3 | 811.3 | 3.5 | 6.8 | 5.9 |
| Illinois ....................... | 9,862,059 | 9,148,129 | 8,549,064 | 7,989,026 | 818.8 | 769.0 | 721.7 | 675.3 | 7.8 | 7.0 | 7.0 |
| Indiana ...................... | 5,883,074 | 5,507,860 | 5,091,091 | 5,114,661 | 997.3 | 939.3 | 871.7 | 881.4 | 6.8 | 8.2 | -0.5 |
| Iowa .......................... | 2,794,519 | 2,869,259 | 2,672,320 | 2,586,535 | 976.4 | 1,006.1 | 937.1 | 910.1 | -2.6 | 7.4 | 3.3 |
| Kansas ....................... | 2,508,870 | 2,325,562 | 2,262,900 | 2,205,990 | 954.3 | 896.2 | 879.8 | 860.0 | 7.9 | 2.8 | 2.6 |
| Kentucky .................... | 3,006,904 | 2,918,190 | 2,825,097 | 2,790,070 | 763.9 | 746.7 | 727.4 | 722.8 | 3.0 | 3.3 | 1.3 |
| Louisiana ................... | 3,451,053 | 3,170,676 | 3,025,800 | 2,981,314 | 789.9 | 728.6 | 695.5 | 686.6 | 8.8 | 4.8 | 1.5 |
| Maine ........................ | 851,942 | 772,724 | 743,190 | 749,851 | 684.8 | 622.2 | 597.7 | 604.2 | 10.3 | 4.0 | -0.9 |
| Maryland .................... | 3,710,641 | 3,536,070 | 3,238,258 | 3,073,888 | 722.6 | 694.2 | 638.5 | 609.7 | 4.9 | 9.2 | 5.3 |
| Massachusetts ............ | 6,215,380 | 5,636,518 | 5,159,973 | 4,740,411 | 1,011.1 | 921.3 | 847.0 | 780.4 | 10.3 | 9.2 | 8.9 |
| Michigan .................... | 15,430,418 | 14,145,451 | 13,299,101 | 13,590,202 | 1,571.8 | 1,447.3 | 1,386.1 | 1,423.2 | 9.1 | 6.4 | -2.1 |
| Minnesota .................. | 6,022,123 | 6,942,130 | 6,068,273 | 5,628,502 | 1,274.5 | 1,481.5 | 1,302.8 | 1,220.9 | -13.3 | 14.4 | 7.8 |
| Mississippi ................. | 2,876,187 | 2,685,689 | 2,506,429 | 2,278,909 | 1,045.1 | 983.4 | 922.8 | 845.0 | 7.1 | 7.2 | 10.0 |
| Missouri ..................... | 4,176,567 | 3,944,195 | 3,434,437 | 3,461,819 | 767.9 | 730.1 | 640.9 | 650.2 | 5.9 | 14.8 | -0.8 |
| Montana ..................... | 712,620 | 714,924 | 699,428 | 684,581 | 809.8 | 813.3 | 795.4 | 786.9 | -0.3 | 2.2 | 2.2 |
| Nebraska .................... | 1,291,135 | 1,210,235 | 1,175,780 | 1,143,564 | 776.4 | 730.4 | 711.7 | 698.6 | 6.7 | 2.9 | 2.8 |
| Nevada ....................... | 1,915,179 | 1,771,680 | 1,624,270 | 1,424,642 | 1,096.3 | 1,056.5 | 1,013.2 | 931.1 | 8.1 | 9.1 | 14.0 |
| New Hampshire .......... | 454,682 | 413,800 | 392,423 | 374,413 | 383.7 | 352.8 | 337.6 | 326.1 | 9.9 | 5.4 | 4.8 |
| New Jersey ................. | 7,176,343 | 6,382,582 | 7,771,309 | 7,900,814 | 884.3 | 792.6 | 972.9 | 994.4 | 12.4 | -17.9 | -1.6 |
| New Mexico ............... | 2,186,948 | 2,075,053 | 2,055,309 | 1,966,326 | 1,259.0 | 1,199.5 | 1,199.5 | 1,167.0 | 5.4 | 1.0 | 4.5 |
| New York .................... | 27,271,351 | 25,637,864 | 25,417,231 | 25,189,620 | 1,500.5 | 1,413.6 | 1,397.7 | 1,388.9 | 6.4 | 0.9 | 0.9 |
| North Carolina ........... | 7,928,480 | 7,314,766 | 6,653,195 | 6,665,456 | 1,050.7 | 985.2 | 908.6 | 926.4 | 8.4 | 9.9 | -0.2 |
| North Dakota ............. | 541,455 | 540,154 | 411,331 | 437,194 | 848.7 | 842.7 | 639.2 | 682.0 | 0.2 | 31.3 | -5.9 |
| Ohio .......................... | 11,214,371 | 10,441,531 | 10,053,551 | 9,533,638 | 1,000.5 | 933.4 | 899.8 | 855.0 | 7.4 | 3.9 | 5.5 |
| Oklahoma ................... | 2,802,808 | 2,625,134 | 2,536,908 | 2,448,562 | 837.4 | 791.4 | 768.5 | 747.0 | 6.8 | 3.5 | 3.6 |
| Oregon ....................... | 3,706,815 | 3,207,793 | 3,109,619 | 2,979,586 | 1,129.4 | 989.1 | 970.6 | 948.6 | 15.6 | 3.2 | 4.4 |
| Pennsylvania .............. | 10,157,714 | 9,844,265 | 9,675,928 | 9,030,954 | 846.4 | 819.0 | 802.6 | 748.1 | 3.2 | 1.7 | 7.1 |
| Rhode Island .............. | 548,018 | 506,349 | 505,323 | 503,523 | 554.7 | 513.0 | 510.3 | 508.6 | 8.2 | 0.2 | 0.4 |
| South Carolina ........... | 3,142,086 | 2,929,143 | 2,720,441 | 2,366,681 | 819.1 | 779.0 | 735.5 | 644.3 | 7.3 | 7.7 | 14.9 |
| South Dakota .............. | 493,167 | 435,456 | 369,368 | 336,695 | 668.2 | 590.0 | 504.3 | 461.9 | 13.3 | 17.9 | 9.7 |
| Tennessee .................. | 3,923,819 | 3,645,098 | 3,517,419 | 3,262,616 | 722.5 | 679.0 | 661.2 | 620.7 | 7.6 | 3.6 | 7.8 |
| Texas ......................... | 14,026,888 | 12,805,943 | 12,364,495 | 11,797,328 | 709.9 | 658.8 | 646.4 | 630.1 | 9.5 | 3.6 | 4.8 |
| Utah .......................... | 1,716,976 | 1,673,127 | 1,526,766 | 1,446,538 | 817.6 | 812.6 | 763.2 | 741.4 | 2.6 | 9.6 | 5.5 |
| Vermont ..................... | 355,608 | 312,333 | 313,167 | 308,672 | 601.7 | 530.3 | 532.0 | 527.6 | 13.9 | -0.3 | 1.5 |
| Virginia ..................... | 5,660,133 | 5,337,239 | 4,462,682 | 4,296,733 | 833.5 | 792.6 | 668.5 | 649.2 | 6.0 | 19.6 | 3.9 |
| Washington ................ | 6,048,013 | 5,681,708 | 5,429,938 | 5,339,678 | 1,063.1 | 1,012.8 | 981.4 | 983.2 | 6.4 | 4.6 | 1.7 |
| West Virginia ............. | 1,530,110 | 1,625,623 | 1,325,430 | 1,254,636 | 844.9 | 895.2 | 726.0 | 686.3 | -5.9 | 22.6 | 5.6 |
| Wisconsin .................. | 7,481,155 | 6,993,213 | 6,290,232 | 5,722,997 | 1,432.1 | 1,352.7 | 1,219.1 | 1,117.1 | 7.0 | 11.2 | 9.9 |
| Wyoming .................... | 710,559 | 702,317 | 686,672 | 676,463 | 1,477.3 | 1,463.2 | 1,426.4 | 1,409.3 | 1.2 | 2.3 | 1.5 |

Source: U.S. Department of Commerce, Bureau of the Census.
Note: Includes payments to the federal government, primarily state reimbursements for the supplemental security income program.

## Table 9.4
## PER CAPITA STATE INTERGOVERNMENTAL EXPENDITURE,
## BY FUNCTION AND BY STATE: 1997
### (Per capita amounts in dollars)

| State | Total | General local government support | Specified functions | | | | |
|---|---|---|---|---|---|---|---|
| | | | Education | Public welfare | Highways | Health | Miscellaneous and combined |
| United States ................. | $989.1 | $81.6 | $614.5 | $133.9 | $42.8 | $42.5 | $73.8 |
| Alabama ............................ | 762.3 | 25.7 | 654.8 | 0.0 | 42.0 | 2.8 | 37.1 |
| Alaska ................................ | 1,666.8 | 94.2 | 1,018.8 | 176.5 | 50.7 | 96.5 | 230.0 |
| Arizona .............................. | 994.2 | 194.8 | 514.6 | 116.2 | 96.4 | 30.0 | 42.1 |
| Arkansas ........................... | 779.8 | 20.2 | 645.4 | 0.0 | 51.8 | 0.4 | 61.8 |
| California ........................... | 1,538.2 | 91.7 | 751.5 | 482.1 | 49.6 | 99.3 | 64.1 |
| Colorado ........................... | 775.1 | 5.5 | 508.4 | 129.1 | 57.7 | 7.9 | 66.4 |
| Connecticut ....................... | 758.6 | 43.2 | 540.0 | 51.9 | 6.1 | 38.5 | 78.8 |
| Delaware ........................... | 786.7 | 0.0 | 623.3 | 1.2 | 12.2 | 19.1 | 131.0 |
| Florida ............................... | 812.1 | 149.5 | 574.9 | 5.7 | 15.0 | 8.8 | 58.2 |
| Georgia .............................. | 820.3 | 0.0 | 731.1 | 0.0 | 1.6 | 53.5 | 34.1 |
| Hawaii ............................... | 131.5 | 88.1 | 0.0 | 10.5 | 0.0 | 21.5 | 11.3 |
| Idaho ................................. | 882.0 | 84.7 | 681.5 | 0.0 | 81.9 | 8.5 | 25.3 |
| Illinois ............................... | 769.0 | 103.5 | 446.7 | 84.4 | 43.0 | 8.4 | 83.0 |
| Indiana .............................. | 939.3 | 216.3 | 523.5 | 50.4 | 101.7 | 11.7 | 35.6 |
| Iowa .................................. | 1,006.1 | 59.6 | 716.7 | 16.0 | 122.7 | 27.8 | 63.4 |
| Kansas ............................... | 896.2 | 38.7 | 738.3 | 2.5 | 52.7 | 28.8 | 35.1 |
| Kentucky ........................... | 746.7 | 0.0 | 627.7 | 0.0 | 25.5 | 32.1 | 61.4 |
| Louisiana ........................... | 728.6 | 37.4 | 589.1 | 17.9 | 12.2 | 0.6 | 71.4 |
| Maine ................................ | 622.2 | 62.6 | 494.3 | 11.6 | 17.6 | 1.2 | 35.0 |
| Maryland ........................... | 694.2 | 10.0 | 444.1 | 0.1 | 78.9 | 54.0 | 107.1 |
| Massachusetts ................... | 921.3 | 165.0 | 455.1 | 48.2 | 34.0 | 0.1 | 218.9 |
| Michigan ............................ | 1,447.3 | 137.4 | 970.3 | 11.2 | 117.3 | 150.3 | 60.8 |
| Minnesota .......................... | 1,481.5 | 296.7 | 807.5 | 164.1 | 101.2 | 35.4 | 76.6 |
| Mississippi ........................ | 983.4 | 184.4 | 601.7 | 50.9 | 54.5 | 14.2 | 77.7 |
| Missouri ............................. | 730.1 | 1.2 | 598.0 | 5.1 | 49.3 | 2.8 | 73.7 |
| Montana ............................ | 813.3 | 57.5 | 613.5 | 11.8 | 19.1 | 30.3 | 81.2 |
| Nebraska ........................... | 730.4 | 50.7 | 456.4 | 5.6 | 88.0 | 80.3 | 49.3 |
| Nevada .............................. | 1,056.5 | 336.4 | 652.3 | 14.6 | 30.1 | 4.4 | 18.6 |
| New Hampshire ................. | 352.8 | 31.5 | 158.7 | 68.3 | 20.2 | 40.2 | 33.8 |
| New Jersey ......................... | 792.6 | 98.4 | 497.2 | 98.5 | 7.1 | 7.6 | 83.8 |
| New Mexico ....................... | 1,199.5 | 304.7 | 860.8 | 0.0 | 8.9 | 0.1 | 25.0 |
| New York ........................... | 1,413.6 | 35.0 | 578.5 | 567.3 | 3.9 | 62.8 | 166.1 |
| North Carolina .................. | 985.2 | 79.8 | 697.8 | 70.5 | 17.2 | 66.4 | 53.5 |
| North Dakota .................... | 842.7 | 108.7 | 505.8 | 1.5 | 100.0 | 35.2 | 91.5 |
| Ohio .................................. | 933.4 | 131.5 | 540.9 | 89.2 | 71.7 | 57.0 | 43.2 |
| Oklahoma .......................... | 791.4 | 7.1 | 642.5 | 13.9 | 66.3 | 20.4 | 41.2 |
| Oregon .............................. | 989.1 | 41.2 | 691.4 | 14.4 | 125.6 | 60.3 | 56.2 |
| Pennsylvania ...................... | 819.0 | 13.6 | 459.4 | 120.3 | 35.7 | 69.3 | 120.8 |
| Rhode Island ..................... | 513.0 | 40.7 | 447.2 | 23.3 | 0.0 | 0.0 | 1.9 |
| South Carolina .................. | 779.0 | 163.6 | 535.4 | 0.5 | 11.8 | 21.2 | 46.4 |
| South Dakota ..................... | 590.0 | 68.6 | 404.1 | 0.3 | 37.8 | 0.4 | 78.8 |
| Tennessee .......................... | 679.0 | 58.3 | 453.3 | 59.2 | 53.8 | 0.1 | 54.4 |
| Texas ................................. | 658.8 | 3.0 | 575.2 | 32.0 | 2.9 | 22.4 | 23.2 |
| Utah .................................. | 812.6 | 0.0 | 761.7 | 7.8 | 2.6 | 20.7 | 19.8 |
| Vermont ............................. | 530.3 | 8.8 | 429.0 | 17.9 | 42.4 | 0.0 | 32.1 |
| Virginia .............................. | 792.6 | 5.1 | 572.7 | 51.5 | 28.6 | 25.8 | 108.8 |
| Washington ....................... | 1,012.8 | 22.6 | 787.8 | 6.3 | 76.8 | 13.5 | 105.8 |
| West Virginia ..................... | 895.2 | 11.4 | 843.2 | 0.0 | 0.0 | 4.3 | 36.2 |
| Wisconsin .......................... | 1,352.7 | 257.3 | 767.7 | 70.7 | 100.7 | 57.2 | 99.1 |
| Wyoming ........................... | 1,463.2 | 274.1 | 864.9 | 5.5 | 56.9 | 47.8 | 214.0 |

*Source:* U.S. Department of Commerce, Bureau of the Census.
*Note:* Includes payments to the federal government, primarily state reimbursements for the supplemental security income program (under "public welfare").

## Table 9.5
## PER CAPITA STATE INTERGOVERNMENTAL EXPENDITURE,
## BY FUNCTION AND BY STATE: 1998 (Per capita amounts in dollars)

| State | Total | General local government support | Specified functions | | | | |
|---|---|---|---|---|---|---|---|
| | | | Education | Public welfare | Highways | Health | Miscellaneous and combined |
| United States ............... | $1,031.6 | $84.0 | $652.1 | $132.5 | $43.1 | $44.2 | $75.9 |
| Alabama ............................ | 785.8 | 24.3 | 676.1 | 0.0 | 42.4 | 2.8 | 40.1 |
| Alaska ................................ | 1,601.2 | 74.4 | 1,008.8 | 169.7 | 38.0 | 88.1 | 222.2 |
| Arizona ............................. | 1,075.9 | 204.8 | 569.5 | 115.8 | 96.3 | 44.4 | 45.1 |
| Arkansas ........................... | 831.4 | 47.8 | 675.0 | 0.0 | 52.8 | 0.4 | 55.4 |
| California .......................... | 1,562.8 | 96.2 | 795.8 | 470.6 | 46.8 | 105.6 | 47.9 |
| Colorado .......................... | 795.6 | 6.6 | 524.6 | 132.5 | 66.1 | 8.1 | 57.7 |
| Connecticut ...................... | 802.6 | 45.5 | 575.4 | 47.1 | 6.1 | 23.8 | 104.8 |
| Delaware .......................... | 794.7 | 0.0 | 612.3 | 1.2 | 15.3 | 19.3 | 146.6 |
| Florida .............................. | 840.5 | 156.8 | 613.0 | 0.0 | 16.0 | 0.8 | 54.0 |
| Georgia ............................. | 825.8 | 0.0 | 730.8 | 0.0 | 1.2 | 55.3 | 38.5 |
| Hawaii ............................... | 123.3 | 84.5 | 0.0 | 9.9 | 0.0 | 13.5 | 15.3 |
| Idaho ................................. | 898.5 | 82.7 | 693.8 | 0.0 | 88.6 | 7.3 | 26.0 |
| Illinois .............................. | 818.8 | 100.6 | 485.9 | 95.5 | 43.6 | 8.0 | 85.1 |
| Indiana .............................. | 997.3 | 248.9 | 550.7 | 45.2 | 108.1 | 10.1 | 34.3 |
| Iowa .................................. | 976.4 | 50.4 | 709.9 | 14.3 | 118.4 | 32.5 | 50.8 |
| Kansas ............................... | 954.3 | 40.2 | 790.0 | 1.8 | 53.1 | 29.6 | 39.6 |
| Kentucky ........................... | 763.9 | 0.0 | 636.6 | 0.3 | 28.1 | 32.8 | 66.2 |
| Louisiana .......................... | 789.9 | 36.3 | 635.9 | 17.4 | 12.2 | 1.1 | 87.1 |
| Maine ................................ | 684.8 | 71.9 | 539.4 | 11.7 | 15.9 | 0.1 | 45.9 |
| Maryland ........................... | 722.6 | 9.2 | 501.4 | 0.1 | 72.5 | 59.1 | 80.3 |
| Massachusetts ................... | 1,011.1 | 185.1 | 509.1 | 44.6 | 32.3 | 1.3 | 238.8 |
| Michigan ........................... | 1,571.8 | 141.6 | 1,043.2 | 42.6 | 112.0 | 161.2 | 71.3 |
| Minnesota ......................... | 1,274.5 | 169.2 | 794.7 | 107.4 | 88.9 | 24.5 | 89.7 |
| Mississippi ........................ | 1,045.1 | 193.0 | 650.9 | 51.2 | 57.8 | 13.7 | 78.5 |
| Missouri ............................ | 767.9 | 1.2 | 637.7 | 6.1 | 50.3 | 2.9 | 69.7 |
| Montana ............................ | 809.8 | 0.0 | 670.8 | 13.6 | 19.3 | 15.4 | 90.8 |
| Nebraska ........................... | 776.4 | 52.3 | 472.7 | 9.5 | 96.7 | 85.6 | 59.5 |
| Nevada .............................. | 1,096.3 | 337.5 | 683.5 | 14.5 | 32.4 | 4.6 | 23.7 |
| New Hampshire ................. | 383.7 | 34.0 | 188.4 | 73.8 | 20.3 | 23.1 | 44.2 |
| New Jersey ........................ | 884.3 | 98.6 | 597.0 | 98.1 | 30.1 | 0.4 | 60.1 |
| New Mexico ...................... | 1,259.0 | 331.1 | 900.2 | 0.0 | 5.6 | 0.0 | 22.1 |
| New York ........................... | 1,500.5 | 40.4 | 617.9 | 560.3 | 2.5 | 71.5 | 208.0 |
| North Carolina ................. | 1,050.7 | 81.4 | 773.1 | 72.5 | 15.7 | 67.5 | 40.4 |
| North Dakota .................... | 848.7 | 74.0 | 531.8 | 1.7 | 88.4 | 22.3 | 130.5 |
| Ohio .................................. | 1,000.5 | 137.6 | 577.8 | 100.5 | 72.6 | 63.9 | 48.1 |
| Oklahoma ......................... | 837.4 | 12.9 | 673.0 | 13.7 | 67.9 | 19.9 | 50.0 |
| Oregon .............................. | 1,129.4 | 32.6 | 833.3 | 15.1 | 107.8 | 66.8 | 73.9 |
| Pennsylvania ..................... | 846.4 | 13.5 | 477.1 | 117.9 | 39.2 | 72.8 | 125.9 |
| Rhode Island ..................... | 554.7 | 42.0 | 487.4 | 23.7 | 0.0 | 0.0 | 1.6 |
| South Carolina ................. | 819.1 | 174.7 | 564.4 | 2.1 | 14.6 | 19.9 | 43.5 |
| South Dakota .................... | 668.2 | 70.1 | 474.1 | 0.1 | 38.9 | 0.0 | 84.9 |
| Tennessee ......................... | 722.5 | 60.5 | 484.4 | 64.4 | 55.2 | 0.1 | 57.8 |
| Texas ................................. | 709.9 | 3.2 | 616.1 | 36.1 | 3.3 | 23.7 | 27.4 |
| Utah .................................. | 817.6 | 0.0 | 762.3 | 6.8 | 10.7 | 19.2 | 18.6 |
| Vermont ............................ | 601.7 | 5.8 | 475.9 | 17.4 | 58.2 | 0.0 | 44.4 |
| Virginia ............................. | 833.5 | 5.7 | 591.2 | 58.0 | 29.1 | 25.1 | 124.4 |
| Washington ....................... | 1,063.1 | 22.7 | 825.5 | 6.1 | 80.8 | 15.4 | 112.6 |
| West Virginia .................... | 844.9 | 11.8 | 783.1 | 0.0 | 0.0 | 4.4 | 45.6 |
| Wisconsin .......................... | 1,432.1 | 322.5 | 792.9 | 59.8 | 103.3 | 64.9 | 88.6 |
| Wyoming ........................... | 1,477.3 | 293.9 | 916.5 | 4.6 | 58.9 | 45.7 | 157.6 |

*Source:* U.S. Department of Commerce, Bureau of the Census.

*Note:* Includes payments to the federal government, primarily state reimbursements for the supplemental security income program (under "public welfare").

## Table 9.6
## STATE INTERGOVERNMENTAL EXPENDITURE, BY FUNCTION AND BY STATE: 1997
### (In thousands of dollars)

| State | Total | General local government support | Special Function | | | | |
|---|---|---|---|---|---|---|---|
| | | | Education | Public welfare | Highways | Health | Miscellaneous and combined |
| **United States** | $264,207,209 | $21,808,828 | $164,147,715 | $35,754,024 | $11,431,270 | $11,364,601 | $19,700,771 |
| Alabama | 3,292,491 | 110,830 | 2,828,276 | 0 | 181,223 | 12,097 | 160,065 |
| Alaska | 1,015,071 | 57,355 | 620,460 | 107,496 | 30,896 | 58,796 | 140,068 |
| Arizona | 4,528,382 | 887,389 | 2,344,039 | 529,316 | 439,091 | 136,796 | 191,751 |
| Arkansas | 1,967,398 | 51,027 | 1,628,406 | 0 | 130,813 | 1,116 | 156,036 |
| California | 49,635,672 | 2,957,483 | 24,249,940 | 15,554,950 | 1,600,312 | 3,203,007 | 2,069,980 |
| Colorado | 3,017,473 | 21,561 | 1,979,341 | 502,653 | 224,585 | 30,703 | 258,630 |
| Connecticut | 2,480,762 | 141,405 | 1,765,926 | 169,667 | 19,919 | 126,043 | 257,802 |
| Delaware | 575,892 | 0 | 456,228 | 889 | 8,898 | 14,001 | 95,876 |
| Florida | 11,899,912 | 2,190,258 | 8,424,345 | 83,171 | 220,119 | 129,161 | 852,858 |
| Georgia | 6,141,128 | 0 | 5,473,024 | 0 | 11,957 | 400,840 | 255,307 |
| Hawaii | 156,055 | 104,605 | 0 | 12,511 | 0 | 25,471 | 13,468 |
| Idaho | 1,067,190 | 102,451 | 824,624 | 0 | 99,147 | 10,325 | 30,643 |
| Illinois | 9,148,129 | 1,231,194 | 5,314,031 | 1,004,448 | 511,250 | 100,049 | 987,157 |
| Indiana | 5,507,860 | 1,268,618 | 3,069,857 | 295,499 | 596,306 | 68,678 | 208,902 |
| Iowa | 2,869,259 | 169,898 | 2,044,137 | 45,509 | 349,801 | 79,237 | 180,677 |
| Kansas | 2,325,562 | 100,410 | 1,915,867 | 6,555 | 136,862 | 74,790 | 91,078 |
| Kentucky | 2,918,190 | 0 | 2,453,031 | 10 | 99,788 | 125,378 | 239,983 |
| Louisiana | 3,170,676 | 162,829 | 2,563,715 | 77,758 | 53,024 | 2,555 | 310,795 |
| Maine | 772,724 | 77,696 | 613,945 | 14,399 | 21,808 | 1,455 | 43,421 |
| Maryland | 3,536,070 | 50,799 | 2,262,472 | 310 | 401,990 | 274,945 | 545,554 |
| Massachusetts | 5,636,518 | 1,009,658 | 2,784,069 | 294,843 | 208,068 | 650 | 1,339,230 |
| Michigan | 14,145,451 | 1,342,493 | 9,483,541 | 109,918 | 1,146,938 | 1,468,702 | 593,859 |
| Minnesota | 6,942,130 | 1,390,300 | 3,783,972 | 769,021 | 474,315 | 165,779 | 358,743 |
| Mississippi | 2,685,689 | 503,614 | 1,643,138 | 139,105 | 148,739 | 38,808 | 212,285 |
| Missouri | 3,944,195 | 6,595 | 3,230,330 | 27,408 | 266,360 | 15,220 | 398,282 |
| Montana | 714,924 | 50,508 | 539,229 | 10,370 | 16,787 | 26,670 | 71,360 |
| Nebraska | 1,210,235 | 83,973 | 756,332 | 9,349 | 145,858 | 132,975 | 81,748 |
| Nevada | 1,771,680 | 564,155 | 1,093,959 | 24,541 | 50,524 | 7,319 | 31,182 |
| New Hampshire | 413,800 | 36,923 | 186,197 | 80,147 | 23,681 | 47,183 | 39,669 |
| New Jersey | 6,382,582 | 792,543 | 4,003,743 | 793,088 | 57,180 | 61,263 | 674,765 |
| New Mexico | 2,075,053 | 527,177 | 1,489,102 | 0 | 15,395 | 198 | 43,181 |
| New York | 25,637,864 | 635,152 | 10,491,703 | 10,288,538 | 71,608 | 1,139,159 | 3,011,704 |
| North Carolina | 7,314,766 | 592,283 | 5,181,238 | 523,362 | 127,366 | 493,239 | 397,278 |
| North Dakota | 540,154 | 69,664 | 324,233 | 979 | 64,071 | 22,540 | 58,667 |
| Ohio | 10,441,531 | 1,471,070 | 6,050,909 | 997,319 | 801,704 | 637,599 | 482,930 |
| Oklahoma | 2,625,134 | 23,562 | 2,131,303 | 46,204 | 219,957 | 67,541 | 136,567 |
| Oregon | 3,207,793 | 133,675 | 2,242,155 | 46,771 | 407,226 | 195,630 | 182,336 |
| Pennsylvania | 9,844,265 | 162,919 | 5,522,041 | 1,445,416 | 428,554 | 833,408 | 1,451,927 |
| Rhode Island | 506,349 | 40,200 | 441,354 | 22,960 | 0 | 0 | 1,835 |
| South Carolina | 2,929,143 | 615,296 | 2,013,238 | 1,842 | 44,539 | 79,864 | 174,364 |
| South Dakota | 435,456 | 50,606 | 298,216 | 233 | 27,931 | 292 | 58,178 |
| Tennessee | 3,645,098 | 312,855 | 2,433,061 | 317,801 | 288,946 | 522 | 291,913 |
| Texas | 12,805,943 | 58,663 | 11,180,590 | 622,644 | 55,983 | 436,229 | 451,834 |
| Utah | 1,673,127 | 0 | 1,568,337 | 16,138 | 5,389 | 42,528 | 40,735 |
| Vermont | 312,333 | 5,180 | 252,682 | 10,540 | 25,002 | 0 | 18,929 |
| Virginia | 5,337,239 | 34,647 | 3,856,654 | 346,926 | 192,690 | 173,657 | 732,665 |
| Washington | 5,681,708 | 126,688 | 4,419,563 | 35,132 | 430,735 | 75,799 | 593,791 |
| West Virginia | 1,625,623 | 20,765 | 1,531,221 | 0 | 0 | 7,881 | 65,756 |
| Wisconsin | 6,993,213 | 1,330,289 | 3,968,792 | 365,647 | 520,646 | 295,559 | 512,280 |
| Wyoming | 702,317 | 131,567 | 415,149 | 2,641 | 27,289 | 22,944 | · 102,727 |

Source: U.S. Department of Commerce, Bureau of the Census.
Note: Detail may not add to totals due to rounding.

## Table 9.7
## STATE INTERGOVERNMENTAL EXPENDITURE, BY FUNCTION AND BY STATE: 1998
### (In thousands of dollars)

| State | Total | General local government support | Education | Public welfare | Highways | Health | Miscellaneous and combined |
|---|---|---|---|---|---|---|---|
| United States ............ | $278,853,409 | $22,693,158 | $176,250,998 | $35,807,218 | $11,648,853 | $11,937,200 | $20,515,982 |
| Alabama ..................... | 3,419,845 | 105,903 | 2,942,520 | 0 | 184,688 | 12,102 | 174,632 |
| Alaska ....................... | 983,153 | 45,685 | 619,386 | 104,185 | 23,360 | 54,081 | 136,456 |
| Arizona ...................... | 5,023,261 | 956,371 | 2,658,844 | 540,623 | 449,840 | 207,173 | 210,410 |
| Arkansas ................... | 2,109,996 | 121,239 | 1,713,117 | 0 | 133,973 | 1,029 | 140,638 |
| California ................... | 51,053,075 | 3,142,756 | 25,997,110 | 15,372,722 | 1,527,768 | 3,449,507 | 1,563,212 |
| Colorado .................... | 3,159,458 | 26,037 | 2,083,310 | 526,332 | 262,474 | 32,267 | 229,038 |
| Connecticut ................ | 2,627,781 | 148,957 | 1,883,788 | 154,137 | 19,919 | 77,987 | 342,993 |
| Delaware .................... | 591,279 | 0 | 455,550 | 918 | 11,368 | 14,340 | 109,103 |
| Florida ....................... | 12,537,431 | 2,339,137 | 9,143,584 | 0 | 238,341 | 11,200 | 805,169 |
| Georgia ...................... | 6,310,697 | 0 | 5,585,137 | 0 | 8,978 | 422,437 | 294,145 |
| Hawaii ....................... | 147,059 | 100,852 | 0 | 11,815 | 0 | 16,112 | 18,280 |
| Idaho ......................... | 1,104,201 | 101,640 | 852,660 | 0 | 108,906 | 9,027 | 31,968 |
| Illinois ....................... | 9,862,059 | 1,211,291 | 5,852,998 | 1,150,369 | 525,617 | 96,681 | 1,025,103 |
| Indiana ...................... | 5,883,074 | 1,468,343 | 3,248,315 | 266,759 | 637,793 | 59,517 | 202,347 |
| Iowa .......................... | 2,794,519 | 144,385 | 2,031,742 | 41,053 | 338,733 | 93,112 | 145,494 |
| Kansas ...................... | 2,508,870 | 105,584 | 2,076,833 | 4,753 | 139,710 | 77,788 | 104,202 |
| Kentucky .................... | 3,006,904 | 0 | 2,505,514 | 1,018 | 110,614 | 129,124 | 260,634 |
| Louisiana ................... | 3,451,053 | 158,550 | 2,778,319 | 75,987 | 53,117 | 4,747 | 380,333 |
| Maine ........................ | 851,942 | 89,490 | 670,957 | 14,555 | 19,761 | 94 | 57,085 |
| Maryland .................... | 3,710,641 | 47,161 | 2,574,845 | 647 | 372,371 | 303,394 | 412,223 |
| Massachusetts ............ | 6,215,380 | 1,137,935 | 3,129,534 | 273,922 | 198,579 | 7,707 | 1,467,703 |
| Michigan .................... | 15,430,418 | 1,389,824 | 10,240,756 | 418,203 | 1,099,153 | 1,582,049 | 700,433 |
| Minnesota .................. | 6,022,123 | 799,628 | 3,755,033 | 507,701 | 420,052 | 115,975 | 423,734 |
| Mississippi ................. | 2,876,187 | 531,087 | 1,791,333 | 140,878 | 159,034 | 37,725 | 216,130 |
| Missouri ..................... | 4,176,567 | 6,485 | 3,468,342 | 33,145 | 273,674 | 15,606 | 379,315 |
| Montana ..................... | 712,620 | 0 | 590,263 | 11,968 | 16,951 | 13,510 | 79,928 |
| Nebraska .................... | 1,291,135 | 87,047 | 786,129 | 15,866 | 160,791 | 142,410 | 98,892 |
| Nevada ....................... | 1,915,179 | 589,696 | 1,194,130 | 25,338 | 56,678 | 7,983 | 41,354 |
| New Hampshire ............ | 454,682 | 40,245 | 223,226 | 87,440 | 24,057 | 27,393 | 52,321 |
| New Jersey ................. | 7,176,343 | 800,187 | 4,844,525 | 796,179 | 244,497 | 3,330 | 487,625 |
| New Mexico ................ | 2,186,948 | 575,182 | 1,563,611 | 0 | 9,699 | 0 | 38,456 |
| New York ................... | 27,271,351 | 733,364 | 11,230,312 | 10,183,263 | 45,483 | 1,299,103 | 3,779,826 |
| North Carolina ............ | 7,928,480 | 614,475 | 5,833,977 | 547,205 | 118,688 | 509,441 | 304,694 |
| North Dakota .............. | 541,455 | 47,226 | 339,274 | 1,106 | 56,392 | 14,222 | 83,235 |
| Ohio .......................... | 11,214,371 | 1,542,321 | 6,476,726 | 1,126,412 | 813,847 | 715,968 | 539,097 |
| Oklahoma .................. | 2,802,808 | 43,153 | 2,252,588 | 45,863 | 227,279 | 66,544 | 167,381 |
| Oregon ....................... | 3,706,815 | 106,942 | 2,734,882 | 49,405 | 353,842 | 219,281 | 242,463 |
| Pennsylvania .............. | 10,157,714 | 162,418 | 5,725,290 | 1,415,428 | 469,867 | 874,121 | 1,510,590 |
| Rhode Island .............. | 548,018 | 41,467 | 481,516 | 23,452 | 0 | 0 | 1,583 |
| South Carolina ............ | 3,142,089 | 669,989 | 2,164,984 | 8,151 | 55,825 | 76,218 | 166,922 |
| South Dakota .............. | 493,167 | 51,761 | 349,897 | 56 | 28,744 | 26 | 62,683 |
| Tennessee .................. | 3,923,819 | 328,363 | 2,630,664 | 349,829 | 300,034 | 779 | 314,150 |
| Texas ......................... | 14,026,888 | 62,303 | 12,175,008 | 713,021 | 65,917 | 468,484 | 542,155 |
| Utah .......................... | 1,716,976 | 0 | 1,600,768 | 14,233 | 22,532 | 40,424 | 39,019 |
| Vermont ..................... | 355,608 | 3,446 | 281,254 | 10,265 | 34,384 | 0 | 26,259 |
| Virginia ...................... | 5,660,133 | 38,395 | 4,015,025 | 393,947 | 197,707 | 170,407 | 844,652 |
| Washington ................ | 6,048,013 | 129,420 | 4,696,024 | 34,434 | 459,802 | 87,843 | 640,490 |
| West Virginia .............. | 1,530,110 | 21,374 | 1,418,247 | 0 | 0 | 7,881 | 82,608 |
| Wisconsin .................. | 7,481,155 | 1,684,656 | 4,142,295 | 312,441 | 539,661 | 339,085 | 463,017 |
| Wyoming .................... | 710,559 | 141,388 | 440,856 | 2,194 | 28,353 | 21,966 | 75,802 |

*Source:* U.S. Department of Commerce, Bureau of the Census.
*Note:* Detail may not add to totals due to rounding.

## Table 9.8
## STATE INTERGOVERNMENTAL EXPENDITURE, BY TYPE OF RECEIVING
## GOVERNMENT AND BY STATE: 1997
### (In thousands of dollars)

| State | Total intergovernmental expenditure | Federal | School districts | Counties, municipalities, and townships | Special districts | Combined and unallocable |
|---|---|---|---|---|---|---|
| | | | | Type of receiving government | | |
| United States ............... | $264,207,209 | $3,839,942 | $136,979,977 | $111,639,394 | $2,468,384 | $9,279,512 |
| Alabama ............................ | 3,292,491 | 0 | 2,828,276 | 461,593 | 0 | 2,622 |
| Alaska ............................... | 1,015,071 | 107,496 | 0 | 831,600 | 0 | 75,975 |
| Arizona ............................. | 4,528,382 | 0 | 2,337,946 | 2,019,992 | 0 | 170,444 |
| Arkansas .......................... | 1,967,398 | 1,911 | 1,627,615 | 243,316 | 5,525 | 89,031 |
| California .......................... | 49,635,672 | 2,022,217 | 22,759,084 | 23,943,998 | 479,073 | 431,300 |
| Colorado .......................... | 3,017,473 | 7,505 | 1,978,752 | 1,001,425 | 29,791 | 0 |
| Connecticut ...................... | 2,480,762 | 0 | 18,256 | 2,277,000 | 0 | 185,506 |
| Delaware .......................... | 575,892 | 852 | 455,137 | 119,903 | 0 | 0 |
| Florida .............................. | 11,899,912 | 496 | 8,424,345 | 3,475,071 | 0 | 0 |
| Georgia ............................ | 6,141,128 | 0 | 5,473,024 | 587,146 | 17,571 | 63,387 |
| Hawaii .............................. | 156,055 | 12,511 | 0 | 133,201 | 0 | 10,343 |
| Idaho ................................ | 1,067,190 | 0 | 824,624 | 138,075 | 2,863 | 101,628 |
| Illinois .............................. | 9,148,129 | 2,153 | 5,295,600 | 2,961,554 | 461,633 | 427,189 |
| Indiana ............................. | 5,507,860 | 20,652 | 3,069,857 | 1,562,364 | 9,801 | 845,186 |
| Iowa ................................. | 2,869,259 | 35,409 | 2,044,137 | 634,940 | 0 | 154,773 |
| Kansas ............................. | 2,325,562 | 10 | 1,915,867 | 323,887 | 6,200 | 79,598 |
| Kentucky .......................... | 2,918,190 | 0 | 2,453,031 | 442,338 | 0 | 22,821 |
| Louisiana ......................... | 3,170,676 | 0 | 2,556,711 | 452,855 | 0 | 161,110 |
| Maine ............................... | 772,724 | 8,541 | 0 | 151,677 | 0 | 612,506 |
| Maryland .......................... | 3,536,070 | 0 | 0 | 3,346,325 | 0 | 189,745 |
| Massachusetts .................. | 5,636,518 | 181,560 | 403,607 | 4,216,398 | 682,752 | 152,201 |
| Michigan ........................... | 14,145,451 | 60,029 | 9,483,541 | 4,270,558 | 284 | 331,039 |
| Minnesota ........................ | 6,942,130 | 0 | 3,755,623 | 3,041,303 | 47,058 | 98,146 |
| Mississippi ....................... | 2,685,689 | 0 | 1,633,510 | 1,029,705 | 0 | 22,474 |
| Missouri ........................... | 3,944,195 | 0 | 3,230,327 | 423,604 | 7,488 | 282,776 |
| Montana ........................... | 714,924 | 0 | 539,229 | 136,646 | 0 | 39,049 |
| Nebraska .......................... | 1,210,235 | 9,349 | 753,112 | 176,607 | 24,288 | 246,879 |
| Nevada ............................. | 1,771,680 | 5,336 | 1,093,959 | 667,154 | 2,210 | 3,021 |
| New Hampshire ................. | 413,800 | 0 | 20,879 | 154,942 | 925 | 237,054 |
| New Jersey ....................... | 6,382,582 | 58,889 | 3,312,361 | 2,959,738 | 0 | 51,594 |
| New Mexico ...................... | 2,075,053 | 0 | 1,489,102 | 566,674 | 0 | 19,277 |
| New York .......................... | 25,637,864 | 954,602 | 5,135,529 | 19,493,369 | 17,299 | 37,065 |
| North Carolina .................. | 7,314,766 | 0 | 0 | 7,269,986 | 38,908 | 5,872 |
| North Dakota .................... | 540,154 | 0 | 324,100 | 212,225 | 3,427 | 402 |
| Ohio ................................. | 10,441,531 | 3,642 | 6,050,909 | 2,544,474 | 18,999 | 1,823,507 |
| Oklahoma ......................... | 2,625,134 | 40,816 | 2,125,742 | 373,673 | 5,542 | 79,361 |
| Oregon ............................. | 3,207,793 | 0 | 2,240,889 | 924,594 | 17,946 | 24,364 |
| Pennsylvania .................... | 9,844,265 | 107,894 | 5,522,041 | 3,747,434 | 362,451 | 104,445 |
| Rhode Island .................... | 506,349 | 21,314 | 27,123 | 454,032 | 0 | 3,880 |
| South Carolina .................. | 2,929,143 | 0 | 2,009,209 | 916,707 | 1,299 | 1,928 |
| South Dakota .................... | 435,456 | 0 | 298,134 | 131,358 | 1,099 | 4,865 |
| Tennessee ........................ | 3,645,098 | 0 | 145,945 | 3,470,039 | 20,829 | 8,285 |
| Texas ............................... | 12,805,943 | 0 | 11,172,620 | 526,160 | 2,454 | 1,104,709 |
| Utah ................................. | 1,673,127 | 111 | 1,568,337 | 104,679 | 0 | 0 |
| Vermont ........................... | 312,333 | 10,540 | 252,682 | 49,111 | 0 | 0 |
| Virginia ............................ | 5,337,239 | 371 | 0 | 5,324,677 | 12,191 | 0 |
| Washington ...................... | 5,681,708 | 31,874 | 4,415,540 | 1,037,076 | 179,664 | 17,554 |
| West Virginia .................... | 1,625,623 | 0 | 1,531,221 | 76,509 | 339 | 17,554 |
| Wisconsin ......................... | 6,993,213 | 133,087 | 3,968,792 | 1,961,490 | 0 | 929,844 |
| Wyoming .......................... | 702,317 | 775 | 413,652 | 270,212 | 8,475 | 9,203 |

*Source:* U.S. Department of Commerce, Bureau of the Census.
*Note:* Detail may not add to totals due to rounding.

## Table 9.9
## STATE INTERGOVERNMENTAL EXPENDITURE, BY TYPE OF RECEIVING GOVERNMENT AND BY STATE: 1998
(In thousands of dollars)

| State | Total intergovernmental expenditure | Federal | School districts | Counties, municipalities, and townships | Special districts | Combined and unallocable |
|---|---|---|---|---|---|---|
| United States ............... | $278,853,409 | $3,515,734 | $146,232,606 | $116,882,348 | $2,550,914 | $9,671,807 |
| Alabama ............................. | 3,419,845 | 0 | 2,942,520 | 474,493 | 0 | 2,832 |
| Alaska ................................. | 983,153 | 104,185 | 0 | 809,607 | 0 | 69,361 |
| Arizona ............................... | 5,023,261 | 0 | 2,586,129 | 2,220,649 | 0 | 216,483 |
| Arkansas ............................. | 2,109,996 | 1,468 | 1,711,338 | 302,070 | 7,139 | 87,981 |
| California ........................... | 51,053,075 | 2,039,620 | 24,325,430 | 23,769,279 | 442,348 | 476,398 |
| Colorado ............................ | 3,159,458 | 8,921 | 2,082,832 | 1,047,063 | 20,642 | 0 |
| Connecticut ........................ | 2,627,781 | 0 | 18,751 | 2,389,866 | 0 | 219,164 |
| Delaware ............................ | 591,279 | 900 | 454,961 | 135,418 | 0 | 0 |
| Florida ............................... | 12,537,431 | 500 | 9,143,584 | 3,393,347 | 0 | 0 |
| Georgia .............................. | 6,310,697 | 0 | 5,585,137 | 622,970 | 9,387 | 93,203 |
| Hawaii ................................ | 147,059 | 11,815 | 0 | 120,177 | 0 | 15,067 |
| Idaho .................................. | 1,104,201 | 0 | 852,660 | 139,785 | 1,995 | 109,761 |
| Illinois ................................ | 9,862,059 | 2,233 | 5,832,956 | 3,106,887 | 475,339 | 444,644 |
| Indiana ............................... | 5,883,074 | 21,347 | 3,248,315 | 1,724,336 | 6,558 | 882,518 |
| Iowa ................................... | 2,794,519 | 30,286 | 2,031,742 | 613,069 | 0 | 119,422 |
| Kansas ................................ | 2,508,870 | 3 | 2,076,833 | 349,631 | 4,074 | 78,329 |
| Kentucky ............................ | 3,006,904 | 0 | 2,505,514 | 477,772 | 0 | 23,618 |
| Louisiana ............................ | 3,451,053 | 0 | 2,777,370 | 496,736 | 0 | 176,947 |
| Maine ................................. | 851,942 | 8,360 | 0 | 172,803 | 0 | 670,779 |
| Maryland ............................ | 3,710,641 | 0 | 0 | 3,656,634 | 0 | 54,007 |
| Massachusetts .................... | 6,215,380 | 166,798 | 454,324 | 4,654,071 | 723,367 | 216,820 |
| Michigan ............................ | 15,430,418 | 70,498 | 10,240,756 | 4,810,119 | 67 | 308,978 |
| Minnesota .......................... | 6,022,123 | 0 | 3,683,461 | 2,186,881 | 49,351 | 102,430 |
| Mississippi ......................... | 2,876,187 | 0 | 1,782,728 | 1,071,160 | 0 | 22,299 |
| Missouri ............................. | 4,176,567 | 0 | 3,468,333 | 431,840 | 7,519 | 268,875 |
| Montana ............................. | 712,620 | 0 | 590,263 | 97,128 | 0 | 25,229 |
| Nebraska ............................ | 1,291,135 | 9,627 | 781,727 | 190,147 | 28,213 | 281,421 |
| Nevada ............................... | 1,915,179 | 5,609 | 1,194,130 | 706,654 | 7,766 | 1,020 |
| New Hampshire .................. | 454,682 | 0 | 20,901 | 170,693 | 823 | 262,265 |
| New Jersey ......................... | 7,176,343 | 60,538 | 3,885,676 | 3,161,647 | 0 | 68,482 |
| New Mexico ........................ | 2,186,948 | 0 | 1,563,611 | 609,297 | 0 | 14,040 |
| New York ............................ | 27,271,351 | 637,000 | 5,443,507 | 21,139,147 | 1,921 | 49,776 |
| North Carolina ................... | 7,928,480 | 0 | 0 | 7,895,861 | 32,619 | 0 |
| North Dakota ..................... | 541,455 | 0 | 339,055 | 197,490 | 4,448 | 462 |
| Ohio ................................... | 11,214,371 | 3,938 | 6,474,587 | 2,806,983 | 21,573 | 1,907,290 |
| Oklahoma ........................... | 2,802,808 | 40,965 | 2,245,993 | 431,043 | 6,532 | 78,275 |
| Oregon ............................... | 3,706,815 | 0 | 2,729,628 | 914,119 | 52,784 | 10,284 |
| Pennsylvania ...................... | 10,157,714 | 99,203 | 5,725,290 | 3,809,595 | 424,708 | 98,918 |
| Rhode Island ...................... | 548,018 | 21,969 | 25,003 | 496,207 | 0 | 4,839 |
| South Carolina ................... | 3,142,089 | 0 | 2,152,033 | 985,695 | 2,158 | 2,203 |
| South Dakota ..................... | 493,167 | 0 | 349,755 | 142,252 | 591 | 569 |
| Tennessee .......................... | 3,923,819 | 0 | 157,722 | 3,744,533 | 12,195 | 9,369 |
| Texas .................................. | 14,026,888 | 0 | 12,174,553 | 563,927 | 6,328 | 1,282,080 |
| Utah ................................... | 1,716,976 | 80 | 1,600,768 | 116,128 | 0 | 0 |
| Vermont .............................. | 355,608 | 10,265 | 281,254 | 64,089 | 0 | 0 |
| Virginia .............................. | 5,660,133 | 956 | 0 | 5,659,177 | 0 | 0 |
| Washington ........................ | 6,048,013 | 29,118 | 4,692,205 | 1,112,342 | 196,223 | 18,125 |
| West Virginia ..................... | 1,530,110 | 0 | 1,418,247 | 98,535 | 305 | 13,023 |
| Wisconsin ........................... | 7,481,155 | 128,282 | 4,141,641 | 2,331,530 | 0 | 879,702 |
| Wyoming ............................ | 710,559 | 1,250 | 439,383 | 261,466 | 3,941 | 4,519 |

*Source:* U.S. Department of Commerce, Bureau of the Census.
*Note:* Detail may not add to totals due to rounding.

## Table 9.10
## STATE INTERGOVERNMENTAL REVENUE FROM FEDERAL AND LOCAL GOVERNMENTS: 1997
### (In thousands of dollars)

| State | Total intergovernmental revenue | From federal government — Total | Education | Public welfare | Health & hospitals | Highways | From local government — Total | Education | Public welfare | Health & hospitals | Highways |
|---|---|---|---|---|---|---|---|---|---|---|---|
| United States | $230,592,191 | $215,420,924 | $33,663,410 | $123,087,017 | $11,675,522 | $19,346,121 | $15,171,267 | $1,133,766 | $9,475,632 | $677,201 | $946,273 |
| Alabama | 3,553,541 | 3,503,489 | 752,023 | 1,867,300 | 134,962 | 329,107 | 50,052 | 12,914 | 0 | 420 | 17,566 |
| Alaska | 1,042,225 | 1,037,324 | 132,407 | 372,265 | 40,400 | 220,719 | 4,901 | 3,322 | 0 | 81 | 0 |
| Arizona | 3,237,414 | 2,935,503 | 594,582 | 1,662,512 | 142,819 | 311,184 | 301,911 | 12,191 | 221,581 | 56,341 | 771 |
| Arkansas | 2,266,482 | 2,253,121 | 326,208 | 1,349,664 | 47,731 | 292,686 | 11,361 | 5,567 | 0 | 705 | 1,933 |
| California | 30,345,109 | 27,718,760 | 4,722,610 | 15,322,261 | 1,146,698 | 1,721,830 | 2,626,349 | 102,587 | 1,950,765 | 3,666 | 425,639 |
| Colorado | 2,595,939 | 2,577,625 | 664,892 | 1,247,092 | 240,891 | 198,494 | 18,314 | 4,326 | 0 | 0 | 10,062 |
| Connecticut | 2,943,626 | 2,938,089 | 255,106 | 1,815,159 | 192,699 | 419,944 | 5,537 | 2 | 0 | 0 | 0 |
| Delaware | 672,129 | 650,430 | 81,189 | 307,023 | 39,467 | 97,396 | 21,699 | 19,377 | 0 | 0 | 0 |
| Florida | 8,297,195 | 7,947,478 | 1,539,797 | 3,920,347 | 761,499 | 810,153 | 349,717 | 1,901 | 222,637 | 59,379 | 0 |
| Georgia | 6,007,066 | 5,948,627 | 1,066,104 | 3,427,543 | 295,084 | 595,628 | 58,439 | 14,998 | 0 | 0 | 21,159 |
| Hawaii | 1,302,690 | 1,300,079 | 208,743 | 599,210 | 77,277 | 191,726 | 2,611 | 923 | 0 | 0 | 0 |
| Idaho | 849,475 | 839,338 | 125,717 | 359,591 | 68,496 | 137,293 | 10,137 | 137 | 160 | 2,524 | 6,761 |
| Illinois | 8,713,602 | 7,912,414 | 1,418,134 | 4,714,815 | 406,357 | 630,166 | 801,188 | 24,780 | 654,434 | 0 | 43,453 |
| Indiana | 3,859,176 | 3,700,317 | 607,913 | 2,121,793 | 147,131 | 456,385 | 158,859 | 3,520 | 92,853 | 7,117 | 32,307 |
| Iowa | 2,007,968 | 1,919,522 | 433,681 | 948,831 | 198,728 | 119,260 | 88,446 | 1,426 | 48,690 | 31,436 | 5,151 |
| Kansas | 1,839,813 | 1,808,477 | 390,780 | 752,770 | 108,595 | 210,805 | 31,336 | 4,226 | 0 | 0 | 27,110 |
| Kentucky | 3,463,950 | 3,453,819 | 515,628 | 2,144,319 | 123,830 | 284,544 | 10,131 | 7,638 | 0 | 0 | 0 |
| Louisiana | 4,329,084 | 4,287,358 | 731,459 | 2,995,606 | 189,067 | 25,778 | 41,726 | 4,306 | 0 | 9,698 | 5 |
| Maine | 1,299,070 | 1,293,290 | 136,959 | 841,011 | 39,660 | 127,780 | 5,780 | 154 | 0 | 0 | 4,261 |
| Maryland | 3,411,382 | 3,303,543 | 590,484 | 1,677,255 | 146,175 | 396,062 | 107,839 | 18,361 | 0 | 29,829 | 21,597 |
| Massachusetts | 5,808,872 | 5,312,022 | 553,165 | 2,401,437 | 610,929 | 981,863 | 496,850 | 9,331 | 6,273 | 4,397 | 308 |
| Michigan | 8,267,080 | 7,780,140 | 1,340,360 | 4,403,265 | 682,018 | 575,506 | 486,940 | 16,544 | 67,978 | 307,347 | 62,467 |
| Minnesota | 3,625,727 | 3,449,026 | 641,823 | 2,009,814 | 146,635 | 215,848 | 176,701 | 3,330 | 138,054 | 16,287 | 12,120 |
| Mississippi | 2,904,204 | 2,787,879 | 485,768 | 1,704,876 | 120,948 | 218,080 | 116,325 | 4,285 | 102,752 | 0 | 763 |
| Missouri | 3,719,819 | 3,696,605 | 459,232 | 2,190,359 | 240,091 | 429,045 | 23,214 | 2,051 | 26 | 157 | 16,368 |
| Montana | 959,197 | 942,088 | 123,491 | 460,065 | 47,452 | 159,138 | 17,109 | 836 | 14,229 | 0 | 1,709 |
| Nebraska | 1,164,360 | 1,141,336 | 201,756 | 612,793 | 75,850 | 138,348 | 23,024 | 5,138 | 3,301 | 2,998 | 9,670 |
| Nevada | 829,530 | 780,154 | 132,136 | 368,973 | 44,956 | 120,248 | 49,376 | 8,469 | 22,559 | 562 | 6,581 |
| New Hampshire | 988,193 | 839,669 | 92,041 | 422,638 | 17,842 | 99,436 | 148,524 | 4,014 | 127,462 | 0 | 10,164 |
| New Jersey | 6,362,916 | 5,989,056 | 567,518 | 3,208,451 | 323,373 | 795,443 | 373,860 | 238,365 | 38,664 | 10,322 | 1,342 |
| New Mexico | 1,973,080 | 1,926,207 | 369,089 | 1,152,260 | 102,107 | 163,191 | 46,873 | 12,319 | 0 | 33,350 | 0 |
| New York | 30,470,368 | 24,277,716 | 1,945,002 | 16,651,099 | 1,120,378 | 955,092 | 6,192,652 | 133,185 | 4,873,665 | 7,026 | 5,036 |
| North Carolina | 6,318,006 | 5,869,356 | 820,507 | 3,597,604 | 174,426 | 702,651 | 448,650 | 9,510 | 398,703 | 1,293 | 13,772 |
| North Dakota | 812,005 | 775,584 | 138,155 | 316,615 | 23,440 | 129,259 | 36,421 | 183 | 17,020 | 0 | 13,140 |
| Ohio | 8,992,850 | 8,707,719 | 1,101,480 | 5,535,850 | 418,167 | 761,736 | 285,131 | 77,260 | 13,698 | 24,011 | 37,418 |

# STATE INTERGOVERNMENTAL REVENUE FROM FEDERAL AND LOCAL GOVERNMENTS: 1997 — Continued

| State | Total intergovernmental revenue | From federal government | | | | | From local government | | | | |
|---|---|---|---|---|---|---|---|---|---|---|---|
| | | Total | Education | Public welfare | Health & hospitals | Highways | Total (a) | Education | Public welfare | Health & hospitals | Highways |
| Oklahoma | 2,169,755 | 2,094,825 | 447,236 | 1,111,944 | 93,058 | 247,478 | 74,930 | 19,430 | 465 | 529 | 10,924 |
| Oregon | 3,517,946 | 3,420,114 | 531,571 | 1,618,775 | 317,881 | 267,771 | 97,832 | 11,232 | 74,957 | 0 | 10,183 |
| Pennsylvania | 9,420,286 | 9,343,925 | 1,369,218 | 5,761,474 | 469,710 | 843,377 | 76,361 | 43,710 | 0 | 0 | 8,119 |
| Rhode Island | 1,108,615 | 1,051,064 | 114,140 | 688,036 | 44,535 | 94,667 | 57,551 | 20 | 0 | 0 | 44 |
| South Carolina | 3,161,523 | 3,041,328 | 515,136 | 1,810,184 | 174,620 | 243,231 | 120,195 | 26,470 | 50,254 | 6,721 | 261 |
| South Dakota | 673,220 | 665,467 | 88,719 | 281,798 | 33,608 | 120,867 | 7,753 | 0 | 0 | 2,857 | 3,880 |
| Tennessee | 5,065,016 | 5,003,101 | 581,737 | 3,338,026 | 164,129 | 408,192 | 61,915 | 16,961 | 0 | 544 | 19,371 |
| Texas | 13,800,422 | 13,281,155 | 2,631,848 | 7,319,474 | 723,487 | 1,213,423 | 519,267 | 186,047 | 330,731 | 1,637 | 738 |
| Utah | 1,592,311 | 1,576,579 | 375,288 | 738,576 | 126,019 | 146,266 | 15,732 | 1,796 | 3,181 | 59 | 4,915 |
| Vermont | 666,942 | 663,542 | 92,391 | 330,195 | 48,342 | 80,605 | 3,400 | 1,679 | 0 | 0 | 1,721 |
| Virginia | 3,544,685 | 3,392,753 | 761,001 | 1,619,436 | 150,355 | 413,730 | 151,932 | 15,261 | 0 | 41,262 | 28,479 |
| Washington | 4,112,300 | 4,051,773 | 863,205 | 1,933,299 | 409,328 | 428,790 | 60,527 | 26,072 | 0 | 0 | 4,896 |
| West Virginia | 2,040,033 | 2,032,610 | 286,617 | 1,090,668 | 65,413 | 358,749 | 7,423 | 1,576 | 0 | 0 | 0 |
| Wisconsin | 3,636,662 | 3,366,772 | 662,904 | 1,793,877 | 142,815 | 336,478 | 269,890 | 2,338 | 540 | 13,451 | 42,297 |
| Wyoming | 851,332 | 832,756 | 76,460 | 168,789 | 16,044 | 120,673 | 18,576 | 13,698 | 0 | 1,195 | 1,812 |

*Source:* U.S. Department of Commerce, Bureau of the Census.
*Note:* Detail may not add to totals due to rounding.

**Table 9.11**
## STATE INTERGOVERNMENTAL REVENUE FROM FEDERAL AND LOCAL GOVERNMENTS: 1998
*(In thousands of dollars)*

| State | Total intergovernmental revenue | From federal government | | | | | From local government | | | | |
|---|---|---|---|---|---|---|---|---|---|---|---|
| | | Total | Education | Public welfare | Health & hospitals | Highways | Total | Education | Public welfare | Health & hospitals | Highways |
| United States | $240,788,817 | $224,443,723 | $36,137,911 | $127,355,715 | $12,579,317 | $19,659,220 | $16,345,094 | $1,119,574 | $10,189,616 | $635,012 | $977,595 |
| Alabama | 4,021,037 | 3,974,642 | 791,617 | 2,287,340 | 134,240 | 303,076 | 46,395 | 11,288 | 0 | 726 | 14,512 |
| Alaska | 1,079,799 | 1,076,032 | 132,506 | 400,838 | 40,532 | 208,579 | 3,767 | 2,977 | 0 | 117 | 0 |
| Arizona | 3,329,995 | 3,011,159 | 665,674 | 1,694,243 | 141,942 | 267,713 | 318,836 | 21,787 | 211,052 | 70,447 | 5,115 |
| Arkansas | 2,368,339 | 2,357,700 | 353,465 | 1,424,910 | 52,574 | 281,035 | 10,639 | 4,323 | 0 | 688 | 2,314 |
| California | 30,893,821 | 28,413,632 | 5,283,380 | 15,221,943 | 1,158,606 | 1,753,250 | 2,480,189 | 101,458 | 1,785,499 | 4,745 | 420,461 |
| Colorado | 2,788,627 | 2,766,867 | 706,088 | 1,338,419 | 246,040 | 236,884 | 21,760 | 6,174 | 81 | 347 | 12,082 |
| Connecticut | 3,016,337 | 3,010,505 | 287,871 | 1,871,144 | 200,598 | 408,168 | 5,832 | 2 | 0 | 0 | 0 |
| Delaware | 724,706 | 697,214 | 89,179 | 306,221 | 41,217 | 118,604 | 27,492 | 21,861 | 0 | 0 | 0 |
| Florida | 8,301,851 | 7,922,246 | 1,505,106 | 3,880,604 | 897,701 | 695,212 | 379,605 | 0 | 242,255 | 66,464 | 0 |
| Georgia | 5,676,362 | 5,627,185 | 1,089,173 | 3,037,171 | 275,607 | 653,440 | 49,177 | 24,011 | 0 | 0 | 5,849 |
| Hawaii | 1,175,599 | 1,169,448 | 240,874 | 539,390 | 77,166 | 116,804 | 6,151 | 1,205 | 0 | 0 | 0 |
| Idaho | 862,978 | 858,057 | 132,599 | 365,559 | 76,462 | 127,204 | 4,921 | 172 | 109 | 2,450 | 2,134 |
| Illinois | 8,958,993 | 8,208,285 | 1,520,733 | 4,766,945 | 384,451 | 729,231 | 750,708 | 13,849 | 638,459 | 0 | 50,636 |
| Indiana | 3,943,070 | 3,784,729 | 639,929 | 2,176,646 | 162,063 | 416,349 | 158,341 | 4,100 | 85,596 | 6,237 | 30,658 |
| Iowa | 2,215,812 | 2,117,659 | 450,227 | 1,060,588 | 195,343 | 212,801 | 98,153 | 1,937 | 53,382 | 30,791 | 10,268 |
| Kansas | 1,862,929 | 1,831,703 | 405,651 | 837,419 | 111,658 | 195,379 | 31,226 | 4,370 | 0 | 0 | 26,856 |
| Kentucky | 3,602,966 | 3,591,773 | 540,899 | 2,281,678 | 124,474 | 317,708 | 11,193 | 8,534 | 0 | 0 | 0 |
| Louisiana | 4,026,348 | 3,972,738 | 767,345 | 2,598,054 | 184,559 | 33,684 | 53,610 | 7,082 | 0 | 4,599 | 0 |
| Maine | 1,411,320 | 1,405,520 | 131,533 | 906,200 | 52,984 | 125,184 | 5,800 | 67 | 0 | 0 | 4,735 |
| Maryland | 3,533,711 | 3,403,718 | 719,604 | 1,662,219 | 234,637 | 332,294 | 129,993 | 22,428 | 0 | 33,597 | 30,879 |
| Massachusetts | 6,458,265 | 5,928,258 | 544,139 | 2,952,202 | 598,777 | 937,034 | 530,007 | 8,381 | 7,649 | 5,192 | 355 |
| Michigan | 8,557,047 | 8,186,439 | 1,454,690 | 4,576,871 | 700,877 | 697,651 | 370,608 | 15,783 | 28,069 | 244,118 | 47,721 |
| Minnesota | 3,938,396 | 3,888,082 | 748,058 | 2,223,162 | 149,029 | 314,881 | 50,314 | 6,288 | 11,398 | 15,992 | 9,076 |
| Mississippi | 2,947,073 | 2,816,014 | 513,379 | 1,707,736 | 116,220 | 215,624 | 131,059 | 4,715 | 112,639 | 40 | 2,132 |
| Missouri | 4,246,338 | 4,223,856 | 563,765 | 2,563,928 | 245,605 | 489,196 | 22,482 | 1,445 | 22 | 370 | 15,381 |
| Montana | 1,047,919 | 1,031,504 | 141,765 | 483,802 | 61,643 | 175,858 | 16,415 | 341 | 13,931 | 0 | 1,849 |
| Nebraska | 1,282,063 | 1,261,213 | 211,897 | 700,858 | 74,012 | 141,081 | 20,850 | 3,592 | 3,523 | 2,215 | 8,273 |
| Nevada | 911,731 | 855,933 | 149,051 | 403,522 | 49,505 | 123,967 | 55,798 | 8,390 | 24,402 | 482 | 14,987 |
| New Hampshire | 1,023,619 | 863,748 | 99,298 | 429,305 | 19,639 | 94,817 | 159,871 | 4,337 | 140,591 | 0 | 8,129 |
| New Jersey | 6,391,527 | 6,026,980 | 643,342 | 3,323,133 | 429,898 | 703,907 | 364,547 | 245,955 | 27,944 | 2,097 | 3,493 |
| New Mexico | 1,846,136 | 1,795,753 | 389,777 | 992,266 | 104,986 | 185,172 | 50,383 | 13,160 | 0 | 34,561 | 0 |
| New York | 33,790,935 | 26,121,389 | 2,070,251 | 17,943,041 | 1,209,083 | 1,019,853 | 7,669,546 | 107,772 | 5,814,540 | 8,384 | 6,024 |
| North Carolina | 6,817,303 | 6,280,928 | 876,999 | 3,775,380 | 315,808 | 837,353 | 536,375 | 7,764 | 473,580 | 10,333 | 13,376 |
| North Dakota | 892,685 | 862,504 | 132,217 | 314,154 | 22,091 | 181,698 | 30,181 | 162 | 9,900 | 0 | 15,196 |
| Ohio | 8,953,346 | 8,690,875 | 1,127,020 | 5,489,274 | 460,872 | 707,461 | 262,471 | 32,058 | 25,096 | 23,012 | 46,767 |

# STATE INTERGOVERNMENTAL REVENUE FROM FEDERAL AND LOCAL GOVERNMENTS: 1998 — Continued

| State | Total intergovernmental revenue | From federal government | | | | | From local government | | | | |
|---|---|---|---|---|---|---|---|---|---|---|---|
| | | Total | Education | Public welfare | Health & hospitals | Highways | Total | Education | Public welfare | Health & hospitals | Highways |
| Oklahoma | 2,516,285 | 2,436,190 | 510,993 | 1,348,787 | 91,549 | 253,193 | 80,095 | 20,164 | 1,768 | 475 | 11,297 |
| Oregon | 3,364,556 | 3,322,069 | 625,473 | 1,524,026 | 289,268 | 266,227 | 42,487 | 9,613 | 21,090 | 0 | 10,183 |
| Pennsylvania | 9,608,658 | 9,536,818 | 1,493,796 | 5,751,861 | 512,289 | 755,742 | 71,840 | 41,277 | 0 | 0 | 7,649 |
| Rhode Island | 1,146,311 | 1,064,835 | 113,698 | 705,661 | 50,062 | 84,883 | 81,476 | 84 | 0 | 0 | 64 |
| South Carolina | 3,442,418 | 3,312,207 | 580,226 | 2,020,960 | 187,110 | 253,149 | 130,211 | 32,215 | 55,317 | 3,088 | 0 |
| South Dakota | 764,232 | 752,090 | 98,246 | 295,110 | 27,583 | 170,323 | 12,142 | 0 | 0 | 5,926 | 5,028 |
| Tennessee | 5,264,984 | 5,196,529 | 635,423 | 3,372,807 | 162,243 | 490,054 | 68,455 | 17,239 | 0 | 452 | 20,562 |
| Texas | 14,605,424 | 13,998,299 | 2,796,069 | 7,599,733 | 817,167 | 1,245,525 | 607,125 | 204,067 | 401,557 | 779 | 4 |
| Utah | 1,689,850 | 1,673,260 | 400,929 | 837,138 | 111,206 | 147,230 | 16,590 | 1,932 | 126 | 112 | 8,001 |
| Vermont | 729,547 | 727,304 | 83,821 | 350,562 | 51,005 | 110,888 | 2,243 | 576 | 0 | 0 | 1,667 |
| Virginia | 3,780,977 | 3,622,599 | 746,322 | 1,762,586 | 169,341 | 450,218 | 158,378 | 16,496 | 0 | 42,919 | 46,176 |
| Washington | 4,247,049 | 4,177,517 | 884,273 | 1,945,801 | 534,095 | 346,799 | 69,532 | 34,240 | 0 | 0 | 7,048 |
| West Virginia | 2,096,294 | 2,068,954 | 318,420 | 1,148,225 | 64,454 | 312,673 | 27,340 | 2,093 | 0 | 0 | 0 |
| Wisconsin | 3,794,650 | 3,708,821 | 651,493 | 1,992,748 | 144,648 | 301,063 | 85,829 | 2,245 | 41 | 12,026 | 46,574 |
| Wyoming | 838,599 | 811,943 | 79,628 | 163,545 | 16,398 | 113,101 | 26,656 | 19,565 | 0 | 1,231 | 4,084 |

*Source:* U.S. Department of Commerce, Bureau of the Census.
*Note:* Detail may not add to totals due to rounding.

# Chapter Ten

# STATE PAGES

*Everything you always wanted to know about the states —
includes capitals, population, land areas, historical data,
elected executive branch officials, legislative leaders,
judges of high courts, state mottoes, flowers, songs, birds
and other items unique to the states and other
U.S. jurisdictions.*

For additional information on Chapter Ten contact
The States Information Center, at The Council of State Governments,
(859) 244-8253 or E-mail: sic@csg.org.

## Table 10.1
## OFFICIAL NAMES OF STATES AND JURISDICTIONS, CAPITALS, ZIP CODES AND CENTRAL SWITCHBOARDS

| State or other jurisdiction | Name of state capitol (a) | Capital | Zip code | Area code | Central switchboard |
|---|---|---|---|---|---|
| Alabama, State of | State House | Montgomery | 36130 | 334 | 242-7100 |
| Alaska, State of | State Capitol | Juneau | 99801 | 907 | 465-4648 |
| Arizona, State of | State Capitol | Phoenix | 85007 | 602 | 542-4900 |
| Arkansas, State of | State Capitol | Little Rock | 72201 | 501 | 682-3000 |
| California, State of | State Capitol | Sacramento | 95814 | 916 | 657-9900 |
| Colorado, State of | State Capitol | Denver | 80203 | 303 | 866-5000 |
| Connecticut, State of | State Capitol | Hartford | 06106 | 860 | 240-0100 |
| Delaware, State of | Legislative Hall | Dover | 19903 | 302 | 739-4000 |
| Florida, State of | The Capitol | Tallahassee | 32399 | 850 | 488-4441 |
| Georgia, State of | State Capitol | Atlanta | 30334 | 404 | 656-2000 |
| Hawaii, State of | State Capitol | Honolulu | 96813 | 808 | 587-0221 |
| Idaho, State of | State Capitol | Boise | 83720 | 208 | 332-1000 |
| Illinois, State of | State House | Springfield | 62706 | 217 | 782-2000 |
| Indiana, State of | State House | Indianapolis | 46204 | 317 | 232-1000 |
| Iowa, State of | State Capitol | Des Moines | 50319 | 515 | 281-5011 |
| Kansas, State of | Statehouse | Topeka | 66612 | 785 | 296-0111 |
| Kentucky, Commonwealth of | State Capitol | Frankfort | 40601 | 502 | 564-8100 |
| Louisiana, State of | State Capitol | Baton Rouge | 70804 | 225 | 342-4479 |
| Maine, State of | State House Station | Augusta | 04333 | 207 | 582-9500 |
| Maryland, State of | State House | Annapolis | 21401 | 410 | 946-5400 |
| Massachusetts, Commonwealth of | State House | Boston | 02133 | 617 | 722-2000 |
| Michigan, State of | State Capitol | Lansing | 48909 | 517 | 373-0184 |
| Minnesota, State of | State Capitol | St. Paul | 55155 | 651 | 296-6013 |
| Mississippi, State of | New Capitol | Jackson | 39215 | 601 | 359-3770 |
| Missouri, State of | State Capitol | Jefferson City | 65101 | 573 | 751-2000 |
| Montana, State of | State Capitol | Helena | 59620 | 406 | 444-2511 |
| Nebraska, State of | State Capitol | Lincoln | 68509 | 402 | 471-2311 |
| Nevada, State of | State Capitol | Carson City | 89701 | 775 | 684-5670 |
| New Hampshire, State of | State House | Concord | 03301 | 603 | 271-1110 |
| New Jersey, State of | State House | Trenton | 08625 | 609 | 292-6000 |
| New Mexico, State of | State Capitol | Santa Fe | 87501 | 505 | 956-4600 |
| New York, State of | State Capitol | Albany | 12224 | 518 | 455-2800 |
| North Carolina, State of | State Capitol | Raleigh | 27601 | 919 | 733-4111 |
| North Dakota, State of | State Capitol | Bismarck | 58505 | 701 | 328-2000 |
| Ohio, State of | Statehouse | Columbus | 43215 | 614 | 466-2000 |
| Oklamhoma, State of | State Capitol | Oklahoma City | 73105 | 405 | 521-2011 |
| Oregon, State of | State Capitol | Salem | 97310 | 503 | 986-1848 |
| Pennsylvania, Commonwealth of | Main Capitol Building | Harrisburg | 17120 | 717 | 787-2121 |
| Rhode Island and Providence Plantations, State of | State House | Providence | 02903 | 401 | 277-2653 |
| South Carolina, State of | State House | Columbia | 29211 | 803 | 212-6200 |
| South Dakota, State of | State Capitol | Pierre | 57501 | 605 | 773-3011 |
| Tennessee, State of | State Capitol | Nashville | 37243 | 615 | 741-2001 |
| Texas, State of | State Capitol | Austin | 78701 | 512 | 463-0063 |
| Utah, State of | State Capitol | Salt Lake City | 84114 | 801 | 538-3000 |
| Vermont, State of | State House | Montpelier | 05609 | 802 | 828-1110 |
| Virginia, Commonwealth of | State Capitol | Richmond | 23219 | 804 | 786-0000 |
| Washington, State of | Legislative Building | Olympia | 98504 | 360 | 753-5000 |
| West Virginia, State of | State Capitol | Charleston | 25305 | 304 | 558-3456 |
| Wisconsin, State of | State Capitol | Madison | 53702 | 608 | 266-0382 |
| Wyoming, State of | State Capitol | Cheyenne | 82002 | 307 | 777-7220 |
| District of Columbia | District Building | . . . | 20001 | 202 | 724-8000 |
| American Samoa, Territory of | Maota Fono | Pago Pago | 96799 | 684 | 633-4116 |
| Guam, Territory of | Congress Building | Hagatna | 96910 | 671 | 472-8931 |
| No. Mariana Islands, Commonwealth of | Civic Center Building | Saipan | 96950 | 670 | 664-0992 |
| Puerto Rico, Commonwealth of | The Capitol | San Juan | 00901 | 787 | 724-2030 |
| U.S. Virgin Islands, Territory of | Capitol Building | Charlotte Amalie, St. Thomas | 00801 | 340 | 774-0880 |

(a) In some instances the name is not official.

## Table 10.2
## HISTORICAL DATA ON THE STATES

| State or other jurisdiction | Source of state lands | Date organized as territory | Date admitted to Union | Chronological order of admission to Union |
|---|---|---|---|---|
| Alabama | Mississippi Territory, 1798 (a) | March 3, 1817 | Dec. 14, 1819 | 22 |
| Alaska | Purchased from Russia, 1867 | Aug. 24, 1912 | Jan. 3, 1959 | 49 |
| Arizona | Ceded by Mexico, 1848 (b) | Feb. 24, 1863 | Feb. 14, 1912 | 48 |
| Arkansas | Louisiana Purchase, 1803 | March 2, 1819 | June 15, 1836 | 25 |
| California | Ceded by Mexico, 1848 | (c) | Sept. 9, 1850 | 31 |
| Colorado | Louisiana Purchase, 1803 (d) | Feb. 28, 1861 | Aug. 1, 1876 | 38 |
| Connecticut | Fundamental Orders, Jan. 14, 1638; Royal charter, April 23, 1662 (e) | ... | Jan. 9, 1788 (f) | 5 |
| Delaware | Swedish charter, 1638; English charter, 1638 (e) | ... | Dec. 7, 1787 (f) | 1 |
| Florida | Ceded by Spain, 1819 | March 30, 1822 | March 3, 1845 | 27 |
| Georgia | Charter, 1732, from George II to Trustees for Establishing the Colony of Georgia (e) | ... | Jan. 2, 1788 (f) | 4 |
| Hawaii | Annexed, 1898 | June 14, 1900 | Aug. 21, 1959 | 50 |
| Idaho | Treaty with Britain, 1846 | March 4, 1863 | July 3, 1890 | 43 |
| Illinois | Northwest Territory, 1787 | Feb. 3, 1809 | Dec. 3, 1818 | 21 |
| Indiana | Northwest Territory, 1787 | May 7, 1800 | Dec. 11, 1816 | 19 |
| Iowa | Louisiana Purchase, 1803 | June 12, 1838 | Dec. 28, 1846 | 29 |
| Kansas | Louisiana Purchase, 1803 (d) | May 30, 1854 | Jan. 29, 1861 | 34 |
| Kentucky | Part of Virginia until admitted as state | (c) | June 1, 1792 | 15 |
| Louisiana | Louisiana Purchase, 1803 (g) | March 26, 1804 | April 30, 1812 | 18 |
| Maine | Part of Massachusetts until admitted as state | (c) | March 15, 1820 | 23 |
| Maryland | Charter, 1632, from Charles I to Calvert (e) | ... | April 28, 1788 (f) | 7 |
| Massachusetts | Charter to Massachusetts Bay Company, 1629 (e) | ... | Feb. 6, 1788 (f) | 6 |
| Michigan | Northwest Territory, 1787 | Jan. 11, 1805 | Jan. 26, 1837 | 26 |
| Minnesota | Northwest Territory, 1787 (h) | March 3, 1849 | May 11, 1858 | 32 |
| Mississippi | Mississippi Territory (i) | April 7, 1798 | Dec. 10, 1817 | 20 |
| Missouri | Louisiana Purchase, 1803 | June 4, 1812 | Aug. 10, 1821 | 24 |
| Montana | Louisiana Purchase, 1803 (j) | May 26, 1864 | Nov. 8, 1889 | 41 |
| Nebraska | Louisiana Purchase, 1803 | May 30, 1854 | March 1, 1867 | 37 |
| Nevada | Ceded by Mexico, 1848 | March 2, 1861 | Oct. 31, 1864 | 36 |
| New Hampshire | Grants from Council for New England, 1622 and 1629; made Royal province, 1679 (e) | ... | June 21, 1788 (f) | 9 |
| New Jersey | Dutch settlement, 1618; English charter, 1664 (e) | ... | Dec. 18, 1787 (f) | 3 |
| New Mexico | Ceded by Mexico, 1848 (b) | Sept. 9, 1850 | Jan. 6, 1912 | 47 |
| New York | Dutch settlement, 1623; English control, 1664 (e) | ... | July 26, 1788 (f) | 11 |
| North Carolina | Charter, 1663, from Charles II (e) | ... | Nov. 21, 1789 (f) | 12 |
| North Dakota | Louisiana Purchase, 1803 (k) | March 2, 1861 | Nov. 2, 1889 | 39 |
| Ohio | Northwest Territory, 1787 | May 7, 1800 | March 1, 1803 | 17 |
| Oklahoma | Louisiana Purchase, 1803 | May 2, 1890 | Nov. 16, 1907 | 46 |
| Oregon | Settlement and treaty with Britain, 1846 | Aug. 14, 1848 | Feb. 14, 1859 | 33 |
| Pennsylvania | Grant from Charles II to William Penn, 1681 (e) | ... | Dec. 12, 1787 (f) | 2 |
| Rhode Island | Charter, 1663, from Charles II (e) | ... | May 29, 1790 (f) | 13 |
| South Carolina | Charter, 1663, from Charles II (e) | ... | May 23, 1788 (f) | 8 |
| South Dakota | Louisiana Purchase, 1803 | March 2, 1861 | Nov. 2, 1889 | 40 |
| Tennessee | Part of North Carolina until land ceded to U.S. in 1789 | June 8, 1790 (l) | June 1, 1796 | 16 |
| Texas | Republic of Texas, 1845 | (c) | Dec. 29, 1845 | 28 |
| Utah | Ceded by Mexico, 1848 | Sept. 9, 1850 | Jan. 4, 1896 | 45 |
| Vermont | From lands of New Hampshire and New York | (c) | March 4, 1791 | 14 |
| Virginia | Charter, 1609, from James I to London Company (e) | ... | June 25, 1788 (f) | 10 |
| Washington | Oregon Territory, 1848 | March 2, 1853 | Nov. 11, 1889 | 42 |
| West Virginia | Part of Virginia until admitted as state | (c) | June 20, 1863 | 35 |
| Wisconsin | Northwest Territory, 1787 | April 20, 1836 | May 29, 1848 | 30 |
| Wyoming | Louisiana Purchase, 1803 (d,j) | July 25, 1868 | July 10, 1890 | 44 |
| Dist. of Columbia | Maryland (m) | ... | ... | ... |
| American Samoa | ----------------------------------------------Became a territory, 1900---------------------------------------------- | | | |
| Guam | Ceded by Spain, 1898 | Aug. 1, 1950 | ... | ... |
| No. Mariana Islands | ... | 24-Mar-76 | ... | ... |
| Puerto Rico | Ceded by Spain, 1898 | ... | July 25, 1952 (n) | ... |
| Republic of Palau | ... | Jan. 1, 1981 | ... | ... |
| U.S. Virgin Islands | --------------------------------------------Purchased from Denmark, March 31, 1917---------------------------------------- | | | |

# HISTORICAL DATA — Continued

(a) By the Treaty of Paris, 1783, England gave up claim to the 13 original Colonies, and to all land within an area extending along the present Canadian border to the Lake of the Woods, down the Mississippi River to the 31st parallel, east to the Chattahoochee, down that river to the mouth of the Flint, east to the source of the St. Mary's down that river to the ocean. The major part of Alabama was acquired by the Treaty of Paris, and the lower portion from Spain in 1813.

(b) Portion of land obtained by Gadsden Purchase, 1853.

(c) No territorial status before admission to Union.

(d) Portion of land ceded by Mexico, 1848.

(e) One of the original 13 Colonies.

(f) Date of ratification of U.S. Constitution.

(g) West Feliciana District (Baton Rouge) acquired from Spain, 1810; added to Louisiana, 1812.

(h) Portion of land obtained by Louisiana Purchase, 1803.

(i) See footnote (a). The lower portion of Mississippi also was acquired from Spain in 1813.

(j) Portion of land obtained from Oregon Territory, 1848.

(k) The northern portion of the Red River Valley was acquired by treaty with Great Britain in 1818.

(l) Date Southwest Territory (identical boundary as Tennessee's) was created.

(m) Area was originally 100 square miles, taken from Virginia and Maryland. Virginia's portion south of the Potomac was given back to that state in 1846. Site chosen in 1790, city incorporated 1802.

(n) On this date, Puerto Rico became a self-governing commonwealth by compact approved by the U.S. Congress and the voters of Puerto Rico as provided in U.S. Public Law 600 of 1950.

## Table 10.3
## STATE STATISTICS

| State or other jurisdiction | Land area — In square miles | Land area — Rank in nation | Population — Size | Population — Rank in nation | Percentage change 1990 to 1998 | Density per square mile | No. of Representatives in Congress | Capital | Population | Rank in state | Largest city | Population |
|---|---|---|---|---|---|---|---|---|---|---|---|---|
| Alabama | 50,750 | 28 | 4,369,862 | 23 | 8.2 | 85.8 | 7 | Montgomery | 197,014 | 3 | Birmingham | 252,997 |
| Alaska | 570,374 | 1 | 619,500 | 48 | 12.6 | 1.1 | 1 | Juneau | 30,191 | 3 | Anchorage | 254,982 |
| Arizona | 113,642 | 6 | 4,778,332 | 20 | 30.4 | 41.1 | 6 | Phoenix | 1,198,064 | 1 | Phoenix | 1,198,064 |
| Arkansas | 52,075 | 27 | 2,551,373 | 33 | 8.5 | 48.7 | 4 | Little Rock | 175,303 | 1 | Little Rock | 175,303 |
| California | 155,973 | 3 | 33,145,121 | 1 | 11.2 | 209.4 | 52 | Sacramento | 404,168 | 6 | Los Angeles | 3,597,556 |
| Colorado | 103,729 | 8 | 4,056,133 | 24 | 23.1 | 38.3 | 6 | Denver | 499,055 | 1 | Denver | 499,055 |
| Connecticut | 4,845 | 48 | 3,282,031 | 29 | -0.2 | 675.8 | 6 | Hartford | 131,523 | 2 | Bridgeport | 137,425 |
| Delaware | 1,955 | 49 | 753,538 | 45 | 13.1 | 276.2 | 1 | Dover | 30,369 | 2 | Wilmington | 71,678 |
| Florida | 53,997 | 26 | 15,111,244 | 4 | 16.8 | 131.9 | 23 | Tallahassee | 136,628 | 8 | Jacksonville | 693,630 |
| Georgia | 57,919 | 21 | 7,788,240 | 10 | 20.2 | 185.7 | 11 | Atlanta | 403,819 | 1 | Atlanta | 403,819 |
| Hawaii | 6423 | 47 | 1,185,497 | 42 | 7.0 | 185.7 | 2 | Honolulu | 377,059 | 1 | Honolulu | 377,059 |
| Idaho | 82,751 | 11 | 1,251,700 | 45 | 24.3 | 14.8 | 2 | Boise | 157,452 | 1 | Boise | 157,452 |
| Illinois | 55,593 | 24 | 12,128,370 | 5 | 6.1 | 216.7 | 20 | Springfield | 117,098 | 4 | Chicago | 2,802,079 |
| Indiana | 35,870 | 38 | 5,942,901 | 14 | 7.2 | 164.5 | 10 | Indianapolis | 741,304 | 1 | Indianapolis | 741,304 |
| Iowa | 55,875 | 23 | 2,869,413 | 30 | 3.3 | 51.2 | 5 | Des Moines | 191,293 | 1 | Des Moines | 191,293 |
| Kansas | 81,823 | 13 | 2,654,052 | 32 | 7.1 | 32.1 | 4 | Topeka | 118,977 | 4 | Wichita | 329,211 |
| Kentucky | 39,732 | 36 | 3,960,825 | 25 | 7.4 | 99.1 | 6 | Frankfort | 26,418 | 9 | Louisville | 255,045 |
| Louisiana | 43,566 | 33 | 4,372,035 | 22 | 3.6 | 100.3 | 7 | Baton Rouge | 211,551 | 2 | New Orleans | 465,538 |
| Maine | 30,865 | 39 | 1,253,040 | 39 | 2.0 | 40.3 | 2 | Augusta | 19,978 | 7 | Portland | 62,786 |
| Maryland | 9,775 | 42 | 5,171,634 | 19 | 8.2 | 525.3 | 8 | Annapolis | 33,585 | 22 | Baltimore | 645,593 |
| Massachusetts | 7,838 | 45 | 6,175,164 | 13 | 2.6 | 784.3 | 10 | Boston | 555,447 | 1 | Boston | 555,447 |
| Michigan | 56,809 | 22 | 9,863,775 | 8 | 6.1 | 172.8 | 16 | Lansing | 127,825 | 5 | Detroit | 970,196 |
| Minnesota | 79,617 | 14 | 4,775,508 | 21 | 9.1 | 59.4 | 8 | St. Paul | 257,284 | 2 | Minneapolis | 351,731 |
| Mississippi | 46,914 | 31 | 2,768,619 | 31 | 7.5 | 58.7 | 5 | Jackson | 188,419 | 1 | Jackson | 188,419 |
| Missouri | 68,898 | 18 | 5,468,338 | 17 | 6.9 | 78.9 | 9 | Jefferson City | 34,911 | 14 | Kansas City | 441,574 |
| Montana | 145,556 | 4 | 882,779 | 44 | 10.5 | 6.0 | 1 | Helena | 28,306 | 6 | Billings | 91,750 |
| Nebraska | 76,878 | 15 | 1,666,028 | 38 | 5.6 | 21.6 | 3 | Lincoln | 213,088 | 2 | Omaha | 371,291 |
| Nevada | 109,806 | 7 | 1,809,253 | 35 | 50.6 | 15.9 | 2 | Carson City | 49,301 | 6 | Las Vegas | 404,288 |
| New Hampshire | 8,969 | 44 | 1,201,134 | 41 | 8.3 | 132.1 | 2 | Concord | 37,444 | 3 | Manchester | 102,524 |
| New Jersey | 7,419 | 46 | 8,143,412 | 9 | 5.1 | 1,093.8 | 13 | Trenton | 84,494 | 5 | Newark | 267,823 |
| New Mexico | 121,365 | 5 | 1,739,844 | 37 | 14.8 | 14.3 | 3 | Santa Fe | 67,879 | 3 | Albuquerque | 419,311 |
| New York | 47,224 | 30 | 18,196,601 | 3 | 1.1 | 384.9 | 31 | Albany | 94,305 | 6 | New York City | 7,420,166 |
| North Carolina | 48,718 | 29 | 7,650,789 | 11 | 15.4 | 154.9 | 12 | Raleigh | 259,423 | 2 | Charlotte | 504,637 |
| North Dakota | 68,994 | 17 | 633,666 | 47 | -0.8 | 9.3 | 1 | Bismarck | 54,040 | 3 | Fargo | 86,718 |
| Ohio | 40,953 | 35 | 11,256,654 | 7 | 3.8 | 273.7 | 19 | Columbus | 670,234 | 1 | Columbus | 670,234 |
| Oklahoma | 68,679 | 19 | 3,358,044 | 27 | 6.8 | 48.7 | 6 | Oklahoma City | 472,221 | 1 | Oklahoma City | 472,221 |
| Oregon | 96,003 | 10 | 3,316,154 | 28 | 16.7 | 34.2 | 5 | Salem | 126,702 | 3 | Portland | 503,891 |
| Pennsylvania | 44,820 | 32 | 11,994,016 | 6 | 0.9 | 267.8 | 21 | Harrisburg | 49,502 | 9 | Philadelphia | 1,436,287 |
| Rhode Island | 1,045 | 50 | 990,819 | 43 | -1.3 | 945.9 | 2 | Providence | 150,890 | 1 | Providence | 150,890 |
| South Carolina | 30,111 | 40 | 3,885,736 | 26 | 11.5 | 127.4 | 6 | Columbia | 110,840 | 1 | Columbia | 110,840 |

# STATE STATISTICS — Continued

| State or other jurisdiction | Land area In square miles | Land area Rank in nation | Population Size | Population Rank in nation | Percentage change 1990 to 1998 | Density per square mile | No. of Representatives in Congress | Capital | Population | Rank in state | Largest city | Population |
|---|---|---|---|---|---|---|---|---|---|---|---|---|
| South Dakota | 75,896 | 16 | 733,133 | 46 | 5.3 | 9.7 | 1 | Pierre | 12,906 | 7 | Sioux Falls | 116,762 |
| Tennessee | 41,220 | 34 | 5,483,535 | 16 | 12.4 | 131.7 | 9 | Nashville | 488,374 | 2 | Memphis | 603,507 |
| Texas | 261,914 | 2 | 20,044,141 | 2 | 18.0 | 75.4 | 30 | Austin | 465,622 | 5 | Houston | 1,786,691 |
| Utah | 82,168 | 12 | 2,129,836 | 34 | 23.6 | 25.6 | 3 | Salt Lake City | 159,936 | 1 | Salt Lake City | 174,348 |
| Vermont | 9,249 | 43 | 593,740 | 49 | 5.5 | 63.9 | 1 | Montpelier | 8,247 | 6 | Burlington | 38,453 |
| Virginia | 39,598 | 37 | 6,872,912 | 12 | 11.0 | 171.5 | 11 | Richmond | 203,056 | 3 | Virginia Beach | 432,380 |
| Washington | 66,581 | 20 | 5,756,361 | 15 | 18.3 | 85.4 | 9 | Olympia | 33,840 | 18 | Seattle | 536,978 |
| West Virginia | 24,087 | 41 | 1,806,920 | 36 | 0.7 | 75.2 | 3 | Charleston | 57,287 | 1 | Charleston | 55,056 |
| Wisconsin | 54,314 | 25 | 5,250,446 | 18 | 7.3 | 96.2 | 9 | Madison | 191,262 | 2 | Milwaukee | 578,364 |
| Wyoming | 97,105 | 9 | 479,602 | 51 | 5.7 | 5.0 | 1 | Cheyenne | 50,008 | 1 | Cheyenne | 53,640 |
| Dist. of Columbia | 61 | 50 | 523,124 | 50 | -14.5 | 8,575.8 | 1 (a) | … | … | … | … | … |
| American Samoa | 77 | … | 61,819 | … | 42.0 | 802.8 | 1 (a) | Pago Pago | 3,519 | 3 | Tafuna | 5,174 |
| Guam | 210 | … | 160,595 | … | 17.0 | 764.7 | 1 (a) | Hagatna | 1,139 | 18 | Dededo | 31,728 |
| No. Mariana Islands | 179 | … | 53,552 | … | 19.0 | 299.2 | … | Saipan | 38,896 | 1 | Saipan | 38,896 |
| Puerto Rico | 3,339 | … | 3,828,506 | … | 8.0 | 1,146.6 | 1 (a) | San Juan | 426,832 | 1 | San Juan | 426,832 |
| Republic of Palau | 177 | … | 18,827 | … | 20.1 | 106.4 | … | Koror | 9,000 | 1 | Koror | 9,000 |
| U.S. Virgin Islands | 134 | … | 97,240 | … | -4.6 | 725.7 | 1 (a) | Charlotte Amalie, St. Thomas | 12,331 | 1 | Charlotte Amalie, St. Thomas | 12,331 |

Source: U.S. Department of Commerce, Bureau of the Census. (1998 Estimated.)

Key:

… — Not applicable

(a) Delegate with privileges to vote in committees and the Committee of the Whole.

# Alabama

Nickname ................................................................. The Heart of Dixie
Motto ......................................... *Aldemus Jura Nostra Defendere*
(We Dare Defend Our Rights)
Horse ...................................................................... Racking Horse
Flower ................................................................................. Camellia
Bird Yellowhammer
Tree Southern (Longleaf) Pine
Song ......................................................................... *Alabama*
Insect ..................................................... Monarch Butterfly
Rock ........................................................................... Marble
Entered the Union ................................... December 14, 1819
Capital ................................................................ Montgomery

## EXECUTIVE BRANCH OFFICIALS

Governor ......................................................... Don Siegelman
Lieutenant Governor ..................................... Steve Windom
Secretary of State ................................................ Jim Bennett
Attorney General ................................................. Bill Pryor
Treasurer ...................................................... Lucy Baxley

## SUPREME COURT

Perry O. Hooper, Sr., Chief Justice
Hugh Maddox
Jean Brown
John England
Douglas Johnstone
Gorman Houston
Champ Lyons
Ralph D. Cook
Harold See

## LEGISLATURE

President of the Senate ...................... Lt. Gov. Steve Windom
President Pro Tem of the Senate .............. Lowell Ray Barron
Secretary of the Senate .................................. McDowell Lee

Speaker of the House .................................... Seth Hammett
Speaker Pro Tem of the House ........................ Demetrius C. Newton
Clerk of the House ................................... William G. Pappas

## STATISTICS

Land Area (square miles) ................................ 50,750
    Rank in Nation ............................................. 28th
Population ........................................................ 4,369862
    Rank in Nation ............................................. 23rd
    Density per square mile ........................... 79.62
Number of Representatives in Congress ................ 7
Capital City ................................................... Montgomery
    Population ............................................. 197,014
    Rank in State ............................................... 3rd
Largest City .................................................. Birmingham
    Population ............................................. 252,997
Number of Places over 10,000 Population .......... 50

# Alaska

Motto ................................................ *North to the Future*
Flower .......................................................... Forget-Me-Not
Marine Mammal ............................................ Bowhead Whale
Bird ....................................................... Willow Ptarmigan
Tree ............................................................... Sitka Spruce
Song ........................................................ *Alaska's Flag*
Fish ........................................................... King Salmon
Fossil .................................................... Wooly Mammoth
Sport ...................................................... Dog Mushing
Gem ........................................................................ Jade
Mineral .................................................................. Gold
Purchased from Russia by the
United States .................................... March 30, 1867
Entered the Union ................................. January 3, 1959
Capital ............................................................. Juneau

## EXECUTIVE BRANCH OFFICIALS

Governor ............................................................ Tony Knowles
Lieutenant Governor ..................................... Fran Ulmer
Attorney General ........................................ Bruce M. Botelho
Treasurer ..................................................... Ross Kinney

## SUPREME COURT

Warren W. Matthews, Chief Justice
Alexander O. Bryner
Walter Carpeneti
Robert L. Eastaugh
Dana Fabe

## LEGISLATURE

President of the Senate ............................... Drue Pearce
Secretary of the Senate ............................... Heidi Vogel

Speaker of the House ................................... Brian Porter
Chief Clerk of the House ........................... Suzanne Lowell

## STATISTICS

Land Area (square miles) ......................... 570,750
    Rank in Nation ............................................. 1st
Population ........................................................ 619,500
    Rank in Nation ............................................. 48th
    Density per square mile ........................... 1.1
Number of Representatives in Congress ................ 1
Capital City ......................................................... Juneau
    Population ............................................. 30,191
    Rank in State ............................................... 3rd
Largest City ................................................. Anchorage
    Population ............................................. 254,997
Number of Places over 10,000 Population .......... 4

# Arizona

Nickname ......................................................... The Grand Canyon State
Motto ............................................................. *Ditat Deus (God Enriches)*
Flower ................................................. Blossom of the Saguaro Cactus
Bird ................................................................................. Cactus Wren
Tree ................................................................................... Palo Verde
Songs .................................................. *Arizona March Song and Arizona*
Gemstone ............................................................................. Turquoise
Official Neckwear ................................................................. Bola Tie
Entered the Union ....................................... February 14, 1912
Capital ................................................................................. Phoenix

## EXECUTIVE BRANCH OFFICIALS

Governor .................................................................... Jane Dee Hull
Secretary of State ......................................................... Betsey Bayless
Attorney General ....................................................... Janet Napolitano
Treasurer .......................................................................... Carol Springer

## SUPREME COURT

Thomas A. Zlaket, Chief Justice
Stanley Feldman
Frederick J. Martone
Charles E. Jones
Ruth McGregor

## LEGISLATURE

President of the Senate ..................................................... Brenda Burns
President Pro Tem of the Senate ......................................... John Wettaw
Secretary of the Senate ......................................... Charmion Billington

Speaker of the House ........................................................ Jeff Groscost
Speaker Pro Tem of the House ................................................. Joe Hart
Chief Clerk of the House .......................................... Norman L. Moore

## STATISTICS

Land Area (square miles) ........................................... 113,642
    Rank in Nation ................................................................. 6th
Population .......................................................... 4,778,332
    Rank in Nation ................................................................ 20th
    Density per square mile ........................................... 30.4
Number Representatives in Congress .................................... 6
Capital City ....................................................................... Phoenix
    Population ......................................................... 1,198,064
    Rank in State ................................................................... 1st
Largest City ...................................................................... Phoenix
Number of Places over 10,000 Population ......................... 28

# Arkansas

Nickname .................................................................... The Natural State
Motto ............................................... *Regnat Populus (The People Rule)*
Flower ........................................................................ Apple Blossom
Bird ............................................................................... Mockingbird
Tree ........................................................................................... Pine
Song ................................................................................. *Arkansas*
Gem .................................................................................... Diamond
Entered the Union .......................................... June 15, 1836
Capital ........................................................................... Little Rock

## EXECUTIVE BRANCH OFFICIALS

Governor ................................................................ Mike Huckabee
Lieutenant Governor .......................................... Winthrop Rockefeller
Secretary of State ....................................................... Sharon Priest
Attorney General .............................................................. Mark Pryor
Treasurer ................................................... Jimmie Lou Fisher

## SUPREME COURT

W. H. Arnold, Chief Justice
Thomas A. Glaze
Donald L. Corbin
Robert L. Brown
Annabell Clinton Imber
Ray Thornton
Lavenski Smith

## GENERAL ASSEMBLY

President of the Senate ........................... Lt. Gov. Winthrop Rockefeller
President Pro Tem of the Senate ........................................ Jay Bradford
Secretary of the Senate ..................................................... Ann Cornwell

Speaker of the House ........................................................ Bob Johnson
Speaker Pro Tem of the House ................................... Douglas C. Kidd
Chief Clerk of the House ................................................... Jo Renshaw

## STATISTICS

Land Area (square miles) ................................................ 52,075
    Rank in Nation ................................................................ 27th
Population .......................................................... 2,551,373
    Rank in Nation ................................................................ 33rd
    Density per square mile ........................................... 48.7
Number of Representatives in Congress ............................... 4
Capital City ..................................................................... Little Rock
    Population ............................................................. 175,303
    Rank in State ................................................................... 1st
Largest City ..................................................................... Little Rock
Number of Places over 10,000 Population ......................... 27

# California

| | |
|---|---|
| Nickname | The Golden State |
| Motto | *Eureka* (I Have Found It) |
| Animal | Grizzly Bear |
| Flower | Golden Poppy |
| Bird | California Valley Quail |
| Tree | California Redwood |
| Song | *I Love You, California* |
| Fossil | Saber-Toothed Cat |
| Marine Mammal | California Gray Whale |
| Entered the Union | September 9, 1850 |
| Capital | Sacramento |

## EXECUTIVE BRANCH OFFICIALS

| | |
|---|---|
| Governor | Gray Davis |
| Lieutenant Governor | Cruz M. Bustamante |
| Secretary of State | Bill Jones |
| Attorney General | Bill Lockyer |
| Treasurer | Philip N. Angelides |

## SUPREME COURT

Ronald M. George, Chief Justice
Stanley Mosk
Joyce L. Kennard
Marvin R. Baxter
Katherine M. Werdegar
Ming W. Chin
Janice Rogers Brown

## LEGISLATURE

| | |
|---|---|
| President of the Senate | Lt. Gov. Cruz Bustamante |
| President Pro Tem of the Senate | John L. Burton |
| Secretary of the Senate | Gregory Schmidt |
| | |
| Speaker of the Assembly | Robert M. Hertzberg |
| Speaker Pro Tem of the Assembly | Fred Keeley |
| Chief Clerk of the Assembly | E. Dotson Wilson |

## STATISTICS

| | |
|---|---|
| Land Area (square miles) | 155,973 |
|     Rank in Nation | 3rd |
| Population | 33,145,121 |
|     Rank in Nation | 1st |
|     Density per Square Mile | 209.4 |
| Number of Representatives in Congress | 52 |
| Capital City | Sacramento |
|     Population | 404,168 |
|     Rank in State | 7th |
| Largest City | Los Angeles |
|     Population | 3,597,556 |
| Number of Places over 10,000 Population | 383 |

# Colorado

| | |
|---|---|
| Nickname | The Centennial State |
| Motto | *Nil Sine Numine* (Nothing Without Providence) |
| Flower | Columbine |
| Bird | Lark Bunting |
| Tree | Blue Spruce |
| Song | *Where the Columbines Grow* |
| Fossil | Stegosaurus |
| Gemstone | Aquamarine |
| Animal | Bighorn Sheep |
| Entered the Union | August 1, 1876 |
| Capital City | Denver |

## EXECUTIVE BRANCH OFFICIALS

| | |
|---|---|
| Governor | Bill Owens |
| Lieutenant Governor | Joe Rogers |
| Secretary of State | Donetta L. Davidson |
| Attorney General | Ken Salazar |
| Treasurer | Mike Coffman |

## SUPREME COURT

Mary J. Mullarkey, Chief Justice
Gregory K. Scott
Rebecca L. Kourlis
Gregory J. Hobbs Jr.
Alex J. Martinez
Michael L. Bender
Nancy E. Rice

## GENERAL ASSEMBLY

| | |
|---|---|
| President of the Senate | Ray Powers |
| President Pro Tem of the Senate | Doug Lamborn |
| Secretary of the Senate | Patricia K. Dicks |
| | |
| Speaker of the House | Russell George |
| Speaker Pro Tem of the House | William G. Kaufman |
| Chief Clerk of the House | Judith Rodrigue |

## STATISTICS

| | |
|---|---|
| Land Area (square miles) | 103,729 |
|     Rank in Nation | 8th |
| Population | 4,056,133 |
|     Rank in Nation | 24th |
|     Density per square mile | 38.3 |
| Number of Representatives in Congress | 6 |
| Capital City | Denver |
|     Population | 499,055 |
|     Rank in State | 1st |
| Largest City | Denver |
| Number of Places over 10,000 Population | 39 |

# Connecticut

| | |
|---|---|
| Nickname | The Constitution State |
| Motto | *Qui Transtulit Sustinet* |
| | (He Who Transplanted Still Sustains) |
| Animal | Sperm Whale |
| Flower | Mountain Laurel |
| Bird | American Robin |
| Tree | White Oak |
| Song | *Yankee Doodle* |
| Mineral | Garnet |
| Insect | European "Praying" Mantis |
| Entered the Union | January 9, 1788 |
| Capital | Hartford |

## EXECUTIVE BRANCH OFFICIALS

| | |
|---|---|
| Governor | John G. Rowland |
| Lieutenant Governor | M. Jodi Rell |
| Secretary of State | Susan Bysiewicz |
| Attorney General | Richard Blumenthal |
| Treasurer | Denise L. Nappier |

## SUPREME COURT

Francis M. McDonald Jr., Chief Justice
David M. Borden
Robert I. Berdon
Flemming L. Norcott Jr.
Joette Katz
Richard N. Palmer
William J. Sullivan

## GENERAL ASSEMBLY

| | |
|---|---|
| President of the Senate | Lt. Gov. M. Jodi Rell |
| President Pro Tem of the Senate | Kevin B. Sullivan |
| Clerk of the Senate | Thomas P. Sheridan |
| | |
| Speaker of the House | Moira K. Lyons |
| Speaker Pro Tem of the House | Joan V. Hartley |
| Clerk of the House | Garey E. Coleman |

## STATISTICS

| | |
|---|---|
| Land Area (square miles) | 4,845 |
| Rank in Nation | 48th |
| Population | 3,282,031 |
| Rank in Nation | 29th |
| Density per square mile | 675.8 |
| Number of Representatives in Congress | 6 |
| Capital City | Hartford |
| Population | 131,523 |
| Rank in State | 2nd |
| Largest City | Bridgeport |
| Population | 137,425 |
| Number of Places over 10,000 Population | 37 |

# Delaware

| | |
|---|---|
| Nickname | The First State |
| Motto | *Liberty and Independence* |
| Flower | Peach Blossom |
| Bird | Blue Hen Chicken |
| Tree | American Holly |
| Song | *Our Delaware* |
| Fish | Sea Trout |
| Entered the Union | December 7, 1787 |
| Capital | Dover |

## EXECUTIVE BRANCH OFFICIALS

| | |
|---|---|
| Governor | Thomas R. Carper |
| Lieutenant Governor | Ruth Ann Minner |
| Secretary of State | Edward J. Freel |
| Attorney General | M. Jane Brady |
| Treasurer | Jack A. Martell |

## SUPREME COURT

E. Norman Veasey, Chief Justice
Joseph T. Walsh
Randy J. Holland
Maurice A. Hartnett III
Carolyn Berger

## GENERAL ASSEMBLY

| | |
|---|---|
| President of the Senate | Lt. Gov. Ruth Ann Minner |
| President Pro Tem of the Senate | Thomas B. Sharp |
| Secretary of the Senate | Bernard J. Brady |
| | |
| Speaker of the House | Terry R. Spence |
| Speaker Pro Tem of the House | William A. Oberle Jr. |
| Clerk of the House | JoAnn M. Hedrick |

## STATISTICS

| | |
|---|---|
| Land Area (square miles) | 1,955 |
| Rank in Nation | 45th |
| Population | 753,538 |
| Rank in Nation | 45th |
| Density per square mile | 380.4 |
| Number of Representatives in Congress | 1 |
| Capital City | Dover |
| Population | 30,369 |
| Rank in State | 2nd |
| Largest City | Wilmington |
| Population | 71,678 |
| Number of Places over 10,000 Population | 5 |

# Florida

| | |
|---|---|
| Nickname | The Sunshine State |
| Motto | *In God We Trust* |
| Animal | Florida Panther |
| Flower | Orange Blossom |
| Bird | Mockingbird |
| Tree | Sabal Palmetto Palm |
| Song | *The Swannee River (Old Folks at Home)* |
| Marine Mammal | Manatee |
| Saltwater Mammal | Porpoise |
| Gem | Moonstone |
| Shell | Horse Conch |
| Entered the Union | March 3, 1845 |
| Capital | Tallahassee |

## EXECUTIVE BRANCH OFFICIALS

| | |
|---|---|
| Governor | Jeb Bush |
| Lieutenant Governor | Frank T. Bogan |
| Secretary of State | Katherine Harris |
| Attorney General | Robert A. Butterworth |
| Treasurer/Insurance Commr. | C. William Nelson |

## SUPREME COURT

Major B. Harding, Chief Justice
Leander J. Shaw
Charles T. Wells
Harry Lee Anstead
Barbara J. Pariente
R. Fred Lewis
Peggy A. Quince

## LEGISLATURE

| | |
|---|---|
| President of the Senate | Toni Jennings |
| President Pro Tem of the Senate | William G. Meyers |
| Secretary of the Senate | Faye W. Blanton |
| | |
| Speaker of the House | John Thrasher |
| Speaker Pro Tem of the House | Dennis L. Jones |
| Clerk of the House | John B. Phelps |

## STATISTICS

| | |
|---|---|
| Land Area (square miles) | 53,997 |
| Rank in Nation | 26th |
| Population | 15,111,244 |
| Rank in Nation | 4th |
| Density per square mile | 276.2 |
| Number of Representatives in Congress | 23 |
| Capital City | Tallahassee |
| Population | 136,628 |
| Rank in State | 8th |
| Largest City | Jacksonville |
| Population | 693,630 |
| Number of Places over 10,000 Population | 216 |

# Georgia

| | |
|---|---|
| Nickname | The Empire State of the South |
| Motto | *Wisdom, Justice and Moderation* |
| Flower | Cherokee Rose |
| Bird | Brown Thrasher |
| Tree | Live Oak |
| Song | *Georgia on My Mind* |
| Butterfly | Tiger Swallowtail |
| Insect | Honeybee |
| Fish | Largemouth Bass |
| Entered the Union | January 2, 1788 |
| Capital | Atlanta |

## EXECUTIVE BRANCH OFFICIALS

| | |
|---|---|
| Governor | Roy E. Barnes |
| Lieutenant Governor | Mark Taylor |
| Secretary of State | Cathy Cox |
| Attorney General | Thurbert E. Baker |
| Treasurer | W. Daniel Ebersole |

## SUPREME COURT

Robert Benham, Chief Justice
Norman S. Fletcher
Leah J. Sears
Carol W. Hunstein
George H. Carley
Hugh P. Thompson
P. Harris Hines

## GENERAL ASSEMBLY

| | |
|---|---|
| President of the Senate | Lt. Gov. Mark Taylor |
| President Pro Tem of the Senate | Terrell Starr |
| Secretary of the Senate | Frank Eldridge Jr. |
| | |
| Speaker of the House | Thomas B. Murphy |
| Speaker Pro Tem of the House | Jack Connell |
| Clerk of the House | Robert E. Rivers Jr. |

## STATISTICS

| | |
|---|---|
| Land Area (square miles) | 57,919 |
| Rank in Nation | 21st |
| Population | 7,788,240 |
| Rank in Nation | 10th |
| Density per square mile | 131.9 |
| Number of Representatives in Congress | 11 |
| Capital City | Atlanta |
| Population | 403,819 |
| Rank in State | 1st |
| Largest City | Atlanta |
| Number of Places over 10,000 Population | 66 |

# Hawaii

Nickname ................................................................ The Aloha State
Motto ........................................... *Ua Mau Ke Ea O Ka Aina I Ka Pono*
(The Life of the Land Is Perpetuated in Righteousness)
Flower ....................................................... Native Yellow Hibiscus
Bird ................................................................ Hawaiian Goose (Nene)
Tree .............................................................. *Kukue Tree (Candlenut)*
Song .......................................................................... *Hawaii Ponoi*
Entered the Union .......................................... August 21, 1959
Capital ...................................................................... Honolulu

## EXECUTIVE BRANCH OFFICIALS

Governor ........................................... Benjamin J. Cayetano
Lieutenant Governor ........................................ Mazie Hirono
Attorney General ................................................. Earl I. Anzai
Treasurer ...................................................... Neal Miyahira

## SUPREME COURT

Ronald T.Y. Moon, Chief Justice
Robert G. Klein
Steven H. Levinson
Paula A. Nakayama
Mario R. Ramil

## LEGISLATURE

President of the Senate ............................... Norman Mizuguchi
Vice President of the Senate ........................ Avery Chumbley
Chief Clerk of the Senate ........................ Paul T. Kawaguchi

Speaker of the House .................................... Calvin K.Y. Say
Vice Speaker of the House .......................... Marcus R. Oshiro
Chief Clerk of the House ............................... Patricia A. Mau-Shimizu

## STATISTICS

Land Area (square miles) ................................................. 6,423
    Rank in Nation ....................................................... 47th
Population ............................................................ 1,185,497
    Rank in Nation ....................................................... 42nd
    Density per square mile ....................................... 185.7
Number of Representatives in Congress .......................... 2
Capital City ......................................................... Honolulu
    Population ......................................................... 377,059
    Rank in State ........................................................... 1st
Largest City ......................................................... Honolulu
Number of Places over 10,000 Population ......................... 17

# Idaho

Nickname ........................................................ The Gem State
Motto ............................................... *Esto Perpetua* (Let It Be Perpetual)
Flower ................................................................... Syringa
Bird ...................................................... Mountain Bluebird
Tree ............................................................ Western White Pine
Song .......................................................... *Here We Have Idaho*
Horse .................................................................. Appaloosa
Gemstone ................................................... Idaho Start Garnett
Entered the Union ................................................. July 3, 1890
Capital .......................................................................... Boise

## EXECUTIVE BRANCH OFFICIALS

Governor ............................................... Dirk Kempthorne
Lieutenant Governor ................................... C.L. Butch Otter
Secretary of State ................................... Pete T. Cenarrusa
Attorney General .................................... Alan G. Lance
Treasurer ........................................................ Ron G. Crane

## SUPREME COURT

Linda Copple Trout, Chief Justice
Wayne L. Kidwell
Cathy R. Silak
Gerald F. Schroeder
Jesse R. Walters

## LEGISLATURE

President of the Senate ............................... Lt. Gov. C.L. Otter
President Pro Tem of the Senate ................................. Robert L. Geddes
Secretary of the Senate ................................... Jeannine Wood

Speaker of the House .................................... Bruce Newcomb
Chief Clerk of the House ................................... Pamm Juker

## STATISTICS

Land Area (square miles) ............................................. 82,751
    Rank in Nation ....................................................... 11th
Population ............................................................ 1,251,700
    Rank in Nation ....................................................... 40th
Density per square mile ............................................... 14.8
Number of Representatives in Congress .......................... 2
Capital City .......................................................... Boise
    Population ......................................................... 157,452
    Rank in State ........................................................... 1st
Largest City .......................................................... Boise
Number of Places over 10,000 Population ......................... 10

# Illinois

| | |
|---|---|
| Nickname | The Prairie State |
| Motto | *State Sovereignty-National Union* |
| Animal | White-tailed Deer |
| Flower | Native Violet |
| Bird | Cardinal |
| Tree | White Oak |
| Song | *Illinois* |
| Mineral | Fluorite |
| Fish | Bluegill |
| Entered the Union | December 3, 1818 |
| Capital | Springfield |

## EXECUTIVE BRANCH OFFICIALS

| | |
|---|---|
| Governor | George H. Ryan, Sr. |
| Lieutenant Governor | Corinne G. Wood |
| Secretary of State | Jesse White |
| Attorney General | Jim Ryan |
| Treasurer | Judy Baar Topinka |

## SUPREME COURT

Moses W. Harrison, II, Chief Justice
Benjamin Miller
Michael A. Bilandic
James D. Heiple
Mary Ann G. McMorrow
John L. Nickels
Charles E. Feeman
S. Louis Rathje

## GENERAL ASSEMBLY

| | |
|---|---|
| President of the Senate | James Philip |
| Secretary of the Senate | Jim Harry |
| | |
| Speaker of the House | Michael J. Madigan |
| House Chief Clerk | Anthony D. Rossi |

## STATISTICS

| | |
|---|---|
| Land Area (square miles) | 55,593 |
| Rank in Nation | 24th |
| Population | 12,128,370 |
| Rank in Nation | 5th |
| Density per square mile | 216.7 |
| Number of Representatives in Congress | 20 |
| Capital City | Springfield |
| Population | 117,098 |
| Rank in State | 4th |
| Largest City | Chicago |
| Population | 2,802,079 |
| Number of Places over 10,000 Population | 180 |

# Indiana

| | |
|---|---|
| Nickname | The Hoosier State |
| Motto | *Crossroads of America* |
| Flower | Peony |
| Bird | Cardinal |
| Tree | Tulip Poplar |
| Song | *On the Banks of the Wabash, Far Away* |
| Poem | *Indiana* by Franklin Maples |
| Stone | Limestone |
| Entered the Union | December 11, 1816 |
| Capital | Indianapolis |

## EXECUTIVE BRANCH OFFICIALS

| | |
|---|---|
| Governor | Frank L. O'Bannon |
| Lieutenant Governor | Joseph E. Kernan |
| Secretary of State | Sue Anne Gilroy |
| Attorney General | Karen Freeman-Wilson |
| Treasurer | Tim Berry |

## SUPREME COURT

Randall T. Shepard, Chief Justice
Frank Sullivan Jr.
Ted Boehm
Brent E. Dickson
Robert D. Rucker

## GENERAL ASSEMBLY

| | |
|---|---|
| President of the Senate | Lt. Gov. Joseph E. Kernan |
| President Pro Tem of the Senate | Robert D. Garton |
| Principal Secretary of the Senate | Carolyn J. Tinkle |
| | |
| Speaker of the House | John R. Gregg |
| Speaker Pro Tem of the House | Chester F. Dobis |
| Principal Clerk of the House | Lee A. Smith |

## STATISTICS

| | |
|---|---|
| Land Area (square miles) | 35,870 |
| Rank in Nation | 38th |
| Population | 5,942,901 |
| Rank in Nation | 14th |
| Density per square mile | 164.5 |
| Number of Representatives in Congress | 10 |
| Capital City | Indianapolis |
| Population | 741,304 |
| Rank in State | 1st |
| Largest City | Indianapolis |
| Number of Places over 10,000 Population | 64 |

# Iowa

Nickname ............................................................... The Hawkeye State
Motto ........................................................ *Our Liberties We Prize and*
*Our Rights We Will Maintain*
Flower ................................................................................. Wild Rose
Bird ......................................................................... Eastern Goldfinch
Tree ............................................................................................... Oak
Song ................................................................... *The Song of Iowa*
Stone ............................................................................................ Geode
Entered the Union .................................... December 28, 1846
Capital ............................................................................ Des Moines

## EXECUTIVE BRANCH OFFICIALS

Governor ...................................................... Thomas J. Vilsack
Lieutenant Governor ................................. Sally J. Pederson
Secretary of State ............................................... Chet Culver
Attorney General .................................................. Tom Miller
Treasurer ........................................... Michael L. Fitzgerald

## SUPREME COURT

Arthur A. McGiverin, Chief Justice
Jerry L. Larson
James H. Carter
Louis A. Lavorato
Linda K. Neuman
Bruce M. Snell Jr.
Marsha K. Ternus
Mark S. Cady

## GENERAL ASSEMBLY

President of the Senate ................................... Mary E. Kramer
President Pro Tem of the Senate ............................ Donald B. Redfern
Secretary of the Senate ......................... Michael E. Marshall

Speaker of the House ...................................... Brent Siegrist
Speaker Pro Tem of the House ......................... Steve Sukup
Chief Clerk of the House .................... Elizabeth A. Isaacson

## STATISTICS

Land Area (square mile) ................................................. 55,875
Rank in Nation ............................................................. 23rd
Population ............................................................. 2,869,413
Rank in Nation ............................................................. 30th
Density per square mile .............................................. 51.2
Number of Representatives in Congress ............................... 5
Capital City .................................................................... Des Moines
Population ............................................................. 191,293
Rank in State ................................................................. 1st
Largest City .................................................................. Des Moines
Number of Places over 10,000 Population ............................ 30

# Kansas

Nickname ........................................................... The Sunflower State
Motto ................................................................ *Ad Astra per Aspera*
(To the Stars through Difficulties)
Animal ...................................................... American Buffalo
Flower ................................................. Wild Native Sunflower
Bird ..................................................... Western Meadowlark
Tree ..................................................................... Cottonwood
Song ..................................................... *Home on the Range*
Reptile ........................................................ Ornate Box Turtle
Insect ................................................................... Honeybee
Entered the Union ......................................... January 29, 1861
Capital ........................................................................... Topeka

## EXECUTIVE BRANCH OFFICIALS

Governor ............................................................. Bill Graves
Lieutenant Governor ................................... Gary Sherrer
Secretary of State ...................................... Ron Thornburgh
Attorney General .................................... Carla J. Stovall
Treasurer ................................................... Tim Shallenburger

## SUPREME COURT

Kay McFarland, Chief Justice
Tyler C. Lockett
Donald L. Allegrucci
Fred N. Six
Bob Abbott
Robert E. Davis
Edward Larson

## LEGISLATURE

President of the Senate ................................... Richard L. Bond
President Pro Tem of the Senate ................... Alicia Salisbury
Secretary of the Senate ...................................... Pat Saville

Speaker of the House ............................... Robin L. Jennison
Speaker Pro tem of the House ............................. Doug Mays
Chief Clerk of the House ................................. Janet E. Jones

## STATISTICS

Land Area (square miles) ............................................. 81,823
Rank in Nation ............................................................. 13th
Population ............................................................. 2,654,052
Rank in Nation ............................................................. 32nd
Density per square mile .............................................. 32.1
Number of Representatives in Congress ............................... 4
Capital City .................................................................... Topeka
Population ............................................................. 118,977
Rank in State ................................................................. 3rd
Largest City .................................................................. Wichita
Population ............................................................. 329,211
Number of Places over 10,000 Population ............................ 34

# Kentucky

| | |
|---|---|
| Nickname | The Bluegrass State |
| Motto | *United We Stand, Divided We Fall* |
| Animal | Gray Squirrel |
| Flower | Goldenrod |
| Bird | Cardinal |
| Tree | Tulip Poplar |
| Song | *My Old Kentucky Home* |
| Fossil | Brachiopod |
| Fish | Kentucky Bass |
| Entered the Union | June 1, 1792 |
| Capital | Frankfort |

## EXECUTIVE BRANCH OFFICIALS

| | |
|---|---|
| Governor | Paul E. Patton |
| Lieutenant Governor | Stephen Henry |
| Secretary of State | John Y. Brown III |
| Attorney General | Albert Benjamin Chandler III |
| Treasurer | Jonathan Miller |

## SUPREME COURT

Joseph E. Lambert, Chief Justice
William S. Cooper
J. William Graves
Martin E. Johnstone
Janet L. Stumbo
Donald C. Wintersheimer
James Keller

## GENERAL ASSEMBLY

| | |
|---|---|
| President of the Senate | Larry Saunders |
| President Pro Tem of the Senate | Richard L. Roeding |
| Chief Clerk of the Senate | Barbara Ferguson |
| | |
| Speaker of the House | Jody Richards |
| Speaker Pro Tem of the House | Larry Clark |
| Chief Clerk of the House | Lois Pulliam |

## STATISTICS

| | |
|---|---|
| Land Area (square miles) | 39,732 |
| Rank in Nation | 36th |
| Population | 3,960,825 |
| Rank in Nation | 25th |
| Density per square mile | 99.1 |
| Number of Representatives in Congress | 6 |
| Capital City | Frankfort |
| Population | 26,418 |
| Rank in State | 9th |
| Largest City | Louisville |
| Population | 255,045 |
| Number of Places over 10,000 Population | 39 |

# Louisiana

| | |
|---|---|
| Nickname | The Pelican State |
| Motto | *Union, Justice and Confidence* |
| Flower | Magnolia |
| Bird | Eastern Brown Pelican |
| Tree | Bald Cypress |
| Songs | *Give Me Louisiana* and *You Are My Sunshine* |
| Crustacean | Crawfish |
| Dog | Catahoula Leopard |
| Entered the Union | April 30, 1812 |
| Capital | Baton Rouge |

## EXECUTIVE BRANCH OFFICIALS

| | |
|---|---|
| Governor | Mike Foster Jr. |
| Lieutenant Governor | Kathleen B. Blanco |
| Secretary of State | W. Fox McKeithen |
| Attorney General | Richard P. Ieyoub Jr. |
| Treasurer | John Kennedy |

## SUPREME COURT

Pascal F. Calogero Jr., Chief Justice
Harry T. Lemmon
Chet D. Traylor
Walter F. Marcus Jr.
Catherine D. Kimball
Jeffrey P. Victory
Bernette Joshua Johnson
Jaeannette T. Knoll

## LEGISLATURE

| | |
|---|---|
| President of the Senate | John J. Hainkel Jr. |
| President Pro Tem of the Senate | Louis J. Lambert |
| Secretary of Senate | Michael S. Baer III |
| | |
| Speaker of the House | Charles W. Dewitt Jr. |
| Speaker Pro Tem of the House | C.E. Bruneau Jr. |
| Clerk of the House and Chief of Staff | Alfred W. Speer |

## STATISTICS

| | |
|---|---|
| Land Area (square miles) | 43,566 |
| Rank in Nation | 33rd |
| Population | 4,372,035 |
| Rank in Nation | 22nd |
| Density per square mile | 100.3 |
| Number of Representatives in Congress | 7 |
| Capital City | Baton Rouge |
| Population | 211,551 |
| Rank in State | 2nd |
| Largest City | New Orleans |
| Population | 465,538 |
| Number of Places over 10,000 Population | 45 |

# Maine

Nickname ............................................................ The Pine Tree State
Motto .......................................................... *Dirigo* (I Direct or I Lead)
Animal ........................................................................................ Moose
Flower ............................................. White Pine Cone and Tassel
Bird .......................................................................................... Chickadee
Tree ...................................................................................... White Pine
Song .................................................................. *State of Maine Song*
Fish ...................................................................... Landlocked Salmon
Mineral ................................................................................ Tourmaline
Entered the Union ................................................ March 15, 1820
Capital .......................................................................................... Augusta

## EXECUTIVE BRANCH OFFICIALS

Governor ................................................................ Angus S. King Jr.
Secretary of State ........................................ Dan A. Gwadosky
Attorney General ............................................ Andrew Ketterer
Treasurer ...................................................................... Dale McCormick

## SUPREME JUDICIAL COURT

Daniel E. Wathen, Chief Justice
Robert W. Clifford
Howard H. Dana Jr.
Donald G. Alexander
Susan Calkins
Paul L. Rudman
Leigh I. Saufley

## LEGISLATURE

President of the Senate .............................. Mark W. Lawrence
Secretary of the Senate ...................................... Joy O'Brien

Speaker of the House .................................... G. Steven Rowe
Clerk of the House ........................................ Joseph W. Mayo

## STATISTICS

Land Area (square miles) .............................................. 30,865
    Rank in Nation ................................................................ 39th
Population ...................................................................... 1,253,040
    Rank in Nation ................................................................ 39th
    Density per square mile .............................................. 40.3
Number of Representatives in Congress ................................ 2
Capital City .......................................................................... Augusta
Population ................................................................................ 19,978
    Rank in State ...................................................................... 7th
Largest City .......................................................................... Portland
    Population ...................................................................... 62,786
Number of Places over 10,000 Population ............................ 13

# Maryland

Nicknames ......................... The Old Line State and Free State
Motto ........................................................ *Fatti Maschii, Parole Femine*
(Manly Deeds, Womanly Words)
Flower ...................................................................... Black-eyed Susan
Bird.. .................................................................... Baltimore Oriole
Tree.. ............................................................................ White Oak
Song .............................................................. *Maryland, My Maryland*
Dog ............................................ Chesapeake Bay Retriever
Boat ............................................................................ The Skipjack
Fish ................................................................................ Striped Bass
Entered the Union ................................................ April 28, 1788
Capital .......................................................................................... Annapolis

## EXECUTIVE BRANCH OFFICIALS

Governor ........................................................ Parris N. Glendening
Lieutenant Governor .............................. Kathleen Kennedy Townsend
Secretary of State ................................................ John T. Willis
Attorney General ...................................... J. Joseph Curran Jr.
Treasurer ...................................................... Richard N. Dixon

## COURT OF APPEALS

Robert M. Bell, Chief Justice
John C. Eldridge
Lawrence F. Rodowsky
Irma S. Raker
Alan M. Wilner
Dale R. Cathell
Glenn T. Harrell Jr.

## GENERAL ASSEMBLY

President of the Senate ................................ Thomas V. Mike Miller Jr.
President Pro Tem of the Senate ........................ Ida G. Ruben
Secretary of the Senate ................................ William B.C. Addison Jr.

Speaker of the House .............................. Casper R. Taylor Jr.
Speaker Pro Tem of the House ............................ Thomas E. Dewberry
Clerk of the House ........................................ Mary Monahan

## STATISTICS

Land Area (square miles) ................................................ 9,775
    Rank in Nation .............................................................. 42nd
Population ...................................................................... 5,171,634
    Rank in Nation ................................................................ 19th
    Density per square mile .............................................. 525.3
Number of Representatives in Congress ................................ 8
Capital City .......................................................................... Annapolis
    Population ...................................................................... 33,585
    Rank in State .................................................................. 22nd
Largest City .......................................................................... Baltimore
    Population .................................................................... 645,593
Number of Places over 10,000 Population ........................ 99

# Massachusetts

Nickname ............................................................... The Bay State
Motto ................................. *Ense Petit Placidam Sub Libertate Quietem*
(By the Sword We Seek Peace, but Peace Only under Liberty)
Animal ............................................................ Morgan Horse
Flower ................................................................ Mayflower
Bird ...................................................................... Chickadee
Tree ............................................................ American Elm
Song ........................................................ *All Hail to Massachusetts*
Fish .............................................................................. Cod
Marine Mammal ........................................... Right Whale
Insect .................................................................. Ladybug
Dog ........................................................... Boston Terrier
Beverage ............................................... Cranberry Juice
Gem ................................................................ Rhodenite
Mineral ........................................................ Babingtonite
Entered the Union ........................................ February 6, 1788
Capital .................................................................... Boston

## EXECUTIVE BRANCH OFFICIALS

Governor ........................................... Argeo Paul Cellucci
Lieutenant Governor ...................................... Jane M. Swift
Secretary of the Commonwealth .............. William F. Galvin
Attorney General ........................................ Thomas Reilly
Treasurer & Receiver General ............... Shannon P. O'Brien

## SUPREME JUDICIAL COURT

Margaret Marshall, Chief Justice
Ruth I. Abrams
Neil L. Lynch
John M. Greaney
Francis X. Spina
Judith A. Cowin
Roderick L. Ireland

## GENERAL COURT

President of the Senate ...................... Thomas F. Birmingham
Clerk of the Senate .................................... Patrick F. Scanlan

Speaker of the House ........................... Thomas M. Finneran
Clerk of the House ...................................... Steven T. James

## STATISTICS

Land Area (square miles) ................................. 7838
    Rank in Nation .......................................... 45th
Population ...................................... 6,175,164
    Rank in Nation .......................................... 13th
    Density per square mile ........................ 784.3
Number of Representatives in Congress ............................. 10
Capital City ................................................ Boston
    Population .................................... 555,447
    Rank in State .......................................... 1st
Largest City ................................................ Boston
Number of Places over 10,000 Population ........................... 83

# Michigan

Nickname ............................................... The Wolverine State
Motto ............................ *Si Quaeris Peninsulam Amoenam Circumspice*
(If You Seek a Pleasant Peninsula, Look About You)
Flower ........................................................ Apple Blossom
Bird .......................................................................... Robin
Tree ................................................................ White Pine
Song .................................................... *Michigan, My Michigan*
Stone ........................................................ Petoskey Stone
Gem ........................................................... Chlorastrolite
Fish ............................................................. Brook Trout
Reptile .................................................. Painted Turtle
Entered the Union ......................................January 26, 1837
Capital ...................................................................... Lansing

## EXECUTIVE BRANCH OFFICIALS

Governor ....................................................... John Engler
Lieutenant Governor .................................. Dick Posthumus
Secretary of State .................................... Candice Miller
Attorney General ................................ Jennifer M. Granholm
Treasurer ........................................................ Mark A. Murray

## SUPREME COURT

Elizabeth A. Weaver Jr., Chief Justice
Robert P. Young Jr.
James H. Brickley
Michael F. Cavanagh
Patricia J. Boyle
Stephen J. Markman
Marilyn Kelly
Clifford W. Taylor
Maura D. Corrigan

## LEGISLATURE

President of the Senate .................... Lt. Gov. Dick Posthumus
President Pro Tem of the Senate .............................. John J. H. Schwarz
Secretary of the Senate ......................... Carol Morey Viventi

Speaker of the House ........................... Charles R. Perricone
Speaker Pro Tem of the House .................................. Patricia Birkholz
Clerk of the House ......................................... Gary L. Randall

## STATISTICS

Land Area (square miles) .............................. 56,809
    Rank in Nation .......................................... 22nd
Population ...................................... 9,863,775
    Rank in Nation .......................................... 8th
    Density per square mile ........................ 172.8
Number of Representatives in Congress ............................. 16
Capital City ................................................ Lansing
    Population .................................... 127,825
    Rank in State .......................................... 5th
Largest City ................................................ Detroit
    Population .................................... 970,196
Number of Places over 10,000 Population .......................... 110

# Minnesota

Nickname ................................................................. The North Star State
Motto ............................................... *L'Etoile du Nord* (The North Star)
Flower ....................................................... Pink and White Lady-Slipper
Bird ............................................................................. Common Loon
Tree ...................................................................................... Red Pine
Song ................................................................... *Hail! Minnesota*
Fish .......................................................................................... Walleye
Grain ................................................................................. Wild Rice
Mushroom ............................................................................... Morel
Entered the Union ............................................... May 11, 1858
Capital ................................................................................... St. Paul

## EXECUTIVE BRANCH OFFICIALS

Governor ................................................................. Jesse Ventura
Lieutenant Governor ............................................... Mae Schunk
Secretary of State ............................................ Mary Kiffmeyer
Attorney General ...................................................... Mike Hatch
Treasurer ...................................................... Carol C. Johnson

## SUPREME COURT

Kathleen A. Blatz, Chief Justice
Esther M. Tomljanovich
Sandra S. Gardebring
Alan C. Page
Paul Anderson
Edward Stringer
James H. Gilbert
Russell Anderson
Joan Eriksen

## LEGISLATURE

President of the Senate ..................................... Allan H. Spear
Secretary of the Senate ............................. Patrick E. Flahaven

Speaker of the House ............................... Steven A. Sviggum
Speaker Pro Tem of the House .............. Ron Abrams, Lynda Boudreau
Chief Clerk of the House .......................... Edward A. Burdick

## STATISTICS

Land Area (square miles) ................................................. 79,617
    Rank in Nation ....................................................................... 14th
Population ................................................................... 4,775,508
    Rank in Nation ........................................................................ 21st
    Density per square mile .............................................. 59.4
Number of Representatives in Congress ................................ 8
Capital City ................................................................... St. Paul
    Population ....................................................................... 257,284
    Rank in State .......................................................................... 2nd
Largest City ............................................................. Minneapolis
    Population ....................................................................... 351,731
Number of Places over 10,000 Population ........................... 73

# Mississippi

Nickname .................................................................. The Magnolia State
Motto ............................................. *Virtute et Armis* (By Valor and Arms)
Animal .................................................................. White-tailed Deer
Flower .................................................................................... Magnolia
Bird ................................................................................. Mockingbird
Water Mammal .................................................. Bottlenosed Dolphin
Tree ....................................................................................... Magnolia
Song ............................................................... *Go, Mississippi*
Fish ................................................................................. Black Bass
Beverage .................................................................................... Milk
Entered the Union ...................................... December 10, 1817
Capital .................................................................................... Jackson

## EXECUTIVE BRANCH OFFICIALS

Governor ......................................................... Ronnie Musgrove
Lieutenant Governor ................................................. Amy Tuck
Secretary of State ...................................................... Eric Clark
Attorney General ..................................................... Mike Moore
Treasurer ............................................... Marshall G. Bennett

## SUPREME COURT

Lenore L. Prather, Chief Justice
Michael D. Sullivan
Edwin Lloyd Pittman
Fred L. Banks Jr.
Chuck R. McRae
James L. Roberts Jr.
James W. Smith Jr.
Michael P. Mills
William Waller Jr.

## LEGISLATURE

President of the Senate ........................... Lt. Gov. Amy Tuck
President Pro Tem of the Senate ......................... Travis Little
Secretary of the Senate ................................. George P. Smith

Speaker of the House ................................................ Tim Ford
Speaker Pro Tem of the House .................... Robert G. Clark
Clerk of the House ........................................ F. Edwin Perry

## STATISTICS

Land Area (square miles) ................................................. 46,914
    Rank in Nation ....................................................................... 31st
Population ................................................................... 2,768,619
    Rank in Nation ........................................................................ 31st
    Density per square mile .............................................. 58.7
Number of Representatives in Congress ................................ 5
Capital City .................................................................... Jackson
    Population ....................................................................... 188,419
    Rank in State .......................................................................... 1st
Largest City ..................................................................... Jackson
Number of Places over 10,000 Population ........................... 34

# Missouri

Nickname ................................................................... The Show Me State
Motto ......................................................... *Salus Populi Suprema Lex Esto*
        (The Welfare of the People Shall Be the Supreme Law)
Flower ........................................................ White Hawthorn Blossom
Bird ......................................................................................... Bluebird
Insect ..................................................................................... Honeybee
Tree ........................................................................ Flowering Dogwood
Song ......................................................................... *Missouri Waltz*
Rock ........................................................................................ Mozarkite
Mineral ....................................................................................... Galena
Fossil ......................................................................................... Crinoid
Entered the Union ...................................................... August 10, 1821
Capital ......................................................................... Jefferson City

## EXECUTIVE BRANCH OFFICIALS

Governor ...................................................................... Mel Carnahan
Lieutenant Governor ................................................ Roger B. Wilson
Secretary of State ...................................................... Rebecca Cook
Attorney General ............................................... Jeremiah W. Nixon
Treasurer ........................................................................... Bob Holden

## SUPREME COURT

William Ray Price Jr., Chief Justice
Duane Benton
Stephen N. Limbaugh Jr.
Ann K. Covington
John C. Holstein
Ronnie L. White
Michael Wolff

## GENERAL ASSEMBLY

President of the Senate ..................................Lt. Gov. Roger B. Wilson
President Pro Tem of the Senate ................................ Edward E. Quick
Secretary of the Senate ..................................... Terry L. Spieler

Speaker of the House ............................................... Steve Gaw
Speaker Pro Tem of the House .......................................... Jim Kreider
Clerk of the House ................................................... Anne Walker

## STATISTICS

Land Area (square miles) ................................................ 68,898
    Rank in Nation ........................................................ 18th
Population .................................................................. 5,468,338
    Rank in Nation ........................................................ 17th
    Density per square mile ........................................... 78.9
Number of Representatives in Congress ................................ 9
Capital City ....................................................... Jefferson City
    Population .................................................................. 34,911
    Rank in State ............................................................ 15th
Largest City ........................................................... Kansas City
    Population ................................................................ 441,574
Number of Places over 10,000 Population ........................ 64

# Montana

Nickname ...................................................... The Treasure State
Motto ..................................... *Oro y Plata* (Gold and Silver)
Animal .......................................................................... Grizzly Bear
Flower ................................................................................ Bitterroot
Bird ................................................................ Western Meadowlark
Tree .............................................................................. Ponderosa Pine
Song ........................................................................................ *Montana*
State Ballad .............................................................. *Montana Melody*
Gem Stones ................................................... Sapphire and Agate
State Fossil ..................................................... Duck-billed Dinosaur
Entered the Union ...................................... November 8, 1889
Capital ............................................................................... Helena

## EXECUTIVE BRANCH OFFICIALS

Governor ......................................................................... Marc Racicot
Lieutenant Governor ................................................... Judy Martz
Secretary of State ............................................... Mike Cooney
Attorney General ..................................... Joseph P. Mazurek
Treasurer ....................................................... Lois A. Menzies

## SUPREME COURT

Jean A. Turnage, Chief Justice
Karla M. Gray
William Leaphart
William E. Hunt
James C. Nelson
Terry N. Trieweiler
James Regnier

## LEGISLATURE

President of the Senate ................................ Bruce D. Crippen
President Pro Tem of the Senate ............................... Thomas A. Beck
Secretary of the Senate ................................... Rosana Skelton

Speaker of the House ................................... John A. Mercer
Speaker Pro Tem of the House ............................... Marian W. Hanson
Chief Clerk of the House ................................... Marilyn Miller

## STATISTICS

Land Area (square miles) .......................................... 145,556
    Rank in Nation ........................................................... 4th
Population .................................................................... 882,779
    Rank in Nation .......................................................... 44th
    Density per square mile ............................................. 6.0
Number of Representatives in Congress ................................ 1
Capital City ...................................................................... Helena
    Population .................................................................. 28,306
    Rank in State ............................................................. 6th
Largest City ...................................................................... Billings
    Population .................................................................. 91,750
Number of Places over 10,000 Population ......................... 10

# Nebraska

| | |
|---|---|
| Nickname | The Cornhusker State |
| Motto | *Equality Before the Law* |
| Mammal | White-tailed Deer |
| Flower | Goldenrod |
| Bird | Western Meadowlark |
| Tree | Western Cottonwood |
| Song | *Beautiful Nebraska* |
| Insect | Honeybee |
| Gemstone | Blue Agate |
| Entered the Union | March 1, 1867 |
| Capital | Lincoln |

## EXECUTIVE BRANCH OFFICIALS

| | |
|---|---|
| Governor | Mike Johanns |
| Lieutenant Governor | David I. Maurstad |
| Secretary of State | Scott Moore |
| Attorney General | Don B. Stenberg |
| Treasurer | David E. Heineman |

## SUPREME COURT

John Hendry, Chief Justice
John F. Wright
William Connolly
John Gerrard
Kenneth C. Stephan
Michael McCormack
Lindsey Miller-Lerman

## UNICAMERAL LEGISLATURE

| | |
|---|---|
| President of the Legislature | Lt. Gov. David I. Maurstad |
| Speaker of the Legislature | Doug Kristensen |
| Chairman of Executive Board, Legislative Council | George Coordsen |
| Vice Chairman of Executive Board, Legislative Council | Jim Cudaback |
| Clerk of the Legislature | Patrick J. O'Donnell |

## STATISTICS

| | |
|---|---|
| Land Area (square miles) | 76,878 |
| Rank in Nation | 15th |
| Population | 1,666,028 |
| Rank in Nation | 38th |
| Density per square mile | 21.6 |
| Number of Representatives in Congress | 3 |
| Capital City | Lincoln |
| Population | 213,088 |
| Rank in State | 2nd |
| Largest City | Omaha |
| Population | 371,291 |
| Number of Places over 10,000 Population | 14 |

# Nevada

| | |
|---|---|
| Nickname | The Silver State |
| Motto | *All for Our Country* |
| Animal | Desert Bighorn Sheep |
| Flower | Sagebrush |
| Bird | Mountain Bluebird |
| Tree | Bristlecone Pine and Single-leaf Pinon |
| Song | *Home Means Nevada* |
| Fish | Lahontan Cutthroat Trout |
| Fossil | Ichtyosaur |
| Entered the Union | October 31, 1864 |
| Capital | Carson City |

## EXECUTIVE BRANCH OFFICIALS

| | |
|---|---|
| Governor | Kenny C. Guinn |
| Lieutenant Governor | Lorraine T. Hunt |
| Secretary of State | Dean Heller |
| Attorney General | Frankie Sue Del Papa |
| Treasurer | Brian K. Krolicki |

## SUPREME COURT

Robert E. Rose, Chief Justice
Miriam Shearing
Myron Leavitt
Cliff Young
A. William Maupin
Deborah A. Agosti
Nancy A. Becker

## LEGISLATURE

| | |
|---|---|
| President of the Senate | Lt. Gov. Lorraine T. Hunt |
| President Pro Tem of the Senate | Lawrence E. Jacobsen |
| Secretary of the Senate | Claire J. Clift |
| Speaker of the Assembly | Joseph E. Dini Jr. |
| Speaker Pro Tem of the Assembly | Jan Evans |
| Chief Clerk of the Assembly | Jacqueline Sneddon |

## STATISTICS

| | |
|---|---|
| Land Area (square miles) | 109,806 |
| Rank in Nation | 7th |
| Population | 1,809,253 |
| Rank in Nation | 35th |
| Density per square mile | 15.9 |
| Number of Representatives in Congress | 2 |
| Capital City | Carson City |
| Population | 49,301 |
| Rank in State | 6th |
| Largest City | Las Vegas |
| Population | 404,288 |
| Number of Places over 10,000 Population | 14 |

# New Hampshire

| | |
|---|---|
| Nickname | The Granite State |
| Motto | *Live Free or Die* |
| Animal | White-tailed Deer |
| Flower | Purple Lilac |
| Bird | Purple Finch |
| Tree | White Birch |
| Song | *Old New Hampshire* |
| Insect | Ladybug |
| Gem | Smoky Quartz |
| Entered the Union | June 21, 1788 |
| Capital | Concord |

## EXECUTIVE BRANCH OFFICIALS

| | |
|---|---|
| Governor | Jeanne Shaheen |
| Secretary of State | William Gardner |
| Attorney General | Philip T. McLaughlin |
| Treasurer | Georgie A. Thomas |

## SUPREME COURT

David A. Brock, Chief Justice
William R. Johnson
W. Stephen Thayer, III
Sherman D. Horton Jr.
John T. Broderick Jr.

## GENERAL COURT

| | |
|---|---|
| President of the Senate | Beverly A. Hollingsworth |
| President Pro Tem of the Senate | Sylvia B. Larsen |
| Clerk of the Senate | Gloria M. Randlett |
| | |
| Speaker of the House | Donna Sytek |
| Speaker Pro Tem of the House | Alf E. Jacobson |
| Clerk of the House | Karen O. Wadsworth |

## STATISTICS

| | |
|---|---|
| Land Area (square miles) | 8,969 |
|     Rank in Nation | 44th |
| Population | 1,201,134 |
|     Rank in Nation | 41st |
|     Density per square mile | 132.1 |
| Number of Representatives in Congress | 2 |
| Capital City | Concord |
|     Population | 37,444 |
|     Rank in State | 3rd |
| Largest City | Manchester |
|     Population | 102,524 |
| Number of Places over 10,000 Population | 14 |

# New Jersey

| | |
|---|---|
| Nickname | The Garden State |
| Motto | *Liberty and Prosperity* |
| Animal | Horse |
| Flower | Violet |
| Bird | Eastern Goldfinch |
| Tree | Red Oak |
| Insect | Honeybee |
| Entered the Union | December 18, 1787 |
| Capital | Trenton |

## EXECUTIVE BRANCH OFFICIALS

| | |
|---|---|
| Governor | Christine T. Whitman |
| Secretary of State | DeForest B. Soaries Jr. |
| Attorney General | John J. Farmer Jr. |
| Treasurer | Roland M. Machold |

## SUPREME COURT

Deborah Poritz, Chief Justice
Daniel J. O'Hern
Marie L. Garibaldi
Gary S. Stein
James H. Coleman Jr.
Virginia Long
Peter G. Verniero

## LEGISLATURE

| | |
|---|---|
| President of the Senate | Donald T. DiFrancesco |
| President Pro Tem of the Senate | Joseph A. Palaia |
| Secretary of the Senate | Dolores A. Kirk |
| | |
| Speaker of the Assembly | Jack Collins |
| Speaker Pro Tem of the Assembly | Nicholas R. Felice |
| Clerk of the General Assembly | Linda Metzger |

## STATISTICS

| | |
|---|---|
| Land Area (square miles) | 7,419 |
|     Rank in Nation | 46th |
| Population | 8143,412 |
|     Rank in Nation | 9th |
|     Density per square mile | 1,093,.8 |
| Number of Representatives in Congress | 13 |
| Capital City | Trenton |
|     Population | 84,494 |
|     Rank in State | 5th |
| Largest City | Newark |
|     Population | 267,823 |
| Number of Places over 10,000 Population | 162 |

# New Mexico

Nickname ............................................. The Land of Enchantment
Motto ......................................... *Crescit Eundo* (It Grows As It Goes)
Flower ............................................. Yucca (Our Lord's Candles)
Bird .................................................................. Chaparral Bird
Tree ............................................................................. Pinon
Songs ............................................................. *Asi es Nuevo Mexico and*
*O, Fair New Mexico*
Gem ............................................................... Turquoise
Fossil .............................................. Coelophysis Dinosaur
Animal ................................................................ Black Bear
Entered the Union ............................................. January 6, 1912
Capital ........................................................... Santa Fe

## EXECUTIVE BRANCH OFFICIALS

Governor ...................................................... Gary E. Johnson
Lieutenant Governor .................................. Walter D.Bradley
Secretary of State .................................. Rebecca Vigil-Giron
Attorney General ......................................... Patricia Madrid
Treasurer ................................................. Michael A. Montoya

## SUPREME COURT

Pamela B. Minzner, Chief Justice
Joseph E. Baca
Patricio Serna
Gene E. Franchini
Petra Maes

## LEGISLATURE

President of the Senate ................................ Lt. Gov. Walter D. Bradley
President Pro Tem of the Senate .............................. Manny M. Aragon
Chief Clerk of the Senate ......................................... Margaret Larragoite

Speaker of the House .......................................... Raymond G. Sanchez
Chief Clerk of the House ............................................. Stephen R. Arias

## STATISTICS

Land Area (square miles) ........................................................ 121,365
   Rank in Nation ...................................................................... 5th
Population ............................................................................. 1,739,844
   Rank in Nation ..................................................................... 37th
   Density per square mile .......................................................... 14.3
Number of Representatives in Congress ........................................ 3
Capital City ....................................................................... Santa Fe
   Population ................................................................................ 67,879
   Rank in State ........................................................................... 3rd
Largest City ...................................................................... Albuquerque
   Population ................................................................................ 419,311
Number of Places over 10,000 Population ............................................ 19

# New York

Nickname ................................................................. The Empire State
Motto .............................................................. *Excelsior* (Ever Upward)
Animal ................................................................. American Beaver
Fish ............................................................................. Brook Trout
Flower ............................................................................... Rose
Bird ................................................................................ Bluebird
Tree ............................................................................ Sugar Maple
Song* ........................................................................ *I Love New York*
Gem .................................................................................. Garnet
Fossil ............................................................ Eurypterus Remipes
Entered the Union ................................................. July 26, 1788
Capital ...................................................................... Albany

## EXECUTIVE BRANCH OFFICIALS

Governor ..................................................... George E. Pataki
Lieutenant Governor ................................... Mary O. Donohue
Secretary of State .............................. Alexander F. Treadwell
Attorney General ................................................. Eliot Spitzer
Treasurer ............................................... George H. Gasser

## COURT OF APPEALS

Judith S. Kaye, Chief Justice
Joseph W. Bellacosa
George Bundy Smith
Howard A. Levine
Carmen Beaucamp Ciparick
Richard C. Wesley
Albert M. Rosenblatt

## LEGISLATURE

President of the Senate ................................ Lt. Gov. Mary O. Donohue
Temporary President and Majority
   Leader of the Senate ................................... Joseph L. Bruno
Secretary of the Senate ................................... Steven Boggess

Speaker of the Assembly ................................. Sheldon Silver
Speaker Pro Tem of the Assembly ...................... Elizabeth A. Connelly
Clerk of the Assembly .................................. Francine Misasi

## STATISTICS

Land Area (square miles) ............................................... 47,224
   Rank in Nation ....................................................................... 30th
Population ....................................................................... 18,196,601
   Rank in Nation ......................................................................... 3rd
   Density per square mile .......................................................... 384.9
Number of Representatives in Congress ............................................. 31
Capital City ............................................................................... Albany
   Population ................................................................................ 94,305
   Rank in State ........................................................................... 6th
Largest City ...................................................................... New York City
   Population ................................................................... 7,420,166
Number of Places over 10,000 Population ........................................ 180

*unofficial

# North Carolina

Nickname ................................ The Tar Heel State and Old North State
Motto ............................................................ *Esse Quam Videri*
                                (To Be Rather Than to Seem)
Flower ................................................................ Dogwood
Bird ...................................................................... Cardinal
Tree ......................................................... Long Leaf Pine
Song ............................................. *The Old North State*
Mammal ....................................................... Grey Squirrel
Dog ............................................................... Plott Hound
Beverage .................................................................. Milk
Vegetable ......................................................... Sweet Potato
Entered the United States ........................ November 21, 1789
Capital ................................................................... Raleigh

## EXECUTIVE BRANCH OFFICIALS

Governor ...................................................... James B. Hunt Jr.
Lieutenant Governor .................................... Dennis A. Wicker
Secretary of State .................................... Elaine F. Marshall
Attorney General ........................................ Michael F. Easley
Treasurer ......................................................... Harlan E. Boyles

## SUPREME COURT

Henry E. Frye, Chief Justice
Franklin Freeman Jr.
Mark D. Martin
Sarah Parker
I. Beverly Lake Jr.
Robert F. Orr
George Wainwright Jr.

## GENERAL ASSEMBLY

President of the Senate .................................. Lt. Gov. Dennis A. Wicker
President Pro Tem of the Senate .................................... Marc Basnight
Principal Clerk of the Senate ................................................. Janet Pruitt

Speaker of the House ...................................... James B. Black
Speaker Pro Tem of the House ........................................ Joe Hackney
Principal Clerk of the House ............................................ Denise Weeks

## STATISTICS

Land Area (square miles) ................................................ 48,718
     Rank in Nation ......................................................... 29th
Population ...................................................... 7,650,789
     Rank in Nation ........................................................... 11th
     Density per square mile ............................................ 154.9
Number of Representatives in Congress ............................ 12
Capital City ................................................................... Raleigh
Population ...................................................... 259,423
     Rank in State ............................................................. 2nd
Largest City ......................................................... Charlotte
     Population ........................................................... 504,637
Number of Places over 10,000 Population ......................... 52

# North Dakota

Nickname .............................................. Peace Garden State
Motto ......................................... *Liberty and Union, Now and Forever,*
                                *One and Inseparable*
Flower ...................................................... Wild Prairie Rose
Bird .............................................................. Western Meadowlark
Tree ................................................................ American Elm
Song ................................................. *North Dakota Hymn*
March ...................................................... *Spirit of the Land*
Fossil ................................................... Teredo Petrified Wood
Fish ............................................................... Northern Pike
Entered the Union ...................................... November 2, 1889
Capital ................................................................... Bismarck

## EXECUTIVE BRANCH OFFICIALS

Governor ...................................................... Edward T. Schafer
Lieutenant Governor ................................... Rosemarie Myrdal
Secretary of State ........................................ Alvin A. Jaeger
Attorney General ......................................... Heidi Heitkamp
Treasurer .......................................................... Kathi Gilmore

## SUPREME COURT

Gerald W. VandeWalle, Chief Justice
William A. Neumann
Dale V. Sandstrom
Mary Muehlen Maring
Carol Ronning Kapsner

## LEGISLATIVE ASSEMBLY

President of the Senate ............................... Lt. Gov. Rosemarie Myrdal
President Pro Tem of the Senate .................................... Layton Freborg
Secretary of the Senate ................................................. William Parker

Speaker of the House ...................................... Francis J. Wald
Clerk of the House ............................................. Lance Hagen

## STATISTICS

Land Area (square miles) ................................................ 68,994
     Rank in Nation ......................................................... 17th
Population ...................................................... 633,666
     Rank in Nation ........................................................... 47th
     Density per square mile ................................................ 9.3
Number of Representatives in Congress .............................. 1
Capital City ................................................................... Bismarck
Population ........................................................ 54,040
     Rank in State ............................................................. 3rd
Largest City ......................................................... Fargo
     Population ........................................................... 86,718
Number of Places over 10,000 Population ........................... 9

# Ohio

Nickname .................................................................... The Buckeye State
Motto ............................................... *With God, All Things Are Possible*
Animal ...................................................................... White-tailed Deer
Flower ..................................................................... Scarlet Carnation
Bird ........................................................................................ Cardinal
Tree ......................................................................................... Buckeye
Song ........................................................................... *Beautiful Ohio*
Stone ................................................................................. Ohio Flint
Insect ...................................................................................... Ladybug
Entered the Union ............................................... March 1, 1803
Capital ............................................................................... Columbus

## EXECUTIVE BRANCH OFFICIALS

Governor ................................................................. Bob Taft
Lieutenant Governor ................................. Maureen O'Connor
Secretary of State ........................................ J. Kenneth Blackwell
Attorney General ................................. Betty D. Montgomery
Treasurer ....................................................... Joseph T. Deters

## SUPREME COURT

Thomas J. Moyer, Chief Justice
Andrew Douglas
Alice Robie Resnick
Francis E. Sweeney
Paul E. Pfeifer
Deborah L. Cook
Evelyn Lundberg Stratton

## GENERAL ASSEMBLY

President of the Senate ................................... Richard H. Finan
President Pro Tem of the Senate ..................... Robert R. Cupp
Clerk of the Senate ......................................... Matthew Schuler

Speaker of the House ................................... Jo Ann Davidson
Speaker Pro Tem of the House ................... Randall Gardner
Legislative Clerk of the House ................... Laura P. Clemens

## STATISTICS

Land Area (square miles) ............................... 40,953
    Rank in Nation ................................................. 35th
Population ........................................................ 11,256,654
    Rank in Nation ..................................................... 7th
    Density per square mile ................................. 273.7
Number of Representatives in Congress ............................ 19
Capital City ........................................................ Columbus
Population ............................................................ 670,234
    Rank in State ......................................................... 1st
Largest City ........................................................ Columbus
Number of Places over 10,000 Population ....................... 164

# Oklahoma

Nickname .................................................................... The Sooner State
Motto ...................... *Labor Omnia Vincit* (Labor Conquers All Things)
Animal ..................................................................... American Buffalo
Flower ................................................................................... Mistletoe
Bird ............................................................... Scissor-tailed Flycatcher
Tree ........................................................................................... Redbud
Song ................................................................................ *Oklahoma*
Rock ............................................................ Barite Rose (Rose Rock)
Grass ................................................................................ Indiangrass
Entered the Union ............................................... November 16, 1907
Capital ........................................................................ Oklahoma City

## EXECUTIVE BRANCH OFFICIALS

Governor ................................................................. Frank Keating
Lieutenant Governor ........................................... Mary Fallin
Secretary of State ................................................. Mike Hunter
Attorney General ................................. W. A. Drew Edmondson
Treasurer ............................................................... Robert Butkin

## SUPREME COURT

Hardy Summers, Chief Justice
Robert E. Lavender      Ralph B. Hodges
Rudolph Hargrave      Marian P. Opala
Daniel Boudreau      Joseph M. Watt

## LEGISLATURE

President of the Senate .......................... Lt. Gov. Mary Fallin
President Pro Tem of the Senate ..................... Stratton Taylor
Secretary of the Senate ...................................... Lance Ward

Speaker of the House ................................... Loyd L. Benson
Speaker Pro Tem of the House ..................... Larry E. Adair
Chief Clerk/Administrator of the House ........................... Larry Warden

## STATISTICS

Land Area (square miles) ............................... 68,679
    Rank in Nation ................................................. 19th
Population ........................................................ 3,358,044
    Rank in Nation ..................................................... 27th
    Density per square mile ................................... 48.7
Number of Representatives in Congress .............................. 6
Capital City ................................................. Oklahoma City
Population ............................................................ 472,221
    Rank in State ......................................................... 1st
Largest City ................................................. Oklahoma City

# Oregon

Nickname ............................................................... The Beaver State
Motto ...................................................... *She Flies with Her Own Wings*
Animal .................................................................. American Beaver
Flower ....................................................................... Oregon Grape
Bird ................................................................ Western Meadowlark
Tree ............................................................................ Douglas Fir
Song ............................................................ *Oregon, My Oregon*
Gemstone ........................................................................ Sunstone
Insect ................................................. Oregon Swallowtail Butterfly
Entered the Union ..................................... February 14, 1859
Capital .................................................................................. Salem

## EXECUTIVE BRANCH OFFICIALS

Governor ..................................................... John A. Kitzhaber
Secretary of State .............................................. Bill Bradbury
Attorney General ................................................. Hardy Myers
Treasurer ................................................................... Jim Hill

## SUPREME COURT

Wallace P. Carson Jr., Chief Justice
Theodore R. Kulongoski
George A. Van Hommissen
Robert D. Durham
W. Michael Gillette
Susan Leeson
R. William Riggs

## LEGISLATIVE ASSEMBLY

President of the Senate ..................................... Brady Adams
President Pro Tem of the Senate ........................ Randy Miller
Secretary of the Senate ......................................... Judy Hall

Speaker of the House ................................... Lynn Snodgrass
Speaker Pro Tem of the House ........................ Ken Strobeck
Chief Clerk of the House ............................. Ramona Kenady

## STATISTICS

Land Area (square miles) ................................................ 96,003
    Rank in Nation ............................................................... 10th
Population ................................................................. 3,316,154
    Rank in Nation ................................................................ 28th
    Density per square mile ................................................. 34.2
Number of Representatives in Congress ................................. 5
Capital City ........................................................................ Salem
    Population ................................................................. 126,702
    Rank in State ................................................................... 3rd
Largest City ..................................................................... Portland
    Population ................................................................. 503,891
Number of Places over 10,000 Population ........................... 43

# Pennsylvania

Nickname ............................................................. The Keystone State
Motto ............................................... *Virtue, Liberty and Independence*
Animal ................................................................. White-tailed Deer
Flower ...................................................................... Mountain Laurel
Game Bird ..................................................................... Ruffed Grouse
Tree ...................................................................................... Hemlock
Insect ...................................................................................... Firefly
Fossil ............................................................................ Phacops rana
Entered the Union ....................................... December 12, 1787
Capital ................................................................................ Harrisburg

## EXECUTIVE BRANCH OFFICIALS

Governor ............................................................. Tom Ridge
Lieutenant Governor ........................... Mark S. Schweiker
Secretary of State .................................... Kim Pizzingrilli
Attorney General ................................... D. Michael Fisher
Treasurer ......................................................... Barbara Hafer

## SUPREME COURT

John P. Flaherty, Chief Justice
Stephen A. Zappala
Ralph Cappy
Ronald D. Castille
Sandra Schultz Newman
Russell M. Nigro
Thomas G. Saylor

## GENERAL ASSEMBLY

President of the Senate ............................. Lt. Gov. Mark S. Schweiker
President Pro Tem of the Senate ............................ Robert C. Jubelirer
Secretary-Parliamentarian of the Senate ................... Mark R. Corrigan

Speaker of the House ................................... Matthew J. Ryan
Chief Clerk of the House .......................................... Ted Mazia

## STATISTICS

Land Area (square miles) .............................................. 44,820
    Rank in Nation ............................................................. 32nd
Population ................................................................ 11,994,016
    Rank in Nation .................................................................. 6th
    Density per square mile ............................................... 267.8
Number of Representatives in Congress ............................... 21
Capital City ................................................................. Harrisburg
    Population ................................................................... 49,502
    Rank in State ................................................................... 9th
Largest City ............................................................. Philadelphia
    Population ................................................................ 1,436,287
Number of Places over 10,000 Population ......................... 102

# Rhode Island

Nicknames ............................................. Little Rhody and Ocean State
Motto .................................................................................... *Hope*
Animal .................................................................................. Quahaug
Flower ..................................................................................... Violet
Bird ........................................................................ Rhode Island Red
Tree ................................................................................ Red Maple
Song ............................................................................ *Rhode Island*
Rock ............................................................................. Cumberlandite
Mineral ............................................................................... Bowenite
Entered the Union ............................................................ May 29, 1790
Capital ............................................................................ Providence

## EXECUTIVE BRANCH OFFICIALS

Governor .................................................... Lincoln C. Almond
Lieutenant Governor ................................... Charles J. Fogarty
Secretary of State ..................................... James R. Langevin
Attorney General ..................................... Sheldon Whitehouse
Treasurer ...................................................... Paul J. Tavares

## SUPREME COURT

Joseph R. Weisberger, Chief Justice
Victoria Lederberg
John Bourcier
Robert G. Flanders
Maureen P. Goldberg

## GENERAL ASSEMBLY

President of the Senate ................................. Lt. Gov. Charles J. Fogarty
President Pro Tem of the Senate ............................... Charles D. Walton
Clerk of the Senate ........................................... Raymond T. Hoyas Jr.

Speaker of the House ................................................. John B. Harwood
Speaker Pro Tem of the House .............................. Mabel M. Anderson
Reading Clerk of the House ....................................... Louis D'Antuono

## STATISTICS

Land Area (square mile) ........................................................ 1,045
   Rank in Nation ................................................................ 50th
Population ............................................................................ 990,819
   Rank in Nation ................................................................. 43rd
   Density per square mile ...................................................... 945.9
Number of Representatives in Congress ...................................... 2
Capital City ..................................................................... Providence
Population ............................................................................ 150,890
   Rank in State ..................................................................... 1st
Largest City ....................................................................... Providence
Number of Places over 10,000 Population ............................................. 1

# South Carolina

Nickname .................................................................. The Palmetto State
Motto .............................................................. *Animis Opibusque Parati*
(Prepared in Mind and Resources)
and *Dum Spiro Spero* (While I breathe, I Hope)
Animal ...................................................................... White-tailed Deer
Flower ........................................................................ Yellow Jessamine
Bird ................................................................................ Carolina Wren
Tree ..................................................................................... Palmetto
Songs ................................... *Carolina* and *South Carolina on My Mind*
Stone .......................................................................... Blue Granite
Fish ................................................................................ Striped Bass
Entered the Union ............................................................ May 23, 1788
Capital ............................................................................... Columbia

## EXECUTIVE BRANCH OFFICIALS

Governor ................................................... James Hovis Hodges
Lieutenant Governor .............................................. Bob Peeler
Secretary of State ................................................... Jim Miles
Attorney General ............................................. Charlie Condon
Treasurer ........................................... Grady L. Patterson Jr.

## SUPREME COURT

Ernest A. Finney Jr., Chief Justice
E.C. Burnett III
James E. Moore
John H. Waller Jr.
Jean H. Toal

## GENERAL ASSEMBLY

President of the Senate ........................................... Lt. Gov. Bob Peeler
President Pro Tem of the Senate ............................ John W. Drummond
Clerk and Director of Senate Research .................... Frank B. Caggiano

Speaker of the House ................................................. David H. Wilkins
Speaker Pro Tem of the House .................................... Terry E. Haskins
Clerk of the House ............................................. Sandra K. McKinney

## STATISTICS

Land Area (square miles) ............................................... 30,111
   Rank in Nation ................................................................ 40th
Population ......................................................................... 3,885,736
   Rank in Nation ................................................................. 26th
   Density per square mile ...................................................... 127.4
Number of Representatives in Congress ............................................. 6
Capital City .......................................................................... Columbia

Population ........................................................................... 110,840
   Rank in State ..................................................................... 1st
Largest City ........................................................................ Columbia
Number of Places over 10,000 Population ........................................ 39

# South Dakota

| | |
|---|---|
| Nicknames | The Mt. Rushmore State |
| Motto | *Under God the People Rule* |
| Animal | Coyote |
| Flower | American Pasque |
| Bird | Chinese ring-necked pheasant |
| Tree | Black Hills Spruce |
| Song | *Hail, South Dakota* |
| Mineral | Rose Quartz |
| Fish | Walleye |
| Insect | Honeybee |
| Grass | Western Wheat Grass |
| Entered the Union | November 2, 1889 |
| Capital | Pierre |

## EXECUTIVE BRANCH OFFICIALS

| | |
|---|---|
| Governor | William J. Janklow |
| Lieutenant Governor | Carole Hillard |
| Secretary of State | Joyce Hazeltine |
| Attorney General | Mark Barnett |
| Treasurer | Richard D. Butler |

## SUPREME COURT

Robert A. Miller, Chief Justice
Richard W. Sabers
Robert A. Amundson
John K. Konenkamp
David E. Gilbertson

## LEGISLATURE

| | |
|---|---|
| President of the Senate | Lt. Gov. Carole Hillard |
| President Pro Tem of the Senate | Harold W. Halverson |
| Secretary of the Senate | Patricia Adam |
| | |
| Speaker of the House | Roger W. Hunt |
| Speaker Pro Tem of the House | Scott Eccarius |
| Chief Clerk of the House | Karen Gerdes |

## STATISTICS

| | |
|---|---|
| Land Area (square miles) | 75,896 |
| Rank in Nation | 16th |
| Population | 733,133 |
| Rank in Nation | 46th |
| Density per square mile | 9.7 |
| Number of Representatives in Congress | 1 |
| Capital City | Pierre |
| Population | 13,267 |
| Rank in State | 7th |
| Largest City | Sioux Falls |
| Population | 116,762 |
| Number of Places over 10,000 Population | 10 |

# Tennessee

| | |
|---|---|
| Nickname | The Volunteer State |
| Motto | *Agriculture and Commerce* |
| Animal | Raccoon |
| Flower | Iris |
| Bird | Mockingbird |
| Tree | Tulip Poplar |
| Wildflower | Passion Flower |
| Songs | *When It's Iris Time in Tennessee;* *The Tennessee Waltz; My Homeland, Tennessee* *My Tennessee;* and *Rocky Top* |
| Insects | Lady Beetle and Firefly |
| Gem | Freshwater Pearl |
| Rocks | Limestone and Agate |
| Entered the Union | June 1, 1796 |
| Capital | Nashville |

## EXECUTIVE BRANCH OFFICIALS

| | |
|---|---|
| Governor | Don Sundquist |
| Lieutenant Governor | John S. Wilder |
| Secretary of State | Riley Darnell |
| Attorney General | Paul G. Summers |
| Treasurer | Stephen D. Adams |

## SUPREME COURT

E. Riley Anderson, Chief Justice
Adolpho A. Birch Jr.
Frank F. Drowota, III
William M. Barker
Janice Holder

## GENERAL ASSEMBLY

| | |
|---|---|
| Speaker of the Senate | Lt. Gov. John S. Wilder |
| Speaker Pro Tem of the Senate | Robert Rochelle |
| Acting Chief Clerk of the Senate | Russell Humphries |
| | |
| Speaker of the House | James O. Naifeh |
| Speaker Pro Tem of the House | Lois M. DeBerry |
| Chief Clerk of the House | Burney T. Durham |

## STATISTICS

| | |
|---|---|
| Land Area (square miles) | 41,220 |
| Rank in Nation | 34th |
| Population | 5,483,535 |
| Rank in Nation | 16th |
| Density per square mile | 131.7 |
| Number of Representatives in Congress | 9 |
| Capital City | Nashville |
| Population | 510,274 |
| Rank in State | 2nd |
| Largest City | Memphis |
| Population | 603,507 |
| Number of Places over 10,000 Population | 44 |

# Texas

| | |
|---|---|
| Nickname | The Lone Star State |
| Motto | *Friendship* |
| Flower | Bluebonnet (Buffalo Clover, Wolf Flower) |
| Bird | Mockingbird |
| Tree | Pecan |
| Song | *Texas, Our Texas* |
| Stone | Petrified Palmwood |
| Gem | Texas Blue Topaz |
| Grass | Side Oats Grama |
| Dish | Chili |
| Seashell | Lightning Whelk |
| Fish | Guadalupe Bass |
| Entered the Union | December 29, 1845 |
| Capital | Austin |

## EXECUTIVE BRANCH OFFICIALS

| | |
|---|---|
| Governor | George W. Bush |
| Lieutenant Governor | Rick Perry |
| Secretary of State | Elton Bomer |
| Attorney General | John Cornyn |
| Comptroller of Public Accounts | Carole Keeton Rylander |

## SUPREME COURT

Thomas R. Phillips, Chief Justice

| | |
|---|---|
| Raul A. Gonzalez | Nathan L. Hecht |
| Deborah G. Hankinson | Craig Enoch |
| Harriett O'Neill | Priscilla R. Owen |
| James A. Baker | Greg Abbott |

## LEGISLATURE

| | |
|---|---|
| President of the Senate | Lt. Gov. Rick Perry |
| President Pro Tem of the Senate | Rodney Ellis |
| Secretary of the Senate | Betty King |
| | |
| Speaker of the House | James E. Laney |
| Speaker Pro Tem of the House | D. R. Uher |
| Chief Clerk of the House | Sharon Carter |

## STATISTICS

| | |
|---|---|
| Land Area (square miles) | 261,914 |
| Rank in Nation | 2nd |
| Population | 20,044,141 |
| Rank in Nation | 2nd |
| Density per square mile | 75.4 |
| Number of Representatives in Congress | 30 |
| Capital City | Austin |
| Population | 552,434 |
| Rank in State | 5th |
| Largest City | Houston |
| Population | 1,786,691 |
| Number of Places over 10,000 Population | 182 |

# Utah

| | |
|---|---|
| Nickname | The Beehive State |
| Motto | *Industry* |
| Flower | Sego Lily |
| Animal | Rocky Mountain Elk |
| Bird | California Seagull |
| Tree | Blue Spruce |
| Fish | Rainbow Trout |
| Song | *Utah, We Love Thee* |
| Gem | Topaz |
| Insect | Honeybee |
| Entered the Union | January 4, 1896 |
| Capital | Salt Lake City |

## EXECUTIVE BRANCH OFFICIALS

| | |
|---|---|
| Governor | Michael O. Leavitt |
| Lieutenant Governor | Olene S. Walker |
| Attorney General | Jan Graham |
| Treasurer | Edward T. Alter |

## SUPREME COURT

Richard C. Howe, Chief Justice
I. Daniel Stewart
Christine M. Durham
Leonard H. Russon
Michael D. Zimmerman

## LEGISLATURE

| | |
|---|---|
| President of the Senate | R. Lane Beattie |
| Secretary of the Senate | Annette B. Moore |
| | |
| Speaker of the House | Martin R. Stephens |
| Speaker Pro Tem of the House | Bill Wright |
| Chief Clerk of the House | Carole E. Peterson |

## STATISTICS

| | |
|---|---|
| Land Area (square miles) | 82,168 |
| Rank in Nation | 12th |
| Population | 2,129,836 |
| Rank in Nation | 34th |
| Density per square mile | 25.6 |
| Number of Representatives in Congress | 3 |
| Capital City | Salt Lake City |
| Population | 174,348 |
| Rank in State | 1st |
| Largest City | Salt Lake City |
| Number of Places over 10,000 Population | 39 |

# Vermont

| | |
|---|---|
| Nickname | The Green Mountain State |
| Motto | *Freedom and Unity* |
| Animal | Morgan Horse |
| Flower | Red Clover |
| Bird | Hermit Thrush |
| Tree | Sugar Maple |
| Song | *Hail, Vermont!* |
| Insect | Honeybee |
| Beverage | Milk |
| Entered the Union | March 4, 1791 |
| Capital | Montpelier |

## EXECUTIVE BRANCH OFFICIALS

| | |
|---|---|
| Governor | Howard Dean |
| Lieutenant Governor | Douglas A. Racine |
| Secretary of State | Deborah L. Markowitz |
| Attorney General | William H. Sorrell |
| Treasurer | James H. Douglas |

## SUPREME COURT

Jeffrey L. Amestoy, Chief Justice
John A. Dooley III
James L. Morse
Denise R. Johnson
Marilyn S. Skogland

## GENERAL ASSEMBLY

| | |
|---|---|
| President of the Senate | Lt. Gov. Douglas A. Racine |
| President Pro Tem of the Senate | Peter E. Shumlin |
| Secretary of the Senate | David A. Gibson |
| | |
| Speaker of the House | Michael J. Obuchowski |
| Clerk of the House | Donald G. Milne |

## STATISTICS

| | |
|---|---|
| Land Area (square miles) | 9,249 |
| Rank in Nation | 43rd |
| Population | 593,740 |
| Rank in Nation | 49th |
| Density per square mile | 63.9 |
| Number of Representatives in Congress | 1 |
| Capital City | Montpelier |
| Population | 7,734 |
| Rank in State | 6th |
| Largest City | Burlington |
| Population | 38,453 |
| Number of Places over 10,000 Population | 3 |

# Virginia

| | |
|---|---|
| Nickname | The Old Dominion |
| Motto | *Sic Semper Tyrannis* (Thus Always to Tyrants) |
| Animal | Foxhound |
| Flower | Dogwood |
| Bird | Cardinal |
| Tree | Dogwood |
| Song | *Carry Me Back to Old Virginia* |
| Shell | Oyster |
| Entered the Union | June 25, 1788 |
| Capital | Richmond |

## EXECUTIVE BRANCH OFFICIALS

| | |
|---|---|
| Governor | James S. Gilmore III |
| Lieutenant Governor | John H. Hager |
| Secretary of the Commonwealth | Anne P. Petera |
| Attorney General | Mark L. Earley |
| Treasurer | Mary G. Morris |

## SUPREME COURT

Harry L. Carrico, Chief Justice
A. Christian Compton
Elizabeth B. Lacy
Leroy R. Hassell, Sr.
Barbara M. Kennan
Lawrence L. Koontz, Jr
Cynthia D. Kinser

## GENERAL ASSEMBLY

| | |
|---|---|
| President of the Senate | Lt. Gov. James H. Hager |
| President Pro Tem of the Senate | John H. Chichester |
| Clerk of the Senate | Susan Clarke Schaar |
| | |
| Speaker of the House | S. Vance Wilkins Jr. |
| Clerk of the House | Bruce F. Jamerson |

## STATISTICS

| | |
|---|---|
| Land Area (square miles) | 39,598 |
| Rank in Nation | 37th |
| Population | 6,872,912 |
| Rank in Nation | 12th |
| Density per square miles | 171.5 |
| Number of Representatives in Congress | 11 |
| Capital City | Richmond |
| Population | 194,173 |
| Rank in State | 3rd |
| Largest City | Virginia Beach |
| Population | 432,380 |
| Number of Places over 10,000 Population | 76 |

# Washington

Nickname ................................................................. The Evergreen State
Motto ......................... *Alki* (Chinook Indian word meaning By and By)
Flower ..................................................................... Coast Rhododendron
Bird ................................................................................. Willow Goldfinch
Tree ................................................................................ Western Hemlock
Song ................................................................... *Washington, My Home*
Dance ................................................................................. Square Dance
Gem ..................................................................................... Petrified Wood
Entered the Union .................................................. November 11, 1889
Capital ............................................................................................. Olympia

## EXECUTIVE BRANCH OFFICIALS

Governor .............................................................................. Gary Locke
Lieutenant Governor ....................................................... Brad Owen
Secretary of State ........................................................ Ralph Munro
Attorney General ................................................ Christine O. Gregoire
Treasurer ......................................................... Michael J. Murphy

## SUPREME COURT

Richard P. Guy, Chief Justice
Charles Z. Smith
Charles W. Johnson
Barbara A. Madsen
Gerry L. Alexander
Phil Talmadge
Richard B. Sanders
Barbara Durham
Faith Ireland

## LEGISLATURE

President of the Senate ........................................... Lt. Gov. Brad Owen
President Pro Tem of the Senate ............................. R. Lorraine Wojahn
Secretary of the Senate .............................................. Tony Conk

Co-Speakers of the House ......................... Clyde Ballard, Frank Chopp
Co-Speakers Pro Tem of the House ........... Val Ogden, John Pennington
Co-Chief Clerks of the House ....... Timothy A. Martin, Cindy Zehnder

## STATISTICS

Land Area (square miles) ................................................. 66,581
    Rank in Nation ....................................................................... 20th
Population ............................................................................. 5,756,361
    Rank in Nation ......................................................................... 15th
    Density per square mile ........................................................... 85.4
Number of Representatives in Congress ............................................... 9
Capital City .................................................................................. Olympia
    Population ........................................................................... 39,188
    Rank in State ......................................................................... 18th
Largest City .................................................................................. Seattle
    Population ......................................................................... 536,978
Number of Places over 10,000 Population .......................................... 82

# West Virginia

Nickname ................................................................. The Mountain State
Motto ......................................................... *Montani Semper Liberi*
(Mountaineers Are Always Free)
Animal ..................................................................................... Black Bear
Flower .................................................................................. Rhododendron
Bird ............................................................................................... Cardinal
Tree ......................................................................................... Sugar Maple
Songs ......................................... *West Virginia, My Home Sweet Home;*
*The West Virginia Hills;*
and *This is My West Virginia*
Fruit ............................................................................................... Apple
Fish .......................................................................................... Brook Trout
Entered the Union ........................................................... June 20, 1863
Capital ..................................................................................... Charleston

## EXECUTIVE BRANCH OFFICIALS

Governor ............................................................... Cecil H. Underwood
Secretary of State ................................................... Ken Hechler
Attorney General .................................................. Darrell V. McGraw Jr.
Treasurer ........................................................................ John D, Perdue

## SUPREME COURT OF APPEALS

Larry Starcher, Chief Justice
Robin Davis
Elliot Maynard
Warren McGraw
George Scott

## LEGISLATURE

President of the Senate .......................................... Earl Ray Tomblin
President Pro Tem of the Senate .......................... William R. Sharpe Jr.
Clerk of the Senate .................................................. Darrell E. Holmes

Speaker of the House ..................................................... Robert S. Kiss
Speaker Pro Tem of the Senate ............................................. John Pino
Clerk of the House ................................................... Gregory M. Gray

## STATISTICS

Land Area (square miles) .......................................... 24,087
    Rank in Nation ....................................................................... 41st
Population ............................................................................. 1,806,920
    Rank in Nation ......................................................................... 36th
    Density per square mile ........................................................... 75.2
Number of Representatives in Congress ............................................... 3
Capital City .................................................................................. Charleston
    Population ........................................................................... 55,056
    Rank in State ........................................................................... 1st
Largest City .................................................................................. Charleston
Number of Places over 10,000 Population .......................................... 16

# Wisconsin

| | |
|---|---|
| Nickname* | The Badger State |
| Motto | *Forward* |
| Animal | Badger |
| Flower | Wood Violet |
| Bird | Robin |
| Tree | Sugar Maple |
| Song | *On, Wisconsin!* |
| Fish | Muskellunge |
| Mineral | Galena |
| Entered the Union | May 29, 1848 |
| Capitol | Madison |

## EXECUTIVE BRANCH OFFICIALS

| | |
|---|---|
| Governor | Tommy G. Thompson |
| Lieutenant Governor | Scott McCallum |
| Secretary of State | Douglas J. La Follette |
| Attorney General | James E. Doyle |
| Treasurer | Jack C. Voight |

## SUPREME COURT

Shirley S. Abrahamson, Chief Justice
David T. Prosser Jr.
William A. Bablitch
Jon P. Wilcox
Diane S. Sykes
Ann Walsh Bradley
N. Patrick Crooks

## LEGISLATURE

| | |
|---|---|
| President of the Senate | Fred Risser |
| President Pro Tem of the Senate | Gary R. George |
| Chief Clerk of the Senate | Donald J. Schneider |
| | |
| Speaker of the Assembly | Scott R. Jensen |
| Speaker Pro Tem of the Assembly | Stephen J. Freese |
| Chief Clerk of the Assembly | Charles Sanders |

## STATISTICS

| | |
|---|---|
| Land Area (square miles) | 54,314 |
| Rank in Nation | 25th |
| Population | 5,250,446 |
| Rank in Nation | 18th |
| Density per square mile | 96.2 |
| Number of Representatives in Congress | 9 |
| Capital City | Madison |
| Population | 209,306 |
| Rank in State | 2nd |
| Largest City | Milwaukee |
| Population | 578,364 |
| Number of Places over 10,000 Population | 61 |

*unofficial

# Wyoming

| | |
|---|---|
| Nicknames | The Equality State and The Cowboy State |
| Motto | *Equal Rights* |
| Animal | Bison |
| Flower | Indian Paintbrush |
| Bird | Western Meadowlark |
| Tree | Cottonwood |
| Song | *Wyoming* |
| Gem | Jade |
| Entered the Union | July 10, 1890 |
| Capital | Cheyenne |

## EXECUTIVE BRANCH OFFICIALS

| | |
|---|---|
| Governor | Jim Geringer |
| Secretary of State | Joe Meyer |
| Attorney General | Gay Woodhouse |
| Treasurer | Cynthia M. Lummis |

## SUPREME COURT

Larry L. Lehman, Chief Justice
Richard V. Thomas
Richard J. Macy
T. Michael Golden
William U. Hill

## LEGISLATURE

| | |
|---|---|
| President of the Senate | Jim Twiford |
| Vice President of the Senate | April Brimmer Kunz |
| Chief Clerk of the Senate | Liv C. Hanes |
| | |
| Speaker of the House | Eli D. Bebout |
| Speaker Pro Tem of the House | Harry B. Tipton |
| Chief Clerk of the House | A. Marvin Helart |

## STATISTICS

| | |
|---|---|
| Land Area (square miles) | 97,105 |
| Rank in Nation | 9th |
| Population | 479,602 |
| Rank in Nation | 50th |
| Density per square mile | 5.0 |
| Number of Representatives in Congress | 1 |
| Capital City | Cheyenne |
| Population | 53,640 |
| Rank in State | 1st |
| Largest City | Cheyenne |
| Number of Places over 10,000 Population | 8 |

# District of Columbia

Motto .................................................. *Justitia Omnibus* (Justice to All)
Flower ................................................................. American Beauty Rose
Bird ............................................................................... Wood Thrush
Tree ............................................................................... Scarlet Oak
Became U.S. Capital ................................................ December 1, 1800

## EXECUTIVE BRANCH OFFICIALS

Mayor ......................................................................... Anthony Williams
Secretary of the District of Columbia ....................... Beverly D. Rivers
Corporation Counsel ....................................................... Robert Rigsby
Treasurer ......................................................................... William Hall

## DISTRICT OF COLUMBIA COURT OF APPEALS

Annice M. Wagner, Chief Justice
John A. Terry
John M. Steadman
Frank E. Schwelb
Michael W. Farrell
Warren R. King
Vanessa Ruiz
Inez Smith-Reid
Vacancy

## COUNCIL OF THE DISTRICT OF COLUMBIA

Chair ............................................................................ Linda W. Cropp
Chair Pro Tem ...................................................... Charlene Drew Jarvis
Secretary to the Council ....................................................... Phyllis Jones

## STATISTICS

Land Area (square miles) ........................................................... 61
Population ...................................................................... 523,124
   Density per square mile ...................................................... 8,575.8
Delegate to Congress* ................................................................. 1

*Committee voting privileges only.

# American Samoa

Motto ............................ *Samoa-Maumua le Atua* (Samoa, God Is First)
Flower .......................................................................... Paogo (Ula-fala)
Plant ............................................................................................... Ava
Song ....................................................................... *Amerika Samoa*
Became a Territory of the United States ........................................ 1900
Capital ............................................................................... Pago Pago

## EXECUTIVE BRANCH OFFICIALS

Governor ...................................................................... Tauese P. F. Sunia
Lieutenant Governor ............................................... Togiola T. Tulafono
Attorney General ................................................ Toetagata Albert Mailo
Treasurer ............................................................................... Tifi Ale

## HIGH COURT

Michael Kruse, Chief Justice
Lyle Richmond

## LEGISLATURE

President of the Senate .................................... Lutu Tenari S. Fuimaono
President Pro Tem of the Senate ............................ Tuilefana M. Vaelaa
Secretary of the Senate .................................................. Leo'o V. Ma'o

Speaker of the House ......................................... 'Aina Saoluaga T. Nua
Vice Speaker of Administration .................... Tulafono Fagamia Solaita
Vice Speaker of Operations ............................................. Sala E. Samiu
Chief Clerk of the House .............................................. Amioga Palelei

## STATISTICS

Land Area (square miles) ........................................................... 77
Population ...................................................................... 61,819
   Density per square mile ...................................................... 607.74
Delegate to Congress ................................................................. 1
Capital City ............................................................................ Pago Pago
   Population ................................................................... 3,519
   Rank in Territory .................................................................. 3rd
Largest City ............................................................................ Tafuna
   Population ................................................................... 5,174

# Guam

Nickname .................................................................. Hub of the Pacific
Flower ................................................. Puti Tai Nobio (Bougainvillea)
Bird ................................................................... Toto (Fruit Dove)
Tree ............................................................... Ifit (Intsiabijuga)
Song ............................................................. *Stand Ye Guamanians*
Stone ............................................................................. Latte
Animal .......................................................................... Iguana
Ceded to the United States
   by Spain ................................................ December 10, 1898
Became a Territory ........................................... August 1, 1950
Request to become a
   Commonwealth Plebiscite .................................... November 1987
Capital ........................................................................ Hagatna

## EXECUTIVE BRANCH OFFICIALS

Governor ..................................................... Carl T. C. Gutierrez
Lieutenant Governor ......................................... Madeleine Z. Bordallo
Attorney General .............................................. John F. Tarantino
Treasurer ..................................................... Y'Asela A. Pereira

## SUPREME COURT

Benjamin J.F. Cruz, Chief Justice
Peter C. Siguenza

## LEGISLATURE

Speaker ............................................. Antonio Reyes Unpingco
Vice Speaker ................................... Lawrence F. Kasperbauer
Clerk of the Legislature ............................... Josephine Brennan-Badley
Legislative Secretary of the Senate ........................ Joanne M.S. Brown

## STATISTICS

Land Area (square miles) ................................................... 210
Population .................................................................. 160,595
   Density per square mile ........................................ 634.06
Delegate to Congress ........................................................... 1
Capital .................................................................... Hagatna
   Population ............................................................. 1,139
   Rank in Territory ..................................................... 18th
Largest City ............................................................. Dededo
Population ................................................................ 31,728

# Northern Mariana Islands

Flower ...................................................................... Plumeria
Bird ......................................................... Marianas Fruit Dove
Tree ....................................................................... Flame Tree
Song ............................................................. *Gi TaloGi Halom Tasi*
Administered by the United States
   a trusteeship for the United Nations .................... July 18, 1947
Voters approved a proposed constitution ........................... June 1975
U.S. president signed covenant agreeing to
   commonwealth status for
   the islands ............................................... March 24, 1976
Became a self-governing
   Commonwealth ...................................... January 9, 1978
Capital ....................................................................... Saipan

## EXECUTIVE BRANCH OFFICIALS

Governor ..................................................... Pedro P. Tenorio
Lieutenant Governor ..................................... Jesus R. Sablan
Attorney General ............................................. Maya B. Kara
Treasurer ................................................. Antoinette S. Calvo

## COMMONWEALTH SUPREME COURT

Miguel S. Demapan, Chief Justice
Alexandro C. Castro
Vacant

## LEGISLATURE

President of the Senate ............................... Paul M Manglona
Vice President of the Senate ............................. Thomas P. Villagomez
Clerk of the Senate ................................... Nicolasa B. Borja

Speaker of the House ............................... Benigno M. Fitial
Vice Speaker of the House ................................. Alejo M. Mendiola Jr.
Clerk of the House ................................... Evelyn C. Fleming

## STATISTICS

Land Area (square miles) ................................................... 179
Population .................................................................. 53,552
   Density per square mile ........................................ 242.15
Capital City ............................................................... Saipan
   Population ............................................................ 38,896
Largest City ............................................................... Saipan

# Puerto Rico

Nickname ............................................................. Island of Enchantment
Motto .................................................................. *Joannes Est Nomen Ejus*
(John is Thy Name)
Flower ................................................................................................ Maga
Bird .................................................................................................. Reinita
Tree .................................................................................................. Ceiba
Song ................................................................................. *La Borinquena*
Bacame a Territory of the
United States ............................................... December 10, 1898
Became a self-governing Commonwealth ...................... July 25, 1952
Capital ........................................................................................ San Juan

## EXECUTIVE BRANCH OFFICIALS

Governor ........................................................... Pedro J. Rosselló
Secretary of State ................................................. Angel Morey
Attorney General ........................................... Jose A. Fuentes-Agostini
Treasurer ....................................................... Xenia Velez Silva

## SUPREME COURT

Jose A. Andreu-Garcia, Chief Justice
Baltasar Corrada del Rio
Jamie Fuster-Berlingeri
Federico Hernandez-Denton
Miriam Naveira-de Rodon
Antonio Negron-Garcia
Francisco Rebollo-Lopez

## LEGISLATIVE ASSEMBLY

President of the Senate ................................... Charles Rodriguez-Colon
Vice President
of the Senate ................................................ Anibal Marrero-Perez
Secretary of the Senate ................................. Brunilda Ortiz Rodriguez

Speaker of the House ...................................... Edison Misla-Aldarondo
Speaker Pro Tem ............................................. Edwin Mundo-Rios
Clerk of the House ......................................................... Michael Rey

## STATISTICS

Land Area (square miles) ................................................. 3,339
Population ...................................................................... 3,828,506
Density per square mile .......................................... 1,035
Delegate to Congress* ........................................................... 1
Capital City ............................................................. San Juan
Population .......................................................... 426,832
Largest City ............................................................ San Juan
Number of Places over 10,000 Population ........................... 30

*Committee voting privileges only.

# U.S. Virgin Islands

Nickname ........................................................... The American Paradise
Motto ................................................................. United in Pride and Hope
Flower ..................................................................... The Yellow Cedar
Bird ......................................................... Yellow Breast or Banana Quit
Song ......................................................................... *Virgin Islands March*
Purchased from Denmark ........................................... March 31, 1917
Capital ...................................................... Charlotte Amalie, St. Thomas

## EXECUTIVE BRANCH OFFICIALS

Governor ................................................................. Charles W. Turnbull
Lieutenant Governor ............................................ Gerard Luz James II
Attorney General .......................................................... Iver A. Stirdiron
Treasurer ................................................................. Bernice A. Turnbull

## FEDERAL DISTRICT COURT

Thomas Moore, Chief Justice
Raymond L. Finch
Geoffrey W. Barnard
Jeffrey L. Resnick

## LEGISLATURE

President .................................................................. Vargrave A. Richards
Vice President .................................................................. Judy M. Gomez
Secretary of the Senate ...................................... Roosevelt St. C. David

## STATISTICS

Land Area (square miles)* ................................................. 134
St. Croix (square miles) .......................................... 82.2
St. John (square miles) ............................................... 20
St. Thomas (square miles) ........................................... 28
Population ........................................................................ 101,809
St. Croix ................................................................ 50,139
St. John ................................................................. 3,504
St. Thomas .............................................................. 48,166
Density per square mile ....................................... 760.90
Delegate to Congress** .................................................... 1
Capital City ............................................. Charlotte Amalie, St. Thomas
Population ............................................................ 12,331
Largest City ............................................ Charlotte Amalie, St. Thomas

*The U.S. Virgin Islands is comprised of three large islands (St. Croix, St. John, St. Thomas) and 50 smaller islands and cays.
**Committee voting privileges only.

# Chapter Eleven

# STATE GOVERNMENT IN REVIEW

*Selected CSG resource data — includes governors' priorities, state air pollution control programs, incentives to create, attract or retain businesses, gaming, Medicaid managed care and state efforts to retain and recruit information technology employees.*

For additional information on Chapter Eleven contact
The States Information Center, at The Council of State Governments,
(859) 244-8253 or E-mail: sic@csg.org.

## Table 11.1
## GOVERNORS' PRIORITIES 2000, BY REGION

| State | Education | Technology | Government reform | Transportation | Tax cut | Economic development | Healthcare | Environment | School safety |
|---|---|---|---|---|---|---|---|---|---|
| **EAST** | | | | | | | | | |
| Connecticut | ★ | | ★ | | ★ | ★ | | | |
| Delaware | ★ | ★ | ★ | ★ | ★ | ★ | ★ | ★ | ★ |
| Maine | ★ | ★ | | ★ | ★ | | ★ | ★ | ★ |
| Massachusetts | ★ | ★ | | | ★ | | ★ | ★ | |
| New Hampshire | ★ | ★ | ★ | | | ★ | ★ | ★ | |
| New Jersey | ★ | ★ | ★ | | ★ | ★ | ★ | ★ | |
| New York | ★ | ★ | ★ | | ★ | ★ | ★ | ★ | ★ |
| Pennsylvania | ★ | ★ | | | ★ | | ★ | ★ | ★ |
| Rhode Island | ★ | | | | | | ★ | ★ | |
| Vermont | ★ | ★ | | | | ★ | ★ | ★ | ★ |
| U.S. Virgin Islands | ★ | | ★ | ★ | | ★ | | | |
| East Total | 11 | 8 | 6 | 3 | 7 | 8 | 9 | 9 | 5 |
| **SOUTH** | | | | | | | | | |
| Alabama | ★ | ★ | ★ | | | ★ | ★ | | ★ |
| Florida | ★ | ★ | ★ | ★ | ★ | ★ | ★ | ★ | ★ |
| Georgia | ★ | | | ★ | | | | | |
| Kentucky | ★ | ★ | ★ | ★ | | ★ | ★ | ★ | ★ |
| Louisiana | ★ | ★ | ★ | ★ | ★ | ★ | ★ | ★ | |
| Maryland | ★ | | | | ★ | ★ | ★ | ★ | ★ |
| Mississippi | ★ | | | ★ | | ★ | ★ | | |
| Missouri | ★ | ★ | | ★ | ★ | ★ | ★ | | ★ |
| Oklahoma | ★ | ★ | ★ | ★ | ★ | ★ | ★ | | |
| South Carolina | ★ | ★ | | | ★ | ★ | ★ | ★ | ★ |
| Tennessee | ★ | ★ | ★ | ★ | | ★ | ★ | | ★ |
| Virginia | ★ | ★ | ★ | ★ | ★ | | | ★ | ★ |
| West Virginia | ★ | ★ | ★ | ★ | | ★ | ★ | ★ | ★ |
| South Total | 13 | 10 | 8 | 10 | 7 | 11 | 10 | 7 | 9 |
| **MIDWEST** | | | | | | | | | |
| Illinois | ★ | ★ | ★ | ★ | ★ | ★ | ★ | ★ | ★ |
| Indiana | ★ | ★ | | | ★ | ★ | | ★ | |
| Iowa | ★ | ★ | ★ | | ★ | ★ | ★ | ★ | ★ |
| Kansas | ★ | ★ | | ★ | ★ | | ★ | ★ | ★ |
| Michigan | ★ | ★ | ★ | ★ | ★ | ★ | ★ | ★ | ★ |
| Nebraska | ★ | ★ | ★ | | ★ | ★ | ★ | | |
| North Dakota | ★ | ★ | | ★ | ★ | ★ | ★ | | |
| Ohio | ★ | ★ | ★ | | ★ | ★ | ★ | ★ | ★ |
| South Dakota | ★ | ★ | ★ | ★ | ★ | ★ | ★ | ★ | |
| Wisconsin | ★ | ★ | ★ | ★ | ★ | ★ | | ★ | ★ |
| Midwest Total | 10 | 10 | 8 | 6 | 10 | 9 | 8 | 8 | 7 |
| **WEST** | | | | | | | | | |
| Alaska | ★ | | | ★ | | ★ | ★ | ★ | ★ |
| Arizona | ★ | ★ | ★ | ★ | ★ | | ★ | ★ | ★ |
| California | ★ | ★ | | ★ | | | ★ | | ★ |
| Colorado | ★ | | ★ | | ★ | | ★ | ★ | ★ |
| Hawaii | ★ | ★ | ★ | | | ★ | ★ | | ★ |
| Idaho | ★ | | ★ | | | ★ | ★ | ★ | ★ |
| New Mexico | ★ | ★ | ★ | ★ | ★ | ★ | ★ | ★ | ★ |
| Oregon | ★ | ★ | | | | ★ | ★ | ★ | |
| Utah | ★ | ★ | | ★ | ★ | ★ | ★ | ★ | ★ |
| Washington | ★ | | | ★ | ★ | | ★ | | ★ |
| Wyoming | ★ | ★ | ★ | ★ | ★ | ★ | | ★ | ★ |
| West Total | 11 | 7 | 6 | 7 | 6 | 7 | 10 | 8 | 10 |
| National Total | 45 | 35 | 28 | 26 | 30 | 35 | 37 | 32 | 31 |

*Source:* The Council of State Governments, March 2000.

# AIR QUALITY

## State Air Pollution Control Programs

By Barry Tonning
The Council of State Governments

From the lofty heights of Capitol Hill in Washington D.C., it may appear that the federal government makes all the important decisions about clean air policy. After all, US EPA regulations and the detailed provisions of the 1990 Clean Air Act regulate pollutants that float in the air, pollutants released by industrial and mobile sources (cars and trucks), and the type of fines and sanctions levied against violators. From the Capitol Hill perspective, all these national standards and regulations are absolutely necessary. According to the cynics, if left to their own devices the states would adopt weaker and weaker environmental protection laws, creating a "race to the bottom" in which states compete for economic growth by enticing industry with less stringent – and less costly – regulations.

Reality, however, is often at odds with popular perception. In 1998, the Environmental Policy Group at The Council of State Governments and the University of Kentucky Martin School of Public Policy and Administration conducted a survey to review state clean air programs, funding and regulations. Overall, the study found that the Capitol Hill perspective on clean air programs can be misleading. These days, the states conduct most of the important clean air activities, provide the bulk of air program funding and oversee a diverse array of air pollution control activities. Most importantly, despite perceptions to the contrary many states have adopted clean air standards and programs that are more stringent than US EPA requirements due to each state's unique interests. So much for a "race to the bottom."

The states and the US EPA share responsibility for nearly all air pollution control activities in the nation. Each state submits a State Implementation Plan (SIP) to the US EPA outlining its clean air program. For each major clean air activity – setting air quality and emissions standards, monitoring emissions and ambient air, enforcing policy, and issuing permits – the US EPA sets minimum criteria for state programs. If the US EPA determines that a state's program meets these standards, it approves the SIP and grants the state full regulatory authority. If the plan does not meet the minimum criteria, the US EPA can preempt the state program and create its own air pollution program for the state. The US EPA can preempt all or part of the state program, depending on how adequately it addresses the minimum criteria.

The CSG survey asked respondents to indicate whether their states' clean air standards exceeded the US EPA minimum criteria in a variety of areas, from ambient air quality to emission limits for new sources. Ambient air quality standards are target levels which govern pollutant concentrations in the air that people breathe outdoors. The US EPA has set National Ambient Air Quality Standards for six "criteria" pollutants that pose significant health hazards if people breath enough of them. The NAAQS pollutants are ozone, particulate matter, carbon monoxide, sulfur dioxide, nitrogen dioxide and lead.

The states can expand on US EPA criteria by setting more stringent ambient standards for criteria pollutants and by establishing ambient standards for pollutants not listed in the NAAQS. Of the 38 states responding to the CSG survey, six (16 percent) reported that their standards for one of the NAAQS pollutants exceeded the US EPA's minimum criteria, and six more (16 percent) reported that their standards exceeded the criteria for two or more pollutants. Only two states – Michigan and Illinois – indicated that they did not have US EPA authority to implement the NAAQS program, but they expected authorization in the near future. Surprisingly, 24 of the 38 responding states (63 percent) have set ambient standards for pollutants other than those regulated by the US EPA's NAAQS standards. These states have set standards for pollutants such as hydrogen sulfide, calcium oxide and odors.

The survey shows that states are exceeding US EPA standards in other areas. Eight of the 38 responding states (21 percent) reported that their emissions standards for new sources were more stringent than the US EPA's New Source Performance Standards. And 25 states (66 percent) reported that their programs for monitoring ambient air quality exceeded federal minimum requirements.

The states have also made considerable progress regulating hazardous air pollutants, which are thought to pose public health risks. The US EPA has long sought to improve HAP regulations, and the 1990 Clean Air Act created an entirely new regulatory regime for 189 identified hazardous air pollutants. Thirty-three of the 38 responding states (87 percent) have received authority from the US EPA to administer the hazardous air pollutant program, with some states again exceeding federal requirements. Eighteen states (47.4 percent) regulate hazardous air pollutants in addition to those listed by US EPA and another 18 regulate additional sources of hazardous air pollutants.

In a true "race to the bottom," no state would voluntarily enact stricter NAAQS standards or regulate non-mandatory pollutants because doing so would risk losing economic growth to states with more lenient regulations. The CSG study, however, shows that in many different areas of clean air policy states have adopted standards and programs that are more stringent than what the US EPA requires for SIP approval.

Title V of the 1990 Clean Air Act mandated important changes in how states fund their clean air programs. Title V requires states to issue operating permits for every major emissions source specifying allowable levels of pollutant concentrations and the applicable emission control strategies. Title V also requires states to charge a fee of at least $25 for each ton of pollut-

ants emitted to help states fund their clean air programs. The goal of Title V is to facilitate enforcement by centralizing regulations that apply to each source of pollution.

The major categories of funding sources for state air quality programs are state general funds, dedicated state funds (such as lottery proceeds or special environmental taxes), fees (including Title V permit fees), enforcement (fines and penalties), EPA/federal grants, and other (usually mobile source) income. Title V permit fees have become the most important source of state air program funding, accounting for 57 percent of the total. Overall, the states still rely on EPA/federal grants, at 22 percent of the total, the second largest funding category. State general funds are another major source of clean air funding at 12 percent of the total. The other budget source categories – dedicated state fund (7 percent), enforcement (2 percent) and other (1 percent), make up only a small percentage of state clean air funding.

The survey also investigated how states spend their air pollution control funds. On average, states spend 24.7 percent of their budgets on permitting activities, 15.8 percent on ambient air monitoring, 12.8 percent on enforcement, 12.1 percent on administration, 10.3 percent on source monitoring, 6.3 percent on technical assistance/industry outreach, 5 percent on policy analysis, 3.2 percent on environmental science research, 2 percent on community outreach, and 9.4 percent on other categories (usually mobile source issues). Many states estimated income and expenses, since they do not record the budget expenditures and sources in the categories listed in the survey.

The 1990 Clean Air Act contained a series of challenges for state clean air programs. The Title V permit section required many states to restructure their programs, including their regulatory structures and enforcement approaches. The HAP program expanded the scope of state clean air regulations to a vast new array of pollutants and sources. For the most part, states have met these challenges. Title V permit fees have become the most important source of state air program funding, as the 1990 Clean Air Act intended. By 1998, the US EPA had granted the states authority to administer the vast majority of air pollution control programs, including the expansive HAPs program.

Most importantly, however, is the obvious intent of the states to pursue their own environmental protection agenda according to their unique circumstances. The CSG study shows that in many policy areas the states have gone beyond minimum federal requirements to become leaders in establishing and implementing clean air policy. Rather than racing to the bottom, the states seem to be vying for the lead in protecting the health of their citizens and ecological resources in a manner as unique and diverse as the states themselves.

Selected tables from the survey follow this article. Readers can get a copy of the complete report entitled *State Air Pollution Control Survey – 1999* by contacting CSG's States Information Center at 859-244-8253.

## Table 11.2
## STATE AMBIENT AIR QUALITY STANDARDS RELATIVE TO US EPA NATIONAL STANDARDS

| State | PM10 | Sulfur dioxide | Nitrogen dioxide | Ozone | Carbon monoxide | Lead |
|---|---|---|---|---|---|---|
| Alabama | 1 | 1 | 1 | 1 | 1 | 1 |
| Alaska | 1 | 1 | 1 | 1 | 1 | 1 |
| Arizona | 1 | 1 | 1 | 1 | 1 | 1 |
| Arkansas | 1 | 1 | 1 | 1 | 1 | 1 |
| California | 2 | 2 | 2 | 2 | 2 | 2 |
| Colorado | 1 | 1 | 1 | 1 | 1 | 1 |
| Connecticut | 1 | 1 | 1 | 1 | 1 | 1 |
| Delaware | 1 | 1 | 1 | 1 | 1 | 1 |
| Florida | 1 | 2 | 1 | 1 | 1 | 1 |
| Georgia | 1 | 1 | 1 | 1 | 1 | 1 |
| Hawaii | 1 | 1 | 2 | 2 | 2 | 1 |
| Idaho | 1 | 1 | 1 | 1 | 1 | 1 |
| Illinois | 0 | 0 | 0 | 0 | 0 | 0 |
| Iowa | 1 | 1 | 1 | 1 | 1 | 1 |
| Kansas | 1 | 1 | 1 | 1 | 1 | 1 |
| Louisiana | 1 | 1 | 1 | 1 | 1 | 1 |
| Maine | 2 | 2 | 2 | 1 | 1 | 2 |
| Maryland | 1 | 1 | 1 | 1 | 1 | 1 |
| Michigan | 0 | 0 | 0 | 0 | 0 | 0 |
| Minnesota | 1 | 2 | 1 | 1 | 1 | 1 |
| Mississippi | 1 | 1 | 1 | 1 | 1 | 1 |
| Missouri | 1 | 1 | 1 | 1 | 1 | 1 |
| Montana | 1 | 2 | 2 | 2 | 2 | 2 |
| Nebraska | 2 | 1 | 1 | 1 | 1 | 1 |
| Nevada | 1 | 1 | 1 | 1 | 2 | 1 |
| New York | 1 | 1 | 1 | 1 | 1 | 1 |
| North Dakota | 1 | 2 | 1 | 1 | 1 | 1 |
| Oregon | 1 | 2 | 1 | 1 | 1 | 1 |
| Pennsylvania | 1 | 1 | 1 | 1 | 1 | 1 |
| Rhode Island | 1 | 1 | 1 | 1 | 1 | 1 |
| South Carolina | 1 | 1 | 1 | 1 | 1 | 1 |
| South Dakota | 1 | 1 | 1 | 1 | 1 | 1 |
| Texas | 1 | 1 | 1 | 1 | 1 | 1 |
| Utah | 1 | 1 | 1 | 1 | 1 | 1 |
| Vermont | 1 | 1 | 1 | 1 | 1 | 1 |
| Virginia | 1 | 1 | 1 | 1 | 1 | 1 |
| Washington | 2 | 2 | 1 | 1 | 1 | 1 |
| Wyoming | 1 | 2 | 1 | 2 | 1 | 1 |

Source: State Air Pollution Control Program Survey – 1999, The Council of State Governments.
Key:
0 = EPA regulates (i.e., state awaiting US EPA authority).
1 = State standards identical to US EPA standards.
2 = State standards more restrictive than US EPA standards.

## Table 11.3
## OTHER AMBIENT POLLUTANTS REGULATED BY STATES

| State | Pollutants |
|---|---|
| Alabama | |
| Alaska | Ammonia, Total reduced sulfur |
| Arizona | HAPs |
| Arkansas | |
| California | Hydrogen sulfide, Particulate sulfates |
| Colorado | Visibility, Odors, Fugitive dust |
| Connecticut | DioxinAir toxics |
| Delaware | Odors |
| Florida | |
| Georgia | Numerous air toxics |
| Hawaii | Hydrogen sulfide |
| Idaho | Fluorides |
| Illinois | |
| Iowa | Asbestos,VOC |
| Kansas | |
| Louisiana | Air toxics |
| Maine | Toluene, Perchloroethylene, Chromium |
| Maryland | Fluorides |
| Michigan | |
| Minnesota | Hydrogen sulfide |
| Mississippi | Odor, TSPs |
| Missouri | Hydrogen sulfide, Sulfuric acid |
| Montana | Hydrogen sulfide, Visibility, Fluoride in forage |
| Nebraska | Total reduced sulfur |
| Nevada | Hydrogen sulfide |
| New York | Hydrogen sulfide, HC, Beryllium, Fluorides |
| North Dakota | Hydrogen sulfide |
| Oregon | TSPs, Calcium oxide |
| Pennsylvania | |
| Rhode Island | Hydrogen sulfide, HAPs |
| South Carolina | TSPs, Gaseous fluorides |
| South Dakota | |
| Texas | NOX,VOC |
| Utah | |
| Vermont | 54 air toxics, 44 air toxics, 192 air toxics (irritants) |
| Virginia | TSP |
| Washington | Fluorides, TSP |
| Wyoming | |

*Source: State Air Pollution Control Program Survey – 1999, The Council of State Governments.*

## Table 11.4
## STATE NEW SOURCE PERFORMANCE STANDARDS RELATIVE TO US EPA STANDARDS

| State | State standards to US EPA standards | Sources states regulate in addition to those listed in NSPS |
|---|---|---|
| Alabama | 1 | Medical waste incinerators |
| Alaska | 0/1 | |
| Arizona | 1 | Concrete batch, stationary rotating machines, gravel stone, unclassified sand blasting, spray paints, others |
| Arkansas | 1 | |
| California | 1 | |
| Colorado | 1 | Minor sources |
| Connecticut | 1/2 | |
| Delaware | 1 | |
| Florida | 1 | |
| Georgia | 1 | |
| Hawaii | 1 | Diesel engines, concrete batch plants, other sources |
| Idaho | 1 | |
| Illinois | 1 | |
| Iowa | 1 | Hundreds of non-listed sources |
| Kansas | 1 | |
| Louisiana | 1 | |
| Maine | 2 | Case by case basis |
| Maryland | 1 | All types of printing, cold degreasers, bakeries, yeast plants, vinegar plants, tanning |
| Michigan | 1 | |
| Minnesota | 1/2 | |
| Mississippi | 1 | |
| Missouri | 1 | Open burning, fugitive dust |
| Montana | 1 | |
| Nebraska | 1 | |
| Nevada | 1 | |
| New York | 2 | Other sources |
| North Dakota | 1 | Oil and gas wells |
| Oregon | 1 | Lots of other sources |
| Pennsylvania | 1 | |
| Rhode Island | 2 | Any apc equipment, any emission greater than 10 lb/hr or 100 lb/ day |
| South Carolina | 1 | |
| South Dakota | 1 | Wire reclamation furnaces |
| Texas | 1 | |
| Utah | 1 | |
| Vermont | 2 | |
| Virginia | 1 | |
| Washington | 2 | |
| Wyoming | 1 | |

*Source: State Air Pollution Control Program Survey – 1999*, The Council of State Governments.
*Key:*
0 = EPA regulates (i.e., state awaiting US EPA authority).
1 = State standards identical to US EPA standards.
2 = State standards more restrictive than US EPA standards.

## Table 11.5
## STATE HAZARDOUS AIR POLLUTANT PROGRAMS

| State | Does state have US EPA authority for HAP program? | Does state regulate additional HAP pollutants? | Does state regulate additional HAP sources? | Does state apply BACT standards to minor sources?* |
|---|---|---|---|---|
| Alabama | Yes | Yes | No | No |
| Alaska | Yes | No | No | No |
| Arizona | Yes | Yes | Yes | No |
| Arkansas | Yes | No | No | No |
| California | Yes | Yes | Yes | Yes |
| Colorado | Yes | No | No | No |
| Connecticut | Yes | Yes | Yes | Yes |
| Delaware | Yes | No | No | Yes |
| Florida | Yes | No | No | No |
| Georgia | Yes | Yes | Yes | No |
| Hawaii | Yes | No | No | Yes |
| Idaho | Yes | Yes | Yes | No |
| Illinois | Yes | No | No | No |
| Iowa | Yes | No | No | No |
| Kansas | Yes | No | No | No |
| Louisiana | No | Yes | Yes | No |
| Maine | Yes | No | No | No |
| Maryland | No | Yes | Yes | Yes |
| Michigan | No | Yes | Yes | Yes |
| Minnesota | Yes | No | Yes | No |
| Mississippi | Yes | No | Yes | No |
| Missouri | Yes | No | No | No |
| Montana | Yes** | No | No | Yes |
| Nebraska | Yes | No | No | No |
| Nevada | Yes | No | No | No |
| New York | Yes | Yes | Yes | Yes |
| North Dakota | Yes | Yes | No | No |
| Oregon | Yes | Yes | Yes | No |
| Pennsylvania | Yes | No | No | Yes |
| Rhode Island | Yes | Yes | Yes | Yes |
| South Carolina | Yes | Yes | Yes | No |
| South Dakota | Yes | No | No | No |
| Texas | No | No | No | Yes |
| Utah | Yes | Yes | Yes | Yes |
| Vermont | Yes | Yes | Yes | Yes |
| Virginia | Yes | Yes | Yes | Yes |
| Washington | Yes | Yes | Yes | Yes |
| Wyoming | No | No | No | Yes |

*Source: State Air Pollution Control Program Survey – 1999*, The Council of State Governments.
*Key:*
* BACT = Best Available Control Technology.
** Partial.

## Table 11.6a
## PROCEDURES FOR DEVELOPING POLICIES, REGULATIONS AND STANDARDS

| State | Submit to oversight commission | | Submit to legislative committee | | Invite public comment | |
|---|---|---|---|---|---|---|
| | Agency performs? | Required by | Agency performs? | Required by | Agency performs? | Required by |
| Alabama | Yes | 1 | Yes | 1 | Yes | |
| Alaska | No | | Yes | 1 | No | |
| Arizona | No | | Yes | 1 | Yes | 3 |
| Arkansas | Yes | 1 | Yes | 1 | Yes | 1 |
| California | No | | Yes | 1 | Yes | 1 |
| Colorado | Yes | | Yes | 1 | Yes | |
| Connecticut | No | 1 | Yes | 1 | Yes | 1 |
| Delaware | No | | No | | Yes | 1 |
| Florida | No | | No | | Yes | 1,4,5 |
| Georgia | Yes | 1 | No | | Yes | 1,4,5 |
| Hawaii | Yes | 5 | No | | Yes | 1 |
| Idaho | Yes | | Yes | 4 | Yes | 4 |
| Illinois | Yes | 2 | Yes | 1 | Yes | 1,4 |
| Iowa | Yes | 5 | No | | Yes | 5 |
| Kansas | No | | Yes | 1 | Yes | 1 |
| Louisiana | No | | Yes | 1 | Yes | 1 |
| Maine | Yes | 1 | Yes | 1 | Yes | 1 |
| Maryland | Yes | 1 | Yes | 1 | Yes | 1 |
| Michigan | No | | Yes | 1,5 | Yes | 1,5 |
| Minnesota | No | | Yes | 1 | Yes | 1 |
| Mississippi | No | | No | | Yes | 1 |
| Missouri | Yes | 1 | Yes | 5 | Yes | 1,3,4,5 |
| Montana | No | | No | | Yes | 1,5 |
| Nebraska | Yes | 1 | No | | Yes | 1,2,3,4,5 |
| Nevada | Yes | 1 | Yes | 1 | Yes | 1 |
| New York | No | | No | | Yes | |
| North Dakota | Yes | 1 | Yes | 1 | Yes | 1 |
| Oregon | Yes | 1 | No | | Yes | 1 |
| Pennsylvania | Yes | 1,3,4,5 | Yes | 1,4,5 | Yes | 1,4,5 |
| Rhode Island | No | 1 | Yes | | Yes | 3 |
| South Carolina | Yes | 3,4,5 | Yes | 1 | Yes | 1,3,4,5 |
| South Dakota | Yes | 1 | Yes | 1 | Yes | 1 |
| Texas | Yes | 1 | No | | Yes | 1,3,4,5 |
| Utah | Yes | 4,5 | Yes | 1 | Yes | 1 |
| Vermont | No | | Yes | 1 | Yes | |
| Virginia | Yes | 1 | Yes | 1 | Yes | 1 |
| Washington | No | | Yes | | Yes | 1,4 |
| Wyoming | Yes | 1 | No | | Yes | 1 |

Source: State Air Pollution Control Program Survey – 1999, The Council of State Governments.

Key:
1 = Required by state statute.
2 = Executive Order.
3 = Oversight Commission.
4 = State air pollution control agency.
5 = State environmental protection agency.

## Table 11.6b
## PROCEDURES FOR DEVELOPING POLICIES, REGULATIONS AND STANDARDS

| State | Cost benefit analysis | | Risk analysis | | Economic Impact analysis | |
|---|---|---|---|---|---|---|
| | Agency performs? | Required by | Agency performs? | Required by | Agency performs? | Required by |
| Alabama | No | | No | | Yes | 1 |
| Alaska | Yes | 1 | Yes | 1 | Yes | 1 |
| Arizona | No | | No | | Yes | 1 |
| Arkansas | Yes | 1 | Yes | 5 | Yes | 1 |
| California | Yes | 1 | Yes | 1 | Yes | 1 |
| Colorado | Yes | | Yes | | Yes | |
| Connecticut | No | | No | | Yes | 1 |
| Delaware | No | | No | | No | |
| Florida | Yes | 4 | Yes | 4 | Yes | 1,4 |
| Georgia | No | | No | | No | 2 |
| Hawaii | No | | Yes | 2 | Yes | |
| Idaho | No | | No | | No | |
| Illinois | Yes | 3,4 | No | | Yes | 2,3 |
| Iowa | No | | No | | Yes | 1 |
| Kansas | Yes | 1 | Yes | 1 | Yes | 1 |
| Louisiana | Yes | 1 | Yes | 1 | Yes | 1 |
| Maine | No | | Yes | 4 | Yes | 2 |
| Maryland | Yes | 1,2,4 | Yes | 1 | No | |
| Michigan | No | | Yes | 1 | Yes | 2 |
| Minnesota | Yes | 1 | Yes | 1 | Yes | 1 |
| Mississippi | No | | No | | No | |
| Missouri | No | | No | | Yes | 1,2 |
| Montana | Yes | 1,5 | Yes | 1,5 | Yes | 1,5 |
| Nebraska | Yes | 2,4,5 | No | | Yes | 2,4,5 |
| Nevada | No | | No | | Yes | 1 |
| New York | Yes | | Yes | | Yes | |
| North Dakota | Yes | 1 | Yes | 1 | Yes | 1 |
| Oregon | No | | No | | Yes | 1 |
| Pennsylvania | Yes | 1,4,5 | Yes | 4,5 | Yes | 1,4,5 |
| Rhode Island | No | | Yes | 3 | Yes | 1 |
| South Carolina | No | | No | | Yes | 1 |
| South Dakota | No | | No | | Yes | 1 |
| Texas | Yes | 1 | Yes | 3 | Yes | 1 |
| Utah | No | | No | | Yes | 1 |
| Vermont | No | | No | | Yes | 1 |
| Virginia | Yes | 2,3 | No | | Yes | 1,2,3 |
| Washington | Yes | 1,4 | Yes | 4 | Yes | 1,4 |
| Wyoming | No | | No | | No | |

*Source: State Air Pollution Control Program Survey – 1999*, The Council of State Governments.
*Key:*
1 = Required by state statute.
2 = Executive Order.
3 = Oversight Commission.
4 = State air pollution control agency.
5 = State environmental protection agency.

Table 11.6c
## PROCEDURES FOR DEVELOPING POLICIES, REGULATIONS AND STANDARDS

| | Consult with environmental groups | | Consult with industry | |
|---|---|---|---|---|
| State | Agency performs? | Required by | Agency performs? | Required by |
| Alabama | No | | No | |
| Alaska | Yes | 3 | No | |
| Arizona | Yes | 3 | No | |
| Arkansas | Yes | 5 | Yes | 5 |
| California | Yes | 1 | Yes | 1 |
| Colorado | Yes | | Yes | |
| Connecticut | Yes | 4,5 | Yes | 4,5 |
| Delaware | Yes | 4,5 | Yes | 4,5 |
| Florida | Yes | 4,5 | Yes | 4,5 |
| Georgia | Yes | 4,5 | Yes | 4,5 |
| Hawaii | Yes | 1 | Yes | 5 |
| Idaho | Yes | 4 | Yes | 4 |
| Illinois | Yes | 4 | Yes | 4 |
| Iowa | Yes | 5 | Yes | 5 |
| Kansas | Yes | 5 | Yes | 5 |
| Louisiana | Yes | 5 | Yes | 5 |
| Maine | Yes | 4 | Yes | 4 |
| Maryland | Yes | 4 | Yes | 4 |
| Michigan | Yes | 5 | Yes | 5 |
| Minnesota | Yes | 5 | Yes | 5 |
| Mississippi | No | | No | |
| Missouri | Yes | 5 | Yes | 5 |
| Montana | Yes | 4 | Yes | 4 |
| Nebraska | Yes | 4,5 | Yes | 4,5 |
| Nevada | Yes | 1 | Yes | 1 |
| New York | Yes | | Yes | |
| North Dakota | Yes | 5 | Yes | 3,5 |
| Oregon | Yes | 5 | Yes | 5 |
| Pennsylvania | Yes | 4,5 | Yes | 4,5 |
| Rhode Island | Yes | 2 | No | |
| South Carolina | Yes | 3,4,5 | Yes | 3,4,5 |
| South Dakota | Yes | 3,4,5 | Yes | 3,4,5 |
| Texas | Yes | 1 | Yes | 5 |
| Utah | Yes | 1 | Yes | 1 |
| Vermont | Yes | 4,5 | Yes | 4,5 |
| Virginia | Yes | 3 | Yes | 3 |
| Washington | Yes | 4 | Yes | 4 |
| Wyoming | Yes | 1 | Yes | 1 |

*Source: State Air Pollution Control Program Survey – 1999*, The Council of State Governments.

*Key:*
1 = Required by state statute.
2 = Executive Order.
3 = Oversight Commission.
4 = State air pollution control agency.
5 = State environmental protection agency.

## Table 11.7
### LEGAL MECHANISMS FOR IMPLEMENTING STATE AMBIENT AIR QUALITY STANDARDS, NEW SOURCE PERFORMANCE STANDARDS, AND HAZARDOUS AIR POLLUTANT PROGRAMS

| State | Ambient standards | NSPS | HAP programs |
|---|---|---|---|
| Alabama | 1,5 | 1,4 | 1,4 |
| Alaska | 1,3 | 1,3 | 1,3 |
| Arizona | 1,3 | 4 | 1,3 |
| Arkansas | 1 | 5 | 5 |
| California | 1,4 | 4 | 1,4 |
| Colorado | 1,5 | 1,4 | 1,5 |
| Connecticut | 1,3,4 | 1,3,4 | 1,3,4 |
| Delaware | 1,3 | 1,3 | 1,3 |
| Florida | 1 | 1,3 | 1,3 |
| Georgia | 1,5 | 1,4 | 1,4 |
| Hawaii | 1,3 | 1,3 | 1,3 |
| Idaho | 3 | 1,3 | 1,3 |
| Illinois | 1,3,5 | 1 | 1 |
| Iowa | 1,3 | 1 | 3 |
| Kansas | 1,3 | 1,3 | 1,3 |
| Louisiana | 3 | 1 | 3 |
| Maine | 1,3 | 1,3 | 1,3 |
| Maryland | 1,3 | 1,3 | 3 |
| Michigan | | 3 | 3 |
| Minnesota | 4 | 4 | 1,4 |
| Mississippi | 1,3,5 | 1,3,4 | 1,3,5 |
| Missouri | 1,5 | 3 | 5 |
| Montana | 1, 6 | 1, 6 | 1, 6 |
| Nebraska | 1,3 | 1,3,5 | 1,3 |
| Nevada | 5 | | 5 |
| New York | 3 | 3 | 3 |
| North Dakota | 1,3 | 1,3 | 1,3 |
| Oregon | 5 | 5 | 5 |
| Pennsylvania | 1,5 | 3 | 1,5 |
| Rhode Island | 1,3 | 1,3 | 1,3 |
| South Carolina | 1,3 | 1,3 | 1,3 |
| South Dakota | 1 | 1 | 1 |
| Texas | 1,2,3,4 | | |
| Utah | 1,5 | 1,4 | 1,5 |
| Vermont | 1,3,4 | 1,2,3 | 3,4 |
| Virginia | 5 | 4 | 5 |
| Washington | 1,4 | 1,4 | 1,4 |
| Wyoming | 4 | 4 | 4 |

*Source: State Air Pollution Control Program Survey – 1999, The Council of State Governments.*
*Key:*
1 = State statute.
2 = Executive order.
3 = State environmental protection agency regulations.
4 = State clean air agency regulations.
5 = State clean air/environmental commission regulations.
6 = Other.

## Table 11.8
## STATE AIR POLLUTION CONTROL PROGRAM BUDGETS AND BUDGET SOURCES

| State | Total Budget | Sources (percentage of total air quality control program budget) | | | | | |
| --- | --- | --- | --- | --- | --- | --- | --- |
| | | State general fund | Dedicated state fund | Fees* | Enforcement | EPA grants | Other |
| Alabama | 7,700,000 | 0 | 0 | 73 | 5 | 22 | 0 |
| Alaska | 4,495,600 | 20 | 0 | 49 | 0 | 31 | 0 |
| Arizona | 19,368,515 | 4 | 23 | 62 | 0 | 11 | 0 |
| Arkansas | 3,262,252 | 0 | 0 | 78 | 22 | 0 | 0 |
| California | 116,748,000 | 2 | 77 | 11 | 1 | 9 | 0 |
| Colorado | 12,800,000 | 0 | 0 | 79.6 | 20.3 | 0 | 0 |
| Connecticut | 13,900,000 | 14 | 0 | 62 | 0 | 22 | 0 |
| Delaware | 5,447,495 | 20 | 0 | 55 | 0 | 23 | 2 |
| Florida | 26,000,000 | 0 | 60 | 35 | 0 | 4 | 1 |
| Georgia | 14,431,000 | 12.1 | | 63.8 | 0 | 14.4 | 9.4 |
| Hawaii | 4,000,000 | 17 | 0 | 68 | 0 | 15 | 0 |
| Idaho | 3,500,000 | 20 | 0 | 50 | 0 | 30 | 0 |
| Illinois | 98,985,100 | 2.5 | 26.9 | 12.8 | 0.2 | 57.4 | 0 |
| Iowa | 7,861,084 | 0 | 5.6 | 78.3 | 0 | 16.1 | 0 |
| Kansas | 5,095,068 | 9 | 0 | 76 | 1 | 15 | 0 |
| Louisiana | 13,116,240 | 0 | 0 | 77 | 0 | 23 | 0 |
| Maine | 4,000,000 | 20 | 0 | 55 | 0 | 25 | 0 |
| Maryland | 9,738,575 | 5 | 0 | 41 | 4 | 26 | 24 |
| Michigan | 15,422,444 | 38.5 | 0.5 | 47 | 0 | 14 | 0 |
| Minnesota | 18,600,000 | 0 | 3.9 | 83.8 | 0 | 12.3 | 0 |
| Mississippi | 7,245,000 | 15 | 0 | 75 | 0 | 10 | 0 |
| Missouri | 10,200,000 | 7 | 0 | 72 | 0 | 21 | 0 |
| Montana | 3,600,000 | 11 | 0 | 58 | 0 | 31 | 0 |
| Nebraska | 2,573,000 | 13.4 | 0 | 57.4 | 0 | 29.2 | 0 |
| Nevada | 2,220,000 | 0 | 0 | 65 | 0 | 35 | 0 |
| New York | 41,200,000 | 16.6 | 0 | 66.7 | 0 | 16.6 | 0 |
| North Dakota | 1,350,000 | 0 | 0 | 80 | 0 | 20 | 0 |
| Oregon | 15,003,623 | 14 | 0 | 68 | 0 | 18 | 0 |
| Pennsylvania | 29,000,000 | 16 | 0 | 53 | 14 | 16 | 1 |
| Rhode Island | 2,600,000 | 46 | 0 | 27 | 0 | 27 | 0 |
| South Carolina | 10,400,000 | 9 | 0 | 79.9 | 0 | 11.5 | 0 |
| South Dakota | 1,400,000 | 20 | 0 | 30 | 0 | 50 | 0 |
| Texas | 71,202,469 | 0 | 0 | 90 | 0 | 10 | 0 |
| Utah | 4,060,400 | 40 | 0 | 0 | 0 | 60 | 0 |
| Vermont | 2,000,000 | 17.5 | 25 | 20 | 0 | 37.5 | 0 |
| Virginia | 14,660,113 | 20 | 0 | 63 | 1 | 17 | 0 |
| Washington | 15,500,000 | 22 | 43 | 14 | 0.5 | 20 | 0 |
| Wyoming | 2,250,000 | 9.5 | 0 | 70.5 | 0 | 20 | 0 |

Source: State Air Pollution Control Program Survey – 1999, The Council of State Governments.
Key:
* Including permit fees.

## Table 11.9
## STATE AIR POLLUTION CONTROL PROGRAM BUDGET EXPENDITURES

| State | Enforcement | Source monitoring | Ambient Air monitoring | Policy analysis | Environmental research | Technical assistance | Community outreach | Administration | Permitting | Other |
|-------|------|------|------|------|------|------|------|------|------|------|
| *Expenditure categories (percentage of total air quality program expenditures)* | | | | | | | | | | |
| Alabama | 25 | 10 | 15 | 1 | 0 | 2 | 2 | 20 | 25 | 0 |
| Alaska | 14.7 | 13.9 | 11.2 | 0.6 | 0 | 9.7 | 0.6 | 12.2 | 27.8 | 9.3 |
| Arizona | 10.5 | 0.5 | 28.9 | 3.3 | 2.5 | 0.5 | 5.3 | 21.5 | 10.5 | 16.3 |
| Arkansas | | | | | | | | | | |
| California | 14 | 7 | 8 | 2 | 12 | 46 | 1 | 4 | | |
| Colorado | 11.2 | 16.5 | 10.3 | 7 | 15.5 | 3.8 | 3.8 | 16.7 | 15.5 | 0 |
| Connecticut | | | | | | | | | | |
| Delaware | 8.57 | 8.57 | 8.57 | 9.11 | 11.25 | 10.18 | 3.93 | 7.14 | 24.11 | 8.57 |
| Florida | 14 | 3 | 22 | 3 | 8 | 2 | 1 | 13 | 19 | 15 |
| Georgia | 15.9 | 11 | 14.5 | 0.5 | 1 | 3 | 0 | 4 | 26.2 | 23.8 |
| Hawaii | 20 | 15 | 20 | 1 | 3 | 1 | 1 | 10 | 30 | 0 |
| Idaho | | | | | | | | | | |
| Illinois | 22.4 | 1.17 | 8.4 | 7.3 | 0 | 2.2 | 0.5 | 9.8 | 15.3 | 33.2 |
| Iowa | 14 | 2 | 13 | 2 | 1 | 6 | 2 | 11 | 46 | 3 |
| Kansas | 31 | 3 | 13 | 6 | 3 | 11 | 4 | 8 | 21 | 0 |
| Louisiana | 5 | 18 | 18 | 10 | 5 | 6 | 3 | 2 | 20 | 13 |
| Maine | 3 | 19 | 25 | 0 | 0 | 5 | 1 | 9 | 19 | 19 |
| Maryland | 8.5 | 8.5 | 16 | 15 | 0 | 0 | 0 | 10 | 14 | 28 |
| Michigan | 6 | 43 | 6 | 1 | 0 | 2 | 1 | 6 | 25 | 10 |
| Minnesota | 19 | 3 | 18 | 12 | 4 | 3 | 2 | 12 | 24 | 3 |
| Mississippi | 17 | 0 | 7 | 0 | 0 | 0 | 0 | 50 | 26 | 0 |
| Missouri | | | | | | | | | | |
| Montana | 4 | 19 | 10 | 5 | 0 | 7 | 2 | 7 | 26 | 20 |
| Nebraska | | | | | | | | | | |
| Nevada | 5 | 3 | 16 | 2 | 0 | 2 | 0 | 24 | 41 | 7 |
| New York | 10 | 5 | 10 | 5 | 5 | 5 | 5 | 10 | 25 | 20 |
| North Dakota | 5 | 30 | 20 | 3 | 3 | 3 | 1 | 5 | 30 | 0 |
| Oregon | | | | | | | | | | |
| Pennsylvania | | | | | | | | | | |
| Rhode Island | | | | | | | | | | |
| South Carolina | 10 | 10 | 25 | 0 | 0 | 15 | 5 | 5 | 30 | 0 |
| South Dakota | | | | | | | | | | |
| Texas | 23 | 2 | 2 | 23 | 0 | 1 | 1 | 30 | 15 | 3 |
| Utah | 15 | 10 | 25 | 3 | 1 | 5 | 2 | 12 | 25 | 2 |
| Vermont | 10 | 10 | 40 | 0 | 10 | 0 | 0 | 10 | 25 | 0 |
| Virginia | 9 | 0 | 8 | 8 | 0 | 5 | 4 | 0 | 46 | 20 |
| Washington | 10 | 5 | 25 | 5 | 5 | 20 | 5 | 10 | 15 | 0 |
| Wyoming | 48 | 12 | 8 | 0 | 0 | 0 | 2 | 7 | 23 | 0 |

*Source: State Air Pollution Control Program Survey – 1999, The Council of State Governments.*

# ECONOMIC DEVELOPMENT

## State Business Incentives: Trends

By Keon S. Chi and Daniel J. Hofmann
The Council of State Governments

"Business incentives" can be broadly defined as public subsidies, including, but not limited to, tax abatement and financial assistance programs. They are designed to create, retain or lure businesses for job creation. The term can be used interchangeably as "industrial" or "development incentives." "Tax incentives" broadly refers to any credits or abatements of corporate income, personal income, sales-and-use, property or other taxes to create, retain or lure business. 'Financial incentives" broadly refers to any type of direct loan, loan guarantec grant, infrastructure development, or job training assistance offered to help create, retain or lure businesses.

During the past two decades, states have offered various business incentive programs to create, retain or expand jobs. In addition to tax and financial incentives, some states have used customized, company-specific incentives to engage in bidding wars with other states. Others have offered incentives to recruit business from abroad.

Since the 1970s, the number of states providing tax incentives to businesses has steadily increased. For example, by 1998, more than 40 states offered tax concessions or credits to businesses for equipment and machinery, goods in transition, manufacturers' inventories, raw materials in manufacturing and job creation. Other tax exemption programs that are becoming increasingly popular in the states are linked to corporate income, personal income, and research and development.

Similarly, the number of states with financial-incentive programs also increased over the past two decades. By 1998, more than 40 states offered special low-interest loans for building construction, equipment, machinery, plant expansion and establishment of industrial plants in areas of high unemployment.

In recent years, most state legislatures have enacted laws to strengthen their business incentive programs. Legislative actions have centered on tax and financial incentives, new economic development organizations, economic zones and worker's compensation. In the next five years, a majority of the states are likely to maintain or increase their incentive activities at current levels.

However, as interstate competition for industries and businesses intensifies, state and local government officials and observers of business incentive practices are questioning the effectiveness of business incentives. Proponents maintain that business incentives have a positive effect on business-location decisions, finance, job creation, are cost-effective, help foster competitiveness and are politically popular. Opponents say that tax and financial incentives are not the most important factor considered in business-location decisions. They suggest that business incentives are ineffective in creating jobs; raise questions about equity in the treatment of existing businesses; pull dollars away from the improvement of public services, such as education and infrastructure; and create a self-defeating zero-sum game between states.

Right or wrong, business incentives are not going away in the near future.

The attached tables summarize state financial incentives for business, state tax incentives for businesses, state job training programs, state enterprise zones, and selected public/private economic development partnership programs, through 1998. They are part of *State Business Incentives: Trends and Options for the Future, Second Edition - 2000*. Readers can contact CSG at 1-800-800-1910 to order a copy or visit www.csg.org/store/.

## Table 11.10
## STATE FINANCIAL INCENTIVES FOR BUSINESS, 1998

| State | State-sponsored industrial development authority | Privately-sponsored development credit corporation | State authority or agency revenue bond financing | State authority or agency general obligation bond financing | City and/or county revenue bond financing | City and/or county general obligation bond financing | State loans for building construction | State loans for equipment, machinery | City and/or county loans for building costruction | City and/or county loans for equipment, machinery | State loan guarantees for building construction | State loan guarantees for equipment, machinery | State financing aid for existing plant expansion | State matching funds for city and/or county industrial financing programs | State incentives for establishing industrial plants in areas of high unemployment | City and/or county incentives for establishing industrial plants in areas of high unemployment |
|---|---|---|---|---|---|---|---|---|---|---|---|---|---|---|---|---|
| Alabama | ★ | ★ | ★ | ... | ★ | ★ | ★ | ★ | ★ | ★ | ... | ★ | ★ | ... | ★ | ★ |
| Alaska | ★ | ★ | ★ | ★ | ★ | ★ | ★ | ★ | ★ | ★ | ★ | ★ | ★ | ★ | ★ | ★ |
| Arizona | ... | ... | ... | ... | ★ | ★ | ★ | ★ | ... | ... | ★ | ★ | ★ | ... | ★ | ★ |
| Arkansas | ★ | ★ | ★ | ★ | ★ | ★ | ★ | ★ | ★ | ★ | ★ | ★ | ★ | ... | ★ | ★ |
| California | ★ | ★ | ★ | ★ | ... | ★ | ★ | ★ | ★ | ★ | ★ | ★ | ★ | ... | ★ | ★ |
| Colorado | ★ | ★ | ... | ... | ★ | ... | ★ | ★ | ★ | ★ | ... | ★ | ★ | ★ | ★ | ★ |
| Connecticut | ★ | ★ | ★ | ★ | ★ | ★ | ★ | ★ | ★ | ★ | ★ | ★ | ★ | ★ | ★ | ★ |
| Delaware | ★ | ★ | ★ | ... | ★ | ... | ★ | ★ | ★ | ★ | ... | ... | ★ | ★ | ★ | ★ |
| Florida | ... | ★ | ★ | ... | ★ | ★ | ★ | ★ | ★ | ★ | ... | ... | ★ | ... | ★ | ★ |
| Georgia | ★ | ★ | ★ | ... | ★ | ★ | ★ | ... | ★ | ... | ★ | ... | ... | ... | ★ | ★ |
| Hawaii | ★ | ... | ★ | ... | ★ | ★ | ★ | ... | ★ | ... | ... | ... | ★ | ... | ★ | ★ |
| Idaho | ... | ★ | ... | ... | ★ | ★ | ... | ... | ★ | ★ | ... | ... | ... | ... | ★ | ★ |
| Illinois | ★ | ★ | ★ | ... | ★ | ... | ★ | ★ | ★ | ★ | ★ | ... | ★ | ... | ★ | ★ |
| Indiana | ★ | ★ | ★ | ... | ★ | ★ | ★ | ★ | ★ | ★ | ★ | ★ | ★ | ★ | ★ | ★ |
| Iowa | ★ | ★ | ★ | ... | ★ | ★ | ... | ★ | ★ | ★ | ★ | ★ | ★ | ★ | ★ | ★ |
| Kansas | ... | ... | ★ | ★ | ★ | ★ | ... | ★ | ★ | ★ | ... | ★ | ★ | ... | ★ | ★ |
| Kentucky | ★ | ... | ★ | ★ | ★ | ★ | ★ | ★ | ★ | ★ | ★ | ★ | ★ | ★ | ★ | ★ |
| Louisiana | ... | ★ | ★ | ★ | ★ | ★ | ★ | ★ | ★ | ★ | ★ | ★ | ★ | ★ | ★ | ★ |
| Maine | ★ | ... | ★ | ... | ★ | ★ | ★ | ★ | ★ | ★ | ★ | ★ | ★ | ★ | ★ | ★ |
| Maryland | ★ | ★ | ★ | ★ | ★ | ★ | ★ | ★ | ★ | ★ | ★ | ★ | ★ | ★ | ★ | ★ |
| Massachusetts | ★ | ★ | ★ | ... | ★ | ★ | ★ | ★ | ★ | ★ | ★ | ★ | ★ | ★ | ★ | ★ |
| Michigan | ★ | ★ | ★ | ... | ★ | ★ | ★ | ★ | ★ | ★ | ★ | ... | ★ | ★ | ★ | ★ |
| Minnesota | ★ | ★ | ★ | ★ | ★ | ★ | ★ | ★ | ★ | ★ | ★ | ... | ★ | ★ | ★ | ... |
| Mississippi | ★ | ★ | ★ | ★ | ★ | ★ | ★ | ★ | ★ | ★ | ★ | ★ | ★ | ★ | ... | ... |
| Missouri | ★ | ★ | ★ | ... | ★ | ★ | ★ | ★ | ★ | ★ | ★ | ★ | ★ | ... | ★ | ★ |
| Montana | ... | ★ | ★ | ★ | ★ | ★ | ★ | ★ | ★ | ★ | ... | ... | ★ | ... | ★ | ★ |
| Nebraska | ★ | ★ | ★ | ★ | ... | ★ | ★ | ★ | ★ | ★ | ★ | ★ | ★ | ★ | ★ | ★ |
| Nevada | ★ | ★ | ★ | ★ | ★ | ... | ... | ... | ★ | ★ | ... | ... | ... | ... | ★ | ★ |
| New Hampshire | ★ | ★ | ★ | ... | ★ | ... | ★ | ... | ... | ★ | ★ | ★ | ★ | ★ | ... | ... |
| New Jersey | ★ | ... | ... | ... | ★ | ★ | ★ | ★ | ★ | ★ | ★ | ★ | ★ | ... | ★ | ★ |
| New Mexico | ★ | ★ | ★ | ★ | ★ | ★ | ★ | ★ | ★ | ★ | ★ | ★ | ★ | ... | ★ | ★ |
| New York | ★ | ★ | ★ | ★ | ★ | ★ | ★ | ★ | ★ | ★ | ★ | ★ | ★ | ... | ★ | ★ |
| North Carolina | ★ | ... | ... | ... | ★ | ★ | ... | ... | ★ | ★ | ... | ... | ★ | ... | ★ | ... |
| North Dakota | ... | ★ | ★ | ★ | ★ | ★ | ★ | ★ | ★ | ★ | ★ | ★ | ★ | ★ | ★ | ★ |
| Ohio | ★ | ★ | ★ | ... | ★ | ... | ★ | ★ | ★ | ★ | ... | ... | ★ | ★ | ★ | ★ |
| Oklahoma | ★ | ... | ★ | ★ | ★ | ★ | ★ | ★ | ★ | ★ | ★ | ★ | ★ | ★ | ★ | ★ |
| Oregon | ★ | ★ | ★ | ★ | ★ | ★ | ★ | ★ | ★ | ★ | ★ | ★ | ★ | ★ | ★ | ★ |
| Pennsylvania | ★ | ★ | ★ | ★ | ★ | ★ | ★ | ★ | ★ | ★ | ★ | ★ | ★ | ★ | ★ | ★ |
| Rhode Island | ★ | ★ | ★ | ★ | ★ | ★ | ★ | ★ | ★ | ★ | ★ | ★ | ★ | ★ | ★ | ★ |
| South Carolina | ★ | ★ | ★ | ... | ★ | ★ | ★ | ★ | ★ | ★ | ... | ... | ★ | ... | ★ | ★ |
| South Dakota | ★ | ... | ★ | ★ | ★ | ★ | ★ | ★ | ★ | ★ | ... | ... | ★ | ★ | ... | ... |
| Tennessee | ... | ... | ★ | ★ | ★ | ★ | ★ | ★ | ★ | ★ | ★ | ★ | ★ | ★ | ... | ... |
| Texas | ★ | ★ | ★ | ★ | ★ | ★ | ★ | ★ | ... | ★ | ★ | ★ | ★ | ... | ★ | ... |
| Utah | ★ | ★ | ... | ... | ★ | ★ | ... | ... | ★ | ★ | ... | ... | ★ | ★ | ★ | ... |
| Vermont | ★ | ★ | ★ | ... | ★ | ★ | ★ | ★ | ★ | ★ | ★ | ★ | ★ | ★ | ... | ... |
| Virginia | ★ | ★ | ★ | ... | ★ | ★ | ★ | ★ | ★ | ★ | ... | ... | ★ | ... | ★ | ★ |
| Washington | ★ | ★ | ★ | ... | ★ | ... | ... | ★ | ... | ... | ★ | ... | ★ | ★ | ★ | ... |
| West Virginia | ★ | ★ | ★ | ... | ★ | ... | ★ | ★ | ... | ★ | ★ | ★ | ★ | ★ | ... | ... |
| Wisconsin | ★ | ... | ★ | ... | ★ | ★ | ★ | ★ | ★ | ★ | ... | ... | ... | ... | ★ | ... |
| Wyoming | ★ | ★ | ★ | ... | ★ | ★ | ★ | ★ | ★ | ★ | ★ | ★ | ★ | ★ | ... | ... |
| **State totals** | 42 | 39 | 45 | 24 | 49 | 41 | 42 | 43 | 47 | 47 | 28 | 30 | 44 | 27 | 43 | 37 |

Source: Compiled by The Council of State Governments from October 1998 issue of *Site Selection*, Conway Data, Inc.

Key:
★ — Yes
... — No

## Table 11.11
## STATE TAX INCENTIVES FOR BUSINESS, 1998

| State | Corporate income tax exemption | Personal income tax exemption | Excise tax exemption | Tax exemption or moratorium on equipment machinery | Tax exemption or moratorium on equipment, machinery | Inventory tax exemption on goods in transit (Freeport) | Tax exemption on manufacturers inventories | Sales/use tax exemption on new equipment | Tax exemption on raw materials used in manufacturing | Tax incentive for creation of jobs | Tax incentive for industrial investment | Tax credits for use of specified state products | Tax stabilization agreements for specified industries | Tax exemption to encourage research and development | Accelerated depreciation of industrial equipment |
|---|---|---|---|---|---|---|---|---|---|---|---|---|---|---|---|
| Alabama | ★ | ★ | ★ | ★ | ★ | ★ | ★ | ★ | ★ | ★ | ★ | … | … | … | ★ |
| Alaska | … | ★ | ★ | ★ | … | … | … | ★ | ★ | … | ★ | ★ | … | … | ★ |
| Arizona | ★ | ★ | … | ★ | ★ | ★ | ★ | ★ | ★ | ★ | ★ | … | … | ★ | ★ |
| Arkansas | ★ | … | ★ | ★ | ★ | … | ★ | ★ | ★ | ★ | ★ | … | ★ | ★ | ★ |
| California | … | ★ | ★ | ★ | ★ | ★ | ★ | ★ | ★ | ★ | ★ | … | … | ★ | ★ |
| Colorado | ★ | … | ★ | … | ★ | ★ | ★ | ★ | ★ | ★ | ★ | … | … | ★ | … |
| Connecticut | ★ | … | … | ★ | ★ | ★ | ★ | ★ | ★ | ★ | ★ | … | … | ★ | ★ |
| Delaware | ★ | ★ | ★ | ★ | ★ | ★ | ★ | ★ | ★ | ★ | ★ | … | … | ★ | ★ |
| Florida | ★ | ★ | … | ★ | ★ | ★ | ★ | ★ | ★ | ★ | ★ | … | … | ★ | ★ |
| Georgia | … | … | … | ★ | ★ | ★ | ★ | ★ | ★ | ★ | ★ | … | … | ★ | … |
| Hawaii | ★ | ★ | ★ | ★ | … | … | ★ | ★ | ★ | ★ | … | … | ★ | ★ | ★ |
| Idaho | ★ | … | … | ★ | ★ | ★ | ★ | ★ | ★ | ★ | ★ | … | … | ★ | ★ |
| Illinois | ★ | ★ | ★ | ★ | ★ | ★ | ★ | ★ | ★ | ★ | ★ | … | … | ★ | ★ |
| Indiana | ★ | ★ | … | ★ | ★ | ★ | ★ | ★ | ★ | ★ | ★ | … | … | ★ | ★ |
| Iowa | ★ | ★ | ★ | ★ | ★ | ★ | ★ | ★ | ★ | ★ | ★ | … | … | ★ | ★ |
| Kansas | ★ | ★ | … | ★ | ★ | ★ | ★ | ★ | ★ | ★ | ★ | … | … | ★ | ★ |
| Kentucky | … | … | … | ★ | ★ | ★ | ★ | ★ | ★ | ★ | ★ | … | … | ★ | ★ |
| Louisiana | ★ | ★ | … | ★ | ★ | ★ | ★ | … | ★ | ★ | ★ | … | ★ | ★ | ★ |
| Maine | ★ | ★ | … | ★ | ★ | ★ | ★ | ★ | ★ | ★ | ★ | … | … | ★ | ★ |
| Maryland | ★ | ★ | ★ | ★ | ★ | ★ | ★ | ★ | ★ | ★ | ★ | … | … | ★ | ★ |
| Massachusetts | ★ | ★ | ★ | ★ | ★ | ★ | ★ | ★ | ★ | ★ | ★ | … | ★ | ★ | ★ |
| Michigan | ★ | ★ | … | ★ | ★ | ★ | ★ | ★ | ★ | ★ | ★ | … | … | ★ | … |
| Minnesota | … | … | ★ | ★ | ★ | ★ | ★ | ★ | ★ | ★ | ★ | … | ★ | ★ | ★ |
| Mississippi | ★ | ★ | … | ★ | ★ | ★ | ★ | ★ | ★ | ★ | ★ | … | … | ★ | ★ |
| Missouri | ★ | ★ | ★ | … | ★ | ★ | ★ | ★ | ★ | ★ | ★ | … | … | ★ | ★ |
| Montana | ★ | ★ | … | ★ | ★ | ★ | ★ | ★ | ★ | ★ | ★ | ★ | ★ | ★ | ★ |
| Nebraska | … | ★ | … | ★ | ★ | … | ★ | ★ | ★ | ★ | ★ | … | … | … | ★ |
| Nevada | ★ | ★ | ★ | … | … | ★ | ★ | ★ | ★ | ★ | ★ | … | … | … | … |
| New Hampshire | … | ★ | … | … | ★ | ★ | ★ | ★ | ★ | ★ | ★ | … | … | … | ★ |
| New Jersey | ★ | ★ | … | ★ | ★ | ★ | ★ | ★ | ★ | ★ | ★ | … | … | ★ | ★ |
| New Mexico | … | … | … | ★ | ★ | ★ | ★ | ★ | ★ | ★ | … | … | ★ | ★ | ★ |
| New York | ★ | ★ | ★ | ★ | ★ | ★ | ★ | ★ | ★ | ★ | ★ | … | … | ★ | … |
| North Carolina | … | … | … | … | ★ | ★ | ★ | ★ | ★ | ★ | ★ | … | … | ★ | … |
| North Dakota | ★ | … | ★ | ★ | ★ | ★ | ★ | ★ | ★ | ★ | ★ | … | … | ★ | … |
| Ohio | ★ | ★ | … | ★ | ★ | ★ | ★ | ★ | ★ | ★ | ★ | … | … | ★ | … |
| Oklahoma | ★ | ★ | ★ | ★ | ★ | ★ | … | ★ | ★ | ★ | ★ | ★ | ★ | ★ | ★ |
| Oregon | … | ★ | ★ | ★ | ★ | ★ | ★ | ★ | ★ | ★ | ★ | … | … | ★ | ★ |
| Pennsylvania | ★ | … | ★ | ★ | ★ | ★ | ★ | ★ | ★ | ★ | ★ | ★ | … | ★ | ★ |
| Rhode Island | … | ★ | ★ | ★ | ★ | … | ★ | ★ | ★ | ★ | ★ | ★ | ★ | ★ | ★ |
| South Carolina | ★ | … | ★ | ★ | ★ | ★ | ★ | ★ | ★ | ★ | ★ | … | … | ★ | ★ |
| South Dakota | ★ | ★ | ★ | ★ | … | ★ | ★ | … | ★ | ★ | ★ | … | … | ★ | ★ |
| Tennessee | ★ | ★ | ★ | ★ | ★ | ★ | ★ | ★ | ★ | ★ | ★ | … | … | ★ | ★ |
| Texas | ★ | ★ | … | ★ | ★ | ★ | ★ | … | ★ | ★ | ★ | … | … | … | ★ |
| Utah | … | … | … | … | ★ | ★ | ★ | ★ | ★ | ★ | ★ | … | … | … | ★ |
| Vermont | … | … | ★ | … | … | ★ | ★ | ★ | ★ | … | … | … | ★ | … | ★ |
| Virginia | ★ | ★ | … | ★ | ★ | ★ | ★ | ★ | ★ | ★ | ★ | … | … | ★ | ★ |
| Washington | ★ | ★ | ★ | … | … | ★ | ★ | ★ | ★ | ★ | ★ | … | … | ★ | ★ |
| West Virginia | ★ | ★ | … | ★ | … | ★ | … | ★ | ★ | ★ | ★ | ★ | ★ | ★ | ★ |
| Wisconsin | ★ | ★ | … | … | ★ | ★ | ★ | ★ | ★ | ★ | ★ | … | … | ★ | ★ |
| Wyoming | ★ | ★ | ★ | … | ★ | ★ | ★ | ★ | ★ | ★ | ★ | … | … | … | … |
| **State totals** | 37 | 34 | 26 | 38 | 42 | 48 | 46 | 47 | 50 | 43 | 43 | 7 | 9 | 38 | 41 |

*Source:* Compiled by The Council of State Governments from October 1998 issue of *Site Selection*, Conway Data, Inc.
*Key:*
★ — Yes
… — No

## Table 11.12
## STATE JOB TRAINING PROGRAMS

| State | Program | Description |
|-------|---------|-------------|
| Alabama | The Alabama Industrial Development Training Program | Provides free job training for companies if certain qualifications for starting wages and job creation are met. Support for on-the-job training is available to companies that meet other criteria. |
| Arizona | The Workforce Recruitment and Job Training Grant Program | Provides grants for short-term training for new employees. The training must be job and business specific. The program is funded annually at $4.5 million. Fifteen percent of the fund goes to businesses with fewer than 100 employees and 15 percent of the fund for businesses located in a rural community. |
| Arkansas | The Existing Workforce Training Program (EWTP) | Provided to manufacturing industries in Arkansas for upgrading workforce skills. The program is administered by the Department of Higher Education, the Vocational-Technical Division of the Department of Education and the Arkansas Industrial Development Commission. The focus of this program is to upgrade skills specific to a company's current workforce at any level. |
| | The Arkansas Industrial Development Commission Industry Training Program (ITP) | Provides intensive pre-employment training for Arkansas workers to meet the increasing technical employment needs of the state's new and expanding industry. AIDC provides training on the company's equipment at its site, or if its in the construction phase, at an off-site facility. |
| California | The Employment Training Panel (ETP) | Assists businesses in acquiring and retaining a highly skilled workforce to increase competitiveness and productivity. The ETP is a program supported by California employers through a small contribution to the California Employment Training Fund. |
| Colorado | The Colorado FIRST and Existing Industries Programs | Offer short-term, fast track job training assistance to qualified Colorado employers. Customized job training assistance is available to new and existing businesses that create primary jobs in the manufacturing and business service sectors. |
| Connecticut | Connecticut Job Training Finance Program | Encourages banks to make loans up to $250,000 to manufacturers to train their production workers. Connecticut Development Authority provides a grant of the lesser of 25 percent of the loan or $25,000 upon completion of training, which is used to pay down the bank loan. |
| Delaware | Venture Capital Program | The Delaware Economic Development Office has access to more than 60 recognized educational resources to provide company-specific skill training. Training contracts may be arranged with Delaware colleges, vocational schools, specialized training centers and independent agencies that provide business, industrial and service-related instruction. |
| Florida | Quick Response Training Program | Provides rapid, effective start-up training tailored to benefit specific companies. Quick Response is administered by the Department of Commerce, in cooperation with community colleges, vocational-technical centers, state universities and private institutions. |
| | The Seaport Employment Training Grant Program | Funds job skills training programs designed to improve the movement of cargo or passengers. |
| Georgia | Quick Start | Provides complete training services free-of-charge to companies opening new facilities in Georgia or expanding existing operations. Training is customized to each company's specific needs and focuses on entry-level job skills. |
| Hawaii | The Employment and Training Fund (ETF) | Assists qualified businesses in recruiting, hiring and training employees quickly, with the assistance of state and local resources and services. The program is administered by the Department of Labor and Industrial Relations. |
| Idaho | The Workforce Development Training Fund | Provides skills training necessary for specific economic opportunities and industry expansion initiatives. It also upgrades the skills of currently employed workers who are at risk of being permanently laid off. |
| | The New Industry Training | Provides customized job training for new and expanding industries. The State Department of Employment assists in recruiting, screening and testing potential trainees and pays for qualified instructors. |
| Illinois | The Industrial Training Program (ITP) | Assists Illinois companies in training new workers or upgrading the skills of existing workers. ITP grants may be awarded to individual companies, multi-company efforts and intermediary organizations offering multi-company training. |
| Indiana | Training 2000 | Indiana's Training 2000 Program is designed to provide financial assistance to new and expanding industries committed to training their workforce. Companies can receive reimbursement not to exceed $200,000 for retraining existing workers. |
| Iowa | New Jobs and Income Program | The Iowa New Jobs and Income Program (NJIP) provides a package of tax credits and exemptions to businesses making a capital investment of at least $10.38 million and creating 50 or more jobs meeting wage and benefit targets. |
| Kansas | Kansas Industrial Training (KIT) | Provides pre-employment training for new an expanding businesses creating at least five jobs. |
| | Kansas Industrial Retraining (KIR) | Provides on-the-job training for restructuring companies whose employees are likely to be displaced due to obsolete or inadequate job skills. This program requires matching funds from the company. |
| | State of Kansas Investments in Lifelong Learning (SKILL) | Provides pre-employment training for new and expanding businesses, or consortiums of business, that are creating large number of new jobs or new jobs paying above average wages. |

See footnotes at end of table.

## STATE JOB TRAINING PROGRAMS — Continued

| State | Program | Description |
|---|---|---|
| Kentucky | The Bluegrass State Skills Corporation (BSSC) | BSSC, an independent dejure corporation within the Cabinet for Economic Development, provides grants for customized skills training of workers for new, expanding and existing businesses and industries in Kentucky. |
| Maryland | The Maryland Industrial Training Program (MITP) <br> The Partnership for Workforce Quality (PWQ) | MITP provides incentive grants for the development and training of new employees in firms locating or expanding their workforce in Maryland. <br> The rapid rate of technological change and increasing domestic and international competition demand a skilled workforce. PWQ targets training grants and technical assistance to resident Maryland manufacturing and technology companies to upgrade the skills of the existing workforce. |
| Massachusetts | Corporation for Business, Work, and Learning | The Corporation provides a variety of worker training services including support for defense firms seeking to enter commercial markets and support for firms adding jobs and developing new training methods. |
| Mississippi | Basic Skills Training Tax Credit | Provides a tax credit to new or existing businesses that pay for certain basic skills training or retraining for their employees. The credit is equal to 25 percent of qualified training expenses. Training programs must be certified by the state Department of Education to qualify for this credit. |
| Nevada | Customized Job Training | Nevada offers a customized job training program to qualified businesses that meet established criteria. This program may be used prior to a plant opening and up to 90 days following. |
| New Hampshire | | New Hampshire offers subsidized training to privately owned companies through state technical colleges and institutes. |
| New Jersey | Workforce Training Grants | New Jersey, through its nationally recognized Workforce Development Partnership, offers customized skills training, education and support services to workers and employers. |
| North Dakota | The Job Training Partnership Act (JTPA) | JTPA provides eligible individuals with an opportunity to get training or retraining so they may gain the skills necessary to obtain employment. There are several ways in which a person may become eligible for JTPA. |
| Rhode Island | Job Development and Training | The Rhode Island Job Training Tax Credit allows companies to take a tax credit up to $5,000 per employee over any three year period against their state business tax. The tax credit is equal to 50 percent of approved worker training expenses up to $5,000 per individual employee over any three-year period. Up to $1,000 of the $5,000 may be for employee wages. Plans must be filed with the Rhode Island Human Resources Investment Council for approval prior to the training. |
| South Carolina | Workforce Training | The State of South Carolina, through its highly regarded network of Technical Colleges, will recruit, screen, test and train workers needed to fill new manufacturing jobs. This training is done in concert with the company's human resources department and is designed specifically to meet the needs of the company. |
| South Dakota | Workforce Development Program | The South Dakota Workforce Development Program is an opportunity to extend training and educational resources so that South Dakota employers will be provided with a well-trained and skilled workforce. Training is provided in conjunction with an educational institution approved by the Workforce Development Coordinator. Technical instructors, curriculum materials, instructional materials and equipment are available through the coordinating educational institution to help deliver quality programs. |
| Tennessee | Appalachian Regional Commission Program (ARC) | All 50 Appalachian counties are eligible. Eligible activities include: infrastructure projects (water, wastewater, roads, rail) required to secure the creation, expansion or retention of job opportunities; job training programs; basic skills development in reading, writing, computation and computer literacy; housing projects; and, multi-jurisdictional programs in enterprise development assistance demonstration projects. State maximum ability to pay is $500,000. |
| Texas | Smart Jobs Fund | The Smart Jobs Fund provides grants to employers to train their employees. The fund is a business incentive program designed to increase the competitiveness of Texas businesses in the global economy. The program is "employer driven," which means the employer determines which employees they will train, what type of training will be performed, and who will administer the training. The legislature has appropriated $108 million for the 1998-99 biennium. The maximum grant amount available to a single employer is $1.5 million per state fiscal year. |
| Vermont | Workforce Development Tax Credit | A person may receive a credit against income tax liability in the amount of 10 percent of his/her qualified training, education and workforce development expenditures. A 20% credit may be taken for qualified training, education and workforce development expenditures for the benefit of welfare to work participants. |
| Virginia | Governor's Opportunity Fund | The Governor's Opportunity Fund supports economic development projects that create new jobs and investment in accordance with criteria established by state legislation. Funds can be used for such activities as site acquisition and development; transportation access; training; construction and build-out of publicly owned buildings; or grants and loans to industrial development authorities. |

See footnotes at end of table.

| State | Program | Description |
|-------|---------|-------------|
| **Washington** | Employee Training Business and Occupation Tax Credits | A B&O tax credit is available to businesses which have received approval for the Distressed Area Sales and Use Tax Deferral/Exemption Program and provide employee job training to their employees at no cost to the employee. The maximum annual credit a business may use is $5,000. The credit is computed by multiplying the approved training cost by 20 percent. |
| **West Virginia** | The Governor's Guaranteed Work Force Program (GGWFP) | The GGWFP is a nationally recognized award-winning customized industry-specific training program. The program provides business and industrial job training assistance to companies essentially guaranteeing that a qualified work force will be available. The program assists both new companies entering the state and existing companies that are either expanding operations or requiring skill enhancement due to technological innovation. The GGWFP can provide up to $1,000 of training assistance per employee and will guarantee the training to the satisfaction of the customer. |
| **Wisconsin** | ISO 14000 Training Program | The ISO 14000 Training program was designed to assist companies that are attempting to obtain ISO 14000 certification. This pilot program provides 50 percent of eligible costs up to $5,000 to train employees on new environmental management systems. The program's primary goal is to help Wisconsin manufacturers maintain their competitive edge by obtaining the ISO 14000 certification. The award will be provided in the form of a forgivable loan, with the undertsanding that if ISO 14001 certification is obtained within two and one-half years, the loan will be forgiven. |
| **Wyoming** | Community Development Block Grant Program | Provides grants to local governments to provide job training programs. |

*Source:* Compiled by The Council of State Governments from CSG's 1999 national survey of state economic development and business-incentive leaders (50 states and three territories responding).

## Table 11.13
## STATE ENTERPRISE ZONE PROGRAMS

| State | Program | Description |
|---|---|---|
| Alabama | Enterprise Zone Credit | Twenty-seven Enterprise Zones across the state encourage economic growth in areas considered to have depressed economies. Each area offers innovative packages of local tax and non-tax incentives to encourage businesses to locate in their Enterprise Zones. |
| Arizona | Enterprise Zone Program | The program has two incentive components (At least 35 percent of the workforce must be hired within the boundaries of the zone in order to qualify for either incentive). In addition: 1) Income Tax Credits are available to any non-retail business that creates net new quality jobs. A "quality job" is full-time and permanent, pays on hourly wage above a certain level and provides at least 50 percent of the health insurance costs for the employee. Businesses can receive up to $3,000 in tax credits per job retained over three years. A five-year carry forward is allowed for unused credits. 2) Property Tax Reclassification is available to manufacturing businesses that are either women or minority owned or "independently owned and operated" and "small." These businesses must make at least a $2 million investment in fixed capital assets. All property is reclassified from a 25 percent assessment ratio to a 5 percent assessment ratio for five years. |
| Arkansas | Arkansas Enterprise Zone Program Incentives | The Enterprise Zone Program offers three incentives: (1) a state income tax credit for each new position or job created based on the average wage of new workers multiplied by 100 in areas with unemployment rates equal to or in excess of 50 percent of the state's average unemployment rate for the previous calendar year. The above formula used is 400 times the average hourly wage. The cap is $6000 per employee in high unemployment counties. Cap is $3000 per employee in other counties; (2) a refund of sales and use taxes on the purchase of materials used in construction of a new facility or expansion of an existing facility; and (3) a refund of sales and use taxes on machinery and equipment to be used in connection with the business. To qualify for the Arkansas Enterprise Zone Program, a company must meet job creation criteria and prove the new employees are Arkansas residents during the year in which the credits are earned. |
| California | Enterprise Zones | These provide the following various tax credits and benefits:<br>I) Tax credits for sales or use taxes paid on up to $20 million of qualified machinery purchased per year.<br>II) A hiring credit of $26,894 or more for each qualified employee during the employee's first 60 months on the job.<br>III) A 15 year carryover of up to 100 percent of net operating losses.<br>IV) Expensing up to $40,000 of certain depreciable property.<br>V) Lender interest income deductions for loans made to zone businesses.<br>VI) Preference points on state contracts. |
| Colorado | Enterprise Zone Credits | The Enterprise Zone includes the following credits: Three percent investment tax credit, $500 job tax credit, double job tax credit for agricultural processing, $200 job tax credit for employer health insurance, research and development tax credit, credit to rehabilitate vacant buildings, credit for contributions to zones, ten percent job training credit, Exemption from state sales and use tax for manufacturing and mining equipment, and local government tax incentives. |
| Connecticut | Targeted Investment Community (TIC) Benefits | (Any community with an Enterprise Zone) 80% for 5-year real property and personal property tax exemptions for manufacturers. Forty to 80 percent for 5-year real property and personal property exemptions for service facilities, depending on amount invested. Fifty percent to 80 percent for 5-year tax exemption for personal property when part of a process technology upgrade, depending on the asset acquired. |
| | Enterprise Corridor Zone Benefits | Selected communities bordering Route 8 and I-395 are eligible for full Enterprise Zone Level benefits. |
| Delaware | Targeted Area Tax Credits | Firms which qualify as a Targeted Industry and locate in one of the targeted areas qualify for corporate income tax credits of $650 for each new employee and $650 for each new $100,000 investment. |
| Florida | Florida Enterprise Zone Program | The Florida Enterprise Zone Program provides a credit against either its sales or corporate income tax to a business located within or hiring from within the zones. There are also credits for building materials used in the zone and other activities in the zone. |
| Georgia | Job Tax Credit | Effective January 1, 1999, job tax credits are available to businesses of any nature, including retail businesses, in counties recognized and designated as the 40 least developed counties.<br>Counties and certain census tracts in the state are ranked and placed in economic tiers using the following factors:<br>1. Highest unemployment;<br>2. Lowest per capita income;<br>3. Highest percentage of residents whose incomes are below the poverty level; and<br>4. Average weekly manufacturing wage. |

See footnotes at end of table.

| State | Program | Description |
|---|---|---|
| Hawaii | Enterprise Zone Program | Established to increase business activity and create jobs in areas with above normal unemployment and/or below average income levels. |
| Illinois | Corporate Income Enterprise Zone Incentives | These incentives include a 0.5 percent investment tax credit; a $500 per job, jobs tax credit; a deduction for dividends paid by a corporation operating in an Illinois enterprise zone; and a deduction for interest paid on loans to businesses operating in an Illinois enterprise zone. |
| | Sales Tax Enterprise Zone Incentives | These exemptions include: a sales tax exemption for building materials to be used in an enterprise zone if bought in the municipality or county which created the zone; a sales tax exemption for materials consumed in a manufacturing process; and, a utility tax exemption on gas, electricity, and telephone. |
| Iowa | Enterprise Zone Program | Eligible businesses locating or expanding in an Enterprise Zone area may receive property tax exemptions and expanded state tax credits. Twenty-eight counties and eighteen cities qualify for the program under the 1997 law's provisions by having areas which meet legislative definitions of economic distress. |
| Kansas | Enterprise Zone Incentives | Enterprise zone incentives are available to qualifying businesses throughout the state, based on the location of the facility, the type of facility (manufacturing, non-manufacturing or retail), the capital investment and the number of jobs created. A sales tax exemption is available on the materials, equipment and services purchased when building, expanding or renovating a business facility. State income tax credits are available for job creation and capital investment. |
| Kentucky | Enterprise Zone Program | State and local tax incentives are offered to businesses located or locating in zones, and some regulations are eased to make development in the area more attractive. A zone remains in effect for 20 years after the date of designation. |
| Louisiana | Enterprise Zones | Qualified businesses locating or expanding in Louisiana enterprise zones are eligible for a one-time tax credit of $2,500 for each net new employee added to the payroll. The credit may be used to satisfy state income and corporate franchise tax obligations. If the entire credit cannot be used in the year claimed, the remainder may be applied against the income tax or franchise tax for the succeeding 10 taxable years, or until the entire credit is used, whichever occurs first. |
| Maryland | Enterprise Zone Tax Credits (Property and Income Tax Credits) | Maryland was a pioneer in the development of enterprise zones. It was one of the first states to enact its own enterprise zone program, and to designate zones. Advantages of a Maryland enterprise zone location include: <br>• Property tax credits — Ten-year credit against local property taxes on a portion of real property improvements. <br>• Credit is 80 percent the first five years, and decreases 10 percent annually there after to 30 percent in the tenth and last year. <br>• Income tax credits — One- to three-year credits for wages paid to new employees in the zone. The general credit is a one-time $500 credit per new worker. For economically disadvantaged employees, the credit increases to a total of $3,000 per worker distributed over three years. <br>• Priority access to Maryland's financing programs — There are thirty-five Maryland enterprise zones. |
| | Enterprise Zone "Focus Area" Tax Credits | The Maryland General Assembly has passed legislation to create "focus area" within enterprise zones. This legislation became effective October 1, 1999. "Focus areas" are especially distressed portions of enterprise zones. Businesses in these "focus areas" receive new and enhanced tax credits. |
| Massachusettts | Economic Development Incentive Program (EDIP) | This program was initiated to stimulate economic development in distressed areas, attract new businesses and encourage existing business to expand in Massachusetts. There are 33 designated Economic Target Areas throughout Massachusetts. Certified projects within Economic Opportunity Areas can qualify for additional investment incentives, including a 5 percent state investment tax credit, a 10% abandoned building tax deduction, priority for state capital funding and municipal tax benefits that include a special tax assessment and tax increment financing. |
| Michigan | Michigan Renaissance Zone Program | Michigan's Tax-Free Renaissance Zones are regions of the state designated as virtually tax free for any business or resident presently moving in to a zone. The zones are designed to provide selected communities with the most powerful market based incentive — No Taxes — to spur new jobs and investment. |
| Minnesota | Enterprise Zone Program | The Enterprise Zone Program provides tax credits to qualifying businesses which create investment, development, job creation or retention in the Enterprise Zone cities. Tax credits are allocated by the State to Enterprise Zone cities and businesses that apply for tax credits through the city Enterprise Zone coordinator. The type of tax credits include: property tax credits, debt financing credit on new construction, sales tax credit on construction equipment and materials, and new or existing employee credits. |

See footnotes at end of table.

# STATE ENTERPRISE ZONE PROGRAMS — Continued

| State | Program | Description |
|---|---|---|
| Mississippi | Economic Development Highway Program | Assist political subdivisions with the construction or improvement of highway projects that encourage high economic benefit projects to locate in a specific area. A high economic benefit project is any new private investment of $50 million or more by a company in land, buildings or depreciable fixed assets, or an investment of at least $20 million by a company that has statewide capital investments of at least $1 billion. |
| Missouri | Enterprise Zone Credit | You may be eligible for this credit if you established a new facility or expanded an existing facility in an enterprise zone and created new jobs and new investment. |
| Nebraska | Enterprise Zone Act | The Enterprise Zone Act provides tax credits for qualifying businesses that, during any tax year, increase investment by at least $75,000 and increase net employment by an average of two or more full-time positions during a taxable year. Credits may be used to reduce a portion of the taxpayer's income tax liability or to obtain a refund of sales-and-use taxes paid. |
| New Jersey | Urban Enterprise Zone | In promoting growth and development within the state's economically distressed areas, New Jersey has created 27 Urban Enterprise Zones (UEZ's). Companies that locate within one of the designated zones and create jobs are eligible for a number of benefits and zone incentives. |
| New Mexico | Enterprise Zones | The Enterprise Zone was enacted to stimulate the creation of new jobs and revitalize economically distressed areas. It authorizes local governments (municipality, county, Indian nation, tribe or pueblo), based on public input, to designate as an Enterprise Zone an area within its jurisdiction not exceeding 25 percent of its land area or encompassing more than 25 percent of its population. |
| New York | Economic Development Zone (EDZ) Investment Tax Credit | A credit against the corporation franchise tax or personal income tax is available for new capital invested in buildings and/or depreciable tangible personal property used primarily in production by manufacturing, processing, assembling, pollution-control and certain other activities in a designated Economic Development Zone. |
| | EDZ Employment Incentive Credit | An additional credit, at 30 percent of the Zone Investment Tax Credit is deductible from the tax payable in each of next three years succeeding the firm's eligible investment, if the firm maintains an average employment in the Zone of 101 percent of the average number of employees employed by the taxpayer in the Zone in the year immediately preceding the year of the eligible investment in the Zone. |
| | EDZ Wage Tax Credit | A credit against the corporation franchise tax, personal income tax, insurance tax or bank tax is available to eligible firms who create full-time jobs in Economic Development Zones. |
| | EDZ Capital Credit | A credit is allowed against the corporation franchise tax or the personal income tax for up to 25 percent of any of the following investments or contributions: Investments in or contributions to EDZ capital corporations; Qualifying investments in certified Zone businesses that employ no more than 250 persons within New York State (not counting general executive officers), investments made by or on behalf of a partner proprietor or stockholder in the business are not eligible for the credit; cash contributions to community development projects in an EDZ. |
| | EDZ Sales/Use Tax Credit | Purchases of building materials that will become an integral part of non-retail commercial or industrial real property located in an economic development zone are exempt from the State sales/use tax and may also be exempt from the local sales/use tax if a local law authorizes such an exemption. |
| | EDZ Real Property Tax Credit | Under Section 485-e of the Real Property Tax Law, businesses or homeowners constructing, reconstructing or improving real property located within an economic development zone may be eligible for a partial exemption from real property taxes for up to ten years. |
| North Carolina | Development Zone Enhancements | Taxpayers located in development zones gain additional tax credit enhancements. The taxpayer must already qualify for credit under Article III A of the Act. |
| Ohio | Enterprise Zone Program | This includes local and state tax incentives for businesses that expand or locate in Ohio. In municipalities, up to a 75% exemption of the value of real property improvements and/or new tangible personal property for up to 10 years. In unincorporated areas, incentives can be up to a 60 percent exemption of the value of new real and/or personal property for up to 10 years. Business must agree to retain or create employment and establish, expand, renovate or occupy a facility in an Enterprise Zone. Retail projects are not eligible. |
| Oklahoma | Enterprise Zones | Enterprise Zones can be designated in either disadvantaged counties, cities or portions of cities. These zones provide extra incentives for business. Double the Investment/New Jobs Tax Credit is allowed and low interest loans may be made available through enterprise district loan funds. |
| Oregon | Enterprise Zone Program | If you locate your facility in an enterprise zone, new construction and most of the equipment installed in the plant would receive a 100% property tax abatement for a minimum of three years. Manufacturing and distribution companies are eligible activities. |

See footnotes at end of table.

## STATE ENTERPRISE ZONE PROGRAMS — Continued

| State | Program | Description |
|---|---|---|
| **Pennsylvania** | Enterprise Zone Credit | These credits are available to businesses making investments in the rehabilitation, expansion, or improvement of buildings or land in enterprise zones. Businesses that are interested must develop a plan that describes their activities, the benefits that will result, a budget itemizing costs, and make a commitment to avoid dislocation of current residents. |
| **Rhode Island** | Enterprise Zones Tax Incentives | A business which has been certified by the Enterprise Zone Council is allowed a credit against chapters 44-11, 44-14, 44-17 and 44-30; Rhode Island General Laws. The credit is 50 percent of the Rhode Island salaries and wages paid only to those newly hired enterprise job workers comprising the employees included in the "5 percent growth test" used for certification by the council. |
| **South Carolina** | Economic Impact Zone Investment Tax Credit | In order to help offset the impact of federal downsizing in the state, legislation was passed to spur economic growth in 26 of the state's 46 counties surrounding the Charleston Naval Base, Myrtle Beach Air Force Base and the Savannah River Site. This legislation allows manufacturers locating in "Economic Impact Zones" a one-time credit against the company's corporate income tax of up to 5 percent of the company's investment in new production equipment. The actual value of the credit depends on the applicable recovery period for property under the Internal Revenue Code. |
| **Tennessee** | Enterprise Zone Contributions | Corporations are entitled to reimbursements of up to 50 percent of their excise tax payments for net new employment in an enterprise zone ($1,000 per new employee) and for 1.3 percent of the purchase price of industrial machinery for use in such a zone. If the reimbursement on account of industrial machinery exceeds the 50 percent limit, it may be carried forward for two years. |
| **Texas** | Enterprise Zone Program | Enterprise projects are eligible for a refund of state sales or use taxes paid on machinery and equipment, building materials, labor for the rehabilitation of existing buildings, and electricity and natural gas purchased for use in the enterprise zone. The refund is based on $2,000 for each permanent job the project creates or retains during the five-year designation period. The maximum number of jobs for which a refund may be received is based upon commitments made in the project application. Each project is limited to a maximum refund of $1.25 million, or $250,000 per year over the five-year period. |
| **Utah** | Enterprise Zones | The act passed by the Utah State Legislature provides tax credits for manufacturing companies locating in rural areas that qualify for assistance. A $750 tax credit is given for all new jobs created plus a credit of $1,250 for jobs paying at least 125 percent of the average wage for the industry. In addition, investment tax credits are available for all investment in new plant and equipment as follows: 10 percent for first $100,000; 5 percent of next $250,000. Tax credits can be carried forward for 3 years. Enterprise Zones benefits are only available in certain non-metro counties. |
| **Virginia** | Enterprise Zone Program | Qualified businesses locating or expanding in an enterprise zone are eligible for the following incentives: A 10-year general credit against state tax liability; a credit against state tax equal to 30 percent of qualified zone real property improvements is available for rehabilitation projects investing at least $50,000 or an amount equal to the current assessed value of the real property, whichever is greater; large projects that invest at least $100 million and create at least 200 jobs are eligible for a negotiable credit of up to 5 percent of the total investment (real property, machinery and equipment); and, businesses creating new, full-time positions are eligible to receive grants of up to $500 per person filling a position and up to $1,000 per zone resident filling a position for three years. |
| **Washington** | Distressed Area Business and Occupation | A $2,000 or $4,000 (if wages and benefits exceed $40,000) credit against the business and occupation tax is available Tax Credit for each new employment position created and filled by certain businesses located in eligible areas. |
| **Wisconsin** | Enterprise Development Zone | The 1995-97 state budget act established up to 50 enterprise development zones in the state. Eligible businesses locating in the zones would be able to claim up to $3 million worth of tax credits. The available tax credits include all of the existing credits under the Community Development Zone Program. Each enterprise development zone will have a minimum of one business eligible to claim the available tax benefits and will be site specific. |

*Source:* Compiled by The Council of State Governments from CSG's 1999 national survey of state economic development and business-incentive leaders (50 states and three territories responding).

## Table 11.14
## SELECTED PUBLIC/PRIVATE PARTNERSHIP PROGRAMS

| State | Program | Description |
|---|---|---|
| Alabama | The Retirement Fund | The Retirement Systems of Alabama is a public/private partnership that totals $22 billion for the Public Pension Fund. |
| Arizona | The Governor's Strategic Partnership for Economic Development (GSPED) | The Governor's Strategic Partnership for Economic Development (GSPED) is a public/private partnership that enhances the competitiveness of Arizona's economy through export-driven industry clusters and linking activities with workforce development. |
| Arkansas | The Arkansas Capital Corporation (ACC) | The Arkansas Capital Corporation (ACC) is a privately owned, non-profit organization established in 1957 to serve as an alternative source of financing for businesses in Arkansas. Its main goal is to improve the economic climate in the state by providing long-term, fixed-rate loans to Arkansas businesses. As a preferred lender for the Small Business Administration, ACC makes loans to existing operations and business start-ups for everything from new construction and equipment to working capital. ACC loans may be used in combination with bank loans, municipal bond issues, or other sources of financing. |
| Delaware | Delaware ACCESS Program | The Delaware Access Program is designed to give banks a flexible and extremely non-bureaucratic tool to make business loans that are somewhat riskier than a conventional bank loan, in a manner consistent with safety and soundness. It is designed to use a small amount of public resources to generate a large amount of private bank financing, thus providing access to bank financing for many Delaware businesses that might otherwise not be able to obtain such access. |
| Florida | Enterprise Florida Innovation Public/Private Partnership | The Innovation Partnership is a nonprofit corporation that centers on the creation and expansion of innovative, technology-based firms in the state such as biochemical, computer, microelectronics and software development. The partnership provides seed capital, expertise and direct production problem assistance. The partnership created Innovation and Commercialization Corporations (ICCs), which provide management, financial and marketing services for the commercialization of technologies developed at universities, federal laboratories and private firms. |
| Hawaii | Strategic Development Corporation | The Hawaii Strategic Development Corporation provides equity funding to private limited partnership venture capitalists who, in turn, invest in Hawaii companies. |
| Indiana | | The Indiana Department of Commerce partners with public utilities to promote economic development. |
| Kansas | Kansas Venture Capital, Inc. (KVCI) | The KVCI is a state-wide risk capital system designed to meet the special needs of businesses throughout Kansas. The system seeks to create private risk capital for investment in smaller Kansas businesses. All funds invested by KVCI must be invested in Kansas businesses solely for the purpose of enhancing productive capacity within the state, or for the purpose of adding value to goods or services produced or processed within the state. Most corporate businesses that meet the Small Business Administration's definition of a small business qualify for KVCI assistance. Any type of business can apply to the KVCI for assistance. |
| Maine | Maine & Company | Maine & Company, a private non-profit corporation dedicated to attracting new businesses into the state, oversees the Maine Investment Exchange (MIX). MIX is a joint venture project created by private businesses from throughout Maine. Their mission is to provide a regularly scheduled forum to bring together providers of risk capital with qualified entrepreneurs seeking capital. The monthly forum provides for prospective investors to hear several presentations given by qualified entrepreneurs seeking investment capital. Investors include: personal investors, personal advisor, venture capital firms, corporations and banks. |
| Massachusetts | Capital Access Program | The program provides participating banks with a cash collateral guarantee. The program is designed to encourage banks to makes loans to small businesses and is available to Massachusetts companies with annual sales less than $5 million that have borrowing needs up to $500,000. |
| | Massachusetts Capital Resource Company | This private company established in conjunction with the state acts as an economic catalyst by providing capital to businesses throughout the commonwealth. |
| | Massachusetts Business Development Corporation | This private corporation under state charter provides loans to firms unable to obtain full financing from conventional lenders. |
| Michigan | Capital Access Program | Participating banks throughout Michigan offer the Capital Access Program directly to companies that need credit enhancement. Similar to loan loss reserve fund, the bank, company and the Michigan Economic Development Corporation place a small percentage of the loan into a reserve that makes it possible for the company to receive fixed asset and working capital financing. |

See footnotes at end of table.

| State | Program | Description |
|-------|---------|-------------|
| Minnesota | Capital Access Program | This program is used to encourage loans from private lending institutions to businesses, particularly small-and medium sized-businesses, to foster economic development. When loans are enrolled in the program by participating lending institutions, the lender obtains additional financial protection through a special fund created by the lender, borrower and the State. The lender and borrower contribute between 3 percent and 7 percent of the loan to the fund. The amount of funds contributed by the borrower/lender must be equal; however, the funds contributed by the bank may be recovered from the borrower as additional fees or through interest rates |
| Mississippi | The Mississippi Department of Economic and Community Development (MDECD) International Development Division | The MDECD and local economic development organizations partner frequently on business recruitment and expansion projects. The public/private partnership also includes: individual businesses participating in foreign investment and trade missions, business leaders serve on Workforce Development Councils (created under the Workforce and Education Act of 1994) to help direct worker training efforts; MDECD and universities are partnering with companies in the MS Space Commerce Initiative to build a remote sensing based industry sector in the state; State agencies and universities partner with private sector controlled non-profit technology development corporations. |
| Missouri | Missouri FIRST Linked Deposit For Small Businesses | The State Treasurer has reserved a portion of available linked deposit funds for small businesses. State funds are deposited with participating lending institutions at up to 3% below the one-year Treasury Bill rate, with the lender passing on this interest savings to the small business borrower. A company must have less than 25 employees, be headquartered in Missouri, and be operating for profit. Small Business MISSOURI FIRST Linked Deposit loans are available for working capital. The maximum loan amount is $100,000. |
| Montana | | The State Commerce Department Regional Development Officers assist clients with finding private capital. |
| Nebraska | The Nebraska Investment Finance Authority (NIFA) | The Nebraska Investment Finance Authority (NIFA) provides low interest financing for eligible industrial projects. NIFA was created by state law, and its Board of Directors is chaired by the Director of the Department of Economic Development, The Department of Economic Development also uses Nebraska's Community Development Block Grant (CDBG) funds to provide loan guarantees for bank financing of projects it favors. |
| New Jersey | Statewide Loan Pool for Business | The Statewide Loan Pool for Business targets businesses that create or maintain jobs; are located in a financially targeted municipality; or represent a targeted industry such as manufacturing, industrial, agricultural or one of the other sectors targeted for assistance by the EDA. Through an arrangement between EDA and New Jersey banks, loans from $50,000 up to $1 million for fixed assets and up to $500,000 for working capital are available. |
| New York | Project Long Island | Project Long Island was begun last year by the LIA to identify and strengthen the high technology manufacturing industries already on Long Island that have the best chance of rapid growth and rapid job creation during the next five years. The industries are biotechnology/bioengineering, emerging electronics, graphic communications, medical imaging and health information systems, and computer software. |
| | New York-Interamerican Commerce for Consulting Engineers (NYICCE) | This is a trade development initiative including partnerships between ESD, the American Consulting Engineers, and it's New York member organization, the Consulting Engineers Council of New York State, Inc., the New York Association of Consulting Engineers, Inc., The US Department of Commerce and the Pan-American Federation of Consulting Engineers. The three year initiative is designed to build business relationships between consulting engineering firms in New York and Latin America to increase exports of their services. |
| | New York State's Energy Research and Development Authority (NYSERDA) | This program advances network technologies and applications that enable collaboration and promote technology transfer for research and education, expand these to government, industry, and the broader community. New York State's Energy Research and NYSERDA provides grants to NYS firms seeking to develop or commercialize Development Authority (NYSERDA) innovative products or processes that will lead to improvements in energy or waste minimization. |
| | Emerging Industry or NYS | This six-member association (NY Biotechnology Association, NY New Media Assoc., Photonics Development Corp. Environmental Business Association of NYS, NY Software Industry Association, Aerospace Diversification & Defense Conversion Association) represents the dynamic high technology sectors of NYS's economy. Each is partially funded by ESD and involved in a number of initiatives to facilitate the job growth and economic prosperity of their constituents. |
| North Carolina | | These partnerships are a joint public/private economic development initiative comprised of North Carolina counties. The counties of North Carolina have been organized into seven regional partnerships for economic development. North Carolina's regional partnerships enable regions to compete effectively for new investment and to devise effective economic development strategies based on regional opportunities and advantages. |

See footnotes at end of table.

## SELECTED PUBLIC/PRIVATE PARTNERSHIP PROGRAMS — Continued

| State | Program | Description |
|---|---|---|
| Oklahoma | Capital Access Program | The Oklahoma Capital Investment Board manages this easy-to-use economic service that encourages additional business lending activity. It provides a "credit insurance" reserve for Oklahoma banks through a fee-matching arrangement for loans enrolled in the program. It gives banks additional resources to finance economic development and community reinvestment activities. |
| Oregon | Capital Access Program | The Capital Access Program is designed to increase the availability of loans from banks to small businesses in Oregon. The program provides a form of loan portfolio insurance so lenders may make business loans that carry higher than conventional risks, but that are within the soundness and safety requirements of federal and state banking regulations. |
| Pennsylvania | Team Pennsylvania | Team Pennsylvania, headquartered in Harrisburg just minutes from the State Capitol's Complex, is a dynamic public-private partnership that brings together Pennsylvania's businesses, its government and community and economic development leaders. Guided by a board of directors chaired by Governor Ridge, Team Pennsylvania builds a vision for the future in the Commonwealth by providing the resources businesses need to launch or expand business success in the Commonwealth. |
| Puerto Rico | The Government Development Bank | The Government Development Bank's Low interest industrial revenue bonds (AFICA is the Spanish acronym) AFICA program for Puerto Rico tax exempt industrial revenue bonds, as well financing for privatization and infrastructure projects. |
|  | The Economic Development Bank | The Economic Development Bank offers financing to small businesses and collaborates with the Puerto Rico Industrial Development Corporation in the Venture Capital Initiative that develops public/private-financing packages for high technology venture capital financing. |
|  |  | Special Fund money may be used for research and development, management buy-outs, venture capital enterprises, financing of strategic industries and risk-sharing programs with small business. |
| Texas |  | These partnerships are through the Texas Capital Access Fund, Texas Linked Deposit Fund, and the Industrial Revenue Bond Program. |
| Virginia | Job Training Partnership | The Virginia Economic Development Department is an authority that can partner with private sector to support economic development. |
| Washington | The State Business Development Team | The State Business Development Team works in partnership with local Economic Development Councils, local and state government agencies, port authorities, and utility companies on business development activities such as arranging site visits by potential business investors, and assisting businesses in accessing local business recruitment incentives. |

*Source:* Compiled by The Council of State Governments from CSG's 1999 national survey of state economic development and business-incentive leaders (50 states and three territories responding).

# GAMING

## Regulating Lotteries and Casinos

By Keon S. Chi and Drew Leatherby
The Council of State Governments

Until recently, legalized gambling spread across the states rapidly. Seen as an effective way to create jobs, promote economic development, help community revitalization, expand tourism, and raise state and local revenues, legislatures in all but two states (Hawaii and Utah) passed laws allowing a variety of gaming activity. During the past few years, however, legislators and voters in many states have been reluctant to legalize more games, and, as a result, most legislative efforts have been defeated either in legislative chambers or by referenda. In 1996, for example, only one gambling bill passed, and in 1997, although gambling was a legislative issue in 23 states, gambling bills were defeated in 14 states. In states such as Iowa, Louisiana, South Carolina and West Virginia, which have legalized gambling, voters have been reluctant to repeal it.

According to recent polls, a vast majority of U.S. adults believe gambling is acceptable behavior. Most adults have played some types of gaming. In Connecticut, for example, nearly nine out of 10 adults gambled at least once in 1995. More than 60 percent of adults in Kentucky played the state lottery at least once since its inception in 1989. About 70 percent of adult Texans purchased at least one Texas Lottery ticket in 1996.

Several states report economic gains from lotteries and casinos. The gambling industry contends that it has created jobs and raised tax revenues for most state and local jurisdictions. But behind the euphoria legalized gambling has created in much of the public and private sectors lies the social costs associated with gaming. Critics say that certain social ills have resulted from the proliferation of lotteries and casinos: a sharp increase in underage and compulsive gambling, fraud, loan-sharking, money laundering,

the introduction of organized and violent crime, and corruption in the political system. They also contend that gambling, especially casino-type, has brought considerable damage to existing businesses.

Federal or state control over gaming is also an issue. State policy-makers insist that states continue to exercise their constitutional authority to regulate legalized gaming. States regulate virtually every other enterprise, and legalized gambling should be no different. Legislators should and can set sound gaming policies that address key issues and challenges associated with legalized gambling, and state gaming officials should enforce such public policies. Some types of gaming, such as Indian and Internet gambling, cannot be regulated effectively by states without congressional actions and cooperation from appropriate federal agencies. But it is the responsibility and duty of individual states, not the federal government, to regulate lotteries and casinos within their borders.

Amidst this debate on positive and negative impacts of legalized gaming is a growing need for state policy-makers to effectively regulate casinos and lotteries so that their benefits can be expanded and their potential social costs minimized.

In 1998, CSG surveyed state gaming officials about trends and issues concerning state-run lotteries and casinos. Subsequently, CSG convened a panel of experts to make recommendations about the issue. These efforts resulted in the following policy options and recommendations to the states:

• Lotteries. Set clear policy on advertising and location of lotteries. Reassess lottery revenue earmarks. Ensure integrity of lottery operations. Study the feasibility of privatizing lottery operations.

• Casinos. Clearly define purposes and objectives in permitting casinos. Maintain gaming commissions independent of the industry. To ensure integrity of casino operations, consider strict regulations for licensing standards and regulators.

• Indian gaming. Encourage Congress to amend the federal law on Indian gaming by paying attention to the definition of Indian lands, regulation, "good faith" negotiation, integrity of gaming and partnership.

• Internet gambling. Propose that Congress ban Internet gambling. Most states don't have laws to regulate Internet gambling operations. Although gaming officials have various proposals, governors and attorneys general are seeking a federal action on this issue.

• Compulsive and underage gamblers. Implement strategic planning to deal with compulsive and underage gamblers by focusing on funding sources, training programs, credit control, penalties and information clearinghouses.

• Reassess purposes and objectives in operating lotteries and casinos;

• Ensure integrity and regulation of lotteries and casinos;

• Encourage Congress to clarify or amend the Indian Gambling Regulatory Act;

• Propose that Congress ban Internet gambling; and

• Implement strategic planning to deal with compulsive and underage gamblers.

The tables that follow this article highlight the number of casino sites in the states as of 1998, state lottery revenue allocations, and state lottery revenue earmarks. They are part of "States Ante Up: Regulating Lotteries and Casinos," *Solutions*, October 1998, Vol. 6, Issue 2. That *Solutions* issue was compiled from a CSG survey on "Gaming and the States," 1998, interviews with state officials by CSG staff, and LaFleur's 1996 *World Gambling Abstract*. Readers can contact CSG at 1-800-800-1910 to order a copy of Vol. 6 Issue 2 of *Solutions* or visit www.csg.org/store/.

## Table 11.15
## NUMBER OF CASINO SITES - 1998

| State | Number of Casino Sites (Figures may include card rooms and/or slots only locations) |
|---|---|
| **Alabama (I)** | Indian casinos operating with no compacts. |
| **Arizona (I)** | Indian — 16 |
| **California I** | State — 165<br>Indian — 25 |
| **Colorado I** | State — 50<br>Indian — 2 |
| **Connecticut (I)** | Indian — 2 |
| **Florida I** | State — 12 non-banking card rooms at racetracks; $10/hand poker<br>Indian — 5 facilities with slots and card games |
| **Idaho (I)** | Indian — 5 facilities with bingo and electronic pulltabs only |
| **Illinois** | State — 10 |
| **Indiana** | State — 8 |
| **Iowa I** | State — 13 (10 riverboat casinos; 3 racetracks with slots)<br>Indian — 3 |
| **Kansas (I)** | Indian — 4 |
| **Louisiana I** | State — 14<br>Indian — 3 |
| **Michigan I** | State — authorized but not yet implemented<br>Indian — 16 |
| **Minnesota (I)** | Indian — 17 |
| **Mississippi I** | State — 29<br>Indian — 1 |
| **Missouri** | State — 10 (*16 licenses) *There are some sites with riverboat and barge casinos at the same location. |
| **Montana I** | State — 1,660 separate locations (e.g. taverns) that operate slots and live games<br>Indian — Unknown (slots-only locations) |
| **Nebraska (I)** | Indian — 1 (slots only; operating in violation of closure order) |
| **Nevada I** | State — 429 full-scale casinos; 1,978 additional slots-only locations<br>Indian — 1 (compacts signed for 4 additional Indian casinos) |
| **New Jersey** | State — 12 |
| **New Mexico (I)** | Indian — 11 |
| **New York (I)** | Indian — 1 (existing casino operated by the Oneida Indian Nation; St. Regis Mohawk Tribe contemplating a casino for 1999) |
| **North Dakota I** | State — 1,000<br>Indian — 6 |
| **Oregon I** | State — non-banking social card games allowed; regulated by cities and counties; total number unknown<br>Indian — 7 |
| **Puerto Rico** | State — 19 |
| **South Carolina** | State — 8,000 (video poker locations; 5 per location) |
| **South Dakota I** | State — 96<br>Indian — 8 |
| **Texas (I)** | Indian casinos operating with no compacts |
| **Washington I** | State — 21 house-banked card rooms under new trial project; new card rooms will be added every month until trial ends and permanent rules are adopted<br>Indian — 12 |
| **Wisconsin (I)** | Indian — 26, soon to be 27 |

*Source:* "States Ante Up: Regulating Lotteries and Casinos," *Solutions,* October 1998, Vol. 6, Issue 2; from a CSG survey on "Gaming and the States," 1998 and Interviews with state officials by CSG staff; LaFleur's 1996 World Gambling Abstract.

*Key:*
**I** — States that also have Indian casinos.
**(I)** — *States that only have Indian casinos.*

## Table 11.16
## LOTTERY REVENUE ALLOCATIONS (percent)

| State or other jurisdiction | State | Prizes | Administration Costs | Retailers | Other |
|---|---|---|---|---|---|
| Arizona | 29 (a); 21.5 (b) | at least 50 | 18.5 | max. 7 | |
| California | 34 | 51.5 | 7.9 | 6.6 | |
| Colorado | 26.1 | 59.3 | 8.9 | 5.7 | |
| Connecticut | 32.6 | 58.5 | 3.4 | 5.3 | 0.2 (c) |
| Delaware | at least 30; 26.8 (d) | at least 45; 11.2 (d) | up to 20; 0.6 (d) | at least 5; 49.8 (d) | 11.6 (e) |
| Florida | 38 | 50 | 6.5 | 5.5 | |
| Georgia | 35 | 51 | 7 | 7 | |
| Idaho | varies | at least 45 | max. 15 | 5 | max. 3.5 |
| Illinois | 37 | 54 | balance | 5 to 6 | |
| Indiana | 30 | 56 | 2 | 10 | 2 |
| Iowa | 28 | 54 | 12 | 6 | |
| Kansas | 31.25 | 53 | 10.15 | 5.6 | |
| Kentucky | 27.1 | 59.7 | 5.7 | 6 | 1.5 (f) |
| Louisiana | 35 | 50 | 10 | 5 | |
| Maine | 27.8 | 56.2 | 8.4 | 6.9 | 0.7 (g) |
| Maryland | 37.68 | 52.75 | 4.29 | 5.28 | |
| Massachusetts | 22 | 70 | 2.2 | 5.8 | |
| Michigan | 37 | 51 | 3 | 7 | 2(h) |
| Minnesota | variable | variable | max. 15 | 6 | |
| Missouri | 31 | 55 | 7.75 | 6.25 | |
| Montana | 23 (i) | 51 (j) | 10 (k) | 5 (l) | 11 (m) |
| Nebraska | 25 | 53 | 2 | 5 | 15 (n) |
| New Hampshire | 30 | — | 2 | — | 68 (o) |
| New Jersey | 41 | 51 | 1 | 7 | |
| New Mexico | (p) | at least 50 | unlimited | — | 2(q) |
| New York | 38 | 51 | 5 | 6 | |
| Ohio | 32.5 | 56.98 | 4.02 | 6.28 | 0.22(r) |
| Oregon | 22 (s); 56 (t) | 62 (s); 89.9 (u) | 5 (s); 10 (t) | (v) | 5 (w) |
| Pennsylvania | 40 (x) | 50 | 3 | 5 | 2 (y) |
| Puerto Rico | 35 | 50 | 10 | 5 | |
| Rhode Island | at least 30; | 67.61 | .60; 31(d) | 8 (a); 5 (b) (z); | 1(aa) |
| South Dakota | 20 (b); 25 (bb); 49.5 (d) | 6.5 (b); 50-55 (bb); (cc) | 9.5 (b); 19.5 (bb); 0.5 (d) | 5.5 (b); 5.5 (bb); (dd) | |
| Texas | 35 | 53 | 7 | 5 | |
| Vermont | 30.7 | 59.6 | 1.1 | 5.3 | 3.3 (o) |
| Virginia | 30 to 35 | 50 to 55 | less than 10 | 5 to 6 | |
| Washington | 22.4 | 63.3 | 7.5 | 6.1 | 0.7 (ee) |
| West Virginia | 30 to 40 | 50 to 60 | 11 | 6.25 | 22 (ff) |
| Wisconsin | 32.7 | 56 | 6.1 | 5.2 | |
| *Average | 32.1 | 53.62 | 6.98 | 6.54 | |
| *Median | 32.5 | 53 | 7 | 6 | |

Source: CSG Survey on "Gaming in the States," 1998.

Key:

\* For states with a range or breakdown by type of lottery game, figures are averaged; figures do not include states with an undefined variable rate.

(a) online sales
(b) instant sales
(c) misc./ Wet Inc.
(d) video lottery
(e) video vendors
(f) ticket costs
(g) Outdoor Heritage Fund
(h) game-related expenses
(i) after prizes, admin. and retailer costs
(j) min. of 45 percent
(k) no limit
(l) no more than 10 percent
(m) cost of tickets and vendor fees
(n) vendors and marketing
(o) cost of sales
(p) of net revenues: 60 percent to critical capital outlay for schools; 40 percent to scholarships

(q) to reserve fund
(r) non-operational revenue 0.07 percent; net income 0.15 percent
(s) of gross for traditional lottery
(t) of net for video lottery
(u) of gross for video lottery
(v) increasing base of 5 percent of gross for traditional; decreasing base of 3.5 percent of gross for video (sliding scales based on retailers' sales)
(w) to vendors of gross for traditional and fixed lease rates for video
(x) Older Pennsylvanians' Benefits
(y) commissions to vendors and bonuses
(z) plus 1 percent bonus for prize earnings exceeding $1,000
(aa) video lottery for cities and towns
(bb) lotto tickets
(cc) other costs are paid after prizes for video lottery
(dd) remainder to operators and establishments for video lottery
(ee) baseball stadium construction
(ff) vendor fees; 6 percent of on-line gross sales and 16.25 percent of all gross net sales

## Table 11.17
## LOTTERY REVENUE EARMARKS

| State | Lottery profits earmarking | State | Lottery profits earmarking |
|-------|---------------------------|-------|---------------------------|
| Arizona | Transportation<br>General Fund<br>County Assistance<br>Economic Development<br>Heritage Fund | Missouri | Education |
| | | Montana | General Fund |
| California | Education | Nebraska | Education Innovation Fund<br>Environmental Trust Fund<br>Solid Waste Landfill Closure<br>  Assistance Fund<br>Compulsive Gamblers<br>  Assistance Fund |
| Colorado | Parks<br>Recreation<br>Wildlife<br>Open Space<br>Public Buildings | New Hampshire | Education |
| | | New Jersey | Education<br>State Institutions |
| Connecticut | General Fund | New Mexico | Education (60% Capital<br>  Improvements 40%<br>Tuition Assistance) |
| Delaware | General Fund | | |
| Florida | Educational Enhancement Fund | New York | Education |
| Georgia | Education | Ohio | Education |
| Idaho | Education<br>State Permanent Building Fund | Oregon | Education<br>Economic Development |
| Illinois | Education | | |
| Indiana | Education<br>Police/Fireman Pensions<br>Teachers Retirement<br>Capital Projects | Pennsylvania | Senior Citizens Program |
| | | Rhode Island | General Fund |
| | | South Dakota | Capital Construction Fund<br>Property Tax Reduction Fund |
| Iowa | General Fund | | |
| Kansas | Economic Development (90%)<br>Prisons (10%) | Texas | Foundation School Fund |
| | | Vermont | General Fund |
| Kentucky | *General Fund | Virginia | General Fund |
| Louisiana | General Fund | Washington | General Fund<br>Stadium Construction |
| Maine | General Fund<br>Outdoor Heritage Fund | West Virginia | Education<br>Senior Citizens<br>Tourism |
| Maryland | General Fund<br>Maryland Stadium Authority | | |
| Massachusetts | Revenue Sharing (Cities and Towns) | Wisconsin | Property Tax Relief |
| Michigan | Education | | |
| Minnesota | Environment & Natural<br>Resources Fund<br>General Fund<br>Sales Tax | | |

*Source:* CSG survey on "Gaming and the States," 1998; *LaFleurs Lottery World Online.*

*Key:*

* Since July 1, 1998 funds are being dedicated on a phase-in basis over a seven year period to college scholarship programs.

# HEALTH CARE

## Medicaid Managed Care

By Trudi L. Mathews
The Council of State Governments

The Medicaid program was enacted in 1965 as a joint federal and state government program to provide health care for the nation's poorest people. Rising health costs over the three decades since its implementation have caused policy-makers repeatedly to examine ways to rein in expenditures. State governments began experimenting with managed care programs for their Medicaid populations decades ago, but due to greater federal government flexibility in recent years, the number of state Medicaid managed care programs has exploded. Less than 10 percent of the Medicaid population was enrolled in some form of managed care before 1992. Over 54 percent of the Medicaid population is now enrolled in managed care, according to the most recent Health Care Financing Administration figures.

While some policy-makers saw Medicaid managed care as the magic answer to double-digit increases in health-care costs, others feared that the emphasis on cost savings hurt the quality of care provided to Medicaid beneficiaries. Critics say that managed care, with its use of fixed payments prior to care, contains an inherent incentive to deny care and underserve patients. Due to the amount of money states spend on Medicaid and the special needs of many Medicaid enrollees, policy-makers have been particularly concerned with providing adequate protections for Medicaid recipients enrolled in managed care plans.

Many state and federal agencies as well as private organizations have developed methods to assess the quality of care provided to patients enrolled in managed care, both private and government-funded. As a way to deal with concerns about quality, states are using quality assurance techniques from other organizations and supplementing them with their own quality measures and programs.

These quality assurance/improvement programs for the Medicaid managed care population are fairly new, and there are tremendous differences between state programs. These differences, coupled with the ever-changing landscape in the field of quality assurance, make describing, analyzing and comparing the quality assurance efforts of Medicaid managed care programs difficult. Like measuring the course of a river, the study of Medicaid managed care quality assurance is the study of a system constantly in flux.

CSG surveyed the states about Medicaid managed care. The results showed that states use a number of different measures in their quality assurance programs for Medicaid managed care, including:

- Reviewing and approving plans' quality assurance/improvement programs.
- Requiring periodic plan reports of utilization information, performance measures/quality indicators, health outcomes measures, enrollment/disenrollment figures, consumer satisfaction information, and/or financial information (e.g., information on solvency).
- External quality reviews.
- Random medical audits/chart reviews.
- Focused quality of care reviews.
- Site visits.
- Provider feedback.
- Consumer satisfaction surveys.
- Monitoring enrollment and disenrollment figures.
- Monitoring and investigation of complaints and grievances.
- Dissemination of information to plan members about procedures and rights.
- Consumer participation on plan boards.
- Toll-free hotlines for complaints and grievances.

- Advocate/ombudsman services.
- Certification of plans.
- Accreditation of plans.

Each state uses some combination of the above measures. These practices may be carried out in conjunction with one another and may be performed by a state agency, a health plan or other entity that contracts with the state agency responsible for the Medicaid program.

From the analysis of original data and the use of existing studies of Medicaid managed care, several conclusions emerge. First, one of the biggest obstacles to assessing the quality of care in Medicaid managed care is the tremendous difference between state quality assurance programs. It is difficult to provide a nationwide analysis of Medicaid managed care without commonly accepted benchmarks of quality used by all programs.

Despite this problem, stakeholders in the debate over quality — government officials, health plans, providers and consumer groups — are working on the foundational elements of what constitutes quality care and how to measure it for Medicaid populations. Collaborative efforts between the National Committee on Quality Assurance and the National Association of State Medicaid Directors, as well as initiatives by the Health Care Financing Administration are steps toward the development of some common measures of quality.

In addition, the overarching consensus from studies on Medicaid managed care is that it provides comparable quality to traditional fee-for-service Medicaid. While this is encouraging on one hand, on the other, the hope was that managed care would actually improve care for Medicaid recipients because they would see the same doctors that individuals with private insurance see. Also, there are several features of Medicaid that make any comparisons of fee-for-service and managed care Medicaid preliminary in nature, including short enrollment times of recipients and differing reporting requirements among states.

Based on the analysis and findings of this report, adopting one or more of the following recommendations could improve the quality of care for Medicaid recipients enrolled in managed care:

- Adoption of 12-month continuous eligibility for Medicaid enrollees.
- Offering user-friendly, easily accessible guides on plan performance and provider qualifications for Medicaid beneficiaries to use in selecting a plan and a primary care provider. Funds should also be provided to translate educational materials for non-English speakers. Plans also need to provide user-friendly, culturally sensitive information on accessing care and on patient rights.
- An ombudsman/advocate and/or a well-publicized multiple-language hotline should be available to assist Medicaid beneficiaries with questions regarding selection of providers, access to care, negotiating managed care arrangements, and the resolution of complaints and grievances.
- Adequate funding, recruitment of staff and competitive pay for quality assurance programs.
- Broad dissemination of consumer-friendly, easy-to-understand comparative reports of plan quality based on plan performance information.
- Periodic objective assessments of the reasons some providers do not participate in Medicaid managed care programs as well as the level of satisfaction of participating providers with the programs
- Aggressive steps to address any provider concerns raised through the assessments.
- Carefully scrutiny of the causes of commercial plan exits from the Medicaid market. Low plan participation rates may indicate that payments to plans are too low and/or administrative requirements too burdensome.
- Review of capitated payments to providers and plans and increases in payments where necessary to maintain provider and plan participation, program competitiveness and quality of care.
- Established procedures and adequate personnel to investigate complaints promptly. When a pattern of poor quality care appears, states must take appropriate and prompt action to protect Medicaid recipients.

The tables that follow this article highlight Medicaid managed care plan types by state and state use of assurance techniques to measure the quality of Medicaid managed care. They are part of *Measuring the Quality of Medicaid Managed Care: An Introduction to State Efforts - 2000,* The Council of State Governments. Readers can contact CSG at 1-800-800-1910 to order a copy or visit www.csg.org/store/.

## Table 11.18
## MEDICAID MANAGED CARE PLAN TYPES AND ENROLLMENT BY STATE, 1998

| State | Comprehensive HIO | Medicaid Only MCO | MCO | PCCM | PHP | Other | Enrollees |
|---|---|---|---|---|---|---|---|
| Alabama | 0 | 1 | 0 | 24 | 1 | 0 | 362,272 |
| Arizona | 0 | 2 | 30 | 0 | 1 | 0 | 368,344 |
| Arkansas | 0 | 0 | 0 | 1 | 1 | 0 | 186,215 |
| California | 5 | 19 | 11 | 2 | 9 | 5 | 2,246,406 |
| Colorado | 1 | 5 | 1 | 1 | 1 | 0 | 215,936 |
| Connecticut | 0 | 5 | 2 | 0 | 0 | 0 | 220,803 |
| Delaware | 0 | 3 | 9 | 0 | 0 | 0 | 62,010 |
| District of Columbia | 0 | 7 | 1 | 1 | 0 | 0 | 51,022 |
| Florida | 0 | 16 | 0 | 1 | 1 | 0 | 915,554 |
| Georgia | 0 | 2 | 0 | 1 | 2 | 0 | 673, 528 |
| Hawaii | 0 | 8 | 2 | 0 | 0 | 0 | 131,761 |
| Idaho | 0 | 0 | 0 | 1 | 0 | 0 | 30,866 |
| Illinois | 0 | 6 | 4 | 0 | 6 | 0 | 175,649 |
| Indiana | 0 | 3 | 0 | 1 | 0 | 0 | 233,065 |
| Iowa | 0 | 5 | 0 | 1 | 2 | 0 | 190,692 |
| Kansas | 0 | 2 | 1 | 1 | 0 | 0 | 84,437 |
| Kentucky | 0 | 0 | 2 | 1 | 1 | 0 | 325,233 |
| Louisiana | 0 | 0 | 0 | 1 | 0 | 0 | 40,729 |
| Maine | 0 | 1 | 0 | 1 | 0 | 0 | 16,295 |
| Maryland | 0 | 3 | 6 | 0 | 0 | 0 | 306,474 |
| Massachusetts | 0 | 1 | 11 | 1 | 0 | 0 | 532,971 |
| Michigan | 0 | 15 | 11 | 1 | 0 | 0 | 752,568 |
| Minnesota | 0 | 7 | 1 | 1 | 0 | 0 | 225,498 |
| Mississippi | 0 | 4 | 0 | 1 | 0 | 0 | 153,562 |
| Missouri | 0 | 7 | 4 | 0 | 0 | 0 | 252,097 |
| Montana | 0 | 2 | 0 | 1 | 1 | 0 | 66,331 |
| Nebraska | 0 | 2 | 0 | 1 | 1 | 0 | 110,606 |
| Nevada | 0 | 4 | 0 | 2 | 0 | 0 | 35,089 |
| New Hampshire | 0 | 4 | 0 | 0 | 0 | 0 | 7,368 |
| New Jersey | 0 | 8 | 2 | 0 | 0 | 0 | 376,839 |
| New Mexico | 0 | 3 | 0 | 0 | 0 | 0 | 193,818 |
| New York | 0 | 21 | 17 | 1 | 8 | 2 | 634,233 |
| North Carolina | 0 | 6 | 0 | 1 | 1 | 0 | 559,035 |
| North Dakota | 0 | 1 | 0 | 1 | 0 | 0 | 22,045 |
| Ohio | 0 | 11 | 2 | 0 | 0 | 0 | 292,819 |
| Oklahoma | 0 | 5 | 0 | 1 | 0 | 0 | 154,270 |
| Oregon | 0 | 13 | 6 | 0 | 22 | 0 | 299,826 |
| Pennsylvania | 0 | 5 | 5 | 2 | 3 | 0 | 904,701 |
| Puerto Rico | 0 | 4 | 0 | 0 | 0 | 0 | 813,791 |
| Rhode Island | 0 | 4 | 0 | 0 | 0 | 0 | 74,446 |
| South Carolina | 0 | 3 | 0 | 0 | 0 | 2 | 15,823 |
| South Dakota | 0 | 0 | 0 | 1 | 0 | 0 | 43,834 |
| Tennessee | 0 | 9 | 0 | 0 | 2 | 0 | 1,268,769 |
| Texas | 0 | 6 | 5 | 1 | 0 | 0 | 437,898 |
| Utah | 0 | 6 | 0 | 1 | 8 | 0 | 112,803 |
| Vermont | 0 | 2 | 0 | 0 | 0 | 0 | 52,153 |
| Virginia | 0 | 6 | 0 | 1 | 0 | 0 | 299,266 |
| Washington | 0 | 15 | 0 | 1 | 14 | 0 | 718,023 |
| West Virginia | 0 | 3 | 0 | 1 | 0 | 0 | 131,349 |
| Wisconsin | 0 | 18 | 3 | 0 | 6 | 2 | 194,874 |
| TOTALS | 6 | 283 | 136 | 58 | 91 | 11 | 16,573,996 |

*Note:* The number of enrollees includes individuals enrolled in state health-care reform programs that expand eligibility beyond traditional eligibility standards. Alaska, Guam, U.S. Virgin Islands and Wyoming are not included because they do not have Medicaid managed care programs.
*Source: Health Care Financing Administration.*

## Table 11.19
# STATE USE OF ASSURANCE TECHNIQUES TO MEASURE THE QUALITY OF MEDICAID MANAGED CARE

| State | Surveys Medicaid recipients (a) | Surveys participating physicians | Requires ombudsman/ consumer advocate (b) | Requires HEDIS data reporting (c) | Uses CAHPS for satisfaction survey (d) |
|---|---|---|---|---|---|
| Alabama | ★ | ★ | ... | ★ | ... |
| Alaska (e) | | | | | |
| Arizona | ★ | ★ | ★ | ★ | ... |
| Arkansas | ★ | ★ | ... | ... | ★ |
| California | ★ | ... | ★ | ★ | ★ (f) |
| Colorado | ★ | ... | ★ | ★ | ★ |
| Connecticut | ★ | ... | ... | ★ | ★ (g) |
| Delaware | ★ | ... | ★ | ★ | ★ |
| Florida | ★ (h) | ... | ★ | ★ | ... |
| Georgia | ★ | ★ | ... | ★ | ... |
| Hawaii | ★ | ★ | ... | ★ | ... |
| Idaho | ★ | ★ | ... | ... | ... |
| Illinois | ★ | ... | ★ | ★ | ... |
| Indiana | ★ | ★ | ... | ★ | ... |
| Iowa | ★ | ★ | ★ | ★ | ★ |
| Kansas | ★ | ★ | ... | ★ | ★ |
| Kentucky | ★ | ★ | ★ | ★ | ... |
| Louisiana | ★ | ... | ★ | ... | ... |
| Maine | ★ | ... | ★ | ★ | ... |
| Maryland | ★ | ★ | ★ | ★ | ★ |
| Massachusetts | ★ | ... | ... | ★ | ★ |
| Michigan | ★ | ... | ★ | ★ | ★ |
| Minnesota | ★ | ... | ★ | ★ | ★ |
| Mississippi | ★ | ... | ... | ★ | ★ |
| Missouri | ★ | ★ | ★ | ★ | ... |
| Montana | ★ | ... | ★ | ★ | ... |
| Nebraska | ★ | ★ | ★ | ★ | ★ |
| Nevada | ★ | ★ | ★ | ... | ... |
| New Hampshire | ★ | ... | ... | ★ | ★ (i) |
| New Jersey | ★ | ★ | ... | ★ | ★ |
| New Mexico | ★ | ★ | ... | ★ | ★ |
| New York | ★ | ... | ★ | ★ | ... |
| North Carolina | ★ | ★ | ... | ★ | ★ |
| North Dakota | ★ | ★ | ... | ... | ... |
| Ohio | ★ | ... | ... | ★ | ★ |
| Oklahoma | ★ | ... | ... | ★ | ★ |
| Oregon | ★ | ... | ★ | ★ | ★ |
| Pennsylvania | ★ | ★ | ... | ★ | ... |
| Rhode Island | ★ | ... | ★ | ★ | ★ |
| South Carolina | ★ (h) | ... | ★ | ★ | ... |
| South Dakota | ★ | ★ | ... | ... | ... |
| Tennessee | ★ | ★ | ★ | ★ | ... |
| Texas | ★ | ★ | ★ | ★ | ★ |
| Utah | ★ | ... | ★ | ★ | ★ |
| Vermont | ★ | ... | ★ | ... | ★ |
| Virginia | ★ | ★ | ... | ... | ... |
| Washington | ★ | ★ | ★ | ★ | ★ |
| West Virginia | ★ | ★ | ★ | ... | ... |
| Wisconsin | ★ | ★ | ★ | ★ | ... |
| Wyoming (e) | | | | | |
| District of Columbia | ★ | ★ | ★ | ★ | ★ |
| Puerto Rico | ★ | ... | ... | ★ | ... |

*Source:* Data on surveys of recipients and physicians are from original data collected by The Council of State Governments; Ombudsman, HEDIS and CAHPS data are from the National Academy for State Health Policy.

*Key:*

★ — Yes

... — No

(a) Surveys of Medicaid recipients may be performed either by plans, EQRO's, or Medicaid agencies.

(b) Ombudsman programs may be either internal to managed care plans or external to plans, i.e., they are part of a state agency.

(c) Information only applies to risk-based plans; PCCM programs that require HEDIS measures are not included in this table; HEDIS data may be collected only for certain populations in Medicaid managed care and not for all Medicaid managed care enrollees.

(d) CAHPS may be used for all enrollees or for only certain populations within a state Medicaid program; states may use other instruments to assess consumer/plan member satisfaction, but these states are not listed here.

(e) Alaska, Guam, the U.S. Virgin Islands, and Wyoming are not included in this table because they do not have any Medicaid beneficiaries enrolled in managed care programs or plans.

(f) California plans to use CAHPS in 1999.

(g) Data from the NASHP did not indicate that Connecticut used CAHPS; but, Connecticut's response on CSG's survey indicated that it did.

(h) Florida and South Carolina indicated on CSG's survey that they do not survey Medicaid recipients; plans are required to do so, however.

(i) New Hampshire has a CAHPS pilot, administered by contracted plans, underway.

# INFORMATION TECHNOLOGY

## Recruiting and Retaining Information Technology Employees in State Government

### By Ed Janairo
### The Council of State Governments

Trends indicate a tight labor market for Information Technology (IT) professionals in the United States. For example, a report by the Information Technology Association of America and Virginia Tech estimates there are 346,000 vacancies in core IT positions.[1] Surveys of the private sector show that the recruiting and retaining IT professionals remains a difficult task in light of the increasing demand for employees, the apparent lack of qualified workers and the dynamics of hi-tech industries.

Experts expect the situation to worsen in the near future. The U.S. Department of Commerce indicates that between 1996 and 2006, 1,134,000 new IT positions will be created, and an additional 240,000 existing IT positions will have to be filled due to retirements.[2]

Unfortunately, the tight market for information technology professionals affects state governments more acutely than the private sector because state governments do not have the financial resources that the private sector has to attract and retain quality IT staff. A *Computerworld* salary survey showed that in 22 of 23 job classifications relevant to government IT workers, the average government worker's compensation was lower than the average for all workers in that classification, and as much as 19% lower than the average for all workers of a given classification.[3] Thus, state governments are not only faced with a shortage of information technology workers, but also are losing out to corporations in the competition to hire these workers.

The Council of State Governments, in conjunction with the National Association of State Information Resource Executives, National Association of State Personnel Executives, National Association of State Telecommunications Directors and the National Association of State Chief Administrators, conducted its own survey on the issue in 1999. Significant findings indicate that:

• Forty-seven of the forty-nine responding states of have a shortage of IT workers.

• Ninety percent of the responding states describe the shortage of IT workers as either Chronic or Regular.

• Two-fifths of the states have an IT vacancy rate between 6 percent and 10 percent.

• Two-fifths have more than a 10 percent vacancy rate.

• Eighty percent of the states indicate that they resort to short-term, long-term and project specific outsourcing.

• The three most commonly cited obstacles to recruiting IT professionals are low base salary, lack of qualified applicants, and a poor image of civil service.

• Thirty states indicate that they have restructured their classification/compensation system for IT staff in order to attract candidates, and an additional nine plan to do so as well.

• Over one-third of the states have an IT turnover rate greater than 10 percent, three of which report turnover rates greater than 20 percent (AZ, FL, TX).

• Twenty-eight states have restructured their classification/compensation system to help retain their current IT staff. The most common changes made include salary increases, bonus programs, allowing for flex-time and telecommuting, and increased opportunity for advancement.

• The most commonly cited obstacles to retaining IT personnel are the inability to compete with the private sector, low base salary, and insufficient reward system.

A compilation of the tables from the CSG survey follows this article. They are part of *Re-cruitment and Retention of Technical Employees in State Government,* The Council of State Governments. Readers can contact CSG's States Information Center at (859) 244-8253 to get a copy of the complete report.

---

[1] *Help Wanted 1998: A Call for Collaborative Action for the New Millennium,* Information Technology Association of America (ITAA) and Virginia Polytechnic Institute and State University (March 1998). This report is a follow-up of an earlier ITAA report, *Help Wanted: The IT Workforce Gap at the Dawn of the New Century* (1997). In the ITAA report, "core IT positions" include the following three categories: programmers, systems analysts, computer scientists/engineers).

[2] *The Digital Work Force: Building Infotech Skills at the Speed of Innovation,* United States Department of Commerce, Office of Technology Policy (June 1999).

[3] "Computerworld's 13th Annual Salary Survey: Return to Sanity," *Computerworld,* September 6, 1999, (http://www.computerworld.com/home/print.nsf/all/990906BFA6).

## Table 11.20
## INFORMATION TECHNOLOGY (IT) EMPLOYEE SHORTAGES IN STATE GOVERNMNENT: 1999

*IT Employee Shortages in State Government*

| | |
|---|---|
| Yes | AL, AK, AR, AZ, CA, CO, CT, DE, FL, GA, HI, ID, IL, IN, IA, KS, KY, ME, MD, MA, MI, MN, MS, MO, MT, NV, NH, NJ, NM, NC, ND, NY, OH, OR, PA, PR, RI, SC, SD, TN, TX, UT, VA, WA, DC, WV, WI, WY |
| No Shortage | LA |

*Severity of Shortage of State IT Employees*

| | |
|---|---|
| Chronic | AK, AZ, DE, FL, GA, IL, IN, MD, MA, MN, NH, NM, PA, RI, TN, TX, UT, VA |
| Regular | AL, AR, CA, CO, CT, HI, ID, IA, KY, ME, MI, MS, MO, MT, NV, MC, MD, OH, OR, PR, SC, SD, DC, WV, WI, WY |
| Occasional | KS, NJ, NY, WA |

*IT Shortages by Level of Employment*

| | |
|---|---|
| Entry Level | AL, CA, DE, FL, GA, HI, IL, IN, KY, LA, MI, MS, MO, NH, NJ, NM, PA, RI, TN, TX, UT, VA, WA, WI |
| Intermediate Level | AL, AK, AZ, CA, CO, DE, FL, GA, HI, ID, IL, IN, IA, KS, KY, MD, MA, MI, MN, MS, MO, MT, NV, NH, NJ, NM, ND, OH, PA, PR, RI, SD, TN, TX, UT, VA, WA, WI |
| Advanced Level/Managerial | AL, AK, AZ, AR, CA, CT, DE, FL, ID, IN, IA, KY, ME, MD, MA, MI, MN, MO, MT, NH, NJ, NM, NY, OR, PR, RI, SC, SD, TN, TX, UT, VA, WA, DC, WV, WI, WY |

*Percentage of IT Positions That are Typically Vacant*

| | |
|---|---|
| Less than 5 percent | IL, NY, OH, PA, SD |
| 6 percent to 10 percent | AK, CA, CT, HI, ID, KS, KY, ME, MD, MN, MO, NV, NH, NJ, ND, UT, WA, WV, WY |
| 11 percent to 15 percent | DE, FL, OR, SC, TN, VA |
| 16 percent to 20 percent | AL, AZ, AR, CO, IA, MA, MS, MT, MN, PR, RI |
| More than 20 percent | GA, IN, NC |
| None are open at this time | DC |

*Estimated Annual Turnover of IT Employees:*

| | |
|---|---|
| Less than 5 percent | CT, IL, ME, MA, MS, NH, NJ, NY, OR, PA, RI, DC |
| 6 percent to 10 percent | AL, AR, GA, ID, IN, IA, KS, KY, MD, MI, NC, ND, OH, PR, SD, TN, WA |
| 11 percent to 15 percent | AK, DE, MO, MT, SC, UT, WV, WY |
| 16 percent to 20 percent | CO, LA, MN, NV, NM, VA, WI |
| More than 20 percent | AZ, FL, TX |

*Primary Factors that Contribute to IT Employee Turnover*

| | |
|---|---|
| Unable to compete with private sector | AZ, AR, CO, CT, DE, FL, GA, HI, ID, IL, IN, IA, KY, ME, MD, MA, MI, MN, MS, MO, MT, NV, NH, NJ, NM, NC, ND, OR, PR, SC, SD, TN, TX, UT, WA, WV, WI, WY |
| Not enough high profile projects to keep staff interested | AZ, CO, MN, NV, OH, RI, TX |
| Lack of advancement opportunities | AZ, AR, DE, IL, IN, IA, KY, MN, MT, NJ, NM, OH, PA, RI, TN, TX, VA |
| Base salary too low | AK, AZ, AR, CA, CO, DE, FL, GA, HI, ID, IA, KY, LA, MD, MA, MI, MN, MO, MT, NV, NH, NM, NC, OR, PA, RI, SC, SD, TN, TX, UT, VA, WA, WV, WI, WY |
| Insufficient reward system | AK, AZ, AR, CO, CT, DE, GA, HI, IL, KY, LA, ME, MA, MN, MS, MO, MT, NV, NH, NM, ND, OH, OR, PA, SD, TN, UT, WA, WV, WI, WY |

*Typical Career Path for IT Employees Who Leave State Employment*

| | |
|---|---|
| Private Sector companies | AZ, AR, CA, CO, CT, DE, FL, GA, HI, ID, IL, IN, IA, KS, KY, LA, ME, MD, MA, MI, MN, MS, MO, MT, NV, NH, NJ, NM, NC, ND, OH, OR, PA, PR, RI, SC, SD, TN, TX, UT, WA, DC, WV, WI, WY |
| Start up own company | FL, MS, WV |
| Other state agencies | CO, CT, DE, FL, IL, KY, LA, MN, NV, NJ, NY, OH, OR, PA, RI, TX, UT, VA, WA, WI |
| Retirement | AL, DE, HI, KS, KY, NJ, NY, OH, OR, PA, RI, WY |
| Not Known | AK |

*Source:* The Council of State Governments in conjunction with the National Association of State Information Resource Executives, National Association of State Personnel Executives, National Association of State Telecommunications Directors, and the National Association of Chief State Administrators. This table was compiled from information in *Recruitment and Retention of Technical Employees in State Government*.

## Table 11.21
## STATE ACTIONS TO RETAIN INFORMATION TECHNOLOGY (IT) EMPLOYEES: 1999

| | |
|---|---|
| *Restructured Classification/Compensation System* | |
| Yes | AR, CA, FL, HI, IN, IA, KS, KY, LA, ME, MA, MI, MN, MS, MO, NV, NC, ND, OH, OR, SD, TN, TX, WA, WV, WI, WY |
| No | AL, AK, AZ, CO, CT, DE, GA, ID, IL, MT, NH, NJ, NM, NY, PA, PR, RI, SC, VA, DC |
| *Restructured Classification/Compensation System by Category* | |
| Salary increases | AR, FL, IN, KY, MA, MI, MN, MS, NV, NJ, NC, ND, OH, OR, PA, SD, TN, TX, WA, WV, WI, WY |
| Unclassifying positions to allow contracting opportunities with the state | AZ, KS, MI, NJ |
| Bonus programs | CA, FL, KS, MA, MI, MN, NV, OH, TX, VA, WI |
| Enhanced benefits programs | MI, WA |
| Employee development programs | AZ, FL, KS, MN, NJ, NC, OH, OR, TN, TX |
| Alternate schedules/flex-time | AZ, FL, KS, KY, MN, MO, NC, TX, VA, WA, WI |
| Higher profile projects | AZ, FL, KS |
| Telecommuting | AZ, AR, FL, KS, KY, MN, MO, OR, TN, TX, UT, VA, WI, WY |
| Enhanced IT training programs | AZ, FL, KS, NV, NJ, ND, OR, TN, WV, WI |
| Support for continuing education | AZ, FL, KS, MN, MO, NJ, NC, TN, VA |
| Increased opportunity for advancement | AZ, FL, KS, MI, MS, NJ, NC, ND, OR, TX, WY |

*Source:* The Council of State Governments in conjunction with the National Association of State Information Resource Executives, National Association of State Personnel Executives, National Association of State Telecommunications Directors, and the National Association of State Chief Administrators. This table was compiled from information in *Recruitment and Retention of Technical Employees in State Government.*

## Table 11.22
## STATE ACTIONS TO RECRUIT INFORMATION TECHNOLOGY (IT) EMPLOYEES: 1999

| | |
|---|---|
| *Restructured Classification/Compensation System* | |
| Yes | AR, FL, HI, IN, KS, KY, LA, MA, MI, MN, MS, MO, MT, NV, NJ, NM, NY, NC, ND, OH, OR, PA, PR, SD, TN, TX, UT, VA, WA, WV, WI, WY |
| No | AL, AK, AZ, CA, CO, CT, DE, GA, ID, IL, IA, ME, MD, NH, RI, SC, DC |
| | |
| *Restructured Classification/Compensation System by Category* | |
| Increased base pay | FL, IN, KS, KY, MN, MS, MT, NV, NJ, NM, NY, NC, ND, OH, OR, PR, TN, WA, WV, WI, WY |
| Enhanced benefits package | MI, NV |
| Alternate schedules/flex-time | FL, KS, MO, NM, NY, NC, OH, TX, VA, WI, WY |
| Telecommuting | FL, KS, KY, MO, NY, OR, TN, TX, UT, VA, WI, WY |
| Education reimbursement | FL, KS, MO, NJ, NM, OH, PR, TN, TX, WI, WY |
| Unique pay structure for IT positions | AZ, AR, KS, KY, MA, MI, MN, MS, MT, NV, NY, NC, OH, SD, VA, WI |

*Source:* The Council of State Governments in conjunction with the National Association of State Information Resource Executives, National Association of State Personnel Executives, National Association of State Telecommunications Directors, and the National Association of State Chief Administrators. This table was compiled from information in *Recruitment and Retention of Technical Employees in State Government.*

## Table 11.23
## OUTSOURCING STATE INFORMATION TECHNOLOGY (IT) FUNCTIONS: 1999

*Typical Outsourced IT Functions*

| | |
|---|---|
| Programming | AL, AK, AZ, AR, CA, CO, CT, DE, FL, GA, HI, ID, IL, IN, IA, KS, KY, ME, MD, MA, MI, MN, MS, MO, MT, NV, NH, NJ, NM, NY, NC, ND, OH, PA, PR, RI, SC, SD, TN, TX, UT, VA, WA, WV, WI |
| Systems Analyst | AL, AK, CA, CO, CT, DE, GA, HI, ID, IL, IN, IA, KS, KY, ME, MI, MN, MO, MT, NV, NH, NM, NY, NC, ND, OH, PA, TN, TX, UT, VA, WA, WV |
| Database Administration | CA, CT, DE, FL, HI, ID, IN, KY, ME, MD, MA, MI, MN, MO, MT, NH, NM, NY, PA, PR, RI, TN, TX, VA, WI |
| Web Page/Internet Administration | AZ, CA, CT, DE, FL, ID, IN, ME, MD, MI, MT, NV, NH, NJ, NM, NY, ND, PA, PR, TN, TX, UT, VA |
| None | LA, DC |

*Percentage of IT Staff Outsourced During Fiscal Year 1998/99:*

| | |
|---|---|
| Less than 5 percent | HI, KS, ME, NH, PA, SC, DC |
| 6 percent to 10 percent | AK, AR, CT, MS, NM, ND, SD, WA, WV |
| 11 percent to 15 percent | CO, ID, IL, MA, MN, MT, NJ, NC, TN, UT, VA |
| 16 percent to 20 percent | KY, NY, RI |
| More than 20 percent | AL, AZ, GA, IN, MI, MO, NV, PR, WY |
| Our state does not outsource IT personnel | DE |

*Duration of Outsourced IT Functions*

| | |
|---|---|
| Short-term (less than 6 months) | AL, AK, AZ, AR, CA, CT, DE, FL, GA, HI, ID, IL, IN, IA, KS, ME, MA, MN, MS, MO, MT, NV, NH, NJ, NM, NY, NC, OH, OR, PA, PR, RI, SC, TN, TX, UT, VA, WA, WV, WI |
| Long-term (longer than 6 months) | AL, AZ, CA, CO, CT, DE, FL, GA, ID, IL, IN, IA, ME, MD, MA, MI, MN, MS, MO, MT, NV, NH, NJ, NM, NY, NC, ND, OH, OR, PA, PR, RI, SD, TN, TX, UT, VA, WV, WI |
| Project specific (Length determined by project schedule/needs) | AL, AR, CA, CO, CT, DE, FL, GA, ID, IL, IN, KY, ME, MD, MA, MI, MN, MS, MO, MT, NV, NH, NJ, NM, NY, NC, ND, OH, PA, RI, SC, TN, TX, UT, VA, WA, DC, WV, WI, WY |

*Source:* The Council of State Governments in conjunction with the National Association of State Information Resource Executives, National Association of State Personnel Executives, National Association of State Telecommuni- cations Directors, and the National Association of State Chief Administrators. This table was compiled from information in *Recruitment and Retention of Technical Employees in State Government.*

# Index

# — NOTES —

## — NOTES —

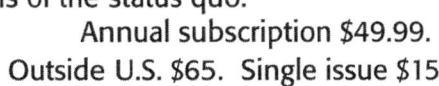
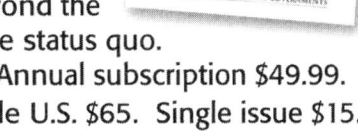